The Almanac of American Education

2022

The Almanac of American Education

2022

Fourteenth Edition

Edited by Hannah Anderson Krog

Lanham • Boulder • New York • London

Published by Bernan Press
An imprint of The Rowman & Littlefield Publishing Group, Inc.
4501 Forbes Boulevard, Suite 200, Lanham, Maryland 20706
www.rowman.com

86-90 Paul Street, London EC2A 4NE

ISBN 978-1-63671-066-2 (paperback) | ISBN 978-1-63671-067-9 (ebook)

Contents

Tables

PART A—NATIONAL EDUCATION STATISTICS

ENROLLMENT TABLES

HISTORICAL ENROLLMENT TABLES

ATTAINMENT TABLES

HISTORICAL ATTAINMENT TABLES

PART B—REGION AND STATE EDUCATION STATISTICS

ATTAINMENT TABLES

POPULATION, SCHOOL, AND STUDENT CHARACTERISTICS TABLES

PART C—COUNTY EDUCATION STATISTICS

POPULATION CHARACTERISTICS, ENROLLMENT, AND ATTAINMENT TABLES

Figures

PART C—LOCAL AREA EDUCATION STATISTICS

Preface

The Almanac of American Education serves as a guide to understanding and comparing the quality of education at the national, state, and local (county and school district) levels. Compiled from data released by the U.S. Census Bureau and the National Center for Education Statistics (NCES), the *Almanac* contains historical and current data, insightful analysis, and useful graphics that provide a detailed picture of the state of education in the United States, at the current moment and over time. With some of the tables in this fourteenth edition containing data from 2020 and 2021, we can just begin to see how the COVID-19 pandemic has affected education in the United States.

The fourteenth edition of the *Almanac* includes tables and figures updated from the thirteenth edition alongside several new tables. Due to the impact of the COVID-19 pandemic on data collection for the American Community Survey (ACS), the U.S. Census Bureau will not be releasing ACS 1-year estimates for the year 2020. We typically use ACS estimates for many of the tables in the *Almanac*, so you may notice that this edition still contains some tables with 2019 data and includes more new tables than usual. We rely on the ACS estimates for county-level education data and for that reason have replaced several of the county tables in Part C with more recent data for the largest school districts in each state.

The *Almanac* is organized into three sections: Part A—National Education Statistics; Part B—Region and State Education Statistics; and Part C—Local Area Education Statistics. Most of the tables presented in Part A are available from Census.gov and excerpted from the *Digest of Education Statistics* from the NCES. The data in Parts B and C have been specially tabulated for this publication from data obtained from the NCES and the Census Bureau.

The *Almanac*'s content allows users to ask—and answer—important questions about historic and current trends in U.S. education, including:

- Is the earnings gap between high-school graduates and college graduates growing or shrinking?
- What are the racial disparities in educational attainment, and are these disparities growing or shrinking over time?
- Which states have the highest and lowest high-school dropout rates?
- Is there a relationship between childhood poverty rates and state-level expenditures per student?
- Which states have the largest county-to-county variation in high-school graduation rates?
- How has the COVID-19 pandemic affected education in various states and communities?

The data in this volume meet the publication standards of the federal statistical agencies from which they were obtained. Every effort has been made to select accurate, meaningful, and useful data. All statistical data are subject to error arising from sampling variability, reporting errors, incomplete coverage, imputation, and other causes. The responsibility of the editor and publisher of this volume is limited to reasonable care in the reproduction and presentation of data obtained from established sources.

Hannah Anderson Krog edits several titles for Bernan Press including *State Profiles: The Population and Economy of Each U.S. State* and *Patterns of Economic Change.* She earned her bachelor of arts in journalism from the University of Maryland.

Much appreciation is due to the federal agency personnel who prepared the original data used in this book.

PART A
NATIONAL EDUCATION STATISTICS

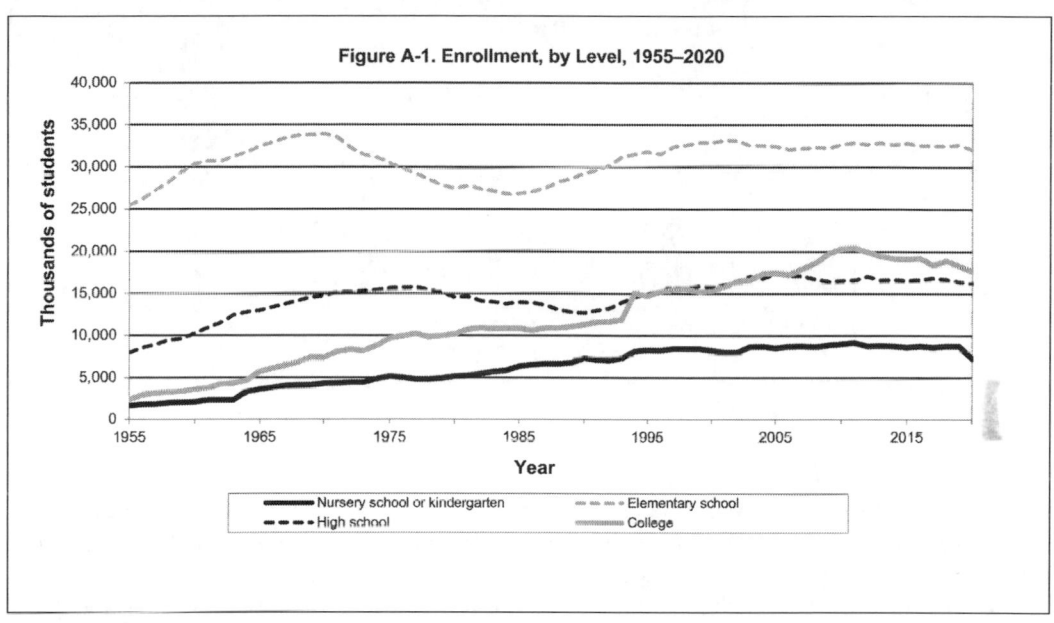

Figure A-1. Enrollment, by Level, 1955–2020

More than 73.2 million people were enrolled in school in 2020, which was a large decrease from the 76.1 million who were enrolled in 2019. Total school enrollment decreased in the late 1970s and early 1980s, but it began to rise again by 1985. Enrollment peaked in 2011, with more than 79 million students enrolled in school. Enrollment has been trending downward since then. College enrollment peaked at 20.4 million students in 2011. Elementary school enrollment has remained between 32.0 and 33.2 million since 1997 (32.0 million in 2020), similar to the baby boom levels of the 1960s but never quite reaching the 33.9 million elementary school enrollees of 1970. High-school enrollment in 2020 was 16.3 million students. High school enrollment has hovered around 16.5 million since 2013. College enrollment decreased by 615,000 students from 2019 to 2020. (Table A-1 and A-10)

In 2020, 23.3 percent of people age 3 years and over were enrolled in school. For the population 3 to 4 years old, 40.3 percent were enrolled in nursery school or kindergarten, and 59.7 percent were not enrolled in school. Among the population 18 to 24 years old, 45.8 percent were enrolled in school, as were 10.5 percent of 25- to 29-year-olds. The proportion of 30- to 34-year-olds enrolled in school was 5.8 percent. (Table A-1)

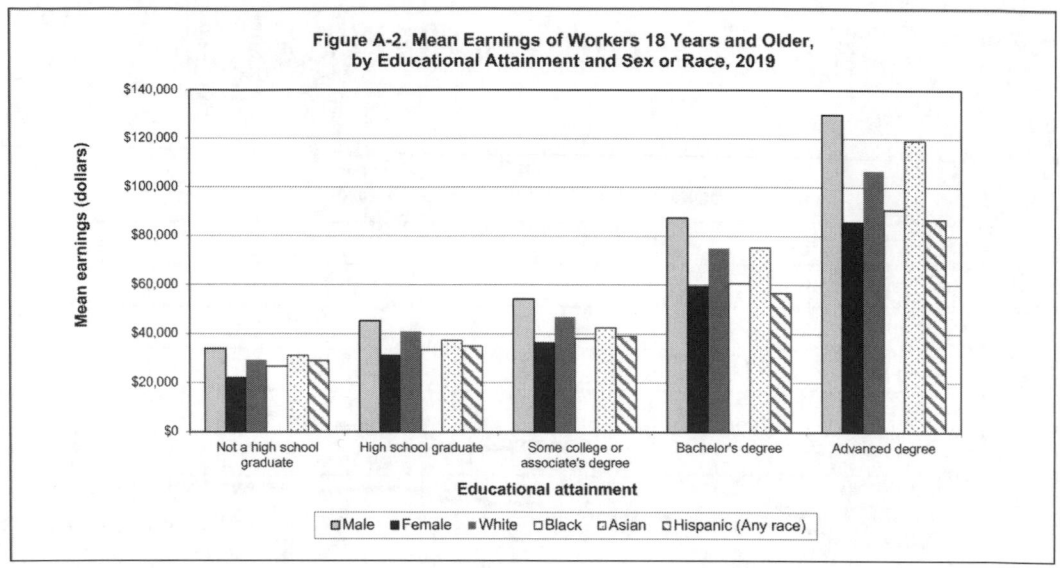

Figure A-2. Mean Earnings of Workers 18 Years and Older, by Educational Attainment and Sex or Race, 2019

In 2019, the wage gap between males and females age 18 years and older was seen for all levels of educational attainment. On average, women earned 28.7 percent less than men. The largest gap was between males and females with less than a high school diploma: the mean earnings for women without a high school diploma were 35.3 percent less than men who had that level of educational attainment ($21,869 versus $33,824).

The wage gap between racial/ethnic groups was also seen across most levels of educational attainment. Among people age 18 years and older with a bachelor's degree, the mean earnings of those who identified as black were 19.2 percent less than the mean earnings of people who identified as white. People age 18 years and older with a bachelor's degree who identified as Hispanic earned 26.7 percent less than those who identified as non-Hispanic white. (Table A-34)

In 2020, the median annual earnings for men 25 years old and over was $48,917; for women it was $31,663, with half of the men or women earning more than this amount and half earning less. For those who attended but did not finish high school, the median annual earnings were $25,102 for men, $15,177 for women. For high school graduates, including those with a GED, median earnings were $36,271 for men and $21,835 for women. Men with bachelor's degrees had median earnings of $70,653, while women with bachelor's degrees had median earnings of $46,686. Workers with a professional degree had the highest median earnings, $110,937 for men and $82,015 for women. Men earned at least 26 percent more than women at all levels of educational attainment. (Table A-35)

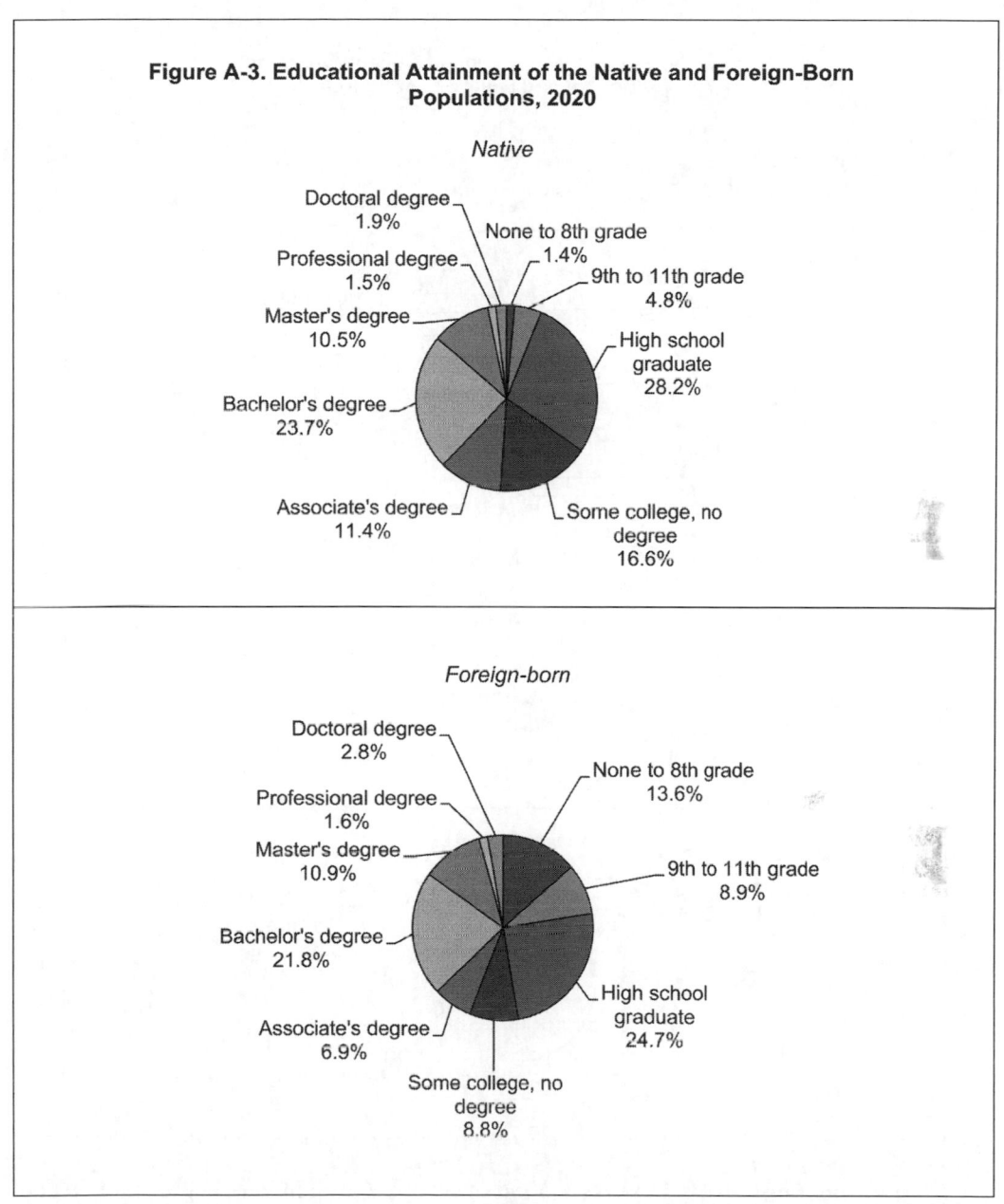

Figure A-3. Educational Attainment of the Native and Foreign-Born Populations, 2020

Native

Foreign-born

In 2020, 82.3 percent of the population age 25 years and older in the United States was native-born, and 17.7 percent of the population was foreign-born. The foreign-born population had a much larger proportion of people with less than a 9th-grade education, with 13.6 percent of the foreign-born population in this category, compared to 1.4 percent of the native population. However, the foreign-born population also had a higher percent of people with doctoral degrees than the native population (2.8 percent, compared to 1.9 percent of natives). (Table A-30)

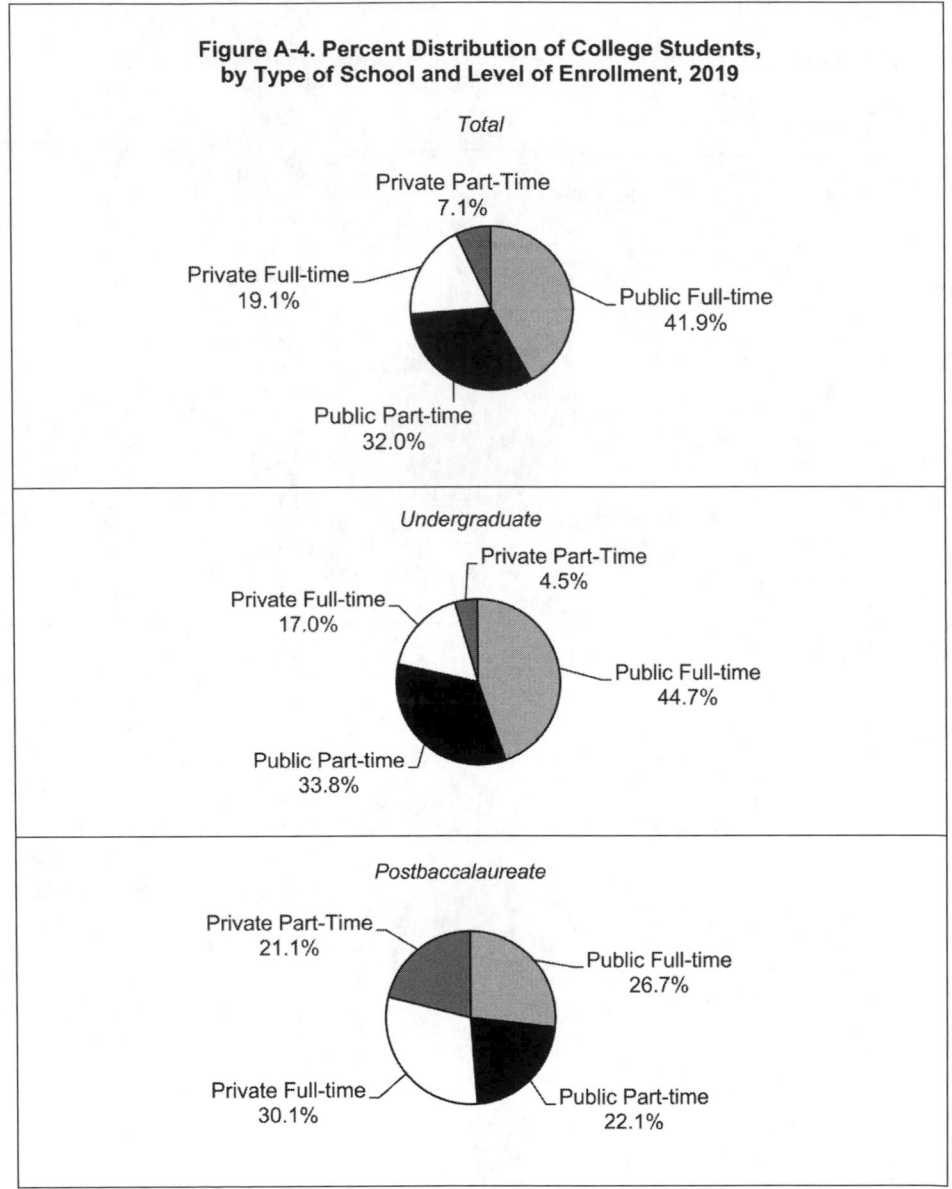

Figure A-4. Percent Distribution of College Students, by Type of School and Level of Enrollment, 2019

Total

Private Part-Time 7.1%
Private Full-time 19.1%
Public Full-time 41.9%
Public Part-time 32.0%

Undergraduate

Private Part-Time 4.5%
Private Full-time 17.0%
Public Full-time 44.7%
Public Part-time 33.8%

Postbaccalaureate

Private Part-Time 21.1%
Public Full-time 26.7%
Private Full-time 30.1%
Public Part-time 22.1%

In 2020, 17.7 million students 15 years old and over were enrolled in colleges and universities. Approximately 13.8 million of them were undergraduates. A higher percent of undergraduates attending four-year colleges were full-time students (85.8 percent) compared to those attending two-year colleges (68.1 percent full-time). The proportion of full-time to part-time college students decreased as age increased. Among students 15 to 19 years old enrolled in college, 91.9 percent were full-time students, followed by 86.1 percent of 20- to 24-year-olds, 65.8 percent of 25- to 34-year-olds, and 43.3 percent of students age 35 years and older. Among graduate students, 66.9 percent were full-time students in 2020. Since 2008 there have been more full-time graduate students than part-time, but prior to 2008 the reverse was usually true: part-time students outnumbered full-time in graduate programs most years. (Table A-5 and A-17)

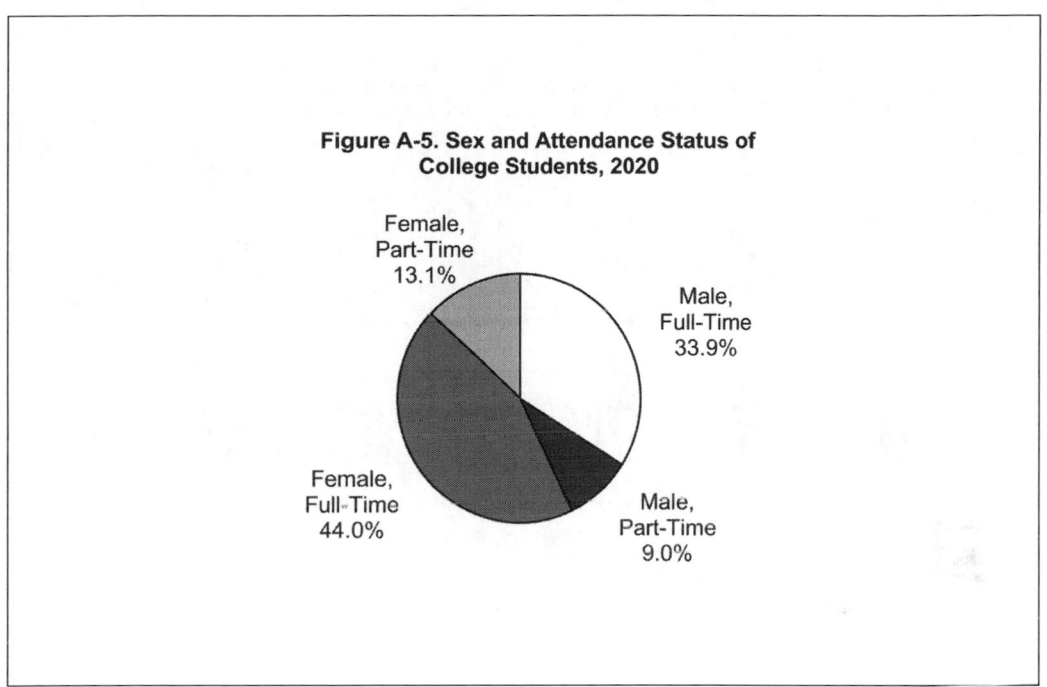

Figure A-5. Sex and Attendance Status of College Students, 2020

In 2020, women made up 57.1 percent of all undergraduate students, which is the highest proportion of all time. By contrast, only 42.2 percent of all undergraduate students in 1970 were women. By the end of the 1970s, the proportions of men and women were more equal; since then, women's share has steadily increased, staying above 55 percent in most years since the early 1990s. (Table A-17)

In 2019, 63.8 percent of college students who identified as Black were female. Among Hispanic college students, 59.1 percent were female, and females comprised 54.0 percent of the Asian/Pacific Islander college population. Among graduate students, women accounted for 60.5 percent of enrollment in 2019. (Table A-22)

In 2020, 42.6 percent of full-time college students were employed—either full- or part-time—and 78.5 percent of part-time college students were employed. Among those who were enrolled in vocational courses, 66.7 percent were employed, either full-time or part-time. (Tables A–5 and A-6)

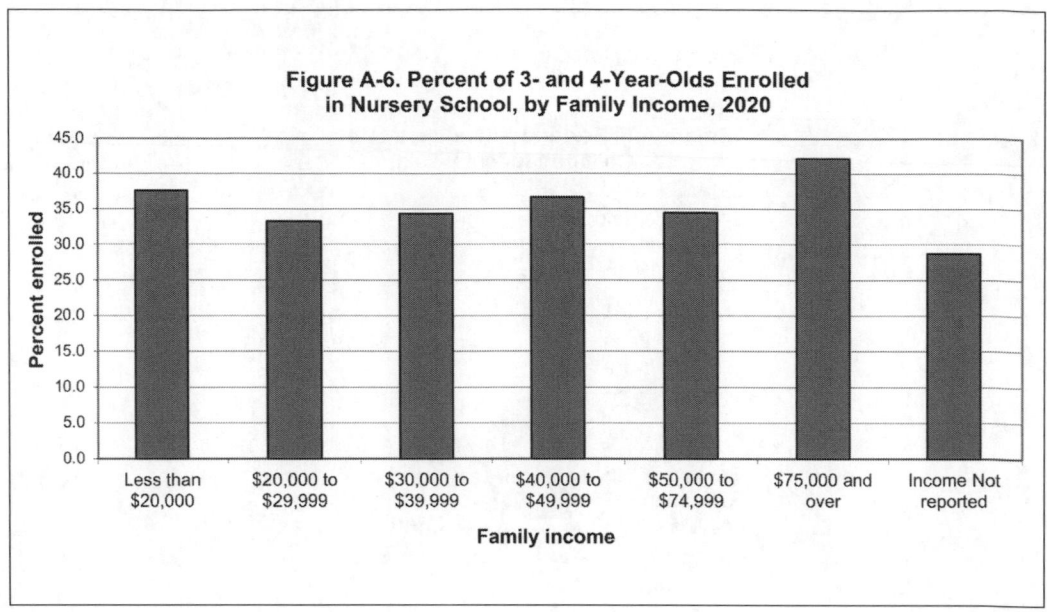

Figure A-6. Percent of 3- and 4-Year-Olds Enrolled in Nursery School, by Family Income, 2020

In 2020, families with incomes of $75,000 and over had the highest percent of 3- and 4-year-olds enrolled in nursery school (42.1 percent), followed by families with incomes of less than $20,000 (37.6 percent) and families in the $40,000 to $49,999 income range (36.7 percent). (Table A-3)

In 2020, 90.9 percent of Americans 25 years old and over had completed high school, and 37.5 percent had completed college. For people age 25 to 29 years, 94.8 percent had completed high school and 39.2 percent had completed college. Women 25 years of age and older had slightly higher rates of high school attainment and college attainment, at 91.3 percent and 38.3 percent, respectively. For women age 25 to 29 years, 94.9 percent had completed high school and 43.8 percent had completed college. Among race and ethnic groups (age 25 and older) in 2020, those who identified as non-Hispanic White had the highest

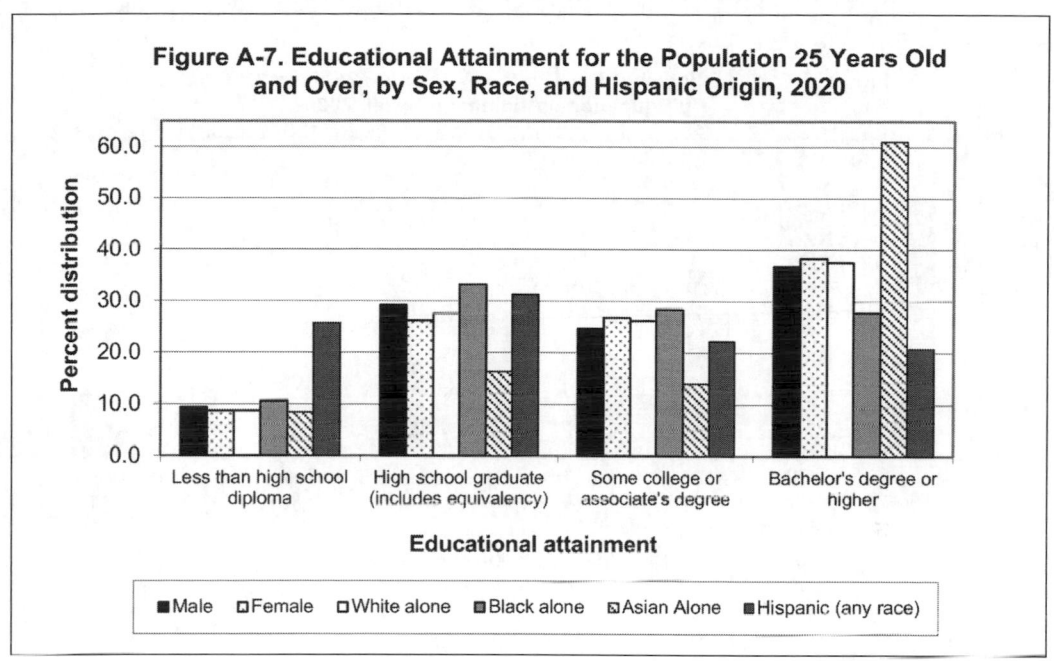

Figure A-7. Educational Attainment for the Population 25 Years Old and Over, by Sex, Race, and Hispanic Origin, 2020

high school completion rate (95.1 percent), followed by Asian (91.6 percent), White (91.3 percent), Black (89.4 percent), and Hispanic (74.3 percent) individuals. The highest percent of people who identified as Asian had completed college (61.1 percent), followed by those who identified as non-Hispanic White (41.3 percent), White (37.5 percent), Black (27.8 percent), and Hispanic (20.8 percent). (People who identified as Hispanic may be of any race.) (Tables A-32)

In 2020, 60.8 percent of the population 25 years and older were employed, 2.8 percent were unemployed, and 36.4 percent were not in the labor force. Of people age 25 and older with bachelor's degrees as their highest level of educational attainment, 70.3 percent were employed, 2.3 percent were unemployed, and 27.4 percent were not in the labor force. (Table A-27)

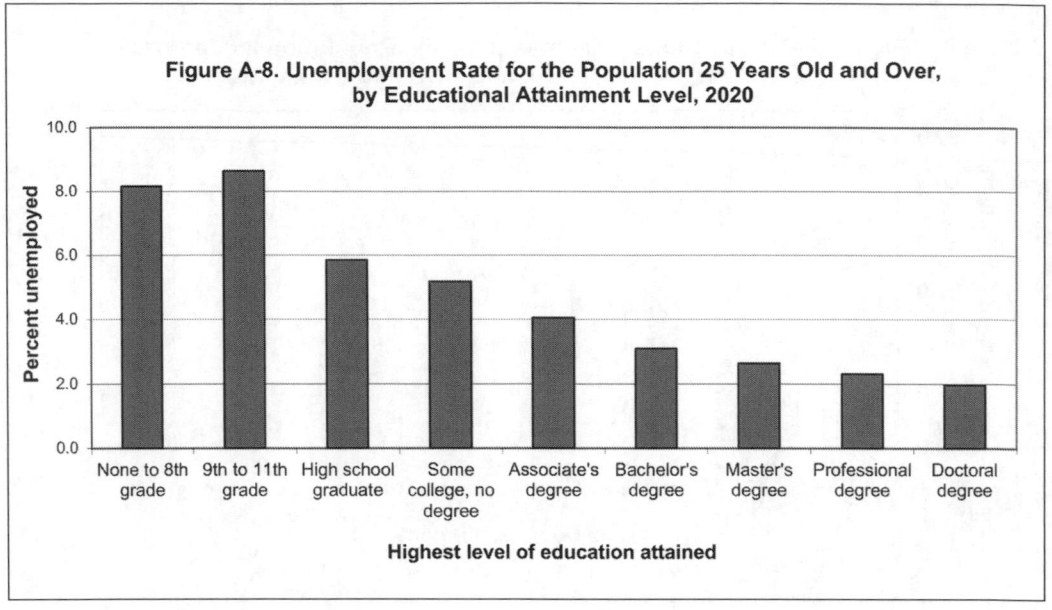

Figure A-8. Unemployment Rate for the Population 25 Years Old and Over, by Educational Attainment Level, 2020

Unemployment data for 2020 show once again that the more education a person has obtained, the less likely he or she will be unemployed. The unemployment rate for the population age 25 and over with a 9th to 11th grade education was 8.6 percent in 2020. For high-school graduates, the rate of unemployment was 5.9 percent; for civilians with a bachelor's degree, it was 3.1 percent. With a professional degree, this percentage dropped to 2.3; and the lowest unemployment rate was for those with a doctoral degree (2.0 percent). The overall unemployment rate in 2020 was 4.4 percent. The unemployment rate for men (4.7 percent) was higher than that for women (4.2 percent). However, there were fewer women than men in the work force. In 2020, the labor force participation rate was 69.9 percent for men, and 57.8 percent for women. (Table A-27)

For persons 25 years old and over, professional and related occupations provided the most jobs in 2020. This category includes teachers, lawyers, scientists, artists, doctors, nurses, and other healthcare professionals. Of individuals employed in professional and related occupations, 76.0 percent held a bachelor's degree or more. In contrast, 9.2 percent of people employed in construction and extraction occupations and 12.7 percent of those employed in farming, forestry, and fishing occupations had a bachelor's degree or more. Farming, forestry, and fishing employed the greatest percent of people without a high-school diploma (36.4 percent), and service occupations employed the highest number of people without a high-school diploma (2.5 million). (Table A-28)

The educational and health services industry was the largest employer in the United States and employed nearly 32.3 million people in 2020. More than half (59.4 percent) of the population in the education and health services industry held a bachelor's degree or higher, and 30.8 percent of workers in this field had a master's degree or higher. Mining was the smallest industry in terms of employment, with 742,000 workers, of whom 36.1 percent held a bachelor's degree or higher. (Table A-29)

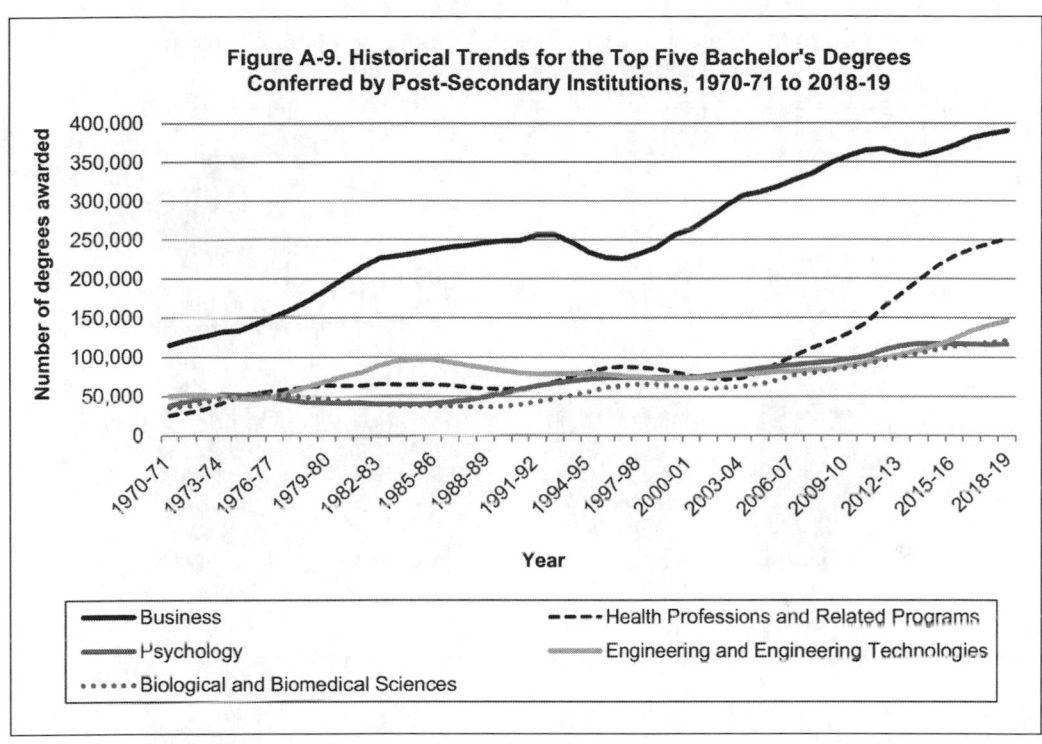

Figure A-9. Historical Trends for the Top Five Bachelor's Degrees Conferred by Post-Secondary Institutions, 1970-71 to 2018-19

The top five bachelor's degrees conferred by post-secondary institutions in the United States during the 2018–19 school year were: business (390,564 bachelor's degrees conferred), health professions and related programs (251,355 bachelor's degrees), engineering and engineering technologies (146,307 bachelor's degrees), biological and biomedical sciences (121,191 bachelor's degrees), and psychology (116,536 bachelor's degrees). The top three master's degrees granted in 2018–19 were in: business (197,089 master's degrees conferred), education (146,432 master's degrees conferred), and health professions and related programs (131,569 master's degrees conferred). (Table A-37)

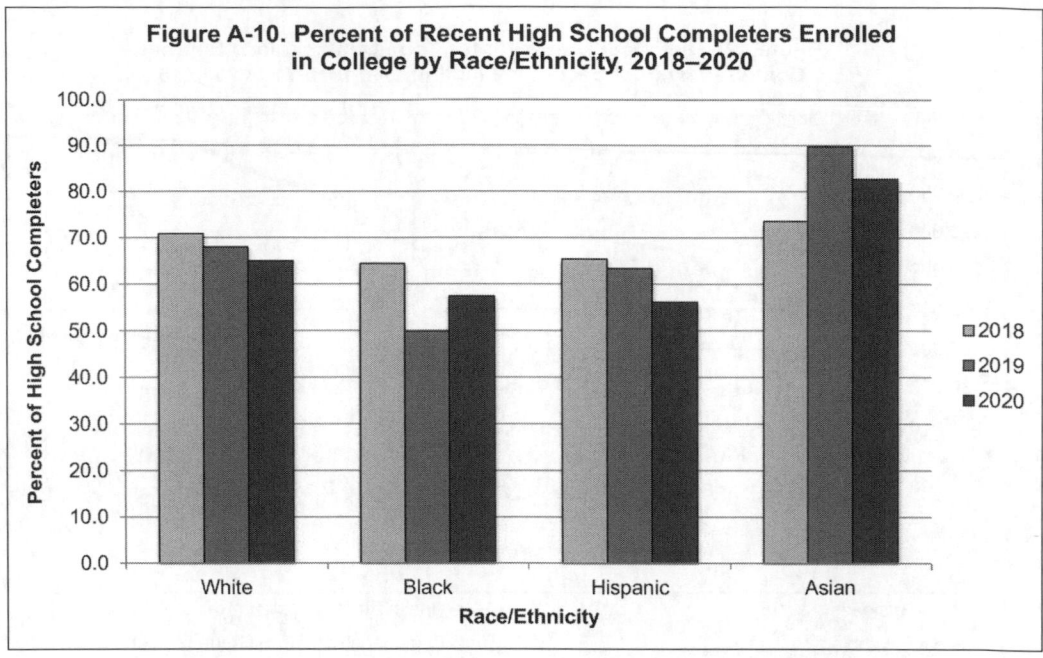

The past three years saw an increase in the percent of Hispanic and Asian college students, and a decrease in the percent of college students who identified as White or Black. In 2017, 56.0 percent of college students identified as White, 13.6 percent identified as Black, 18.9 percent identified as Hispanic, and 6.8 percent identified as Asian. In 2019, the proportions were 54.3 percent White, 13.3 percent Black, 20.3 percent Hispanic, and 7.1 percent Asian. (Table A-22)

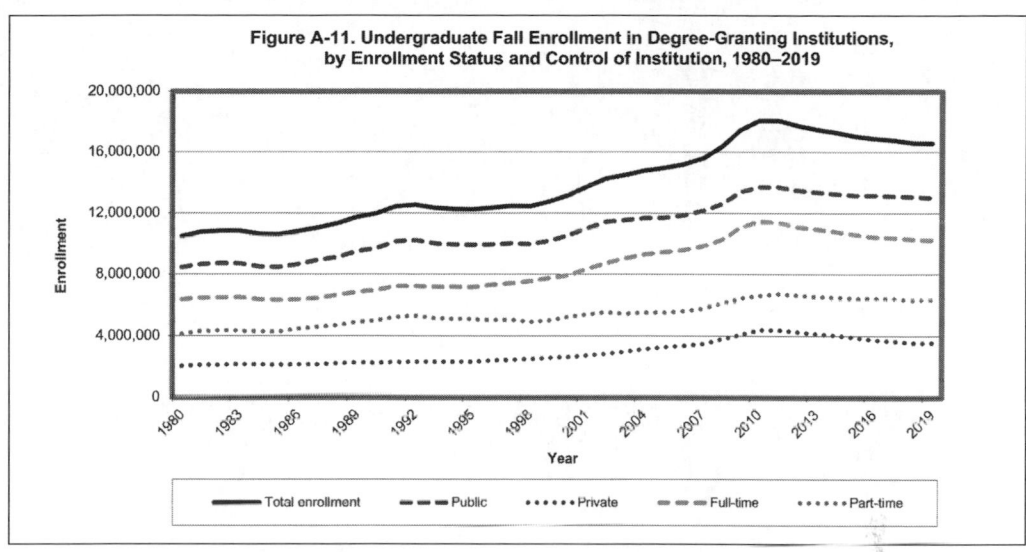

Figure A-11. Undergraduate Fall Enrollment in Degree-Granting Institutions, by Enrollment Status and Control of Institution, 1980–2019

College enrollment increased 37.3 percent between 2000 and 2010, but it has decreased each year since 2010. In 2019, 19.6 million students were enrolled in college, with 14.5 million of them enrolled in public institutions. Enrollment in private colleges peaked at nearly 5.9 million students in 2011, but private college enrollment has decreased each year since then. There were about 5.1 million students enrolled in private colleges in 2019. Public 4-year colleges continued to enroll the most students, with 9.1 million students enrolled in 2019. Both public 2-year colleges saw a decrease in enrollment from 2018 to 2019, with 157,986 fewer students enrolled in public, 2-year colleges. There have been more females than males enrolled in college since 1979. Women comprised 57.4 percent of college students in 2019, which matched the previous peak of female enrollment in 2005. (Tables A-18 and A-19)

PART A
NATIONAL EDUCATION STATISTICS

■ **Enrollment Tables**

Table A-1. Enrollment Status of the Population 3 Years Old and Over, by Sex, Age, Race, Hispanic Origin, Foreign Born, and Foreign-Born Parentage, October 2020

(Numbers in thousands; percent; civilian noninstitutionalized population.)

| Age, sex, race, Hispanic origin, and nativity | Population | Enrolled in school | | | | | | | |
| | | Total | | Nursery or kindergarten | | Elementary | | High school | |
	Number	Number	Percent	Number	Percent	Number	Percent	Number	Percent
ALL RACES									
Both Sexes									
Total	313,928	73,222	23.3	7,243	2.3	32,046	10.2	16,259	5.2
3 and 4 years old	7,913	3,189	40.3	3,189	40.3	*	*	*	*
5 and 6 years old	8,145	7,268	89.2	4,002	49.1	3,266	40.1	*	*
7 to 9 years old	12,081	11,543	95.5	51	0.4	11,492	95.1	*	*
10 to 13 years old	16,523	16,030	97.0	*	*	15,842	95.9	188	1.1
14 and 15 years old	8,340	8,159	97.8	*	*	1,319	15.8	6,802	81.6
16 and 17 years old	8,309	7,671	92.3	*	*	73	0.9	7,466	89.9
18 and 19 years old	8,242	5,484	66.5	*	*	5	0.1	1,442	17.5
20 and 21 years old	8,753	4,621	52.8	*	*	6	0.1	153	1.7
22 to 24 years old	12,164	3,236	26.6	*	*	8	0.1	62	0.5
25 to 29 years old	22,473	2,366	10.5	*	*	4	*	20	0.1
30 to 34 years old	22,394	1,301	5.8	*	*	8	*	25	0.1
35 to 44 years old	41,513	1,381	3.3	*	*	11	*	48	0.1
45 to 54 years old	39,787	661	1.7	*	*	7	*	41	0.1
55 years old and over	97,290	311	0.3	*	*	5	*	13	*
Male									
Total	153,256	35,899	23.4	3,640	2.4	16,491	10.8	8,191	5.3
3 and 4 years old	4,014	1,557	38.8	1,557	38.8	*	*	*	*
5 and 6 years old	4,203	3,767	89.6	2,049	48.7	1,718	40.9	*	*
7 to 9 years old	6,138	5,885	95.9	33	0.5	5,851	95.3	*	*
10 to 13 years old	8,431	8,158	96.8	*	*	8,094	96.0	64	0.8
14 and 15 years old	4,253	4,131	97.1	*	*	736	17.3	3,371	79.3
16 and 17 years old	4,215	3,867	91.7	*	*	48	1.1	3,753	89.0
18 and 19 years old	4,149	2,567	61.9	*	*	4	0.1	853	20.6
20 and 21 years old	4,435	2,186	49.3	*	*	6	0.1	73	1.6
22 to 24 years old	6,009	1,392	23.2	*	*	8	0.1	13	0.2
25 to 29 years old	11,257	939	8.3	*	*	4	*	3	*
30 to 34 years old	11,146	601	5.4	*	*	4	*	16	0.1
35 to 44 years old	20,441	529	2.6	*	*	10	*	19	0.1
45 to 54 years old	19,456	192	1.0	*	*	4	*	13	0.1
55 years old and over	45,109	128	0.3	*	*	5	*	13	*
Female									
Total	160,671	37,323	23.2	3,603	2.2	15,554	9.7	8,068	5.0
3 and 4 years old	3,899	1,632	41.9	1,632	41.9	*	*	*	*
5 and 6 years old	3,942	3,501	88.8	1,953	49.6	1,548	39.3	*	*
7 to 9 years old	5,943	5,658	95.2	18	0.3	5,641	94.9	*	*
10 to 13 years old	8,093	7,872	97.3	*	*	7,748	95.7	124	1.5
14 and 15 years old	4,087	4,028	98.5	*	*	583	14.3	3,431	83.9
16 and 17 years old	4,093	3,804	92.9	*	*	25	0.6	3,712	90.7
18 and 19 years old	4,094	2,916	71.2	*	*	*	*	589	14.4
20 and 21 years old	4,318	2,436	56.4	*	*	*	*	80	1.9
22 to 24 years old	6,155	1,844	30.0	*	*	*	*	49	0.8
25 to 29 years old	11,216	1,427	12.7	*	*	*	*	17	0.2
30 to 34 years old	11,248	700	6.2	*	*	4	*	9	0.1
35 to 44 years old	21,072	852	4.0	*	*	2	*	29	0.1
45 to 54 years old	20,331	469	2.3	*	*	3	*	28	0.1
55 years old and over	52,181	183	0.4	*	*	*	*	*	*
WHITE ALONE OR IN COMBINATION									
Both Sexes									
Total	247,097	55,721	22.6	5,561	2.3	24,662	10.0	12,514	5.1
3 and 4 years old	6,055	2,424	40.0	2,424	40.0	*	*	*	*
5 and 6 years old	6,201	5,530	89.2	3,103	50.0	2,427	39.1	*	*
7 to 9 years old	9,404	8,982	95.5	33	0.4	8,948	95.2	*	*
10 to 13 years old	12,673	12,303	97.1	*	*	12,146	95.8	158	1.2
14 and 15 years old	6,436	6,276	97.5	*	*	1,033	16.1	5,223	81.2
16 and 17 years old	6,468	5,961	92.2	*	*	64	1.0	5,816	89.9
18 and 19 years old	6,350	4,115	64.8	*	*	5	0.1	1,067	16.8
20 and 21 years old	6,648	3,508	52.8	*	*	6	0.1	115	1.7
22 to 24 years old	9,380	2,358	25.1	*	*	8	0.1	40	0.4
25 to 29 years old	16,831	1,698	10.1	*	*	4	*	9	0.1
30 to 34 years old	16,930	894	5.3	*	*	8	*	16	0.1

* = Quantity equals zero or rounds to zero.

Table A-1. Enrollment Status of the Population 3 Years Old and Over, by Sex, Age, Race, Hispanic Origin, Foreign Born, and Foreign-Born Parentage, October 2020— *Continued*

(Numbers in thousands; percent; civilian noninstitutionalized population.)

Age, sex, race, Hispanic origin, and nativity	Enrolled in school — College undergraduate or graduate		Not enrolled in school — Total		High school graduate		Not high school graduate	
	Number	Percent	Number	Percent	Number	Percent	Number	Percent
ALL RACES								
Both Sexes								
Total	17,674	5.6	240,706	76.7	212,261	67.6	28,445	9.1
3 and 4 years old	*	*	4,724	59.7	*	*	4,724	59.7
5 and 6 years old	*	*	877	10.8	*	*	877	10.8
7 to 9 years old	*	*	538	4.5	*	*	538	4.5
10 to 13 years old	*	*	494	3.0	*	*	494	3.0
14 and 15 years old	38	0.5	181	2.2	*	*	181	2.2
16 and 17 years old	133	1.6	638	7.7	165	2.0	473	5.7
18 and 19 years old	4,037	49.0	2,759	33.5	2,325	28.2	434	5.3
20 and 21 years old	4,463	51.0	4,132	47.2	3,673	42.0	459	5.2
22 to 24 years old	3,166	26.0	8,928	73.4	8,313	68.3	614	5.1
25 to 29 years old	2,342	10.4	20,107	89.5	18,833	83.8	1,274	5.7
30 to 34 years old	1,268	5.7	21,093	94.2	19,676	87.9	1,416	6.3
35 to 44 years old	1,322	3.2	40,132	96.7	36,420	87.7	3,712	8.9
45 to 54 years old	613	1.5	39,126	98.3	35,723	89.8	3,403	8.6
55 years old and over	293	0.3	96,978	99.7	87,133	89.6	9,846	10.1
Male								
Total	7,577	4.9	117,357	76.6	102,727	67.0	14,630	9.5
3 and 4 years old	*	*	2,457	61.2	*	*	2,457	61.2
5 and 6 years old	*	*	437	10.4	*	*	437	10.4
7 to 9 years old	*	*	253	4.1	*	*	253	4.1
10 to 13 years old	*	*	273	3.2	*	*	273	3.2
14 and 15 years old	24	0.6	121	2.9	*	*	121	2.9
16 and 17 years old	66	1.6	348	8.3	87	2.1	261	6.2
18 and 19 years old	1,710	41.2	1,581	38.1	1,343	32.4	239	5.8
20 and 21 years old	2,107	47.5	2,250	50.7	1,963	44.3	287	6.5
22 to 24 years old	1,370	22.8	4,617	76.8	4,238	70.5	379	6.3
25 to 29 years old	932	8.3	10,318	91.7	9,620	85.5	699	6.2
30 to 34 years old	582	5.2	10,545	94.6	9,804	88.0	741	6.6
35 to 44 years old	501	2.4	19,912	97.4	17,859	87.4	2,053	10.0
45 to 54 years old	174	0.9	19,265	99.0	17,477	89.8	1,788	9.2
55 years old and over	110	0.2	44,981	99.7	40,336	89.4	4,644	10.3
Female								
Total	10,097	6.3	123,348	76.8	109,534	68.2	13,814	8.6
3 and 4 years old	*	*	2,267	58.1	*	*	2,267	58.1
5 and 6 years old	*	*	441	11.2	*	*	441	11.2
7 to 9 years old	*	*	285	4.8	*	*	285	4.8
10 to 13 years old	*	*	221	2.7	*	*	221	2.7
14 and 15 years old	14	0.3	60	1.5	*	*	60	1.5
16 and 17 years old	67	1.6	289	7.1	78	1.9	211	5.2
18 and 19 years old	2,327	56.8	1,177	28.8	982	24.0	195	4.8
20 and 21 years old	2,355	54.6	1,882	43.6	1,710	39.6	172	4.0
22 to 24 years old	1,795	29.2	4,311	70.0	4,075	66.2	236	3.8
25 to 29 years old	1,410	12.6	9,789	87.3	9,213	82.1	576	5.1
30 to 34 years old	686	6.1	10,548	93.8	9,873	87.8	675	6.0
35 to 44 years old	821	3.9	20,220	96.0	18,561	88.1	1,659	7.9
45 to 54 years old	439	2.2	19,862	97.7	18,246	89.7	1,616	7.9
55 years old and over	183	0.4	51,998	99.6	46,796	89.7	5,201	10.0
WHITE ALONE OR IN COMBINATION								
Both Sexes								
Total	12,985	5.3	191,377	77.4	169,252	68.5	22,124	9.0
3 and 4 years old	*	*	3,631	60.0	*	*	3,631	60.0
5 and 6 years old	*	*	671	10.8	*	*	671	10.8
7 to 9 years old	*	*	422	4.5	*	*	422	4.5
10 to 13 years old	*	*	370	2.9	*	*	370	2.9
14 and 15 years old	20	0.3	159	2.5	*	*	159	2.5
16 and 17 years old	81	1.3	507	7.8	121	1.9	386	6.0
18 and 19 years old	3,043	47.9	2,235	35.2	1,890	29.8	344	5.4
20 and 21 years old	3,387	50.9	3,140	47.2	2,751	41.4	389	5.9
22 to 24 years old	2,309	24.6	7,022	74.9	6,520	69.5	502	5.4
25 to 29 years old	1,684	10.0	15,133	89.9	14,145	84.0	988	5.9
30 to 34 years old	871	5.1	16,035	94.7	14,906	88.0	1,130	6.7

* = Quantity equals zero or rounds to zero.

Table A-1. Enrollment Status of the Population 3 Years Old and Over, by Sex, Age, Race, Hispanic Origin, Foreign Born, and Foreign-Born Parentage, October 2020— *Continued*

(Numbers in thousands; percent; civilian noninstitutionalized population.)

Age, sex, race, Hispanic origin, and nativity	Population	Enrolled in school							
		Total		Nursery or kindergarten		Elementary		High school	
	Number	Number	Percent	Number	Percent	Number	Percent	Number	Percent
35 to 44 years old	31,825	973	3.1	*	*	5	*	31	0.1
45 to 54 years old	31,194	479	1.5	*	*	7	*	29	0.1
55 years old and over	80,704	219	0.3	*	*	1	*	10	*
Male									
Total	121,814	27,439	22.5	2,812	2.3	12,736	10.5	6,332	5.2
3 and 4 years old	3,115	1,205	38.7	1,205	38.7	*	*	*	*
5 and 6 years old	3,148	2,850	90.5	1,582	50.2	1,268	40.3	*	*
7 to 9 years old	4,833	4,639	96.0	25	0.5	4,614	95.5	*	*
10 to 13 years old	6,461	6,246	96.7	*	*	6,192	95.8	55	0.8
14 and 15 years old	3,290	3,180	96.6	*	*	583	17.7	2,580	78.4
16 and 17 years old	3,282	3,013	91.8	*	*	44	1.3	2,938	89.5
18 and 19 years old	3,199	1,905	59.6	*	*	4	0.1	629	19.7
20 and 21 years old	3,404	1,650	48.5	*	*	6	0.2	63	1.9
22 to 24 years old	4,695	1,022	21.8	*	*	8	0.2	12	0.2
25 to 29 years old	8,509	705	8.3	*	*	4	*	*	*
30 to 34 years old	8,549	415	4.9	*	*	4	*	16	0.2
35 to 44 years old	15,921	386	2.4	*	*	3	*	18	0.1
45 to 54 years old	15,531	139	0.9	*	*	4	*	13	0.1
55 years old and over	37,877	84	0.2	*	*	1	*	10	*
Female									
Total	125,284	28,282	22.6	2,749	2.2	11,926	9.5	6,181	4.9
3 and 4 years old	2,940	1,219	41.5	1,219	41.5	*	*	*	*
5 and 6 years old	3,053	2,680	87.8	1,522	49.9	1,158	37.9	*	*
7 to 9 years old	4,571	4,343	95.0	9	0.2	4,334	94.8	*	*
10 to 13 years old	6,213	6,057	97.5	*	*	5,954	95.8	103	1.7
14 and 15 years old	3,145	3,096	98.5	*	*	450	14.3	2,643	84.0
16 and 17 years old	3,185	2,947	92.5	*	*	20	0.6	2,878	90.3
18 and 19 years old	3,151	2,210	70.1	*	*	*	*	439	13.9
20 and 21 years old	3,244	1,859	57.3	*	*	*	*	52	1.6
22 to 24 years old	4,685	1,336	28.5	*	*	*	*	29	0.6
25 to 29 years old	8,322	992	11.9	*	*	*	*	9	0.1
30 to 34 years old	8,381	479	5.7	*	*	4	0.1	*	*
35 to 44 years old	15,904	587	3.7	*	*	2	*	13	0.1
45 to 54 years old	15,663	340	2.2	*	*	3	*	16	0.1
55 years old and over	42,827	136	0.3	*	*	*	*	*	*
BLACK ALONE OR IN COMBINATION									
Both Sexes									
Total	45,507	13,001	28.6	1,365	3.0	5,862	12.9	2,925	6.4
3 and 4 years old	1,464	619	42.3	619	42.3	*	*	*	*
5 and 6 years old	1,552	1,398	90.1	736	47.4	662	42.6	*	*
7 to 9 years old	2,276	2,159	94.9	9	0.4	2,149	94.4	*	*
10 to 13 years old	2,979	2,878	96.6	*	*	2,857	95.9	21	0.7
14 and 15 years old	1,444	1,429	99.0	*	*	189	13.1	1,225	84.9
16 and 17 years old	1,413	1,304	92.3	*	*	5	0.4	1,259	89.1
18 and 19 years old	1,351	947	70.1	*	*	*	*	318	23.6
20 and 21 years old	1,527	642	42.0	*	*	*	*	42	2.8
22 to 24 years old	1,963	505	25.8	*	*	*	*	18	0.9
25 to 29 years old	3,779	384	10.2	*	*	*	*	5	0.1
30 to 34 years old	3,510	260	7.4	*	*	*	*	5	0.1
35 to 44 years old	5,948	253	4.3	*	*	*	*	17	0.3
45 to 54 years old	5,413	144	2.7	*	*	*	*	11	0.2
55 years old and over	10,889	79	0.7	*	*	*	*	3	*
Male									
Total	21,426	6,295	29.4	626	2.9	3,025	14.1	1,449	6.8
3 and 4 years old	719	277	38.5	277	38.5	*	*	*	*
5 and 6 years old	786	699	88.9	344	43.7	356	45.2	*	*
7 to 9 years old	1,174	1,124	95.7	5	0.4	1,119	95.3	*	*
10 to 13 years old	1,502	1,449	96.5	*	*	1,439	95.8	9	0.6
14 and 15 years old	739	732	99.1	*	*	109	14.7	616	83.4
16 and 17 years old	703	641	91.2	*	*	3	0.5	610	86.7
18 and 19 years old	658	443	67.4	*	*	*	*	187	28.5
20 and 21 years old	790	325	41.2	*	*	*	*	18	2.3
22 to 24 years old	952	205	21.5	*	*	*	*	1	0.1

* = Quantity equals zero or rounds to zero.

Table A-1. Enrollment Status of the Population 3 Years Old and Over, by Sex, Age, Race, Hispanic Origin, Foreign Born, and Foreign-Born Parentage, October 2020— *Continued*

(Numbers in thousands; percent; civilian noninstitutionalized population.)

Age, sex, race, Hispanic origin, and nativity	Enrolled in school — College undergraduate or graduate		Not enrolled in school — Total		High school graduate		Not high school graduate	
	Number	Percent	Number	Percent	Number	Percent	Number	Percent
35 to 44 years old	937	2.9	30,852	96.9	27,941	87.8	2,911	9.1
45 to 54 years old	442	1.4	30,715	98.5	27,954	89.6	2,761	8.9
55 years old and over	209	0.3	80,485	99.7	73,024	90.5	7,460	9.2
Male								
Total	5,559	4.6	94,375	77.5	82,792	68.0	11,583	9.5
3 and 4 years old	*	*	1,910	61.3	*	*	1,910	61.3
5 and 6 years old	*	*	298	9.5	*	*	298	9.5
7 to 9 years old	*	*	194	4.0	*	*	194	4.0
10 to 13 years old	*	*	214	3.3	*	*	214	3.3
14 and 15 years old	17	0.5	111	3.4	*	*	111	3.4
16 and 17 years old	31	0.9	269	8.2	54	1.7	215	6.5
18 and 19 years old	1,272	39.8	1,294	40.4	1,112	34.8	182	5.7
20 and 21 years old	1,581	46.4	1,755	51.5	1,505	44.2	250	7.3
22 to 24 years old	1,002	21.3	3,673	78.2	3,382	72.0	291	6.2
25 to 29 years old	701	8.2	7,803	91.7	7,227	84.9	577	6.8
30 to 34 years old	396	4.6	8,134	95.1	7,530	88.1	603	7.1
35 to 44 years old	365	2.3	15,535	97.6	13,909	87.4	1,626	10.2
45 to 54 years old	121	0.8	15,392	99.1	13,927	89.7	1,465	9.4
55 years old and over	73	0.2	37,793	99.8	34,146	90.2	3,647	9.6
Female								
Total	7,426	5.9	97,002	77.4	86,460	69.0	10,541	8.4
3 and 4 years old	*	*	1,721	58.5	*	*	1,721	58.5
5 and 6 years old	*	*	372	12.2	*	*	372	12.2
7 to 9 years old	*	*	228	5.0	*	*	228	5.0
10 to 13 years old	*	*	156	2.5	*	*	156	2.5
14 and 15 years old	4	0.1	49	1.5	*	*	49	1.5
16 and 17 years old	50	1.6	238	7.5	67	2.1	171	5.4
18 and 19 years old	1,771	56.2	941	29.9	779	24.7	162	5.1
20 and 21 years old	1,806	55.7	1,385	42.7	1,246	38.4	140	4.3
22 to 24 years old	1,307	27.9	3,349	71.5	3,138	67.0	211	4.5
25 to 29 years old	983	11.8	7,330	88.1	6,918	83.1	411	4.9
30 to 34 years old	475	5.7	7,902	94.3	7,375	88.0	526	6.3
35 to 44 years old	572	3.6	15,317	96.3	14,031	88.2	1,285	8.1
45 to 54 years old	321	2.0	15,323	97.8	14,027	89.6	1,296	8.3
55 years old and over	136	0.3	42,692	99.7	38,878	90.8	3,813	8.9
BLACK ALONE OR IN COMBINATION								
Both Sexes								
Total	2,849	6.3	32,507	71.4	28,007	61.5	4,499	9.9
3 and 4 years old	*	*	845	57.7	*	*	845	57.7
5 and 6 years old	*	*	154	9.9	*	*	154	9.9
7 to 9 years old	*	*	117	5.1	*	*	117	5.1
10 to 13 years old	*	*	101	3.4	*	*	101	3.4
14 and 15 years old	15	1.0	15	1.0	*	*	15	1.0
16 and 17 years old	40	2.8	109	7.7	51	3.6	59	4.2
18 and 19 years old	629	46.6	404	29.9	345	25.6	58	4.3
20 and 21 years old	600	39.3	885	58.0	808	52.9	77	5.1
22 to 24 years old	487	24.8	1,457	74.2	1,371	69.9	86	4.4
25 to 29 years old	379	10.0	3,395	89.8	3,182	84.2	213	5.6
30 to 34 years old	255	7.3	3,250	92.0	3,043	86.7	208	5.9
35 to 44 years old	236	4.0	5,694	95.7	5,171	86.9	523	8.8
45 to 54 years old	132	2.4	5,270	97.3	4,862	89.8	408	7.5
55 years old and over	75	0.7	10,810	99.3	9,175	84.3	1,636	15.0
Male								
Total	1,194	5.6	15,131	70.6	12,919	60.3	2,212	10.3
3 and 4 years old	*	*	442	61.5	*	*	442	61.5
5 and 6 years old	*	*	87	11.1	*	*	87	11.1
7 to 9 years old	*	*	50	4.3	*	*	50	4.3
10 to 13 years old	*	*	53	3.5	*	*	53	3.5
14 and 15 years old	7	1.0	7	0.9	*	*	7	0.9
16 and 17 years old	28	4.0	62	8.8	27	3.8	35	5.0
18 and 19 years old	256	38.9	214	32.6	184	28.0	30	4.6
20 and 21 years old	307	38.9	465	58.8	421	53.3	44	5.5
22 to 24 years old	204	21.4	747	78.5	680	71.5	67	7.0

* = Quantity equals zero or rounds to zero.

Table A-1. Enrollment Status of the Population 3 Years Old and Over, by Sex, Age, Race, Hispanic Origin, Foreign Born, and Foreign-Born Parentage, October 2020—*Continued*

(Numbers in thousands; percent; civilian noninstitutionalized population.)

Age, sex, race, Hispanic origin, and nativity	Population Number	Enrolled in school Total Number	Total Percent	Nursery or kindergarten Number	Nursery or kindergarten Percent	Elementary Number	Elementary Percent	High school Number	High school Percent
25 to 29 years old	1,846	120	6.5	*	*	*	*	3	0.1
30 to 34 years old	1,654	115	7.0	*	*	*	*	*	*
35 to 44 years old	2,737	87	3.2	*	*	*	*	1	*
45 to 54 years old	2,472	40	1.6	*	*	*	*	*	*
55 years old and over	4,694	38	0.8	*	*	*	*	3	0.1
Female									
Total	24,082	6,706	27.8	739	3.1	2,836	11.8	1,476	6.1
3 and 4 years old	745	342	46.0	342	46.0	*	*	*	*
5 and 6 years old	765	698	91.2	392	51.2	306	40.0	*	*
7 to 9 years old	1,102	1,035	93.9	4	0.4	1,031	93.5	*	*
10 to 13 years old	1,477	1,430	96.8	*	*	1,418	96.0	12	0.8
14 and 15 years old	705	697	98.9	*	*	80	11.4	609	86.4
16 and 17 years old	710	663	93.3	*	*	2	0.3	649	91.4
18 and 19 years old	693	504	72.7	*	*	*	*	131	18.9
20 and 21 years old	737	316	42.9	*	*	*	*	24	3.2
22 to 24 years old	1,011	301	29.7	*	*	*	*	17	1.7
25 to 29 years old	1,933	264	13.7	*	*	*	*	2	0.1
30 to 34 years old	1,856	145	7.8	*	*	*	*	5	0.3
35 to 44 years old	3,211	167	5.2	*	*	*	*	16	0.5
45 to 54 years old	2,941	104	3.5	*	*	*	*	11	0.4
55 years old and over	6,195	41	0.7	*	*	*	*	*	*
ASIAN ALONE OR IN COMBINATION									
Both Sexes									
Total	21,555	5,877	27.3	514	2.4	2,357	10.9	1,040	4.8
3 and 4 years old	586	233	39.7	233	39.7	*	*	*	*
5 and 6 years old	591	515	87.1	271	45.8	244	41.3	*	*
7 to 9 years old	838	812	96.9	10	1.2	802	95.7	*	*
10 to 13 years old	1,252	1,214	96.9	*	*	1,200	95.8	14	1.1
14 and 15 years old	561	555	98.9	*	*	94	16.8	458	81.6
16 and 17 years old	526	495	94.2	*	*	4	0.8	474	90.3
18 and 19 years old	591	460	77.8	*	*	*	*	69	11.7
20 and 21 years old	683	555	81.3	*	*	6	0.8	11	1.6
22 to 24 years old	885	393	44.4	*	*	*	*	4	0.4
25 to 29 years old	1,828	294	16.1	*	*	*	*	6	0.3
30 to 34 years old	1,883	141	7.5	*	*	*	*	5	0.2
35 to 44 years old	3,387	154	4.5	*	*	7	0.2	*	*
45 to 54 years old	2,889	34	1.2	*	*	*	*	*	*
55 years old and over	5,055	23	0.5	*	*	*	*	*	*
Male									
Total	10,260	2,907	28.3	273	2.7	1,184	11.5	530	5.2
3 and 4 years old	277	101	36.6	101	36.6	*	*	*	*
5 and 6 years old	350	295	84.4	167	47.7	128	36.7	*	*
7 to 9 years old	395	380	96.2	5	1.2	375	95.0	*	*
10 to 13 years old	639	631	98.9	*	*	625	97.9	6	1.0
14 and 15 years old	291	287	98.7	*	*	43	14.9	244	83.8
16 and 17 years old	264	246	93.2	*	*	*	*	237	89.9
18 and 19 years old	316	239	75.6	*	*	*	*	37	11.5
20 and 21 years old	328	267	81.6	*	*	6	1.7	6	1.7
22 to 24 years old	414	174	41.9	*	*	*	*	*	*
25 to 29 years old	893	131	14.6	*	*	*	*	*	*
30 to 34 years old	913	74	8.1	*	*	*	*	*	*
35 to 44 years old	1,579	59	3.7	*	*	7	0.4	*	*
45 to 54 years old	1,347	11	0.8	*	*	*	*	*	*
55 years old and over	2,253	12	0.5	*	*	*	*	*	*
Female									
Total	11,295	2,970	26.3	241	2.1	1,173	10.4	510	4.5
3 and 4 years old	309	131	42.5	131	42.5	*	*	*	*
5 and 6 years old	242	220	91.1	104	43.2	116	47.9	*	*
7 to 9 years old	443	432	97.4	5	1.1	427	96.3	*	*
10 to 13 years old	614	583	95.0	*	*	575	93.7	8	1.3
14 and 15 years old	270	267	99.1	*	*	51	19.0	214	79.2
16 and 17 years old	262	249	95.1	*	*	4	1.5	237	90.6
18 and 19 years old	275	221	80.3	*	*	*	*	33	11.8

* = Quantity equals zero or rounds to zero.

Table A-1. Enrollment Status of the Population 3 Years Old and Over, by Sex, Age, Race, Hispanic Origin, Foreign Born, and Foreign-Born Parentage, October 2020— Continued

(Numbers in thousands; percent; civilian noninstitutionalized population.)

	Enrolled in school		Not enrolled in school					
	College undergraduate or graduate		Total		High school graduate		Not high school graduate	
Age, sex, race, Hispanic origin, and nativity	Number	Percent	Number	Percent	Number	Percent	Number	Percent
25 to 29 years old	117	6.4	1,726	93.5	1,654	89.6	72	3.9
30 to 34 years old	115	7.0	1,539	93.0	1,443	87.3	95	5.8
35 to 44 years old	85	3.1	2,650	96.8	2,378	86.9	273	10.0
45 to 54 years old	40	1.6	2,432	98.4	2,237	90.5	195	7.9
55 years old and over	34	0.7	4,657	99.2	3,894	82.9	763	16.2
Female								
Total	1,654	6.9	17,376	72.2	15,089	62.7	2,287	9.5
3 and 4 years old	*	*	403	54.0	*	*	403	54.0
5 and 6 years old	*	*	67	8.8	*	*	67	8.8
7 to 9 years old	*	*	67	6.1	*	*	67	6.1
10 to 13 years old	*	*	47	3.2	*	*	47	3.2
14 and 15 years old	8	1.1	8	1.1	*	*	8	1.1
16 and 17 years old	12	1.7	47	6.7	24	3.3	24	3.3
18 and 19 years old	373	53.8	189	27.3	161	23.2	28	4.1
20 and 21 years old	293	39.7	421	57.1	387	52.5	34	4.6
22 to 24 years old	284	28.1	710	70.3	691	68.4	19	1.9
25 to 29 years old	262	13.5	1,669	86.3	1,528	79.0	141	7.3
30 to 34 years old	140	7.5	1,712	92.2	1,599	86.2	112	6.0
35 to 44 years old	151	4.7	3,044	94.8	2,794	87.0	251	7.8
45 to 54 years old	92	3.1	2,837	96.5	2,624	89.2	213	7.2
55 years old and over	41	0.7	6,154	99.3	5,281	85.2	873	14.1
ASIAN ALONE OR IN COMBINATION								
Both Sexes								
Total	1,967	9.1	15,678	72.7	14,052	65.2	1,626	7.5
3 and 4 years old	*	*	354	60.3	*	*	354	60.3
5 and 6 years old	*	*	76	12.9	*	*	76	12.9
7 to 9 years old	*	*	26	3.1	*	*	26	3.1
10 to 13 years old	*	*	38	3.1	*	*	38	3.1
14 and 15 years old	2	0.4	6	1.1	*	*	6	1.1
16 and 17 years old	17	3.2	31	5.8	11	2.0	20	3.8
18 and 19 years old	391	66.1	131	22.2	109	18.4	23	3.9
20 and 21 years old	539	78.9	127	18.7	113	16.6	14	2.1
22 to 24 years old	389	44.0	492	55.6	482	54.5	10	1.1
25 to 29 years old	288	15.8	1,535	83.9	1,498	81.9	37	2.0
30 to 34 years old	136	7.2	1,742	92.5	1,693	89.9	50	2.6
35 to 44 years old	147	4.4	3,233	95.5	3,028	89.4	205	6.1
45 to 54 years old	34	1.2	2,855	98.8	2,691	93.1	164	5.7
55 years old and over	23	0.5	5,032	99.5	4,429	87.6	603	11.9
Male								
Total	920	9.0	7,353	71.7	6,655	64.9	697	6.8
3 and 4 years old	*	*	176	63.4	*	*	176	63.4
5 and 6 years old	*	*	55	15.6	*	*	55	15.6
7 to 9 years old	*	*	15	3.8	*	*	15	3.8
10 to 13 years old	*	*	7	1.1	*	*	7	1.1
14 and 15 years old	*	*	4	1.3	*	*	4	1.3
16 and 17 years old	9	3.3	18	6.8	11	4.0	7	2.8
18 and 19 years old	203	64.0	77	24.4	61	19.3	16	5.1
20 and 21 years old	256	78.1	60	18.4	53	16.2	7	2.3
22 to 24 years old	174	41.9	241	58.1	233	56.2	8	1.8
25 to 29 years old	131	14.6	763	85.4	741	83.0	21	2.4
30 to 34 years old	74	8.1	839	91.9	817	89.5	22	2.4
35 to 44 years old	52	3.3	1,520	96.3	1,423	90.1	97	6.1
45 to 54 years old	11	0.8	1,336	99.2	1,251	92.8	86	6.3
55 years old and over	12	0.5	2,241	99.5	2,065	91.7	176	7.8
Female								
Total	1,047	9.3	8,325	73.7	7,396	65.5	929	8.2
3 and 4 years old	*	*	178	57.5	*	*	178	57.5
5 and 6 years old	*	*	21	8.9	*	*	21	8.9
7 to 9 years old	*	*	11	2.6	*	*	11	2.6
10 to 13 years old	*	*	31	5.0	*	*	31	5.0
14 and 15 years old	2	0.9	3	0.9	*	*	3	0.9
16 and 17 years old	8	3.0	13	4.9	*	*	13	4.9
18 and 19 years old	188	68.5	54	19.7	47	17.3	7	2.4

* = Quantity equals zero or rounds to zero.

Table A-1. Enrollment Status of the Population 3 Years Old and Over, by Sex, Age, Race, Hispanic Origin, Foreign Born, and Foreign-Born Parentage, October 2020— *Continued*

(Numbers in thousands; percent; civilian noninstitutionalized population.)

| | | | | Enrolled in school | | | | | |
| | Population | Total | | Nursery or kindergarten | | Elementary | | High school | |
Age, sex, race, Hispanic origin, and nativity	Number	Number	Percent	Number	Percent	Number	Percent	Number	Percent
20 and 21 years old	355	288	81.1	*	*	*	*	5	1.4
22 to 24 years old	470	219	46.6	*	*	*	*	4	0.8
25 to 29 years old	935	163	17.4	*	*	*	*	6	0.6
30 to 34 years old	970	67	6.9	*	*	*	*	5	0.5
35 to 44 years old	1,808	95	5.3	*	*	*	*	*	*
45 to 54 years old	1,542	23	1.5	*	*	*	*	*	*
55 years old and over	2,802	11	0.4	*	*	*	*	*	*
HISPANIC (OF ANY RACE)									
Both Sexes									
Total	58,214	17,524	30.1	1,641	2.8	8,302	14.3	4,029	6.9
3 and 4 years old	2,046	674	32.9	674	32.9	*	*	*	*
5 and 6 years old	2,093	1,821	87.0	956	45.7	865	41.3	*	*
7 to 9 years old	3,162	2,986	94.4	11	0.4	2,975	94.1	*	*
10 to 13 years old	4,317	4,179	96.8	*	*	4,095	94.9	84	1.9
14 and 15 years old	2,115	2,075	98.1	*	*	331	15.6	1,740	82.3
16 and 17 years old	1,987	1,815	91.3	*	*	26	1.3	1,756	88.4
18 and 19 years old	2,054	1,289	62.7	*	*	*	*	359	17.5
20 and 21 years old	2,092	1,000	47.8	*	*	*	*	49	2.3
22 to 24 years old	2,722	578	21.2	*	*	*	*	*	*
25 to 29 years old	4,849	494	10.2	*	*	*	*	8	0.2
30 to 34 years old	4,598	186	4.0	*	*	*	*	7	0.1
35 to 44 years old	8,672	287	3.3	*	*	3	*	19	0.2
45 to 54 years old	7,259	89	1.2	*	*	7	0.1	3	*
55 years old and over	10,249	50	0.5	*	*	*	*	4	*
Male									
Total	29,134	8,641	29.7	838	2.9	4,298	14.8	2,069	7.1
3 and 4 years old	1,054	360	34.1	360	34.1	*	*	*	*
5 and 6 years old	1,070	938	87.6	472	44.1	466	43.6	*	*
7 to 9 years old	1,607	1,547	96.2	6	0.4	1,540	95.8	*	*
10 to 13 years old	2,217	2,133	96.2	*	*	2,112	95.2	21	0.9
14 and 15 years old	1,061	1,034	97.5	*	*	157	14.8	872	82.2
16 and 17 years old	1,040	946	91.0	*	*	15	1.4	923	88.7
18 and 19 years old	999	567	56.8	*	*	*	*	209	20.9
20 and 21 years old	1,027	452	44.0	*	*	*	*	19	1.9
22 to 24 years old	1,395	230	16.5	*	*	*	*	*	*
25 to 29 years old	2,464	214	8.7	*	*	*	*	*	*
30 to 34 years old	2,376	76	3.2	*	*	*	*	7	0.3
35 to 44 years old	4,432	93	2.1	*	*	3	0.1	10	0.2
45 to 54 years old	3,631	18	0.5	*	*	4	0.1	3	0.1
55 years old and over	4,761	33	0.7	*	*	*	*	4	0.1
Female									
Total	29,079	8,884	30.6	803	2.8	4,004	13.8	1,960	6.7
3 and 4 years old	992	314	31.7	314	31.7	*	*	*	*
5 and 6 years old	1,023	883	86.3	484	47.3	399	39.0	*	*
7 to 9 years old	1,555	1,440	92.6	5	0.3	1,435	92.2	*	*
10 to 13 years old	2,099	2,047	97.5	*	*	1,984	94.5	63	3.0
14 and 15 years old	1,054	1,041	98.7	*	*	173	16.4	868	82.3
16 and 17 years old	947	868	91.7	*	*	11	1.2	834	88.1
18 and 19 years old	1,055	721	68.4	*	*	*	*	150	14.2
20 and 21 years old	1,065	548	51.5	*	*	*	*	29	2.8
22 to 24 years old	1,327	348	26.2	*	*	*	*	*	*
25 to 29 years old	2,385	281	11.8	*	*	*	*	8	0.3
30 to 34 years old	2,221	110	4.9	*	*	*	*	*	*
35 to 44 years old	4,240	194	4.6	*	*	*	*	8	0.2
45 to 54 years old	3,628	72	2.0	*	*	3	0.1	*	*
55 years old and over	5,489	17	0.3	*	*	*	*	*	*
FOREIGN–BORN									
Both Sexes									
Total	43,835	4,336	9.9	177	0.4	1,278	2.9	888	2.0
3 and 4 years old	165	45	27.5	45	27.5	*	*	*	*
5 and 6 years old	247	217	87.7	131	53.1	86	34.6	*	*
7 to 9 years old	487	467	95.9	*	*	467	95.9	*	*

* = Quantity equals zero or rounds to zero.

Table A-1. Enrollment Status of the Population 3 Years Old and Over, by Sex, Age, Race, Hispanic Origin, Foreign Born, and Foreign-Born Parentage, October 2020—
Continued

(Numbers in thousands; percent; civilian noninstitutionalized population.)

Age, sex, race, Hispanic origin, and nativity	Enrolled in school — College undergraduate or graduate		Not enrolled in school — Total		High school graduate		Not high school graduate	
	Number	Percent	Number	Percent	Number	Percent	Number	Percent
20 and 21 years old	283	79.7	67	18.9	60	16.9	7	1.9
22 to 24 years old	215	45.8	251	53.4	249	52.9	3	0.5
25 to 29 years old	157	16.8	772	82.6	756	80.9	16	1.7
30 to 34 years old	62	6.4	903	93.1	876	90.3	28	2.8
35 to 44 years old	95	5.3	1,712	94.7	1,604	88.8	108	6.0
45 to 54 years old	23	1.5	1,518	98.5	1,440	93.4	78	5.1
55 years old and over	11	0.4	2,791	99.6	2,364	84.4	427	15.2
HISPANIC (OF ANY RACE)								
Both Sexes								
Total	3,553	6.1	40,689	69.9	29,079	50.0	11,610	19.9
3 and 4 years old	*	*	1,372	67.1	*	*	1,372	67.1
5 and 6 years old	*	*	272	13.0	*	*	272	13.0
7 to 9 years old	*	*	176	5.6	*	*	176	5.6
10 to 13 years old	*	*	137	3.2	*	*	137	3.2
14 and 15 years old	5	0.2	40	1.9	*	*	40	1.9
16 and 17 years old	32	1.6	172	8.7	43	2.2	129	6.5
18 and 19 years old	930	45.3	765	37.3	653	31.8	112	5.5
20 and 21 years old	952	46.5	1,092	52.2	914	43.7	178	8.5
22 to 24 years old	578	21.2	2,143	78.8	1,910	70.2	234	8.6
25 to 29 years old	486	10.0	4,354	89.8	3,781	78.0	573	11.8
30 to 34 years old	179	3.9	4,412	96.0	3,631	79.0	780	17.0
35 to 44 years old	266	3.1	8,385	96.7	6,267	72.3	2,119	24.4
45 to 54 years old	80	1.1	7,170	98.8	5,247	72.3	1,923	26.5
55 years old and over	46	0.4	10,200	99.5	6,634	64.7	3,566	34.8
Male								
Total	1,436	4.9	20,494	70.3	14,487	49.7	6,007	20.6
3 and 4 years old	*	*	694	65.9	*	*	694	65.9
5 and 6 years old	*	*	132	12.4	*	*	132	12.4
7 to 9 years old	*	*	61	3.8	*	*	61	3.8
10 to 13 years old	*	*	84	3.8	*	*	84	3.8
14 and 15 years old	5	0.4	26	2.5	*	*	26	2.5
16 and 17 years old	9	0.8	94	9.0	20	1.9	74	7.1
18 and 19 years old	358	35.9	432	43.2	373	37.3	59	5.9
20 and 21 years old	433	42.2	575	56.0	460	44.8	114	11.1
22 to 24 years old	230	16.5	1,165	83.5	1,017	73.0	147	10.5
25 to 29 years old	214	8.7	2,250	91.3	1,912	77.6	338	13.7
30 to 34 years old	69	2.9	2,300	96.8	1,863	78.4	437	18.4
35 to 44 years old	80	1.8	4,339	97.9	3,158	71.2	1,182	26.7
45 to 54 years old	11	0.3	3,613	99.5	2,633	72.5	981	27.0
55 years old and over	28	0.6	4,728	99.3	3,051	64.1	1,677	35.2
Female								
Total	2,116	7.3	20,196	69.4	14,593	50.2	5,603	19.3
3 and 4 years old	*	*	678	68.3	*	*	678	68.3
5 and 6 years old	*	*	140	13.7	*	*	140	13.7
7 to 9 years old	*	*	116	7.4	*	*	116	7.4
10 to 13 years old	*	*	53	2.5	*	*	53	2.5
14 and 15 years old	*	*	13	1.3	*	*	13	1.3
16 and 17 years old	24	2.5	78	8.3	24	2.5	54	5.8
18 and 19 years old	571	54.2	333	31.6	280	26.6	53	5.0
20 and 21 years old	518	48.7	517	48.5	453	42.6	64	6.0
22 to 24 years old	348	26.2	979	73.8	892	67.2	87	6.5
25 to 29 years old	273	11.4	2,104	88.2	1,869	78.4	235	9.9
30 to 34 years old	110	4.9	2,112	95.1	1,768	79.6	344	15.5
35 to 44 years old	186	4.4	4,046	95.4	3,109	73.3	937	22.1
45 to 54 years old	69	1.9	3,556	98.0	2,614	72.1	942	26.0
55 years old and over	17	0.3	5,471	99.7	3,583	65.3	1,888	34.4
FOREIGN–BORN								
Both Sexes								
Total	1,993	4.5	39,500	90.1	30,315	69.2	9,184	21.0
3 and 4 years old	*	*	120	72.5	*	*	120	72.5
5 and 6 years old	*	*	30	12.3	*	*	30	12.3
7 to 9 years old	*	*	20	4.1	*	*	20	4.1

* – Quantity equals zero or rounds to zero.

Table A-1. Enrollment Status of the Population 3 Years Old and Over, by Sex, Age, Race, Hispanic Origin, Foreign Born, and Foreign-Born Parentage, October 2020— *Continued*

(Numbers in thousands; percent; civilian noninstitutionalized population.)

| Age, sex, race, Hispanic origin, and nativity | Population | Enrolled in school | | | | | | | |
| | | Total | | Nursery or kindergarten | | Elementary | | High school | |
	Number	Number	Percent	Number	Percent	Number	Percent	Number	Percent
10 to 13 years old	710	681	95.9	*	*	673	94.8	8	1.1
14 and 15 years old	405	396	97.6	*	*	35	8.7	360	88.9
16 and 17 years old	422	372	88.1	*	*	4	0.9	348	82.5
18 and 19 years old	599	378	63.2	*	*	*	*	120	20.0
20 and 21 years old	737	378	51.3	*	*	*	*	12	1.6
22 to 24 years old	1,309	347	26.5	*	*	*	*	7	0.5
25 to 29 years old	3,194	341	10.7	*	*	*	*	14	0.4
30 to 34 years old	3,891	244	6.3	*	*	*	*	5	0.1
35 to 44 years old	8,977	299	3.3	*	*	7	0.1	7	0.1
45 to 54 years old	8,607	110	1.3	*	*	7	0.1	3	0.0
55 years old and over	14,084	61	0.4	*	*	*	*	4	0.0

Male

Age, sex, race, Hispanic origin, and nativity	Population	Total		Nursery or kindergarten		Elementary		High school	
Total	21,114	1,987	9.4	84	0.4	622	2.9	480	2.3
3 and 4 years old	97	17	17.9	17	17.9	*	*	*	*
5 and 6 years old	118	101	85.7	66	56.0	35	29.6	*	*
7 to 9 years old	221	214	97.0	*	*	214	97.0	*	*
10 to 13 years old	364	344	94.5	*	*	344	94.5	*	*
14 and 15 years old	216	208	96.2	*	*	14	6.5	194	89.7
16 and 17 years old	222	199	89.7	*	*	4	1.7	184	82.9
18 and 19 years old	334	200	59.8	*	*	*	*	84	25.3
20 and 21 years old	307	144	46.8	*	*	*	*	3	1.0
22 to 24 years old	631	121	19.2	*	*	*	*	3	0.4
25 to 29 years old	1,558	161	10.3	*	*	*	*	*	*
30 to 34 years old	1,960	109	5.6	*	*	*	*	*	*
35 to 44 years old	4,354	97	2.2	*	*	7	0.2	4	0.1
45 to 54 years old	4,240	40	1.0	*	*	4	0.1	3	0.1
55 years old and over	6,491	31	0.5	*	*	*	*	4	0.1

Female

Age, sex, race, Hispanic origin, and nativity	Population	Total		Nursery or kindergarten		Elementary		High school	
Total	22,722	2,348	10.3	93	0.4	656	2.9	408	1.8
3 and 4 years old	68	28	41.4	28	41.4	*	*	*	*
5 and 6 years old	129	116	89.6	65	50.4	51	39.2	*	*
7 to 9 years old	266	253	95.0	*	*	253	95.0	*	*
10 to 13 years old	346	337	97.4	*	*	329	95.1	8	2.3
14 and 15 years old	189	188	99.2	*	*	21	11.2	166	88.0
16 and 17 years old	200	172	86.3	*	*	*	*	164	81.9
18 and 19 years old	266	179	67.4	*	*	*	*	36	13.4
20 and 21 years old	430	235	54.6	*	*	*	*	9	2.0
22 to 24 years old	677	225	33.3	*	*	*	*	4	0.6
25 to 29 years old	1,637	180	11.0	*	*	*	*	14	0.8
30 to 34 years old	1,931	135	7.0	*	*	*	*	5	0.2
35 to 44 years old	4,623	201	4.4	*	*	*	*	3	0.1
45 to 54 years old	4,367	70	1.6	*	*	3	0.1	*	*
55 years old and over	7,593	30	0.4	*	*	*	*	*	*

CHILDREN OF FOREIGN–BORN PARENTS

Both Sexes

Age, sex, race, Hispanic origin, and nativity	Population	Total		Nursery or kindergarten		Elementary		High school	
Total	81,400	20,309	25.0	1,721	2.1	8,511	10.5	4,522	5.6
3 and 4 years old	1,986	708	35.6	708	35.6	*	*	*	*
5 and 6 years old	2,079	1,853	89.1	990	47.6	863	41.5	*	*
7 to 9 years old	3,093	2,949	95.3	23	0.8	2,925	94.6	*	*
10 to 13 years old	4,572	4,411	96.5	*	*	4,336	94.9	74	1.6
14 and 15 years old	2,288	2,236	97.7	*	*	351	15.3	1,877	82.0
16 and 17 years old	2,327	2,150	92.4	*	*	19	0.8	2,066	88.8
18 and 19 years old	2,432	1,727	71.0	*	*	*	*	387	15.9
20 and 21 years old	2,379	1,410	59.3	*	*	*	*	45	1.9
22 to 24 years old	3,306	916	27.7	*	*	*	*	26	0.8
25 to 29 years old	6,371	787	12.3	*	*	*	*	14	0.2
30 to 34 years old	6,522	413	6.3	*	*	4	0.1	10	0.1
35 to 44 years old	12,658	485	3.8	*	*	7	0.1	15	0.1
45 to 54 years old	11,307	167	1.5	*	*	7	0.1	3	0.0
55 years old and over	20,079	99	0.5	*	*	*	*	4	0.0

Male

Age, sex, race, Hispanic origin, and nativity	Population	Total		Nursery or kindergarten		Elementary		High school	
Total	39,671	9,882	24.9	853	2.2	4,441	11.2	2,279	5.7
3 and 4 years old	985	317	32.2	317	32.2	*	*	*	*
5 and 6 years old	1,126	980	87.0	518	46.0	462	41.0	*	*

* = Quantity equals zero or rounds to zero.

Table A-1. Enrollment Status of the Population 3 Years Old and Over, by Sex, Age, Race, Hispanic Origin, Foreign Born, and Foreign-Born Parentage, October 2020— *Continued*

(Numbers in thousands; percent; civilian noninstitutionalized population.)

Age, sex, race, Hispanic origin, and nativity	Enrolled in school — College undergraduate or graduate		Not enrolled in school — Total		High school graduate		Not high school graduate	
	Number	Percent	Number	Percent	Number	Percent	Number	Percent
10 to 13 years old	*	*	29	4.1	*	*	29	4.1
14 and 15 years old	*	*	10	2.4	*	*	10	2.4
16 and 17 years old	20	4.7	50	11.9	17	4.1	33	7.8
18 and 19 years old	258	43.1	221	36.8	173	28.9	48	8.0
20 and 21 years old	367	49.8	358	48.7	282	38.3	76	10.3
22 to 24 years old	340	25.9	962	73.5	809	61.8	153	11.7
25 to 29 years old	327	10.2	2,854	89.3	2,430	76.1	424	13.3
30 to 34 years old	240	6.2	3,647	93.7	3,057	78.6	590	15.2
35 to 44 years old	285	3.2	8,678	96.7	6,739	75.1	1,939	21.6
45 to 54 years old	100	1.2	8,497	98.7	6,591	76.6	1,906	22.1
55 years old and over	56	0.4	14,023	99.6	10,217	72.5	3,807	27.0
Male								
Total	802	3.8	19,126	90.6	14,503	68.7	4,624	21.9
3 and 4 years old	*	*	80	82.1	*	*	80	82.1
5 and 6 years old	*	*	17	14.3	*	*	17	14.3
7 to 9 years old	*	*	7	3.0	*	*	7	3.0
10 to 13 years old	*	*	20	5.5	*	*	20	5.5
14 and 15 years old	*	*	8	3.8	*	*	8	3.8
16 and 17 years old	11	5.0	23	10.3	8	3.4	15	6.9
18 and 19 years old	115	34.5	134	40.2	103	30.8	31	9.4
20 and 21 years old	141	45.8	163	53.2	117	38.1	46	15.1
22 to 24 years old	118	18.7	510	80.8	403	63.8	108	17.1
25 to 29 years old	161	10.3	1,397	89.7	1,157	74.3	240	15.4
30 to 34 years old	109	5.6	1,851	94.4	1,530	78.1	321	16.4
35 to 44 years old	87	2.0	4,257	97.8	3,212	73.8	1,045	24.0
45 to 54 years old	33	0.8	4,200	99.0	3,219	75.9	981	23.1
55 years old and over	27	0.4	6,460	99.5	4,755	73.2	1,705	26.3
Female								
Total	1,191	5.2	20,373	89.7	15,813	69.6	4,561	20.1
3 and 4 years old	*	*	40	58.6	*	*	40	58.6
5 and 6 years old	*	*	13	10.4	*	*	13	10.4
7 to 9 years old	*	*	13	5.0	*	*	13	5.0
10 to 13 years old	*	*	9	2.6	*	*	9	2.6
14 and 15 years old	*	*	1	0.8	*	*	1	0.8
16 and 17 years old	9	4.4	27	13.7	10	4.8	18	8.9
18 and 19 years old	143	54.0	87	32.6	70	26.4	16	6.2
20 and 21 years old	226	52.6	195	45.4	165	38.4	30	7.0
22 to 24 years old	221	32.7	452	66.7	407	60.1	45	6.7
25 to 29 years old	166	10.1	1,457	89.0	1,273	77.8	184	11.2
30 to 34 years old	130	6.8	1,796	93.0	1,527	79.1	269	13.9
35 to 44 years old	198	4.3	4,421	95.6	3,527	76.3	895	19.4
45 to 54 years old	67	1.5	4,297	98.4	3,372	77.2	925	21.2
55 years old and over	30	0.4	7,564	99.6	5,462	71.9	2,102	27.7
CHILDREN OF FOREIGN–BORN PARENTS								
Both Sexes								
Total	5,555	6.8	61,090	75.0	48,838	60.0	12,253	15.1
3 and 4 years old	*	*	1,278	64.4	*	*	1,278	64.4
5 and 6 years old	*	*	227	10.9	*	*	227	10.9
7 to 9 years old	*	*	145	4.7	*	*	145	4.7
10 to 13 years old	*	*	161	3.5	*	*	161	3.5
14 and 15 years old	8	0.4	52	2.3	*	*	52	2.3
16 and 17 years old	65	2.8	176	7.6	52	2.2	124	5.3
18 and 19 years old	1,340	55.1	705	29.0	589	24.2	117	4.8
20 and 21 years old	1,364	57.4	969	40.7	821	34.5	148	6.2
22 to 24 years old	890	26.9	2,390	72.3	2,144	64.8	246	7.4
25 to 29 years old	773	12.1	5,584	87.7	5,023	78.8	562	8.8
30 to 34 years old	399	6.1	6,109	93.7	5,342	81.9	767	11.8
35 to 44 years old	463	3.7	12,173	96.2	9,985	78.9	2,188	17.3
45 to 54 years old	157	1.4	11,140	98.5	9,112	80.6	2,028	17.9
55 years old and over	95	0.5	19,980	99.5	15,771	78.5	4,209	21.0
Male								
Total	2,308	5.8	29,789	75.1	23,568	59.4	6,221	15.7
3 and 4 years old	*	*	668	67.8	*	*	668	67.8
5 and 6 years old	*	*	146	13.0	*	*	146	13.0

* = Quantity equals zero or rounds to zero.

Table A-1. Enrollment Status of the Population 3 Years Old and Over, by Sex, Age, Race, Hispanic Origin, Foreign Born, and Foreign-Born Parentage, October 2020— *Continued*

(Numbers in thousands; percent; civilian noninstitutionalized population.)

| Age, sex, race, Hispanic origin, and nativity | Population | Enrolled in school | | | | | | | |
| | | Total | | Nursery or kindergarten | | Elementary | | High school | |
	Number	Number	Percent	Number	Percent	Number	Percent	Number	Percent
7 to 9 years old	1,537	1,496	97.3	18	1.2	1,478	96.1	*	*
10 to 13 years old	2,416	2,327	96.3	*	*	2,308	95.5	19	0.8
14 and 15 years old	1,134	1,095	96.5	*	*	171	15.1	922	81.3
16 and 17 years old	1,200	1,107	92.2	*	*	12	1.0	1,063	88.6
18 and 19 years old	1,206	781	64.7	*	*	*	*	240	19.9
20 and 21 years old	1,108	616	55.6	*	*	*	*	14	1.3
22 to 24 years old	1,606	339	21.1	*	*	*	*	3	0.2
25 to 29 years old	3,159	352	11.1	*	*	*	*	*	*
30 to 34 years old	3,204	192	6.0	*	*	*	*	5	0.2
35 to 44 years old	6,157	162	2.6	*	*	7	0.1	7	0.1
45 to 54 years old	5,585	68	1.2	*	*	4	0.1	3	0.1
55 years old and over	9,248	52	0.6	*	*	*	*	4	0.0
Female									
Total	41,729	10,427	25.0	868	2.1	4,070	9.8	2,242	5.4
3 and 4 years old	1,001	391	39.0	391	39.0	*	*	*	*
5 and 6 years old	954	873	91.5	472	49.5	401	42.0	*	*
7 to 9 years old	1,556	1,452	93.4	5	0.3	1,447	93.0	*	*
10 to 13 years old	2,156	2,084	96.7	*	*	2,028	94.1	55	2.6
14 and 15 years old	1,153	1,141	98.9	*	*	179	15.5	955	82.8
16 and 17 years old	1,127	1,044	92.6	*	*	7	0.6	1,004	89.1
18 and 19 years old	1,226	946	77.2	*	*	*	*	148	12.0
20 and 21 years old	1,271	793	62.4	*	*	*	*	31	2.4
22 to 24 years old	1,701	577	33.9	*	*	*	*	24	1.4
25 to 29 years old	3,212	435	13.5	*	*	*	*	14	0.4
30 to 34 years old	3,318	222	6.7	*	*	4	0.1	5	0.1
35 to 44 years old	6,501	323	5.0	*	*	*	*	8	0.1
45 to 54 years old	5,723	100	1.7	*	*	3	0.0	*	*
55 years old and over	10,832	47	0.4	*	*	*	*	*	*

* = Quantity equals zero or rounds to zero.

Table A-1. Enrollment Status of the Population 3 Years Old and Over, by Sex, Age, Race, Hispanic Origin, Foreign Born, and Foreign-Born Parentage, October 2020— *Continued*

(Numbers in thousands; percent; civilian noninstitutionalized population.)

Age, sex, race, Hispanic origin, and nativity	Enrolled in school — College undergraduate or graduate		Not enrolled in school — Total		High school graduate		Not high school graduate	
	Number	Percent	Number	Percent	Number	Percent	Number	Percent
7 to 9 years old	*	*	41	2.7	*	*	41	2.7
10 to 13 years old	*	*	89	3.7	*	*	89	3.7
14 and 15 years old	1	0.1	40	3.5	*	*	40	3.5
16 and 17 years old	33	2.7	93	7.8	31	2.6	62	5.2
18 and 19 years old	541	44.9	425	35.3	354	29.3	72	5.9
20 and 21 years old	602	54.3	491	44.4	398	35.9	93	8.4
22 to 24 years old	336	20.9	1,267	78.9	1,115	69.4	152	9.5
25 to 29 years old	352	11.1	2,808	88.9	2,479	78.5	328	10.4
30 to 34 years old	187	5.8	3,012	94.0	2,584	80.6	428	13.4
35 to 44 years old	148	2.4	5,996	97.4	4,819	78.3	1,177	19.1
45 to 54 years old	60	1.1	5,517	98.8	4,484	80.3	1,033	18.5
55 years old and over	48	0.5	9,195	99.4	7,304	79.0	1,892	20.5
Female								
Total	3,247	7.8	31,301	75.0	25,270	60.6	6,031	14.5
3 and 4 years old	*	*	610	61.0	*	*	610	61.0
5 and 6 years old	*	*	81	8.5	*	*	81	8.5
7 to 9 years old	*	*	103	6.6	*	*	103	6.6
10 to 13 years old	*	*	72	3.3	*	*	72	3.3
14 and 15 years old	7	0.6	12	1.1	*	*	12	1.1
16 and 17 years old	32	2.9	83	7.4	21	1.9	62	5.5
18 and 19 years old	799	65.1	280	22.8	235	19.1	45	3.7
20 and 21 years old	763	60.0	478	37.6	423	33.3	55	4.3
22 to 24 years old	554	32.6	1,123	66.1	1,029	60.5	94	5.5
25 to 29 years old	421	13.1	2,777	86.5	2,543	79.2	233	7.3
30 to 34 years old	212	6.4	3,097	93.3	2,758	83.1	339	10.2
35 to 44 years old	315	4.8	6,177	95.0	5,166	79.5	1,011	15.6
45 to 54 years old	97	1.7	5,623	98.3	4,627	80.9	996	17.4
55 years old and over	47	0.4	10,785	99.6	8,467	78.2	2,318	21.4

* = Quantity equals zero or rounds to zero.

Table A-2. Single Grade of Enrollment and High School Graduation Status for Population 3 Years Old and Over, by Sex, Age (Single Years for 3 to 24 Years), Race, and Hispanic Origin, October 2020

(Numbers in thousands; percent; civilian noninstitutionalized population.)

Age, sex, race, and Hispanic origin	Population[1]	Enrolled				Enrolled								
									Elementary grades					
		Number	Percent	Nursery	Kinder-garten	1	2	3	4	5	6	7	8
ALL RACES														
Both Sexes														
Total	313,928	73,222	23.3	3,545	3,698	4,072	3,814	4,073	3,878	4,009	4,056	4,317	3,827
3 years old	3,847	1,143	29.7	1,074	69	*	*	*	*	*	*	*	*
4 years old	4,066	2,047	50.3	1,813	234	*	*	*	*	*	*	*	*
5 years old	3,945	3,327	84.3	601	2,580	113	33	*	*	*	*	*	*
6 years old	4,201	3,941	93.8	57	764	2,964	126	29	*	*	*	*	*
7 years old	3,973	3,755	94.5	*	51	913	2,586	186	18	*	*	*	*
8 years old	4,114	3,930	95.5	*	*	70	993	2,726	126	14	*	*	*
9 years old	3,994	3,859	96.6	*	*	10	70	1,013	2,591	150	25	*	*
10 years old	4,060	3,916	96.5	*	*	*	6	117	1,018	2,651	116	8	*
11 years old	4,075	3,954	97.1	*	*	*	*	2	115	1,031	2,677	107	22
12 years old	4,315	4,208	97.5	*	*	*	*	*	10	128	1,045	2,834	168
13 years old	4,074	3,951	97.0	*	*	*	*	*	*	34	130	1,136	2,486
14 years old	4,136	4,051	97.9	*	*	*	*	*	*	*	43	142	1,038
15 years old	4,204	4,108	97.7	*	*	*	*	*	*	*	*	34	62
16 years old	4,122	3,856	93.5	*	*	*	*	*	*	*	*	24	36
17 years old	4,187	3,815	91.1	*	*	*	*	*	*	*	*	2	11
18 years old	4,185	2,959	70.7	*	*	*	*	*	*	*	*	5	*
19 years old	4,057	2,524	62.2	*	*	*	*	*	*	*	*	*	*
20 years old	4,512	2,564	56.8	*	*	*	*	*	*	*	*	6	*
21 years old	4,241	2,058	48.5	*	*	*	*	*	*	*	*	*	*
22 years old	4,003	1,415	35.3	*	*	*	*	*	*	*	*	*	*
23 years old	4,019	936	23.3	*	*	*	*	*	*	*	*	8	*
24 years old	4,143	885	21.4	*	*	*	*	*	*	*	*	*	*
25 to 29 years old	22,473	2,366	10.5	*	*	*	*	*	*	*	4	*	*
30 to 34 years old	22,394	1,301	5.8	*	*	*	*	*	*	*	8	*	*
35 to 39 years old	21,409	791	3.7	*	*	*	*	*	*	*	*	4	*
40 to 44 years old	20,103	590	2.9	*	*	*	*	*	*	*	3	1	4
45 to 49 years old	19,559	371	1.9	*	*	*	*	*	*	*	*	3	*
50 to 54 years old	20,228	290	1.4	*	*	*	*	*	*	*	*	4	*
55 to 59 years old	21,174	142	0.7	*	*	*	*	*	*	*	1	*	*
60 to 64 years old	20,999	109	0.5	*	*	*	*	*	*	*	4	*	*
65 years and over	55,116	61	0.1	*	*	*	*	*	*	*	*	*	*
Male														
Total	153,256	35,899	23.4	1,762	1,878	2,142	1,834	2,174	1,954	2,056	2,082	2,276	1,972
3 years old	1,953	540	27.7	518	23	*	*	*	*	*	*	*	*
4 years old	2,062	1,017	49.3	893	124	*	*	*	*	*	*	*	*
5 years old	2,032	1,728	85.0	326	1,322	61	19	*	*	*	*	*	*
6 years old	2,172	2,039	93.9	25	376	1,556	63	19	*	*	*	*	*
7 years old	1,992	1,875	94.1	*	33	485	1,232	116	8	*	*	*	*
8 years old	2,058	1,977	96.1	*	*	40	480	1,383	63	10	*	*	*
9 years old	2,088	2,033	97.4	*	*	*	35	574	1,318	88	18	*	*
10 years old	2,039	1,974	96.8	*	*	*	5	80	488	1,329	69	3	*
11 years old	2,111	2,036	96.5	*	*	*	*	2	74	561	1,337	58	5
12 years old	2,240	2,175	97.1	*	*	*	*	*	3	59	554	1,462	88
13 years old	2,041	1,973	96.7	*	*	*	*	*	*	10	66	601	1,242
14 years old	2,062	2,007	97.3	*	*	*	*	*	*	*	23	89	566
15 years old	2,191	2,125	97.0	*	*	*	*	*	*	*	*	21	38
16 years old	2,073	1,923	92.8	*	*	*	*	*	*	*	*	16	19
17 years old	2,143	1,944	90.7	*	*	*	*	*	*	*	*	1	11
18 years old	2,147	1,481	69.0	*	*	*	*	*	*	*	*	4	*
19 years old	2,001	1,086	54.3	*	*	*	*	*	*	*	*	*	*
20 years old	2,258	1,165	51.6	*	*	*	*	*	*	*	*	6	*
21 years old	2,177	1,021	46.9	*	*	*	*	*	*	*	*	*	*
22 years old	1,962	628	32.0	*	*	*	*	*	*	*	*	*	*
23 years old	2,081	431	20.7	*	*	*	*	*	*	*	*	8	*
24 years old	1,966	332	16.9	*	*	*	*	*	*	*	*	*	*
25 to 29 years old	11,257	939	8.3	*	*	*	*	*	*	*	4	*	*
30 to 34 years old	11,146	601	5.4	*	*	*	*	*	*	*	4	*	*
35 to 39 years old	10,568	312	3.0	*	*	*	*	*	*	*	*	3	*
40 to 44 years old	9,873	217	2.2	*	*	*	*	*	*	*	3	*	4
45 to 49 years old	9,559	101	1.1	*	*	*	*	*	*	*	*	*	*
50 to 54 years old	9,897	91	0.9	*	*	*	*	*	*	*	*	4	*
55 to 59 years old	10,274	57	0.6	*	*	*	*	*	*	*	1	*	*

* = Quantity zero or rounds to zero.

Table A-2. Single Grade of Enrollment and High School Graduation Status for Population 3 Years Old and Over, by Sex, Age (Single Years for 3 to 24 Years), Race, and Hispanic Origin, October 2020—*Continued*

(Numbers in thousands; percent; civilian noninstitutionalized population.)

Age, sex, race, and Hispanic origin	Enrolled – High school 9	10	11	12	Undergraduate college 1	2	3	4	Graduate school 1	2+	Not enrolled H.S. grad	Not grad	Not enrolled Number	Percent
ALL RACES														
Both Sexes														
Total	4,019	4,287	3,674	4,279	4,060	3,864	3,376	2,525	1,416	2,433	212,261	28,445	240,706	76.7
3 years old	*	*	*	*	*	*	*	*	*	*	*	2,705	2,705	70.3
4 years old	*	*	*	*	*	*	*	*	*	*	*	2,019	2,019	49.7
5 years old	*	*	*	*	*	*	*	*	*	*	*	617	617	15.7
6 years old	*	*	*	*	*	*	*	*	*	*	*	260	260	6.2
7 years old	*	*	*	*	*	*	*	*	*	*	*	218	218	5.5
8 years old	*	*	*	*	*	*	*	*	*	*	*	184	184	4.5
9 years old	*	*	*	*	*	*	*	*	*	*	*	135	135	3.4
10 years old	*	*	*	*	*	*	*	*	*	*	*	144	144	3.5
11 years old	*	*	*	*	*	*	*	*	*	*	*	120	120	2.9
12 years old	23	*	*	*	*	*	*	*	*	*	*	107	107	2.5
13 years old	125	40	*	*	*	*	*	*	*	*	*	123	123	3.0
14 years old	2,570	238	20	*	*	*	*	*	*	*	*	85	85	2.1
15 years old	1,133	2,520	278	42	13	*	9	*	16	*	*	96	96	2.3
16 years old	82	1,202	2,206	284	10	*	*	*	12	*	36	230	266	6.5
17 years old	17	195	979	2,501	86	11	6	*	7	*	129	242	371	8.9
18 years old	9	24	134	1,044	1,598	116	20	*	7	3	1,002	224	1,226	29.3
19 years old	1	19	13	196	861	1,175	217	23	12	6	1,323	209	1,533	37.8
20 years old	12	11	4	68	369	982	973	117	21	*	1,705	243	1,948	43.2
21 years old	7	*	11	39	147	423	593	711	34	92	1,968	215	2,184	51.5
22 years old	6	4	*	13	133	184	322	491	156	106	2,441	147	2,588	64.7
23 years old	8	*	*	16	87	98	192	228	134	164	2,810	273	3,083	76.7
24 years old	*	*	*	15	58	126	152	179	181	174	3,063	194	3,257	78.6
25 to 29 years old	4	*	7	10	238	294	332	361	350	767	18,833	1,274	20,107	89.5
30 to 34 years old	*	13	*	12	155	163	239	156	178	378	19,676	1,416	21,093	94.2
35 to 39 years old	7	4	*	5	106	111	99	72	98	285	18,781	1,837	20,618	96.3
40 to 44 years old	1	12	8	11	64	67	103	86	60	172	17,639	1,875	19,513	97.1
45 to 49 years old	*	5	6	14	73	41	44	39	46	101	17,577	1,611	19,188	98.1
50 to 54 years old	8	*	4	4	31	46	26	32	55	79	18,146	1,792	19,938	98.6
55 to 59 years old	4	*	*	*	5	17	19	13	20	63	19,082	1,951	21,033	99.3
60 to 64 years old	*	*	4	3	20	6	16	12	21	23	18,992	1,899	20,891	99.5
65 years and over	1	*	*	*	6	5	13	5	9	22	49,059	5,996	55,055	99.9
Male														
Total	1,982	2,140	1,890	2,179	1,816	1,699	1,494	1,058	549	960	102,727	14,630	117,357	76.6
3 years old	*	*	*	*	*	*	*	*	*	*	*	1,412	1,412	72.3
4 years old	*	*	*	*	*	*	*	*	*	*	*	1,045	1,045	50.7
5 years old	*	*	*	*	*	*	*	*	*	*	*	304	304	15.0
6 years old	*	*	*	*	*	*	*	*	*	*	*	133	133	6.1
7 years old	*	*	*	*	*	*	*	*	*	*	*	117	117	5.9
8 years old	*	*	*	*	*	*	*	*	*	*	*	81	81	3.9
9 years old	*	*	*	*	*	*	*	*	*	*	*	55	55	2.6
10 years old	*	*	*	*	*	*	*	*	*	*	*	65	65	3.2
11 years old	*	*	*	*	*	*	*	*	*	*	*	74	74	3.5
12 years old	10	*	*	*	*	*	*	*	*	*	*	64	64	2.9
13 years old	40	14	*	*	*	*	*	*	*	*	*	68	68	3.3
14 years old	1,220	103	7	*	*	*	*	*	*	*	*	55	55	2.7
15 years old	622	1,247	156	16	11	*	9	*	4	*	*	66	66	3.0
16 years old	51	638	1,049	131	6	*	*	*	12	*	18	132	150	7.2
17 years old	5	83	556	1,241	40	*	*	*	7	*	69	129	199	9.3
18 years old	9	15	91	594	713	52	4	*	*	*	565	100	666	31.0
19 years old	1	18	10	115	400	455	78	3	3	3	777	138	915	45.7
20 years old	6	11	*	33	171	471	405	49	13	*	941	153	1,094	48.4
21 years old	1	*	6	16	76	224	333	297	11	57	1,022	134	1,156	53.1
22 years old	*	*	*	2	74	85	135	229	49	55	1,245	89	1,334	68.0
23 years old	*	*	*	11	37	50	98	114	47	65	1,483	167	1,650	79.3
24 years old	*	*	*	*	29	60	65	77	69	32	1,510	124	1,633	83.1
25 to 29 years old	*	*	2	1	90	115	141	152	129	304	9,620	699	10,318	91.7
30 to 34 years old	*	8	*	0	09	79	128	50	79	177	9,804	741	10,545	94.6
35 to 39 years old	3	4	*	*	35	48	49	34	39	98	9,261	995	10,256	97.0
40 to 44 years old	1	*	8	4	21	33	25	27	17	75	8,598	1,057	9,656	97.8
45 to 49 years old	*	*	1	3	25	12	13	3	25	18	8,624	834	9,458	98.9
50 to 54 years old	8	*	*	1	9	8	3	12	21	25	8,853	953	9,806	99.1
55 to 59 years old	4	*	*	*	4	5	2	1	9	30	9,181	1,036	10,217	99.4

* = Quantity zero or rounds to zero.

Table A-2. Single Grade of Enrollment and High School Graduation Status for Population 3 Years Old and Over, by Sex, Age (Single Years for 3 to 24 Years), Race, and Hispanic Origin, October 2020—*Continued*

(Numbers in thousands; percent; civilian noninstitutionalized population.)

						Enrolled								
		Enrolled			Kinder-	Elementary grades								
Age, sex, race, and Hispanic origin	Population¹	Number	Percent	Nursery	garten	1	2	3	4	5	6	7	8
60 to 64 years old	10,052	37	0.4	*	*	*	*	*	*	*	4	*	*
65 years and over	24,784	35	0.1	*	*	*	*	*	*	*	*	*	*
Female													
Total	160,671	37,323	23.2	1,783	1,820	1,930	1,980	1,899	1,925	1,953	1,974	2,041	1,854
3 years old	1,895	602	31.8	556	46	*	*	*	*	*	*	*	*
4 years old	2,004	1,030	51.4	920	110	*	*	*	*	*	*	*	*
5 years old	1,913	1,600	83.6	275	1,258	53	14	*	*	*	*	*	*
6 years old	2,029	1,902	93.7	32	388	1,408	62	11	*	*	*	*	*
7 years old	1,981	1,880	94.9	*	18	428	1,354	70	10	*	*	*	*
8 years old	2,056	1,953	95.0	*	*	31	512	1,343	64	4	*	*	*
9 years old	1,906	1,826	95.8	*	*	10	35	439	1,272	62	7	*	*
10 years old	2,021	1,942	96.1	*	*	*	1	37	530	1,323	47	4	*
11 years old	1,964	1,918	97.7	*	*	*	*	*	41	470	1,340	50	17
12 years old	2,076	2,033	97.9	*	*	*	*	*	7	69	491	1,372	80
13 years old	2,032	1,978	97.3	*	*	*	*	*	*	24	64	535	1,244
14 years old	2,075	2,044	98.5	*	*	*	*	*	*	*	20	53	473
15 years old	2,013	1,983	98.5	*	*	*	*	*	*	*	*	14	24
16 years old	2,049	1,933	94.3	*	*	*	*	*	*	*	*	7	17
17 years old	2,044	1,871	91.5	*	*	*	*	*	*	*	*	1	*
18 years old	2,038	1,478	72.5	*	*	*	*	*	*	*	*	*	*
19 years old	2,056	1,439	70.0	*	*	*	*	*	*	*	*	*	*
20 years old	2,253	1,399	62.1	*	*	*	*	*	*	*	*	*	*
21 years old	2,064	1,036	50.2	*	*	*	*	*	*	*	*	*	*
22 years old	2,040	786	38.5	*	*	*	*	*	*	*	*	*	*
23 years old	1,938	505	26.0	*	*	*	*	*	*	*	*	*	*
24 years old	2,177	553	25.4	*	*	*	*	*	*	*	*	*	*
25 to 29 years old	11,216	1,427	12.7	*	*	*	*	*	*	*	*	*	*
30 to 34 years old	11,248	700	6.2	*	*	*	*	*	*	*	4	*	*
35 to 39 years old	10,841	479	4.4	*	*	*	*	*	*	*	*	1	*
40 to 44 years old	10,231	373	3.6	*	*	*	*	*	*	*	*	1	*
45 to 49 years old	10,000	270	2.7	*	*	*	*	*	*	*	*	3	*
50 to 54 years old	10,331	199	1.9	*	*	*	*	*	*	*	*	*	*
55 to 59 years old	10,900	85	0.8	*	*	*	*	*	*	*	*	*	*
60 to 64 years old	10,947	71	0.7	*	*	*	*	*	*	*	*	*	*
65 years and over	30,333	27	0.1	*	*	*	*	*	*	*	*	*	*
WHITE ALONE NON-HISPANIC													
Both Sexes													
Total	188,296	37,264	19.8	1,900	1,881	1,982	1,919	1,990	1,952	1,909	2,019	2,175	1,855
3 years old	1,926	667	34.6	618	49	*	*	*	*	*	*	*	*
4 years old	1,956	1,016	51.9	920	96	*	*	*	*	*	*	*	*
5 years old	1,988	1,721	86.6	339	1,285	77	19	*	*	*	*	*	*
6 years old	2,015	1,891	93.8	23	426	1,396	34	11	*	*	*	*	*
7 years old	1,993	1,889	94.8	*	26	471	1,304	72	16	*	*	*	*
8 years old	1,991	1,907	95.8	*	*	38	514	1,304	49	3	*	*	*
9 years old	2,006	1,942	96.8	*	*	*	42	537	1,292	60	10	*	*
10 years old	2,018	1,944	96.3	*	*	*	5	64	538	1,290	39	8	*
11 years old	1,954	1,902	97.3	*	*	*	*	2	56	492	1,307	36	8
12 years old	2,133	2,075	97.2	*	*	*	*	*	*	40	581	1,387	66
13 years old	2,001	1,943	97.1	*	*	*	*	*	*	25	47	622	1,181
14 years old	2,102	2,053	97.7	*	*	*	*	*	*	*	20	68	559
15 years old	2,118	2,048	96.7	*	*	*	*	*	*	*	*	23	23
16 years old	2,184	2,058	94.2	*	*	*	*	*	*	*	*	14	14
17 years old	2,176	1,997	91.8	*	*	*	*	*	*	*	*	2	4
18 years old	2,072	1,499	72.4	*	*	*	*	*	*	*	*	5	*
19 years old	2,184	1,327	60.8	*	*	*	*	*	*	*	*	*	*
20 years old	2,250	1,359	60.4	*	*	*	*	*	*	*	*	*	*
21 years old	2,235	1,119	50.1	*	*	*	*	*	*	*	*	*	*
22 years old	2,110	759	36.0	*	*	*	*	*	*	*	*	*	*
23 years old	2,310	548	23.7	*	*	*	*	*	*	*	*	8	*
24 years old	2,173	450	20.7	*	*	*	*	*	*	*	*	*	*
25 to 29 years old	12,025	1,204	10.0	*	*	*	*	*	*	*	4	*	*
30 to 34 years old	12,382	711	5.7	*	*	*	*	*	*	*	8	*	*
35 to 39 years old	12,060	403	3.3	*	*	*	*	*	*	*	*	1	*
40 to 44 years old	11,407	297	2.6	*	*	*	*	*	*	*	*	1	*

* = Quantity zero or rounds to zero.

Table A-2. Single Grade of Enrollment and High School Graduation Status for Population 3 Years Old and Over, by Sex, Age (Single Years for 3 to 24 Years), Race, and Hispanic Origin, October 2020—*Continued*

(Numbers in thousands; percent; civilian noninstitutionalized population.)

Age, sex, race, and Hispanic origin	Enrolled										Not enrolled		Not enrolled	
	High school				Undergraduate college				Graduate school		H.S. grad	Not grad		
	9	10	11	12	1	2	3	4	1	2+			Number	Percent
60 to 64 years old	*	*	4	3	4	*	7	4	11	1	9,016	999	10,015	99.6
65 years and over	1	*	*	*	1	3	*	5	4	20	22,139	2,610	24,749	99.9
Female														
Total	2,038	2,147	1,784	2,100	2,244	2,165	1,882	1,467	867	1,472	109,534	13,814	123,348	76.8
3 years old	*	*	*	*	*	*	*	*	*	*	*	1,293	1,293	68.2
4 years old	*	*	*	*	*	*	*	*	*	*	*	974	974	48.6
5 years old	*	*	*	*	*	*	*	*	*	*	*	314	314	16.4
6 years old	*	*	*	*	*	*	*	*	*	*	*	127	127	6.3
7 years old	*	*	*	*	*	*	*	*	*	*	*	101	101	5.1
8 years old	*	*	*	*	*	*	*	*	*	*	*	103	103	5.0
9 years old	*	*	*	*	*	*	*	*	*	*	*	81	81	4.2
10 years old	*	*	*	*	*	*	*	*	*	*	*	78	78	3.9
11 years old	*	*	*	*	*	*	*	*	*	*	*	46	46	2.3
12 years old	13	*	*	*	*	*	*	*	*	*	*	43	43	2.1
13 years old	85	25	*	*	*	*	*	*	*	*	*	55	55	2.7
14 years old	1,351	135	13	*	*	*	*	*	*	*	*	30	30	1.5
15 years old	511	1,273	122	26	2	*	*	*	11	*	*	29	29	1.5
16 years old	31	565	1,156	153	4	*	*	*	*	*	18	98	117	5.7
17 years old	12	112	422	1,201	46	11	6	*	*	*	60	113	173	8.5
18 years old	*	10	43	450	885	64	15	*	7	3	436	124	560	27.5
19 years old	*	2	3	81	462	720	139	20	8	3	546	71	617	30.0
20 years old	7	*	4	34	198	511	568	68	9	*	764	90	854	37.9
21 years old	7	*	5	23	70	199	261	414	23	35	946	82	1,028	49.8
22 years old	6	4	*	11	59	99	187	263	108	51	1,195	58	1,254	61.5
23 years old	8	*	*	5	50	48	94	114	87	99	1,327	106	1,433	74.0
24 years old	*	*	*	15	29	67	87	101	112	142	1,553	71	1,624	74.6
25 to 29 years old	4	*	5	9	148	179	191	209	221	463	9,213	576	9,789	87.3
30 to 34 years old	*	5	*	5	86	84	111	106	99	201	9,873	675	10,548	93.8
35 to 39 years old	5	*	*	5	71	63	51	38	59	187	9,521	842	10,362	95.6
40 to 44 years old	*	12	*	7	43	34	79	58	43	97	9,040	818	9,858	96.4
45 to 49 years old	*	5	5	10	48	29	32	36	21	82	8,953	777	9,730	97.3
50 to 54 years old	*	*	4	3	22	38	23	21	34	54	9,293	839	10,132	98.1
55 to 59 years old	*	*	*	*	1	12	18	11	10	32	9,901	915	10,816	99.2
60 to 64 years old	*	*	*	*	16	6	9	8	10	22	9,976	900	10,876	99.3
65 years and over	*	*	*	*	5	2	13	*	5	2	26,920	3,386	30,306	99.9
WHITE ALONE NON-HISPANIC														
Both Sexes														
Total	2,058	2,079	1,945	2,175	1,951	1,848	1,845	1,570	852	1,356	140,163	10,869	151,032	80.2
3 years old	*	*	*	*	*	*	*	*	*	*	*	1,260	1,260	65.4
4 years old	*	*	*	*	*	*	*	*	*	*	*	940	940	48.1
5 years old	*	*	*	*	*	*	*	*	*	*	*	267	267	13.4
6 years old	*	*	*	*	*	*	*	*	*	*	*	124	124	6.2
7 years old	*	*	*	*	*	*	*	*	*	*	*	103	103	5.2
8 years old	*	*	*	*	*	*	*	*	*	*	*	84	84	4.2
9 years old	*	*	*	*	*	*	*	*	*	*	*	64	64	3.2
10 years old	*	*	*	*	*	*	*	*	*	*	*	74	74	3.7
11 years old	*	*	*	*	*	*	*	*	*	*	*	52	52	2.7
12 years old	*	*	*	*	*	*	*	*	*	*	*	59	59	2.8
13 years old	59	8	*	*	*	*	*	*	*	*	*	58	58	2.9
14 years old	1,292	109	4	*	*	*	*	*	*	*	*	49	49	2.3
15 years old	620	1,222	128	17	*	*	9	*	7	*	*	70	70	3.3
16 years old	42	623	1,234	129	*	*	*	*	3	*	16	110	126	5.8
17 years old	8	83	515	1,338	38	7	*	*	1	*	58	121	179	8.2
18 years old	*	11	34	551	831	47	16	*	4	*	468	104	572	27.6
19 years old	1	14	10	60	446	631	143	9	12	*	739	117	857	39.2
20 years old	2	4	*	25	163	479	619	52	15	*	778	113	891	39.6
21 years old	7	*	4	12	64	179	348	431	24	50	1,019	97	1,116	49.9
22 years old	6	*	*	2	50	70	128	363	92	48	1,289	63	1,351	64.0
23 years old	8	*	*	14	65	37	91	137	81	106	1,629	133	1,762	76.3
24 years old	*	*	*	5	17	66	53	111	94	104	1,641	81	1,722	79.3
25 to 29 years old	1	*	*	*	77	133	148	227	203	410	10,388	432	10,821	90.0
30 to 34 years old	*	3	*	6	74	69	147	84	96	224	11,286	385	11,671	94.3
35 to 39 years old	2	*	*	3	33	59	39	48	74	144	11,157	500	11,657	96.7
40 to 44 years old	*	*	3	4	26	20	43	50	46	103	10,679	431	11,110	97.4

* = Quantity zero or rounds to zero.

Table A-2. Single Grade of Enrollment and High School Graduation Status for Population 3 Years Old and Over, by Sex, Age (Single Years for 3 to 24 Years), Race, and Hispanic Origin, October 2020—*Continued*

(Numbers in thousands; percent; civilian noninstitutionalized population.)

Age, sex, race, and Hispanic origin	Population[1]	Enrolled		Enrolled										
		Number	Percent	Nursery	Kinder-garten	Elementary grades							
						1	2	3	4	5	6	7	8
45 to 49 years old	11,419	211	1.8	*	*	*	*	*	*	*	*	*	*
50 to 54 years old	12,630	162	1.3	*	*	*	*	*	*	*	*	*	*
55 to 59 years old	14,208	78	0.5	*	*	*	*	*	*	*	1	*	*
60 to 64 years old	14,677	52	0.4	*	*	*	*	*	*	*	*	*	*
65 years and over	41,594	35	0.1	*	*	*	*	*	*	*	*	*	*
Male													
Total	92,391	18,352	19.9	959	960	1,018	951	1,066	991	952	1,068	1,129	986
3 years old	987	315	31.9	294	21	*	*	*	*	*	*	*	*
4 years old	997	496	49.8	442	54	*	*	*	*	*	*	*	*
5 years old	1,022	902	88.3	201	644	42	15	*	*	*	*	*	*
6 years old	1,032	979	94.9	21	223	712	15	8	*	*	*	*	*
7 years old	1,015	949	93.5	*	17	243	634	48	6	*	*	*	*
8 years old	1,021	979	95.9	*	*	20	258	675	23	3	*	*	*
9 years old	1,025	994	96.9	*	*	*	24	296	634	34	6	*	*
10 years old	1,014	967	95.4	*	*	*	5	38	289	612	20	3	*
11 years old	1,028	998	97.1	*	*	*	*	2	39	274	671	11	2
12 years old	1,133	1,101	97.2	*	*	*	*	*	*	22	330	700	48
13 years old	996	964	96.8	*	*	*	*	*	*	8	19	332	578
14 years old	1,079	1,052	97.5	*	*	*	*	*	*	*	13	47	327
15 years old	1,084	1,026	94.7	*	*	*	*	*	*	*	*	9	20
16 years old	1,098	1,033	94.0	*	*	*	*	*	*	*	*	13	8
17 years old	1,105	1,011	91.5	*	*	*	*	*	*	*	*	1	4
18 years old	1,058	730	69.0	*	*	*	*	*	*	*	*	4	*
19 years old	1,127	601	53.3	*	*	*	*	*	*	*	*	*	*
20 years old	1,119	605	54.1	*	*	*	*	*	*	*	*	*	*
21 years old	1,208	578	47.8	*	*	*	*	*	*	*	*	*	*
22 years old	1,078	352	32.7	*	*	*	*	*	*	*	*	*	*
23 years old	1,183	240	20.3	*	*	*	*	*	*	*	*	8	*
24 years old	996	190	19.1	*	*	*	*	*	*	*	*	*	*
25 to 29 years old	6,049	491	8.1	*	*	*	*	*	*	*	4	*	*
30 to 34 years old	6,197	337	5.4	*	*	*	*	*	*	*	4	*	*
35 to 39 years old	6,015	181	3.0	*	*	*	*	*	*	*	*	*	*
40 to 44 years old	5,668	116	2.1	*	*	*	*	*	*	*	*	*	*
45 to 49 years old	5,686	61	1.1	*	*	*	*	*	*	*	*	*	*
50 to 54 years old	6,270	55	0.9	*	*	*	*	*	*	*	*	*	*
55 to 59 years old	6,997	18	0.3	*	*	*	*	*	*	*	1	*	*
60 to 64 years old	7,060	8	0.1	*	*	*	*	*	*	*	*	*	*
65 years and over	19,043	20	0.1	*	*	*	*	*	*	*	*	*	*
Female													
Total	95,905	18,912	19.7	941	922	965	968	924	961	957	951	1,046	869
3 years old	939	351	37.4	324	28	*	*	*	*	*	*	*	*
4 years old	958	519	54.2	478	41	*	*	*	*	*	*	*	*
5 years old	966	819	84.8	138	641	35	5	*	*	*	*	*	*
6 years old	983	911	92.7	2	203	684	20	3	*	*	*	*	*
7 years old	978	941	96.2	*	9	228	670	24	10	*	*	*	*
8 years old	970	929	95.7	*	*	18	256	629	26	*	*	*	*
9 years old	981	948	96.7	*	*	*	18	241	659	26	4	*	*
10 years old	1,004	977	97.3	*	*	*	*	26	249	678	20	4	*
11 years old	926	903	97.5	*	*	*	*	18	218	636	25	6	
12 years old	1,000	974	97.3	*	*	*	*	*	18	251	687	18	
13 years old	1,005	979	97.4	*	*	*	*	*	17	28	291	603	
14 years old	1,023	1,000	97.8	*	*	*	*	*	*	7	21	232	
15 years old	1,035	1,022	98.8	*	*	*	*	*	*	*	14	3	
16 years old	1,086	1,025	94.4	*	*	*	*	*	*	*	1	6	
17 years old	1,071	986	92.1	*	*	*	*	*	*	*	1		
18 years old	1,014	769	75.9	*	*	*	*	*	*	*	*	*	*
19 years old	1,057	726	68.7	*	*	*	*	*	*	*	*	*	*
20 years old	1,130	753	66.7	*	*	*	*	*	*	*	*	*	*
21 years old	1,026	541	52.7	*	*	*	*	*	*	*	*	*	*
22 years old	1,033	407	39.4	*	*	*	*	*	*	*	*	*	*
23 years old	1,126	308	27.3	*	*	*	*	*	*	*	*	*	*
24 years old	1,177	260	22.1	*	*	*	*	*	*	*	*	*	*
25 to 29 years old	5,975	713	11.9	*	*	*	*	*	*	*	*	*	*
30 to 34 years old	6,184	373	6.0	*	*	*	*	*	*	*	4	*	*
35 to 39 years old	6,045	223	3.7	*	*	*	*	*	*	*	*	1	*

* = Quantity zero or rounds to zero.

Table A-2. Single Grade of Enrollment and High School Graduation Status for Population 3 Years Old and Over, by Sex, Age (Single Years for 3 to 24 Years), Race, and Hispanic Origin, October 2020—*Continued*

(Numbers in thousands; percent; civilian noninstitutionalized population.)

| | Enrolled | | | | | | | | | | Not enrolled | | | |
| | High school | | | | Undergraduate college | | | | Graduate school | | | | Not enrolled | |
Age, sex, race, and Hispanic origin	9	10	11	12	1	2	3	4	1	2+	H.S. grad	Not grad	Number	Percent
45 to 49 years old	*	*	6	4	36	17	31	25	38	55	10,748	460	11,208	98.2
50 to 54 years old	8	*	4	4	13	20	9	17	33	52	11,980	488	12,468	98.7
55 to 59 years old	*	*	*	*	2	11	11	9	11	32	13,453	678	14,130	99.5
60 to 64 years old	*	*	4	*	16	*	4	2	13	13	13,948	677	14,625	99.6
65 years and over	1	*	*	*	1	2	5	5	5	15	38,889	2,671	41,559	99.9
Male														
Total	1,016	1,042	981	1,114	904	833	852	672	322	536	68,239	5,800	74,039	80.1
3 years old	*	*	*	*	*	*	*	*	*	*	*	672	672	68.1
4 years old	*	*	*	*	*	*	*	*	*	*	*	501	501	50.2
5 years old	*	*	*	*	*	*	*	*	*	*	*	120	120	11.7
6 years old	*	*	*	*	*	*	*	*	*	*	*	53	53	5.1
7 years old	*	*	*	*	*	*	*	*	*	*	*	66	66	6.5
8 years old	*	*	*	*	*	*	*	*	*	*	*	42	42	4.1
9 years old	*	*	*	*	*	*	*	*	*	*	*	32	32	3.1
10 years old	*	*	*	*	*	*	*	*	*	*	*	47	47	4.6
11 years old	*	*	*	*	*	*	*	*	*	*	*	30	30	2.9
12 years old	*	*	*	*	*	*	*	*	*	*	*	32	32	2.8
13 years old	19	8	*	*	*	*	*	*	*	*	*	32	32	3.2
14 years old	623	42	*	*	*	*	*	*	*	*	*	27	27	2.5
15 years old	339	580	61	6	*	*	9	*	3	*	*	57	57	5.3
16 years old	21	348	586	55	*	*	*	*	3	*	7	58	66	6.0
17 years old	4	32	287	665	17	*	*	*	1	*	27	67	94	8.5
18 years old	*	11	25	307	370	13	1	*	*	*	281	47	328	31.0
19 years old	1	13	10	35	236	247	52	3	3	*	448	79	526	46.7
20 years old	*	4	*	17	57	234	265	19	9	*	449	65	514	45.9
21 years old	*	*	4	7	32	97	209	184	8	37	562	68	630	52.2
22 years old	*	*	*	2	30	37	63	168	33	20	685	40	725	67.3
23 years old	*	*	*	9	32	18	44	64	32	32	871	72	943	79.7
24 years old	*	*	*	*	11	41	25	52	42	19	763	43	806	80.9
25 to 29 years old	*	*	*	*	30	51	61	91	74	180	5,307	251	5,558	91.9
30 to 34 years old	*	3	*	6	42	36	73	37	42	95	5,669	191	5,860	94.6
35 to 39 years old	*	*	*	*	17	30	21	22	31	60	5,574	260	5,835	97.0
40 to 44 years old	*	*	3	4	8	13	13	16	12	47	5,275	276	5,551	97.9
45 to 49 years old	*	*	1	*	12	8	11	3	17	9	5,352	273	5,625	98.9
50 to 54 years old	8	*	*	1	9	4	3	7	8	14	5,937	278	6,215	99.1
55 to 59 years old	*	*	*	*	1	5	*	1	1	9	6,565	414	6,979	99.7
60 to 64 years old	*	*	4	*	*	*	1	*	3	1	6,691	360	7,052	99.9
65 years and over	1	*	*	*	*	*	*	5	*	13	17,775	1,248	19,023	99.9
Female														
Total	1,042	1,036	964	1,061	1,047	1,016	993	897	531	820	71,925	5,068	76,993	80.3
3 years old	*	*	*	*	*	*	*	*	*	*	*	588	588	62.6
4 years old	*	*	*	*	*	*	*	*	*	*	*	439	439	45.8
5 years old	*	*	*	*	*	*	*	*	*	*	*	147	147	15.2
6 years old	*	*	*	*	*	*	*	*	*	*	*	71	71	7.3
7 years old	*	*	*	*	*	*	*	*	*	*	*	37	37	3.8
8 years old	*	*	*	*	*	*	*	*	*	*	*	42	42	4.3
9 years old	*	*	*	*	*	*	*	*	*	*	*	33	33	3.3
10 years old	*	*	*	*	*	*	*	*	*	*	*	27	27	2.7
11 years old	*	*	*	*	*	*	*	*	*	*	*	23	23	2.5
12 years old	*	*	*	*	*	*	*	*	*	*	*	27	27	2.7
13 years old	40	*	*	*	*	*	*	*	*	*	*	27	27	2.6
14 years old	669	67	4	*	*	*	*	*	*	*	*	23	23	2.2
15 years old	281	642	67	11	*	*	*	*	4	*	*	13	13	1.2
16 years old	22	275	647	74	*	*	*	*	*	*	9	52	61	5.6
17 years old	4	50	228	673	21	7	*	*	*	*	31	54	85	7.9
18 years old	*	*	9	244	461	35	15	*	4	*	187	58	245	24.1
19 years old	*	2	*	25	210	384	91	6	8	*	292	39	330	31.3
20 years old	2	*	*	8	106	245	354	32	6	*	329	48	377	33.3
21 years old	7	*	*	5	32	82	139	247	16	13	456	29	486	47.3
22 years old	6	*	*	*	19	34	65	195	59	28	603	23	626	60.6
23 years old	8	*	*	5	33	20	47	72	49	74	757	61	818	72.7
24 years old	*	*	*	5	6	25	28	59	52	84	878	39	917	77.9
25 to 29 years old	1	*	*	*	47	82	88	136	129	230	5,082	181	5,263	88.1
30 to 34 years old	*	*	*	*	32	33	73	47	54	130	5,617	194	5,811	94.0
35 to 39 years old	2	*	*	3	16	29	18	26	44	84	5,582	240	5,822	96.3

* = Quantity zero or rounds to zero.

Table A-2. Single Grade of Enrollment and High School Graduation Status for Population 3 Years Old and Over, by Sex, Age (Single Years for 3 to 24 Years), Race, and Hispanic Origin, October 2020—*Continued*

(Numbers in thousands; percent; civilian noninstitutionalized population.)

Age, sex, race, and Hispanic origin	Population¹	Enrolled Number	Enrolled Percent	Nursery	Kinder-garten	1	2	3	4	5	6	7	8
40 to 44 years old	5,739	180	3.1	*	*	*	*	*	*	*	*	1	*
45 to 49 years old	5,733	150	2.6	*	*	*	*	*	*	*	*	*	*
50 to 54 years old	6,360	106	1.7	*	*	*	*	*	*	*	*	*	*
55 to 59 years old	7,210	59	0.8	*	*	*	*	*	*	*	*	*	*
60 to 64 years old	7,618	44	0.6	*	*	*	*	*	*	*	*	*	*
65 years and over	22,551	15	0.1	*	*	*	*	*	*	*	*	*	*
BLACK ALONE													
Both Sexes													
Total	41,485	11,014	26.5	512	597	619	535	647	526	721	590	625	550
3 years old	588	183	31.2	175	8	*	*	*	*	*	*	*	*
4 years old	636	307	48.4	267	40	*	*	*	*	*	*	*	*
5 years old	563	467	82.9	64	399	5	*	*	*	*	*	*	*
6 years old	716	684	95.6	5	141	487	47	4	*	*	*	*	*
7 years old	555	526	94.7	*	9	119	353	44	*	*	*	*	*
8 years old	634	593	93.5	*	*	5	121	433	30	4	*	*	*
9 years old	591	575	97.3	*	*	3	14	148	356	49	5	*	*
10 years old	628	613	97.7	*	*	*	*	17	122	459	15	*	*
11 years old	604	594	98.3	*	*	*	*	*	8	185	383	17	*
12 years old	713	680	95.4	*	*	*	*	*	9	23	166	443	32
13 years old	565	533	94.4	*	*	*	*	*	*	2	18	145	354
14 years old	627	620	98.9	*	*	*	*	*	*	*	3	18	137
15 years old	612	604	98.7	*	*	*	*	*	*	*	*	1	22
16 years old	608	589	96.8	*	*	*	*	*	*	*	*	*	2
17 years old	589	527	89.4	*	*	*	*	*	*	*	*	*	3
18 years old	655	474	72.3	*	*	*	*	*	*	*	*	*	*
19 years old	556	393	70.8	*	*	*	*	*	*	*	*	*	*
20 years old	704	334	47.4	*	*	*	*	*	*	*	*	*	*
21 years old	623	217	34.9	*	*	*	*	*	*	*	*	*	*
22 years old	616	193	31.3	*	*	*	*	*	*	*	*	*	*
23 years old	574	133	23.1	*	*	*	*	*	*	*	*	*	*
24 years old	561	145	25.9	*	*	*	*	*	*	*	*	*	*
25 to 29 years old	3,462	339	9.8	*	*	*	*	*	*	*	*	*	*
30 to 34 years old	3,265	244	7.5	*	*	*	*	*	*	*	*	*	*
35 to 39 years old	2,875	121	4.2	*	*	*	*	*	*	*	*	*	*
40 to 44 years old	2,705	124	4.6	*	*	*	*	*	*	*	*	*	*
45 to 49 years old	2,571	70	2.7	*	*	*	*	*	*	*	*	*	*
50 to 54 years old	2,594	67	2.6	*	*	*	*	*	*	*	*	*	*
55 to 59 years old	2,450	26	1.1	*	*	*	*	*	*	*	*	*	*
60 to 64 years old	2,709	31	1.1	*	*	*	*	*	*	*	*	*	*
65 years and over	5,335	7	0.1	*	*	*	*	*	*	*	*	*	*
Male													
Total	19,336	5,248	27.1	232	291	309	244	320	289	383	277	362	267
3 years old	271	68	25.2	67	1	*	*	*	*	*	*	*	*
4 years old	316	152	48.1	135	17	*	*	*	*	*	*	*	*
5 years old	280	215	76.8	29	187	*	*	*	*	*	*	*	*
6 years old	383	371	97.0	2	81	255	29	4	*	*	*	*	*
7 years old	265	241	91.1	*	5	53	153	29	*	*	*	*	*
8 years old	285	276	96.9	*	*	*	55	203	14	4	*	*	*
9 years old	336	327	97.3	*	*	*	7	71	213	32	5	*	*
10 years old	318	315	99.0	*	*	*	*	13	51	242	8	*	*
11 years old	306	295	96.6	*	*	*	*	*	8	94	177	17	*
12 years old	367	346	94.2	*	*	*	*	*	3	9	76	245	7
13 years old	279	267	95.5	*	*	*	*	*	*	2	11	86	166
14 years old	317	310	97.8	*	*	*	*	*	*	*	2	13	75
15 years old	308	308	100.0	*	*	*	*	*	*	*	*	1	15
16 years old	294	276	93.9	*	*	*	*	*	*	*	*	*	1
17 years old	303	274	90.5	*	*	*	*	*	*	*	*	*	3
18 years old	334	242	72.6	*	*	*	*	*	*	*	*	*	*
19 years old	261	162	62.1	*	*	*	*	*	*	*	*	*	*
20 years old	350	163	46.7	*	*	*	*	*	*	*	*	*	*
21 years old	312	103	33.1	*	*	*	*	*	*	*	*	*	*
22 years old	261	63	24.1	*	*	*	*	*	*	*	*	*	*
23 years old	291	63	21.5	*	*	*	*	*	*	*	*	*	*
24 years old	270	49	18.0	*	*	*	*	*	*	*	*	*	*

* = Quantity zero or rounds to zero.

Table A-2. Single Grade of Enrollment and High School Graduation Status for Population 3 Years Old and Over, by Sex, Age (Single Years for 3 to 24 Years), Race, and Hispanic Origin, October 2020—*Continued*

(Numbers in thousands; percent; civilian noninstitutionalized population.)

Age, sex, race, and Hispanic origin	Enrolled										Not enrolled		Not enrolled	
	High school				Undergraduate college				Graduate school		H.S. grad	Not grad	Number	Percent
	9	10	11	12	1	2	3	4	1	2+				
40 to 44 years old	*	*	*	*	18	6	30	35	35	56	5,404	155	5,559	96.9
45 to 49 years old	*	*	5	4	24	9	20	22	21	46	5,396	187	5,583	97.4
50 to 54 years old	*	*	4	3	4	16	6	9	25	38	6,043	211	6,253	98.3
55 to 59 years old	*	*	*	*	1	6	11	8	10	23	6,887	264	7,151	99.2
60 to 64 years old	*	*	*	*	16	*	4	2	10	12	7,257	317	7,574	99.4
65 years and over	*	*	*	*	1	2	5	*	5	2	21,114	1,423	22,537	99.9
BLACK ALONE														
Both Sexes														
Total	580	612	599	711	711	590	508	270	157	356	26,391	4,080	30,471	73.5
3 years old	*	*	*	*	*	*	*	*	*	*	*	404	404	68.8
4 years old	*	*	*	*	*	*	*	*	*	*	*	328	328	51.6
5 years old	*	*	*	*	*	*	*	*	*	*	*	96	96	17.1
6 years old	*	*	*	*	*	*	*	*	*	*	*	31	31	4.4
7 years old	*	*	*	*	*	*	*	*	*	*	*	30	30	5.3
8 years old	*	*	*	*	*	*	*	*	*	*	*	41	41	6.5
9 years old	*	*	*	*	*	*	*	*	*	*	*	16	16	2.7
10 years old	*	*	*	*	*	*	*	*	*	*	*	14	14	2.3
11 years old	*	*	*	*	*	*	*	*	*	*	*	10	10	1.7
12 years old	7	*	*	*	*	*	*	*	*	*	*	33	33	4.6
13 years old	6	8	*	*	*	*	*	*	*	*	*	32	32	5.6
14 years old	413	45	4	*	*	*	*	*	*	*	*	7	7	1.1
15 years old	140	374	42	11	6	*	*	*	9	*	*	8	8	1.3
16 years old	8	140	362	61	5	*	*	*	10	*	3	17	20	3.2
17 years old	*	27	125	347	19	*	2	*	4	*	30	32	62	10.6
18 years old	*	*	53	174	234	13	*	*	*	*	147	34	181	27.7
19 years old	*	1	3	62	132	176	16	*	*	2	150	12	162	29.2
20 years old	*	*	*	9	84	131	92	18	*	*	351	20	370	52.6
21 years old	*	*	7	12	27	65	57	44	*	5	376	30	406	65.1
22 years old	*	*	*	7	28	46	69	32	6	4	391	32	423	68.7
23 years old	*	*	*	1	11	15	36	30	13	26	410	32	441	76.9
24 years old	*	*	*	10	28	8	40	35	13	12	400	16	416	74.1
25 to 29 years old	2	*	2	1	38	54	71	46	45	81	2,925	198	3,123	90.2
30 to 34 years old	*	5	*	*	32	43	51	25	26	61	2,822	199	3,021	92.5
35 to 39 years old	3	*	*	2	27	4	29	8	*	48	2,532	222	2,755	95.8
40 to 44 years old	1	7	*	4	19	11	23	17	4	37	2,329	252	2,582	95.4
45 to 49 years old	*	5	*	7	7	11	5	*	2	34	2,357	144	2,501	97.3
50 to 54 years old	*	*	*	*	6	4	8	9	18	22	2,297	230	2,527	97.4
55 to 59 years old	*	*	*	*	3	2	3	*	5	13	2,149	275	2,424	98.9
60 to 64 years old	*	*	*	3	*	6	6	6	*	9	2,311	368	2,678	98.9
65 years and over	*	*	*	*	4	*	*	*	3	*	4,411	917	5,327	99.9
Male														
Total	298	263	310	348	310	277	174	99	62	133	12,101	1,988	14,088	72.9
3 years old	*	*	*	*	*	*	*	*	*	*	*	203	203	74.8
4 years old	*	*	*	*	*	*	*	*	*	*	*	164	164	51.9
5 years old	*	*	*	*	*	*	*	*	*	*	*	65	65	23.2
6 years old	*	*	*	*	*	*	*	*	*	*	*	12	12	3.0
7 years old	*	*	*	*	*	*	*	*	*	*	*	24	24	8.9
8 years old	*	*	*	*	*	*	*	*	*	*	*	9	9	3.1
9 years old	*	*	*	*	*	*	*	*	*	*	*	9	9	2.7
10 years old	*	*	*	*	*	*	*	*	*	*	*	3	3	1.0
11 years old	*	*	*	*	*	*	*	*	*	*	*	10	10	3.4
12 years old	7	*	*	*	*	*	*	*	*	*	*	21	21	5.8
13 years old	1	1	*	*	*	*	*	*	*	*	*	13	13	4.5
14 years old	208	12	*	*	*	*	*	*	*	*	*	7	7	2.2
15 years old	74	170	35	6	6	*	*	*	1	*	*	*	*	*
16 years old	6	66	172	16	5	*	*	*	10	*	3	16	18	6.1
17 years old	*	13	59	187	9	*	*	*	4	*	19	10	29	9.5
18 years old	*	*	39	91	99	13	*	*	*	*	73	18	91	27.4
19 years old	*	1	*	36	51	61	11	*	*	2	87	12	99	37.9
20 years old	*	*	*	4	47	73	28	11	*	*	172	14	186	53.3
21 years old	*	*	2	3	23	48	10	13	*	4	194	15	209	66.9
22 years old	*	*	*	*	10	25	16	5	3	4	175	23	198	75.9
23 years old	*	*	*	1	*	11	17	17	4	12	203	26	229	78.5
24 years old	*	*	*	*	10	*	19	13	7	1	210	11	221	82.0

* = Quantity zero or rounds to zero.

Table A-2. Single Grade of Enrollment and High School Graduation Status for Population 3 Years Old and Over, by Sex, Age (Single Years for 3 to 24 Years), Race, and Hispanic Origin, October 2020—*Continued*

(Numbers in thousands; percent; civilian noninstitutionalized population.)

Age, sex, race, and Hispanic origin	Population[1]	Enrolled Number	Enrolled Percent	Nursery	Kinder-garten	1	2	3	4	5	6	7	8
25 to 29 years old	1,678	98	5.8	*	*	*	*	*	*	*	*	*	*
30 to 34 years old	1,543	111	7.2	*	*	*	*	*	*	*	*	*	*
35 to 39 years old	1,324	38	2.9	*	*	*	*	*	*	*	*	*	*
40 to 44 years old	1,229	45	3.7	*	*	*	*	*	*	*	*	*	*
45 to 49 years old	1,158	17	1.5	*	*	*	*	*	*	*	*	*	*
50 to 54 years old	1,183	23	1.9	*	*	*	*	*	*	*	*	*	*
55 to 59 years old	1,144	15	1.4	*	*	*	*	*	*	*	*	*	*
60 to 64 years old	1,197	9	0.8	*	*	*	*	*	*	*	*	*	*
65 years and over	2,173	3	0.2	*	*	*	*	*	*	*	*	*	*
Female													
Total	22,149	5,766	26.0	279	306	310	291	327	237	338	312	263	283
3 years old	316	115	36.3	108	7	*	*	*	*	*	*	*	*
4 years old	320	156	48.6	132	23	*	*	*	*	*	*	*	*
5 years old	283	252	89.0	35	212	5	*	*	*	*	*	*	*
6 years old	333	313	94.1	4	60	232	18	*	*	*	*	*	*
7 years old	290	284	98.0	*	4	66	199	15	*	*	*	*	*
8 years old	349	317	90.8	*	*	5	66	230	16	*	*	*	*
9 years old	255	248	97.3	*	*	3	7	77	143	17	*	*	*
10 years old	309	298	96.4	*	*	*	*	5	71	216	6	*	*
11 years old	298	298	100.0	*	*	*	*	*	*	91	207	1	*
12 years old	346	334	96.6	*	*	*	*	*	6	14	90	198	25
13 years old	286	266	93.3	*	*	*	*	*	*	*	8	59	188
14 years old	310	310	100.0	*	*	*	*	*	*	*	1	5	62
15 years old	304	296	97.4	*	*	*	*	*	*	*	*	*	7
16 years old	314	313	99.5	*	*	*	*	*	*	*	*	*	2
17 years old	286	252	88.3	*	*	*	*	*	*	*	*	*	*
18 years old	322	232	72.1	*	*	*	*	*	*	*	*	*	*
19 years old	295	232	78.6	*	*	*	*	*	*	*	*	*	*
20 years old	354	170	48.1	*	*	*	*	*	*	*	*	*	*
21 years old	311	114	36.6	*	*	*	*	*	*	*	*	*	*
22 years old	355	130	36.7	*	*	*	*	*	*	*	*	*	*
23 years old	283	70	24.8	*	*	*	*	*	*	*	*	*	*
24 years old	291	96	33.2	*	*	*	*	*	*	*	*	*	*
25 to 29 years old	1,785	242	13.5	*	*	*	*	*	*	*	*	*	*
30 to 34 years old	1,722	134	7.8	*	*	*	*	*	*	*	*	*	*
35 to 39 years old	1,551	82	5.3	*	*	*	*	*	*	*	*	*	*
40 to 44 years old	1,477	78	5.3	*	*	*	*	*	*	*	*	*	*
45 to 49 years old	1,413	53	3.7	*	*	*	*	*	*	*	*	*	*
50 to 54 years old	1,411	45	3.2	*	*	*	*	*	*	*	*	*	*
55 to 59 years old	1,306	10	0.8	*	*	*	*	*	*	*	*	*	*
60 to 64 years old	1,512	21	1.4	*	*	*	*	*	*	*	*	*	*
65 years and over	3,162	4	0.1	*	*	*	*	*	*	*	*	*	*
ASIAN ALONE													
Both Sexes													
Total	19,474	4,771	24.5	178	219	209	205	197	220	227	227	230	286
3 years old	187	55	29.6	43	12	*	*	*	*	*	*	*	*
4 years old	246	120	48.8	105	15	*	*	*	*	*	*	*	*
5 years old	235	187	79.9	29	152	7	*	*	*	*	*	*	*
6 years old	238	224	93.9	*	32	174	17	*	*	*	*	*	*
7 years old	170	158	93.0	*	9	28	118	4	*	*	*	*	*
8 years old	236	225	95.3	*	*	*	63	152	6	4	*	*	*
9 years old	213	210	98.5	*	*	*	7	32	163	7	2	*	*
10 years old	254	238	93.6	*	*	*	*	10	44	175	9	*	*
11 years old	227	219	96.3	*	*	*	*	*	7	37	168	7	1
12 years old	220	220	100.0	*	*	*	*	*	1	1	39	136	44
13 years old	281	277	98.6	*	*	*	*	*	*	4	5	75	185
14 years old	177	171	96.4	*	*	*	*	*	*	*	5	9	46
15 years old	254	254	100.0	*	*	*	*	*	*	*	*	*	3
16 years old	176	168	95.7	*	*	*	*	*	*	*	*	*	4
17 years old	244	230	94.2	*	*	*	*	*	*	*	*	*	*
18 years old	245	197	80.4	*	*	*	*	*	*	*	*	*	*
19 years old	266	208	78.2	*	*	*	*	*	*	*	*	*	*
20 years old	303	257	84.6	*	*	*	*	*	*	*	*	*	*
21 years old	256	215	83.9	*	*	*	*	*	*	*	*	*	*

* = Quantity zero or rounds to zero.

Table A-2. Single Grade of Enrollment and High School Graduation Status for Population 3 Years Old and Over, by Sex, Age (Single Years for 3 to 24 Years), Race, and Hispanic Origin, October 2020—*Continued*

(Numbers in thousands; percent; civilian noninstitutionalized population.)

Age, sex, race, and Hispanic origin	Enrolled										Not enrolled		Not enrolled	
	High school				Undergraduate college				Graduate school		H.S. grad	Not grad		
	9	10	11	12	1	2	3	4	1	2+			Number	Percent
25 to 29 years old	*	*	2	1	13	18	15	19	7	22	1,518	61	1,580	94.2
30 to 34 years old	*	*	*	*	9	23	25	7	6	40	1,337	95	1,432	92.8
35 to 39 years old	*	*	*	*	12	*	17	*	*	9	1,173	113	1,286	97.1
40 to 44 years old	1	*	*	*	9	5	9	8	*	14	1,046	137	1,183	96.3
45 to 49 years old	*	*	*	*	5	*	1	*	2	9	1,079	62	1,141	98.5
50 to 54 years old	*	*	*	*	*	*	*	4	11	8	1,046	115	1,160	98.1
55 to 59 years old	*	*	*	*	3	*	*	*	5	8	991	138	1,129	98.6
60 to 64 years old	*	*	*	3	*	*	6	*	*	*	977	210	1,187	99.2
65 years and over	*	*	*	*	*	*	*	*	3	*	1,798	371	2,169	99.8
Female														
Total	283	349	289	363	400	313	334	171	95	223	14,291	2,092	16,383	74.0
3 years old	*	*	*	*	*	*	*	*	*	*	*	202	202	63.7
4 years old	*	*	*	*	*	*	*	*	*	*	*	164	164	51.4
5 years old	*	*	*	*	*	*	*	*	*	*	*	31	31	11.0
6 years old	*	*	*	*	*	*	*	*	*	*	*	20	20	5.9
7 years old	*	*	*	*	*	*	*	*	*	*	*	6	6	2.0
8 years old	*	*	*	*	*	*	*	*	*	*	*	32	32	9.2
9 years old	*	*	*	*	*	*	*	*	*	*	*	7	7	2.7
10 years old	*	*	*	*	*	*	*	*	*	*	*	11	11	3.6
11 years old	*	*	*	*	*	*	*	*	*	*	*	*	*	*
12 years old	*	*	*	*	*	*	*	*	*	*	*	12	12	3.4
13 years old	5	7	*	*	*	*	*	*	*	*	*	19	19	6.7
14 years old	204	33	4	*	*	*	*	*	*	*	*	*	*	*
15 years old	66	204	6	5	*	*	*	*	8	*	*	8	8	2.6
16 years old	2	74	190	45	*	*	*	*	*	*	*	1	1	0.5
17 years old	*	14	66	160	10	*	2	*	*	*	11	22	33	11.7
18 years old	*	*	14	83	135	*	*	*	*	*	74	16	90	27.9
19 years old	*	*	3	26	82	115	6	*	*	*	63	1	63	21.4
20 years old	*	*	*	5	37	58	63	6	*	*	179	5	184	51.9
21 years old	*	*	5	9	4	17	47	31	*	2	182	15	197	63.4
22 years old	*	*	*	7	18	22	54	27	4	*	217	8	225	63.3
23 years old	*	*	*	*	11	4	19	13	9	14	207	6	213	75.2
24 years old	*	*	*	10	18	8	21	22	6	11	189	5	194	66.8
25 to 29 years old	2	*	*	*	24	36	56	26	38	59	1,407	136	1,543	86.5
30 to 34 years old	*	5	*	*	23	20	26	18	20	22	1,485	104	1,588	92.2
35 to 39 years old	3	*	*	2	15	4	12	8	*	38	1,360	109	1,469	94.7
40 to 44 years old	*	7	*	4	11	7	14	9	4	24	1,283	115	1,398	94.7
45 to 49 years old	*	5	*	7	2	11	4	*	*	25	1,278	82	1,360	96.3
50 to 54 years old	*	*	*	*	6	4	8	5	8	14	1,251	115	1,367	96.8
55 to 59 years old	*	*	*	*	*	2	3	*	*	5	1,159	137	1,295	99.2
60 to 64 years old	*	*	*	*	6	*	6	*	9	1,334	157	1,491	98.6
65 years and over	*	*	*	*	4	*	*	*	*	*	2,613	545	3,158	99.9
ASIAN ALONE														
Both Sexes														
Total	157	238	189	231	353	371	268	228	189	348	13,223	1,480	14,703	75.5
3 years old	*	*	*	*	*	*	*	*	*	*	*	131	131	70.4
4 years old	*	*	*	*	*	*	*	*	*	*	*	126	126	51.2
5 years old	*	*	*	*	*	*	*	*	*	*	*	47	47	20.1
6 years old	*	*	*	*	*	*	*	*	*	*	*	15	15	6.1
7 years old	*	*	*	*	*	*	*	*	*	*	*	12	12	7.0
8 years old	*	*	*	*	*	*	*	*	*	*	*	11	11	4.7
9 years old	*	*	*	*	*	*	*	*	*	*	*	3	3	1.5
10 years old	*	*	*	*	*	*	*	*	*	*	*	16	16	6.4
11 years old	*	*	*	*	*	*	*	*	*	*	*	8	8	3.7
12 years old	*	*	*	*	*	*	*	*	*	*	*	*	*	*
13 years old	4	4	*	*	*	*	*	*	*	*	*	4	4	1.4
14 years old	107	4	*	*	*	*	*	*	*	*	*	6	6	3.6
15 years old	46	163	36	3	2	*	*	*	*	*	*	*	*	*
16 years old	*	51	97	15	1	*	*	*	*	*	*	8	8	4.3
17 years old	*	12	49	157	9	*	*	*	2	*	11	4	14	5.8
18 years old	*	*	6	27	139	16	4	*	3	3	32	16	48	19.6
19 years old	*	*	*	12	46	123	22	1	*	4	51	7	58	21.8
20 years old	*	*	*	5	44	95	79	33	*	*	40	7	47	15.4
21 years old	*	*	*	*	12	49	57	86	3	7	34	7	41	16.1

* = Quantity zero or rounds to zero.

Table A-2. Single Grade of Enrollment and High School Graduation Status for Population 3 Years Old and Over, by Sex, Age (Single Years for 3 to 24 Years), Race, and Hispanic Origin, October 2020—*Continued*

(Numbers in thousands; percent; civilian noninstitutionalized population.)

Age, sex, race, and Hispanic origin	Population[1]	Enrolled		Nursery	Kinder-garten	Elementary grades							
		Number	Percent			1	2	3	4	5	6	7	8
22 years old	260	163	62.5	*	*	*	*	*	*	*	*	*	*
23 years old	244	88	36.1	*	*	*	*	*	*	*	*	*	*
24 years old	281	101	35.8	*	*	*	*	*	*	*	*	*	*
25 to 29 years old	1,644	271	16.5	*	*	*	*	*	*	*	*	*	*
30 to 34 years old	1,734	130	7.5	*	*	*	*	*	*	*	*	*	*
35 to 39 years old	1,670	90	5.4	*	*	*	*	*	*	*	*	3	*
40 to 44 years old	1,526	42	2.7	*	*	*	*	*	*	*	*	*	4
45 to 49 years old	1,498	16	1.1	*	*	*	*	*	*	*	*	*	*
50 to 54 years old	1,267	17	1.4	*	*	*	*	*	*	*	*	*	*
55 to 59 years old	1,180	15	1.3	*	*	*	*	*	*	*	*	*	*
60 to 64 years old	1,069	8	0.7	*	*	*	*	*	*	*	*	*	*
65 years and over	2,673	*	*	*	*	*	*	*	*	*	*	*	*
Male													
Total	9,229	2,329	25.2	94	115	105	82	85	123	83	119	148	129
3 years old	73	20	28.0	20	*	*	*	*	*	*	*	*	*
4 years old	132	58	43.8	54	4	*	*	*	*	*	*	*	*
5 years old	148	115	77.7	19	89	7	*	*	*	*	*	*	*
6 years old	121	106	88.0	*	19	82	5	*	*	*	*	*	*
7 years old	74	69	93.0	*	4	17	49	*	*	*	*	*	*
8 years old	101	95	93.7	*	*	*	26	66	3	*	*	*	*
9 years old	109	105	97.0	*	*	*	2	11	86	7	*	*	*
10 years old	111	107	96.7	*	*	*	*	7	28	63	9	*	*
11 years old	120	117	97.5	*	*	*	*	*	7	13	90	7	*
12 years old	131	131	100.0	*	*	*	*	*	*	*	18	97	16
13 years old	129	129	100.0	*	*	*	*	*	*	*	1	34	94
14 years old	88	84	95.6	*	*	*	*	*	*	*	1	7	15
15 years old	141	141	100.0	*	*	*	*	*	*	*	*	*	*
16 years old	79	79	100.0	*	*	*	*	*	*	*	*	*	*
17 years old	136	122	89.6	*	*	*	*	*	*	*	*	*	*
18 years old	143	114	79.4	*	*	*	*	*	*	*	*	*	*
19 years old	140	100	71.7	*	*	*	*	*	*	*	*	*	*
20 years old	129	102	79.3	*	*	*	*	*	*	*	*	*	*
21 years old	128	114	88.9	*	*	*	*	*	*	*	*	*	*
22 years old	118	86	72.9	*	*	*	*	*	*	*	*	*	*
23 years old	118	38	31.8	*	*	*	*	*	*	*	*	*	*
24 years old	127	30	23.4	*	*	*	*	*	*	*	*	*	*
25 to 29 years old	825	125	15.1	*	*	*	*	*	*	*	*	*	*
30 to 34 years old	833	67	8.0	*	*	*	*	*	*	*	*	*	*
35 to 39 years old	782	32	4.1	*	*	*	*	*	*	*	*	3	*
40 to 44 years old	714	20	2.8	*	*	*	*	*	*	*	*	*	4
45 to 49 years old	688	2	0.3	*	*	*	*	*	*	*	*	*	*
50 to 54 years old	604	9	1.5	*	*	*	*	*	*	*	*	*	*
55 to 59 years old	519	4	0.8	*	*	*	*	*	*	*	*	*	*
60 to 64 years old	524	8	1.4	*	*	*	*	*	*	*	*	*	*
65 years and over	1,143	*	*	*	*	*	*	*	*	*	*	*	*
Female													
Total	10,246	2,442	23.8	84	104	103	123	113	97	144	108	82	157
3 years old	114	35	30.5	23	12	*	*	*	*	*	*	*	*
4 years old	115	63	54.6	51	11	*	*	*	*	*	*	*	*
5 years old	86	72	83.7	10	63	*	*	*	*	*	*	*	*
6 years old	117	117	100.0	*	14	92	12	*	*	*	*	*	*
7 years old	96	89	93.0	*	5	11	69	4	*	*	*	*	*
8 years old	134	129	96.5	*	*	*	37	86	3	4	*	*	*
9 years old	105	105	100.0	*	*	*	5	21	77	*	2	*	*
10 years old	144	131	91.1	*	*	*	*	2	17	112	*	*	*
11 years old	107	102	95.1	*	*	*	*	*	1	24	78	*	1
12 years old	89	89	100.0	*	*	*	*	*	1	1	20	39	28
13 years old	152	148	97.3	*	*	*	*	*	*	4	5	41	91
14 years old	89	87	97.2	*	*	*	*	*	*	*	3	2	31
15 years old	113	113	100.0	*	*	*	*	*	*	*	*	*	3
16 years old	96	89	92.2	*	*	*	*	*	*	*	*	*	4
17 years old	108	108	100.0	*	*	*	*	*	*	*	*	*	*
18 years old	102	84	81.6	*	*	*	*	*	*	*	*	*	*
19 years old	126	108	85.3	*	*	*	*	*	*	*	*	*	*
20 years old	175	154	88.5	*	*	*	*	*	*	*	*	*	*

* = Quantity zero or rounds to zero.

Table A-2. Single Grade of Enrollment and High School Graduation Status for Population 3 Years Old and Over, by Sex, Age (Single Years for 3 to 24 Years), Race, and Hispanic Origin, October 2020—*Continued*

(Numbers in thousands; percent; civilian noninstitutionalized population.)

| Age, sex, race, and Hispanic origin | Enrolled | | | | | | | | | | Not enrolled | | Not enrolled | |
| | High school | | | | Undergraduate college | | | | Graduate school | | H.S. grad | Not grad | Number | Percent |
	9	10	11	12	1	2	3	4	1	2+				
22 years old	*	4	*	*	18	20	25	24	43	28	95	3	98	37.5
23 years old	*	*	*	*	1	8	26	22	20	10	152	4	156	63.9
24 years old	*	*	*	*	5	15	14	4	30	32	176	4	180	64.2
25 to 29 years old	*	*	*	6	23	23	16	29	35	139	1,339	34	1,373	83.5
30 to 34 years old	*	*	*	5	4	5	16	10	31	58	1,555	50	1,605	92.5
35 to 39 years old	*	*	*	*	27	*	4	8	5	43	1,485	94	1,580	94.6
40 to 44 years old	*	*	*	*	9	1	*	4	6	18	1,380	105	1,485	97.3
45 to 49 years old	*	*	*	*	6	4	*	3	*	3	1,401	81	1,482	98.9
50 to 54 years old	*	*	*	*	3	9	*	*	3	3	1,167	83	1,250	98.6
55 to 59 years old	*	*	*	*	*	4	4	4	4	*	1,052	113	1,165	98.7
60 to 64 years old	*	*	*	*	4	*	*	*	3	*	968	94	1,062	99.3
65 years and over	*	*	*	*	*	*	*	*	*	*	2,285	388	2,673	100.0
Male														
Total	82	126	102	115	199	157	134	102	77	151	6,269	631	6,900	74.8
3 years old	*	*	*	*	*	*	*	*	*	*	*	52	52	72.0
4 years old	*	*	*	*	*	*	*	*	*	*	*	74	74	56.2
5 years old	*	*	*	*	*	*	*	*	*	*	*	33	33	22.3
6 years old	*	*	*	*	*	*	*	*	*	*	*	15	15	12.0
7 years old	*	*	*	*	*	*	*	*	*	*	*	5	5	7.0
8 years old	*	*	*	*	*	*	*	*	*	*	*	6	6	6.3
9 years old	*	*	*	*	*	*	*	*	*	*	*	3	3	3.0
10 years old	*	*	*	*	*	*	*	*	*	*	*	4	4	3.3
11 years old	*	*	*	*	*	*	*	*	*	*	*	3	3	2.5
12 years old	*	*	*	*	*	*	*	*	*	*	*	*	*	*
13 years old	*	*	*	*	*	*	*	*	*	*	*	*	*	*
14 years old	57	4	*	*	*	*	*	*	*	*	*	4	4	4.4
15 years old	25	92	24	*	*	*	*	*	*	*	*	*	*	*
16 years old	*	27	39	12	1	*	*	*	*	*	*	*	*	*
17 years old	*	2	33	80	4	*	*	*	2	*	11	4	14	10.4
18 years old	*	*	6	10	81	13	4	*	*	*	20	10	29	20.6
19 years old	*	*	*	12	30	54	4	*	*	*	33	7	39	28.3
20 years old	*	*	*	*	38	33	28	4	*	*	20	7	27	20.7
21 years old	*	*	*	*	3	19	40	45	3	3	14	*	14	11.1
22 years old	*	*	*	*	16	10	17	17	12	14	32	*	32	27.1
23 years old	*	*	*	*	*	4	17	10	2	4	77	4	81	68.2
24 years old	*	*	*	*	5	5	7	1	4	9	93	4	97	76.6
25 to 29 years old	*	*	*	*	11	10	8	19	22	54	681	19	700	84.9
30 to 34 years old	*	*	*	*	*	4	10	*	20	33	745	22	767	92.0
35 to 39 years old	*	*	*	*	*	*	*	8	1	20	691	60	751	95.9
40 to 44 years old	*	*	*	*	4	1	*	*	1	10	658	36	694	97.2
45 to 49 years old	*	*	*	*	2	*	*	*	*	*	651	34	686	99.7
50 to 54 years old	*	*	*	*	*	4	*	*	3	3	544	51	595	98.5
55 to 59 years old	*	*	*	*	*	*	*	*	4	*	481	34	515	99.2
60 to 64 years old	*	*	*	*	4	*	*	*	3	*	489	28	517	98.6
65 years and over	*	*	*	*	*	*	*	*	*	*	1,030	113	1,143	100.0
Female														
Total	75	112	87	116	154	215	134	126	111	198	6,955	848	7,803	76.2
3 years old	*	*	*	*	*	*	*	*	*	*	*	79	79	69.5
4 years old	*	*	*	*	*	*	*	*	*	*	*	52	52	45.4
5 years old	*	*	*	*	*	*	*	*	*	*	*	14	14	16.3
6 years old	*	*	*	*	*	*	*	*	*	*	*	*	*	*
7 years old	*	*	*	*	*	*	*	*	*	*	*	7	7	7.0
8 years old	*	*	*	*	*	*	*	*	*	*	*	5	5	3.5
9 years old	*	*	*	*	*	*	*	*	*	*	*	*	*	*
10 years old	*	*	*	*	*	*	*	*	*	*	*	13	13	8.9
11 years old	*	*	*	*	*	*	*	*	*	*	*	5	5	4.9
12 years old	*	*	*	*	*	*	*	*	*	*	*	*	*	*
13 years old	4	4	*	*	*	*	*	*	*	*	*	4	4	2.7
14 years old	50	*	*	*	*	*	*	*	*	*	*	3	3	2.8
15 years old	21	71	13	3	2	*	*	*	*	*	*	*	*	*
16 years old	*	24	58	3	*	*	*	*	*	*	*	8	8	7.8
17 years old	*	10	16	77	4	*	*	*	*	*	*	*	*	*
18 years old	*	*	*	17	68	3	*	*	3	3	12	6	19	18.4
19 years old	*	*	*	*	16	70	18	1	*	3	18	*	18	14.7
20 years old	*	*	*	5	6	62	52	29	*	*	20	*	20	11.5

* = Quantity zero or rounds to zero.

Table A-2. Single Grade of Enrollment and High School Graduation Status for Population 3 Years Old and Over, by Sex, Age (Single Years for 3 to 24 Years), Race, and Hispanic Origin, October 2020—*Continued*

(Numbers in thousands; percent; civilian noninstitutionalized population.)

						Enrolled								
		Enrolled					Elementary grades							
Age, sex, race, and Hispanic origin	Population[1]	Number	Percent	Nursery	Kinder-garten	1	2	3	4	5	6	7	8
21 years old	128	101	78.9	*	*	*	*	*	*	*	*	*	*
22 years old	142	77	53.9	*	*	*	*	*	*	*	*	*	*
23 years old	125	50	40.3	*	*	*	*	*	*	*	*	*	*
24 years old	154	71	46.0	*	*	*	*	*	*	*	*	*	*
25 to 29 years old	819	146	17.8	*	*	*	*	*	*	*	*	*	*
30 to 34 years old	901	63	7.0	*	*	*	*	*	*	*	*	*	*
35 to 39 years old	888	58	6.6	*	*	*	*	*	*	*	*	*	*
40 to 44 years old	812	22	2.7	*	*	*	*	*	*	*	*	*	*
45 to 49 years old	810	14	1.8	*	*	*	*	*	*	*	*	*	*
50 to 54 years old	663	8	1.2	*	*	*	*	*	*	*	*	*	*
55 to 59 years old	661	11	1.7	*	*	*	*	*	*	*	*	*	*
60 to 64 years old	545	*	*	*	*	*	*	*	*	*	*	*	*
65 years and over	1,530	*	*	*	*	*	*	*	*	*	*	*	*
HISPANIC (OF ANY RACE)													
Both Sexes													
Total	58,214	17,524	30.1	751	890	1,059	977	1,048	1,034	1,016	1,054	1,154	961
3 years old	1,009	217	21.5	209	8	*	*	*	*	*	*	*	*
4 years old	1,037	457	44.1	381	76	*	*	*	*	*	*	*	*
5 years old	1,005	828	82.4	136	658	20	14	*	*	*	*	*	*
6 years old	1,088	993	91.3	24	137	786	39	7	*	*	*	*	*
7 years old	1,012	951	93.9	*	11	223	669	48	*	*	*	*	*
8 years old	1,091	1,025	93.9	*	*	30	246	708	36	4	*	*	*
9 years old	1,059	1,011	95.4	*	*	*	10	268	686	40	8	*	*
10 years old	1,011	978	96.8	*	*	*	1	16	273	636	52	*	*
11 years old	1,134	1,094	96.5	*	*	*	*	*	39	284	726	38	7
12 years old	1,124	1,097	97.6	*	*	*	*	*	*	49	212	797	23
13 years old	1,049	1,011	96.4	*	*	*	*	*	*	4	39	251	650
14 years old	1,058	1,035	97.9	*	*	*	*	*	*	*	14	41	255
15 years old	1,057	1,040	98.3	*	*	*	*	*	*	*	*	11	10
16 years old	988	906	91.7	*	*	*	*	*	*	*	*	10	16
17 years old	998	909	91.0	*	*	*	*	*	*	*	*	*	*
18 years old	1,101	735	66.8	*	*	*	*	*	*	*	*	*	*
19 years old	953	554	58.1	*	*	*	*	*	*	*	*	*	*
20 years old	1,120	550	49.1	*	*	*	*	*	*	*	*	*	*
21 years old	972	451	46.4	*	*	*	*	*	*	*	*	*	*
22 years old	884	252	28.5	*	*	*	*	*	*	*	*	*	*
23 years old	808	159	19.7	*	*	*	*	*	*	*	*	*	*
24 years old	1,030	167	16.2	*	*	*	*	*	*	*	*	*	*
25 to 29 years old	4,849	494	10.2	*	*	*	*	*	*	*	*	*	*
30 to 34 years old	4,598	186	4.0	*	*	*	*	*	*	*	*	*	*
35 to 39 years old	4,454	164	3.7	*	*	*	*	*	*	*	*	*	*
40 to 44 years old	4,219	123	2.9	*	*	*	*	*	*	*	3	*	*
45 to 49 years old	3,855	57	1.5	*	*	*	*	*	*	*	*	3	*
50 to 54 years old	3,404	32	0.9	*	*	*	*	*	*	*	*	4	*
55 to 59 years old	2,978	23	0.8	*	*	*	*	*	*	*	*	*	*
60 to 64 years old	2,332	9	0.4	*	*	*	*	*	*	*	*	*	*
65 years and over	4,940	18	0.4	*	*	*	*	*	*	*	*	*	*
Male													
Total	29,134	8,641	29.7	374	464	594	448	590	471	565	509	609	511
3 years old	516	107	20.7	107	*	*	*	*	*	*	*	*	*
4 years old	538	253	47.1	213	40	*	*	*	*	*	*	*	*
5 years old	509	434	85.3	52	366	12	4	*	*	*	*	*	*
6 years old	561	504	89.8	2	51	435	15	*	*	*	*	*	*
7 years old	507	486	95.8	*	6	130	317	33	*	*	*	*	*
8 years old	545	519	95.2	*	*	17	107	372	20	4	*	*	*
9 years old	555	542	97.7	*	*	*	6	174	327	28	8	*	*
10 years old	518	508	98.0	*	*	*	*	12	109	356	31	*	*
11 years old	577	545	94.4	*	*	*	*	*	16	162	341	23	3
12 years old	561	546	97.3	*	*	*	*	*	*	15	103	406	19
13 years old	561	535	95.3	*	*	*	*	*	*	*	17	140	359
14 years old	517	500	96.6	*	*	*	*	*	*	*	6	21	119
15 years old	543	534	98.3	*	*	*	*	*	*	*	*	11	*
16 years old	543	494	91.1	*	*	*	*	*	*	*	*	4	11
17 years old	497	452	90.9	*	*	*	*	*	*	*	*	*	*

* = Quantity zero or rounds to zero.

Table A-2. Single Grade of Enrollment and High School Graduation Status for Population 3 Years Old and Over, by Sex, Age (Single Years for 3 to 24 Years), Race, and Hispanic Origin, October 2020—*Continued*

(Numbers in thousands; percent; civilian noninstitutionalized population.)

Age, sex, race, and Hispanic origin	Enrolled										Not enrolled		Not enrolled	
	High school				Undergraduate college				Graduate school		H.S. grad	Not grad	Number	Percent
	9	10	11	12	1	2	3	4	1	2+				
21 years old	*	*	*	*	8	29	18	41	*	4	20	7	27	21.1
22 years old	*	4	*	*	3	10	8	7	31	14	63	3	66	46.1
23 years old	*	*	*	*	1	4	9	12	18	6	75	*	75	59.7
24 years old	*	*	*	*	*	10	7	4	27	23	83	*	83	54.0
25 to 29 years old	*	*	*	6	11	13	8	10	13	85	658	15	673	82.2
30 to 34 years old	*	*	*	5	4	1	6	10	12	25	810	28	838	93.0
35 to 39 years old	*	*	*	*	27	*	4	*	4	23	795	34	829	93.4
40 to 44 years old	*	*	*	*	5	*	*	4	5	8	722	69	790	97.3
45 to 49 years old	*	*	*	*	4	4	*	3	*	3	750	46	796	98.2
50 to 54 years old	*	*	*	*	3	5	*	4	*	*	623	32	655	98.8
55 to 59 years old	*	*	*	*	*	4	4	4	*	*	570	79	650	98.3
60 to 64 years old	*	*	*	*	*	*	*	*	*	*	479	66	545	100.0
65 years and over	*	*	*	*	*	*	*	*	*	*	1,256	274	1,530	100.0

HISPANIC (OF ANY RACE)

Both Sexes

Age, sex, race, and Hispanic origin	9	10	11	12	1	2	3	4	1	2+	H.S. grad	Not grad	Number	Percent
Total	1,002	1,235	820	971	976	976	716	394	172	319	29,079	11,610	40,689	69.9
3 years old	*	*	*	*	*	*	*	*	*	*	*	792	792	78.5
4 years old	*	*	*	*	*	*	*	*	*	*	*	580	580	55.9
5 years old	*	*	*	*	*	*	*	*	*	*	*	177	177	17.6
6 years old	*	*	*	*	*	*	*	*	*	*	*	95	95	8.7
7 years old	*	*	*	*	*	*	*	*	*	*	*	62	62	6.1
8 years old	*	*	*	*	*	*	*	*	*	*	*	66	66	6.1
9 years old	*	*	*	*	*	*	*	*	*	*	*	48	48	4.6
10 years old	*	*	*	*	*	*	*	*	*	*	*	33	33	3.2
11 years old	*	*	*	*	*	*	*	*	*	*	*	40	40	3.5
12 years old	17	*	*	*	*	*	*	*	*	*	*	26	26	2.4
13 years old	53	14	*	*	*	*	*	*	*	*	*	38	38	3.6
14 years old	644	70	11	*	*	*	*	*	*	*	*	22	22	2.1
15 years old	238	696	68	12	5	*	*	*	*	*	*	17	17	1.7
16 years old	23	356	434	63	4	*	*	*	*	*	15	67	82	8.3
17 years old	6	63	248	564	24	*	5	*	*	*	28	61	90	9.0
18 years old	9	12	45	228	408	33	*	*	*	*	310	56	366	33.2
19 years old	*	4	*	61	201	241	33	14	*	*	343	56	399	41.9
20 years old	4	7	4	24	74	252	153	26	6	*	471	99	570	50.9
21 years old	1	*	*	9	44	123	119	126	*	30	442	79	521	53.6
22 years old	*	*	*	*	23	48	95	52	14	20	587	45	632	71.5
23 years old	*	*	*	*	10	33	47	43	16	10	546	102	648	80.3
24 years old	*	*	*	*	9	32	44	17	44	22	776	87	863	83.8
25 to 29 years old	*	*	5	3	98	79	99	52	56	102	3,781	573	4,354	89.8
30 to 34 years old	*	5	*	2	30	46	25	20	16	42	3,631	780	4,412	96.0
35 to 39 years old	3	4	*	*	16	43	26	12	9	51	3,271	1,019	4,290	96.3
40 to 44 years old	*	5	4	3	13	27	38	13	4	13	2,995	1,100	4,095	97.1
45 to 49 years old	*	*	*	3	14	9	9	10	6	4	2,861	936	3,797	98.5
50 to 54 years old	*	*	*	*	4	8	9	6	*	1	2,386	986	3,372	99.1
55 to 59 years old	4	*	*	*	*	*	2	*	*	17	2,100	855	2,955	99.2
60 to 64 years old	*	*	*	*	*	*	5	4	*	*	1,578	745	2,323	99.6
65 years and over	*	*	*	*	*	3	8	*	*	7	2,956	1,966	4,922	99.6

Male

Age, sex, race, and Hispanic origin	9	10	11	12	1	2	3	4	1	2+	H.S. grad	Not grad	Number	Percent
Total	493	631	453	491	363	415	310	152	72	124	14,487	6,007	20,494	70.3
3 years old	*	*	*	*	*	*	*	*	*	*	*	410	410	79.3
4 years old	*	*	*	*	*	*	*	*	*	*	*	285	285	52.9
5 years old	*	*	*	*	*	*	*	*	*	*	*	75	75	14.7
6 years old	*	*	*	*	*	*	*	*	*	*	*	57	57	10.2
7 years old	*	*	*	*	*	*	*	*	*	*	*	21	21	4.2
8 years old	*	*	*	*	*	*	*	*	*	*	*	26	26	4.8
9 years old	*	*	*	*	*	*	*	*	*	*	*	13	13	2.3
10 years old	*	*	*	*	*	*	*	*	*	*	*	11	11	2.0
11 years old	*	*	*	*	*	*	*	*	*	*	*	32	32	5.6
12 years old	3	*	*	*	*	*	*	*	*	*	*	15	15	2.7
13 years old	18	*	*	*	*	*	*	*	*	*	*	26	26	4.7
14 years old	304	42	7	*	*	*	*	*	*	*	*	17	17	3.4
15 years old	131	351	33	4	5	*	*	*	*	*	*	9	9	1.7
16 years old	20	186	236	38	*	*	*	*	*	*	7	41	48	8.9
17 years old	1	30	149	263	9	*	*	*	*	*	12	33	45	9.1

* – Quantity zero or rounds to zero.

Table A-2. Single Grade of Enrollment and High School Graduation Status for Population 3 Years Old and Over, by Sex, Age (Single Years for 3 to 24 Years), Race, and Hispanic Origin, October 2020—*Continued*

(Numbers in thousands; percent; civilian noninstitutionalized population.)

						Enrolled								
		Enrolled				Elementary grades								
Age, sex, race, and Hispanic origin	Population[1]	Number	Percent	Nursery	Kinder-garten	1	2	3	4	5	6	7	8
18 years old	556	356	63.9	*	*	*	*	*	*	*	*	*	*
19 years old	443	212	47.8	*	*	*	*	*	*	*	*	*	*
20 years old	588	261	44.4	*	*	*	*	*	*	*	*	*	*
21 years old	439	191	43.5	*	*	*	*	*	*	*	*	*	*
22 years old	424	92	21.6	*	*	*	*	*	*	*	*	*	*
23 years old	445	83	18.6	*	*	*	*	*	*	*	*	*	*
24 years old	527	56	10.6	*	*	*	*	*	*	*	*	*	*
25 to 29 years old	2,464	214	8.7	*	*	*	*	*	*	*	*	*	*
30 to 34 years old	2,376	76	3.2	*	*	*	*	*	*	*	*	*	*
35 to 39 years old	2,289	60	2.6	*	*	*	*	*	*	*	*	*	*
40 to 44 years old	2,144	33	1.5	*	*	*	*	*	*	*	3	*	*
45 to 49 years old	1,925	14	0.7	*	*	*	*	*	*	*	*	*	*
50 to 54 years old	1,706	4	0.2	*	*	*	*	*	*	*	*	4	*
55 to 59 years old	1,412	19	1.4	*	*	*	*	*	*	*	*	*	*
60 to 64 years old	1,183	4	0.3	*	*	*	*	*	*	*	*	*	*
65 years and over	2,166	10	0.5	*	*	*	*	*	*	*	*	*	*
Female													
Total	29,079	8,884	30.6	377	426	465	529	458	562	452	545	545	450
3 years old	493	110	22.4	103	8	*	*	*	*	*	*	*	*
4 years old	499	204	40.8	168	36	*	*	*	*	*	*	*	*
5 years old	496	394	79.4	84	292	8	10	*	*	*	*	*	*
6 years old	527	489	92.9	22	86	351	23	7	*	*	*	*	*
7 years old	505	465	92.0	*	5	93	352	15	*	*	*	*	*
8 years old	546	506	92.7	*	*	13	139	337	17	*	*	*	*
9 years old	504	469	93.0	*	*	*	4	94	359	12	*	*	*
10 years old	493	470	95.5	*	*	*	1	4	164	280	21	*	*
11 years old	556	549	98.7	*	*	*	*	*	23	122	385	15	4
12 years old	563	552	98.0	*	*	*	*	*	*	34	109	391	4
13 years old	488	476	97.5	*	*	*	*	*	*	4	21	111	290
14 years old	540	536	99.1	*	*	*	*	*	*	*	8	19	135
15 years old	514	506	98.3	*	*	*	*	*	*	*	*	*	10
16 years old	446	412	92.4	*	*	*	*	*	*	*	*	6	5
17 years old	501	457	91.2	*	*	*	*	*	*	*	*	*	*
18 years old	544	379	69.7	*	*	*	*	*	*	*	*	*	*
19 years old	510	342	67.1	*	*	*	*	*	*	*	*	*	*
20 years old	532	288	54.2	*	*	*	*	*	*	*	*	*	*
21 years old	533	260	48.7	*	*	*	*	*	*	*	*	*	*
22 years old	460	160	34.8	*	*	*	*	*	*	*	*	*	*
23 years old	363	76	21.0	*	*	*	*	*	*	*	*	*	*
24 years old	503	111	22.1	*	*	*	*	*	*	*	*	*	*
25 to 29 years old	2,385	281	11.8	*	*	*	*	*	*	*	*	*	*
30 to 34 years old	2,221	110	4.9	*	*	*	*	*	*	*	*	*	*
35 to 39 years old	2,165	104	4.8	*	*	*	*	*	*	*	*	*	*
40 to 44 years old	2,075	91	4.4	*	*	*	*	*	*	*	*	*	*
45 to 49 years old	1,929	44	2.3	*	*	*	*	*	*	*	*	3	*
50 to 54 years old	1,698	28	1.7	*	*	*	*	*	*	*	*	*	*
55 to 59 years old	1,566	4	0.2	*	*	*	*	*	*	*	*	*	*
60 to 64 years old	1,149	5	0.5	*	*	*	*	*	*	*	*	*	*
65 years and over	2,774	8	0.3	*	*	*	*	*	*	*	*	*	*

* = Quantity zero or rounds to zero.

Table A-2. Single Grade of Enrollment and High School Graduation Status for Population 3 Years Old and Over, by Sex, Age (Single Years for 3 to 24 Years), Race, and Hispanic Origin, October 2020—*Continued*

(Numbers in thousands; percent; civilian noninstitutionalized population.)

Age, sex, race, and Hispanic origin	Enrolled										Not enrolled		Not enrolled	
	High school				Undergraduate college				Graduate school		H.S. grad	Not grad	Number	Percent
	9	10	11	12	1	2	3	4	1	2+				
18 years old	9	4	25	137	170	12	*	*	*	*	180	21	201	36.1
19 years old	*	4	*	31	72	93	12	*	*	*	193	38	231	52.2
20 years old	*	7	*	12	28	132	69	10	4	*	256	71	327	55.6
21 years old	1	*	*	*	17	57	62	41	*	14	205	43	248	56.5
22 years old	*	*	*	*	7	9	39	21	*	16	310	22	332	78.4
23 years old	*	*	*	*	5	13	28	27	5	6	298	64	362	81.4
24 years old	*	*	*	*	4	14	14	3	17	4	410	61	471	89.4
25 to 29 years old	*	*	*	*	26	34	56	29	26	42	1,912	338	2,250	91.3
30 to 34 years old	*	5	*	2	16	16	14	2	11	11	1,863	437	2,300	96.8
35 to 39 years old	3	4	*	*	6	18	10	12	*	8	1,663	565	2,228	97.4
40 to 44 years old	*	*	4	*	*	11	2	4	4	4	1,494	617	2,111	98.5
45 to 49 years old	*	*	*	3	*	4	1	*	6	*	1,442	470	1,911	99.3
50 to 54 years old	*	*	*	*	*	*	*	*	*	*	1,191	511	1,702	99.8
55 to 59 years old	4	*	*	*	*	*	2	*	*	13	963	430	1,393	98.6
60 to 64 years old	*	*	*	*	*	*	*	4	*	*	778	401	1,179	99.7
65 years and over	*	*	*	*	*	3	*	*	*	7	1,310	846	2,156	99.5
Female														
Total	509	604	367	480	613	560	406	242	99	195	14,593	5,603	20,196	69.4
3 years old	*	*	*	*	*	*	*	*	*	*	*	383	383	77.6
4 years old	*	*	*	*	*	*	*	*	*	*	*	295	295	59.2
5 years old	*	*	*	*	*	*	*	*	*	*	*	102	102	20.6
6 years old	*	*	*	*	*	*	*	*	*	*	*	38	38	7.1
7 years old	*	*	*	*	*	*	*	*	*	*	*	40	40	8.0
8 years old	*	*	*	*	*	*	*	*	*	*	*	40	40	7.3
9 years old	*	*	*	*	*	*	*	*	*	*	*	35	35	7.0
10 years old	*	*	*	*	*	*	*	*	*	*	*	22	22	4.5
11 years old	*	*	*	*	*	*	*	*	*	*	*	7	7	1.3
12 years old	13	*	*	*	*	*	*	*	*	*	*	11	11	2.0
13 years old	35	14	*	*	*	*	*	*	*	*	*	12	12	2.5
14 years old	341	28	4	*	*	*	*	*	*	*	*	5	5	0.9
15 years old	107	345	35	7	*	*	*	*	*	*	*	8	8	1.7
16 years old	4	170	199	24	4	*	*	*	*	*	8	26	34	7.6
17 years old	5	32	99	301	15	*	5	*	*	*	16	28	44	8.8
18 years old	*	9	20	91	238	21	*	*	*	*	130	35	165	30.3
19 years old	*	*	*	30	129	148	21	14	*	*	151	17	168	32.9
20 years old	4	*	4	12	46	120	83	16	3	*	216	28	244	45.8
21 years old	*	*	*	9	27	66	57	85	*	16	238	36	273	51.3
22 years old	*	*	*	*	16	39	56	31	14	5	277	23	300	65.2
23 years old	*	*	*	*	5	20	19	16	12	4	249	38	287	79.0
24 years old	*	*	*	*	5	18	29	14	27	18	366	26	392	77.9
25 to 29 years old	*	*	5	3	72	46	43	23	30	61	1,869	235	2,104	88.2
30 to 34 years old	*	*	*	*	14	30	11	19	5	31	1,768	344	2,112	95.1
35 to 39 years old	*	*	*	*	10	25	17	*	9	43	1,608	454	2,062	95.2
40 to 44 years old	*	5	*	3	13	16	36	9	*	9	1,501	483	1,984	95.6
45 to 49 years old	*	*	*	*	14	4	8	10	*	4	1,419	467	1,886	97.7
50 to 54 years old	*	*	*	*	4	8	9	6	*	1	1,195	475	1,670	98.3
55 to 59 years old	*	*	*	*	*	*	9	*	*	4	1,137	425	1,562	99.8
60 to 64 years old	*	*	*	*	*	*	5	*	*	*	800	344	1,144	99.5
65 years and over	*	*	*	*	*	*	8	*	*	*	1,646	1,120	2,766	99.7

* = Quantity zero or rounds to zero.

Table A-3. Nursery and Primary School Enrollment of Population 3 to 6 Years Old, by Control of School, Attendance Status, Age, Race, Hispanic Origin, Mother's Labor Force Status and Education, and Family Income, October 2020

(Numbers in thousands; civilian noninstitutionalized population.)

Characteristic	Total	Not enrolled	Enrolled in nursery school								
			Total			Public			Private		
			Total	Part-day	Full-day	Total	Part-day	Full-day	Total	Part-day	Full-day
3 TO 6 YEARS OLD											
Total..	16,058	5,601	3,545	1,622	1,923	2,094	1,098	996	1,451	524	927
Race and Hispanic origin											
White alone...............................	11,465	4,027	2,553	1,173	1,380	1,429	769	660	1,124	404	720
White alone non-Hispanic........................	7,885	2,591	1,900	887	1,013	969	537	432	931	350	581
Black alone...............................	2,502	860	512	220	291	382	181	201	130	40	90
Asian alone...............................	906	319	178	97	81	104	59	45	73	38	35
Hispanic (of any race).....................	4,139	1,644	751	326	424	534	271	264	216	56	161
Labor force status of mother											
Children not living with mother.....................	1,854	629	403	199	204	298	164	134	106	35	71
Mother employed part-time	2,075	703	458	216	242	276	142	134	182	75	107
Mother employed full-time....................	6,462	2,048	1,595	620	975	779	395	384	816	226	591
Mother unemployed.........................	586	164	127	47	80	73	22	52	54	25	29
Mother not in the labor force	5,081	2,057	962	540	422	668	376	292	293	164	130
Education of mother											
Children not living with mother.....................	1,854	629	403	199	204	298	164	134	106	35	71
Elementary: 0 to 8 years	519	208	72	37	34	56	29	27	15	8	7
High school: 9 to 11 years	737	287	176	60	117	138	57	81	38	3	35
High school graduate.........................	3,169	1,271	578	299	279	463	255	208	115	44	71
Some college or associate's degree	3,578	1,220	777	350	427	493	252	241	284	98	186
Bachelor's degree or more	6,201	1,986	1,539	677	862	646	341	305	893	336	557
Family income											
Less than $20,000	1,439	503	350	173	177	260	137	123	90	36	54
$20,000 to $29,999	1,008	425	237	121	116	196	105	91	40	16	25
$30,000 to $39,999	1,028	357	212	85	127	181	76	105	31	8	22
$40,000 to $49,999	886	275	165	86	80	121	75	46	45	11	34
$50,000 to $74,999	2,102	795	450	199	251	289	134	156	160	65	95
$75,000 and over.........................	5,950	1,858	1,546	670	876	669	352	316	878	318	560
Not reported.........................	3,645	1,388	585	289	296	378	219	159	208	70	138
3 AND 4 YEARS OLD											
Total..	7,913	4,724	2,887	1,299	1,588	1,622	846	776	1,265	453	812
Race and Hispanic origin											
White alone..............................	5,666	3,400	2,047	931	1,117	1,073	583	490	974	348	627
White alone non-Hispanic........................	3,882	2,200	1,538	700	838	737	399	338	801	301	500
Black alone...............................	1,223	733	442	182	260	328	149	179	115	33	81
Asian alone...............................	433	257	149	74	75	85	44	41	64	30	34
Hispanic (of any race).....................	2,046	1,372	590	265	325	399	217	183	191	48	143
Labor force status of mother											
Children not living with mother.....................	918	534	329	165	164	235	129	105	94	35	59
Mother employed part-time	966	592	356	168	188	194	104	91	162	64	98
Mother employed full-time..........................	3,217	1,766	1,317	477	840	586	279	307	731	198	532
Mother unemployed.........................	252	132	102	44	58	57	19	38	46	25	21
Mother not in the labor force	2,560	1,701	783	445	338	550	315	235	233	130	102
Education of mother											
Children not living with mother.....................	918	534	329	165	164	235	129	105	94	35	59
Elementary: 0 to 8 years	221	150	64	33	31	48	25	24	15	8	7
High school: 9 to 11 years	360	230	129	51	78	98	51	47	31	*	31
High school graduate.........................	1,590	1,071	464	229	236	371	196	175	93	33	61
Some college or associate's degree	1,726	1,018	649	291	358	395	202	193	254	89	165
Bachelor's degree or more	3,098	1,721	1,252	531	721	475	243	232	778	288	489
Family income											
Less than $20,000	747	443	281	143	138	201	114	87	80	30	51
$20,000 to $29,999	535	337	178	98	80	143	87	55	36	11	25
$30,000 to $39,999	492	305	169	58	111	138	50	88	31	8	22
$40,000 to $49,999	409	240	150	79	72	106	68	38	45	11	34
$50,000 to $74,999	1,076	662	371	162	209	230	101	129	141	62	79
$75,000 and over.........................	2,981	1,615	1,256	528	728	498	247	251	758	280	478
Not reported.........................	1,673	1,122	481	230	250	307	180	127	174	51	123
5 YEARS OLD											
Total..	3,945	617	601	304	297	425	239	185	176	65	112
Race and Hispanic origin											
White alone..............................	2,896	432	458	231	228	316	178	138	142	53	90
White alone non-Hispanic........................	1,988	267	339	178	161	213	133	80	126	45	81
Black alone................................	563	96	64	35	29	52	32	20	12	3	9

* = Quantity zero or rounds to zero.

Table A-3. Nursery and Primary School Enrollment of Population 3 to 6 Years Old, by Control of School, Attendance Status, Age, Race, Hispanic Origin, Mother's Labor Force Status and Education, and Family Income, October 2020—*Continued*

(Numbers in thousands; civilian noninstitutionalized population.)

Characteristic	Enrolled in kindergarten									Enrolled in elementary school		
	Total			Public			Private					
	Total	Part-day	Full-day	Total	Part-day	Full-day	Total	Part-day	Full-day	Total	Public	Private
3 TO 6 YEARS OLD												
Total	3,646	768	2,879	3,079	660	2,419	568	108	460	3,266	2,842	424
Race and Hispanic origin												
White alone	2,619	550	2,069	2,213	458	1,754	406	92	315	2,267	1,992	275
White alone non-Hispanic	1,855	373	1,482	1,512	282	1,230	344	92	252	1,538	1,312	226
Black alone	588	104	484	482	100	382	107	5	102	543	473	70
Asian alone	211	62	148	171	55	116	40	8	32	198	165	33
Hispanic (of any race)	879	218	661	809	218	591	70	*	70	865	795	70
Labor force status of mother												
Children not living with mother	466	105	361	428	99	329	38	6	32	355	339	16
Mother employed part-time	472	116	356	370	91	279	102	25	76	442	402	40
Mother employed full-time	1,469	280	1,189	1,198	226	971	272	54	218	1,350	1,174	176
Mother unemployed	169	30	139	147	24	123	22	6	16	125	95	30
Mother not in the labor force	1,070	236	833	936	220	716	134	16	118	993	831	162
Education of mother												
Children not living with mother	466	105	361	428	99	329	38	6	32	355	339	16
Elementary: 0 to 8 years	146	25	122	146	25	122	*	*	*	93	71	22
High school: 9 to 11 years	132	19	112	111	19	92	21	*	21	142	117	25
High school graduate	672	158	514	601	151	450	72	7	64	648	597	50
Some college or associate's degree	820	142	678	674	124	550	146	18	128	761	640	121
Bachelor's degree or more	1,410	318	1,092	1,119	242	877	290	76	215	1,266	1,077	189
Family income												
Less than $20,000	326	49	277	295	45	250	30	4	27	260	242	18
$20,000 to $29,999	184	52	132	175	48	127	8	4	5	163	153	10
$30,000 to $39,999	224	41	182	199	36	163	25	6	20	235	227	9
$40,000 to $49,999	218	69	149	201	65	137	17	5	12	228	161	66
$50,000 to $74,999	419	65	354	360	61	299	59	4	55	440	399	41
$75,000 and over	1,365	292	1,073	1,102	241	861	263	51	212	1,180	983	197
Not reported	912	200	712	747	165	582	165	36	130	760	677	83
3 AND 4 YEARS OLD												
Total	303	67	235	245	49	196	58	19	39	*	*	*
Race and Hispanic origin												
White alone	219	47	172	170	28	142	49	19	30	*	*	*
White alone non-Hispanic	144	34	110	101	15	86	43	19	24	*	*	*
Black alone	48	15	33	44	15	29	4	*	4	*	*	*
Asian alone	27	4	22	22	4	18	5	*	5	*	*	*
Hispanic (of any race)	84	12	71	78	12	65	6	*	6	*	*	*
Labor force status of mother												
Children not living with mother	56	16	39	50	16	34	5	*	5	*	*	*
Mother employed part-time	18	6	13	14	1	12	5	4	*	*	*	*
Mother employed full-time	133	26	107	100	19	81	34	8	26	*	*	*
Mother unemployed	18	*	18	18	*	18	*	*	*	*	*	*
Mother not in the labor force	77	19	58	63	12	51	14	7	7	*	*	*
Education of mother												
Children not living with mother	56	16	39	50	16	34	5	*	5	*	*	*
Elementary: 0 to 8 years	7	*	7	7	*	7	*	*	*	*	*	*
High school: 9 to 11 years	2	1	*	2	1	*	*	*	*	*	*	*
High school graduate	54	8	46	52	6	45	3	2	*	*	*	*
Some college or associate's degree	59	15	44	52	10	42	7	4	2	*	*	*
Bachelor's degree or more	125	27	98	82	14	68	43	12	31	*	*	*
Family income												
Less than $20,000	23	2	21	23	2	21	*	*	*	*	*	*
$20,000 to $29,999	19	8	10	19	8	10	*	*	*	*	*	*
$30,000 to $39,999	19	9	9	16	7	9	2	2	*	*	*	*
$40,000 to $49,999	19	4	15	19	4	15	*	*	*	*	*	*
$50,000 to $74,999	43	9	34	43	9	34	*	*	*	*	*	*
$75,000 and over	110	14	96	70	6	63	41	8	33	*	*	*
Not reported	70	21	49	55	12	43	15	9	6	*	*	*
5 YEARS OLD												
Total	2,580	528	2,052	2,189	467	1,723	390	61	329	146	127	19
Race and Hispanic origin												
White alone	1,875	392	1,483	1,597	341	1,257	278	51	227	130	121	10
White alone non-Hispanic	1,285	258	1,027	1,057	206	851	227	51	176	96	87	10
Black alone	399	57	341	328	55	273	71	3	68	5	5	*

* = Quantity zero or rounds to zero.

Table A-3. Nursery and Primary School Enrollment of Population 3 to 6 Years Old, by Control of School, Attendance Status, Age, Race, Hispanic Origin, Mother's Labor Force Status and Education, and Family Income, October 2020—*Continued*

(Numbers in thousands; civilian noninstitutionalized population.)

Characteristic	Total	Not enrolled	Enrolled in nursery school								
			Total			Public			Private		
			Total	Part-day	Full-day	Total	Part-day	Full-day	Total	Part-day	Full-day
Asian alone	235	47	29	23	6	19	15	4	10	8	1
Hispanic (of any race)	1,005	177	136	59	77	114	51	63	22	7	14
Labor force status of mother											
Children not living with mother	480	65	70	30	40	58	30	28	12	*	12
Mother employed part-time	528	73	75	42	33	58	34	23	17	8	10
Mother employed full-time	1,546	181	270	137	133	188	113	75	82	24	59
Mother unemployed	173	23	22	3	19	15	3	12	7	*	7
Mother not in the labor force	1,218	276	164	92	72	106	59	47	58	33	25
Education of mother											
Children not living with mother	480	65	70	30	40	58	30	28	12	*	12
Elementary: 0 to 8 years	190	46	8	5	3	8	5	3	*	*	*
High school: 9 to 11 years	191	46	32	5	27	28	5	23	5	*	5
High school graduate	776	147	110	70	40	89	59	30	22	11	10
Some college or associate's degree	870	153	112	52	60	85	42	43	27	9	17
Bachelor's degree or more	1,439	160	268	142	126	157	98	59	112	44	68
Family income											
Less than $20,000	338	39	62	23	39	55	19	36	7	3	3
$20,000 to $29,999	256	73	51	18	33	46	13	33	4	4	*
$30,000 to $39,999	248	36	43	26	16	43	26	16	*	*	*
$40,000 to $49,999	199	16	14	7	7	14	7	7	*	*	*
$50,000 to $74,999	523	112	72	35	37	54	32	22	18	3	15
$75,000 and over	1,396	151	269	139	130	153	105	48	116	34	82
Not reported	985	191	90	56	35	59	36	23	31	19	12
6 YEARS OLD											
Total	4,201	260	57	19	38	47	13	34	10	6	4
Race and Hispanic origin											
White alone	2,903	194	47	12	35	40	8	32	7	3	4
White alone non-Hispanic	2,015	124	23	9	14	20	5	14	3	3	*
Black alone	716	31	5	3	2	2	*	2	3	3	*
Asian alone	238	15	*	*	*	*	*	*	*	*	*
Hispanic (of any race)	1,088	95	24	3	21	21	3	17	4	*	4
Labor force status of mother											
Children not living with mother	456	31	5	5	*	5	5	*	*	*	*
Mother employed part-time	581	38	27	7	20	24	4	20	3	3	*
Mother employed full-time	1,700	101	8	6	2	5	2	2	3	3	*
Mother unemployed	161	10	3	*	3	2	*	2	1	*	1
Mother not in the labor force	1,303	81	15	2	13	12	2	10	3	*	3
Education of mother											
Children not living with mother	456	31	5	5	*	5	5	*	*	*	*
Elementary: 0 to 8 years	109	12	*	*	*	*	*	*	*	*	*
High school: 9 to 11 years	186	11	15	4	11	12	1	11	3	3	*
High school graduate	803	53	3	*	3	3	*	3	*	*	*
Some college or associate's degree	982	49	16	7	9	13	7	5	4	*	4
Bachelor's degree or more	1,664	105	18	3	15	15	*	15	3	3	*
Family income											
Less than $20,000	354	21	7	7	*	4	4	*	3	3	*
$20,000 to $29,999	218	14	7	5	3	7	5	3	*	*	*
$30,000 to $39,999	287	17	*	*	*	*	*	*	*	*	*
$40,000 to $49,999	278	19	1	*	1	1	*	1	*	*	*
$50,000 to $74,999	504	21	7	1	5	5	1	4	1	*	1
$75,000 and over	1,573	93	21	3	18	18	*	18	3	3	*
Not reported	986	74	15	3	11	12	3	9	3	*	3

* = Quantity zero or rounds to zero.

Table A-3. Nursery and Primary School Enrollment of Population 3 to 6 Years Old, by Control of School, Attendance Status, Age, Race, Hispanic Origin, Mother's Labor Force Status and Education, and Family Income, October 2020—*Continued*

(Numbers in thousands; civilian noninstitutionalized population.)

Characteristic	Enrolled in kindergarten									Enrolled in elementary school		
	Total			Public			Private					
	Total	Part-day	Full-day	Total	Part-day	Full-day	Total	Part-day	Full-day	Total	Public	Private
Asian alone	152	42	109	125	39	86	27	4	24	7	2	5
Hispanic (of any race)	658	153	505	600	153	447	58	*	58	34	34	*
Labor force status of mother												
Children not living with mother	312	71	241	294	71	224	18	*	18	33	33	*
Mother employed part-time	369	83	286	284	62	222	86	21	64	11	11	*
Mother employed full-time	1,040	195	845	857	169	688	183	26	157	55	50	5
Mother unemployed	122	18	104	99	12	88	22	6	16	7	*	7
Mother not in the labor force	737	161	576	655	153	502	82	7	74	41	34	7
Education of mother												
Children not living with mother	312	71	241	294	71	224	18	*	18	33	33	*
Elementary: 0 to 8 years	130	17	113	130	17	113	*	*	*	5	5	*
High school: 9 to 11 years	107	12	95	86	12	74	21	*	21	5	5	*
High school graduate	489	99	391	435	95	340	54	3	51	29	25	4
Some college or associate's degree	573	109	464	468	95	373	105	14	91	32	27	5
Bachelor's degree or more	968	221	747	776	177	599	192	44	148	42	32	10
Family income												
Less than $20,000	228	33	195	204	33	172	23	*	23	10	10	*
$20,000 to $29,999	122	30	92	114	26	87	8	4	5	10	8	3
$30,000 to $39,999	161	25	135	143	22	121	18	3	15	9	9	*
$40,000 to $49,999	156	47	109	143	47	96	13	*	12	13	8	5
$50,000 to $74,999	318	54	264	271	50	221	47	4	44	21	21	*
$75,000 and over	932	213	719	770	178	592	162	35	128	43	33	10
Not reported	664	126	538	545	111	434	119	15	104	40	39	1
6 YEARS OLD												
Total	764	172	592	644	145	500	119	27	92	3,119	2,714	405
Race and Hispanic origin												
White alone	525	111	414	446	90	356	79	21	58	2,136	1,871	265
White alone non-Hispanic	426	81	345	353	60	293	73	21	52	1,442	1,225	217
Black alone	141	32	109	109	30	80	32	2	30	538	468	70
Asian alone	32	16	17	24	11	13	8	4	3	191	163	28
Hispanic (of any race)	137	52	85	131	52	79	6	*	6	831	761	70
Labor force status of mother												
Children not living with mother	99	18	81	84	12	72	15	6	9	322	307	16
Mother employed part-time	84	27	57	73	27	45	11	*	11	431	391	40
Mother employed full-time	296	58	238	241	39	202	55	19	35	1,295	1,124	171
Mother unemployed	30	12	18	30	12	18	*	*	*	119	95	23
Mother not in the labor force	256	57	199	218	55	163	38	2	36	952	797	155
Education of mother												
Children not living with mother	99	18	81	84	12	72	15	6	9	322	307	16
Elementary: 0 to 8 years	9	8	1	9	8	1	*	*	*	88	66	22
High school: 9 to 11 years	23	6	17	23	6	17	*	*	*	137	112	25
High school graduate	129	51	77	114	50	64	15	2	13	619	572	47
Some college or associate's degree	188	18	169	153	18	135	34	*	34	729	612	117
Bachelor's degree or more	317	70	246	262	51	211	55	19	35	1,224	1,045	179
Family income												
Less than $20,000	75	14	61	68	10	58	7	4	4	251	232	18
$20,000 to $29,999	43	13	30	43	13	30	*	*	*	153	146	7
$30,000 to $39,999	44	7	37	39	7	32	5	*	5	226	217	9
$40,000 to $49,999	43	18	25	39	14	25	4	4	*	215	154	61
$50,000 to $74,999	57	2	56	46	2	44	12	*	12	419	378	41
$75,000 and over	322	65	257	262	57	206	60	8	52	1,137	950	188
Not reported	178	53	125	147	42	105	31	11	20	719	638	82

* = Quantity zero or rounds to zero.

Table A-4. Current Grade for People 15 to 24 Years Old Enrolled in School, and Highest Grade Completed for People with Selected Enrollment and Completion Status, by Sex, Age, Race, and Hispanic Origin, October 2020

(Numbers in thousands; civilian noninstitutionalized population.)

| Age, sex, race, and Hispanic origin | Total | Enrolled — Current grade | | | | | | | Not enrolled — Enrolled last year — Highest grade completed | | | | | | Not enrolled last year |
		Less than 9th grade	9th grade	10th grade	11th grade	12th grade	College (graduated this year)	Other college	Less than 9th grade	9th grade	10th grade	11th or 12th, no diploma	New HS graduate	Other[1]	
ALL RACES															
Both Sexes															
Total......................	41,671	188	1,275	3,976	3,625	4,219	1,962	9,874	32	69	177	328	1,162	2,142	12,641
15 years old	4,204	96	1,133	2,520	278	42	7	31	13	6	12	*	*	*	64
16 years old	4,122	60	82	1,202	2,206	284	6	16	9	25	97	56	23	*	56
17 years old	4,187	13	17	195	979	2,501	64	47	*	15	57	134	67	15	84
18 years old	4,185	5	9	24	134	1,044	1,288	456	6	5	1	87	665	78	384
19 years old	4,057	*	1	19	13	196	459	1,835	4	5	5	38	278	268	935
20 to 24 years old	20,917	14	33	14	16	151	139	7,489	*	13	5	13	129	1,781	11,119
Male															
Total......................	20,999	124	695	2,011	1,869	2,159	942	4,336	26	47	104	178	643	1,013	6,851
15 years old	2,191	59	622	1,247	156	16	4	19	11	3	12	*	*	*	40
16 years old	2,073	36	51	638	1,049	131	2	16	5	21	57	24	10	*	32
17 years old	2,143	12	5	83	556	1,241	33	14	*	15	26	68	30	4	55
18 years old	2,147	4	9	15	91	594	603	165	6	*	*	39	368	44	209
19 years old	2,001	*	1	18	10	115	220	721	4	*	4	37	176	123	573
20 to 24 years old	10,444	14	6	11	6	62	78	3,399	*	8	5	10	60	843	5,942
Female															
Total......................	20,672	63	581	1,966	1,756	2,060	1,020	5,538	6	22	74	150	519	1,128	5,790
15 years old	2,013	37	511	1,273	122	26	2	11	2	3	*	*	*	*	25
16 years old	2,049	24	31	565	1,156	153	4	*	4	4	40	32	13	*	24
17 years old	2,044	1	12	112	422	1,261	30	33	*	*	31	65	37	11	28
18 years old	2,038	*	*	10	43	450	684	290	*	5	1	48	297	34	175
19 years old	2,056	*	*	2	3	81	238	1,114	*	5	2	1	102	145	362
20 to 24 years old	10,473	*	27	4	10	89	61	4,090	*	5	*	3	70	938	5,176
WHITE ALONE															
Total......................	30,491	139	958	2,914	2,606	3,016	1,450	7,065	32	58	113	243	854	1,635	9,408
15 years old	3,032	66	845	1,807	186	23	*	20	13	6	12	*	*	*	52
16 years old	3,036	54	66	911	1,599	191	4	3	9	21	58	49	21	*	52
17 years old	3,037	6	14	143	736	1,832	42	28	*	15	36	96	35	11	43
18 years old	3,022	5	4	23	66	770	957	304	6	5	1	56	501	52	270
19 years old	3,041	*	1	18	10	114	362	1,313	4	5	5	31	232	219	726
20 to 24 years old	15,323	8	28	11	8	85	86	5,396	*	6	1	11	65	1,354	8,264
WHITE ALONE NON-HISPANIC															
Total......................	21,811	92	695	1,958	1,925	2,154	1,085	5,255	24	24	82	148	584	1,232	6,553
15 years old	2,118	45	620	1,222	128	17	*	16	10	6	12	*	*	*	42
16 years old	2,184	28	42	623	1,234	129	*	3	8	13	28	27	10	*	41
17 years old	2,176	6	8	83	515	1,338	30	17	*	3	35	69	30	11	30
18 years old	2,072	5	*	11	34	551	729	170	6	*	*	27	339	29	171
19 years old	2,184	*	1	14	10	60	289	952	*	*	5	24	156	163	509
20 to 24 years old	11,077	8	23	4	4	59	38	4,098	*	2	1	1	49	1,029	5,760
BLACK ALONE															
Total......................	6,098	28	148	542	593	694	265	1,338	*	7	20	33	201	213	2,016
15 years old	612	23	140	374	42	17	4	11	*	*	*	*	*	*	8
16 years old	608	2	8	140	362	61	2	13	*	4	8	3	3	*	2
17 years old	589	3	*	27	125	347	12	13	*	*	12	14	10	*	26
18 years old	655	*	*	*	53	174	169	78	*	*	*	15	93	12	61
19 years old	556	*	*	1	3	62	53	274	*	*	*	1	39	15	107
20 to 24 years old	3,078	*	*	*	7	40	25	950	*	3	*	*	55	185	1,813
ASIAN ALONE															
Total......................	2,528	7	46	230	189	221	161	1,027	*	*	11	20	32	146	441
15 years old	254	3	46	163	36	3	2	*	*	*	*	*	*	*	*
16 years old	176	4	*	51	97	15	1	*	*	*	8	*	*	*	*

[1]Other includes people whose response to questions on educational attainment did not fall into one of the listed categories (e.g., completed high school (not last year), but enrolled in college or some other type of school last year).

* = Quantity zero or rounds to zero.

Table A-4. Current Grade for People 15 to 24 Years Old Enrolled in School, and Highest Grade Completed for People with Selected Enrollment and Completion Status, by Sex, Age, Race, and Hispanic Origin, October 2020—*Continued*

(Numbers in thousands; civilian noninstitutionalized population.)

Age, sex, race, and Hispanic origin	Total	Enrolled — Current grade							Not enrolled — Enrolled last year						Not enrolled last year
									Highest grade completed						
		Less than 9th grade	9th grade	10th grade	11th grade	12th grade	College (graduated this year)	Other college	Less than 9th grade	9th grade	10th grade	11th or 12th, no diploma	New HS graduate	Other[1]	Not enrolled last year
17 years old	244	*	*	12	49	157	9	2	*	*	*	4	*	4	6
18 years old	245	*	*	*	6	27	114	50	*	*	*	10	23	4	11
19 years old	266	*	*	*	*	12	15	181	*	*	*	7	5	9	38
20 to 24 years old	1,344	*	*	4	*	5	20	794	*	^	4	*	4	129	386
HISPANIC (OF ANY RACE)															
Total	9,911	47	281	1,137	800	960	429	2,067	9	34	36	103	335	447	3,226
15 years old	1,057	21	238	696	68	12	*	5	4	*	*	*	*	*	14
16 years old	908	26	23	356	434	63	4	*	1	8	29	22	11	*	11
17 years old	998	*	6	63	248	564	17	11	*	12	5	35	21	*	17
18 years old	1,101	*	9	12	45	228	275	165	*	5	1	30	198	23	109
19 years old	953	*	*	4	*	61	78	411	4	5	*	7	82	63	238
20 to 24 years old	4,814	*	5	7	4	33	55	1,475	*	4	*	10	23	361	2,837

[1]Other includes people whose response to questions on educational attainment did not fall into one of the listed categories (e.g., completed high school (not last year), but enrolled in college or some other type of school last year).

* = Quantity zero or rounds to zero.

Table A-5. Type of College and Year Enrolled for College Students 15 Years Old and Over, by Age, Sex, Race, Attendance Status, Control of School, Disability Status, and Enrollment Status, October 2020

(Numbers in thousands; civilian noninstitutionalized population.)

Characteristic	Total enrolled	Undergraduate college								Graduate school	
		All colleges				Two-year college		Four-year college			
		1st year	2nd year	3rd year	4th year	1st year	2nd or higher	1st year	2nd or higher	1st year	2nd or higher
BOTH SEXES	17,674	4,060	3,864	3,376	2,525	1,674	2,068	2,386	7,697	1,416	2,433
Full-Time Students											
Total	13,774	3,296	3,120	2,739	2,043	1,182	1,366	2,114	6,536	927	1,649
Age											
15–19 years old	3,867	2,333	1,201	246	23	719	267	1,615	1,203	55	9
20–24 years old	6,566	577	1,520	2,005	1,590	244	731	333	4,384	429	446
25–34 years old	2,377	240	278	333	328	124	248	117	691	337	861
35 years old and over	965	146	122	154	102	96	120	50	258	107	334
Race											
White alone	9,649	2,280	2,149	2,025	1,510	811	990	1,468	4,693	611	1,075
White alone non-Hispanic	7,360	1,613	1,521	1,550	1,276	474	627	1,139	3,720	531	868
Black alone	1,967	524	493	389	210	171	220	353	872	123	229
Asian alone	1,475	286	330	227	202	84	78	202	681	149	281
Hispanic (of any race)	2,656	801	707	523	304	404	418	397	1,115	91	230
Employment Status											
Full time	2,065	304	344	302	314	145	245	159	714	246	555
Part time	3,799	680	897	873	707	319	470	360	2,008	190	451
Not employed	7,911	2,312	1,879	1,563	1,023	718	651	1,594	3,814	491	643
Control of School											
Public	10,761	2,664	2,631	2,245	1,633	1,050	1,258	1,614	5,252	632	956
Private	3,013	632	489	494	410	132	108	500	1,284	295	694
Disability Status											
No disability	13,435	3,193	3,062	2,676	2,010	1,151	1,332	2,042	6,416	887	1,607
Any disability	340	103	57	63	34	31	34	72	120	40	43
Part-Time Students											
Total	3,900	764	744	637	482	491	702	273	1,161	489	784
Age											
15–19 years old	341	235	101	6	*	178	65	57	42	*	*
20–24 years old	1,062	217	294	228	135	116	256	101	401	97	91
25–34 years old	1,233	153	178	238	189	113	202	40	403	191	284
35 years old and over	1,263	159	171	166	158	85	179	74	316	201	409
Race											
White alone	2,848	498	576	437	371	341	523	157	861	402	564
White alone non-Hispanic	2,064	338	327	295	293	219	309	119	606	321	488
Black alone	624	187	97	119	60	112	95	75	181	35	127
Asian alone	284	67	42	42	26	32	42	35	67	40	67
Hispanic (of any race)	897	175	269	193	90	137	247	38	305	80	90
Employment Status											
Full time	2,213	270	305	337	298	148	310	121	629	380	624
Part time	848	211	242	159	100	155	193	56	309	71	64
Not employed	839	283	197	141	84	188	199	95	224	38	95
Control of School											
Public	3,156	688	684	551	395	452	670	236	959	314	526
Private	743	76	60	86	87	40	32	37	203	175	258
Disability Status											
No disability	3,709	719	693	610	444	459	664	260	1,083	475	768
Any disability	191	45	51	27	38	32	38	13	78	14	15
MALE	7,577	1,816	1,699	1,494	1,058	746	879	1,070	3,372	549	960
Full-Time Students											
Total	5,994	1,465	1,415	1,202	868	519	598	946	2,887	363	680
Age											
15–19 years old	1,624	1,051	452	87	3	329	105	722	437	28	3
20–24 years old	3,001	279	768	916	703	121	328	159	2,059	153	182
25–34 years old	1,011	93	134	154	129	47	110	46	307	137	363
35 years old and over	359	41	62	45	32	23	55	19	84	46	133
Race											
White alone	4,172	981	968	916	622	355	403	626	2,103	243	441
White alone non-Hispanic	3,284	741	702	727	550	243	245	498	1,734	215	350
Black alone	815	234	239	122	76	75	96	159	342	49	95
Asian alone	693	160	145	118	91	36	54	124	299	63	116
Hispanic (of any race)	1,064	295	307	216	111	130	208	165	425	33	103
Employment Status											
Full time	808	152	170	90	103	72	97	80	266	75	218

* = Quantity zero or rounds to zero.

Table A-5. Type of College and Year Enrolled for College Students 15 Years Old and Over, by Age, Sex, Race, Attendance Status, Control of School, Disability Status, and Enrollment Status, October 2020—*Continued*

(Numbers in thousands; civilian noninstitutionalized population.)

Characteristic	Total enrolled	Undergraduate college								Graduate school	
		All colleges				Two-year college		Four-year college			
		1st year	2nd year	3rd year	4th year	1st year	2nd or higher	1st year	2nd or higher	1st year	2nd or higher
Part time	1,449	234	371	355	259	114	194	120	790	54	177
Not employed	3,737	1,079	874	758	506	333	306	746	1,832	234	286
Control of School											
Public	4,658	1,164	1,203	981	699	459	566	704	2,317	254	357
Private	1,336	302	212	221	169	60	31	242	570	110	324
Disability Status											
No disability	5,811	1,394	1,394	1,169	851	499	590	895	2,824	350	654
Any disability	182	71	21	33	17	21	8	51	63	14	26
Part-Time Students											
Total	1,583	351	284	292	190	227	282	124	485	186	280
Age											
15–19 years old	177	118	55	4	*	89	49	29	9	*	*
20–24 years old	477	108	123	121	63	50	105	58	202	35	28
25–34 years old	503	66	60	115	73	54	77	13	170	71	118
35 years old and over	427	59	47	52	54	35	51	24	103	80	134
Race											
White alone	1,172	231	219	211	156	167	227	83	360	146	208
White alone non-Hispanic	835	164	131	125	122	109	141	54	237	107	186
Black alone	240	77	38	52	22	33	31	44	81	14	38
Asian alone	129	39	12	16	12	25	20	15	20	15	35
Hispanic (of any race)	372	68	109	94	41	59	98	9	146	39	22
Employment Status											
Full time	922	133	121	159	124	77	127	57	277	153	232
Part time	336	72	104	75	40	50	94	22	125	27	18
Not employed	325	146	59	58	27	100	61	46	83	6	30
Control of School											
Public	1,313	306	269	258	172	213	282	94	416	120	189
Private	270	45	16	34	19	14	*	30	68	65	91
Disability Status											
No disability	1,501	322	263	281	177	209	269	114	453	179	278
Any disability	82	29	21	10	14	18	13	10	32	6	2
FEMALE	10,097	2,244	2,165	1,882	1,467	927	1,189	1,316	4,325	867	1,472
Full-Time Students											
Total	7,780	1,831	1,705	1,536	1,176	663	768	1,168	3,649	564	969
Age											
15–19 years old	2,243	1,282	749	159	20	390	162	892	765	27	6
20–24 years old	3,566	297	752	1,089	887	123	403	174	2,326	276	264
25–34 years old	1,366	147	144	179	199	77	138	70	384	200	498
35 years old and over	606	104	60	110	70	73	65	31	174	61	202
Race											
White alone	5,477	1,299	1,180	1,108	889	457	587	842	2,590	368	634
White alone non-Hispanic	4,075	873	819	823	726	232	382	641	1,986	316	518
Black alone	1,152	290	254	267	134	96	124	194	530	74	134
Asian alone	782	126	185	109	112	48	23	78	382	86	165
Hispanic (of any race)	1,591	506	400	307	193	274	211	232	690	58	127
Employment Status											
Full time	1,257	152	174	212	211	73	148	79	449	171	337
Part time	2,350	446	527	519	448	205	276	241	1,218	136	275
Not employed	4,173	1,233	1,005	805	517	385	345	848	1,982	256	357
Control of School											
Public	6,103	1,500	1,428	1,264	934	591	692	909	2,934	378	599
Private	1,677	331	277	273	241	72	77	259	714	185	370
Disability Status											
No disability	7,623	1,799	1,669	1,507	1,159	653	742	1,146	3,592	537	953
Any disability	157	32	36	30	17	10	26	21	57	26	16
Part-Time Students											
Total	2,317	413	460	346	292	265	420	148	676	303	503
Age											
15–19 years old	164	117	46	2	*	89	15	28	33	*	*
20–24 years old	585	110	171	107	72	67	152	43	199	62	63
25–34 years old	731	87	119	123	116	59	125	28	233	120	166
36 years old and over	837	100	124	114	103	50	128	50	212	121	274

* = Quantity zero or rounds to zero.

Table A-5. Type of College and Year Enrolled for College Students 15 Years Old and Over, by Age, Sex, Race, Attendance Status, Control of School, Disability Status, and Enrollment Status, October 2020—*Continued*

(Numbers in thousands; civilian noninstitutionalized population.)

Characteristic	Total enrolled	Undergraduate college									Graduate school	
		All colleges				Two-year college		Four-year college				
		1st year	2nd year	3rd year	4th year	1st year	2nd or higher	1st year	2nd or higher	1st year	2nd or higher	
Race												
White alone	1,677	268	357	226	215	173	296	94	501	256	356	
White alone non-Hispanic	1,229	174	196	170	172	109	168	65	370	215	302	
Black alone	384	110	60	67	37	79	63	31	101	21	89	
Asian alone	155	28	30	25	14	7	22	21	47	25	32	
Hispanic (of any race)	525	108	160	99	49	78	149	29	159	41	68	
Employment Status												
Full time	1,291	137	183	178	174	72	184	65	352	227	392	
Part time	512	139	138	84	60	105	98	34	184	44	47	
Not employed	514	138	138	83	58	88	138	50	141	32	65	
Control of School												
Public	1,843	381	415	293	223	239	389	142	542	194	337	
Private	474	32	45	53	69	25	32	6	134	110	167	
Disability Status												
No disability	2,207	396	430	328	268	250	395	146	631	295	490	
Any disability	109	17	30	17	24	14	25	2	46	8	13	

* = Quantity zero or rounds to zero.

Table A-6. Employment Status and Enrollment in Vocational Courses for the Population 15 Years Old and Over, by Sex, Age, Educational Attainment, and College Enrollment, October 2020[1]

(Numbers in thousands; percent; civilian noninstitutionalized population.)

Characteristic	Total	Enrolled in vocational courses		Employed full-time	Enrolled in vocational courses		Employed part-time	Enrolled in vocational courses		Not employed	Enrolled in vocational courses	
	Total	Number	Percent	Total	Number	Percent	Total	Number	Percent	Total	Number	Percent
BOTH SEXES												
Total......................................	265,129	3,785	1.4	125,032	1,937	1.5	26,714	586	2.2	113,382	1,262	1.1
Age												
15 to 19 years old	20,755	322	1.6	1,546	64	4.2	3,799	95	2.5	15,410	163	1.1
20 to 24 years old	20,917	616	2.9	8,660	207	2.4	4,477	132	2.9	7,780	277	3.6
25 to 34 years old	44,867	1,050	2.3	30,071	628	2.1	4,275	116	2.7	10,522	306	2.9
35 to 44 years old	41,513	629	1.5	28,509	430	1.5	3,602	54	1.5	9,402	145	1.5
45 to 64 years old	81,961	924	1.1	49,549	550	1.1	6,832	122	1.8	25,579	251	1.0
65 years and over	55,116	245	0.4	6,698	58	0.9	3,729	67	1.8	44,689	120	0.3
Educational attainment												
Not a high school graduate	34,939	110	0.3	7,573	44	0.6	3,766	11	0.3	23,599	55	0.2
High school graduate only	73,761	643	0.9	32,421	276	0.9	6,744	94	1.4	34,596	273	0.8
Some college or associate's degree...................................	69,748	1,369	2.0	31,889	570	1.8	8,835	297	3.4	29,023	502	1.7
Bachelor's degree or more	86,681	1,663	1.9	53,148	1,047	2.0	7,369	184	2.5	26,164	432	1.7
College enrollment												
Enrolled in college....................	17,674	1,138	6.4	4,278	375	8.8	4,647	246	5.3	8,749	517	5.9
Not enrolled in college	247,454	2,647	1.1	120,754	1,562	1.3	22,067	339	1.5	104,633	746	0.7
MALE												
Total...................................	128,409	1,697	1.3	70,427	929	1.3	9,924	228	2.3	48,057	539	1.1
Age												
15 to 19 years old	10,555	183	1.7	953	43	4.5	1,696	41	2.4	7,906	99	1.3
20 to 24 years old	10,444	296	2.8	4,774	125	2.6	1,856	61	3.3	3,813	110	2.9
25 to 34 years old	22,403	506	2.3	16,735	319	1.9	1,604	53	3.3	4,064	134	3.3
35 to 44 years old	20,441	251	1.2	16,273	193	1.2	997	11	1.1	3,171	47	1.5
45 to 64 years old	39,782	344	0.9	27,595	220	0.8	2,046	36	1.8	10,141	87	0.9
65 years and over	24,784	116	0.5	4,098	29	0.7	1,725	26	1.5	18,961	61	0.3
Educational attainment												
Not a high school graduate	17,966	48	0.3	5,355	31	0.6	1,707	-	-	10,905	17	0.2
High school graduate only	37,926	334	0.9	20,650	161	0.8	2,721	45	1.7	14,554	128	0.9
Some college or associate's degree...................................	32,298	627	1.9	17,308	299	1.7	3,082	117	3.8	11,907	212	1.8
Bachelor's degree or more	40,219	688	1.7	27,114	438	1.6	2,414	66	2.8	10,692	183	1.7
College enrollment												
Enrolled in college....................	7,577	484	6.4	1,730	150	8.7	1,784	101	5.7	4,062	233	5.7
Not enrolled in college	120,832	1,212	1.0	68,697	779	1.1	8,140	127	1.6	43,995	306	0.7
FEMALE												
Total...................................	136,720	2,088	1.5	54,605	1,008	1.8	16,790	357	2.1	65,325	723	1.1
Age												
15 to 19 years old	10,200	138	1.4	593	22	3.6	2,104	53	2.5	7,503	64	0.8
20 to 24 years old	10,473	320	3.1	3,885	82	2.1	2,620	71	2.7	3,967	167	4.2
25 to 34 years old	22,464	544	2.4	13,336	309	2.3	2,671	63	2.3	6,458	172	2.7
35 to 44 years old	21,072	378	1.8	12,236	237	1.9	2,605	44	1.7	6,231	97	1.6
45 to 64 years old	42,179	580	1.4	21,954	330	1.5	4,786	86	1.8	15,438	164	1.1
65 years and over	30,333	129	0.4	2,600	29	1.1	2,004	41	2.1	25,729	59	0.2
Educational attainment												
Not a high school graduate	16,972	62	0.4	2,219	13	0.6	2,060	11	0.5	12,694	39	0.3
High school graduate only	35,835	309	0.9	11,771	115	1.0	4,022	49	1.2	20,042	145	0.7
Some college or associate's degree...................................	37,450	742	2.0	14,581	271	1.9	5,753	180	3.1	17,116	290	1.7
Bachelor's degree or more	46,462	974	2.1	26,034	608	2.3	4,955	118	2.4	15,473	248	1.6
College enrollment												
Enrolled in college....................	10,097	653	6.5	2,548	225	8.8	2,862	145	5.1	4,687	283	6.0
Not enrolled in college	126,623	1,435	1.1	52,057	783	1.5	13,927	212	1.5	60,638	440	0.7

[1]People enrolled in vocational courses are not considered to be enrolled in school for all tables. People enrolled in regular school below the college level are not asked about vocational enrollment in the CPS. They are counted in this table as not enrolled in vocational courses.

Table A-7. Enrollment Status of High School Graduates 15 to 24 Years Old, by Type of School, Attendance Status, and Sex, October 2020

(Numbers in thousands; civilian noninstitutionalized population.)

Characteristic	Total	Enrolled in college or vocational school						Not enrolled	
		2-year college		4-year college		Graduate school	Vocational school	Employed	Not employed
		Full-time	Part-time	Full-time	Part-time				
ALL RACES									
Both sexes	26,243	1,937	610	7,494	600	1,126	273	10,330	3,873
Graduated this year	3,125	518	96	1,301	34	13	43	610	509
Graduated earlier	23,119	1,419	514	6,194	566	1,113	230	9,720	3,364
Male	12,873	873	292	3,351	299	428	175	5,530	1,925
Graduated this year	1,585	253	51	616	22	*	30	334	280
Graduated earlier	11,288	620	241	2,735	276	428	146	5,197	1,645
Female	13,370	1,064	317	4,144	301	698	97	4,800	1,948
Graduated this year	1,539	266	45	685	12	13	14	276	229
Graduated earlier	11,831	798	273	3,459	289	685	84	4,523	1,719
WHITE ALONE									
Both sexes	19,208	1,406	445	5,385	442	791	208	7,897	2,635
Graduated this year	2,304	395	67	960	22	6	30	480	344
Graduated earlier	16,904	1,011	377	4,425	420	784	179	7,417	2,291
Male	9,478	600	226	2,378	213	305	146	4,288	1,321
Graduated this year	1,162	192	39	420	13	*	25	280	193
Graduated earlier	8,316	408	186	1,958	200	305	122	4,007	1,129
Female	9,730	806	219	3,007	229	485	62	3,610	1,314
Graduated this year	1,143	204	28	540	8	6	5	200	151
Graduated earlier	8,588	602	191	2,467	220	479	57	3,409	1,162
WHITE ALONE, NON-HISPANIC									
Both sexes	13,957	864	235	4,297	283	641	176	5,746	1,715
Graduated this year	1,669	226	43	805	12	*	22	360	202
Graduated earlier	12,287	638	192	3,492	271	641	154	5,386	1,513
Male	6,952	383	118	1,970	145	242	123	3,073	897
Graduated this year	876	121	29	363	12	*	21	212	118
Graduated earlier	6,076	262	89	1,607	133	242	103	2,862	779
Female	7,005	481	117	2,326	138	399	53	2,673	818
Graduated this year	793	104	14	441	*	*	1	148	84
Graduated earlier	6,211	376	103	1,885	138	399	51	2,525	734
BLACK ALONE									
Both sexes	3,850	289	110	981	107	105	44	1,421	793
Graduated this year	466	74	23	164	4	*	14	77	110
Graduated earlier	3,385	215	87	818	102	105	31	1,344	683
Male	1,829	131	32	413	65	51	27	709	401
Graduated this year	214	34	6	81	4	*	5	32	51
Graduated earlier	1,615	96	26	332	60	51	22	677	350
Female	2,022	158	78	568	42	54	17	712	392
Graduated this year	252	39	17	83	*	*	9	45	59
Graduated earlier	1,770	119	61	486	42	54	9	667	333
ASIAN ALONE									
Both sexes	1,769	106	45	814	27	186	8	418	165
Graduated this year	192	5	5	142	8	*	*	13	18
Graduated earlier	1,577	100	40	672	19	186	8	405	147
Male	861	70	33	399	6	54	*	217	82
Graduated this year	134	4	5	100	5	*	*	8	12
Graduated earlier	727	66	28	300	1	54	*	210	69
Female	908	35	12	415	21	132	8	201	83
Graduated this year	58	1	*	42	4	*	*	6	6
Graduated earlier	850	34	12	373	18	132	8	196	78
HISPANIC (OF ANY RACE)									
Both sexes	5,980	624	229	1,275	170	162	37	2,426	1,057
Graduated this year	764	196	24	186	10	13	8	149	178
Graduated earlier	5,216	428	205	1,088	160	149	30	2,276	879
Male	2,883	264	120	485	79	64	28	1,355	487
Graduated this year	345	80	11	69	1	*	4	79	101
Graduated earlier	2,538	184	109	417	78	64	24	1,275	386
Female	3,098	360	109	789	91	98	9	1,071	570
Graduated this year	419	116	13	118	8	13	4	70	77
Graduated earlier	2,679	244	96	672	82	85	5	1,001	493

* = Quantity zero or rounds to zero.

Table A-8. Enrollment Status for Families with Children 5 to 24 Years Old, by Control of School, Race, Type of Family, and Family Income, October 2020

(Numbers in thousands; civilian noninstitutionalized population.)

| Characteristic | Total | Families with no dependents 5 to 24 years old[1] | Families with dependents 5 to 24 years old[1] | | | | | | |
| | | | Kindergarten, elementary, and high school enrollment status | | | | College enrollment status | | |
			None enrolled in elementary or high school	Public only	Public and private	Private only	None enrolled in college	One enrolled in college	Two or more enrolled in college
ALL RACES									
All Families	83,993	45,581	8,516	26,591	748	2,556	31,923	5,433	1,056
Less than $20,000	4,917	2,075	485	2,221	33	102	2,577	248	16
$20,000 to $74,999	26,277	14,308	2,395	8,821	171	581	10,376	1,306	207
$75,000 and over	30,585	16,234	3,368	9,351	334	1,299	11,289	2,469	593
Not reported	22,214	12,964	2,268	6,198	210	574	7,680	1,330	240
Married-couple families	61,502	37,054	4,951	16,972	585	1,940	19,961	3,678	809
Less than $20,000	1,864	1,095	85	630	10	44	674	95	*
$20,000 to $74,999	17,010	10,880	1,042	4,595	114	379	5,298	707	124
$75,000 and over	26,590	14,691	2,559	7,905	310	1,125	9,360	2,049	489
Not reported	16,039	10,389	1,265	3,841	151	392	4,629	826	195
Unmarried householder[2]	22,491	8,527	3,565	9,620	164	616	11,962	1,756	247
Less than $20,000	3,053	981	400	1,591	23	58	1,903	154	16
$20,000 to $74,999	9,267	3,428	1,353	4,226	58	202	5,078	678	83
$75,000 and over	3,995	1,543	809	1,446	24	174	1,929	420	103
Not reported	6,175	2,575	1,003	2,357	59	181	3,051	504	45
WHITE ALONE									
All Families	65,756	37,205	6,446	19,554	588	1,963	23,755	4,002	794
Less than $20,000	3,066	1,393	304	1,299	12	58	1,513	152	8
$20,000 to $74,999	20,168	11,457	1,749	6,406	128	429	7,566	999	146
$75,000 and over	25,411	13,969	2,689	7,407	284	1,062	9,060	1,915	466
Not reported	17,111	10,386	1,704	4,442	165	414	5,615	936	173
Married-couple families	50,945	31,483	4,053	13,329	498	1,583	15,900	2,904	659
Less than $20,000	1,366	820	73	434	4	35	482	64	*
$20,000 to $74,999	14,017	9,201	829	3,587	95	306	4,154	561	100
$75,000 and over	22,586	12,830	2,159	6,398	271	928	7,705	1,641	411
Not reported	12,976	8,632	992	2,910	128	314	3,558	638	148
Unmarried householder[2]	14,811	5,722	2,393	6,225	90	380	7,856	1,098	135
Less than $20,000	1,701	573	231	865	8	23	1,031	89	8
$20,000 to $74,999	6,151	2,256	920	2,819	33	123	3,412	437	46
$75,000 and over	2,824	1,139	530	1,009	13	134	1,356	275	55
Not reported	4,134	1,754	712	1,532	37	100	2,057	297	26
WHITE ALONE NON-HISPANIC									
All Families	53,225	32,439	4,838	13,760	459	1,728	17,304	2,876	605
Less than $20,000	1,992	1,006	210	715	3	58	892	86	8
$20,000 to $74,999	14,917	9,625	1,133	3,763	74	322	4,709	510	73
$75,000 and over	22,610	12,800	2,296	6,276	249	989	7,825	1,598	387
Not reported	13,706	9,008	1,199	3,007	133	359	3,878	682	137
Married-couple families	42,958	28,249	3,190	9,735	394	1,391	12,015	2,183	512
Less than $20,000	906	615	40	216	*	35	259	32	*
$20,000 to $74,999	10,813	7,974	540	2,020	53	225	2,508	289	43
$75,000 and over	20,363	11,922	1,881	5,456	237	868	6,704	1,383	354
Not reported	10,877	7,738	729	2,043	104	263	2,544	479	115
Unmarried householder[2]	10,266	4,190	1,648	4,026	65	337	5,289	694	93
Less than $20,000	1,086	390	171	499	3	23	633	55	8
$20,000 to $74,999	4,105	1,652	593	1,743	21	96	2,201	221	31
$75,000 and over	2,247	879	415	820	12	121	1,121	215	33
Not reported	2,829	1,270	470	964	29	96	1,334	203	22
BLACK ALONE									
All Families	10,545	4,704	1,233	4,208	113	286	4,931	812	97
Less than $20,000	1,400	475	157	723	11	34	851	67	7
$20,000 to $74,999	3,837	1,767	424	1,528	36	82	1,824	221	25
$75,000 and over	2,206	919	290	879	32	86	989	260	38
Not reported	3,102	1,544	363	1,078	34	83	1,268	263	26

* = Quantity zero or rounds to zero.
[1] Unmarried (or married with spouse absent) child, grandchild, brother/sister or other relative.
[2] No spouse present.
[3] May be of any race.

Table A-8. Enrollment Status for Families with Children 5 to 24 Years Old, by Control of School, Race, Type of Family, and Family Income, October 2020—*Continued*

(Numbers in thousands; civilian noninstitutionalized population.)

Characteristic	Total	Families with no dependents 5 to 24 years old[1]	Families with dependents 5 to 24 years old[1]						
			Kindergarten, elementary, and high school enrollment status				College enrollment status		
			None enrolled in elementary or high school	Public only	Public and private	Private only	None enrolled in college	One enrolled in college	Two or more enrolled in college
Married-couple families	4,902	2,706	377	1,651	45	123	1,808	351	37
Less than $20,000	254	137	12	100	*	5	101	17	*
$20,000 to $74,999	1,557	925	109	490	12	21	571	56	6
$75,000 and over.....................	1,510	687	114	622	22	65	625	178	21
Not reported............................	1,580	957	142	439	12	31	512	100	11
Unmarried householder[2]	5,643	1,998	857	2,557	68	163	3,123	462	60
Less than $20,000	1,146	338	146	623	11	28	750	50	7
$20,000 to $74,999	2,280	842	315	1,038	24	61	1,253	166	20
$75,000 and over.....................	696	232	175	257	10	22	364	83	17
Not reported............................	1,521	587	221	639	22	52	756	163	16
ASIAN ALONE									
All Families	5,077	2,567	581	1,687	37	205	1,913	460	136
Less than $20,000	209	118	9	74	4	4	87	4	*
$20,000 to $74,999	1,258	679	140	411	8	21	428	129	23
$75,000 and over.....................	2,194	1,021	297	742	16	119	868	224	82
Not reported............................	1,415	750	135	460	10	60	530	103	32
Married-couple families	4,069	2,114	384	1,374	33	165	1,530	323	103
Less than $20,000	160	94	*	63	*	4	66	*	*
$20,000 to $74,999	876	491	76	285	8	17	288	80	17
$75,000 and over.....................	1,904	921	208	653	16	105	757	168	58
Not reported............................	1,129	608	99	374	10	39	419	75	28
Unmarried householder[2]	1,007	454	198	312	4	40	383	137	33
Less than $20,000	49	24	9	12	4	*	21	4	*
$20,000 to $74,999	382	188	64	127	*	5	141	49	5
$75,000 and over.....................	291	100	88	88	*	14	111	56	24
Not reported............................	286	142	36	86	*	21	111	28	4
HISPANIC[3]									
All Families...................................	14,078	5,331	1,755	6,583	129	280	7,290	1,244	213
Less than $20,000	1,211	431	112	652	9	7	691	82	7
$20,000 to $74,999	5,920	2,062	675	3,005	54	125	3,264	516	78
$75,000 and over.....................	3,174	1,301	418	1,335	35	86	1,425	356	92
Not reported............................	3,773	1,538	551	1,591	32	62	1,909	290	36
Married-couple families	8,848	3,589	925	4,006	104	224	4,333	778	148
Less than $20,000	505	224	34	244	4	*	243	38	*
$20,000 to $74,999	3,572	1,375	299	1,758	42	98	1,859	279	59
$75,000 and over.....................	2,476	1,008	288	1,072	34	74	1,130	280	57
Not reported............................	2,295	982	304	933	24	52	1,100	181	32
Unmarried householder[2]	5,230	1,742	830	2,577	25	56	2,957	465	65
Less than $20,000	706	207	79	408	5	7	448	43	7
$20,000 to $74,999	2,348	687	375	1,247	12	27	1,405	237	19
$75,000 and over.....................	698	293	130	263	0	13	295	76	35
Not reported............................	1,478	556	247	658	8	9	809	110	4

* = Quantity zero or rounds to zero.
[1]Unmarried (or married with spouse absent) child, grandchild, brother/sister or other relative.
[2]No spouse present.
[3]May be of any race.

Table A-9. Total Fall Enrollment in Degree-Granting Postsecondary Institutions, by Level of Enrollment, Sex of Student, Level and Control of Institution, and Attendance Status of Student, 2019

(Number.)

Level and control of institution and attendance status of student	Total			Undergraduate			Postbaccalaureate		
	Total	Males	Females	Total	Males	Females	Total	Males	Females
Total.................................	19,637,499	8,362,890	11,274,609	16,565,066	7,148,530	9,416,536	3,072,433	1,214,360	1,858,073
Full-time.....................................	11,966,494	5,276,895	6,689,599	10,219,934	4,544,189	5,675,745	1,746,560	732,706	1,013,854
Part-time.....................................	7,671,005	3,085,995	4,585,010	6,345,132	2,604,341	3,740,791	1,325,873	481,654	844,219
4-Year.................................	14,038,455	5,989,207	8,049,248	10,966,022	4,774,847	6,191,175	3,072,433	1,214,360	1,858,073
Full-time.....................................	9,911,369	4,356,539	5,554,830	8,164,809	3,623,833	4,540,976	1,746,560	732,706	1,013,854
Part-time.....................................	4,127,086	1,632,668	2,494,418	2,801,213	1,151,014	1,650,199	1,325,873	481,654	844,219
2-Year.................................	5,599,044	2,373,683	3,225,361	5,599,044	2,373,683	3,225,361	NA	NA	NA
Full-time.....................................	2,055,125	920,356	1,134,769	2,055,125	920,356	1,134,769	NA	NA	NA
Part-time.....................................	3,543,919	1,453,327	2,090,592	3,543,919	1,453,327	2,090,592	NA	NA	NA
PUBLIC	14,501,057	6,324,820	8,176,237	13,001,543	5,708,358	7,293,185	1,499,514	616,462	883,052
Full-time.....................................	8,220,295	3,730,816	4,489,479	7,398,491	3,373,788	4,024,703	821,804	357,028	464,776
Part-time.....................................	6,280,762	2,594,004	3,686,758	5,603,052	2,334,570	3,268,482	677,710	259,434	418,276
Public 4-Year	9,102,958	4,019,019	5,083,939	7,603,444	3,402,557	4,200,887	1,499,514	616,462	883,052
Full-time............................	6,351,051	2,873,997	3,477,054	5,529,247	2,516,969	3,012,278	821,804	357,028	464,776
Part-time............................	2,751,907	1,145,022	1,606,885	2,074,197	885,588	1,188,609	677,710	259,434	418,276
Public 2-Year	5,398,099	2,305,801	3,092,298	5,398,099	2,305,801	3,092,298	NA	NA	NA
Full-time............................	1,869,244	856,819	1,012,425	1,869,244	856,819	1,012,425	NA	NA	NA
Part-time............................	3,528,855	1,448,982	2,079,873	3,528,855	1,448,982	2,079,873	NA	NA	NA
PRIVATE	5,136,442	2,038,070	3,098,372	3,563,523	1,440,172	2,123,351	1,572,919	597,898	975,021
Full-time.....................................	3,746,199	1,546,079	2,200,120	2,821,443	1,170,401	1,651,042	924,756	375,678	549,078
Part-time.....................................	1,390,243	491,991	898,252	742,080	269,771	472,309	648,163	222,220	425,943
Private 4-Year	4,935,497	1,970,188	2,965,309	3,362,578	1,372,290	1,990,288	1,572,919	597,898	975,021
Full-time............................	3,560,318	1,482,542	2,077,776	2,635,562	1,106,864	1,528,698	924,756	375,678	549,078
Part-time............................	1,375,179	487,646	887,533	727,016	265,426	461,590	648,163	222,220	425,943
Private 2-Year	200,945	67,882	133,063	200,945	67,882	133,063	NA	NA	NA
Full-time............................	185,881	63,537	122,344	185,881	63,537	122,344	NA	NA	NA
Part-time............................	15,064	4,345	10,719	15,064	4,345	10,719	NA	NA	NA
Nonprofit........................	4,145,263	1,714,053	2,431,210	2,804,878	1,179,520	1,625,358	1,340,385	534,533	805,852
Full-time.....................................	3,137,088	1,332,751	1,804,337	2,313,494	988,879	1,324,615	823,594	343,872	479,722
Part-time.....................................	1,008,175	381,302	626,873	491,384	190,641	300,743	516,791	190,661	326,130
Nonprofit 4-year..............	4,100,619	1,702,973	2,397,646	2,760,234	1,168,440	1,591,794	1,340,385	534,533	805,852
Full-time......................	3,099,183	1,323,354	1,775,829	2,275,589	979,482	1,296,107	823,594	343,872	479,722
Part-time......................	1,001,436	379,619	621,817	484,645	188,958	295,687	516,791	190,661	326,130
Nonprofit 2-year..............	44,644	11,080	33,564	44,644	11,080	33,564	NA	NA	NA
Full-time......................	37,905	9,397	28,508	37,905	9,397	28,508	NA	NA	NA
Part-time......................	6,739	1,683	5,056	6,739	1,683	5,056	NA	NA	NA
For-profit........................	991,179	324,017	667,162	758,645	260,652	497,993	232,534	63,365	169,169
Full-time............................	609,111	213,328	395,783	507,949	181,522	326,427	101,162	31,806	69,356
Part-time............................	382,068	110,689	271,379	250,696	79,130	171,566	131,372	31,559	99,813
For-profit 4-year..............	834,878	267,215	567,663	602,344	203,850	398,494	232,534	63,365	169,169
Full-time......................	461,135	159,188	301,947	359,973	127,382	232,591	101,162	31,806	69,356
Part-time......................	373,743	108,027	265,716	242,371	76,468	165,903	131,372	31,559	99,813
For-profit 2-year..............	156,301	56,802	99,499	156,301	56,802	99,499	NA	NA	NA
Full-time......................	147,976	54,140	93,836	147,976	54,140	93,836	NA	NA	NA
Part-time......................	8,325	2,662	5,663	8,325	2,662	5,663	NA	NA	NA

NA = Not applicable

Note: Degree-granting institutions grant associate's or higher degrees and participate in Title IV federal financial aid programs.

PART A
NATIONAL EDUCATION STATISTICS

■ **Historical Enrollment Tables**

Table A-10. School Enrollment of the Population 3 Years Old and Over, by Level and Control of School, Selected Race, and Hispanic Origin, October 1955–2019

(Numbers in thousands; civilian noninstitutionalized population.)

Year, race, and Hispanic origin	Total enrolled	Nursery school			Kindergarten			Elementary school		
		Total	Public	Private	Total	Public	Private	Total	Public	Private
ALL RACES										
2019	76,089	4,728	2,614	2,114	4,057	3,531	525	32,619	29,754	2,866
2018	76,840	4,836	2,763	2,073	3,908	3,529	379	32,483	29,665	2,818
2017	76,409	4,676	2,782	1,894	3,964	3,542	422	32,530	29,873	2,656
2016	77,232	4,746	2,806	1,941	4,017	3,654	364	32,604	29,978	2,627
2015	77,066	4,532	2,610	1,922	4,073	3,644	428	32,826	30,173	2,653
2014	77,214	4,694	2,693	2,001	4,069	3,617	453	32,622	29,805	2,817
2013	77,772	4,682	2,558	2,124	4,150	3,725	425	32,873	30,171	2,702
2012	78,426	4,628	2,732	1,896	4,138	3,684	454	32,683	29,865	2,818
2011	79,043	4,946	2,904	2,042	4,214	3,732	482	32,872	29,965	2,907
2010	78,519	4,835	2,776	2,059	4,172	3,764	408	32,663	29,841	2,822
2009	77,288	4,708	2,744	1,964	4,132	3,767	365	32,238	29,365	2,874
2008	76,353	4,614	2,632	1,982	4,047	3,578	469	32,344	29,162	3,182
2007	75,967	4,628	2,570	2,058	4,132	3,656	476	32,169	29,052	3,117
2006	75,197	4,688	2,519	2,169	4,039	3,552	487	32,089	28,975	3,113
2005	75,780	4,603	2,480	2,123	3,912	3,349	563	32,438	29,072	3,366
2004	75,461	4,739	2,487	2,252	3,992	3,417	575	32,556	29,166	3,389
2003	74,911	4,928	2,567	2,361	3,719	3,098	622	32,565	29,204	3,361
2002	74,046	4,471	2,246	2,225	3,571	2,976	594	33,132	29,658	3,474
2001	73,124	4,289	2,161	2,128	3,737	3,145	591	33,166	29,800	3,366
2000	72,214	4,401	2,217	2,184	3,832	3,173	659	32,898	29,378	3,520
1999	72,395	4,578	2,269	2,309	3,825	3,167	658	32,873	29,264	3,609
1998	72,109	4,577	2,265	2,313	3,828	3,128	700	32,573	29,124	3,449
1997	72,031	4,500	2,254	2,246	3,933	3,271	663	32,369	29,308	3,061
1996	70,297	4,212	1,868	2,344	4,034	3,353	681	31,515	28,153	3,362
1995	69,769	4,399	2,012	2,387	3,877	3,174	704	31,815	28,384	3,431
1994[1]	69,272	4,259	1,940	2,319	3,863	3,278	585	31,512	28,131	3,381
1993r	64,414	3,032	1,258	1,774	4,275	3,589	686	31,219	28,278	2,941
1993	62,730	3,018	1,230	1,788	4,180	3,499	681	30,604	27,688	2,914
1992	62,082	2,899	1,098	1,801	4,130	3,507	623	30,165	27,066	3,102
1991	61,276	2,933	1,094	1,839	4,152	3,531	621	29,591	26,632	2,958
1990	60,588	3,401	1,212	2,188	3,899	3,332	567	29,265	26,591	2,674
1989	59,236	2,877	971	1,906	3,868	3,293	575	28,637	25,897	2,740
1988	58,847	2,639	868	1,770	3,958	3,420	538	28,223	25,443	2,778
1987	58,691	2,587	848	1,739	4,018	3,423	595	27,524	24,760	2,765
1986	58,153	2,554	835	1,719	3,961	3,328	633	27,121	24,163	2,958
1985	58,014	2,491	854	1,637	3,815	3,221	594	26,866	23,803	3,063
1984	57,313	2,354	761	1,593	3,484	2,953	531	26,838	24,120	2,718
1983	57,745	2,350	809	1,541	3,361	2,706	656	27,198	24,203	2,994
1982	57,905	2,153	729	1,423	3,299	2,746	553	27,412	24,381	3,031
1981	58,390	2,058	663	1,396	3,161	2,616	545	27,795	24,758	3,037
1980	57,348	1,987	633	1,354	3,176	2,690	486	27,449	24,398	3,051
1979	57,854	1,869	636	1,233	3,025	2,593	432	27,865	24,756	3,109
1978	58,616	1,824	587	1,237	2,989	2,493	496	28,490	25,252	3,238
1977	60,013	1,618	562	1,056	3,191	2,665	526	29,234	25,983	3,251
1976	60,482	1,526	476	1,050	3,490	2,962	528	29,774	26,698	3,075
1975	60,969	1,748	574	1,174	3,393	2,851	542	30,446	27,166	3,279
1974	60,259	1,607	423	1,184	3,252	2,726	526	31,126	27,956	3,169
1973	59,392	1,324	400	924	3,074	2,582	493	31,469	28,201	3,268
1972	60,142	1,283	402	881	3,135	2,636	499	32,242	28,693	3,549
1971	61,106	1,066	317	749	3,263	2,689	574	33,507	29,829	3,678
1970	60,357	1,096	333	763	3,183	2,647	536	33,950	30,001	3,949
1969	59,913	860	245	615	3,276	2,682	594	33,788	29,825	3,964
1968	58,791	816	262	554	3,268	2,709	559	33,761	29,527	4,234
1967	57,656	713	230	484	3,312	2,678	635	33,440	28,877	4,562
1966	56,167	688	215	473	3,115	2,527	588	32,916	28,208	4,706
1965	54,701	520	127	393	3,057	2,439	618	32,474	27,596	4,878
1964	52,490	471	91	380	2,830	2,349	481	31,734	26,811	4,923
1963	50,356	NA	NA	NA	2,340	1,936	404	31,245	26,502	4,742
1962	48,704	NA	NA	NA	2,319	1,914	405	30,661	26,148	4,513
1961	47,708	NA	NA	NA	2,299	1,926	373	30,718	26,221	4,497
1960	46,260	NA	NA	NA	2,092	1,691	401	30,349	25,814	4,535
1959	44,370	NA	NA	NA	2,032	1,678	354	29,382	24,680	4,702
1958	42,900	NA	NA	NA	1,991	1,569	422	28,184	23,800	4,385
1957	41,166	NA	NA	NA	1,824	1,471	353	27,248	23,076	4,172

NA = Not available.
r = Revised, controlled to 1990 census based population estimates; previous 1993 data controlled to 1980 census based population estimates.
[1]Prior to 1994, total enrolled does not include the 35 and over population.
[2]Starting in 2003 respondents could identify more than one race. Except as noted, the race data in this table from 2003 onward represent those respondents who indicated only one race category.
[3]Data shown for 1955 to 1966 for the Black population are for Black and Other races.
[4]The data shown prior to 2003 consists of those identifying themselves as "Asian or Pacific Islanders."

Table A-10. School Enrollment of the Population 3 Years Old and Over, by Level and Control of School, Selected Race, and Hispanic Origin, October 1955–2019—*Continued*

(Numbers in thousands; civilian noninstitutionalized population.)

Year, race, and Hispanic origin	High school			College			
	Total	Public	Private	Total	Public	Private	Full-time
ALL RACES							
2019............................	16,395	15,208	1,187	18,289	14,746	3,543	13,849
2018............................	16,706	15,519	1,187	18,908	15,234	3,674	14,204
2017............................	16,841	15,546	1,295	18,398	14,806	3,592	13,606
2016............................	16,668	15,330	1,338	19,196	14,971	4,225	14,421
2015............................	16,535	15,358	1,177	19,101	15,175	3,926	14,236
2014............................	16,654	15,379	1,275	19,175	15,325	3,850	14,400
2013............................	16,601	15,468	1,133	19,467	15,514	3,953	14,228
2012............................	17,047	15,704	1,343	19,930	15,778	4,152	14,602
2011............................	16,613	15,426	1,187	20,397	16,134	4,263	14,903
2010............................	16,574	15,338	1,236	20,275	16,153	4,122	14,600
2009............................	16,445	15,269	1,177	19,764	15,722	4,042	14,364
2008............................	16,715	15,397	1,319	18,632	14,739	3,893	13,245
2007............................	17,082	15,804	1,278	17,956	14,072	3,884	12,656
2006............................	17,149	15,617	1,532	17,232	13,466	3,766	12,070
2005............................	17,354	15,934	1,420	17,472	13,435	4,037	12,237
2004............................	16,791	15,498	1,293	17,383	13,652	3,731	11,990
2003............................	17,062	15,785	1,276	16,638	13,109	3,529	11,490
2002............................	16,374	15,064	1,310	16,497	12,834	3,664	11,141
2001............................	16,059	14,830	1,230	15,873	12,421	3,452	10,404
2000............................	15,770	14,431	1,339	15,314	12,008	3,305	10,159
1999............................	15,916	14,638	1,278	15,203	11,659	3,544	10,112
1998............................	15,584	14,299	1,285	15,547	11,984	3,563	10,184
1997............................	15,793	14,634	1,159	15,436	12,091	3,345	10,236
1996............................	15,309	14,113	1,197	15,226	12,014	3,212	9,839
1995............................	14,963	13,750	1,213	14,715	11,372	3,343	9,544
1994[1]........................	14,616	13,539	1,077	15,022	11,694	3,329	9,573
1993r..........................	13,989	12,985	1,004	11,901	9,440	2,461	8,706
1993............................	13,522	12,542	977	11,409	9,031	2,374	8,308
1992............................	13,219	12,268	952	11,671	9,282	2,386	8,503
1991............................	13,010	12,069	945	11,589	9,078	2,511	8,461
1990............................	12,719	11,818	903	11,306	8,889	2,417	8,154
1989............................	12,786	11,980	806	11,066	8,576	2,490	7,905
1988............................	13,093	12,095	998	10,937	8,663	2,278	7,771
1987............................	13,647	12,577	1,070	10,915	8,556	2,361	7,560
1986............................	13,912	12,746	1,166	10,605	8,153	2,452	7,507
1985............................	13,979	12,764	1,215	10,863	8,379	2,483	7,720
1984............................	13,777	12,721	1,057	10,859	8,467	2,392	7,822
1983............................	14,010	12,792	1,218	10,825	8,185	2,640	7,711
1982............................	14,123	13,004	1,118	10,919	8,354	2,565	7,736
1981............................	14,642	13,523	1,119	10,734	8,159	2,576	7,569
1980............................	14,556	NA	NA	10,180	NA	NA	7,147
1979............................	15,116	13,994	1,122	9,978	7,699	2,280	7,010
1978............................	15,475	14,231	1,244	9,838	7,427	2,410	6,979
1977............................	15,753	14,505	1,248	10,217	7,925	2,292	7,196
1976............................	15,742	14,541	1,201	9,950	7,739	2,211	7,176
1975............................	15,683	14,503	1,180	9,697	7,704	1,994	7,105
1974............................	15,447	14,275	1,172	8,827	6,905	1,922	6,351
1973............................	15,347	14,162	1,184	8,179	6,224	1,955	6,089
1972............................	15,169	14,015	1,155	8,313	6,337	1,976	6,314
1971............................	15,183	14,057	1,126	8,087	6,271	1,816	6,204
1970............................	14,715	13,545	1,170	7,413	5,699	1,714	5,763
1969............................	14,553	13,400	1,153	7,435	5,439	1,995	5,810
1968............................	14,145	12,793	1,352	6,801	4,948	1,854	5,357
1967............................	13,790	12,498	1,292	6,401	4,540	1,861	4,976
1966............................	13,364	11,985	1,377	6,085	4,178	1,908	4,847
1965............................	12,975	11,517	1,457	5,675	3,840	1,835	4,114
1964............................	12,812	11,403	1,410	4,643	3,025	1,618	3,556
1963............................	12,438	11,186	1,251	4,336	2,897	1,439	3,260
1962............................	11,516	10,431	1,085	4,208	2,820	1,388	3,237
1961............................	10,959	9,817	1,141	3,731	2,376	1,354	2,902
1960............................	10,249	9,215	1,033	3,570	2,307	1,262	2,681
1959............................	9,616	8,571	1,045	3,340	2,120	1,220	2,464
1958............................	9,482	8,485	998	3,242	2,088	1,155	NA
1957............................	8,956	8,059	897	3,138	2,054	1,084	NA

NA = Not available.
r = Revised, controlled to 1990 census based population estimates; previous 1993 data controlled to 1980 census based population estimates.
[1]Prior to 1994, total enrolled does not include the 35 and over population.
[2]Starting in 2003 respondents could identify more than one race. Except as noted, the race data in this table from 2003 onward represent those respondents who indicated only one race category.
[3]Data shown for 1955 to 1966 for the Black population are for Black and Other races.
[4]The data shown prior to 2003 consists of those identifying themselves as "Asian or Pacific Islanders."

Table A-10. School Enrollment of the Population 3 Years Old and Over, by Level and Control of School, Selected Race, and Hispanic Origin, October 1955–2019—*Continued*

(Numbers in thousands; civilian noninstitutionalized population.)

Year, race, and Hispanic origin	Total enrolled	Nursery school Total	Nursery school Public	Nursery school Private	Kindergarten Total	Kindergarten Public	Kindergarten Private	Elementary school Total	Elementary school Public	Elementary school Private
1956.............................	39,353	NA	NA	NA	1,758	1,566	192	26,169	22,474	3,695
1955.............................	37,426	NA	NA	NA	1,628	1,365	263	25,458	22,078	3,379
WHITE ALONE										
2019.............................	54,352	3,352	1,756	1,596	2,895	2,533	362	23,385	21,129	2,257
2018.............................	55,199	3,509	1,943	1,565	2,831	2,510	321	23,379	21,215	2,164
2017.............................	55,148	3,315	1,885	1,430	2,918	2,580	338	23,411	21,385	2,026
2016.............................	56,007	3,445	1,984	1,461	2,859	2,578	281	23,732	21,786	1,946
2015.............................	56,056	3,230	1,778	1,452	2,970	2,630	340	23,863	21,776	2,088
2014.............................	56,343	3,354	1,814	1,540	2,866	2,557	309	23,886	21,677	2,209
2013.............................	56,914	3,346	1,740	1,606	2,933	2,588	345	24,238	22,090	2,148
2012.............................	57,702	3,393	1,925	1,468	2,940	2,584	355	24,187	21,928	2,260
2011.............................	59,647	3,624	1,997	1,627	3,198	2,806	393	24,864	22,419	2,445
2010.............................	59,236	3,659	1,992	1,668	3,069	2,745	324	24,680	22,395	2,284
2009.............................	58,586	3,404	1,832	1,572	3,154	2,860	293	24,575	22,257	2,319
2008.............................	58,244	3,479	1,830	1,649	3,121	2,748	373	24,552	21,986	2,565
2007.............................	58,021	3,545	1,880	1,665	3,223	2,836	387	24,431	21,869	2,562
2006.............................	57,419	3,624	1,815	1,809	3,084	2,701	382	24,472	21,923	2,549
2005.............................	58,013	3,542	1,767	1,775	3,056	2,611	445	24,652	21,858	2,795
2004.............................	57,585	3,566	1,703	1,863	3,043	2,571	472	24,773	21,889	2,883
2003[2].............................	57,391	3,909	1,918	1,990	2,866	2,367	499	24,711	21,893	2,818
2002.............................	57,501	3,473	1,613	1,860	2,760	2,240	520	25,625	22,703	2,922
2001.............................	56,649	3,278	1,484	1,794	2,893	2,394	499	25,729	22,848	2,881
2000.............................	56,344	3,392	1,539	1,853	2,998	2,453	545	25,562	22,538	3,024
1999.............................	56,713	3,590	1,571	2,019	2,956	2,422	534	25,628	22,552	3,076
1998.............................	56,515	3,549	1,598	1,951	2,933	2,356	577	25,489	22,547	2,942
1997.............................	56,587	3,489	1,572	1,917	3,078	2,532	546	25,289	22,679	2,610
1996.............................	55,378	3,284	1,314	1,970	3,163	2,596	567	24,692	21,785	2,907
1995.............................	55,186	3,553	1,435	2,118	3,032	2,440	592	24,963	22,010	2,954
1994[1].............................	54,823	3,376	1,330	2,046	3,010	2,505	505	24,786	21,903	2,883
1993r.............................	51,034	2,434	851	1,583	3,323	2,730	593	24,637	22,078	2,559
1993.............................	49,985	2,447	843	1,604	3,273	2,681	592	24,249	21,714	2,535
1992.............................	49,713	2,387	785	1,602	3,256	2,727	529	23,932	21,213	2,718
1991.............................	49,156	2,447	810	1,637	3,274	2,766	508	23,547	20,948	2,599
1990.............................	48,897	2,830	869	1,961	3,081	2,609	472	23,343	20,984	2,359
1989.............................	47,923	2,393	712	1,681	3,118	2,611	506	22,867	20,468	2,399
1988.............................	47,672	2,234	651	1,583	3,192	2,722	471	22,541	20,086	2,455
1987.............................	47,471	2,204	630	1,574	3,120	2,591	529	22,037	19,538	2,498
1986.............................	47,267	2,144	601	1,543	3,161	2,589	572	21,761	19,090	2,671
1985.............................	47,452	2,087	617	1,470	3,060	2,545	515	21,593	18,817	2,776
1984.............................	46,941	1,915	543	1,372	2,788	2,319	469	21,730	19,282	2,449
1983.............................	47,423	1,932	563	1,369	2,769	2,181	588	22,054	19,340	2,714
1982.............................	47,662	1,783	504	1,279	2,677	2,189	489	22,297	19,583	2,713
1981.............................	48,169	1,685	447	1,238	2,597	2,130	467	22,663	19,924	2,739
1980.............................	47,673	1,637	432	1,205	2,595	2,172	423	22,510	19,743	2,768
1979.............................	48,225	1,537	428	1,110	2,437	2,069	368	22,959	20,174	2,785
1978.............................	48,843	1,456	351	1,105	2,452	2,009	444	23,524	20,551	2,973
1977.............................	50,151	1,314	372	942	2,611	2,153	458	24,262	21,312	2,950
1976.............................	50,761	1,246	318	929	2,881	2,423	457	24,776	21,947	2,829
1975.............................	51,430	1,432	392	1,040	2,845	2,363	483	25,412	22,351	3,059
1974.............................	50,992	1,340	293	1,048	2,745	2,268	477	26,051	23,063	2,990
1973.............................	50,617	1,087	242	845	2,584	2,139	445	26,531	23,506	3,025
1972.............................	51,314	1,079	285	794	2,633	2,185	448	27,185	23,869	3,316
1971.............................	52,081	888	225	664	2,735	2,207	527	28,187	24,720	3,466
1970.............................	51,719	893	198	695	2,706	2,233	473	28,638	24,923	3,715
1969.............................	51,465	676	136	539	2,803	2,289	515	28,572	24,803	3,768
1968.............................	50,608	664	163	501	2,775	2,272	504	28,634	24,580	4,054
1967.............................	49,721	564	134	429	2,840	2,254	587	28,415	24,044	4,371
1966.............................	48,620	564	127	437	2,693	2,163	530	28,012	23,469	4,542
1965.............................	47,451	451	93	358	2,648	2,086	562	27,679	22,976	4,703
1964.............................	44,850	NA	NA	NA	2,157	1,795	362	27,099	22,381	4,718
1963.............................	43,815	NA	NA	NA	2,064	1,699	365	26,709	22,181	4,527
1962.............................	42,501	NA	NA	NA	2,025	1,667	358	26,272	21,922	4,350
1961.............................	42,498	NA	NA	NA	1,968	1,618	350	26,294	22,014	4,281
1960.............................	40,348	NA	NA	NA	1,849	1,485	364	26,035	21,696	4,339

NA = Not available.

r = Revised, controlled to 1990 census based population estimates; previous 1993 data controlled to 1980 census based population estimates.

[1]Prior to 1994, total enrolled does not include the 35 and over population.

[2]Starting in 2003 respondents could identify more than one race. Except as noted, the race data in this table from 2003 onward represent those respondents who indicated only one race category.

[3]Data shown for 1955 to 1966 for the Black population are for Black and Other races.

[4]The data shown prior to 2003 consists of those identifying themselves as "Asian or Pacific Islanders."

Table A-10. School Enrollment of the Population 3 Years Old and Over, by Level and Control of School, Selected Race, and Hispanic Origin, October 1955–2019—*Continued*

(Numbers in thousands; civilian noninstitutionalized population.)

Year, race, and Hispanic origin	High school			College			
	Total	Public	Private	Total	Public	Private	Full-time
1956.............................	8,543	7,668	875	2,883	1,824	1,059	NA
1955.............................	7,961	7,181	780	2,379	1,515	864	NA
WHITE ALONE							
2019.............................	11,936	11,065	870	12,783	10,217	2,567	9,652
2018.............................	12,157	11,174	983	13,323	10,670	2,653	9,989
2017.............................	12,281	11,306	975	13,224	10,524	2,700	9,623
2016.............................	12,071	11,017	1,053	13,901	10,846	3,054	10,373
2015.............................	12,133	11,199	934	13,859	11,039	2,821	10,254
2014.............................	12,283	11,315	969	13,953	11,227	2,727	10,506
2013.............................	12,157	11,270	887	14,240	11,378	2,862	10,281
2012.............................	12,554	11,494	1,060	14,628	11,530	3,098	10,694
2011.............................	12,548	11,542	1,007	15,412	12,161	3,251	11,205
2010.............................	12,570	11,525	1,045	15,258	12,179	3,079	10,818
2009.............................	12,425	11,419	1,006	15,027	11,948	3,079	10,847
2008.............................	12,687	11,585	1,103	14,405	11,432	2,973	10,256
2007.............................	12,986	11,886	1,100	13,835	10,855	2,979	9,696
2006.............................	12,966	11,694	1,273	13,273	10,338	2,936	9,236
2005.............................	13,296	12,109	1,187	13,466	10,303	3,163	9,392
2004.............................	12,823	11,684	1,138	13,381	10,478	2,904	9,257
2003[2]	13,036	11,939	1,097	12,870	10,101	2,769	8,855
2002.............................	12,862	11,730	1,132	12,781	9,774	3,007	8,613
2001.............................	12,540	11,473	1,067	12,208	9,503	2,705	7,909
2000.............................	12,392	11,259	1,133	11,999	9,364	2,636	7,945
1999.............................	12,487	11,374	1,113	12,053	9,185	2,868	7,886
1998.............................	12,142	11,013	1,130	12,401	9,518	2,883	8,012
1997.............................	12,290	11,287	1,003	12,442	9,713	2,729	8,127
1996.............................	12,052	10,999	1,053	12,188	9,567	2,622	7,849
1995.............................	11,617	10,574	1,042	12,021	9,311	2,711	7,773
1994[1]	11,430	10,514	916	12,222	9,472	2,751	7,722
1993r	10,960	10,124	836	9,685	7,695	1,990	6,996
1993.............................	10,651	9,834	819	9,366	7,428	1,940	6,739
1992.............................	10,480	9,648	833	9,658	7,653	2,001	6,985
1991.............................	10,309	9,467	841	9,579	7,464	2,118	6,919
1990.............................	10,177	9,370	807	9,466	7,411	2,056	6,776
1989.............................	10,172	9,443	730	9,374	7,219	2,158	6,650
1988.............................	10,462	9,571	890	9,245	7,302	1,940	6,488
1987.............................	10,967	10,019	947	9,143	7,113	2,034	6,275
1986.............................	11,259	10,229	1,030	8,943	6,821	2,122	6,253
1985.............................	11,378	10,258	1,120	9,334	7,131	2,203	6,597
1984.............................	11,240	10,266	974	9,269	7,163	2,105	6,672
1983.............................	11,425	10,339	1,086	9,242	6,949	2,293	6,532
1982.............................	11,577	10,541	1,036	9,328	7,102	2,227	6,579
1981.............................	12,062	11,035	1,027	9,162	6,906	2,256	6,452
1980.............................	12,056	NA	NA	8,875	NA	NA	6,212
1979.............................	12,583	11,549	1,033	8,709	6,672	2,037	6,058
1978.............................	12,897	11,741	1,156	8,514	6,368	2,145	5,974
1977.............................	13,152	11,980	1,172	8,812	6,743	2,069	6,165
1976.............................	13,214	12,093	1,121	8,644	6,657	1,987	6,170
1975.............................	13,224	12,112	1,112	8,516	6,724	1,792	6,183
1974.............................	13,073	11,966	1,107	7,781	6,049	1,732	5,575
1973.............................	13,091	11,967	1,124	7,324	5,550	1,773	5,408
1972.............................	12,959	11,876	1,083	7,458	5,644	1,814	5,678
1971.............................	12,998	11,937	1,061	7,273	5,624	1,650	5,560
1970.............................	12,723	11,599	1,124	6,759	5,168	1,591	5,221
1969.............................	12,588	11,502	1,085	6,827	4,967	1,860	5,307
1968.............................	12,280	11,007	1,272	6,255	4,501	1,753	4,919
1967.............................	11,997	10,769	1,228	5,905	4,155	1,750	4,604
1966.............................	11,643	10,312	1,329	5,708	3,914	1,795	4,556
1965.............................	11,356	9,961	1,395	5,317	3,568	1,749	4,111
1964.............................	11,257	9,898	1,359	4,338	2,798	1,540	NA
1963.............................	10,994	9,782	1,212	4,050	2,680	1,370	NA
1962.............................	10,270	9,217	1,053	3,934	2,620	1,314	NA
1961.............................	9,737	8,635	1,102	3,498	2,205	1,293	NA
1960.............................	9,122	8,124	999	3,342	2,126	1,215	NA

NA = Not available.
r = Revised, controlled to 1990 census based population estimates; previous 1993 data controlled to 1980 census based population estimates.
[1]Prior to 1994, total enrolled does not include the 35 and over population.
[2]Starting in 2003 respondents could identify more than one race. Except as noted, the race data in this table from 2003 onward represent those respondents who indicated only one race category.
[3]Data shown for 1955 to 1966 for the Black population are for Black and Other races.
[4]The data shown prior to 2003 consists of those identifying themselves as "Asian or Pacific Islanders."

Table A-10. School Enrollment of the Population 3 Years Old and Over, by Level and Control of School, Selected Race, and Hispanic Origin, October 1955–2019—*Continued*

(Numbers in thousands; civilian noninstitutionalized population.)

Year, race, and Hispanic origin	Total enrolled	Nursery school			Kindergarten			Elementary school		
		Total	Public	Private	Total	Public	Private	Total	Public	Private
1959	38,857	NA	NA	NA	1,758	1,434	324	25,395	20,854	4,541
1958	37,662	NA	NA	NA	1,769	1,383	386	24,380	20,178	4,203
1957	36,132	NA	NA	NA	1,595	1,258	337	23,610	19,595	4,015
1956	34,641	NA	NA	NA	1,544	1,364	180	22,740	19,186	3,554
1955	32,929	NA	NA	NA	1,484	1,244	240	22,185	18,947	3,238
WHITE ALONE NON-HISPANIC										
2019	38,673	2,399	1,094	1,306	1,963	1,684	279	16,186	14,265	1,921
2018	39,679	2,550	1,221	1,329	1,972	1,726	246	16,272	14,419	1,854
2017	39,649	2,461	1,211	1,250	1,955	1,699	256	16,272	14,594	1,679
2016	40,606	2,499	1,275	1,224	1,956	1,697	259	16,640	14,939	1,701
2015	41,145	2,410	1,143	1,268	2,022	1,748	273	16,879	15,095	1,783
2014	41,456	2,477	1,159	1,317	1,990	1,726	264	16,904	15,008	1,897
2013	42,025	2,531	1,089	1,442	1,968	1,691	277	17,309	15,379	1,930
2012	42,776	2,509	1,227	1,283	2,011	1,691	320	17,413	15,401	2,012
2011	44,951	2,743	1,332	1,411	2,238	1,903	335	17,830	15,670	2,160
2010	44,968	2,766	1,274	1,492	2,120	1,842	278	17,942	15,960	1,981
2009	45,470	2,575	1,188	1,387	2,252	1,990	262	18,244	16,198	2,046
2008	45,373	2,710	1,213	1,497	2,206	1,884	323	18,349	16,029	2,320
2007	45,334	2,711	1,225	1,486	2,279	1,929	351	18,306	15,998	2,307
2006	45,386	2,769	1,152	1,616	2,288	1,940	348	18,622	16,322	2,301
2005	46,338	2,810	1,211	1,599	2,308	1,936	372	18,858	16,335	2,523
2004	46,095	2,840	1,153	1,687	2,325	1,917	408	19,093	16,447	2,646
2003[2]	46,440	3,184	1,382	1,802	2,245	1,804	440	19,252	16,735	2,517
2002	46,725	2,881	1,172	1,709	2,065	1,585	480	20,124	17,495	2,628
2001	46,110	2,725	1,054	1,671	2,203	1,781	422	20,298	17,693	2,605
2000	46,660	2,854	1,149	1,705	2,346	1,846	500	20,574	17,747	2,827
1999	47,292	3,044	1,146	1,898	2,307	1,839	468	20,779	17,960	2,819
1998	47,386	2,964	1,136	1,828	2,336	1,790	547	20,806	18,107	2,699
1997	47,776	2,956	1,143	1,813	2,456	1,970	486	20,839	18,426	2,413
1996	46,947	2,767	922	1,845	2,590	2,081	509	20,447	17,808	2,639
1995	48,019	3,104	1,129	1,975	2,551	2,047	504	21,256	18,518	2,738
1994[1]	47,679	3,024	1,090	1,934	2,522	2,059	462	21,170	18,555	2,615
1993	43,827	2,277	720	1,557	2,779	2,239	540	20,961	18,617	2,344
BLACK ALONE[3]										
2019	11,551	714	520	194	642	557	85	4,991	4,651	341
2018	11,690	680	459	221	555	541	14	4,991	4,694	297
2017	11,609	754	576	178	507	477	30	5,048	4,739	309
2016	11,684	620	457	163	668	631	37	4,855	4,522	333
2015	11,544	703	501	202	618	596	23	4,883	4,647	236
2014	11,796	746	557	189	690	605	86	4,844	4,587	257
2013	11,824	683	465	218	736	691	46	4,848	4,625	224
2012	11,918	708	516	193	646	598	48	4,856	4,583	273
2011	12,037	794	562	232	559	503	56	4,902	4,658	245
2010	11,969	698	522	175	736	682	54	4,795	4,498	298
2009	11,748	811	640	171	619	578	41	4,749	4,424	325
2008	11,421	706	548	158	601	545	56	4,993	4,665	329
2007	11,475	700	485	215	605	548	56	4,926	4,572	353
2006	11,400	715	513	202	608	536	71	4,952	4,608	344
2005	11,384	719	542	177	538	486	52	5,106	4,747	359
2004	11,540	825	600	224	596	535	61	5,159	4,905	254
2003[2]	11,408	697	484	212	558	495	63	5,245	4,942	302
2002	11,703	725	503	221	598	543	55	5,545	5,210	335
2001	11,630	787	537	250	605	536	69	5,478	5,160	318
2000	11,503	726	531	195	629	547	82	5,481	5,133	347
1999	11,282	729	569	160	632	558	74	5,388	5,002	386
1998	11,411	761	528	233	689	592	97	5,332	5,031	301
1997	11,270	796	582	214	632	571	61	5,332	5,049	284
1996	10,851	702	459	243	634	545	89	5,171	4,846	325
1995	10,753	663	478	185	653	564	89	5,185	4,845	340
1994[1]	10,702	721	513	208	662	603	59	5,086	4,709	378
1993r	9,786	433	320	113	721	649	72	5,009	4,733	276
1993	9,470	414	307	107	687	618	69	4,865	4,599	266

NA = Not available.

r = Revised, controlled to 1990 census based population estimates; previous 1993 data controlled to 1980 census based population estimates.

[1]Prior to 1994, total enrolled does not include the 35 and over population.

[2]Starting in 2003 respondents could identify more than one race. Except as noted, the race data in this table from 2003 onward represent those respondents who indicated only one race category.

[3]Data shown for 1955 to 1966 for the Black population are for Black and Other races.

[4]The data shown prior to 2003 consists of those identifying themselves as "Asian or Pacific Islanders."

Table A-10. School Enrollment of the Population 3 Years Old and Over, by Level and Control of School, Selected Race, and Hispanic Origin, October 1955–2019—*Continued*

(Numbers in thousands; civilian noninstitutionalized population.)

Year, race, and Hispanic origin	High school			College			
	Total	Public	Private	Total	Public	Private	Full-time
1959..............................	8,586	7,572	1,014	3,118	1,960	1,158	NA
1958..............................	8,484	7,501	982	3,030	1,928	1,101	NA
1957..............................	7,995	7,121	874	2,932	1,924	1,006	NA
1956..............................	7,670	6,825	845	2,687	1,704	983	NA
1955..............................	7,036	6,303	733	2,224	1,429	795	NA
WHITE ALONE NON-HISPANIC							
2019..............................	8,447	7,718	729	9,677	7,497	2,180	7,410
2018..............................	8,637	7,817	820	10,248	7,973	2,274	7,748
2017..............................	8,905	8,051	854	10,055	7,736	2,319	7,404
2016..............................	8,760	7,839	921	10,749	8,219	2,530	8,135
2015..............................	8,931	8,087	843	10,904	8,526	2,377	8,226
2014..............................	9,018	8,155	862	11,068	8,775	2,292	8,456
2013..............................	8,869	8,109	760	11,348	8,889	2,459	8,362
2012..............................	9,193	8,252	941	11,650	8,977	2,672	8,604
2011..............................	9,437	8,535	902	12,703	9,842	2,861	9,333
2010..............................	9,528	8,598	930	12,613	9,900	2,713	9,122
2009..............................	9,573	8,655	919	12,826	10,022	2,803	9,368
2008..............................	9,783	8,798	986	12,324	9,630	2,694	8,925
2007..............................	10,171	9,204	966	11,867	9,141	2,726	8,379
2006..............................	10,222	9,072	1,150	11,485	8,821	2,664	8,105
2005..............................	10,647	9,566	1,081	11,715	8,852	2,863	8,246
2004..............................	10,266	9,221	1,044	11,571	8,928	2,643	8,082
2003[2]..............................	10,463	9,473	990	11,295	8,742	2,553	7,810
2002..............................	10,419	9,388	1,031	11,236	8,488	2,749	7,673
2001..............................	10,281	9,331	950	10,602	8,133	2,469	6,980
2000..............................	10,250	9,222	1,029	10,636	8,202	2,434	7,105
1999..............................	10,344	9,314	1,030	10,818	8,158	2,660	7,162
1998..............................	10,170	9,131	1,039	11,109	8,435	2,674	7,251
1997..............................	10,280	9,358	922	11,245	8,688	2,558	7,378
1996..............................	10,107	9,148	959	11,034	8,584	2,450	7,178
1995..............................	10,084	9,094	991	11,024	8,439	2,585	7,194
1994[1]..............................	9,786	8,951	835	11,178	8,568	2,610	7,152
1993..............................	9,216	8,449	767	8,594	6,772	1,822	6,247
BLACK ALONE[4]							
2019..............................	2,355	2,167	189	2,848	2,330	517	2,001
2018..............................	2,456	2,380	76	3,009	2,475	534	2,143
2017..............................	2,488	2,366	122	2,812	2,414	398	2,034
2016..............................	2,656	2,556	100	2,885	2,271	614	2,064
2015..............................	2,515	2,420	95	2,826	2,260	566	2,045
2014..............................	2,581	2,451	130	2,934	2,284	650	2,055
2013..............................	2,699	2,588	111	2,857	2,340	517	2,092
2012..............................	2,669	2,528	141	3,038	2,507	531	2,168
2011..............................	2,635	2,545	91	3,146	2,541	605	2,279
2010..............................	2,657	2,552	105	3,083	2,495	587	2,223
2009..............................	2,680	2,592	89	2,889	2,322	567	2,061
2008..............................	2,639	2,524	115	2,481	1,975	506	1,690
2007..............................	2,743	2,627	116	2,501	1,968	533	1,683
2006..............................	2,792	2,628	165	2,334	1,816	518	1,628
2005..............................	2,723	2,592	131	2,298	1,800	498	1,526
2004..............................	2,660	2,584	76	2,301	1,831	470	1,504
2003[2]..............................	2,765	2,691	74	2,144	1,773	371	1,416
2002..............................	2,558	2,451	107	2,278	1,868	410	1,468
2001..............................	2,531	2,412	119	2,230	1,766	463	1,475
2000..............................	2,502	2,350	152	2,164	1,721	443	1,351
1999..............................	2,536	2,427	109	1,998	1,587	411	1,372
1998..............................	2,614	2,515	99	2,016	1,595	421	1,284
1997..............................	2,605	2,516	89	1,903	1,546	357	1,280
1996..............................	2,443	2,338	105	1,901	1,519	381	1,179
1995..............................	2,481	2,370	111	1,772	1,353	419	1,117
1994[1]..............................	2,434	2,313	121	1,800	1,439	361	1,147
1993r..............................	2,317	2,197	120	1,305	1,006	299	951
1993..............................	2,244	2,128	115	1,261	973	288	914

NA = Not available.
r = Revised, controlled to 1990 census based population estimates; previous 1993 data controlled to 1980 census based population estimates.
[1] Prior to 1994, total enrolled does not include the 35 and over population.
[2] Starting in 2003 respondents could identify more than one race. Except as noted, the race data in this table from 2003 onward represent those respondents who indicated only one race category.
[3] Data shown for 1955 to 1966 for the Black population are for Black and Other races.
[4] The data shown prior to 2003 consists of those identifying themselves as "Asian or Pacific Islanders."

Table A-10. School Enrollment of the Population 3 Years Old and Over, by Level and Control of School, Selected Race, and Hispanic Origin, October 1955–2019—*Continued*

(Numbers in thousands; civilian noninstitutionalized population.)

Year, race, and Hispanic origin	Total enrolled	Nursery school			Kindergarten			Elementary school		
		Total	Public	Private	Total	Public	Private	Total	Public	Private
1992	9,150	374	250	124	688	625	63	4,730	4,494	234
1991	9,031	360	244	117	676	598	79	4,672	4,445	229
1990	8,854	431	283	148	636	574	62	4,627	4,428	199
1989	8,707	366	216	150	601	557	44	4,528	4,296	232
1988	8,609	286	168	118	591	547	44	4,538	4,289	250
1987	8,712	277	164	113	699	658	41	4,402	4,206	194
1986	8,556	315	200	115	647	600	47	4,326	4,134	193
1985	8,444	332	212	120	625	562	63	4,307	4,131	175
1984	8,226	340	179	161	563	513	51	4,123	3,947	177
1983	8,199	326	215	111	476	427	48	4,153	3,964	189
1982	8,262	305	192	113	508	463	45	4,194	3,974	220
1981	8,350	284	182	102	474	412	62	4,291	4,087	204
1980	8,251	294	180	115	490	440	50	4,259	4,058	202
1979	8,317	278	185	95	497	443	54	4,296	4,053	243
1978	8,416	312	210	102	451	414	38	4,356	4,154	202
1977	8,564	250	171	78	496	447	50	4,387	4,166	221
1976	8,518	226	146	80	542	482	60	4,430	4,256	175
1975	8,400	276	171	105	468	426	42	4,509	4,344	165
1974	8,215	227	121	106	463	416	47	4,585	4,455	131
1973	7,834	210	146	64	423	391	32	4,473	4,277	196
1972	7,959	185	113	72	448	402	46	4,573	4,382	191
1971	8,179	151	90	61	464	422	42	4,877	4,712	165
1970	7,829	178	129	49	426	374	53	4,868	4,668	200
1969	7,680	170	102	68	425	361	64	4,785	4,633	151
1968	7,448	132	89	43	448	397	51	4,716	4,569	146
1967	7,196	140	92	47	418	375	44	4,618	4,444	173
1966	7,547	125	88	37	420	364	56	4,904	4,739	165
1965	7,252	72	37	35	407	353	54	4,796	4,620	176
1964	6,807	NA	NA	NA	312	275	37	4,634	4,430	205
1963	6,541	NA	NA	NA	276	237	39	4,536	4,321	215
1962	6,203	NA	NA	NA	294	247	47	4,389	4,226	163
1961	6,210	NA	NA	NA	331	308	23	4,424	4,207	216
1960	5,910	NA	NA	NA	243	206	37	4,313	4,118	195
1959	5,513	NA	NA	NA	274	244	30	3,987	3,826	161
1958	5,238	NA	NA	NA	222	186	36	3,804	3,621	182
1957	5,034	NA	NA	NA	229	213	16	3,638	3,483	155
1956	4,712	NA	NA	NA	214	202	12	3,429	3,287	142
1955	4,498	NA	NA	NA	144	121	23	3,273	3,131	142
ASIAN ALONE[3]										
2019	5,023	260	118	142	256	197	58	1,800	1,684	116
2018	4,779	263	129	134	220	208	12	1,720	1,551	170
2017	4,636	253	123	130	239	204	35	1,632	1,478	154
2016	4,720	304	138	166	214	188	26	1,781	1,658	123
2015	4,567	244	102	142	215	188	27	1,704	1,552	152
2014	4,449	257	105	152	179	147	32	1,643	1,476	167
2013	4,375	242	113	129	165	149	16	1,576	1,402	174
2012	4,275	208	90	118	224	196	28	1,540	1,388	152
2011	3,779	212	120	92	209	189	21	1,469	1,336	133
2010	3,815	223	97	127	196	181	15	1,488	1,358	130
2009	3,515	239	107	132	167	146	21	1,296	1,170	125
2008	3,545	205	110	95	144	119	24	1,356	1,168	188
2007	3,470	171	77	94	137	112	25	1,421	1,305	115
2006	3,287	143	65	78	162	149	13	1,235	1,105	130
2005	3,377	185	80	105	138	99	39	1,228	1,137	91
2004	3,409	165	72	93	164	152	12	1,239	1,153	86
2003[2]	3,312	138	56	82	122	93	29	1,258	1,122	136
2002	3,787	217	85	132	157	137	20	1,431	1,237	195
2001	3,803	161	91	70	181	161	20	1,409	1,263	146
2000	3,442	222	91	132	152	124	28	1,350	1,257	93
1999	3,621	205	96	109	195	148	47	1,461	1,343	118
1998	3,386	196	77	118	145	120	25	1,380	1,190	189
1997	3,261	168	59	108	161	110	51	1,329	1,186	144
1996	3,258	183	63	120	177	158	19	1,255	1,144	111
1995	1,863	76	28	47	75	62	13	697	622	74

NA = Not available.

r = Revised, controlled to 1990 census based population estimates; previous 1993 data controlled to 1980 census based population estimates.

[1]Prior to 1994, total enrolled does not include the 35 and over population.

[2]Starting in 2003 respondents could identify more than one race. Except as noted, the race data in this table from 2003 onward represent those respondents who indicated only one race category.

[3]Data shown for 1955 to 1966 for the Black population are for Black and Other races.

[4]The data shown prior to 2003 consists of those identifying themselves as "Asian or Pacific Islanders."

Table A-10. School Enrollment of the Population 3 Years Old and Over, by Level and Control of School, Selected Race, and Hispanic Origin, October 1955–2019—*Continued*

(Numbers in thousands; civilian noninstitutionalized population.)

Year, race, and Hispanic origin	High school			College			
	Total	Public	Private	Total	Public	Private	Full-time
1992	2,152	2,072	72	1,217	980	237	904
1991	2,100	2,044	56	1,220	1,004	217	900
1990	1,975	1,909	65	1,188	963	227	869
1989	2,069	2,027	42	1,139	932	208	833
1988	2,079	2,016	62	1,114	894	220	801
1987	2,140	2,056	84	1,193	977	218	852
1986	2,130	2,040	91	1,138	896	242	859
1985	2,131	2,068	63	1,049	860	190	767
1984	2,061	2,002	59	1,138	918	220	810
1983	2,143	2,057	86	1,102	858	245	806
1982	2,128	2,073	55	1,127	865	263	800
1981	2,168	2,102	65	1,133	898	235	815
1980	2,200	NA	NA	1,007	NA	NA	723
1979	2,245	2,171	74	1,002	814	188	748
1978	2,276	2,211	65	1,020	822	199	753
1977	2,327	2,269	59	1,103	916	187	803
1976	2,258	2,187	71	1,062	887	175	817
1975	2,199	2,140	59	948	782	166	742
1974	2,125	2,072	54	814	659	155	589
1973	2,044	1,988	56	685	537	147	536
1972	2,025	1,971	54	727	582	145	525
1971	2,006	1,951	55	680	532	148	534
1970	1,834	1,794	41	522	422	100	427
1969	1,808	1,751	57	492	372	120	401
1968	1,718	1,656	62	434	359	75	338
1967	1,651	1,605	46	370	280	90	271
1966	1,721	1,673	48	282	NA	NA	210
1965	1,619	1,556	62	358	272	86	218
1964	1,556	1,505	51	306	227	78	NA
1963	1,444	1,404	39	286	217	69	NA
1962	1,246	1,214	32	274	200	74	NA
1961	1,222	1,182	39	233	171	61	NA
1960	1,127	1,092	34	227	180	46	NA
1959	1,030	999	31	222	160	62	NA
1958	998	981	17	212	160	53	NA
1957	961	939	22	206	132	74	NA
1956	873	843	30	196	120	76	NA
1955	926	878	48	155	86	69	NA
ASIAN ALONE[3]							
2019	938	901	37	1,768	1,443	325	1,503
2018	886	851	34	1,691	1,336	355	1,439
2017	931	853	78	1,581	1,219	362	1,330
2016	837	776	62	1,585	1,163	421	1,349
2015	787	727	60	1,616	1,232	384	1,340
2014	827	766	61	1,543	1,202	341	1,247
2013	817	741	76	1,576	1,144	432	1,260
2012	857	778	79	1,447	1,078	369	1,175
2011	685	635	50	1,204	936	268	963
2010	586	542	43	1,322	969	353	1,090
2009	582	530	53	1,231	950	282	972
2008	620	564	56	1,220	918	301	917
2007	638	616	23	1,103	841	261	896
2006	663	611	51	1,084	862	223	866
2005	642	596	46	1,184	904	279	948
2004	650	619	31	1,191	928	263	881
2003[2]	632	585	47	1,162	833	328	901
2002	723	664	59	1,258	1,040	218	951
2001	771	736	35	1,280	1,026	254	921
2000	668	622	46	1,049	831	218	792
1999	719	666	53	1,041	779	261	787
1998	650	599	51	1,016	783	233	821
1997	656	600	57	947	712	235	721
1996	644	606	38	999	816	183	710
1995	399	375	24	617	470	147	456

NA = Not available.
r = Revised, controlled to 1990 census based population estimates; previous 1993 data controlled to 1980 census based population estimates.
[1]Prior to 1994, total enrolled does not include the 35 and over population.
[2]Starting in 2003 respondents could identify more than one race. Except as noted, the race data in this table from 2003 onward represent those respondents who indicated only one race category.
[3]Data shown for 1955 to 1966 for the Black population are for Black and Other races.
[4]The data shown prior to 2003 consists of those identifying themselves as "Asian or Pacific Islanders."

Table A-10. School Enrollment of the Population 3 Years Old and Over, by Level and Control of School, Selected Race, and Hispanic Origin, October 1955–2019—*Continued*

(Numbers in thousands; civilian noninstitutionalized population.)

Year, race, and Hispanic origin	Total enrolled	Nursery school			Kindergarten			Elementary school		
		Total	Public	Private	Total	Public	Private	Total	Public	Private
1994[1]	2,057	76	27	50	74	60	14	785	707	78
1993	2,321	100	38	62	139	125	14	1,012	930	82
HISPANIC (OF ANY RACE)										
2019	18,204	1,115	775	340	1,038	939	99	8,396	8,021	375
2018	18,080	1,149	864	285	970	891	79	8,305	7,929	375
2017	17,974	1,007	751	257	1,116	1,032	83	8,340	7,924	416
2016	17,865	1,079	791	287	1,034	1,008	26	8,148	7,835	313
2015	17,362	933	735	198	1,090	1,020	70	8,187	7,824	364
2014	17,122	1,016	769	248	1,044	991	54	8,085	7,699	386
2013	16,971	991	781	210	1,090	1,018	73	7,942	7,680	262
2012	17,043	988	781	206	1,050	1,009	41	7,841	7,566	275
2011	16,131	1,010	766	244	1,042	984	58	7,716	7,401	315
2010	15,670	994	794	200	1,050	1,002	49	7,403	7,052	351
2009	14,528	930	717	213	965	933	32	7,058	6,716	342
2008	13,967	844	668	177	961	910	51	6,742	6,450	292
2007	13,708	905	711	194	990	954	37	6,582	6,299	284
2006	13,111	911	707	205	846	798	48	6,394	6,109	285
2005	12,809	797	601	196	804	725	79	6,330	5,991	339
2004	12,509	787	591	196	769	699	70	6,184	5,895	290
2003	11,929	768	561	206	694	633	61	5,974	5,651	322
2002	11,544	637	476	161	727	688	39	5,909	5,585	324
2001	11,163	593	452	141	728	641	87	5,779	5,478	301
2000	10,163	574	419	154	687	639	48	5,224	5,012	213
1999	9,936	585	458	127	666	594	73	5,088	4,829	259
1998	9,528	618	492	126	639	608	31	4,831	4,568	262
1997	9,220	548	436	112	648	589	59	4,644	4,427	217
1996	8,818	533	403	130	602	539	63	4,443	4,162	281
1995	8,563	510	350	160	558	465	93	4,434	4,165	269
1994[1]	8,183	400	278	122	559	516	43	4,162	3,848	314
1993r	7,651	231	169	62	639	576	63	4,027	3,779	248
1993	6,689	194	142	52	538	484	53	3,534	3,317	217
1992	6,598	209	139	70	554	493	60	3,525	3,271	252
1991	6,306	215	146	69	552	525	27	3,461	3,240	221
1990	6,072	242	153	88	475	446	29	3,301	3,107	197
1989	5,722	181	95	86	404	382	21	3,219	3,031	188
1988	5,588	151	111	40	461	445	16	3,160	2,954	207
1987	5,619	226	138	88	439	399	39	3,048	2,861	187
1986	5,513	179	114	65	465	421	44	2,995	2,787	208
1985	5,070	168	105	63	364	315	49	2,803	2,607	196
1984	4,284	117	78	39	293	267	26	2,384	2,218	166
1983	4,618	108	60	48	335	285	50	2,548	2,323	225
1982	4,478	83	46	37	329	291	37	2,501	2,276	225
1981	4,551	131	68	63	306	282	24	2,474	2,239	235
1980	4,263	146	70	75	263	234	30	2,363	2,134	228
1979	3,608	89	50	39	226	210	16	1,934	1,745	189
1978	3,455	87	47	39	231	198	33	1,893	1,704	188
1977	3,516	75	30	46	220	206	14	1,874	1,654	220
1976	3,623	68	38	30	262	242	20	1,934	1,768	165
1975	3,741	85	47	39	235	218	17	2,062	1,858	204
1974	3,620	85	37	48	225	207	18	2,040	1,780	260
1973	3,171	68	41	27	171	165	6	1,884	1,712	172
1972	3,257	61	43	18	241	227	14	1,879	1,705	173
WHITE ALONE OR IN COMBINATION										
2019	57,879	3,637	1,904	1,732	3,107	2,726	382	25,033	22,672	2,361
2018	58,796	3,785	2,088	1,697	3,034	2,684	350	25,102	22,789	2,313
2017	58,381	3,576	2,022	1,554	3,137	2,780	356	25,040	22,895	2,145
2016	58,973	3,695	2,119	1,576	3,046	2,746	300	25,148	23,034	2,114
2015	59,162	3436	1890	1546	3133	2762	371	25,493	23,271	2223
2014	59,281	3,575	1,942	1,634	3,125	2,791	334	25,391	23,054	2,337
2013	60,066	3,650	1,896	1,754	3,166	2,813	353	25,776	23,510	2,266
2012	60,618	3601	2058	1543	3177	2799	378	25,613	23,244	2369

NA = Not available.

r = Revised, controlled to 1990 census based population estimates; previous 1993 data controlled to 1980 census based population estimates.

[1] Prior to 1994, total enrolled does not include the 35 and over population.

[2] Starting in 2003 respondents could identify more than one race. Except as noted, the race data in this table from 2003 onward represent those respondents who indicated only one race category.

[3] Data shown for 1955 to 1966 for the Black population are for Black and Other races.

[4] The data shown prior to 2003 consists of those identifying themselves as "Asian or Pacific Islanders."

Table A-10. School Enrollment of the Population 3 Years Old and Over, by Level and Control of School, Selected Race, and Hispanic Origin, October 1955–2019—*Continued*

(Numbers in thousands; civilian noninstitutionalized population.)

Year, race, and Hispanic origin	High school			College			
	Total	Public	Private	Total	Public	Private	Full-time
1994[1]	399	365	34	723	548	174	530
1993	428	390	37	641	519	122	542
HISPANIC (OF ANY RACE)							
2019	4,101	3,900	201	3,555	3,133	421	2,568
2018	4,082	3,901	181	3,574	3,116	458	2,578
2017	3,936	3,769	167	3,574	3,133	442	2,510
2016	3,943	3,787	156	3,661	3,050	612	2,571
2015	3,777	3,658	120	3,374	2,861	514	2,343
2014	3,681	3,545	136	3,295	2,799	496	2,352
2013	3,729	3,596	133	3,219	2,768	452	2,179
2012	3,765	3,633	131	3,400	2,948	451	2,397
2011	3,410	3,294	116	2,953	2,515	438	2,041
2010	3,344	3,219	125	2,879	2,478	401	1,868
2009	3,142	3,052	90	2,434	2,122	312	1,651
2008	3,192	3,066	126	2,227	1,919	308	1,434
2007	3,058	2,902	156	2,172	1,888	284	1,459
2006	2,990	2,856	134	1,968	1,664	304	1,246
2005	2,937	2,824	113	1,942	1,625	316	1,255
2004	2,793	2,685	108	1,975	1,676	299	1,276
2003	2,779	2,667	112	1,714	1,480	235	1,139
2002	2,614	2,513	101	1,656	1,374	283	1,004
2001	2,363	2,246	117	1,700	1,445	255	1,005
2000	2,253	2,144	108	1,426	1,219	207	873
1999	2,290	2,200	91	1,307	1,093	214	765
1998	2,077	1,978	98	1,363	1,137	226	801
1997	2,119	2,035	84	1,260	1,079	181	797
1996	2,018	1,922	96	1,223	1,031	192	708
1995	1,854	1,772	83	1,207	1,037	170	709
1994[1]	1,874	1,781	92	1,187	1,019	169	640
1993r	1,722	1,653	69	1,029	872	157	686
1993	1,556	1,496	60	867	731	134	573
1992	1,494	1,435	59	813	710	104	487
1991	1,357	1,299	61	721	607	115	481
1990	1,437	1,374	64	617	515	100	380
1989	1,278	1,231	48	642	557	82	416
1988	1,163	1,113	49	654	592	60	414
1987	1,239	1,160	80	668	551	115	414
1986	1,197	1,116	81	677	540	137	418
1985	1,156	1,090	67	579	464	116	381
1984	966	909	57	524	433	91	356
1983	1,104	1,027	77	523	441	82	335
1982	1,072	995	77	493	398	96	312
1981	1,130	1,056	74	510	398	112	343
1980	1,048	NA	NA	443	NA	NA	294
1979	920	875	45	440	365	75	314
1978	868	825	43	377	315	62	231
1977	928	836	92	418	357	60	287
1976	932	867	65	427	354	73	297
1975	948	886	61	411	358	53	287
1974	916	858	59	354	297	57	247
1973	758	707	51	290	247	43	201
1972	834	784	50	242	213	29	178
WHITE ALONE OR IN COMBINATION							
2019	12,727	11,812	915	13,375	10,712	2,662	10,127
2018	12,991	11,928	1,063	13,885	11,123	2,761	10,402
2017	12,926	11,869	1,056	13,703	10,897	2,805	10,029
2016	12,728	11,627	1,102	14,355	11,223	3,132	10,731
2015	12,805	11,813	992	14,295	11,365	2930	10,581
2014	12,879	11,824	1,055	14,310	11,503	2,807	10,778
2013	12,732	11,803	929	14,743	11,768	2,975	10,647
2012	13,110	12,010	1101	15,117	11,919	3198	11,038

NA = Not available.
r = Revised, controlled to 1990 census based population estimates; previous 1993 data controlled to 1980 census based population estimates.
[1]Prior to 1994, total enrolled does not include the 35 and over population.
[2]Starting in 2003 respondents could identify more than one race. Except as noted, the race data in this table from 2003 onward represent those respondents who indicated only one race category.
[3]Data shown for 1955 to 1966 for the Black population are for Black and Other races.
[4]The data shown prior to 2003 consists of those identifying themselves as "Asian or Pacific Islanders."

Table A-10. School Enrollment of the Population 3 Years Old and Over, by Level and Control of School, Selected Race, and Hispanic Origin, October 1955–2019—*Continued*

(Numbers in thousands; civilian noninstitutionalized population.)

Year, race, and Hispanic origin	Total enrolled	Nursery school			Kindergarten			Elementary school		
		Total	Public	Private	Total	Public	Private	Total	Public	Private
2011.............................	61,979	3,833	2,132	1,702	3,393	2,988	405	25,989	23,474	2,516
2010.............................	61,498	3,880	2,130	1,749	3,188	2,848	339	25,844	23,469	2,375
2009.............................	60,778	3,582	1,931	1,651	3,271	2,974	298	25,629	23,238	2,391
2008.............................	60,309	3,642	1,927	1,715	3,247	2,863	385	25,498	22,849	2,649
2007.............................	59,896	3,689	1,959	1,730	3,339	2,946	393	25,321	22,689	2,632
2006.............................	59,391	3,765	1,895	1,871	3,213	2,820	393	25,424	22,809	2,615
2005.............................	60,035	3,642	1,819	1,823	3,179	2,715	463	25,682	22,794	2,888
2004.............................	59,427	3,682	1,762	1,920	3,169	2,670	498	25,691	22,682	3,009
2003.............................	59,184	4,039	1,989	2,050	3,002	2,477	525	25,581	22,686	2,895
BLACK ALONE OR IN COMBINATION										
2019.............................	13,679	911	640	271	761	671	90	6,015	5,638	377
2018.............................	13,654	835	558	277	685	663	22	5,960	5,590	370
2017.............................	13,598	909	663	246	651	615	36	6,087	5,695	391
2016.............................	13,507	792	561	231	797	749	48	5,749	5,332	417
2015.............................	13,248	820	594	226	710	680	29	5,883	5,598	285
2014.............................	13,387	840	624	216	830	739	91	5,720	5,409	312
2013.............................	13,517	852	560	291	855	804	51	5,637	5,378	259
2012.............................	13,534	834	613	221	799	744	55	5,603	5,299	305
2011.............................	13,288	904	649	255	696	628	68	5,524	5,253	271
2010.............................	13,105	798	589	210	809	743	66	5,402	5,069	333
2009.............................	12,825	894	687	206	674	632	42	5,295	4,942	353
2008.............................	12,542	776	589	187	668	609	59	5,593	5,225	368
2007.............................	12,401	788	546	242	673	617	57	5,395	5,030	365
2006.............................	12,261	801	568	234	678	607	71	5,365	5,002	363
2005.............................	12,118	763	563	200	593	531	62	5,504	5,122	382
2004.............................	12,303	864	622	242	676	606	70	5,540	5,251	289
2003.............................	12,144	787	526	262	637	559	78	5,604	5,276	327
ASIAN ALONE OR IN COMBINATION										
2019.............................	6,094	341	142	199	322	249	73	2,253	2,078	175
2018.............................	5,857	339	157	183	273	237	36	2,216	1,955	262
2017.............................	5,708	356	172	184	305	257	48	2,165	1,952	213
2016.............................	5,669	402	170	232	266	233	34	2,207	1,990	217
2015.............................	5,417	334	125	209	256	211	44	2,047	1,830	217
2014.............................	5,353	320	122	198	255	214	41	2,078	1,857	221
2013.............................	5,399	367	157	210	240	214	26	2,026	1,780	246
2012.............................	5,154	268	118	150	270	232	38	1,939	1,733	206
2011.............................	4,571	273	139	134	257	235	22	1,860	1,686	173
2010.............................	4,591	297	132	165	230	212	18	1,876	1,696	180
2009.............................	4,117	316	140	175	195	170	25	1,571	1,410	160
2008.............................	4,122	267	143	123	188	156	32	1,570	1,351	219
2007.............................	4,025	219	94	125	179	151	28	1,664	1,513	151
2006.............................	3,849	189	78	111	203	181	22	1,497	1,331	166
2005.............................	3,964	220	94	126	159	118	41	1,495	1,362	133
2004.............................	3,943	208	82	127	191	169	21	1,497	1,350	148
2003.............................	3,817	164	73	90	148	111	38	1,507	1,346	161

NA = Not available.

r = Revised, controlled to 1990 census based population estimates; previous 1993 data controlled to 1980 census based population estimates.

[1]Prior to 1994, total enrolled does not include the 35 and over population.

[2]Starting in 2003 respondents could identify more than one race. Except as noted, the race data in this table from 2003 onward represent those respondents who indicated only one race category.

[3]Data shown for 1955 to 1966 for the Black population are for Black and Other races.

[4]The data shown prior to 2003 consists of those identifying themselves as "Asian or Pacific Islanders."

Table A-10. School Enrollment of the Population 3 Years Old and Over, by Level and Control of School, Selected Race, and Hispanic Origin, October 1955–2019—*Continued*

(Numbers in thousands; civilian noninstitutionalized population.)

Year, race, and Hispanic origin	High school			College			
	Total	Public	Private	Total	Public	Private	Full-time
2011.............................	12,979	11,952	1,027	15,785	12,449	3,336	11,476
2010.............................	13,001	11,924	1,077	15,586	12,460	3,127	11,062
2009.............................	12,905	11,877	1,029	15,391	12,236	3,155	11,150
2008.............................	13,184	12,050	1,133	14,738	11,692	3,046	10,511
2007.............................	13,433	12,302	1,131	14,114	11,058	3,056	9,912
2006.............................	13,425	12,115	1,309	13,564	10,569	2,995	9,433
2005.............................	13,741	12,516	1,225	13,791	10,561	3,230	9,618
2004.............................	13,218	12,047	1,170	13,668	10,711	2,957	9,468
2003.............................	13,398	12,267	1,131	13,164	10,366	2,798	9,048
BLACK ALONE OR IN COMBINATION							
2019.............................	2,852	2,629	222	3,142	2,577	564	2,215
2018.............................	2,902	2,802	100	3,272	2,694	579	2,331
2017.............................	2,884	2,727	157	3,068	2,609	459	2,261
2016.............................	3,090	2,959	131	3,079	2,435	644	2,219
2015.............................	2,850	2,730	120	2,985	2,364	621	2,163
2014.............................	2,898	2,730	168	3,099	2,405	694	2,185
2013.............................	3,055	2,921	134	3,118	2,542	577	2,297
2012.............................	2,962	2,816	146	3,335	2,752	583	2,373
2011.............................	2,847	2,752	95	3,317	2,676	641	2,401
2010.............................	2,846	2,724	122	3,250	2,641	610	2,354
2009.............................	2,932	2,836	97	3,030	2,434	596	2,178
2008.............................	2,886	2,769	118	2,619	2,065	554	1,770
2007.............................	2,915	2,792	122	2,630	2,059	571	1,774
2006.............................	2,971	2,798	174	2,444	1,907	537	1,702
2005.............................	2,870	2,729	141	2,387	1,866	521	1,585
2004.............................	2,811	2,726	85	2,412	1,922	490	1,591
2003.............................	2,889	2,800	89	2,227	1,846	381	1,482
ASIAN ALONE OR IN COMBINATION							
2019.............................	1,178	1,115	63	1,999	1,642	358	1,711
2018.............................	1,109	1,042	67	1,919	1,531	388	1,634
2017.............................	1,132	1,015	117	1,750	1,356	394	1,460
2016.............................	1,014	922	92	1,780	1,324	455	1,512
2015.............................	960	879	81	1,821	1,385	436	1,501
2014.............................	988	893	96	1,712	1,337	375	1,392
2013.............................	1,000	909	91	1,766	1,295	471	1,412
2012.............................	1,060	949	111	1,617	1,201	415	1,300
2011.............................	825	757	68	1,356	1,053	302	1,063
2010.............................	722	668	54	1,467	1,089	378	1,205
2009.............................	701	636	65	1,334	1,033	301	1,061
2008.............................	758	690	68	1,340	1,009	331	1,009
2007.............................	760	718	42	1,204	917	287	988
2006.............................	806	743	63	1,154	918	235	900
2005.............................	792	726	67	1,297	993	305	1,036
2004.............................	786	743	43	1,260	980	281	936
2003.............................	736	674	62	1,262	925	337	965

NA = Not available.

r = Revised, controlled to 1990 census based population estimates; previous 1993 data controlled to 1980 census based population estimates.

[1]Prior to 1994, total enrolled does not include the 35 and over population.

[2]Starting in 2003 respondents could identify more than one race. Except as noted, the race data in this table from 2003 onward represent those respondents who indicated only one race category.

[3]Data shown for 1955 to 1966 for the Black population are for Black and Other races.

[4]The data shown prior to 2003 consists of those identifying themselves as "Asian or Pacific Islanders."

Table A-11. Percentage of the Population 3 Years Old and Over Enrolled in School, by Age, Sex, Race, and Hispanic Origin, October 1947–2019

(Percent; civilian noninstitutionalized population.)

Year, sex, race, and Hispanic origin	Total enrolled 3 to 34 years old	Total enrolled 3 years old and over	Age											
			3 and 4	5 and 6	7 to 9	10 to 13	14 and 15	16 and 17	18 and 19	20 and 21	22 to 24	25 to 29	30 to 34	35 and over
ALL RACES														
Both Sexes														
2019	54.1	24.3	53.7	93.6	97.5	98.0	97.9	92.7	67.3	53.5	28.6	11.0	6.0	1.4
2018	54.6	24.6	54.0	93.5	97.0	98.2	98.6	92.3	69.1	54.6	28.0	12.7	6.3	1.5
2017	54.6	24.7	53.8	93.5	97.1	97.8	98.2	92.9	68.2	55.0	28.4	12.1	5.9	1.5
2016	55.2	25.1	53.8	93.3	97.8	98.5	98.0	93.0	69.5	55.5	28.4	13.2	6.4	1.5
2015	55.2	25.3	52.7	94.2	97.3	98.0	98.0	93.7	68.5	53.3	28.8	13.2	6.6	1.6
2014	55.2	25.6	54.5	93.4	97.7	97.5	97.8	92.9	68.4	51.4	29.6	13.1	6.4	1.8
2013	55.8	25.9	54.9	93.8	97.9	98.2	98.4	93.7	67.1	52.8	29.7	13.3	6.7	1.8
2012	56.6	26.4	53.5	93.2	98.0	98.0	98.2	95.8	69.0	54.0	30.7	14.0	7.5	1.9
2011	56.8	26.9	52.4	95.1	98.0	98.5	98.6	95.7	71.1	52.7	31.1	14.8	7.7	2.0
2010	56.5	26.9	53.2	94.5	97.7	98.2	98.1	96.1	69.2	52.4	28.9	14.6	8.3	2.1
2009	56.5	26.7	52.4	94.1	97.7	98.5	98.0	94.6	68.9	51.7	30.4	13.5	8.1	2.1
2008	56.2	26.6	52.8	93.8	98.3	98.9	98.6	95.2	66.0	50.1	28.2	13.2	7.3	2.0
2007	56.1	26.6	54.5	94.7	98.1	98.6	98.7	94.3	66.8	48.4	27.3	12.4	7.2	1.9
2006	56.2	26.7	55.7	94.6	98.2	98.3	98.3	94.5	65.5	47.5	26.7	11.7	7.2	1.9
2005	56.5	27.1	53.6	95.4	98.6	98.6	98.0	95.1	67.6	48.7	27.3	11.9	6.9	2.0
2004	56.2	27.2	54.0	95.4	98.1	98.6	98.5	94.5	64.4	48.9	26.3	13.0	6.6	2.0
2003	56.2	27.2	55.1	94.5	98.1	98.4	97.5	94.9	64.5	48.3	27.8	11.8	6.8	1.9
2002	56.1	27.3	54.5	95.2	98.0	98.5	98.4	94.3	63.3	47.8	25.6	12.1	6.6	2.1
2001	55.7	27.2	52.2	95.3	98.2	98.4	98.1	93.4	61.0	45.5	25.1	11.7	6.8	2.0
2000	55.9	27.5	52.1	95.6	98.1	98.3	98.7	92.8	61.2	44.1	24.6	11.4	6.7	1.9
1999	56.0	27.7	54.2	96.0	98.5	98.8	98.2	93.6	60.6	45.3	24.5	11.1	6.2	2.1
1998	55.8	27.9	52.1	95.6	98.8	99.0	98.4	93.9	62.2	44.8	24.9	11.9	6.6	2.1
1997	55.6	28.3	52.6	96.6	98.8	99.3	98.9	94.3	61.5	45.9	26.4	11.8	5.7	2.3
1996	54.1	27.8	48.3	94.0	97.2	98.1	98.0	92.8	61.5	44.4	24.8	11.9	6.1	2.3
1995	53.7	27.8	48.7	96.0	98.7	99.1	98.9	93.6	59.4	44.9	23.2	11.6	6.0	2.2
1994	53.3	27.9	47.3	96.7	99.3	99.4	98.8	94.4	60.2	44.9	24.1	10.8	6.7	2.3
1993r	51.9	NA	40.1	95.3	99.5	99.5	98.9	93.9	61.4	42.6	23.5	10.2	5.9	NA
1993	51.8	26.9	40.4	95.4	99.5	99.5	98.9	94.0	61.6	42.7	23.6	10.2	5.9	2.2
1992	51.4	26.9	39.7	95.5	99.4	99.4	99.1	94.1	61.4	44.0	23.7	9.8	6.1	2.1
1991	50.7	26.9	40.5	95.4	99.6	99.7	98.8	93.3	59.6	42.0	22.2	10.2	6.2	2.2
1990	50.2	26.8	44.4	96.5	99.7	99.6	99.0	92.5	57.3	39.7	21.0	9.7	5.8	2.1
1989	49.1	26.4	39.1	95.2	99.2	99.4	98.8	92.7	56.0	38.5	19.9	9.3	5.7	2.0
1988	48.7	26.5	38.2	96.0	99.6	99.7	98.9	91.6	55.7	39.1	18.3	8.3	5.9	2.1
1987	48.6	26.6	38.3	95.1	99.6	99.5	98.6	91.7	55.6	38.7	17.5	9.0	5.9	1.8
1986	48.2	26.6	39.0	95.3	99.3	99.1	97.6	92.3	54.6	33.0	17.9	8.8	6.0	1.8
1985	48.3	26.8	38.9	96.1	99.1	99.3	98.1	91.7	51.6	35.3	16.9	9.2	6.1	1.7
1984	47.9	26.6	36.3	94.5	99.0	99.4	97.8	91.5	50.1	33.9	17.3	9.1	6.3	1.5
1983	48.4	27.1	37.6	95.4	98.9	99.4	98.3	91.7	50.4	32.5	16.6	9.6	6.4	1.7
1982	48.6	27.4	36.4	95.0	99.2	99.1	98.5	90.6	47.8	34.0	16.8	9.6	6.3	1.6
1981	48.9	27.9	36.0	94.0	99.2	99.3	98.0	90.6	49.0	31.6	16.5	9.0	6.9	1.7
1980	49.7	28.2	36.7	95.7	99.1	99.4	98.2	89.0	46.4	31.0	16.3	9.3	6.5	1.6
1979	50.3	28.7	35.1	95.8	99.2	99.1	98.1	89.2	45.0	30.2	15.8	9.6	6.4	1.7
1978	51.2	29.3	34.2	95.3	99.3	99.0	98.4	89.1	45.4	29.5	16.3	9.4	6.4	1.6
1977	52.5	NA	32.0	95.8	99.5	99.4	98.5	88.9	46.2	31.8	16.5	10.8	6.9	NA
1976	53.1	31.7	31.3	95.5	99.2	99.2	98.2	89.1	46.2	32.0	17.1	10.0	6.0	3.9
1975	53.7	NA	31.5	94.7	99.3	99.3	98.2	89.0	46.9	31.2	16.2	10.1	6.6	NA
1974	53.6	NA	28.8	94.2	99.1	99.5	97.9	87.9	43.1	30.2	15.1	9.6	5.7	NA
1973	53.5	NA	24.2	92.5	99.1	99.2	97.5	88.3	42.9	30.1	14.5	8.5	4.5	NA
1972	54.9	NA	24.4	91.9	99.0	99.3	97.6	88.9	46.3	31.4	14.8	8.6	4.6	NA
1971	56.2	NA	21.2	91.6	99.1	99.2	98.6	90.2	49.2	32.2	15.4	8.0	4.9	NA
1970	56.4	NA	20.5	89.5	99.3	99.2	98.1	90.0	47.7	31.9	14.9	7.5	4.2	NA
1969	57.0	NA	16.1	88.4	99.3	99.1	98.1	89.7	50.2	34.1	15.4	7.9	4.8	NA
1968	56.7	NA	15.7	87.6	99.1	99.1	98.0	90.2	50.4	31.2	13.8	7.0	3.9	NA
1967	56.6	NA	14.2	87.4	99.4	99.1	98.2	88.8	47.6	33.3	13.6	6.6	4.0	NA
1966	56.1	NA	12.5	85.1	99.3	99.3	98.6	88.5	47.2	29.9	13.2	6.5	2.7	NA
1965	55.5	NA	10.6	84.4	99.3	99.4	98.9	87.4	46.3	27.6	13.2	6.1	3.2	NA
1964	54.5	NA	9.5	83.3	99.0	99.0	98.6	87.7	41.6	26.3	9.9	5.2	2.6	NA
1963	58.5	NA	NA	82.7	99.4	99.3	98.4	87.1	40.9	25.0	11.4	4.9	2.5	NA
1962	57.8	NA	NA	82.2	99.2	99.3	98.0	84.3	41.8	23.0	10.3	5.0	2.6	NA

Note: Data shown for 1947 to 1966 for the Black population are for Black and other races. Data for 1947 to 1963 exclude kindergarten. Nursery school was first collected in 1964.
* = Quantity zero or rounds to zero.
NA = Not available.
r = Revised, controlled to 1990 census based population estimates; previous 1993 data controlled to 1980 census based population estimates.
[1]Starting in 2003, respondents could identify more than one race. Except as noted, the race data in this table from 2003 onward represent those respondents who indicated only one race category.
[2]The data shown prior to 2003 consists of those identifying themselves as "Asian or Pacific Islanders."

Table A-11. Percentage of the Population 3 Years Old and Over Enrolled in School, by Age, Sex, Race, and Hispanic Origin, October 1947–2019—*Continued*

(Percent; civilian noninstitutionalized population.)

Year, sex, race, and Hispanic origin	Total enrolled 3 to 34 years old	Total enrolled 3 years old and over	Age 3 and 4	5 and 6	7 to 9	10 to 13	14 and 15	16 and 17	18 and 19	20 and 21	22 to 24	25 to 29	30 to 34	35 and over
1961	56.8	NA	NA	81.7	99.4	99.3	97.6	83.6	38.0	21.5	8.4	4.4	2.0	NA
1960	56.4	NA	NA	80.7	99.6	99.5	97.8	82.6	38.4	19.4	8.7	4.9	2.4	NA
1959	55.5	NA	NA	80.0	99.4	99.4	97.5	82.9	36.8	18.8	8.6	5.1	2.2	NA
1958	54.8	NA	NA	80.4	99.5	99.5	96.9	80.6	37.6	------13.4------		5.7	2.2	NA
1957	53.6	NA	NA	78.6	99.5	99.5	97.1	80.5	34.9	------14.0------		5.5	1.8	NA
1956	52.3	NA	NA	77.6	99.4	99.2	96.9	78.4	35.4	------12.8------		5.1	1.9	NA
1955	50.8	NA	NA	78.1	99.2	99.2	95.9	77.4	31.5	------11.1------		4.2	1.6	NA
1954	50.0	NA	NA	77.3	99.2	99.5	95.8	78.0	32.4	------11.2------		4.1	1.5	NA
1953	48.8	NA	NA	55.7	99.4	99.4	96.5	74.7	31.2	------11.1------		2.9	1.7	NA
1952	46.8	NA	NA	54.7	98.7	98.9	96.2	73.4	28.7	--------9.5------		2.6	1.1	NA
1951	45.4	NA	NA	54.5	99.0	99.2	94.8	75.1	26.3	--------8.3------		2.5	NA	NA
1950	44.2	NA	NA	58.2	98.9	98.6	94.7	71.3	29.4	--------9.0------		3.0	NA	NA
1949	43.9	NA	NA	59.3	98.5	98.7	93.5	69.5	25.3	--------9.2------		3.8	1.1	NA
1948	43.1	NA	NA	56.0	98.3	98.0	92.7	71.2	26.9	--------9.7------		2.6	0.9	NA
1947	42.3	NA	NA	58.0	98.4	98.6	91.6	67.6	24.3	------10.2------		3.0	1.0	NA
Male														
2019	53.6	24.7	53.3	94.4	98.2	97.8	98.0	92.6	65.7	50.1	25.4	10.1	4.7	1.2
2018	54.1	25.0	53.6	93.3	97.1	98.1	98.8	93.7	66.1	50.9	26.1	11.2	5.4	1.1
2017	54.0	25.1	53.4	92.8	97.1	97.8	98.2	92.3	65.1	50.8	26.8	10.9	6.2	1.1
2016	54.8	25.0	54.1	92.7	97.5	98.3	98.7	92.7	68.2	51.4	27.6	11.8	5.5	1.2
2015	54.9	25.7	53.6	93.5	97.5	98.3	97.9	93.1	65.7	50.2	27.5	11.7	5.5	1.2
2014	54.8	25.9	53.5	94.0	97.5	96.9	97.5	92.1	64.9	49.1	28.1	12.2	5.3	1.4
2013	55.2	26.2	53.2	93.8	97.9	98.1	98.2	93.3	65.1	48.5	27.6	12.2	5.3	1.4
2012	55.9	26.6	52.7	93.2	97.7	98.2	98.3	95.7	65.8	49.5	29.4	11.9	5.8	1.3
2011	56.2	27.2	52.8	95.1	98.1	98.6	98.4	95.4	68.8	49.2	30.3	12.9	6.4	1.5
2010	55.9	27.1	53.0	93.7	97.6	97.9	98.0	94.9	66.9	49.2	27.0	13.5	6.7	1.6
2009	55.7	26.9	51.6	93.9	97.6	98.6	97.6	94.5	65.0	48.7	29.0	11.7	6.9	1.5
2008	55.6	26.9	52.3	93.8	98.0	98.7	99.0	94.9	64.0	47.4	26.3	12.1	6.3	1.4
2007	55.4	26.9	54.4	94.0	98.1	98.4	98.4	94.4	66.3	43.7	25.4	10.2	6.4	1.5
2006	55.5	27.0	56.0	94.4	98.1	98.2	98.2	94.1	63.6	44.0	25.0	10.4	5.9	1.5
2005	55.8	27.4	52.8	94.8	98.2	98.4	97.5	95.1	66.5	45.3	25.2	9.6	5.9	1.5
2004	55.0	27.6	54.7	95.5	97.8	98.5	98.7	94.9	60.3	46.6	24.1	11.5	5.6	1.6
2003	55.9	27.8	55.9	94.7	97.9	98.3	97.5	95.0	62.4	43.4	26.1	10.8	6.3	1.5
2002	55.8	27.9	54.6	95.3	98.1	98.3	98.4	94.0	61.8	44.8	23.8	10.7	5.5	1.7
2001	55.4	27.8	51.6	95.2	98.5	98.1	98.1	93.0	58.9	44.0	23.8	10.3	5.7	1.5
2000	55.8	28.0	50.8	95.1	98.0	98.3	98.7	92.7	58.3	41.0	23.9	10.0	5.6	1.5
1999	56.6	28.6	53.3	95.9	98.3	98.7	98.0	93.7	60.3	44.7	23.6	10.7	5.8	1.6
1998	55.9	28.6	53.3	95.2	98.7	99.0	98.3	93.5	60.1	42.7	24.6	10.9	5.5	1.6
1997	55.8	28.8	51.9	96.7	98.6	99.4	99.1	94.2	60.6	44.4	25.4	11.7	4.7	1.6
1996	54.4	28.5	46.9	93.8	97.2	98.0	98.5	93.2	60.8	43.9	25.2	11.4	4.9	1.8
1995	54.3	28.7	49.4	95.3	98.9	99.1	99.0	94.5	59.5	44.7	22.8	11.0	5.4	1.8
1994	53.7	28.7	47.6	97.0	99.2	99.4	98.8	94.3	60.4	42.7	24.2	10.5	5.9	1.7
1993r	52.6	NA	41.1	95.5	99.5	99.6	99.0	94.9	61.1	42.3	25.3	9.6	5.2	NA
1993	52.6	27.9	41.5	95.5	99.5	99.6	99.0	95.0	61.0	42.6	25.5	9.6	5.2	1.6
1992	51.9	27.7	40.3	95.7	99.5	99.5	99.2	95.4	61.6	41.7	23.8	9.1	5.2	1.5
1991	51.5	27.9	39.9	95.0	99.7	99.8	99.1	93.7	59.8	41.8	24.0	10.6	5.6	1.6
1990	50.9	27.7	43.9	96.5	99.7	99.6	99.1	92.7	58.2	40.3	22.3	9.2	4.8	1.5
1989	49.7	27.3	38.8	95.1	99.3	99.2	99.2	93.2	56.6	37.3	20.4	9.3	5.0	1.4
1988	49.6	27.6	38.3	95.9	99.6	99.7	98.9	92.1	56.2	39.0	20.5	8.1	5.5	1.5
1987	49.9	27.9	40.0	95.7	99.7	99.7	98.7	92.3	57.9	41.2	18.7	9.1	5.0	1.3
1986	49.3	27.8	38.8	96.0	99.4	98.9	97.6	92.3	57.1	33.4	19.0	9.4	5.6	1.3
1985	49.2	27.9	36.8	95.3	99.1	99.2	98.3	92.4	52.2	36.5	18.8	9.4	5.4	1.3
1984	49.1	28.0	35.9	94.0	98.8	99.3	97.5	91.8	52.4	36.2	20.1	9.6	5.8	1.1
1983	49.7	28.6	38.1	95.1	98.8	99.3	98.4	91.8	50.4	35.2	10.4	10.7	5.0	1.2
1982	49.7	28.8	36.4	94.7	99.2	99.0	98.7	91.3	48.9	35.2	18.5	10.1	5.6	1.2
1981	50.2	29.3	36.8	94.2	98.9	99.2	98.2	90.7	50.5	32.1	19.2	9.6	6.2	1.2
1980	50.9	29.6	37.8	95.0	99.0	99.4	98.7	89.1	47.0	32.6	17.8	9.8	5.9	1.2
1979	51.8	30.2	34.6	96.3	99.0	98.9	98.3	90.8	46.6	31.6	17.6	10.4	6.0	1.3
1978	52.9	31.0	34.0	95.1	99.1	98.8	98.4	89.5	47.8	31.7	19.1	10.9	6.5	1.3
1977	54.3	NA	32.1	94.7	99.5	99.2	98.7	90.0	48.4	34.6	19.7	12.6	7.1	NA
1976	55.1	33.6	30.9	95.6	98.9	99.1	98.6	90.5	48.2	33.6	20.7	13.0	6.8	3.6

Note: Data shown for 1947 to 1966 for the Black population are for Black and other races. Data for 1947 to 1963 exclude kindergarten. Nursery school was first collected in 1964.
* = Quantity zero or rounds to zero.
NA = Not available.
r = Revised, controlled to 1990 census based population estimates; previous 1993 data controlled to 1980 census based population estimates.
[1]Starting in 2003, respondents could identify more than one race. Except as noted, the race data in this table from 2003 onward represent those respondents who indicated only one race category.
[2]The data shown prior to 2003 consists of those identifying themselves as "Asian or Pacific Islanders."

Table A-11. Percentage of the Population 3 Years Old and Over Enrolled in School, by Age, Sex, Race, and Hispanic Origin, October 1947–2019—*Continued*

(Percent; civilian noninstitutionalized population.)

Year, sex, race, and Hispanic origin	Total enrolled 3 to 34 years old	Total enrolled 3 years old and over	Age											
			3 and 4	5 and 6	7 to 9	10 to 13	14 and 15	16 and 17	18 and 19	20 and 21	22 to 24	25 to 29	30 to 34	35 and over
1975	56.0	NA	30.6	94.3	99.2	98.9	98.4	90.7	49.9	35.3	20.0	13.1	7.7	NA
1974	56.0	NA	28.1	94.4	99.1	99.3	98.0	88.6	45.8	34.8	19.4	12.7	6.7	NA
1973	56.1	NA	24.5	92.2	99.0	99.2	97.9	89.4	47.9	34.4	19.1	11.8	5.6	NA
1972	57.8	NA	24.4	91.7	98.9	99.3	97.7	90.2	51.2	37.3	21.3	12.1	5.8	NA
1971	59.3	NA	20.0	90.9	99.0	98.8	98.7	91.7	55.4	38.9	23.3	11.9	6.3	NA
1970	59.7	NA	21.2	88.9	99.3	98.8	98.2	91.3	54.4	42.7	21.2	11.0	5.3	NA
1969	60.5	NA	15.5	87.7	99.0	98.9	98.1	91.6	59.4	46.5	22.9	11.4	5.9	NA
1968	60.4	NA	15.4	87.3	98.9	98.9	98.2	91.7	60.4	45.0	20.5	10.8	5.0	NA
1967	60.0	NA	14.2	86.6	99.4	98.9	98.3	91.0	56.3	44.3	21.0	9.9	5.4	NA
1966	59.7	NA	12.3	84.5	99.2	99.1	98.7	89.9	57.8	41.4	21.3	9.6	3.8	NA
1965	58.8	NA	10.2	84.4	99.3	99.3	99.0	88.0	55.6	37.6	21.1	9.4	4.5	NA
1964	57.5	NA	8.9	83.4	98.7	98.9	99.0	89.8	50.9	34.4	16.1	8.1	3.6	NA
1963	62.3	NA	NA	82.7	99.2	99.0	98.7	89.4	51.0	33.6	19.5	7.8	3.7	NA
1962	61.7	NA	NA	82.6	99.1	99.2	98.7	87.1	51.2	31.3	17.7	8.5	3.9	NA
1961	60.4	NA	NA	82.0	99.5	99.2	98.1	84.7	48.6	29.5	13.9	7.1	2.9	NA
1960	60.0	NA	NA	80.8	99.6	99.4	97.9	84.5	47.8	27.1	15.0	8.4	3.7	NA
1959	59.1	NA	NA	79.5	99.2	99.4	97.8	84.8	45.6	28.3	13.7	8.9	3.3	NA
1958	58.7	NA	NA	80.6	99.6	99.4	96.9	83.8	47.5	------21.0------		9.5	2.9	NA
1957	57.5	NA	NA	78.3	99.4	99.6	98.0	82.8	43.3	------21.3------		9.5	2.6	NA
1956	56.3	NA	NA	77.1	99.2	99.1	97.1	79.9	45.1	------20.6------		8.9	2.7	NA
1955	54.9	NA	NA	78.1	99.1	99.4	95.7	81.1	42.5	------18.1------		7.0	2.1	NA
1954	54.0	NA	NA	76.3	99.0	99.4	96.1	80.9	40.6	------19.1------		6.7	1.9	NA
1953	50.2	NA	NA	55.0	99.3	99.1	96.4	76.5	37.7	------18.5------		5.5	2.0	NA
1952	49.4	NA	NA	54.8	98.6	98.9	96.2	73.9	37.2	------16.9------		4.7	1.7	NA
1951	56.8	NA	NA	55.1	99.1	99.1	95.1	74.3	32.4	------14.3------		4.2	NA	NA
1950	54.8	NA	NA	56.8	98.8	98.7	95.2	72.8	35.7	------14.3------		5.9	NA	NA
1949	45.8	NA	NA	60.1	98.5	98.6	93.9	70.8	31.6	------15.4------		6.8	1.9	NA
1948	44.8	NA	NA	55.1	99.5	98.1	92.0	72.1	34.3	------16.5------		5.1	1.5	NA
1947	44.3	NA	NA	57.4	98.5	98.7	90.3	67.6	31.4	------17.0------		5.8	1.7	NA
Female														
2019	54.6	23.9	54.0	92.8	96.8	98.2	97.8	92.8	68.9	57.0	31.8	11.9	7.2	1.7
2018	55.1	24.3	54.4	93.8	96.9	98.4	98.3	90.8	72.2	58.4	29.9	14.2	7.2	1.8
2017	55.2	24.4	54.1	94.2	97.0	97.8	98.3	93.5	71.3	59.2	30.0	13.4	6.5	1.8
2016	55.6	24.7	53.5	93.8	98.1	98.7	97.3	93.3	70.7	59.7	30.0	14.7	7.2	1.7
2015	55.6	24.9	51.8	94.9	97.2	97.6	98.1	94.4	71.4	56.5	30.1	14.6	7.7	1.9
2014	55.7	25.2	55.5	92.8	97.9	98.1	98.2	93.8	72.1	53.9	31.0	14.0	7.4	2.1
2013	56.4	25.7	56.7	93.7	97.9	98.2	98.6	94.1	69.2	57.3	31.7	14.4	8.1	2.3
2012	57.4	26.2	54.4	93.3	98.4	97.8	98.2	95.9	72.3	58.3	32.1	16.0	9.2	2.3
2011	57.4	26.5	52.1	95.2	97.9	98.4	98.9	96.0	73.5	56.4	32.0	16.8	8.9	2.4
2010	57.4	26.7	53.4	95.3	98.0	98.6	98.3	97.3	71.5	56.0	30.8	15.8	9.9	2.6
2009	57.3	26.6	53.2	94.4	97.9	98.4	98.5	94.7	72.9	54.9	31.8	15.3	9.3	2.7
2008	56.7	26.3	53.3	93.7	98.7	99.2	98.2	95.4	68.1	53.0	30.1	14.3	8.3	2.5
2007	56.8	26.3	54.7	95.3	98.1	98.7	99.0	94.1	67.2	53.3	29.2	14.7	7.9	2.4
2006	56.6	26.3	55.4	94.8	98.3	98.4	98.4	95.0	67.4	51.1	28.5	13.0	8.5	2.3
2005	57.2	26.8	54.4	96.1	99.0	98.9	98.4	95.1	68.8	52.3	29.2	14.2	7.9	2.4
2004	56.5	26.8	53.2	95.3	98.5	98.7	98.3	94.1	68.5	51.3	28.4	14.4	7.7	2.5
2003	56.4	26.6	54.1	94.4	98.3	98.6	97.5	94.8	66.6	52.9	29.5	12.8	7.3	2.2
2002	56.4	26.8	54.4	95.1	97.9	98.7	98.5	94.7	65.0	50.9	27.3	13.5	7.7	2.5
2001	55.9	26.7	52.9	95.4	97.8	98.8	98.2	93.8	63.2	46.9	26.5	13.0	7.9	2.5
2000	56.0	26.9	53.4	96.1	98.2	98.3	98.6	92.9	64.2	47.3	25.3	12.7	7.7	2.3
1999	55.5	27.0	55.2	96.1	98.7	98.9	98.3	93.5	60.9	45.8	25.4	11.4	6.6	2.4
1998	55.6	27.3	50.9	95.9	98.8	99.1	98.5	94.3	64.4	47.2	25.2	12.9	7.7	2.6
1997	55.4	27.6	53.2	96.4	99.1	99.3	98.7	94.4	62.4	47.4	27.4	11.9	6.6	2.9
1996	53.8	27.1	49.8	94.3	97.3	98.2	97.5	92.4	62.2	44.8	24.5	12.5	7.3	2.8
1995	53.2	27.0	48.1	96.8	98.5	99.1	98.8	92.6	59.2	45.1	23.6	12.2	6.5	2.7
1994	52.9	27.2	46.9	96.4	99.5	99.4	98.7	94.4	60.0	47.0	23.9	11.1	7.5	2.8
1993r	51.1	NA	39.0	95.2	99.4	99.5	98.7	92.8	61.7	42.8	21.7	10.8	6.6	NA
1993	51.0	25.9	39.3	95.2	99.4	99.5	98.7	92.9	61.7	42.9	21.8	10.8	6.6	2.6
1992	51.0	26.1	39.1	95.2	99.2	99.2	99.1	92.7	61.2	46.1	23.6	10.5	7.0	2.6
1991	49.9	26.0	41.1	95.8	99.5	99.6	98.4	92.8	59.4	42.2	20.4	9.8	6.8	2.8
1990	49.5	25.9	44.9	96.4	99.6	99.7	98.9	92.4	56.3	39.2	19.9	10.2	6.9	2.7

Note: Data shown for 1947 to 1966 for the Black population are for Black and other races. Data for 1947 to 1963 exclude kindergarten. Nursery school was first collected in 1964.
* = Quantity zero or rounds to zero.
NA = Not available.
r = Revised, controlled to 1990 census based population estimates; previous 1993 data controlled to 1980 census based population estimates.
[1]Starting in 2003, respondents could identify more than one race. Except as noted, the race data in this table from 2003 onward represent those respondents who indicated only one race category.
[2]The data shown prior to 2003 consists of those identifying themselves as "Asian or Pacific Islanders."

Table A-11. Percentage of the Population 3 Years Old and Over Enrolled in School, by Age, Sex, Race, and Hispanic Origin, October 1947–2019—*Continued*

(Percent; civilian noninstitutionalized population.)

Year, sex, race, and Hispanic origin	Total enrolled 3 to 34 years old	Total enrolled 3 years old and over	Age 3 and 4	5 and 6	7 to 9	10 to 13	14 and 15	16 and 17	18 and 19	20 and 21	22 to 24	25 to 29	30 to 34	35 and over
1989	48.4	25.5	39.5	95.2	99.2	99.6	98.4	92.2	55.5	39.7	19.5	9.3	6.4	2.5
1988	47.7	25.5	38.1	96.0	99.6	99.7	98.8	91.2	55.2	39.1	16.2	8.6	6.4	2.6
1987	47.4	25.3	36.6	94.5	99.5	99.2	98.4	91.1	53.4	36.4	16.5	9.0	6.7	2.2
1986	47.1	25.4	39.0	94.6	99.2	99.3	97.5	92.3	52.1	32.7	16.8	8.2	6.4	2.2
1985	47.4	25.7	41.2	97.0	99.2	99.4	97.9	90.9	51.0	34.1	15.1	9.1	6.8	2.1
1984	46.6	25.3	36.7	95.1	99.3	99.4	98.2	91.2	48.0	31.7	14.6	8.6	6.7	1.9
1983	47.0	25.7	36.9	95.8	99.0	99.5	98.2	91.6	50.3	29.9	13.9	8.5	7.0	2.0
1982	47.5	26.1	36.4	95.3	99.2	99.3	98.3	89.9	46.8	32.9	15.1	9.0	6.9	1.9
1981	47.7	26.6	35.2	93.8	99.5	99.4	97.7	90.5	47.5	31.2	13.9	8.4	7.5	2.0
1980	48.5	26.9	35.5	96.4	99.2	99.4	97.7	88.8	45.8	29.5	14.9	8.8	7.0	1.9
1979	49.0	27.3	35.6	95.2	99.4	99.4	97.9	87.6	43.4	28.9	14.1	8.8	6.7	2.0
1978	49.5	27.8	34.5	95.5	99.5	99.2	98.4	88.8	43.0	27.5	13.6	7.9	6.2	2.0
1977	50.7	NA	32.0	96.9	99.5	99.6	98.3	87.7	44.0	29.1	13.6	9.1	6.7	NA
1976	51.0	29.8	31.6	95.5	99.4	99.3	97.8	87.7	44.4	30.6	13.8	7.3	5.2	4.2
1975	51.5	NA	32.4	95.2	99.5	99.6	98.0	87.2	44.2	27.4	12.6	7.2	5.6	NA
1974	51.3	NA	29.5	93.9	99.2	99.7	97.9	87.1	40.7	26.0	11.1	6.7	4.6	NA
1973	50.9	NA	23.8	92.9	99.3	99.2	97.1	87.2	38.2	26.3	10.2	5.4	3.6	NA
1972	52.0	NA	24.4	92.2	99.1	99.4	97.5	87.6	41.8	26.3	8.9	5.3	3.6	NA
1971	53.2	NA	22.4	92.3	99.2	99.5	98.5	88.7	43.4	26.8	8.4	4.4	3.6	NA
1970	53.2	NA	19.8	90.2	99.3	99.5	98.0	88.6	41.6	23.6	9.4	4.3	3.1	NA
1969	53.6	NA	16.8	80.1	99.0	99.4	98.2	87.7	41.8	25.3	9.1	4.6	3.8	NA
1968	53.2	NA	16.1	88.0	99.3	99.3	97.8	88.7	41.3	21.5	8.3	3.4	2.9	NA
1967	53.3	NA	14.1	88.2	99.5	99.3	98.2	86.7	40.3	24.9	7.4	3.6	2.8	NA
1966	52.7	NA	12.7	85.7	99.4	99.5	98.4	87.1	37.7	20.9	6.6	3.6	1.7	NA
1965	52.3	NA	10.9	84.4	99.3	99.5	98.7	86.9	37.7	19.5	6.5	3.1	2.1	NA
1964	51.5	NA	10.2	83.2	99.3	99.2	98.2	85.6	33.7	19.5	4.4	2.6	1.6	NA
1963	54.9	NA	NA	82.6	99.6	99.6	98.0	84.8	32.3	17.8	4.4	2.4	1.5	NA
1962	54.0	NA	NA	81.7	99.3	99.4	97.3	81.5	33.7	16.1	3.9	1.8	1.4	NA
1961	53.4	NA	NA	81.4	99.3	99.4	97.2	82.4	28.6	14.9	3.7	1.9	1.2	NA
1960	52.8	NA	NA	80.6	99.6	99.5	97.6	80.6	30.0	13.1	3.4	1.8	1.2	NA
1959	52.0	NA	NA	80.5	99.6	99.5	97.1	81.0	29.2	11.1	4.4	1.7	1.3	NA
1958	51.0	NA	NA	80.2	99.4	99.5	96.9	77.3	29.4	------7.3------		2.2	1.5	NA
1957	50.0	NA	NA	79.0	99.6	99.5	96.2	78.1	28.1	------8.2------		1.9	1.1	NA
1956	48.7	NA	NA	78.2	99.5	99.4	96.8	76.9	27.4	------6.8------		1.7	1.2	NA
1955	47.0	NA	NA	78.1	99.3	99.0	96.1	73.8	22.5	------6.1------		1.8	1.1	NA
1954	46.3	NA	NA	78.3	99.5	99.7	95.4	75.2	25.4	------6.0------		1.7	1.1	NA
1953	43.0	NA	NA	56.6	99.5	99.7	96.6	72.9	25.9	------6.4------		0.5	1.4	NA
1952	41.9	NA	NA	54.6	98.9	98.9	96.6	72.9	22.1	------4.9------		0.6	0.7	NA
1951	49.1	NA	NA	54.0	90.9	99.3	94.5	75.4	21.3	------4.3------		1.0	NA	NA
1950	48.4	NA	NA	59.5	99.0	98.4	94.3	69.8	24.3	------4.6------		0.4	NA	NA
1949	39.2	NA	NA	58.4	98.5	98.8	93.1	68.2	19.9	------3.7------		1.1	0.4	NA
1948	38.4	NA	NA	56.8	98.2	97.8	93.5	70.3	20.3	------3.4------		0.4	0.4	NA
1947	38.0	NA	NA	58.7	98.4	98.5	92.8	67.5	18.5	3.9------		0.4	0.3	NA
WHITE ALONE														
Both Sexes														
2019	53.3	22.7	52.6	93.9	97.6	97.8	97.7	92.8	66.9	52.9	27.2	9.7	5.2	1.2
2018	53.9	23.1	54.7	93.7	96.8	98.4	98.6	93.3	68.9	53.9	26.8	11.3	5.6	1.3
2017	53.9	23.2	53.4	93.5	96.9	97.5	98.4	93.1	67.8	54.7	26.9	11.5	5.6	1.3
2016	54.7	23.6	53.7	93.8	98.0	98.4	98.4	92.4	69.4	56.2	27.5	12.7	5.9	1.3
2015	54.6	23.8	52.2	94.1	97.5	97.8	97.8	93.8	68.6	53.8	27.7	12.8	6.1	1.4
2014	54.6	24.0	53.6	93.6	97.6	97.5	97.7	93.5	68.3	53.0	28.6	12.4	5.9	1.5
2013	55.0	24.3	54.0	93.9	98.1	98.2	98.4	93.6	65.6	52.2	28.9	12.2	6.4	1.6
2012	55.8	24.8	54.0	93.3	98.2	97.7	98.3	96.0	68.7	54.4	29.5	13.4	6.5	1.6
2011	56.2	25.5	51.4	95.7	98.2	98.6	98.6	95.5	70.3	53.8	30.9	14.0	6.9	1.7
2010	55.8	25.4	52.1	94.2	97.7	98.1	98.0	96.2	70.0	51.6	28.1	13.9	7.8	1.9
2009	55.7	25.3	51.1	94.0	97.9	98.7	98.1	94.4	68.7	52.6	28.9	12.9	7.3	1.9
2008	55.5	25.3	52.0	94.0	98.2	98.9	98.7	95.4	67.1	51.2	28.1	12.3	6.2	1.8
2007	55.5	25.3	54.1	94.8	98.0	98.7	98.7	94.6	67.1	50.1	26.3	11.5	6.6	1.8
2006	55.5	25.3	55.6	95.0	98.4	98.4	98.4	95.0	64.9	48.2	25.5	11.3	6.7	1.7
2005	55.9	25.7	54.2	95.3	98.6	98.7	98.3	95.4	68.0	49.3	26.0	11.3	6.2	1.8

Note: Data shown for 1947 to 1966 for the Black population are for Black and other races. Data for 1947 to 1963 exclude kindergarten. Nursery school was first collected in 1964.
* = Quantity zero or rounds to zero.
NA = Not available.
r – Revised, controlled to 1990 census based population estimates; previous 1993 data controlled to 1980 census based population estimates.
[1]Starting in 2003, respondents could identify more than one race. Except as noted, the race data in this table from 2003 onward represent those respondents who indicated only one race category.
[2]The data shown prior to 2003 consists of those identifying themselves as "Asian or Pacific Islanders."

Table A-11. Percentage of the Population 3 Years Old and Over Enrolled in School, by Age, Sex, Race, and Hispanic Origin, October 1947–2019—*Continued*

(Percent; civilian noninstitutionalized population.)

Year, sex, race, and Hispanic origin	Total enrolled 3 to 34 years old	Total enrolled 3 years old and over	Age											
			3 and 4	5 and 6	7 to 9	10 to 13	14 and 15	16 and 17	18 and 19	20 and 21	22 to 24	25 to 29	30 to 34	35 and over
2004	55.5	25.7	52.8	95.5	98.1	98.3	98.5	94.2	64.9	49.3	25.3	12.2	6.4	1.8
2003[1]	55.4	25.8	55.3	94.7	98.0	98.4	97.3	95.0	64.4	48.2	26.7	11.0	6.2	1.8
2002	55.4	26.0	53.9	95.1	98.0	98.5	98.5	94.6	63.8	47.4	24.6	11.4	5.9	2.0
2001	54.8	25.8	51.7	94.8	98.3	98.7	98.2	93.5	60.4	45.9	23.3	10.7	6.0	1.8
2000	55.1	26.1	50.2	95.3	98.2	98.3	98.4	92.8	61.3	44.9	23.7	10.4	6.0	1.8
1999	55.2	26.4	53.7	95.6	98.5	98.8	98.2	93.5	60.5	45.6	24.1	10.5	5.8	1.9
1998	55.0	26.6	50.7	95.4	98.8	99.1	98.6	94.1	61.9	44.8	24.1	11.0	6.2	2.0
1997	54.8	26.8	50.9	96.8	98.8	99.3	98.8	94.5	61.5	46.4	25.8	11.3	5.4	2.2
1996	53.4	26.4	47.9	94.8	97.1	98.2	98.0	92.8	62.5	44.9	24.6	11.3	5.7	2.2
1995	53.2	26.6	49.6	96.2	98.9	99.0	98.8	93.7	59.3	46.2	23.1	11.5	5.5	2.1
1994	52.6	26.6	47.0	96.6	99.2	99.3	98.7	94.3	60.9	46.2	23.5	10.4	6.6	2.2
1993r	51.2	NA	40.4	95.4	99.5	99.5	98.9	93.9	61.4	43.7	23.1	9.7	5.9	NA
1993	51.1	25.7	40.8	95.5	99.5	99.5	98.9	94.1	61.7	44.0	23.3	9.8	5.9	2.1
1992	50.7	NA	40.1	95.4	99.4	99.3	99.2	94.2	61.7	45.3	23.3	9.6	6.0	NA
1991	50.0	NA	41.3	95.3	99.6	99.7	98.7	93.3	59.7	43.2	21.7	9.9	6.0	NA
1990	49.5	NA	44.9	96.5	99.7	99.6	99.1	92.5	57.1	41.0	20.2	9.9	5.9	NA
1989	48.4	NA	39.4	95.2	99.2	99.4	98.8	92.3	56.4	39.5	20.0	9.4	5.6	NA
1988	48.0	NA	38.9	96.1	99.7	99.7	98.8	91.4	55.8	40.2	18.6	8.2	5.9	NA
1987	47.7	NA	38.2	94.8	99.6	99.4	98.5	91.8	55.3	39.6	17.3	8.7	5.7	NA
1986	47.7	NA	39.1	95.3	99.3	97.8	99.0	92.2	55.3	33.9	17.7	9.1	6.2	NA
1985	47.8	NA	38.6	96.4	99.3	99.3	98.1	91.6	52.4	36.1	17.0	9.2	5.9	NA
1984	47.3	NA	36.0	94.6	99.0	99.4	97.8	91.2	51.1	34.3	17.2	9.1	6.2	NA
1983	47.7	NA	37.6	95.7	98.9	99.3	98.4	91.4	50.9	33.4	16.4	9.4	6.1	NA
1982	47.9	NA	35.9	94.9	99.2	99.2	98.6	90.3	47.9	35.1	16.2	9.6	6.2	NA
1981	48.2	NA	35.6	93.9	99.3	99.3	98.1	90.4	48.5	32.6	16.2	8.5	6.1	NA
1980	48.9	NA	36.3	95.8	99.0	99.4	98.3	88.6	46.3	31.9	16.4	9.2	6.3	NA
1979	49.6	NA	33.9	95.8	99.2	99.2	98.2	89.0	44.5	31.1	15.7	9.7	6.3	NA
1978	50.3	NA	32.7	95.4	99.3	99.0	98.4	88.7	44.9	29.6	16.1	9.4	6.2	NA
1977	51.6	NA	31.1	95.6	99.5	99.4	98.5	88.5	45.5	31.8	16.3	10.6	6.6	NA
1976	52.3	NA	30.4	95.8	99.1	99.2	98.1	89.1	45.4	32.5	17.0	10.0	5.7	NA
1975	53.1	NA	30.9	94.8	99.4	99.3	98.3	89.3	46.5	31.8	16.8	10.0	6.6	NA
1974	53.0	NA	28.6	94.4	99.2	99.4	98.1	87.9	42.6	30.7	15.2	9.6	5.5	NA
1973	53.1	NA	23.2	93.0	99.1	99.3	97.6	88.3	43.4	31.3	14.6	8.7	4.5	NA
1972	54.4	NA	23.8	92.2	99.1	99.3	97.6	88.9	46.6	32.6	15.0	8.7	4.5	NA
1971	55.8	NA	20.9	91.9	99.1	99.2	98.7	90.5	49.4	32.7	15.9	8.1	4.8	NA
1970	56.2	NA	19.9	90.3	99.3	99.1	98.2	90.6	48.7	33.1	15.7	7.7	4.2	NA
1969	56.8	NA	15.1	89.2	99.4	99.2	98.2	90.2	50.9	35.4	16.2	8.2	5.0	NA
1968	56.6	NA	15.0	88.5	99.1	99.1	98.1	90.8	50.9	32.8	14.5	7.4	3.9	NA
1967	56.5	NA	13.3	88.2	99.5	99.2	98.5	89.5	48.4	34.7	14.1	6.7	4.1	NA
1966	56.1	NA	12.3	85.7	99.3	99.3	98.8	89.0	48.2	32.2	14.0	6.9	2.7	NA
1965	55.5	NA	10.3	85.3	99.4	99.4	99.0	87.8	47.1	29.4	14.1	6.5	3.2	NA
1964	54.4	NA	9.3	84.0	99.0	99.0	98.8	88.3	42.3	27.8	10.6	5.4	2.6	NA
1963	58.4	NA	NA	83.7	99.5	99.3	98.5	87.8	41.0	26.2	12.2	5.2	2.6	NA
1962	57.9	NA	NA	83.2	99.3	99.4	98.2	85.9	43.0	24.1	10.9	5.2	2.7	NA
1961	56.9	NA	NA	82.2	99.6	99.5	98.0	84.5	39.0	22.4	9.0	4.6	2.1	NA
1960	56.4	NA	NA	82.0	99.7	99.5	98.1	83.3	38.9	20.6	9.3	5.2	2.6	NA
1959	55.5	NA	NA	81.0	99.5	99.5	97.9	83.8	37.3	19.9	8.9	5.4	2.3	NA
1958	54.9	NA	NA	81.4	------99.6------		------90.0------		38.1	------14.1------		5.9	2.3	NA
1957	53.7	NA	NA	79.3	------99.7------		------90.1------		34.6	------14.7------		5.7	1.9	NA
1956	52.5	NA	NA	78.4	------99.4------		------89.2------		35.9	------13.4------		5.4	2.1	NA
1955	50.8	NA	NA	79.2	------99.3------		------87.5------		32.1	------11.6------		4.2	1.6	NA
1954	50.2	NA	NA	78.6	------99.6------		------88.3------		33.6	------12.0------		4.0	1.5	NA
1953	46.6	NA	NA	67.1	------99.7------		------86.4------		31.7	------11.9------		3.1	1.8	NA
1952	45.4	NA	NA	54.8	------99.1------		------86.1------		28.9	------9.8------		2.7	1.2	NA
1951	52.8	NA	NA	54.5	------99.3------		------86.3------		26.9	------8.8------		2.8	NA	NA
1950	51.6	NA	NA	------89.0------			------84.4------		30.5	------9.5------		3.0	NA	NA
1949	42.6	NA	NA	------88.8------			------83.0------		25.9	------9.6------		4.0	1.2	NA
1948	41.8	NA	NA	------87.8------			------83.9------		27.3	------10.0------		2.8	0.9	NA
1947	41.2	NA	NA	------88.7------			------80.2------		24.8	------10.5------		3.0	1.1	NA
Male														
2019	52.6	22.9	51.7	94.4	98.2	97.5	97.6	92.8	64.7	48.8	24.3	8.8	4.3	1.0
2018	53.3	23.4	55.4	93.4	97.0	98.5	98.7	93.7	65.5	49.3	25.0	9.9	5.3	1.0

Note: Data shown for 1947 to 1966 for the Black population are for Black and other races. Data for 1947 to 1963 exclude kindergarten. Nursery school was first collected in 1964.
* = Quantity zero or rounds to zero.
NA = Not available.
r = Revised, controlled to 1990 census based population estimates; previous 1993 data controlled to 1980 census based population estimates.
[1]Starting in 2003, respondents could identify more than one race. Except as noted, the race data in this table from 2003 onward represent those respondents who indicated only one race category.
[2]The data shown prior to 2003 consists of those identifying themselves as "Asian or Pacific Islanders."

Table A-11. Percentage of the Population 3 Years Old and Over Enrolled in School, by Age, Sex, Race, and Hispanic Origin, October 1947–2019—*Continued*

(Percent; civilian noninstitutionalized population.)

Year, sex, race, and Hispanic origin	Total enrolled 3 to 34 years old	Total enrolled 3 years old and over	Age											
			3 and 4	5 and 6	7 to 9	10 to 13	14 and 15	16 and 17	18 and 19	20 and 21	22 to 24	25 to 29	30 to 34	35 and over
2017	53.2	23.4	52.1	92.9	97.3	97.6	98.4	92.6	65.1	50.8	25.1	10.3	5.1	1.0
2016	54.0	23.9	55.6	93.8	97.9	98.2	98.8	92.2	67.9	51.2	25.8	10.9	4.9	1.0
2015	53.9	24.0	53.0	93.5	97.5	98.0	97.5	92.9	65.1	50.8	25.7	11.5	5.3	1.1
2014	53.9	24.2	52.3	93.7	97.2	96.8	97.3	92.5	64.8	50.4	26.8	11.6	5.0	1.2
2013	54.1	24.4	52.2	93.7	98.0	98.2	98.3	92.8	66.0	47.2	26.1	11.1	5.3	1.2
2012	54.9	24.9	52.9	93.1	98.0	98.0	98.3	95.8	66.0	48.5	28.3	11.6	5.5	1.2
2011	55.5	25.8	52.0	95.5	98.4	98.6	98.5	95.5	67.6	50.3	30.1	12.3	6.0	1.4
2010	54.9	25.5	51.8	93.2	97.3	97.6	90.0	95.0	67.5	48.2	25.9	13.0	6.5	1.5
2009	54.8	25.4	50.0	93.7	97.7	98.9	97.9	94.1	64.6	48.8	28.3	11.2	6.4	1.4
2008	54.8	25.5	51.8	93.8	97.9	98.7	99.0	94.9	64.3	48.4	26.5	11.5	5.5	1.3
2007	54.4	25.4	52.9	94.1	97.9	98.6	98.3	94.5	66.4	44.6	24.2	9.6	5.7	1.4
2006	54.6	25.5	55.9	94.8	98.3	98.4	98.2	94.7	62.7	43.8	24.0	10.2	5.5	1.3
2005	54.9	25.9	53.1	94.6	98.2	98.6	98.3	95.1	66.1	45.1	24.4	8.9	5.5	1.4
2004	54.8	26.0	53.4	95.8	97.9	98.2	98.8	94.5	60.0	46.0	23.3	11.2	5.5	1.4
2003[1]	54.8	26.2	56.2	95.0	97.6	98.2	97.2	95.3	61.7	43.2	25.6	9.9	5.6	1.4
2002	54.9	26.5	54.0	95.0	98.0	98.3	98.4	94.2	62.5	44.1	23.5	10.2	5.0	1.6
2001	54.3	26.2	51.8	94.7	98.6	98.4	98.0	92.8	58.2	43.6	21.5	9.8	5.0	1.4
2000	54.8	26.5	49.1	94.8	97.8	98.3	98.4	93.1	58.5	41.8	23.2	9.5	4.9	1.4
1999	55.5	27.1	53.5	95.4	98.5	98.6	98.2	93.1	60.0	44.5	23.7	10.3	5.4	1.5
1998	54.9	27.1	52.4	94.9	98.8	99.1	98.7	93.3	59.7	42.1	24.5	10.2	5.2	1.6
1997	54.7	27.3	50.4	97.4	98.5	99.4	99.1	94.2	60.0	45.0	24.9	10.8	4.3	1.5
1996	53.3	27.0	46.5	94.6	96.9	98.0	98.6	93.0	60.9	43.6	25.4	10.6	4.3	1.7
1995	53.5	27.3	49.6	95.5	99.0	99.0	98.8	94.2	59.4	46.3	22.7	11.3	5.0	1.7
1994	52.7	27.2	46.2	97.0	99.1	99.3	98.7	94.3	61.3	43.4	23.6	9.9	5.8	1.7
1993r	51.6	NA	41.2	95.1	99.5	99.5	98.9	95.0	60.1	44.4	24.5	9.1	5.2	NA
1993	51.6	26.4	41.7	95.2	99.5	99.5	99.0	95.1	60.6	44.8	24.9	9.1	5.2	1.5
1992	50.8	NA	39.8	95.1	99.5	99.5	99.0	99.5	60.7	44.0	23.6	8.6	5.2	NA
1991	50.4	NA	40.6	94.9	99.7	99.8	98.9	94.2	58.4	42.4	23.3	10.0	5.4	NA
1990	50.0	NA	44.9	96.7	99.7	99.6	99.2	92.3	57.3	41.2	21.8	9.4	4.9	NA
1989	48.9	NA	38.7	95.4	99.3	99.2	99.3	92.6	57.3	39.3	20.4	9.3	5.0	NA
1988	48.7	NA	39.0	96.1	99.7	99.6	98.9	91.6	56.5	40.9	20.7	7.8	5.4	NA
1987	48.8	NA	39.8	95.2	99.6	99.7	98.8	92.5	57.3	42.1	18.4	8.6	5.0	NA
1986	48.6	NA	39.3	95.6	99.4	99.0	99.1	92.1	57.5	34.2	19.2	9.6	5.7	NA
1985	48.5	NA	37.3	95.7	99.3	99.2	98.2	92.5	51.9	37.2	19.0	9.5	5.4	NA
1984	48.3	NA	35.8	94.1	98.7	99.3	97.6	91.5	52.6	36.3	20.2	9.2	5.4	NA
1983	48.9	NA	38.2	95.1	98.8	99.3	98.3	91.6	50.7	36.6	19.2	10.4	5.6	NA
1982	48.9	NA	36.3	94.8	99.2	99.1	98.8	91.0	48.5	36.5	18.0	10.2	5.4	NA
1981	49.2	NA	36.8	94.3	99.1	99.2	98.3	90.5	49.2	33.3	19.1	9.1	5.5	NA
1980	50.0	NA	38.0	95.2	98.8	99.4	98.7	88.8	47.5	33.7	18.2	9.6	5.6	NA
1979	50.7	NA	33.5	96.3	99.0	99.0	98.3	90.3	46.1	32.2	17.6	10.5	5.9	NA
1978	51.9	NA	33.1	95.3	99.2	98.9	98.3	88.9	47.2	32.0	19.2	10.9	6.4	NA
1977	53.3	NA	31.7	94.3	99.6	99.3	98.7	89.5	47.7	34.7	19.4	12.6	6.8	NA
1976	54.2	NA	29.9	95.8	98.8	99.1	98.5	90.6	46.9	34.2	20.4	12.9	6.5	NA
1975	55.4	NA	30.8	94.3	99.2	99.0	98.5	91.0	49.6	36.3	20.5	13.1	7.5	NA
1974	55.2	NA	27.7	94.8	99.1	99.2	98.2	88.2	45.5	35.0	19.2	12.8	6.4	NA
1973	55.6	NA	23.5	92.7	99.0	99.3	98.0	89.4	48.4	35.7	19.6	12.1	5.4	NA
1972	57.3	NA	23.4	91.7	98.9	99.2	97.7	90.4	51.5	38.4	21.6	12.5	5.8	NA
1971	59.0	NA	20.1	91.2	99.0	98.9	98.9	92.0	55.9	39.7	24.6	12.1	6.2	NA
1970	59.6	NA	20.7	89.7	99.3	98.8	98.3	92.2	56.0	45.0	22.6	11.2	5.4	NA
1969	60.5	NA	14.5	88.5	99.1	98.9	98.2	92.2	60.9	48.9	24.2	12.2	6.2	NA
1968	60.4	NA	14.8	87.9	99.0	99.0	98.2	92.1	61.5	47.8	21.9	11.4	5.0	NA
1967	60.0	NA	13.6	87.5	99.5	99.0	98.5	91.4	57.2	46.9	22.0	10.5	5.4	NA
1966	59.8	NA	12.2	85.0	99.2	99.1	98.8	90.3	59.0	44.9	23.0	10.3	3.8	NA
1965	59.0	NA	10.4	84.8	99.3	99.3	99.1	88.6	56.6	39.9	23.3	10.0	4.5	NA
1964	57.6	NA	8.8	84.0	98.8	98.9	99.0	90.4	52.4	36.6	17.7	8.3	3.6	NA
1963	62.3	NA	NA	84.1	99.4	99.0	98.8	89.8	51.6	35.2	21.1	8.2	3.8	NA
1962	61.9	NA	NA	83.9	99.1	99.3	98.7	88.5	52.7	33.7	18.8	8.9	4.2	NA
1961	60.4	NA	NA	82.6	99.7	99.4	98.3	85.5	49.6	31.1	15.0	7.5	3.1	NA
1960	60.3	NA	NA	82.3	99.7	99.5	98.1	85.2	49.5	29.2	16.3	8.9	4.0	NA
1959	59.2	NA	NA	80.1	99.3	99.4	98.1	85.9	47.1	30.8	14.1	9.5	3.4	NA
1958	58.8	NA	NA	81.5	------99.6------		------91.1------		48.1	------22.3------		9.9	3.0	NA
1957	57.7	NA	NA	79.1	------99.7------		------91.9------		44.0	------22.9------		9.9	2.7	NA
1956	56.5	NA	NA	78.2	------99.4------		------90.1------		46.4	------21.8------		9.3	2.9	NA

Note: Data shown for 1947 to 1960 for the Black population are for Black and other races. Data for 1947 to 1963 exclude kindergarten. Nursery school was first collected in 1964.
* = Quantity zero or rounds to zero.
NA = Not available.
r = Revised, controlled to 1990 census based population estimates; previous 1993 data controlled to 1980 census based population estimates.
[1]Starting in 2003, respondents could identify more than one race. Except as noted, the race data in this table from 2003 onward represent those respondents who indicated only one race category.
[2]The data shown prior to 2003 consists of those identifying themselves as "Asian or Pacific Islanders."

Table A-11. Percentage of the Population 3 Years Old and Over Enrolled in School, by Age, Sex, Race, and Hispanic Origin, October 1947–2019—*Continued*

(Percent; civilian noninstitutionalized population.)

Year, sex, race, and Hispanic origin	Total enrolled 3 to 34 years old	Total enrolled 3 years old and over	Age											
			3 and 4	5 and 6	7 to 9	10 to 13	14 and 15	16 and 17	18 and 19	20 and 21	22 to 24	25 to 29	30 to 34	35 and over
1955	54.9	NA	NA	79.0	------99.4------		------89.1------		43.9	------19.3------		7.1	2.2	NA
1954	54.3	NA	NA	78.0	------99.4------		------89.6------		43.3	------20.5------		6.5	1.9	NA
1953	50.5	NA	NA	56.8	------99.4------		------87.9------		38.1	------20.3------		5.7	2.2	NA
1952	49.4	NA	NA	55.2	------99.1------		------87.0------		38.3	------17.8------		5.0	1.6	NA
1951	56.8	NA	NA	55.4	------99.3------		------86.6------		33.8	------14.9------		4.2	NA	NA
1950	54.7	NA	NA		----------88.6----------		------85.0------		37.3	------14.6------		5.9	NA	NA
1949	45.9	NA	NA		----------89.1----------		------84.1------		32.1	------15.7------		7.1	2.0	NA
1948	45.3	NA	NA		----------87.6----------		------84.4------		35.9	------17.2------		5.3	1.5	NA
1947	44.4	NA	NA		----------88.6----------		----79.6----		32.6	------17.4------		5.9	1.8	NA
Female														
2019	54.0	22.5	53.5	93.3	97.0	98.2	97.7	92.8	69.1	57.4	30.1	10.6	6.1	1.4
2018	54.6	22.8	53.9	94.0	96.7	98.2	98.5	92.9	72.5	58.7	28.5	12.8	5.9	1.5
2017	54.6	23.0	54.8	94.2	96.6	97.5	98.4	93.7	70.7	58.6	28.7	12.8	6.2	1.6
2016	55.3	23.4	51.7	93.7	98.0	98.7	97.9	92.7	71.0	61.3	29.3	14.6	7.0	1.5
2015	55.2	23.5	51.4	94.9	97.4	97.5	98.0	94.8	72.2	56.9	29.8	14.1	6.8	1.7
2014	55.4	23.8	55.0	93.6	97.9	98.3	98.1	94.5	72.0	56.1	30.3	13.2	6.9	1.8
2013	55.9	24.3	55.8	94.0	98.1	98.2	98.5	94.5	69.2	57.5	31.6	13.3	7.5	2.0
2012	56.7	24.7	55.1	93.6	98.3	97.4	98.4	96.1	71.6	60.1	30.7	15.2	7.5	2.0
2011	56.9	25.2	50.8	96.0	97.9	98.5	98.8	95.6	73.2	57.5	31.7	15.8	7.9	2.0
2010	56.8	25.3	52.5	95.1	98.0	98.5	98.1	97.4	72.5	55.5	30.2	14.9	9.0	2.2
2009	56.7	25.2	52.2	94.3	98.1	98.4	98.4	94.8	73.0	56.6	29.5	14.7	8.3	2.4
2008	56.3	25.1	52.3	94.2	98.6	99.1	98.5	95.9	69.9	54.3	29.8	13.1	6.9	2.3
2007	56.7	25.2	55.4	95.6	98.1	98.8	99.2	94.7	67.8	55.7	28.5	13.6	7.6	2.2
2006	56.3	25.1	55.3	95.2	98.5	98.5	98.7	95.3	67.2	52.6	27.1	12.4	8.0	2.1
2005	57.0	25.6	55.4	96.0	98.9	98.8	98.4	95.7	70.1	53.8	27.7	13.8	7.0	2.2
2004	56.2	25.4	52.0	95.2	98.4	98.5	98.2	93.9	69.8	52.6	27.4	13.3	7.2	2.2
2003[1]	55.9	25.4	54.3	94.4	98.4	98.6	97.4	94.8	67.3	53.1	27.8	12.1	6.8	2.1
2002	55.8	25.6	53.7	95.1	98.0	98.7	98.5	95.0	65.1	50.8	25.7	12.7	6.9	2.3
2001	55.3	25.4	51.5	94.9	97.9	98.9	98.4	94.3	62.7	48.2	25.1	11.7	7.0	2.2
2000	55.4	25.7	51.4	95.8	98.5	98.4	98.3	92.5	64.2	48.2	24.2	11.3	7.1	2.2
1999	55.0	25.8	53.9	95.8	98.7	98.9	98.3	93.8	60.9	46.8	24.5	10.7	6.3	2.3
1998	55.0	26.0	49.0	96.0	98.8	99.2	98.5	94.9	64.2	47.9	23.8	11.9	7.2	2.4
1997	54.9	26.3	51.3	96.2	99.1	99.2	98.6	94.8	63.1	47.9	26.7	11.8	6.4	2.8
1996	53.5	25.9	49.3	95.0	97.4	98.3	97.3	92.7	64.1	46.1	23.6	12.0	7.1	2.6
1995	52.9	25.8	49.6	96.9	98.8	99.1	98.8	93.3	59.2	46.0	23.6	11.7	6.0	2.6
1994	52.6	26.0	47.9	96.1	99.4	99.4	98.8	94.4	60.5	49.0	23.5	11.0	7.4	2.7
1993r	50.7	NA	39.5	95.7	99.5	99.5	98.9	92.8	62.8	43.0	21.7	10.4	6.5	NA
1993	50.6	24.9	39.9	95.8	99.5	99.5	98.9	93.0	62.9	43.3	21.8	10.4	6.5	2.6
1992	50.5	NA	40.4	95.7	99.2	99.1	99.4	92.8	62.7	46.6	22.9	10.6	6.7	NA
1991	49.5	NA	42.0	95.7	99.5	99.6	98.5	92.5	60.9	43.9	20.2	9.7	6.7	NA
1990	49.0	NA	44.8	96.4	99.7	99.7	98.9	92.8	57.0	40.9	18.7	10.4	6.9	NA
1989	47.8	NA	40.2	94.9	99.2	99.6	98.1	92.1	55.6	39.7	19.6	9.6	6.3	NA
1988	47.2	NA	38.8	96.1	99.6	99.8	98.8	91.1	55.1	39.6	16.5	8.6	6.3	NA
1987	46.7	NA	36.4	94.4	99.5	99.2	98.3	91.0	53.3	37.3	16.2	8.7	6.4	NA
1986	46.8	NA	39.0	94.9	99.1	99.3	98.8	92.2	53.0	33.7	16.2	8.7	6.7	NA
1985	47.0	NA	39.9	97.1	99.3	99.3	97.9	90.8	52.9	35.0	15.0	9.0	6.4	NA
1984	46.3	NA	36.1	95.2	99.3	99.4	98.0	91.0	49.6	32.3	14.2	8.9	6.9	NA
1983	46.6	NA	36.0	96.5	99.0	99.4	98.4	91.2	51.1	30.5	13.6	8.5	6.7	NA
1982	46.9	NA	35.5	95.0	99.2	99.4	98.4	89.6	47.4	33.7	14.5	9.0	6.9	NA
1981	47.1	NA	34.3	93.5	99.5	99.4	97.8	90.4	47.8	31.9	13.4	7.9	6.7	NA
1980	47.9	NA	34.6	96.4	99.2	99.4	97.8	88.4	45.1	30.2	14.8	8.9	7.0	NA
1979	48.4	NA	34.4	95.3	99.5	99.5	98.1	87.7	43.0	30.0	13.9	9.0	6.7	NA
1978	48.7	NA	32.2	95.6	99.5	99.2	98.5	88.4	42.7	27.4	13.0	7.9	6.0	NA
1977	49.9	NA	30.5	96.9	99.5	99.6	98.4	87.4	43.4	29.0	13.3	8.8	6.3	NA
1976	50.4	NA	31.0	95.8	99.5	99.3	97.6	87.7	44.0	30.9	13.7	7.1	4.8	NA
1975	50.9	NA	30.9	95.3	99.5	99.6	98.1	87.5	43.5	27.5	12.2	7.0	5.7	NA
1974	50.9	NA	29.5	94.0	99.3	99.7	97.9	87.6	39.9	26.6	11.4	6.5	4.6	NA
1973	50.5	NA	22.9	93.2	99.3	99.3	97.1	87.3	38.7	27.4	9.9	5.4	3.6	NA
1972	51.5	NA	24.4	92.7	99.2	99.4	97.5	87.3	41.9	27.5	8.9	5.1	3.2	NA
1971	52.6	NA	21.7	92.6	99.3	99.5	98.4	88.9	43.2	27.0	8.1	4.3	3.5	NA
1970	52.9	NA	19.1	90.9	99.3	99.5	98.1	89.0	41.8	24.1	9.7	4.4	3.1	NA

Note: Data shown for 1947 to 1966 for the Black population are for Black and other races. Data for 1947 to 1963 exclude kindergarten. Nursery school was first collected in 1964.

* = Quantity zero or rounds to zero.

NA = Not available.

r = Revised, controlled to 1990 census based population estimates; previous 1993 data controlled to 1980 census based population estimates.

[1]Starting in 2003, respondents could identify more than one race. Except as noted, the race data in this table from 2003 onward represent those respondents who indicated only one race category.

[2]The data shown prior to 2003 consists of those identifying themselves as "Asian or Pacific Islanders."

Table A-11. Percentage of the Population 3 Years Old and Over Enrolled in School, by Age, Sex, Race, and Hispanic Origin, October 1947–2019—*Continued*

(Percent; civilian noninstitutionalized population.)

Year, sex, race, and Hispanic origin	Total enrolled 3 to 34 years old	Total enrolled 3 years old and over	Age 3 and 4	5 and 6	7 to 9	10 to 13	14 and 15	16 and 17	18 and 19	20 and 21	22 to 24	25 to 29	30 to 34	35 and over
1969	53.2	NA	15.8	89.8	99.6	99.5	98.2	88.2	41.8	25.8	9.4	4.5	3.7	NA
1968	52.9	NA	15.2	89.0	99.3	99.3	98.0	89.4	41.3	22.3	8.2	3.7	2.8	NA
1967	53.0	NA	13.1	89.0	99.6	99.4	98.5	87.4	41.0	25.6	7.5	3.3	2.9	NA
1966	52.5	NA	12.4	86.4	99.5	99.5	98.7	87.6	38.6	22.3	6.6	3.9	1.7	NA
1965	52.2	NA	10.3	85.7	99.4	99.5	98.9	87.0	38.3	20.9	6.3	3.2	2.0	NA
1964	51.3	NA	9.9	83.9	99.2	99.1	98.6	86.1	33.7	20.3	4.5	2.6	1.6	NA
1963	54.7	NA	NA	83.8	99.7	99.5	98.2	85.7	32.1	18.6	4.4	2.4	1.5	NA
1962	54.0	NA	NA	82.4	99.5	99.5	97.6	83.3	34.6	16.3	4.1	1.8	1.4	NA
1961	53.4	NA	NA	81.7	99.5	99.5	97.7	83.5	29.7	15.3	3.8	2.1	1.3	NA
1960	52.7	NA	NA	81.6	99.7	99.6	98.1	81.4	29.7	13.5	3.5	1.8	1.2	NA
1959	52.0	NA	NA	81.9	99.7	99.6	97.7	81.6	28.8	11.1	4.6	1.7	1.3	NA
1958	51.1	NA	NA	81.2	------99.6------		------88.9------		29.9	------7.5------		2.2	1.6	NA
1957	49.8	NA	NA	79.5	------99.7------		------88.2------		27.0	------8.3------		1.7	1.1	NA
1956	48.6	NA	NA	78.6	------99.5------		------88.2------		27.3	------7.0------		1.8	1.3	NA
1955	46.9	NA	NA	79.5	------99.3------		------85.9------		22.4	------6.2------		1.5	1.0	NA
1954	46.4	NA	NA	79.1	------99.8------		------87.0------		25.3	------6.4------		1.7	1.1	NA
1953	42.9	NA	NA	57.4	------99.9------		------84.9------		26.5	------6.5------		0.6	1.5	NA
1952	41.7	NA	NA	54.3	------99.1------			85.3	21.1	------4.3------		0.6	0.7	NA
1951	49.0	NA	NA	53.6	------99.4------		------86.0------		21.7	------4.3------		0.9	NA	NA
1950	48.6	NA	NA	---------89.4---------			------83.7------		24.2	------4.8------		0.4	NA	NA
1949	39.4	NA	NA	---------88.6---------			------81.9------		20.5	------3.0------		1.2	0.4	NA
1948	38.4	NA	NA	---------87.9---------			------83.4------		19.7	------3.5------		0.4	0.4	NA
1947	38.1	NA	NA	---------88.9---------			------80.8------		18.3	------4.1------		0.4	0.4	NA
WHITE ALONE NON-HISPANIC														
Both Sexes														
2019	52.7	20.5	54.4	94.0	98.2	98.1	97.9	93.4	68.1	54.4	27.7	9.8	5.2	1.2
2018	53.6	21.0	58.2	93.9	96.7	98.6	98.8	93.9	71.3	57.5	27.5	11.3	5.9	1.2
2017	53.2	21.0	56.0	93.0	97.0	97.8	98.5	93.3	67.8	58.1	27.2	11.3	5.8	1.2
2016	54.1	21.5	55.5	93.9	98.0	98.5	98.7	92.2	70.4	57.3	27.7	13.3	6.6	1.2
2015	54.4	21.8	56.0	94.1	97.5	98.1	98.3	94.4	70.1	55.5	28.9	13.1	6.5	1.3
2014	54.4	21.9	57.6	93.4	97.3	97.5	97.8	93.4	69.3	56.1	29.9	12.9	6.3	1.4
2013	54.7	22.3	57.4	93.6	97.9	98.5	98.4	93.6	69.6	55.2	29.1	12.9	6.5	1.6
2012	55.6	22.7	56.5	93.8	98.1	97.5	98.2	96.4	68.8	55.9	30.2	14.6	6.6	1.6
2011	56.4	23.6	56.2	95.8	98.2	98.5	98.9	95.9	72.1	56.2	32.9	15.2	7.8	1.7
2010	56.1	23.6	56.1	94.2	97.4	98.3	98.0	96.2	71.0	55.5	29.1	14.6	8.5	1.8
2009	56.8	23.9	55.5	94.1	98.4	98.9	98.3	95.0	72.4	56.4	31.1	14.0	8.1	1.9
2008	56.7	23.9	56.0	94.9	98.8	98.9	98.8	95.9	70.0	55.8	30.3	13.3	6.9	1.8
2007	56.6	23.9	56.3	95.0	98.6	98.6	98.8	95.6	69.7	54.5	28.4	12.5	7.4	1.8
2006	56.8	24.0	58.2	95.6	98.5	98.6	98.4	95.9	67.9	52.9	27.4	12.5	7.4	1.7
2005	57.6	24.6	58.5	95.9	99.0	99.0	98.6	96.1	71.6	54.4	27.8	12.5	6.9	1.8
2004	56.9	24.5	56.0	96.2	98.3	98.6	98.5	95.1	68.1	54.0	27.0	13.5	6.7	1.8
2003[1]	57.0	24.7	58.8	95.8	98.2	98.5	97.5	95.6	67.9	51.8	29.4	12.5	6.8	1.8
2002	56.8	24.9	57.8	95.3	98.1	98.6	98.6	95.3	67.1	53.1	27.3	12.2	6.3	1.9
2001	56.2	24.7	55.1	95.3	98.5	98.8	98.2	94.6	64.2	50.8	25.5	11.7	6.4	1.8
2000	56.0	25.0	54.6	95.5	98.4	98.5	98.9	94.0	63.9	49.2	24.9	11.1	6.1	1.8
1999	56.2	25.4	58.6	96.0	98.5	98.9	98.4	94.5	64.1	50.0	26.3	10.9	5.9	1.9
1998	55.9	25.6	54.0	96.1	98.8	99.2	98.9	95.1	66.6	49.2	26.1	11.5	6.3	2.0
1997	55.6	25.9	54.9	96.9	98.9	99.2	98.9	95.1	64.1	49.9	27.8	12.2	5.6	2.2
1996	54.0	25.5	50.3	96.1	97.3	98.3	98.2	93.6	65.5	48.9	25.9	11.8	5.8	2.2
1995	53.8	25.9	52.3	96.6	99.0	99.0	98.8	94.4	61.8	49.7	24.4	12.3	5.7	2.1
1994	54.5	25.9	50.1	96.7	99.2	99.3	99.2	95.1	62.6	50.1	24.9	10.8	6.7	2.2
1993	51.4	25.0	43.1	95.7	99.5	99.5	99.1	95.0	63.6	46.1	24.9	10.2	6.0	2.1
Male														
2019	52.0	20.8	52.1	95.3	98.2	98.0	98.1	93.2	65.4	49.8	25.3	8.7	4.5	0.9
2018	53.2	21.4	58.1	94.0	96.8	98.7	99.0	93.8	68.3	53.4	26.2	9.9	5.5	1.0
2017	52.8	21.3	54.3	92.5	97.2	97.9	98.6	92.8	65.4	54.6	25.9	10.5	5.0	0.9
2016	53.8	21.9	56.6	94.2	98.0	98.3	98.8	91.9	69.4	52.8	26.8	11.7	5.5	1.0
2015	54.1	22.1	57.1	93.2	97.8	98.3	98.3	93.8	67.2	53.3	26.9	12.3	5.9	1.0

Note: Data shown for 1947 to 1966 for the Black population are for Black and other races. Data for 1947 to 1963 exclude kindergarten. Nursery school was first collected in 1964.

* = Quantity zero or rounds to zero.

NA = Not available.

r = Revised, controlled to 1990 census based population estimates; previous 1993 data controlled to 1980 census based population estimates.

[1]Starting in 2003, respondents could identify more than one race. Except as noted, the race data in this table from 2003 onward represent those respondents who indicated only one race category.

[2]The data shown prior to 2003 consists of those identifying themselves as "Asian or Pacific Islanders."

Table A-11. Percentage of the Population 3 Years Old and Over Enrolled in School, by Age, Sex, Race, and Hispanic Origin, October 1947–2019—*Continued*

(Percent; civilian noninstitutionalized population.)

Year, sex, race, and Hispanic origin	Total enrolled 3 to 34 years old	Total enrolled 3 years old and over	Age											
			3 and 4	5 and 6	7 to 9	10 to 13	14 and 15	16 and 17	18 and 19	20 and 21	22 to 24	25 to 29	30 to 34	35 and over
2014	54.1	22.3	56.5	93.7	96.9	96.8	97.1	92.7	66.0	55.3	28.3	12.1	5.8	1.1
2013	54.1	22.4	55.2	93.7	97.8	98.4	98.4	92.8	68.6	51.0	26.2	11.4	5.6	1.1
2012	55.0	22.9	55.6	93.6	97.7	97.7	97.9	96.0	65.4	49.7	29.6	13.0	6.1	1.2
2011	56.1	23.9	56.4	95.5	98.3	98.5	98.4	95.8	69.9	53.0	33.1	13.2	7.0	1.3
2010	55.5	23.9	55.9	93.3	97.1	97.7	98.0	94.7	67.8	52.1	27.8	13.8	7.2	1.4
2009	56.2	24.2	54.9	93.3	98.2	99.0	97.9	94.7	68.4	53.2	30.8	12.4	7.1	1.4
2008	56.5	24.3	57.2	94.7	98.5	98.7	99.1	95.5	66.8	52.4	29.1	12.6	6.2	1.3
2007	56.0	24.2	53.8	94.0	98.5	98.5	98.3	95.2	69.3	49.9	26.9	10.6	6.7	1.3
2006	56.4	24.4	58.3	95.9	98.5	98.6	97.9	95.5	65.4	49.2	26.2	11.9	6.3	1.3
2005	57.1	24.9	56.8	95.4	98.9	99.1	98.4	95.9	69.8	50.5	26.4	10.2	6.5	1.3
2004	56.7	25.0	57.2	96.2	98.2	98.4	98.7	95.6	63.8	50.6	25.1	12.7	6.2	1.4
2003[1]	57.1	25.4	60.6	96.2	97.7	98.2	97.4	96.1	65.4	47.9	28.9	11.7	6.3	1.4
2002	56.8	25.5	57.8	94.9	98.1	98.5	98.5	95.2	66.3	49.2	27.6	11.1	5.5	1.6
2001	56.0	25.2	54.4	94.8	98.8	98.4	97.8	94.0	62.7	49.1	23.7	10.8	5.3	1.3
2000	55.8	25.5	54.1	94.5	98.1	98.2	98.8	94.7	61.2	45.8	25.0	10.5	4.7	1.4
1999	56.7	26.2	59.2	96.1	98.4	98.7	98.2	94.3	63.7	48.9	26.8	10.7	5.8	1.5
1998	55.7	26.3	54.8	95.5	98.8	99.0	99.0	94.4	65.2	46.4	27.4	10.9	5.3	1.6
1997	55.9	26.5	54.9	97.4	98.8	99.3	99.0	94.5	63.3	48.5	27.5	12.0	4.6	1.5
1996	54.2	26.1	48.0	95.5	97.2	98.1	98.8	93.5	63.7	48.7	27.3	11.4	4.3	1.6
1995	54.2	26.6	51.1	95.9	99.0	99.0	98.9	95.0	61.9	50.0	24.1	12.2	5.0	1.6
1994	53.5	26.6	49.0	97.1	99.2	99.4	99.4	95.4	62.5	47.6	25.5	10.3	6.0	1.6
1993	52.2	25.9	44.1	95.4	99.5	99.6	99.3	96.2	62.5	47.0	26.7	9.9	5.2	1.5
Female														
2019	53.3	20.3	56.8	92.7	98.2	98.3	97.8	93.6	71.1	59.2	30.0	10.9	5.8	1.4
2018	53.9	20.6	58.2	93.8	96.5	98.5	98.5	94.0	74.3	61.8	28.9	12.8	6.2	1.5
2017	53.6	20.7	57.8	93.5	96.8	97.6	98.4	93.8	70.3	61.8	28.4	12.1	6.6	1.5
2016	54.4	21.1	54.3	93.5	97.9	98.8	98.6	92.5	71.6	62.0	28.5	14.9	7.8	1.4
2015	54.6	21.4	54.8	95.1	97.2	97.9	98.4	95.0	73.1	57.7	30.9	14.0	7.1	1.6
2014	54.7	21.6	58.8	93.1	97.7	98.1	98.5	94.1	72.9	57.0	31.4	13.6	6.9	1.7
2013	55.4	22.1	59.7	93.5	98.0	98.5	98.4	94.5	70.8	59.6	31.9	14.3	7.4	2.0
2012	56.2	22.5	57.4	94.0	98.5	97.3	98.4	96.8	72.3	61.7	30.8	16.2	7.1	2.0
2011	56.8	23.3	56.1	96.1	98.1	98.5	99.3	95.9	74.3	59.5	32.7	17.3	8.5	2.0
2010	56.7	23.4	56.3	95.2	97.7	98.9	98.1	97.8	74.3	59.2	30.4	15.4	9.8	2.2
2009	57.4	23.7	56.2	95.0	98.7	98.7	98.7	95.4	76.5	59.8	31.4	15.6	9.0	2.4
2008	57.0	23.5	54.8	95.0	99.1	99.2	98.4	96.3	73.4	59.5	31.5	14.0	7.6	2.2
2007	57.3	23.7	58.9	96.0	98.8	98.7	99.2	96.0	70.1	59.2	29.9	14.4	8.0	2.2
2006	57.1	23.7	58.1	95.3	98.6	98.5	99.0	96.2	70.5	56.5	28.7	13.2	8.5	2.1
2005	58.0	24.3	60.3	96.3	99.0	98.8	98.7	96.3	73.5	58.5	29.1	14.7	7.4	2.2
2004	57.1	24.1	54.7	96.2	98.5	98.7	98.3	94.5	72.5	57.4	28.8	14.4	7.2	2.1
2003[1]	57.0	24.1	56.9	95.3	98.6	98.8	97.6	95.1	70.3	55.6	29.9	13.2	7.3	2.1
2002	56.8	24.3	57.7	95.6	98.0	98.6	98.6	95.5	67.9	57.0	27.0	13.4	7.2	2.2
2001	56.4	24.2	55.9	95.9	98.3	99.1	98.6	95.3	65.8	52.4	27.3	12.5	7.4	2.2
2000	56.1	24.6	55.2	96.4	98.6	98.8	99.0	93.3	66.7	52.7	24.8	11.8	7.4	2.1
1999	55.7	24.7	57.9	96.0	98.5	99.1	98.6	94.8	64.6	51.1	25.7	11.0	6.1	2.3
1998	55.7	25.0	53.1	96.7	98.7	99.3	98.8	95.7	68.0	52.2	24.8	12.1	7.3	2.4
1997	55.2	25.4	55.0	96.4	99.0	99.1	98.8	95.7	64.9	51.3	28.1	12.4	6.6	2.9
1996	53.8	25.0	52.9	96.7	97.3	98.6	97.7	93.7	67.3	49.0	24.5	12.1	7.3	2.6
1995	53.4	25.1	53.5	97.4	98.9	99.0	98.7	93.8	61.8	49.3	24.8	12.3	6.3	2.5
1994	52.9	25.3	51.3	96.3	99.3	99.3	98.9	94.8	62.7	52.4	24.3	11.4	7.3	2.7
1993	50.6	24.3	42.0	96.0	99.5	99.5	98.9	93.7	64.8	45.2	23.1	10.5	6.7	2.6
BLACK ALONE														
Both Sexes														
2019	54.1	28.0	55.4	93.0	96.0	97.7	97.7	91.4	60.7	48.1	27.9	13.7	7.8	2.6
2018	55.3	28.6	54.5	93.4	97.1	98.4	97.5	87.9	65.8	52.7	28.1	16.1	8.3	2.6
2017	55.1	28.7	57.7	91.5	96.8	98.9	96.6	90.7	67.0	47.5	27.5	13.5	7.7	2.7
2016	55.4	29.2	50.8	93.5	97.4	98.6	96.1	94.9	67.2	48.2	28.0	12.7	8.7	2.9
2015	55.3	29.2	52.7	93.7	95.4	98.3	98.7	94.4	64.5	43.7	27.5	13.1	8.2	2.8
2014	56.0	30.2	57.5	94.5	98.8	97.7	98.9	91.8	65.2	41.1	24.5	14.6	9.1	3.8
2013	57.2	30.7	57.2	94.4	96.7	97.8	98.7	92.8	64.2	47.9	27.0	16.7	8.6	3.1

Note: Data shown for 1947 to 1966 for the Black population are for Black and other races. Data for 1947 to 1963 exclude kindergarten. Nursery school was first collected in 1964.
* = Quantity zero or rounds to zero.
NA = Not available.
r = Revised, controlled to 1990 census based population estimates; previous 1993 data controlled to 1980 census based population estimates.
[1]Starting in 2003, respondents could identify more than one race. Except as noted, the race data in this table from 2003 onward represent those respondents who indicated only one race category.
[2]The data shown prior to 2003 consists of those identifying themselves as "Asian or Pacific Islanders."

Table A-11. Percentage of the Population 3 Years Old and Over Enrolled in School, by Age, Sex, Race, and Hispanic Origin, October 1947–2019—*Continued*

(Percent; civilian noninstitutionalized population.)

Year, sex, race, and Hispanic origin	Total enrolled 3 to 34 years old	Total enrolled 3 years old and over	Age											
			3 and 4	5 and 6	7 to 9	10 to 13	14 and 15	16 and 17	18 and 19	20 and 21	22 to 24	25 to 29	30 to 34	35 and over
2012............................	58.3	31.4	53.1	91.5	97.2	98.9	97.3	94.2	68.6	49.4	27.9	16.1	12.2	3.2
2011............................	58.4	32.3	55.2	92.0	97.1	98.5	98.5	95.7	74.1	41.1	31.2	18.1	11.4	3.8
2010............................	58.4	32.5	56.2	94.3	97.1	98.6	98.5	95.5	62.7	50.2	29.0	16.0	10.9	4.0
2009............................	58.5	32.4	57.7	93.6	97.4	98.6	97.8	94.1	65.2	44.7	31.9	14.6	11.0	3.7
2008............................	57.8	31.7	54.6	93.1	98.9	99.0	97.9	94.2	59.2	40.3	24.9	14.7	11.5	2.8
2007............................	58.4	32.2	58.5	94.0	98.2	97.9	99.0	93.4	61.7	38.7	28.0	15.0	9.4	3.0
2006............................	58.1	32.3	59.2	92.6	97.1	97.2	97.5	93.3	64.7	39.1	27.2	11.8	8.6	3.1
2005............................	58.4	32.7	52.2	95.9	98.6	98.6	95.8	93.1	62.8	37.6	28.0	11.7	10.0	3.1
2004............................	59.0	33.4	59.6	94.1	97.5	99.4	99.0	95.7	59.2	40.0	25.1	14.3	7.2	3.3
2003[1].........................	59.2	33.4	55.5	94.4	98.3	98.2	97.9	94.3	61.9	41.4	27.4	12.2	8.6	2.8
2002............................	59.6	34.1	57.5	95.7	98.1	98.1	98.2	93.3	57.7	43.5	23.5	13.6	9.8	3.1
2001............................	59.5	34.3	58.8	96.0	97.8	97.0	97.6	92.1	59.6	37.2	26.0	12.2	11.5	3.2
2000............................	59.0	34.0	59.9	96.3	97.5	98.4	99.6	91.4	57.2	36.6	24.2	14.3	9.6	2.6
1999............................	58.1	33.7	56.3	97.5	98.2	98.7	98.2	93.3	57.4	39.4	21.7	10.4	7.8	2.5
1998............................	58.9	34.6	58.5	95.3	98.7	98.6	98.9	92.9	60.2	39.2	21.5	13.6	8.5	2.6
1997............................	58.4	34.6	60.0	95.8	99.2	99.4	99.2	93.4	58.2	35.9	25.4	10.7	6.5	2.8
1996............................	56.2	33.8	49.9	90.5	97.4	97.4	98.9	92.1	52.8	37.0	21.0	13.7	7.1	3.0
1995............................	56.1	33.9	47.5	95.5	97.7	99.2	99.0	92.9	57.4	37.4	19.9	10.0	7.8	2.7
1994............................	56.4	34.4	51.9	97.2	99.7	99.6	99.2	95.4	54.0	34.9	22.6	10.5	7.2	2.9
1993r..........................	53.8	NA	39.8	94.5	99.0	99.8	98.5	94.8	57.6	30.1	18.0	10.4	5.5	NA
1993............................	53.6	32.4	39.8	94.6	99.0	99.8	98.5	94.7	57.7	30.0	18.1	10.4	5.5	2.6
1992............................	53.0	NA	38.6	95.9	99.4	99.7	99.4	93.0	56.2	33.3	20.3	7.9	5.3	NA
1991............................	52.5	NA	37.2	95.8	99.6	100.0	99.1	91.7	55.6	30.0	18.2	8.7	6.5	NA
1990............................	51.9	NA	41.6	96.3	99.9	99.9	99.2	91.7	55.2	28.4	20.0	6.1	4.4	NA
1989............................	51.3	NA	38.9	94.9	99.0	99.4	99.4	93.7	50.2	30.7	17.2	6.4	4.9	NA
1988............................	50.6	NA	33.4	95.5	99.7	99.7	98.9	91.5	50.3	28.1	13.2	7.2	5.6	NA
1987............................	51.7	NA	36.8	95.8	99.7	99.8	98.3	91.5	53.2	28.7	15.0	9.3	6.0	NA
1986............................	51.6	NA	38.6	95.4	99.8	99.0	98.3	93.9	50.7	25.6	17.1	8.0	6.2	NA
1985............................	50.9	NA	42.7	95.7	98.4	99.5	97.9	91.7	44.1	27.7	13.7	7.5	5.9	NA
1984............................	50.1	NA	38.2	94.1	99.5	99.3	97.9	92.4	44.3	27.7	15.7	7.4	5.1	NA
1983............................	50.8	NA	36.2	94.7	99.1	99.7	97.8	92.6	46.1	23.4	15.6	7.4	6.5	NA
1982............................	51.6	NA	38.6	95.4	99.2	98.9	98.1	91.6	43.6	24.3	17.0	7.8	7.6	NA
1981............................	52.5	NA	36.7	94.5	98.8	99.4	97.1	91.3	48.2	23.4	14.7	8.4	7.0	NA
1980............................	53.9	NA	38.2	95.4	99.4	99.4	97.9	90.6	45.7	23.4	13.6	8.8	6.8	NA
1979............................	55.0	NA	40.8	96.0	99.4	98.7	97.4	90.8	46.6	23.7	15.0	7.9	6.8	NA
1978............................	56.3	NA	41.3	93.9	99.5	98.9	98.5	91.2	46.2	25.6	15.0	8.7	7.9	NA
1977............................	57.7	NA	35.2	96.5	99.3	99.0	98.8	90.8	48.3	29.5	15.2	11.3	9.0	NA
1976............................	57.9	NA	34.5	94.0	99.3	98.8	99.0	89.0	50.4	28.2	16.4	9.4	8.1	NA
1975............................	57.7	NA	33.5	94.3	99.3	99.2	97.4	86.9	47.1	27.1	14.2	9.4	7.1	NA
1974............................	57.3	NA	29.1	92.8	99.2	99.8	97.0	87.1	44.0	23.4	12.1	8.9	6.9	NA
1973............................	55.8	NA	28.9	89.9	99.2	99.0	96.7	87.7	37.8	20.5	12.4	6.1	5.0	NA
1972............................	57.8	NA	28.3	90.0	98.7	99.3	97.4	89.5	42.8	22.0	13.1	6.5	5.9	NA
1971............................	58.6	NA	21.5	89.8	99.0	98.8	98.4	89.2	46.6	27.3	11.4	6.2	5.2	NA
1970............................	57.4	NA	22.7	84.9	99.3	99.3	97.6	85.7	40.1	22.8	8.0	4.8	3.4	NA
1969............................	57.8	NA	21.2	84.1	98.8	99.1	97.9	85.8	44.5	23.3	8.6	4.3	3.4	NA
1968............................	57.4	NA	18.7	82.7	99.2	99.0	97.7	86.4	45.4	18.2	7.9	3.1	3.3	NA
1967............................	56.8	NA	17.7	82.2	99.1	98.7	86.1	84.1	40.7	21.2	7.2	5.0	2.4	NA
1966............................	55.5	NA	13.7	80.8	99.2	99.2	97.4	85.2	37.7	11.6	6.1	2.3	2.3	NA
1965............................	55.6	NA	11.8	79.1	98.9	99.3	98.1	83.9	39.6	12.8	6.2	2.1	2.4	NA
1964............................	54.5	NA	10.5	80.3	99.0	99.0	96.9	82.4	35.6	14.0	3.8	3.1	2.9	NA
1963............................	58.8	NA	NA	76.6	98.5	99.5	97.6	82.0	39.8	16.2	5.5	3.3	2.0	NA
1962............................	57.1	NA	NA	76.0	98.6	98.8	97.1	73.2	33.4	14.9	6.1	3.8	1.5	NA
1961............................	56.8	NA	NA	79.1	98.0	98.3	95.1	76.8	30.6	15.9	4.3	2.4	1.1	NA
1960............................	55.9	NA	NA	73.3	99.3	99.0	95.9	76.9	34.6	11.9	4.4	2.9	1.0	NA
1959............................	55.1	NA	NA	74.3	98.9	99.1	93.9	76.3	33.6	11.6	6.3	2.8	1.3	NA
1958............................	54.0	NA	NA	73.9	------98.8		------82.8------		34.3	------8.7------		3.9	1.3	NA
1957............................	53.5	NA	NA	74.3	------98.2------		------84.8------		36.7	------8.8------		4.6	1.2	NA
1956............................	51.5	NA	NA	72.8	------98.4------		------81.2------		31.8	------8.7------		3.1	0.7	NA
1955............................	50.7	NA	NA	71.1	------98.2------		------82.8------		27.6	------7.2------		4.9	1.8	NA
1954............................	48.6	NA	NA	68.8	------98.0------		------78.8------		24.0	------5.8------		4.8	1.4	NA
1953............................	45.5	NA	NA	46.3	------97.3------		------82.3------		27.6	------5.4------		1.7	0.8	NA
1952............................	46.4	NA	NA	54.0	------96.4------		------77.3------		------------------6.3------------------					NA

Note: Data shown for 1947 to 1966 for the Black population are for Black and other races. Data for 1947 to 1963 exclude kindergarten. Nursery school was first collected in 1964.
* = Quantity zero or rounds to zero.
NA = Not available.
r = Revised, controlled to 1990 census based population estimates; previous 1993 data controlled to 1980 census based population estimates.
[1] Starting in 2003, respondents could identify more than one race. Except as noted, the race data in this table from 2003 onward represent those respondents who indicated only one race category.
[2] The data shown prior to 2003 consists of those identifying themselves as "Asian or Pacific Islanders."

Table A-11. Percentage of the Population 3 Years Old and Over Enrolled in School, by Age, Sex, Race, and Hispanic Origin, October 1947–2019—*Continued*

(Percent; civilian noninstitutionalized population.)

Year, sex, race, and Hispanic origin	Total enrolled 3 to 34 years old	Total enrolled 3 years old and over	3 and 4	5 and 6	7 to 9	10 to 13	14 and 15	16 and 17	18 and 19	20 and 21	22 to 24	25 to 29	30 to 34	35 and over
1951	53.4	NA	NA	54.9	------97.3-----		------77.1-----		20.8	------6.2------		2.7	NA	NA
1950	51.2	NA	NA	--------------86.8----------			------75.5-----		23.3	------6.3-----		3.0	NA	NA
1949	40.9	NA	NA	--------------83.7----------			------69.5-----		20.0	------6.2-----		1.8	0.5	NA
1948	39.2	NA	NA	--------------80.1----------			------66.8-----		24.6	------6.3-----		1.5	0.6	NA
1947	41.0	NA	NA	--------------84.8----------			------71.9-----		20.2	------6.9-----		2.5	0.5	NA
Male														
2019	54.0	29.1	56.1	92.4	97.8	98.0	98.7	90.1	60.1	46.7	23.2	12.1	4.9	2.1
2018	54.8	29.3	50.0	92.3	97.2	98.1	98.7	92.0	65.2	52.2	23.8	13.7	4.5	1.7
2017	54.7	29.7	59.7	90.0	96.0	98.8	95.4	89.0	63.2	42.6	24.0	12.3	6.2	2.1
2016	56.0	30.5	46.6	91.2	96.1	98.6	98.9	95.7	66.6	46.2	26.8	12.9	7.4	2.3
2015	55.6	30.3	51.0	92.1	95.8	99.2	99.5	94.7	63.3	39.6	30.4	10.1	4.5	1.8
2014	56.2	31.2	58.0	96.1	98.6	97.3	98.7	92.6	60.3	41.8	22.2	11.6	7.0	2.7
2013	56.8	31.5	54.1	94.4	96.5	97.8	98.8	94.3	59.9	43.2	25.2	13.1	5.2	2.4
2012	58.1	31.9	51.1	92.1	97.0	98.9	98.5	95.5	60.5	48.8	26.8	11.5	7.3	1.9
2011	57.9	33.0	53.4	92.4	97.5	98.5	97.8	94.0	72.6	38.0	29.8	14.2	7.5	2.7
2010	57.9	33.1	55.5	93.7	97.5	98.4	97.7	93.5	60.8	44.5	28.5	13.2	6.5	2.7
2009	58.0	32.9	56.3	93.7	96.8	98.5	96.4	95.2	60.5	42.2	26.6	11.7	7.9	2.2
2008	58.0	32.7	53.3	95.5	98.5	98.5	98.9	94.0	57.9	37.8	23.2	10.6	8.5	1.5
2007	59.5	33.9	59.6	93.9	98.3	97.2	99.2	95.2	61.9	37.8	28.0	10.4	9.4	2.0
2006	58.7	33.7	56.6	93.5	97.2	96.8	97.7	91.8	63.9	38.0	24.2	9.3	6.9	2.5
2005	58.9	34.0	54.0	94.8	97.7	97.7	93.6	93.6	67.2	35.1	23.4	9.3	6.3	2.4
2004	59.2	34.6	61.1	93.7	96.7	99.2	98.8	96.5	58.1	37.8	20.2	8.7	4.0	2.2
2003[1]	60.0	34.9	56.5	92.4	98.8	98.1	98.3	94.0	61.5	34.3	23.5	9.7	7.4	1.9
2002	60.2	35.4	57.5	96.2	99.1	97.9	97.6	92.9	54.9	39.5	16.6	10.1	7.5	2.1
2001	60.1	35.7	55.4	95.6	98.3	96.0	99.0	93.2	57.3	36.2	22.7	8.2	8.3	2.3
2000	59.5	35.3	57.6	95.8	98.3	98.7	99.6	89.1	52.4	30.5	21.8	11.3	8.3	2.2
1999	59.9	35.8	53.0	98.4	97.7	99.0	97.9	94.4	60.3	42.3	16.1	9.0	6.5	2.0
1998	60.1	36.2	57.8	95.0	98.5	98.6	97.7	93.9	58.2	40.7	15.1	12.6	5.6	1.8
1997	59.5	36.2	57.3	94.2	98.7	99.1	99.6	93.9	56.7	34.1	21.5	10.5	5.6	2.0
1996	57.8	35.7	47.0	90.1	98.1	97.2	98.1	93.7	55.2	39.0	18.6	12.8	5.4	2.4
1995	58.3	36.2	51.5	94.7	98.2	99.5	99.6	95.2	59.1	36.1	20.3	6.1	6.7	2.3
1994	58.4	36.5	56.8	97.1	99.6	99.5	99.7	95.3	53.4	33.7	21.3	10.8	5.7	2.1
1993r	56.0	NA	41.6	96.8	99.3	100.0	99.0	96.1	63.4	23.7	19.6	10.4	3.1	NA
1993	55.8	34.8	41.7	96.9	99.3	100.0	99.0	96.0	63.6	23.9	19.6	10.3	3.1	2.0
1992	54.8	NA	41.3	97.6	99.9	99.7	99.9	94.5	60.7	27.1	18.7	7.6	3.3	NA
1991	54.5	NA	35.2	95.4	99.8	100.0	100.0	90.4	62.2	30.1	19.3	8.6	4.8	NA
1990	53.9	NA	38.3	96.1	99.9	99.9	99.7	93.2	60.7	31.1	20.0	4.6	2.3	NA
1989	52.6	NA	40.2	92.9	98.9	98.8	99.3	96.5	51.0	23.2	15.5	5.5	3.2	NA
1988	52.4	NA	34.5	96.0	99.6	100.0	99.1	93.2	49.7	20.7	14.7	6.3	4.1	NA
1987	54.0	NA	39.0	97.4	100.0	99.8	98.1	91.8	58.7	30.3	15.5	8.4	3.4	NA
1986	53.8	NA	38.7	97.1	99.6	98.8	98.4	94.7	54.1	25.4	17.3	7.1	5.9	NA
1985	52.6	NA	34.6	94.6	98.2	99.1	98.2	91.8	49.5	29.7	13.2	6.9	5.7	NA
1984	52.6	NA	37.2	92.8	99.5	99.1	96.9	93.2	48.6	29.7	17.5	5.7	3.9	NA
1983	52.9	NA	37.1	95.8	98.9	99.4	98.4	91.8	46.4	23.5	17.2	9.1	6.6	NA
1982	53.2	NA	37.4	93.9	99.3	98.4	97.8	92.2	46.5	20.9	17.4	8.5	7.1	NA
1981	54.5	NA	34.8	94.5	98.5	99.2	97.3	92.1	51.9	20.6	14.7	8.4	5.6	NA
1980	56.1	NA	36.6	94.1	99.5	99.4	98.5	90.8	42.8	23.0	13.3	10.6	7.3	NA
1979	57.8	NA	40.4	96.6	99.0	98.4	98.5	94.6	48.0	26.9	14.6	8.1	6.3	NA
1978	58.7	NA	37.9	93.2	99.4	98.8	99.0	92.8	50.5	25.2	14.7	9.5	7.8	NA
1977	60.3	NA	32.4	96.0	99.1	98.6	99.0	92.5	50.5	31.0	18.5	12.1	9.2	NA
1976	61.1	NA	36.3	94.4	99.5	98.8	99.5	90.9	54.9	28.0	18.7	11.0	8.8	NA
1975	60.3	NA	29.5	94.6	99.3	99.0	97.6	88.2	49.9	28.7	14.7	11.8	8.6	NA
1974	60.7	NA	30.3	91.8	99.5	99.6	96.1	90.1	46.1	27.7	16.0	10.4	9.7	NA
1973	58.6	NA	29.2	89.0	99.2	99.1	96.9	89.0	43.5	24.5	13.9	6.9	6.5	NA
1972	60.9	NA	32.1	90.8	98.4	99.4	97.6	88.9	47.7	27.1	18.4	7.3	5.2	NA
1971	60.4	NA	19.0	88.7	99.1	98.1	97.7	90.0	50.7	31.3	12.9	8.5	6.4	NA
1970	59.5	NA	22.3	84.2	99.2	99.1	98.0	85.4	41.3	27.8	9.6	6.1	3.6	NA
1969	60.0	NA	21.3	83.1	98.3	98.9	98.0	87.4	49.5	28.4	10.7	2.8	2.9	NA
1968	60.0	NA	16.9	84.1	98.8	98.4	98.5	88.5	53.1	23.4	7.5	5.2	3.4	NA
1967	59.2	NA	17.0	81.0	99.0	98.3	96.5	86.7	48.6	24.5	9.0	3.5	3.5	NA
1966	58.1	NA	12.7	80.0	99.1	99.0	98.2	87.4	46.3	14.4	9.1	2.6	2.7	NA

Note: Data shown for 1947 to 1966 for the Black population are for Black and other races. Data for 1947 to 1963 exclude kindergarten. Nursery school was first collected in 1964.

* = Quantity zero or rounds to zero.

NA = Not available.

r = Revised, controlled to 1990 census based population estimates; previous 1993 data controlled to 1980 census based population estimates.

[1] Starting in 2003, respondents could identify more than one race. Except as noted, the race data in this table from 2003 onward represent those respondents who indicated only one race category.

[2] The data shown prior to 2003 consists of those identifying themselves as "Asian or Pacific Islanders."

Table A-11. Percentage of the Population 3 Years Old and Over Enrolled in School, by Age, Sex, Race, and Hispanic Origin, October 1947–2019—*Continued*

(Percent; civilian noninstitutionalized population.)

Year, sex, race, and Hispanic origin	Total enrolled 3 to 34 years old	Total enrolled 3 years old and over	Age											
			3 and 4	5 and 6	7 to 9	10 to 13	14 and 15	16 and 17	18 and 19	20 and 21	22 to 24	25 to 29	30 to 34	35 and over
1965	57.7	NA	9.5	81.0	99.3	99.4	98.7	82.2	47.5	18.5	4.3	2.6	2.3	NA
1964	56.8	NA	9.4	80.7	98.2	98.7	98.8	84.3	39.9	14.2	3.8	3.5	4.0	NA
1963	61.9	NA	NA	74.3	97.7	99.2	98.2	85.9	46.5	21.7	7.1	4.7	2.7	NA
1962	60.4	NA	NA	74.5	98.9	98.6	99.1	77.1	40.3	15.0	10.1	5.8	1.7	NA
1961	60.0	NA	NA	78.7	98.4	97.6	96.6	78.6	41.7	19.9	6.1	4.0	1.9	NA
1960	58.3	NA	NA	71.8	99.4	98.7	97.0	79.1	36.9	13.7	6.3	3.9	1.0	NA
1959	58.0	NA	NA	76.0	98.7	99.1	95.8	76.3	35.5	12.5	10.6	4.5	1.8	NA
1958	58.0	NA	NA	74.2	------98.8-----		------87.6------		43.4	-------11.8------		6.3	2.4	NA
1957	55.9	NA	NA	73.1	------98.2-----		------84.7------		38.5	-------10.3------		6.0	1.2	NA
1956	54.3	NA	NA	70.4	------97.6-----		------81.3------		36.8	------12.5------		5.3	0.9	NA
1955	54.4	NA	NA	72.8	------98.2-----		------85.2------		32.9	--------9.8------		6.2	1.9	NA
1954	52.0	NA	NA	64.7	------97.5-----		------82.8------		21.6	-------10.1------		7.9	1.9	NA
1953	47.8	NA	NA	41.6	------97.1-----		------79.1------		34.6	--------5.8------		3.3	0.9	NA
1952	49.7	NA	NA	51.4	------96.0-----		------72.5------		----------------6.0-------------					NA
1951	56.9	NA	NA	52.8	------98.0-----		------74.9------		23.6	--------9.0------		4.3	NA	NA
1950	56.0	NA	NA	-----------87.0----------			------79.3------		19.9	-------11.1------		6.1	NA	NA
1949	45.0	NA	NA	-----------83.1----------			------68.8------		26.1	-------11.8------		3.3	1.1	NA
1948	40.4	NA	NA	-----------78.9----------			------63.9------		24.0	-------10.5------		2.5	1.4	NA
1947	45.1	NA	NA	-----------84.6----------			------72.6------		20.7	-------12.3------		5.1	0.8	NA
Female														
2019	54.2	27.0	54.5	93.7	94.2	97.5	96.7	92.7	61.2	49.4	32.2	15.2	10.4	3.0
2018	55.7	28.1	58.6	94.5	97.1	98.8	96.3	83.8	66.4	53.1	32.2	18.3	11.7	3.4
2017	55.4	27.9	55.4	93.1	97.7	98.9	97.8	92.5	70.7	52.5	30.7	14.7	8.9	3.1
2016	54.9	28.0	55.1	95.9	98.7	98.6	93.2	94.0	67.8	50.3	29.0	12.5	9.8	3.4
2015	55.0	28.3	54.6	95.3	94.9	97.4	97.8	94.1	65.6	47.7	24.8	15.7	11.2	3.6
2014	55.7	29.4	57.0	92.9	98.9	98.0	99.1	91.0	70.1	40.5	26.8	17.2	10.8	4.6
2013	57.6	30.0	60.2	94.4	96.8	97.8	98.6	91.3	68.3	52.1	28.7	19.8	11.5	3.6
2012	58.6	30.9	55.1	90.9	97.3	98.9	96.1	92.8	76.6	50.0	28.9	20.0	16.1	4.2
2011	58.9	31.7	57.1	91.5	96.8	98.6	99.3	97.3	75.6	44.6	32.2	21.7	14.7	4.8
2010	58.8	31.9	56.8	95.0	96.8	98.8	99.3	97.5	64.5	55.4	29.6	18.5	14.6	4.9
2009	58.9	31.9	59.0	93.6	98.0	98.8	99.3	92.9	69.7	47.3	36.2	17.2	13.5	4.8
2008	57.6	30.9	55.8	90.8	99.4	99.4	96.9	94.4	60.5	42.6	26.3	18.3	13.8	3.8
2007	57.4	30.8	57.3	94.2	98.1	98.6	98.8	91.7	61.6	39.5	27.9	18.9	9.4	3.8
2006	57.6	31.1	61.5	91.7	96.9	97.6	97.2	94.7	65.4	40.2	30.0	14.0	9.9	3.6
2005	57.9	31.5	50.6	97.1	99.5	99.5	98.0	92.5	58.5	40.1	31.8	13.8	13.0	3.6
2004	58.7	32.3	57.7	94.5	98.2	99.6	99.1	94.8	60.2	41.9	29.5	19.0	9.8	4.2
2003[1]	58.4	32.1	54.5	96.4	97.7	98.3	97.5	94.6	62.2	47.4	30.8	14.2	9.6	3.5
2002	59.1	33.0	57.4	95.2	97.2	98.3	98.8	93.7	60.6	47.1	28.8	16.3	11.7	3.8
2001	58.9	33.1	62.1	96.5	97.2	98.1	96.2	91.0	62.0	37.9	29.0	15.3	14.0	3.9
2000	58.7	32.9	62.3	96.8	96.8	98.2	99.6	93.8	61.5	41.3	26.4	16.5	10.7	2.9
1999	56.5	32.0	59.1	96.5	98.7	98.6	98.5	92.1	54.7	36.9	25.9	11.5	8.9	2.9
1998	57.8	33.2	59.1	95.6	98.9	98.7	100.0	91.8	62.2	37.8	26.2	14.4	10.9	3.2
1997	57.4	33.3	62.9	97.2	99.8	99.7	98.9	92.9	59.6	37.3	28.7	10.8	7.2	3.5
1996	54.7	32.2	52.6	90.0	96.7	97.8	99.6	90.4	50.5	35.5	23.2	14.4	8.6	3.5
1995	54.1	31.9	43.6	96.3	97.2	99.0	98.3	90.4	55.9	38.5	19.5	13.0	8.7	3.0
1994	54.4	32.5	47.0	97.2	99.7	99.7	98.6	95.5	54.6	35.9	23.6	10.3	8.5	3.4
1993r	51.6	NA	37.9	92.0	98.7	99.7	97.9	93.4	52.0	35.3	16.6	10.5	7.4	NA
1993	51.6	30.4	37.8	92.1	98.7	99.7	97.9	93.4	51.9	35.1	16.7	10.5	7.5	3.0
1992	51.3	NA	35.8	94.1	98.9	99.6	98.8	91.5	51.8	38.6	21.6	8.2	6.9	NA
1991	50.6	NA	39.5	96.1	99.5	100.0	98.2	93.1	49.4	29.9	17.3	8.8	7.9	NA
1990	50.1	NA	45.0	96.5	99.8	99.8	98.7	90.2	50.0	26.0	20.1	7.3	6.2	NA
1989	50.1	NA	37.6	97.1	99.2	99.9	99.5	91.7	49.4	37.3	18.6	7.1	6.3	NA
1988	49.0	NA	32.3	94.9	99.8	99.3	98.6	89.8	50.9	34.3	11.9	7.9	6.9	NA
1987	49.6	NA	34.4	94.1	99.3	99.7	98.6	91.2	48.2	27.4	14.6	10.0	8.1	NA
1986	49.5	NA	38.6	93.7	100.0	99.3	98.2	93.1	47.6	25.7	16.9	8.6	6.5	NA
1985	49.4	NA	50.2	97.1	98.7	99.9	97.6	91.6	39.0	26.0	14.1	7.9	6.1	NA
1984	47.8	NA	39.2	95.3	99.5	99.4	99.0	91.7	40.3	25.9	14.1	8.8	6.2	NA
1983	48.8	NA	35.2	93.6	99.3	100.0	97.1	93.4	45.7	23.3	14.2	6.0	6.5	NA
1982	50.2	NA	39.8	97.0	99.1	99.5	98.3	91.0	41.0	27.2	16.6	7.2	8.0	NA
1981	50.6	NA	38.7	94.4	99.1	99.6	97.0	90.5	44.9	25.7	14.7	8.4	8.1	NA
1980	52.0	NA	39.7	96.7	99.3	99.3	97.4	90.4	48.2	23.7	13.9	7.4	6.5	NA

Note: Data shown for 1947 to 1966 for the Black population are for Black and other races. Data for 1947 to 1963 exclude kindergarten. Nursery school was first collected in 1964.
* = Quantity zero or rounds to zero.
NA – Not available.
r = Revised, controlled to 1990 census based population estimates; previous 1993 data controlled to 1980 census based population estimates.
[1]Starting in 2003, respondents could identify more than one race. Except as noted, the race data in this table from 2003 onward represent those respondents who indicated only one race category.
[2]The data shown prior to 2003 consists of those identifying themselves as "Asian or Pacific Islanders."

Table A-11. Percentage of the Population 3 Years Old and Over Enrolled in School, by Age, Sex, Race, and Hispanic Origin, October 1947–2019—*Continued*

(Percent; civilian noninstitutionalized population.)

Year, sex, race, and Hispanic origin	Total enrolled 3 to 34 years old	Total enrolled 3 years old and over	Age											
			3 and 4	5 and 6	7 to 9	10 to 13	14 and 15	16 and 17	18 and 19	20 and 21	22 to 24	25 to 29	30 to 34	35 and over
1979	52.5	NA	41.2	95.5	99.7	99.0	96.4	87.1	45.4	21.1	15.3	7.7	7.3	NA
1978	54.1	NA	44.8	94.7	99.6	99.1	98.0	89.6	42.4	26.0	15.2	8.1	8.0	NA
1977	55.4	NA	38.1	97.0	99.4	99.4	98.5	89.1	46.3	28.2	12.6	10.7	8.9	NA
1976	55.0	NA	32.6	93.6	99.1	98.8	98.4	87.0	46.4	28.4	14.5	8.1	7.6	NA
1975	55.3	NA	37.6	93.9	99.3	99.4	97.2	85.6	44.7	25.8	13.8	7.5	5.9	NA
1974	54.2	NA	28.0	93.8	98.9	100.0	97.9	84.2	42.1	20.1	9.0	7.7	4.8	NA
1973	53.3	NA	28.5	90.9	99.2	98.9	96.5	86.4	32.8	17.3	11.1	5.5	3.8	NA
1972	54.9	NA	24.5	89.1	99.0	99.3	97.3	90.1	38.7	17.9	8.5	5.9	6.5	NA
1971	56.9	NA	24.1	90.9	98.9	99.4	99.0	88.4	43.1	24.1	10.1	4.2	4.2	NA
1970	55.5	NA	23.2	85.7	99.5	99.5	97.2	85.9	38.9	18.9	6.7	3.6	3.3	NA
1969	55.8	NA	21.1	85.0	99.4	99.2	97.7	84.3	40.1	19.6	6.9	5.5	3.7	NA
1968	54.9	NA	20.5	81.3	99.7	99.5	96.9	84.3	38.6	14.5	8.3	1.5	3.2	NA
1967	54.6	NA	18.5	83.4	99.2	99.0	95.8	81.6	34.0	18.5	5.6	6.1	1.5	NA
1966	53.2	NA	14.7	81.6	99.3	99.4	96.5	83.1	30.3	9.3	3.6	2.0	2.0	NA
1965	53.6	NA	14.1	77.3	98.6	99.2	97.6	85.6	32.5	8.0	7.8	1.7	2.4	NA
1964	52.5	NA	11.7	79.9	99.9	99.3	95.0	80.6	31.7	13.7	3.8	2.8	2.0	NA
1963	56.0	NA	NA	79.0	99.2	99.8	96.9	78.2	33.9	11.5	4.3	2.2	1.5	NA
1962	54.1	NA	NA	77.5	98.3	99.1	95.2	69.5	27.3	14.9	3.0	2.2	1.3	NA
1961	53.8	NA	NA	79.5	97.6	99.0	93.5	75.1	20.6	12.4	2.7	1.0	0.4	NA
1960	53.7	NA	NA	74.9	99.1	99.3	94.8	74.7	32.2	10.4	2.8	2.1	1.0	NA
1959	52.4	NA	NA	72.5	99.2	99.1	92.0	76.4	31.9	10.8	2.7	1.4	1.0	NA
1958	50.3	NA	NA	73.7	------98.7------		------78.1------		26.4	------6.0------		1.9	0.4	NA
1957	51.3	NA	NA	75.6	------98.2------		------85.0------		35.1	------7.6------		3.5	1.1	NA
1956	49.0	NA	NA	75.2	------99.1------		------81.1------		27.5	------5.7------		1.3	0.6	NA
1955	47.4	NA	NA	69.4	------98.1------		------80.5------		23.1	------5.5------		3.8	1.7	NA
1954	45.6	NA	NA	73.0	------98.6------		------74.7------		25.7	------2.9------		2.3	0.9	NA
1953	43.5	NA	NA	51.1	------97.6------		------85.5------		21.6	------5.0------		0.3	0.7	NA
1952	43.6	NA	NA	56.3	------97.0------		------82.3------		------------------6.4------------------					NA
1951	50.3	NA	NA	57.1	------96.5------		------79.2------		17.9	------4.3------		1.5	NA	NA
1950	47.0	NA	NA	NA	-----------86.5-----------		------71.9------		25.7	------3.0------		0.6	NA	NA
1949	37.3	NA	NA	--------------84.5----------			------70.0------		14.5	------1.9------		0.7	-	NA
1948	38.2	NA	NA	--------------81.3----------			------69.6------		25.2	------2.7------		0.6	-	NA
1947	37.3	NA	NA	--------------84.9----------			------71.3------		19.9	------2.5------		0.3	0.3	NA
ASIAN²														
Both Sexes														
2019	55.8	26.0	58.3	92.5	98.3	100.0	99.5	94.0	86.2	78.4	47.0	17.6	9.5	1.4
2018	53.9	25.2	50.9	90.4	99.0	97.1	100.0	90.0	79.1	74.4	45.5	18.7	9.2	1.5
2017	55.1	25.4	56.5	94.8	98.2	98.5	100.0	93.8	82.4	79.7	50.5	16.7	5.8	1.1
2016	54.7	25.9	62.8	89.5	97.8	98.5	97.9	94.2	77.1	75.6	46.5	21.0	6.4	1.4
2015	56.4	26.6	56.2	95.4	97.4	98.3	99.7	86.8	83.7	83.8	49.7	20.2	8.6	1.5
2014	55.8	26.9	53.9	90.5	96.3	97.5	95.5	94.5	88.1	75.8	56.5	19.2	5.4	1.9
2013	56.6	27.4	57.5	91.7	96.9	98.8	98.8	96.8	83.8	81.7	47.3	18.9	8.0	2.1
2012	57.2	27.6	54.1	93.5	99.9	98.3	98.7	97.3	81.0	74.6	53.0	18.8	8.6	1.8
2011	56.8	26.9	51.8	96.7	97.4	96.7	97.9	97.2	84.5	79.0	42.6	16.4	8.3	2.0
2010	58.6	27.9	61.8	96.5	98.5	98.4	97.6	95.3	82.3	80.2	46.5	20.9	10.3	1.8
2009	57.8	26.9	52.4	94.7	96.4	95.4	96.2	96.6	94.1	73.0	56.7	19.3	10.8	2.0
2008	57.3	27.4	55.8	90.8	98.0	99.5	98.7	92.4	85.4	81.1	43.1	23.4	11.5	2.4
2007	55.6	26.9	53.4	94.3	98.2	99.2	99.8	92.6	86.5	66.5	47.4	19.0	9.9	1.7
2006	54.7	26.9	48.3	96.7	99.1	99.2	99.5	92.2	83.0	74.7	44.8	17.8	8.7	2.2
2005	55.6	28.2	55.0	94.7	99.5	97.6	98.8	98.3	88.3	80.5	42.7	21.0	9.3	2.2
2004	56.8	29.3	58.3	97.2	99.9	99.1	97.5	98.6	82.6	79.7	46.8	21.5	9.5	2.6
2003¹	56.8	29.3	54.5	89.4	99.0	99.3	99.0	97.6	87.3	79.8	48.1	22.5	9.2	2.2
2002	57.3	30.8	56.1	95.6	96.9	98.8	98.4	94.9	78.9	72.8	49.5	18.3	8.3	2.4
2001	57.7	31.7	41.9	99.4	96.3	99.6	98.4	95.7	84.0	72.6	50.8	22.6	7.8	2.2
2000	58.3	32.6	56.0	97.6	97.8	97.6	99.6	98.4	78.8	66.2	45.3	18.7	8.9	2.8
1999	60.9	34.3	55.8	98.9	99.6	100.0	95.8	97.3	78.5	61.7	45.6	20.3	7.8	3.0
1998	59.9	34.2	53.4	97.9	97.9	98.1	95.3	95.6	83.3	70.6	49.0	21.3	8.7	2.6
1997	60.6	34.6	62.4	94.0	97.7	100.0	99.4	94.7	80.2	73.2	41.8	24.2	9.6	2.7
1996	58.6	35.0	50.4	95.7	98.9	99.3	96.8	94.3	78.3	65.8	39.5	18.6	9.9	3.6
1995	57.3	32.5	42.1	95.9	99.5	99.8	100.0	95.9	83.1	63.4	46.7	21.2	11.1	3.2

Note: Data shown for 1947 to 1966 for the Black population are for Black and other races. Data for 1947 to 1963 exclude kindergarten. Nursery school was first collected in 1964.

* = Quantity zero or rounds to zero.
NA = Not available.
r = Revised, controlled to 1990 census based population estimates; previous 1993 data controlled to 1980 census based population estimates.
¹Starting in 2003, respondents could identify more than one race. Except as noted, the race data in this table from 2003 onward represent those respondents who indicated only one race category.
²The data shown prior to 2003 consists of those identifying themselves as "Asian or Pacific Islanders."

Table A-11. Percentage of the Population 3 Years Old and Over Enrolled in School, by Age, Sex, Race, and Hispanic Origin, October 1947–2019—*Continued*

(Percent; civilian noninstitutionalized population.)

Year, sex, race, and Hispanic origin	Total enrolled 3 to 34 years old	Total enrolled 3 years old and over	Age											
			3 and 4	5 and 6	7 to 9	10 to 13	14 and 15	16 and 17	18 and 19	20 and 21	22 to 24	25 to 29	30 to 34	35 and over
1994	60.9	33.1	42.3	97.8	99.5	99.7	100.0	97.3	81.8	67.4	53.5	23.8	8.4	2.7
1993	62.2	34.7	39.6	97.1	99.7	100.0	99.9	91.1	82.5	76.1	55.3	21.0	8.6	3.4
Male														
2019	56.6	27.6	55.8	95.3	98.0	100.0	100.0	96.7	89.0	79.4	45.0	18.9	8.6	1.6
2018	54.0	26.4	51.1	91.0	98.1	94.7	100.0	95.0	75.3	73.9	47.4	18.7	7.9	1.4
2017	55.5	26.7	53.7	93.3	97.7	98.0	100.0	94.4	78.2	78.6	54.5	16.3	4.4	0.8
2016	56.2	27.8	60.5	86.4	98.0	98.8	98.8	91.7	75.1	77.6	51.4	22.3	7.0	1.7
2015	57.1	27.6	60.4	97.8	97.6	98.4	99.7	85.3	80.5	81.8	47.2	20.2	8.4	1.1
2014	57.4	28.7	53.9	91.2	97.8	97.2	94.7	93.3	87.5	74.0	62.2	22.0	3.7	1.8
2013	58.4	29.0	60.1	94.5	97.7	99.0	98.0	95.2	83.0	86.6	48.4	22.3	6.1	1.7
2012	57.9	28.8	48.7	93.0	99.7	97.9	97.5	97.4	83.1	74.8	52.8	19.9	7.0	1.5
2011	57.7	28.0	51.6	96.9	96.8	98.2	98.4	96.5	89.2	80.5	39.4	15.8	8.1	1.3
2010	59.8	29.4	63.2	97.5	98.8	97.8	97.1	96.0	77.6	82.9	42.7	22.8	10.8	1.8
2009	58.0	28.2	51.9	94.2	95.6	94.5	97.3	95.1	92.6	71.8	56.9	19.6	9.5	2.3
2008	57.1	27.9	54.2	91.1	96.8	99.1	100.0	96.0	89.0	74.1	38.0	25.2	10.3	1.9
2007	57.2	28.6	56.7	96.9	99.0	99.0	99.7	93.5	91.8	67.6	46.0	18.1	10.3	1.9
2006	55.5	28.3	56.7	96.8	98.3	98.8	99.4	91.0	79.7	76.1	42.2	16.3	8.5	2.4
2005	56.9	29.7	53.2	96.8	99.8	96.9	97.8	97.8	85.2	84.0	42.6	21.1	10.3	2.0
2004	59.3	31.9	58.3	96.0	99.7	99.8	96.5	99.0	85.9	84.2	49.8	24.1	11.4	2.9
2003[1]	59.6	31.8	53.3	90.8	97.9	99.9	97.8	100.0	90.4	77.0	47.8	28.9	11.9	2.3
2002	58.7	32.3	54.1	97.7	95.6	98.4	99.5	94.3	80.0	70.2	50.1	20.6	9.5	2.4
2001	59.1	33.6	35.9	99.6	96.0	100.0	97.1	94.5	83.3	74.9	58.9	22.9	10.6	1.7
2000	60.5	35.0	56.0	96.8	99.5	97.0	99.3	97.8	75.5	67.2	49.1	16.0	10.2	2.7
1999	62.0	35.8	53.5	97.9	99.2	100.0	93.7	98.7	74.4	59.6	50.5	21.4	10.6	3.1
1998	60.8	35.2	51.5	100.0	97.9	98.5	95.0	96.8	74.8	68.0	51.3	21.4	11.1	2.2
1997	63.4	36.6	61.3	89.7	99.4	100.0	98.6	95.5	88.2	71.6	46.9	31.0	10.6	2.5
1996	62.1	38.0	51.0	94.0	99.0	99.6	97.9	93.7	81.0	70.7	37.3	24.4	14.4	3.6
1995	60.0	35.6	38.0	94.5	98.9	99.6	100.0	96.9	81.9	60.3	47.8	24.8	15.7	3.5
1994	64.7	35.8	45.5	98.2	99.0	100.0	100.0	96.9	81.5	70.9	57.0	31.3	10.7	2.1
1993	65.9	37.9	43.0	95.9	99.8	99.9	100.0	93.4	79.4	78.5	65.4	21.0	11.2	3.4
Female														
2019	55.1	24.5	61.1	90.0	98.6	100.0	99.0	91.6	83.4	77.4	49.3	16.4	10.4	1.3
2018	53.8	24.1	50.7	89.8	100.0	99.7	100.0	86.2	83.1	75.1	43.6	18.7	10.4	1.5
2017	54.7	24.3	59.4	96.3	98.7	99.0	100.0	93.3	86.8	80.8	46.4	17.0	7.1	1.4
2016	53.3	24.2	65.4	92.8	97.5	98.2	97.1	96.3	79.3	73.7	41.2	19.5	5.9	1.2
2015	55.7	25.7	51.9	92.6	97.1	98.2	99.7	88.2	86.9	85.6	52.5	20.1	8.9	1.9
2014	54.2	25.4	53.8	89.8	94.9	97.8	96.3	95.5	88.7	77.8	50.7	16.7	7.0	2.0
2013	54.9	26.0	54.6	88.8	96.2	98.5	99.6	98.0	84.6	76.3	46.0	15.7	9.6	2.5
2012	56.5	26.6	59.0	94.0	100.0	98.6	100.0	97.3	78.7	74.4	53.3	17.7	10.0	2.1
2011	55.9	25.9	52.0	96.5	98.0	95.3	97.3	98.0	79.2	77.5	46.0	17.0	8.5	2.5
2010	57.3	26.5	60.5	95.6	98.2	99.0	98.1	94.3	87.2	77.8	50.3	19.1	9.9	1.8
2009	57.5	25.8	53.1	95.3	97.3	96.2	94.5	98.3	95.8	74.1	56.5	19.1	12.0	1.8
2008	57.4	26.8	57.8	90.4	99.0	100.0	97.5	88.7	81.8	89.5	47.5	21.7	12.7	2.9
2007	54.0	25.3	49.1	91.9	97.3	99.5	100.0	91.7	81.0	65.4	48.5	19.8	9.6	1.5
2006	53.8	25.6	39.1	96.5	100.0	99.5	99.0	93.3	87.3	72.9	47.0	19.1	8.9	2.0
2005	54.4	26.8	56.8	92.3	99.3	98.3	100.0	98.8	91.7	75.9	42.9	20.9	8.4	2.4
2004	54.1	26.9	58.4	99.1	100.0	98.2	98.5	98.1	79.0	74.7	43.9	19.1	7.6	2.4
2003[1]	54.0	27.1	55.8	87.4	100.0	98.4	100.0	94.9	84.6	82.5	48.3	16.6	6.7	2.1
2002	56.1	29.5	58.1	93.4	97.9	99.2	97.5	95.5	77.9	75.8	48.9	16.1	7.2	2.3
2001	56.2	29.9	47.7	99.1	96.6	99.2	100.0	97.2	84.6	70.0	42.5	22.3	5.1	2.6
2000	56.0	30.4	55.9	98.6	96.2	98.2	100.0	99.1	82.0	65.1	41.7	20.6	7.5	2.9
1999	59.8	32.9	57.8	100.0	100.0	100.0	97.6	95.8	82.0	63.7	42.2	19.4	5.2	2.9
1998	59.0	33.2	55.0	95.6	97.8	97.7	95.6	94.4	81.5	73.6	46.6	21.2	0.5	3.0
1997	57.9	32.7	59.5	98.4	95.5	100.0	100.0	93.8	71.6	74.3	36.5	17.4	8.8	2.9
1996	54.9	32.0	49.5	97.9	98.8	99.0	95.5	95.0	75.4	80.8	42.2	13.5	6.1	3.7
1995	54.5	29.6	46.0	98.1	100.0	100.0	100.0	94.8	84.4	67.0	46.2	17.8	6.8	3.1
1994	57.3	30.6	39.0	97.4	100.0	99.4	100.0	97.7	81.9	64.2	49.3	16.9	6.7	3.2
1993	58.6	31.9	36.1	98.5	99.6	100.0	99.8	88.7	87.0	74.5	43.4	20.9	6.3	3.4

Note: Data shown for 1947 to 1966 for the Black population are for Black and other races. Data for 1947 to 1963 exclude kindergarten. Nursery school was first collected in 1964.

* = Quantity zero or rounds to zero.

NA = Not available.

r = Revised, controlled to 1990 census based population estimates; previous 1993 data controlled to 1980 census based population estimates.

[1]Starting in 2003, respondents could identify more than one race. Except as noted, the race data in this table from 2003 onward represent those respondents who indicated only one race category.

[2]The data shown prior to 2003 consists of those identifying themselves as "Asian or Pacific Islanders."

Table A-11. Percentage of the Population 3 Years Old and Over Enrolled in School, by Age, Sex, Race, and Hispanic Origin, October 1947–2019—*Continued*

(Percent; civilian noninstitutionalized population.)

Year, sex, race, and Hispanic origin	Total enrolled 3 to 34 years old	Total enrolled 3 years old and over	Age											
			3 and 4	5 and 6	7 to 9	10 to 13	14 and 15	16 and 17	18 and 19	20 and 21	22 to 24	25 to 29	30 to 34	35 and over
HISPANIC ORIGIN (OF ANY RACE)														
Both Sexes														
2019	55.7	31.6	49.8	93.3	96.8	97.5	97.4	90.7	63.7	48.1	26.5	10.2	5.4	1.5
2018	55.7	31.9	47.9	93.5	96.9	97.8	98.1	91.7	63.5	46.0	24.8	12.0	4.9	1.6
2017	56.4	32.6	47.9	95.0	97.0	97.3	98.4	92.7	67.2	46.0	25.9	12.3	4.8	1.8
2016	56.8	32.9	49.5	93.0	97.0	98.4	97.6	93.6	68.4	51.7	26.7	11.3	4.7	1.6
2015	55.8	32.7	44.1	93.7	97.9	97.1	96.7	92.6	65.2	48.8	25.2	11.2	4.6	1.7
2014	55.4	33.1	45.5	94.4	98.2	97.3	97.1	92.2	64.7	44.7	24.0	10.7	5.3	1.9
2013	55.5	33.4	45.4	93.9	98.4	97.7	98.3	93.9	59.3	43.9	26.7	10.4	5.7	2.0
2012	56.4	34.2	46.3	92.1	98.1	98.3	98.5	94.8	68.1	49.5	27.1	9.4	6.2	1.8
2011	55.6	34.0	41.6	95.6	98.2	98.5	98.2	94.6	65.2	45.7	23.6	10.5	4.5	1.6
2010	55.1	33.8	44.2	94.3	98.5	97.3	97.9	96.0	66.2	37.0	23.8	11.4	5.7	2.3
2009	52.8	32.3	41.9	93.7	96.5	98.0	97.9	92.6	57.1	37.2	20.4	9.5	5.6	2.2
2008	51.9	31.9	43.6	91.8	97.1	98.6	98.7	93.8	55.1	32.1	19.8	9.2	4.2	2.2
2007	51.7	32.1	48.2	94.3	96.3	99.0	98.4	90.6	57.2	32.3	18.8	8.3	4.5	2.1
2006	51.3	31.9	48.8	93.4	98.1	98.2	98.4	91.1	53.4	30.6	17.9	7.3	5.3	1.8
2005	50.9	32.1	43.0	93.8	97.4	97.9	97.3	92.6	54.3	30.0	19.5	7.8	4.2	2.0
2004	50.7	32.4	43.9	93.0	97.6	97.5	98.2	90.2	50.1	32.2	19.4	8.1	5.3	2.2
2003	49.6	31.6	43.7	91.6	97.5	98.3	96.7	92.1	50.5	33.7	16.1	6.2	4.6	1.8
2002	49.9	32.3	41.0	94.4	97.9	98.1	98.1	90.9	50.6	24.6	15.3	8.4	4.4	2.4
2001	49.5	32.4	39.7	93.6	97.4	98.3	97.8	88.2	45.5	27.9	15.5	7.7	4.4	2.5
2000	51.3	32.6	35.9	94.3	97.5	97.4	96.2	87.0	49.5	26.1	18.2	7.4	5.6	2.0
1999	51.1	32.9	36.9	93.9	99.0	98.3	97.6	88.1	44.5	22.6	15.0	9.1	5.6	2.3
1998	50.4	32.6	36.7	98.2	98.8	99.1	96.8	89.1	40.3	25.6	16.3	8.7	5.5	2.3
1997	50.8	32.7	36.6	96.6	98.6	99.6	98.4	91.1	49.4	28.9	16.4	7.3	3.7	1.8
1996	50.3	32.8	38.1	89.5	96.6	97.6	96.6	88.7	47.0	25.3	17.6	8.6	5.0	2.5
1995	49.7	32.9	36.9	93.9	98.5	99.2	98.9	88.2	46.1	27.1	15.6	7.1	4.7	2.7
1994	49.0	32.6	30.8	96.1	99.2	99.4	96.1	88.3	51.4	24.9	15.1	8.1	5.7	2.7
1993r	48.6	NA	26.8	93.6	99.6	99.2	97.6	88.1	50.0	31.8	13.8	7.7	5.1	NA
1993	48.9	31.6	26.8	93.8	99.6	99.2	97.6	88.3	50.0	31.8	13.7	7.7	5.1	1.9
1992	49.2	NA	28.8	96.0	99.5	99.1	98.8	87.2	53.7	30.1	14.5	6.7	6.0	NA
1991	47.9	NA	30.6	92.4	99.9	99.4	97.2	82.6	47.9	26.4	11.6	6.9	5.9	NA
1990	47.4	NA	29.8	94.8	99.6	99.2	99.0	85.4	44.1	27.2	9.9	6.3	3.1	NA
1989	45.8	NA	23.8	92.8	98.0	99.3	96.5	86.4	44.6	18.8	12.0	6.6	3.5	NA
1988	46.0	NA	24.5	95.7	99.6	99.8	98.8	78.8	44.1	16.7	12.1	5.8	6.2	NA
1987	47.2	NA	30.7	93.0	99.2	99.4	97.6	87.1	39.1	26.5	12.3	7.5	4.9	NA
1986	48.2	NA	28.8	93.7	99.4	99.3	97.2	84.0	46.0	21.4	13.7	9.2	5.6	NA
1985	47.7	NA	27.0	94.5	99.4	99.4	96.1	84.5	41.8	24.0	11.6	8.6	5.6	NA
1984	47.7	NA	24.2	93.9	98.7	99.4	94.9	85.7	39.9	28.1	11.3	6.6	7.5	NA
1983	49.3	NA	23.5	95.1	98.5	99.7	96.0	88.6	44.3	24.0	12.5	7.1	5.7	NA
1982	49.4	NA	21.8	92.2	98.7	98.8	96.9	85.5	39.2	22.7	10.4	8.2	4.4	NA
1981	49.0	NA	24.5	90.4	99.2	99.1	94.0	82.8	37.8	20.6	12.3	8.0	4.7	NA
1980	49.8	NA	28.5	94.5	98.4	99.7	94.3	81.8	37.8	19.5	11.7	6.9	4.1	NA
1979	48.6	NA	22.5	92.5	98.7	99.0	96.3	82.3	39.9	22.6	10.0	7.8	7.1	NA
1978	48.3	NA	22.5	91.4	99.5	98.0	95.2	83.0	35.7	16.8	11.8	8.0	4.1	NA
1977	50.8	NA	19.5	93.7	99.0	99.3	97.6	83.6	40.6	23.1	10.8	9.3	5.6	NA
1976	51.8	NA	22.2	95.0	97.5	99.1	95.4	81.3	45.2	24.0	14.8	7.9	2.7	NA
1975	54.8	NA	27.3	92.1	99.6	99.2	95.6	86.2	44.0	27.5	14.1	8.3	4.1	NA
1974	54.3	NA	25.3	92.1	98.8	99.2	96.1	78.3	45.2	23.2	11.3	6.7	2.2	NA
1973	52.8	NA	18.8	90.7	98.7	99.1	94.4	80.2	39.2	21.5	10.0	6.8	1.3	NA
1972	53.0	NA	20.5	90.0	98.7	99.1	96.7	83.9	41.4	17.0	9.9	5.2	3.5	NA
Male														
2019	54.7	31.5	51.8	93.5	98.4	96.6	96.9	90.7	63.5	44.8	21.8	8.9	3.4	1.3
2018	54.7	31.8	48.2	92.8	96.8	97.9	97.8	93.4	59.4	42.1	21.4	10.7	5.1	1.4
2017	55.0	32.1	47.1	94.6	97.5	97.4	98.2	91.7	63.3	40.9	23.0	9.9	5.0	1.4
2016	55.4	32.6	50.7	91.8	96.3	98.1	98.4	93.4	66.3	46.0	23.4	9.3	3.6	1.3
2015	54.4	32.4	44.3	93.6	97.5	97.3	96.0	91.7	59.9	44.4	24.2	9.2	3.3	1.6
2014	53.6	32.6	43.1	94.6	97.8	96.7	97.8	89.3	61.6	37.4	21.5	10.0	3.2	1.9
2013	54.0	33.1	44.2	93.6	98.6	97.7	97.9	93.5	55.4	38.0	24.4	10.8	3.9	1.6

Note: Data shown for 1947 to 1966 for the Black population are for Black and other races. Data for 1947 to 1963 exclude kindergarten. Nursery school was first collected in 1964.
* = Quantity zero or rounds to zero.
NA = Not available.
r = Revised, controlled to 1990 census based population estimates; previous 1993 data controlled to 1980 census based population estimates.
[1]Starting in 2003, respondents could identify more than one race. Except as noted, the race data in this table from 2003 onward represent those respondents who indicated only one race category.
[2]The data shown prior to 2003 consists of those identifying themselves as "Asian or Pacific Islanders."

Table A-11. Percentage of the Population 3 Years Old and Over Enrolled in School, by Age, Sex, Race, and Hispanic Origin, October 1947–2019—*Continued*

(Percent; civilian noninstitutionalized population.)

Year, sex, race, and Hispanic origin	Total enrolled 3 to 34 years old	Total enrolled 3 years old and over	Age											
			3 and 4	5 and 6	7 to 9	10 to 13	14 and 15	16 and 17	18 and 19	20 and 21	22 to 24	25 to 29	30 to 34	35 and over
2012	54.7	33.9	45.4	92.2	98.2	98.6	98.9	95.1	65.7	44.4	24.7	7.4	3.3	1.8
2011	54.1	33.9	43.6	95.9	98.8	98.8	98.7	94.6	61.0	43.1	21.0	9.9	3.4	1.6
2010	52.9	32.8	43.3	93.4	98.1	96.9	97.5	96.0	64.9	34.0	18.6	9.6	4.9	1.9
2009	50.9	31.3	39.4	94.1	96.2	98.8	98.1	92.5	51.8	32.1	18.6	7.8	5.2	1.6
2008	50.0	31.1	40.5	91.0	96.7	98.6	98.6	93.1	54.7	30.8	16.6	8.2	4.1	1.6
2007	49.4	31.1	50.7	94.1	96.4	99.0	97.8	91.1	55.2	24.6	14.4	6.7	3.1	1.8
2006	49.0	30.9	49.1	91.7	97.7	97.9	99.0	91.7	51.5	24.1	16.0	5.4	3.5	1.2
2005	48.4	31.0	43.0	92.4	96.0	97.2	97.8	92.5	51.8	25.2	17.5	5.6	2.6	1.6
2004	48.5	31.5	43.8	93.9	97.2	97.5	99.0	89.2	43.9	30.6	17.2	6.7	3.3	1.5
2003	47.3	30.8	42.9	91.3	97.5	98.4	96.7	90.4	47.0	27.2	13.3	4.9	3.8	1.3
2002	48.1	31.9	41.7	95.1	97.8	97.6	98.2	88.8	48.4	24.5	11.5	7.0	3.1	2.2
2001	48.4	32.2	42.9	94.9	97.9	98.6	98.4	87.8	40.0	24.4	14.6	6.5	3.5	2.2
2000	50.5	32.5	31.9	95.4	96.6	98.4	96.9	85.7	48.0	24.2	15.2	5.1	5.7	1 4
1999	50.3	32.9	33.5	92.8	98.8	98.5	98.1	87.9	45.3	21.5	11.2	8.6	3.9	2.0
1998	49.0	32.4	44.9	92.8	98.8	99.3	97.0	88.0	33.7	24.6	12.9	6.9	4.7	1.8
1997	49.0	32.3	35.5	97.7	97.7	99.8	99.5	92.5	45.4	27.6	14.0	5.9	2.7	1.6
1996	49.2	33.0	39.6	91.0	95.4	97.9	98.0	90.4	46.8	19.5	16.2	6.8	4.3	2.6
1995	49.1	33.1	40.8	93.6	98.8	98.8	98.4	88.4	47.4	24.8	14.8	5.6	4.5	2.1
1994	48.0	32.5	32.6	96.5	98.6	99.3	94.6	86.6	54.2	23.7	14.0	7.1	4.2	2.3
1993r	46.6	NA	26.9	93.4	99.8	98.8	96.9	88.7	47.8	31.6	13.0	5.5	5.4	NA
1993	47.4	31.5	27.0	93.6	99.8	98.8	96.9	89.1	47.7	31.6	12.8	5.5	5.4	1.5
1992	47.9	NA	24.9	96.5	100.0	99.2	98 1	89 2	52.6	24.3	13.8	5.3	3.5	NA
1991	46.4	NA	30.7	92.3	99.8	99.7	97.8	83.6	42.1	20.8	9.9	6.8	3.3	NA
1990	47.1	NA	27.3	95.6	99.5	99.0	99.1	85.5	40.7	21.7	11.2	4.6	4.0	NA
1989	45.8	NA	21.3	92.5	97.7	98.6	98.0	88.7	44.2	17.1	12.2	7.3	4.1	NA
1988	46.2	NA	27.9	96.7	99.2	100.0	98.1	80.9	44.7	21.6	12.5	4.5	5.0	NA
1987	47.8	NA	30.5	92.8	99.7	100.0	98.1	90.9	42.3	30.1	11.4	7.8	5.1	NA
1986	47.3	NA	29.4	93.0	100.0	99.4	96.8	85.0	45.8	19.2	13.0	9.1	4.4	NA
1985	47.5	NA	26.4	95.3	98.9	99.1	96.2	88.9	38.6	20.3	12.6	8.7	3.8	NA
1984	48.6	NA	20.0	93.6	98.2	100.0	95.7	85.1	38.8	27.5	12.3	8.2	4.0	NA
1983	50.7	NA	25.0	91.9	98.8	99.6	97.8	88.2	40.4	26.2	15.1	6.9	4.6	NA
1982	50.4	NA	25.2	90.3	99.6	98.4	96.8	87.8	39.7	21.6	11.2	10.8	3.1	NA
1981	49.6	NA	25.5	89.6	98.8	99.0	92.3	84.5	36.0	24.4	11.4	8.3	4.3	NA
1980	49.9	NA	30.1	94.0	97.7	99.4	96.7	81.5	36.9	21.4	10.7	6.8	6.2	NA
1979	51.0	NA	22.8	93.8	98.7	99.0	96.6	85.1	42.6	24.0	12.4	8.7	6.1	NA
1978	50.5	NA	22.6	93.2	99.1	97.8	94.0	80.4	40.0	18.1	13.6	9.5	4.4	NA
1977	54.2	NA	23.2	91.4	100.0	98.7	99.1	89.4	43.1	22.8	16.0	13.1	6.4	NA
1976	55.0	NA	22.1	94.6	97 4	98.5	97.3	85.5	46.3	27.1	18.6	11.4	5.6	NA
1975	58.1	NA	26.7	89.7	99.6	98.8	97.4	88.3	51.9	31.3	15.9	11.9	7.2	NA
1974	56.0	NA	23.5	93.1	98.3	98.5	97.9	78.6	46.8	22.3	14.5	8.4	7.4	NA
1973	55.5	NA	23.1	92.4	99.1	99.1	96.5	86.6	45.8	23.8	10.8	9.9	6.7	NA
1972	54.7	NA	20.4	90.3	98.8	99.1	98.1	87.8	40.5	20.0	13.9	5.8	2.5	NA
Female														
2019	56.0	31.7	47.6	93.1	95.1	98.3	97.9	90.7	63.9	51.6	31.2	11.6	7.4	1.7
2018	56.9	32.0	47.6	94.3	96.9	97.7	98.3	90.1	67.9	50.0	28.2	13.3	4.7	1.8
2017	57.8	33.0	48.8	95.5	96.5	97.3	98.6	93.6	71.1	50.7	29.2	14.7	4.6	2.2
2016	58.3	33.2	48.2	94.2	97.6	98.8	96.8	93.9	70.5	57.5	30.2	13.3	5.9	1.9
2015	55.7	32.9	44.0	93.9	98.4	96.9	97.4	93.7	70.1	53.2	26.3	13.2	5.9	1.8
2014	57.4	33.6	47.8	94.2	98.6	97.9	96.4	95.3	67.8	53.8	26.3	11.5	7.6	2.0
2013	57.0	33.7	46.7	94.1	98.2	97.7	98.8	94.3	63.2	50.6	29.1	10.0	7.6	2.3
2012	58.2	34.5	47.1	92.1	98.1	98.0	98.1	94.5	70.7	55.0	29.7	11.5	9.3	1.9
2011	57.2	34.1	39.6	95.3	97.6	98.2	97.6	94.6	70.3	48.8	26.6	11.2	5.8	1.6
2010	57.4	34.8	45.0	92.5	98.9	97.7	98.3	96.0	67.6	40.5	29.2	13.6	6.6	2.7
2009	55.0	33.3	44.4	93.2	96.7	97.2	97.6	92.6	62.5	43.1	22.2	11.6	6.0	2.8
2008	53.9	32.8	46.9	92.6	97.4	98.7	98.8	94.5	55.5	33.5	23.4	10.4	4.4	2.7
2007	54.3	33.1	45.6	94.5	96.2	99.0	99.1	90.0	59.2	41.0	23.7	10.3	6.1	2.3
2006	53.9	33.1	48.5	95.3	98.5	98.6	97.7	90.4	55.4	37.5	20.1	9.7	7.3	2.3
2005	58.0	33.3	43.0	95.3	98.8	98.6	96.7	92.6	57.2	35.3	21.8	10.4	6.1	2.4
2004	53.1	33.3	44.0	92.2	97.9	97.5	97.5	91.3	56.9	34.0	22.0	9.7	7.5	2.8
2003	52.2	32.5	44.7	92.0	97.5	98.2	96.8	93.8	54.4	41.1	19.4	7.9	5.6	2.2
2002	51.8	32.8	40.3	93.8	98.1	98.7	97.9	92.8	53.2	24.6	20.2	9.9	6.0	2.7

Note: Data shown for 1947 to 1966 for the Black population are for Black and other races. Data for 1947 to 1963 exclude kindergarten. Nursery school was first collected in 1964.
* = Quantity zero or rounds to zero.
NA = Not available.
r – Revised, controlled to 1990 census based population estimates; previous 1993 data controlled to 1900 census based population estimates.
[1]Starting in 2003, respondents could identify more than one race. Except as noted, the race data in this table from 2003 onward represent those respondents who indicated only one race category.
[2]The data shown prior to 2003 consists of those identifying themselves as "Asian or Pacific Islanders."

Table A-11. Percentage of the Population 3 Years Old and Over Enrolled in School, by Age, Sex, Race, and Hispanic Origin, October 1947–2019—*Continued*

(Percent; civilian noninstitutionalized population.)

Year, sex, race, and Hispanic origin	Total enrolled 3 to 34 years old	Total enrolled 3 years old and over	Age											
			3 and 4	5 and 6	7 to 9	10 to 13	14 and 15	16 and 17	18 and 19	20 and 21	22 to 24	25 to 29	30 to 34	35 and over
2001	50.6	32.6	36.3	92.4	96.9	98.1	97.2	88.7	51.1	31.6	16.7	9.1	5.3	2.8
2000	52.2	32.8	40.0	93.1	98.4	96.4	95.4	88.3	51.1	28.1	21.6	9.5	5.5	2.6
1999	52.1	32.8	40.5	95.0	99.3	98.0	96.9	88.3	43.6	23.6	19.2	9.5	7.3	2.7
1998	51.9	32.8	34.3	93.7	98.8	98.9	96.7	90.5	46.8	26.8	20.0	10.6	6.5	2.8
1997	52.7	33.0	37.7	95.7	99.6	99.5	97.3	89.6	53.9	30.4	19.2	8.8	4.9	2.0
1996	51.4	32.7	36.8	87.8	97.9	97.4	95.0	86.9	47.2	31.1	19.3	10.5	5.7	2.5
1995	50.3	32.7	32.7	94.3	98.2	99.6	99.4	88.0	44.8	29.2	16.6	8.7	4.9	3.2
1994	50.2	32.7	28.9	95.7	99.8	99.4	97.6	90.2	48.6	26.4	16.5	9.1	7.3	3.0
1993r	50.7	NA	26.7	93.9	99.4	99.6	98.2	87.3	51.9	31.9	14.7	10.2	4.7	NA
1993	50.6	31.6	26.7	93.9	99.4	99.6	98.2	87.4	51.9	32.0	14.5	10.2	4.8	2.2
1992	50.6	NA	32.7	95.4	99.0	99.1	99.6	85.0	54.9	35.6	15.4	8.2	6.0	NA
1991	49.5	NA	30.5	92.6	100.0	99.2	96.6	81.5	53.7	32.0	13.6	7.0	5.9	NA
1990	47.7	NA	32.3	93.9	99.7	99.4	98.8	85.3	47.2	33.1	8.4	8.1	3.1	NA
1989	45.9	NA	26.5	93.3	98.3	100.0	95.1	83.7	45.0	20.8	11.9	5.8	3.5	NA
1988	45.8	NA	20.7	94.6	100.0	99.6	99.6	76.6	43.5	11.2	11.5	7.2	6.2	NA
1987	46.5	NA	30.8	93.2	98.7	98.9	97.1	82.6	36.2	22.0	13.2	7.3	4.9	NA
1986	49.0	NA	28.2	94.4	98.7	99.2	97.5	83.0	46.2	23.7	14.5	9.2	5.6	NA
1985	47.9	NA	27.7	93.7	98.0	99.7	96.0	80.0	44.7	27.4	10.4	8.6	5.6	NA
1984	46.8	NA	28.2	94.2	99.2	98.7	94.0	86.3	40.8	28.7	10.4	4.9	7.5	NA
1983	48.0	NA	22.0	98.3	98.1	99.8	94.1	89.1	47.6	21.7	10.1	7.4	5.7	NA
1982	48.4	NA	16.3	93.9	97.8	99.2	97.1	82.8	38.7	23.7	9.7	5.7	4.4	NA
1981	48.4	NA	23.4	91.3	99.6	99.3	95.7	80.8	39.4	16.8	13.1	7.7	4.7	NA
1980	49.8	NA	26.6	94.9	99.0	99.9	92.1	82.2	38.8	17.6	12.6	6.9	4.1	NA
1979	46.3	NA	22.3	91.1	98.7	98.9	95.9	79.5	37.1	21.5	7.8	7.0	7.1	NA
1978	46.2	NA	22.5	89.4	100.0	98.2	96.6	86.2	31.9	15.7	10.1	6.5	4.1	NA
1977	47.6	NA	15.8	96.3	97.9	99.9	95.9	77.4	38.5	23.4	6.2	5.9	5.6	NA
1976	48.8	NA	22.3	95.5	97.6	99.7	93.6	77.6	44.2	21.4	12.1	4.8	2.7	NA
1975	51.7	NA	27.9	94.4	99.5	99.7	93.8	84.0	37.1	24.3	12.5	5.3	4.1	NA
1974	52.5	NA	27.4	91.1	99.2	100.0	94.1	77.9	43.7	23.9	8.4	4.9	2.2	NA
1973	50.1	NA	14.0	88.9	98.3	99.1	92.5	74.9	32.9	19.4	9.2	3.9	1.3	NA
1972	51.4	NA	20.5	89.7	98.5	99.0	95.4	80.0	42.4	14.6	6.8	4.7	3.5	NA
WHITE ALONE OR IN COMBINATION														
Both Sexes														
2019	54.0	23.4	53.1	94.0	97.7	97.9	97.8	92.9	67.4	53.0	27.3	9.8	5.3	1.2
2018	54.6	23.9	54.5	93.7	97.0	98.3	98.6	93.2	69.2	53.9	26.7	11.4	5.6	1.3
2017	54.5	23.9	53.2	93.7	97.0	97.6	98.4	93.3	68.1	54.6	26.8	11.5	5.6	1.3
2016	55.2	24.2	53.8	93.7	98.0	98.5	98.4	92.6	69.7	56.0	27.4	12.7	5.9	1.3
2015	55.2	24.4	52.1	94.2	97.6	97.9	97.9	94.0	68.5	53.4	27.7	12.7	6.1	1.4
2014	55.1	24.6	54.0	93.4	97.7	97.5	97.7	93.4	68.1	52.3	28.6	12.3	5.9	1.5
2013	55.5	25.0	54.4	93.9	98.2	98.2	98.5	93.7	67.0	52.3	29.1	12.2	6.3	1.6
2012	56.2	25.4	53.6	93.7	98.1	97.8	98.3	96.1	68.4	54.0	29.5	13.3	6.7	1.7
2011	56.5	25.9	51.6	95.6	98.2	98.6	98.7	95.7	70.2	53.7	30.8	14.1	7.0	1.7
2010	56.1	25.8	52.3	94.3	97.8	98.1	98.1	96.2	70.0	51.4	28.0	14.0	7.7	1.9
2009	56.0	25.7	51.3	94.2	98.0	98.7	98.1	94.6	68.4	52.5	28.8	13.0	7.4	1.9
2008	55.9	25.7	52.4	94.0	98.2	98.9	98.7	95.5	67.0	51.0	28.1	12.4	6.3	1.8
2007	55.7	25.7	54.0	94.8	98.0	98.7	98.7	94.6	67.1	49.7	26.2	16.2	9.4	1.8
2006	55.8	25.7	55.5	94.8	98.4	98.5	98.4	94.9	65.0	47.9	25.6	11.4	6.8	1.7
2005	56.2	26.1	53.9	95.3	98.6	98.7	98.3	95.3	67.7	49.3	26.2	11.3	6.2	1.8
2004	55.7	26.1	52.7	95.5	98.2	98.4	98.5	94.0	64.8	49.4	25.2	12.2	6.4	1.8
2003	55.6	26.1	55.2	94.8	98.0	98.4	97.4	95.0	64.2	48.3	26.8	11.0	6.3	1.7
Male														
2019	53.3	23.7	52.4	94.8	98.3	97.6	97.7	93.0	65.3	49.3	24.1	8.9	4.4	1.0
2018	53.9	24.1	54.8	93.6	97.2	98.5	98.8	93.9	65.8	49.2	25.0	10.0	5.3	1.0
2017	53.8	24.1	52.2	93.2	97.2	97.7	98.5	92.9	65.5	50.5	25.0	10.2	5.1	1.0
2016	54.5	24.5	55.3	93.7	97.9	98.2	98.7	92.2	68.4	51.0	25.7	10.7	4.9	1.0
2015	54.6	24.7	53.4	93.4	97.7	98.1	97.6	93.2	65.3	50.6	25.4	11.5	5.3	1.1
2014	54.4	24.9	52.6	93.8	97.4	96.8	97.3	92.4	64.6	49.4	26.7	11.5	5.1	1.2
2013	54.7	25.1	52.7	93.9	98.1	98.2	98.4	93.0	65.4	47.4	26.6	11.2	5.2	1.2

Note: Data shown for 1947 to 1966 for the Black population are for Black and other races. Data for 1947 to 1963 exclude kindergarten. Nursery school was first collected in 1964.

* = Quantity zero or rounds to zero.

NA = Not available.

r = Revised, controlled to 1990 census based population estimates; previous 1993 data controlled to 1980 census based population estimates.

[1]Starting in 2003, respondents could identify more than one race. Except as noted, the race data in this table from 2003 onward represent those respondents who indicated only one race category.

[2]The data shown prior to 2003 consists of those identifying themselves as "Asian or Pacific Islanders."

Table A-11. Percentage of the Population 3 Years Old and Over Enrolled in School, by Age, Sex, Race, and Hispanic Origin, October 1947–2019—Continued

(Percent; civilian noninstitutionalized population.)

Year, sex, race, and Hispanic origin	Total enrolled 3 to 34 years old	Total enrolled 3 years old and over	Age											
			3 and 4	5 and 6	7 to 9	10 to 13	14 and 15	16 and 17	18 and 19	20 and 21	22 to 24	25 to 29	30 to 34	35 and over
2012	55.3	25.5	52.8	93.6	97.8	98.1	98.2	95.9	65.6	48.2	28.2	11.5	5.6	1.3
2011	55.9	26.3	52.5	95.6	98.4	98.7	98.5	95.6	67.4	50.3	30.1	12.5	6.2	1.4
2010	55.2	26.0	52.2	93.4	97.4	97.7	98.1	95.0	67.5	48.2	25.9	13.1	6.4	1.5
2009	55.1	25.8	50.5	93.8	97.8	98.9	97.8	94.3	64.3	49.2	27.9	11.3	6.5	1.4
2008	55.2	25.9	52.1	93.6	97.9	98.7	99.0	95.0	64.4	48.1	26.4	11.6	5.7	1.3
2007	54.6	25.8	53.2	94.0	97.9	98.6	98.3	94.4	66.4	44.1	24.0	12.9	9.4	1.4
2006	54.9	25.9	56.0	94.5	98.3	98.4	98.2	94.7	62.7	43.5	24.1	10.3	5.6	1.3
2005	55.2	26.2	52.6	94.7	98.2	98.6	98.3	95.2	65.7	45.1	24.6	8.9	5.4	1.4
2004	55.0	26.3	53.4	95.8	98.0	98.2	98.8	94.3	59.9	46.5	23.2	11.1	5.5	1.4
2003	55.0	26.5	55.9	95.2	97.7	98.2	97.3	95.1	61.6	43.4	25.5	9.8	5.7	1.4
Female														
2019	54.7	23.2	53.8	93.2	97.1	98.2	97.9	92.8	69.6	56.9	30.3	10.7	6.2	1.5
2018	55.3	23.6	54.2	93.8	96.8	98.2	98.5	92.5	72.8	58.7	28.4	12.8	5.9	1.5
2017	55.1	23.7	54.2	94.2	96.7	97.4	98.4	93.7	70.7	58.9	28.7	12.8	6.1	1.6
2016	55.9	24.0	52.3	93.7	98.2	98.8	98.0	93.0	71.0	61.2	29.0	14.8	6.9	1.5
2015	55.7	24.2	50.9	95.1	97.6	97.6	98.1	94.8	71.8	56.2	30.0	14.0	6.9	1.7
2014	55.8	24.3	55.4	92.9	98.0	98.2	98.1	94.4	71.7	55.7	30.3	13.1	6.8	1.8
2013	56.4	24.9	56.1	94.0	98.3	98.3	98.6	94.5	68.8	57.6	31.7	13.2	7.4	2.0
2012	57.2	25.3	54.5	93.8	98.4	97.5	98.5	96.3	71.4	59.6	31.0	16.1	7.8	2.0
2011	57.2	25.6	50.7	95.7	98.0	98.5	98.8	95.7	73.1	57.4	31.6	15.9	7.9	2.0
2010	57.1	25.7	52.5	95.2	98.1	98.5	98.1	97.4	72.5	55.0	30.1	15.0	9.1	2.3
2009	57.0	25.7	52.1	94.5	98.1	98.4	98.4	94.8	72.7	56.0	29.7	14.8	8.3	2.4
2008	56.6	25.5	52.7	94.4	98.6	99.1	98.5	96.0	69.7	54.0	29.8	13.2	7.0	2.3
2007	56.9	25.6	54.9	95.6	98.1	98.7	99.2	94.9	67.9	55.5	28.4	19.2	9.4	2.2
2006	56.6	25.5	55.0	95.2	98.5	98.5	98.6	95.2	67.3	52.4	27.1	12.4	8.1	2.1
2005	57.4	26.0	55.3	96.0	98.9	98.8	98.4	95.5	70.0	53.8	27.9	13.8	7.1	2.3
2004	56.5	25.8	51.9	95.3	98.4	98.5	98.2	93.8	69.7	52.4	27.1	13.4	7.3	2.2
2003	56.3	25.7	54.4	94.5	98.3	98.7	97.5	94.9	66.8	53.1	28.1	12.2	7.0	2.1
BLACK ALONE OR IN COMBINATION														
Both Sexes														
2019	56.1	30.2	56.7	93.5	96.7	97.9	98.1	92.0	61.6	47.7	28.3	13.8	7.9	2.6
2018	56.5	30.5	53.3	93.4	97.3	98.1	97.7	88.5	67.1	50.9	28.0	15.6	7.9	2.7
2017	56.9	30.9	56.7	92.1	97.1	98.8	96.8	91.4	66.9	47.9	27.6	13.6	7.3	2.7
2016	57.1	31.1	52.4	93.2	97.7	98.8	96.3	95.0	67.2	47.6	27.2	12.6	8.7	2.9
2015	56.6	31.0	51.2	93.7	96.2	98.5	98.3	95	64.7	42.4	26.8	12.6	8.3	2.8
2014	57.1	31.8	56.9	94.6	98.8	97.8	98.7	91.7	64.8	39.7	24.7	14.2	9.0	3.7
2013	58.5	32.5	58.4	94.3	97.1	98.0	98.7	92.9	64.0	49.1	27.4	16.7	8.2	3.0
2012	59.5	33.2	51.8	92.4	96.7	99.0	97.6	94.6	68.7	49.6	29.3	15.7	12.2	3.3
2011	59.3	33.6	53.9	92.1	97.3	98.5	98.7	96.0	74.1	41.8	31.0	18.1	11.3	3.8
2010	59.2	33.6	55.8	94.8	97.5	98.7	98.6	95.7	63.2	49.9	28.9	16.0	10.8	3.9
2009	59.4	33.5	57.1	93.8	97.4	98.6	97.7	94.4	64.7	44.2	31.6	14.7	11.1	3.7
2008	58.8	33.0	54.5	92.9	98.8	99.1	98.1	94.5	59.7	40.4	24.8	15.1	11.4	2.8
2007	59.0	33.2	58.2	94.2	98.2	98.0	99.1	93.7	62.0	38.1	27.3	15.3	9.6	3.0
2006	58.8	33.3	59.0	92.4	96.9	97.2	97.4	93.2	64.9	38.9	27.8	11.9	8.9	3.2
2005	59.0	33.5	51.3	96.1	98.5	98.6	95.9	92.9	62.5	38.1	27.8	11.7	9.9	3.1
2004	59.6	34.3	58.6	94.5	97.4	99.4	98.6	95.3	59.7	40.8	25.3	14.8	7.0	3.3
2003	59.8	34.2	56.5	94.6	98.1	98.3	98.0	94.2	60.9	42.1	27.2	12.4	8.4	2.8
Male														
2019	56.5	31.6	57.3	93.7	98.2	98.1	98.9	91.3	61.6	48.5	22.9	12.1	5.6	2.1
2018	55.8	31.2	48.4	93.1	97.7	97.8	98.9	93.4	66.9	50.9	23.4	13.1	4.6	1.7
2017	56.3	31.8	58.3	91.2	96.0	98.8	95.9	90.7	62.8	41.4	23.8	12.1	6.0	2.2
2016	57.4	32.4	48.1	90.8	96.6	98.8	98.5	95.4	66.9	44.2	25.8	12.3	7.3	2.2
2015	57.2	32.2	50.6	92.4	96.5	99.3	99.1	95.2	64.6	39.4	29.3	9.7	4.6	1.8
2014	57.4	32.8	56.4	95.7	98.8	97.8	98.4	91.7	61.1	39.2	21.9	11.6	7.2	2.6
2013	58.5	33.5	55.4	94.6	97.0	97.8	98.6	95.0	59.4	44.6	26.2	13.7	4.9	2.4
2012	59.0	33.7	48.8	93.5	95.8	99.1	98.7	95.6	61.4	49.4	27.2	11.1	7.2	2.1
2011	59.0	34.5	52.8	92.8	97.5	98.6	97.9	94.5	71.6	38.9	30.0	14.1	7.7	2.7

Note: Data shown for 1947 to 1966 for the Black population are for Black and other races. Data for 1947 to 1963 exclude kindergarten. Nursery school was first collected in 1964.
* = Quantity zero or rounds to zero.
NA = Not available.
r – Revised, controlled to 1990 census based population estimates; previous 1993 data controlled to 1980 census based population estimates.
[1]Starting in 2003, respondents could identify more than one race. Except as noted, the race data in this table from 2003 onward represent those respondents who indicated only one race category.
[2]The data shown prior to 2003 consists of those identifying themselves as "Asian or Pacific Islanders."

Table A-11. Percentage of the Population 3 Years Old and Over Enrolled in School, by Age, Sex, Race, and Hispanic Origin, October 1947–2019—*Continued*

(Percent; civilian noninstitutionalized population.)

Year, sex, race, and Hispanic origin	Total enrolled 3 to 34 years old	Total enrolled 3 years old and over	3 and 4	5 and 6	7 to 9	10 to 13	14 and 15	16 and 17	18 and 19	20 and 21	22 to 24	25 to 29	30 to 34	35 and over
2010	58.8	34.4	55.0	94.2	97.7	98.6	97.8	93.8	62.0	44.9	28.0	12.9	6.3	2.7
2009	58.9	34.0	57.4	93.8	97.2	98.3	95.9	95.6	60.4	42.3	25.7	11.5	8.1	2.2
2008	58.8	34.0	53.1	94.0	98.3	98.7	99.0	94.3	58.0	38.1	22.7	11.0	8.6	1.6
2007	60.1	35.0	60.5	93.9	98.1	97.5	99.2	95.2	61.5	37.8	27.8	10.7	9.7	2.0
2006	59.5	34.8	57.0	92.5	97.0	97.1	97.8	91.9	64.1	38.8	25.6	9.5	7.0	2.5
2005	59.2	34.6	52.5	95.1	97.5	97.9	93.8	93.8	66.2	34.9	23.9	9.3	6.1	2.3
2004	59.7	35.3	59.9	93.9	96.8	99.2	98.8	96.3	57.9	38.2	21.0	9.3	3.9	2.2
2003	60.6	35.7	57.6	93.2	98.8	98.2	98.3	93.8	61.1	35.6	23.4	9.4	7.2	1.9
Female														
2019	55.8	29.0	56.0	93.4	95.2	97.6	97.2	92.8	61.6	47.0	33.4	15.3	10.0	3.1
2018	57.1	29.9	58.0	93.8	97.0	98.4	96.4	83.6	67.4	50.9	32.5	18.0	11.0	3.5
2017	57.4	30.2	54.9	93.1	98.1	98.7	97.6	92.1	70.9	54.6	31.1	15.0	8.5	3.0
2016	56.8	29.9	56.6	95.6	98.9	98.8	93.9	94.6	67.6	51.1	28.5	12.8	9.9	3.4
2015	56.1	29.9	51.9	94.9	95.8	97.6	97.6	94.8	64.8	45.2	24.6	15.1	11.5	3.6
2014	56.8	31.0	57.4	93.6	98.9	97.9	99.1	91.6	68.4	40.1	27.5	16.4	10.5	4.5
2013	58.6	31.7	61.2	94.0	97.3	98.1	98.8	91.0	68.4	53.1	28.6	19.1	10.9	3.5
2012	59.9	32.7	54.7	91.3	97.7	99.0	96.5	93.7	76.4	49.7	31.2	19.6	16.3	4.3
2011	59.5	32.8	55.0	91.3	97.2	98.4	99.4	97.5	76.5	45.0	31.7	21.7	14.4	4.7
2010	59.6	33.0	56.7	95.4	97.2	98.8	99.4	97.6	64.3	54.2	29.7	18.7	14.5	4.9
2009	59.8	33.0	56.9	93.9	97.6	98.9	99.4	93.1	68.9	46.1	36.5	17.5	13.5	4.8
2008	58.8	32.1	55.7	91.7	99.4	99.5	97.2	94.7	61.3	42.5	26.6	18.6	13.8	3.8
2007	57.9	31.7	55.7	94.5	98.2	98.4	98.9	92.2	62.6	38.5	26.8	19.4	9.5	3.8
2006	58.2	32.0	60.9	92.3	96.9	97.4	97.0	94.6	65.6	39.0	29.8	14.0	10.5	3.6
2005	58.8	32.4	50.0	97.1	99.4	99.3	97.8	92.0	59.1	41.3	31.1	13.8	12.8	3.7
2004	59.6	33.4	57.0	95.0	98.1	99.6	98.4	94.2	61.3	43.1	29.3	19.3	9.5	4.2
2003	59.1	32.9	55.3	95.9	97.3	98.4	97.6	94.5	60.7	47.5	30.7	14.7	9.4	3.5
ASIAN ALONE OR IN COMBINATION														
Both Sexes														
2019	58.0	28.6	57.8	93.0	98.6	98.9	99.6	94.6	86.2	78.6	45.4	17.1	9.8	1.4
2018	56.5	28.1	51.8	91.7	98.0	97.6	100.0	91.8	80.9	74.3	43.0	19.2	8.7	1.5
2017	57.6	28.5	54.9	96.0	98.1	98.6	100.0	94.5	83.1	77.0	49.0	16.6	6.1	1.2
2016	57.0	28.6	63.2	90.7	98.1	98.8	98.2	94.0	78.4	73.7	46.7	20.6	6.4	1.4
2015	58.0	28.8	59.9	95.6	97.8	98.2	98.2	88.1	83.3	83.1	48.4	19.8	9.0	1.5
2014	57.4	29.4	54.2	89.3	97.0	97.7	96.3	93.8	85.9	73.7	53.9	19.5	5.6	2.0
2013	58.7	30.3	57.4	92.5	97.7	98.5	99.0	97.4	83.0	80.3	46.2	18.1	7.8	2.2
2012	59.1	30.1	56.7	93.9	99.9	98.6	99.0	97.8	79.4	72.8	52.2	18.5	8.4	1.8
2011	58.8	29.7	55.4	96.6	97.9	97.4	98.2	97.6	80.4	77.1	41.4	17.2	9.1	2.1
2010	60.5	30.6	62.4	96.7	98.9	98.4	98.0	96.1	81.9	76.9	46.5	21.3	10.1	1.8
2009	59.3	29.0	55.3	95.6	97.2	95.8	96.8	97.0	90.1	73.6	53.5	18.7	10.8	2.1
2008	59.2	29.5	57.4	92.6	98.3	99.6	98.8	93.5	85.9	79.4	43.0	23.0	11.9	2.5
2007	57.0	28.8	54.1	93.9	98.4	99.3	99.7	93.4	86.3	64.3	45.9	19.6	9.5	1.8
2006	56.3	29.0	51.5	94.6	99.0	99.3	99.6	92.0	82.3	72.2	43.1	17.3	8.8	2.2
2005	57.6	30.5	54.4	95.5	99.6	97.5	98.7	98.2	86.2	77.1	44.4	20.9	9.4	2.3
2004	58.5	31.4	57.7	97.6	99.9	99.2	98.0	97.1	79.9	77.7	46.2	20.8	9.3	2.7
2003	58.2	31.3	51.4	89.3	99.2	99.4	99.1	95.7	87.1	77.0	48.1	21.6	9.4	2.2
Male														
2019	58.4	30.0	58.7	96.3	98.4	99.6	100.0	96.1	88.8	79.9	45.4	17.9	9.0	1.5
2018	56.2	29.1	51.0	92.9	96.3	95.5	100.0	95.6	76.6	73.3	45.5	19.0	7.3	1.4
2017	58.2	29.8	53.7	94.7	98.3	98.2	100.0	94.7	80.0	76.0	53.0	15.6	5.6	1.0
2016	58.7	30.6	60.1	87.5	98.2	98.9	99.0	91.1	76.3	76.9	52.1	21.4	7.2	1.6
2015	58.5	29.8	65.2	96.6	98.0	98.6	97.9	87.5	81.4	82.3	44.7	19.8	8.4	1.1
2014	59.0	31.1	55.3	92.0	98.3	97.7	95.6	94.0	85.2	71.3	59.2	21.6	4.1	1.9
2013	59.6	31.3	57.8	94.1	98.2	98.3	98.3	96.1	82.4	84.2	47.9	20.4	5.6	1.6
2012	59.5	31.2	57.8	94.2	99.8	98.3	98.0	97.8	82.3	72.6	49.4	19.6	6.3	1.5
2011	59.4	30.7	55.9	97.4	97.3	98.6	98.6	96.9	83.3	79.5	39.1	17.0	9.5	1.4
2010	61.5	32.2	63.1	97.9	99.0	98.0	97.6	96.5	78.1	80.7	43.1	23.5	10.3	1.7
2009	59.5	30.5	54.9	95.3	96.6	95.3	97.8	96.1	91.4	74.3	51.5	17.9	9.7	2.3

Note: Data shown for 1947 to 1966 for the Black population are for Black and other races. Data for 1947 to 1963 exclude kindergarten. Nursery school was first collected in 1964.
* = Quantity zero or rounds to zero.
NA = Not available.
r = Revised, controlled to 1990 census based population estimates; previous 1993 data controlled to 1980 census based population estimates.
[1]Starting in 2003, respondents could identify more than one race. Except as noted, the race data in this table from 2003 onward represent those respondents who indicated only one race category.
[2]The data shown prior to 2003 consists of those identifying themselves as "Asian or Pacific Islanders."

Table A-11. Percentage of the Population 3 Years Old and Over Enrolled in School, by Age, Sex, Race, and Hispanic Origin, October 1947–2019—*Continued*

(Percent; civilian noninstitutionalized population.)

Year, sex, race, and Hispanic origin	Total enrolled 3 to 34 years old	Total enrolled 3 years old and over	3 and 4	5 and 6	7 to 9	10 to 13	14 and 15	16 and 17	18 and 19	20 and 21	22 to 24	25 to 29	30 to 34	35 and over
2008............................	59.4	30.2	56.1	92.8	97.3	99.2	100.0	96.4	89.7	74.2	39.0	24.5	11.3	2.0
2007............................	58.6	30.4	58.9	95.4	99.1	99.1	99.7	93.5	90.6	62.7	47.0	19.5	9.8	2.1
2006............................	57.0	30.2	60.4	94.7	98.2	99.0	100.0	90.1	78.1	74.6	43.0	14.9	8.5	2.4
2005............................	58.3	31.7	51.1	97.4	99.7	96.5	98.0	97.3	83.6	82.1	42.2	20.2	9.9	2.0
2004............................	60.8	33.9	57.2	96.5	99.8	99.9	97.1	96.9	83.5	83.6	49.6	23.0	10.9	2.9
2003............................	60.2	33.4	49.3	91.9	98.2	99.9	98.2	95.9	89.6	74.0	47.3	27.9	12.1	2.4
Female														
2019............................	57.6	27.2	56.7	90.2	98.9	98.2	99.2	93.3	83.9	77.4	45.4	16.3	10.6	1.2
2018............................	56.9	27.2	52.6	90.6	99.8	99.7	100.0	88.8	85.5	75.3	40.4	19.4	9.9	1.5
2017............................	56.9	27.3	56.1	97.2	98.0	98.9	100.0	94.4	86.4	78.0	44.8	17.5	6.6	1.4
2016............................	55.3	26.8	66.4	94.0	98.0	98.6	97.6	96.7	80.4	70.6	40.4	19.7	5.8	1.2
2015............................	57.4	28.0	54.4	94.4	97.5	97.8	98.5	88.7	85.2	83.8	52.5	19.8	9.6	1.9
2014............................	55.8	27.9	53.2	86.4	95.6	97.8	97.1	93.6	86.5	76.2	48.6	17.6	7.0	2.0
2013............................	57.8	29.4	57.0	90.5	97.2	98.7	99.7	98.4	83.6	76.0	44.4	15.8	9.6	2.7
2012............................	58.7	29.2	55.5	93.7	100.0	98.8	100.0	97.9	76.3	72.9	55.3	17.5	10.2	2.1
2011............................	58.3	28.7	54.9	95.7	98.5	96.2	97.9	98.3	77.1	74.8	44.0	17.4	8.7	2.6
2010............................	59.4	29.1	61.7	95.5	98.7	98.9	98.4	95.7	86.2	73.1	50.0	19.1	9.9	2.0
2009............................	59.2	27.7	55.8	95.9	97.8	96.3	95.2	98.1	88.8	73.0	55.6	19.5	11.9	1.9
2008............................	58.9	28.8	59.1	92.3	99.2	100.0	97.5	90.8	82.4	85.7	46.8	21.7	12.5	2.9
2007............................	55.5	27.4	48.3	92.5	97.6	99.5	99.7	93.2	82.2	66.1	45.0	19.7	9.2	1.5
2006............................	55.7	27.9	41.4	94.5	100.0	99.6	99.1	93.6	87.8	69.4	43.2	19.4	9.0	2.1
2005............................	57.0	29.3	57.5	93.2	99.5	98.5	99.7	99.1	89.2	71.2	46.2	21.6	8.9	2.5
2004............................	56.1	29.0	58.4	99.2	99.9	98.5	98.9	97.2	76.3	71.5	42.9	18.8	7.8	2.5
2003............................	56.2	29.3	54.2	86.0	100.0	98.7	100.0	95.4	85.1	79.7	48.8	15.8	6.9	2.1

Note: Data shown for 1947 to 1966 for the Black population are for Black and other races. Data for 1947 to 1963 exclude kindergarten. Nursery school was first collected in 1964.
* = Quantity zero or rounds to zero.
NA = Not available.
r = Revised, controlled to 1990 census based population estimates; previous 1993 data controlled to 1980 census based population estimates.
[1]Starting in 2003, respondents could identify more than one race. Except as noted, the race data in this table from 2003 onward represent those respondents who indicated only one race category.
[2]The data shown prior to 2003 consists of those identifying themselves as "Asian or Pacific Islanders."

Table A-12. Population 6 to 17 Years Old Enrolled Below Modal Grade, 1971–2019

(Numbers in thousands; percent; civilian noninstitutionalized population.)

Year, sex, race, and Hispanic origin	Percent below modal grade				Dropout rate, 15 to 17 years	Population in age group			
	6 to 8 years	9 to 11 years	12 to 14 years	15 to 17 years		6 to 8 years	9 to 11 years	12 to 14 years	15 to 17 years
ALL RACES									
Both Sexes									
2019............................	25.1	29.9	29.9	31.4	4.2	11,998	12,378	12,551	12,551
2018............................	25.5	30.0	29.4	33.1	4.4	12,231	12,353	12,474	12,547
2017............................	24.7	30.2	30.1	33.6	3.6	12,196	12,463	12,363	12,687
2016............................	24.6	30.0	30.1	31.9	3.8	12,152	12,497	12,326	12,663
2015............................	24.0	29.7	31.0	32.0	3.2	12,182	12,520	12,361	12,663
2014............................	23.3	28.6	30.8	32.7	4.1	12,320	12,286	12,433	12,502
2013............................	23.0	26.5	31.1	32.9	3.7	12,405	12,246	12,448	12,422
2012............................	24.0	28.2	30.7	34.5	2.4	12,185	12,236	12,435	12,554
2011............................	22.8	28.8	29.8	32.5	2.3	12,643	12,408	11,834	12,282
2010............................	18.8	25.1	29.1	29.8	2.2	12,618	12,190	11,963	12,273
2009............................	19.4	26.8	30.1	30.8	3.0	12,305	11,819	12,030	12,391
2008............................	20.2	27.3	31.3	31.7	2.7	12,104	11,793	12,128	12,746
2007............................	20.1	26.2	27.9	30.0	2.9	12,011	11,805	12,398	12,857
2006............................	20.1	26.1	27.9	30.5	3.0	11,776	11,902	12,473	12,926
2005............................	20.7	25.4	28.3	30.6	2.8	11,784	11,998	12,689	13,204
2004............................	21.7	25.4	28.2	32.0	3.5	11,799	12,034	12,870	12,766
2003............................	21.3	28.1	28.8	30.6	3.2	11,866	12,124	12,951	12,753
2002............................	18.0	25.5	27.1	30.1	3.3	12,029	12,421	12,592	12,187
2001............................	18.6	23.7	25.9	29.7	3.8	11,972	12,738	12,357	12,031
2000............................	19.2	24.0	27.8	30.2	4.3	12,079	12,713	12,003	11,933
1999............................	17.4	25.3	26.5	30.8	4.0	12,159	12,537	11,921	12,048
1998............................	19.0	23.8	26.7	31.9	3.8	12,364	12,098	11,739	11,850
1997............................	18.6	24.2	28.5	32.1	3.6	12,325	11,866	11,650	11,953
1996............................	17.9	23.3	28.8	31.0	4.8	12,191	11,845	11,653	11,617
1995............................	17.5	25.6	30.8	32.8	4.1	11,728	11,812	11,582	11,401
1994............................	18.9	26.2	31.3	30.9	3.8	11,601	11,528	11,462	10,560
1993r...........................	18.7	28.1	31.0	32.3	3.8	11,363	11,283	10,981	10,247
1993............................	18.7	28.0	30.8	32.0	3.7	11,363	11,283	10,981	10,247
1992............................	19.4	28.4	30.9	30.5	3.6	11,260	11,183	10,723	10,114
1991............................	21.2	26.9	29.6	30.0	4.6	11,120	11,099	10,440	9,923
1990............................	21.5	27.6	31.0	30.1	4.7	11,015	10,914	10,152	9,912
1989............................	21.4	29.0	31.8	28.0	4.5	11,007	10,673	9,928	10,020
1988............................	20.4	28.4	28.7	26.2	5.1	10,906	10,350	9,869	10,379
1987............................	20.9	26.7	27.6	24.8	5.1	10,702	10,053	9,795	10,944
1986............................	19.2	26.5	27.3	25.8	4.9	10,389	9,959	9,908	11,149
1985............................	17.9	24.9	25.7	25.5	5.1	10,076	9,673	10,442	11,024
1984............................	16.6	23.9	27.0	24.6	5.3	9,707	9,594	10,858	10,711
1983............................	15.4	24.4	24.8	23.7	5.2	9,605	9,730	11,123	10,768
1982............................	16.6	22.8	23.9	23.0	5.4	9,492	10,169	10,989	11,131
1981............................	14.4	23.3	23.0	23.8	6.1	9,519	10,657	10,712	11,757
1980............................	14.3	20.3	22.6	22.5	6.6	9,350	10,681	10,537	11,835
1979............................	13.0	20.2	20.3	21.6	6.5	9,804	10,545	10,886	12,190
1978............................	12.4	19.5	19.2	21.8	6.5	10,246	10,448	11,391	12,346
1977............................	10.7	18.9	18.9	21.2	6.4	10,449	10,537	11,826	12,472
1976............................	10.6	18.1	19.8	22.2	6.3	10,334	10,872	12,137	12,550
1975............................	11.1	17.4	21.3	22.5	6.4	10,256	11,343	12,372	12,531
1974............................	10.3	17.8	21.7	21.6	7.1	10,343	11,789	12,415	12,566
1973............................	10.7	18.4	21.5	21.3	7.1	10,614	11,946	12,542	12,309
1972............................	10.7	19.6	21.9	22.3	6.6	11,119	12,152	12,451	12,283
1971............................	11.1	19.7	22.0	22.5	5.7	11,938	12,648	12,429	11,906
Male									
2019............................	25.4	30.3	30.9	34.1	3.9	6,117	6,290	6,398	6,388
2018............................	27.7	31.7	31.6	36.8	3.6	6,288	6,277	6,335	6,396
2017............................	25.6	31.7	32.4	36.8	4.1	6,244	6,341	6,295	6,460
2016............................	26.0	31.3	33.5	35.4	4.1	6,197	6,358	6,296	6,413
2015............................	24.8	31.0	31.5	35.6	3.3	6,201	6,398	6,302	6,464
2014............................	24.7	30.3	33.3	35.6	4.7	6,269	6,316	6,346	6,375
2013............................	24.3	30.0	34.0	37.0	3.9	6,264	6,272	6,347	6,328
2012............................	26.4	31.1	34.9	38.5	2.6	6,252	6,251	6,347	6,423
2011............................	25.2	32.2	32.7	37.1	2.4	6,478	6,326	6,067	6,256
2010............................	20.7	28.1	31.3	32.9	2.9	6,451	6,213	6,104	6,300
2009............................	20.5	30.2	33.0	34.8	3.2	6,260	6,058	6,144	6,334
2008............................	22.5	28.9	34.4	34.6	2.8	6,174	6,005	6,220	6,502
2007............................	23.0	28.1	29.8	33.7	2.9	6,159	6,031	6,310	6,572
2006............................	21.7	28.2	31.1	35.0	3.3	5,991	6,115	6,374	6,574

* = Quantity zero or rounds to zero.
r = Revised, controlled to 1990 census based population estimates; previous 1993 data controlled to 1980 census based population estimates.
[1]Starting in 2003, respondents could identify more than one race. Except as noted, the race data in this table from 2003 onward represent those respondents who indicated only one race category.
[2]The data shown prior to 2003 consists of those identifying themselves as "Asian or Pacific Islanders."

Table A-12. Population 6 to 17 Years Old Enrolled Below Modal Grade, 1971–2019—*Continued*

(Numbers in thousands; percent; civilian noninstitutionalized population.)

Year, sex, race, and Hispanic origin	Percent below modal grade				Dropout rate, 15 to 17 years	Population in age group			
	6 to 8 years	9 to 11 years	12 to 14 years	15 to 17 years		6 to 8 years	9 to 11 years	12 to 14 years	15 to 17 years
2005............................	23.2	28.6	30.7	34.3	3.0	6,014	6,126	6,523	6,645
2004............................	23.9	28.2	31.7	36.8	3.5	6,075	6,120	6,685	6,395
2003............................	23.9	32.0	31.8	35.1	3.4	6,198	6,331	6,426	6,569
2002............................	20.3	29.2	31.0	35.6	3.5	6,156	6,349	6,436	6,210
2001............................	22.1	26.1	28.7	34.0	4.3	6,147	6,540	6,311	6,182
2000............................	22.1	27.2	31.3	34.3	4.5	6,181	6,504	6,148	6,136
1999............................	18.8	28.9	30.2	36.2	3.9	6,211	6,471	6,048	6,195
1998............................	21.4	26.6	30.4	37.4	4.1	6,341	6,206	5,971	6,082
1997............................	21.9	27.7	33.4	37.8	3.7	6,295	6,112	5,932	6,126
1996............................	20.7	26.0	33.9	36.9	4.5	6,268	6,043	5,934	5,985
1995............................	20.2	28.0	35.2	38.5	3.5	5,999	6,027	5,930	5,840
1994............................	21.1	28.0	35.6	35.7	3.9	5,894	6,026	5,874	5,640
1993r..........................	21.2	32.1	35.4	40.3	3.3	5,837	5,736	5,629	5,262
1993............................	21.1	32.0	35.0	38.7	3.1	5,837	5,736	5,629	5,262
1992............................	21.6	32.6	37.0	35.2	2.7	5,738	5,742	5,502	5,166
1991............................	24.0	30.7	34.7	35.5	4.3	5,674	5,704	5,343	5,085
1990............................	23.9	32.0	36.2	35.3	4.6	5,629	5,603	5,200	5,078
1989............................	25.1	32.9	36.7	33.4	4.3	5,632	5,472	5,088	5,151
1988............................	23.5	33.2	33.7	30.6	4.8	5,580	5,298	5,065	5,286
1987............................	23.7	31.8	31.8	29.2	4.6	5,496	5,147	5,036	5,535
1986............................	22.9	30.4	32.2	30.2	4.9	5,311	5,113	5,066	5,697
1985............................	20.6	28.3	29.0	30.2	4.9	5,159	4,946	5,340	5,623
1984............................	18.8	27.7	31.1	30.2	5.5	4,963	4,905	5,521	5,469
1983............................	17.8	28.7	30.3	28.5	5.3	4,913	4,974	5,690	5,463
1982............................	19.2	26.4	28.0	27.9	5.2	4,852	5,198	5,566	5,688
1981............................	17.2	27.9	25.6	28.1	6.2	4,866	5,447	5,510	5,914
1980............................	16.4	23.4	27.3	26.8	6.4	4,774	5,453	5,282	6,067
1979............................	15.5	23.4	24.1	27.4	5.9	5,004	5,379	5,555	6,174
1978............................	14.7	22.9	22.9	26.2	6.7	5,227	5,326	5,797	6,265
1977............................	12.5	22.4	22.6	25.3	6.1	5,327	5,371	6,044	6,297
1976............................	12.5	20.9	23.4	27.5	5.7	5,265	5,540	6,185	6,356
1975............................	12.6	21.2	25.8	26.8	5.7	5,223	5,782	6,336	6,309
1974............................	12.2	21.2	25.9	26.3	7.0	5,267	6,011	6,329	6,352
1973............................	12.8	20.8	25.2	26.4	6.8	5,403	6,082	6,397	6,215
1972............................	12.5	23.3	26.8	26.8	6.2	5,662	6,188	6,322	6,232
1971............................	13.5	22.8	26.1	27.2	5.0	6,088	6,440	6,293	6,019
Female									
2019............................	24.8	29.5	28.9	28.6	4.4	5,880	6,088	6,153	6,163
2018............................	23.2	28.4	27.1	29.1	5.2	5,943	6,076	6,139	6,150
2017............................	23.7	28.8	27.8	30.3	3.1	5,952	6,122	6,068	6,227
2016............................	23.2	28.7	26.5	28.3	3.5	5,955	6,140	6,030	6,250
2015............................	23.1	28.3	30.6	28.3	3.0	5,981	6,123	6,060	6,199
2014............................	21.8	26.9	28.1	29.8	3.4	6,050	5,970	6,087	6,126
2013............................	21.6	22.8	28.0	28.7	3.4	6,141	5,974	6,100	6,095
2012............................	21.5	25.2	26.4	30.3	2.1	5,933	5,985	6,087	6,132
2011............................	20.4	25.2	26.8	27.8	2.1	6,165	6,082	5,767	6,026
2010............................	16.8	22.1	26.9	26.6	1.5	6,166	5,977	5,860	5,973
2009............................	18.2	23.2	27.2	26.7	2.8	6,046	5,761	5,886	6,057
2008............................	17.9	25.8	28.1	28.7	2.7	5,930	5,787	5,908	6,244
2007............................	17.2	24.1	25.9	26.2	2.9	5,852	5,773	6,088	6,285
2006............................	18.4	23.9	24.6	25.9	2.6	5,785	5,787	6,099	6,352
2005............................	18.2	22.0	25.8	26.8	2.6	5,769	5,872	6,167	6,559
2004............................	19.4	22.5	24.4	27.1	3.5	5,724	5,914	6,185	6,371
2003............................	18.5	23.8	25.8	25.8	3.0	5,668	5,793	6,524	6,184
2002............................	15.6	21.7	23.0	24.4	3.1	5,872	6,072	6,156	5,977
2001............................	14.9	21.3	23.0	25.2	3.3	5,825	6,197	6,046	5,849
2000............................	16.1	20.6	24.2	25.8	4.2	5,807	6,200	5,855	5,797
1990............................	16.1	21.6	22.7	25.1	4.2	5,948	6,066	5,872	5,852
1998............................	16.5	20.9	22.8	26.2	3.5	6,023	5,892	5,768	5,768
1997............................	15.1	20.4	23.3	26.1	3.5	6,030	5,754	5,718	5,827
1996............................	14.9	20.4	23.4	24.7	5.3	5,923	5,802	5,719	5,632
1995............................	14.6	23.1	26.0	26.7	4.4	5,728	5,786	5,653	5,552
1994............................	16.5	24.2	26.7	24.8	3.6	5,705	5,644	5,666	5,384
1993r..........................	16.3	24.0	26.4	26.4	4.4	5,526	5,545	5,353	4,984
1993............................	16.1	23.9	26.2	24.9	4.3	5,526	5,545	5,353	4,984
1992............................	17.1	23.5	24.6	25.6	4.5	5,523	5,441	5,220	4,947
1991............................	18.2	22.8	24.6	24.2	5.1	5,445	5,395	5,098	4,838

* = Quantity zero or rounds to zero.
r = Revised, controlled to 1990 census based population estimates; previous 1993 data controlled to 1980 census based population estimates.
[1]Starting in 2003, respondents could identify more than one race. Except as noted, the race data in this table from 2003 onward represent those respondents who indicated only one race category.
[2]The data shown prior to 2003 consists of those identifying themselves as "Asian or Pacific Islanders."

Table A-12. Population 6 to 17 Years Old Enrolled Below Modal Grade, 1971–2019—*Continued*

(Numbers in thousands; percent; civilian noninstitutionalized population.)

Year, sex, race, and Hispanic origin	Percent below modal grade				Dropout rate, 15 to 17 years	Population in age group			
	6 to 8 years	9 to 11 years	12 to 14 years	15 to 17 years		6 to 8 years	9 to 11 years	12 to 14 years	15 to 17 years
1990	19.1	23.2	25.7	24.7	4.7	5,387	5,312	4,951	4,834
1989	18.1	22.6	26.6	22.3	4.6	5,375	5,201	4,840	4,869
1988	17.3	23.6	23.4	21.7	5.4	5,327	5,052	4,803	5,093
1987	17.8	21.5	23.2	20.2	5.6	5,206	4,906	4,759	5,408
1986	15.2	22.4	22.1	21.1	4.9	5,078	4,846	4,842	5,452
1985	15.1	21.4	22.1	20.6	5.5	4,917	4,727	5,102	5,401
1984	14.2	19.8	22.9	18.7	5.1	4,744	4,689	5,337	5,242
1983	12.9	19.9	19.1	18.6	5.2	4,692	4,756	5,433	5,305
1982	13.8	19.0	19.7	17.9	5.7	4,640	4,971	5,423	5,443
1981	11.6	18.4	20.1	19.6	6.1	4,653	5,210	5,202	5,843
1980	12.1	17.0	17.8	18.0	6.7	4,576	5,228	5,255	5,768
1979	10.4	16.9	16.4	15.6	7.1	4,800	5,166	5,331	6,016
1978	10.1	16.0	15.3	17.2	6.4	5,019	5,122	5,594	6,081
1977	8.9	15.2	15.0	17.1	6.6	5,122	5,166	5,782	6,175
1976	8.6	15.1	16.0	16.8	7.0	5,069	5,332	5,952	6,194
1975	9.4	13.5	16.7	18.2	7.2	5,033	5,561	6,036	6,222
1974	8.3	14.4	17.4	16.8	7.1	5,076	5,778	6,086	6,214
1973	8.7	15.8	16.5	16.1	7.4	5,211	5,864	6,145	6,094
1972	8.9	15.7	17.0	17.7	7.1	5,457	5,964	6,129	6,051
1971	8.7	12.3	17.8	17.6	6.5	5,850	6,208	6,136	5,887
WHITE ALONE									
Both Sexes									
2019	25.9	30.6	29.6	31.3	4.2	8,673	8,834	9,111	9,115
2018	25.1	30.1	30.0	32.6	3.8	8,723	8,925	9,095	9,147
2017	25.4	30.0	30.3	33.3	3.6	8,720	9,036	9,077	9,210
2016	25.2	30.1	30.6	32.2	4.1	8,772	9,060	9,073	9,267
2015	24.5	30.0	31.4	32.0	3.2	8,865	9,038	9,095	9,271
2014	24.0	28.3	29.9	31.9	3.9	8,983	9,035	9,181	9,220
2013	23.2	27.1	31.8	33.3	3.7	9,014	9,034	9,236	9,228
2012	24.4	28.3	31.3	33.7	2.4	9,006	9,067	9,247	9,291
2011	23.6	28.7	30.6	32.5	2.2	9,488	9,401	9,020	9,337
2010	19.7	25.3	28.8	29.4	2.3	9,455	9,276	9,110	9,344
2009	19.6	26.7	29.4	29.9	3.3	9,377	9,006	9,167	9,495
2008	20.8	27.5	29.7	30.8	2.6	9,288	8,967	9,250	9,658
2007	21.3	26.2	27.6	28.3	2.8	9,118	9,021	9,432	9,834
2006	20.6	25.5	26.8	29.9	3.0	8,981	9,074	9,542	9,813
2005	21.4	23.8	28.0	29.5	2.6	8,929	9,194	9,680	10,131
2004	22.4	25.6	27.6	30.7	3.8	9,051	9,173	9,853	9,784
2003[1]	21.5	27.6	28.3	29.4	3.2	9,102	9,112	9,875	9,889
2002	18.1	25.7	26.2	29.6	3.1	9,230	9,682	9,832	9,520
2001	19.2	22.7	25.2	28.9	3.8	9,330	9,826	9,651	9,480
2000	19.4	23.7	26.3	29.7	4.5	9,404	9,937	9,368	9,449
1999	18.3	24.6	25.8	30.0	4.2	9,539	9,768	9,323	9,428
1998	19.5	23.5	25.8	30.5	3.8	9,624	9,508	9,219	9,341
1997	18.8	24.0	27.9	30.3	3.5	9,555	9,390	9,167	9,352
1996	18.1	22.6	27.6	30.1	4.9	9,458	9,420	9,184	9,135
1995	17.7	24.9	29.2	31.0	3.9	9,221	9,340	9,130	8,933
1994	19.4	25.8	30.1	29.6	3.7	9,087	9,261	9,121	8,668
1993r	18.8	27.3	29.4	31.2	3.9	9,018	8,967	8,728	8,160
1993	18.7	27.2	29.2	29.7	3.6	9,074	9,017	8,783	8,159
1992	19.5	27.5	29.6	28.1	3.5	8,956	8,996	8,520	8,031
1991	21.3	25.7	27.7	27.2	4.7	8,874	8,840	8,328	7,903
1990	21.9	26.8	28.4	27.3	4.6	8,860	8,752	8,140	7,909
1989	22.4	26.8	29.9	25.7	4.6	8,858	8,527	7,994	8,026
1988	21.0	27.6	27.2	23.9	5.4	8,758	8,323	7,929	8,353
1987	21.1	25.9	26.0	22.7	5.1	8,606	8,117	7,846	8,887
1986	19.1	25.1	25.3	23.7	5.0	8,395	8,000	8,054	9,037
1985	18.0	23.3	23.3	23.0	5.3	8,136	7,840	8,429	9,045
1984	16.3	22.1	24.7	22.7	5.6	7,915	7,781	8,827	8,853
1983	15.5	22.4	23.1	21.1	5.4	7,821	7,906	9,152	8,831
1982	16.4	21.8	22.1	21.1	5.6	7,729	8,294	9,035	9,184
1981	14.7	22.2	21.0	21.6	6.1	7,782	8,741	8,813	9,762
1980	14.1	19.0	21.1	19.3	6.7	7,635	8,823	8,739	10,132
1979	12.9	18.4	18.5	19.4	6.5	8,041	8,747	9,026	10,239
1978	12.4	18.0	17.9	19.3	6.8	8,460	8,686	9,522	10,358
1977	10.6	17.7	17.5	19.3	6.6	8,675	8,771	9,918	10,510

* = Quantity zero or rounds to zero.
r = Revised, controlled to 1990 census based population estimates; previous 1993 data controlled to 1980 census based population estimates.
[1]Starting in 2003, respondents could identify more than one race. Except as noted, the race data in this table from 2003 onward represent those respondents who indicated only one race category.
[2]The data shown prior to 2003 consists of those identifying themselves as "Asian or Pacific Islanders."

Table A-12. Population 6 to 17 Years Old Enrolled Below Modal Grade, 1971–2019—*Continued*

(Numbers in thousands; percent; civilian noninstitutionalized population.)

Year, sex, race, and Hispanic origin	Percent below modal grade				Dropout rate, 15 to 17 years	Population in age group			
	6 to 8 years	9 to 11 years	12 to 14 years	15 to 17 years		6 to 8 years	9 to 11 years	12 to 14 years	15 to 17 years
1976	10.5	17.2	18.7	19.7	6.3	8,612	9,066	10,187	10,622
1975	11.0	16.0	20.0	20.4	6.3	8,566	9,486	10,466	10,583
1974	10.2	16.5	19.7	19.4	6.9	8,656	9,912	10,508	10,678
1973	10.6	17.3	19.9	19.1	7.0	8,929	10,117	10,704	10,481
1972	10.3	18.2	20.1	20.0	6.6	9,359	10,313	10,606	10,506
1971	10.5	18.3	20.4	19.9	5.5	9,988	10,692	10,682	10,231
Male									
2019	26.0	31.0	31.1	33.6	3.8	4,440	4,517	4,662	4,655
2018	27.8	32.7	31.6	36.6	3.6	4,465	4,564	4,656	4,671
2017	26.9	32.7	32.7	35.7	4.0	4,460	4,622	4,643	4,704
2016	27.2	31.0	33.5	36.7	4.3	4,486	4,637	4,639	4,737
2015	26.3	31.5	32.2	35.7	3.6	4,535	4,628	4,650	4,742
2014	25.5	30.0	32.3	35.2	4.5	4,600	4,629	4,703	4,721
2013	25.6	30.6	34.7	37.2	4.2	4,618	4,626	4,733	4,726
2012	26.2	30.9	36.0	38.2	2.8	4,615	4,642	4,741	4,764
2011	26.2	31.9	33.5	37.7	2.2	4,861	4,816	4,626	4,809
2010	22.1	28.0	30.9	32.4	3.0	4,825	4,746	4,666	4,805
2009	20.9	29.8	32.2	33.4	3.5	4,816	4,611	4,697	4,866
2008	23.1	29.8	32.9	34.2	2.7	4,764	4,568	4,748	4,966
2007	24.3	28.4	29.5	31.8	2.9	4,671	4,620	4,851	5,022
2006	22.5	27.0	29.8	34.2	3.3	4,596	4,652	4,900	5,011
2005	24.3	27.4	31.0	33.2	2.7	4,576	4,715	4,995	5,116
2004	24.9	28.0	31.4	35.2	3.8	4,706	4,647	5,168	4,905
2003[1]	24.4	31.6	31.2	34.0	3.4	4,785	4,795	4,961	5,026
2002	21.7	29.5	30.4	34.7	3.2	4,737	4,965	5,044	4,875
2001	22.7	25.3	28.3	32.8	4.4	4,789	5,040	4,949	4,862
2000	22.5	27.6	29.6	34.0	4.4	4,815	5,094	4,798	4,861
1999	19.9	28.2	29.7	35.8	4.2	4,883	5,009	4,777	4,851
1998	21.9	26.4	30.2	36.2	4.4	4,930	4,879	4,728	4,815
1997	22.3	27.8	32.7	37.0	3.8	4,897	4,819	4,702	4,821
1996	20.8	25.9	32.3	36.5	4.5	4,849	4,836	4,706	4,694
1995	20.5	28.0	33.4	36.5	3.8	4,727	4,797	4,680	4,592
1994	22.0	27.9	34.4	35.2	4.0	4,659	4,758	4,679	4,457
1993r	21.4	31.8	33.8	37.6	3.2	4,625	4,601	4,476	4,178
1993	21.4	31.6	33.6	36.1	3.1	4,662	4,614	4,485	4,178
1992	21.5	31.8	35.8	32.4	2.8	4,602	4,607	4,359	4,115
1991	24.4	29.1	32.5	32.5	4.2	4,556	4,568	4,270	4,047
1990	24.6	31.3	33.3	32.6	4.8	4,555	4,482	4,186	4,054
1989	26.0	32.1	35.0	30.8	4.6	4,544	4,378	4,112	4,107
1988	24.7	32.8	32.2	28.8	5.1	4,493	4,272	4,062	4,281
1987	24.6	30.5	30.4	26.6	4.5	4,416	4,167	4,009	4,504
1986	22.9	28.9	30.1	27.9	5.2	4,307	4,108	4,125	4,624
1985	21.1	26.5	26.7	28.0	4.9	4,175	4,024	4,307	4,634
1984	18.1	25.8	28.7	28.1	5.8	4,061	3,994	4,501	4,542
1983	18.1	26.3	28.0	26.3	5.6	4,002	4,054	4,697	4,481
1982	19.3	26.2	26.2	26.1	5.3	3,956	4,260	4,591	4,711
1981	17.3	26.9	24.2	25.4	6.3	3,990	4,480	4,556	4,937
1980	16.3	21.9	25.7	23.9	6.7	3,907	4,517	4,399	5,066
1979	15.4	20.8	22.3	24.8	6.2	4,114	4,475	4,616	5,201
1978	14.7	21.2	22.0	23.1	7.2	4,328	4,441	4,843	5,287
1977	12.5	21.1	21.2	23.5	6.3	4,436	4,484	5,079	5,325
1976	12.6	20.2	22.1	24.8	5.6	4,402	4,632	5,200	5,398
1975	12.9	19.7	24.7	24.7	5.4	4,376	4,848	5,385	5,332
1974	12.1	19.5	23.7	23.8	7.0	4,422	5,066	5,383	5,402
1973	12.5	19.6	23.1	24.0	6.6	4,559	5,165	5,469	5,319
1972	12.2	21.9	24.6	24.3	6.1	4,778	5,266	5,410	5,340
1971	12.6	21.6	23.9	24.4	4.6	5,106	5,461	5,455	5,185
Female									
2019	25.8	30.2	28.1	28.8	4.5	4,233	4,317	4,449	4,461
2018	22.3	27.3	28.4	28.4	4.0	4,259	4,361	4,440	4,476
2017	23.8	27.2	27.7	30.9	3.1	4,260	4,414	4,434	4,500
2016	23.1	29.2	27.6	27.5	3.9	4,286	4,423	4,434	4,530
2015	22.7	28.4	30.6	28.1	2.7	4,330	4,410	4,445	4,529
2014	22.3	26.4	27.5	28.5	3.4	4,383	4,406	4,479	4,500
2013	20.6	23.4	28.7	29.2	3.1	4,397	4,408	4,502	4,502
2012	22.6	25.6	26.3	29.0	2.0	4,392	4,425	4,506	4,527

* = Quantity zero or rounds to zero.

r = Revised, controlled to 1990 census based population estimates; previous 1993 data controlled to 1980 census based population estimates.

[1]Starting in 2003, respondents could identify more than one race. Except as noted, the race data in this table from 2003 onward represent those respondents who indicated only one race category.

[2]The data shown prior to 2003 consists of those identifying themselves as "Asian or Pacific Islanders."

Table A-12. Population 6 to 17 Years Old Enrolled Below Modal Grade, 1971–2019—*Continued*

(Numbers in thousands; percent; civilian noninstitutionalized population.)

Year, sex, race, and Hispanic origin	Percent below modal grade				Dropout rate, 15 to 17 years	Population in age group			
	6 to 8 years	9 to 11 years	12 to 14 years	15 to 17 years		6 to 8 years	9 to 11 years	12 to 14 years	15 to 17 years
2011............................	20.8	25.4	27.6	27.0	2.2	4,627	4,585	4,394	4,528
2010............................	17.3	22.5	26.6	26.3	1.4	4,630	4,530	4,444	4,539
2009............................	18.2	23.3	26.5	26.2	3.0	4,561	4,394	4,470	4,629
2008............................	18.4	25.0	26.3	27.2	2.4	4,524	4,398	4,502	4,692
2007............................	18.2	23.9	25.7	24.6	2.7	4,447	4,401	4,582	4,812
2006............................	18.6	24.0	23.8	25.5	2.6	4,385	4,422	4,643	4,801
2005............................	18.3	20.1	24.8	25.8	2.5	4,353	4,479	4,685	5,015
2004............................	19.7	23.3	23.4	26.1	3.8	4,345	4,527	4,686	4,878
2003[1]........................	18.3	23.1	25.3	24.7	3.0	4,317	4,317	4,914	4,863
2002............................	14.4	21.7	21.9	24.3	3.0	4,493	4,717	4,788	4,645
2001............................	15.5	20.0	21.8	24.9	3.1	4,541	4,786	4,701	4,618
2000............................	16.1	19.7	22.9	25.2	4.5	4,587	4,843	4,570	4,588
1999............................	16.7	20.7	21.8	23.9	4.1	4,655	4,579	4,546	4,578
1998............................	16.9	20.5	21.2	24.4	3.2	4,694	4,629	4,491	4,527
1997............................	15.1	20.0	22.7	23.2	3.3	4,658	4,571	4,464	4,530
1996............................	15.3	19.2	22.7	23.2	5.3	4,609	4,583	4,477	4,441
1995............................	14.7	21.6	24.8	25.0	4.1	4,494	4,543	4,449	4,342
1994............................	16.7	23.5	25.7	23.6	3.4	4,427	4,504	4,443	4,212
1993r..........................	15.9	22.6	24.8	24.4	4.3	4,393	4,366	4,252	3,982
1993............................	15.8	22.5	24.6	23.1	4.2	4,412	4,404	4,298	3,982
1992............................	17.3	22.9	23.2	23.6	4.3	4,354	4,389	4,161	3,916
1991............................	18.1	22.1	22.6	21.5	5.2	4,318	4,272	4,058	3,856
1990............................	19.0	22.2	23.2	21.8	4.5	4,305	4,270	3,954	3,855
1989............................	18.6	21.3	24.5	20.3	4.7	4,314	4,149	3,882	3,919
1988............................	17.1	22.2	21.9	18.8	5.6	4,265	4,051	3,867	4,072
1987............................	17.3	21.0	21.3	18.7	5.8	4,191	3,950	3,777	4,383
1986............................	15.0	21.1	20.2	19.3	4.8	4,088	3,892	3,929	4,413
1985............................	14.8	19.9	19.7	17.6	5.7	3,961	3,816	4,122	4,411
1984............................	14.3	18.3	20.5	17.0	5.4	3,854	3,787	4,326	4,311
1983............................	12.7	18.3	17.9	15.8	5.2	3,819	3,852	4,455	4,350
1982............................	13.4	17.2	17.8	15.8	6.0	3,773	4,034	4,444	4,473
1981............................	11.9	17.3	17.6	17.6	5.9	3,792	4,261	4,257	4,825
1980............................	11.7	16.0	16.5	14.7	6.6	3,728	4,306	4,340	5,066
1979............................	10.3	15.8	14.5	13.8	6.9	3,927	4,272	4,410	5,038
1978............................	10.0	14.7	13.7	15.2	6.4	4,132	4,245	4,679	5,071
1977............................	8.5	14.1	13.7	14.9	6.8	4,239	4,287	4,839	5,185
1976............................	8.4	14.1	15.1	14.5	6.9	4,210	4,434	4,987	5,224
1975............................	9.1	12.2	15.1	16.0	7.1	4,190	4,638	5,081	5,251
1974............................	8.2	13.4	15.5	15.0	6.7	4,234	4,846	5,125	5,276
1973............................	8.5	14.8	16.5	14.0	7.4	4,370	4,952	5,235	5,162
1972............................	8.3	14.2	15.4	15.5	7.2	4,581	5,047	5,196	5,166
1971............................	8.4	14.9	16.6	15.2	6.3	4,882	5,231	5,227	5,046
WHITE ALONE NON-HISPANIC									
Both Sexes									
2019............................	26.7	30.8	30.5	30.0	3.7	5,955	6,102	6,338	6,501
2018............................	25.4	31.8	31.2	30.8	3.5	5,998	6,188	6,394	6,594
2017............................	26.3	32.0	28.4	33.5	3.3	5,968	6,291	6,497	6,739
2016............................	25.6	29.8	30.8	31.4	4.4	6,038	6,340	6,533	6,757
2015............................	25.6	29.9	30.8	30.8	2.7	6,185	6,411	6,574	6,806
2014............................	24.6	28.6	29.5	30.7	4.0	6,300	6,443	6,656	6,829
2013............................	23.2	25.8	30.9	32.1	3.6	6,287	6,489	6,752	6,865
2012............................	25.2	28.1	31.5	32.3	2.2	6,366	6,552	6,812	6,916
2011............................	25.0	29.0	31.1	30.8	1.8	6,648	6,765	6,750	7,033
2010............................	21.0	25.3	28.5	27.6	2.2	6,707	6,836	6,821	7,243
2009............................	19.9	26.6	29.7	29.0	2.8	6,768	6,755	6,989	7,437
2008............................	21.6	28.0	29.8	29.4	2.2	6,798	6,768	7,008	7,534
2007............................	21.3	25.3	26.5	26.8	2.1	6,763	6,783	7,182	7,784
2006............................	20.5	24.5	25.1	28.6	2.3	6,748	6,887	7,368	7,827
2005............................	22.4	23.2	26.3	29.0	2.1	6,728	7,052	7,584	8,150
2004	22.7	25.1	27.0	29.8	3.3	6,878	7,090	7,768	7,892
2003[1]........................	21.8	27.1	27.3	28.7	2.8	7,006	7,102	7,889	7,980
2002............................	18.9	24.9	25.8	28.1	2.5	7,118	7,627	7,913	7,803
2001............................	19.9	23.1	25.3	28.1	3.1	7,325	7,726	7,773	7,829
2000............................	19.4	23.7	26.1	28.8	3.5	7,418	8,045	7,727	7,852
1999............................	18.9	24.2	25.3	28.9	3.6	7,717	7,938	7,669	7,879
1998............................	20.5	23.7	26.0	28.9	3.0	7,755	7,794	7,697	7,859

* = Quantity zero or rounds to zero.
r = Revised, controlled to 1990 census based population estimates; previous 1993 data controlled to 1980 census based population estimates.
[1]Starting in 2003, respondents could identify more than one race. Except as noted, the race data in this table from 2003 onward represent those respondents who indicated only one race category.
[2]The data shown prior to 2003 consists of those identifying themselves as "Asian or Pacific Islanders."

Table A-12. Population 6 to 17 Years Old Enrolled Below Modal Grade, 1971–2019—*Continued*

(Numbers in thousands; percent; civilian noninstitutionalized population.)

Year, sex, race, and Hispanic origin	Percent below modal grade				Dropout rate, 15 to 17 years	Population in age group			
	6 to 8 years	9 to 11 years	12 to 14 years	15 to 17 years		6 to 8 years	9 to 11 years	12 to 14 years	15 to 17 years
1997............................	19.7	24.6	27.3	28.4	3.2	7,729	7,775	7,789	7,866
1996............................	18.8	22.7	26.2	28.6	4.2	7,803	7,792	7,731	7,716
1995............................	18.2	24.5	28.0	29.2	3.4	7,853	8,000	7,872	7,795
1994............................	19.8	25.6	30.0	28.0	3.1	7,779	7,864	7,845	7,490
1993............................	18.8	27.2	28.8	29.5	3.0	7,736	7,802	7,600	7,022
Male									
2019............................	27.3	31.4	32.8	31.9	3.5	3,055	3,128	3,235	3,327
2018............................	27.9	35.4	33.4	34.3	3.5	3,104	3,176	3,276	3,383
2017............................	28.8	34.6	31.2	36.9	3.6	3,064	3,225	3,323	3,447
2016............................	28.2	31.7	33.2	35.0	4.9	3,086	3,251	3,360	3,467
2015............................	28.3	32.3	31.3	34.4	2.9	3,150	3,289	3,390	3,479
2014............................	25.8	29.6	32.3	33.4	4.6	3,218	3,303	3,412	3,487
2013............................	25.5	29.0	33.6	36.8	4.2	3,232	3,320	3,474	3,515
2012............................	26.6	31.7	36.9	37.7	2.8	3,264	3,371	3,518	3,545
2011............................	28.7	32.8	34.4	36.9	1.9	3,394	3,473	3,472	3,619
2010............................	24.3	28.5	31.2	31.7	3.1	3,414	3,498	3,487	3,728
2009............................	22.4	30.3	32.4	33.4	3.1	3,489	3,453	3,593	3,793
2008............................	24.8	30.3	33.6	33.0	2.4	3,485	3,459	3,599	3,862
2007............................	24.1	28.4	28.1	30.3	2.2	3,457	3,473	3,715	3,970
2006............................	23.1	26.0	27.6	32.4	2.9	3,449	3,537	3,775	3,984
2005............................	25.4	26.8	28.2	32.5	2.2	3,450	3,618	3,902	4,136
2004	25.0	27.9	30.6	35.0	3.4	3,548	3,605	4,054	3,994
2003[1].........................	24.6	31.7	30.7	33.4	2.9	3,668	3,725	3,960	4,101
2002............................	22.7	29.0	30.7	33.6	2.4	3,667	3,969	4,005	4,038
2001............................	23.1	26.2	28.5	31.6	3.7	3,808	3,971	3,920	4,020
2000............................	22.5	27.7	30.0	33.4	3.4	3,795	4,135	3,970	4,034
1999............................	20.3	27.7	29.7	35.1	3.5	3,955	4,076	3,913	4,058
1998............................	23.1	26.5	30.8	34.3	3.6	4,016	4,003	3,894	3,981
1997............................	24.1	29.0	32.5	35.3	3.8	3,977	3,971	3,996	4,020
1996............................	22.5	25.9	30.8	35.1	4.1	3,964	4,035	3,957	3,959
1995............................	22.1	27.3	31.9	34.9	3.1	4,038	4,094	4,017	4,010
1994............................	22.8	28.0	34.3	33.6	2.9	3,993	4,010	4,030	3,866
1993............................	22.0	31.5	33.2	35.6	2.4	3,952	4,021	3,889	3,578
Female									
2019............................	26.2	30.3	28.2	27.9	4.0	2,900	2,973	3,102	3,175
2018............................	22.7	28.0	28.9	27.1	3.5	2,894	3,011	3,118	3,211
2017............................	23.6	29.2	25.5	29.9	3.0	2,904	3,066	3,173	3,293
2016............................	22.9	27.7	28.2	27.6	3.9	2,952	3,089	3,173	3,290
2015............................	22.7	27.4	30.2	27.2	2.6	3,035	3,122	3,184	3,327
2014............................	23.4	27.5	26.7	28.0	3.3	3,082	3,141	3,245	3,342
2013............................	20.7	22.4	28.1	27.3	3.0	3,055	3,169	3,279	3,350
2012............................	23.8	24.4	25.7	26.8	1.5	3,102	3,181	3,295	3,371
2011............................	21.1	24.9	27.5	24.3	1.7	3,254	3,292	3,278	3,414
2010............................	17.6	22.0	25.8	23.4	1.3	3,294	3,338	3,334	3,515
2009............................	17.3	22.8	26.8	24.4	2.4	3,280	3,301	3,396	3,644
2008............................	18.3	25.5	25.7	25.6	2.1	3,313	3,309	3,408	3,673
2007............................	18.4	22.0	24.7	23.1	2.0	3,306	3,310	3,467	3,814
2006............................	17.6	22.8	22.6	24.6	1.8	3,299	3,350	3,593	3,843
2005............................	19.2	19.4	24.2	25.3	2.0	3,277	3,434	3,682	4,014
2004	20.3	22.2	23.1	24.5	3.3	3,330	3,485	3,714	3,898
2003[1].........................	18.6	22.2	24.0	23.7	2.6	3,337	3,377	3,929	3,878
2002............................	14.8	20.4	20.9	22.2	2.6	3,451	3,658	3,908	3,765
2001............................	16.4	19.8	22.0	24.4	2.6	3,517	3,755	3,853	3,809
2000............................	16.2	19.6	21.9	23.9	3.7	3,623	3,910	3,757	3,818
1999............................	17.4	20.5	20.8	22.3	3.6	3,761	3,864	3,757	3,840
1998............................	17.6	20.8	21.2	23.5	2.5	3,740	3,791	3,803	3,878
1997............................	15.0	19.9	21.8	21.3	2.6	3,752	3,804	3,793	3,846
1996............................	15.0	19.3	21.3	21.7	4.3	3,839	3,757	3,773	3,757
1995............................	14.1	21.5	23.8	23.1	3.0	3,815	3,906	3,854	3,784
1994............................	16.6	23.1	25.5	22.1	3.2	3,786	3,854	3,814	3,624
1993............................	15.4	22.6	24.2	23.1	3.6	3,784	3,782	3,710	3,444
BLACK ALONE									
Both Sexes									
2019............................	22.3	30.1	35.7	33.8	4.7	1,816	1,884	1,881	1,807
2018............................	28.5	32.0	28.3	37.4	7.5	1,862	1,901	1,847	1,830

* = Quantity zero or rounds to zero.
r = Revised, controlled to 1990 census based population estimates; previous 1993 data controlled to 1980 census based population estimates.
[1]Starting in 2003, respondents could identify more than one race. Except as noted, the race data in this table from 2003 onward represent those respondents who indicated only one race category.
[2]The data shown prior to 2003 consists of those identifying themselves as "Asian or Pacific Islanders."

Table A-12. Population 6 to 17 Years Old Enrolled Below Modal Grade, 1971–2019—*Continued*

(Numbers in thousands; percent; civilian noninstitutionalized population.)

Year, sex, race, and Hispanic origin	Percent below modal grade				Dropout rate, 15 to 17 years	Population in age group			
	6 to 8 years	9 to 11 years	12 to 14 years	15 to 17 years		6 to 8 years	9 to 11 years	12 to 14 years	15 to 17 years
2017	23.8	32.8	32.7	37.4	4.4	1,962	1,814	1,818	1,873
2016	24.2	33.9	30.9	33.2	2.8	1,877	1,878	1,817	1,895
2015	22.3	28.9	32.3	35.6	3.1	1,794	1,913	1,831	1,899
2014	22.2	32.2	35.5	38.1	5.2	1,772	1,822	1,871	1,869
2013	24.7	28.0	32.2	36.0	4.6	1,885	1,781	1,892	1,865
2012	25.3	28.5	35.6	38.3	2.6	1,719	1,828	1,897	1,879
2011	20.9	30.6	29.4	33.6	2.7	1,882	1,831	1,773	1,855
2010	17.2	26.8	33.4	32.7	2.2	1,871	1,710	1,809	1,911
2009	20.5	31.6	33.1	36.5	2.7	1,692	1,814	1,801	1,943
2008	19.1	27.6	41.6	39.4	3.1	1,781	1,797	1,851	1,994
2007	17.7	28.1	33.0	39.2	3.0	1,797	1,770	1,937	2,021
2006	19.1	29.9	35.7	35.7	3.1	1,813	1,811	1,960	2,059
2005	20.8	35.6	34.1	38.8	4.2	1,806	1,826	2,011	2,085
2004	19.8	27.4	34.1	40.1	2.3	1,775	1,906	2,034	1,992
2003[1]	22.7	34.2	33.9	37.4	3.7	1,760	2,043	2,110	1,950
2002	19.6	28.6	32.8	36.2	3.9	2,017	2,048	2,036	1,943
2001	17.3	29.7	31.1	35.6	4.0	1,937	2,144	1,998	1,823
2000	19.6	26.9	37.8	34.6	4.7	1,976	2,082	1,961	1,852
1999	16.1	30.2	31.7	34.8	3.5	1,948	2,108	1,912	1,911
1998	18.3	26.6	31.4	38.4	3.6	2,068	1,968	1,868	1,892
1997	18.4	26.1	33.5	40.0	3.8	2,061	1,908	1,845	1,938
1996	18.4	29.2	36.8	36.9	4.8	2,054	1,847	1,839	1,858
1995	16.8	31.1	38.3	41.3	4.1	1,909	1,890	1,822	1,851
1994	18.4	35.1	36.1	37.7	3.3	1,912	1,795	1,835	1,809
1993r	20.0	33.6	34.8	45.1	3.6	1,767	1,763	1,747	1,641
1993	19.9	33.4	38.8	43.3	3.6	1,709	1,710	1,695	1,642
1992	20.6	28.7	38.0	40.6	4.2	1,761	1,635	1,686	1,621
1991	21.0	34.3	40.7	43.4	5.3	1,674	1,701	1,643	1,574
1990	21.9	33.1	46.1	42.9	5.2	1,645	1,712	1,574	1,571
1989	19.6	34.0	41.3	39.3	3.9	1,642	1,682	1,554	1,618
1988	18.6	33.1	37.6	38.4	4.7	1,680	1,629	1,545	1,637
1987	19.8	33.1	35.6	35.3	5.1	1,679	1,554	1,552	1,654
1986	12.7	34.6	38.5	38.3	4.6	1,611	1,542	1,530	1,692
1985	18.0	33.9	37.9	37.7	4.6	1,568	1,498	1,635	1,627
1984	17.9	32.3	38.1	34.6	4.1	1,445	1,442	1,652	1,536
1983	15.3	34.9	34.4	35.8	4.7	1,429	1,450	1,601	1,617
1982	17.2	27.1	32.5	32.6	4.6	1,765	1,874	1,953	1,947
1981	13.9	26.2	33.7	36.1	6.3	1,437	1,594	1,615	1,679
1980	14.9	27.8	30.5	37.6	5.1	1,460	1,606	1,568	1,728
1979	12.5	29.5	29.2	34.3	6.4	1,515	1,576	1,636	1,722
1978	12.6	27.8	26.6	35.4	5.7	1,557	1,523	1,664	1,764
1977	11.3	24.9	26.3	32.2	5.4	1,552	1,558	1,698	1,754
1976	10.5	23.2	26.1	35.6	6.7	1,493	1,633	1,724	1,726
1975	11.9	26.1	29.2	34.9	8.0	1,489	1,656	1,720	1,760
1974	11.6	26.2	33.2	34.4	8.2	1,509	1,684	1,750	1,682
1973	12.0	25.8	31.7	35.4	8.2	1,525	1,650	1,671	1,671
1972	13.2	30.5	33.1	37.3	6.6	1,585	1,638	1,691	1,636
1971	14.2	27.9	34.7	40.2	7.0	1,794	1,787	1,638	1,533
Male									
2019	25.7	30.7	33.4	39.2	5.7	896	939	951	905
2018	31.8	31.2	32.5	39.7	5.0	950	960	934	917
2017	23.8	31.6	35.9	43.0	5.4	990	908	919	939
2016	22.2	36.2	36.6	31.0	2.4	962	931	918	952
2015	18.9	30.1	33.9	39.4	2.2	903	971	927	954
2014	23.2	34.1	38.3	40.2	4.6	883	959	948	939
2013	22.1	30.2	36.8	41.8	3.8	921	905	961	936
2012	29.3	33.6	37.7	40.3	1.4	918	911	963	943
2011	21.5	35.7	32.9	36.3	4.1	977	902	898	927
2010	17.4	31.5	35.2	37.0	3.0	954	856	912	961
2009	19.4	35.8	35.1	44.4	2.6	805	954	911	980
2008	19.8	26.6	47.0	43.1	3.4	917	908	934	992
2007	22.7	31.6	35.4	43.5	2.2	946	886	964	1,027
2006	20.3	35.1	40.3	43.9	3.3	929	920	991	1,032
2005	22.6	37.9	35.8	43.0	5.2	912	913	1,011	1,041
2004	21.0	31.4	37.8	46.5	2.0	885	992	1,012	1,009
2003[1]	23.6	36.8	38.7	43.4	3.9	927	1,059	975	1,047
2002	17.5	32.5	37.0	44.7	5.0	1,044	1,036	1,012	973

* = Quantity zero or rounds to zero.
r = Revised, controlled to 1990 census based population estimates; previous 1993 data controlled to 1980 census based population estimates.
[1]Starting in 2003, respondents could identify more than one race. Except as noted, the race data in this table from 2003 onward represent those respondents who indicated only one race category.
[2]The data shown prior to 2003 consists of those identifying themselves as "Asian or Pacific Islanders."

Table A-12. Population 6 to 17 Years Old Enrolled Below Modal Grade, 1971–2019—*Continued*

(Numbers in thousands; percent; civilian noninstitutionalized population.)

Year, sex, race, and Hispanic origin	Percent below modal grade				Dropout rate, 15 to 17 years	Population in age group			
	6 to 8 years	9 to 11 years	12 to 14 years	15 to 17 years		6 to 8 years	9 to 11 years	12 to 14 years	15 to 17 years
2001..............................	21.1	31.1	33.3	42.8	3.5	978	1,108	1,010	924
2000..............................	20.8	27.5	43.3	37.0	6.4	1,003	1,057	994	941
1999..............................	15.9	34.2	36.3	37.6	3.0	964	1,085	969	992
1998..............................	20.9	29.3	33.3	41.9	3.0	1,054	994	946	968
1997..............................	21.3	29.3	39.4	43.8	3.1	1,019	994	934	979
1996..............................	21.3	30.4	45.1	43.2	4.5	1,054	925	931	943
1995..............................	18.8	31.2	45.0	47.5	2.9	982	944	922	952
1994..............................	19.4	30.3	39.9	39.8	3.2	951	928	928	898
1993r.............................	21.8	36.5	44.3	53.0	2.5	903	884	891	832
1993..............................	21.6	36.5	44.2	51.8	2.5	864	857	867	832
1992..............................	24.5	28.7	44.5	47.0	2.8	864	862	860	813
1991..............................	22.9	39.6	46.2	50.6	5.4	846	878	839	790
1990..............................	23.2	37.3	52.7	49.1	4.3	828	877	791	795
1989..............................	21.7	38.8	44.8	46.7	2.8	831	858	785	828
1988..............................	18.9	37.2	43.7	41.4	4.1	851	828	780	828
1987..............................	21.6	41.1	39.7	42.3	4.9	861	770	802	818
1986..............................	15.0	39.0	45.2	45.9	4.0	806	792	770	855
1985..............................	19.5	38.2	41.4	40.3	5.4	778	775	830	816
1984..............................	24.1	38.1	42.5	42.8	4.2	729	727	832	769
1983..............................	16.8	42.0	43.1	40.6	4.4	721	723	808	799
1982..............................	18.8	27.5	36.2	36.9	4.8	898	937	975	977
1981..............................	17.7	34.2	33.3	42.4	5.4	723	811	814	832
1980r.............................	16.8	31.8	36.2	43.3	4.9	736	807	770	876
1979..............................	14.7	37.3	33.8	43.6	4.0	762	796	828	853
1978..............................	15.4	33.0	30.3	43.1	4.1	774	767	847	870
1977..............................	12.1	29.8	31.1	35.3	4.8	776	782	858	868
1976..............................	11.5	26.1	30.9	43.3	5.7	755	816	870	855
1975..............................	12.8	30.7	32.5	40.2	7.6	743	849	845	879
1974..............................	13.5	31.0	40.9	41.1	7.2	747	858	861	849
1973..............................	14.1	29.5	38.0	42.0	8.5	752	831	837	824
1972..............................	14.5	36.8	41.3	43.8	6.6	787	828	836	818
1971..............................	18.1	30.9	38.5	47.6	7.4	890	900	810	757
Female									
2019..............................	18.7	29.5	38.1	28.6	3.8	920	945	929	903
2018..............................	25.1	32.8	23.9	34.9	9.9	912	941	914	913
2017..............................	23.8	33.9	29.5	31.9	3.3	972	906	899	933
2016..............................	26.2	31.6	25.0	35.6	3.3	915	947	899	943
2015..............................	25.8	27.6	30.7	31.8	3.9	891	942	905	945
2014..............................	21.2	30.1	32.7	36.0	5.8	890	863	923	930
2013..............................	27.1	25.7	27.5	29.9	5.4	904	877	931	929
2012..............................	20.7	23.4	33.4	36.2	3.9	801	917	934	935
2011..............................	20.2	25.5	25.8	31.0	1.4	905	930	875	928
2010..............................	16.9	22.0	31.6	28.6	1.4	917	853	897	951
2009..............................	21.5	26.9	31.1	28.5	2.8	887	860	891	963
2008..............................	18.3	28.6	36.0	35.8	2.9	864	889	917	1,003
2007..............................	12.2	24.7	30.5	34.5	3.9	851	885	972	993
2006..............................	17.7	24.7	31.0	27.5	2.8	884	891	968	1,027
2005..............................	19.0	33.3	32.4	34.7	3.3	893	913	999	1,044
2004..............................	18.6	23.1	30.5	33.4	2.6	890	914	1,022	983
2003¹.............................	21.7	31.5	39.8	30.3	3.4	833	983	1,135	903
2002..............................	22.0	24.7	28.7	27.8	2.8	973	1,012	1,024	970
2001..............................	13.3	28.2	29.0	27.9	4.5	959	1,036	988	900
2000..............................	18.2	26.4	32.0	32.3	2.9	974	1,025	968	911
1999..............................	16.3	25.8	27.0	31.6	4.0	984	1,022	944	919
1998..............................	15.6	23.8	29.6	34.6	4.3	1,014	974	922	924
1997..............................	15.9	22.8	27.4	36.0	4.5	1,041	915	911	959
1996..............................	13.4	28.1	28.4	30.3	4.9	1,000	922	909	915
1995..............................	14.8	23.6	30.9	34.6	5.3	928	946	901	898
1994..............................	17.5	29.1	32.3	35.4	3.6	961	867	908	911
1993r.............................	18.0	30.8	33.1	36.6	4.7	864	879	856	809
1993..............................	18.1	30.3	33.2	34.6	4.7	844	854	828	809
1992..............................	16.7	28.7	31.2	34.2	5.6	897	773	826	808
1991..............................	19.0	28.6	35.0	36.0	5.2	828	823	804	776
1990..............................	20.7	28.7	39.3	36.6	6.1	817	835	783	776
1989..............................	17.5	29.0	37.7	31.5	5.1	811	824	769	790
1988..............................	18.2	28.8	31.4	35.2	5.3	829	801	765	809
1987..............................	18.0	25.2	31.3	28.5	5.3	818	775	750	836

* = Quantity zero or rounds to zero.

r = Revised, controlled to 1990 census based population estimates; previous 1993 data controlled to 1980 census based population estimates.

¹Starting in 2003, respondents could identify more than one race. Except as noted, the race data in this table from 2003 onward represent those respondents who indicated only one race category.

²The data shown prior to 2003 consists of those identifying themselves as "Asian or Pacific Islanders."

Table A-12. Population 6 to 17 Years Old Enrolled Below Modal Grade, 1971–2019—*Continued*

(Numbers in thousands; percent; civilian noninstitutionalized population.)

Year, sex, race, and Hispanic origin	Percent below modal grade				Dropout rate, 15 to 17 years	Population in age group			
	6 to 8 years	9 to 11 years	12 to 14 years	15 to 17 years		6 to 8 years	9 to 11 years	12 to 14 years	15 to 17 years
1985.............................	16.6	29.3	34.2	35.1	3.8	790	723	805	811
1984.............................	11.5	26.4	33.5	26.3	4.0	716	715	820	767
1983.............................	13.8	27.8	25.5	31.2	5.0	708	727	793	818
1982.............................	15.5	26.7	28.7	28.1	4.3	867	937	978	970
1981.............................	10.1	17.9	34.2	29.9	7.1	714	783	801	847
1980.............................	12.8	23.8	25.1	31.7	5.3	724	799	798	852
1979.............................	10.4	21.5	24.5	25.2	8.7	753	780	808	869
1978.............................	9.8	22.6	22.6	27.9	7.2	783	756	817	894
1977.............................	10.6	20.0	21.3	29.1	6.0	776	776	840	886
1976.............................	9.5	20.3	21.2	28.1	7.7	738	817	854	871
1975.............................	11.0	21.3	25.9	29.6	8.3	746	807	875	881
1974.............................	9.7	21.3	25.8	27.5	9.2	762	826	889	833
1973.............................	10.0	22.1	25.4	28.9	7.9	773	819	834	847
1972.............................	11.9	24.1	25.1	30.9	6.6	798	810	855	818
1971.............................	10.4	24.9	31.0	33.1	6.7	904	887	828	776
ASIAN ALONE[2]									
Both Sexes									
2019.............................	24.7	22.4	22.2	24.7	3.5	680	631	727	704
2018.............................	20.6	25.9	22.4	22.8	5.5	713	605	651	684
2017.............................	20.3	30.0	22.7	26.8	3.8	602	664	632	717
2016.............................	21.8	22.5	22.9	27.3	2.9	642	700	628	681
2015.............................	25.2	22.2	22.5	25.5	4.8	605	691	619	644
2014.............................	13.0	25.1	26.7	28.1	1.4	618	611	625	650
2013.............................	15.1	15.0	21.3	18.7	1.2	606	630	542	615
2012.............................	17.1	19.1	17.6	30.5	1.6	590	560	591	624
2011.............................	17.4	23.7	25.0	26.5	2.4	602	582	481	536
2010.............................	9.1	20.5	22.7	19.9	3.1	618	575	495	424
2009.............................	9.3	12.2	26.8	20.6	1.5	522	491	448	421
2008.............................	17.8	23.0	26.8	20.1	4.4	491	517	482	507
2007.............................	11.3	21.9	17.0	24.2	3.7	545	534	497	463
2006.............................	15.2	19.7	20.9	23.0	3.2	425	472	490	476
2005.............................	12.8	12.2	16.3	19.1	1.2	502	429	486	457
2004	12.1	11.4	20.9	23.6	1.7	417	468	490	491
2003[1]	7.5	13.6	19.7	24.5	1.6	486	453	459	458
2002.............................	11.1	12.3	20.4	18.6	2.7	602	490	530	553
2001.............................	11.9	17.9	20.3	21.0	2.8	503	565	523	565
2000.............................	10.7	15.5	17.5	22.2	0.6	524	490	490	475
1999.............................	7.5	16.5	17.9	25.5	3.2	533	496	560	555
Male									
2019.............................	25.2	23.2	28.3	21.0	1.2	347	324	376	338
2018.............................	20.2	23.3	24.4	21.0	2.7	367	328	301	340
2017.............................	24.5	29.0	21.3	30.8	3.5	298	353	318	356
2016.............................	24.0	28.0	25.4	29.2	3.3	337	360	313	307
2015.............................	22.4	20.6	17.2	26.1	4.9	299	352	285	327
2014.............................	18.5	25.0	31.6	30.6	2.9	316	306	323	303
2013.............................	13.0	18.5	23.9	21.5	1.4	297	298	281	287
2012.............................	19.2	19.3	17.0	30.2	2.4	300	259	307	327
2011.............................	17.1	25.8	25.3	29.7	2.3	324	293	249	266
2010.............................	8.1	20.2	24.4	21.8	2.6	327	296	247	237
2009.............................	9.7	13.2	26.6	22.0	0.7	272	232	227	233
2008.............................	25.1	20.8	24.5	17.9	2.4	227	257	249	253
2007.............................	7.6	20.5	18.2	26.0	4.0	278	272	240	246
2006.............................	14.3	18.4	23.5	21.7	3.3	206	256	264	227
2005.............................	12.3	13.8	13.2	18.1	1.6	261	202	265	228
2004	10.9	16.0	20.9	23.5	2.4	220	216	282	231
2003[1]	7.3	15.9	20.3	19.3	-	226	223	261	231
2002.............................	9.6	12.4	23.3	18.9	1.7	274	239	267	287
2001.............................	15.2	16.6	19.0	22.2	4.9	265	294	256	313
2000.............................	14.7	14.2	16.1	30.3	1.0	286	243	267	261
1999.............................	8.4	16.4	17.6	30.3	2.2	277	269	246	276
Female									
2019.............................	24.2	21.5	15.7	28.2	5.6	333	307	351	366
2018.............................	21.0	28.9	20.7	24.6	8.2	346	276	350	344
2017.............................	16.1	31.1	24.1	22.9	4.0	304	311	314	362

* = Quantity zero or rounds to zero.
r = Revised, controlled to 1990 census based population estimates; previous 1993 data controlled to 1980 census based population estimates.
[1]Starting in 2003, respondents could identify more than one race. Except as noted, the race data in this table from 2003 onward represent those respondents who indicated only one race category.
[2]The data shown prior to 2003 consists of those identifying themselves as "Asian or Pacific Islanders."

Table A-12. Population 6 to 17 Years Old Enrolled Below Modal Grade, 1971–2019—*Continued*

(Numbers in thousands; percent; civilian noninstitutionalized population.)

Year, sex, race, and Hispanic origin	Percent below modal grade				Dropout rate, 15 to 17 years	Population in age group			
	6 to 8 years	9 to 11 years	12 to 14 years	15 to 17 years		6 to 8 years	9 to 11 years	12 to 14 years	15 to 17 years
2016............................	19.3	16.6	20.5	25.8	2.5	305	340	315	374
2015............................	27.9	24.0	26.8	24.8	4.8	305	339	334	318
2014............................	7.1	25.3	21.5	25.9	0.1	302	306	302	346
2013............................	17.2	12.0	18.6	16.3	1.0	309	332	262	327
2012............................	15.0	18.8	18.3	30.9	0.7	290	301	284	296
2011............................	17.6	21.5	24.6	23.3	2.6	278	289	232	270
2010............................	10.4	20.7	20.9	17.5	3.7	290	279	248	187
2009............................	8.7	11.4	27.0	18.9	2.4	251	259	220	188
2008............................	11.7	25.1	29.3	22.4	6.5	264	260	233	254
2007............................	15.2	23.5	15.8	22.2	3.4	268	263	257	217
2006............................	16.1	21.2	17.9	24.2	3.1	218	216	226	249
2005............................	13.4	10.8	20.0	20.1	0.9	241	227	221	229
2004	13.5	7.3	20.0	23.7	1.1	196	253	208	260
2003[1].........................	7.6	11.3	18.8	29.9	3.2	259	230	198	227
2002............................	12.4	12.2	17.5	18.2	3.7	327	251	263	266
2001............................	8.3	19.3	21.4	19.6	0.2	238	270	268	252
2000............................	5.9	16.7	19.2	12.3	0.1	239	247	224	215
1999............................	6.6	16.7	18.5	20.6	4.0	256	227	314	278
HISPANIC (OF ANY RACE)									
Both Sexes									
2019............................	23.5	30.9	26.5	33.7	5.4	3,132	3,251	3,164	3,050
2018............................	23.7	26.4	26.7	36.7	4.8	3,196	3,205	3,161	2,933
2017............................	22.9	25.6	34.2	33.6	3.9	3,164	3,215	2,999	2,913
2016............................	24.1	29.6	29.1	34.3	3.0	3,104	3,173	2,956	2,978
2015............................	21.5	30.7	31.5	34.4	4.0	3,134	3,165	2,909	2,871
2014............................	22.0	27.5	30.5	34.4	4.5	3,159	2,967	2,901	2,703
2013............................	22.5	29.8	32.9	36.0	3.6	3,117	2,926	2,868	2,662
2012............................	22.8	28.6	29.0	38.2	3.0	3,025	2,954	2,791	2,661
2011............................	20.2	28.4	29.0	37.8	3.3	3,161	2,847	2,496	2,502
2010............................	16.0	24.0	28.5	35.5	2.5	3,046	2,681	2,494	2,307
2009............................	18.6	26.7	28.9	34.1	4.7	2,893	2,524	2,418	2,254
2008............................	18.4	25.8	29.4	35.8	3.5	2,690	2,402	2,422	2,321
2007............................	20.9	28.9	31.1	34.0	5.7	2,541	2,414	2,418	2,211
2006............................	20.6	29.2	32.6	35.3	5.7	2,441	2,382	2,361	2,165
2005............................	18.1	26.2	33.2	32.1	4.9	2,390	2,317	2,322	2,202
2004	21.5	28.1	30.0	34.6	6.1	2,382	2,250	2,283	2,072
2003............................	20.2	28.7	31.3	32.7	5.2	2,280	2,221	2,167	2,063
2002............................	15.5	28.4	27.9	36.6	5.9	2,258	2,204	2,079	1,841
2001............................	16.7	22.1	25.0	34.6	6.9	2,143	2,198	2,011	1,733
2000............................	19.4	23.2	27.3	34.4	8.8	2,067	1,965	1,744	1,671
1999............................	15.7	25.9	27.9	36.5	7.3	1,902	1,922	1,734	1,653
1998............................	15.4	23.2	24.6	33.8	7.6	1,940	1,767	1,561	1,549
1997............................	15.2	21.5	31.0	41.4	5.5	1,909	1,666	1,444	1,575
1996............................	14.9	22.9	35.5	39.0	8.4	1,711	1,680	1,550	1,478
1995............................	14.4	26.1	38.5	43.6	7.4	1,597	1,628	1,496	1,373
1994............................	16.8	28.4	32.3	39.9	8.8	1,526	1,593	1,442	1,347
1993[r]..........................	18.9	29.2	33.2	42.2	8.2	1,390	1,255	1,204	1,225
1993............................	18.9	29.2	32.7	38.3	7.9	1,455	1,295	1,243	1,226
1992............................	16.2	25.3	34.3	39.9	8.1	1,272	1,371	1,141	1,110
1991............................	21.8	30.7	35.8	38.4	11.3	1,290	1,356	1,088	1,023
1990............................	21.5	34.0	37.7	39.8	9.0	1,270	1,230	1,095	1,062
1989............................	21.9	33.8	39.9	39.5	10.6	1,257	1,154	1,079	1,001
1988............................	23.2	37.0	45.0	36.8	13.7	1,248	1,107	1,052	953
1987............................	16.9	31.2	38.9	37.3	9.1	1,181	1,054	1,063	981
1986............................	19.1	33.3	42.5	35.5	11.0	1,067	1,119	1,025	1,018
1985............................	18.7	32.4	35.8	35.7	11.3	1,035	1,047	957	946
1984............................	20.2	32.7	34.7	38.5	10.7	901	829	806	816
1983............................	20.2	32.7	39.5	38.0	8.3	903	909	949	860
1982............................	21.9	32.6	37.3	37.0	10.9	823	875	924	883
1981............................	17.9	34.7	34.9	34.9	13.3	882	939	866	963
1980............................	20.8	26.1	34.8	35.8	12.6	881	949	863	889
1979............................	18.2	33.6	33.0	30.3	10.9	729	712	697	755
1978............................	19.8	29.1	33.6	37.8	12.3	723	684	666	751
1977............................	13.0	24.1	25.1	35.2	11.0	676	693	662	773

* = Quantity zero or rounds to zero.

r = Revised, controlled to 1990 census based population estimates; previous 1993 data controlled to 1980 census based population estimates.

[1] Starting in 2003, respondents could identify more than one race. Except as noted, the race data in this table from 2003 onward represent those respondents who indicated only one race category.

[2] The data shown prior to 2003 consists of those identifying themselves as "Asian or Pacific Islanders."

Table A-12. Population 6 to 17 Years Old Enrolled Below Modal Grade, 1971–2019—*Continued*

(Numbers in thousands; percent; civilian noninstitutionalized population.)

Year, sex, race, and Hispanic origin	Percent below modal grade				Dropout rate, 15 to 17 years	Population in age group			
	6 to 8 years	9 to 11 years	12 to 14 years	15 to 17 years		6 to 8 years	9 to 11 years	12 to 14 years	15 to 17 years
Male									
2019	23.5	30.4	25.5	37.4	5.1	1,613	1,660	1,593	1,567
2018	26.1	27.0	27.4	42.2	4.0	1,639	1,619	1,629	1,463
2017	22.6	27.2	36.1	35.2	5.1	1,641	1,604	1,559	1,461
2016	25.3	28.5	32.4	41.0	2.7	1,570	1,620	1,507	1,530
2015	21.0	31.0	32.1	37.3	4.6	1,595	1,608	1,492	1,512
2014	23.8	31.2	31.8	38.1	5.5	1,594	1,510	1,481	1,402
2013	24.5	34.7	35.3	38.4	4.0	1,579	1,507	1,458	1,373
2012	26.4	29.5	32.2	40.7	2.7	1,571	1,513	1,408	1,382
2011	21.0	30.7	30.5	39.6	3.0	1,605	1,465	1,290	1,294
2010	16.7	24.9	29.1	35.0	3.1	1,544	1,381	1,290	1,178
2009	16.8	28.4	32.3	34.5	4.9	1,458	1,322	1,216	1,165
2008	18.4	27.4	31.2	38.1	3.7	1,377	1,218	1,233	1,198
2007	24.3	28.5	34.1	37.4	5.9	1,302	1,252	1,217	1,130
2006	20.0	31.0	37.7	40.6	4.9	1,251	1,214	1,208	1,111
2005	20.5	29.2	39.2	37.0	4.7	1,219	1,192	1,202	1,087
2004	25.2	28.8	34.3	36.6	6.4	1,247	1,142	1,202	1,001
2003	23.0	31.2	32.3	35.9	6.2	1,205	1,178	1,081	1,020
2002	17.4	31.6	28.7	38.5	7.4	1,140	1,090	1,137	911
2001	21.2	23.4	27.8	40.8	7.7	1,065	1,128	1,093	895
2000	23.1	26.7	27.7	36.9	9.0	1,048	993	875	872
1999	17.9	29.5	29.7	38.9	7.6	973	990	893	854
1998	16.8	26.6	26.9	44.9	8.1	950	900	849	869
1997	15.3	22.3	33.7	45.8	3.7	969	863	735	836
1996	13.5	25.8	40.5	45.1	6.8	914	808	798	764
1995	11.4	31.1	42.4	47.6	7.5	794	839	776	697
1994	16.4	27.5	36.3	45.1	11.4	778	845	721	676
1993r	19.1	35.1	37.2	50.4	7.6	722	612	618	658
1993	19.1	34.3	36.9	46.0	7.3	778	637	648	658
1992	15.6	27.2	42.5	46.2	6.8	636	687	602	576
1991	22.7	31.5	43.9	42.6	10.7	651	691	544	521
1990	22.2	36.4	40.2	43.8	9.0	676	616	590	564
1989	23.7	36.1	40.0	45.2	7.8	642	584	560	511
1988	26.9	42.0	53.8	40.5	12.4	676	566	470	523
1987	19.8	31.7	44.8	38.7	6.4	600	524	569	517
1986	22.2	38.0	49.3	37.8	10.8	544	555	535	471
1985	16.7	36.8	38.4	43.4	7.8	521	527	502	449
1984	18.3	35.7	33.1	42.8	10.0	443	420	423	432
1983	22.2	38.8	45.7	41.8	8.2	445	479	479	428
1982	23.1	36.4	39.1	43.4	10.1	428	426	466	477
1981	19.9	39.8	38.0	40.0	14.3	438	480	439	495
1980	22.5	29.9	40.5	40.7	13.5	418	481	415	445
1979	19.0	34.6	36.4	31.3	8.8	368	358	349	386
1978	23.5	29.9	33.9	37.3	13.6	388	335	339	413
1977	11.5	31.4	23.3	38.4	6.7	365	325	330	406
Female									
2019	23.5	31.5	27.5	29.9	5.6	1,519	1,591	1,571	1,483
2018	21.3	25.8	25.9	31.1	5.5	1,557	1,586	1,532	1,470
2017	23.1	24.0	32.2	32.1	2.6	1,524	1,611	1,440	1,452
2016	22.8	30.8	25.7	27.2	3.3	1,534	1,553	1,449	1,448
2015	22.0	30.4	30.8	31.3	3.4	1,539	1,556	1,417	1,359
2014	20.2	23.7	29.2	30.5	3.5	1,565	1,457	1,420	1,301
2013	20.5	24.5	30.5	33.4	3.0	1,539	1,420	1,410	1,289
2012	18.9	27.6	25.8	35.5	3.3	1,454	1,441	1,382	1,279
2011	19.5	25.9	27.4	35.8	3.7	1,556	1,382	1,206	1,209
2010	15.2	23.0	27.9	36.1	2.0	1,502	1,301	1,204	1,129
2009	20.5	24.9	25.4	33.6	4.6	1,435	1,202	1,202	1,089
2008	18.4	24.1	27.5	33.3	3.2	1,313	1,184	1,189	1,123
2007	17.3	29.4	28.2	30.5	5.4	1,239	1,162	1,202	1,080
2006	21.3	27.4	27.3	29.5	6.5	1,190	1,168	1,153	1,054
2005	15.6	23.0	26.7	27.3	5.1	1,171	1,126	1,119	1,115
2004	17.6	27.3	25.1	32.8	5.7	1,135	1,108	1,080	1,070
2003	17.1	25.7	30.3	29.7	4.3	1,075	1,043	1,086	1,042
2002	13.6	25.3	27.0	32.7	4.5	1,118	1,115	942	930
2001	12.2	20.8	21.6	28.0	6.0	1,078	1,070	918	838
2000	15.7	19.7	26.9	31.8	8.6	1,020	974	869	800
1999	13.5	22.0	26.1	33.8	6.9	930	932	841	800

* = Quantity zero or rounds to zero.
r = Revised, controlled to 1990 census based population estimates; previous 1993 data controlled to 1980 census based population estimates.
[1]Starting in 2003, respondents could identify more than one race. Except as noted, the race data in this table from 2003 onward represent those respondents who indicated only one race category.
[2]The data shown prior to 2003 consists of those identifying themselves as "Asian or Pacific Islanders."

Table A-12. Population 6 to 17 Years Old Enrolled Below Modal Grade, 1971–2019—*Continued*

(Numbers in thousands; percent; civilian noninstitutionalized population.)

Year, sex, race, and Hispanic origin	Percent below modal grade				Dropout rate, 15 to 17 years	Population in age group			
	6 to 8 years	9 to 11 years	12 to 14 years	15 to 17 years		6 to 8 years	9 to 11 years	12 to 14 years	15 to 17 years
1998.............................	14.1	19.7	21.8	31.1	7.0	990	867	712	680
1997.............................	15.0	20.4	28.8	36.1	7.4	939	803	710	739
1996.............................	16.6	20.3	30.4	32.4	10.4	798	871	753	712
1995.............................	17.5	20.6	34.5	39.5	7.2	802	789	721	677
1994.............................	17.2	29.2	28.5	34.9	6.1	748	747	722	671
1993r...........................	18.9	24.2	29.0	32.3	8.7	667	643	586	567
1993.............................	18.7	24.3	28.3	29.3	8.6	678	658	597	567
1992.............................	16.8	23.4	25.0	33.1	9.6	636	684	539	534
1991.............................	20.8	29.8	27.6	34.1	12.0	639	665	544	502
1990.............................	20.7	33.2	34.9	35.3	9.0	594	614	505	498
1989.............................	20.0	31.4	39.7	33.5	13.5	615	570	519	490
1988.............................	18.7	31.8	37.8	32.3	15.3	572	541	582	430
1987.............................	13.8	30.8	32.2	35.8	12.1	581	530	494	464
1986.............................	15.9	20.7	35.1	33.5	11.2	523	564	490	547
1985.............................	20.8	27.9	33.0	28.8	14.5	514	520	455	497
1984.............................	22.1	29.6	36.6	33.6	11.5	458	409	383	384
1983.............................	18.1	25.8	33.2	34.3	8.3	458	430	470	432
1982.............................	20.8	29.0	35.6	29.6	11.8	495	449	458	406
1981.............................	16.0	29.4	31.6	29.5	12.2	444	459	427	468
1980.............................	19.2	22.2	29.5	30.9	11.7	463	468	448	444
1979.............................	17.5	32.5	29.6	29.3	13.0	361	354	348	369
1978.............................	15.5	28.4	33.3	38.5	10.7	335	349	327	338
1977.............................	14.8	17.7	26.8	31.6	15.8	311	368	332	367
WHITE ALONE OR IN COMBINATION									
Both Sexes									
2019.............................	25.4	30.1	29.3	31.2	4.1	9,268	9,497	9,686	9,730
2018.............................	25.0	30.0	30.0	32.7	3.7	9,361	9,594	9,736	9,762
2017.............................	25.1	29.7	30.3	33.3	3.4	9,320	9,694	9,618	9,720
2016.............................	24.9	29.8	30.5	32.0	4.0	9,274	9,615	9,586	9,779
2015.............................	24.4	30.3	31.2	31.9	3.1	9,492	9,632	9,658	9,802
2014.............................	24.2	28.2	29.9	32.1	3.9	9,623	9,586	9,679	9,679
2013.............................	23.1	27.3	31.3	33.1	3.6	9,664	9,574	9,754	9,681
2012.............................	24.4	28.5	30.8	33.6	2.4	9,007	9,630	9,685	9,740
2011.............................	23.6	28.8	30.4	32.6	2.1	9,956	9,824	9,378	9,652
2010.............................	19.6	25.2	28.6	29.4	2.2	9,935	9,712	9,435	9,699
2009.............................	19.7	26.7	29.6	30.0	3.2	9,887	9,345	9,515	9,832
2008.............................	20.6	27.5	29.6	30.7	2.5	9,680	9,298	9,577	10,043
2007.............................	21.1	26.1	27.4	28.5	2.8	9,502	9,326	9,734	10,169
2006.............................	20.6	25.6	26.7	29.9	3.0	9,346	9,444	9,850	10,175
2005.............................	21.1	23.9	27.9	29.4	2.6	9,314	9,588	10,026	10,479
2004.............................	22.4	25.6	27.4	30.5	3.9	9,422	9,506	10,175	10,079
2003.............................	21.7	27.4	28.1	29.4	3.2	9,447	9,446	10,194	10,151
Male									
2019.............................	25.2	30.5	30.7	33.8	3.8	4,759	4,823	4,937	4,961
2018.............................	27.3	32.5	31.7	37.1	3.4	4,780	4,858	4,977	4,969
2017.............................	26.3	31.8	32.5	35.7	3.9	4,758	4,943	4,921	4,968
2016.............................	26.8	30.7	33.4	36.5	4.3	4,731	4,923	4,922	4,998
2015.............................	26.2	31.8	31.8	35.7	3.4	4,855	4,935	4,968	5,003
2014.............................	25.6	29.7	32.3	35.4	4.6	4,945	4,931	4,960	4,948
2013.............................	25.6	31.0	34.0	36.8	4.1	4,911	4,940	4,965	4,951
2012.............................	26.5	31.1	35.6	37.9	2.8	4,898	4,966	4,935	4,979
2011.............................	26.3	31.9	33.2	37.6	2.1	5,089	5,042	4,820	4,956
2010.............................	22.0	28.0	30.7	32.3	3.0	5,039	4,970	4,824	4,996
2009.............................	21.1	29.8	32.8	33.3	3.4	5,072	4,776	4,866	5,039
2008.............................	22.8	29.7	32.6	33.7	2.7	4,963	4,744	4,934	5,163
2007.............................	24.0	28.2	29.1	32.0	2.9	4,857	4,770	4,997	5,203
2006.............................	22.4	27.2	29.6	34.1	3.4	4,769	4,842	5,042	5,193
2005.............................	23.9	27.3	30.9	33.1	2.7	4,751	4,925	5,151	5,268
2004.............................	24.9	28.1	31.2	35.1	3.9	4,876	4,823	5,318	5,043
2003.............................	24.5	31.6	31.0	33.8	3.4	4,965	4,946	5,108	5,172
Female									
2019.............................	25.6	29.7	27.9	28.4	4.5	4,509	4,674	4,749	4,768
2018.............................	22.6	27.4	28.1	28.1	4.0	4,581	4,736	4,760	4,793

* = Quantity zero or rounds to zero.
r = Revised, controlled to 1990 census based population estimates; previous 1993 data controlled to 1980 census based population estimates.
[1]Starting in 2003, respondents could identify more than one race. Except as noted, the race data in this table from 2003 onward represent those respondents who indicated only one race category.
[2]The data shown prior to 2003 consists of those identifying themselves as "Asian or Pacific Islanders."

Table A-12. Population 6 to 17 Years Old Enrolled Below Modal Grade, 1971–2019—*Continued*

(Numbers in thousands; percent; civilian noninstitutionalized population.)

Year, sex, race, and Hispanic origin	Percent below modal grade				Dropout rate, 15 to 17 years	Population in age group			
	6 to 8 years	9 to 11 years	12 to 14 years	15 to 17 years		6 to 8 years	9 to 11 years	12 to 14 years	15 to 17 years
2017............................	23.9	27.5	28.1	30.7	3.0	4,562	4,750	4,697	4,753
2016............................	22.9	28.8	27.3	27.4	3.7	4,543	4,692	4,664	4,782
2015............................	22.6	28.6	30.5	27.9	2.8	4,636	4,697	4,690	4,799
2014............................	22.8	26.6	27.3	28.8	3.2	4,678	4,655	4,718	4,731
2013............................	20.6	23.3	28.5	29.3	3.1	4,753	4,633	4,789	4,729
2012............................	22.2	25.7	25.7	29.1	1.9	4,709	4,664	4,751	4,761
2011............................	20.8	25.5	27.4	27.3	2.2	4,867	4,782	4,558	4,696
2010............................	17.1	22.4	26.5	26.4	1.4	4,896	4,743	4,610	4,703
2009............................	18.2	23.4	26.3	26.5	2.9	4,815	4,569	4,649	4,792
2008............................	18.3	25.3	26.3	27.5	2.4	4,717	4,554	4,643	4,880
2007............................	18.1	23.9	25.5	24.7	2.7	4,646	4,555	4,737	4,966
2006............................	18.7	23.8	23.6	25.5	2.6	4,577	4,602	4,808	4,982
2005............................	18.2	20.2	24.7	25.7	2.6	4,563	4,663	4,875	5,211
2004............................	19.6	23.0	23.2	25.9	3.9	4,545	4,683	4,857	5,037
2003............................	18.6	22.7	25.2	24.8	3.0	4,482	4,500	5,086	4,979
BLACK ALONE OR IN COMBINATION									
Both Sexes									
2019............................	22.3	28.6	34.0	33.4	4.3	2,210	2,303	2,188	2,201
2018............................	27.8	31.6	27.8	37.6	6.8	2,253	2,289	2,179	2,175
2017............................	23.0	31.8	32.6	36.9	4.0	2,395	2,245	2,098	2,187
2016............................	24.2	33.4	30.6	32.8	2.8	2,217	2,212	2,130	2,238
2015............................	22.4	30.4	32.3	35.6	2.7	2,146	2,321	2,148	2,144
2014............................	23.0	31.7	35.1	37.9	5.2	2,157	2,130	2,131	2,133
2013............................	24.2	28.2	30.9	35.7	4.5	2,235	2,055	2,163	2,145
2012............................	25.9	28.8	33.7	38.1	2.4	2,066	2,094	2,139	2,113
2011............................	21.6	30.7	28.6	34.2	2.5	2,186	2,061	1,945	2,003
2010............................	17.4	26.3	32.7	32.7	2.1	2,122	1,938	1,971	2,067
2009............................	21.2	30.9	33.2	36.4	2.5	1,939	2,006	2,001	2,116
2008............................	18.7	27.2	40.0	38.6	3.0	2,026	2,002	2,036	2,179
2007............................	17.6	27.3	32.1	38.8	2.8	1,998	1,950	2,071	2,146
2006............................	18.9	28.3	34.8	35.0	3.1	1,982	1,988	2,074	2,202
2005............................	20.3	34.8	33.4	37.9	4.4	1,970	1,982	2,137	2,194
2004............................	20.3	27.0	33.2	39.1	2.5	1,950	2,022	2,174	2,107
2003............................	23.2	33.5	33.4	36.8	3.8	1,921	2,183	2,220	2,034
Male									
2019............................	23.7	28.9	32.6	39.4	4.7	1,093	1,170	1,107	1,122
2018............................	29.3	31.4	32.1	41.1	4.2	1,171	1,118	1,102	1,086
2017............................	21.2	29.2	34.3	42.2	4.7	1,210	1,115	1,049	1,090
2016............................	22.4	36.2	35.5	31.8	2.7	1,138	1,093	1,083	1,135
2015............................	20.2	30.9	33.3	39.3	2.0	1,058	1,187	1,105	1,075
2014............................	22.6	33.7	38.5	40.1	5.3	1,055	1,122	1,097	1,053
2013............................	22.0	31.3	35.3	39.9	3.3	1,088	1,050	1,100	1,061
2012............................	31.0	32.4	36.1	39.4	1.4	1,095	1,061	1,085	1,047
2011............................	23.6	35.4	32.2	36.8	3.8	1,135	1,017	991	994
2010............................	17.3	30.9	34.5	36.1	3.0	1,085	961	978	1,041
2009............................	21.4	34.1	36.9	43.3	2.4	934	1,042	1,006	1,059
2008............................	20.2	26.0	45.4	41.3	3.3	1,026	1,020	1,032	1,090
2007............................	21.7	29.9	34.4	42.6	2.1	1,053	983	1,034	1,086
2006............................	20.0	33.5	39.0	42.8	3.5	1,013	1,018	1,050	1,094
2005............................	22.1	37.0	35.5	41.8	5.0	981	999	1,061	1,082
2004............................	21.1	30.6	37.3	45.3	1.9	966	1,042	1,065	1,056
2003............................	24.2	36.6	38.5	42.9	4.0	1,014	1,116	1,033	1,083
Female									
2019............................	20.8	28.2	35.4	27.3	3.7	1,117	1,133	1,081	1,079
2018............................	26.2	31.8	23.4	33.7	9.3	1,082	1,170	1,077	1,089
2017............................	24.8	34.3	30.9	31.7	3.4	1,184	1,130	1,050	1,097
2016............................	25.9	30.7	25.6	33.8	2.8	1,079	1,119	1,047	1,103
2015............................	24.5	29.9	31.4	31.8	3.5	1,088	1,134	1,044	1,069
2014............................	23.4	29.5	31.6	35.8	5.1	1,102	1,008	1,033	1,080
2013............................	26.3	24.8	26.4	31.5	5.6	1,147	1,005	1,063	1,085
2012............................	20.2	25.1	31.2	36.8	3.4	971	1,032	1,054	1,066
2011............................	19.5	26.0	24.8	31.7	1.3	1,051	1,044	954	1,009
2010............................	17.4	21.8	31.0	29.4	1.3	1,037	977	993	1,026

* = Quantity zero or rounds to zero.

r = Revised, controlled to 1990 census based population estimates; previous 1993 data controlled to 1980 census based population estimates.

[1]Starting in 2003, respondents could identify more than one race. Except as noted, the race data in this table from 2003 onward represent those respondents who indicated only one race category.

[2]The data shown prior to 2003 consists of those identifying themselves as "Asian or Pacific Islanders."

Table A-12. Population 6 to 17 Years Old Enrolled Below Modal Grade, 1971–2019—*Continued*

(Numbers in thousands; percent; civilian noninstitutionalized population.)

Year, sex, race, and Hispanic origin	Percent below modal grade				Dropout rate, 15 to 17 years	Population in age group			
	6 to 8 years	9 to 11 years	12 to 14 years	15 to 17 years		6 to 8 years	9 to 11 years	12 to 14 years	15 to 17 years
2009	21.0	27.5	29.5	29.5	2.5	1,004	965	995	1,058
2008	17.2	28.3	34.4	35.9	2.7	1,000	982	1,004	1,089
2007	13.2	24.6	29.9	34.8	3.6	945	967	1,037	1,061
2006	17.8	23.0	30.6	27.3	2.7	969	969	1,024	1,108
2005	18.6	32.6	31.4	34.1	3.7	990	983	1,076	1,112
2004	17.8	23.0	30.6	27.3	2.7	969	969	1,024	1,108
2003	22.0	30.4	29.0	29.8	3.4	907	1,067	1,187	951
ASIAN ALONE OR IN COMBINATION									
Both Sexes									
2019	23.5	22.0	21.4	26.4	2.8	848	844	885	888
2018	19.8	26.5	23.1	24.8	4.5	898	782	838	847
2017	19.7	26.8	22.9	25.3	3.4	802	866	817	869
2016	23.3	21.2	22.5	25.3	3.0	784	890	761	813
2015	26.1	23.7	22.1	24.0	4.5	761	793	765	772
2014	15.5	23.9	25.5	28.1	1.3	801	783	756	760
2013	17.2	16.5	21.3	18.8	1.0	825	772	693	734
2012	17.0	19.2	17.7	30.9	1.3	751	707	738	768
2011	17.5	22.5	25.7	27.8	2.0	744	718	614	650
2010	10.9	19.8	22.5	19.9	2.5	779	728	603	532
2009	9.5	13.6	26.9	19.8	1.2	690	563	513	508
2008	16.9	23.7	24.8	20.8	3.9	599	587	558	603
2007	11.4	20.6	15.6	25.3	3.6	650	613	600	548
2006	15.0	19.9	19.2	22.2	3.2	528	574	574	603
2005	13.0	12.3	16.5	18.4	1.2	600	531	576	581
2004	13.9	12.4	20.3	24.6	2.6	494	576	585	599
2003	8.8	14.9	18.4	23.5	2.4	579	548	552	543
Male									
2019	21.9	23.0	25.7	24.4	0.9	426	434	431	421
2018	18.1	26.4	24.3	23.8	2.5	457	422	393	412
2017	21.9	26.1	23.9	28.3	3.5	411	444	414	437
2016	24.7	26.6	24.9	25.9	3.9	411	460	389	382
2015	24.0	22.1	17.4	25.0	4.1	377	402	358	388
2014	20.5	21.1	30.0	31.6	2.5	414	395	373	348
2013	16.3	19.8	22.2	21.1	1.2	383	373	339	343
2012	18.9	20.6	17.5	32.9	2.0	376	341	368	397
2011	17.5	23.0	27.0	30.8	2.0	380	368	324	300
2010	9.7	19.6	25.2	21.8	2.1	307	385	309	291
2009	10.5	16.9	26.0	20.6	0.6	363	269	271	285
2008	22.3	23.0	20.6	15.9	2.1	285	291	299	289
2007	8.4	20.2	16.7	28.4	4.3	316	307	287	289
2006	15.4	15.4	15.4	15.4	4.1	259	311	291	285
2005	12.5	13.2	14.5	16.5	1.6	318	254	307	286
2004	12.4	16.2	19.3	22.3	3.6	254	278	324	286
2003	9.3	19.8	19.4	19.2	1.8	263	268	299	277
Female									
2019	25.1	20.9	17.2	28.4	4.5	421	410	454	467
2018	21.5	26.8	22.1	25.9	6.5	441	360	445	435
2017	17.5	27.6	22.0	22.2	3.3	391	422	403	432
2016	21.7	15.5	19.9	24.7	2.2	373	430	372	432
2015	28.2	25.5	26.1	22.9	4.9	383	392	407	384
2014	10.2	26.9	21.2	25.1	0.3	388	389	383	411
2013	18.1	13.6	20.4	16.7	0.8	442	400	354	391
2012	15.1	17.9	18.0	28.8	0.5	376	366	370	371
2011	17.4	22.0	24.3	25.2	2.0	364	350	290	350
2010	12.1	20.0	19.6	17.6	2.9	382	344	294	242
2009	8.4	10.6	27.0	18.8	2.1	326	293	242	223
2008	12.2	24.4	29.6	25.6	5.5	314	295	259	314
2007	14.3	21.1	14.6	21.8	2.9	334	306	314	259
2006	14.6	20.6	15.4	22.2	2.4	269	263	283	318
2005	13.7	11.5	18.8	20.2	0.9	282	276	269	295
2004	15.5	8.8	21.6	26.7	1.6	241	298	261	313
2003	8.4	10.3	17.2	28.0	3.1	316	280	253	266

* = Quantity zero or rounds to zero.
r = Revised, controlled to 1990 census based population estimates; previous 1993 data controlled to 1980 census based population estimates.
[1]Starting in 2003, respondents could identify more than one race. Except as noted, the race data in this table from 2003 onward represent those respondents who indicated only one race category.
[2]The data shown prior to 2003 consists of those identifying themselves as "Asian or Pacific Islanders."

Table A-13. Annual High School Dropout Rates of 15 to 24 Year Olds by Sex, Race, Grade, and Hispanic Origin, October 1967–2019

(Numbers in thousands; percent; civilian noninstitutionalized population.)

Year, grade, race, and Hispanic origin	Total[1]			Male			Female		
	Total students	Dropouts	Dropout rate	Total students	Dropouts	Dropout rate	Total students	Dropouts	Dropout rate
ALL RACES									
Grades 10–12									
2019.............................	11,694	473	4.0	5,859	227	3.9	5,835	246	4.2
2018.............................	11,638	518	4.5	5,973	236	4.0	5,665	282	5.0
2017.............................	11,719	523	4.5	5,971	307	5.1	5,748	215	3.7
2016.............................	11,807	532	4.5	5,939	305	5.1	5,868	227	3.9
2015.............................	11,646	535	4.6	5,894	283	4.8	5,752	252	4.4
2014.............................	11,634	567	4.9	5,932	300	5.1	5,702	267	4.7
2013.............................	11,495	508	4.4	5,844	267	4.6	5,651	241	4.3
2012.............................	11,962	386	3.2	5,997	201	3.4	5,965	184	3.1
2011.............................	11,726	375	3.2	6,010	206	3.4	5,716	169	2.9
2010.............................	11,647	326	2.8	6,006	172	2.9	5,641	154	2.7
2009.............................	11,651	373	3.2	5,798	189	3.3	5,853	184	3.1
2008.............................	11,750	390	3.3	5,999	174	2.9	5,751	216	3.8
2007.............................	11,584	383	3.3	5,879	206	3.5	5,705	177	3.1
2006.............................	11,604	407	3.5	5,932	227	3.8	5,672	180	3.2
2005.............................	11,494	414	3.6	5,843	233	4.0	5,651	181	3.2
2004.............................	11,166	486	4.4	5,624	266	4.7	5,542	220	4.0
2003.............................	11,378	429	3.8	5,705	225	4.0	5,674	203	3.6
2002.............................	10,989	367	3.3	5,504	193	3.5	5,484	174	3.2
2001.............................	10,777	507	4.7	5,534	293	5.3	5,243	214	4.1
2000.............................	10,773	488	4.5	5,417	280	5.2	5,356	208	3.9
1999.............................	11,067	520	4.7	5,659	243	4.3	5,411	277	5.1
1998.............................	10,791	479	4.4	5,486	237	4.3	5,305	243	4.6
1997.............................	10,645	454	4.3	5,330	251	4.7	5,313	203	3.8
1996.............................	10,249	485	4.7	5,175	240	4.6	5,072	244	4.8
1995.............................	10,106	544	5.4	5,161	297	5.8	4,946	247	5.0
1994.............................	9,922	497	5.0	5,048	249	4.9	4,873	247	5.1
1993r............................	9,430	404	4.3	4,787	211	4.4	4,640	192	4.1
1993.............................	9,021	382	4.2	4,570	199	4.4	4,452	183	4.1
1992.............................	8,939	384	4.3	4,580	175	3.8	4,357	207	4.8
1991.............................	8,612	348	4.0	4,380	167	3.8	4,231	180	4.3
1990.............................	8,679	347	4.0	4,356	177	4.1	4,323	170	3.9
1989.............................	8,974	404	4.5	4,519	203	4.5	4,453	199	4.5
1988.............................	9,590	461	4.8	4,960	256	5.2	4,628	206	4.5
1987.............................	9,802	403	4.1	4,921	215	4.4	4,879	187	3.8
1986.............................	9,829	421	4.3	4,910	213	4.3	4,917	208	4.2
1985.............................	9,704	504	5.2	4,831	259	5.4	4,874	245	5.0
1984.............................	10,041	507	5.0	4,986	268	5.4	5,054	238	4.7
1983.............................	10,331	535	5.2	5,130	294	5.7	5,200	241	4.6
1982.............................	10,611	577	5.4	5,310	305	5.7	5,301	271	5.1
1981.............................	10,868	639	5.9	5,379	322	6.0	5,487	316	5.8
1980.............................	10,891	658	6.0	5,445	362	6.6	5,448	296	5.4
1979.............................	11,136	744	6.7	5,479	369	6.7	5,658	377	6.7
1978.............................	11,116	743	6.7	5,558	415	7.5	5,558	328	5.9
1977.............................	11,300	734	6.5	5,657	392	6.9	5,643	342	6.1
1976.............................	10,996	644	5.9	5,534	360	6.5	5,463	285	5.2
1975.............................	11,033	639	5.8	5,485	296	5.4	5,548	343	6.2
1974.............................	11,026	742	6.7	5,421	402	7.4	5,605	340	6.1
1973.............................	10,851	683	6.3	5,407	370	6.8	5,444	313	5.7
1972.............................	10,664	659	6.2	5,305	317	6.0	5,358	341	6.4
1971.............................	10,451	562	5.4	5,193	297	5.7	5,258	266	5.1
1970.............................	10,281	588	5.7	5,145	288	5.6	5,138	302	5.9
1969.............................	10,212	551	5.4	5,069	273	5.4	5,142	278	5.4
1968.............................	9,814	506	5.2	4,831	247	5.1	4,983	259	5.2
1967.............................	9,350	486	5.2	4,605	237	5.1	4,745	249	5.2
Grade 10									
2019.............................	3,964	65	1.6	2,059	15	0.7	1,905	50	2.6
2018.............................	3,950	66	1.7	2,045	23	1.1	1,905	43	2.3
2017.............................	3,975	41	1.0	2,153	35	1.6	1,822	6	0.3
2016.............................	3,985	69	1.7	2,013	36	1.8	1,972	33	1.7
2015.............................	3,994	61	1.5	2,016	24	1.2	1,979	37	1.9
2014.............................	4,026	73	1.8	2,095	58	2.8	1,931	16	0.8
2013.............................	3,971	35	0.9	1,996	19	0.9	1,976	16	0.8
2012.............................	4,226	34	0.8	2,104	20	1.0	2,122	14	0.7

* = Quantity zero or rounds to zero.
r = Revised, controlled to 1990 census based population estimates; previous 1993 data controlled to 1980 census based population estimates.
[1]Starting in 2003 respondents could identify more than one race. Except as noted, the race data in this table from 2003 onward represent those respondents who indicated only one race category.
[2]The data shown prior to 2003 consists of those identifying themselves as "Asian or Pacific Islanders."

Table A-13. Annual High School Dropout Rates of 15 to 24 Year Olds by Sex, Race, Grade, and Hispanic Origin, October 1967–2019—*Continued*

(Numbers in thousands; percent; civilian noninstitutionalized population.)

Year, grade, race, and Hispanic origin	Total[1] Total students	Dropouts	Dropout rate	Male Total students	Dropouts	Dropout rate	Female Total students	Dropouts	Dropout rate
2011	3,998	48	1.2	2,009	26	1.3	1,989	22	1.1
2010	3,983	27	0.7	2,008	17	0.8	1,976	10	0.5
2009	3,983	50	1.2	1,993	28	1.4	1,989	22	1.1
2008	4,154	56	1.4	2,104	25	1.2	2,050	31	1.5
2007	4,064	63	1.6	2,027	32	1.6	2,037	31	1.5
2006	4,179	31	0.7	2,053	19	0.9	2,126	12	0.5
2005	4,483	72	1.6	2,244	49	2.2	2,239	23	1.0
2004	4,028	99	2.5	2,096	56	2.7	1,931	42	2.2
2003	4,107	64	1.6	2,111	26	1.2	1,995	37	1.9
2002	3,896	55	1.4	1,963	36	1.8	1,934	19	1.0
2001	3,900	90	2.3	1,988	50	2.5	1,913	41	2.1
2000	3,957	77	1.9	2,036	48	2.4	1,920	28	1.5
1999	3,910	104	2.7	2,036	54	2.7	1,875	50	2.7
1998	3,883	90	2.3	1,971	36	1.8	1,911	54	2.8
1997	3,738	79	2.1	1,894	44	2.3	1,843	35	1.9
1996	3,691	94	2.5	1,906	50	2.6	1,784	43	2.4
1995	3,552	88	2.5	1,823	40	2.2	1,728	47	2.7
1994	3,474	76	2.2	1,793	45	2.5	1,681	31	1.8
1993r	3,265	86	2.6	1,696	52	3.1	1,567	33	2.1
1993	3,139	81	2.6	1,627	50	3.1	1,513	31	2.0
1992	3,197	81	2.5	1,657	37	2.2	1,539	43	2.8
1991	3,132	105	3.4	1,571	46	2.9	1,561	59	3.8
1990	3,215	90	2.8	1,660	43	2.6	1,555	47	3.0
1989	3,071	99	3.2	1,567	56	3.6	1,504	43	2.9
1988	3,308	112	3.4	1,716	63	3.7	1,592	49	3.1
1987	3,492	106	3.0	1,818	45	2.5	1,674	61	3.6
1986	3,555	119	3.3	1,820	56	3.1	1,734	63	3.6
1985	3,491	143	4.1	1,797	74	4.1	1,695	69	4.1
1984	3,415	135	4.0	1,735	76	4.4	1,680	59	3.5
1983	3,468	129	3.7	1,755	70	4.0	1,713	59	3.4
1982	3,540	144	4.1	1,792	69	3.9	1,747	74	4.2
1981	3,735	144	3.9	1,816	65	3.6	1,918	78	4.1
1980	3,817	166	4.3	1,957	95	4.9	1,861	71	3.8
1979	3,920	217	5.5	1,985	102	5.1	1,934	114	5.9
1978	3,878	185	4.8	1,943	96	4.9	1,935	89	4.6
1977	3,970	177	4.5	2,021	96	4.8	1,949	81	4.2
1976	3,914	145	3.7	1,960	79	4.0	1,955	67	3.4
1975	3,983	183	4.6	2,017	87	4.3	1,967	97	4.9
1974	3,901	223	5.7	1,951	122	6.3	1,940	101	5.2
1973	3,899	210	5.4	1,930	112	5.8	1,969	98	5.0
1972	3,008	203	5.2	1,940	106	5.5	1,928	97	5.0
1971	3,762	174	4.6	1,925	95	4.9	1,838	79	4.3
1970	3,686	186	5.0	1,865	90	4.8	1,822	97	5.3
1969	3,485	159	4.6	1,756	84	4.8	1,729	75	4.3
1968	3,615	151	4.2	1,849	75	4.1	1,767	76	4.3
1967	3,370	129	3.8	1,726	64	3.7	1,644	65	4.0
Grade 11									
2019	4,290	141	3.3	2,194	69	3.2	2,096	72	3.4
2018	4,210	140	3.3	2,137	49	2.3	2,074	91	4.4
2017	4,510	137	3.0	2,327	86	3.7	2,183	51	2.3
2016	4,261	126	3.0	2,191	78	3.6	2,070	48	2.3
2015	4,338	137	3.2	2,198	63	2.9	2,140	74	3.4
2014	4,274	151	3.5	2,189	89	4.1	2,085	63	3.0
2013	4,232	149	3.5	2,172	89	4.1	2,060	60	2.9
2012	4,378	66	1.5	2,228	28	1.2	2,150	39	1.8
2011	4,358	84	1.9	2,234	52	2.3	2,124	32	1.5
2010	4,247	84	2.0	2,201	50	2.3	2,046	34	1.7
2009	4,444	106	2.4	2,226	51	2.3	2,218	55	2.5
2008	4,186	96	2.3	2,113	60	2.9	2,073	36	1.7
2007	4,388	118	2.7	2,280	64	2.8	2,108	55	2.6
2006	4,323	112	2.6	2,271	62	2.7	2,053	50	2.4
2005	4,080	72	1.8	2,184	46	2.1	1,896	26	1.4
2004	4,010	141	3.5	2,012	76	3.8	1,998	65	3.3
2003	4,327	117	2.7	2,158	68	3.2	2,169	49	2.3
2002	4,137	99	2.4	2,111	54	2.6	2,026	45	2.2

* = Quantity zero or rounds to zero.
r = Revised, controlled to 1990 census based population estimates; previous 1993 data controlled to 1980 census based population estimates.
[1]Starting in 2003 respondents could identify more than one race. Except as noted, the race data in this table from 2003 onward represent those respondents who indicated only one race category.
[2]The data shown prior to 2003 consists of those identifying themselves as "Asian or Pacific Islanders."

Table A-13. Annual High School Dropout Rates of 15 to 24 Year Olds by Sex, Race, Grade, and Hispanic Origin, October 1967–2019—*Continued*

(Numbers in thousands; percent; civilian noninstitutionalized population.)

Year, grade, race, and Hispanic origin	Total[1]			Male			Female		
	Total students	Dropouts	Dropout rate	Total students	Dropouts	Dropout rate	Total students	Dropouts	Dropout rate
2001	4,114	139	3.4	2,134	72	3.4	1,979	67	3.4
2000	3,833	170	4.4	1,933	78	4.0	1,901	93	4.9
1999	4,036	150	3.7	2,052	69	3.4	1,984	81	4.0
1998	3,735	110	2.9	1,902	55	2.9	1,833	55	3.0
1997	3,882	142	3.7	1,957	71	3.6	1,925	71	3.7
1996	3,606	138	3.8	1,828	76	4.2	1,778	62	3.5
1995	3,568	159	4.5	1,846	89	4.8	1,724	71	4.1
1994	3,587	132	3.7	1,864	61	3.3	1,722	70	4.1
1993r	3,375	106	3.1	1,725	43	2.5	1,650	63	3.8
1993	3,218	100	3.1	1,643	40	2.4	1,575	60	3.8
1992	3,213	120	3.7	1,642	52	3.2	1,570	67	4.3
1991	3,083	101	3.3	1,598	42	2.6	1,484	58	3.9
1990	2,976	98	3.3	1,462	57	3.9	1,514	41	2.7
1989	3,302	125	3.8	1,683	67	4.0	1,618	57	3.5
1988	3,447	161	4.7	1,819	89	4.9	1,627	72	4.4
1987	3,566	122	3.4	1,766	71	4.0	1,800	51	2.8
1986	3,433	116	3.4	1,700	51	3.0	1,733	65	3.8
1985	3,274	139	4.2	1,618	70	4.3	1,656	69	4.2
1984	3,328	163	4.9	1,682	87	5.2	1,646	76	4.6
1983	3,601	162	4.5	1,825	87	4.8	1,775	75	4.2
1982	3,694	218	5.9	1,872	122	6.5	1,822	96	5.3
1981	3,787	262	6.9	1,937	144	7.4	1,850	118	6.4
1980	3,670	225	6.1	1,832	120	6.6	1,839	105	5.7
1979	3,718	229	6.2	1,840	102	5.5	1,879	128	6.8
1978	3,708	230	6.2	1,905	113	5.9	1,803	117	6.5
1977	3,832	244	6.4	1,964	133	6.8	1,867	110	5.9
1976	3,786	227	6.0	1,955	123	6.3	1,831	104	5.7
1975	3,596	230	6.4	1,828	103	5.6	1,767	126	7.1
1974	3,721	237	6.4	1,819	123	6.8	1,902	114	6.0
1973	3,631	237	6.5	1,877	126	6.7	1,754	111	6.3
1972	3,581	241	6.7	1,825	107	5.9	1,756	134	7.6
1971	3,585	185	5.2	1,772	82	4.6	1,811	103	5.7
1970	3,456	198	5.7	1,750	96	5.5	1,706	102	6.0
1969	3,489	190	5.4	1,779	100	5.6	1,710	90	5.3
1968	3,255	179	5.5	1,640	91	5.5	1,614	88	5.5
1967	3,068	169	5.5	1,557	76	4.9	1,511	93	6.2
Grade 12									
2019	3,440	266	7.7	1,606	142	8.8	1,835	124	6.8
2018	3,478	312	9.0	1,791	164	9.2	1,687	148	8.8
2017	3,234	344	10.6	1,491	186	12.5	1,744	158	9.1
2016	3,561	337	9.5	1,735	191	11.0	1,826	146	8.0
2015	3,315	337	10.2	1,680	196	11.7	1,634	141	8.6
2014	3,334	343	10.3	1,648	154	9.3	1,686	189	11.2
2013	3,291	325	9.9	1,675	159	9.5	1,615	166	10.3
2012	3,358	285	8.5	1,665	154	9.2	1,693	131	7.7
2011	3,370	243	7.2	1,767	129	7.3	1,603	114	7.1
2010	3,417	215	6.3	1,798	106	5.9	1,620	110	6.8
2009	3,224	217	6.7	1,578	109	6.9	1,646	108	6.5
2008	3,409	237	7.0	1,781	89	5.0	1,628	149	9.1
2007	3,133	202	6.4	1,572	111	7.0	1,561	91	5.8
2006	3,101	265	8.5	1,608	146	9.1	1,492	119	8.0
2005	2,931	270	9.2	1,415	138	9.7	1,516	132	8.7
2004	3,130	247	7.9	1,516	133	8.8	1,614	114	7.1
2003	2,945	248	8.4	1,435	131	9.1	1,510	117	7.7
2002	2,956	214	7.2	1,432	104	7.3	1,524	110	7.2
2001	2,762	277	10.0	1,411	171	12.1	1,351	106	7.8
2000	2,983	241	8.1	1,447	154	10.6	1,535	87	5.7
1999	3,121	266	8.5	1,571	120	7.6	1,552	146	9.4
1998	3,173	279	8.8	1,613	146	9.0	1,560	133	8.5
1997	3,025	233	7.7	1,479	136	9.2	1,545	97	6.3
1996	2,952	253	8.6	1,441	114	7.9	1,510	139	9.2
1995	2,986	297	9.9	1,492	168	11.3	1,494	129	8.6
1994	2,861	289	10.1	1,391	143	10.3	1,470	146	9.9
1993r	2,790	212	7.6	1,366	116	8.5	1,423	96	6.7
1993	2,664	201	7.5	1,300	109	8.4	1,364	92	6.7

* = Quantity zero or rounds to zero.
r = Revised, controlled to 1990 census based population estimates; previous 1993 data controlled to 1980 census based population estimates.
[1]Starting in 2003 respondents could identify more than one race. Except as noted, the race data in this table from 2003 onward represent those respondents who indicated only one race category.
[2]The data shown prior to 2003 consists of those identifying themselves as "Asian or Pacific Islanders."

Table A-13. Annual High School Dropout Rates of 15 to 24 Year Olds by Sex, Race, Grade, and Hispanic Origin, October 1967–2019—*Continued*

(Numbers in thousands; percent; civilian noninstitutionalized population.)

Year, grade, race, and Hispanic origin	Total[1]			Male			Female		
	Total students	Dropouts	Dropout rate	Total students	Dropouts	Dropout rate	Total students	Dropouts	Dropout rate
1992............................	2,529	183	7.2	1,281	86	6.7	1,248	97	7.8
1991............................	2,397	142	5.9	1,211	79	6.5	1,186	63	5.3
1990............................	2,488	159	6.4	1,234	77	6.2	1,254	82	6.5
1989............................	2,601	180	6.9	1,269	80	6.3	1,331	99	7.4
1988............................	2,835	188	6.6	1,425	104	7.3	1,409	85	6.0
1987............................	2,744	175	6.4	1,337	99	7.4	1,405	75	5.3
1986............................	2,841	186	6.5	1,390	106	7.6	1,450	80	5.5
1985............................	2,939	222	7.6	1,416	115	8.1	1,523	107	7.0
1984............................	3,298	209	6.3	1,569	105	6.7	1,728	103	6.0
1983............................	3,262	244	7.5	1,550	137	8.8	1,712	107	6.3
1982............................	3,377	215	6.4	1,646	114	6.9	1,732	101	5.8
1981............................	3,346	233	7.0	1,626	113	6.9	1,719	120	7.0
1980............................	3,404	267	7.8	1,656	147	8.9	1,748	120	6.9
1979............................	3,498	298	8.5	1,654	164	9.9	1,845	135	7.3
1978............................	3,530	328	9.3	1,710	206	12.0	1,820	122	6.7
1977............................	3,498	313	8.9	1,672	163	9.7	1,827	151	8.3
1976............................	3,296	272	8.3	1,619	158	9.8	1,677	114	6.8
1975............................	3,454	226	6.5	1,640	106	6.5	1,814	120	6.6
1974............................	3,404	282	8.3	1,651	157	9.5	1,754	125	7.1
1973............................	3,321	236	7.1	1,600	132	8.3	1,721	104	6.0
1972............................	3,215	215	6.7	1,540	104	6.8	1,674	110	6.6
1971............................	3,104	203	6.5	1,496	120	8.0	1,609	84	5.2
1970............................	3,139	204	6.5	1,530	102	6.7	1,610	103	6.4
1969............................	3,238	202	6.2	1,534	89	5.8	1,703	113	6.6
1968............................	2,944	176	6.0	1,342	81	6.0	1,602	95	5.9
1967............................	2,912	188	6.5	1,322	97	7.3	1,590	91	5.7
WHITE ALONE									
Grades 10–12									
2019............................	8,562	353	4.1	4,334	169	3.9	4,228	185	4.4
2018............................	8,428	348	4.1	4,293	175	4.1	4,135	173	4.2
2017............................	8,528	369	4.3	4,401	209	4.8	4,126	159	3.9
2016............................	8,541	371	4.3	4,303	211	4.0	4,238	159	3.8
2015............................	8,605	369	4.3	4,382	213	4.9	4,223	156	3.7
2014............................	8,594	434	5.0	4,379	218	5.0	4,215	216	5.1
2013............................	8,501	386	4.5	4,391	216	4.9	4,110	171	4.2
2012............................	8,767	207	2.4	4,479	126	2.8	4,288	81	1.9
2011............................	8,815	261	3.0	4,559	145	3.2	4,256	116	2.7
2010............................	8,793	221	2.5	4,592	127	2.8	4,201	94	2.2
2009............................	8,886	269	3.0	4,459	146	3.3	4,427	123	2.8
2008............................	8,942	246	2.8	4,588	123	2.7	4,353	123	2.8
2007............................	8,927	246	2.8	4,518	126	2.8	4,409	120	2.7
2006............................	8,924	311	3.5	4,568	177	3.9	4,355	133	3.1
2005............................	8,855	271	3.1	4,472	151	3.4	4,382	120	2.7
2004............................	8,585	359	4.2	4,344	211	4.9	4,241	148	3.5
2003[1]............................	8,781	321	3.7	4,434	172	3.9	4,347	148	3.4
2002............................	8,636	259	3.0	4,371	133	3.0	4,265	126	3.0
2001............................	8,490	388	4.6	4,363	230	5.3	4,126	158	3.8
2000............................	8,540	371	4.3	4,368	204	4.7	4,172	167	4.0
1999............................	8,665	380	4.4	4,426	180	4.1	4,238	198	4.7
1998............................	8,487	371	4.4	4,306	188	4.4	4,181	183	4.4
1997............................	8,402	355	4.2	4,220	208	4.9	4,180	145	3.5
1996............................	8,005	361	4.5	4,077	198	4.8	3,928	163	4.1
1995............................	7,926	402	5.1	4,079	220	5.4	3,849	183	4.8
1994............................	7,862	371	4.7	4,014	184	4.6	3,848	188	4.9
1993r............................	7,442	306	4.1	3,790	157	4.1	3,654	150	4.1
1993............................	7,152	290	4.1	3,623	147	4.1	3,530	143	4.1
1992............................	7,077	292	4.1	3,646	140	3.8	3,430	151	4.4
1991............................	6,856	254	3.7	3,514	127	3.6	3,343	120	3.8
1990............................	6,984	266	3.8	3,522	144	4.1	3,462	122	3.5
1989............................	7,243	286	3.9	3,653	149	4.1	3,589	136	3.8
1988............................	7,727	362	4.7	4,016	203	5.1	3,712	161	4.3
1987............................	7,979	299	3.7	4,023	163	4.1	3,953	135	3.4
1986............................	8,011	333	4.2	4,007	168	4.2	4,007	166	4.1
1985............................	7,967	384	4.8	3,963	195	4.9	4,003	188	4.7

* = Quantity zero or rounds to zero.
r = Revised, controlled to 1990 census based population estimates; previous 1993 data controlled to 1980 census based population estimates.
[1]Starting in 2003 respondents could identify more than one race. Except as noted, the race data in this table from 2003 onward represent those respondents who indicated only one race category.
[2]The data shown prior to 2003 consists of those identifying themselves as "Asian or Pacific Islanders."

Table A-13. Annual High School Dropout Rates of 15 to 24 Year Olds by Sex, Race, Grade, and Hispanic Origin, October 1967–2019—*Continued*

(Numbers in thousands; percent; civilian noninstitutionalized population.)

Year, grade, race, and Hispanic origin	Total[1] Total students	Dropouts	Dropout rate	Male Total students	Dropouts	Dropout rate	Female Total students	Dropouts	Dropout rate
1984	8,221	410	5.0	4,119	220	5.3	4,101	190	4.6
1983	8,531	410	4.8	4,264	232	5.4	4,264	177	4.2
1982	8,769	444	5.1	4,381	231	5.3	4,390	214	4.9
1981	9,067	478	5.3	4,532	254	5.6	4,536	224	4.9
1980	9,177	517	5.6	4,624	294	6.4	4,554	224	4.9
1979	9,437	588	6.2	4,694	311	6.6	4,742	277	5.8
1978	9,360	574	6.1	4,747	329	6.9	4,611	244	5.3
1977	9,536	594	6.2	4,766	327	6.9	4,770	267	5.6
1976	9,362	532	5.7	4,708	297	6.3	4,654	235	5.0
1975	9,440	507	5.4	4,709	234	5.0	4,732	274	5.8
1974	9,403	566	6.0	4,650	326	7.0	4,754	241	5.1
1973	9,359	537	5.7	4,708	288	6.1	4,649	248	5.3
1972	9,173	520	5.7	4,588	247	5.4	4,583	272	5.9
1971	9,140	470	5.1	4,577	244	5.3	4,562	226	5.0
1970	8,959	449	5.0	4,496	212	4.7	4,462	237	5.3
1969	8,878	429	4.8	4,438	208	4.7	4,439	221	5.0
1968	8,580	387	4.5	4,246	190	4.5	4,331	196	4.5
1967	8,186	379	4.6	4,060	189	4.7	4,126	190	4.6
WHITE ALONE, NON-HISPANIC									
Grades 10–12									
2019	6,198	234	3.8	3,161	115	3.6	3,037	119	3.9
2018	6,097	213	3.5	3,112	113	3.6	2,984	100	3.3
2017	6,224	235	3.8	3,231	132	4.1	2,993	103	3.4
2016	6,230	273	4.4	3,234	164	5.1	2,996	109	3.6
2015	6,382	233	3.6	3,289	145	4.4	3,092	87	2.8
2014	6,397	285	4.5	3,288	154	4.7	3,109	131	4.2
2013	6,268	256	4.1	3,236	144	4.5	3,031	112	3.7
2012	6,436	95	1.5	3,257	61	1.9	3,179	34	1.1
2011	6,647	171	2.6	3,404	89	2.6	3,243	82	2.5
2010	6,851	150	2.2	3,568	97	2.7	3,284	53	1.6
2009	6,944	160	2.3	3,491	91	2.6	3,453	68	2.0
2008	7,079	156	2.2	3,638	83	2.3	3,441	73	2.1
2007	7,274	155	2.1	3,684	82	2.2	3,590	73	2.0
2006	7,171	200	2.8	3,693	120	3.2	3,478	80	2.3
2005	7,227	196	2.7	3,652	103	2.8	3,575	93	2.6
2004	7,015	245	3.5	3,582	130	3.6	3,434	115	3.4
2003[1]	7,139	214	3.0	3,665	116	3.2	3,474	98	2.8
2002	7,124	173	2.4	3,620	84	2.3	3,504	89	2.6
2001	7,070	272	3.8	3,647	173	4.7	3,423	98	2.9
2000	7,159	276	3.9	3,648	150	4.1	3,511	126	3.6
1999	7,265	274	3.8	3,744	130	3.5	3,523	145	4.1
1998	7,174	266	3.7	3,605	130	3.6	3,570	137	3.8
1997	7,090	242	3.4	3,533	140	4.0	3,558	103	2.9
1996	6,850	267	3.9	3,511	145	4.1	3,337	121	3.6
1995	6,905	296	4.3	3,564	164	4.6	3,341	131	3.9
1994	6,839	274	4.0	3,496	137	3.9	3,343	137	4.1
1993	6,277	237	3.8	3,229	128	4.0	3,047	108	3.5
BLACK ALONE									
Grades 10–12									
2019	1,710	70	4.1	815	34	4.1	894	36	4.1
2018	1,769	113	6.4	946	41	4.3	823	73	8.8
2017	1,784	88	5.0	879	58	6.6	905	31	3.4
2016	1,815	98	5.4	919	49	5.3	897	49	5.5
2015	1,735	112	6.4	842	49	5.8	893	63	7.0
2014	1,757	83	4.7	905	44	4.9	852	39	4.5
2013	1,791	88	4.9	859	37	4.3	931	51	5.5
2012	1,949	124	6.4	897	49	5.5	1,052	75	7.1
2011	1,944	78	4.0	965	54	5.6	978	24	2.4
2010	1,898	62	3.2	946	36	3.8	952	26	2.7
2009	1,797	81	4.5	870	38	4.4	927	42	4.6
2008	1,868	114	6.1	925	42	4.6	943	72	7.6

* = Quantity zero or rounds to zero.
r = Revised, controlled to 1990 census based population estimates; previous 1993 data controlled to 1980 census based population estimates.
[1]Starting in 2003 respondents could identify more than one race. Except as noted, the race data in this table from 2003 onward represent those respondents who indicated only one race category.
[2]The data shown prior to 2003 consists of those identifying themselves as "Asian or Pacific Islanders."

Table A-13. Annual High School Dropout Rates of 15 to 24 Year Olds by Sex, Race, Grade, and Hispanic Origin, October 1967–2019—*Continued*

(Numbers in thousands; percent; civilian noninstitutionalized population.)

Year, grade, race, and Hispanic origin	Total[1]			Male			Female		
	Total students	Dropouts	Dropout rate	Total students	Dropouts	Dropout rate	Total students	Dropouts	Dropout rate
2007	1,781	76	4.3	914	45	4.9	867	31	3.6
2006	1,767	65	3.7	902	29	3.2	864	37	4.3
2005	1,763	122	6.9	943	71	7.5	820	51	6.2
2004	1,716	90	5.2	833	40	4.8	883	50	5.7
2003[1]	1,698	76	4.5	812	33	4.1	886	43	4.9
2002	1,664	73	4.4	782	40	5.1	882	33	3.8
2001	1,655	95	5.7	828	51	6.2	827	45	5.4
2000	1,706	96	5.6	819	62	7.6	888	34	3.8
1999	1,794	107	6.0	925	48	5.2	870	59	6.8
1998	1,759	88	5.0	918	42	4.6	841	46	5.5
1997	1,678	80	4.8	813	33	4.1	866	49	5.7
1996	1,704	107	6.3	803	37	4.6	901	70	7.8
1995	1,598	97	6.1	797	63	7.9	802	35	4.4
1994	1,559	96	6.1	763	50	6.5	795	45	5.7
1993r	1,499	80	5.3	740	43	5.8	758	37	4.9
1993	1,447	78	5.4	724	41	5.7	722	36	5.0
1992	1,422	70	4.9	702	23	3.3	720	48	6.7
1991	1,366	85	6.2	685	38	5.5	683	48	7.0
1990	1,303	66	5.1	636	26	4.1	666	40	6.0
1989	1,384	106	7.7	684	47	6.9	701	60	8.6
1988	1,468	93	6.3	751	50	6.7	717	43	6.0
1987	1,463	93	6.4	730	45	6.2	732	47	6.4
1986	1,449	68	4.7	711	34	4.8	737	34	4.6
1985	1,422	110	7.7	703	58	8.3	719	52	7.2
1984	1,524	88	5.8	711	44	6.2	813	43	5.3
1983	1,498	103	6.9	687	48	7.0	810	55	6.8
1982	1,553	121	7.8	786	71	9.0	767	50	6.5
1981	1,516	146	9.6	704	66	9.4	815	83	10.2
1980	1,496	124	8.3	714	57	8.0	781	66	8.5
1979	1,479	142	9.6	679	51	7.5	802	92	11.5
1978	1,542	160	10.4	706	78	11.0	835	81	9.7
1977	1,588	133	8.4	746	62	8.3	789	71	9.0
1976	1,449	105	7.2	729	62	8.5	721	45	6.2
1975	1,416	123	8.7	673	56	8.3	743	67	9.0
1974	1,441	167	11.6	679	73	10.8	761	93	12.2
1973	1,372	138	10.1	650	78	12.0	725	61	8.4
1972	1,373	133	9.7	644	65	10.1	756	68	9.0
1971	1,195	87	7.3	552	51	9.2	643	37	5.8
1970	1,192	133	11.2	587	74	12.6	606	60	9.9
1969	1,209	110	9.3	562	58	10.3	646	55	8.5
1968	1,123	113	10.1	523	52	9.9	600	61	10.2
1967	1,066	106	9.9	485	47	9.7	578	58	10.0
ASIAN[2]									
Grades 10–12									
2019	630	18	2.8	313	7	2.3	317	11	3.3
2018	617	28	4.5	310	9	3.0	308	19	6.1
2017	657	42	6.3	323	22	6.8	334	20	5.9
2016	594	20	3.3	281	11	3.9	313	9	2.8
2015	552	34	6.2	263	20	7.5	288	14	5.0
2014	566	5	0.9	259	3	1.2	307	2	0.6
2013	604	10	1.7	279	4	1.5	324	6	1.8
2012	592	19	3.2	331	9	2.7	261	10	3.8
2011	495	17	3.5	272	4	1.5	223	13	6.0
2010	419	12	2.8	220	6	2.9	199	5	2.6
2009	426	7	1.7	215	2	0.8	210	5	2.6
2008	429	17	3.9	219	-	0.2	210	16	7.8
2007	404	30	7.5	202	13	6.6	202	17	8.3
2006	445	19	4.2	237	11	4.5	208	8	3.7
2005	425	6	1.5	219	5	2.4	206	1	0.5
2004	452	4	0.9	233	-	-	219	4	1.9
2003[1]	457	11	2.4	237	3	1.4	221	7	3.4
2002	515	12	2.3	266	8	3.0	249	4	1.6
2001	470	10	2.1	274	9	3.3	197	1	0.5
2000	399	13	3.3	178	12	6.7	221	1	0.5
1999	523	25	4.8	269	13	4.8	253	12	4.7

* = Quantity zero or rounds to zero.
r = Revised, controlled to 1990 census based population estimates; previous 1993 data controlled to 1980 census based population estimates.
[1]Starting in 2003 respondents could identify more than one race. Except as noted, the race data in this table from 2003 onward represent those respondents who indicated only one race category.
[2]The data shown prior to 2003 consists of those identifying themselves as "Asian or Pacific Islanders."

Table A-13. Annual High School Dropout Rates of 15 to 24 Year Olds by Sex, Race, Grade, and Hispanic Origin, October 1967–2019—*Continued*

(Numbers in thousands; percent; civilian noninstitutionalized population.)

Year, grade, race, and Hispanic origin	Total[1]			Male			Female		
	Total students	Dropouts	Dropout rate	Total students	Dropouts	Dropout rate	Total students	Dropouts	Dropout rate
HISPANIC ORIGIN (OF ANY RACE)									
Grades 10–12									
2019	2,744	147	5.3	1,395	72	5.2	1,350	74	5.5
2018	2,736	153	5.6	1,385	67	4.8	1,351	86	6.4
2017	2,650	161	6.1	1,357	104	7.7	1,293	56	4.4
2016	2,747	118	4.3	1,331	67	5.1	1,416	51	3.6
2015	2,599	148	5.7	1,314	67	5.1	1,285	80	6.3
2014	2,490	179	7.2	1,254	86	6.8	1,236	93	7.5
2013	2,509	132	5.3	1,291	71	5.5	1,218	61	5.0
2012	2,671	136	5.1	1,377	76	5.5	1,294	60	4.6
2011	2,376	100	4.2	1,260	56	4.4	1,116	44	4.0
2010	2,130	80	3.8	1,113	30	2.7	1,018	51	5.0
2009	2,129	114	5.3	1,039	55	5.3	1,090	59	5.4
2008	2,062	101	4.9	1,052	44	4.2	1,011	57	5.6
2007	1,785	99	5.5	904	49	5.5	882	49	5.6
2006	1,923	124	6.4	958	61	6.3	965	63	6.6
2005	1,814	86	4.7	910	51	5.6	904	35	3.9
2004	1,723	138	8.0	842	97	11.5	881	40	4.6
2003	1,792	116	6.5	846	65	7.7	945	51	5.4
2002	1,614	86	5.3	801	50	6.2	814	36	4.4
2001	1,487	121	8.1	755	57	7.5	732	64	8.7
2000	1,465	100	6.8	761	54	7.1	704	46	6.5
1999	1,482	105	7.1	729	50	6.9	751	55	7.3
1998	1,368	115	8.4	731	63	8.6	637	52	8.2
1997	1,377	119	8.6	710	74	10.4	668	45	6.7
1996	1,195	100	8.4	588	54	9.2	608	46	7.6
1995	1,251	145	11.6	644	70	10.9	608	76	12.5
1994	1,179	109	9.2	607	51	8.4	572	58	10.1
1993r	1,061	69	6.5	488	25	5.1	573	44	7.5
1993	943	60	6.4	436	21	4.8	508	39	7.7
1992	917	72	7.9	468	27	5.8	441	38	8.6
1991	809	59	7.3	396	41	10.4	417	20	4.8
1990	811	65	8.0	379	33	8.7	428	31	7.2
1989	762	59	7.7	394	30	7.6	366	28	7.7
1988	730	77	10.5	398	49	12.3	333	28	8.4
1987	769	43	5.6	380	19	5.0	389	24	6.2
1986	764	91	11.9	376	44	11.7	388	48	12.4
1985	729	71	9.7	333	31	9.3	396	39	9.8
1984	706	77	10.9	311	38	12.2	396	40	10.1
1983	691	68	9.8	351	48	13.7	340	21	6.2
1982	692	65	9.4	370	35	9.5	321	29	9.0
1981	717	77	10.7	350	37	10.6	367	40	10.9
1980	646	74	11.5	295	50	16.9	350	24	6.9
1979	593	58	9.8	295	30	10.2	298	27	9.1
1978	567	70	12.3	295	46	15.6	271	23	8.5
1977	627	50	8.0	341	35	10.3	287	15	5.2
1976	638	46	7.2	300	22	7.3	336	23	6.8
1975	614	67	10.9	317	32	10.1	294	34	11.6
1974	547	53	9.7	271	34	12.5	278	20	7.2
1973	499	50	10.0	240	19	7.9	259	31	12.0
1972	498	55	11.0	253	28	11.1	247	27	10.9
WHITE ALONE OR IN COMBINATION									
Grades 10–12									
2019	9,098	374	4.1	4,582	177	3.9	4,516	197	4.4
2018	8,983	364	4.0	4,553	180	4.0	4,430	184	4.1
2017	8,968	375	4.2	4,619	212	4.6	4,348	163	3.7
2016	9,054	385	4.3	4,566	224	4.9	4,488	161	3.6
2015	9,037	378	4.2	4,610	213	4.6	4,427	165	3.7
2014	9,005	446	5.0	4,580	229	5.0	4,424	217	4.9
2013	8,854	404	4.6	4,577	226	4.9	4,276	178	4.2
2012	9,101	220	2.4	4,629	137	3.0	4,473	83	1.9

* = Quantity zero or rounds to zero.
r = Revised, controlled to 1990 census based population estimates; previous 1993 data controlled to 1980 census based population estimates.
[1]Starting in 2003 respondents could identify more than one race. Except as noted, the race data in this table from 2003 onward represent those respondents who indicated only one race category.
[2]The data shown prior to 2003 consists of those identifying themselves as "Asian or Pacific Islanders."

Table A-13. Annual High School Dropout Rates of 15 to 24 Year Olds by Sex, Race, Grade, and Hispanic Origin, October 1967–2019—*Continued*

(Numbers in thousands; percent; civilian noninstitutionalized population.)

Year, grade, race, and Hispanic origin	Total[1]			Male			Female		
	Total students	Dropouts	Dropout rate	Total students	Dropouts	Dropout rate	Total students	Dropouts	Dropout rate
2011	9,087	272	3.0	4,696	145	3.1	4,391	127	2.9
2010	9,112	242	2.7	4,764	130	2.7	4,348	112	2.6
2009	9,216	280	3.0	4,610	148	3.2	4,606	132	2.9
2008	9,277	257	2.8	4,766	129	2.7	4,511	128	2.8
2007	9,199	251	2.7	4,664	131	2.8	4,535	120	2.7
2006	9,212	320	3.5	4,695	185	3.9	4,517	136	3.0
2005	9,158	281	3.1	4,610	155	3.4	4,548	126	2.8
2004	8,821	382	4.3	4,464	222	5.0	4,357	160	3.7
2003	9,045	335	3.7	4,573	183	4.0	4,471	151	3.4
BLACK ALONE OR IN COMBINATION									
Grades 10–12									
2019	2,000	76	3.8	962	36	3.7	1,038	41	3.9
2018	2,085	129	6.2	1,093	41	3.7	992	88	8.9
2017	2,084	95	4.6	1,022	58	5.7	1,062	37	3.4
2016	2,142	106	4.9	1,077	56	5.2	1,066	49	4.6
2015	1,950	112	5.7	951	49	5.1	999	63	6.3
2014	2,012	95	4.7	1,019	55	5.4	993	40	4.0
2013	1,989	98	4.9	962	42	4.3	1,027	56	5.4
2012	2,124	129	6.1	976	52	5.3	1,148	77	6.7
2011	2,051	82	4.0	1,024	54	5.3	1,027	28	2.8
2010	2,038	76	3.7	1,021	38	3.7	1,017	39	3.8
2009	1,985	86	4.3	958	40	4.2	1,026	46	4.5
2008	2,033	121	5.9	1,012	46	4.5	1,021	75	7.3
2007	1,900	78	4.1	977	47	4.8	923	31	3.4
2006	1,891	66	3.5	952	29	3.0	939	38	4.0
2005	1,870	129	6.9	979	71	7.3	890	58	6.5
2004	1,797	99	5.5	869	40	4.6	928	59	6.3
2003	1,808	79	4.4	853	36	4.2	955	43	4.5
ASIAN ALONE OR IN COMBINATION									
Grades 10–12									
2019	783	19	2.4	370	7	1.9	413	11	2.7
2018	758	30	3.9	372	11	3.0	386	19	4.8
2017	796	44	5.5	397	24	6.2	398	20	4.9
2016	731	25	3.4	353	16	4.4	378	9	2.3
2015	661	38	5.7	312	20	6.3	349	18	5.2
2014	660	5	0.8	300	3	1.0	361	2	0.5
2013	744	10	1.4	339	4	1.2	405	6	1.5
2012	696	19	2.7	368	9	2.5	328	10	3.1
2011	579	17	3.0	303	4	1.3	275	13	4.9
2010	520	16	3.2	270	6	2.4	250	10	4.0
2009	525	8	1.4	255	2	0.8	270	5	2.0
2008	511	17	3.3	256	-	0.2	255	16	6.4
2007	483	30	6.2	233	13	5.8	250	17	6.7
2006	542	23	4.2	279	15	5.4	263	8	3.0
2005	525	8	1.5	270	6	2.3	255	2	0.6
2004	516	8	1.6	273	3	1.2	243	5	2.1
2003	533	17	3.1	278	8	3.0	254	8	3.3

* = Quantity zero or rounds to zero.
r = Revised, controlled to 1990 census based population estimates; previous 1993 data controlled to 1980 census based population estimates.
[1]Starting in 2003 respondents could identify more than one race. Except as noted, the race data in this table from 2003 onward represent those respondents who indicated only one race category.
[2]The data shown prior to 2003 consists of those identifying themselves as "Asian or Pacific Islanders."

Table A-14. Population 14 to 24 Years Old, by High School Graduate Status, College Enrollment, Attainment, Sex, Race, and Hispanic Origin, October 1967–2019

(Numbers in thousands; percent; civilian noninstitutionalized population.)

Year, race, and Hispanic origin	Population 18 to 24 years old								High school graduates, 14 to 24 years old		
		High school graduates			Percent			High school dropouts		Percent	
	Total	Total	Enrolled in college	High school graduates	Enrolled in college	Of high school graduates enrolled in college	Number	Percent	All graduates	Enrolled in college	Enrolled or completed some college
Both Sexes											
2019	29,343	25,999	11,934	88.6	40.7	45.9	1,515	5.2	26,410	46.1	71.1
2018	29,553	26,039	12,097	88.1	40.9	46.5	1,673	5.7	26,412	46.6	72.2
2017	29,538	25,831	11,937	87.5	40.4	46.2	1,772	6.0	26,248	46.4	72.0
2016	29,893	26,123	12,320	87.4	41.2	47.2	1,911	6.4	26,571	47.3	72.3
2015	30,037	26,248	12,152	87.4	40.5	46.3	1,917	6.4	26,673	46.4	72.2
2014	30,304	26,311	12,132	86.8	40.0	46.1	2,090	6.9	26,700	46.3	72.0
2013	30,556	26,317	12,202	86.1	39.9	46.4	2,215	7.3	26,734	46.8	71.8
2012	30,377	25,866	12,456	85.1	41.0	48.2	2,319	7.6	26,255	48.5	72.9
2011	29,943	25,435	12,570	84.9	42.0	49.4	2,481	8.3	25,765	49.6	73.1
2010	29,659	25,224	12,213	85.0	41.2	48.4	2,590	8.7	25,564	48.7	72.6
2009	29,223	24,647	12,073	84.3	41.3	49.0	2,733	9.4	25,015	49.1	72.0
2008	28,950	24,568	11,466	84.9	39.6	46.7	2,702	9.3	24,922	47.0	70.6
2007	28,778	24,146	11,161	83.9	38.8	46.2	2,937	10.2	24,491	46.3	69.7
2006	28,372	23,430	10,586	82.6	37.3	45.2	3,128	11.0	23,800	45.4	69.3
2005	27,855	23,103	10,834	82.9	38.9	46.9	3,154	11.3	23,445	47.0	69.8
2004	27,948	23,086	10,611	82.6	38.0	46.0	3,836	12.1	23,379	46.2	69.0
2003	27,404	22,603	10,364	82.5	37.8	45.9	3,228	11.8	22,898	45.9	68.8
2002	27,367	22,319	10,033	81.6	36.7	45.0	3,375	12.3	22,639	45.2	67.6
2001	26,965	21,836	9,629	81.0	35.7	44.1	3,519	13.0	22,136	44.1	66.7
2000	26,658	21,822	9,452	81.9	35.5	43.3	3,315	12.4	22,080	43.5	66.7
1999	26,041	21,127	9,259	81.1	35.6	43.8	3,413	13.1	21,390	44.0	67.2
1998	25,507	20,567	9,322	80.6	36.6	45.3	3,544	13.9	20,775	45.5	68.0
1997	24,973	20,338	9,204	81.4	36.9	45.2	3,236	13.0	20,577	45.6	67.3
1996	24,671	20,131	8,767	81.6	35.5	43.5	3,147	12.8	20,465	44.0	67.2
1995	24,900	20,125	8,539	80.8	34.3	42.4	3,471	13.9	20,359	42.7	67.1
1994	25,254	20,581	8,729	81.5	34.6	42.4	3,365	13.3	20,779	42.7	66.9
1993r	25,522	20,844	8,630	81.7	33.8	41.4	3,349	13.1	21,060	41.6	65.3
1993	24,100	19,772	8,193	82.0	34.0	41.4	3,070	12.7	19,979	41.6	65.4
1992	24,278	19,921	8,343	82.1	34.4	41.9	3,083	12.7	20,194	42.3	65.6
1991	24,572	19,883	8,172	80.9	33.3	41.1	3,486	14.2	20,065	41.4	60.7
1990	24,852	20,311	7,964	82.3	32.0	39.1	3,379	13.6	20,571	39.6	58.9
1989	25,261	20,461	7,804	81.0	30.9	38.1	3,644	14.4	20,749	38.5	57.9
1988	25,733	20,900	7,791	81.2	30.3	37.3	3,749	14.6	21,204	37.6	57.4
1987	25,950	21,118	7,693	81.4	29.6	36.4	3,751	14.5	21,477	36.9	56.2
1986	26,512	21,768	7,477	82.1	28.2	34.3	3,687	13.9	22,086	34.8	55.0
1985	27,122	22,349	7,537	82.4	27.8	33.7	3,687	13.9	22,722	34.3	54.3
1984	28,031	22,870	7,591	81.6	27.1	33.2	4,142	14.8	23,252	33.7	53.0
1983	28,580	22,988	7,477	80.4	26.2	32.5	4,410	15.4	23,359	33.1	52.8
1982	28,846	23,291	7,678	80.7	26.6	33.0	4,500	15.6	23,708	33.5	52.7
1981	28,965	23,343	7,575	80.6	26.2	32.5	4,520	15.6	23,705	32.9	51.7
1980	28,957	23,413	7,400	80.9	25.6	31.6	4,515	15.6	23,856	32.1	51.1
1979	27,974	22,421	6,991	80.1	25.0	31.2	4,560	16.3	22,911	31.9	51.6
1978	27,647	22,309	6,995	80.7	25.3	31.4	4,388	15.9	22,759	31.9	51.4
1977	27,331	22,008	7,142	80.5	26.1	32.5	4,313	15.8	22,499	33.0	52.0
1976	26,919	21,677	7,181	80.5	26.7	33.1	4,276	15.9	22,158	33.7	53.4
1975	26,387	21,326	6,935	80.8	26.3	32.5	4,110	15.6	21,824	33.1	52.5
1974	25,670	20,725	6,316	80.7	24.6	30.5	4,070	15.9	21,267	31.2	51.3
1973	25,237	20,377	6,055	80.7	24.0	29.7	3,973	15.7	20,895	30.4	50.7
1972	24,579	19,618	6,257	79.8	25.5	31.9	4,068	16.6	20,107	32.6	52.9
1971	23,668	18,691	6,210	79.0	26.2	33.2	4,025	17.0	19,130	33.9	53.1
1970	22,552	17,768	5,805	78.8	25.7	32.7	3,908	17.3	18,218	33.5	52.3
1969	21,362	16,703	5,840	78.2	27.3	35.0	3,769	17.6	17,152	35.7	52.5
1968	20,562	15,683	5,356	76.3	26.0	34.2	3,929	19.1	16,165	35.2	51.5
1967	20,009	15,114	5,100	75.5	25.5	33.7	3,967	19.8	15,642	34.9	50.5
Male											
2019	14,700	12,741	5,442	86.7	37.0	42.7	898	6.1	12,943	42.8	66.2
2018	14,845	12,816	5,586	86.3	37.6	43.6	995	6.7	12,956	43.8	67.5

r = Revised, controlled to 1990 census based population estimates; previous 1993 data controlled to 1980 census based population estimates.
Note: The change in the educational attainment question and the college completion categories from "4 or more years of college" to "at least some college," in 1992 caused an increase in the proportion of 14-to-24-year-old high school graduates enrolled in college or completed some college, of approximately 5 percentage points. High school graduates are people who have completed 4 years of high school or more, for 1967 to 1991. Beginning in 1992, they were people whose highest degree was a high school diploma (including equivalency) or higher.
[1]Starting in 2003 respondents could identify more than one race. Except as noted, the race data in this table from 2003 onward represent those respondents who indicated only one race category.
[2]The data shown prior to 2003 consists of those identifying themselves as "Asian or Pacific Islanders."

Table A-14. Population 14 to 24 Years Old, by High School Graduate Status, College Enrollment, Attainment, Sex, Race, and Hispanic Origin, October 1967–2019—*Continued*

(Numbers in thousands; percent; civilian noninstitutionalized population.)

Year, race, and Hispanic origin	Population 18 to 24 years old								High school graduates, 14 to 24 years old		
		High school graduates		Percent			High school dropouts			Percent	
	Total	Total	Enrolled in college	High school graduates	Enrolled in college	Of high school graduates enrolled in college	Number	Percent	All graduates	Enrolled in college	Enrolled or completed some college
2017	14,833	12,697	5,460	85.6	36.8	43.0	1,019	6.9	12,873	43.1	67.8
2016	15,042	12,851	5,800	85.4	38.6	45.1	1,134	7.5	13,014	45.2	68.1
2015	15,074	13,031	5,694	86.5	37.8	43.7	1,034	6.9	13,256	43.8	68.0
2014	15,234	13,019	5,676	85.5	37.3	43.6	1,132	7.4	13,225	43.9	67.7
2013	15,379	13,051	5,630	84.9	36.6	43.1	1,183	7.7	13,254	43.6	67.0
2012	15,252	12,753	5,731	83.6	37.6	44.9	1,300	8.5	12,940	45.3	68.4
2011	15,211	12,659	5,953	83.2	39.1	47.0	1,374	9.0	12,834	47.2	69.0
2010	14,887	12,371	5,698	83.1	38.3	46.1	1,473	9.9	12,540	46.2	68.4
2009	14,677	12,111	5,640	82.5	38.4	46.6	1,568	10.7	12,277	46.7	68.5
2008	14,559	12,181	5,383	83.7	37.0	44.2	1,445	9.9	12,374	44.6	66.7
2007	14,515	11,825	5,156	81.5	35.5	43.6	1,680	11.6	11,972	43.7	66.0
2006	14,300	11,508	4,874	80.5	34.1	42.4	1,741	12.2	11,659	42.5	65.1
2005	14,077	11,182	4,973	79.4	35.3	44.5	1,852	13.2	11,330	44.4	65.9
2004	14,018	11,258	4,865	80.3	34.7	43.2	1,942	13.9	11,364	43.5	65.0
2003	13,681	10,919	4,697	79.8	34.3	43.0	1,875	13.7	11,040	43.1	65.0
2002	13,744	10,823	4,629	78.7	33.7	42.8	1,925	14.0	10,975	42.9	64.6
2001	13,434	10,461	4,437	77.9	33.0	42.4	2,028	15.1	10,587	42.4	63.9
2000	13,338	10,622	4,343	79.6	32.6	40.9	1,837	13.8	10,736	41.0	63.1
1999	12,905	10,201	4,396	79.1	34.0	43.1	1,818	14.9	10,331	43.3	64.5
1998	12,764	9,915	4,403	77.7	34.5	44.4	2,018	15.8	10,006	44.5	64.9
1997	12,513	9,933	4,374	79.4	35.0	44.0	1,765	14.1	10,025	44.2	64.9
1996	12,285	9,815	4,187	80.0	34.1	42.6	1,628	13.2	9,960	43.0	65.6
1995	12,351	9,789	4,089	79.3	33.1	41.8	1,791	14.5	9,884	42.1	64.2
1994	12,557	9,970	4,152	79.4	33.1	41.6	1,804	14.4	10,051	41.9	64.9
1993r	12,712	10,142	4,237	79.8	33.3	41.8	1,745	13.7	10,229	42.0	63.9
1993	11,898	9,541	3,994	80.2	33.6	41.9	1,575	13.2	9,625	42.0	64.1
1992	11,965	9,576	3,912	80.0	32.7	40.9	1,617	13.5	9,706	41.3	64.1
1991	12,036	9,493	3,954	78.9	32.9	41.7	1,810	15.0	9,564	41.9	59.2
1990	12,134	9,778	3,922	80.6	32.3	40.1	1,689	13.9	9,894	40.5	58.0
1989	12,325	9,700	3,717	78.7	30.2	38.3	1,941	15.7	9,810	38.6	57.2
1988	12,491	9,832	3,770	78.7	30.2	38.3	1,950	15.6	9,947	38.5	56.5
1987	12,626	10,030	3,867	79.4	30.6	38.6	1,948	15.4	10,207	39.0	56.0
1986	12,921	10,338	3,702	80.0	28.7	35.8	1,924	14.9	10,465	36.2	54.4
1985	13,199	10,614	3,749	80.4	28.4	35.3	2,015	15.3	10,784	36.0	54.6
1984	13,744	10,914	3,929	79.4	28.6	36.0	2,184	15.9	11,052	36.4	53.6
1983	14,003	10,906	3,820	77.9	27.3	35.0	2,379	17.0	10,959	35.5	52.7
1982	14,083	11,120	3,837	79.0	27.2	34.5	2,329	16.5	11,295	35.0	53.0
1981	14,127	11,052	3,833	78.2	27.1	34.7	2,424	17.2	11,203	35.1	52.1
1980	14,107	11,125	3,717	78.9	26.3	33.4	2,390	16.9	11,309	33.7	51.4
1979	13,571	10,657	3,508	78.5	25.8	32.9	2,320	17.1	10,838	33.6	52.4
1978	13,385	10,614	3,621	79.3	27.1	34.1	2,200	16.4	10,789	34.5	52.6
1977	13,218	10,440	3,712	79.0	28.1	35.6	2,170	16.4	10,626	36.0	54.2
1976	13,012	10,312	3,673	79.2	28.2	35.6	2,109	16.2	10,492	36.0	55.7
1975	12,724	10,214	3,693	80.3	29.0	36.2	1,928	15.2	10,415	36.7	56.1
1974	12,315	9,835	3,411	79.9	27.7	34.7	1,958	15.9	10,073	35.3	55.6
1973	12,111	9,716	3,360	80.2	27.7	34.6	1,853	15.3	9,908	35.1	55.4
1972	11,712	9,247	3,534	79.0	30.2	38.2	1,898	16.2	9,461	38.8	59.0
1971	11,092	8,669	3,599	78.2	32.4	41.5	1,865	16.8	8,855	42.1	60.1
1970	10,385	8,087	3,331	77.9	32.1	41.2	1,746	16.8	8,279	41.8	59.2
1969	9,649	7,445	3,392	77.2	35.2	45.6	1,640	17.0	7,609	46.2	61.2
1968	9,251	6,864	3,152	74.2	34.1	45.9	1,777	19.2	8,038	46.7	61.1
1967	8,999	6,678	2,982	74.2	33.1	44.7	1,804	20.0	6,829	45.1	58.8
Female											
2019	14,643	13,258	6,492	90.5	44.3	49.0	617	4.2	13,466	49.3	75.7
2018	14,708	13,223	6,511	89.9	44.3	49.2	679	4.6	13,456	49.3	76.8
2017	14,705	13,134	6,477	89.3	44.0	49.3	754	5.1	13,375	49.6	76.1
2016	14,851	13,273	6,521	89.4	43.9	49.1	778	5.2	13,557	49.3	76.4
2015	14,963	13,217	6,459	88.3	43.2	48.9	883	5.9	13,418	49.0	76.3

r = Revised, controlled to 1990 census based population estimates; previous 1993 data controlled to 1980 census based population estimates.
Note: The change in the educational attainment question and the college completion categories from "4 or more years of college" to "at least some college," in 1992 caused an increase in the proportion of 14-to-24-year-old high school graduates enrolled in college or completed some college, of approximately 5 percentage points. High school graduates are people who have completed 4 years of high school or more, for 1967 to 1991. Beginning in 1992, they were people whose highest degree was a high school diploma (including equivalency) or higher.
[1]Starting in 2003 respondents could identify more than one race. Except as noted, the race data in this table from 2003 onward represent those respondents who indicated only one race category.
[2]The data shown prior to 2003 consists of those identifying themselves as "Asian or Pacific Islanders."

Table A-14. Population 14 to 24 Years Old, by High School Graduate Status, College Enrollment, Attainment, Sex, Race, and Hispanic Origin, October 1967–2019—*Continued*

(Numbers in thousands; percent; civilian noninstitutionalized population.)

Year, race, and Hispanic origin	Population 18 to 24 years old								High school graduates, 14 to 24 years old		
		High school graduates		Percent			High school dropouts			Percent	
	Total	Total	Enrolled in college	High school graduates	Enrolled in college	Of high school graduates enrolled in college	Number	Percent	All graduates	Enrolled in college	Enrolled or completed some college
2014	15,070	13,293	6,456	88.2	42.8	48.6	958	6.4	13,475	48.7	76.3
2013	15,177	13,266	6,573	87.4	43.3	49.5	1,033	6.8	13,480	49.9	76.6
2012	15,125	13,113	6,725	86.7	44.5	51.3	1,019	6.7	13,316	51.6	77.2
2011	14,732	12,776	6,617	86.7	44.9	51.8	1,107	7.5	12,930	51.9	77.2
2010	14,772	12,854	6,515	87.0	44.1	50.7	1,116	7.6	13,024	51.1	76.7
2009	14,546	12,536	6,432	86.2	44.2	51.3	1,165	8.0	12,738	51.4	75.5
2008	14,391	12,387	6,083	86.1	42.3	49.1	1,257	8.7	12,548	49.3	74.5
2007	14,263	12,321	6,005	86.4	42.1	48.7	1,256	8.8	12,519	48.8	73.3
2006	14,073	11,922	5,712	84.7	40.6	47.9	1,387	9.9	12,141	48.1	73.3
2005	13,778	11,921	5,861	86.5	42.5	49.2	1,302	9.5	12,115	49.4	73.4
2004	13,930	11,828	5,746	84.9	41.2	48.6	1,444	10.4	12,015	48.8	72.8
2003	13,724	11,684	5,667	85.1	41.3	48.5	1,354	9.9	11,858	48.5	72.2
2002	13,623	11,496	5,404	84.4	39.7	47.0	1,450	10.6	11,664	47.3	70.3
2001	13,531	11,375	5,192	84.1	38.4	45.7	1,491	11.0	11,549	45.7	69.4
2000	13,319	11,200	5,109	84.1	38.4	45.6	1,478	11.1	11,344	45.8	70.1
1999	13,136	10,926	4,863	83.2	37.0	44.5	1,594	12.1	11,058	44.6	69.8
1998	12,743	10,651	4,919	83.6	38.6	46.2	1,526	12.0	10,768	46.4	70.7
1997	12,460	10,403	4,829	83.5	38.8	46.4	1,471	11.8	10,549	46.8	69.6
1996	12,386	10,317	4,582	83.3	37.0	44.4	1,519	12.3	10,507	44.9	68.6
1995	12,548	10,338	4,452	82.4	35.5	43.1	1,679	13.4	10,477	43.4	69.8
1994	12,696	10,611	4,576	83.6	36.0	43.1	1,561	12.3	10,729	43.4	68.7
1993r	12,810	10,702	4,393	83.5	34.3	41.0	1,604	12.5	10,831	41.3	66.6
1993	12,202	10,232	4,199	83.9	34.4	41.0	1,494	12.2	10,355	41.2	66.7
1992	12,313	10,344	4,429	84.0	36.0	42.8	1,466	11.9	10,486	43.3	66.9
1991	12,536	10,391	4,218	82.9	33.6	40.6	1,676	13.4	10,502	41.0	62.1
1990	12,718	10,533	4,042	82.8	31.8	38.4	1,690	13.3	10,676	38.7	59.8
1989	12,936	10,758	4,085	83.2	31.6	38.0	1,702	13.2	10,936	38.4	58.6
1988	13,242	11,068	4,021	83.6	30.4	36.3	1,799	13.5	11,257	36.8	58.2
1987	13,324	11,086	3,826	83.2	28.7	34.5	1,803	13.5	11,268	35.0	56.4
1986	13,591	11,430	3,775	84.1	27.8	33.0	1,751	12.9	11,623	33.5	55.5
1985	13,923	11,736	3,788	84.3	27.2	32.3	1,804	13.0	11,937	32.8	54.0
1984	14,287	11,956	3,662	83.7	25.6	30.6	1,958	13.7	12,199	31.3	52.4
1983	14,577	12,082	3,657	82.9	25.1	30.3	2,031	13.9	12,294	31.0	52.8
1982	14,763	12,171	3,841	82.4	26.0	31.6	2,171	14.7	12,411	32.1	52.4
1981	14,838	12,290	3,741	82.8	25.2	30.4	2,097	14.1	12,503	31.0	51.3
1980	14,851	12,287	3,682	82.7	24.8	30.0	2,124	14.3	12,547	30.6	50.8
1979	14,403	11,763	3,482	81.7	24.2	29.6	2,240	15.6	12,074	30.4	50.8
1978	14,262	11,694	3,373	82.0	23.7	28.8	2,188	15.3	11,969	29.6	50.3
1977	14,113	11,569	3,431	82.0	24.3	29.7	2,143	15.2	11,875	30.3	50.0
1976	13,907	11,365	3,508	81.7	25.2	30.9	2,168	15.6	11,666	31.6	51.4
1975	13,663	11,113	3,243	81.3	23.7	29.2	2,181	16.0	11,407	29.9	49.2
1974	13,355	10,889	2,905	81.5	21.8	26.7	2,112	15.8	11,194	27.4	47.5
1973	13,126	10,663	2,696	81.2	20.5	25.3	2,119	16.1	10,986	26.1	46.5
1972	12,867	10,371	2,724	80.6	21.2	26.3	2,170	16.9	10,644	27.0	47.4
1971	12,576	10,020	2,610	79.7	20.8	26.0	2,159	17.2	10,272	26.9	47.1
1970	12,167	9,680	2,474	79.6	20.3	25.6	2,163	17.8	9,908	26.3	46.6
1969	11,713	9,259	2,448	79.0	20.9	26.4	2,128	18.2	9,499	27.1	45.7
1968	11,311	8,820	2,205	78.0	19.5	25.0	2,150	19.0	9,072	25.9	44.4
1967	11,011	8,436	2,117	76.6	19.2	25.1	2,162	19.6	8,694	26.0	44.7
WHITE ALONE											
Both Sexes											
2019	21,574	19,132	8,603	88.7	39.9	45.0	1,109	5.1	19,409	45.1	70.0
2018	21,717	19,133	8,771	88.1	40.4	45.8	1,284	5.9	19,413	46.1	71.8
2017	21,789	19,069	8,690	87.5	39.9	45.6	1,358	6.2	19,351	45.7	72.1
2016	22,018	19,373	9,106	88.0	41.4	47.0	1,381	6.3	19,673	47.1	72.7
2015	22,244	19,451	8,969	87.4	40.3	46.1	1,430	6.4	19,747	46.2	72.6

r = Revised, controlled to 1990 census based population estimates; previous 1993 data controlled to 1980 census based population estimates.
Note: The change in the educational attainment question and the college completion categories from "4 or more years of college" to "at least some college," in 1992 caused an increase in the proportion of 14-to-24-year-old high school graduates enrolled in college or completed some college, of approximately 5 percentage points. High school graduates are people who have completed 4 years of high school or more, for 1967 to 1991. Beginning in 1992, they were people whose highest degree was a high school diploma (including equivalency) or higher.
[1]Starting in 2003 respondents could identify more than one race. Except as noted, the race data in this table from 2003 onward represent those respondents who indicated only one race category.
[2]The data shown prior to 2003 consists of those identifying themselves as "Asian or Pacific Islanders."

Table A-14. Population 14 to 24 Years Old, by High School Graduate Status, College Enrollment, Attainment, Sex, Race, and Hispanic Origin, October 1967–2019—*Continued*

(Numbers in thousands; percent; civilian noninstitutionalized population.)

| Year, race, and Hispanic origin | Population 18 to 24 years old | | | | | | | | High school graduates, 14 to 24 years old | | |
| | Total | High school graduates | | | Percent | | High school dropouts | | | Percent | |
		Total	Enrolled in college	High school graduates	Enrolled in college	Of high school graduates enrolled in college	Number	Percent	All graduates	Enrolled in college	Enrolled or completed some college
2014	22,507	19,541	9,077	86.8	40.3	46.4	1,599	7.1	19,786	46.6	72.1
2013	22,658	19,660	9,049	86.8	39.9	46.0	1,599	7.1	19,985	46.5	72.1
2012	22,712	19,555	9,302	86.1	41.0	47.6	1,641	7.2	19,831	47.9	73.5
2011	23,089	19,760	9,813	85.6	42.5	49.7	1,885	8.2	20,007	49.8	74.0
2010	22,851	19,517	9,325	85.4	40.8	47.8	1,941	8.5	19,741	48.0	73.0
2009	22,606	19,241	9,327	85.1	41.3	48.5	2,059	9.1	19,512	48.6	72.1
2008	22,530	19,334	9,141	85.8	40.6	47.3	1,991	8.8	19,586	47.5	71.6
2007	22,392	18,913	8,780	84.5	39.2	46.4	2,248	10.0	19,170	46.5	70.3
2006	22,169	18,489	8,298	83.4	37.4	44.9	2,399	10.8	18,751	45.1	69.9
2005	21,777	18,130	8,498	83.3	39.0	46.9	2,466	11.3	18,352	46.9	70.0
2004	21,896	18,213	8,351	82.6	38.0	45.9	2,599	11.9	18,414	46.1	69.1
2003[1]	21,502	17,901	8,150	83.3	37.9	45.5	2,489	11.6	18,123	45.5	69.1
2002	21,704	17,793	7,921	82.0	36.5	44.5	2,641	12.2	17,995	44.6	67.5
2001	21,372	17,348	7,548	81.2	35.3	43.5	2,865	13.4	17,547	43.5	67.0
2000	21,257	17,512	7,566	82.4	35.6	43.2	2,598	12.2	17,714	43.4	66.9
1999	20,866	17,052	7,447	81.7	35.7	43.7	2,680	12.8	17,220	43.8	67.5
1998	20,465	16,701	7,541	81.6	36.9	45.2	2,810	13.7	16,855	45.3	68.3
1997	20,020	16,557	7,495	82.7	37.4	45.3	2,476	12.4	16,733	45.6	67.7
1996	19,676	16,199	7,123	82.3	36.2	44.0	2,458	12.5	16,436	44.3	68.4
1995	19,866	16,269	7,011	81.9	35.3	43.1	2,711	13.6	16,439	43.4	68.3
1994	20,171	16,670	7,118	82.6	35.3	42.7	2,553	12.7	16,814	42.9	67.6
1993r	20,493	16,989	7,074	82.9	34.5	41.6	2,595	12.7	17,161	41.8	66.5
1993	19,430	16,196	6,763	83.4	34.8	41.8	2,369	12.2	16,361	41.9	66.7
1992	19,671	16,379	6,916	83.3	35.2	42.2	2,398	12.2	16,586	42.7	67.0
1991	19,980	16,324	6,813	81.7	34.1	41.7	2,845	14.2	16,467	42.0	62.3
1990	20,393	16,823	6,635	82.5	32.5	39.4	2,751	13.5	17,022	39.8	60.1
1989	20,825	17,089	6,631	82.1	31.8	38.8	2,926	14.1	17,329	39.1	58.9
1988	21,261	17,491	6,659	82.3	31.3	38.1	3,012	14.2	17,720	30.4	58.5
1987	21,493	17,689	6,483	82.3	30.2	36.6	3,042	14.2	17,982	37.1	56.8
1986	22,020	18,291	6,307	83.1	28.6	34.5	2,961	13.4	18,554	34.9	55.5
1985	22,632	18,916	6,500	83.6	28.7	34.4	3,050	13.5	19,229	35.0	55.3
1984	23,347	19,373	6,526	83.0	28.0	33.7	3,281	14.1	19,686	34.2	53.8
1983	23,899	19,643	6,463	82.2	27.0	32.9	3,428	14.3	19,948	33.6	53.4
1982	24,208	19,944	6,694	82.4	27.2	33.1	3,523	14.6	20,292	33.6	53.1
1981	24,486	20,123	6,549	82.2	26.7	32.5	3,590	14.7	20,439	33.0	52.1
1980	24,482	20,214	6,423	82.6	26.2	31.8	3,525	14.4	20,583	32.3	51.4
1979	23,895	19,616	6,120	82.1	25.6	31.2	3,571	14.9	20,033	31.8	51.7
1978	23,650	19,526	6,077	82.6	25.7	31.1	3,464	14.6	19,911	31.7	51.3
1977	23,430	19,291	6,209	82.3	26.5	32.2	3,445	14.7	19,712	32.6	52.1
1976	23,119	19,045	6,276	82.4	27.1	33.0	3,407	14.7	19,462	33.5	53.5
1975	22,703	18,883	6,116	83.2	26.9	32.4	3,149	13.9	19,298	33.0	52.7
1974	22,141	18,318	5,509	82.7	25.2	30.5	3,212	14.5	18,794	31.2	51.7
1973	21,766	18,023	5,438	82.8	25.0	30.2	3,085	14.2	18,470	30.8	51.6
1972	21,315	17,410	5,624	81.7	26.4	32.3	3,241	15.2	17,838	33.0	53.9
1971	20,533	16,593	5,594	81.3	27.2	33.5	3,156	15.4	17,087	34.2	54.1
1970	19,608	15,960	5,305	81.4	27.1	33.2	2,974	15.2	16,334	33.9	53.4
1969	18,606	15,031	5,347	80.8	28.7	35.6	2,915	15.7	15,383	36.2	53.5
1968	17,951	14,127	4,929	78.7	27.5	34.9	3,107	17.3	14,506	35.7	52.5
1967	17,500	13,657	4,708	78.0	26.9	34.5	3,141	17.9	14,022	35.2	51.4
Male											
2019	10,880	9,440	3,922	86.8	36.0	41.5	666	6.1	9,573	41.6	64.8
2018	10,972	9,478	4,045	86.4	36.9	42.7	765	7.0	9,588	42.8	66.3
2017	11,012	9,408	3,973	85.4	36.1	42.2	780	7.1	9,536	42.3	67.6
2016	11,139	9,014	4,267	86.3	38.3	44.4	818	7.3	9,734	44.4	67.7
2015	11,251	9,714	4,189	86.3	37.2	43.1	791	7.0	9,875	43.2	67.6
2014	11,397	9,781	4,296	85.8	37.7	43.9	866	7.6	9,904	44.1	67.4
2013	11,475	9,792	4,131	85.3	36.0	42.2	855	7.5	9,956	42.6	66.7

r = Revised, controlled to 1990 census based population estimates; previous 1993 data controlled to 1980 census based population estimates.

Note: The change in the educational attainment question and the college completion categories from "4 or more years of college" to "at least some college," in 1992 caused an increase in the proportion of 14-to-24-year-old high school graduates enrolled in college or completed some college, of approximately 5 percentage points. High school graduates are people who have completed 4 years of high school or more, for 1967 to 1991. Beginning in 1992, they were people whose highest degree was a high school diploma (including equivalency) or higher.

[1] Starting in 2003 respondents could identify more than one race. Except as noted, the race data in this table from 2003 onward represent those respondents who indicated only one race category.

[2] The data shown prior to 2003 consists of those identifying themselves as "Asian or Pacific Islanders."

Table A-14. Population 14 to 24 Years Old, by High School Graduate Status, College Enrollment, Attainment, Sex, Race, and Hispanic Origin, October 1967–2019—*Continued*

(Numbers in thousands; percent; civilian noninstitutionalized population.)

Year, race, and Hispanic origin	Population 18 to 24 years old								High school graduates, 14 to 24 years old		
		High school graduates		Percent			High school dropouts			Percent	
	Total	Total	Enrolled in college	High school graduates	Enrolled in college	Of high school graduates enrolled in college	Number	Percent	All graduates	Enrolled in college	Enrolled or completed some college
2012	11,499	9,692	4,261	84.3	37.1	44.0	937	8.1	9,810	44.3	68.0
2011	11,850	9,928	4,685	83.8	39.5	47.2	1,077	9.1	10,061	47.3	70.0
2010	11,579	9,651	4,369	83.3	37.7	45.3	1,124	9.7	9,754	45.4	68.6
2009	11,449	9,535	4,404	83.3	38.5	46.2	1,201	10.5	9,662	46.4	68.3
2008	11,432	9,646	4,340	84.4	38.0	45.0	1,122	9.8	9,784	45.2	67.8
2007	11,387	9,311	4,040	81.8	35.5	43.4	1,333	11.7	9,430	43.5	66.0
2006	11,264	9,139	3,842	81.1	34.1	42.0	1,396	12.4	9,237	42.2	66.0
2005	11,116	8,885	3,924	79.9	35.3	44.1	1,469	13.2	8,986	44.1	65.9
2004	11,107	9,001	3,855	81.0	34.7	42.8	1,524	13.7	9,067	43.1	64.4
2003[1]	10,885	8,763	3,726	80.5	34.2	42.5	1,452	13.3	8,862	42.6	65.1
2002	10,986	8,717	3,701	79.4	33.7	42.5	1,506	13.7	8,833	42.5	64.6
2001	10,817	8,490	3,521	78.5	32.6	41.5	1,659	15.3	8,582	41.5	64.0
2000	10,739	8,603	3,522	80.1	32.8	40.9	1,450	13.5	8,690	41.1	63.5
1999	10,532	8,382	3,585	79.6	34.0	42.7	1,462	13.9	8,457	42.8	64.8
1998	10,400	8,194	3,634	78.8	34.9	44.3	1,628	15.7	8,256	44.4	65.5
1997	10,173	8,204	3,633	80.6	35.7	44.3	1,406	13.8	8,274	44.5	65.3
1996	9,897	8,000	3,419	80.8	34.5	42.7	1,275	12.9	8,104	43.0	66.0
1995	9,980	8,001	3,398	80.2	34.0	42.5	1,430	14.3	8,067	42.7	65.3
1994	10,123	8,168	3,406	80.7	33.6	41.7	1,377	13.6	8,227	41.9	65.4
1993r	10,294	8,338	3,498	81.0	34.0	42.0	1,388	13.5	8,411	42.1	65.1
1993	9,641	7,857	3,313	81.5	34.4	42.2	1,379	12.9	7,926	42.3	65.4
1992	9,744	7,911	3,291	81.2	33.8	41.6	1,300	13.3	8,016	42.1	65.8
1991	9,896	7,843	3,270	79.3	33.0	41.7	1,520	15.4	7,899	41.9	59.9
1990	10,053	8,157	3,292	81.1	32.7	40.3	1,430	14.2	8,246	40.7	58.8
1989	10,240	8,177	3,223	79.9	31.5	39.4	1,572	15.4	8,271	39.7	58.5
1988	10,380	8,268	3,260	79.7	31.4	39.4	1,594	15.4	8,365	39.6	57.8
1987	10,549	8,498	3,289	80.6	31.2	38.7	1,593	15.1	8,647	39.2	56.4
1986	10,814	8,780	3,168	81.2	29.3	36.1	1,575	14.6	8,886	36.4	55.1
1985	11,108	9,077	3,254	81.7	29.3	35.8	1,637	14.7	9,229	36.6	55.5
1984	11,521	9,348	3,406	81.1	29.6	36.4	1,744	15.1	9,459	36.8	54.2
1983	11,787	9,411	3,335	79.8	28.3	35.4	1,865	15.8	9,534	35.9	53.5
1982	11,874	9,611	3,308	80.9	27.9	34.4	1,810	15.2	9,761	34.9	53.2
1981	12,040	9,619	3,340	79.9	27.7	34.7	1,960	16.3	9,754	35.1	52.8
1980	12,011	9,686	3,275	80.6	27.3	33.8	1,883	15.7	9,838	34.1	51.8
1979	11,721	9,457	3,104	80.7	26.5	32.8	1,830	15.6	9,615	33.4	52.7
1978	11,572	9,438	3,195	81.6	27.6	33.9	1,722	14.9	9,582	34.3	52.5
1977	11,445	9,263	3,286	80.9	28.7	35.5	1,779	15.5	9,422	35.8	54.5
1976	11,279	9,186	3,250	81.4	28.8	35.4	1,691	15.0	9,340	35.7	55.9
1975	11,050	9,139	3,326	82.7	30.1	36.4	1,490	13.5	9,310	36.9	56.6
1974	10,722	8,768	3,035	81.8	28.3	34.6	1,579	14.7	8,980	35.2	55.9
1973	10,511	8,637	3,032	82.2	28.8	35.1	1,453	13.8	8,817	35.6	56.5
1972	10,212	8,278	3,195	81.1	31.3	38.6	1,506	14.7	8,462	39.2	60.1
1971	9,653	7,807	3,284	80.9	34.0	42.1	1,429	14.8	7,978	42.6	61.4
1970	9,053	7,324	3,096	80.9	34.2	42.3	1,297	14.3	7,496	42.9	60.9
1969	8,420	6,740	3,146	80.0	37.4	46.7	1,248	14.8	6,882	47.3	62.8
1968	8,084	6,221	2,949	77.0	36.5	47.4	1,401	17.3	6,372	48.1	62.7
1967	7,864	6,073	2,761	77.2	35.1	45.5	1,391	17.7	6,210	45.9	60.0
Female											
2019	10,694	9,692	4,680	90.6	43.8	48.3	443	4.1	9,837	48.6	75.1
2018	10,744	9,655	4,725	89.9	44.0	48.9	518	4.8	9,825	49.2	77.2
2017	10,777	9,661	4,717	89.6	43.8	48.8	578	5.4	9,814	49.0	76.4
2016	10,879	9,759	4,839	89.7	44.5	49.6	563	5.2	9,939	49.8	77.5
2015	10,993	9,736	4,780	88.6	43.5	49.1	639	5.8	9,872	49.1	77.5
2014	11,110	9,760	4,780	87.9	43.0	49.0	733	6.6	9,882	49.2	76.8
2013	11,183	9,868	4,919	88.2	44.0	49.8	744	6.7	10,029	50.2	77.5
2012	11,214	9,863	5,041	88.0	45.0	51.1	704	6.3	10,021	51.5	78.8
2011	11,238	9,832	5,128	87.5	45.6	51.8	808	7.2	9,946	52.2	78.0

r = Revised, controlled to 1990 census based population estimates; previous 1993 data controlled to 1980 census based population estimates.
Note: The change in the educational attainment question and the college completion categories from "4 or more years of college" to "at least some college," in 1992 caused an increase in the proportion of 14-to-24-year-old high school graduates enrolled in college or completed some college, of approximately 5 percentage points. High school graduates are people who have completed 4 years of high school or more, for 1967 to 1991. Beginning in 1992, they were people whose highest degree was a high school diploma (including equivalency) or higher.
[1]Starting in 2003 respondents could identify more than one race. Except as noted, the race data in this table from 2003 onward represent those respondents who indicated only one race category.
[2]The data shown prior to 2003 consists of those identifying themselves as "Asian or Pacific Islanders."

Table A-14. Population 14 to 24 Years Old, by High School Graduate Status, College Enrollment, Attainment, Sex, Race, and Hispanic Origin, October 1967–2019—*Continued*

(Numbers in thousands; percent; civilian noninstitutionalized population.)

| Year, race, and Hispanic origin | Population 18 to 24 years old | | | | | | | | High school graduates, 14 to 24 years old | | |
| | Total | High school graduates | | Percent | | | High school dropouts | | | Percent | |
		Total	Enrolled in college	High school graduates	Enrolled in college	Of high school graduates enrolled in college	Number	Percent	All graduates	Enrolled in college	Enrolled or completed some college
2010	11,271	9,867	4,956	87.5	44.0	50.2	817	7.2	9,987	50.6	77.3
2009	11,157	9,706	4,923	87.0	44.1	50.7	858	7.7	9,850	50.8	75.8
2008	11,098	9,688	4,801	87.3	43.3	49.6	869	7.8	9,802	49.9	75.4
2007	11,005	9,603	4,741	87.3	43.1	49.4	915	8.3	9,741	49.5	74.4
2006	10,905	9,350	4,456	85.7	40.9	47.7	1,003	9.2	9,513	47.9	73.7
2005	10,661	9,245	4,574	86.7	42.9	49.5	997	9.4	9,366	49.7	73.9
2004	10,789	9,212	4,496	85.4	41.7	48.8	1,075	10.0	9,347	49.0	73.5
2003[1]	10,617	9,138	4,424	86.1	41.7	48.4	1,037	9.8	9,260	48.3	72.9
2002	10,718	9,075	4,220	84.7	39.4	46.5	1,135	10.6	9,162	46.6	70.4
2001	10,555	8,859	4,027	83.9	38.1	45.5	1,206	11.4	8,965	45.5	69.8
2000	10,517	8,909	4,044	84.7	38.5	45.4	1,148	10.9	9,024	45.6	70.2
1999	10,334	8,671	3,862	83.9	37.4	44.5	1,218	11.8	8,763	44.7	70.1
1998	10,065	8,507	3,907	84.5	38.8	45.9	1,181	11.7	8,599	46.2	71.0
1997	9,847	8,352	3,863	84.8	39.2	46.3	1,072	10.9	8,458	46.6	70.1
1996	9,778	8,200	3,705	83.9	37.9	45.2	1,182	12.1	8,333	45.6	70.7
1995	9,886	8,271	3,615	83.7	36.6	43.7	1,281	13.0	8,376	44.0	71.3
1994	10,048	8,503	3,714	84.6	37.0	43.7	1,175	11.7	8,588	43.9	69.7
1993r	10,199	8,651	3,576	84.8	35.1	41.3	1,207	11.8	8,750	41.5	67.9
1993	9,790	8,339	3,450	85.2	35.2	41.4	1,125	11.5	8,435	41.6	68.0
1992	9,928	8,468	3,625	85.3	36.5	42.8	1,098	11.1	8,569	43.2	68.1
1991	10,119	8,481	3,544	83.8	35.0	41.8	1,324	13.1	8,568	42.1	64.5
1990	10,340	8,666	3,344	83.8	32.3	38.6	1,322	12.8	8,775	38.9	61.4
1989	10,586	8,913	3,409	84.2	32.2	38.2	1,354	12.8	9,059	38.6	59.2
1988	10,881	9,223	3,399	84.8	31.2	36.9	1,418	13.0	9,355	37.3	59.1
1987	10,944	9,189	3,192	84.0	29.2	34.7	1,449	13.2	9,334	36.2	57.2
1986	11,205	9,509	3,139	84.9	28.0	33.0	1,388	12.4	9,667	33.6	55.8
1985	11,524	9,840	3,247	85.4	28.2	33.0	1,413	12.3	10,001	33.6	55.2
1984	11,826	10,026	3,120	84.8	26.4	31.1	1,535	13.0	10,089	31.8	53.4
1983	12,112	10,233	3,129	84.5	25.8	30.6	1,563	12.9	10,233	31.3	53.4
1982	12,332	10,333	3,285	83.8	26.6	31.8	1,713	13.0	10,530	32.3	52.9
1981	12,446	10,504	3,208	84.4	25.8	30.5	1,629	13.1	10,687	31.1	51.6
1980	12,471	10,528	3,147	84.4	25.2	29.9	1,642	13.2	10,749	30.6	50.9
1979	12,174	10,157	3,015	83.4	24.8	29.7	1,741	14.3	10,417	30.3	60.8
1978	12,078	10,088	2,882	83.5	23.9	28.6	1,742	14.4	10,327	29.3	50.3
1977	11,985	10,029	2,923	83.7	24.4	29.1	1,666	13.9	10,292	29.7	50.0
1976	11,840	9,860	3,026	83.3	25.6	30.7	1,717	14.5	10,118	31.4	51.3
1975	11,653	9,743	2,790	83.6	23.9	28.6	1,658	14.2	9,986	29.4	49.1
1974	11,419	9,551	2,555	83.6	22.4	26.8	1,633	14.3	9,811	27.5	47.8
1973	11,255	9,387	2,406	83.4	21.4	25.6	1,632	14.5	9,653	26.4	47.1
1972	11,103	9,132	2,428	82.2	21.9	26.6	1,735	15.6	9,377	27.4	48.3
1971	10,880	8,887	2,310	81.7	21.2	26.0	1,726	15.9	9,107	26.8	47.7
1970	10,555	8,634	2,209	81.8	20.9	25.6	1,675	15.9	8,837	26.3	47.2
1969	10,186	8,291	2,200	81.4	21.6	26.5	1,668	16.4	8,501	27.2	46.3
1968	9,866	7,906	1,980	80.1	20.1	25.0	1,706	17.3	8,135	26.0	45.1
1967	9,637	7,586	1,949	78.7	20.2	25.7	1,750	18.2	7,815	26.6	45.7
WHITE ALONE NON-HISPANIC											
Both Sexes											
2019	15,637	14,007	6,430	89.6	41.1	45.9	710	4.5	14,220	46.1	72.0
2018	15,789	14,183	6,671	89.8	42.3	47.0	704	4.5	14,374	47.2	73.8
2017	15,945	14,251	6,544	89.4	41.0	45.9	747	4.7	14,442	45.9	74.3
2016	16,363	14,641	6,895	89.5	42.1	47.1	822	5.0	14,816	47.1	74.6
2015	16,615	14,812	6,938	89.1	41.8	46.8	816	4.9	15,025	46.9	74.6
2014	16,723	14,877	7,054	89.0	42.2	47.4	890	5.3	15,066	47.6	74.9
2013	16,962	15,135	7,065	89.2	41.6	46.7	876	5.2	15,394	47.1	75.0
2012	17,072	15,216	7,189	89.1	42.1	47.2	819	4.8	15,421	47.6	75.0

r = Revised, controlled to 1990 census based population estimates; previous 1993 data controlled to 1980 census based population estimates.
Note: The change in the educational attainment question and the college completion categories from "4 or more years of college" to "at least some college," in 1992 caused an increase in the proportion of 14-to-24-year-old high school graduates enrolled in college or completed some college, of approximately 5 percentage points. High school graduates are people who have completed 4 years of high school or more, for 1967 to 1991. Beginning in 1992, they were people whose highest degree was a high school diploma (including equivalency) or higher.
[1] Starting in 2003 respondents could identify more than one race. Except as noted, the race data in this table from 2003 onward represent those respondents who indicated only one race category.
[2] The data shown prior to 2003 consists of those identifying themselves as "Asian or Pacific Islanders."

Table A-14. Population 14 to 24 Years Old, by High School Graduate Status, College Enrollment, Attainment, Sex, Race, and Hispanic Origin, October 1967–2019—*Continued*

(Numbers in thousands; percent; civilian noninstitutionalized population.)

Year, race, and Hispanic origin	Population 18 to 24 years old								High school graduates, 14 to 24 years old		
		High school graduates		Percent			High school dropouts			Percent	
	Total	Total	Enrolled in college	High school graduates	Enrolled in college	Of high school graduates enrolled in college	Number	Percent	All graduates	Enrolled in college	Enrolled or completed some college
2011	17,627	15,565	7,882	88.3	44.7	50.6	1,002	5.7	15,752	50.7	76.2
2010	17,693	15,761	7,663	89.1	43.3	48.6	1,003	5.7	15,927	48.8	75.4
2009	17,750	15,839	7,983	89.2	45.0	50.4	1,029	5.8	16,051	50.5	75.2
2008	17,839	16,038	7,894	89.9	44.2	49.2	960	5.4	16,224	49.4	74.2
2007	17,669	15,727	7,533	89.0	42.6	47.9	1,064	6.0	15,921	48.0	72.9
2006	17,565	15,452	7,200	88.0	41.0	46.6	1,189	6.8	15,642	46.8	72.5
2005	17,293	15,187	7,393	87.8	42.8	48.7	1,216	7.0	15,368	48.7	72.6
2004	17,326	15,224	7,228	87.9	41.7	47.5	1,313	7.6	15,382	47.7	71.8
2003[1]	17,158	15,070	7,129	87.8	41.6	47.3	1,267	7.4	15,255	47.3	71.5
2002	17,131	14,910	7,004	87.0	40.9	47.0	1,289	7.5	15,089	47.1	70.4
2001	16,721	14,480	6,565	86.6	39.3	45.3	1,390	8.3	14,646	45.3	69.7
2000	17,327	15,187	6,709	87.7	38.7	44.2	1,316	7.6	15,344	44.3	69.0
1999	17,080	14,812	6,735	86.7	39.4	45.5	1,404	8.2	14,952	45.6	70.2
1998	16,634	14,402	6,757	86.6	40.6	46.9	1,491	9.0	14,542	47.0	70.6
1997	16,575	14,414	6,728	87.0	40.6	46.7	1,432	8.6	14,527	46.9	70.0
1996	16,339	14,288	6,447	87.5	39.5	45.1	1,303	8.0	14,501	45.5	70.7
1995	16,867	14,523	6,393	86.1	37.9	44.0	1,647	9.8	14,672	44.3	70.2
1994	17,114	14,916	6,521	87.2	38.1	43.7	1,505	8.8	15,049	44.0	69.2
1993	16,895	14,665	6,221	86.8	36.8	42.4	1,524	9.0	14,801	42.6	68.1
Male											
2019	7,922	6,920	2,929	87.4	37.0	42.3	438	5.5	7,019	42.4	66.8
2018	7,977	7,044	3,123	88.3	39.1	44.3	416	5.2	7,125	44.5	68.3
2017	8,096	7,098	3,057	87.7	37.8	43.1	409	5.1	7,187	43.0	69.8
2016	8,259	7,279	3,288	88.1	39.8	45.2	463	5.6	7,348	45.2	69.6
2015	8,401	7,396	3,284	88.0	39.1	44.4	451	5.4	7,512	44.4	69.7
2014	8,446	7,426	3,391	87.9	40.2	45.7	485	5.7	7,526	45.8	70.5
2013	8,562	7,526	3,260	87.9	38.1	43.3	462	5.4	7,658	43.8	70.2
2012	8,598	7,552	3,290	87.8	38.3	43.6	455	5.3	7,637	43.9	69.5
2011	8,864	7,697	3,754	86.8	42.4	48.8	554	6.2	7,794	48.9	72.7
2010	8,919	7,808	3,617	87.5	40.6	46.3	569	6.4	7,884	46.4	70.9
2009	8,957	7,818	3,787	87.3	42.3	48.4	632	7.1	7,915	48.5	71.9
2008	9,032	8,028	3,766	88.9	41.7	46.9	546	6.0	8,126	47.1	70.4
2007	8,940	7,786	3,541	87.1	39.6	45.5	622	7.0	7,883	45.5	68.8
2006	8,842	7,660	3,354	86.6	37.9	43.8	647	7.3	7,734	43.9	68.4
2005	8,700	7,443	3,429	85.5	39.4	46.1	685	7.9	7,526	46.0	68.6
2004	8,644	7,527	3,322	87.1	38.4	44.1	691	8.0	7,576	44.4	66.7
2003[2]	8,538	7,325	3,291	85.8	38.5	44.9	721	8.4	7,401	45.0	68.5
2002	8,453	7,244	3,287	85.7	38.9	45.4	668	7.9	7,352	45.5	67.9
2001	8,343	7,112	3,094	85.3	37.1	43.4	741	8.9	7,191	43.4	67.1
2000	8,670	7,493	3,136	86.4	36.2	41.9	677	7.8	7,556	42.0	65.4
1999	8,580	7,301	3,284	85.1	38.3	45.0	753	8.8	7,369	45.0	67.7
1998	8,380	7,094	3,300	84.7	39.4	46.5	826	9.9	7,151	46.6	68.2
1997	8,326	7,112	3,276	85.4	39.3	46.1	797	9.6	7,154	46.3	68.1
1996	8,168	7,050	3,130	86.3	38.3	44.4	651	8.0	7,143	44.7	68.6
1995	8,399	7,089	3,105	84.4	37.0	43.8	883	10.5	7,147	44.0	67.3
1994	8,457	7,261	3,126	85.9	37.0	43.1	777	9.2	7,317	43.3	67.0
1993	8,403	7,138	3,071	84.9	36.6	43.0	811	9.7	7,191	43.2	67.1
Female											
2019	7,715	7,087	3,502	91.9	45.4	49.4	272	3.5	7,201	49.7	77.0
2018	7,812	7,139	3,549	91.4	45.4	49.7	287	3.7	7,250	49.9	79.3
2017	7,849	7,154	3,487	91.1	44.4	48.7	338	4.3	7,255	48.8	78.8
2016	8,104	7,362	3,606	90.8	44.5	49.0	360	4.4	7,468	49.0	79.5
2015	8,215	7,416	3,654	90.3	44.5	49.3	365	4.4	7,513	49.3	79.5
2014	8,278	7,451	3,663	90.0	44.2	49.2	404	4.9	7,541	49.3	79.3
2013	8,400	7,609	3,804	90.6	45.3	50.0	414	4.9	7,736	50.4	79.8
2012	8,474	7,664	3,899	90.4	46.0	50.9	364	4.3	7,784	51.2	80.5

r = Revised, controlled to 1990 census based population estimates; previous 1993 data controlled to 1980 census based population estimates.
Note: The change in the educational attainment question and the college completion categories from "4 or more years of college" to "at least some college," in 1992 caused an increase in the proportion of 14-to-24-year-old high school graduates enrolled in college or completed some college, of approximately 5 percentage points. High school graduates are people who have completed 4 years of high school or more, for 1967 to 1991. Beginning in 1992, they were people whose highest degree was a high school diploma (including equivalency) or higher.
[1]Starting in 2003 respondents could identify more than one race. Except as noted, the race data in this table from 2003 onward represent those respondents who indicated only one race category.
[2]The data shown prior to 2003 consists of those identifying themselves as "Asian or Pacific Islanders."

Table A-14. Population 14 to 24 Years Old, by High School Graduate Status, College Enrollment, Attainment, Sex, Race, and Hispanic Origin, October 1967–2019—*Continued*

(Numbers in thousands; percent; civilian noninstitutionalized population.)

Year, race, and Hispanic origin	Total	High school graduates — Total	High school graduates — Enrolled in college	Percent — High school graduates	Percent — Enrolled in college	Percent — Of high school graduates enrolled in college	High school dropouts — Number	High school dropouts — Percent	All graduates	Percent — Enrolled in college	Percent — Enrolled or completed some college
2011............................	8,763	7,868	4,128	89.8	47.1	52.5	448	5.1	7,958	52.5	79.6
2010............................	8,774	7,953	4,046	90.6	46.1	50.9	434	4.9	8,044	51.2	79.8
2009............................	8,793	8,021	4,195	91.2	47.7	52.3	398	4.5	8,136	52.4	78.3
2008............................	8,808	8,010	4,127	90.9	46.9	51.5	414	4.7	8,099	51.7	78.0
2007............................	8,728	7,941	3,992	91.0	45.7	50.3	442	5.1	8,039	50.4	76.9
2006............................	8,724	7,791	3,846	89.3	44.1	49.4	542	6.2	7,908	49.5	76.4
2005............................	8,593	7,744	3,964	90.1	46.1	51.2	531	6.2	7,842	51.4	76.4
2004............................	8,628	7,697	3,906	89.2	45.3	50.7	622	7.2	7,805	50.9	76.8
2003[1]............................	8,620	7,745	3,838	89.9	44.5	49.6	546	6.3	7,854	49.5	74.4
2002............................	8,678	7,666	3,717	88.3	42.8	48.5	621	7.2	7,736	48.6	72.8
2001............................	8,378	7,368	3,471	87.9	41.4	47.2	648	7.7	7,455	47.2	72.3
2000............................	8,657	7,693	3,573	88.9	41.3	46.4	638	7.4	7,789	46.6	72.5
1999............................	8,500	7,510	3,451	88.4	40.6	46.0	651	7.7	7,583	46.2	72.5
1998............................	8,254	7,308	3,457	88.5	41.9	47.3	665	8.1	7,391	47.5	73.0
1997............................	8,249	7,302	3,452	88.5	41.9	47.3	636	7.7	7,373	47.5	71.9
1996............................	8,171	7,238	3,317	88.6	40.6	45.8	652	8.0	7,358	46.3	72.8
1995............................	8,467	7,433	3,288	87.8	38.8	44.2	764	9.0	7,525	44.6	73.1
1994............................	8,657	7,655	3,395	88.4	39.2	44.4	728	8.4	7,732	44.6	71.3
1993............................	8,492	7,527	3,150	88.6	37.1	41.9	714	8.4	7,610	42.0	69.1
BLACK ALONE											
Both Sexes											
2019............................	4,344	3,784	1,588	87.1	36.5	42.0	270	6.2	3,850	42.4	66.4
2018............................	4,415	3,852	1,670	87.2	37.8	43.3	216	4.9	3,894	43.3	67.8
2017............................	4,458	3,807	1,595	85.4	35.8	41.9	270	6.1	3,885	41.9	65.4
2016............................	4,551	3,857	1,644	84.7	36.1	42.6	314	6.9	3,937	42.5	65.6
2015............................	4,635	3,971	1,636	85.7	35.3	41.2	347	7.5	4,019	41.3	64.5
2014............................	4,704	3,993	1,528	84.9	32.5	38.3	345	7.3	4,061	39.0	65.9
2013............................	4,746	3,885	1,600	81.9	33.7	41.2	393	8.3	3,929	41.5	65.7
2012............................	4,714	3,754	1,689	79.6	35.8	45.0	467	9.9	3,816	45.0	66.6
2011............................	4,503	3,649	1,639	81.0	36.4	44.9	399	8.9	3,702	45.3	66.3
2010............................	4,457	3,669	1,692	82.3	38.0	46.1	450	10.1	3,731	40.2	66.2
2009............................	4,346	3,458	1,604	79.6	36.9	46.4	505	11.6	3,532	46.4	67.5
2008............................	4,265	3,387	1,349	79.4	31.6	40.0	548	12.1	3,445	40.2	60.7
2007............................	4,182	3,423	1,396	81.8	33.4	40.8	425	10.2	3,483	40.9	61.4
2006............................	4,085	3,156	1,321	77.3	32.3	41.9	532	13.0	3,224	41.9	60.8
2005............................	3,964	3,137	1,297	79.1	32.7	41.3	512	12.9	3,212	41.3	63.5
2004............................	3,940	3,050	1,238	77.4	31.4	40.6	596	15.1	3,112	41.1	63.2
2003[1]............................	3,837	2,948	1,225	76.8	31.9	41.6	545	14.2	2,997	41.8	62.5
2002............................	3,924	3,040	1,226	77.5	31.3	40.3	571	14.5	3,117	41.1	61.2
2001............................	3,916	3,016	1,206	77.0	30.8	40.0	540	13.8	3,095	40.0	59.0
2000............................	4,013	3,090	1,216	77.0	30.3	39.4	615	15.3	3,129	39.5	61.0
1999............................	3,827	2,911	1,145	76.1	29.9	39.4	613	16.0	2,985	39.9	60.4
1998............................	3,745	2,747	1,116	73.4	29.8	40.6	642	17.1	2,790	40.8	61.8
1997............................	3,650	2,725	1,085	74.7	29.7	39.8	611	16.7	2,762	40.2	60.0
1996............................	3,637	2,738	983	75.3	27.0	35.9	581	16.0	2,805	36.6	54.6
1995............................	3,625	2,788	988	76.9	27.3	35.4	522	14.4	2,828	35.8	58.0
1994............................	3,661	2,818	1,001	77.0	27.3	35.5	568	15.5	2,859	36.3	59.2
1993r............................	3,666	2,747	897	74.9	24.5	32.7	600	16.4	2,771	32.8	54.0
1993............................	3,516	2,629	861	74.8	24.5	32.8	578	16.4	2,653	32.9	53.9
1992............................	3,521	2,625	886	74.6	25.2	33.8	575	16.3	2,668	34.3	53.3
1991............................	3,504	2,630	828	75.1	23.6	31.5	545	15.6	2,658	31.8	46.0
1990............................	3,520	2,710	894	77.0	25.4	33.0	530	15.1	2,759	33.7	48.0
1989............................	3,559	2,708	835	76.1	23.5	30.8	583	16.4	2,750	31.5	49.2
1988............................	3,568	2,680	752	75.1	21.1	28.1	631	17.7	2,741	28.6	46.3
1987............................	3,603	2,739	823	76.0	22.8	30.0	611	17.0	2,790	30.6	48.1
1986............................	3,653	2,795	812	76.5	22.2	29.1	617	16.8	2,837	29.3	47.8

r = Revised, controlled to 1990 census based population estimates; previous 1993 data controlled to 1980 census based population estimates.
Note: The change in the educational attainment question and the college completion categories from "4 or more years of college" to "at least some college," in 1992 caused an increase in the proportion of 14-to-24-year-old high school graduates enrolled in college or completed some college, of approximately 5 percentage points. High school graduates are people who have completed 4 years of high school or more, for 1967 to 1991. Beginning in 1992, they were people whose highest degree was a high school diploma (including equivalency) or higher.
[1]Starting in 2003 respondents could identify more than one race. Except as noted, the race data in this table from 2003 onward represent those respondents who indicated only one race category.
[2]The data shown prior to 2003 consists of those identifying themselves as "Asian or Pacific Islanders."

Table A-14. Population 14 to 24 Years Old, by High School Graduate Status, College Enrollment, Attainment, Sex, Race, and Hispanic Origin, October 1967–2019—*Continued*

(Numbers in thousands; percent; civilian noninstitutionalized population.)

| Year, race, and Hispanic origin | Population 18 to 24 years old | | | | | | | | High school graduates, 14 to 24 years old | | |
| | | High school graduates | | Percent | | | High school dropouts | | | Percent | |
	Total	Total	Enrolled in college	High school graduates	Enrolled in college	Of high school graduates enrolled in college	Number	Percent	All graduates	Enrolled in college	Enrolled or completed some college
1985	3,716	2,810	734	75.6	19.8	26.1	655	17.6	2,848	26.5	43.8
1984	3,862	2,885	786	74.7	20.4	27.2	712	18.4	2,950	28.0	45.2
1983	3,865	2,740	741	70.9	19.2	27.0	832	21.5	2,790	27.7	45.0
1982	3,872	2,744	767	70.9	19.8	28.0	851	22.0	2,793	28.2	45.5
1981	3,778	2,678	750	70.9	19.9	28.0	821	21.7	2,718	28.7	44.8
1980	3,721	2,592	715	69.7	19.2	27.6	876	23.5	2,656	28.1	45.9
1979	3,510	2,356	696	67.1	19.8	29.5	895	25.5	2,415	30.6	48.4
1978	3,452	2,340	694	67.8	20.1	29.7	850	24.6	2,396	30.6	47.8
1977	3,387	2,286	721	67.5	21.3	31.5	808	23.9	2,342	32.4	46.9
1976	3,315	2,239	749	67.5	22.6	33.5	803	24.2	2,291	34.2	50.4
1975	3,213	2,081	665	64.8	20.7	32.0	877	27.3	2,149	32.6	48.1
1974	3,105	2,083	555	67.1	17.9	26.6	780	25.1	2,145	27.5	44.8
1973	3,114	2,079	498	66.8	16.0	24.0	826	26.5	2,139	25.0	41.6
1972	2,986	1,992	540	66.7	18.1	27.1	782	26.2	2,044	28.0	42.0
1971	2,866	1,789	522	62.4	18.2	29.2	825	28.8	1,833	30.0	42.3
1970	2,692	1,602	416	59.5	15.5	26.0	897	33.3	1,635	26.7	39.4
1969	2,542	1,497	407	58.9	16.0	27.2	828	32.6	1,547	27.5	40.1
1968	2,421	1,399	352	57.8	14.5	25.2	799	33.0	1,432	26.0	38.1
1967	2,283	1,276	297	55.9	13.0	23.3	788	34.5	1,316	23.7	35.0
Male											
2019	2,109	1,790	695	84.9	32.9	38.8	152	7.2	1,826	39.3	63.1
2018	2,148	1,819	736	84.7	34.2	40.4	129	6.0	1,827	40.6	63.2
2017	2,172	1,821	695	83.8	32.0	38.2	163	7.5	1,857	38.1	60.4
2016	2,218	1,774	728	80.0	32.8	41.0	204	9.2	1,795	41.2	61.4
2015	2,257	1,923	779	85.2	34.5	40.5	165	7.3	1,947	40.6	63.3
2014	2,289	1,889	633	82.5	27.6	33.5	166	7.3	1,934	34.7	61.1
2013	2,303	1,847	690	80.2	30.0	37.4	221	9.6	1,865	38.0	61.7
2012	2,278	1,787	760	78.4	33.4	42.5	258	11.3	1,820	42.7	63.8
2011	2,165	1,701	717	78.6	33.1	42.2	205	9.5	1,732	42.7	60.9
2010	2,140	1,692	734	79.1	34.3	43.4	258	12.1	1,730	43.2	61.4
2009	2,082	1,592	673	76.5	32.3	42.3	289	13.9	1,617	42.0	63.5
2008	2,045	1,641	595	80.2	29.1	36.3	210	10.2	1,668	36.9	54.8
2007	2,011	1,622	649	80.6	32.3	40.0	202	10.0	1,642	40.1	59.3
2006	1,959	1,488	541	76.0	27.6	36.4	219	11.2	1,519	36.3	53.4
2005	1,897	1,393	530	73.4	27.9	38.0	280	14.8	1,420	37.9	58.4
2004	1,852	1,341	479	72.4	25.9	35.7	331	17.9	1,363	36.1	60.9
2003[1]	1,801	1,331	499	73.9	27.7	37.5	300	16.7	1,346	37.8	57.1
2002	1,843	1,354	475	73.5	25.8	35.1	311	16.9	1,372	35.6	56.1
2001	1,818	1,287	470	70.8	25.8	36.4	308	16.9	1,310	36.4	53.1
2000	1,885	1,389	470	73.7	24.9	33.8	329	17.4	1,409	34.1	53.5
1999	1,747	1,292	501	73.9	28.7	38.8	285	16.3	1,336	40.2	57.7
1998	1,724	1,163	445	67.5	25.8	38.2	354	20.5	1,186	38.5	57.5
1997	1,701	1,214	425	71.4	25.0	35.0	297	17.5	1,232	35.1	56.3
1996	1,682	1,199	422	71.3	25.1	35.2	292	17.4	1,225	35.8	53.7
1995	1,660	1,247	430	75.1	25.9	34.4	235	14.2	1,262	35.1	56.2
1994	1,733	1,277	440	73.7	25.4	34.5	303	17.5	1,293	35.3	57.9
1993r	1,703	1,240	387	72.8	22.7	31.2	266	15.6	1,247	31.4	50.1
1993	1,659	1,207	379	72.8	22.8	31.4	258	15.6	1,214	31.5	50.0
1992	1,676	1,211	356	72.3	21.2	29.4	259	15.5	1,226	29.7	49.4
1991	1,635	1,174	378	71.8	23.1	32.2	252	15.4	1,188	32.4	47.0
1990	1,634	1,240	426	75.9	26.1	34.4	223	13.6	1,260	35.1	48.8
1989	1,654	1,195	324	72.2	19.6	27.1	307	18.6	1,207	27.5	45.8
1988	1,653	1,189	297	71.9	18.0	25.0	312	18.9	1,205	25.1	42.5
1987	1,666	1,188	377	71.3	22.6	31.7	312	18.7	1,209	32.3	48.0
1986	1,687	1,220	349	72.3	20.7	28.6	300	17.8	1,239	29.1	44.4
1985	1,720	1,244	345	72.3	20.1	27.7	323	18.8	1,258	28.2	43.6
1984	1,811	1,272	367	70.2	20.3	28.9	362	20.2	1,295	29.6	45.2

r = Revised, controlled to 1990 census based population estimates; previous 1993 data controlled to 1980 census based population estimates.

Note: The change in the educational attainment question and the college completion categories from "4 or more years of college" to "at least some college," in 1992 caused an increase in the proportion of 14-to-24-year-old high school graduates enrolled in college or completed some college, of approximately 5 percentage points. High school graduates are people who have completed 4 years of high school or more, for 1967 to 1991. Beginning in 1992, they were people whose highest degree was a high school diploma (including equivalency) or higher.

[1]Starting in 2003 respondents could identify more than one race. Except as noted, the race data in this table from 2003 onward represent those respondents who indicated only one race category.

[2]The data shown prior to 2003 consists of those identifying themselves as "Asian or Pacific Islanders."

Table A-14. Population 14 to 24 Years Old, by High School Graduate Status, College Enrollment, Attainment, Sex, Race, and Hispanic Origin, October 1967–2019—*Continued*

(Numbers in thousands; percent; civilian noninstitutionalized population.)

Year, race, and Hispanic origin	Population 18 to 24 years old								High school graduates, 14 to 24 years old		
		High school graduates		Percent			High school dropouts			Percent	
	Total	Total	Enrolled in college	High school graduates	Enrolled in college	Of high school graduates enrolled in college	Number	Percent	All graduates	Enrolled in college	Enrolled or completed some college
1983	1,807	1,202	331	66.5	18.3	27.5	435	24.1	1,228	27.9	43.6
1982	1,786	1,171	331	65.6	18.5	28.3	458	25.6	1,188	28.6	44.5
1981	1,730	1,154	325	66.7	18.8	28.2	419	24.2	1,165	28.5	42.3
1980	1,690	1,115	293	66.0	17.3	26.3	440	26.0	1,141	26.9	44.1
1979	1,577	973	304	61.7	19.3	31.2	457	29.0	988	32.0	46.7
1978	1,554	956	305	61.5	19.6	31.9	451	29.0	981	32.4	49.3
1977	1,528	970	309	63.5	20.2	31.9	369	24.1	991	33.0	47.6
1976	1,503	936	331	62.3	22.0	35.4	393	26.1	952	35.9	50.3
1975	1,451	897	294	61.8	20.3	32.8	404	27.8	923	33.4	50.5
1974	1,396	919	280	65.8	20.1	30.5	346	24.8	941	31.1	47.3
1973	1,434	952	266	66.4	18.5	27.9	371	25.9	962	28.4	44.2
1972	1,373	870	287	63.4	20.9	33.0	373	27.2	897	34.0	47.4
1971	1,318	769	262	58.3	19.9	34.1	416	31.6	783	34.9	45.8
1970	1,220	668	192	54.8	15.7	28.7	436	35.7	684	29.5	41.4
1969	1,141	631	202	55.3	17.7	32.0	383	33.6	653	32.5	44.6
1968	1,087	582	170	53.5	15.6	29.2	370	34.0	600	30.3	43.2
1967	1,032	525	167	50.9	16.2	31.8	397	38.5	539	32.3	41.6
Female											
2019	2,235	1,993	893	89.2	40.0	44.8	118	5.3	2,023	45.1	69.5
2018	2,267	2,034	934	89.7	41.2	45.9	86	3.8	2,067	45.6	71.9
2017	2,286	1,986	900	86.9	39.3	45.3	107	4.7	2,028	45.4	70.1
2016	2,333	2,083	916	89.3	39.3	44.0	111	4.7	2,142	43.6	69.1
2015	2,378	2,048	857	86.1	36.1	41.9	182	7.7	2,071	42.0	65.6
2014	2,415	2,104	895	87.2	37.1	42.5	179	7.4	2,128	42.9	70.2
2013	2,442	2,038	909	83.4	37.2	44.6	173	7.1	2,064	44.7	69.3
2012	2,436	1,967	929	80.8	38.1	47.2	209	8.6	1,996	47.0	69.2
2011	2,339	1,949	921	83.3	39.4	47.3	194	8.3	1,970	47.6	71.0
2010	2,317	1,977	958	85.3	41.3	48.4	192	8.3	2,001	48.8	70.4
2009	2,263	1,865	931	82.4	41.1	49.9	216	9.5	1,915	50.1	70.9
2008	2,220	1,746	754	78.7	34.0	43.2	304	13.7	1,777	43.3	66.2
2007	2,171	1,801	747	82.9	34.4	41.5	223	10.3	1,841	41.5	63.3
2006	2,126	1,668	780	78.5	36.7	46.7	313	14.7	1,705	46.9	67.0
2005	2,067	1,745	767	84.4	37.1	44.0	232	11.2	1,793	44.0	67.5
2004	2,088	1,709	759	81.8	36.3	44.4	266	12.7	1,749	44.9	65.0
2003[1]	2,035	1,618	726	79.5	35.7	44.9	245	12.0	1,652	45.1	66.8
2002	2,081	1,686	751	81.0	36.1	44.5	260	12.5	1,745	45.5	65.2
2001	2,098	1,729	736	82.4	35.1	42.7	232	11.0	1,785	42.7	63.3
2000	2,128	1,700	747	79.9	35.1	43.9	287	13.5	1,720	43.9	67.1
1999	2,080	1,619	644	77.9	31.0	39.8	327	15.7	1,650	39.6	62.6
1998	2,021	1,584	671	78.4	33.2	42.4	288	14.3	1,604	42.4	65.0
1997	1,949	1,511	659	77.5	33.8	43.6	314	16.1	1,529	43.1	63.0
1996	1,956	1,539	561	78.7	28.7	36.4	288	14.7	1,580	37.3	55.3
1995	1,965	1,541	558	78.4	28.4	36.2	287	14.6	1,566	36.3	59.5
1994	1,928	1,542	561	80.0	29.1	36.4	265	13.7	1,567	37.1	60.3
1993r	1,965	1,508	511	76.7	26.0	33.9	337	17.2	1,626	34.1	57.2
1993	1,857	1,425	484	76.7	26.1	34.0	319	17.2	1,441	34.1	57.1
1992	1,845	1,417	531	76.8	28.8	37.5	315	17.1	1,446	38.2	56.6
1991	1,869	1,455	450	77.8	24.1	30.9	296	15.8	1,468	31.4	45.2
1990	1,886	1,468	467	77.8	24.8	31.8	306	16.2	1,498	32.4	47.3
1989	1,905	1,511	511	79.3	26.8	33.8	277	14.5	1,541	34.7	51.8
1988	1,915	1,492	455	77.9	23.8	30.5	318	16.6	1,538	31.3	49.2
1987	1,937	1,550	445	80.0	23.0	28.7	298	15.4	1,579	20.4	48.9
1986	1,966	1,574	462	80.1	23.5	29.4	306	15.6	1,598	29.3	50.4
1985	1,996	1,565	389	78.4	19.5	24.9	332	16.6	1,592	25.1	44.0
1984	2,052	1,613	419	78.6	20.4	26.0	349	17.0	1,655	26.8	45.1
1983	2,058	1,539	411	74.8	20.0	26.7	398	19.3	1,561	27.5	46.3
1982	2,086	1,572	436	75.4	20.9	27.7	393	18.0	1,604	27.9	46.3

r = Revised, controlled to 1990 census based population estimates; previous 1993 data controlled to 1980 census based population estimates.
Note: The change in the educational attainment question and the college completion categories from "4 or more years of college" to "at least some college," in 1992 caused an increase in the proportion of 14-to-24-year-old high school graduates enrolled in college or completed some college, of approximately 5 percentage points. High school graduates are people who have completed 4 years of high school or more, for 1967 to 1991. Beginning in 1992, they were people whose highest degree was a high school diploma (including equivalency) or higher.
[1] Starting in 2003 respondents could identify more than one race. Except as noted, the race data in this table from 2003 onward represent those respondents who indicated only one race category.
[2] The data shown prior to 2003 consists of those identifying themselves as "Asian or Pacific Islanders."

Table A-14. Population 14 to 24 Years Old, by High School Graduate Status, College Enrollment, Attainment, Sex, Race, and Hispanic Origin, October 1967–2019—*Continued*

(Numbers in thousands; percent; civilian noninstitutionalized population.)

Year, race, and Hispanic origin	Population 18 to 24 years old								High school graduates, 14 to 24 years old		
		High school graduates		Percent			High school dropouts			Percent	
	Total	Total	Enrolled in college	High school graduates	Enrolled in college	Of high school graduates enrolled in college	Number	Percent	All graduates	Enrolled in college	Enrolled or completed some college
1981	2,049	1,526	424	74.5	20.7	27.8	402	19.6	1,554	28.8	46.6
1980	2,031	1,475	422	72.6	20.8	28.6	436	21.5	1,511	29.1	47.4
1979	1,934	1,383	392	71.5	20.3	28.3	439	22.7	1,426	29.7	49.8
1978	1,897	1,384	390	73.0	20.6	28.2	398	21.0	1,415	29.3	46.7
1977	1,859	1,317	413	70.8	22.2	31.4	439	23.6	1,354	31.9	46.2
1976	1,813	1,302	417	71.8	23.0	32.0	410	22.6	1,338	32.9	50.3
1975	1,761	1,182	372	67.1	21.1	31.5	473	26.9	1,224	32.0	46.4
1974	1,709	1,167	277	68.3	16.2	23.7	434	25.4	1,207	24.8	42.9
1973	1,681	1,125	231	66.9	13.7	20.5	456	27.1	1,177	22.2	39.4
1972	1,613	1,123	253	69.6	15.7	22.5	408	25.3	1,150	23.2	37.9
1971	1,547	1,019	259	65.9	16.7	25.4	409	26.4	1,049	26.4	39.8
1970	1,471	935	225	63.6	15.3	24.1	461	31.3	955	24.7	39.3
1969	1,402	867	206	61.8	14.7	23.8	444	31.7	896	24.0	38.6
1968	1,334	819	183	61.4	13.7	22.3	430	32.2	834	22.9	35.9
1967	1,249	751	130	60.1	10.4	17.3	391	31.3	778	17.9	33.2
ASIAN ALONE[2]											
Both Sexes											
2019	1,826	1,700	1,131	93.1	61.9	66.5	41	2.3	1,744	66.9	93.6
2018	1,842	1,719	1,079	93.3	58.6	62.8	51	2.8	1,742	63.0	88.4
2017	1,753	1,658	1,101	94.6	62.8	66.4	28	1.6	1,694	66.9	90.6
2016	1,768	1,628	1,003	92.1	56.7	61.6	53	3.0	1,661	61.5	87.7
2015	1,634	1,514	1,026	92.6	62.8	67.8	38	2.3	1,560	67.1	91.9
2014	1,590	1,504	1,023	94.6	64.3	68.0	17	1.1	1,541	67.6	91.7
2013	1,639	1,495	1,001	91.2	61.1	66.9	61	3.7	1,530	67.4	86.8
2012	1,537	1,385	915	90.1	59.5	66.0	54	3.5	1,418	66.3	84.9
2011	1,252	1,123	748	89.8	59.7	66.5	65	5.2	1,149	66.9	88.1
2010	1,303	1,193	811	91.5	62.2	68.0	64	4.9	1,232	68.4	89.8
2009	1,181	1,080	768	91.4	65.0	71.1	26	2.2	1,096	71.0	91.8
2008	1,113	1,021	655	91.8	58.9	64.1	42	3.8	1,056	64.6	90.4
2007	1,165	1,010	658	86.7	56.4	65.1	86	7.4	1,026	65.1	91.6
2006	1,148	1,046	661	91.1	57.6	63.2	46	4.0	1,064	63.0	87.0
2005	1,145	1,072	693	93.6	60.5	64.6	34	3.0	1,098	65.1	87.0
2004	1,152	1,066	695	92.5	60.3	65.2	49	4.3	1,090	65.7	89.1
2003[1]	1,144	1,030	693	90.1	60.6	67.3	56	4.9	1,046	67.7	88.2
2002	1,339	1,230	803	91.8	60.0	65.3	57	4.2	1,265	65.7	86.9
2001	1,312	1,197	794	91.2	60.5	66.5	47	3.6	1,218	66.5	87.6
2000	1,143	1,038	639	90.8	55.9	61.6	52	4.6	1,053	61.8	83.9
1999	1,130	1,019	626	90.2	55.4	61.4	58	5.1	1,035	62.0	85.5
Male											
2019	906	839	552	92.6	60.9	65.8	20	2.2	865	66.4	91.1
2018	950	888	558	93.5	58.8	62.9	27	2.8	901	63.4	89.1
2017	895	842	561	94.1	62.7	66.7	12	1.3	849	66.9	89.4
2016	914	842	533	92.1	58.3	63.3	21	2.3	854	63.0	87.1
2015	819	758	493	92.6	60.2	65.0	24	2.9	783	64.2	90.0
2014	809	771	549	95.3	67.9	71.2	13	1.6	793	71.0	91.1
2013	859	795	534	92.5	62.2	67.2	18	2.1	806	67.2	86.1
2012	776	695	455	89.6	58.6	65.4	21	2.6	713	65.9	84.7
2011	639	573	379	89.6	59.3	66.2	30	4.7	582	66.1	87.6
2010	651	597	390	91.7	59.9	65.3	29	4.5	619	65.7	87.5
2009	590	546	383	92.4	64.9	70.2	7	1.2	559	69.9	90.1
2008	547	487	295	89.1	53.9	60.5	21	3.9	510	62.0	89.9
2007	560	481	318	85.8	56.9	66.3	38	6.8	483	66.4	91.8
2006	591	525	338	88.8	57.2	64.4	34	5.8	536	64.0	84.0
2005	590	552	366	93.5	62.0	66.3	17	2.9	565	66.4	88.2
2004	586	549	373	93.7	63.6	67.9	15	2.5	561	68.4	88.2

r = Revised, controlled to 1990 census based population estimates; previous 1993 data controlled to 1980 census based population estimates.
Note: The change in the educational attainment question and the college completion categories from "4 or more years of college" to "at least some college," in 1992 caused an increase in the proportion of 14-to-24-year-old high school graduates enrolled in college or completed some college, of approximately 5 percentage points. High school graduates are people who have completed 4 years of high school or more, for 1967 to 1991. Beginning in 1992, they were people whose highest degree was a high school diploma (including equivalency) or higher.
[1]Starting in 2003 respondents could identify more than one race. Except as noted, the race data in this table from 2003 onward represent those respondents who indicated only one race category.
[2]The data shown prior to 2003 consists of those identifying themselves as "Asian or Pacific Islanders."

Table A-14. Population 14 to 24 Years Old, by High School Graduate Status, College Enrollment, Attainment, Sex, Race, and Hispanic Origin, October 1967–2019—*Continued*

(Numbers in thousands; percent; civilian noninstitutionalized population.)

Year, race, and Hispanic origin	Population 18 to 24 years old								High school graduates, 14 to 24 years old		
		High school graduates		Percent			High school dropouts			Percent	
	Total	Total	Enrolled in college	High school graduates	Enrolled in college	Of high school graduates enrolled in college	Number	Percent	All graduates	Enrolled in college	Enrolled or completed some college
2003[1]	543	483	337	88.9	62.0	69.8	43	7.8	486	69.9	90.0
2002	707	637	417	90.0	59.0	65.5	38	5.4	652	65.3	86.7
2001	661	583	417	88.1	63.1	72.0	35	5.3	594	72.0	88.9
2000	571	521	337	91.1	58.9	64.7	34	6.0	527	64.7	85.6
1999	505	443	284	87.8	56.2	64.0	39	7.7	454	64.9	82.5
Female											
2019	920	861	579	93.6	62.9	67.2	22	2.4	880	67.5	96.1
2018	892	831	520	93.1	58.3	62.6	24	2.7	841	62.5	87.7
2017	859	816	540	95.0	62.8	66.1	17	1.9	844	66.9	91.9
2016	854	787	469	92.2	55.0	59.7	32	3.8	808	60.0	88.3
2015	816	756	533	92.6	65.4	70.6	14	1.7	776	70.0	93.8
2014	780	732	473	93.9	60.6	64.6	4	0.5	748	63.9	92.3
2013	780	700	467	89.8	59.8	66.6	43	5.5	723	67.5	87.5
2012	761	690	460	90.7	60.4	66.6	33	4.3	704	66.8	85.1
2011	612	551	369	89.9	60.2	66.9	35	5.8	567	67.8	88.7
2010	653	596	422	91.3	64.6	70.7	35	5.3	614	71.2	92.1
2009	591	534	384	90.4	65.1	72.0	19	3.3	538	72.2	93.7
2008	566	534	360	94.4	63.7	67.5	21	3.6	546	67.0	90.9
2007	605	529	339	87.4	56.0	64.1	48	7.9	543	63.9	91.5
2006	557	521	324	93.6	58.1	62.2	11	2.1	528	61.9	90.0
2005	555	521	327	93.8	58.9	62.8	17	3.0	533	63.7	85.8
2004	567	517	323	91.3	56.9	62.4	35	6.1	529	62.8	90.0
2003[1]	601	547	356	91.2	59.3	65.1	13	2.2	561	65.9	86.7
2002	632	593	386	93.8	61.0	65.1	19	2.9	613	66.1	87.2
2001	651	614	377	94.3	57.9	61.3	12	1.8	625	61.3	86.3
2000	572	517	302	90.4	52.9	58.5	18	3.1	526	58.9	82.3
1999	626	576	342	92.1	54.7	59.4	19	3.1	582	59.7	87.8
HISPANIC (OF ANY RACE)											
Both Sexes											
2019	6,811	5,799	2,469	85.1	36.3	42.6	509	7.5	5,879	42.7	64.7
2018	6,762	5,661	2,430	83.7	35.9	42.9	656	9.7	5,755	43.2	66.6
2017	6,053	5,457	2,410	82.0	36.2	44.2	703	10.6	5,571	44.7	65.9
2016	6,539	5,477	2,565	83.8	39.2	46.8	648	9.9	5,608	47.3	67.2
2015	6,464	5,366	2,368	83.0	36.6	44.1	669	10.3	5,460	44.2	66.6
2014	6,568	5,324	2,282	81.1	34.7	42.9	777	11.8	5,409	43.1	62.8
2013	6,489	5,118	2,193	78.9	33.8	42.8	889	13.7	5,190	43.1	62.3
2012	6,416	4,902	2,403	76.4	37.5	49.0	972	15.1	4,987	49.4	68.1
2011	5,974	4,569	2,079	76.5	34.8	45.5	975	16.3	4,630	45.7	65.4
2010	5,685	4,138	1,814	72.8	31.9	43.8	1,050	18.5	4,199	44.2	63.2
2009	5,332	3,747	1,465	70.3	27.5	39.1	1,112	20.8	3,813	39.6	57.8
2008	5,176	3,618	1,338	69.9	25.8	37.0	1,155	22.3	3,691	37.7	58.7
2007	5,175	3,487	1,375	67.4	26.6	39.4	1,310	25.3	3,553	39.9	58.0
2006	5,006	3,301	1,182	65.9	23.6	35.8	1,313	26.2	3,379	36.6	57.2
2005	4,898	3,230	1,215	66.0	24.8	37.6	1,335	27.3	3,280	38.0	57.3
2004	4,941	3,244	1,221	65.6	24.7	37.7	1,386	28.0	3,287	37.9	55.9
2003	4,754	3,096	1,115	65.1	23.5	36.0	1,353	28.4	3,135	36.0	56.5
2002	4,918	3,078	979	62.6	19.9	31.8	1,479	30.1	3,109	32.0	53.1
2001	4,892	3,031	1,035	62.0	21.1	34.2	1,548	31.7	3,068	34.2	52.8
2000	4,134	2,462	899	59.6	21.7	36.5	1,335	32.3	2,509	36.8	53.1
1999	3,953	2,325	739	58.8	18.7	31.8	1,340	33.9	2,359	31.7	49.6
1998	4,014	2,403	820	59.8	20.4	34.1	1,383	34.4	2,419	34.3	53.2
1997	3,606	2,236	806	62.0	22.4	36.0	1,103	30.6	2,302	37.1	54.3
1996	3,510	2,019	706	57.5	20.1	35.0	1,210	34.5	2,046	34.5	52.5
1995	3,603	2,112	745	58.6	20.7	35.3	1,250	34.7	2,142	35.7	55.8

r = Revised, controlled to 1990 census based population estimates; previous 1993 data controlled to 1980 census based population estimates.

Note: The change in the educational attainment question and the college completion categories from "4 or more years of college" to "at least some college," in 1992 caused an increase in the proportion of 14-to-24-year-old high school graduates enrolled in college or completed some college, of approximately 5 percentage points. High school graduates are people who have completed 4 years of high school or more, for 1967 to 1991. Beginning in 1992, they were people whose highest degree was a high school diploma (including equivalency) or higher.

[1]Starting in 2003 respondents could identify more than one race. Except as noted, the race data in this table from 2003 onward represent those respondents who indicated only one race category.

[2]The data shown prior to 2003 consists of those identifying themselves as "Asian or Pacific Islanders."

Table A-14. Population 14 to 24 Years Old, by High School Graduate Status, College Enrollment, Attainment, Sex, Race, and Hispanic Origin, October 1967–2019—*Continued*

(Numbers in thousands; percent; civilian noninstitutionalized population.)

| Year, race, and Hispanic origin | Population 18 to 24 years old | | | | | | | | High school graduates, 14 to 24 years old | | |
| | | High school graduates | | Percent | | | High school dropouts | | | Percent | |
	Total	Total	Enrolled in college	High school graduates	Enrolled in college	Of high school graduates enrolled in college	Number	Percent	All graduates	Enrolled in college	Enrolled or completed some college
1994	3,523	1,995	662	56.6	18.8	33.2	1,224	34.7	2,009	33.4	54.3
1993r	3,363	2,049	728	60.9	21.6	35.5	1,103	32.8	2,081	35.8	55.6
1993	2,772	1,682	602	60.7	21.7	35.8	907	32.7	1,712	36.0	55.8
1992	2,754	1,579	586	57.3	21.3	37.1	936	33.9	1,603	37.6	55.0
1991	2,874	1,498	516	52.1	18.0	34.4	1,139	39.6	1,519	34.6	47.6
1990	2,749	1,498	435	54.5	15.8	29.0	1,025	37.3	1,523	29.4	44.7
1989	2,818	1,576	453	55.9	16.1	28.7	1,062	37.7	1,600	29.4	43.6
1988	2,642	1,458	450	55.2	17.0	30.9	1,046	39.6	1,481	31.3	47.0
1987	2,592	1,597	455	61.6	17.6	28.5	849	32.8	1,612	28.7	44.0
1986	2,514	1,507	458	59.9	18.2	30.4	864	34.4	1,535	30.9	45.6
1985	2,221	1,396	375	62.9	16.9	26.9	700	31.5	1,419	27.6	46.7
1984	2,018	1,212	362	60.1	17.9	29.9	691	34.2	1,223	30.0	46.0
1983	2,025	1,110	349	54.8	17.2	31.4	759	37.5	1,134	32.3	48.4
1982	2,001	1,153	337	57.6	16.8	29.2	740	37.0	1,173	30.0	47.3
1981	2,052	1,144	342	55.8	16.7	29.9	790	38.5	1,166	30.5	45.8
1980	2,033	1,099	327	54.1	16.1	29.8	820	40.3	1,117	30.1	47.3
1979	1,754	968	292	55.2	16.6	30.2	687	39.2	1,001	31.2	45.7
1978	1,672	935	254	55.9	15.2	27.2	656	39.2	965	28.0	43.2
1977	1,609	880	277	54.7	17.2	31.5	622	38.7	900	32.4	43.8
1976	1,551	862	309	55.6	19.9	35.8	566	36.5	891	36.3	48.9
1975	1,446	832	295	57.5	20.4	35.5	505	34.9	849	36.5	50.8
1974	1,506	842	272	55.9	18.1	32.3	558	37.1	858	33.1	47.8
1973	1,285	709	206	55.2	16.0	29.1	500	38.9	732	30.3	43.0
1972	1,338	694	179	51.9	13.4	25.8	541	40.4	709	27.2	36.7
Male											
2019	3,424	2,878	1,127	84.1	32.9	39.1	279	8.1	2,918	39.0	59.4
2018	3,442	2,787	1,089	81.0	31.6	39.1	406	11.8	2,816	39.3	61.9
2017	3,355	2,648	1,045	78.9	31.1	39.5	429	12.8	2,690	40.0	62.1
2016	3,291	2,674	1,148	81.3	34.9	42.9	395	12.0	2,729	43.1	63.0
2015	3,246	2,661	1,063	82.0	32.8	40.0	360	11.1	2,711	40.1	61.3
2014	3,354	2,667	1,016	79.5	30.3	38.1	429	12.8	2,700	38.1	57.7
2013	3,329	2,564	968	77.0	29.1	37.7	491	14.7	2,597	38.0	55.7
2012	3,311	2,455	1,109	74.1	33.5	45.2	560	16.9	2,496	45.5	63.2
2011	3,250	2,421	1,006	74.5	31.0	41.6	568	17.5	2,458	41.9	60.2
2010	2,930	2,034	819	69.4	27.9	40.2	623	21.3	2,065	40.6	58.5
2009	2,741	1,894	663	69.1	24.2	35.0	616	22.5	1,925	35.6	51.3
2008	2,675	1,797	615	67.2	23.0	34.2	649	24.3	1,841	35.1	54.4
2007	2,706	1,689	560	62.4	20.7	33.1	790	29.2	1,711	33.6	52.2
2006	2,618	1,600	523	61.1	20.0	32.7	812	31.0	1,628	33.2	53.2
2005	2,613	1,569	540	60.1	20.7	34.4	838	32.1	1,589	34.6	52.4
2004	2,648	1,597	574	60.3	21.7	36.0	888	33.5	1,614	35.9	53.0
2003	2,541	1,548	465	60.9	18.3	30.0	805	31.7	1,571	30.0	48.7
2002	2,707	1,562	439	57.7	16.2	28.1	914	33.8	1,572	28.1	48.4
2001	2,596	1,455	449	56.1	17.3	31.0	962	37.1	1,468	31.0	48.1
2000	2,171	1,172	401	54.0	18.5	34.2	800	36.8	1,197	34.5	50.8
1999	2,045	1,122	322	54.9	15.8	28.7	746	36.4	1,131	28.7	45.7
1998	2,109	1,146	346	54.3	16.4	30.2	838	39.7	1,153	30.0	47.2
1997	1,937	1,140	371	58.9	19.2	32.5	643	33.2	1,168	33.0	49.2
1996	1,815	994	300	54.8	16.5	30.2	657	36.2	1,005	30.6	48.8
1995	1,907	1,106	356	58.0	18.7	32.2	653	34.2	1,022	36.2	52.3
1994	1,896	1,021	312	53.8	16.5	30.6	685	36.1	1,026	30.7	52.7
1993r	1,710	1,005	338	58.8	19.8	33.6	591	34.6	1,023	33.7	51.2
1993	1,354	786	266	58.1	19.6	33.8	470	34.7	803	33.9	51.1
1992	1,384	720	247	52.0	17.8	34.3	531	38.4	736	34.8	52.2
1991	1,503	719	211	47.8	14.0	29.3	668	44.4	728	29.7	42.2
1990	1,403	753	214	53.7	15.3	28.4	559	39.8	770	29.4	46.5
1989	1,439	756	211	52.5	14.7	27.9	580	40.3	767	28.2	42.7

r = Revised, controlled to 1990 census based population estimates; previous 1993 data controlled to 1980 census based population estimates.

Note: The change in the educational attainment question and the college completion categories from "4 or more years of college" to "at least some college," in 1992 caused an increase in the proportion of 14-to-24-year-old high school graduates enrolled in college or completed some college, of approximately 5 percentage points. High school graduates are people who have completed 4 years of high school or more, for 1967 to 1991. Beginning in 1992, they were people whose highest degree was a high school diploma (including equivalency) or higher.

[1] Starting in 2003 respondents could identify more than one race. Except as noted, the race data in this table from 2003 onward represent those respondents who indicated only one race category.

[2] The data shown prior to 2003 consists of those identifying themselves as "Asian or Pacific Islanders."

Table A-14. Population 14 to 24 Years Old, by High School Graduate Status, College Enrollment, Attainment, Sex, Race, and Hispanic Origin, October 1967–2019—*Continued*

(Numbers in thousands; percent; civilian noninstitutionalized population.)

Year, race, and Hispanic origin	Population 18 to 24 years old								High school graduates, 14 to 24 years old		
		High school graduates		Percent			High school dropouts			Percent	
	Total	Total	Enrolled in college	High school graduates	Enrolled in college	Of high school graduates enrolled in college	Number	Percent	All graduates	Enrolled in college	Enrolled or completed some college
1988	1,375	724	228	52.7	16.6	31.5	553	40.2	736	32.2	48.3
1987	1,337	795	247	59.5	18.5	31.1	461	34.5	803	31.1	45.1
1986	1,339	769	233	57.4	17.4	30.3	499	37.3	776	30.5	44.4
1985	1,132	659	168	58.2	14.8	25.5	405	35.8	675	26.4	44.9
1984	956	549	154	57.4	16.1	28.1	338	35.4	554	28.2	45.7
1983	968	476	152	49.2	15.7	31.9	396	40.9	489	33.1	47.4
1982	944	519	141	55.0	14.9	27.2	347	36.8	525	28.0	44.8
1981	988	498	164	50.4	16.6	32.9	428	43.3	506	33.6	48.6
1980	1,012	518	160	51.2	15.8	30.9	431	42.6	521	31.1	49.5
1979	837	454	153	54.2	18.3	33.7	328	39.2	469	34.3	49.5
1978	781	420	126	53.8	16.1	30.0	313	40.1	438	30.4	46.3
1977	754	396	139	52.5	18.4	35.1	295	39.1	404	35.9	46.5
1976	701	378	150	53.9	21.4	39.7	253	36.1	403	39.8	51.8
1975	678	383	145	56.5	21.4	37.9	221	32.6	390	37.9	55.4
1974	720	390	141	54.2	19.6	36.2	279	38.8	401	36.7	51.4
1973	625	348	105	55.7	16.8	30.2	228	36.5	361	32.1	45.4
1972	609	301	92	49.4	15.1	30.6	253	41.5	309	32.0	44.3
Female											
2019	3,386	2,920	1,342	86.2	39.6	46.0	230	6.8	2,961	46.3	70.0
2018	3,320	2,874	1,342	86.6	40.4	46.7	250	7.5	2,939	47.1	71.1
2017	3,298	2,810	1,365	85.2	41.4	48.6	274	8.3	2,801	49.1	69.4
2016	3,248	2,803	1,417	86.3	43.6	50.6	253	7.8	2,879	51.3	71.2
2015	3,218	2,704	1,305	84.0	40.5	48.2	309	9.6	2,750	48.2	71.9
2014	3,214	2,657	1,265	82.7	39.4	47.6	348	10.8	2,709	48.2	67.9
2013	3,160	2,554	1,225	80.8	38.8	48.0	398	12.6	2,593	48.1	69.0
2012	3,105	2,447	1,294	78.8	41.7	52.9	411	13.2	2,491	53.3	72.9
2011	2,724	2,147	1,073	78.8	39.4	50.0	407	15.0	2,173	50.0	71.4
2010	2,755	2,104	995	76.4	36.1	47.3	426	15.5	2,134	47.7	67.8
2009	2,591	1,853	803	71.5	31.0	43.3	496	19.1	1,888	43.6	64.5
2008	2,501	1,821	723	72.8	28.9	39.7	506	20.2	1,850	40.3	63.1
2007	2,469	1,798	816	72.8	33.0	45.4	520	21.1	1,842	45.6	63.4
2006	2,388	1,701	660	71.2	27.6	38.8	501	21.0	1,751	39.7	61.0
2005	2,285	1,661	675	72.7	29.5	40.6	498	21.8	1,691	41.2	62.0
2004	2,293	1,647	647	71.8	28.2	39.3	498	21.7	1,673	39.8	58.6
2003	2,213	1,548	651	69.9	29.4	42.1	548	24.7	1,563	41.9	64.4
2002	2,211	1,516	540	68.6	24.4	35.6	565	25.6	1,537	35.9	57.9
2001	2,296	1,576	585	68.6	25.5	37.1	586	25.5	1,600	37.1	57.0
2000	1,963	1,290	498	65.7	25.4	38.6	535	27.3	1,312	38.9	55.2
1999	1,908	1,203	417	63.0	21.8	34.7	593	31.1	1,228	34.4	53.3
1998	1,906	1,257	474	66.0	24.9	37.7	545	28.6	1,266	38.2	58.7
1997	1,669	1,097	436	65.7	26.1	39.7	460	27.6	1,135	41.4	59.6
1996	1,694	1,026	406	60.6	24.0	39.6	554	32.7	1,043	40.4	56.0
1995	1,696	1,011	389	59.6	22.9	38.4	598	35.4	1,022	38.6	59.6
1994	1,628	973	350	59.8	21.5	36.0	539	33.1	983	36.2	55.9
1993r	1,652	1,045	390	63.3	23.6	37.3	510	30.9	1,050	37.8	60.1
1993	1,418	895	336	63.1	23.7	37.5	439	31.0	907	38.0	60.4
1992	1,369	860	339	62.8	24.8	39.4	405	29.6	867	39.9	57.4
1991	1,372	780	305	56.9	22.2	39.1	473	34.5	791	39.2	52.5
1990	1,346	745	221	55.3	16.4	29.7	465	34.5	753	29.5	43.0
1989	1,377	823	244	59.8	17.7	29.6	482	35.0	836	30.5	44.5
1988	1,267	736	224	58.1	17.7	30.4	492	38.8	747	30.5	45.8
1987	1,256	801	208	63.8	16.6	26.0	387	30.8	808	26.4	43.2
1986	1,175	739	226	62.9	19.2	30.6	365	31.1	759	31.4	46.0
1985	1,091	734	205	67.3	18.8	27.9	295	27.0	743	28.4	48.0
1984	1,061	661	207	62.3	19.5	31.3	353	33.2	667	31.5	46.6
1983	1,057	634	198	60.0	18.7	31.2	363	34.3	644	31.8	49.7
1982	1,056	634	196	60.0	18.6	30.9	393	37.2	648	31.8	49.2

r = Revised, controlled to 1990 census based population estimates; previous 1993 data controlled to 1980 census based population estimates.

Note. The change in the educational attainment question and the college completion categories from "4 or more years of college" to "at least some college," in 1992 caused an increase in the proportion of 14-to-24-year-old high school graduates enrolled in college or completed some college, of approximately 5 percentage points. High school graduates are people who have completed 4 years of high school or more, for 1967 to 1991. Beginning in 1992, they were people whose highest degree was a high school diploma (including equivalency) or higher.

[1] Starting in 2003 respondents could identify more than one race. Except as noted, the race data in this table from 2003 onward represent those respondents who indicated only one race category.

[2] The data shown prior to 2003 consists of those identifying themselves as "Asian or Pacific Islanders."

Table A-14. Population 14 to 24 Years Old, by High School Graduate Status, College Enrollment, Attainment, Sex, Race, and Hispanic Origin, October 1967–2019—*Continued*

(Numbers in thousands; percent; civilian noninstitutionalized population.)

| Year, race, and Hispanic origin | Population 18 to 24 years old | | | | | | | | High school graduates, 14 to 24 years old | | |
| | | High school graduates | | Percent | | | High school dropouts | | | Percent | |
	Total	Total	Enrolled in college	High school graduates	Enrolled in college	Of high school graduates enrolled in college	Number	Percent	All graduates	Enrolled in college	Enrolled or completed some college
1981	1,064	646	178	60.7	16.7	27.6	362	34.0	662	28.2	43.4
1980	1,021	579	165	56.7	16.2	28.5	389	38.1	595	29.1	45.4
1979	917	516	140	56.3	15.3	27.1	358	39.0	534	28.1	42.3
1978	891	516	128	57.9	14.4	24.8	343	38.5	528	25.8	40.0
1977	855	483	139	56.5	16.3	28.8	326	38.1	495	29.7	41.6
1976	850	483	160	56.8	18.8	33.1	313	36.8	489	33.5	46.5
1975	769	449	150	58.4	19.5	33.4	283	36.8	460	34.8	46.7
1974	786	451	129	57.4	16.4	28.6	280	35.6	459	29.2	43.4
1973	658	362	102	55.0	15.5	28.2	272	41.3	372	28.8	41.1
1972	728	394	88	54.1	12.1	22.3	288	39.6	402	23.6	31.1
WHITE ALONE OR IN COMBINATION											
Both Sexes											
2019	22,581	20,033	9,041	88.7	40.0	45.1	1,144	5.1	20,321	45.3	70.3
2018	22,681	19,953	9,174	88.0	40.5	46.0	1,356	6.0	20,259	46.2	71.9
2017	22,651	19,846	9,048	87.6	39.9	45.6	1,390	6.1	20,145	45.7	72.0
2016	22,830	20,100	9,446	88.0	41.4	47.0	1,419	6.2	20,416	47.2	72.6
2015	23,067	20,193	9,268	87.5	40.2	45.9	1,464	6.3	20,507	46.0	72.5
2014	23,327	20,258	9,329	86.8	40.0	46.1	1,638	7.0	20,520	46.2	72.0
2013	23,539	20,436	9,422	86.8	40.0	46.1	1,679	7.1	20,773	46.5	72.1
2012	23,516	20,257	9,614	86.1	40.9	47.5	1,710	7.3	20,546	47.8	73.4
2011	23,679	20,256	10,043	85.5	42.4	49.6	1,941	8.2	20,504	49.7	73.9
2010	23,381	19,949	9,524	85.3	40.7	47.7	2,013	8.6	20,180	48.0	72.9
2009	23,256	19,784	9,562	85.1	41.1	48.3	2,127	9.1	20,060	48.5	72.0
2008	23,120	19,810	9,360	85.7	40.5	47.2	2,072	9.0	20,067	47.5	71.6
2007	22,928	19,330	8,958	84.3	39.1	46.3	2,338	10.2	19,595	46.5	70.3
2006	22,670	18,882	8,465	83.3	37.3	44.8	2,458	10.8	19,153	45.1	69.9
2005	22,345	18,583	8,721	83.2	39.0	47.1	2,539	11.4	18,818	47.0	70.0
2004	22,411	18,663	8,544	83.3	38.1	45.8	2,639	11.8	18,868	46.0	69.0
2003	22,029	18,335	8,358	83.2	37.9	45.6	2,558	11.6	18,565	45.6	69.0
Male											
2019	11,358	9,846	4,116	86.7	36.2	41.8	694	6.1	9,978	41.8	65.1
2018	11,446	9,872	4,225	86.2	36.9	42.8	809	7.1	9,989	43.0	66.5
2017	11,424	9,769	4,116	85.5	36.0	42.1	796	7.0	9,898	42.2	67.5
2016	11,534	9,967	4,432	86.4	38.4	44.5	845	7.3	10,093	44.5	67.9
2015	11,635	10,059	4,319	86.5	37.1	42.9	812	7.0	10,224	43.0	67.6
2014	11,801	10,108	4,397	85.7	37.3	43.5	900	7.6	10,237	43.7	67.4
2013	11,921	10,185	4,323	85.4	36.3	42.4	896	7.5	10,357	42.9	66.7
2012	11,925	10,045	4,399	84.2	36.9	43.8	991	8.3	10,174	44.2	68.1
2011	12,153	10,175	4,789	83.7	39.4	47.1	1,105	9.1	10,308	47.2	69.7
2010	11,832	9,869	4,472	83.4	37.8	45.3	1,152	9.7	9,976	45.4	68.5
2009	11,774	9,824	4,513	83.4	38.3	45.9	1,224	10.4	9,952	46.1	68.3
2008	11,738	9,891	4,444	84.3	37.9	44.9	1,165	9.9	10,031	45.2	67.8
2007	11,670	9,511	4,116	81.5	35.3	43.3	1,397	12.0	9,634	43.4	66.0
2006	11,502	9,331	3,923	81.1	34.1	42.0	1,427	12.4	9,435	42.2	66.1
2005	11,394	9,086	4,018	79.7	35.3	43.5	1,519	13.3	9,193	44.2	60.0
2004	11,371	9,227	3,956	81.1	34.8	42.9	1,548	13.6	9,296	43.1	64.4
2003	11,147	8,967	3,815	80.4	34.2	42.5	1,493	13.4	9,070	42.6	65.1
Female											
2019	11,223	10,187	4,925	90.8	43.9	48.3	450	4.0	10,343	48.7	75.3
2018	11,234	10,081	4,950	89.7	44.1	49.1	547	4.9	10,270	49.3	77.0
2017	11,228	10,077	4,931	89.8	43.9	48.9	593	5.3	10,248	49.1	76.4
2016	11,296	10,133	5,014	89.7	44.4	49.5	574	5.1	10,323	49.7	77.3
2015	11,433	10,134	4,949	88.6	43.3	48.8	653	5.7	10,283	48.9	77.4

r = Revised, controlled to 1990 census based population estimates; previous 1993 data controlled to 1980 census based population estimates.

Note: The change in the educational attainment question and the college completion categories from "4 or more years of college" to "at least some college," in 1992 caused an increase in the proportion of 14-to-24-year-old high school graduates enrolled in college or completed some college, of approximately 5 percentage points. High school graduates are people who have completed 4 years of high school or more, for 1967 to 1991. Beginning in 1992, they were people whose highest degree was a high school diploma (including equivalency) or higher.

[1]Starting in 2003 respondents could identify more than one race. Except as noted, the race data in this table from 2003 onward represent those respondents who indicated only one race category.

[2]The data shown prior to 2003 consists of those identifying themselves as "Asian or Pacific Islanders."

Table A-14. Population 14 to 24 Years Old, by High School Graduate Status, College Enrollment, Attainment, Sex, Race, and Hispanic Origin, October 1967–2019—*Continued*

(Numbers in thousands; percent; civilian noninstitutionalized population.)

| Year, race, and Hispanic origin | Population 18 to 24 years old | | | | | | | | High school graduates, 14 to 24 years old | | |
| | High school graduates | | | | Percent | | High school dropouts | | | Percent | |
	Total	Total	Enrolled in college	High school graduates	Enrolled in college	Of high school graduates enrolled in college	Number	Percent	All graduates	Enrolled in college	Enrolled or completed some college
2014	11,526	10,151	4,932	88.1	42.8	48.6	739	6.4	10,283	48.8	76.5
2013	11,617	10,251	5,099	88.2	43.9	49.7	783	6.7	10,415	50.1	77.4
2012	11,590	10,212	5,215	88.1	45.0	51.1	719	6.2	10,372	51.4	78.5
2011	11,525	10,081	5,254	87.5	45.6	52.1	836	7.3	10,196	52.1	78.1
2010	11,549	10,080	5,052	87.3	43.7	50.1	861	7.5	10,204	50.5	77.1
2009	11,482	9,960	5,049	86.7	44.0	50.7	903	7.9	10,108	50.8	75.6
2008	11,381	9,919	4,916	87.2	43.2	49.6	908	8.0	10,036	49.9	75.4
2007	11,258	9,820	4,842	87.2	43.0	49.3	941	8.4	9,960	49.4	74.4
2006	11,168	9,551	4,542	85.5	40.7	47.6	1,032	9.2	9,718	47.8	73.6
2005	10,952	9,497	4,702	86.7	42.9	49.4	1,020	9.3	9,625	49.7	73.9
2004	11,040	9,436	4,588	85.5	41.6	48.6	1,091	9.9	9,572	48.8	73.5
2003	10,882	9,367	4,543	86.1	41.7	48.5	1,065	9.8	9,495	48.5	72.7
BLACK ALONE OR IN COMBINATION											
Both Sexes											
2019	4,877	4,257	1,791	87.3	36.7	42.1	287	5.9	4,327	42.4	67.2
2018	4,865	4,214	1,840	86.6	37.8	43.7	270	5.5	4,275	43.6	68.6
2017	4,935	4,219	1,782	85.5	36.1	42.2	296	6.0	4,314	42.4	65.7
2016	4,978	4,216	1,782	84.7	35.8	42.3	342	6.9	4,305	42.2	65.5
2015	5,032	4,316	1,741	85.8	34.6	40.3	359	7.1	4,367	40.5	64.2
2014	5,121	4,352	1,645	85.0	32.1	37.8	366	7.1	4,426	38.4	65.7
2013	5,199	4,297	1,806	82.7	34.7	42.0	422	8.1	4,345	42.4	66.4
2012	5,142	4,119	1,891	80.1	36.8	45.9	500	9.7	4,187	45.9	67.2
2011	4,793	3,902	1,759	81.4	36.7	45.1	424	8.8	3,955	45.5	67.3
2010	4,745	3,898	1,808	82.1	38.1	46.4	493	10.4	3,965	46.6	66.7
2009	4,623	3,688	1,699	79.8	36.8	46.1	532	11.5	3,766	46.0	67.2
2008	4,531	3,588	1,435	79.2	31.7	40.0	548	12.1	3,646	40.3	60.9
2007	4,425	3,603	1,468	81.4	33.2	40.7	477	10.8	3,671	40.9	61.8
2006	4,264	3,287	1,387	77.1	32.5	42.2	560	13.1	3,359	42.2	61.1
2005	4,158	3,303	1,371	79.4	33.0	31.7	530	12.7	3,378	41.5	63.5
2004	4,115	3,190	1,318	77.5	32.0	41.3	620	15.1	3,253	41.8	60.5
2003	4,016	3,091	1,285	77.0	32.0	41.6	563	14.0	3,141	41.9	62.0
Male											
2019	2,375	2,012	796	84.7	33.5	39.6	169	7.1	2,052	40.0	64.3
2018	2,385	2,016	822	84.5	34.5	40.8	155	6.5	2,029	41.1	65.0
2017	2,413	2,032	767	84.2	31.8	37.8	176	7.3	2,068	37.7	60.2
2016	2,407	1,924	777	79.9	32.3	40.4	226	9.4	1,948	40.6	61.2
2015	2,421	2,067	833	85.4	34.4	40.3	172	7.1	2,094	40.5	63.2
2014	2,451	2,008	660	81.9	26.9	32.8	183	7.4	2,055	34.0	60.6
2013	2,491	2,020	780	81.1	31.3	38.6	230	9.2	2,042	39.3	62.5
2012	2,500	1,972	859	78.9	34.4	43.6	279	11.2	2,009	43.8	65.0
2011	2,289	1,800	762	78.6	33.3	42.4	218	9.5	1,831	42.9	61.4
2010	2,250	1,781	779	79.2	34.6	43.7	269	11.9	1,823	43.7	61.9
2009	2,211	1,702	712	76.9	32.2	41.0	301	13.6	1,726	41.6	63.7
2008	2,190	1,743	633	79.6	28.9	36.3	235	10.7	1,770	36.9	54.9
2007	2,132	1,703	686	79.9	32.2	40.3	234	11.0	1,728	40.4	59.6
2006	2,032	1,545	577	76.0	28.4	37.3	225	11.0	1,576	37.2	54.5
2005	1,988	1,466	557	73.7	28.0	38.0	290	14.6	1,492	37.9	58.2
2004	1,951	1,418	521	72.7	26.7	36.7	347	17.8	1,442	37.0	61.3
2003	1,868	1,382	525	74.0	28.1	38.0	311	16.6	1,397	38.3	57.4
Female											
2019	2,502	2,244	994	89.7	39.7	44.3	118	4.7	2,275	44.6	69.9
2018	2,401	2,198	1,017	88.6	41.0	46.3	115	4.6	2,245	45.9	71.8
2017	2,522	2,187	1,014	86.7	40.2	46.4	120	4.8	2,246	46.7	70.7

r = Revised, controlled to 1990 census based population estimates; previous 1993 data controlled to 1980 census based population estimates.

Note: The change in the educational attainment question and the college completion categories from "4 or more years of college" to "at least some college," in 1992 caused an increase in the proportion of 14-to-24-year-old high school graduates enrolled in college or completed some college, of approximately 5 percentage points. High school graduates are people who have completed 4 years of high school or more, for 1967 to 1991. Beginning in 1992, they were people whose highest degree was a high school diploma (including equivalency) or higher.

¹Starting in 2003 respondents could identify more than one race. Except as noted, the race data in this table from 2003 onward represent those respondents who indicated only one race category.

²The data shown prior to 2003 consists of those identifying themselves as "Asian or Pacific Islanders."

Table A-14. Population 14 to 24 Years Old, by High School Graduate Status, College Enrollment, Attainment, Sex, Race, and Hispanic Origin, October 1967–2019—*Continued*

(Numbers in thousands; percent; civilian noninstitutionalized population.)

Year, race, and Hispanic origin	Population 18 to 24 years old								High school graduates, 14 to 24 years old		
		High school graduates			Percent		High school dropouts			Percent	
	Total	Total	Enrolled in college	High school graduates	Enrolled in college	Of high school graduates enrolled in college	Number	Percent	All graduates	Enrolled in college	Enrolled or completed some college
2016..............	2,571	2,292	1,004	89.1	39.1	43.8	116	4.5	2,357	43.5	69.1
2015..............	2,612	2,249	908	86.1	34.8	40.4	188	7.2	2,273	40.6	65.2
2014..............	2,670	2,344	985	87.8	36.9	42.0	183	6.9	2,371	42.3	70.1
2013..............	2,708	2,277	1,026	84.1	37.9	45.0	192	7.1	2,303	45.1	69.9
2012..............	2,642	2,147	1,032	81.3	39.1	48.1	221	8.4	2,178	47.9	69.4
2011..............	2,504	2,102	997	84.0	39.8	47.4	206	8.2	2,124	47.7	72.3
2010..............	2,495	2,117	1,029	84.8	41.3	48.6	224	9.0	2,142	49.0	70.7
2009..............	2,411	1,987	987	82.4	40.9	49.7	231	9.6	2,040	49.8	70.1
2008..............	2,341	1,845	802	78.8	34.2	43.5	313	13.4	1,876	43.5	66.5
2007..............	2,293	1,900	782	82.9	34.1	41.2	243	10.6	1,942	41.3	63.7
2006..............	2,232	1,742	810	78.1	36.3	46.5	335	15.0	1,783	46.5	66.8
2005..............	2,170	1,837	814	84.7	37.5	44.4	240	11.1	1,885	44.3	67.7
2004..............	2,164	1,772	797	81.9	36.8	45.0	272	12.6	1,811	45.5	65.3
2003..............	2,148	1,708	760	79.5	35.4	44.5	252	11.7	1,744	44.7	65.7
ASIAN ALONE OR IN COMBINATION											
Both Sexes											
2019..............	2,138	1,993	1,312	93.2	61.4	65.8	41	1.9	2,051	66.2	92.6
2018..............	2,180	2,036	1,265	93.4	58.0	62.2	58	2.6	2,059	62.4	88.1
2017..............	1,989	1,875	1,223	94.2	61.5	65.2	33	1.6	1,910	65.7	90.1
2016..............	2,025	1,867	1,161	92.2	57.3	62.2	61	3.0	1,903	62.1	87.3
2015..............	1,889	1,747	1,182	92.5	62.6	67.7	52	2.8	1,795	67.0	91.5
2014..............	1,844	1,737	1,132	94.2	61.4	65.2	17	0.9	1,781	64.6	90.2
2013..............	1,947	1,765	1,156	90.6	59.4	65.5	70	3.6	1,801	65.9	86.5
2012..............	1,780	1,610	1,043	90.5	58.6	64.8	61	3.4	1,650	65.2	85.2
2011..............	1,435	1,295	833	90.2	58.0	64.3	67	4.6	1,321	64.7	88.1
2010..............	1,465	1,338	904	91.3	61.7	67.6	80	5.5	1,382	68.0	88.9
2009..............	1,345	1,231	844	91.5	62.8	68.5	29	2.1	1,249	68.5	90.8
2008..............	1,251	1,153	738	92.1	59.0	64.0	42	3.4	1,188	64.4	89.7
2007..............	1,293	1,126	720	87.1	55.7	63.9	94	7.3	1,143	63.9	90.3
2006..............	1,270	1,158	705	91.2	55.5	60.9	49	3.9	1,180	60.6	86.1
2005..............	1,299	1,214	773	93.5	59.5	63.7	38	2.9	1,243	64.2	86.0
2004..............	1,263	1,167	750	92.5	59.4	64.3	53	4.2	1,191	64.6	87.6
2003..............	1,280	1,162	774	90.8	60.5	66.6	56	4.4	1,184	66.9	87.8
Male											
2019..............	1,039	964	638	92.8	61.4	66.2	20	1.9	994	66.5	90.3
2018..............	1,114	1,033	641	92.7	57.6	62.1	33	3.0	1,046	62.5	88.4
2017..............	1,003	934	613	93.1	61.1	65.6	16	1.6	941	65.8	89.3
2016..............	1,045	969	624	92.7	59.7	64.4	25	2.3	984	64.1	87.3
2015..............	937	869	561	92.8	59.9	64.6	30	3.2	896	63.9	89.2
2014..............	932	882	600	94.6	64.3	68.0	13	1.4	904	67.9	89.8
2013..............	1,009	927	612	91.9	60.7	66.1	22	2.2	939	66.1	84.8
2012..............	900	807	510	89.7	56.7	63.2	28	3.1	832	63.9	84.5
2011..............	747	673	429	90.1	57.4	63.7	31	4.2	682	63.7	87.6
2010..............	750	685	453	91.4	60.4	66.1	40	5.3	711	66.5	87.4
2009..............	673	624	418	92.8	62.2	67.0	7	1.1	637	66.8	89.8
2008..............	626	560	340	89.4	54.4	60.8	22	3.4	582	62.2	89.2
2007..............	560	481	318	85.8	56.9	66.3	38	6.8	483	66.4	91.8
2006..............	649	578	362	89.1	55.8	62.7	34	5.3	591	62.3	83.8
2005..............	653	603	392	92.4	59.9	65.0	20	3.1	621	65.1	86.3
2004..............	634	588	398	92.8	62.7	67.7	18	2.9	601	68.0	87.8
2003..............	609	545	370	89.5	60.8	67.9	43	7.1	551	67.7	88.7
Female											
2019..............	1,098	1,029	674	93.7	61.4	65.5	22	2.0	1,058	66.0	94.8
2018..............	1,066	1,003	624	94.1	58.6	62.2	24	2.3	1,014	62.1	87.9

r = Revised, controlled to 1990 census based population estimates; previous 1993 data controlled to 1980 census based population estimates.
Note: The change in the educational attainment question and the college completion categories from "4 or more years of college" to "at least some college," in 1992 caused an increase in the proportion of 14-to-24-year-old high school graduates enrolled in college or completed some college, of approximately 5 percentage points. High school graduates are people who have completed 4 years of high school or more, for 1967 to 1991. Beginning in 1992, they were people whose highest degree was a high school diploma (including equivalency) or higher.
[1]Starting in 2003 respondents could identify more than one race. Except as noted, the race data in this table from 2003 onward represent those respondents who indicated only one race category.
[2]The data shown prior to 2003 consists of those identifying themselves as "Asian or Pacific Islanders."

Table A-14. Population 14 to 24 Years Old, by High School Graduate Status, College Enrollment, Attainment, Sex, Race, and Hispanic Origin, October 1967–2019—*Continued*

(Numbers in thousands; percent; civilian noninstitutionalized population.)

| Year, race, and Hispanic origin | Population 18 to 24 years old | | | | | | | | High school graduates, 14 to 24 years old | | |
| | | High school graduates | | Percent | | | High school dropouts | | | Percent | |
	Total	Total	Enrolled in college	High school graduates	Enrolled in college	Of high school graduates enrolled in college	Number	Percent	All graduates	Enrolled in college	Enrolled or completed some college
2017............................	986	941	611	95.4	61.9	64.9	17	1.7	969	65.6	90.9
2016............................	980	898	536	91.6	54.7	59.7	36	3.7	919	60.0	87.3
2015............................	952	878	621	92.2	65.2	70.7	22	2.3	899	70.2	93.8
2014............................	911	855	533	93.8	58.5	62.3	4	0.5	877	61.3	90.6
2013............................	938	838	544	89.3	58.0	64.9	48	5.1	861	65.7	88.4
2012............................	880	803	533	91.2	60.6	66.4	33	3.7	817	66.5	85.8
2011............................	688	622	403	90.4	58.7	64.9	35	5.1	638	65.7	88.7
2010............................	715	652	451	91.2	63.1	69.1	41	5.7	671	69.7	90.4
2009............................	673	607	426	90.3	63.3	70.1	21	3.2	611	70.2	91.8
2008............................	625	593	397	94.9	63.6	67.0	21	3.3	605	66.5	90.3
2007............................	605	529	339	87.4	56.0	64.1	48	7.9	543	63.9	91.5
2006............................	621	580	343	93.4	55.3	59.2	14	2.3	589	58.8	88.5
2005............................	645	610	381	94.6	59.1	62.5	17	2.7	622	63.3	85.8
2004............................	628	579	352	92.1	56.0	60.8	35	5.5	591	61.2	87.5
2003............................	671	617	404	92.0	60.2	65.5	13	1.9	633	66.3	87.0

r = Revised, controlled to 1990 census based population estimates; previous 1993 data controlled to 1980 census based population estimates.

Note: The change in the educational attainment question and the college completion categories from "4 or more years of college" to "at least some college," in 1992 caused an increase in the proportion of 14-to-24-year-old high school graduates enrolled in college or completed some college, of approximately 5 percentage points. High school graduates are people who have completed 4 years of high school or more, for 1967 to 1991. Beginning in 1992, they were people whose highest degree was a high school diploma (including equivalency) or higher.

[1]Starting in 2003 respondents could identify more than one race. Except as noted, the race data in this table from 2003 onward represent those respondents who indicated only one race category.

[2]The data shown prior to 2003 consists of those identifying themselves as "Asian or Pacific Islanders."

Table A-15. Population 18 and 19 Years Old, by School Enrollment Status, Sex, Race, and Hispanic Origin, October 1967–2019

(Numbers in thousands; percent; civilian noninstitutionalized population.)

Year, race, and Hispanic origin	Total	Still in high school	Percent	Dropped out	Percent	High school graduate only	Percent	In college	Percent
ALL RACES									
Both Sexes									
2019	8,306	1,582	19.1	481	5.8	2,238	26.9	4,004	48.2
2018	8,359	1,556	18.6	528	6.3	2,055	24.6	4,220	50.5
2017	8,222	1,663	20.2	568	6.9	2,049	24.9	3,943	48.0
2016	8,266	1,570	19.0	532	6.4	1,993	24.1	4,171	50.5
2015	8,158	1,613	19.8	611	7.5	1,957	24.0	3,978	48.8
2014	8,261	1,618	19.6	588	7.1	2,019	24.4	4,036	48.9
2013	8,473	1,736	20.5	529	6.2	2,257	26.6	3,951	46.6
2012	8,484	1,840	21.7	605	7.1	2,025	23.9	4,015	47.3
2011	8,465	1,775	21.0	545	6.4	1,903	22.5	4,242	50.1
2010	8,529	1,540	18.1	622	7.3	2,003	23.5	4,364	51.2
2009	8,615	1,645	19.1	736	8.5	1,944	22.6	4,289	49.8
2008	8,492	1,481	17.4	750	8.8	2,134	25.1	4,126	48.6
2007	8,338	1,491	17.9	675	8.1	2,097	25.2	4,075	48.9
2006	8,102	1,560	19.3	743	9.2	2,053	25.3	3,746	46.2
2005	7,559	1,372	18.1	661	8.7	1,694	22.4	3,727	49.3
2004	7,701	1,266	16.4	840	10.9	1,910	24.8	3,685	47.8
2003	7,533	1,345	17.9	817	10.8	1,859	24.7	3,512	46.6
2002	7,907	1,427	18.0	884	11.2	2,015	25.5	3,581	45.3
2001	7,985	1,394	17.5	1,034	12.9	2,079	26.0	3,478	43.6
2000	8,045	1,327	16.5	1,012	12.6	2,107	26.2	3,599	44.7
1999	7,991	1,321	16.5	1,047	13.1	2,103	26.3	3,520	44.0
1998	7,902	1,244	15.7	1,104	14.0	1,884	23.8	3,670	46.4
1997	7,510	1,256	16.7	1,038	13.8	1,854	24.7	3,362	44.8
1996	7,376	1,230	16.7	940	12.7	1,897	25.7	3,309	44.9
1995	7,198	1,173	16.3	1,051	14.6	1,873	26.0	3,101	43.1
1994	6,946	1,129	16.3	929	13.4	1,837	26.4	3,051	43.9
1993	6,594	1,137	17.2	778	11.8	1,753	26.6	2,926	44.4
1992	6,535	1,121	17.2	780	11.9	1,742	26.7	2,892	44.3
1991	6,664	1,040	15.6	889	13.3	1,806	27.1	2,929	44.0
1990	7,064	1,024	14.5	1,003	14.2	2,018	28.6	3,019	42.7
1989	7,361	1,058	14.4	1,033	14.0	2,204	29.9	3,066	41.7
1988	7,294	1,013	13.9	1,063	14.6	2,172	29.8	3,046	41.8
1987	7,160	937	13.1	954	13.3	2,224	31.1	3,045	42.5
1986	7,095	930	13.1	872	12.3	2,351	33.1	2,942	41.5
1985	7,204	809	11.2	1,031	14.3	2,457	34.1	2,907	40.4
1984	7,428	857	11.5	1,129	15.2	2,575	34.7	2,867	38.6
1983	7,819	999	12.8	1,132	14.5	2,748	35.1	2,940	37.6
1982	8,023	908	11.3	1,336	16.7	2,850	35.5	2,929	36.5
1981	8,115	932	11.5	1,299	16.0	2,840	35.0	3,044	37.5
1980	8,160	855	10.5	1,284	15.7	3,088	37.8	2,933	35.9
1979	8,214	849	10.3	1,382	16.8	3,139	38.2	2,844	34.6
1978	8,153	801	9.8	1,361	16.7	3,092	37.9	2,899	35.6
1977	8,151	849	10.4	1,355	16.6	3,034	37.2	2,913	35.7
1976	8,148	831	10.2	1,355	16.6	3,025	37.1	2,937	36.0
1975	8,024	822	10.2	1,286	16.0	2,973	37.1	2,943	36.7
1974	7,822	777	9.9	1,302	16.6	3,146	40.2	2,597	33.2
1973	7,649	766	10.0	1,228	16.1	3,138	41.0	2,517	32.9
1972	7,462	778	10.4	1,100	14.7	2,904	38.9	2,680	35.9
1971	7,231	830	11.5	1,108	15.3	2,567	35.5	2,726	37.7
1970	6,958	728	10.5	1,125	16.2	2,511	36.1	2,594	37.3
1969	6,677	749	11.2	1,007	15.1	2,320	34.7	2,601	39.0
1968	6,587	816	12.4	1,033	15.7	2,237	34.0	2,501	38.0
1967	6,358	741	11.7	1,086	17.1	2,245	35.3	2,286	36.0
Male									
2019	4,182	924	22.1	270	6.5	1,165	27.9	1,822	43.6
2018	4,233	886	20.9	340	8.0	1,097	25.9	1,911	45.1
2017	4,153	957	23.1	346	8.3	1,103	26.6	1,746	42.1
2016	4,192	916	21.9	303	7.2	1,028	24.5	1,944	46.4
2015	4,106	860	20.9	359	8.7	1,050	25.6	1,838	44.7
2014	4,183	935	22.4	323	7.7	1,146	27.4	1,779	42.5
2013	4,319	1,004	23.2	272	6.3	1,235	28.6	1,809	41.9

* = Quantity zero or rounds to zero.

Note: High school graduates are people who have completed 4 years of high school or more, for 1967 to 1991. Beginning in 1992, they were people whose highest degree was a high school diploma (including equivalency) or higher.

[1]Starting in 2003 respondents could identify more than one race. Except as noted, the race data in this table from 2003 onward represent those respondents who indicated only one race category.

[2]The data shown prior to 2003 consists of those identifying themselves as "Asian or Pacific Islanders."

Table A-15. Population 18 and 19 Years Old, by School Enrollment Status, Sex, Race, and Hispanic Origin, October 1967–2019—*Continued*

(Numbers in thousands; percent; civilian noninstitutionalized population.)

Year, race, and Hispanic origin	Total	Population 18 and 19 years old							
		Still in high school	Percent	Dropped out	Percent	High school graduate only	Percent	In college	Percent
2012	4,310	1,033	23.7	359	8.3	1,114	25.9	1,803	41.8
2011	4,341	1,038	23.9	293	6.8	1,060	24.4	1,949	44.9
2010	4,296	867	20.2	347	8.1	1,073	25.0	2,009	46.8
2009	4,352	899	20.7	410	9.4	1,114	25.6	1,928	44.3
2008	4,289	834	19.5	376	8.8	1,169	27.3	1,909	44.5
2007	4,222	895	21.2	354	8.4	1,070	25.3	1,903	45.1
2006	4,103	907	22.1	414	10.1	1,079	26.3	1,703	41.5
2005	3,880	899	23.2	392	10.1	914	23.6	1,675	43.2
2004	3,861	714	18.5	522	13.5	1,015	26.3	1,610	41.7
2003	3,764	781	20.7	480	12.8	935	24.8	1,568	41.7
2002	4,042	862	21.3	523	12.9	1,022	25.3	1,635	40.5
2001	4,027	801	19.9	614	15.2	1,042	25.9	1,570	39.0
2000	4,037	783	19.4	571	14.1	1,113	27.6	1,570	38.9
1999	4,026	780	19.4	550	13.7	1,048	26.0	1,648	40.9
1998	3,994	732	18.3	611	15.3	984	24.6	1,667	41.7
1997	3,816	750	19.7	585	15.3	920	24.1	1,561	40.9
1996	3,711	769	20.7	488	13.2	965	26.0	1,489	40.1
1995	3,611	719	19.9	532	14.7	929	25.7	1,431	39.6
1994	3,485	688	19.7	499	14.3	882	25.3	1,416	40.6
1993	3,329	712	21.4	403	12.1	877	26.3	1,337	40.2
1992	3,275	694	21.2	400	12.2	856	26.1	1,325	40.5
1991	3,307	650	19.7	453	13.7	878	26.5	1,326	40.1
1990	3,503	595	17.0	512	14.6	953	27.2	1,443	41.2
1989	3,640	640	17.6	531	14.6	1,047	28.8	1,422	39.1
1988	3,618	666	18.4	566	15.6	1,021	28.2	1,365	37.7
1987	3,537	564	15.9	493	13.9	997	28.2	1,483	41.9
1986	3,502	594	17.0	459	13.1	1,045	29.8	1,404	40.1
1985	3,550	503	14.2	580	16.3	1,118	31.5	1,349	38.0
1984	3,674	551	15.0	594	16.2	1,156	31.5	1,373	37.4
1983	3,877	616	15.9	630	16.2	1,291	33.3	1,340	34.6
1982	3,961	562	14.2	709	17.9	1,314	33.2	1,376	34.7
1981	3,996	567	14.2	706	17.7	1,273	31.9	1,450	36.3
1980	3,993	510	12.8	673	16.9	1,441	36.1	1,369	34.3
1979	4,023	533	13.2	739	18.4	1,410	35.0	1,341	33.3
1978	3,975	511	12.9	692	17.4	1,381	34.7	1,391	35.0
1977	3,961	522	13.2	702	17.7	1,341	33.9	1,396	35.2
1976	3,957	516	13.0	684	17.3	1,366	34.5	1,391	35.2
1975	3,891	514	13.2	603	15.5	1,348	34.6	1,426	36.6
1974	3,782	469	12.4	706	18.7	1,345	35.6	1,262	33.4
1973	3,720	490	13.2	589	15.8	1,348	36.2	1,293	34.8
1972	3,630	492	13.6	555	15.3	1,217	33.5	1,366	37.6
1971	3,503	496	14.2	551	15.7	1,012	28.9	1,444	41.2
1970	3,349	485	14.5	537	16.0	981	29.3	1,346	40.2
1969	3,173	489	15.4	473	14.9	814	25.7	1,397	44.0
1968	3,133	535	17.1	485	15.5	756	24.1	1,357	43.3
1967	2,908	438	15.1	500	17.2	772	26.5	1,198	41.2
Female									
2019	4,124	658	16.0	211	5.1	1,073	26.0	2,181	52.9
2018	4,126	671	16.3	188	4.5	958	23.2	2,309	56.0
2017	4,070	705	17.3	222	5.5	946	23.2	2,197	54.0
2016	4,075	654	16.0	229	5.6	965	23.7	2,227	54.7
2015	4,052	752	18.6	252	6.2	907	22.4	2,141	52.8
2014	4,079	683	16.7	265	6.5	873	21.4	2,257	55.3
2013	4,154	732	17.6	257	6.2	1,022	24.6	2,142	51.6
2012	4,174	807	18.9	245	5.9	911	21.8	2,212	53.0
2011	4,124	737	17.9	252	6.1	843	20.4	2,293	55.6
2010	4,233	673	15.9	275	6.5	930	22.0	2,355	55.6
2009	4,263	746	17.5	325	7.6	830	19.5	2,361	55.4
2008	4,203	647	15.4	374	8.9	965	23.0	2,217	52.7
2007	4,116	595	14.5	321	7.8	1,027	25.0	2,172	52.8
2006	3,999	654	16.3	328	8.2	974	24.4	2,043	51.1
2005	3,679	472	12.8	269	7.3	886	24.1	2,052	55.8
2004	3,840	553	14.4	318	8.3	806	23.3	2,074	54.0
2003	3,769	565	15.0	337	8.9	923	24.5	1,944	51.6

* = Quantity zero or rounds to zero.
Note: High school graduates are people who have completed 4 years of high school or more, for 1967 to 1991. Beginning in 1992, they were people whose highest degree was a high school diploma (including equivalency) or higher.
[1] Starting in 2003 respondents could identify more than one race. Except as noted, the race data in this table from 2003 onward represent those respondents who indicated only one race category.
[2] The data shown prior to 2003 consists of those identifying themselves as "Asian or Pacific Islanders."

Table A-15. Population 18 and 19 Years Old, by School Enrollment Status, Sex, Race, and Hispanic Origin, October 1967–2019—*Continued*

(Numbers in thousands; percent; civilian noninstitutionalized population.)

Year, race, and Hispanic origin	Total	Population 18 and 19 years old							
		Still in high school	Percent	Dropped out	Percent	High school graduate only	Percent	In college	Percent
2002.............................	3,865	565	14.6	361	9.3	993	25.7	1,946	50.3
2001.............................	3,958	594	15.0	420	10.6	1,037	26.2	1,907	48.2
2000.............................	4,008	544	13.6	440	11.0	995	24.8	2,029	50.6
1999.............................	3,965	540	13.6	497	12.5	1,056	26.6	1,872	47.2
1998.............................	3,908	513	13.1	492	12.6	900	23.0	2,003	51.3
1997.............................	3,694	506	13.7	453	12.3	934	25.3	1,801	48.8
1996.............................	3,665	460	12.6	452	12.3	932	25.4	1,821	49.7
1995.............................	3,587	453	12.6	519	14.5	944	26.3	1,671	46.6
1994.............................	3,461	440	12.7	430	12.4	956	27.6	1,635	47.2
1993.............................	3,265	425	13.0	375	11.5	877	26.9	1,588	48.6
1992.............................	3,260	428	13.1	380	11.7	886	27.2	1,566	48.0
1991.............................	3,357	389	11.6	436	13.0	929	27.7	1,603	47.8
1990.............................	3,561	429	12.0	491	13.8	1,065	29.9	1,576	44.3
1989.............................	3,721	421	11.3	501	13.5	1,156	31.1	1,643	44.2
1988.............................	3,676	346	9.4	497	13.5	1,151	31.3	1,682	45.8
1987.............................	3,623	374	10.3	461	12.7	1,226	33.8	1,562	43.1
1986.............................	3,593	337	9.4	413	11.5	1,306	36.3	1,537	42.8
1985.............................	3,654	304	8.3	451	12.3	1,340	36.7	1,559	42.7
1984.............................	3,754	306	8.2	535	14.3	1,419	37.8	1,494	39.8
1983.............................	3,942	383	9.7	502	12.7	1,457	37.0	1,600	40.6
1982.............................	4,062	346	8.5	627	15.4	1,536	37.8	1,553	38.2
1981.............................	4,119	364	8.8	594	14.4	1,567	38.0	1,594	38.7
1980.............................	4,167	345	8.3	611	14.7	1,646	39.5	1,565	37.6
1979.............................	4,191	317	7.6	643	15.3	1,728	41.2	1,503	35.9
1978.............................	4,178	291	7.0	669	16.0	1,711	41.0	1,507	36.1
1977.............................	4,190	326	7.8	654	15.6	1,693	40.4	1,517	36.2
1976.............................	4,191	314	7.5	672	16.0	1,659	39.6	1,546	36.9
1975.............................	4,133	308	7.5	683	16.5	1,625	39.3	1,517	36.7
1974.............................	4,040	309	7.6	596	14.8	1,800	44.6	1,335	33.0
1973.............................	3,929	276	7.0	638	16.2	1,791	45.6	1,224	31.2
1972.............................	3,832	287	7.5	545	14.2	1,686	44.0	1,314	34.3
1971.............................	3,728	337	9.0	556	14.9	1,554	41.7	1,281	34.4
1970.............................	3,609	253	7.0	589	16.3	1,519	42.1	1,248	34.6
1969.............................	3,504	260	7.4	534	15.2	1,506	43.0	1,204	34.4
1968.............................	3,454	281	8.1	548	15.9	1,481	42.9	1,144	33.1
1967.............................	3,450	302	8.8	586	17.0	1,474	42.7	1,088	31.5
WHITE									
Both Sexes									
2019.............................	6,165	1,174	19.0	356	5.8	1,685	27.3	2,949	47.8
2018.............................	6,198	1,092	17.6	419	6.8	1,509	24.3	3,178	51.3
2017.............................	6,153	1,192	19.4	450	7.3	1,529	24.8	2,982	48.5
2016.............................	6,144	1,097	17.9	370	6.0	1,506	24.5	3,170	51.6
2015.............................	6,147	1,159	18.9	474	7.7	1,456	23.7	3,057	49.7
2014.............................	6,213	1,182	19.0	451	7.3	1,517	24.4	3,064	49.3
2013.............................	6,294	1,219	19.4	390	6.2	1,652	26.2	3,033	48.2
2012.............................	6,372	1,303	20.1	418	6.6	1,575	24.7	3,077	48.3
2011.............................	6,501	1,274	19.6	449	6.9	1,480	22.8	3,298	50.7
2010.............................	6,523	1,168	17.9	435	6.7	1,522	23.3	3,398	52.1
2009.............................	6,594	1,194	18.1	526	8.0	1,536	23.3	3,337	50.6
2008.............................	6,589	1,067	16.2	558	8.5	1,611	24.4	3,353	50.9
2007.............................	6,446	1,083	16.8	517	8.0	1,605	24.9	3,242	50.3
2006.............................	6,321	1,121	17.7	600	9.5	1,619	25.6	2,982	47.2
2005.............................	5,893	1,023	17.4	515	8.7	1,383	23.5	2,972	50.4
2004	6,043	963	15.9	634	10.5	1,500	24.8	2,946	48.8
2003[1]	5,915	979	16.6	659	11.1	1,444	24.4	2,833	47.9
2002.............................	6,252	1,096	17.5	663	10.6	1,602	25.6	2,891	46.2
2001.............................	6,254	1,022	16.3	843	13.5	1,634	26.1	2,755	44.1
2000.............................	6,399	1,010	15.8	795	12.4	1,680	26.3	2,914	45.5
1999.............................	6,383	1,009	15.8	810	12.7	1,715	26.9	2,849	44.6
1998.............................	6,266	884	14.1	848	13.5	1,540	24.6	2,994	47.8
1997.............................	5,995	896	14.9	816	13.6	1,491	24.9	2,792	46.6
1996.............................	5,833	914	15.7	735	12.6	1,453	24.9	2,731	46.8
1995.............................	5,698	803	14.1	809	14.2	1,509	26.5	2,577	45.2

* = Quantity zero or rounds to zero.
Note: High school graduates are people who have completed 4 years of high school or more, for 1967 to 1991. Beginning in 1992, they were people whose highest degree was a high school diploma (including equivalency) or higher.
[1]Starting in 2003 respondents could identify more than one race. Except as noted, the race data in this table from 2003 onward represent those respondents who indicated only one race category.
[2]The data shown prior to 2003 consists of those identifying themselves as "Asian or Pacific Islanders."

Table A-15. Population 18 and 19 Years Old, by School Enrollment Status, Sex, Race, and Hispanic Origin, October 1967–2019—Continued

(Numbers in thousands; percent; civilian noninstitutionalized population.)

Year, race, and Hispanic origin	Total	Population 18 and 19 years old							
		Still in high school	Percent	Dropped out	Percent	High school graduate only	Percent	In college	Percent
1994............................	5,559	817	14.7	681	12.3	1,493	26.9	2,568	46.2
1993............................	5,252	786	15.0	628	12.0	1,382	26.3	2,456	46.8
1992............................	5,203	793	15.2	582	11.2	1,409	27.1	2,419	46.5
1991............................	5,358	709	13.2	722	13.5	1,440	26.9	2,487	46.4
1990............................	5,725	724	12.6	799	14.0	1,654	28.9	2,548	44.5
1989............................	6,013	744	12.4	819	13.6	1,802	30.0	2,648	44.0
1988............................	5,981	699	11.7	855	14.3	1,788	29.9	2,639	44.1
1987............................	5,845	667	11.4	762	13.0	1,852	31.7	2,564	43.9
1986............................	5,825	669	11.5	693	11.9	1,940	33.3	2,523	43.3
1985............................	5,922	566	9.6	815	13.8	2,002	33.8	2,539	42.9
1984............................	6,139	594	9.7	913	14.9	2,091	34.1	2,541	41.4
1983............................	6,452	688	10.7	884	13.7	2,283	35.4	2,597	40.3
1982............................	6,666	647	9.7	1,051	15.8	2,419	36.3	2,549	38.2
1981............................	6,794	656	9.7	1,054	15.5	2,445	36.0	2,639	38.8
1980............................	6,913	621	9.0	1,032	14.9	2,682	38.8	2,578	37.3
1979............................	6,980	607	8.7	1,115	16.0	2,760	39.5	2,498	35.8
1978............................	6,933	560	8.1	1,082	15.6	2,738	39.5	2,553	36.8
1977............................	6,944	581	8.4	1,103	15.9	2,681	38.6	2,579	37.1
1976............................	6,951	581	8.4	1,131	16.3	2,662	38.3	2,577	37.1
1975............................	6,855	572	8.3	1,005	14.7	2,665	38.9	2,613	38.1
1974............................	6,707	551	8.2	1,045	15.6	2,803	41.8	2,308	34.4
1973............................	6,559	568	8.7	962	14.7	2,748	41.9	2,281	34.8
1972............................	6,424	582	9.1	857	13.3	2,574	40.1	2,411	37.5
1971............................	6,243	596	9.5	875	14.0	2,287	36.6	2,485	39.8
1970............................	6,009	563	9.4	845	14.1	2,240	37.3	2,361	39.3
1969............................	5,762	557	9.7	772	13.4	2,056	35.7	2,377	41.3
1968............................	5,692	614	10.8	822	14.4	1,972	34.6	2,284	40.1
1967............................	5,506	558	10.1	875	15.9	1,968	35.7	2,105	38.2
Male									
2019............................	3,122	687	22.0	211	6.8	890	28.5	1,334	42.7
2018............................	3,147	630	20.0	281	8.9	806	25.6	1,430	45.4
2017............................	3,123	717	22.9	273	8.7	816	26.1	1,317	42.2
2016............................	3,119	649	20.8	202	6.5	798	25.6	1,470	47.1
2015............................	3,123	621	19.9	282	9.0	806	25.8	1,414	45.3
2014............................	3,165	653	20.6	236	7.5	879	27.8	1,397	44.1
2013............................	3,212	732	22.8	196	6.1	898	27.9	1,386	43.2
2012............................	3,259	763	23.1	237	7.3	872	26.8	1,387	42.6
2011............................	3,352	748	22.3	240	7.2	845	25.2	1,520	45.3
2010............................	3,316	667	20.1	246	7.4	830	25.0	1,573	47.4
2009............................	3,349	652	19.5	291	8.7	894	26.7	1,511	45.1
2008............................	3,350	589	17.6	299	8.9	896	26.7	1,566	46.7
2007............................	3,277	668	20.4	281	8.6	819	25.0	1,508	46.0
2006............................	3,211	645	20.1	351	10.9	848	26.4	1,367	42.6
2005............................	3,049	665	21.8	304	10.0	737	24.2	1,343	44.1
2004[1]........................	3,062	524	17.1	406	13.3	824	26.9	1,308	42.7
2003[1]........................	3,003	594	19.8	381	12.7	770	25.6	1,258	41.9
2002............................	3,186	661	20.7	366	11.5	830	26.1	1,329	41.7
2001............................	3,192	585	18.3	494	15.5	840	26.3	1,273	39.9
2000............................	3,248	612	18.8	447	13.8	900	27.7	1,289	39.7
1999............................	3,242	609	18.8	423	13.0	874	27.0	1,336	41.2
1998............................	3,197	533	16.7	472	14.8	816	25.5	1,376	43.0
1997............................	3,060	523	17.1	473	15.5	750	24.5	1,314	42.9
1996............................	2,953	575	19.5	382	12.9	773	26.2	1,223	41.4
1995............................	2,886	519	18.0	408	14.1	764	26.5	1,195	41.4
1994............................	2,813	512	18.2	355	12.6	734	26.1	1,212	43.1
1993............................	2,641	497	18.8	338	12.8	703	26.6	1,103	41.8
1992............................	2,608	482	18.5	304	11.7	720	27.6	1,102	42.3
1991............................	2,677	451	16.8	381	14.2	733	27.4	1,112	41.5
1990............................	2,852	416	14.6	421	14.8	797	27.9	1,218	42.7
1989............................	2,997	463	15.4	433	14.4	848	28.3	1,253	41.8
1988............................	2,976	487	16.4	461	15.5	834	28.0	1,194	40.1
1987............................	2,906	404	13.9	400	13.8	842	29.0	1,260	43.4
1986............................	2,888	411	14.2	370	12.8	866	30.0	1,241	43.0
1985............................	2,937	349	11.9	478	16.3	934	31.8	1,176	40.0

* = Quantity zero or rounds to zero.
Note: High school graduates are people who have completed 4 years of high school or more, for 1967 to 1991. Beginning in 1992, they were people whose highest degree was a high school diploma (including equivalency) or higher.
[1]Starting in 2003 respondents could identify more than one race. Except as noted, the race data in this table from 2003 onward represent those respondents who indicated only one race category
[2]The data shown prior to 2003 consists of those identifying themselves as "Asian or Pacific Islanders."

Table A-15. Population 18 and 19 Years Old, by School Enrollment Status, Sex, Race, and Hispanic Origin, October 1967–2019—*Continued*

(Numbers in thousands; percent; civilian noninstitutionalized population.)

Year, race, and Hispanic origin	Total	Still in high school	Percent	Dropped out	Percent	High school graduate only	Percent	In college	Percent
						Population 18 and 19 years old			
1984............................	3,047	378	12.4	480	15.8	965	31.7	1,224	40.2
1983............................	3,216	434	13.5	500	15.5	1,085	33.7	1,197	37.2
1982............................	3,301	412	12.5	549	16.6	1,151	34.9	1,189	36.0
1981............................	3,356	394	11.7	599	17.8	1,104	32.9	1,259	37.5
1980............................	3,407	385	11.3	549	16.1	1,241	36.4	1,232	36.2
1979............................	3,445	395	11.5	610	17.7	1,248	36.2	1,192	34.6
1978............................	3,405	368	10.8	554	16.3	1,244	36.5	1,239	36.4
1977............................	3,396	348	10.2	577	17.0	1,199	35.3	1,272	37.5
1976............................	3,393	348	10.3	582	17.2	1,219	35.9	1,244	36.7
1975............................	3,343	374	11.2	458	13.7	1,228	36.7	1,283	38.4
1974............................	3,265	343	10.5	568	17.4	1,211	37.1	1,143	35.0
1973............................	3,208	375	11.7	454	14.2	1,202	37.5	1,177	36.7
1972............................	3,137	374	11.9	423	13.5	1,098	35.0	1,242	39.6
1971............................	3,035	367	12.1	432	14.2	908	29.9	1,328	43.8
1970............................	2,901	374	12.9	384	13.2	892	30.7	1,251	43.1
1969............................	2,745	374	13.6	345	12.6	728	26.5	1,298	47.3
1968............................	2,710	403	14.9	387	14.3	658	24.3	1,262	46.6
1967............................	2,511	340	13.5	386	15.4	688	27.4	1,097	43.7
Female									
2019............................	3,043	488	16.0	145	4.8	795	26.1	1,615	53.1
2018............................	3,051	462	15.2	137	4.5	703	23.0	1,749	57.3
2017............................	3,029	476	15.7	177	5.8	712	23.5	1,665	54.9
2016............................	3,025	448	14.8	168	5.6	709	23.4	1,700	56.2
2015............................	3,024	538	17.8	192	6.3	650	21.5	1,644	54.4
2014............................	3,049	529	17.4	215	7.1	638	20.9	1,667	54.7
2013............................	3,083	487	15.8	195	6.3	754	24.5	1,646	53.4
2012............................	3,113	540	16.9	181	5.8	702	22.6	1,690	54.3
2011............................	3,148	526	16.7	209	6.6	635	20.2	1,779	56.5
2010............................	3,206	501	15.6	188	5.9	692	21.6	1,825	56.9
2009............................	3,245	542	16.7	235	7.2	642	19.8	1,826	56.3
2008............................	3,239	478	14.8	259	8.0	715	22.1	1,787	55.2
2007............................	3,169	414	13.1	235	7.4	785	24.8	1,734	54.7
2006............................	3,111	476	15.3	249	8.0	771	24.8	1,615	51.9
2005............................	2,844	358	12.6	210	7.4	647	22.7	1,629	57.3
2004............................	2,980	440	14.7	227	7.6	675	22.7	1,638	55.0
2003¹..........................	2,913	385	13.2	279	9.6	674	23.1	1,575	54.1
2002............................	3,066	435	14.2	297	9.7	772	25.2	1,562	50.9
2001............................	3,062	438	14.3	349	11.4	794	25.9	1,481	48.4
2000............................	3,151	397	12.6	348	11.0	781	24.8	1,625	51.6
1999............................	3,141	400	12.7	387	12.3	841	26.8	1,513	48.2
1998............................	3,069	351	11.4	376	12.3	724	23.6	1,618	52.7
1997............................	2,934	371	12.6	344	11.7	740	25.2	1,479	50.4
1996............................	2,879	338	11.7	353	12.3	680	23.6	1,508	52.4
1995............................	2,812	283	10.1	401	14.3	745	26.5	1,383	49.2
1994............................	2,746	305	11.1	325	11.8	759	27.6	1,357	49.4
1993............................	2,611	289	11.1	290	11.1	679	26.0	1,353	51.8
1992............................	2,595	311	12.0	278	10.7	689	26.6	1,317	50.8
1991............................	2,681	259	9.7	341	12.7	706	26.3	1,375	51.3
1990............................	2,873	307	10.7	378	13.2	857	29.8	1,331	46.3
1989............................	3,016	281	9.3	386	12.8	954	31.6	1,395	46.3
1988............................	3,005	212	7.1	394	13.1	954	31.7	1,445	48.1
1987............................	2,939	263	8.9	362	12.3	1,010	34.4	1,304	44.4
1986............................	2,937	257	8.8	323	11.0	1,074	36.6	1,283	43.7
1985............................	2,985	217	7.3	337	11.3	1,068	35.8	1,363	45.7
1984............................	3,092	216	7.0	432	14.0	1,127	36.4	1,317	42.6
1983............................	3,236	255	7.9	383	11.8	1,198	37.0	1,400	43.3
1982............................	3,365	234	7.0	502	14.9	1,269	37.7	1,360	40.4
1981............................	3,438	262	7.6	454	13.2	1,342	39.0	1,380	40.1
1980............................	3,506	237	6.8	483	13.8	1,440	41.1	1,346	38.4
1979............................	3,535	213	6.0	505	14.3	1,511	42.7	1,306	36.9
1978............................	3,528	193	5.5	528	15.0	1,493	42.3	1,314	37.2
1977............................	3,548	232	6.5	526	14.8	1,483	41.8	1,307	36.8
1976............................	3,558	230	6.5	550	15.5	1,444	40.6	1,334	37.5
1975............................	3,512	199	5.7	547	15.6	1,436	40.9	1,330	37.9

* = Quantity zero or rounds to zero.
Note: High school graduates are people who have completed 4 years of high school or more, for 1967 to 1991. Beginning in 1992, they were people whose highest degree was a high school diploma (including equivalency) or higher.
¹Starting in 2003 respondents could identify more than one race. Except as noted, the race data in this table from 2003 onward represent those respondents who indicated only one race category.
²The data shown prior to 2003 consists of those identifying themselves as "Asian or Pacific Islanders."

Table A-15. Population 18 and 19 Years Old, by School Enrollment Status, Sex, Race, and Hispanic Origin, October 1967–2019—*Continued*

(Numbers in thousands; percent; civilian noninstitutionalized population.)

Year, race, and Hispanic origin	Total	Population 18 and 19 years old								
		Still in high school	Percent	Dropped out	Percent	High school graduate only	Percent	In college	Percent
1974	3,442	207	6.0	477	13.9	1,592	46.3	1,166	33.9
1973	3,351	192	5.7	508	15.2	1,547	46.2	1,104	32.9
1972	3,287	208	6.3	434	13.2	1,476	44.9	1,169	35.6
1971	3,208	229	7.1	442	13.8	1,380	43.0	1,157	36.1
1970	3,108	190	6.1	460	14.8	1,348	43.4	1,110	35.7
1969	3,017	183	6.1	427	14.2	1,328	44.0	1,079	35.8
1968	2,981	210	7.0	435	14.6	1,314	44.1	1,022	34.3
1967	2,996	218	7.3	489	16.3	1,280	42.7	1,009	33.7
WHITE NON-HISPANIC									
Both Sexes									
2019	4,410	836	19.0	228	5.2	1,177	26.7	2,169	49.2
2018	4,404	756	17.2	222	5.0	1,043	23.7	2,382	54.1
2017	4,400	853	19.4	294	6.7	1,124	25.5	2,129	48.4
2016	4,563	775	17.0	242	5.3	1,106	24.2	2,439	53.5
2015	4,575	839	18.3	305	6.7	1,063	23.2	2,368	51.8
2014	4,555	860	18.9	290	6.4	1,106	24.3	2,299	50.5
2013	4,645	856	18.4	248	5.3	1,162	25.0	2,379	51.2
2012	4,748	905	18.6	249	5.2	1,232	26.0	2,363	49.8
2011	4,889	937	19.2	291	5.9	1,074	22.0	2,588	52.9
2010	4,935	804	16.3	277	5.6	1,156	23.4	2,699	54.7
2009	5,068	826	16.3	288	5.7	1,112	21.9	2,842	56.1
2008	5,185	780	15.0	296	5.7	1,258	24.3	2,850	55.0
2007	5,067	793	15.7	283	5.6	1,252	24.7	2,739	54.1
2006	5,018	843	16.8	361	7.2	1,251	24.9	2,564	51.1
2005	4,770	790	16.6	297	6.2	1,065	22.3	2,618	54.9
2004	4,885	731	15.0	363	7.4	1,195	24.5	2,596	53.1
2003[1]	4,780	758	15.9	379	7.9	1,157	24.2	2,486	52.0
2002	5,016	817	16.3	369	7.4	1,281	25.5	2,549	50.8
2001	4,928	780	15.8	467	9.5	1,298	26.3	2,383	48.4
2000	5,221	757	14.5	500	9.6	1,384	26.5	2,580	49.4
1999	5,228	779	14.9	491	9.4	1,384	26.5	2,574	49.2
1998	5,080	691	13.6	475	9.4	1,211	23.8	2,703	53.2
Male									
2019	2,262	508	22.4	131	5.8	653	28.9	971	42.9
2018	2,239	443	19.8	152	6.8	557	24.0	1,086	48.5
2017	2,262	528	23.4	174	7.7	608	26.9	952	42.1
2016	2,351	463	19.7	123	5.2	597	25.4	1,168	49.7
2015	2,350	460	19.6	181	7.7	589	25.1	1,121	47.7
2014	2,334	490	21.0	147	6.3	646	27.7	1,050	45.0
2013	2,392	516	21.6	123	5.2	629	26.3	1,124	47.0
2012	2,412	527	21.4	124	5.1	710	29.4	1,051	43.6
2011	2,470	543	22.0	145	5.9	599	24.2	1,184	47.9
2010	2,516	470	18.7	166	6.6	645	25.6	1,236	49.1
2009	2,573	473	18.4	173	6.7	641	24.9	1,286	50.0
2008	2,649	423	16.0	170	6.4	709	26.8	1,346	50.8
2007	2,587	496	19.2	150	5.8	643	24.9	1,298	50.2
2006	2,553	501	19.6	204	8.0	679	26.6	1,168	45.7
2005	2,449	515	21.0	168	6.9	573	23.4	1,193	48.7
2004	2,443	408	16.7	204	8.4	681	27.9	1,150	47.1
2003[1]	2,407	460	19.1	230	9.6	602	25.0	1,115	46.3
2002	2,502	481	19.2	182	7.3	660	26.4	1,179	47.1
2001	2,526	453	17.9	257	10.2	685	27.1	1,131	44.8
2000	2,628	471	17.9	274	10.4	745	28.3	1,138	43.3
1999	2,648	473	17.9	255	9.6	706	26.7	1,214	45.8
1998	2,613	432	16.5	254	9.7	653	25.0	1,274	48.8
Female									
2019	1,252	221	17.7	83	6.6	409	32.7	538	43.0
2018	2,165	312	14.4	70	3.2	486	22.5	1,296	59.9
2017	2,138	325	15.2	120	5.6	515	24.1	1,178	55.1
2016	2,212	312	14.1	119	5.4	610	23.1	1,271	57.5
2015	2,225	379	17.1	124	5.6	474	21.3	1,248	56.1

* = Quantity zero or rounds to zero.
Note: High school graduates are people who have completed 4 years of high school or more, for 1967 to 1991. Beginning in 1992, they were people whose highest degree was a high school diploma (including equivalency) or higher.
[1]Starting in 2003 respondents could identify more than one race. Except as noted, the race data in this table from 2003 onward represent those respondents who indicated only one race category.
[2]The data shown prior to 2003 consists of those identifying themselves as "Asian or Pacific Islanders."

Table A-15. Population 18 and 19 Years Old, by School Enrollment Status, Sex, Race, and Hispanic Origin, October 1967–2019—*Continued*

(Numbers in thousands; percent; civilian noninstitutionalized population.)

Year, race, and Hispanic origin	Total	Population 18 and 19 years old							
		Still in high school	Percent	Dropped out	Percent	High school graduate only	Percent	In college	Percent
2014..............................	2,222	370	16.6	143	6.4	460	20.7	1,249	56.2
2013..............................	2,253	340	15.1	125	5.5	533	23.7	1,254	55.7
2012..............................	2,336	377	15.7	125	5.3	522	22.3	1,312	56.2
2011..............................	2,419	394	16.3	146	6.0	475	19.6	1,404	58.1
2010..............................	2,419	334	13.8	111	4.6	511	21.1	1,463	60.5
2009..............................	2,495	353	14.1	115	4.6	471	18.9	1,556	62.4
2008..............................	2,536	357	14.1	126	5.0	549	21.7	1,504	59.3
2007..............................	2,480	298	12.0	132	5.3	609	24.6	1,441	58.1
2006..............................	2,466	341	13.8	157	6.4	571	23.2	1,396	56.6
2005..............................	2,321	275	11.9	129	5.6	491	21.2	1,425	61.4
2004..............................	2,441	323	13.2	159	6.5	513	21.0	1,446	59.2
2003[1]..........................	2,373	298	12.6	149	6.3	555	23.4	1,371	57.8
2002..............................	2,514	336	13.4	187	7.4	621	24.7	1,370	54.5
2001..............................	2,402	328	13.7	209	8.7	613	25.5	1,252	52.1
2000..............................	2,593	286	11.0	225	8.7	639	24.6	1,443	55.6
1999..............................	2,580	307	11.9	236	9.1	677	26.2	1,360	52.7
1998..............................	2,467	259	10.5	221	9.0	558	22.6	1,429	57.9

BLACK

Both Sexes

Year, race, and Hispanic origin	Total	Still in high school	Percent	Dropped out	Percent	High school graduate only	Percent	In college	Percent
2019..............................	1,252	221	17.7	83	6.6	409	32.7	538	43.0
2018..............................	1,264	302	23.9	71	5.6	361	28.6	530	42.0
2017..............................	1,246	310	24.9	64	5.2	346	27.8	525	42.1
2016..............................	1,244	305	24.5	87	7.0	321	25.8	530	42.6
2015..............................	1,233	286	23.2	84	6.8	354	28.7	509	41.3
2014..............................	1,251	307	24.5	94	7.5	341	27.3	510	40.7
2013..............................	1,305	386	29.6	92	7.1	375	28.8	451	34.6
2012..............................	1,356	400	29.2	110	8.1	315	23.2	531	39.1
2011..............................	1,316	396	30.1	60	4.5	281	21.3	580	44.0
2010..............................	1,336	271	20.3	144	10.8	355	26.5	567	42.4
2009..............................	1,346	319	23.7	180	13.4	288	21.4	559	41.5
2008..............................	1,335	311	23.3	145	10.8	400	30.0	479	35.9
2007..............................	1,284	300	23.4	112	8.7	380	29.6	492	38.3
2006..............................	1,230	332	27.0	103	8.3	332	27.0	464	37.7
2005..............................	1,126	256	22.7	110	9.8	309	27.4	451	40.0
2004	1,112	218	19.6	162	14.5	292	26.3	440	39.6
2003[1]..........................	1,052	277	26.3	128	12.2	273	26.0	374	35.6
2002..............................	1,181	251	21.3	180	15.2	320	27.1	430	36.4
2001..............................	1,246	299	24.0	152	12.2	351	28.2	444	35.6
2000..............................	1,251	262	20.9	187	14.9	348	27.8	454	36.3
1999..............................	1,199	259	21.6	190	15.8	320	26.7	430	35.9
1998..............................	1,246	290	23.3	224	18.0	271	21.7	461	37.0
1997..............................	1,133	278	24.5	172	15.2	302	26.7	381	33.6
1996..............................	1,161	268	23.1	175	15.1	373	32.1	345	29.7
1995..............................	1,099	287	26.1	177	16.1	291	26.5	344	31.3
1994..............................	1,017	239	23.5	199	19.6	269	26.5	310	30.5
1993..............................	1,040	290	27.9	133	12.8	306	29.4	311	29.9
1992..............................	1,007	275	27.3	166	16.5	275	27.3	291	28.9
1991..............................	1,041	276	26.5	146	14.0	316	30.4	303	29.1
1990..............................	1,079	246	22.8	178	16.5	306	28.4	349	32.3
1989..............................	1,078	239	22.2	194	18.0	343	31.8	302	28.0
1988..............................	1,057	251	23.7	189	17.9	336	31.8	281	26.6
1987..............................	1,043	213	20.4	166	15.9	323	31.0	341	32.7
1986..............................	1,048	212	20.2	156	14.9	374	35.7	306	29.2
1985..............................	1,072	213	19.9	186	17.4	414	38.6	259	24.2
1984..............................	1,092	218	20.0	186	17.0	423	38.7	265	24.3
1983..............................	1,134	265	23.4	199	17.5	412	36.3	258	22.8
1982..............................	1,146	226	19.7	253	22.1	393	34.3	274	23.9
1981..............................	1,128	238	21.1	218	19.3	366	32.4	306	27.1
1980..............................	1,081	211	19.5	229	21.2	358	33.1	283	26.2
1979..............................	1,072	221	20.6	246	22.9	326	30.4	279	26.0
1978..............................	1,065	221	20.8	258	24.2	316	29.7	270	25.4
1977..............................	1,072	249	23.2	235	21.9	319	29.8	269	25.1

* = Quantity zero or rounds to zero.

Note: High school graduates are people who have completed 4 years of high school or more, for 1967 to 1991. Beginning in 1992, they were people whose highest degree was a high school diploma (including equivalency) or higher.

[1]Starting in 2003 respondents could identify more than one race. Except as noted, the race data in this table from 2003 onward represent those respondents who indicated only one race category.

[2]The data shown prior to 2003 consists of those identifying themselves as "Asian or Pacific Islanders."

Table A-15. Population 18 and 19 Years Old, by School Enrollment Status, Sex, Race, and Hispanic Origin, October 1967–2019—*Continued*

(Numbers in thousands; percent; civilian noninstitutionalized population.)

Year, race, and Hispanic origin	Total	Population 18 and 19 years old							
		Still in high school	Percent	Dropped out	Percent	High school graduate only	Percent	In college	Percent
1976	1,055	230	21.8	211	20.0	312	29.6	302	28.6
1975	1,030	225	21.8	262	25.4	283	27.5	260	25.2
1974	1,004	209	20.8	235	23.4	327	32.6	233	23.2
1973	997	182	18.3	252	25.3	369	37.0	194	19.5
1972	958	181	18.9	229	23.9	319	33.3	229	23.9
1971	908	219	24.1	219	24.1	266	29.3	204	22.5
1970	878	161	18.3	274	31.2	252	28.7	191	21.0
1969	837	179	21.4	227	27.1	238	28.4	193	23.1
1968	830	195	23.5	202	24.3	251	30.2	182	21.9
1967	780	175	22.4	203	26.0	261	33.5	141	18.1
Male									
2019	616	128	20.7	41	6.7	205	33.2	243	39.4
2018	623	173	27.7	31	5.0	186	29.8	234	37.5
2017	615	155	25.3	45	7.4	181	29.4	234	38.0
2016	612	193	31.5	56	9.2	148	24.2	215	35.1
2015	606	155	25.5	49	8.0	173	28.6	229	37.8
2014	617	197	31.9	56	9.1	189	30.6	175	28.4
2013	646	201	31.1	58	8.9	201	31.1	186	28.9
2012	673	201	29.9	87	12.9	179	26.6	206	30.6
2011	645	226	35.0	39	6.0	138	21.4	242	37.6
2010	654	159	24.4	83	12.6	174	26.5	238	36.4
2009	659	174	26.4	102	15.5	158	24.0	225	34.1
2008	653	173	26.5	53	8.1	222	34.0	205	31.4
2007	628	161	25.7	54	8.6	186	29.6	227	36.2
2006	600	210	35.0	42	7.0	174	29.0	174	28.9
2005	552	178	32.2	60	10.9	121	21.9	193	35.0
2004	519	137	26.4	91	17.6	126	24.3	165	31.7
2003[1]	502	143	28.5	77	15.3	116	23.1	166	33.1
2002	608	155	25.5	123	20.2	151	24.8	179	29.4
2001	624	179	28.7	97	15.5	169	27.1	179	28.7
2000	593	148	25.0	105	17.7	177	29.8	163	27.5
1999	586	144	24.6	97	16.6	136	23.2	209	35.7
1998	613	163	26.6	128	20.9	128	20.9	194	31.6
1997	554	172	31.0	90	16.2	150	27.1	142	25.6
1996	564	167	29.6	90	16.0	162	28.7	145	25.7
1995	519	162	31.2	94	18.1	118	22.7	145	27.9
1994	497	134	27.0	116	23.3	115	23.1	132	26.6
1993	517	181	35.0	53	10.3	135	26.1	148	28.6
1992	499	180	36.1	82	16.4	114	22.8	123	24.6
1991	504	176	34.9	62	12.3	129	25.6	137	27.2
1990	520	152	29.2	80	15.4	124	23.8	164	31.5
1989	516	137	26.6	90	17.4	163	31.6	126	24.4
1988	510	145	28.4	92	18.0	165	32.4	108	21.2
1987	501	140	27.9	80	16.0	127	25.3	154	30.7
1986	506	149	29.4	74	14.6	165	32.6	118	23.3
1985	518	135	26.1	92	17.8	170	32.8	121	23.4
1984	524	143	27.3	103	19.7	166	31.7	112	21.4
1983	539	158	29.3	106	19.7	182	33.8	93	17.3
1982	549	132	24.0	145	26.4	148	27.0	124	22.6
1981	538	145	27.0	102	19.0	158	29.4	133	24.7
1980	503	118	23.5	114	22.7	173	34.4	98	19.5
1979	497	128	25.8	122	24.5	137	27.6	110	22.1
1978	493	135	27.4	127	25.8	117	23.7	114	23.1
1977	496	161	32.5	118	23.8	127	25.6	90	18.1
1976	499	153	30.7	96	19.2	129	25.9	121	24.2
1975	476	127	26.7	132	27.7	106	22.3	111	23.3
1974	474	116	24.5	128	27.0	128	27.0	102	21.5
1973	467	106	22.7	130	27.8	135	28.9	96	20.6
1972	445	110	24.7	121	27.2	112	25.2	102	22.9
1971	423	120	28.4	110	26.0	99	23.4	94	22.2
1970	414	98	23.7	151	36.5	92	22.2	73	17.6
1969	394	109	27.7	124	31.5	75	19.0	86	21.8
1968	390	124	31.8	93	23.8	90	23.1	83	21.3

* = Quantity zero or rounds to zero.
Note: High school graduates are people who have completed 4 years of high school or more, for 1967 to 1991. Beginning in 1992, they were people whose highest degree was a high school diploma (including equivalency) or higher.
[1] Starting in 2003 respondents could identify more than one race. Except as noted, the race data in this table from 2003 onward represent those respondents who indicated only one race category.
[2] The data shown prior to 2003 consists of those identifying themselves as "Asian or Pacific Islanders."

Table A-15. Population 18 and 19 Years Old, by School Enrollment Status, Sex, Race, and Hispanic Origin, October 1967–2019—*Continued*

(Numbers in thousands; percent; civilian noninstitutionalized population.)

Year, race, and Hispanic origin	Total	Still in high school	Percent	Dropped out	Percent	High school graduate only	Percent	In college	Percent
					Population 18 and 19 years old				
1967..............................	356	95	26.7	109	30.6	74	20.8	78	21.9
Female									
2019..............................	636	94	14.7	42	6.5	205	32.2	295	46.5
2018..............................	640	129	20.2	39	6.1	176	27.4	296	46.3
2017..............................	631	155	24.6	19	3.1	165	26.2	291	46.1
2016..............................	631	112	17.8	31	4.9	173	27.4	316	50.0
2015..............................	627	131	20.9	36	5.7	180	28.8	280	44.6
2014..............................	635	110	17.4	38	6.0	152	24.0	334	52.7
2013..............................	659	186	28.2	35	5.2	174	26.4	265	40.1
2012..............................	683	198	28.5	23	3.4	136	20.0	325	47.6
2011..............................	671	170	25.4	21	3.1	143	21.3	337	50.3
2010..............................	682	111	16.3	61	9.0	181	26.5	329	48.2
2009..............................	687	145	21.1	78	11.3	130	19.0	334	48.6
2008..............................	681	138	20.3	92	13.5	178	26.1	274	40.2
2007..............................	655	139	21.2	58	8.8	194	29.6	265	40.4
2006..............................	631	122	19.3	60	9.6	158	25.0	291	46.1
2005..............................	574	78	13.6	49	8.6	189	32.9	258	44.9
2004	593	81	13.7	70	11.9	167	28.2	275	46.5
2003[1]..............................	550	133	24.2	51	9.3	157	28.5	209	38.0
2002..............................	574	97	16.9	57	9.9	169	29.4	251	43.7
2001..............................	623	122	19.6	54	8.7	182	29.2	265	42.5
2000..............................	658	113	17.2	82	12.5	172	26.1	291	44.2
1999..............................	613	114	18.6	94	15.3	184	30.0	221	36.1
1998..............................	633	127	20.1	96	15.2	143	22.6	267	42.2
1997..............................	579	107	18.5	82	14.2	152	26.3	238	41.1
1996..............................	597	102	17.1	85	14.2	211	35.3	199	33.3
1995..............................	581	126	21.7	83	14.3	173	29.8	199	34.3
1994..............................	520	105	20.2	83	16.0	154	29.6	178	34.2
1993..............................	523	108	20.7	80	15.3	172	32.9	163	31.2
1992..............................	508	95	18.7	84	16.5	161	31.7	168	33.1
1991..............................	537	99	18.4	85	15.8	187	34.8	166	30.9
1990..............................	559	95	17.0	98	17.5	181	32.4	185	33.1
1989..............................	562	102	18.1	104	18.5	180	32.0	176	31.3
1988..............................	547	105	19.2	97	17.7	172	31.4	173	31.6
1987..............................	542	75	13.8	85	15.7	196	36.2	186	34.3
1986..............................	542	62	11.4	83	15.3	209	38.6	188	34.7
1985..............................	554	78	14.1	94	17.0	244	44.0	138	24.9
1984..............................	568	76	13.4	82	14.4	257	45.2	153	26.9
1983..............................	595	108	18.2	93	15.6	230	38.7	164	27.6
1982..............................	597	95	15.9	108	18.1	244	40.9	150	25.1
1981..............................	590	93	15.8	116	19.7	209	35.4	172	29.2
1980..............................	578	93	16.1	115	19.9	185	32.0	185	32.0
1979..............................	576	93	16.1	125	21.7	189	32.8	169	29.3
1978..............................	572	88	15.4	130	22.7	199	34.8	155	27.1
1977..............................	576	88	15.3	117	20.3	192	33.3	179	31.1
1976..............................	556	77	13.8	115	20.7	183	32.9	181	32.6
1975..............................	553	97	17.5	130	23.5	176	31.8	150	27.1
1974..............................	530	92	17.4	107	20.2	200	37.7	131	24.7
1973..............................	530	77	14.5	122	23.0	234	44.2	97	18.3
1972..............................	513	71	13.8	108	21.1	207	40.4	127	24.8
1971..............................	485	100	20.6	109	22.5	167	34.4	109	22.5
1970..............................	464	62	13.4	124	26.7	160	34.5	118	25.4
1969..............................	443	70	15.8	102	23.0	163	36.8	108	24.4
1968..............................	439	69	15.7	109	24.8	161	36.7	100	22.8
1967..............................	424	81	19.1	93	21.9	187	44.1	63	14.9
ASIAN ALONE[2]									
Both Sexes									
2019..............................	473	85	17.9	22	4.8	43	9.1	323	68.2
2018..............................	439	57	13.0	11	2.5	81	18.4	291	66.1
2017..............................	376	49	13.1	11	3.0	55	14.6	260	69.3
2016..............................	405	57	14.1	16	4.1	76	18.9	255	63.0

* = Quantity zero or rounds to zero.
Note: High school graduates are people who have completed 4 years of high school or more, for 1967 to 1991. Beginning in 1992, they were people whose highest degree was a high school diploma (including equivalency) or higher.
[1]Starting in 2003 respondents could identify more than one race. Except as noted, the race data in this table from 2003 onward represent those respondents who indicated only one race category.
[2]The data shown prior to 2003 consists of those identifying themselves as "Asian or Pacific Islanders."

Table A-15. Population 18 and 19 Years Old, by School Enrollment Status, Sex, Race, and Hispanic Origin, October 1967–2019—*Continued*

(Numbers in thousands; percent; civilian noninstitutionalized population.)

Year, race, and Hispanic origin	Total	Population 18 and 19 years old							
		Still in high school	Percent	Dropped out	Percent	High school graduate only	Percent	In college	Percent
2015	358	65	18.1	17	4.7	41	11.5	235	65.6
2014	352	40	11.3	*	*	42	11.9	270	76.8
2013	442	68	15.5	4	0.9	68	15.3	302	68.3
2012	388	61	15.7	23	5.8	51	13.1	253	65.3
2011	337	44	13.2	13	3.7	40	11.8	240	71.3
2010	331	38	11.5	12	3.7	46	14.0	234	70.8
2009	327	64	19.7	2	0.7	17	5.2	243	74.4
2008	259	49	19.0	7	2.7	31	12.0	172	66.4
2007	296	55	18.4	12	4.2	27	9.3	201	68.1
2006	297	43	14.4	9	3.0	41	14.0	204	68.6
2005	251	34	13.4	4	1.5	25	10.0	188	74.9
2004	257	31	11.9	10	3.8	34	13.2	182	70.7
2003[1]	286	41	14.3	3	1.0	33	11.5	209	73.1
2002	353	42	11.9	14	4.0	61	17.3	236	66.9
2001	353	50	14.2	18	5.1	38	10.8	247	70.0
2000	326	45	13.8	17	5.2	52	16.0	212	65.0
1999	339	43	12.7	22	6.5	51	15.0	223	65.8
Male									
2019	233	47	20.2	7	3.1	18	7.8	161	68.8
2018	221	27	12.2	8	3.6	47	21.1	139	63.1
2017	194	30	15.5	3	1.5	39	20.2	122	62.7
2016	215	27	12.6	10	4.4	44	20.5	135	62.5
2015	178	31	17.4	14	8.0	20	11.5	112	63.1
2014	177	19	11.0	*	*	22	12.5	136	76.5
2013	230	37	16.2	1	0.3	38	16.7	154	66.9
2012	200	37	18.7	14	7.1	20	9.7	129	64.5
2011	178	28	15.4	*	*	19	10.8	131	73.7
2010	170	16	9.6	8	5.0	30	17.4	116	68.1
2009	178	31	17.6	*	*	13	7.4	134	75.0
2008	128	39	30.2	6	5.1	8	5.9	75	58.9
2007	150	33	22.1	2	1.1	11	7.1	104	69.7
2006	167	20	12.2	8	4.7	26	15.7	113	67.5
2005	131	21	16.3	3	2.0	17	13.0	90	68.9
2004	133	22	16.7	1	0.7	18	13.5	92	69.3
2003[1]	129	14	10.9	3	2.3	9	7.0	103	79.8
2002	179	22	12.3	10	5.6	26	14.5	121	67.6
2001	168	27	16.1	14	8.3	14	0.3	113	67.3
2000	162	14	8.6	14	8.6	26	16.0	108	66.7
1999	156	23	14.7	17	10.9	23	14.7	93	59.6
Female									
2019	239	38	15.7	15	6.3	25	10.3	162	67.7
2018	218	30	13.8	3	1.3	34	15.7	151	69.3
2017	182	19	10.5	8	4.6	16	8.7	138	76.3
2016	189	30	15.7	7	3.6	32	17.0	120	63.6
2015	180	34	18.7	3	1.5	21	11.6	123	68.2
2014	175	20	11.6	*	*	20	11.3	134	77.0
2013	212	31	14.8	3	1.6	29	13.8	148	69.8
2012	188	24	12.6	8	4.5	32	16.8	124	66.2
2011	158	17	10.7	13	7.9	20	12.8	109	68.6
2010	161	22	13.6	4	2.4	17	10.4	118	73.6
2009	149	33	22.2	2	1.6	4	2.7	109	73.6
2008	132	11	8.0	*	0.4	24	17.9	97	73.7
2007	146	21	14.6	11	7.5	17	11.5	97	66.4
2006	130	23	17.3	1	0.9	15	11.8	91	70.0
2005	120	12	10.3	1	0.9	9	7.5	98	81.4
2004	124	8	6.8	9	7.1	18	14.5	89	72.2
2003[1]	157	26	16.6	*	*	24	15.3	107	68.2
2002	173	20	11.6	3	1.7	35	20.2	115	66.5
2001	185	23	12.4	4	2.2	24	13.0	134	72.4
2000	164	30	18.3	4	2.4	26	15.9	104	63.4
1999	183	20	10.9	5	2.7	28	15.3	130	71.0

* = Quantity zero or rounds to zero.
Note: High school graduates are people who have completed 4 years of high school or more, for 1967 to 1991. Beginning in 1992, they were people whose highest degree was a high school diploma (including equivalency) or higher.
[1]Starting in 2003 respondents could identify more than one race. Except as noted, the race data in this table from 2003 onward represent those respondents who indicated only one race category.
[2]The data shown prior to 2003 consists of those identifying themselves as "Asian or Pacific Islanders."

Table A-15. Population 18 and 19 Years Old, by School Enrollment Status, Sex, Race, and Hispanic Origin, October 1967–2019—*Continued*

(Numbers in thousands; percent; civilian noninstitutionalized population.)

Year, race, and Hispanic origin	Total	Still in high school	Percent	Dropped out	Percent	High school graduate only	Percent	In college	Percent
HISPANIC (OF ANY RACE)									
Both Sexes									
2019	2,032	422	20.8	170	8.4	568	27.9	872	42.9
2018	2,006	383	19.1	209	10.4	523	26.1	890	44.4
2017	1,965	390	19.9	181	9.2	463	23.6	931	47.4
2016	1,825	364	19.9	146	8.0	430	23.6	884	48.5
2015	1,760	372	21.1	181	10.3	432	24.5	776	44.1
2014	1,908	377	19.8	183	9.6	491	25.7	857	44.9
2013	1,889	393	20.8	184	9.7	585	31.0	727	38.5
2012	1,871	449	23.8	222	11.9	374	20.0	827	44.2
2011	1,743	371	21.3	166	9.5	441	25.3	765	43.9
2010	1,768	389	22.0	179	10.1	418	23.6	783	44.3
2009	1,680	409	24.3	261	15.5	460	27.4	550	32.7
2008	1,539	320	20.8	296	19.3	395	25.7	528	34.3
2007	1,523	311	20.4	254	16.7	399	26.2	559	36.7
2006	1,406	307	21.8	253	18.0	402	28.6	444	31.6
2005	1,253	272	21.7	227	18.1	348	27.8	406	32.4
2004	1,270	244	19.2	296	23.3	346	27.2	384	30.2
2003	1,214	229	18.9	291	24.0	315	25.9	379	31.2
2002	1,309	303	23.1	310	23.7	336	25.7	360	27.5
2001	1,391	246	17.7	399	28.7	359	25.8	387	27.8
2000	1,248	268	21.5	311	24.9	320	25.6	349	28.0
1999	1,220	246	20.2	337	27.6	340	27.9	297	24.3
1998	1,209	199	16.5	402	33.3	320	26.5	288	23.8
1997	1,087	221	20.3	274	25.2	276	25.4	316	29.1
1996	1,000	229	22.9	295	29.5	236	23.6	240	24.0
1995	1,012	203	20.1	312	30.8	233	23.0	264	26.1
1994	925	250	27.0	237	25.6	213	23.0	225	24.3
1993	710	159	22.4	201	28.3	155	21.8	195	27.5
1992	778	188	24.2	197	25.3	163	21.0	230	29.6
1991	823	206	25.0	269	32.7	160	19.4	188	22.8
1990	746	181	24.3	255	34.2	162	21.7	148	19.8
1989	733	150	20.5	205	28.0	201	27.4	177	24.1
1988	734	121	16.5	229	31.2	181	24.7	203	27.7
1987	699	121	17.3	195	27.9	231	33.0	152	21.7
1986	614	114	18.6	164	26.7	171	27.9	165	26.9
1985	570	111	19.5	175	30.7	157	27.5	127	22.3
1984	561	88	15.7	146	26.0	191	34.0	136	24.2
1983	573	119	20.8	166	29.0	154	26.9	134	23.4
1982	600	92	15.3	198	33.0	167	27.8	143	23.8
1981	606	100	16.5	220	36.3	157	25.9	129	21.3
1980	597	89	14.9	233	39.0	138	23.1	137	22.9
1979	507	78	15.4	157	31.0	148	29.2	124	24.5
1978	478	61	12.8	183	38.3	125	26.2	109	22.8
1977	515	86	16.7	168	32.6	138	26.8	123	23.9
1976	534	98	18.4	164	30.7	129	24.2	143	26.8
1975	489	97	19.8	147	30.1	127	26.0	118	24.1
1974	467	99	21.2	139	29.8	117	25.1	112	24.0
1973	387	70	18.1	142	36.7	93	24.0	82	21.2
1972	381	88	23.1	117	30.7	106	27.8	70	18.4
Male									
2019	1,014	235	23.2	102	10.0	268	26.5	409	40.4
2018	1,036	222	21.5	139	13.4	282	27.2	392	37.9
2017	982	209	21.3	113	11.5	247	25.1	413	42.0
2016	894	210	23.4	90	10.0	212	23.7	383	42.8
2015	849	194	22.8	108	12.8	232	27.3	315	37.1
2014	958	206	21.5	105	10.9	263	27.4	385	40.2
2013	953	233	24.4	98	10.3	326	34.2	295	31.0
2012	950	252	26.5	143	15.1	183	19.2	372	39.2
2011	952	229	24.1	102	10.7	269	28.3	351	36.9
2010	896	201	22.4	97	10.9	217	24.2	381	42.5

* = Quantity zero or rounds to zero.

Note: High school graduates are people who have completed 4 years of high school or more, for 1967 to 1991. Beginning in 1992, they were people whose highest degree was a high school diploma (including equivalency) or higher.

[1]Starting in 2003 respondents could identify more than one race. Except as noted, the race data in this table from 2003 onward represent those respondents who indicated only one race category.

[2]The data shown prior to 2003 consists of those identifying themselves as "Asian or Pacific Islanders."

Table A-15. Population 18 and 19 Years Old, by School Enrollment Status, Sex, Race, and Hispanic Origin, October 1967–2019—*Continued*

(Numbers in thousands; percent; civilian noninstitutionalized population.)

Year, race, and Hispanic origin	Total	Still in high school	Percent	Dropped out	Percent	High school graduate only	Percent	In college	Percent
						Population 18 and 19 years old			
2009............................	853	200	23.4	129	15.2	282	33.0	242	28.4
2008............................	779	190	24.4	141	18.1	212	27.2	236	30.3
2007............................	780	185	23.7	145	18.5	205	26.3	246	31.5
2006............................	708	152	21.4	150	21.2	193	27.3	213	30.1
2005............................	663	166	25.1	144	21.7	180	27.1	173	26.2
2004............................	668	117	17.5	214	32.0	166	24.9	171	25.6
2003	635	142	22.4	161	25.4	179	28.2	153	24.1
2002............................	716	191	26.7	200	27.9	169	23.6	156	21.8
2001............................	701	131	18.7	254	36.2	167	23.8	149	21.3
2000............................	656	154	23.5	183	27.9	159	24.2	160	24.4
1999............................	642	148	23.1	180	28.0	171	26.6	143	22.3
1998............................	598	104	17.4	234	39.1	163	27.3	97	16.2
1997............................	579	130	22.5	162	28.0	154	26.6	133	23.0
1996............................	506	139	27.5	154	30.4	115	22.7	98	19.4
1995............................	535	132	24.7	145	27.1	137	25.6	121	22.6
1994............................	454	157	34.6	118	26.0	90	19.8	89	19.6
1993............................	325	86	26.5	105	32.3	65	20.0	69	21.2
1992............................	385	110	28.6	99	25.7	83	21.6	93	24.2
1991............................	416	107	25.7	161	38.7	80	19.2	68	16.3
1990............................	358	76	21.2	141	39.4	71	19.8	70	19.6
1989............................	371	89	24.0	96	25.9	111	29.9	75	20.2
1988............................	364	88	24.2	128	35.2	73	20.1	75	20.6
1987............................	333	66	19.8	105	31.5	86	25.8	76	22.8
1986............................	326	58	17.8	95	29.1	86	26.4	87	26.7
1985............................	275	62	22.5	116	42.2	53	19.3	44	16.0
1984............................	249	55	22.1	65	26.1	87	34.9	42	16.9
1983............................	266	66	24.8	87	32.7	72	27.1	41	15.4
1982............................	304	69	22.7	106	34.9	77	25.3	52	17.1
1981............................	288	47	16.3	127	44.1	57	19.8	57	19.8
1980............................	310	46	14.8	134	43.2	62	20.0	68	21.9
1979............................	256	42	16.4	89	34.8	58	22.7	67	26.2
1978............................	221	35	15.8	81	36.7	52	23.5	53	24.0
1977............................	238	49	20.6	80	33.6	55	23.1	54	22.7
1976............................	258	51	19.8	82	31.8	56	21.7	69	26.7
1975............................	229	66	28.8	60	26.2	50	21.8	53	23.1
1974............................	222	49	22.1	78	35.1	40	18.0	55	24.8
1973............................	190	48	25.3	62	32.6	41	21.6	39	20.5
1972............................	190	49	25.8	67	35.3	46	24.2	28	14.7
Female									
2019............................	1,018	187	18.4	69	6.7	299	29.4	463	45.5
2018............................	970	161	16.6	70	7.2	241	24.9	498	51.3
2017............................	983	181	18.4	67	6.9	216	22.0	518	52.7
2016............................	930	154	16.6	56	6.1	218	23.5	501	53.9
2015............................	912	179	19.6	72	7.9	200	21.9	461	50.5
2014............................	950	172	18.1	78	8.2	228	24.0	472	49.7
2013............................	936	160	17.1	86	9.1	259	27.6	432	46.2
2012............................	921	197	21.0	79	8.6	191	20.7	454	49.3
2011............................	791	142	17.9	64	8.1	172	21.7	414	52.4
2010............................	872	188	21.5	82	9.4	201	23.0	402	46.1
2009............................	827	209	25.3	132	15.9	179	21.6	308	37.2
2008............................	760	130	17.1	156	20.5	183	24.0	292	38.4
2007............................	743	126	17.0	109	14.7	193	26.1	313	42.2
2006............................	698	156	22.3	102	14.7	209	30.0	231	33.1
2005............................	591	105	17.8	83	14.0	171	28.9	232	30.3
2004	602	127	21.1	82	13.6	180	29.9	213	35.4
2003............................	579	87	15.0	130	22.5	136	23.5	226	39.0
2002............................	593	112	18.9	110	18.5	167	28.2	204	34.4
2001............................	691	116	16.8	145	21.0	192	27.8	238	34.4
2000............................	591	114	19.3	128	21.7	161	27.2	188	31.8
1999............................	577	99	17.2	157	27.2	168	29.1	153	26.5
1998............................	611	95	15.5	169	27.7	156	25.5	191	31.3
1997............................	508	91	17.9	112	22.0	122	24.0	183	36.0
1996............................	494	91	18.4	140	28.3	121	24.5	142	28.7

* = Quantity zero or rounds to zero.

Note: High school graduates are people who have completed 4 years of high school or more, for 1967 to 1991. Beginning in 1992, they were people whose highest degree was a high school diploma (including equivalency) or higher.

[1]Starting in 2003 respondents could identify more than one race. Except as noted, the race data in this table from 2003 onward represent those respondents who indicated only one race category.

[2]The data shown prior to 2003 consists of those identifying themselves as "Asian or Pacific Islanders."

Table A-15. Population 18 and 19 Years Old, by School Enrollment Status, Sex, Race, and Hispanic Origin, October 1967–2019—*Continued*

(Numbers in thousands; percent; civilian noninstitutionalized population.)

Year, race, and Hispanic origin	Total	Population 18 and 19 years old							
		Still in high school	Percent	Dropped out	Percent	High school graduate only	Percent	In college	Percent
1995	478	71	14.9	167	34.9	97	20.3	143	29.9
1994	471	93	19.7	119	25.3	123	26.1	136	28.9
1993	385	74	19.2	96	24.9	89	23.1	126	32.7
1992	393	78	19.8	98	24.9	80	20.4	137	34.9
1991	407	98	24.1	109	26.8	80	19.7	120	29.5
1990	388	105	27.1	114	29.4	91	23.5	78	20.1
1989	362	60	16.6	108	29.8	91	25.1	103	28.5
1988	370	32	8.6	101	27.3	108	29.2	129	34.9
1987	367	58	15.8	89	24.3	144	39.2	76	20.7
1986	288	54	18.8	69	24.0	86	29.9	79	27.4
1985	296	51	17.2	59	19.9	104	35.1	82	27.7
1984	311	33	10.6	81	26.0	103	33.1	94	30.2
1983	307	53	17.3	79	25.7	82	26.7	93	30.3
1982	296	23	7.8	92	31.1	90	30.4	91	30.7
1981	318	53	16.7	93	29.2	100	31.4	72	22.6
1980	287	44	15.3	99	34.5	76	26.5	68	23.7
1979	251	35	13.9	68	27.1	90	35.9	58	23.1
1978	257	26	10.1	102	39.7	73	28.4	56	21.8
1977	277	37	13.4	88	31.8	82	29.6	70	25.3
1976	276	49	17.8	81	29.3	72	26.1	74	26.8
1975	261	32	12.3	87	33.3	77	29.5	65	24.9
1974	245	50	20.4	62	25.3	77	31.4	56	22.9
1973	197	21	10.7	80	40.6	52	26.4	44	22.3
1972	191	37	19.4	50	26.2	61	31.9	43	22.5
WHITE ALONE OR IN COMBINATION									
Both Sexes									
2019	6,425	1,231	19.2	363	5.6	1,732	26.9	3,100	48.3
2018	6,488	1,157	17.8	432	6.7	1,563	24.1	3,336	51.4
2017	6,408	1,241	19.4	461	7.2	1,585	24.7	3,121	48.7
2016	6,392	1,139	17.8	383	6.0	1,554	24.3	3,316	51.9
2015	6,376	1,204	18.9	489	7.7	1,519	23.8	3,163	49.6
2014	6,450	1,238	19.2	467	7.2	1,592	24.7	3,154	48.9
2013	6,502	1,235	19.0	414	6.4	1,728	26.6	3,124	48.0
2012	6,539	1,331	20.0	437	6.7	1,627	24.9	3,144	48.1
2011	6,686	1,309	19.6	455	6.8	1,540	23.0	3,381	50.6
2010	6,679	1,195	17.9	450	6.7	1,556	23.3	3,478	52.1
2009	6,780	1,227	18.1	538	7.9	1,601	23.6	3,414	50.3
2008	6,762	1,093	16.2	581	8.6	1,647	24.4	3,440	50.9
2007	6,595	1,108	16.8	525	8.0	1,644	24.9	3,318	50.3
2006	6,466	1,160	17.9	615	9.5	1,648	25.5	3,043	47.1
2005	6,078	1,064	17.5	537	8.8	1,434	23.6	3,043	50.1
2004	6,191	988	16.0	643	10.4	1,548	25.0	3,012	48.7
2003	6,093	994	16.3	675	11.1	1,519	24.9	2,905	47.7
Male									
2019	3,240	726	22.4	218	6.7	908	28.0	1,389	42.9
2018	3,299	661	20.0	289	8.8	839	25.4	1,510	45.8
2017	3,233	747	23.1	276	8.5	839	26.0	1,370	42.4
2016	3,233	664	20.5	209	6.5	813	25.1	1,547	47.8
2015	3,232	639	19.8	289	8.9	832	25.7	1,472	45.5
2014	3,292	694	21.1	252	7.7	913	27.7	1,433	43.5
2013	3,327	743	22.3	209	6.3	943	28.3	1,433	43.1
2012	3,364	779	22.9	254	7.5	902	26.8	1,429	42.5
2011	3,457	776	22.4	247	7.1	881	25.5	1,554	44.9
2010	3,396	674	19.8	251	7.4	852	25.1	1,620	47.7
2009	3,422	665	19.4	297	8.7	925	27.0	1,535	44.9
2008	3,435	605	17.6	305	8.9	917	26.7	1,607	46.8
2007	3,350	684	20.4	284	8.5	842	25.1	1,540	46.0
2006	3,278	657	20.0	357	10.9	864	26.4	1,399	42.7
2005	3,149	692	22.0	321	10.2	765	24.3	1,371	43.5
2004	3,129	538	17.2	415	13.3	845	27.0	1,331	42.5
2003	3,078	604	19.6	390	12.7	801	26.0	1,283	41.7

* = Quantity zero or rounds to zero.

Note: High school graduates are people who have completed 4 years of high school or more, for 1967 to 1991. Beginning in 1992, they were people whose highest degree was a high school diploma (including equivalency) or higher.

[1]Starting in 2003 respondents could identify more than one race. Except as noted, the race data in this table from 2003 onward represent those respondents who indicated only one race category.

[2]The data shown prior to 2003 consists of those identifying themselves as "Asian or Pacific Islanders."

Table A-15. Population 18 and 19 Years Old, by School Enrollment Status, Sex, Race, and Hispanic Origin, October 1967–2019—*Continued*

(Numbers in thousands; percent; civilian noninstitutionalized population.)

Year, race, and Hispanic origin	Total	Population 18 and 19 years old							
		Still in high school	Percent	Dropped out	Percent	High school graduate only	Percent	In college	Percent
Female									
2019	3,185	505	15.9	145	4.5	824	25.9	1,712	53.7
2018	3,189	496	15.5	143	4.5	724	22.7	1,826	57.3
2017	3,174	494	15.6	185	5.8	745	23.5	1,751	55.1
2016	3,159	475	15.0	174	5.5	741	23.5	1,770	56.0
2015	3,144	565	18.0	200	6.4	687	21.9	1,691	53.8
2014	3,159	544	17.2	215	6.8	679	21.5	1,720	54.5
2013	3,174	492	15.5	206	6.5	786	24.7	1,691	53.3
2012	3,175	552	16.9	183	5.8	725	22.8	1,715	54.0
2011	3,228	533	16.5	209	6.5	659	20.4	1,828	56.6
2010	3,282	521	15.9	200	6.1	704	21.4	1,858	56.6
2009	3,358	562	16.7	242	7.2	676	20.1	1,879	55.9
2008	3,328	488	14.7	277	8.3	730	21.9	1,833	55.1
2007	3,245	424	13.1	241	7.4	801	24.7	1,779	54.8
2006	3,188	503	15.8	258	8.1	784	24.6	1,643	51.5
2005	2,929	372	12.7	216	7.4	669	22.8	1,672	57.1
2004	3,062	450	14.7	228	7.4	702	22.9	1,682	54.9
2003	3,015	390	12.9	284	9.4	719	23.8	1,622	53.8
BLACK ALONE OR IN COMBINATION									
Both Sexes									
2019	1,373	255	18.5	84	6.1	444	32.4	591	43.0
2018	1,411	336	23.8	76	5.4	388	27.5	611	43.3
2017	1,414	349	24.7	78	5.5	391	27.6	597	42.2
2016	1,399	338	24.2	99	7.1	360	25.7	602	43.1
2015	1,370	326	23.8	90	6.5	394	28.8	560	40.8
2014	1,384	345	24.9	106	7.7	380	27.5	553	39.9
2013	1,420	399	28.1	101	7.1	411	29.0	509	35.9
2012	1,461	426	28.9	117	8.0	340	23.3	579	39.6
2011	1,381	409	29.6	65	4.7	292	21.2	615	44.5
2010	1,439	287	20.0	158	11.0	371	25.8	622	43.2
2009	1,450	335	23.1	191	13.1	321	22.1	604	41.7
2008	1,431	339	23.7	155	10.8	422	29.5	515	36.0
2007	1,347	306	22.7	116	8.6	395	29.3	530	39.3
2006	1,287	343	26.6	111	8.6	341	26.5	492	38.2
2005	1,195	266	22.3	112	9.4	336	28.1	481	40.2
2004	1,163	229	19.7	163	14.0	305	26.2	466	40.1
2003	1,129	288	25.5	131	11.6	310	27.5	400	35.4
Male									
2019	677	150	22.1	42	6.2	218	32.2	267	39.4
2018	692	186	26.9	31	4.5	198	28.6	277	40.0
2017	701	172	24.5	53	7.5	208	29.7	269	38.3
2016	686	208	30.4	64	9.3	163	23.8	250	36.5
2015	661	167	25.3	49	7.4	186	28.1	259	39.2
2014	679	222	32.8	66	9.7	198	29.2	192	28.4
2013	700	206	29.4	62	8.9	222	31.7	210	30.0
2012	744	213	28.6	94	12.6	194	26.0	244	32.7
2011	681	238	35.0	44	6.5	149	21.9	250	36.6
2010	700	170	24.3	86	12.3	180	25.7	264	37.7
2009	708	182	25.8	110	15.5	171	24.1	245	34.6
2008	706	191	27.0	58	8.3	238	33.7	219	31.1
2007	657	164	25.0	56	8.5	197	30.0	240	36.5
2006	623	213	34.3	45	7.3	178	28.6	186	29.8
2005	586	187	31.8	62	10.7	136	23.2	201	34.3
2004	549	142	25.9	93	17.0	139	25.3	175	31.9
2003	525	146	27.8	81	15.4	123	23.4	175	33.3
Female									
2019	696	105	15.0	42	6.0	226	32.5	324	46.5
2018	719	150	20.8	45	6.2	190	26.4	334	46.6
2017	713	177	24.0	25	3.5	182	25.6	328	46.0
2016	713	130	18.2	35	4.9	197	27.6	352	49.3

* = Quantity zero or rounds to zero.
Note: High school graduates are people who have completed 4 years of high school or more, for 1967 to 1991. Beginning in 1992, they were people whose highest degree was a high school diploma (including equivalency) or higher.
[1]Starting in 2003 respondents could identify more than one race. Except as noted, the race data in this table from 2003 onward represent those respondents who indicated only one race category.
[2]The data shown prior to 2003 consists of those identifying themselves as "Asian or Pacific Islanders."

Table A-15. Population 18 and 19 Years Old, by School Enrollment Status, Sex, Race, and Hispanic Origin, October 1967–2019—*Continued*

(Numbers in thousands; percent; civilian noninstitutionalized population.)

Year, race, and Hispanic origin	Total	Population 18 and 19 years old							
		Still in high school	Percent	Dropped out	Percent	High school graduate only	Percent	In college	Percent
2015	709	159	22.4	41	5.8	209	29.5	300	42.3
2014	705	122	17.3	41	5.7	182	25.8	360	51.1
2013	720	193	26.8	38	5.3	189	26.3	299	41.6
2012	717	213	29.1	23	3.2	146	20.4	335	46.7
2011	699	170	24.3	21	3.0	143	20.5	365	52.2
2010	739	117	15.9	72	9.8	192	25.9	358	48.4
2009	742	152	20.5	81	11.3	150	20.2	359	48.4
2008	724	148	20.5	96	13.3	184	25.4	296	40.8
2007	690	142	20.6	61	8.8	198	28.6	290	42.0
2006	665	130	19.5	66	9.9	163	24.5	307	46.1
2005	609	80	13.1	49	8.1	200	32.8	280	45.9
2004	615	86	14.0	70	11.4	169	27.5	290	47.2
2003	604	142	23.5	51	8.4	186	30.8	225	37.3
ASIAN ALONE OR IN COMBINATION									
Both Sexes									
2019	546	102	18.7	22	4.1	53	9.7	368	67.5
2018	523	63	12.0	11	2.1	89	17.0	360	68.9
2017	433	63	14.5	11	2.6	62	14.3	297	68.7
2016	487	69	14.2	17	3.6	88	18.1	313	64.2
2015	430	71	16.5	24	5.6	48	11.1	287	66.8
2014	407	53	13.0	*	*	58	14.1	296	72.8
2013	529	89	16.7	9	1.7	81	15.4	350	66.2
2012	436	71	16.4	23	5.2	67	15.4	274	63.0
2011	399	55	13.6	13	3.1	66	16.4	267	66.8
2010	369	39	10.5	13	3.6	53	14.4	264	71.5
2009	384	74	19.3	3	0.9	35	9.0	271	70.8
2008	309	52	16.8	7	2.3	37	11.8	214	69.1
2007	336	58	17.2	12	3.7	34	10.0	232	69.1
2006	318	47	14.8	9	2.8	47	14.9	215	67.5
2005	286	42	14.7	4	1.3	36	12.6	204	71.5
2004	299	36	12.0	14	4.5	46	15.4	203	67.9
2003	320	43	13.4	3	1.1	38	11.9	236	73.8
Male									
2019	255	54	21.3	7	2.9	21	8.3	172	67.5
2018	268	33	12.2	8	3.0	55	20.5	172	64.3
2017	220	43	19.4	3	1.3	41	18.7	133	60.6
2016	244	27	11.2	10	3.9	48	19.8	159	65.2
2015	213	32	15.1	18	8.3	22	10.3	141	66.3
2014	206	29	14.3	*	*	30	14.8	146	71.0
2013	265	48	18.0	1	0.2	46	17.3	171	64.5
2012	225	42	18.6	14	6.3	26	11.4	143	63.7
2011	214	33	15.5	*	*	36	16.7	145	67.9
2010	196	17	8.6	9	4.6	34	17.2	136	69.5
2009	188	34	18.3	1	0.3	16	8.3	138	73.2
2008	150	41	27.6	6	4.3	9	6.0	93	62.1
2007	161	33	20.7	2	1.0	14	8.4	113	69.9
2006	179	22	12.4	8	4.3	31	17.5	118	65.8
2005	152	30	19.5	3	1.7	22	14.5	97	64.1
2004	149	27	18.1	5	3.2	20	13.4	97	65.1
2003	144	17	11.8	3	2.3	12	8.3	112	77.8
Female									
2019	291	48	16.4	15	5.2	32	10.9	196	67.5
2018	255	30	11.8	3	1.1	34	13.4	187	73.7
2017	213	20	9.4	8	3.9	21	9.7	164	77.1
2016	243	42	17.2	8	3.2	40	16.3	153	63.3
2015	217	39	18.0	6	2.9	26	11.9	146	67.3
2014	201	24	11.8	*	*	27	13.5	150	74.7
2013	263	41	15.5	8	3.1	35	13.4	179	68.0
2012	210	30	14.1	8	4.0	41	19.7	131	62.2

* = Quantity zero or rounds to zero.
Note: High school graduates are people who have completed 4 years of high school or more, for 1967 to 1991. Beginning in 1992, they were people whose highest degree was a high school diploma (including equivalency) or higher.
[1]Starting in 2003 respondents could identify more than one race. Except as noted, the race data in this table from 2003 onward represent those respondents who indicated only one race category.
[2]The data shown prior to 2003 consists of those identifying themselves as "Asian or Pacific Islanders."

Table A-15. Population 18 and 19 Years Old, by School Enrollment Status, Sex, Race, and Hispanic Origin, October 1967–2019—*Continued*

(Numbers in thousands; percent; civilian noninstitutionalized population.)

Year, race, and Hispanic origin	Total	Population 18 and 19 years old							
		Still in high school	Percent	Dropped out	Percent	High school graduate only	Percent	In college	Percent
2011............................	186	21	11.6	13	6.8	30	16.1	122	65.6
2010............................	174	22	12.6	4	2.5	20	11.3	128	73.7
2009............................	196	40	20.4	3	1.5	19	9.7	134	68.4
2008............................	159	11	6.6	*	0.3	28	17.3	121	75.8
2007............................	174	24	13.9	11	6.3	20	11.5	119	68.3
2006............................	139	25	18.0	1	0.8	16	11.4	97	69.7
2005............................	134	12	9.2	1	0.9	14	10.4	107	80.0
2004............................	150	8	5.3	9	5.9	27	18.0	106	70.7
2003............................	176	25	14.2	*	*	27	15.3	124	70.5

* = Quantity zero or rounds to zero.
Note: High school graduates are people who have completed 4 years of high school or more, for 1967 to 1991. Beginning in 1992, they were people whose highest degree was a high school diploma (including equivalency) or higher.
[1]Starting in 2003 respondents could identify more than one race. Except as noted, the race data in this table from 2003 onward represent those respondents who indicated only one race category.
[2]The data shown prior to 2003 consists of those identifying themselves as "Asian or Pacific Islanders."

Table A-16. Age Distribution of College Students 14 Years Old and Over, by Sex, October 1947–2019

(Numbers in thousands; civilian noninstitutionalized population.)

Year, sex, race, and Hispanic origin	All students								Male				
	Total	14 to 17 years	18 and 19 years	20 and 21 years	22 to 24 years	25 to 29 years	30 to 34 years	35 years and over	Total	14 to 17 years	18 and 19 years	20 and 21 years	22 to 24 years
ALL RACES													
2019	18,289	251	4,004	4,495	3,436	2,456	1,290	2,358	8,067	102	1,822	2,123	1,497
2018	18,908	212	4,220	4,396	3,481	2,862	1,338	2,399	8,373	86	1,911	2,076	1,600
2017	18,398	236	3,943	4,367	3,627	2,674	1,207	2,346	8,112	85	1,746	2,025	1,688
2016	19,196	241	4,171	4,417	3,733	2,882	1,336	2,417	8,644	80	1,944	2,085	1,771
2015	19,101	222	3,978	4,505	3,669	2,805	1,370	2,551	8,484	108	1,838	2,113	1,743
2014	19,175	234	4,036	4,218	3,878	2,722	1,267	2,820	8,629	126	1,779	2,090	1,808
2013	19,467	308	3,951	4,326	3,925	2,715	1,351	2,891	8,536	148	1,809	2,001	1,819
2012	19,930	269	4,015	4,562	3,879	2,817	1,516	2,871	8,602	130	1,803	2,049	1,878
2011	20,397	203	4,242	4,459	3,869	3,066	1,551	3,007	9,132	108	1,949	2,127	1,877
2010	20,275	229	4,364	4,348	3,501	2,992	1,632	3,210	9,007	94	2,009	2,108	1,580
2009	19,764	206	4,289	4,034	3,749	2,769	1,524	3,193	8,642	89	1,928	1,943	1,770
2008	18,632	241	4,126	3,920	3,420	2,657	1,356	2,911	8,311	133	1,909	1,908	1,566
2007	17,956	186	4,075	3,794	3,292	2,496	1,342	2,772	7,826	76	1,903	1,729	1,524
2006	17,232	212	3,746	3,675	3,166	2,312	1,346	2,776	7,506	79	1,703	1,682	1,489
2005	17,472	181	3,727	3,945	3,162	2,291	1,309	2,857	7,539	62	1,675	1,878	1,420
2004	17,383	198	3,685	3,777	3,149	2,403	1,287	2,884	7,575	75	1,610	1,811	1,444
2003[1]	16,638	150	3,512	3,533	3,320	2,164	1,330	2,630	7,318	61	1,568	1,551	1,578
2002	16,497	195	3,581	3,525	2,927	2,093	1,308	2,867	7,240	80	1,635	1,640	1,354
2001	15,873	138	3,478	3,421	2,731	2,084	1,337	2,685	6,875	54	1,570	1,579	1,287
2000	15,314	149	3,599	3,169	2,683	1,962	1,244	2,507	6,682	61	1,570	1,472	1,300
1999	15,203	151	3,520	3,120	2,620	1,940	1,155	2,697	6,956	78	1,648	1,525	1,224
1998	15,546	123	3,670	3,092	2,561	2,148	1,266	2,685	6,905	48	1,667	1,517	1,219
1997	15,436	171	3,362	3,143	2,699	2,154	1,116	2,791	6,843	59	1,561	1,521	1,292
1996	15,226	237	3,309	2,907	2,551	2,215	1,228	2,778	6,820	97	1,489	1,379	1,319
1995	14,715	158	3,101	2,940	2,498	2,143	1,206	2,669	6,703	68	1,431	1,423	1,235
1994[2]	15,022	150	3,051	3,028	2,650	2,026	1,393	2,725	6,764	65	1,416	1,414	1,322
1993r	14,394	130	3,070	2,892	2,668	1,914	1,226	2,493	6,599	55	1,407	1,405	1,425
1993	13,898	123	2,926	2,734	2,533	1,867	1,227	2,488	6,324	52	1,337	1,312	1,345
1992	14,035	205	2,892	2,938	2,512	1,829	1,296	2,364	6,192	97	1,325	1,344	1,243
1991	14,057	132	2,929	2,939	2,304	1,983	1,302	2,468	6,439	49	1,326	1,390	1,238
1990	13,621	178	3,019	2,767	2,178	1,927	1,235	2,319	6,192	86	1,443	1,364	1,115
1989	13,180	183	3,066	2,570	2,168	1,889	1,192	2,112	5,950	73	1,422	1,228	1,067
1988	13,116	182	3,046	2,681	2,064	1,735	1,228	2,179	5,950	58	1,365	1,295	1,110
1987	12,719	239	3,045	2,642	2,006	1,826	1,159	1,802	6,030	116	1,483	1,350	1,034
1986	12,651	201	2,967	2,374	2,136	1,860	1,245	1,867	5,957	82	1,421	1,161	1,120
1985	12,524	262	2,907	2,616	2,014	1,884	1,180	1,661	5,906	131	1,349	1,313	1,087
1984	12,304	253	2,867	2,597	2,127	1,857	1,158	1,445	5,989	91	1,373	1,337	1,219
1983	12,320	260	2,940	2,495	2,042	1,921	1,167	1,495	6,010	108	1,340	1,310	1,170
1982	12,308	254	2,929	2,689	2,060	1,859	1,129	1,389	5,899	112	1,376	1,346	1,115
1981	12,127	232	3,044	2,545	1,986	1,717	1,211	1,393	5,825	96	1,450	1,239	1,144
1980	11,387	249	2,933	2,423	1,870	1,641	1,062	1,207	5,430	96	1,369	1,246	989
1979	11,380	311	2,844	2,353	1,794	1,679	996	1,402	5,480	129	1,341	1,192	975
1978	11,141	274	2,899	2,298	1,798	1,619	950	1,303	5,580	106	1,391	1,202	1,028
1977	11,546	274	2,913	2,430	1,799	1,809	992	1,329	5,889	112	1,396	1,280	1,036
1976	11,139	281	2,937	2,398	1,846	1,686	803	1,189	5,785	105	1,391	1,209	1,073
1975	10,880	293	2,943	2,313	1,679	1,616	853	1,183	5,911	128	1,426	1,256	1,011
1974	9,852	309	2,597	2,192	1,527	1,482	720	1,025	5,402	145	1,262	1,206	943
1973	8,966	295	2,517	2,073	1,465	1,278	551	787	5,048	121	1,293	1,130	937
1972	9,096	295	2,680	2,116	1,461	1,229	531	783	5,218	141	1,366	1,170	998
1971	8,087	284	2,726	1,997	1,487	1,067	527	NA	4,850	129	1,444	1,090	1,065
1970	7,413	260	2,594	1,857	1,354	939	410	NA	4,401	130	1,346	1,083	902
1969	7,435	242	2,601	1,945	1,294	918	435	NA	4,448	120	1,397	1,112	883
1968	6,801	281	2,501	1,826	1,029	790	373	NA	4,124	134	1,357	1,093	702
1967	6,401	239	2,286	1,816	998	707	356	NA	3,841	96	1,198	1,066	718
1966	6,085	254	2,440	1,472	987	679	254	NA	3,749	105	1,355	899	722
1965	5,675	264	2,215	1,326	940	614	316	NA	3,503	113	1,218	804	699
1964	4,643	291	1,616	1,287	670	523	256	NA	2,888	165	866	769	510
1963	4,336	180	1,504	1,212	717	482	241	NA	2,742	99	796	734	574
1962	4,208	233	1,612	996	630	486	251	NA	2,742	125	891	617	508

NA = Not available.

r = Revised, controlled to 1990 census based population estimates; previous 1993 data controlled to 1980 census based population estimates.

[1]Starting in 2003 respondents could identify more than one race. Except as noted, the race data in this table from 2003 onward represent those respondents who indicated only one race category.

[2]The data shown prior to 2003 consists of those identifying themselves as "Asian or Pacific Islanders."

[3]Total excludes age groups where "NA" appears in the column. This applies to people 35 and over prior to 1972 for the total population, prior to 1973 for the White alone population and the Black alone population, and prior to 1986 for the Hispanic population. Data for 1950 exclude persons aged 30 and over.

[4]Data for 1955 to 1963 are for Black and other races.

[5]This series was discontinued in 2006.

Table A-16. Age Distribution of College Students 14 Years Old and Over, by Sex, October 1947–2019—*Continued*

(Numbers in thousands; civilian noninstitutionalized population.)

Year, sex, race, and Hispanic origin	Male 25 to 29 years	Male 30 to 34 years	Male 35 years and over	Female Total	Female 14 to 17 years	Female 18 and 19 years	Female 20 and 21 years	Female 22 to 24 years	Female 25 to 29 years	Female 30 to 34 years	Female 35 years and over
ALL RACES											
2019	1,133	508	880	10,223	149	2,181	2,372	1,939	1,322	782	1,478
2018	1,280	562	858	10,534	126	2,309	2,320	1,881	1,582	776	1,540
2017	1,188	526	853	10,287	151	2,197	2,341	1,939	1,486	681	1,492
2016	1,264	574	927	10,551	161	2,227	2,331	1,962	1,618	762	1,490
2015	1,238	565	878	10,617	113	2,141	2,392	1,927	1,567	805	1,673
2014	1,283	509	1,036	10,546	108	2,257	2,128	2,070	1,439	758	1,784
2013	1,253	522	983	10,931	159	2,142	2,325	2,105	1,462	829	1,908
2012	1,194	576	972	11,327	139	2,212	2,513	2,001	1,623	940	1,900
2011	1,343	643	1,084	11,266	95	2,293	2,333	1,992	1,722	908	1,923
2010	1,396	659	1,160	11,268	135	2,355	2,240	1,920	1,596	973	2,049
2009	1,194	649	1,069	11,123	116	2,361	2,091	1,980	1,575	875	2,124
2008	1,229	577	989	10,321	108	2,217	2,013	1,854	1,428	779	1,922
2007	1,029	596	968	10,130	109	2,172	2,065	1,768	1,466	746	1,804
2006	1,033	537	982	9,726	133	2,043	1,993	1,677	1,278	809	1,793
2005	923	562	1,019	9,934	119	2,052	2,067	1,742	1,368	747	1,838
2004	1,068	533	1,033	9,808	123	2,074	1,966	1,705	1,335	753	1,850
2003[1]	982	607	970	9,319	89	1,944	1,982	1,742	1,181	723	1,660
2002	918	542	1,071	9,258	116	1,946	1,885	1,573	1,175	766	1,797
2001	917	559	908	8,998	84	1,907	1,841	1,444	1,167	778	1,776
2000	844	517	918	8,631	88	2,029	1,697	1,383	1,118	728	1,589
1999	911	547	1,023	8,247	73	1,872	1,595	1,396	1,029	608	1,674
1998	979	521	953	8,641	74	2,003	1,574	1,342	1,170	745	1,732
1997	1,052	457	899	8,593	112	1,801	1,622	1,406	1,102	658	1,892
1996	1,038	485	1,013	8,406	140	1,821	1,528	1,233	1,177	743	1,765
1995	1,008	553	985	8,013	90	1,671	1,518	1,263	1,135	653	1,684
1994[2]	972	617	958	8,258	85	1,635	1,613	1,328	1,054	776	1,766
1993r	892	534	880	7,795	75	1,663	1,487	1,243	1,022	692	1,613
1993	872	534	873	7,574	71	1,588	1,422	1,189	995	693	1,616
1992	845	547	789	7,844	107	1,566	1,594	1,269	984	748	1,575
1991	1,018	587	832	7,618	83	1,603	1,549	1,066	965	715	1,636
1990	910	502	772	7,429	91	1,576	1,403	1,063	1,017	732	1,546
1989	926	517	716	7,231	110	1,643	1,342	1,100	964	675	1,396
1988	835	560	727	7,166	124	1,682	1,386	953	900	668	1,452
1987	921	500	625	6,689	123	1,562	1,292	972	905	659	1,176
1986	968	577	628	6,694	120	1,546	1,213	1,016	892	667	1,240
1985	942	522	561	6,618	129	1,559	1,303	926	941	658	1,100
1984	965	527	476	6,315	161	1,494	1,260	908	892	630	970
1983	1,055	521	506	6,310	153	1,600	1,185	872	865	645	989
1982	968	492	490	6,410	141	1,553	1,343	945	891	637	900
1981	909	533	453	6,303	136	1,594	1,305	842	808	677	940
1980	853	472	405	5,957	153	1,565	1,178	882	788	590	802
1979	893	463	487	5,900	183	1,503	1,161	818	786	533	914
1978	922	474	457	5,559	168	1,507	1,096	770	697	476	845
1977	1,035	511	520	5,657	162	1,517	1,151	763	774	481	809
1976	1,067	451	489	5,354	176	1,546	1,189	773	619	352	700
1975	1,025	496	569	4,969	164	1,517	1,058	668	590	357	614
1974	951	420	476	4,449	165	1,335	986	584	531	300	548
1973	867	329	371	3,918	174	1,224	944	528	411	222	416
1972	848	330	365	3,877	153	1,314	946	464	381	200	418
1971	787	334	NA	3,236	154	1,281	906	423	280	192	NA
1970	684	256	NA	3,013	130	1,248	774	452	255	154	NA
1969	671	265	NA	2,987	122	1,204	833	411	247	171	NA
1968	603	236	NA	2,677	147	1,144	733	328	187	138	NA
1967	524	239	NA	2,560	143	1,088	749	280	183	117	NA
1966	494	174	NA	2,337	149	1,085	573	265	185	80	NA
1965	458	211	NA	2,172	151	997	522	241	156	105	NA
1964	396	182	NA	1,755	126	750	510	160	127	74	NA
1963	365	174	NA	1,594	81	708	478	143	117	67	NA
1962	406	195	NA	1,466	108	721	379	122	80	56	NA

NA – Not available.

r = Revised, controlled to 1990 census based population estimates; previous 1993 data controlled to 1980 census based population estimates.

[1]Starting in 2003 respondents could identify more than one race. Except as noted, the race data in this table from 2003 onward represent those respondents who indicated only one race category.

[2]The data shown prior to 2003 consists of those identifying themselves as "Asian or Pacific Islanders."

[3]Total excludes age groups where "NA" appears in the column. This applies to people 35 and over prior to 1972 for the total population, prior to 1973 for the White alone population and the Black alone population, and prior to 1986 for the Hispanic population. Data for 1950 exclude persons aged 30 and over.

[4]Data for 1955 to 1963 are for Black and other races.

[5]This series was discontinued in 2006.

Table A-16. Age Distribution of College Students 14 Years Old and Over, by Sex, October 1947–2019—*Continued*

(Numbers in thousands; civilian noninstitutionalized population.)

Year, sex, race, and Hispanic origin	All students								Male				
	Total	14 to 17 years	18 and 19 years	20 and 21 years	22 to 24 years	25 to 29 years	30 to 34 years	35 years and over	Total	14 to 17 years	18 and 19 years	20 and 21 years	22 to 24 years
1961	3,731	213	1,470	892	507	437	212	NA	2,356	84	834	554	393
1960	3,570	222	1,299	790	509	491	259	NA	2,339	99	734	503	411
1959	3,340	210	1,175	739	489	503	224	NA	2,187	92	651	501	355
1958	3,242	167	1,114	----1,221----		534	206	NA	2,129	73	621	----850----	
1957	3,138	176	989	----1,236----		553	184	NA	2,028	77	538	----827----	
1956	2,883	167	934	----1,105----		494	183	NA	1,932	77	512	----781----	
1955	2,379	147	745	----931----		406	150	NA	1,579	57	432	----647----	
1950	2,175	180	733	----939----		324	NA	NA	1,474	74	395	----692----	
1947	2,311	188	620	----1,088----		321	94	NA	1,687	87	343	----872----	
WHITE ALONE													
2019	12,783	157	2,949	3,262	2,391	1,587	824	1,613	5,661	56	1,334	1,539	1,050
2018	13,323	169	3,178	3,154	2,438	1,862	875	1,647	5,980	61	1,430	1,485	1,130
2017	13,224	156	2,982	3,178	2,530	1,845	861	1,672	5,864	64	1,317	1,484	1,172
2016	13,901	166	3,170	3,289	2,647	2,041	925	1,663	6,222	55	1,470	1,549	1,247
2015	13,859	149	3,057	3,308	2,604	2,021	945	1,776	6,253	78	1,414	1,586	1,189
2014	13,953	148	3,064	3,232	2,781	1,942	888	1,898	6,398	67	1,397	1,621	1,278
2013	14,240	234	3,033	3,160	2,857	1,879	970	2,107	6,241	115	1,386	1,452	1,292
2012	14,628	204	3,077	3,427	2,798	2,048	1,002	2,072	6,392	87	1,387	1,497	1,377
2011	15,412	141	3,298	3,545	2,970	2,254	1,085	2,120	7,054	78	1,520	1,679	1,486
2010	15,258	154	3,398	3,297	2,629	2,217	1,197	2,366	6,883	59	1,573	1,624	1,172
2009	15,027	160	3,337	3,205	2,784	2,066	1,097	2,377	6,681	77	1,511	1,533	1,360
2008	14,405	171	3,353	3,119	2,669	1,952	907	2,234	6,570	85	1,566	1,524	1,250
2007	13,835	141	3,242	3,053	2,485	1,817	952	2,144	6,050	62	1,508	1,359	1,172
2006	13,273	161	2,982	2,958	2,358	1,740	985	2,090	5,829	57	1,367	1,344	1,131
2005	13,466	116	2,972	3,176	2,350	1,708	939	2,205	5,843	38	1,343	1,488	1,092
2004	13,381	134	2,946	3,016	2,389	1,776	974	2,146	5,944	49	1,308	1,437	1,110
2003[1]	12,870	100	2,833	2,796	2,521	1,585	960	2,075	5,714	48	1,258	1,236	1,232
2002	12,781	109	2,891	2,810	2,220	1,582	933	2,236	5,719	57	1,329	1,306	1,066
2001	12,208	88	2,755	2,774	2,019	1,514	956	2,103	5,383	36	1,273	1,305	943
2000	11,999	117	2,914	2,590	2,062	1,433	906	1,978	5,311	47	1,289	1,225	1,008
1999	12,053	87	2,849	2,520	2,077	1,475	870	2,174	5,562	33	1,336	1,226	1,024
1998	12,401	93	2,994	2,537	2,011	1,604	964	2,199	5,602	30	1,376	1,256	1,002
1997	12,442	127	2,792	2,602	2,101	1,666	856	2,298	5,552	48	1,314	1,289	1,030
1996	12,189	167	2,731	2,362	2,030	1,704	940	2,254	5,453	70	1,223	1,117	1,079
1995	12,021	116	2,577	2,437	1,997	1,745	941	2,208	5,535	44	1,195	1,201	1,002
1994[2]	12,222	101	2,568	2,459	2,091	1,592	1,143	2,267	5,524	44	1,212	1,140	1,054
1993r	11,735	103	2,566	2,356	2,152	1,507	1,003	2,049	5,403	44	1,157	1,196	1,145
1993	11,434	98	2,456	2,243	2,064	1,490	1,015	2,068	5,222	41	1,103	1,120	1,090
1992	11,710	158	2,419	2,466	2,031	1,512	1,070	2,053	5,210	82	1,102	1,162	1,027
1991	11,686	104	2,487	2,449	1,877	1,598	1,063	2,107	5,304	41	1,112	1,146	1,012
1990	11,488	132	2,548	2,341	1,746	1,638	1,060	2,023	5,235	63	1,218	1,151	923
1989	11,243	147	2,648	2,170	1,813	1,611	986	1,868	5,136	63	1,253	1,070	900
1988	11,140	137	2,639	2,270	1,750	1,425	1,023	1,896	5,078	50	1,194	1,114	952
1987	10,731	194	2,564	2,254	1,665	1,483	985	1,584	5,104	97	1,260	1,156	873
1986	10,707	173	2,549	2,015	1,743	1,580	1,037	1,609	5,074	69	1,254	982	932
1985	10,781	229	2,539	2,257	1,704	1,590	1,014	1,448	5,103	120	1,176	1,137	941
1984	10,520	209	2,541	2,206	1,779	1,566	967	1,252	5,111	73	1,224	1,143	1,039
1983	10,565	214	2,597	2,161	1,705	1,603	961	1,324	5,162	87	1,197	1,149	989
1982	10,551	216	2,549	2,348	1,697	1,581	938	1,222	5,077	95	1,189	1,188	931
1981	10,353	197	2,639	2,239	1,671	1,390	1,027	1,190	5,010	86	1,259	1,104	977
1980	9,925	212	2,578	2,131	1,625	1,413	915	1,051	4,804	79	1,232	1,114	878
1979	9,956	256	2,498	2,079	1,543	1,474	859	1,247	4,823	110	1,192	1,058	854
1978	9,661	229	2,553	1,993	1,531	1,399	808	1,148	4,913	90	1,239	1,056	900
1977	9,962	227	2,579	2,099	1,531	1,550	827	1,149	5,156	91	1,272	1,124	890
1976	9,679	237	2,577	2,108	1,591	1,458	673	1,035	5,084	89	1,244	1,073	933
1975	9,546	252	2,613	2,042	1,461	1,410	737	1,031	5,263	111	1,283	1,134	909
1974	8,689	271	2,308	1,940	1,341	1,308	613	908	4,782	128	1,143	1,067	825
1973	8,014	253	2,281	1,865	1,292	1,152	481	690	4,218	111	1,177	1,017	838
1972	7,458	259	2,411	1,917	1,296	1,119	456	NA	4,395	120	1,242	1,062	891

NA = Not available.

r = Revised, controlled to 1990 census based population estimates; previous 1993 data controlled to 1980 census based population estimates.

[1]Starting in 2003 respondents could identify more than one race. Except as noted, the race data in this table from 2003 onward represent those respondents who indicated only one race category.

[2]The data shown prior to 2003 consists of those identifying themselves as "Asian or Pacific Islanders."

[3]Total excludes age groups where "NA" appears in the column. This applies to people 35 and over prior to 1972 for the total population, prior to 1973 for the White alone population and the Black alone population, and prior to 1986 for the Hispanic population. Data for 1950 exclude persons aged 30 and over.

[4]Data for 1955 to 1963 are for Black and other races.

[5]This series was discontinued in 2006.

Table A-16. Age Distribution of College Students 14 Years Old and Over, by Sex, October 1947–2019—*Continued*

(Numbers in thousands; civilian noninstitutionalized population.)

Year, sex, race, and Hispanic origin	Male			Female							
	25 to 29 years	30 to 34 years	35 years and over	Total	14 to 17 years	18 and 19 years	20 and 21 years	22 to 24 years	25 to 29 years	30 to 34 years	35 years and over
1961	337	154	NA	1,375	129	636	338	114	100	58	NA
1960	399	193	NA	1,231	123	565	287	98	92	66	NA
1959	422	166	NA	1,153	118	524	238	134	81	58	NA
1958	439	146	NA	1,113	94	493	----371----		95	60	NA
1957	459	127	NA	1,110	99	451	----409----		94	57	NA
1956	429	133	NA	951	90	422	----324----		65	50	NA
1955	337	107	NA	800	90	313	----285----		69	43	NA
1950	314	NA	NA	701	106	338	----247----		10	NA	NA
1947	301	84	NA	624	101	277	----216----		20	10	NA

WHITE ALONE

Year, sex, race, and Hispanic origin	Male			Female							
	25 to 29 years	30 to 34 years	35 years and over	Total	14 to 17 years	18 and 19 years	20 and 21 years	22 to 24 years	25 to 29 years	30 to 34 years	35 years and over
2019	723	343	616	7,123	101	1,615	1,724	1,341	863	482	997
2018	830	414	629	7,343	108	1,749	1,668	1,308	1,032	460	1,018
2017	825	396	606	7,360	92	1,665	1,695	1,358	1,020	465	1,066
2016	872	385	644	7,678	112	1,700	1,740	1,400	1,169	540	1,019
2015	920	415	651	7,607	71	1,644	1,721	1,415	1,101	530	1,124
2014	927	374	733	7,555	81	1,667	1,611	1,502	1,015	514	1,165
2013	867	406	721	7,999	119	1,646	1,707	1,565	1,011	564	1,386
2012	892	428	725	8,236	117	1,690	1,930	1,421	1,156	574	1,347
2011	1,013	470	808	8,358	63	1,779	1,866	1,484	1,241	615	1,311
2010	1,051	511	893	8,375	95	1,825	1,673	1,458	1,166	686	1,472
2009	904	483	814	8,346	84	1,826	1,672	1,424	1,162	614	1,564
2008	938	413	794	7,835	85	1,787	1,595	1,419	1,014	493	1,440
2007	770	413	766	7,785	80	1,734	1,694	1,313	1,047	539	1,378
2006	799	396	734	7,445	104	1,615	1,613	1,227	941	588	1,355
2005	685	420	777	7,624	79	1,629	1,688	1,258	1,024	519	1,428
2004	837	421	782	7,438	86	1,638	1,579	1,279	939	553	1,364
2003[1]	723	435	783	7,155	53	1,575	1,560	1,289	862	525	1,291
2002	712	394	855	7,062	52	1,562	1,504	1,154	870	539	1,381
2001	693	401	731	6,826	52	1,481	1,468	1,077	820	555	1,372
2000	662	367	713	6,689	70	1,625	1,365	1,054	770	539	1,266
1999	715	414	816	6,491	55	1,513	1,296	1,053	760	455	1,359
1998	746	396	795	6,799	63	1,618	1,281	1,008	858	567	1,405
1997	802	345	725	6,890	79	1,479	1,313	1,071	864	511	1,573
1996	797	357	811	6,735	97	1,508	1,246	951	906	583	1,443
1995	857	432	804	6,486	72	1,383	1,237	995	887	508	1,404
1994[?]	749	512	815	6,698	57	1,357	1,320	1,037	844	631	1,453
1993r	705	451	705	6,331	59	1,409	1,160	1,007	802	552	1,344
1993	699	457	711	6,212	57	1,353	1,123	974	791	558	1,357
1992	689	471	678	6,499	76	1,317	1,303	1,005	823	599	1,376
1991	809	480	703	6,382	63	1,375	1,304	865	789	583	1,404
1990	782	434	665	6,253	69	1,331	1,190	823	856	627	1,358
1989	789	438	623	6,107	84	1,395	1,101	913	822	548	1,245
1988	685	470	613	6,063	87	1,445	1,156	798	740	554	1,283
1987	740	436	541	5,627	97	1,304	1,097	791	743	550	1,044
1986	835	475	528	5,632	105	1,295	1,033	811	745	562	1,081
1985	812	449	468	5,679	110	1,363	1,120	764	778	565	979
1984	796	434	402	5,410	136	1,317	1,063	740	770	533	851
1983	876	421	444	5,404	127	1,400	1,012	717	728	540	880
1982	831	415	428	5,472	120	1,360	1,159	766	749	523	795
1981	745	448	391	5,342	111	1,380	1,134	694	646	578	799
1980	735	400	366	5,121	133	1,346	1,017	747	678	514	686
1979	788	398	423	5,131	146	1,306	1,021	688	686	461	823
1978	810	413	405	4,748	139	1,314	937	631	590	395	742
1977	907	433	439	4,806	135	1,307	975	641	643	394	711
1976	936	382	427	4,593	147	1,334	1,034	658	521	291	608
1975	911	426	489	4,284	141	1,330	908	552	500	311	542
1974	855	350	414	3,907	143	1,166	873	516	453	263	493
1973	789	286	NA	3,107	142	1,104	848	454	363	196	NA
1972	784	296	NA	3,061	138	1,169	855	404	334	160	NA

NA = Not available.

r = Revised, controlled to 1990 census based population estimates, previous 1993 data controlled to 1980 census based population estimates.

[1]Starting in 2003 respondents could identify more than one race. Except as noted, the race data in this table from 2003 onward represent those respondents who indicated only one race category.

[2]The data shown prior to 2003 consists of those identifying themselves as "Asian or Pacific Islanders."

[3]Total excludes age groups where "NA" appears in the column. This applies to people 35 and over prior to 1972 for the total population, prior to 1973 for the White alone population and the Black alone population, and prior to 1988 for the Hispanic population. Data for 1950 exclude persons aged 30 and over.

[4]Data for 1955 to 1963 are for Black and other races.

[5]This series was discontinued in 2006.

Table A-16. Age Distribution of College Students 14 Years Old and Over, by Sex, October 1947–2019—*Continued*

(Numbers in thousands; civilian noninstitutionalized population.)

Year, sex, race, and Hispanic origin	All students								Male				
	Total	14 to 17 years	18 and 19 years	20 and 21 years	22 to 24 years	25 to 29 years	30 to 34 years	35 years and over	Total	14 to 17 years	18 and 19 years	20 and 21 years	22 to 24 years
1971	7,273	251	2,485	1,758	1,351	965	463	NA	4,407	117	1,328	964	992
1970	6,759	230	2,361	1,684	1,260	853	371	NA	4,066	117	1,251	995	850
1969	6,827	222	2,377	1,762	1,208	855	404	NA	4,146	110	1,298	1,021	827
1968	6,255	251	2,284	1,691	954	741	333	NA	3,843	117	1,262	1,021	666
1967	5,905	220	2,105	1,688	915	646	329	NA	3,560	88	1,097	998	666
1966	5,708	233	2,293	----2,313----		----869----		NA	3,536	93	1,281	----1,541----	
1965	5,317	233	2,074	----2,139----		----871----		NA	3,326	104	1,152	----1,441----	
1964	4,337	257	1,519	----1,850----		----711----		NA	2,720	147	823	----1,226----	
1963	4,050	171	1,391	----1,817----		----671----		NA	2,593	94	746	----1,246----	
1962	3,934	217	1,509	----1,517----		----691----		NA	2,586	120	836	----1,066----	
1961	3,498	204	1,388	----1,296----		----610----		NA	2,208	79	786	------883----	
1960	3,342	214	1,211	----1,209----		----709----		NA	2,214	97	691	------859----	
1959	3,118	193	1,101	----1,134----		----690----		NA	2,067	88	620	------798----	
1958	3,030	155	1,044	----1,136----		----695----		NA	1,999	68	577	------802----	
1957	2,932	161	921	----1,165----		----685----		NA	1,938	68	510	------797----	
1956	2,687	152	869	----1,025----		----641----		NA	1,808	68	474	------733----	
1955	2,224	125	715	------880----		----504----		NA	1,495	47	418	------621----	
WHITE ALONE NON-HISPANIC													
2019	9,677	121	2,169	2,491	1,770	1,175	621	1,329	4,261	46	971	1,170	787
2018	10,248	116	2,382	2,420	1,869	1,384	684	1,392	4,616	45	1,086	1,161	875
2017	10,055	89	2,129	2,510	1,905	1,379	691	1,351	4,518	34	952	1,206	899
2016	10,749	82	2,439	2,465	1,990	1,615	789	1,368	4,879	30	1,168	1,168	952
2015	10,904	106	2,368	2,517	2,053	1,593	777	1,489	4,970	54	1,121	1,234	930
2014	11,068	113	2,299	2,545	2,209	1,545	742	1,613	5,115	58	1,050	1,310	1,031
2013	11,348	193	2,379	2,456	2,230	1,529	764	1,798	4,944	97	1,124	1,135	1,001
2012	11,650	150	2,363	2,620	2,207	1,734	778	1,799	5,074	61	1,051	1,126	1,113
2011	12,703	105	2,588	2,867	2,427	1,892	936	1,888	5,731	55	1,184	1,349	1,221
2010	12,613	114	2,699	2,813	2,152	1,818	996	2,022	5,673	39	1,236	1,395	986
2009	12,826	120	2,842	2,755	2,385	1,736	913	2,074	5,709	54	1,286	1,327	1,174
2008	12,324	121	2,850	2,734	2,309	1,625	779	1,906	5,602	58	1,346	1,322	1,098
2007	11,867	104	2,739	2,677	2,117	1,509	816	1,904	5,269	45	1,298	1,223	1,021
2006	11,485	114	2,564	2,606	2,030	1,494	830	1,848	5,085	41	1,168	1,208	979
2005	11,715	93	2,618	2,769	2,006	1,445	806	1,977	5,114	30	1,193	1,308	928
2004	11,571	111	2,596	2,618	2,014	1,513	814	1,905	5,146	44	1,150	1,242	930
2003[1]	11,295	90	2,486	2,419	2,225	1,371	832	1,872	5,067	41	1,115	1,082	1,094
2002	11,236	97	2,549	2,525	1,931	1,317	812	2,007	5,060	57	1,179	1,162	947
2001	10,602	74	2,383	2,450	1,732	1,283	827	1,854	4,691	30	1,131	1,170	794
2000	10,636	92	2,580	2,333	1,796	1,275	770	1,790	4,716	35	1,138	1,109	890
1999	10,818	80	2,574	2,324	1,837	1,283	755	1,965	5,033	30	1,214	1,141	929
1998	11,109	84	2,715	2,281	1,760	1,408	840	2,020	5,084	30	1,280	1,123	897
1997	11,246	81	2,491	2,361	1,876	1,504	779	2,153	5,024	33	1,184	1,161	930
1996	11,034	147	2,504	2,156	1,788	1,514	834	2,091	4,961	61	1,136	1,039	955
1995	11,024	103	2,372	2,226	1,796	1,618	859	2,051	5,068	36	1,111	1,103	892
1994[2]	11,178	93	2,362	2,255	1,904	1,444	1,018	2,101	5,053	41	1,132	1,039	955
1993	10,554	83	2,270	2,026	1,924	1,367	923	1,960	4,838	36	1,038	1,016	1,017
BLACK ALONE[4]													
2019	2,848	43	538	550	499	461	238	518	1,171	24	243	252	199
2018	3,009	15	530	600	540	561	246	518	1,183	6	234	282	220
2017	2,812	35	525	546	524	455	219	509	1,175	13	234	251	210
2016	2,885	30	530	572	542	405	247	559	1,217	12	215	276	237
2015	2,826	25	509	575	553	404	223	537	1,147	12	229	252	298
2014	2,934	54	510	537	482	414	242	695	1,132	38	175	244	214
2013	2,857	32	451	633	515	461	225	539	1,116	18	186	268	236
2012	3,038	27	531	636	522	443	326	553	1,152	18	206	316	238
2011	3,146	38	580	489	570	511	307	651	1,212	23	242	243	232
2010	3,083	33	567	622	503	438	277	643	1,185	14	238	262	234

NA = Not available.

r = Revised, controlled to 1990 census based population estimates; previous 1993 data controlled to 1980 census based population estimates.

[1]Starting in 2003 respondents could identify more than one race. Except as noted, the race data in this table from 2003 onward represent those respondents who indicated only one race category.

[2]The data shown prior to 2003 consists of those identifying themselves as "Asian or Pacific Islanders."

[3]Total excludes age groups where "NA" appears in the column. This applies to people 35 and over prior to 1972 for the total population, prior to 1973 for the White alone population and the Black alone population, and prior to 1986 for the Hispanic population. Data for 1950 exclude persons aged 30 and over.

[4]Data for 1955 to 1963 are for Black and other races.

[5]This series was discontinued in 2006.

Table A-16. Age Distribution of College Students 14 Years Old and Over, by Sex, October 1947–2019—*Continued*

(Numbers in thousands; civilian noninstitutionalized population.)

Year, sex, race, and Hispanic origin	Male			Female							
	25 to 29 years	30 to 34 years	35 years and over	Total	14 to 17 years	18 and 19 years	20 and 21 years	22 to 24 years	25 to 29 years	30 to 34 years	35 years and over
1971	712	293	NA	2,867	134	1,157	794	359	252	170	NA
1970	622	231	NA	2,693	113	1,110	689	410	231	140	NA
1969	637	252	NA	2,681	112	1,079	741	380	218	151	NA
1968	564	213	NA	2,412	134	1,022	670	288	177	120	NA
1967	494	217	NA	2,345	133	1,009	690	250	152	112	NA
1966	-----621----		NA	2,172	140	1,012	----772-----		----248-----		NA
1965	-----629----		NA	1,991	129	922	----698-----		----242-----		NA
1964	-----524----		NA	1,617	110	696	----624-----		----187-----		NA
1963	-----507----		NA	1,457	77	645	----571-----		--- 164-----		NA
1962	-----564----		NA	1,348	97	673	----451-----		----127-----		NA
1961	-----460----		NA	1,290	125	602	----413-----		----150-----		NA
1960	-----567----		NA	1,128	117	520	----350-----		----142-----		NA
1959	-----561----		NA	1,051	105	481	----336-----		----129-----		NA
1958	-----552----		NA	1,031	87	467	----334-----		----143-----		NA
1957	-----563----		NA	994	93	411	----368-----		----122-----		NA
1956	-----533----		NA	879	84	395	----292-----		----108----		NA
1955	-----409----		NA	729	78	297	----259-----		------95-----		NA

WHITE ALONE NON-HISPANIC

Year, sex, race, and Hispanic origin	Male			Female							
2019	521	271	494	5,416	76	1,198	1,321	982	653	350	835
2018	611	315	522	5,632	71	1,296	1,258	994	773	370	870
2017	637	304	486	5,537	55	1,178	1,304	1,006	742	387	865
2016	702	327	531	5,870	52	1,271	1,297	1,038	913	463	837
2015	744	353	534	5,934	52	1,248	1,283	1,123	849	424	954
2014	728	337	600	5,953	55	1,249	1,235	1,179	817	405	1,013
2013	668	322	597	6,404	95	1,254	1,321	1,229	861	442	1,201
2012	761	356	606	6,575	88	1,312	1,494	1,094	973	422	1,193
2011	817	417	689	6,972	50	1,404	1,517	1,206	1,075	519	1,199
2010	854	416	747	6,940	75	1,463	1,417	1,166	964	581	1,275
2009	765	397	706	7,116	66	1,556	1,429	1,211	971	516	1,368
2008	766	347	664	6,722	63	1,504	1,412	1,211	859	432	1,242
2007	639	370	674	6,598	59	1,441	1,455	1,096	870	447	1,230
2006	702	347	640	6,400	73	1,396	1,398	1,051	792	483	1,208
2005	590	373	692	6,601	63	1,425	1,461	1,078	855	433	1,285
2004	710	372	698	6,425	67	1,446	1,375	1,085	803	442	1,207
2003[1]	639	386	710	6,228	49	1,371	1,337	1,130	732	446	1,163
2002	596	350	770	6,177	40	1,370	1,364	984	721	462	1,237
2001	587	348	632	5,912	44	1,252	1,280	938	695	479	1,222
2000	603	296	646	5,921	57	1,443	1,224	906	672	474	1,145
1999	627	368	722	5,785	49	1,360	1,183	908	656	387	1,241
1998	668	348	738	6,025	54	1,435	1,158	863	740	493	1,282
1997	732	314	669	6,222	48	1,307	1,200	946	771	465	1,485
1996	727	303	740	6,073	86	1,367	1,117	833	787	531	1,352
1995	799	380	749	5,956	67	1,261	1,123	904	819	479	1,302
1994[2]	689	457	741	6,124	53	1,229	1,216	950	755	561	1,361
1993	663	399	670	5,715	48	1,232	1,010	907	704	524	1,290

BLACK ALONE[4]

Year, sex, race, and Hispanic origin	Male			Female							
2019	208	69	176	1,676	20	295	298	300	253	169	342
2018	228	63	151	1,826	9	296	318	320	332	183	367
2017	193	81	192	1,637	22	291	295	314	262	138	316
2016	192	97	188	1,669	18	316	296	305	212	151	372
2015	145	57	154	1,679	13	280	323	255	259	166	383
2014	162	79	220	1,802	17	334	293	268	252	164	475
2013	172	54	182	1,740	14	265	365	280	289	171	357
2012	142	85	148	1,886	10	325	320	284	301	241	406
2011	189	92	191	1,934	16	337	246	338	322	215	460
2010	180	77	180	1,898	20	329	360	269	258	199	463

NA = Not available.

r = Revised, controlled to 1990 census based population estimates; previous 1993 data controlled to 1980 census based population estimates.

[1] Starting in 2003 respondents could identify more than one race. Except as noted, the race data in this table from 2003 onward represent those respondents who indicated only one race category.

[2] The data shown prior to 2003 consists of those identifying themselves as "Asian or Pacific Islanders."

[3] Total excludes age groups where "NA" appears in the column. This applies to people 35 and over prior to 1972 for the total population, prior to 1973 for the White alone population and the Black alone population, and prior to 1986 for the Hispanic population. Data for 1960 exclude persons aged 30 and over.

[4] Data for 1955 to 1963 are for Black and other races.

[5] This series was discontinued in 2006.

Table A-16. Age Distribution of College Students 14 Years Old and Over, by Sex, October 1947–2019—*Continued*

(Numbers in thousands; civilian noninstitutionalized population.)

Year, sex, race, and Hispanic origin	All students Total	14 to 17 years	18 and 19 years	20 and 21 years	22 to 24 years	25 to 29 years	30 to 34 years	35 years and over	Male Total	14 to 17 years	18 and 19 years	20 and 21 years	22 to 24 years
2009	2,889	34	559	495	550	410	253	587	1,058	5	225	237	212
2008	2,481	36	479	463	408	377	269	451	919	21	205	217	174
2007	2,501	27	492	436	468	400	229	449	1,016	10	227	213	209
2006	2,334	30	464	416	441	303	199	480	896	10	174	182	186
2005	2,217	28	431	393	435	282	217	430	832	6	182	178	153
2004	2,301	40	440	398	400	352	170	501	776	13	165	169	146
2003[1]	2,144	28	374	415	435	289	214	388	798	10	166	153	180
2002	2,278	56	430	418	379	301	241	454	802	14	179	175	121
2001	2,230	33	444	383	379	283	279	429	781	7	179	137	153
2000	2,164	19	454	375	387	325	242	361	815	10	163	137	169
1999	1,998	45	430	389	325	254	199	354	833	34	210	193	98
1998	2,016	22	461	354	300	328	211	340	770	12	194	162	88
1997	1,903	24	381	321	383	258	165	372	723	7	142	137	146
1996	1,901	45	345	346	292	337	182	354	764	17	145	155	122
1995	1,772	24	344	339	305	233	193	334	710	13	145	142	143
1994	1,800	36	310	347	344	256	184	323	745	16	132	161	147
1993r	1,599	13	322	311	264	253	143	293	652	4	151	109	127
1993	1,545	13	311	297	253	245	141	284	636	4	148	107	124
1992	1,424	28	291	316	279	170	132	208	527	8	123	114	119
1991	1,477	18	303	302	223	216	157	257	629	7	137	138	103
1990	1,393	35	349	287	258	150	108	207	587	16	164	151	111
1989	1,287	32	302	290	243	156	119	146	480	8	126	104	94
1988	1,321	33	281	273	198	188	142	206	494	6	108	90	99
1987	1,351	32	341	264	218	220	121	155	587	13	154	124	99
1986	1,359	19	308	242	262	187	143	198	580	12	120	111	118
1985	1,263	21	259	274	201	183	112	213	552	10	121	140	84
1984	1,332	40	265	274	247	182	131	193	618	16	112	129	126
1983	1,273	31	258	242	241	179	151	171	560	12	93	112	126
1982	1,294	22	274	242	251	196	142	167	544	9	124	92	115
1981	1,335	31	306	232	212	219	132	203	566	7	133	92	100
1980	1,163	30	283	225	180	176	113	156	476	14	98	101	79
1979	1,156	43	279	224	193	150	112	155	498	12	110	110	84
1978	1,175	38	270	238	186	167	121	155	504	13	114	106	85
1977	1,284	37	269	262	190	210	136	180	571	18	90	115	104
1976	1,217	34	302	252	195	171	109	154	551	11	121	113	97
1975	1,099	34	260	237	168	151	97	152	523	14	111	107	76
1974	930	34	233	190	132	136	88	117	485	13	102	100	78
1973	781	37	194	164	140	89	60	97	358	7	96	93	77
1972	727	32	229	168	143	87	68	NA	384	18	102	91	94
1971	680	29	204	199	119	79	50	NA	363	11	94	106	62
1970	522	21	191	152	73	54	31	NA	253	10	73	81	38
1969	492	19	193	149	65	39	26	NA	236	10	86	75	41
1968	434	20	182	112	58	33	29	NA	221	12	83	61	26
1967	370	16	141	105	51	42	15	NA	199	7	78	57	32
1966	282	17	112	-----112-----		-----41-----		NA	154	10	47	-----72-----	
1965	274	30	111	------99-----		------34-----		NA	126	8	52	------47-----	
1964	234	30	78	------79-----		------47-----		NA	120	16	35	-----36-----	
1963	286	9	113	-----112-----		------52-----		NA	149	5	50	------62-----	
1962	274	16	103	-----109-----		------46-----		NA	156	5	55	-----59-----	
1961	233	9	82	-----103-----		------39-----		NA	148	5	48	------64-----	
1960	227	8	88	------90-----		------41-----		NA	125	2	43	-----55-----	
1959	222	17	74	------94-----		------37-----		NA	120	4	31	-----58-----	
1958	212	12	70	------85-----		------45-----		NA	130	5	44	-----48-----	
1957	206	15	68	------71-----		------52-----		NA	90	9	28	-----30-----	
1956	196	15	65	------80-----		------36-----		NA	124	9	38	-----48-----	
1955	155	21	31	------51-----		------52-----		NA	84	9	15	-----25-----	
BLACK ALONE NON-HISPANIC[5]													
2005	2,217	28	431	393	435	282	217	430	832	6	182	178	153

NA = Not available.

r = Revised, controlled to 1990 census based population estimates; previous 1993 data controlled to 1980 census based population estimates.

[1]Starting in 2003 respondents could identify more than one race. Except as noted, the race data in this table from 2003 onward represent those respondents who indicated only one race category.

[2]The data shown prior to 2003 consists of those identifying themselves as "Asian or Pacific Islanders."

[3]Total excludes age groups where "NA" appears in the column. This applies to people 35 and over prior to 1972 for the total population, prior to 1973 for the White alone population and the Black alone population, and prior to 1986 for the Hispanic population. Data for 1950 exclude persons aged 30 and over.

[4]Data for 1955 to 1963 are for Black and other races.

[5]This series was discontinued in 2006.

Table A-16. Age Distribution of College Students 14 Years Old and Over, by Sex, October 1947–2019—*Continued*

(Numbers in thousands; civilian noninstitutionalized population.)

Year, sex, race, and Hispanic origin	Male 25 to 29 years	Male 30 to 34 years	Male 35 years and over	Female Total	Female 14 to 17 years	Female 18 and 19 years	Female 20 and 21 years	Female 22 to 24 years	Female 25 to 29 years	Female 30 to 34 years	Female 35 years and over
2009	151	81	147	1,831	29	334	258	338	259	172	441
2008	115	82	106	1,562	15	274	246	234	261	188	345
2007	126	102	130	1,485	18	265	223	259	274	127	320
2006	112	70	163	1,438	20	291	234	255	191	130	318
2005	99	64	150	1,385	22	249	215	282	183	153	281
2004	92	41	151	1,525	27	275	229	254	259	130	350
2003[1]	100	84	105	1,346	19	209	262	255	188	130	283
2002	97	83	133	1,476	42	251	243	257	204	158	321
2001	88	90	126	1,449	26	265	245	226	195	190	302
2000	110	92	133	1,349	9	201	238	218	215	150	228
1999	93	79	123	1,164	10	221	196	227	161	120	229
1998	140	67	105	1,247	9	267	192	212	188	144	234
1997	110	65	117	1,180	17	238	184	237	149	100	255
1996	142	64	120	1,136	28	199	192	170	195	119	234
1995	65	80	122	1,062	11	199	197	162	168	113	212
1994	118	72	99	1,054	21	178	186	197	138	112	224
1993r	118	36	107	947	9	172	202	137	135	107	186
1993	116	36	102	909	8	163	191	130	129	106	182
1992	73	37	54	897	21	168	202	161	97	95	154
1991	99	55	90	848	11	166	164	120	118	102	167
1990	52	26	65	807	19	185	136	146	98	82	141
1989	65	37	47	807	24	176	186	149	91	82	99
1988	75	48	68	827	27	173	183	99	113	94	138
1987	99	37	62	764	19	186	140	119	121	84	93
1986	81	64	74	779	7	187	131	144	106	79	124
1985	64	40	93	712	11	138	134	117	119	72	121
1984	99	62	74	714	24	153	145	121	83	69	119
1983	91	64	62	714	19	164	131	116	88	87	109
1982	91	51	62	750	12	150	150	136	105	92	105
1981	115	57	62	769	24	172	140	112	105	75	141
1980	92	53	39	686	16	185	124	101	84	60	116
1979	71	47	64	659	31	169	114	109	79	66	91
1978	82	52	52	671	25	155	133	102	85	68	103
1977	101	62	81	712	19	179	147	87	108	74	98
1976	90	57	62	665	23	181	139	97	81	52	92
1975	82	53	80	577	20	150	130	92	69	44	72
1974	70	60	62	448	22	131	91	55	66	28	55
1973	49	36	NA	325	30	97	71	63	40	24	NA
1972	49	30	NA	343	14	127	77	49	38	38	NA
1971	58	31	NA	317	18	109	93	57	21	19	NA
1970	33	19	NA	269	11	118	71	36	22	11	NA
1969	15	10	NA	256	9	108	74	24	25	17	NA
1968	27	13	NA	213	8	100	51	32	7	15	NA
1967	15	11	NA	171	9	63	48	19	27	4	NA
1966	-----25-----		NA	128	7	65	-----40-----			-----16-----	NA
1965	-----19-----		NA	148	22	59	-----52-----			-----15-----	NA
1964	-----33-----		NA	114	14	43	-----43-----			-----14-----	NA
1963	-----32-----		NA	137	4	63	-----50-----			-----20-----	NA
1962	-----37-----		NA	118	11	48	-----50-----			-----9-----	NA
1961	-----31-----		NA	85	4	34	-----39-----			-----8-----	NA
1960	-----25-----		NA	102	6	45	-----35-----			-----16-----	NA
1959	-----27-----		NA	102	13	43	-----36-----			-----10-----	NA
1958	-----33-----		NA	82	7	26	-----37-----			-----12-----	NA
1957	-----23-----		NA	116	6	40	-----41-----			-----29-----	NA
1956	-----29-----		NA	72	6	27	-----32-----			-----7-----	NA
1955	-----35-----		NA	71	12	16	-----26-----			-----17-----	NA
BLACK ALONE NON-HISPANIC[5]											
2005	99	64	150	1,385	22	249	215	282	183	153	281

NA = Not available.

r = Revised, controlled to 1990 census based population estimates; previous 1993 data controlled to 1980 census based population estimates.

[1]Starting in 2003 respondents could identify more than one race. Except as noted, the race data in this table from 2003 onward represent those respondents who indicated only one race category.

[2]The data shown prior to 2003 consists of those identifying themselves as "Asian or Pacific Islanders."

[3]Total excludes age groups where "NA" appears in the column. This applies to people 35 and over prior to 1972 for the total population, prior to 1973 for the White alone population and the Black alone population, and prior to 1986 for the Hispanic population. Data for 1950 exclude persons aged 30 and over.

[4]Data for 1955 to 1963 are for Black and other races.

[5]This series was discontinued in 2006.

Table A-16. Age Distribution of College Students 14 Years Old and Over, by Sex, October 1947–2019—*Continued*

(Numbers in thousands; civilian noninstitutionalized population.)

Year, sex, race, and Hispanic origin	All students								Male				
	Total	14 to 17 years	18 and 19 years	20 and 21 years	22 to 24 years	25 to 29 years	30 to 34 years	35 years and over	Total	14 to 17 years	18 and 19 years	20 and 21 years	22 to 24 years
2004	2,231	40	430	392	379	344	163	483	760	13	161	166	143
2003[1]	2,090	28	368	399	423	282	205	385	773	10	166	145	177
2002	2,217	56	428	410	358	293	233	439	782	14	177	174	113
2001	2,173	33	430	373	375	263	275	423	759	7	174	137	150
2000	2,119	19	439	373	370	321	242	355	798	10	154	137	164
1999	1,952	45	413	390	320	250	192	342	811	35	192	193	99
1998	1,971	22	453	351	282	322	211	331	752	12	194	159	83
1997	1,868	21	371	314	378	253	161	369	712	7	138	137	143
1996	1,863	41	342	342	281	329	176	350	750	17	142	155	122
1995	1,745	24	332	337	302	231	189	330	699	13	136	142	143
1994	1,783	36	308	347	342	253	182	314	734	16	131	161	145
1993	1,505	13	310	291	246	232	134	279	615	4	149	105	121
ASIAN[2]													
2019	1,768	37	323	430	379	302	166	133	870	22	161	205	186
2018	1,691	19	291	414	374	314	152	128	846	13	139	226	193
2017	1,581	32	260	430	411	262	90	95	750	7	122	213	227
2016	1,585	19	255	358	390	328	108	127	835	4	135	177	222
2015	1,616	20	235	421	370	291	135	143	752	10	112	193	188
2014	1,543	19	270	305	447	273	80	148	797	14	136	158	255
2013	1,576	30	302	340	359	261	111	174	789	8	154	188	193
2012	1,447	26	253	289	372	247	116	143	700	15	129	140	185
2011	1,204	21	240	281	227	189	99	147	567	6	131	141	107
2010	1,322	32	234	308	269	237	117	126	647	17	116	150	124
2009	1,231	11	243	216	308	197	114	141	613	8	134	97	153
2008	1,220	27	172	247	236	245	137	156	567	22	75	123	96
2007	1,103	10	201	204	252	206	123	105	533	2	104	106	108
2006	1,084	8	204	215	242	187	103	125	535	5	113	121	104
2005	1,184	22	188	272	234	226	114	129	605	10	90	163	113
2004	1,191	20	182	245	269	217	113	146	636	11	92	135	145
2003[1]	1,162	16	209	219	264	228	108	116	606	3	103	104	130
2002	1,258	28	236	269	299	182	105	140	649	8	121	137	160
2001	1,280	17	247	245	302	265	90	115	664	10	113	127	177
2000	1,049	12	212	200	227	188	81	130	517	4	108	109	120
1999	1,041	16	223	192	211	187	71	142	506	11	93	95	96
HISPANIC (OF ANY RACE)													
2019	3,555	40	872	867	730	485	229	333	1,559	11	409	408	310
2018	3,574	58	890	885	656	562	218	306	1,613	17	392	405	292
2017	3,574	80	931	769	710	530	187	368	1,529	30	413	311	321
2016	3,661	89	884	948	732	491	191	326	1,582	28	383	437	327
2015	3,374	43	776	930	663	459	189	315	1,484	23	315	421	327
2014	3,295	52	857	797	628	441	189	332	1,441	11	385	356	275
2013	3,219	43	727	773	692	417	222	345	1,438	19	295	352	321
2012	3,400	61	827	912	664	365	257	313	1,510	26	372	421	316
2011	2,953	36	765	740	574	407	175	256	1,438	23	351	376	279
2010	2,879	41	783	517	514	424	228	373	1,302	19	381	242	196
2009	2,434	43	550	482	433	373	217	336	1,080	23	242	221	200
2008	2,227	53	528	407	402	359	141	337	1,042	31	236	210	169
2007	2,172	41	559	412	404	332	155	269	880	16	246	154	160
2006	1,968	54	444	386	353	271	190	271	808	19	213	146	164
2005	1,942	31	406	420	389	288	150	257	804	10	173	183	183
2004	1,975	23	384	431	407	280	179	271	852	5	171	212	191
2003	1,714	12	379	407	329	224	156	207	703	7	153	167	145
2002	1,656	15	360	303	316	274	140	249	705	3	156	151	132
2001	1,700	14	387	342	306	255	136	260	731	6	149	145	156
2000	1,426	24	349	268	282	167	142	194	619	12	160	118	123
1999	1,307	7	297	197	247	207	127	225	568	2	143	84	96

NA = Not available.
r = Revised, controlled to 1990 census based population estimates; previous 1993 data controlled to 1980 census based population estimates.
[1]Starting in 2003 respondents could identify more than one race. Except as noted, the race data in this table from 2003 onward represent those respondents who indicated only one race category.
[2]The data shown prior to 2003 consists of those identifying themselves as "Asian or Pacific Islanders."
[3]Total excludes age groups where "NA" appears in the column. This applies to people 35 and over prior to 1972 for the total population, prior to 1973 for the White alone population and the Black alone population, and prior to 1986 for the Hispanic population. Data for 1950 exclude persons aged 30 and over.
[4]Data for 1955 to 1963 are for Black and other races.
[5]This series was discontinued in 2006.

Table A-16. Age Distribution of College Students 14 Years Old and Over, by Sex, October 1947–2019—*Continued*

(Numbers in thousands; civilian noninstitutionalized population.)

Year, sex, race, and Hispanic origin	Male			Female							
	25 to 29 years	30 to 34 years	35 years and over	Total	14 to 17 years	18 and 19 years	20 and 21 years	22 to 24 years	25 to 29 years	30 to 34 years	35 years and over
2004	92	38	147	1,471	27	268	227	237	251	125	336
2003[1]	93	80	102	1,317	19	202	254	246	188	125	283
2002	95	83	126	1,435	42	251	237	244	198	150	313
2001	78	90	123	1,414	26	256	236	226	186	185	300
2000	110	92	130	1,321	9	285	235	206	211	150	225
1999	91	76	125	1,141	10	221	196	221	159	117	218
1998	134	67	102	1,219	9	259	192	199	180	144	229
1997	105	65	117	1,156	14	233	177	235	149	96	252
1996	134	64	117	1,113	25	199	188	160	195	113	234
1995	65	80	120	1,046	11	196	195	159	167	109	210
1994	116	72	93	1,049	21	178	186	197	138	109	221
1993	104	33	100	890	8	161	186	125	128	102	179
ASIAN[2]											
2019	162	71	63	898	14	162	224	193	140	94	70
2018	166	61	48	844	6	151	188	181	148	91	80
2017	127	30	25	831	25	138	217	184	135	60	71
2016	177	53	68	749	15	120	181	168	151	55	59
2015	138	61	49	864	10	123	229	182	153	74	94
2014	149	26	59	746	5	134	147	192	124	55	89
2013	151	38	58	787	22	148	152	166	110	73	116
2012	131	44	55	747	11	124	148	187	116	72	88
2011	92	45	45	637	16	109	140	120	97	54	101
2010	126	58	57	676	15	118	158	145	111	59	69
2009	96	53	73	619	4	109	120	155	101	61	68
2008	132	61	58	653	5	97	123	140	113	76	98
2007	98	60	54	569	8	97	98	144	108	63	51
2006	80	51	61	549	3	91	94	139	107	52	64
2005	110	61	58	579	12	98	109	120	116	53	71
2004	116	65	71	556	9	89	110	124	101	48	75
2003[1]	141	67	59	556	13	107	115	134	88	42	57
2002	101	56	67	609	19	115	132	139	82	49	73
2001	134	63	40	616	6	134	118	125	131	27	75
2000	66	51	60	532	8	104	91	107	122	30	69
1999	97	47	67	534	5	130	97	115	89	24	74
HISPANIC (OF ANY RACE)											
2019	211	73	137	1,996	29	463	459	420	274	155	195
2018	261	116	131	1,960	41	498	480	364	301	102	175
2017	219	104	132	2,045	50	518	457	390	312	83	236
2016	210	76	120	2,079	60	501	511	405	281	115	206
2015	192	69	136	1,890	20	461	508	336	267	120	179
2014	222	47	144	1,855	40	472	441	352	219	142	188
2013	237	84	130	1,781	24	432	421	371	180	138	215
2012	155	72	148	1,890	35	454	491	348	211	185	166
2011	212	67	130	1,515	13	414	364	294	196	108	126
2010	197	108	159	1,576	21	402	275	319	227	119	213
2009	159	108	127	1,354	20	308	261	234	214	108	209
2008	186	76	135	1,185	23	292	197	233	173	65	202
2007	145	57	102	1,292	25	313	258	244	187	98	167
2006	109	64	94	1,161	36	231	240	189	162	126	177
2005	111	52	92	1,137	21	232	237	206	178	90	165
2004	131	53	89	1,123	19	213	219	216	150	126	182
2003	93	61	77	1,011	5	226	240	185	131	95	130
2002	118	49	97	951	12	204	152	184	156	92	152
2001	116	57	102	969	8	238	197	150	139	80	157
2000	61	75	70	807	13	188	150	160	106	67	124
1999	94	54	95	739	5	154	113	151	113	73	130

NA = Not available.

r = Revised, controlled to 1990 census based population estimates; previous 1993 data controlled to 1980 census based population estimates.

[1]Starting in 2003 respondents could identify more than one race. Except as noted, the race data in this table from 2003 onward represent those respondents who indicated only one race category.

[2]The data shown prior to 2003 consists of those identifying themselves as "Asian or Pacific Islanders."

[3]Total excludes age groups where "NA" appears in the column. This applies to people 35 and over prior to 1972 for the total population, prior to 1973 for the White alone population and the Black alone population, and prior to 1986 for the Hispanic population. Data for 1950 exclude persons aged 30 and over.

[4]Data for 1955 to 1963 are for Black and other races.

[5]This series was discontinued in 2006.

Table A-16. Age Distribution of College Students 14 Years Old and Over, by Sex, October 1947–2019—*Continued*

(Numbers in thousands; civilian noninstitutionalized population.)

Year, sex, race, and Hispanic origin	All students								Male				
	Total	14 to 17 years	18 and 19 years	20 and 21 years	22 to 24 years	25 to 29 years	30 to 34 years	35 years and over	Total	14 to 17 years	18 and 19 years	20 and 21 years	22 to 24 years
1998	1,363	9	288	263	269	206	130	198	550	—	97	139	110
1997	1,260	49	316	254	236	174	80	151	555	15	133	132	106
1996	1,223	22	240	213	253	198	112	184	529	8	98	78	124
1995	1,207	20	264	245	236	153	97	193	568	14	121	111	124
1994	1,187	9	225	230	207	180	132	205	529	3	89	115	108
1993r	1,169	17	222	299	207	178	106	139	539	7	81	154	103
1993	995	15	195	241	166	149	100	129	442	6	69	118	79
1992	918	17	230	200	156	124	90	102	388	9	93	80	74
1991	830	10	188	203	125	124	72	109	347	5	68	79	64
1990	748	13	148	188	99	109	59	130	364	12	70	80	64
1989	754	17	177	134	142	112	58	114	353	5	75	66	70
1988	747	13	203	110	137	118	73	93	355	9	75	76	77
1987	739	8	152	155	148	137	67	73	390	3	76	100	71
1986	794	16	171	146	141	164	67	89	377	4	92	67	74
1985	580	16	127	128	120	111	78	NA	279	10	44	53	71
1984	524	5	136	133	93	100	57	NA	231	2	42	63	49
1983	521	17	134	124	91	114	41	NA	253	10	41	61	50
1982	494	16	143	104	90	94	47	NA	216	6	52	47	42
1981	510	15	129	123	90	103	50	NA	258	6	57	68	39
1980	443	10	137	94	84	69	49	NA	222	2	68	52	34
1979	439	18	124	95	73	73	56	NA	225	8	67	43	43
1978	377	15	109	68	77	78	30	NA	196	7	53	30	43
1977	417	14	123	95	59	81	45	NA	224	6	54	45	40
1976	426	13	143	83	83	73	31	NA	223	3	69	39	42
1975	411	13	118	101	76	68	35	NA	218	3	53	52	40
1974	354	11	112	96	64	39	32	NA	195	6	55	44	42
1973	289	15	82	69	55	45	23	NA	168	11	39	37	29
1972	242	14	70	60	49	34	15	NA	126	7	28	35	29
WHITE ALONE OR IN COMBINATION													
2019	13,375	167	3,100	3,436	2,504	1,657	858	1,652	5,903	56	1,389	1,641	1,086
2018	13,885	178	3,336	3,316	2,522	1,935	900	1,697	6,229	67	1,510	1,543	1,172
2017	13,703	168	3,121	3,306	2,621	1,904	885	1,698	6,059	64	1,370	1,533	1,212
2016	14,355	180	3,316	3,418	2,712	2,099	942	1,687	6,415	60	1,547	1,602	1,284
2015	14,295	165	3,163	3,416	2,689	2,072	972	1,818	6,425	81	1,472	1,627	1,220
2014	14,310	154	3,154	3,299	2,877	1,982	910	1,935	6,549	73	1,433	1,646	1,318
2013	14,743	246	3,124	3,292	3,005	1,942	988	2,145	6,500	123	1,433	1,521	1,369
2012	15,117	216	3,144	3,574	2,897	2,099	1,058	2,130	6,612	98	1,429	1,547	1,423
2011	15,785	141	3,381	3,631	3,031	2,316	1,124	2,160	7,239	78	1,554	1,719	1,517
2010	15,586	157	3,478	3,359	2,687	2,287	1,220	2,399	7,030	60	1,620	1,656	1,196
2009	15,391	160	3,414	3,289	2,859	2,125	1,133	2,411	6,848	77	1,535	1,591	1,387
2008	14,738	175	3,440	3,181	2,738	2,003	936	2,264	6,730	87	1,607	1,550	1,286
2007	14,114	147	3,318	3,111	2,529	1,857	978	2,174	6,169	64	1,540	1,390	1,186
2006	13,564	166	3,043	3,006	2,416	1,791	1,016	2,125	5,966	61	1,399	1,363	1,161
2005	13,791	125	3,043	3,244	2,433	1,740	954	2,251	5,978	43	1,371	1,519	1,128
2004	13,668	135	3,012	3,106	2,425	1,807	989	2,192	6,068	49	1,331	1,494	1,131
2003	13,164	106	2,905	2,868	2,584	1,613	989	2,099	5,837	48	1,283	1,274	1,257
BLACK ALONE OR IN COMBINATION													
2019	3,142	43	591	636	564	506	261	540	1,309	24	267	310	220
2018	3,272	23	611	643	586	595	258	557	1,305	11	277	305	241
2017	3,068	47	597	606	579	493	225	520	1,273	13	269	267	231
2016	3,079	35	602	607	572	430	261	572	1,283	14	250	280	247
2015	2,985	28	560	602	580	421	244	551	1,216	14	259	269	305
2014	3,099	56	553	562	530	432	259	707	1,181	40	192	244	223
2013	3,118	36	509	716	581	499	228	550	1,238	22	210	306	263
2012	3,335	33	579	721	592	465	348	598	1,292	22	244	353	263

NA = Not available.

r = Revised, controlled to 1990 census based population estimates; previous 1993 data controlled to 1980 census based population estimates.

[1]Starting in 2003 respondents could identify more than one race. Except as noted, the race data in this table from 2003 onward represent those respondents who indicated only one race category.

[2]The data shown prior to 2003 consists of those identifying themselves as "Asian or Pacific Islanders."

[3]Total excludes age groups where "NA" appears in the column. This applies to people 35 and over prior to 1972 for the total population, prior to 1973 for the White alone population and the Black alone population, and prior to 1986 for the Hispanic population. Data for 1950 exclude persons aged 30 and over.

[4]Data for 1955 to 1963 are for Black and other races.

[5]This series was discontinued in 2006.

Table A-16. Age Distribution of College Students 14 Years Old and Over, by Sex, October 1947–2019—*Continued*

(Numbers in thousands; civilian noninstitutionalized population.)

Year, sex, race, and Hispanic origin	Male			Female							
	25 to 29 years	30 to 34 years	35 years and over	Total	14 to 17 years	18 and 19 years	20 and 21 years	22 to 24 years	25 to 29 years	30 to 34 years	35 years and over
1998	86	54	64	814	9	191	124	159	120	77	134
1997	78	31	60	704	34	183	123	130	96	49	91
1996	79	54	90	693	15	142	136	128	119	59	95
1995	71	55	73	639	6	143	134	112	82	42	120
1994	73	55	86	659	6	136	115	99	106	78	119
1993r	71	67	56	630	10	141	145	104	107	40	83
1993	57	63	51	553	9	126	123	87	93	38	78
1992	57	35	40	530	7	137	120	82	67	55	62
1991	64	30	37	483	5	120	124	61	59	42	72
1990	39	30	67	384	1	78	108	35	70	29	63
1989	63	31	42	401	11	103	69	72	49	27	71
1988	48	29	43	391	4	129	35	60	70	43	51
1987	77	42	21	349	5	76	56	76	60	25	51
1986	80	26	34	417	12	79	80	67	84	41	54
1985	72	29	NA	299	6	82	75	48	39	49	NA
1984	49	26	NA	292	3	94	70	43	51	31	NA
1983	74	17	NA	270	7	93	64	41	40	25	NA
1982	49	20	NA	278	10	91	57	48	45	27	NA
1981	55	33	NA	252	9	72	55	51	48	17	NA
1980	36	30	NA	221	8	63	42	50	33	20	NA
1979	39	25	NA	215	10	58	52	30	34	31	NA
1978	49	14	NA	181	8	56	38	34	29	16	NA
1977	56	23	NA	194	8	70	50	19	25	22	NA
1976	50	20	NA	203	9	74	45	41	23	11	NA
1975	45	25	NA	193	10	65	49	36	23	10	NA
1974	24	24	NA	157	5	56	51	22	15	8	NA
1973	32	20	NA	123	5	44	33	25	13	3	NA
1972	20	7	NA	117	7	43	25	20	14	8	NA
WHITE ALONE OR IN COMBINATION											
2019	753	358	619	7,471	111	1,712	1,795	1,418	904	500	1,032
2018	866	424	647	7,655	111	1,826	1,773	1,350	1,069	476	1,050
2017	847	409	623	7,644	104	1,751	1,772	1,408	1,057	476	1,076
2016	876	396	651	7,940	121	1,770	1,816	1,428	1,224	546	1,036
2015	942	423	658	7,870	84	1,691	1,780	1,469	1,129	548	1,160
2014	947	385	748	7,761	81	1,720	1,653	1,559	1,036	525	1,187
2013	905	411	738	8,243	123	1,691	1,771	1,637	1,037	577	1,407
2012	915	442	759	8,505	119	1,715	2,027	1,473	1,184	615	1,372
2011	1,046	496	830	8,545	63	1,828	1,912	1,514	1,270	627	1,330
2010	1,080	516	902	8,556	97	1,858	1,702	1,491	1,207	703	1,497
2009	930	501	826	8,544	84	1,879	1,698	1,473	1,195	631	1,585
2008	966	426	807	8,008	88	1,833	1,631	1,452	1,037	510	1,457
2007	789	425	774	7,945	82	1,779	1,721	1,343	1,068	553	1,400
2006	827	411	744	7,598	105	1,643	1,643	1,255	964	605	1,382
2005	696	424	796	7,813	82	1,672	1,725	1,305	1,044	530	1,454
2004	847	425	792	7,600	86	1,682	1,612	1,295	960	564	1,401
2003	730	446	798	7,328	57	1,622	1,594	1,327	883	543	1,302
BLACK ALONE OR IN COMBINATION											
2019	224	87	178	1,833	20	324	326	345	282	174	362
2018	243	73	156	1,968	12	334	338	345	352	185	401
2017	208	82	203	1,794	34	320	339	347	286	144	317
2016	195	102	194	1,797	21	352	328	325	234	159	378
2015	150	63	156	1,770	14	300	332	275	271	181	396
2014	173	88	220	1,919	17	360	318	307	259	171	486
2013	192	54	190	1,880	14	299	409	317	306	174	360
2012	149	89	174	2,043	11	335	368	329	316	259	424

NA = Not available.

r = Revised, controlled to 1990 census based population estimates; previous 1993 data controlled to 1980 census based population estimates.

[1]Starting in 2003 respondents could identify more than one race. Except as noted, the race data in this table from 2003 onward represent those respondents who indicated only one race category.

[2]The data shown prior to 2003 consists of those identifying themselves as "Asian or Pacific Islanders."

[3]Total excludes age groups where "NA" appears in the column. This applies to people 35 and over prior to 1972 for the total population, prior to 1973 for the White alone population and the Black alone population, and prior to 1986 for the Hispanic population. Data for 1950 exclude persons aged 30 and over.

[4]Data for 1955 to 1963 are for Black and other races.

[5]This series was discontinued in 2006.

Table A-16. Age Distribution of College Students 14 Years Old and Over, by Sex, October 1947–2019—*Continued*

(Numbers in thousands; civilian noninstitutionalized population.)

Year, sex, race, and Hispanic origin	All students								Male				
	Total	14 to 17 years	18 and 19 years	20 and 21 years	22 to 24 years	25 to 29 years	30 to 34 years	35 years and over	Total	14 to 17 years	18 and 19 years	20 and 21 years	22 to 24 years
2011.........................	3,317	39	615	540	605	533	321	665	1,279	23	250	264	249
2010.........................	3,250	38	622	653	533	463	286	655	1,241	19	264	271	244
2009.........................	3,030	34	604	520	574	428	268	601	1,109	5	245	250	217
2008.........................	2,619	36	515	490	429	400	278	470	983	21	219	229	184
2007.........................	2,630	33	530	459	479	432	243	455	1,077	12	240	229	217
2006.........................	2,444	30	492	423	471	318	217	493	951	10	186	186	206
2005.........................	2,387	31	481	428	462	299	229	458	895	9	201	189	167
2004.........................	2,412	40	466	436	416	371	170	512	827	13	175	187	159
2003.........................	2,227	30	400	440	445	303	214	395	826	10	175	165	186
ASIAN ALONE OR IN COMBINATION													
2019.........................	1,999	47	368	525	419	326	181	134	977	22	172	256	210
2018.........................	1,919	19	360	504	402	350	152	133	951	13	172	258	211
2017.........................	1,750	32	297	488	438	286	101	108	822	7	133	236	243
2016.........................	1,780	22	313	421	427	346	118	133	937	7	159	211	254
2015.........................	1,821	21	287	488	407	315	156	147	840	11	141	218	202
2014.........................	1,712	19	296	347	490	310	90	161	878	14	146	175	278
2013.........................	1,766	31	350	394	412	274	117	188	872	8	171	221	221
2012.........................	1,617	33	274	348	421	266	124	151	774	21	143	165	202
2011.........................	1,356	21	267	323	243	220	121	161	658	6	145	162	123
2010.........................	1,467	37	264	343	298	268	125	133	740	20	136	177	141
2009.........................	1,334	11	271	242	330	207	122	150	656	8	138	115	165
2008.........................	1,340	27	214	265	259	260	149	167	632	22	93	134	113
2007.........................	1,204	11	232	220	268	232	126	116	592	2	113	116	123
2006.........................	1,154	9	215	227	263	198	110	131	566	6	118	122	122
2005.........................	1,297	25	204	292	277	240	122	137	640	13	97	170	124
2003.........................	1,262	19	236	248	290	232	117	121	649	3	112	115	143

NA = Not available.

r = Revised, controlled to 1990 census based population estimates; previous 1993 data controlled to 1980 census based population estimates.

[1]Starting in 2003 respondents could identify more than one race. Except as noted, the race data in this table from 2003 onward represent those respondents who indicated only one race category.

[2]The data shown prior to 2003 consists of those identifying themselves as "Asian or Pacific Islanders."

[3]Total excludes age groups where "NA" appears in the column. This applies to people 35 and over prior to 1972 for the total population, prior to 1973 for the White alone population and the Black alone population, and prior to 1986 for the Hispanic population. Data for 1950 exclude persons aged 30 and over.

[4]Data for 1955 to 1963 are for Black and other races.

[5]This series was discontinued in 2006.

Table A-16. Age Distribution of College Students 14 Years Old and Over, by Sex, October 1947–2019—*Continued*

(Numbers in thousands; civilian noninstitutionalized population.)

Year, sex, race, and Hispanic origin	Male			Female							
	25 to 29 years	30 to 34 years	35 years and over	Total	14 to 17 years	18 and 19 years	20 and 21 years	22 to 24 years	25 to 29 years	30 to 34 years	35 years and over
2011.............................	196	100	198	2,037	16	365	276	356	337	221	467
2010.............................	186	78	180	2,009	20	358	383	289	277	208	474
2009.............................	155	88	149	1,921	29	359	270	357	274	180	451
2008.............................	127	85	116	1,636	15	296	261	245	272	193	354
2007.............................	139	110	130	1,553	20	290	230	263	292	133	325
2006.............................	120	74	170	1,493	20	307	238	265	198	143	323
2005.............................	109	66	154	1,493	22	280	239	295	190	164	303
2004.............................	100	41	153	1,584	27	290	249	258	271	130	359
2003.............................	100	84	107	1,401	20	225	275	260	203	130	288
ASIAN ALONE OR IN COMBINATION											
2019.............................	174	81	63	1,022	24	196	269	209	153	100	71
2018.............................	182	61	53	968	6	187	246	191	168	91	80
2017.............................	131	40	32	928	25	164	252	195	155	60	76
2016.............................	178	59	70	843	15	153	209	174	169	60	63
2015.............................	151	67	49	981	10	146	270	205	164	88	98
2014.............................	166	30	68	834	5	150	171	212	145	60	92
2013.............................	153	38	60	894	22	179	173	191	121	78	128
2012.............................	140	44	58	843	11	131	183	219	126	80	94
2011.............................	110	60	53	697	16	122	161	121	110	61	108
2010.............................	149	61	57	721	17	128	166	157	119	63	76
2009.............................	98	57	76	678	4	134	127	165	109	65	74
2008.............................	135	70	65	708	5	121	131	146	125	79	102
2007.............................	113	61	64	612	9	119	104	145	110	65	52
2006.............................	81	55	62	588	3	97	105	141	117	55	69
2005.............................	113	63	60	657	12	107	122	153	128	59	77
2003.............................	142	72	61	613	16	124	133	147	89	44	60

NA = Not available.

r = Revised, controlled to 1990 census based population estimates; previous 1993 data controlled to 1980 census based population estimates.

[1] Starting in 2003 respondents could identify more than one race. Except as noted, the race data in this table from 2003 onward represent those respondents who indicated only one race category.

[2] The data shown prior to 2003 consists of those identifying themselves as "Asian or Pacific Islanders."

[3] Total excludes age groups where "NA" appears in the column. This applies to people 35 and over prior to 1972 for the total population, prior to 1973 for the White alone population and the Black alone population, and prior to 1986 for the Hispanic population. Data for 1950 exclude persons aged 30 and over.

[4] Data for 1955 to 1963 are for Black and other races.

[5] This series was discontinued in 2006.

Table A-17. College Enrollment of Students 14 Years Old and Over, by Type of College, Attendance Status, Age, and Sex, October 1970–2019

(Numbers in thousands; civilian noninstitutionalized population.)

Year and type of college	All students Total	14 to 19 years	20 to 21 years	22 to 24 years	25 to 34 years	35 years and over	Public	Private	Male Total	Full-time	Part-time	Female Total	Full-time	Part-time
ALL UNDERGRADUATES														
2019	14,586	4,212	4,307	2,543	2,202	1,322	12,317	2,268	6,567	5,244	1,323	8,019	6,237	1,782
2018	14,827	4,393	4,237	2,607	2,322	1,269	12,457	2,370	6,727	5,494	1,233	8,100	6,231	1,869
2017	14,589	4,126	4,261	2,615	2,295	1,293	12,236	2,353	6,581	5,210	1,371	8,008	6,125	1,884
2016	15,497	4,369	4,295	2,916	2,489	1,427	12,523	2,974	7,075	5,630	1,445	8,422	6,486	1,936
2015	15,433	4,165	4,371	2,774	2,570	1,553	12,762	2,671	7,002	5,477	1,525	8,431	6,438	1,992
2014	15,498	4,249	4,075	2,978	2,438	1,759	12,877	2,620	7,071	5,713	1,358	8,427	6,524	1,903
2013	15,738	4,202	4,159	3,052	2,598	1,727	13,129	2,609	7,097	5,606	1,492	8,641	6,507	2,133
2012	16,170	4,236	4,420	3,025	2,783	1,706	13,451	2,719	7,107	5,603	1,505	9,063	6,789	2,274
2011	16,625	4,435	4,368	3,000	3,019	1,802	13,816	2,809	7,515	5,830	1,685	9,110	6,908	2,202
2010	16,354	4,546	4,225	2,671	2,912	2,000	13,701	2,653	7,300	5,582	1,718	9,054	6,773	2,282
2009	16,012	4,463	3,965	2,849	2,737	1,999	13,356	2,656	7,121	5,632	1,488	8,891	6,686	2,205
2008	14,955	4,347	3,862	2,600	2,430	1,716	12,340	2,616	6,737	5,220	1,517	8,218	6,158	2,060
2007	14,365	4,237	3,732	2,513	2,277	1,605	11,811	2,554	6,405	5,053	1,353	7,959	5,813	2,146
2006	13,854	3,940	3,591	2,437	2,178	1,709	11,269	2,585	6,135	4,686	1,450	7,719	5,695	2,024
2005	14,169	3,901	3,847	2,588	2,142	1,690	11,292	2,876	6,189	4,799	1,391	7,979	5,852	2,127
2004	14,004	3,863	3,700	2,431	2,257	1,753	11,384	2,620	6,156	4,714	1,442	7,848	5,704	2,144
2003	13,370	3,633	3,449	2,687	2,094	1,506	10,980	2,389	5,902	4,476	1,425	7,468	5,391	2,077
2002	13,426	3,743	3,457	2,355	2,106	1,764	10,830	2,595	5,929	4,462	1,467	7,497	5,273	2,223
2001	12,552	3,568	3,329	2,136	1,979	1,540	10,188	2,364	5,522	4,057	1,464	7,030	4,949	2,082
2000	12,401	3,710	3,093	2,113	1,988	1,498	10,044	2,357	5,520	4,059	1,461	6,881	4,832	2,049
1999	12,046	3,625	3,043	2,000	1,885	1,493	9,689	2,357	5,554	4,143	1,411	6,492	4,548	1,945
1998	12,509	3,749	3,019	2,025	2,101	1,616	10,100	2,410	5,621	4,051	1,570	6,888	4,765	2,123
1997	12,409	3,504	3,080	2,137	1,970	1,718	10,074	2,335	5,539	4,165	1,375	6,870	4,752	2,118
1996	12,305	3,526	2,856	2,017	2,226	1,680	10,121	2,183	5,533	4,032	1,502	6,772	4,502	2,269
1995	11,966	3,251	2,881	2,033	2,151	1,651	9,570	2,396	5,413	3,911	1,501	6,554	4,433	2,121
1994	12,410	3,192	3,006	2,099	2,281	1,832	9,983	2,427	5,526	3,969	1,557	6,883	4,480	2,404
1993r	11,959	3,197	2,879	2,131	2,118	1,634	9,706	2,253	5,442	4,020	1,422	6,517	4,346	2,171
1993	11,507	3,045	2,721	2,020	2,088	1,633	9,330	2,176	5,194	3,812	1,382	6,313	4,182	2,130
1992	11,643	3,097	2,902	2,004	2,090	1,550	9,519	2,124	5,091	3,724	1,365	6,553	4,338	2,214
1991	11,374	3,061	2,902	1,757	2,120	1,534	9,257	2,117	5,120	3,724	1,395	6,254	4,145	2,109
1990	11,108	3,194	2,740	1,681	2,067	1,425	9,031	2,076	5,030	3,628	1,402	6,077	3,967	2,109
1989	10,661	3,250	2,529	1,658	1,921	1,304	8,633	2,027	4,730	3,436	1,295	5,931	3,880	2,051
1988	10,605	3,229	2,645	1,600	1,865	1,266	8,617	1,988	4,763	3,441	1,322	5,842	3,816	2,026
1987	10,304	3,283	2,585	1,512	1,848	1,076	8,306	1,998	4,878	3,476	1,403	5,426	3,445	1,981
1986	10,036	3,158	2,298	1,583	1,932	1,065	7,955	2,081	4,663	3,350	1,312	5,373	3,474	1,899
1985	10,097	3,169	2,586	1,475	1,884	984	8,042	2,055	4,667	3,454	1,213	5,430	3,578	1,852
1984	9,910	3,120	2,564	1,547	1,826	852	7,944	1,966	4,725	3,573	1,152	5,185	3,419	1,766
1983	9,925	3,200	2,464	1,475	1,873	914	7,808	2,117	4,759	3,472	1,287	5,166	3,424	1,742
1982	9,952	3,183	2,657	1,526	1,745	843	7,908	2,044	4,703	3,485	1,218	5,249	3,480	1,769
1981	9,969	3,276	2,511	1,458	1,808	916	7,789	2,180	4,724	3,452	1,273	5,245	3,490	1,755
1980	9,279	3,182	2,393	1,316	1,598	791	NA	NA	4,353	3,247	1,105	4,927	3,210	1,717
1979	9,193	3,156	2,308	1,297	1,526	905	7,331	1,861	4,387	3,219	1,168	4,805	3,163	1,642
1978	8,947	3,173	2,246	1,233	1,505	790	7,008	1,939	4,445	3,269	1,176	4,502	3,031	1,471
1977[1]	8,408	3,184	2,376	1,206	1,640	NA	6,683	1,724	4,372	3,304	1,068	4,027	3,002	1,025
1976	8,988	3,216	2,358	1,224	1,472	718	7,196	1,787	4,569	3,353	1,213	4,419	3,166	1,253
1975	8,108	3,237	2,255	1,072	1,546	NA	6,598	1,510	4,393	3,394	999	3,715	2,902	813
1974	7,338	2,906	2,131	1,028	1,272	NA	5,843	1,494	4,030	3,128	902	3,307	2,561	746
1973	6,794	2,812	2,031	924	1,028	NA	5,279	1,516	3,791	3,035	756	3,004	2,423	581
1972	6,992	2,974	2,065	944	1,011	NA	5,460	1,532	3,982	3,231	751	3,010	2,445	565
1971	6,895	3,008	1,936	1,019	931	NA	5,472	1,423	4,017	3,240	777	2,878	2,348	530
1970	6,274	2,854	1,803	866	750	NA	4,910	1,363	3,627	3,045	582	2,646	2,164	482
TWO-YEAR COLLEGE STUDENTS														
2019	4,330	1,323	991	604	833	579	4,053	277	2,041	1,342	699	2,289	1,469	820
2018	4,272	1,488	878	558	818	530	3,986	285	1,828	1,246	582	2,444	1,512	932
2017	4,272	1,292	956	644	888	491	3,979	293	1,988	1,317	671	2,284	1,372	912
2016	4,346	1,363	876	692	903	512	4,054	293	2,040	1,350	690	2,306	1,432	875
2015	4,717	1,433	1,104	632	912	637	4,344	373	2,124	1,379	745	2,593	1,669	924
2014	4,841	1,432	989	734	973	714	4,410	431	2,056	1,363	693	2,786	1,839	946
2013	5,270	1,502	1,052	938	1,008	770	4,920	350	2,390	1,617	772	2,881	1,865	1,016
2012	5,830	1,624	1,307	892	1,205	802	5,377	453	2,509	1,665	844	3,321	2,119	1,201

* = Quantity equals zero or rounds to zero.
NA = Not available.
r = Revised, controlled to 1990 census based population estimates; previous 1993 data controlled to 1980 census based population estimates.
[1]Data for 1970–1975 and 1977 do not include people ages 35 and over.

Table A-17. College Enrollment of Students 14 Years Old and Over, by Type of College, Attendance Status, Age, and Sex, October 1970–2019—*Continued*

(Numbers in thousands; civilian noninstitutionalized population.)

Year and type of college	Full time						Part time					
	Total	14 to 19 years	20 to 21 years	22 to 24 years	25 to 34 years	35 years and over	Total	14 to 19 years	20 to 21 years	22 to 24 years	25 to 34 years	35 years and over
ALL UNDERGRADUATES												
2019	11,480	3,915	3,739	1,955	1,291	580	3,105	298	568	588	911	741
2018	11,725	4,062	3,746	2,024	1,283	611	3,102	331	491	583	1,039	658
2017	11,334	3,768	3,832	1,962	1,268	505	3,255	358	429	654	1,027	788
2016	12,116	4,011	3,757	2,314	1,398	637	3,381	359	539	602	1,091	790
2015	11,915	3,751	3,848	2,170	1,424	722	3,518	414	523	604	1,146	831
2014	12,237	3,943	3,620	2,338	1,542	794	3,260	306	465	640	895	964
2013	12,113	3,823	3,627	2,250	1,608	805	3,625	379	532	802	990	922
2012	12,391	3,820	3,804	2,369	1,675	723	3,779	416	616	655	1,109	983
2011	12,738	4,059	3,855	2,235	1,758	832	3,887	376	514	766	1,261	970
2010	12,354	4,032	3,653	2,071	1,674	924	4,000	514	572	599	1,237	1,077
2009	12,318	4,128	3,534	2,276	1,547	833	3,694	335	431	573	1,189	1,165
2008	11,378	3,999	3,445	2,017	1,240	676	3,577	347	417	583	1,190	1,040
2007	10,866	3,879	3,282	1,858	1,285	562	3,499	358	450	656	992	1,043
2006	10,380	3,567	3,150	1,810	1,242	612	3,474	373	441	627	936	1,097
2005	10,651	3,540	3,369	1,977	1,139	625	3,518	360	479	611	1,003	1,065
2004	10,418	3,533	3,251	1,836	1,150	648	3,586	330	449	595	1,107	1,105
2003	9,868	3,299	2,992	1,948	1,081	547	3,502	334	457	739	1,013	959
2002	9,735	3,356	3,058	1,737	1,073	511	3,690	387	399	619	1,033	1,253
2001	9,006	3,190	2,840	1,524	976	476	3,546	378	489	612	1,003	1,064
2000	8,891	3,368	2,658	1,479	930	457	3,510	342	435	633	1,058	1,041
1999	8,691	3,280	2,625	1,485	888	412	3,355	345	418	514	997	1,081
1998	8,816	3,327	2,619	1,461	956	452	3,693	421	400	563	1,145	1,164
1997	8,917	3,144	2,704	1,576	960	532	3,492	360	376	560	1,010	1,186
1996	8,534	3,131	2,480	1,516	990	437	3,771	394	396	501	1,236	1,243
1995	8,344	2,902	2,462	1,444	1,004	533	3,622	349	419	589	1,147	1,118
1994	8,449	2,843	2,585	1,455	981	586	3,961	350	421	644	1,300	1,245
1993r	8,366	2,866	2,513	1,513	941	533	3,593	332	366	619	1,176	1,102
1993	7,994	2,732	2,380	1,429	927	527	3,513	314	342	590	1,161	1,106
1992	8,063	2,838	2,506	1,427	834	458	3,580	259	396	578	1,255	1,092
1991	7,869	2,809	2,534	1,248	878	400	3,505	252	368	509	1,242	1,134
1990	7,597	2,912	2,333	1,165	824	363	3,511	282	408	515	1,244	1,062
1989	7,314	2,989	2,209	1,122	655	341	3,346	260	321	536	1,266	963
1988	7,257	2,925	2,275	1,079	691	285	3,348	303	371	521	1,173	981
1987	6,920	2,892	2,179	1,005	610	235	3,384	391	406	507	1,238	841
1986	6,825	2,880	1,973	1,055	680	237	3,212	278	324	528	1,254	828
1985	7,033	2,900	2,237	1,017	701	178	3,065	269	349	457	1,184	806
1984	6,992	2,846	2,221	1,067	689	170	2,918	274	344	480	1,139	683
1983	6,896	2,895	2,124	993	718	166	3,029	305	340	482	1,153	748
1982	6,965	2,880	2,286	979	662	159	2,987	302	372	547	1,083	684
1981	6,942	2,983	2,157	986	613	202	3,027	293	353	471	1,195	715
1980	6,457	2,897	2,107	810	500	142	2,822	283	287	505	1,098	649
1979	6,383	2,892	1,994	815	523	158	2,810	264	314	482	1,003	748
1978	6,300	2,872	1,918	820	559	132	2,647	302	328	412	947	658
1977[1]	6,304	2,855	2,075	775	598	NA	2,104	329	301	431	1,042	NA
1976	6,519	2,963	2,033	821	563	138	2,466	253	325	403	909	577
1975	6,296	2,987	1,958	696	655	NA	1,812	250	297	376	891	NA
1974	5,689	2,661	1,842	697	488	NA	1,649	245	289	331	784	NA
1973	5,460	2,629	1,801	630	398	NA	1,334	183	230	294	630	NA
1972	5,678	2,797	1,845	624	412	NA	1,314	177	220	320	599	NA
1971	5,588	2,801	1,729	700	357	NA	1,307	207	207	319	574	NA
1970	5,208	2,685	1,628	591	301	NA	1,066	169	175	275	449	NA
TWO-YEAR COLLEGE STUDENTS												
2019	2,811	1,133	672	361	418	227	1,519	190	319	242	415	353
2018	2,758	1,280	612	317	351	199	1,513	208	266	241	467	332
2017	2,689	1,039	732	391	405	122	1,583	253	225	253	483	369
2016	2,782	1,125	587	416	446	207	1,565	238	290	276	457	304
2015	3,048	1,142	792	403	457	254	1,669	291	312	229	454	383
2014	3,202	1,225	665	474	559	279	1,639	207	324	259	415	434
2013	3,482	1,254	748	571	535	374	1,788	240	305	367	472	396
2012	3,784	1,312	938	568	631	336	2,046	312	369	324	574	466

* = Quantity equals zero or rounds to zero.
NA = Not available.
r = Revised, controlled to 1990 census based population estimates; previous 1993 data controlled to 1980 census based population estimates.
[1]Data for 1970, 1975 and 1977 do not include people ages 35 and over.

Table A-17. College Enrollment of Students 14 Years Old and Over, by Type of College, Attendance Status, Age, and Sex, October 1970–2019—*Continued*

(Numbers in thousands; civilian noninstitutionalized population.)

Year and type of college	Total	All students 14 to 19 years	20 to 21 years	22 to 24 years	25 to 34 years	35 years and over	Public	Private	Male Total	Male Full-time	Male Part-time	Female Total	Female Full-time	Female Part-time
2011	5,705	1,596	1,187	845	1,237	840	5,265	440	2,453	1,664	790	3,252	2,053	1,199
2010	5,904	1,754	1,230	836	1,170	915	5,450	454	2,693	1,803	890	3,211	2,066	1,144
2009	5,551	1,636	960	813	1,221	920	5,095	456	2,363	1,573	790	3,188	2,060	1,128
2008	5,345	1,731	1,001	726	1,095	792	5,006	339	2,331	1,487	844	3,014	1,910	1,104
2007	4,814	1,496	856	774	963	725	4,418	396	2,061	1,322	739	2,753	1,666	1,087
2006	4,294	1,367	788	573	836	731	3,878	416	1,788	1,169	620	2,506	1,531	975
2005	4,327	1,259	833	603	882	751	3,890	437	1,866	1,197	669	2,462	1,436	1,026
2004	4,340	1,243	802	568	898	829	3,939	401	1,756	1,141	615	2,584	1,461	1,123
2003	4,384	1,178	746	843	834	784	3,999	385	1,782	1,055	726	2,603	1,507	1,095
2002	4,378	1,227	777	656	880	838	3,948	431	1,884	1,102	783	2,494	1,363	1,131
2001	4,159	1,200	776	605	832	746	3,749	410	1,802	1,057	745	2,357	1,252	1,105
2000	3,881	1,232	710	525	673	741	3,590	291	1,655	969	686	2,226	1,224	1,002
1999	3,794	1,187	715	460	683	749	3,482	312	1,637	949	688	2,157	1,157	1,000
1998	4,234	1,301	701	619	839	774	3,865	369	1,845	1,049	796	2,389	1,287	1,103
1997	4,078	1,178	760	528	806	807	3,780	298	1,663	983	680	2,415	1,307	1,108
1996	4,174	1,223	669	515	922	845	3,890	284	1,752	974	778	2,423	1,235	1,187
1995	3,882	1,028	608	593	892	761	3,553	330	1,626	898	728	2,256	1,124	1,132
1994	4,208	1,063	623	621	1,011	890	3,846	362	1,704	937	766	2,504	1,234	1,270
1993r	4,345	1,131	745	648	978	843	4,024	321	1,825	1,061	764	2,520	1,317	1,203
1993	4,196	1,077	696	614	965	844	3,884	311	1,748	1,006	742	2,448	1,268	1,179
1992	4,239	1,084	789	581	988	797	3,937	302	1,688	936	751	2,551	1,268	1,283
1991	4,277	1,120	732	560	1,084	781	4,025	252	1,798	973	825	2,479	1,239	1,239
1990	3,965	1,059	689	475	967	775	3,689	276	1,624	849	775	2,340	1,103	1,237
1989	3,627	1,048	557	467	880	676	3,382	245	1,464	777	688	2,163	949	1,214
1988	3,837	1,134	665	497	879	662	3,609	228	1,542	847	695	2,295	1,054	1,241
1987	3,648	1,111	624	457	851	605	3,405	243	1,522	780	742	2,127	937	1,190
1986	3,391	1,023	506	427	875	559	3,089	302	1,466	752	714	1,924	856	1,068
1985	3,289	959	558	403	851	518	3,009	281	1,336	702	634	1,954	914	1,040
1984	3,172	994	525	442	795	417	2,875	298	1,436	834	601	1,738	829	909
1983	3,416	1,050	595	405	882	485	3,136	280	1,498	807	691	1,919	897	1,022
1982	3,448	1,088	604	494	826	437	3,164	283	1,477	854	623	1,971	961	1,011
1981	3,347	1,144	566	414	768	455	3,091	255	1,475	837	638	1,872	909	963
1980	3,107	1,079	450	417	721	441	NA	NA	1,331	768	563	1,777	798	979
1979	2,897	933	403	407	664	490	2,710	187	1,251	684	567	1,646	725	921
1978	2,904	966	427	391	670	451	2,686	218	1,368	698	669	1,537	701	835
1977¹	2,510	933	455	380	741	NA	2,362	148	1,253	681	572	1,256	691	565
1976	2,854	907	444	367	718	419	2,688	165	1,400	760	640	1,454	743	711
1975	2,561	1,024	431	354	752	NA	2,437	123	1,412	850	562	1,148	717	431
1974	2,072	834	369	305	565	NA	1,917	154	1,172	709	463	899	528	371
1973	1,797	816	278	254	449	NA	1,669	128	1,012	629	383	785	471	314
1972	1,910	883	334	267	426	NA	1,816	94	1,125	770	355	785	484	301
1971	1,830	928	307	263	331	NA	1,726	105	1,087	726	361	743	473	270
1970	1,692	895	281	234	283	NA	1,559	133	1,001	726	275	691	452	239
GRADUATE STUDENTS														
2019	3,704	42	188	893	1,544	1,037	2,429	1,275	1,500	1,004	496	2,204	1,365	839
2018	4,080	38	159	875	1,878	1,130	2,777	1,304	1,646	1,048	598	2,434	1,431	1,003
2017	3,809	53	105	1,012	1,586	1,053	2,570	1,239	1,531	994	537	2,278	1,278	1,000
2016	3,699	42	121	817	1,729	990	2,448	1,251	1,569	1,071	498	2,130	1,234	896
2015	3,668	35	134	895	1,605	998	2,413	1,255	1,482	1,043	439	2,186	1,278	908
2014	3,677	22	143	900	1,551	1,061	2,447	1,230	1,559	957	602	2,119	1,205	913
2013	3,729	57	168	873	1,468	1,164	2,385	1,344	1,439	933	506	2,291	1,182	1,108
2012	3,760	48	142	854	1,550	1,165	2,327	1,433	1,495	910	585	2,265	1,301	964
2011	3,773	11	91	868	1,598	1,205	2,318	1,454	1,617	905	712	2,156	1,261	895
2010	3,921	47	123	830	1,712	1,209	2,453	1,468	1,708	1,050	658	2,214	1,196	1,017
2009	3,752	32	70	901	1,556	1,194	2,366	1,386	1,521	852	669	2,232	1,194	1,038
2008	3,676	20	58	819	1,583	1,195	2,399	1,277	1,574	880	694	2,103	987	1,116
2007	3,591	24	62	779	1,560	1,166	2,261	1,330	1,420	819	601	2,171	971	1,200
2006	3,378	18	84	729	1,480	1,067	2,197	1,181	1,371	692	678	2,007	998	1,009
2005	3,304	7	98	574	1,458	1,167	2,143	1,161	1,349	711	638	1,955	875	1,079
2004	3,378	20	77	718	1,433	1,131	2,267	1,111	1,419	726	693	1,959	845	1,114
2003	3,268	29	84	632	1,399	1,123	2,129	1,139	1,416	774	643	1,852	849	1,003
2002	3,072	33	68	572	1,296	1,104	2,003	1,068	1,311	632	679	1,761	774	987
2001	3,321	48	91	595	1,442	1,145	2,233	1,088	1,353	614	739	1,968	784	1,184

* = Quantity equals zero or rounds to zero.
NA = Not available.
r = Revised, controlled to 1990 census based population estimates; previous 1993 data controlled to 1980 census based population estimates.
¹Data for 1970–1975 and 1977 do not include people ages 35 and over.

Table A-17. College Enrollment of Students 14 Years Old and Over, by Type of College, Attendance Status, Age, and Sex, October 1970–2019—*Continued*

(Numbers in thousands; civilian noninstitutionalized population.)

| Year and type of college | Full time | | | | | | Part time | | | | | |
	Total	14 to 19 years	20 to 21 years	22 to 24 years	25 to 34 years	35 years and over	Total	14 to 19 years	20 to 21 years	22 to 24 years	25 to 34 years	35 years and over
2011	3,716	1,341	882	458	672	363	1,989	255	306	387	564	477
2010	3,870	1,422	868	554	654	372	2,034	332	362	282	516	542
2009	3,633	1,409	689	540	641	354	1,918	227	271	274	580	566
2008	3,397	1,450	763	455	466	263	1,948	281	239	271	628	529
2007	2,988	1,276	627	425	443	219	1,826	221	230	349	520	506
2006	2,699	1,145	600	312	401	241	1,595	221	188	261	435	490
2005	2,632	1,031	605	373	393	231	1,695	228	228	230	489	520
2004	2,602	1,027	553	327	425	269	1,738	216	249	241	472	560
2003	2,563	973	516	306	429	258	1,822	205	230	457	404	526
2002	2,464	975	571	344	374	200	1,914	252	206	312	506	638
2001	2,310	951	529	301	307	222	1,850	250	247	304	524	525
2000	2,193	993	507	278	230	184	1,688	239	202	247	444	557
1999	2,105	955	498	261	230	161	1,688	231	217	199	453	588
1998	2,336	1,024	495	331	302	184	1,899	277	206	288	537	591
1997	2,290	947	522	283	327	212	1,788	231	238	245	479	595
1996	2,209	995	457	271	315	171	1,965	227	212	244	607	674
1995	2,022	810	397	298	321	195	1,860	218	211	295	571	565
1994	2,172	848	407	319	341	256	2,036	215	216	302	669	634
1993r	2,378	891	515	348	365	259	1,967	240	230	300	613	585
1993	2,274	850	483	325	360	256	1,922	227	213	288	605	588
1992	2,205	897	528	287	304	188	2,034	187	261	294	683	609
1991	2,212	915	476	269	361	191	2,065	205	256	291	723	589
1990	1,953	847	408	227	310	160	2,012	212	281	247	657	615
1989	1,725	860	368	160	210	128	1,902	188	189	307	669	548
1988	1,901	926	410	209	227	128	1,936	207	256	288	651	534
1987	1,716	830	360	192	212	105	1,932	272	256	264	639	500
1986	1,608	814	296	170	223	105	1,783	209	210	257	652	454
1985	1,615	779	341	174	244	78	1,674	180	217	229	607	440
1984	1,663	812	330	190	247	84	1,509	182	195	252	548	333
1983	1,703	855	374	159	250	65	1,713	195	221	245	631	420
1982	1,814	883	381	214	260	77	1,634	205	223	280	566	356
1981	1,745	927	357	170	188	102	1,601	217	209	243	579	353
1980	1,566	884	287	160	167	67	1,542	195	163	256	554	374
1979	1,408	749	251	156	185	68	1,489	184	152	251	480	423
1978	1,400	776	243	157	167	57	1,505	190	184	234	503	394
1977¹	1,372	718	283	162	208	NA	1,138	216	172	218	533	NA
1976	1,503	764	261	177	228	74	1,351	143	183	190	490	346
1975	1,567	865	274	155	274	NA	994	159	157	199	478	NA
1974	1,237	702	233	151	152	NA	835	132	136	154	413	NA
1973	1,100	702	164	121	111	NA	697	114	113	133	338	NA
1972	1,255	772	223	134	126	NA	655	111	111	133	300	NA
1971	1,199	797	209	124	70	NA	631	131	98	139	261	NA
1970	1,177	786	197	114	80	NA	515	109	84	120	203	NA
GRADUATE STUDENTS												
2019	2,368	42	161	755	1,018	392	1,335	*	27	138	526	644
2018	2,479	38	134	684	1,184	439	1,601	*	26	190	693	691
2017	2,272	53	85	837	946	351	1,537	*	20	175	640	702
2016	2,305	42	95	693	1,103	372	1,094	*	26	123	627	618
2015	2,321	35	105	749	1,051	381	1,347	*	29	146	555	617
2014	2,163	22	111	739	911	380	1,515	*	32	161	640	682
2013	2,115	38	143	702	866	366	1,614	18	25	171	602	790
2012	2,211	45	122	699	924	420	1,549	3	21	155	625	745
2011	2,165	6	77	604	955	444	1,607	5	14	185	643	761
2010	2,246	35	120	697	1,027	367	1,675	12	4	133	685	842
2009	2,046	26	49	704	916	351	1,707	6	20	197	641	843
2008	1,867	20	53	646	851	296	1,810	*	5	173	732	899
2007	1,790	23	59	569	815	324	1,801	1	4	210	745	842
2006	1,690	16	70	542	809	254	1,688	3	14	187	671	813
2005	1,587	4	98	423	767	294	1,717	3	*	150	691	873
2004	1,571	20	76	548	675	252	1,807	*	1	170	757	878
2003	1,622	26	76	479	738	304	1,646	3	8	153	662	820
2002	1,406	31	61	432	631	251	1,666	2	6	140	666	852
2001	1,398	38	77	455	630	197	1,923	10	14	139	812	947

* = Quantity equals zero or rounds to zero.
NA = Not available.
r = Revised, controlled to 1990 census based population estimates; previous 1993 data controlled to 1980 census based population estimates.
¹Data for 1970–1975 and 1977 do not include people ages 35 and over.

Table A-17. College Enrollment of Students 14 Years Old and Over, by Type of College, Attendance Status, Age, and Sex, October 1970–2019—*Continued*

(Numbers in thousands; civilian noninstitutionalized population.)

Year and type of college	All students								Male			Female		
	Total	14 to 19 years	20 to 21 years	22 to 24 years	25 to 34 years	35 years and over	Public	Private	Total	Full-time	Part-time	Total	Full-time	Part-time
2000	2,913	38	77	571	1,218	1,009	1,965	948	1,162	546	616	1,750	722	1,028
1999	3,157	45	77	620	1,211	1,205	1,970	1,188	1,403	699	703	1,755	722	1,033
1998	3,037	45	73	536	1,313	1,070	1,884	1,153	1,284	614	669	1,753	758	995
1997	3,027	30	63	562	1,299	1,073	2,016	1,010	1,304	651	653	1,723	668	1,055
1996	2,922	21	52	534	1,217	1,098	1,893	1,029	1,288	650	638	1,634	655	979
1995	2,749	8	60	465	1,198	1,018	1,802	947	1,290	646	644	1,459	554	905
1994	2,613	9	21	551	1,138	893	1,710	902	1,238	619	619	1,375	505	870
1993r	2,435	3	14	537	1,022	859	1,611	824	1,156	601	555	1,278	458	820
1993	2,391	3	13	514	1,006	856	1,580	812	1,130	579	551	1,261	446	815
1992	2,392	*	36	508	1,035	814	1,546	846	1,102	606	496	1,291	521	770
1991	2,683	*	37	547	1,165	934	1,824	859	1,320	688	631	1,364	491	872
1990	2,514	2	27	497	1,095	893	1,722	792	1,162	569	593	1,352	531	820
1989	2,520	*	40	509	1,161	809	1,662	857	1,219	626	594	1,300	515	786
1988	2,511	*	36	464	1,098	913	1,716	795	1,187	522	666	1,324	435	889
1987	2,415	1	57	494	1,137	725	1,655	760	1,152	579	573	1,263	462	801
1986	2,365	*	44	530	1,057	732	1,624	741	1,184	596	589	1,181	479	702
1985	2,427	*	31	540	1,179	678	1,652	775	1,239	607	632	1,188	395	793
1984	2,395	*	32	580	1,190	594	1,648	747	1,263	654	610	1,132	440	692
1983	2,442	*	32	568	1,214	629	1,614	829	1,279	665	614	1,163	438	725
1982	2,393	1	31	534	1,244	584	1,587	806	1,216	626	590	1,178	421	756
1981	2,205	*	34	528	1,120	523	1,478	726	1,127	546	581	1,078	347	731
1980	2,173	2	31	554	1,104	481	NA	NA	1,106	526	581	1,066	372	694
1979	2,214	*	45	497	1,149	523	1,537	678	1,105	503	602	1,109	355	754
1978	2,217	*	51	565	1,064	536	1,454	762	1,149	516	633	1,068	366	702
1977[1]	1,810	2	53	593	1,161	NA	1,241	568	995	548	447	813	338	475
1976	2,152	*	40	622	1,017	472	1,516	634	1,216	576	638	937	292	644
1975	1,590	*	59	607	923	NA	1,105	484	949	542	407	640	267	373
1974	1,490	*	61	499	930	NA	1,061	428	897	457	440	593	205	388
1973	1,385	*	42	541	801	NA	945	439	887	467	420	498	163	335
1972	1,320	1	52	517	749	NA	877	443	872	481	391	450	155	295
1971	1,192	1	60	468	663	NA	799	393	833	480	353	359	136	223
1970	1,140	*	54	488	599	NA	789	351	774	432	342	366	123	243

* = Quantity equals zero or rounds to zero.
NA = Not available.
r = Revised, controlled to 1990 census based population estimates; previous 1993 data controlled to 1980 census based population estimates.
[1]Data for 1970–1975 and 1977 do not include people ages 35 and over.

Table A-17. College Enrollment of Students 14 Years Old and Over, by Type of College, Attendance Status, Age, and Sex, October 1970–2019—*Continued*

(Numbers in thousands; civilian noninstitutionalized population.)

Year and type of college	Full time						Part time					
	Total	14 to 19 years	20 to 21 years	22 to 24 years	25 to 34 years	35 years and over	Total	14 to 19 years	20 to 21 years	22 to 24 years	25 to 34 years	35 years and over
2000	1,268	32	67	414	544	211	1,645	6	10	156	674	798
1999	1,421	38	71	487	539	287	1,736	8	6	133	672	918
1998	1,372	45	58	429	579	262	1,665	*	15	107	734	808
1997	1,319	26	57	401	605	229	1,708	3	6	160	694	844
1996	1,305	18	42	420	570	254	1,617	3	9	114	647	844
1995	1,199	8	43	352	571	225	1,550	*	17	112	627	793
1994	1,124	9	19	377	544	175	1,489	*	2	174	594	718
1993r	1,059	3	11	376	482	186	1,376	*	3	161	540	673
1993	1,025	3	10	358	469	184	1,366	*	3	156	536	672
1992	1,126	*	33	387	478	228	1,266	*	3	120	557	586
1991	1,180	*	29	423	539	188	1,504	*	8	124	626	746
1990	1,100	2	25	376	518	180	1,413	*	2	121	577	714
1989	1,140	*	33	375	525	208	1,380	*	7	135	637	601
1988	956	*	31	304	465	157	1,555	*	5	160	634	756
1987	1,041	1	52	343	477	167	1,374	*	5	151	660	558
1986	1,074	*	40	412	465	157	1,291	*	4	120	593	575
1985	1,002	*	27	385	449	141	1,424	*	4	155	728	537
1984	1,093	*	27	427	544	95	1,302	*	6	153	644	498
1983	1,103	*	32	420	530	121	1,339	*	*	140	685	507
1982	1,047	*	20	381	522	116	1,346	1	4	153	721	467
1981	893	*	28	355	447	64	1,312	*	6	173	673	459
1980	898	2	24	403	403	66	1,275	*	6	152	702	415
1979	858	*	32	358	397	72	1,356	*	14	140	752	451
1978	882	*	38	396	376	71	1,335	*	14	169	688	465
1977[1]	886	2	43	382	459	NA	922	*	10	211	702	NA
1976	869	*	35	405	355	73	1,282	*	5	217	662	398
1975	809	*	43	382	386	NA	780	*	16	225	537	NA
1974	662	*	41	289	330	NA	828	*	20	210	600	NA
1973	630	*	33	350	248	NA	755	*	9	191	553	NA
1972	636	1	44	332	262	NA	686	*	8	185	487	NA
1971	616	1	57	299	261	NA	576	*	3	169	402	NA
1970	555	*	42	304	212	NA	585	*	12	184	387	NA

* = Quantity equals zero or rounds to zero.
NA = Not available.
r = Revised, controlled to 1990 census based population estimates; previous 1993 data controlled to 1980 census based population estimates.
[1]Data for 1970 1975 and 1977 do not include people ages 35 and over.

Table A-18. Total Fall Enrollment in Degree-Granting Institutions, by Attendance Status, Sex of Student, and Control of Institution, Selected Years, 1947–2019

(Number; percent.)

Year	Total enrolled	Attendance status Full-time	Part-time	Percent part-time	Sex of student Male	Female	Percent Female	Control of institution Public	Private Total	Nonprofit	For-profit
2019	19,637,499	11,966,494	7,671,005	39.1	8,362,890	11,274,609	57.4	14,501,057	5,136,442	4,145,263	991,179
2018	19,651,412	11,989,569	7,661,843	39.0	8,444,614	11,206,798	57.0	14,539,257	5,112,155	4,131,846	980,309
2017	19,778,151	12,076,141	7,702,010	38.9	8,571,314	11,206,837	56.7	14,571,739	5,206,412	4,108,489	1,097,923
2016	19,846,904	12,125,314	7,721,590	38.9	8,638,422	11,208,482	56.5	14,585,840	5,261,064	4,078,956	1,182,108
2015	19,988,204	12,287,512	7,700,692	38.5	8,723,819	11,264,385	56.4	14,572,843	5,415,361	4,065,891	1,349,470
2014	20,209,092	12,454,464	7,754,628	38.4	8,797,530	11,411,562	56.5	14,654,660	5,554,432	3,997,249	1,557,183
2013	20,376,677	12,596,610	7,780,067	38.2	8,861,197	11,515,480	56.5	14,746,848	5,629,829	3,971,390	1,658,439
2012	20,644,478	12,734,404	7,910,074	38.3	8,919,006	11,725,472	56.8	14,884,667	5,759,811	3,951,388	1,808,423
2011	21,010,590	13,002,531	8,008,059	38.1	9,034,256	11,976,334	57.0	15,116,303	5,894,287	3,926,819	1,967,468
2010	21,019,438	13,087,182	7,932,256	37.7	9,045,759	11,973,679	57.0	15,142,171	5,877,267	3,854,482	2,022,785
2009	20,313,594	12,605,355	7,708,239	37.9	8,732,953	11,580,641	57.0	14,810,768	5,502,826	3,767,672	1,735,154
2008	19,102,814	11,747,743	7,355,071	38.5	8,188,895	10,913,919	57.1	13,972,153	5,130,661	3,661,519	1,469,142
2007	18,248,128	11,269,892	6,978,236	38.2	7,815,914	10,432,214	57.2	13,490,780	4,757,348	3,571,150	1,186,198
2006	17,758,870	10,957,305	6,801,565	38.3	7,574,815	10,184,055	57.3	13,180,133	4,578,737	3,512,866	1,065,871
2005	17,487,475	10,797,011	6,690,464	38.3	7,455,925	10,031,550	57.4	13,021,834	4,465,641	3,454,692	1,010,949
2004	17,272,044	10,610,177	6,661,867	38.6	7,387,262	9,884,782	57.2	12,980,112	4,291,932	3,411,685	880,247
2003	16,911,481	10,326,133	6,585,348	38.9	7,260,264	9,651,217	57.1	12,858,698	4,052,783	3,341,048	711,735
2002	16,611,711	9,946,359	6,665,352	40.1	7,202,116	9,409,595	56.6	12,751,993	3,859,718	3,265,476	594,242
2001	15,927,987	9,447,502	6,480,485	40.7	6,960,815	8,967,172	56.3	12,233,156	3,694,831	3,167,330	527,501
2000	15,312,289	9,009,600	6,302,689	41.2	6,721,769	8,590,520	56.1	11,752,786	3,559,503	3,109,419	450,084
1999	14,849,691	8,803,139	6,046,552	40.7	6,515,164	8,334,527	56.1	11,375,739	3,473,952	3,055,029	418,923
1998	14,506,967	8,563,338	5,943,629	41.0	6,369,265	8,137,702	56.1	11,137,769	3,369,198	3,004,925	364,273
1997	14,502,334	8,438,062	6,064,272	41.8	6,396,028	8,106,306	55.9	11,196,119	3,306,215	2,977,614	328,601
1996	14,367,520	8,302,953	6,064,567	42.2	6,352,825	8,014,695	55.8	11,120,499	3,247,021	2,942,556	304,465
1995	14,261,781	8,128,802	6,132,979	43.0	6,342,539	7,919,242	55.5	11,092,374	3,169,407	2,929,044	240,363
1994	14,278,790	8,137,776	6,141,014	43.0	6,371,898	7,906,892	55.4	11,133,680	3,145,110	2,910,107	235,003
1993	14,304,803	8,127,618	6,177,185	43.2	6,427,450	7,877,353	55.1	11,189,088	3,115,715	2,888,897	226,818
1992	14,487,359	8,162,118	6,325,241	43.7	6,523,989	7,963,370	55.0	11,384,567	3,102,792	2,872,523	230,269
1991	14,358,953	8,115,329	6,243,624	43.5	6,501,844	7,857,109	54.7	11,309,563	3,049,390	2,819,041	230,349
1990	13,818,637	7,820,985	5,997,652	43.4	6,283,909	7,534,728	54.5	10,844,717	2,973,920	2,760,227	213,693
1989	13,538,560	7,660,950	5,877,610	43.4	6,190,015	7,348,545	54.3	10,577,963	2,960,597	2,731,174	229,423
1988	13,055,337	7,436,768	5,618,569	43.0	6,001,896	7,053,441	54.0	10,161,388	2,893,949	2,673,567	220,382
1987	12,766,642	7,231,085	5,535,557	43.4	5,932,056	6,834,586	53.5	9,973,254	2,793,388	2,602,350	191,038 3
1986	12,503,511	7,119,550	5,383,961	43.1	5,884,515	6,618,996	52.9	9,713,893	2,789,618	2,572,479	217,139 3
1985	12,247,055	7,075,221	5,171,834	42.2	5,818,450	6,428,605	52.5	9,479,273	2,767,782	2,571,791	195,991
1984	12,241,940	7,098,388	5,143,552	42.0	5,863,574	6,378,366	52.1	9,477,370	2,764,570	2,574,419	190,151
1983	12,464,661	7,261,050	5,203,611	41.7	6,023,725	6,440,936	51.7	9,682,734	2,781,927	2,589,187	192,740
1982	12,425,780	7,220,618	5,205,162	41.9	6,031,384	6,394,396	51.5	9,696,087	2,729,693	2,552,739	176,954 2
1981	12,371,672	7,181,250	5,190,422	42.0	5,975,056	6,396,616	51.7	9,647,032	2,724,640	2,572,405	152,235 2
1980	12,096,895	7,097,958	4,998,937	41.3	5,874,374	6,222,521	51.4	9,457,394	2,639,501	2,527,787	152,235 2
1979	11,569,899	6,794,039	4,775,860	41.3	5,682,877	5,887,022	50.9	9,036,822	2,533,077	2,461,773	71,304
1978	11,260,092	6,667,657	4,592,435	40.8	5,640,998	5,619,094	49.9	8,785,893	2,474,199	2,408,331	65,868
1977	11,285,787	6,792,925	4,492,862	39.8	5,789,016	5,496,771	48.7	8,846,993	2,438,794	2,386,652	52,142
1976	11,012,137	6,717,058	4,295,079	39.0	5,810,828	5,201,309	47.2	8,653,477	2,358,660	2,314,298	44,362
1975	11,184,859	6,841,334	4,343,525	38.8	6,148,997	5,035,862	45.0	8,834,508	2,350,351	2,311,448	38,903
1974	10,223,729	6,370,273	3,853,456	37.7	5,622,429	4,601,300	45.0	7,988,500	2,235,229	2,200,963	34,266
1973	9,602,123	6,189,493	3,412,630	35.5	5,371,052	4,231,071	44.1	7,419,516	2,182,607	2,148,784	33,823
1972	9,214,860	6,072,389	3,142,471	34.1	5,238,757	3,976,103	43.1	7,070,635	2,144,225	2,123,245	20,980
1971	8,948,644	6,077,232	2,871,412	32.1	5,207,004	3,741,640	41.8	6,804,309	2,144,335	2,121,913	22,422
1970	8,580,887	5,816,290	2,764,597	32.2	5,043,642	3,537,245	41.2	6,428,134	2,152,753	2,134,420	18,333
1969	8,004,660	5,498,883	2,505,777	31.3	4,746,201	3,258,459	40.7	5,896,868	2,107,792	2,087,653	20,139
1968	7,513,091	5,210,155	2,302,936	30.7	4,477,649	3,035,442	40.4	5,430,652	2,082,439	2,061,211	21,228
1967	6,911,748	4,793,128	2,118,620	30.7	4,132,800	2,778,948	40.2	4,816,028	2,095,720	2,074,041	21,679
1966	6,389,872	4,438,606	1,951,266	30.5	3,856,216	2,533,656	39.7	4,348,917	2,040,955	NA	NA
1965	5,920,864	4,095,728	1,825,136	30.8	3,630,020	2,290,844	38.7	3,969,596	1,951,268	NA	NA
1964	5,280,020	3,573,238	1,706,782	32.3	3,248,713	2,031,307	38.5	3,467,708	1,812,312	NA	NA
1963	4,779,609	3,183,833	1,595,776	33.4	2,961,540	1,818,069	38.0	3,081,279	1,698,330	NA	NA
1961	4,145,065	2,785,133	1,359,932	32.8	2,585,821	1,559,244	37.6	2,561,447	1,583,618	NA	NA

Note: Data through 1995 are for institutions of higher education, while later data are for degree-granting institutions. Degree-granting institutions grant associate's or higher degrees and participate in Title IV federal financial aid programs. The degree-granting classification is very similar to the earlier higher education classification, but it includes more 2-year colleges and excludes a few higher education institutions that did not grant degrees. Some data have been revised from previously published figures.
NA = Not available.

Table A-18. Total Fall Enrollment in Degree-Granting Institutions, by Attendance Status, Sex of Student, and Control of Institution, Selected Years, 1947–2019—*Continued*

(Number; percent.)

Year	Total enrolled	Attendance status			Sex of student			Control of institution			
		Full-time	Part-time	Percent part-time	Male	Female	Percent Female	Public	Private		
									Total	Nonprofit	For-profit
1959...............	3,639,847	2,421,016	1,218,831	33.5	2,332,617	1,307,230	35.9	2,180,982	1,458,865	NA	NA
1957...............	3,323,783	NA	NA	NA	2,170,765	1,153,018	34.7	1,972,673	1,351,110	NA	NA
1956...............	2,918,212	NA	NA	NA	1,911,458	1,006,754	34.5	1,656,402	1,261,810	NA	NA
1955...............	2,653,034	NA	NA	NA	1,733,184	919,850	34.7	1,476,282	1,176,752	NA	NA
1954...............	2,446,693	NA	NA	NA	1,563,382	883,311	36.1	1,353,531	1,093,162	NA	NA
1953...............	2,231,054	NA	NA	NA	1,422,598	808,456	36.2	1,185,876	1,045,178	NA	NA
1952...............	2,134,242	NA	NA	NA	1,380,357	753,885	35.3	1,101,240	1,033,002	NA	NA
1951...............	2,101,962	NA	NA	NA	1,390,740	711,222	33.8	1,037,938	1,064,024	NA	NA
1950...............	2,281,298	NA	NA	NA	1,560,392	720,906	31.6	1,139,699	1,141,599	NA	NA
1949...............	2,444,900	NA	NA	NA	1,721,572	723,328	29.6	1,207,151	1,237,749	NA	NA
1948...............	2,403,396	NA	NA	NA	1,709,367	694,029	28.9	1,185,588	1,217,808	NA	NA
1947...............	2,338,226	NA	NA	NA	1,659,249	678,977	29.0	1,152,377	1,185,849	NA	NA

Note: Data through 1995 are for institutions of higher education, while later data are for degree-granting institutions. Degree-granting institutions grant associate's or higher degrees and participate in Title IV federal financial aid programs. The degree-granting classification is very similar to the earlier higher education classification, but it includes more 2-year colleges and excludes a few higher education institutions that did not grant degrees. Some data have been revised from previously published figures.
NA = Not available.

Table A-19. Total Fall Enrollment in Degree-Granting Institutions, by Control and Type of Institution, 1970–2019

(Numbers in thousands.)

Year	All institutions			Public institutions			Private institutions		
	Total	4-year	2-year	Total	4-year	2-year	Total	4-year	2-year
2019	19,637	14,038	5,599	14,501	9,103	5,398	5,136	4,935	201
2018	19,651	13,898	5,753	14,539	8,983	5,556	5,112	4,915	197
2017	19,778	13,825	5,953	14,572	8,854	5,717	5,206	4,971	235
2016	19,847	13,754	6,092	14,586	8,743	5,843	5,261	5,012	250
2015	19,988	13,489	6,499	14,573	8,349	6,224	5,415	5,140	275
2014	20,209	13,494	6,715	14,655	8,257	6,398	5,554	5,237	317
2013	20,377	13,406	6,971	14,747	8,120	6,626	5,630	5,286	344
2012	20,644	13,477	7,168	14,885	8,093	6,792	5,760	5,384	376
2011	21,011	13,499	7,511	15,116	8,048	7,068	5,894	5,451	443
2010	21,019	13,336	7,684	15,142	7,924	7,218	5,877	5,412	466
2009	20,314	12,791	7,523	14,811	7,709	7,102	5,503	5,082	421
2008	19,103	12,131	6,971	13,972	7,332	6,640	5,131	4,800	331
2007	18,248	11,630	6,618	13,491	7,167	6,324	4,757	4,464	294
2006	17,759	11,240	6,519	13,180	6,955	6,225	4,579	4,285	293
2005	17,487	10,999	6,488	13,022	6,838	6,184	4,466	4,162	304
2004	17,272	10,726	6,546	12,980	6,737	6,244	4,292	3,990	302
2003	16,911	10,417	6,494	12,859	6,649	6,209	4,053	3,768	285
2002	16,612	10,082	6,529	12,752	6,482	6,270	3,860	3,601	259
2001	15,928	9,677	6,251	12,233	6,236	5,997	3,695	3,441	254
2000	15,312	9,364	5,948	11,753	6,055	5,697	3,560	3,308	251
1999	14,850	9,196	5,654	11,376	5,978	5,398	3,474	3,218	255
1998	14,507	9,018	5,489	11,138	5,892	5,246	3,369	3,126	243
1997	14,502	8,897	5,606	11,196	5,835	5,361	3,306	3,061	245
1996	14,368	8,804	5,563	11,120	5,806	5,314	3,247	2,998	249
1995	14,262	8,769	5,493	11,092	5,815	5,278	3,169	2,955	215
1994	14,279	8,749	5,530	11,134	5,825	5,308	3,145	2,924	221
1993	14,305	8,739	5,566	11,189	5,852	5,337	3,116	2,887	229
1992	14,487	8,765	5,722	11,385	5,900	5,485	3,103	2,865	238
1991	14,359	8,707	5,652	11,310	5,905	5,405	3,049	2,802	247
1990	13,819	8,579	5,240	10,845	5,848	4,996	2,974	2,730	244
1989	13,539	8,388	5,151	10,578	5,694	4,884	2,961	2,693	267
1988	13,055	8,180	4,875	10,161	5,546	4,615	2,894	2,634	260
1987	12,767	7,990	4,776	9,973	5,432	4,541	2,793	2,558	235[2]
1986	12,504	7,824	4,680	9,714	5,300	4,414	2,790	2,524	265[2]
1985	12,247	7,716	4,531	9,479	5,210	4,270	2,768	2,506	261
1984	12,242	7,711	4,531	9,477	5,198	4,279	2,765	2,513	252
1983	12,465	7,741	4,723	9,683	5,223	4,459	2,782	2,518	264
1982	12,426	7,654	4,772	9,696	5,176	4,520	2,730	2,478	264[1]
1981	12,372	7,655	4,716	9,647	5,166	4,481	2,725	2,489	264[1]
1980	12,097	7,571	4,526	9,457	5,129	4,329	2,640	2,442	264[1]
1979	11,570	7,353	4,217	9,037	4,980	4,057	2,533	2,373	160
1978	11,260	7,232	4,028	8,786	4,912	3,874	2,474	2,319	155
1977	11,286	7,243	4,043	8,847	4,945	3,902	2,439	2,298	141
1976	11,012	7,129	3,883	8,653	4,902	3,752	2,359	2,227	132
1975	11,185	7,215	3,970	8,835	4,998	3,836	2,350	2,217	134
1974	10,224	6,820	3,404	7,989	4,703	3,285	2,235	2,117	119
1973	9,602	6,590	3,012	7,420	4,530	2,890	2,183	2,060	122
1972	9,215	6,459	2,756	7,071	4,430	2,641	2,144	2,029	115
1971	8,949	6,369	2,579	6,804	4,347	2,457	2,144	2,022	122
1970	8,581	6,262	2,319	6,428	4,233	2,195	2,153	2,029	124

Note: Data through 1995 are for institutions of higher education, while later data are for degree-granting institutions. Degree-granting institutions grant associate's or higher degrees and participate in Title IV federal financial aid programs. The degree-granting classification is very similar to the earlier higher education classification, but it includes more 2-year colleges and excludes a few higher education institutions that did not grant degrees. A university is an institution of higher education consisting of a liberal arts college, a diverse graduate program, and usually two or more professional schools or faculties. It is empowered to confer degrees in various fields of study; for purposes of maintaining trend data in this publication, the selection of university institutions has not been revised since 1982. Some data have been revised from previously published figures.
[1]Large increases are due to the addition of schools accredited by the Accrediting Commission of Career Schools and Colleges of Technology.
[2]Because of imputation techniques, data are not consistent with figures for other years.

Table A-20. Total Undergraduate Fall Enrollment in Degree-Granting Four-Year Institutions, by Attendance Status, Sex of Student, and Control of Institution, Selected Years 1970–2019

(Number.)

Year	Total	Full-time	Part-time	Males	Females	Males Full-time	Males Part-time
2019	16,565,066	10,219,934	6,345,132	7,148,530	9,416,536	4,544,189	2,604,341
2018	16,616,370	10,266,392	6,349,978	7,228,148	9,388,222	4,601,834	2,626,314
2017	16,773,036	10,371,863	6,401,173	7,351,259	9,421,777	4,683,715	2,667,544
2016	16,874,649	10,430,068	6,444,581	7,416,859	9,457,790	4,725,510	2,691,349
2015	17,046,673	10,603,030	6,443,643	7,502,254	9,544,419	4,809,098	2,693,156
2014	17,294,136	10,784,392	6,509,744	7,586,299	9,707,837	4,877,531	2,708,768
2013	17,476,304	10,939,276	6,537,028	7,660,140	9,816,164	4,950,210	2,709,930
2012	17,735,638	11,097,092	6,638,546	7,714,938	10,020,700	4,984,389	2,730,549
2011	18,077,303	11,365,175	6,712,128	7,822,992	10,254,311	5,070,553	2,752,439
2010	18,082,427	11,457,040	6,625,387	7,836,282	10,246,145	5,118,975	2,717,307
2009	17,464,179	11,038,275	6,425,904	7,563,176	9,901,003	4,942,120	2,621,056
2008	16,365,738	10,254,930	6,110,808	7,066,623	9,299,115	4,577,431	2,489,192
2007	15,603,771	9,840,978	5,762,793	6,727,600	8,876,171	4,396,868	2,330,732
2006	15,184,302	9,571,079	5,613,223	6,513,756	8,670,546	4,264,606	2,249,150
2005	14,963,964	9,446,430	5,517,534	6,408,871	8,555,093	4,200,863	2,208,008
2004	14,780,630	9,284,336	5,496,294	6,340,048	8,440,582	4,140,628	2,199,420
2003	14,480,364	9,045,253	5,435,111	6,227,372	8,252,992	4,048,682	2,178,690
2002	14,257,077	8,734,252	5,522,825	6,192,390	8,064,687	3,934,168	2,258,222
2001	13,715,610	8,327,640	5,387,970	6,004,431	7,711,179	3,768,630	2,235,801
2000	13,155,393	7,922,926	5,232,467	5,778,268	7,377,125	3,588,246	2,190,022
1999	12,739,445	7,753,548	4,985,897	5,584,234	7,155,211	3,524,586	2,059,648
1998	12,436,937	7,538,711	4,898,226	5,446,133	6,990,804	3,428,161	2,017,972
1997	12,450,587	7,418,598	5,031,989	5,468,532	6,982,055	3,379,597	2,088,935
1996	12,326,948	7,298,839	5,028,100	5,420,072	6,906,276	3,339,108	2,081,564
1995	12,231,719	7,145,268	5,086,451	5,401,130	6,830,589	3,296,610	2,104,520
1994	12,262,608	7,168,706	5,093,902	5,422,113	6,840,495	3,341,591	2,080,522
1993	12,323,959	7,179,482	5,144,477	5,483,682	6,840,277	3,381,997	2,101,685
1992	12,537,700	7,244,442	5,293,258	5,582,936	6,954,764	3,424,739	2,158,197
1991	12,439,287	7,221,412	5,217,875	5,571,003	6,868,284	3,435,526	2,135,477
1990	11,959,106	6,976,030	4,983,076	5,379,759	6,579,347	3,336,535	2,043,224
1989	11,742,531	6,840,696	4,901,835	5,310,990	6,431,541	3,278,647	2,032,343
1988	11,316,548	6,642,428	4,674,120	5,137,644	6,178,904	3,206,442	1,931,202
1987	11,046,235	6,462,549	4,583,686	5,068,457	5,977,778	3,163,676	1,904,781
1986	10,797,975	6,352,073	4,445,902	5,017,505	5,780,470	3,146,330	1,871,175
1985	10,596,674	6,319,592	4,277,082	4,962,080	5,634,594	3,156,446	1,805,634
1984	10,618,071	6,347,653	4,270,418	5,006,813	5,611,258	3,194,930	1,811,883
1983	10,845,995	6,514,034	4,331,961	5,158,300	5,687,695	3,304,247	1,854,053
1982	10,825,062	6,483,805	4,341,257	5,170,494	5,654,568	3,299,436	1,871,058
1981	10,754,522	6,449,068	4,305,454	5,108,271	5,646,251	3,260,473	1,847,798
1980	10,475,055	6,361,744	4,113,311	5,000,177	5,474,878	3,226,857	1,773,320
1975	9,679,455	6,168,396	3,511,059	5,257,005	4,422,450	3,459,328	1,797,677
1970	7,368,644	5,280,064	2,088,580	4,249,702	3,118,942	3,096,371	1,153,331

NA = Not available.
Note: Data include unclassified undergraduate students. Data through 1995 are for institutions of higher education, while later data are for degree-granting institutions. Degree-granting institutions grant associate's or higher degrees and participate in Title IV federal financial aid programs. The degree-granting classification is very similar to the earlier higher education classification, but it includes more 2-year colleges and excludes a few higher education institutions that did not grant degrees. Some data have been revised from previously published figures. Details may not sum to totals because of rounding.

Table A-20. Total Undergraduate Fall Enrollment in Degree-Granting Four-Year Institutions, by Attendance Status, Sex of Student, and Control of Institution, Selected Years 1970–2019—*Continued*

(Number.)

Year	Females		Public	Private		
	Full-time	Part-time		Total	Nonprofit	For-profit
2019	5,675,745	3,740,791	13,001,543	3,563,523	2,804,878	758,645
2018	5,664,558	3,723,664	13,059,760	3,556,610	2,819,406	737,204
2017	5,688,148	3,733,629	13,112,594	3,660,442	2,819,080	841,362
2016	5,704,558	3,753,232	13,143,979	3,730,670	2,813,742	916,928
2015	5,793,932	3,750,487	13,150,823	3,895,850	2,822,122	1,073,728
2014	5,906,861	3,800,976	13,244,533	4,049,603	2,772,065	1,277,538
2013	5,989,066	3,827,098	13,348,292	4,128,012	2,755,463	1,372,549
2012	6,112,703	3,907,997	13,478,100	4,257,538	2,744,400	1,513,138
2011	6,294,622	3,959,689	13,694,899	4,382,404	2,718,923	1,663,481
2010	6,338,065	3,908,080	13,703,000	4,379,427	2,652,993	1,726,434
2009	6,096,155	3,804,848	13,386,375	4,077,804	2,595,171	1,482,633
2008	5,677,499	3,621,616	12,591,217	3,774,521	2,536,532	1,237,989
2007	5,444,110	3,432,061	12,137,583	3,466,188	2,470,327	995,861
2006	5,306,473	3,364,073	11,847,426	3,336,876	2,448,240	888,636
2005	5,245,567	3,309,526	11,697,730	3,266,234	2,418,368	847,866
2004	5,143,708	3,296,874	11,650,580	3,130,050	2,389,366	740,684
2003	4,996,571	3,256,421	11,523,103	2,957,261	2,346,673	610,588
2002	4,800,084	3,264,603	11,432,855	2,824,222	2,306,091	518,131
2001	4,559,010	3,152,169	10,985,871	2,729,739	2,257,718	472,021
2000	4,334,680	3,042,445	10,539,322	2,616,071	2,213,180	402,891
1999	4,228,962	2,926,249	10,174,228	2,565,217	2,185,290	379,927
1998	4,110,550	2,880,254	9,950,212	2,486,725	2,152,655	334,070
1997	4,039,001	2,943,054	10,007,479	2,443,108	2,139,824	303,284
1996	3,959,731	2,946,545	9,935,283	2,391,665	2,112,318	279,347
1995	3,848,658	2,981,931	9,903,626	2,328,093	2,104,693	223,400
1994	3,827,115	3,013,380	9,945,128	2,317,480	2,100,465	217,015
1993	3,797,485	3,042,792	10,011,787	2,312,172	2,099,197	212,975
1992	3,819,703	3,135,061	10,216,297	2,321,403	2,101,721	219,682
1991	3,785,886	3,082,398	10,147,957	2,291,330	2,072,354	218,976
1990	3,639,495	2,939,852	9,709,596	2,249,510	2,043,407	206,103
1989	3,562,049	2,869,492	9,487,742	2,254,789	NA	NA
1988	3,435,986	2,742,918	9,103,146	2,213,402	NA	NA
1987	3,298,873	2,678,905	8,918,589	2,127,646	1,939,942	187,704
1986	3,205,743	2,574,727	8,660,716	2,137,259	1,928,294	208,965
1985	3,163,146	2,471,448	8,477,125	2,119,549	1,928,996	190,553
1984	3,152,723	2,458,535	8,493,491	2,124,580	1,940,310	184,270
1983	3,209,787	2,477,908	8,697,118	2,148,877	1,961,076	187,801
1982	3,184,369	2,470,199	8,713,073	2,111,989	1,939,389	172,600
1981	3,188,595	2,457,656	8,648,363	2,106,159	1,958,848	147,311
1980	3,134,887	2,339,991	8,441,955	2,033,100	1,926,703	106,397
1975	2,709,068	1,713,382	7,826,032	1,853,423	1,814,844	38,579
1970	2,183,693	935,249	5,620,255	1,748,389	1,730,133	18,256

NA = Not available.

Note: Data include unclassified undergraduate students. Data through 1995 are for institutions of higher education, while later data are for degree-granting institutions. Degree-granting institutions grant associate's or higher degrees and participate in Title IV federal financial aid programs. The degree-granting classification is very similar to the earlier higher education classification, but it includes more 2-year colleges and excludes a few higher education institutions that did not grant degrees. Some data have been revised from previously published figures. Details may not sum to totals because of rounding.

Table A-21. Total Postbaccalaureate Fall Enrollment in Degree-Granting Institutions, by Attendance Status, Sex of Student, and Control of Institution, 1967–2019

(Number.)

Year	Total	Full-time	Part-time	Males	Females	Males Full-time	Males Part-time
2019	3,072,433	1,746,560	1,325,873	1,214,360	1,858,073	732,706	481,654
2018	3,035,042	1,723,177	1,311,865	1,216,466	1,818,576	735,576	480,890
2017	3,005,115	1,704,278	1,300,837	1,220,055	1,785,060	740,240	479,815
2016	2,972,255	1,695,246	1,277,009	1,221,563	1,750,692	747,288	474,275
2015	2,941,531	1,684,482	1,257,049	1,221,565	1,719,966	749,349	472,216
2014	2,914,956	1,670,072	1,244,884	1,211,231	1,703,725	742,247	468,984
2013	2,900,373	1,657,334	1,243,039	1,201,057	1,699,316	732,112	468,945
2012	2,908,840	1,637,312	1,271,528	1,204,068	1,704,772	724,017	480,051
2011	2,933,287	1,637,356	1,295,931	1,211,264	1,722,023	722,265	488,999
2010	2,937,011	1,630,142	1,306,869	1,209,477	1,727,534	719,408	490,069
2009	2,849,415	1,567,080	1,282,335	1,169,777	1,679,638	689,977	479,800
2008	2,737,076	1,492,813	1,244,263	1,122,272	1,614,804	656,926	465,346
2007	2,644,357	1,428,914	1,215,443	1,088,314	1,556,043	632,576	455,738
2006	2,574,568	1,386,226	1,188,342	1,061,059	1,513,509	614,709	446,350
2005	2,523,511	1,350,581	1,172,930	1,047,054	1,476,457	602,525	444,529
2004	2,491,414	1,325,841	1,165,573	1,047,214	1,444,200	598,727	448,487
2003	2,431,117	1,280,880	1,150,237	1,032,892	1,398,225	589,190	443,702
2002	2,354,634	1,212,107	1,142,527	1,009,726	1,344,908	566,930	442,796
2001	2,212,377	1,119,862	1,092,515	956,384	1,255,993	531,260	425,124
2000	2,156,896	1,086,674	1,070,222	943,501	1,213,395	522,847	420,654
1999	2,110,246	1,049,591	1,060,655	930,930	1,179,316	508,930	422,000
1998	2,070,030	1,024,627	1,045,403	923,132	1,146,898	505,492	417,640
1997	2,051,747	1,019,464	1,032,283	927,496	1,124,251	510,845	416,651
1996	2,040,572	1,004,114	1,036,458	932,153	1,108,419	512,100	420,053
1995	2,030,062	983,534	1,046,528	941,409	1,088,653	510,782	430,627
1994	2,016,182	969,070	1,047,112	949,785	1,066,397	613,592	436,193
1993	1,980,844	948,136	1,032,708	943,768	1,037,076	508,574	435,194
1992	1,949,659	917,676	1,031,983	941,053	1,008,606	502,166	438,887
1991	1,919,666	893,917	1,025,749	930,841	988,825	493,849	436,992
1990	1,859,531	844,955	1,014,576	904,150	955,381	471,217	432,933
1989	1,796,029	820,254	975,775	879,025	917,004	461,596	417,429
1988	1,738,789	794,340	944,449	864,252	874,537	455,337	408,915
1987	1,720,407	768,536	951,871	863,599	856,808	447,212	416,387
1986	1,705,536	767,477	938,059	867,010	838,526	452,717	414,293
1985	1,650,381	755,629	894,752	856,370	794,011	451,274	405,096
1984	1,623,869	750,735	873,134	856,761	767,108	452,579	404,182
1983	1,618,666	747,016	871,650	865,425	753,241	455,540	409,885
1982	1,600,718	736,813	863,905	860,890	739,828	453,519	407,371
1981	1,617,150	732,182	884,968	866,785	750,365	452,364	414,421
1980	1,621,840	736,214	885,626	874,197	747,643	462,387	411,810
1979	1,571,922	714,624	857,298	862,754	709,168	456,197	406,557
1978	1,575,693	704,831	870,862	879,931	695,762	458,865	421,066
1977	1,569,084	698,902	870,182	891,819	677,265	462,038	429,781
1976	1,577,546	683,825	893,721	904,551	672,995	459,286	445,265
1975	1,505,404	672,938	832,466	891,992	613,412	467,425	424,567
1974	1,425,001	643,927	781,074	856,847	568,154	454,706	402,141
1973	1,342,452	610,935	731,517	833,453	508,999	444,219	389,234
1972	1,272,421	583,299	689,122	810,164	462,257	436,533	373,631
1971	1,204,390	564,236	640,154	789,131	415,259	428,167	360,964
1970	1,212,243	536,226	676,017	793,940	418,303	407,724	386,216
1969	1,120,175	506,833	613,342	738,673	381,502	383,630	355,043
1968	1,037,377	469,747	567,630	696,649	340,728	358,686	337,963
1967	806,065	448,238	447,827	630,701	265,364	354,628	276,073

NA = Not available.
Note: Data include unclassified graduate students. Data through 1995 are for institutions of higher education, while later data are for degree-granting institutions. Degree-granting institutions grant associate's or higher degrees and participate in Title IV federal financial aid programs. The degree-granting classification is very similar to the earlier higher education classification, but it includes more 2-year colleges and excludes a few higher education institutions that did not grant degrees. Some data have been revised from previously published figures.

Table A-21. Total Postbaccalaureate Fall Enrollment in Degree-Granting Institutions, by Attendance Status, Sex of Student, and Control of Institution, 1967–2019—*Continued*

(Number.)

Year	Females		Public	Private		
	Full-time	Part-time		Total	Nonprofit	For-profit
2019..................................	1,013,854	844,219	1,499,514	1,572,919	1,340,385	232,534
2018..................................	987,601	830,975	1,479,497	1,555,545	1,312,440	243,105
2017..................................	964,038	821,022	1,459,145	1,545,970	1,289,409	256,561
2016..................................	947,958	802,734	1,441,861	1,530,394	1,265,214	265,180
2015..................................	935,133	784,833	1,422,020	1,519,511	1,243,769	275,742
2014..................................	927,825	775,900	1,410,127	1,504,829	1,225,184	279,645
2013..................................	925,222	774,094	1,398,556	1,501,817	1,215,927	285,890
2012..................................	913,295	791,477	1,406,567	1,502,273	1,206,988	295,285
2011..................................	915,091	806,932	1,421,404	1,511,883	1,207,896	303,987
2010..................................	910,734	816,800	1,439,171	1,497,840	1,201,489	296,351
2009..................................	877,103	802,535	1,424,393	1,425,022	1,172,501	252,521
2008..................................	835,887	778,917	1,380,936	1,356,140	1,124,987	231,153
2007..................................	796,338	759,705	1,353,197	1,291,160	1,100,823	190,337
2006..................................	771,517	741,992	1,332,707	1,241,861	1,064,626	177,235
2005..................................	748,056	728,401	1,324,104	1,199,407	1,036,324	163,083
2004..................................	727,114	717,086	1,329,532	1,161,882	1,022,319	139,563
2003..................................	691,690	706,535	1,335,595	1,095,522	994,375	101,147
2002..................................	645,177	699,731	1,319,138	1,035,496	959,385	76,111
2001..................................	588,602	667,391	1,247,285	965,092	909,612	55,480
2000..................................	563,827	649,568	1,213,464	943,432	896,239	47,193
1999..................................	540,661	638,655	1,201,511	908,735	869,739	38,996
1998..................................	519,135	627,763	1,187,557	882,473	852,270	30,203
1997..................................	508,619	615,632	1,188,640	863,107	837,790	25,317
1996..................................	492,014	616,405	1,185,216	855,356	830,238	25,118
1995..................................	472,752	615,901	1,188,748	841,314	824,351	16,963
1994..................................	455,478	610,919	1,188,552	827,630	809,642	17,988
1993..................................	439,562	597,514	1,177,301	803,543	789,700	13,843
1992..................................	415,510	593,096	1,168,270	781,389	770,802	10,587
1991..................................	400,068	588,757	1,161,606	758,060	746,687	11,373
1990..................................	373,738	581,643	1,135,121	724,410	716,820	7,590
1989..................................	358,658	558,346	1,090,221	705,808	NA	NA
1988..................................	339,003	535,534	1,058,242	680,547	NA	NA
1987..................................	321,324	535,484	1,054,665	665,742	662,408	3,334
1986..................................	314,760	523,766	1,053,177	652,359	644,185	8,174
1985..................................	304,355	489,656	1,002,148	648,233	642,795	5,438
1984..................................	298,156	468,952	983,879	639,990	634,109	5,881
1983..................................	291,476	461,765	985,616	633,050	628,111	4,939
1982..................................	283,294	456,534	983,014	617,704	613,350	4,354
1981..................................	279,818	470,547	998,669	618,481	613,557	4,924
1980..................................	273,827	473,816	1,015,439	606,401	601,084	5,317
1979..................................	258,427	450,741	989,991	581,931	578,425	3,506
1978..................................	245,966	449,796	998,608	577,085	573,563	3,522
1977..................................	236,864	440,401	1,004,013	565,071	561,384	3,687
1976..................................	224,539	448,456	1,033,115	544,431	541,064	3,367
1975..................................	205,513	407,899	1,008,476	496,928	496,604	324
1974..................................	189,221	378,933	956,770	468,231	467,950	281
1973..................................	166,716	342,283	897,104	445,348	445,205	143
1972..................................	146,766	315,491	848,031	424,390	424,278	112
1971..................................	136,069	279,190	796,516	407,874	407,804	70
1970..................................	128,502	289,801	807,879	404,364	404,287	77
1969..................................	123,203	258,299	738,551	381,624	381,558	66
1968..................................	111,061	229,667	648,657	388,720	388,681	39
1967..................................	93,610	171,754	522,623	373,442	373,336	106

NA = Not available.
Note: Data include unclassified graduate students. Data through 1995 are for institutions of higher education, while later data are for degree-granting institutions. Degree-granting institutions grant associate's or higher degrees and participate in Title IV federal financial aid programs. The degree-granting classification is very similar to the earlier higher education classification, but it includes more 2-year colleges and excludes a few higher education institutions that did not grant degrees. Some data have been revised from previously published figures.

This page is intentionally left blank

Table A-22. Total Fall Enrollment in Degree-Granting Institutions, by Race/Ethnicity, Sex, Attendance Status, and Level of Student, Selected Years 1976–2019

(Numbers in thousands; percent.)

Race/ethnicity, sex, attendance status, and level of student	1976 Number	1976 Percent	1990 Number	1990 Percent	2000 Number	2000 Percent	2010 Number	2010 Percent	2013 Number	2013 Percent
All students, total	10,986	100.0	13,819	100.0	15,312	100.0	21,019	100.0	20,377	100.0
White	9,076	84.3	10,722	79.9	10,462	70.8	12,721	62.6	11,589	59.3
Black	1,033	9.6	1,247	9.3	1,730	11.7	3,039	15.0	2,872	14.7
Hispanic	384	3.6	782	5.8	1,462	9.9	2,749	13.5	3,093	15.8
Asian/Pacific Islander	198	1.8	572	4.3	978	6.6	1,282	6.3	1,260	6.4
Asian	NA	NA	NA	NA	NA	NA	1,218	6.0	1,199	6.1
Pacific Islander	NA	NA	NA	NA	NA	NA	64	0.3	61	0.3
American Indian/Alaska Native	76	0.7	103	0.8	151	1.0	196	1.0	162	0.8
Two or more races	NA	NA	NA	NA	NA	NA	325	1.6	560	2.9
Nonresident alien	219	X	391	X	529	X	708	X	840	X
Male	5,794	100.0	6,284	100.0	6,722	100.0	9,046	100.0	8,861	100.0
White	4,814	85.3	4,861	80.5	4,635	72.1	5,606	64.7	5,132	61.1
Black	470	8.3	485	8.0	635	9.9	1,089	12.6	1,065	12.7
Hispanic	210	3.7	354	5.9	627	9.8	1,158	13.4	1,308	15.6
Asian/Pacific Islander	108	1.9	295	4.9	466	7.3	601	6.9	594	7.1
Asian	NA	NA	NA	NA	NA	NA	572	6.6	567	6.8
Pacific Islander	NA	NA	NA	NA	NA	NA	29	0.3	27	0.3
American Indian/Alaska Native	39	0.7	43	0.7	61	1.0	79	0.9	65	0.8
Two or more races	NA	NA	NA	NA	NA	NA	134	1.6	237	2.8
Nonresident alien	154	X	246	X	297	X	380	X	460	X
Female	5,191	100.0	7,535	100.0	8,591	100.0	11,974	100.0	11,515	100.0
White	4,262	83.1	5,861	79.3	5,827	69.7	7,115	61.1	6,457	58.0
Black	563	11.0	762	10.3	1,095	13.1	1,950	16.7	1,807	16.2
Hispanic	174	3.4	429	5.8	835	10.0	1,591	13.7	1,785	16.0
Asian/Pacific Islander	89	1.7	278	3.8	512	6.1	681	5.8	665	6.0
Asian	NA	NA	NA	NA	NA	NA	646	5.5	632	5.7
Pacific Islander	NA	NA	NA	NA	NA	NA	35	0.3	34	0.3
American Indian/Alaska Native	38	0.7	60	0.8	90	1.1	118	1.0	98	0.9
Two or more races	NA	NA	NA	NA	NA	NA	191	1.6	323	2.9
Nonresident alien	65	X	145	X	231	X	328	X	380	X
Full-time	6,704	100.0	7,821	100.0	9,010	100.0	13,087	100.0	12,597	100.0
White	5,513	84.2	6,016	79.9	6,231	72.5	8,053	64.3	7,238	60.8
Black	659	10.1	718	9.5	983	11.4	1,811	14.5	1,669	14.0
Hispanic	211	3.2	395	5.2	710	8.3	1,501	12.0	1,702	14.3
Asian/Pacific Islander	118	1.8	347	4.6	591	6.9	821	6.6	821	6.9
Asian	NA	NA	NA	NA	NA	NA	783	6.3	786	6.6
Pacific Islander	NA	NA	NA	NA	NA	NA	38	0.3	36	0.3
American Indian/Alaska Native	43	0.7	54	0.7	84	1.0	118	0.9	94	0.8
Two or more races	NA	NA	NA	NA	NA	NA	217	1.7	378	3.2
Nonresident alien	160	X	290	X	410	X	565	X	695	X
Part-time	4,282	100.0	5,998	100.0	6,303	100.0	7,932	100.0	7,780	100.0
White	3,563	84.4	4,706	79.8	4,231	68.4	4,667	59.9	4,352	57.0
Black	374	8.9	529	9.0	748	12.1	1,228	15.8	1,203	15.8
Hispanic	173	4.1	388	6.6	751	12.2	1,248	16.0	1,391	18.2
Asian/Pacific Islander	80	1.9	225	3.8	387	6.3	461	5.9	438	5.7
Asian	NA	NA	NA	NA	NA	NA	435	5.6	413	5.4
Pacific Islander	NA	NA	NA	NA	NA	NA	26	0.3	25	0.3
American Indian/Alaska Native	33	0.8	48	0.8	67	1.1	78	1.0	68	0.9
Two or more races	NA	NA	NA	NA	NA	NA	108	1.4	183	2.4
Nonresident alien	59	X	102	X	119	X	142	X	145	X
Undergraduate, total	9,419	100.0	11,959	100.0	13,155	100.0	18,082	100.0	17,476	100.0
White	7,740	83.4	9,273	79.0	8,983	69.8	10,896	61.6	9,898	58.2
Black	943	10.2	1,147	9.8	1,549	12.0	2,677	15.1	2,505	14.7
Hispanic	353	3.8	725	6.2	1,351	10.5	2,551	14.4	2,872	16.9
Asian/Pacific Islander	169	1.8	500	4.3	846	6.6	1,087	6.1	1,064	6.3

NA = Not available.
X = Not applicable.
Note: Race categories exclude persons of Hispanic ethnicity. Because of underreporting and nonreporting of racial/ethnic data, some figures are slightly lower than corresponding data in other tables. Data through 1990 are for institutions of higher education, while later data are for degree-granting institutions. Degree-granting institutions grant associate's or higher degrees and participate in Title IV federal financial aid programs. The degree-granting classification is very similar to the earlier higher education classification, but it includes more 2-year colleges and excludes a few higher education institutions that did not grant degrees. Some data have been revised from previously published figures. Detail may not sum to totals because of rounding.

Table A-22. Total Fall Enrollment in Degree-Granting Institutions, by Race/Ethnicity, Sex, Attendance Status, and Level of Student, Selected Years 1976–2019—*Continued*

(Numbers in thousands; percent.)

Race/ethnicity, sex, attendance status, and level of student	2014 Number	2014 Percent	2015 Number	2015 Percent	2016 Number	2016 Percent	2017 Number	2017 Percent	2018 Number	2018 Percent	2019 Number	2019 Percent
All students, total	20,209	100.0	19,988	100.0	19,847	100.0	19,778	100.0	19,651	100.0	19,637	100.0
White	11,239	58.3	10,939	57.6	10,717	56.9	10,517	56.0	10,305	55.2	10,142	54.3
Black	2,793	14.5	2,681	14.1	2,589	13.7	2,550	13.6	2,496	13.4	2,474	13.3
Hispanic	3,192	16.5	3,298	17.4	3,428	18.2	3,546	18.9	3,643	19.5	3,783	20.3
Asian/Pacific Islander	1,272	6.6	1,284	6.8	1,307	6.9	1,328	7.1	1,355	7.3	1,378	7.4
Asian	1,214	6.3	1,229	6.5	1,253	6.7	1,276	6.8	1,305	7.0	1,327	7.1
Pacific Islander	58	0.3	55	0.3	53	0.3	52	0.3	50	0.3	51	0.3
American Indian/Alaska Native	153	0.8	146	0.8	142	0.8	137	0.7	133	0.7	130	0.7
Two or more races	642	3.3	658	3.5	666	3.5	700	3.7	729	3.9	756	4.1
Nonresident alien	918	X	982	X	998	X	1,000	X	990	X	974	X
Male	8,798	100.0	8,724	100.0	8,638	100.0	8,571	100.0	8,445	100.0	8,363	100.0
White	4,974	60.0	4,848	59.3	4,736	58.6	4,632	57.8	4,502	57.0	4,395	56.1
Black	1,035	12.5	999	12.2	959	11.9	942	11.7	911	11.5	895	11.4
Hispanic	1,348	16.3	1,389	17.0	1,439	17.8	1,479	18.4	1,507	19.1	1,548	19.8
Asian/Pacific Islander	599	7.2	603	7.4	610	7.5	617	7.7	627	7.9	635	8.1
Asian	573	6.9	578	7.1	586	7.3	594	7.4	604	7.6	613	7.8
Pacific Islander	26	0.3	25	0.3	24	0.3	23	0.3	22	0.3	22	0.3
American Indian/Alaska Native	61	0.7	58	0.7	56	0.7	54	0.7	51	0.6	49	0.6
Two or more races	270	3.3	278	3.4	282	3.5	295	3.7	305	3.9	313	4.0
Nonresident alien	510	X	549	X	556	X	552	X	542	X	528	X
Female	11,412	100.0	11,264	100.0	11,208	100.0	11,207	100.0	11,207	100.0	11,275	100.0
White	6,265	56.9	6,091	56.2	5,981	55.6	5,885	54.7	5,803	53.9	5,747	56.1
Black	1,758	16.0	1,682	15.5	1,630	15.1	1,607	14.9	1,585	14.7	1,580	11.4
Hispanic	1,844	16.8	1,908	17.6	1,989	18.5	2,067	19.2	2,136	19.9	2,236	19.8
Asian/Pacific Islander	673	6.1	681	6.3	697	6.5	710	6.6	728	6.8	744	8.1
Asian	641	5.8	651	6.0	667	6.2	682	6.3	700	6.5	715	7.8
Pacific Islander	32	0.3	30	0.3	30	0.3	29	0.3	28	0.3	29	0.3
American Indian/Alaska Native	92	0.8	88	0.8	86	0.8	84	0.8	82	0.8	81	0.6
Two or more races	373	3.4	380	3.5	384	3.6	405	3.8	424	3.9	443	4.0
Nonresident alien	408	X	434	X	443	X	448	X	448	X	446	X
Full-time	12,454	100.0	12,288	100.0	12,125	100.0	12,076	100.0	11,990	100.0	11,966	100.0
White	6,983	59.7	6,784	59.1	6,611	58.5	6,482	57.6	6,360	56.9	6,244	55.9
Black	1,600	13.7	1,537	13.4	1,470	13.0	1,454	12.9	1,418	12.7	1,405	12.6
Hispanic	1,748	14.9	1,786	15.6	1,843	16.3	1,914	17.0	1,961	17.6	2,049	18.4
Asian/Pacific Islander	832	7.1	844	7.4	857	7.6	870	7.7	888	7.9	907	8.1
Asian	798	6.8	812	7.1	827	7.3	841	7.5	860	7.7	879	7.9
Pacific Islander	34	0.3	32	0.3	30	0.3	29	0.3	28	0.3	28	0.3
American Indian/Alaska Native	88	0.8	83	0.7	80	0.7	76	0.7	73	0.7	71	0.6
Two or more races	440	3.8	440	3.8	435	3.9	455	4.0	472	4.2	487	4.4
Nonresident alien	763	X	813	X	828	X	825	X	817	X	804	X
Part-time	7,755	100.0	7,701	100.0	7,722	100.0	7,702	100.0	7,662	100.0	7,671	100.0
White	4,256	56.0	4,155	55.2	4,105	54.4	4,035	53.6	3,946	52.7	3,898	52.0
Black	1,192	15.7	1,144	15.2	1,120	14.8	1,096	14.6	1,078	14.4	1,070	14.3
Hispanic	1,444	19.0	1,511	20.1	1,585	21.0	1,632	21.7	1,681	22.5	1,734	23.1
Asian/Pacific Islander	440	5.8	440	5.8	449	5.9	458	6.1	467	6.2	471	6.3
Asian	416	5.5	417	5.5	427	5.6	435	5.8	445	5.9	449	6.0
Pacific Islander	24	0.3	24	0.3	23	0.3	23	0.3	22	0.3	23	0.3
American Indian/Alaska Native	65	0.9	63	0.8	62	0.8	61	0.8	60	0.8	59	0.8
Two or more races	202	2.7	217	2.9	230	3.1	245	3.3	257	3.4	269	3.6
Nonresident alien	155	X	169	X	170	X	175	X	173	X	170	X
Undergraduate, total	17,294	100.0	17,047	100.0	16,875	100.0	16,773	100.0	16,616	100.0	16,565	100.0
White	9,583	57.2	9,304	56.4	9,086	55.7	8,883	54.8	8,668	54.0	8,500	53.1
Black	2,427	14.5	2,317	14.1	2,226	13.7	2,184	13.5	2,131	13.3	2,107	13.2
Hispanic	2,962	17.7	3,055	18.5	3,168	19.4	3,271	20.2	3,351	20.9	3,476	21.7
Asian/Pacific Islander	1,075	6.4	1,084	6.6	1,100	6.7	1,114	6.9	1,134	7.1	1,147	7.2

NA = Not available.
X = Not applicable.
Note: Race categories exclude persons of Hispanic ethnicity. Because of underreporting and nonreporting of racial/ethnic data, some figures are slightly lower than corresponding data in other tables. Data through 1990 are for institutions of higher education, while later data are for degree-granting institutions. Degree-granting institutions grant associate's or higher degrees and participate in Title IV federal financial aid programs. The degree-granting classification is very similar to the earlier higher education classification, but it includes more 2-year colleges and excludes a few higher education institutions that did not grant degrees. Some data have been revised from previously published figures. Detail may not sum to totals because of rounding.

Table A-22. Total Fall Enrollment in Degree-Granting Institutions, by Race/Ethnicity, Sex, Attendance Status, and Level of Student, Selected Years 1976–2019—*Continued*

(Numbers in thousands; percent.)

Race/ethnicity, sex, attendance status, and level of student	1976 Number	1976 Percent	1990 Number	1990 Percent	2000 Number	2000 Percent	2010 Number	2010 Percent	2013 Number	2013 Percent
Asian	NA	NA	NA	NA	NA	NA	1,030	5.8	1,010	5.9
Pacific Islander	NA	NA	NA	NA	NA	NA	58	0.3	54	0.3
American Indian/Alaska Native	70	0.8	95	0.8	139	1.1	179	1.0	147	0.9
Two or more races	NA	NA	NA	NA	NA	NA	294	1.7	506	3.0
Nonresident alien	143	X	219	X	288	X	398	X	484	X
Undergraduate, male	4,897	100.0	5,380	100.0	5,778	100.0	7,836	100.0	7,660	100.0
White	4,052	84.4	4,184	79.6	4,010	71.3	4,861	63.7	4,439	60.0
Black	431	9.0	448	8.5	577	10.3	983	12.9	955	12.9
Hispanic	192	4.0	327	6.2	583	10.4	1,083	14.2	1,224	16.5
Asian/Pacific Islander	91	1.9	254	4.8	402	7.1	513	6.7	507	6.9
Asian	NA	NA	NA	NA	NA	NA	487	6.4	483	6.5
Pacific Islander	NA	NA	NA	NA	NA	NA	26	0.3	25	0.3
American Indian/Alaska Native	35	0.7	40	0.8	56	1.0	72	0.9	59	0.8
Two or more races	NA	NA	NA	NA	NA	NA	122	1.6	217	2.9
Nonresident alien	96	X	126	X	150	X	201	X	258	X
Undergraduate, female	4,522	100.0	6,579	100.0	7,377	100.0	10,246	100.0	9,816	100.0
White	3,688	82.4	5,088	78.4	4,973	68.7	6,035	60.1	5,459	56.9
Black	513	11.5	699	10.8	972	13.4	1,694	16.9	1,549	16.2
Hispanic	161	3.6	398	6.1	768	10.6	1,468	14.6	1,648	17.2
Asian/Pacific Islander	78	1.7	246	3.8	444	6.1	574	5.7	557	5.8
Asian	NA	NA	NA	NA	NA	NA	542	5.4	527	5.5
Pacific Islander	NA	NA	NA	NA	NA	NA	32	0.3	30	0.3
American Indian/Alaska Native	35	0.8	56	0.9	82	1.1	107	1.1	88	0.9
Two or more races	NA	NA	NA	NA	NA	NA	171	1.7	289	3.0
Nonresident alien	47	X	93	X	138	X	197	X	225	X
Postbaccalaureate, total	1,567	100.0	1,860	100.0	2,157	100.0	2,937	100.0	2,900	100.0
White	1,336	89.6	1,450	86.0	1,479	77.2	1,825	69.4	1,691	66.5
Black	90	6.0	100	5.9	181	9.5	362	13.8	367	14.4
Hispanic	31	2.1	58	3.4	111	5.8	198	7.5	221	8.7
Asian/Pacific Islander	29	1.9	72	4.3	133	6.9	194	7.4	195	7.7
Asian	NA	NA	NA	NA	NA	NA	188	7.1	188	7.4
Pacific Islander	NA	NA	NA	NA	NA	NA	6	0.2	7	0.3
American Indian/Alaska Native	6	0.4	7	0.4	13	0.7	17	0.7	15	0.6
Two or more races	NA	NA	NA	NA	NA	NA	32	1.2	54	2.1
Nonresident alien	75	X	173	X	241	X	309	X	357	X
Postbaccalaureate, male	898	100.0	904	100.0	944	100.0	1,209	100.0	1,201	100.0
White	762	90.7	677	86.3	625	78.4	745	72.2	693	69.4
Black	39	4.7	37	4.7	58	7.3	106	10.3	110	11.0
Hispanic	18	2.2	27	3.4	45	5.6	75	7.2	84	8.4
Asian/Pacific Islander	17	2.1	40	5.2	64	8.0	87	8.5	87	8.7
Asian	NA	NA	NA	NA	NA	NA	85	8.2	84	8.4
Pacific Islander	NA	NA	NA	NA	NA	NA	3	0.2	3	0.3
American Indian/Alaska Native	4	0.4	3	0.4	5	0.6	6	0.6	5	0.5
Two or more races	NA	NA	NA	NA	NA	NA	12	1.2	21	2.1
Nonresident alien	58	X	120	X	147	X	178	X	202	X
Postbaccalaureate, female	669	100.0	955	100.0	1,213	100.0	1,728	100.0	1,699	100.0
White	574	88.1	773	85.6	854	76.3	1,080	67.7	998	64.6
Black	50	7.7	63	7.0	123	11.0	256	16.0	258	16.7
Hispanic	13	2.0	31	3.4	66	5.9	123	7.7	137	8.9
Asian/Pacific Islander	11	1.7	32	3.5	69	6.1	107	6.7	108	7.0
Asian	NA	NA	NA	NA	NA	NA	103	6.5	104	6.7
Pacific Islander	NA	NA	NA	NA	NA	NA	4	0.2	4	0.3
American Indian/Alaska Native	3	0.4	4	0.5	8	0.7	11	0.7	9	0.6
Two or more races	NA	NA	NA	NA	NA	NA	20	1.2	34	2.2
Nonresident alien	18	X	53	X	94	X	131	X	155	X

NA = Not available.
X = Not applicable.
Note: Race categories exclude persons of Hispanic ethnicity. Because of underreporting and nonreporting of racial/ethnic data, some figures are slightly lower than corresponding data in other tables. Data through 1990 are for institutions of higher education, while later data are for degree-granting institutions. Degree-granting institutions grant associate's or higher degrees and participate in Title IV federal financial aid programs. The degree-granting classification is very similar to the earlier higher education classification, but it includes more 2-year colleges and excludes a few higher education institutions that did not grant degrees. Some data have been revised from previously published figures. Detail may not sum to totals because of rounding.

Table A-22. Total Fall Enrollment in Degree-Granting Institutions, by Race/Ethnicity, Sex, Attendance Status, and Level of Student, Selected Years 1976–2019—*Continued*

(Numbers in thousands; percent.)

Race/ethnicity, sex, attendance status, and level of student	2014 Number	2014 Percent	2015 Number	2015 Percent	2016 Number	2016 Percent	2017 Number	2017 Percent	2018 Number	2018 Percent	2019 Number	2019 Percent
Asian	1,023	6.1	1,035	6.3	1,053	6.5	1,068	6.6	1,090	6.8	1,102	6.9
Pacific Islander	52	0.3	49	0.3	47	0.3	46	0.3	45	0.3	45	0.3
American Indian/Alaska Native	139	0.8	132	0.8	129	0.8	124	0.8	119	0.7	116	0.7
Two or more races	580	3.5	590	3.6	595	3.7	624	3.9	648	4.0	670	4.2
Nonresident alien	529	X	565	X	570	X	574	X	565	X	548	X
Undergraduate, male	7,586	100.0	7,502	100.0	7,417	100.0	7,351	100.0	7,228	100.0	7,149	100.0
White	4,299	58.9	4,188	58.2	4,087	57.5	3,990	56.7	3,860	55.8	3,770	55.0
Black	925	12.7	888	12.3	849	12.0	832	11.8	802	11.6	786	11.5
Hispanic	1,262	17.3	1,298	18.0	1,343	18.9	1,379	19.6	1,402	20.2	1,439	21.0
Asian/Pacific Islander	512	7.0	515	7.2	521	7.3	525	7.5	533	7.7	537	7.8
Asian	488	6.7	492	6.8	499	7.0	504	7.2	513	7.4	517	7.5
Pacific Islander	24	0.3	23	0.3	21	0.3	21	0.3	20	0.3	20	0.3
American Indian/Alaska Native	56	0.8	53	0.7	52	0.7	49	0.7	47	0.7	45	0.7
Two or more races	246	3.4	252	3.5	255	3.6	267	3.8	275	4.0	282	4.1
Nonresident alien	287	X	307	X	310	X	309	X	302	X	290	X
Undergraduate, female	9,708	100.0	9,544	100.0	9,458	100.0	9,422	100.0	9,388	100.0	9,417	100.0
White	5,283	55.8	5,116	55.1	4,999	54.3	4,893	53.4	4,799	52.6	4,730	51.6
Black	1,502	15.9	1,428	15.4	1,377	15.0	1,352	14.8	1,329	14.6	1,321	14.4
Hispanic	1,701	18.0	1,757	18.9	1,825	19.8	1,892	20.7	1,950	21.4	2,037	22.2
Asian/Pacific Islander	563	6.0	569	6.1	580	6.3	588	6.4	602	6.6	610	6.7
Asian	535	5.6	543	5.8	554	6.0	563	6.2	577	6.3	585	6.4
Pacific Islander	29	0.3	26	0.3	26	0.3	25	0.3	25	0.3	25	0.3
American Indian/Alaska Native	83	0.9	79	0.9	77	0.8	75	0.8	73	0.8	72	0.8
Two or more races	334	3.5	338	3.6	340	3.7	357	3.9	373	4.1	388	4.2
Nonresident alien	242	X	258	X	261	X	265	X	264	X	258	X
Postbaccalaureate, total	2,915	100.0	2,942	100.0	2,972	100.0	3,005	100.0	3,035	100.0	3,072	100.0
White	1,657	65.6	1,635	64.8	1,631	64.1	1,635	63.4	1,638	62.7	1,642	62.0
Black	366	14.5	364	14.4	363	14.3	365	14.2	365	14.0	367	13.9
Hispanic	229	9.1	243	9.6	260	10.2	275	10.7	291	11.1	307	11.6
Asian/Pacific Islander	197	7.8	200	7.9	206	8.1	214	8.3	221	8.5	231	8.7
Asian	191	7.6	194	7.7	200	7.9	208	8.1	215	8.2	225	8.5
Pacific Islander	6	0.3	6	0.2	6	0.2	6	0.2	6	0.2	6	0.2
American Indian/Alaska Native	14	0.6	14	0.6	14	0.5	14	0.5	14	0.5	13	0.5
Two or more races	63	2.5	67	2.7	71	2.8	70	2.9	82	3.1	86	3.2
Nonresident alien	388	X	417	X	428	X	426	X	425	X	426	X
Postbaccalaureate, male	1,211	100.0	1,222	100.0	1,222	100.0	1,220	100.0	1,216	100.0	1,214	100.0
White	675	68.3	660	67.4	649	66.5	642	65.7	633	64.9	625	64.1
Black	110	11.1	111	11.3	110	11.3	110	11.3	109	11.2	109	11.2
Hispanic	86	8.7	91	9.3	96	9.8	100	10.3	105	10.7	109	11.1
Asian/Pacific Islander	87	8.8	88	9.0	89	9.2	92	9.4	94	9.6	98	10.0
Asian	85	8.6	86	8.7	87	8.9	90	9.2	92	9.4	95	9.8
Pacific Islander	3	0.3	2	0.2	2	0.2	2	0.2	2	0.2	2	0.2
American Indian/Alaska Native	5	0.5	5	0.5	5	0.5	5	0.5	5	0.5	4	0.5
Two or more races	24	2.4	26	2.6	27	2.7	28	2.9	30	3.1	31	3.2
Nonresident alien	223	X	241	X	246	X	242	X	240	X	239	X
Postbaccalaureate, female	1,704	100.0	1,720	100.0	1,751	100.0	1,785	100.0	1,819	100.0	1,858	100.0
White	981	63.8	975	63.1	982	62.6	992	62.0	1,004	61.5	1,017	60.9
Black	256	16.6	254	16.4	253	16.1	255	15.9	256	15.7	258	15.5
Hispanic	143	9.3	152	9.8	164	10.4	175	10.9	186	11.4	199	11.9
Asian/Pacific Islander	110	7.1	112	7.3	117	7.5	122	7.6	127	7.8	133	8.0
Asian	106	6.9	109	7.0	113	7.2	118	7.4	123	7.5	129	7.7
Pacific Islander	4	0.3	4	0.2	4	0.2	4	0.2	4	0.2	4	0.2
American Indian/Alaska Native	9	0.6	9	0.6	9	0.6	9	0.6	9	0.6	9	0.5
Two or more races	39	2.5	42	2.7	44	2.8	48	3.0	51	3.1	55	3.3
Nonresident alien	165	X	176	X	182	X	184	X	185	X	187	X

NA = Not available.

X = Not applicable.

Note: Race categories exclude persons of Hispanic ethnicity. Because of underreporting and nonreporting of racial/ethnic data, some figures are slightly lower than corresponding data in other tables. Data through 1990 are for institutions of higher education, while later data are for degree-granting institutions. Degree-granting institutions grant associate's or higher degrees and participate in Title IV federal financial aid programs. The degree-granting classification is very similar to the earlier higher education classification, but it includes more 2-year colleges and excludes a few higher education institutions that did not grant degrees. Some data have been revised from previously published figures. Detail may not sum to totals because of rounding.

Table A-23. Percentage of Recent High School Completers Enrolled in College, by Race/Ethnicity, 1972–2020

(Percent.)

Year	Percent of recent high school completers¹ enrolled in college² (annual data)					3-year moving averages³ — Percent of recent high school completers enrolled in college					3-year moving averages³ — Difference between percent enrolled		
	Total	White	Black	Hispanic	Asian⁴	Total	White	Black	Hispanic	Asian⁴	White-Black	White-Hispanic	White-Asian⁴
2020	62.7	65.0	57.5	56.2	82.7	64.5	66.6	53.6	59.6	86.3	13.0	7.0	-19.7
2019	66.2	68.0	49.8	63.4	89.8	67.7	69.4	57.5	64.5	81.8	12.0	NA	-12.3
2018	69.1	70.9	64.5	65.4	73.6	67.4	69.3	58.1	63.4	82.1	11.2	5.9	-12.7
2017	66.7	69.1	59.4	61.0	82.7	68.6	69.9	60.7	66.5	82.0	9.2	NA	-12.1
2016	69.8	69.7	57.3	72.0	91.9	68.6	70.1	57.5	67.6	85.7	12.6	NA	-15.7
2015	69.2	71.3	55.6	68.9	83.2	69.1	69.6	60.8	69.0	88.5	8.8	NA	-18.9
2014	68.4	67.7	70.2	65.2	90.9	67.8	69.3	60.6	64.7	84.2	8.8	NA	-14.9
2013	65.9	68.8	56.7	59.8	80.1	66.8	67.4	60.7	65.5	83.6	6.7	NA	-16.2
2012	66.2	65.7	56.4	70.3	81.5	66.8	67.6	60.5	65.9	82.3	7.1	NA	-14.7
2011	68.2	68.3	67.1	66.6	86.1	67.5	68.2	62.1	66.1	83.9	6.1	NA	-15.7
2010	68.1	70.5	62.0	59.7	84.7	68.8	70.1	66.1	62.3	87.4	NA	7.8	-17.3
2009	70.1	71.3	69.5	59.3	92.1	68.9	71.2	62.4	60.9	88.1	8.8	10.3	-16.9
2008	68.6	71.7	55.7	63.9	88.4	68.6	70.8	60.3	62.3	90.1	10.5	8.6	-19.2
2007	67.2	69.5	55.7	64.0	88.8	67.3	70.0	55.7	62.0	85.8	14.3	8.0	-15.8
2006	66.0	68.5	55.5	57.9	82.3	67.2	70.4	55.6	58.5	85.1	14.7	11.9	-14.7
2005	68.6	73.2	55.7	54.0	86.7	67.1	70.2	58.2	57.5	80.9	12.0	12.6	-10.7
2004	66.7	68.8	62.5	61.8	75.6	66.4	69.4	58.8	57.7	81.6	10.6	11.7	-12.2
2003⁵	63.9	66.2	57.5	58.6	84.1	65.3	68.0	59.9	57.7	74.2	8.1	10.3	NA
2002	65.2	69.1	59.4	53.6	63.7	63.7	66.5	57.3	54.8	71.9	9.3	11.7	NA
2001	61.8	64.3	55.0	51.7	73.8	63.5	66.3	56.4	52.8	78.4	10.0	13.5	-12.0
2000	63.3	65.7	54.9	52.9	81.0	62.7	65.4	56.4	48.6	81.3	9.1	16.9	-15.8
1999	62.9	66.3	58.9	42.3	78.3	64.0	66.8	58.6	47.4	81.1	8.3	19.5	-14.3
1998	65.6	68.5	61.9	47.4	85.5	65.2	67.7	59.8	51.9	83.8	7.9	15.7	-16.1
1997	67.0	68.2	58.5	65.6	80.5	65.9	68.1	58.8	55.3	83.0	9.3	12.8	-15.0
1996	65.0	67.4	56.0	50.8	85.3	64.7	66.6	55.4	57.6	82.7	11.3	9.0	-16.0
1995	61.9	64.3	51.2	53.7	83.0	63.0	65.4	52.9	51.6	82.7	12.5	13.8	-17.3
1994	61.9	64.5	50.8	49.1	78.3	62.1	64.0	52.4	55.0	82.2	11.5	NA	-18.2
1993	62.6	62.9	55.6	62.2	86.2	62.1	63.9	51.3	55.7	82.5	12.6	NA	-18.6
1992	61.9	64.3	48.2	55.0	81.7	62.3	64.2	50.0	58.2	80.9	14.2	NA	-16.7
1991	62.5	65.4	46.4	57.2	78.9	61.5	64.2	47.2	52.6	80.6	17.0	11.7	-16.3
1990	60.1	63.0	46.8	42.7	81.7	60.7	63.0	48.9	52.5	81.4	14.0	NA	-18.5
1989	59.6	60.7	53.4	55.1	81.1	59.5	61.6	48.0	52.7	81.4	13.6	NA	-19.8
1988	58.9	61.1	44.4	57.1	NA	58.4	60.1	49.7	48.5	NA	10.4	11.6	NA
1987	56.8	58.6	52.2	33.5	NA	56.5	58.8	44.2	45.0	NA	14.6	13.8	NA
1986	53.8	56.8	36.9	44.0	NA	56.1	58.5	43.5	42.3	NA	15.0	16.2	NA
1985	57.7	60.1	42.2	51.0	NA	55.5	58.6	39.5	46.1	NA	19.1	12.5	NA
1984	55.2	59.0	39.8	44.3	NA	55.1	57.9	39.9	49.3	NA	18.0	NA	NA
1983	52.7	55.0	38.2	54.2	NA	52.8	55.5	38.0	46.7	NA	17.5	NA	NA
1982	50.6	52.7	35.8	43.2	NA	52.4	54.2	38.8	49.4	NA	15.4	NA	NA
1981	53.9	54.9	42.7	52.1	NA	51.3	52.4	40.3	48.7	NA	12.2	NA	NA
1980	49.3	49.8	42.7	52.3	NA	50.8	51.5	44.0	49.6	NA	7.5	NA	NA
1979	49.3	49.9	46.7	45.0	NA	49.6	50.1	45.2	46.3	NA	NA	NA	NA
1978	50.1	50.5	46.4	42.0	NA	50.0	50.4	47.5	46.1	NA	NA	NA	NA
1977	50.6	50.8	49.5	50.8	NA	49.9	50.1	46.8	48.8	NA	NA	NA	NA
1976	48.8	48.8	44.4	52.7	NA	50.1	50.3	45.3	53.6	NA	NA	NA	NA
1975	50.7	51.1	41.7	58.0	NA	49.1	49.1	44.5	52.7	NA	NA	NA	NA
1974	47.6	47.2	47.2	46.9	NA	48.3	48.7	40.5	53.1	NA	8.3	NA	NA
1973	46.6	47.8	32.5	54.1	NA	47.8	48.2	41.4	48.8	NA	6.8	NA	NA
1972	49.2	49.7	44.6	45.0	NA	49.7	50.5	38.4	49.9	NA	12.1	NA	NA

NA = Not available.
¹Individuals ages 16 to 24 who graduated from high school or completed a GED or other high school equivalency credential.
²Enrollment in college as of October of each year for individuals ages 16 to 24 who had completed high school earlier in the calendar year.
³A 3-year moving average is a weighted average of the year indicated, the year immediately preceding, and the year immediately following. For the first and final years of available data, a 2-year moving average is used: The moving average for 1960 reflects an average of 1960 and 1961; for Black and Hispanic data, the moving average for 1972 reflects an average of 1972 and 1973; for Asian-only data, the moving average for 2003 reflects an average of 2003 and 2004; and the moving average for 2019 reflects an average of 2018 and 2019. Moving averages are used to produce more stable estimates.
⁴Prior to 2003, Asian data include Pacific Islanders.
⁵After 2002, White, Black, and Asian data exclude persons of Two or more races.

PART A
NATIONAL EDUCATION STATISTICS

■ **Attainment Tables**

Table A-24. Educational Attainment of the Population 18 Years Old and Over, by Age, Sex, Race, and Hispanic Origin, 2020

(Numbers in thousands; civilian noninstitutionalized population.[1])

Age, sex, race, and Hispanic origin	Total	None	1st to 4th grade	5th to 6th grade	7th to 8th grade	9th grade	10th grade	11th grade[2]	High school graduate
ALL RACES									
Both Sexes									
18 years old and over	252,117	771	1,414	2,933	3,093	3,049	3,631	9,736	70,199
18 to 24 years old	29,059	46	33	89	149	245	491	3,368	8,602
25 years old and over	223,058	725	1,381	2,844	2,944	2,805	3,140	6,369	61,597
25 to 29 years old	23,027	25	35	67	141	140	203	596	6,387
30 to 34 years old	22,233	58	51	170	179	218	218	593	5,410
35 to 39 years old	21,560	61	88	235	234	280	302	538	5,104
40 to 44 years old	19,852	66	96	289	271	301	260	576	4,949
45 to 49 years old	19,621	73	112	290	254	294	218	525	4,780
50 to 54 years old	19,967	57	130	291	268	296	267	508	5,427
55 to 59 years old	21,142	60	164	315	241	292	313	691	6,384
60 to 64 years old	21,015	76	148	266	250	223	349	678	6,493
65 to 69 years old	17,700	49	131	259	221	192	266	496	5,002
70 to 74 years old	14,569	66	157	235	225	176	220	344	4,115
75 years old and over	22,373	134	270	427	661	391	524	824	7,545
Male									
18 years old and over	122,151	378	717	1,435	1,540	1,530	1,869	5,097	36,124
18 to 24 years old	14,634	27	16	45	76	136	285	1,824	4,770
25 years old and over	107,517	351	702	1,389	1,464	1,393	1,584	3,273	31,355
25 to 29 years old	11,682	11	10	39	62	62	98	346	3,762
30 to 34 years old	11,101	34	39	93	92	118	111	329	3,134
35 to 39 years old	10,720	30	56	127	135	137	174	295	2,883
40 to 44 years old	9,746	44	56	150	130	163	148	315	2,732
45 to 49 years old	9,474	40	64	161	142	158	117	296	2,534
50 to 54 years old	9,652	34	70	128	137	157	160	264	2,898
55 to 59 years old	10,162	33	78	148	125	156	186	386	3,236
60 to 64 years old	10,104	29	72	140	144	105	176	366	3,229
65 to 69 years old	8,307	22	56	120	108	94	130	226	2,278
70 to 74 years old	6,876	27	68	95	104	80	75	139	1,744
75 years old and over	9,694	48	133	188	286	161	209	312	2,922
Female									
18 years old and over	129,966	393	697	1,499	1,553	1,520	1,761	4,639	34,075
18 to 24 years old	14,426	19	18	44	73	108	205	1,543	3,833
25 years old and over	115,540	374	680	1,455	1,480	1,411	1,556	3,096	30,243
25 to 29 years old	11,345	15	24	29	79	78	105	250	2,624
30 to 34 years old	11,132	24	12	77	87	100	107	265	2,276
35 to 39 years old	10,840	31	32	108	99	143	128	243	2,221
40 to 44 years old	10,107	23	40	140	141	137	112	261	2,217
45 to 49 years old	10,147	34	49	128	112	136	100	229	2,246
50 to 54 years old	10,314	23	60	164	131	139	107	244	2,530
55 to 59 years old	10,980	27	85	167	116	136	128	305	3,147
60 to 64 years old	10,910	47	76	126	106	118	173	312	3,264
65 to 69 years old	9,393	26	75	139	113	98	136	270	2,724
70 to 74 years old	7,693	39	89	140	120	97	145	205	2,371
75 years old and over	12,679	85	137	238	375	230	315	512	4,623
WHITE ALONE									
Both Sexes									
18 years old and over	195,592	530	1,119	2,414	2,384	2,403	2,669	6,963	54,211
18 to 24 years old	21,310	40	23	62	131	186	334	2,463	6,183
25 years old and over	174,282	490	1,096	2,352	2,252	2,217	2,335	4,500	48,027
25 to 29 years old	16,719	18	18	54	126	102	158	409	4,619
30 to 34 years old	16,345	40	40	145	150	177	163	403	3,843
35 to 39 years old	16,245	48	77	219	184	232	236	419	3,866
40 to 44 years old	14,938	41	83	257	209	260	178	404	3,757
45 to 49 years old	14,896	53	90	250	190	224	162	389	3,610
50 to 54 years old	15,588	45	113	264	208	253	174	362	4,142
55 to 59 years old	16,907	40	135	255	194	231	252	499	5,008
60 to 64 years old	16,884	41	114	230	182	171	251	461	5,194
65 to 69 years old	14,496	32	112	171	147	140	189	304	4,119
70 to 74 years old	12,260	49	118	188	171	135	175	247	3,404
75 years old and over	19,004	83	197	320	491	291	397	602	6,465

* = Quantity zero or rounds to zero.
[1]Civilian noninstitutionalized population, plus armed forces living off post or with their families on post.
[2]Population who attained the 12th grade but received no diploma are included in this category.

Table A-24. Educational Attainment of the Population 18 Years Old and Over, by Age, Sex, Race, and Hispanic Origin, 2020—*Continued*

(Numbers in thousands; civilian noninstitutionalized population.[1])

Age, sex, race, and Hispanic origin	Educational attainment						
	Some college, no degree	Associate's degree, occupational	Associate's degree, academic	Bachelor's degree	Master's degree	Professional degree	Doctoral degree
ALL RACES							
Both Sexes							
18 years old and over..........................	44,109	10,555	14,908	55,791	23,857	3,387	4,683
18 to 24 years old	10,122	678	1,219	3,627	340	25	25
25 years old and over..........................	33,986	9,877	13,689	52,164	23,516	3,362	4,659
25 to 29 years old	3,922	1,010	1,478	6,862	1,824	162	176
30 to 34 years old	3,378	942	1,449	6,304	2,404	365	494
35 to 39 years old	3,044	992	1,318	5,805	2,692	353	512
40 to 44 years old	2,750	838	1,331	4,840	2,493	336	456
45 to 49 years old	2,754	952	1,311	4,762	2,421	330	544
50 to 54 years old	2,874	954	1,184	4,685	2,292	314	418
55 to 59 years old	3,160	1,069	1,350	4,495	1,932	283	394
60 to 64 years old	3,359	925	1,401	4,308	1,901	273	367
65 to 69 years old	2,931	811	1,095	3,591	1,926	319	410
70 to 74 years old	2,495	630	878	2,708	1,661	278	380
75 years old and over.......................	3,320	754	894	3,804	1,970	349	507
Male							
18 years old and over..........................	21,126	5,001	6,211	26,156	10,364	1,966	2,637
18 to 24 years old	4,886	364	508	1,535	140	9	12
25 years old and over..........................	16,240	4,637	5,704	24,621	10,223	1,957	2,624
25 to 29 years old	2,062	508	665	3,219	688	92	59
30 to 34 years old	1,696	441	719	2,903	1,000	174	217
35 to 39 years old	1,490	525	555	2,812	1,037	190	273
40 to 44 years old	1,346	404	601	2,263	1,005	137	251
45 to 49 years old	1,307	444	564	2,134	1,060	166	285
50 to 54 years old	1,345	470	429	2,171	980	183	228
55 to 59 years old	1,420	506	506	2,068	879	188	247
60 to 64 years old	1,614	416	534	1,996	907	166	210
65 to 69 years old	1,449	343	410	1,781	848	200	241
70 to 74 years old	1,165	276	360	1,441	853	199	250
75 years old and over.......................	1,345	303	362	1,832	965	261	364
Female							
18 years old and over..........................	22,983	5,554	8,697	29,635	13,493	1,421	2,047
18 to 24 years old	5,236	314	711	2,093	200	16	12
25 years old and over..........................	17,746	5,240	7,985	27,542	13,293	1,405	2,034
25 to 29 years old	1,860	502	812	3,643	1,136	71	117
30 to 34 years old	1,682	500	730	3,401	1,405	191	276
35 to 39 years old	1,553	468	762	2,993	1,656	163	239
40 to 44 years old	1,404	434	730	2,577	1,488	199	205
45 to 49 years old	1,447	508	748	2,627	1,361	164	260
50 to 54 years old	1,529	484	756	2,514	1,312	131	190
55 to 59 years old	1,741	563	845	2,426	1,053	95	147
60 to 64 years old	1,744	508	867	2,312	993	107	158
65 to 69 years old	1,482	468	685	1,810	1,078	118	170
70 to 74 years old	1,329	355	518	1,268	808	80	130
75 years old and over.......................	1,975	451	532	1,972	1,005	87	143
WHITE ALONE							
Both Sexes							
18 years old and over..........................	33,891	8,640	11,958	43,760	18,450	2,663	3,539
18 to 24 years old	7,350	569	962	2,753	226	16	12
25 years old and over..........................	26,540	8,070	10,996	41,008	18,225	2,647	3,527
25 to 29 years old	2,697	825	1,148	5,102	1,211	106	125
30 to 34 years old	2,435	733	1,162	4,704	1,753	246	351
35 to 39 years old	2,220	753	1,037	4,406	1,901	257	389
40 to 44 years old	2,110	655	1,000	3,662	1,779	232	313
45 to 49 years old	2,139	722	1,022	3,659	1,785	249	353
50 to 54 years old	2,230	805	957	3,725	1,770	242	298
55 to 59 years old	2,549	915	1,102	3,622	1,582	240	283
60 to 64 years old	2,670	790	1,120	3,524	1,600	239	297
65 to 69 years old	2,417	691	916	2,992	1,639	277	350
70 to 74 years old	2,145	534	748	2,291	1,473	253	329
75 years old and over.......................	2,929	648	783	3,320	1,732	206	440

* – Quantity zero or rounds to zero.
[1]Civilian noninstitutionalized population, plus armed forces living off post or with their families on post.
[2]Population who attained the 12th grade but received no diploma are included in this category.

Table A-24. Educational Attainment of the Population 18 Years Old and Over, by Age, Sex, Race, and Hispanic Origin, 2020—*Continued*

(Numbers in thousands; civilian noninstitutionalized population.[1])

Age, sex, race, and Hispanic origin	Total	None	1st to 4th grade	5th to 6th grade	7th to 8th grade	9th grade	10th grade	11th grade[2]	High school graduate
Male									
18 years old and over	95,967	297	597	1,217	1,196	1,207	1,361	3,710	28,145
18 to 24 years old	10,836	24	12	38	70	103	180	1,357	3,524
25 years old and over	85,131	273	585	1,180	1,126	1,104	1,181	2,352	24,621
25 to 29 years old	8,562	11	4	31	55	45	83	225	2,775
30 to 34 years old	8,269	25	31	90	76	99	78	224	2,262
35 to 39 years old	8,283	25	52	120	103	108	142	238	2,227
40 to 44 years old	7,477	31	48	138	98	139	100	219	2,130
45 to 49 years old	7,294	34	49	143	107	121	95	228	1,964
50 to 54 years old	7,667	28	63	117	112	132	95	216	2,257
55 to 59 years old	8,163	25	72	127	99	121	146	284	2,542
60 to 64 years old	8,301	19	58	118	112	89	132	261	2,610
65 to 69 years old	6,898	18	52	77	70	71	87	127	1,858
70 to 74 years old	5,870	23	52	76	78	62	60	108	1,454
75 years old and over	8,347	35	105	141	215	119	163	222	2,542
Female									
18 years old and over	99,625	232	522	1,197	1,188	1,195	1,309	3,253	26,065
18 to 24 years old	10,474	16	12	24	61	83	154	1,106	2,659
25 years old and over	89,151	216	511	1,172	1,126	1,112	1,155	2,148	23,407
25 to 29 years old	8,158	8	14	22	72	58	74	184	1,844
30 to 34 years old	8,075	15	9	54	74	78	84	180	1,581
35 to 39 years old	7,962	23	25	99	81	124	95	181	1,639
40 to 44 years old	7,462	10	35	119	111	121	78	185	1,627
45 to 49 years old	7,602	19	41	107	83	102	67	161	1,646
50 to 54 years old	7,921	17	50	147	96	121	79	146	1,885
55 to 59 years old	8,744	15	63	129	95	111	107	215	2,466
60 to 64 years old	8,583	21	56	112	70	82	119	200	2,585
65 to 69 years old	7,598	14	60	94	77	69	102	177	2,261
70 to 74 years old	6,389	26	66	112	92	73	114	139	1,950
75 years old and over	10,657	48	93	178	276	173	235	380	3,923
BLACK ALONE									
Both Sexes									
18 years old and over	32,115	83	112	229	374	371	598	1,890	10,762
18 to 24 years old	4,292	*	5	13	11	34	96	545	1,516
25 years old and over	27,822	83	108	215	363	337	502	1,345	9,246
25 to 29 years old	3,551	1	12	*	8	22	28	110	1,247
30 to 34 years old	3,210	12	9	12	16	17	33	147	1,134
35 to 39 years old	2,886	3	*	9	13	32	40	91	845
40 to 44 years old	2,668	17	2	19	28	23	56	118	828
45 to 49 years old	2,587	10	10	21	20	46	26	94	794
50 to 54 years old	2,582	3	2	7	29	16	54	112	878
55 to 59 years old	2,497	3	11	24	23	30	35	140	889
60 to 64 years old	2,584	7	13	17	33	27	55	165	872
65 to 69 years old	1,954	9	6	40	46	28	60	132	607
70 to 74 years old	1,318	3	18	16	28	32	36	73	454
75 years old and over	1,985	13	25	50	119	64	79	164	700
Male									
18 years old and over	14,643	29	45	102	177	192	344	922	5,477
18 to 24 years old	2,068	*	2	*	2	18	66	291	785
25 years old and over	12,576	29	43	102	175	173	278	630	4,693
25 to 29 years old	1,740	*	6	*	5	9	11	74	676
30 to 34 years old	1,528	9	6	*	7	10	24	76	639
35 to 39 years old	1,324	*	*	*	10	17	16	44	463
40 to 44 years old	1,211	8	*	9	9	17	37	63	434
45 to 49 years old	1,157	*	5	9	16	28	14	45	380
50 to 54 years old	1,168	3	*	5	13	12	46	34	443
55 to 59 years old	1,140	3	*	12	13	16	22	69	474
60 to 64 years old	1,131	2	4	10	16	12	29	82	433
65 to 69 years old	888	4	1	23	22	11	40	66	300
70 to 74 years old	538	*	11	9	14	14	12	14	204
75 years old and over	751	*	10	24	50	27	27	62	246
Female									
18 years old and over	17,471	54	67	126	197	179	255	968	5,285
18 to 24 years old	2,225	*	3	13	9	16	30	253	731

* = Quantity zero or rounds to zero.
[1]Civilian noninstitutionalized population, plus armed forces living off post or with their families on post.
[2]Population who attained the 12th grade but received no diploma are included in this category.

Table A-24. Educational Attainment of the Population 18 Years Old and Over, by Age, Sex, Race, and Hispanic Origin, 2020—*Continued*

(Numbers in thousands; civilian noninstitutionalized population.[1])

Age, sex, race, and Hispanic origin	Educational attainment						
	Some college, no degree	Associate's degree, occupational	Associate's degree, academic	Bachelor's degree	Master's degree	Professional degree	Doctoral degree
Male							
18 years old and over	16,355	4,228	5,018	20,907	8,101	1,616	2,012
18 to 24 years old	3,540	318	387	1,178	100	3	2
25 years old and over	12,816	3,910	4,630	19,728	8,001	1,613	2,010
25 to 29 years old	1,410	436	526	2,440	414	56	50
30 to 34 years old	1,237	382	583	2,186	730	118	150
35 to 39 years old	1,134	408	457	2,176	727	147	220
40 to 44 years old	1,060	345	463	1,732	717	91	165
45 to 49 years old	1,043	331	438	1,639	784	129	187
50 to 54 years old	1,018	416	343	1,788	776	147	161
55 to 59 years old	1,176	439	401	1,686	703	168	175
60 to 64 years old	1,336	362	446	1,669	765	156	166
65 to 69 years old	1,204	303	342	1,550	753	185	200
70 to 74 years old	1,024	236	314	1,242	749	178	213
75 years old and over	1,173	251	317	1,621	883	239	323
Female							
18 years old and over	17,535	4,412	6,941	22,854	10,348	1,047	1,527
18 to 24 years old	3,811	251	575	1,574	125	14	10
25 years old and over	13,725	4,161	6,366	21,279	10,223	1,033	1,517
25 to 29 years old	1,286	389	622	2,662	797	50	75
30 to 34 years old	1,198	351	579	2,518	1,023	129	202
35 to 39 years old	1,086	345	580	2,230	1,174	111	169
40 to 44 years old	1,050	310	537	1,930	1,062	140	148
45 to 49 years old	1,096	391	583	2,020	1,001	119	165
50 to 54 years old	1,212	389	614	1,937	995	95	137
55 to 59 years old	1,373	475	702	1,936	879	72	108
60 to 64 years old	1,334	428	673	1,855	835	83	131
65 to 69 years old	1,213	388	574	1,442	886	92	150
70 to 74 years old	1,121	298	433	1,049	724	75	116
75 years old and over	1,756	398	467	1,699	849	67	117
BLACK ALONE							
Both Sexes							
18 years old and over	6,528	1,260	1,769	5,344	2,177	283	335
18 to 24 years old	1,490	71	119	347	33	6	7
25 years old and over	5,038	1,189	1,650	4,997	2,144	277	328
25 to 29 years old	812	118	203	803	155	24	8
30 to 34 years old	617	117	187	650	187	45	28
35 to 39 years old	570	165	154	596	302	39	28
40 to 44 years old	393	114	210	542	247	36	35
45 to 49 years old	382	159	183	474	274	30	65
50 to 54 years old	437	106	142	498	235	29	32
55 to 59 years old	436	111	165	415	165	17	32
60 to 64 years old	530	98	167	387	172	13	30
65 to 69 years old	365	81	99	262	179	17	23
70 to 74 years old	248	58	72	164	89	4	22
75 years old and over	248	61	68	205	140	24	25
Male							
18 years old and over	2,951	492	668	2,275	688	128	153
18 to 24 years old	679	31	52	119	10	6	7
25 years old and over	2,272	460	616	2,156	679	122	147
25 to 29 years old	429	44	80	347	42	17	*
30 to 34 years old	270	25	85	284	51	22	9
35 to 39 years old	266	85	37	272	101	11	2
40 to 44 years old	176	29	88	239	60	20	22
45 to 49 years old	151	83	79	218	86	9	33
50 to 54 years old	229	30	58	199	77	12	8
55 to 59 years old	154	46	61	183	65	6	16
60 to 64 years old	202	44	43	163	71	3	17
65 to 69 years old	184	21	39	106	54	0	10
70 to 74 years old	83	24	25	67	40	4	15
75 years old and over	117	29	22	79	33	10	14
Female							
18 years old and over	3,577	768	1,101	3,069	1,488	156	181
18 to 24 years old	811	40	67	228	23	*	*

* = Quantity zero or rounds to zero.
[1]Civilian noninstitutionalized population, plus armed forces living off post or with their families on post.
[2]Population who attained the 12th grade but received no diploma are included in this category.

Table A-24. Educational Attainment of the Population 18 Years Old and Over, by Age, Sex, Race, and Hispanic Origin, 2020—*Continued*

(Numbers in thousands; civilian noninstitutionalized population.[1])

Age, sex, race, and Hispanic origin	Total	None	1st to 4th grade	5th to 6th grade	7th to 8th grade	9th grade	10th grade	11th grade[2]	High school graduate
25 years old and over	15,247	54	64	113	187	163	224	715	4,554
25 to 29 years old	1,811	1	5	*	3	13	17	36	571
30 to 34 years old	1,683	3	3	12	9	6	9	70	495
35 to 39 years old	1,561	3	*	9	3	14	24	48	381
40 to 44 years old	1,457	9	2	10	19	6	20	55	394
45 to 49 years old	1,430	10	5	12	4	18	12	49	413
50 to 54 years old	1,414	*	2	2	16	5	8	77	435
55 to 59 years old	1,357	*	11	12	11	14	13	71	415
60 to 64 years old	1,453	5	9	7	16	15	26	82	438
65 to 69 years old	1,067	5	4	17	24	18	21	66	307
70 to 74 years old	780	3	7	7	14	17	24	59	250
75 years old and over	1,234	13	15	26	69	37	52	101	454
ASIAN ALONE									
Both Sexes									
18 years old and over	16,010	141	120	167	216	151	199	398	2,664
18 to 24 years old	1,775	6	5	5	2	11	21	145	323
25 years old and over	14,235	135	115	162	213	141	178	253	2,341
25 to 29 years old	1,675	6	6	1	3	8	10	23	178
30 to 34 years old	1,744	2	2	8	9	5	12	18	173
35 to 39 years old	1,661	8	2	2	17	6	11	9	200
40 to 44 years old	1,518	8	5	8	17	6	6	17	171
45 to 49 years old	1,509	6	5	14	25	13	24	23	214
50 to 54 years old	1,241	5	12	9	17	18	23	20	240
55 to 59 years old	1,172	17	12	20	20	14	18	26	264
60 to 64 years old	1,078	28	9	12	27	17	21	36	266
65 to 69 years old	885	6	11	26	20	17	10	29	184
70 to 74 years old	715	14	17	21	21	9	5	13	162
75 years old and over	1,038	34	34	41	36	27	37	38	289
Male									
18 years old and over	7,538	46	44	47	92	68	84	206	1,187
18 to 24 years old	880	3	2	2	*	3	14	69	153
25 years old and over	6,659	43	41	45	92	65	70	137	1,034
25 to 29 years old	846	*	*	*	2	8	4	19	97
30 to 34 years old	844	*	2	3	5	5	2	11	94
35 to 39 years old	754	4	*	2	8	3	5	3	103
40 to 44 years old	724	5	5	2	12	2	5	7	54
45 to 49 years old	725	2	2	7	6	4	8	14	106
50 to 54 years old	562	4	6	1	3	10	13	10	107
55 to 59 years old	586	4	6	4	13	11	11	22	115
60 to 64 years old	472	8	3	4	11	4	10	12	116
65 to 69 years old	344	*	3	5	9	6	1	13	79
70 to 74 years old	341	4	4	6	8	3	*	9	57
75 years old and over	461	13	10	9	14	10	12	17	106
Female									
18 years old and over	8,472	95	76	120	124	83	115	191	1,477
18 to 24 years old	895	3	2	3	2	8	8	76	170
25 years old and over	7,577	92	74	117	122	75	107	116	1,307
25 to 29 years old	829	6	6	1	1	*	6	4	82
30 to 34 years old	899	2	*	5	4	*	11	8	80
35 to 39 years old	907	5	2	*	8	3	6	6	97
40 to 44 years old	794	4	*	5	6	4	1	10	116
45 to 49 years old	785	4	2	7	20	9	16	9	108
50 to 54 years old	679	2	6	7	14	8	10	10	133
55 to 59 years old	586	13	6	16	7	4	6	4	149
60 to 64 years old	606	20	7	8	16	13	12	24	149
65 to 69 years old	541	6	9	22	11	11	10	15	105
70 to 74 years old	374	10	13	15	14	6	5	4	105
75 years old and over	577	21	24	31	22	17	25	20	182
HISPANIC (OF ANY RACE)									
Both Sexes									
18 years old and over	41,994	397	1,047	2,317	1,313	1,483	1,007	2,726	13,279
18 to 24 years old	6,788	20	16	75	28	119	133	854	2,294

* = Quantity zero or rounds to zero.
[1] Civilian noninstitutionalized population, plus armed forces living off post or with their families on post.
[2] Population who attained the 12th grade but received no diploma are included in this category.

Table A-24. Educational Attainment of the Population 18 Years Old and Over, by Age, Sex, Race, and Hispanic Origin, 2020—*Continued*

(Numbers in thousands; civilian noninstitutionalized population.[1])

Age, sex, race, and Hispanic origin	Educational attainment						
	Some college, no degree	Associate's degree, occupational	Associate's degree, academic	Bachelor's degree	Master's degree	Professional degree	Doctoral degree
25 years old and over	2,766	728	1,034	2,841	1,465	156	181
25 to 29 years old	383	74	123	456	113	7	8
30 to 34 years old	338	92	102	367	136	23	18
35 to 39 years old	304	80	116	324	201	28	26
40 to 44 years old	216	85	122	303	186	16	13
45 to 49 years old	231	75	104	256	188	20	31
50 to 54 years old	208	76	84	299	158	18	25
55 to 59 years old	282	66	105	232	100	11	16
60 to 64 years old	327	54	124	225	101	10	13
65 to 69 years old	181	60	61	156	125	9	13
70 to 74 years old	165	35	46	97	49	*	6
75 years old and over	131	32	46	126	106	14	11

ASIAN ALONE

Both Sexes

18 years old and over	1,771	361	652	5,276	2,803	367	727
18 to 24 years old	679	23	82	401	64	2	6
25 years old and over	1,091	338	570	4,875	2,739	364	721
25 to 29 years old	161	29	61	729	404	28	28
30 to 34 years old	102	40	46	720	433	66	106
35 to 39 years old	119	35	48	631	436	45	91
40 to 44 years old	114	37	66	503	403	60	97
45 to 49 years old	112	43	61	498	310	44	116
50 to 54 years old	113	24	54	353	248	28	79
55 to 59 years old	90	22	45	365	161	22	75
60 to 64 years old	83	22	69	323	108	16	40
65 to 69 years old	67	30	61	288	90	17	30
70 to 74 years old	53	25	37	214	77	21	24
75 years old and over	79	30	21	251	70	18	34

Male

18 years old and over	898	167	290	2,349	1,421	201	438
18 to 24 years old	367	9	44	181	28	*	4
25 years old and over	530	158	246	2,168	1,393	201	434
25 to 29 years old	95	16	27	346	207	18	9
30 to 34 years old	58	17	27	330	205	33	54
35 to 39 years old	45	15	22	280	188	25	51
40 to 44 years old	52	12	28	244	211	26	58
45 to 49 years old	47	19	26	231	171	25	55
50 to 54 years old	55	14	15	132	117	17	58
55 to 59 years old	45	16	20	153	100	14	52
60 to 64 years old	44	7	31	125	64	7	26
65 to 69 years old	25	11	24	98	35	7	28
70 to 74 years old	24	14	11	111	56	17	17
75 years old and over	40	18	15	119	41	12	24

Female

18 years old and over	873	194	362	2,926	1,381	166	289
18 to 24 years old	312	14	38	220	35	2	2
25 years old and over	561	180	324	2,707	1,346	163	287
25 to 29 years old	66	14	34	384	197	9	19
30 to 34 years old	44	23	19	391	228	33	52
35 to 39 years old	73	20	26	351	248	20	40
40 to 44 years old	61	25	38	259	192	34	39
45 to 49 years old	65	24	34	267	139	20	60
50 to 54 years old	58	10	39	221	131	10	21
55 to 59 years old	44	7	25	212	61	8	23
60 to 64 years old	39	15	38	198	44	9	14
65 to 69 years old	42	19	37	190	56	10	2
70 to 74 years old	29	12	26	103	21	4	7
75 years old and over	39	12	6	131	29	6	10

HISPANIC (OF ANY RACE)

Both Sexes

18 years old and over	7,041	1,448	2,115	5,514	1,766	269	273
18 to 24 years old	2,316	131	311	449	35	*	3

* = Quantity zero or rounds to zero.
[1]Civilian noninstitutionalized population, plus armed forces living off post or with their families on post.
[2]Population who attained the 12th grade but received no diploma are included in this category.

Table A-24. Educational Attainment of the Population 18 Years Old and Over, by Age, Sex, Race, and Hispanic Origin, 2020—*Continued*

(Numbers in thousands; civilian noninstitutionalized population.[1])

Age, sex, race, and Hispanic origin	Total	None	1st to 4th grade	5th to 6th grade	7th to 8th grade	9th grade	10th grade	11th grade[2]	High school graduate
25 years old and over......................	35,206	376	1,031	2,241	1,285	1,365	874	1,872	10,985
25 to 29 years old	4,993	3	16	60	58	67	73	228	1,737
30 to 34 years old	4,478	34	40	152	109	152	98	239	1,543
35 to 39 years old	4,496	24	79	221	165	183	147	232	1,412
40 to 44 years old	4,123	39	82	258	166	212	125	266	1,282
45 to 49 years old	3,838	47	87	253	172	171	98	208	1,261
50 to 54 years old	3,303	40	108	276	159	177	81	176	976
55 to 59 years old	2,970	38	139	268	108	154	67	183	806
60 to 64 years old	2,218	37	126	224	88	72	74	105	639
65 to 69 years old	1,747	34	101	183	89	69	27	86	452
70 to 74 years old	1,307	28	107	146	77	38	37	66	355
75 years old and over......................	1,733	53	146	200	94	70	47	82	522
Male									
18 years old and over......................	20,891	251	538	1,177	655	711	481	1,411	7,067
18 to 24 years old	3,415	12	4	41	26	71	57	440	1,230
25 years old and over......................	17,476	239	533	1,137	629	641	424	970	5,837
25 to 29 years old	2,603	3	4	33	21	33	37	120	991
30 to 34 years old	2,285	19	31	90	49	84	43	134	868
35 to 39 years old	2,330	18	55	125	95	77	82	114	793
40 to 44 years old	2,069	27	44	140	71	110	75	147	703
45 to 49 years old	1,928	38	49	141	101	82	55	112	672
50 to 54 years old	1,632	25	60	126	83	90	39	99	533
55 to 59 years old	1,420	28	69	127	54	67	26	88	407
60 to 64 years old	1,108	18	65	113	51	38	26	59	300
65 to 69 years old	791	18	47	92	38	30	14	40	184
70 to 74 years old	566	19	45	60	31	12	10	29	162
75 years old and over......................	744	27	64	90	34	19	19	28	223
Female									
18 years old and over......................	21,103	146	509	1,139	658	772	526	1,315	6,212
18 to 24 years old	3,373	8	12	35	2	48	75	413	1,064
25 years old and over......................	17,730	138	498	1,104	656	724	450	901	5,148
25 to 29 years old	2,390	*	13	28	36	35	36	108	746
30 to 34 years old	2,193	15	9	61	60	68	55	106	675
35 to 39 years old	2,166	6	24	96	70	106	65	118	619
40 to 44 years old	2,054	13	38	119	95	102	50	119	578
45 to 49 years old	1,911	9	38	112	71	89	43	96	589
50 to 54 years old	1,671	15	49	149	77	87	42	77	443
55 to 59 years old	1,550	10	70	141	54	87	42	95	399
60 to 64 years old	1,110	18	61	111	37	35	48	46	339
65 to 69 years old	956	16	54	91	51	38	14	46	268
70 to 74 years old	741	10	61	85	46	26	27	36	193
75 years old and over......................	989	27	82	110	60	51	29	54	299

* = Quantity zero or rounds to zero.
[1]Civilian noninstitutionalized population, plus armed forces living off post or with their families on post.
[2]Population who attained the 12th grade but received no diploma are included in this category.

Table A-24. Educational Attainment of the Population 18 Years Old and Over, by Age, Sex, Race, and Hispanic Origin, 2020—*Continued*

(Numbers in thousands; civilian noninstitutionalized population.[1])

Age, sex, race, and Hispanic origin	Educational attainment						
	Some college, no degree	Associate's degree, occupational	Associate's degree, academic	Bachelor's degree	Master's degree	Professional degree	Doctoral degree
25 years old and over......................	4,725	1,317	1,801	5,065	1,731	269	270
25 to 29 years old	928	218	362	973	230	20	20
30 to 34 years old	671	196	264	674	240	37	31
35 to 39 years old	637	178	235	706	219	25	34
40 to 44 years old	553	142	200	528	194	45	32
45 to 49 years old	412	149	168	547	205	26	37
50 to 54 years old	379	124	116	440	202	34	15
55 to 59 years old	376	104	171	374	143	18	21
60 to 64 years old	280	73	95	273	97	14	21
65 to 69 years old	205	50	76	245	85	13	25
70 to 74 years old	145	38	67	126	51	11	14
75 years old and over......................	140	39	48	179	66	26	21
Male							
18 years old and over........................	3,408	695	937	2,515	775	154	117
18 to 24 years old	1,133	77	151	159	14	*	*
25 years old and over........................	2,275	618	786	2,356	761	154	117
25 to 29 years old	489	108	166	468	115	13	1
30 to 34 years old	343	89	136	284	82	27	6
35 to 39 years old	307	86	104	352	92	16	15
40 to 44 years old	261	55	77	242	86	18	12
45 to 49 years old	183	74	72	235	84	13	19
50 to 54 years old	165	63	35	213	81	16	4
55 to 59 years old	166	52	67	182	66	7	16
60 to 64 years old	128	35	51	142	59	7	14
65 to 69 years old	105	26	37	100	41	9	10
70 to 74 years old	66	18	19	56	22	8	8
75 years old and over......................	63	12	22	81	32	18	12
Female							
18 years old and over........................	3,633	753	1,178	2,999	991	116	156
18 to 24 years old	1,184	54	163	290	21	*	3
25 years old and over........................	2,450	698	1,015	2,709	970	116	153
25 to 29 years old	438	110	196	506	115	6	19
30 to 34 years old	328	107	128	390	158	9	25
35 to 39 years old	330	92	131	354	127	9	19
40 to 44 years old	292	86	123	285	108	27	21
45 to 49 years old	229	74	96	312	121	13	18
50 to 54 years old	213	61	82	226	121	18	12
55 to 59 years old	210	52	105	193	77	11	4
60 to 64 years old	152	38	44	131	38	7	6
65 to 69 years old	101	31	39	145	44	4	15
70 to 74 years old	80	20	47	70	29	3	6
75 years old and over......................	77	26	26	98	33	8	9

* = Quantity zero or rounds to zero.
[1]Civilian noninstitutionalized population, plus armed forces living off post or with their families on post.
[2]Population who attained the 12th grade but received no diploma are included in this category.

Table A-25. Educational Attainment of the Population 25 Years Old and Over, by Marital Status and Sex, 2020

(Numbers in thousands; percent; civilian noninstitutionalized population.[1])

Sex and marital status	Educational attainment									
	Total		None to 8th grade		9th to 11th grade		High school graduate		Some college, no degree	
	Number	Percent	Number	Percent	Number	Percent	Number	Percent	Number	Percent
BOTH SEXES										
Total...	223,058	100.0	7,895	100.0	12,313	100.0	61,597	100.0	33,986	100.0
Married spouse present	127,930	57.4	4,226	53.5	5,690	46.2	31,970	51.9	18,068	53.2
Married spouse absent, not separated	3,286	1.5	245	3.1	199	1.6	923	1.5	426	1.3
Separated..	4,275	1.9	306	3.9	501	4.1	1,473	2.4	728	2.1
Widowed..	14,712	6.6	1,044	13.2	1,361	11.1	5,335	8.7	2,452	7.2
Divorced..	25,205	11.3	626	7.9	1,571	12.8	7,719	12.5	4,629	13.6
Never married	47,649	21.4	1,448	18.3	2,992	24.3	14,178	23.0	7,683	22.6
MALE										
Total...	107,517	100.0	3,906	100.0	6,250	100.0	31,355	100.0	16,240	100.0
Married spouse present	64,165	59.7	2,303	59.0	3,036	48.6	16,660	53.1	9,141	56.3
Married spouse absent, not separated	1,637	1.5	158	4.0	87	1.4	482	1.5	179	1.1
Separated..	1,734	1.6	147	3.8	200	3.2	661	2.1	260	1.6
Widowed..	3,470	3.2	234	6.0	330	5.3	1,241	4.0	569	3.5
Divorced..	10,626	9.9	262	6.7	772	12.4	3,683	11.7	1,874	11.5
Never married	25,886	24.1	802	20.5	1,825	29.2	8,628	27.5	4,217	26.0
FEMALE										
Total...	115,540	100.0	3,988	100.0	6,063	100.0	30,243	100.0	17,746	100.0
Married spouse present	63,765	55.2	1,922	48.2	2,654	43.8	15,310	50.6	8,927	50.3
Married spouse absent, not separated	1,649	1.4	86	2.2	113	1.9	441	1.5	247	1.4
Separated..	2,542	2.2	160	4.0	300	4.9	812	2.7	468	2.6
Widowed..	11,242	9.7	810	20.3	1,031	17.0	4,094	13.5	1,883	10.6
Divorced..	14,578	12.6	364	9.1	799	13.2	4,036	13.3	2,755	15.5
Never married	21,763	18.8	647	16.2	1,166	19.2	5,550	18.4	3,466	19.5

[1]Plus armed forces living off post or with their families on post.

Table A-25. Educational Attainment of the Population 25 Years Old and Over, by Marital Status and Sex, 2020—*Continued*

(Numbers in thousands; percent; civilian noninstitutionalized population.[1])

Sex and marital status	Educational attainment									
	Associate's degree		Bachelor's degree		Master's degree		Professional degree		Doctoral degree	
	Number	Percent	Number	Percent	Number	Percent	Number	Percent	Number	Percent
BOTH SEXES										
Total..	23,566	100.0	52,164	100.0	23,516	100.0	3,362	100.0	4,659	100.0
Married spouse present	13,714	58.2	32,361	62.0	16,169	68.8	2,354	70.0	3,380	72.5
Married spouse absent, not separated	317	1.3	693	1.3	337	1.4	50	1.5	96	2.1
Separated...................................	384	1.6	575	1.1	237	1.0	46	1.4	24	0.5
Widowed.....................................	1,299	5.5	2,072	4.0	885	3.8	121	3.6	144	3.1
Divorced.....................................	3,319	14.1	4,707	9.0	2,025	8.6	298	8.9	311	6.7
Never married	4,532	19.2	11,755	22.5	3,864	16.4	494	14.7	703	15.1
MALE										
Total..	10,341	100.0	24,621	100.0	10,223	100.0	1,957	100.0	2,624	100.0
Married spouse present	6,305	61.0	15,663	63.6	7,548	73.8	1,443	73.7	2,065	78.7
Married spouse absent, not separated	144	1.4	362	1.5	152	1.5	24	1.2	50	1.9
Separated...................................	118	1.1	225	0.9	82	0.8	28	1.4	13	0.5
Widowed.....................................	260	2.5	503	2.0	217	2.1	55	2.8	60	2.3
Divorced.....................................	1,226	11.9	1,931	7.8	611	6.0	141	7.2	127	4.8
Never married	2,287	22.1	5,938	24.1	1,613	15.8	265	13.5	310	11.8
FEMALE										
Total..	13,225	100.0	27,542	100.0	13,293	100.0	1,405	100.0	2,034	100.0
Married spouse present	7,409	56.0	16,698	60.6	8,621	64.9	910	64.8	1,315	64.7
Married spouse absent, not separated	174	1.3	332	1.2	186	1.4	25	1.0	46	2.3
Separated...................................	266	2.0	351	1.3	155	1.2	18	1.3	11	0.5
Widowed.....................................	1,039	7.9	1,569	5.7	667	5.0	66	4.7	84	4.1
Divorced.....................................	2,093	15.8	2,777	10.1	1,414	10.6	157	11.2	184	9.0
Never married	2,245	17.0	5,817	21.1	2,250	16.9	229	16.3	394	19.4

[1]Plus armed forces living off post or with their families on post.

Table A-26. Educational Attainment of the Population 25 Years Old and Over, by Household Relationship and Sex, 2020

(Numbers in thousands; percent; civilian noninstitutionalized population.[1])

Sex and household relationship	Educational attainment									
	Total		None to 8th grade		9th to 11th grade		High school graduate		Some college, no degree	
	Number	Percent	Number	Percent	Number	Percent	Number	Percent	Number	Percent
BOTH SEXES										
Total..	223,058	100.0	7,895	100.0	12,313	100.0	61,597	100.0	33,986	100.0
Family householder...........................	81,157	36.4	2,438	30.9	4,034	32.8	19,751	32.1	13,407	39.4
Married spouse present...................	61,680	76.0	1,694	69.5	2,500	62.0	13,944	70.6	9,562	71.3
Other family householder................	19,477	24.0	743	30.5	1,534	38.0	5,807	29.4	3,844	28.7
Nonfamily householder......................	42,024	18.8	1,238	15.7	2,611	21.2	11,385	18.5	6,973	20.5
Living alone..................................	34,952	83.2	1,075	86.8	2,256	86.4	9,851	86.5	5,853	83.9
Living with nonrelatives.................	7,072	16.8	164	13.2	355	13.6	1,534	13.5	1,120	16.1
Relative of householder	87,603	39.3	3,771	47.8	4,971	40.4	26,492	43.0	11,737	34.5
Spouse..	61,481	70.2	1,920	50.9	2,782	56.0	16,329	61.6	7,955	67.8
Other..	26,122	29.8	1,851	49.1	2,189	44.0	10,163	38.4	3,782	32.2
Nonrelative....................................	12,274	5.5	447	5.7	697	5.7	3,969	6.4	1,869	5.5
MALE										
Total..	107,517	100.0	3,906	100.0	6,250	100.0	31,355	100.0	16,240	100.0
Family householder...........................	42,500	39.5	1,347	34.5	1,947	31.2	10,267	32.7	6,610	40.7
Married spouse present...................	36,920	86.9	1,107	82.2	1,542	79.2	8,446	82.3	5,521	83.5
Other family householder................	5,580	13.1	240	17.8	405	20.8	1,821	17.7	1,088	16.5
Nonfamily householder......................	19,855	18.5	573	14.7	1,308	20.9	5,643	18.0	3,239	19.9
Living alone..................................	15,600	78.6	462	80.6	1,078	82.4	4,669	82.7	2,514	77.6
Living with nonrelatives.................	4,256	21.4	111	19.4	230	17.6	973	17.2	724	22.4
Relative of householder	38,677	36.0	1,721	44.1	2,524	40.4	13,076	41.7	5,452	33.6
Spouse..	24,841	64.2	863	50.1	1,296	51.3	7,346	56.2	3,354	61.5
Other..	13,836	35.8	858	49.9	1,228	48.7	5,730	43.8	2,099	38.5
Nonrelative....................................	6,485	6.0	266	6.8	471	7.5	2,369	7.6	939	5.8
FEMALE										
Total..	115,540	100.0	3,988	100.0	6,063	100.0	30,243	100.0	17,746	100.0
Family householder...........................	38,657	33.5	1,091	27.4	2,087	34.4	9,484	31.4	6,797	38.3
Married spouse present...................	24,760	64.1	587	53.8	958	45.9	5,498	58.0	4,041	59.5
Other family householder................	13,897	35.9	504	46.2	1,129	54.1	3,986	42.0	2,756	40.5
Nonfamily householder......................	22,168	19.2	666	16.7	1,303	21.5	5,743	19.0	3,735	21.0
Living alone..................................	19,352	87.3	613	92.0	1,178	90.4	5,182	90.2	3,339	89.4
Living with nonrelatives.................	2,816	12.7	53	8.0	125	9.6	561	9.8	396	10.6
Relative of householder	48,926	42.3	2,050	51.4	2,447	40.4	13,416	44.4	6,284	35.4
Spouse..	36,641	74.9	1,056	51.5	1,486	60.7	8,983	67.0	4,601	73.2
Other..	12,286	25.1	993	48.4	961	39.3	4,433	33.0	1,683	26.8
Nonrelative....................................	5,789	5.0	181	4.5	225	3.7	1,600	5.3	931	5.2

Note. Percentages may not sum to total because of rounding.
[1] Civilian noninstitutionalized population, plus armed forces living off post or with their families on post.

Table A-26. Educational Attainment of the Population 25 Years Old and Over, by Household Relationship and Sex, 2020—*Continued*

(Numbers in thousands; percent; civilian noninstitutionalized population.[1])

Sex and household relationship	Educational attainment									
	Associate degree		Bachelor's degree		Master's degree		Professional degree		Doctoral degree	
	Number	Percent	Number	Percent	Number	Percent	Number	Percent	Number	Percent
BOTH SEXES										
Total...	23,566	100.0	52,164	100.0	23,516	100.0	3,362	100.0	4,659	100.0
Family householder............................	9,176	38.9	19,395	37.2	9,661	41.1	1,372	40.8	1,924	41.3
Married spouse present......................	6,692	72.9	16,067	82.8	8,264	85.5	1,211	88.3	1,745	90.7
Other family householder....................	2,484	27.1	3,328	17.2	1,398	14.5	161	11.7	179	9.3
Nonfamily householder.........................	4,340	18.4	9,896	19.0	4,183	17.8	573	17.0	824	17.7
Living alone....................................	3,580	82.5	7,745	78.3	3,443	82.3	475	82.9	675	81.9
Living with nonrelatives	760	17.5	2,151	21.7	740	17.7	98	17.1	149	18.1
Relative of householder	9,001	38.2	19,899	38.1	8,675	36.9	1,314	39.1	1,744	37.4
Spouse..	6,650	73.9	15,539	78.1	7,603	87.6	1,111	84.6	1,593	91.3
Other..	2,351	26.1	4,359	21.9	1,072	12.4	203	15.4	151	8.7
Nonrelative..	1,050	4.5	2,974	5.7	997	4.2	103	3.1	167	3.6
MALE										
Total..	10,341	100.0	24,621	100.0	10,223	100.0	1,957	100.0	2,624	100.0
Family householder.............................	4,319	41.8	10,645	43.2	5,091	49.8	934	47.7	1,341	51.1
Married spouse present......................	3,700	85.7	9,634	90.5	4,809	94.5	880	94.2	1,280	95.5
Other family householder....................	619	14.3	1,011	9.5	281	5.5	54	5.8	61	4.5
Nonfamily householder.........................	1,968	19.0	4,698	19.1	1,704	16.7	328	16.8	397	15.1
Living alone....................................	1,527	77.6	3,465	73.8	1,297	76.1	257	78.4	331	83.4
Living with nonrelatives	441	22.4	1,232	26.2	407	23.9	71	21.6	65	16.4
Relative of householder	3,556	34.4	7,863	31.9	3,014	29.5	653	33.4	818	31.2
Spouse..	2,439	68.6	5,649	71.8	2,598	86.2	543	83.2	753	92.1
Other..	1,117	31.4	2,214	28.2	416	13.8	110	16.8	65	7.9
Nonrelative..	499	4.8	1,416	5.8	415	4.1	42	2.1	69	2.6
FEMALE										
Total..	13,225	100.0	27,542	100.0	13,293	100.0	1,405	100.0	2,034	100.0
Family householder.............................	4,857	36.7	8,749	31.8	4,571	34.4	438	31.2	583	28.7
Married spouse present......................	2,992	61.6	6,433	73.5	3,455	75.6	331	75.6	465	79.8
Other family householder....................	1,865	38.4	2,316	26.5	1,116	24.4	107	24.4	118	20.2
Nonfamily householder.........................	2,372	17.9	5,198	18.9	2,479	18.6	245	17.4	427	21.0
Living alone....................................	2,053	86.6	4,200	82.3	2,146	86.6	218	89.0	343	80.3
Living with nonrelatives	319	13.4	919	17.7	333	13.4	27	11.0	84	19.7
Relative of householder	5,445	41.2	12,036	43.7	5,661	42.6	661	47.0	926	45.5
Spouse..	4,211	77.3	9,891	82.2	5,005	88.4	568	85.9	840	90.7
Other..	1,234	22.7	2,145	17.8	656	11.6	93	14.1	86	9.3
Nonrelative..	551	4.2	1,559	5.7	582	4.4	61	4.3	98	4.8

Note. Percentages may not sum to total because of rounding.
[1]Civilian noninstitutionalized population, plus armed forces living off post or with their families on post.

Table A-27. Educational Attainment of the Population 25 Years Old and Over, by Labor Force Status and Sex, 2020

(Numbers in thousands; percent; civilian noninstitutionalized population.[1])

| Sex and labor force status | Total | Educational attainment | | | | | | | | |
		None to 8th grade	9th to 11th grade	High school graduate	Some college, no degree	Associate's degree	Bachelor's degree	Master's degree	Professional degree	Doctoral degree
BOTH SEXES										
Total..............................	223,058	7,895	12,313	61,597	33,986	23,566	52,164	23,516	3,362	4,659
Employed................................	135,602	3,142	5,194	32,930	19,733	15,403	36,695	16,562	2,495	3,447
Unemployed............................	6,300	279	491	2,048	1,077	652	1175	449	59	69
Unemployment rate..................	4.4	8.2	8.6	5.9	5.2	4.1	3.1	2.6	2.3	2.0
Not in civilian labor force	81,156	4,474	6,628	26,619	13,176	7,511	14,293	6,505	808	1,143
Percent...................................	36.4	56.7	53.8	43.2	38.8	31.9	27.4	27.7	24.0	24.5
MALE										
Total..............................	107,517	3,906	6,250	31,355	16,240	10,341	24,621	10,223	1,957	2,624
Employed................................	71,616	2,086	3,241	19,393	10,381	7,310	18,446	7,408	1,453	1,898
Unemployed............................	3,504	181	305	1,230	581	331	572	233	27	44
Unemployment rate..................	4.7	8.0	8.6	6.0	5.3	4.3	3.0	3.0	1.8	2.3
Not in civilian labor force	32,398	1,640	2,704	10,731	5,278	2,699	5,604	2,582	477	682
Percent...................................	30.1	42.0	43.3	34.2	32.5	26.1	22.8	25.3	24.4	26.0
FEMALE										
Total..............................	115,540	3,988	6,063	30,243	17,746	13,225	27,542	13,293	1,405	2,034
Employed................................	63,986	1,056	1,953	13,537	9,353	8,093	18,249	9,154	1,042	1,549
Unemployed............................	2,796	98	187	818	496	321	604	216	33	24
Unemployment rate..................	4.2	8.5	8.7	5.7	5.0	3.8	3.2	2.3	3.1	1.5
Not in civilian labor force	48,759	2,834	3,923	15,888	7,898	4,812	8,689	3,923	331	461
Percent...................................	42.2	71.1	64.7	52.5	44.5	36.4	31.5	29.5	23.6	22.7

Note. Percentages may not sum to total because of rounding.
[1]Civilian noninstitutionalized population, plus armed forces living off post or with their families on post. May be of any race.

Table A-28. Educational Attainment of Employed Civilians 25 Years Old and Over, by Occupation and Sex, 2020

(Numbers in thousands; percent; civilian noninstitutionalized population.[1])

Occupation and sex	Total		None to 8th grade		9th to 11th grade		High school graduate		Some college, no degree	
	Number	Percent	Number	Percent	Number	Percent	Number	Percent	Number	Percent
BOTH SEXES										
Total Employed Civilians	135,602	100.0	3,142	100.0	5,194	100.0	32,930	100.0	19,733	100.0
Occupation										
Management, business, and financial occupations..........	26,484	19.5	154	4.9	354	6.8	3,690	11.2	3,298	16.7
Professional and related occupations	35,250	26.0	34	1.1	186	3.6	2,044	6.2	2,444	12.4
Service occupations..........................	19,803	14.6	1,052	33.5	1,487	28.6	7,239	22.0	3,651	18.5
Sales and related occupations........................	11,653	8.6	92	2.9	322	6.2	3,153	9.6	2,216	11.2
Office and administrative occupations	13,950	10.3	57	1.8	277	5.3	4,118	12.5	3,289	16.7
Farming, forestry, and fishing occupations......	902	0.7	247	7.9	81	1.6	301	0.9	89	0.5
Construction and extraction occupations..........	6,940	5.1	630	20.1	836	16.1	3,070	9.3	1,082	5.5
Installation, maintenance, and repair occupations..........	4,199	3.1	105	3.3	216	4.2	1,772	5.4	754	3.8
Production occupations	7,031	5.2	392	12.5	555	10.7	3,286	10.0	1,165	5.9
Transportation and material moving occupations....................	9,390	6.9	380	12.1	880	16.9	4,258	12.9	1,746	8.8
MALE										
Total Employed Civilians	71,616	100.0	2,086	100.0	3,241	100.0	19,393	100.0	10,381	100.0
Occupation										
Management, business, and financial occupations..........	14,364	20.1	121	5.8	231	7.1	2,193	11.3	1,794	17.3
Professional and related occupations	15,298	21.4	17	0.8	74	2.3	825	4.3	1,078	10.4
Service occupations...........	8,416	11.8	464	22.2	542	16.7	3,022	15.6	1,591	15.3
Sales and related occupations........................	6,105	8.5	42	2.0	123	3.8	1,569	8.1	1,123	10.8
Office and administrative occupations	3,532	4.9	32	1.5	102	3.1	981	5.1	755	7.3
Farming, forestry, and fishing occupations......	677	0.9	185	8.9	56	1.7	245	1.3	70	0.7
Construction and extraction occupations..........	6,647	9.3	604	29.0	794	24.5	2,967	15.3	1,030	9.9
Installation, maintenance, and repair occupations..........	4,019	5.6	103	4.9	210	6.5	1,719	8.9	708	6.8
Production occupations	5,010	7.0	233	11.2	376	11.6	2,436	12.6	856	8.2
Transportation and material moving occupations....................	7,548	10.5	286	13.7	735	22.7	3,435	17.7	1,376	13.3
FEMALE										
Total Employed Civilians	63,986	100.0	1,056	100.0	1,953	100.0	13,537	100.0	9,353	100.0
Occupation										
Management, business, and financial occupations..........	12,120	18.9	33	3.1	124	6.3	1,496	11.1	1,504	16.1
Professional and related occupations	19,952	31.2	17	1.6	113	5.8	1,219	9.0	1,366	14.6
Service occupations..........................	11,387	17.8	587	55.6	945	48.4	4,217	31.2	2,060	22.0
Sales and related occupations........................	5,548	8.7	51	4.8	200	10.2	1,583	11.7	1,093	11.7
Office and administrative occupations	10,417	16.3	25	2.4	175	9.0	3,137	23.2	2,534	27.1
Farming, forestry, and fishing occupations......	224	0.4	62	5.9	25	1.3	56	0.4	20	0.2
Construction and extraction occupations..........	294	0.5	26	2.5	42	2.2	103	0.8	52	0.6
Installation, maintenance, and repair occupations..........	181	0.3	2	0.2	6	0.3	53	0.4	46	0.5
Production occupations	2,021	3.2	159	15.1	179	9.2	850	6.3	308	3.3
Transportation and material moving occupations....................	1,841	2.9	94	8.9	145	7.4	823	6.1	370	4.0

Note. Percentages may not sum to total because of rounding
^ = Quantity zero or rounds to zero.
[1]Civilian noninstitutionalized population plus armed forces living off post or with their families on post.

Table A-28. Educational Attainment of Employed Civilians 25 Years Old and Over, by Occupation and Sex, 2020—*Continued*

(Numbers in thousands; percent; civilian noninstitutionalized population.[1])

	Educational Attainment									
	Associate's degree		Bachelor's degree		Master's degree		Professional degree		Doctoral degree	
Occupation and sex	Number	Percent	Number	Percent	Number	Percent	Number	Percent	Number	Percent
BOTH SEXES										
Total Employed Civilians	15,403	100.0	36,695	100.0	16,562	100.0	2,495	100.0	3,447	100.0
Occupation										
Management, business, and financial occupations.....	2,391	15.5	10,648	29.0	5,169	31.2	310	12.4	470	13.6
Professional and related occupations	3,760	24.4	13,233	36.1	8,880	53.6	1,945	78.0	2,724	79.0
Service occupations................................	2,614	17.0	3,089	8.4	520	3.1	90	3.6	61	1.8
Sales and related occupations..........................	1,303	8.5	3,668	10.0	773	4.7	54	2.2	72	2.1
Office and administrative occupations	2,102	13.6	3,236	8.8	754	4.6	53	2.1	65	1.9
Farming, forestry, and fishing occupations	68	0.4	94	0.3	21	0.1	*	*	*	*
Construction and extraction occupations..........	685	4.4	542	1.5	84	0.5	3	0.1	7	0.2
Installation, maintenance, and repair occupations.......	883	5.7	397	1.1	51	0.3	13	0.5	8	0.2
Production occupations	797	5.2	688	1.9	126	0.8	3	0.1	19	0.6
Transportation and material moving occupations................................	801	5.2	1098	3.0	182	1.1	24	1.0	20	0.6
MALE										
Total Employed Civilians	7,310	100.0	18,446	100.0	7,408	100.0	1,453	100.0	1,898	100.0
Occupation										
Management, business, and financial occupations.....	1,132	15.5	5,637	30.6	2,795	37.7	196	13.5	265	14.0
Professional and related occupations	1,316	18.0	6,022	32.6	3,346	45.2	1,122	77.2	1,497	78.9
Service occupations................................	999	13.7	1,455	7.9	265	3.6	50	3.4	27	1.4
Sales and related occupations..........................	599	8.2	2,157	11.7	428	5.8	21	1.4	43	2.3
Office and administrative occupations	445	6.1	937	5.1	240	3.2	25	1.7	17	0.9
Farming, forestry, and fishing occupations	52	0.7	53	0.3	17	0.2	*	*	*	*
Construction and extraction occupations..........	659	9.0	502	2.7	81	1.1	3	0.2	6	0.3
Installation, maintenance, and repair occupations.......	858	11.7	357	1.9	43	0.6	13	0.9	8	0.4
Production occupations	603	8.2	424	2.3	68	0.9	1	0.1	13	0.7
Transportation and material moving occupations................................	648	8.9	901	4.9	126	1.7	22	1.5	20	1.1
FEMALE										
Total Employed Civilians	8,093	100.0	18,249	100.0	9,154	100.0	1,042	100.0	1,549	100.0
Occupation										
Management, business, and financial occupations.....	1,259	15.6	5,011	27.5	2,375	25.9	113	10.8	205	13.2
Professional and related occupations	2,443	30.2	7,211	39.5	5,534	60.5	823	79.0	1,227	79.2
Service occupations................................	1,616	20.0	1,634	9.0	255	2.8	40	3.8	34	2.2
Sales and related occupations..........................	704	8.7	1,511	8.3	345	3.8	33	3.2	29	1.9
Office and administrative occupations	1,657	20.5	2,299	12.6	514	5.6	28	2.7	47	3.0
Farming, forestry, and fishing occupations	16	0.2	41	0.2	5	0.1	*	*	*	*
Construction and extraction occupations..........	26	0.3	41	0.2	3	*	*	*	1	0.1
Installation, maintenance, and repair occupations.......	25	0.3	41	0.2	8	0.1	*	*	*	*
Production occupations	194	2.4	263	1.4	58	0.6	2	0.2	6	0.4
Transportation and material moving occupations................................	152	1.9	197	1.1	57	0.6	2	0.2	*	*

Note. Percentages may not sum to total because of rounding.
* = Quantity zero or rounds to zero.
[1]Civilian noninstitutionalized population plus armed forces living off post or with their families on post.

Table A-29. Educational Attainment of the Population 25 Years Old and Over, by Industry and Sex, 2020

(Numbers in thousands; percent; civilian noninstitutionalized population.[1])

Industry and sex	Total		None to 8th grade		9th to 11th grade		High school graduate		Some college, no degree	
	Number	Percent	Number	Percent	Number	Percent	Number	Percent	Number	Percent
BOTH SEXES										
Total Employed Civilians	135,602	100.0	3,142	100.0	5,194	100.0	32,930	100.0	19,733	100.0
Industry										
Agriculture, forestry, fishing, and hunting........	2,040	1.5	313	10.0	123	2.4	686	2.1	266	1.3
Mining..	742	0.5	19	0.6	39	0.8	220	0.7	107	0.5
Construction	9,670	7.1	657	20.9	925	17.8	3,901	11.8	1,524	7.7
Manufacturing..	13,917	10.3	456	14.5	672	12.9	4,401	13.4	2,060	10.4
Wholesale and retail trade...............................	15,487	11.4	275	8.8	726	14.0	5,114	15.5	2,959	15.0
Transportation and utilities..............................	8,110	6.0	135	4.3	391	7.5	3,021	9.2	1,589	8.1
Information	2,614	1.9	7	0.2	42	0.8	317	1.0	399	2.0
Financial activities..	10,214	7.5	50	1.6	98	1.9	1,616	4.9	1,544	7.8
Professional and business services	17,600	13.0	406	12.9	563	10.8	2,690	8.2	1,996	10.1
Educational and health services	32,334	23.8	182	5.8	540	10.4	4,601	14.0	3,523	17.9
Leisure and hospitality....................................	9,191	6.8	432	13.7	666	12.8	3,126	9.5	1,610	8.2
Other services...	6,476	4.8	184	5.9	336	6.5	2,074	6.3	971	4.9
Public administration	7,206	5.3	26	0.8	71	1.4	1,164	3.5	1,187	6.0
MALE										
Total Employed Civilians	71,616	100.0	2,086	100.0	3,241	100.0	19,393	100.0	10,381	100.0
Industry										
Agriculture, forestry, fishing, and hunting........	1,485	2.1	240	11.5	94	2.9	560	2.9	172	1.7
Mining..	624	0.9	19	0.9	37	1.1	198	1.0	101	1.0
Construction	8,552	11.9	627	30.1	872	26.9	3,571	18.4	1,310	12.6
Manufacturing..	9,854	13.8	291	14.0	503	15.5	3,241	16.7	1,487	14.3
Wholesale and retail trade...............................	8,651	12.1	160	7.7	411	12.7	2,875	14.8	1,653	15.9
Transportation and utilities..............................	6,148	8.6	121	5.8	324	10.0	2,330	12.0	1,160	11.2
Information	1,564	2.2	5	0.2	36	1.1	210	1.1	251	2.4
Financial activities..	4,860	6.8	40	1.9	55	1.7	602	3.1	539	5.2
Professional and business services	10,297	14.4	259	12.4	324	10.0	1,561	8.0	1,077	10.4
Educational and health services	8,025	11.2	20	1.0	73	2.3	925	4.8	680	6.6
Leisure and hospitality....................................	4,739	6.6	221	10.6	324	10.0	1,601	8.3	837	8.1
Other services...	3,017	4.2	74	3.5	161	5.0	1,052	5.4	450	4.3
Public administration	3,798	5.3	9	0.4	27	0.8	669	3.4	665	6.4
FEMALE										
Total Employed Civilians	63,986	100.0	1,056	100.0	1,953	100.0	13,537	100.0	9,353	100.0
Industry										
Agriculture, forestry, fishing, and hunting........	555	0.9	73	6.9	29	1.5	126	0.9	94	1.0
Mining..	118	0.2	*	*	2	0.1	22	0.2	6	0.1
Construction	1,118	1.7	31	2.9	53	2.7	331	2.4	215	2.3
Manufacturing..	4,063	6.3	165	15.6	169	8.7	1,161	8.6	573	6.1
Wholesale and retail trade...............................	6,837	10.7	115	10.9	315	16.1	2,239	16.5	1,306	14.0
Transportation and utilities..............................	1,962	3.1	15	1.4	68	3.5	691	5.1	429	4.6
Information	1,050	1.6	2	0.2	6	0.3	107	0.8	147	1.6
Financial activities..	5,354	8.4	10	0.9	43	2.2	1,013	7.5	1,005	10.7
Professional and business services	7,303	11.4	147	13.9	240	12.3	1,129	8.3	919	9.8
Educational and health services	24,309	38.0	162	15.3	468	24.0	3,676	27.2	2,843	30.4
Leisure and hospitality....................................	4,453	7.0	210	19.9	342	17.5	1,525	11.3	773	8.3
Other services...	3,459	5.4	110	10.4	175	9.0	1,022	7.5	521	5.6
Public administration	3,408	5.3	17	1.6	44	2.3	496	3.7	522	5.6

Note. Percentages may not sum to total because of rounding.
* = Quantity zero or rounds to zero.
[1]Civilian noninstitutionalized population plus armed forces living off post or with their families on post.

Table A-29. Educational Attainment of the Population 25 Years Old and Over, by Industry and Sex, 2020—*Continued*

(Numbers in thousands; percent; civilian noninstitutionalized population.[1])

Industry and sex	Educational Attainment										Percent Bachelor's Degree or Higher
	Associate's degree		Bachelor's degree		Master's degree		Professional degree		Doctoral degree		
	Number	Percent	Number	Percent	Number	Percent	Number	Percent	Number	Percent	
BOTH SEXES											
Total Employed Civilians	15,403	100.0	36,695	100.0	16,562	100.0	2,495	100.0	3,447	100.0	43.7
Industry											
Agriculture, forestry, fishing, and hunting........	201	1.3	356	1.0	78	0.5	10	0.4	7	0.2	22.1
Mining...	89	0.6	188	0.5	67	0.4	2	0.1	11	0.3	36.1
Construction...	955	6.2	1,388	3.8	284	1.7	21	0.8	13	0.4	17.6
Manufacturing..	1,597	10.4	3,193	8.7	1,261	7.6	67	2.7	210	6.1	34.0
Wholesale and retail trade................................	1,842	12.0	3,518	9.6	786	4.7	88	3.5	179	5.2	29.5
Transportation and utilities...............................	931	6.0	1,623	4.4	346	2.1	29	1.2	45	1.3	25.2
Information...	255	1.7	1,068	2.9	461	2.8	15	0.6	51	1.5	61.0
Financial activities..	1038	6.7	4,214	11.5	1,471	8.9	87	3.5	97	2.8	57.5
Professional and business services	1,497	9.7	6,444	17.6	2,619	15.8	773	31.0	612	17.8	59.4
Educational and health services	4,275	27.8	9,241	25.2	7,037	42.5	1,070	42.9	1,867	54.2	59.4
Leisure and hospitality	912	5.9	1,927	5.3	423	2.6	51	2.0	45	1.3	26.6
Other services...	820	5.3	1,301	3.5	613	3.7	73	2.9	104	3.0	32.3
Public administration	991	6.4	2,235	6.1	1116	6.7	210	8.4	206	6.0	52.3
MALE											
Total Employed Civilians	7,310	100.0	18,446	100.0	7,408	100.0	1,453	100.0	1,898	100.0	40.8
Industry											
Agriculture, forestry, fishing, and hunting........	137	1.9	222	1.2	46	0.6	10	0.7	5	0.3	19.1
Mining...	80	1.1	133	0.7	47	0.6	2	0.1	8	0.4	30.4
Construction...	813	11.1	1107	6.0	224	3.0	18	1.2	11	0.6	15.9
Manufacturing..	1142	15.6	2,150	11.7	850	11.5	43	3.0	146	7.7	32.4
Wholesale and retail trade................................	962	13.2	1,999	10.8	463	6.3	51	3.5	77	4.1	29.9
Transportation and utilities...............................	705	9.6	1206	6.5	239	3.2	25	1.7	39	2.1	24.5
Information...	176	2.4	611	3.3	242	3.3	7	0.5	25	1.3	56.6
Financial activities..	359	4.9	2,289	12.4	871	11.8	52	3.6	53	2.8	67.2
Professional and business services	791	10.8	3,774	20.5	1,624	21.9	492	33.9	396	20.9	61.0
Educational and health services	812	11.1	2,237	12.1	1,750	23.6	568	39.1	962	50.7	68.7
Leisure and hospitality	437	6.0	1044	5.7	215	2.9	34	2.3	26	1.4	27.8
Other services...	352	4.8	539	2.9	281	3.8	35	2.4	73	3.8	30.8
Public administration	545	7.5	1,134	6.1	556	7.5	117	8.1	76	4.0	49.6
FEMALE											
Total Employed Civilians	8,093	100.0	18,249	100.0	9,154	100.0	1,042	100.0	1,549	100.0	46.9
Industry											
Agriculture, forestry, fishing, and hunting........	65	0.8	135	0.7	32	0.3	*	*	2	0.1	30.5
Mining...	9	0.1	54	0.3	20	0.2	*	*	4	0.3	66.1
Construction...	142	1.8	281	1.5	61	0.7	3	0.3	2	0.1	31.0
Manufacturing..	455	5.6	1,042	5.7	410	4.5	24	2.3	64	4.1	37.9
Wholesale and retail trade................................	881	10.9	1,519	8.3	323	3.5	38	3.6	102	6.6	29.0
Transportation and utilities...............................	226	2.8	417	2.3	107	1.2	4	0.4	5	0.3	27.2
Information...	79	1.0	456	2.5	219	2.4	8	0.8	26	1.7	67.5
Financial activities..	679	8.4	1,925	10.5	601	6.6	34	3.3	44	2.8	48.6
Professional and business services	706	8.7	2,670	14.6	995	10.9	281	27.0	216	13.9	57.0
Educational and health services	3,463	42.8	7,004	38.4	5,287	57.8	502	48.2	905	58.4	56.3
Leisure and hospitality	475	5.9	883	4.8	207	2.3	17	1.6	19	1.2	25.3
Other services...	468	5.8	762	4.2	332	3.6	38	3.6	31	2.0	33.6
Public administration	445	5.5	1,101	6.0	560	6.1	93	8.9	130	8.4	55.3

Note. Percentages may not sum to total because of rounding.
* = Quantity zero or rounds to zero.
[1]Civilian noninstitutionalized population plus armed forces living off post or with their families on post.

Table A-30. Educational Attainment of the Population 25 Years Old and Over, by Citizenship, Nativity, Period of Entry, and Sex, 2020

(Numbers in thousands; percent; civilian noninstitutionalized population.[1])

Citizenship, nativity, period of entry, and sex	Total		None to 8th grade		9th to 11th grade		High school graduate		Some college, no degree	
	Number	Percent	Number	Percent	Number	Percent	Number	Percent	Number	Percent
BOTH SEXES										
Total	223,058	100.0	7,895	100.0	12,313	100.0	61,597	100.0	33,986	100.0
Native..........................	183,560	82.3	2,540	32.2	8,789	71.4	51,826	84.1	30,493	89.7
Foreign-born..........................	39,497	17.7	5,355	67.8	3,524	28.6	9,771	15.9	3,493	10.3
Native										
Native parentage[2]...........................	164,897	89.8	2,184	86.0	7,859	89.4	47,196	91.1	27,411	89.9
Foreign or mixed parentage[3]........................	18,664	10.2	356	14.0	930	10.6	4,631	8.9	3,082	10.1
Foreign-born										
Naturalized citizen..........................	21,276	53.9	1,936	36.2	1,345	38.2	5,153	52.7	2,164	62.0
Not a citizen	18,222	46.1	3,419	63.8	2,180	61.9	4,618	47.3	1,329	38.0
Year of entry										
2010 or later	8,705	22.0	724	13.5	571	16.2	2,009	20.6	642	18.4
2000–2009..........................	9,932	25.1	1,424	26.6	1,036	29.4	2,515	25.7	799	22.9
1990–1999..........................	8,983	22.7	1,298	24.2	935	26.5	2,279	23.3	800	22.9
1980–1989..........................	6,029	15.3	1,027	19.2	558	15.8	1,491	15.3	591	16.9
1970–1979..........................	3,457	8.8	592	11.1	264	7.5	817	8.4	374	10.7
Before 1970	2,391	6.1	291	5.4	160	4.5	660	6.8	286	8.2
MALE										
Total..........................	107,517	100.0	3,906	100.0	6,250	100.0	31,355	100.0	16,240	100.0
Native..........................	88,561	82.4	1,361	34.8	4,485	71.8	26,664	85.0	14,572	89.7
Foreign-born..........................	18,956	17.6	2,546	65.2	1,765	28.2	4,690	15.0	1,668	10.3
Native										
Native parentage[2]..........................	79,106	89.3	1,186	87.1	3,997	89.1	24,102	90.4	13,024	89.4
Foreign or mixed parentage[3]..........................	9,456	10.7	175	12.9	488	10.9	2,563	9.6	1,548	10.6
Foreign-born										
Naturalized citizen..........................	9,840	51.9	820	32.2	654	37.1	2,351	50.1	1,007	60.4
Not a citizen	9,116	48.1	1,726	67.8	1,111	62.9	2,340	49.9	661	39.6
Year of entry										
2010 or later	4,142	21.9	293	11.5	303	17.2	927	19.8	329	19.7
2000–2009..........................	4,763	25.1	678	26.6	507	28.7	1,237	26.4	365	21.9
1990–1999..........................	4,388	23.1	642	25.2	505	28.6	1,118	23.8	402	24.1
1980–1989..........................	3,002	15.8	549	21.6	265	15.0	791	16.9	269	16.1
1970–1979..........................	1,677	8.8	275	10.8	136	7.7	300	8.1	203	12.2
Before 1970	986	5.2	108	4.2	49	2.8	236	5.0	99	5.9
FEMALE										
Total..........................	115,540	100.0	3,988	100.0	6,063	100.0	30,243	100.0	17,746	100.0
Native..........................	94,999	82.2	1,179	29.6	4,304	71.0	25,162	83.2	15,921	89.7
Foreign-born..........................	20,542	17.8	2,809	70.4	1,759	29.0	5,080	16.8	1,825	10.3
Native										
Native parentage[2]..........................	85,791	90.3	998	84.6	3,862	89.7	23,094	91.8	14,387	90.4
Foreign or mixed parentage[3]..........................	9,208	9.7	181	15.4	442	10.3	2,068	8.2	1,534	9.6
Foreign-born										
Naturalized citizen..........................	11,436	55.7	1,116	39.7	691	39.3	2,802	55.2	1,158	63.5
Not a citizen	9,106	44.3	1,693	60.3	1,068	60.7	2,278	44.8	668	36.6
Year of entry										
2010 or later	4,563	22.2	431	15.3	267	15.2	1081	21.3	313	17.2
2000–2009..........................	5,169	25.2	745	26.5	529	30.1	1,278	25.2	434	23.8
1990–1999..........................	4,594	22.4	656	23.4	430	24.4	1,161	22.9	398	21.8
1980–1989..........................	3,027	14.7	478	17.0	293	16.7	700	13.8	322	17.0
1970–1979..........................	1,781	8.7	317	11.3	128	7.3	437	8.6	171	9.4
Before 1970	1,406	6.8	183	6.5	111	6.3	424	8.3	187	10.2

[1]Civilian noninstitutionalized population plus armed forces living off post or with their families on post.
[2]Native parentage: Both parents born in the United States. Percent: percent of native citizens.
[3]Foreign or mixed parentage: One or both parents born outside of the United States.

Table A-30. Educational Attainment of the Population 25 Years Old and Over, by Citizenship, Nativity, Period of Entry, and Sex, 2020—*Continued*

(Numbers in thousands; percent; civilian noninstitutionalized population.[1])

Citizenship, nativity, period of entry, and sex	Educational attainment									
	Associate degree		Bachelor's degree		Master's degree		Professional degree		Doctoral degree	
	Number	Percent	Number	Percent	Number	Percent	Number	Percent	Number	Percent
BOTH SEXES										
Total	23,566	100.0	52,164	100.0	23,516	100.0	3,362	100.0	4,659	100.0
Native.............	20,842	88.4	43,573	83.5	19,209	81.7	2,747	81.7	3,542	76.0
Foreign-born..............	2,724	11.6	8,591	16.5	4,308	18.3	615	18.3	1,117	24.0
Native										
Native parentage[2]	18,811	90.3	38,872	89.2	17,194	89.5	2,312	84.2	3,057	86.3
Foreign or mixed parentage[3]	2,031	9.7	4,701	10.8	2,014	10.5	435	15.8	484	13.7
Foreign-born										
Naturalized citizen	1,860	68.3	5,331	62.1	2,317	53.8	437	71.1	733	65.6
Not a citizen	864	31.7	3,260	37.9	1,991	46.2	178	28.9	384	34.4
Year of entry										
2010 or later	496	18.2	2,409	28.0	1,457	33.8	152	24.7	246	22.0
2000–2009.............	677	24.9	1,963	22.8	1091	25.3	143	23.3	284	25.4
1990–1999.............	613	22.5	1,925	22.4	773	17.9	120	19.5	240	21.5
1980–1989.............	461	16.9	1,146	13.3	490	11.4	99	16.1	165	14.8
1970–1979.............	248	9.1	680	7.9	320	7.4	62	10.1	100	9.0
Before 1970	229	8.4	467	5.4	177	4.1	39	6.3	83	7.4
MALE										
Total.............	10,341	100.0	24,621	100.0	10,223	100.0	1,957	100.0	2,624	100.0
Native.............	9,174	88.7	20,643	83.8	8,087	79.1	1,648	84.2	1,928	73.5
Foreign-born.............	1,167	11.3	3,978	16.2	2,137	20.9	309	15.8	696	26.5
Native										
Native parentage[2]	8,214	89.5	18,330	88.8	7,212	89.2	1,368	83.0	1,673	86.8
Foreign or mixed parentage[3]	960	10.5	2,313	11.2	874	10.8	279	16.9	255	13.2
Foreign-born										
Naturalized citizen	782	67.0	2,443	61.4	1,103	51.6	209	67.6	472	67.8
Not a citizen	385	33.0	1,535	38.6	1,033	48.3	101	32.7	224	32.2
Year of entry										
2010 or later	246	21.1	1095	27.5	732	34.3	75	24.3	142	20.4
2000–2009.............	295	25.3	896	22.5	537	25.1	81	26.2	167	24.0
1990–1999.............	282	24.2	867	21.8	364	17.0	60	19.4	149	21.4
1980–1989.............	182	15.6	559	14.1	246	11.5	35	11.3	105	15.1
1970–1979.............	80	6.9	328	8.2	169	7.9	32	10.4	73	10.5
Before 1970	82	7.0	234	5.9	88	4.1	27	8.7	61	8.8
FEMALE										
Total.............	13,225	100.0	27,542	100.0	13,293	100.0	1,405	100.0	2,034	100.0
Native.............	11,668	88.2	22,930	83.3	11,122	83.7	1,100	78.3	1,614	79.4
Foreign-born.............	1,558	11.8	4,613	16.7	2,171	16.3	306	21.8	421	20.7
Native										
Native parentage[2]	10,597	90.8	20,542	89.6	9,982	89.8	944	85.8	1,384	85.7
Foreign or mixed parentage[3]	1071	9.2	2,388	10.4	1,140	10.2	156	14.2	229	14.2
Foreign-born										
Naturalized citizen	1,078	69.2	2,888	62.6	1,213	55.9	228	74.5	261	62.0
Not a citizen	479	30.7	1,725	37.4	958	44.1	77	25.2	159	37.8
Year of entry										
2010 or later	251	16.1	1,314	28.5	725	33.4	77	25.2	104	24.7
2000–2009.............	382	24.5	1,068	23.2	554	25.5	61	19.9	117	27.8
1990–1999.............	332	21.3	1059	23.0	408	18.8	60	19.6	91	21.6
1980–1989.............	279	17.9	587	12.7	245	11.3	65	21.2	60	14.3
1970–1979.............	168	10.8	353	7.7	150	6.9	30	9.8	27	6.4
Before 1970	147	9.4	233	5.1	88	4.1	12	3.9	22	5.2

[1]Civilian noninstitutionalized population plus armed forces living off post or with their families on post.
[2]Native parentage: Both parents born in the United States. Percent: percent of native citizens.
[3]Foreign or mixed parentage: One or both parents born outside of the United States.

Table A-31. Detailed Years of School Completed by People 25 Years Old and Over, by Sex, Age Groups, Race, and Hispanic Origin, 2020

(Numbers in thousands; civilian noninstitutionalized population.[1])

Detailed years of school	All races Number	All races Percent	Males Number	Males Percent	Females Number	Females Percent	25 to 34 years old Number	25 to 34 years old Percent	35 to 54 years old Number	35 to 54 years old Percent
Total..	223,058	100.0	107,517	100.0	115,540	100.0	45,260	100.0	80,999	100.0
Elementary or High school, no diploma										
Less than 1 year, no diploma	725	0.3	351	0.3	374	0.3	83	0.2	258	0.3
1st-4th grade, no diploma..............................	1,381	0.6	702	0.7	680	0.6	85	0.2	427	0.5
5th-6th grade, no diploma	2,844	1.3	1,389	1.3	1,455	1.3	238	0.5	1,106	1.4
7th-8th grade, no diploma	2,944	1.3	1,464	1.4	1,480	1.3	319	0.7	1,027	1.3
9th grade, no diploma..............................	2,805	1.3	1,393	1.3	1,411	1.2	359	0.8	1,171	1.4
10th grade, no diploma..	3,140	1.4	1,584	1.5	1,556	1.3	421	0.9	1,047	1.3
11th grade, no diploma..............................	3,625	1.6	1,862	1.7	1,763	1.5	558	1.2	1,245	1.5
12th grade, no diploma..............................	2,744	1.2	1,411	1.3	1,332	1.2	631	1.4	902	1.1
Elementary or High school, GED										
Less than 1 year, GED	25	*	13	*	12	*	8	*	11	*
1st-4th grade, GED	120	0.1	74	0.1	47	*	36	0.1	40	*
5th-6th grade, GED	50	*	25	*	24	*	7	*	23	*
7th-8th grade, GED	242	0.1	134	0.1	108	0.1	30	0.1	58	0.1
9th grade, GED..............................	610	0.3	293	0.3	316	0.3	106	0.2	205	0.3
10th grade, GED..............................	1,258	0.6	658	0.6	600	0.5	266	0.6	392	0.5
11th grade, GED..............................	1,746	0.8	960	0.9	786	0.7	303	0.7	693	0.9
12th grade, GED..............................	1,525	0.7	941	0.9	584	0.5	381	0.8	608	0.8
High school diploma	56,022	25.1	28,257	26.3	27,765	24.0	10,661	23.6	18,232	22.5
College, no degree										
Less than 1 year college, no degree.......................	4,512	2.0	2,119	2.0	2,393	2.1	978	2.2	1,459	1.8
One year of college, no degree..............................	10,706	4.8	4,973	4.6	5,733	5.0	2,332	5.2	3,436	4.2
Two years of college, no degree............................	13,894	6.2	6,624	6.2	7,270	6.3	2,755	6.1	4,740	5.9
Three years of college, no degree	3,390	1.5	1,724	1.6	1,665	1.4	844	1.9	1,241	1.5
Four or more years of college, no degree................	1,485	0.7	799	0.7	686	0.6	391	0.9	545	0.7
Associate's degree, vocational										
Less than 1 year college, vocational/associate's	496	0.2	232	0.2	265	0.2	111	0.2	195	0.2
One year of college, vocational/associate's	1,428	0.6	675	0.6	753	0.7	308	0.7	511	0.6
Two years of college, vocational/associate's	6,234	2.8	2,877	2.7	3,357	2.9	1,138	2.5	2,333	2.9
Three years of college, vocational/associate's........	861	0.4	396	0.4	465	0.4	209	0.5	329	0.4
Four or more years of college, vocational/ associate's	858	0.4	457	0.4	401	0.3	185	0.4	368	0.5
Associate's degree, academic										
Less than 1 year college, academic/associate's	137	0.1	47	*	91	0.1	15	*	35	*
One year of college, academic/associate's	722	0.3	300	0.3	422	0.4	155	0.3	257	0.3
Two years of college, academic/associate's	9,453	4.2	3,908	3.6	5,545	4.8	1,903	4.2	3,547	4.4
Three years of college, academic/associate's........	1,697	0.8	747	0.7	949	0.8	407	0.9	619	0.8
Four or more years of college, academic/ associate's	1,680	0.8	702	0.7	978	0.8	446	1.0	686	0.8
Bachelor's degree	52,164	23.4	24,621	22.9	27,542	23.8	13,166	29.1	20,092	24.8
Master's degree[2]	23,516	10.5	10,223	9.5	13,293	11.5	4,228	9.3	9,898	12.2
Professional degree	3,362	1.5	1,957	1.8	1,405	1.2	528	1.2	1,333	1.6
Doctorate degree	4,659	2.1	2,624	2.4	2,034	1.8	670	1.5	1,930	2.4

* = Quantity zero or rounds to zero.
[1]Excluding members of the Armed Forces living in barracks.
[2]Detail on graduate school attendance and length of master's degree program, available in previous years, discontinued due to questionnaire changes in 2015.

Table A-31. Detailed Years of School Completed by People 25 Years Old and Over, by Sex, Age Groups, Race, and Hispanic Origin, 2020—*Continued*

(Numbers in thousands; civilian noninstitutionalized population.[1])

Detailed years of school	55 years and older Number	Percent	White Number	Percent	Non-Hispanic White Number	Percent	Black Number	Percent	Asian Number	Percent	Hispanic (of any race) Number	Percent
Total...	96,798	100.0	174,282	100.0	142,871	100.0	27,822	100.0	14,235	100.0	35,206	100.0
Elementary or High school, no diploma												
Less than 1 year, no diploma	384	0.4	490	0.3	148	0.1	83	0.3	135	0.9	376	1.1
1st-4th grade, no diploma.................................	869	0.9	1,096	0.6	140	0.1	108	0.4	115	0.8	1,031	2.9
5th-6th grade, no diploma.................................	1,501	1.6	2,352	1.3	268	0.2	215	0.8	162	1.1	2,241	6.4
7th-8th grade, no diploma.................................	1,598	1.7	2,252	1.3	1,100	0.8	363	1.3	213	1.5	1,285	3.7
9th grade, no diploma.....................................	1,275	1.3	2,217	1.3	944	0.7	337	1.2	141	1.0	1,365	3.9
10th grade, no diploma....................................	1,672	1.7	2,335	1.3	1,559	1.1	502	1.8	178	1.2	874	2.5
11th grade, no diploma....................................	1,822	1.9	2,567	1.5	1,737	1.2	821	3.0	81	0.6	921	2.6
12th grade, no diploma....................................	1,212	1.3	1,933	1.1	1,090	0.8	524	1.9	172	1.2	951	2.7
Elementary or High school, GED												
Less than 1 year, GED	6	*	17	*	8	*	3.0	*	*	*	11	*
1st-4th grade, GED	44	*	85	*	52	*	24	0.1	4.0	*	33	0.1
5th-6th grade, GED	20	*	31	*	23	*	10.0	*	3.0	*	10	*
7th-8th grade, GED	154	0.2	212	0.1	171	0.1	20	0.1	5	*	50	0.1
9th grade, GED..	298	0.3	497	0.3	408	0.3	92	0.3	3	*	108	0.3
10th grade, GED..	601	0.6	1,037	0.6	877	0.6	136	0.5	15	0.1	181	0.5
11th grade, GED..	750	0.8	1,391	0.8	1,138	0.8	255	0.9	10	0.1	284	0.8
12th grade, GED..	537	0.6	1,181	0.7	817	0.6	231	0.8	50	0.4	405	1.2
High school diploma	27,129	28.0	43,575	25.0	34,682	24.3	8,474	30.5	2,251	15.8	9,902	28.1
College, no degree												
Less than 1 year college, no degree..................	2,075	2.1	3,585	2.1	3,031	2.1	683	2.5	105	0.7	604	1.7
One year of college, no degree.........................	4,938	5.1	8,487	4.9	7,237	5.1	1,510	5.4	267	1.9	1,437	4.1
Two years of college, no degree.......................	6,399	6.6	10,742	6.2	9,093	6.4	2,179	7.8	451	3.2	1,915	5.4
Three years of college, no degree.....................	1,305	1.3	2,574	1.5	2,156	1.5	507	1.8	169	1.2	486	1.4
Four or more years of college, no degree..........	549	0.6	1,151	0.7	908	0.6	160	0.6	99	0.7	283	0.8
Associate's degree, vocational												
Less than 1 year college, vocational/associate's	190	0.2	409	0.2	334	0.2	51	0.2	26	0.2	83	0.2
One year of college, vocational/associate's	608	0.6	1,189	0.7	974	0.7	151	0.5	42	0.3	231	0.7
Two years of college, vocational/associate's	2,762	2.9	5,133	2.9	4,440	3.1	765	2.7	181	1.3	767	2.2
Three years of college, vocational/associate's...	323	0.3	668	0.4	576	0.4	115	0.4	53	0.4	106	0.3
Four or more years of college, vocational/associate's	305	0.3	673	0.4	558	0.4	107	0.4	35	0.2	129	0.4
Associate's degree, academic												
Less than 1 year college, academic/associate's	87	0.1	101	0.1	84	0.1	26	0.1	9	0.1	16	*
One year of college, academic/associate's	310	0.3	561	0.3	436	0.3	98	0.4	38	0.3	131	0.4
Two years of college, academic/associate's	4,004	4.1	7,629	4.4	6,588	4.6	1,145	4.1	385	2.7	1,163	3.3
Three years of college, academic/associate's....	670	0.7	1,349	0.8	1,113	0.8	206	0.7	61	0.4	249	0.7
Four or more years of college, academic/associate's	548	0.6	1,355	0.8	1,143	0.8	176	0.6	77	0.5	242	0.7
Bachelor's degree	18,906	19.5	41,008	23.5	36,595	25.6	4,997	18.0	4,875	34.2	5,065	14.4
Master's degree[2]...................................	9,390	9.7	18,225	10.5	16,697	11.7	2,144	7.7	2,739	19.2	1,731	4.9
Professional degree	1,501	1.6	2,647	1.5	2,450	1.7	277	1.0	364	2.6	269	0.8
Doctorate degree	2,059	2.1	3,527	2.0	3,295	2.3	328	1.2	721	5.1	270	0.8

* = Quantity zero or rounds to zero.
[1]Excluding members of the Armed Forces living in barracks.
[2]Detail on graduate school attendance and length of master's degree program, available in previous years, discontinued due to questionnaire changes in 2015.

PART A
NATIONAL EDUCATION STATISTICS

■ **Historical Attainment Tables**

Table A-32. Percent of People 25 Years Old and Over Who Have Completed High School or College, by Race, Hispanic Origin, and Sex, Selected Years, 1940–2020

(Percent; civilian noninstitutionalized population.)

Age and Year	All races			White			Non-Hispanic White			Black[1]			Asian		
	Total	Male	Female	Total	Male	Female	Total	Male	Female	Total	Male	Female	Total	Male	Female
25 YEARS AND OLDER															
Completed 4 Years of High School or More															
2020	90.9	90.6	91.3	91.3	90.8	91.7	95.1	94.8	95.4	89.4	88.6	90	91.6	92.6	90.7
2019	90.1	89.6	90.5	90.5	89.9	91.0	94.6	94.2	95.0	87.9	87.1	88.6	91.2	92.8	89.8
2018	89.8	89.4	90.2	90.2	89.6	90.8	94.3	93.9	94.7	87.9	87.7	88.1	90.5	92.7	88.6
2017	89.6	89.1	90.0	90.1	89.5	90.6	94.1	93.7	94.5	87.3	86.5	87.9	90.9	92.6	89.4
2016	89.1	88.5	89.6	89.5	88.8	90.1	93.8	93.4	94.3	87.1	86.4	87.7	90.3	91.9	89.0
2015	88.4	88.0	88.8	88.8	88.3	89.3	93.3	93.0	93.5	87.0	86.4	87.6	89.1	91.0	87.4
2014	88.3	87.7	88.9	88.8	88.0	89.6	93.1	92.5	93.7	85.8	85.3	86.2	89.5	91.9	87.4
2013	88.2	87.6	88.6	88.6	88.0	89.2	92.9	92.7	93.2	85.1	84.1	86.0	90.1	91.5	89.0
2012[2]	87.6	87.3	88.0	88.1	87.6	88.5	92.5	92.2	92.7	85.0	84.3	85.5	88.9	90.4	87.6
2011	87.6	87.1	88.0	88.1	87.4	88.6	92.4	92.0	92.8	84.5	83.8	85.0	88.6	90.4	87.1
2010	87.1	86.6	87.6	87.6	86.9	88.2	92.1	91.8	92.3	84.2	83.6	84.6	88.9	91.2	87.0
2009	86.7	86.2	87.1	87.1	86.5	87.7	91.6	91.4	91.9	84.1	84.0	84.1	88.2	90.4	86.2
2008	86.6	85.9	87.2	87.1	86.3	87.8	91.5	91.1	91.8	83.0	81.8	84.0	88.7	90.8	86.9
2007	85.7	85.0	86.4	86.2	85.3	87.1	90.6	90.2	91.0	82.3	81.9	82.6	87.8	89.8	85.9
2006	85.5	85.0	85.9	86.1	85.5	86.7	90.5	90.2	90.8	80.7	80.1	81.2	87.4	89.6	85.5
2005	85.2	84.9	85.5	85.8	85.2	86.2	90.1	89.9	90.3	81.1	81.0	81.2	87.6	90.4	85.2
2004	85.2	84.8	85.4	85.8	85.3	86.3	90.0	89.9	90.1	80.6	80.4	80.8	86.8	88.7	85.0
2003[3]	84.6	84.1	85.0	85.1	84.5	85.7	89.4	89.0	89.7	80.0	79.6	80.3	87.6	89.5	86.0
2002	84.1	83.8	84.4	84.8	84.3	85.2	88.7	88.5	88.9	78.7	78.5	78.9	NA	NA	NA
2001[4]	84.1	84.1	84.2	84.8	84.4	85.1	88.6	88.6	88.6	78.8	79.2	78.5	NA	NA	NA
2000	84.1	84.2	84.0	84.9	84.8	85.0	88.4	88.5	88.4	78.5	78.7	78.3	NA	NA	NA
1999	83.4	83.4	83.4	84.3	84.2	84.3	87.7	87.7	87.7	77.0	76.7	77.2	NA	NA	NA
1998	82.8	82.8	82.9	83.7	83.6	83.8	87.1	87.1	87.1	76.0	75.2	76.7	NA	NA	NA
1997	82.1	82.0	82.2	83.0	82.9	83.2	86.3	86.3	86.3	74.9	73.5	76.0	NA	NA	NA
1996	81.7	81.9	81.6	82.8	82.7	82.8	86.0	86.1	85.9	74.3	74.3	74.2	NA	NA	NA
1995	81.7	81.7	81.6	83.0	83.0	83.0	85.9	86.0	85.8	73.8	73.4	74.1	NA	NA	NA
1994	80.9	81.0	80.7	82.0	82.1	81.9	84.9	85.1	84.7	72.9	71.7	73.8	NA	NA	NA
1993	80.2	80.5	80.0	81.5	81.8	81.3	84.1	84.5	83.8	70.4	69.6	71.1	NA	NA	NA
1992[5]	79.4	79.7	79.2	80.9	81.1	80.7	NA	NA	NA	67.7	67.0	68.2	NA	NA	NA
1991	78.4	78.5	78.3	79.9	79.8	79.9	NA	NA	NA	66.7	66.7	66.7	NA	NA	NA
1990	77.6	77.7	77.5	79.1	79.1	79.0	NA	NA	NA	66.2	65.8	66.5	NA	NA	NA
1989	76.9	77.2	76.6	78.4	78.6	78.2	NA	NA	NA	64.6	64.2	65.0	NA	NA	NA
1988	76.2	76.4	76.0	77.7	77.7	77.6	NA	NA	NA	63.5	63.7	63.4	NA	NA	NA
1987	75.6	76.0	75.3	77.0	77.3	76.7	NA	NA	NA	63.4	63.0	63.7	NA	NA	NA
1986	74.7	75.1	74.4	76.2	76.5	75.9	NA	NA	NA	62.3	61.5	63.0	NA	NA	NA
1985	73.9	74.4	73.5	75.5	76.0	75.1	NA	NA	NA	59.8	58.4	60.8	NA	NA	NA
1984	73.3	73.7	73.0	75.0	75.4	74.6	NA	NA	NA	58.5	57.1	59.7	NA	NA	NA
1983	72.1	72.7	71.5	73.8	74.4	73.3	NA	NA	NA	56.8	56.5	57.1	NA	NA	NA
1982	71.0	71.7	70.3	72.8	73.4	72.3	NA	NA	NA	54.9	55.7	54.3	NA	NA	NA
1981	69.7	70.3	69.1	71.6	72.1	71.2	NA	NA	NA	52.9	53.2	52.6	NA	NA	NA
1980	68.6	69.2	68.1	70.5	71.0	70.1	NA	NA	NA	51.2	51.1	51.3	NA	NA	NA
1979	67.7	68.4	67.1	69.7	70.3	69.2	NA	NA	NA	49.4	49.2	49.5	NA	NA	NA
1978	65.9	66.8	65.2	67.9	68.6	67.2	NA	NA	NA	47.6	47.9	47.3	NA	NA	NA
1977	64.9	65.6	64.4	67.0	67.5	66.5	NA	NA	NA	45.5	45.6	45.4	NA	NA	NA
1976	64.1	64.7	63.5	66.1	66.7	65.5	NA	NA	NA	43.8	42.3	45.0	NA	NA	NA
1975	62.5	63.1	62.1	64.5	65.0	64.1	NA	NA	NA	42.5	41.6	43.3	NA	NA	NA
1974	61.2	61.6	60.9	63.3	63.6	63.0	NA	NA	NA	40.8	39.9	41.5	NA	NA	NA
1973	59.8	60.0	59.6	61.9	62.1	61.7	NA	NA	NA	39.2	38.2	40.1	NA	NA	NA
1972	58.2	58.2	58.2	60.4	60.3	60.5	NA	NA	NA	36.6	35.7	37.2	NA	NA	NA
1971	56.4	56.3	56.6	58.6	58.4	58.8	NA	NA	NA	34.7	33.8	35.4	NA	NA	NA
1970	55.2	55.0	55.4	57.4	57.2	57.6	NA	NA	NA	33.7	32.4	34.8	NA	NA	NA
1969	54.0	53.6	54.4	56.3	55.7	56.7	NA	NA	NA	32.3	31.9	32.6	NA	NA	NA
1968	52.6	52.0	53.2	54.9	54.3	55.5	NA	NA	NA	30.1	28.9	31.0	NA	NA	NA
1967	51.1	50.5	51.7	53.4	52.8	53.8	NA	NA	NA	29.5	27.1	31.5	NA	NA	NA

Note: Starting in 2001, data are from the expanded CPS sample.

NA = Not available

[1] Data in the column labeled "Black" include Black and other races from 1940 to 1962: from 1963 to 2003, data are for the Black population only.

[2] Starting in 2012, data were calculated using population controls based on the 2010 Census.

[3] Starting in 2003, respondents could choose more than one race. The race data in this table for White, non-Hispanic White, Black, and Asian from 2003 onward represent those respondents who indicated only one racial identity. Prior to 2003, Asians were grouped with Pacific Islanders.

[4] Starting in 2001, data were calculated using population controls based on Census 2000.

[5] Begining with data for 1992, a new question results in different categories than for earlier years: Data shown as 'Completed 4 Years of High School or more' is now collected in the category 'High School Graduate.' Data shown as 'College 1 to 3 years' is now collected in the 'Some college' and the two 'Associate degree' categories. Data shown as 'Completed 4 Years of College or more', is now collected in the categories, 'Bachelor's degree,' 'Master's degree,' 'Doctorate degree,' and 'Professional degree'. Due to the change in question format, median years of schooling cannot be derived.

Table A-32. Percent of People 25 Years Old and Over Who Have Completed High School or College, by Race, Hispanic Origin, and Sex, Selected Years, 1940–2020—*Continued*

(Percent; civilian noninstitutionalized population.)

Age and Year	Hispanic (of any race) Total	Male	Female	White alone or in combination Total	Male	Female	Non-Hispanic White alone or in combination Total	Male	Female	Black alone or in combination Total	Male	Female	Asian alone or in combination Total	Male	Female
25 YEARS AND OLDER															
Completed 4 Years of High School or More															
2020	74.3	73.8	74.8	91.2	90.8	91.6	95.1	94.8	95.4	89.5	88.8	90.1	91.7	92.7	90.9
2019	71.8	70.8	72.8	90.4	89.9	91.0	94.6	94.2	94.9	88.0	87.1	88.8	91.5	92.9	90.1
2018	71.6	70.7	72.5	90.2	89.5	90.7	94.3	93.9	94.6	87.9	87.6	88.2	90.7	92.9	88.8
2017	70.5	69.5	71.6	90.0	89.4	90.5	94.1	93.7	94.5	87.2	86.3	88.0	91.1	92.7	89.7
2016	68.5	67.2	69.7	89.4	88.8	90.1	93.8	93.4	94.3	87.2	86.5	87.7	90.6	92.0	89.4
2015	66.7	65.5	67.8	88.7	88.2	89.2	93.3	93.0	93.5	87.1	86.4	87.6	89.3	91.1	87.7
2014	66.5	65.1	67.9	88.7	87.9	89.5	93.1	92.6	93.7	85.8	85.2	86.3	89.9	92.2	87.9
2013	66.2	64.6	67.9	88.6	88.0	89.2	92.9	92.7	93.1	85.1	84.1	85.9	90.3	91.6	89.2
2012[2]	65.0	64.0	66.0	88.1	87.6	88.5	92.5	92.2	92.7	85.1	84.5	85.6	89.0	90.5	87.8
2011	64.3	63.6	65.1	88.0	87.4	88.6	92.4	92.0	92.7	84.6	83.9	85.1	88.9	90.6	87.4
2010	62.9	61.4	64.4	87.6	86.8	88.2	92.0	91.7	92.3	84.2	83.5	84.8	89.1	91.2	87.3
2009	61.9	60.6	63.3	87.1	86.4	87.7	91.6	91.4	91.8	84.1	83.9	84.2	88.3	90.6	86.4
2008	62.3	60.9	63.7	87.1	86.3	87.8	91.4	91.1	91.8	83.2	81.9	84.1	89.0	90.9	87.2
2007	60.3	58.2	62.5	86.2	85.3	87.0	90.6	90.2	91.0	82.4	82.0	82.6	87.8	89.2	86.5
2006	59.3	58.5	60.1	86.1	85.5	86.7	90.5	90.2	90.8	80.8	80.3	81.2	87.6	89.6	85.8
2005	58.5	57.9	59.1	85.7	85.2	86.2	90.1	89.9	90.3	81.3	81.2	81.3	87.9	90.5	85.6
2004	58.4	57.3	59.5	85.8	85.3	86.2	90.0	89.9	90.1	80.6	80.3	80.9	86.9	88.8	85.2
2003[3]	57.0	56.3	57.8	85.1	84.5	85.7	89.4	89.0	89.6	80.0	79.5	80.3	87.8	89.7	86.1
2002	57.0	56.1	57.9	NA	NA	NA	NA	NA	NA	NA	NA	NA	NA	NA	NA
2001[4]	56.8	55.5	58.0	NA	NA	NA	NA	NA	NA	NA	NA	NA	NA	NA	NA
2000	57.0	56.6	57.5	NA	NA	NA	NA	NA	NA	NA	NA	NA	NA	NA	NA
1999	56.1	56.0	56.3	NA	NA	NA	NA	NA	NA	NA	NA	NA	NA	NA	NA
1998	55.5	55.7	55.3	NA	NA	NA	NA	NA	NA	NA	NA	NA	NA	NA	NA
1997	54.7	54.9	54.6	NA	NA	NA	NA	NA	NA	NA	NA	NA	NA	NA	NA
1996	53.1	53.0	53.3	NA	NA	NA	NA	NA	NA	NA	NA	NA	NA	NA	NA
1995	53.4	52.9	53.8	NA	NA	NA	NA	NA	NA	NA	NA	NA	NA	NA	NA
1994	53.3	53.4	53.2	NA	NA	NA	NA	NA	NA	NA	NA	NA	NA	NA	NA
1993	53.1	52.9	53.2	NA	NA	NA	NA	NA	NA	NA	NA	NA	NA	NA	NA
1992[5]	52.6	53.7	51.5	NA	NA	NA	NA	NA	NA	NA	NA	NA	NA	NA	NA
1991	51.3	51.4	51.2	NA	NA	NA	NA	NA	NA	NA	NA	NA	NA	NA	NA
1990	50.8	50.3	51.3	NA	NA	NA	NA	NA	NA	NA	NA	NA	NA	NA	NA
1989	50.9	51.0	50.7	NA	NA	NA	NA	NA	NA	NA	NA	NA	NA	NA	NA
1988	51.0	52.0	50.0	NA	NA	NA	NA	NA	NA	NA	NA	NA	NA	NA	NA
1987	50.9	51.8	50.0	NA	NA	NA	NA	NA	NA	NA	NA	NA	NA	NA	NA
1986	48.5	49.2	47.8	NA	NA	NA	NA	NA	NA	NA	NA	NA	NA	NA	NA
1985	47.9	48.5	47.4	NA	NA	NA	NA	NA	NA	NA	NA	NA	NA	NA	NA
1984	47.1	48.6	45.7	NA	NA	NA	NA	NA	NA	NA	NA	NA	NA	NA	NA
1983	46.2	48.6	44.2	NA	NA	NA	NA	NA	NA	NA	NA	NA	NA	NA	NA
1982	45.9	48.1	44.1	NA	NA	NA	NA	NA	NA	NA	NA	NA	NA	NA	NA
1981	44.5	45.5	43.6	NA	NA	NA	NA	NA	NA	NA	NA	NA	NA	NA	NA
1980	45.3	46.4	44.1	NA	NA	NA	NA	NA	NA	NA	NA	NA	NA	NA	NA
1979	42.0	42.3	41.7	NA	NA	NA	NA	NA	NA	NA	NA	NA	NA	NA	NA
1978	40.8	42.2	39.6	NA	NA	NA	NA	NA	NA	NA	NA	NA	NA	NA	NA
1977	39.6	42.3	37.2	NA	NA	NA	NA	NA	NA	NA	NA	NA	NA	NA	NA
1976	39.3	41.4	37.3	NA	NA	NA	NA	NA	NA	NA	NA	NA	NA	NA	NA
1975	37.9	39.5	36.7	NA	NA	NA	NA	NA	NA	NA	NA	NA	NA	NA	NA
1974	36.5	38.3	34.9	NA	NA	NA	NA	NA	NA	NA	NA	NA	NA	NA	NA
1973	NA	NA	NA	NA	NA	NA	NA	NA	NA	NA	NA	NA	NA	NA	NA
1972	NA	NA	NA	NA	NA	NA	NA	NA	NA	NA	NA	NA	NA	NA	NA
1971	NA	NA	NA	NA	NA	NA	NA	NA	NA	NA	NA	NA	NA	NA	NA
1970	NA	NA	NA	NA	NA	NA	NA	NA	NA	NA	NA	NA	NA	NA	NA
1960	NA	NA	NA	NA	NA	NA	NA	NA	NA	NA	NA	NA	NA	NA	NA
1968	NA	NA	NA	NA	NA	NA	NA	NA	NA	NA	NA	NA	NA	NA	NA
1967	NA	NA	NA	NA	NA	NA	NA	NA	NA	NA	NA	NA	NA	NA	NA

Note: Starting in 2001, data are from the expanded CPS sample.
NA = Not available
[1]Data in the column labeled "Black" include Black and other races from 1940 to 1962; from 1963 to 2003, data are for the Black population only.
[2]Starting in 2012, data were calculated using population controls based on the 2010 Census.
[3]Starting in 2003, respondents could choose more than one race. The race data in this table for White, non-Hispanic White, Black, and Asian from 2003 onward represent those respondents who indicated only one racial identity. Prior to 2003, Asians were grouped with Pacific Islanders.
[4]Starting in 2001, data were calculated using population controls based on Census 2000.
[5]Begining with data for 1992, a new question results in different categories than for earlier years. Data shown as 'Completed 4 Years of High School or more' is now collected in the category 'High School Graduate.' Data shown as 'College 1 to 3 years' is now collected in the 'Some college' and the two 'Associate degree' categories. Data shown as 'Completed 4 Years of College or more', is now collected in the categories, 'Bachelor's degree,' 'Master's degree,' 'Doctorate degree,' and 'Professional degree'. Due to the change in question format, median years of schooling cannot be derived.

Table A-32. Percent of People 25 Years Old and Over Who Have Completed High School or College, by Race, Hispanic Origin, and Sex, Selected Years, 1940–2020—*Continued*

(Percent; civilian noninstitutionalized population.)

Age and Year	All races			White			Non-Hispanic White			Black[1]			Asian		
	Total	Male	Female	Total	Male	Female	Total	Male	Female	Total	Male	Female	Total	Male	Female
1966	49.9	49.0	50.8	52.2	51.3	53.0	NA	NA	NA	27.8	25.8	29.5	NA	NA	NA
1965	49.0	48.0	49.9	51.3	50.2	52.2	NA	NA	NA	27.2	25.8	28.4	NA	NA	NA
1964	48.0	47.0	48.9	50.3	49.3	51.2	NA	NA	NA	25.7	23.7	27.4	NA	NA	NA
1962	46.3	45.0	47.5	48.7	47.4	49.9	NA	NA	NA	24.8	23.2	26.2	NA	NA	NA
1959	43.7	42.2	45.2	46.1	44.5	47.7	NA	NA	NA	20.7	19.6	21.6	NA	NA	NA
1957	41.6	39.7	43.3	43.2	41.1	45.1	NA	NA	NA	18.4	16.9	19.7	NA	NA	NA
1952	38.8	36.9	40.5	NA	NA	NA	NA	NA	NA	15.0	14.0	15.7	NA	NA	NA
1950	34.3	32.6	36.0	NA	NA	NA	NA	NA	NA	13.7	12.5	14.7	NA	NA	NA
1947	33.1	31.4	34.7	35.0	33.2	36.7	NA	NA	NA	13.6	12.7	14.5	NA	NA	NA
1940	24.5	22.7	26.3	26.1	24.2	28.1	NA	NA	NA	7.7	6.9	8.4	NA	NA	NA
Completed 4 Years of College or More															
2020	37.5	36.7	38.3	37.5	36.8	38.2	41.3	41.0	41.7	27.8	24.7	30.5	61.1	63.0	59.4
2019	36.0	35.4	36.6	36.3	35.7	36.8	40.1	39.9	40.3	26.1	24.1	27.7	58.1	60.4	56.1
2018	35.0	34.6	35.3	35.2	34.9	35.5	38.8	38.9	38.8	25.2	23.2	26.9	56.5	59.3	54.0
2017	34.2	33.7	34.6	34.5	34.0	35.0	38.1	37.8	38.3	23.9	22.1	25.4	54.8	56.6	53.2
2016	33.4	33.2	33.7	33.7	33.4	34.0	37.3	37.2	37.3	23.3	21.7	24.6	55.9	58.8	53.4
2015	32.5	32.3	32.7	32.8	32.6	32.9	36.2	36.3	36.1	22.5	20.6	24.0	53.9	56.8	51.5
2014	32.0	31.9	32.0	32.3	32.3	32.3	35.6	35.9	35.3	22.2	20.4	23.7	52.3	54.7	50.3
2013	31.7	32.0	31.4	32.0	32.4	31.6	35.2	36.0	34.4	21.8	19.8	23.3	53.2	56.1	50.8
2012	30.9	31.4	30.6	31.3	31.9	30.8	34.5	35.5	33.5	21.2	19.2	22.9	51.0	53.7	48.8
2011	30.4	30.8	30.1	31.0	31.5	30.5	34.0	35.0	33.1	19.9	18.0	21.4	50.3	53.4	47.7
2010	29.9	30.3	29.6	30.3	30.8	29.9	33.2	34.2	32.4	19.8	17.7	21.4	52.4	55.6	49.5
2009	29.5	30.1	29.1	29.9	30.6	29.3	32.9	33.9	31.9	19.3	17.8	20.6	52.3	55.7	49.3
2008	29.4	30.1	28.8	29.8	30.5	29.1	32.6	33.8	31.5	19.6	18.7	20.4	52.6	55.8	49.8
2007	28.7	29.5	28.0	29.1	29.9	28.3	31.8	33.2	30.6	18.5	18.0	19.0	52.1	55.2	49.3
2006	28.0	29.2	26.9	28.4	29.7	27.1	31.0	32.8	29.3	18.5	17.2	19.4	49.7	52.5	47.1
2005	27.7	28.9	26.5	28.1	29.4	26.8	30.6	32.4	28.9	17.6	16.0	18.8	50.2	54.0	46.8
2004	27.7	29.4	26.1	28.2	30.0	26.4	30.6	32.9	28.4	17.6	16.6	18.5	49.4	53.7	45.6
2003	27.2	28.9	25.7	27.6	29.4	25.9	30.0	32.3	27.9	17.3	16.7	17.8	49.8	53.9	46.1
2002	26.7	28.5	25.1	27.2	29.1	25.4	29.4	31.7	27.3	17.0	16.4	17.5	NA	NA	NA
2001	26.2	28.2	24.3	26.6	28.7	24.6	28.7	31.3	26.3	15.7	15.3	16.1	NA	NA	NA
2000	25.6	27.8	23.6	26.1	28.5	23.9	28.1	30.8	25.5	16.5	16.3	16.7	NA	NA	NA
1999	25.2	27.5	23.1	25.9	28.5	23.5	27.7	30.6	25.0	15.4	14.2	16.4	NA	NA	NA
1998	24.4	26.5	22.4	25.0	27.3	22.8	26.6	29.3	24.1	14.7	13.9	15.4	NA	NA	NA
1997	23.9	26.2	21.7	24.6	27.0	22.3	26.2	29.0	23.7	13.3	12.5	13.9	NA	NA	NA
1996	23.6	26.0	21.4	24.3	26.9	21.8	25.9	28.8	23.2	13.6	12.4	14.6	NA	NA	NA
1995	23.0	26.0	20.2	24.0	27.2	21.0	25.4	28.9	22.1	13.2	13.6	12.9	NA	NA	NA
1994	22.2	25.1	19.6	22.9	26.1	20.0	24.3	27.8	21.1	12.9	12.8	13.0	NA	NA	NA
1993	21.9	24.8	19.2	22.6	25.7	19.7	23.8	27.2	20.7	12.2	11.9	12.4	NA	NA	NA
1992	21.4	24.3	18.6	22.1	25.2	19.1	NA	NA	NA	11.9	11.9	12.0	NA	NA	NA
1991	21.4	24.3	18.8	22.2	25.4	19.3	NA	NA	NA	11.5	11.4	11.6	NA	NA	NA
1990	21.3	24.4	18.4	22.0	25.3	19.0	NA	NA	NA	11.3	11.9	10.8	NA	NA	NA
1989	21.1	24.5	18.1	21.8	25.4	18.5	NA	NA	NA	11.8	11.7	11.9	NA	NA	NA
1988	20.3	24.0	17.0	20.9	25.0	17.3	NA	NA	NA	11.2	11.1	11.4	NA	NA	NA
1987	19.9	23.6	16.5	20.5	24.5	16.9	NA	NA	NA	10.7	11.0	10.4	NA	NA	NA
1986	19.4	23.2	16.1	20.1	24.1	16.4	NA	NA	NA	10.9	11.2	10.7	NA	NA	NA
1985	19.4	23.1	16.0	20.0	24.0	16.3	NA	NA	NA	11.1	11.2	11.0	NA	NA	NA
1984	19.1	22.9	15.7	19.8	23.9	16.0	NA	NA	NA	10.4	10.4	10.4	NA	NA	NA
1983	18.8	23.0	15.1	19.5	24.0	15.4	NA	NA	NA	9.5	10.0	9.2	NA	NA	NA
1982	17.7	21.9	14.0	18.5	23.0	14.4	NA	NA	NA	8.8	9.1	8.5	NA	NA	NA
1981	17.1	21.1	13.4	17.8	22.2	13.8	NA	NA	NA	8.2	8.2	8.2	NA	NA	NA
1980	17.0	20.9	13.6	17.8	22.1	14.0	NA	NA	NA	7.9	7.7	8.1	NA	NA	NA
1979	16.4	20.4	12.9	17.2	21.4	13.3	NA	NA	NA	7.9	8.3	7.5	NA	NA	NA
1978	15.7	19.7	12.2	16.4	20.7	12.6	NA	NA	NA	7.2	7.3	7.1	NA	NA	NA
1977	15.4	19.2	12.0	16.1	20.2	12.4	NA	NA	NA	7.2	7.0	7.4	NA	NA	NA
1976	14.7	18.6	11.3	15.4	19.6	11.6	NA	NA	NA	6.6	6.3	6.8	NA	NA	NA

Note: Starting in 2001, data are from the expanded CPS sample.
NA = Not available
[1]Data in the column labeled "Black" include Black and other races from 1940 to 1962: from 1963 to 2003, data are for the Black population only.
[2]Starting in 2012, data were calculated using population controls based on the 2010 Census.
[3]Starting in 2003, respondents could choose more than one race. The race data in this table for White, non-Hispanic White, Black, and Asian from 2003 onward represent those respondents who indicated only one racial identity. Prior to 2003, Asians were grouped with Pacific Islanders.
[4]Starting in 2001, data were calculated using population controls based on Census 2000.
[5]Begining with data for 1992, a new question results in different categories than for earlier years: Data shown as 'Completed 4 Years of High School or more' is now collected in the category 'High School Graduate.' Data shown as 'College 1 to 3 years' is now collected in the 'Some college' and the two 'Associate degree' categories. Data shown as 'Completed 4 Years of College or more', is now collected in the categories, 'Bachelor's degree,' 'Master's degree,' 'Doctorate degree,' and 'Professional degree'. Due to the change in question format, median years of schooling cannot be derived.

Table A-32. Percent of People 25 Years Old and Over Who Have Completed High School or College, by Race, Hispanic Origin, and Sex, Selected Years, 1940–2020—*Continued*

(Percent; civilian noninstitutionalized population.)

Age and Year	Hispanic (of any race)			White alone or in combination			Non-Hispanic White alone or in combination			Black alone or in combination			Asian alone or in combination		
	Total	Male	Female	Total	Male	Female	Total	Male	Female	Total	Male	Female	Total	Male	Female
1966	NA	NA	NA	NA	NA	NA	NA	NA	NA	NA	NA	NA	NA	NA	NA
1965	NA	NA	NA	NA	NA	NA	NA	NA	NA	NA	NA	NA	NA	NA	NA
1964	NA	NA	NA	NA	NA	NA	NA	NA	NA	NA	NA	NA	NA	NA	NA
1962	NA	NA	NA	NA	NA	NA	NA	NA	NA	NA	NA	NA	NA	NA	NA
1959	NA	NA	NA	NA	NA	NA	NA	NA	NA	NA	NA	NA	NA	NA	NA
1957	NA	NA	NA	NA	NA	NA	NA	NA	NA	NA	NA	NA	NA	NA	NA
1952	NA	NA	NA	NA	NA	NA	NA	NA	NA	NA	NA	NA	NA	NA	NA
1950	NA	NA	NA	NA	NA	NA	NA	NA	NA	NA	NA	NA	NA	NA	NA
1947	NA	NA	NA	NA	NA	NA	NA	NA	NA	NA	NA	NA	NA	NA	NA
1940	NA	NA	NA	NA	NA	NA	NA	NA	NA	NA	NA	NA	NA	NA	NA

Completed 4 Years of College or More

Age and Year	Total	Male	Female	Total	Male	Female	Total	Male	Female	Total	Male	Female	Total	Male	Female
2020	20.8	19.4	22.3	37.4	36.7	38.2	41.2	40.8	41.6	28.1	24.9	30.8	60.3	61.6	59.1
2019	18.8	16.9	20.8	36.2	35.5	36.8	40.0	39.8	40.2	26.3	24.3	28.0	57.7	59.6	56.0
2018	18.3	16.6	20.1	35.1	34.7	35.5	38.7	38.8	38.7	25.4	23.2	27.1	56.0	58.6	53.7
2017	17.2	15.8	18.6	34.4	33.9	34.9	38.0	37.8	38.3	24.2	22.3	25.7	54.4	55.9	53.2
2016	16.4	15.4	17.4	33.6	33.3	33.9	37.2	37.1	37.3	23.5	21.8	24.9	55.4	57.9	53.3
2015	15.5	14.3	16.6	32.7	32.5	32.9	36.2	36.2	36.1	22.7	20.7	24.2	53.7	56.2	51.5
2014	15.2	14.2	16.1	32.2	32.2	32.3	35.5	35.8	35.3	22.7	20.6	24.3	52.2	54.2	50.4
2013	15.1	13.9	16.2	31.9	32.3	31.5	35.1	35.9	34.4	22.0	20.0	23.6	52.8	55.5	50.5
2012	14.5	13.3	15.8	31.2	31.8	30.7	34.4	35.4	33.4	21.4	19.4	22.9	50.4	52.6	48.6
2011	14.1	13.1	15.2	30.9	31.4	30.5	33.9	34.9	33.1	20.1	18.2	21.6	49.9	52.8	47.3
2010	13.9	12.9	14.9	30.2	30.7	29.8	33.2	34.1	32.3	19.9	17.7	21.6	51.8	54.7	49.3
2009	13.2	12.5	14.0	29.8	30.4	29.3	32.8	33.8	31.8	19.4	17.8	20.7	51.8	54.8	49.2
2008	13.3	12.6	14.1	29.7	30.3	29.0	32.6	33.0	31.4	19.8	18.8	20.5	52.0	54.6	49.8
2007	12.7	11.8	13.7	29.0	29.8	28.3	31.7	33.0	30.5	18.7	18.2	19.1	47.1	49.1	45.4
2006	12.4	11.9	12.9	28.3	29.6	27.0	30.9	32.7	29.2	18.7	17.4	19.7	49.0	51.4	46.8
2005	12.0	11.8	12.1	28.0	29.3	26.7	30.5	32.3	28.9	17.6	16.0	18.9	49.8	53.3	46.6
2004	12.1	11.8	12.3	28.0	29.9	26.3	30.5	32.8	28.3	17.7	16.5	18.6	48.9	52.8	45.4
2003	11.4	11.2	11.6	27.5	29.3	25.8	29.9	32.2	27.9	17.5	16.8	18.0	49.2	52.7	46.0
2002	11.1	11.0	11.2	NA	NA	NA	NA	NA	NA	NA	NA	NA	NA	NA	NA
2001	11.1	10.8	11.4	NA	NA	NA	NA	NA	NA	NA	NA	NA	NA	NA	NA
2000	10.6	10.7	10.6	NA	NA	NA	NA	NA	NA	NA	NA	NA	NA	NA	NA
1999	10.9	10.7	11.0	NA	NA	NA	NA	NA	NA	NA	NA	NA	NA	NA	NA
1998	11.0	11.1	10.9	NA	NA	NA	NA	NA	NA	NA	NA	NA	NA	NA	NA
1997	10.3	10.6	10.1	NA	NA	NA	NA	NA	NA	NA	NA	NA	NA	NA	NA
1996	9.3	10.3	8.3	NA	NA	NA	NA	NA	NA	NA	NA	NA	NA	NA	NA
1995	9.3	10.1	8.4	NA	NA	NA	NA	NA	NA	NA	NA	NA	NA	NA	NA
1994	9.1	9.6	8.6	NA	NA	NA	NA	NA	NA	NA	NA	NA	NA	NA	NA
1993	9.0	9.5	8.5	NA	NA	NA	NA	NA	NA	NA	NA	NA	NA	NA	NA
1992	9.3	10.2	8.5	NA	NA	NA	NA	NA	NA	NA	NA	NA	NA	NA	NA
1991	9.7	10.0	9.4	NA	NA	NA	NA	NA	NA	NA	NA	NA	NA	NA	NA
1990	9.2	9.8	8.7	NA	NA	NA	NA	NA	NA	NA	NA	NA	NA	NA	NA
1989	9.9	11.0	8.8	NA	NA	NA	NA	NA	NA	NA	NA	NA	NA	NA	NA
1988	10.1	12.3	8.1	NA	NA	NA	NA	NA	NA	NA	NA	NA	NA	NA	NA
1987	8.6	9.7	7.5	NA	NA	NA	NA	NA	NA	NA	NA	NA	NA	NA	NA
1986	8.4	9.5	7.4	NA	NA	NA	NA	NA	NA	NA	NA	NA	NA	NA	NA
1985	8.5	9.7	7.3	NA	NA	NA	NA	NA	NA	NA	NA	NA	NA	NA	NA
1984	8.2	9.5	7.0	NA	NA	NA	NA	NA	NA	NA	NA	NA	NA	NA	NA
1983	7.9	9.2	6.8	NA	NA	NA	NA	NA	NA	NA	NA	NA	NA	NA	NA
1982	7.8	9.6	6.2	NA	NA	NA	NA	NA	NA	NA	NA	NA	NA	NA	NA
1981	7.7	9.7	5.9	NA	NA	NA	NA	NA	NA	NA	NA	NA	NA	NA	NA
1980	7.9	9.7	6.2	NA	NA	NA	NA	NA	NA	NA	NA	NA	NA	NA	NA
1979	6.7	8.2	5.3	NA	NA	NA	NA	NA	NA	NA	NA	NA	NA	NA	NA
1978	7.0	8.6	5.7	NA	NA	NA	NA	NA	NA	NA	NA	NA	NA	NA	NA
1977	6.2	8.1	4.4	NA	NA	NA	NA	NA	NA	NA	NA	NA	NA	NA	NA
1976	6.1	8.6	4.0	NA	NA	NA	NA	NA	NA	NA	NA	NA	NA	NA	NA

Note: Starting in 2001, data are from the expanded CPS sample.

NA = Not available

[1]Data in the column labeled "Black" include Black and other races from 1940 to 1962; from 1963 to 2003, data are for the Black population only.

[2]Starting in 2012, data were calculated using population controls based on the 2010 Census.

[3]Starting in 2003, respondents could choose more than one race. The race data in this table for White, non-Hispanic White, Black, and Asian from 2003 onward represent those respondents who indicated only one racial identity. Prior to 2003, Asians were grouped with Pacific Islanders.

[4]Starting in 2001, data were calculated using population controls based on Census 2000.

[5]Begining with data for 1992, a new question results in different categories than for earlier years: Data shown as 'Completed 4 Years of High School or more' is now collected in the category 'High School Graduate.' Data shown as 'College 1 to 3 years' is now collected in the 'Some college' and the two 'Associate degree' categories. Data shown as 'Completed 4 Years of College or more', is now collected in the categories, 'Bachelor's degree,' 'Master's degree,' 'Doctorate degree,' and 'Professional degree'. Due to the change in question format, median years of schooling cannot be derived.

Table A-32. Percent of People 25 Years Old and Over Who Have Completed High School or College, by Race, Hispanic Origin, and Sex, Selected Years, 1940–2020—*Continued*

(Percent; civilian noninstitutionalized population.)

Age and Year	All races			White			Non-Hispanic White			Black[1]			Asian		
	Total	Male	Female	Total	Male	Female	Total	Male	Female	Total	Male	Female	Total	Male	Female
1975	13.9	17.6	10.6	14.5	18.4	11.0	NA	NA	NA	6.4	6.7	6.2	NA	NA	NA
1974	13.3	16.9	10.1	14.0	17.7	10.6	NA	NA	NA	5.5	5.7	5.3	NA	NA	NA
1973	12.6	16.0	9.6	13.1	16.8	9.9	NA	NA	NA	6.0	5.9	6.0	NA	NA	NA
1972	12.0	15.4	9.0	12.6	16.2	9.4	NA	NA	NA	5.1	5.5	4.8	NA	NA	NA
1971	11.4	14.6	8.5	12.0	15.5	8.9	NA	NA	NA	4.5	4.7	4.3	NA	NA	NA
1970	11.0	14.1	8.2	11.6	15.0	8.6	NA	NA	NA	4.5	4.6	4.4	NA	NA	NA
1969	10.7	13.6	8.1	11.2	14.3	8.5	NA	NA	NA	4.6	4.8	4.5	NA	NA	NA
1968	10.5	13.3	8.0	11.0	14.1	8.3	NA	NA	NA	4.3	3.7	4.8	NA	NA	NA
1967	10.1	12.8	7.6	10.6	13.6	7.9	NA	NA	NA	4.0	3.4	4.4	NA	NA	NA
1966	9.8	12.5	7.4	10.4	13.3	7.7	NA	NA	NA	3.8	3.9	3.7	NA	NA	NA
1965	9.4	12.0	7.1	9.9	12.7	7.3	NA	NA	NA	4.7	4.9	4.5	NA	NA	NA
1964	9.1	11.7	6.8	9.6	12.3	7.1	NA	NA	NA	3.9	4.5	3.4	NA	NA	NA
1962	8.9	11.4	6.7	9.5	12.2	7.0	NA	NA	NA	4.0	3.9	4.0	NA	NA	NA
1959	8.1	10.3	6.0	8.6	11.0	6.2	NA	NA	NA	3.3	3.8	2.9	NA	NA	NA
1957	7.6	9.6	5.8	8.0	10.1	6.0	NA	NA	NA	2.9	2.7	3.0	NA	NA	NA
1952	7.0	8.3	5.8	NA	NA	NA	NA	NA	NA	2.4	2.0	2.7	NA	NA	NA
1950	6.2	7.3	5.2	NA	NA	NA	NA	NA	NA	2.3	2.1	2.4	NA	NA	NA
1947	5.4	6.2	4.7	5.7	6.6	4.9	NA	NA	NA	2.5	2.4	2.6	NA	NA	NA
1940	4.6	5.5	3.8	4.9	5.9	4.0	NA	NA	NA	1.3	1.4	1.2	NA	NA	NA
25 TO 29 YEARS															
Completed 4 Years of High School or More															
2020	94.8	94.6	94.9	94.7	94.7	94.7	96.4	96.3	96.6	94.9	94.0	95.9	96.6	96.2	97.1
2019	93.5	92.7	94.3	93.8	93.3	94.2	96.3	96.2	96.4	91.0	88.9	93.0	97.0	97.0	97.1
2018	92.9	91.9	94.0	92.9	91.7	94.1	95.6	95.0	96.3	92.0	90.7	93.1	97.5	97.6	97.4
2017	92.5	91.5	93.4	92.4	91.2	93.7	95.6	94.8	96.4	91.8	91.2	92.4	96.8	97.7	95.9
2016	91.7	90.9	92.5	91.6	90.6	92.7	95.2	94.8	95.7	90.6	90.8	90.4	96.5	95.9	97.1
2015	91.2	90.5	91.8	90.8	90.0	91.7	95.4	95.1	95.8	92.2	91.4	93.0	95.5	96.3	94.7
2014	90.8	90.1	91.5	90.9	90.2	91.7	95.6	95.4	95.9	89.8	90.2	89.4	96.7	96.3	97.2
2013	89.9	88.3	91.5	89.5	88.0	91.1	94.1	93.3	94.9	89.8	87.3	92.1	94.7	93.6	95.7
2012	89.7	88.4	91.1	89.6	88.3	90.9	94.6	93.8	95.3	88.5	87.1	89.7	95.7	96.2	95.3
2011	89.0	87.5	90.7	88.9	87.1	90.8	94.4	93.4	95.5	87.7	87.6	87.8	95.2	93.6	96.7
2010	88.8	87.4	90.2	88.5	87.3	89.9	94.5	94.6	94.4	89.0	86.7	91.0	93.2	92.3	94.1
2009	88.6	87.5	89.8	88.4	87.0	89.9	94.6	94.4	94.8	88.9	88.6	89.1	95.2	95.6	94.9
2008	87.8	85.8	89.9	87.6	85.5	89.8	93.7	92.6	94.7	87.4	85.4	89.2	95.6	95.4	95.7
2007	87.0	84.9	89.1	86.5	84.2	89.0	93.5	92.7	94.2	87.4	87.0	87.8	97.2	95.8	98.5
2006	86.4	84.4	88.5	86.1	84.1	88.3	93.4	92.3	94.6	85.6	83.1	87.8	96.6	97.2	96.0
2005	86.2	85.0	87.4	85.7	84.3	87.1	92.8	91.8	93.8	86.5	86.4	86.6	95.5	96.7	94.5
2004	86.6	85.2	88.0	85.9	83.7	88.1	93.3	92.1	94.5	87.9	90.1	86.1	96.2	96.9	95.4
2003	86.5	84.9	88.2	85.7	83.8	87.6	93.7	92.8	94.5	87.6	86.4	88.5	97.1	97.4	96.8
2002	86.4	84.7	88.1	85.9	84.1	87.7	93.0	92.1	93.8	86.6	85.0	88.0	NA	NA	NA
2001	86.8	85.3	88.3	86.4	84.6	88.3	93.4	93.1	93.7	86.3	85.4	87.0	NA	NA	NA
2000	88.1	86.7	89.4	88.3	86.6	90.0	94.0	92.9	95.2	85.9	86.6	85.3	NA	NA	NA
1999	87.8	86.1	89.5	87.6	85.8	89.3	93.0	91.9	94.1	88.2	87.7	88.6	NA	NA	NA
1998	88.1	86.6	89.6	88.1	86.3	90.0	93.6	92.5	94.6	87.6	87.6	87.6	NA	NA	NA
1997	87.4	85.8	88.9	87.6	85.8	89.4	92.9	91.7	94.0	86.2	85.2	87.1	NA	NA	NA
1996	87.3	86.5	88.1	87.5	86.3	88.8	92.6	92.0	93.1	85.6	87.2	84.2	NA	NA	NA
1995	86.8	86.3	87.4	87.4	86.6	88.2	92.5	92.0	93.0	86.5	88.1	85.1	NA	NA	NA
1994	86.1	84.5	87.6	86.5	84.7	88.3	91.1	90.0	92.3	84.1	82.9	85.0	NA	NA	NA
1993	86.7	86.0	87.4	87.3	86.1	88.5	91.2	90.6	91.8	82.8	85.0	80.9	NA	NA	NA
1992	86.3	86.1	86.5	87.0	86.5	87.6	NA	NA	NA	80.9	82.5	79.5	NA	NA	NA
1991	85.4	84.9	85.8	85.8	85.1	86.6	NA	NA	NA	81.7	83.5	80.1	NA	NA	NA
1990	85.7	84.4	87.0	86.3	84.6	88.1	NA	NA	NA	81.7	81.5	81.8	NA	NA	NA
1989	85.5	84.4	86.5	86.0	84.8	87.1	NA	NA	NA	82.2	80.6	83.6	NA	NA	NA
1988	85.7	84.4	87.0	86.5	84.8	88.2	NA	NA	NA	80.7	80.6	80.7	NA	NA	NA
1987	86.0	85.5	86.4	86.3	85.6	87.0	NA	NA	NA	83.3	84.8	82.1	NA	NA	NA

Note: Starting in 2001, data are from the expanded CPS sample.

NA = Not available

[1]Data in the column labeled "Black" include Black and other races from 1940 to 1962: from 1963 to 2003, data are for the Black population only.

[2]Starting in 2012, data were calculated using population controls based on the 2010 Census.

[3]Starting in 2003, respondents could choose more than one race. The race data in this table for White, non-Hispanic White, Black, and Asian from 2003 onward represent those respondents who indicated only one racial identity. Prior to 2003, Asians were grouped with Pacific Islanders.

[4]Starting in 2001, data were calculated using population controls based on Census 2000.

[5]Begining with data for 1992, a new question results in different categories than for earlier years: Data shown as 'Completed 4 Years of High School or more' is now collected in the category 'High School Graduate.' Data shown as 'College 1 to 3 years' is now collected in the 'Some college' and the two 'Associate degree' categories. Data shown as 'Completed 4 Years of College or more', is now collected in the categories, 'Bachelor's degree,' 'Master's degree,' 'Doctorate degree,' and 'Professional degree'. Due to the change in question format, median years of schooling cannot be derived.

Table A-32. Percent of People 25 Years Old and Over Who Have Completed High School or College, by Race, Hispanic Origin, and Sex, Selected Years, 1940–2020—*Continued*

(Percent; civilian noninstitutionalized population.)

Age and Year	Hispanic (of any race)			White alone or in combination			Non-Hispanic White alone or in combination			Black alone or in combination			Asian alone or in combination		
	Total	Male	Female	Total	Male	Female	Total	Male	Female	Total	Male	Female	Total	Male	Female
1975	6.3	8.3	4.6	NA	NA	NA	NA	NA	NA	NA	NA	NA	NA	NA	NA
1974	5.5	7.1	4.0	NA	NA	NA	NA	NA	NA	NA	NA	NA	NA	NA	NA
1973	NA	NA	NA	NA	NA	NA	NA	NA	NA	NA	NA	NA	NA	NA	NA
1972	NA	NA	NA	NA	NA	NA	NA	NA	NA	NA	NA	NA	NA	NA	NA
1971	NA	NA	NA	NA	NA	NA	NA	NA	NA	NA	NA	NA	NA	NA	NA
1970	NA	NA	NA	NA	NA	NA	NA	NA	NA	NA	NA	NA	NA	NA	NA
1969	NA	NA	NA	NA	NA	NA	NA	NA	NA	NA	NA	NA	NA	NA	NA
1968	NA	NA	NA	NA	NA	NA	NA	NA	NA	NA	NA	NA	NA	NA	NA
1967	NA	NA	NA	NA	NA	NA	NA	NA	NA	NA	NA	NA	NA	NA	NA
1966	NA	NA	NA	NA	NA	NA	NA	NA	NA	NA	NA	NA	NA	NA	NA
1965	NA	NA	NA	NA	NA	NA	NA	NA	NA	NA	NA	NA	NA	NA	NA
1964	NA	NA	NA	NA	NA	NA	NA	NA	NA	NA	NA	NA	NA	NA	NA
1962	NA	NA	NA	NA	NA	NA	NA	NA	NA	NA	NA	NA	NA	NA	NA
1959	NA	NA	NA	NA	NA	NA	NA	NA	NA	NA	NA	NA	NA	NA	NA
1957	NA	NA	NA	NA	NA	NA	NA	NA	NA	NA	NA	NA	NA	NA	NA
1952	NA	NA	NA	NA	NA	NA	NA	NA	NA	NA	NA	NA	NA	NA	NA
1950	NA	NA	NA	NA	NA	NA	NA	NA	NA	NA	NA	NA	NA	NA	NA
1947	NA	NA	NA	NA	NA	NA	NA	NA	NA	NA	NA	NA	NA	NA	NA
1940	NA	NA	NA	NA	NA	NA	NA	NA	NA	NA	NA	NA	NA	NA	NA

25 TO 29 YEARS

Completed 4 Years of High School or More

Age and Year	Total	Male	Female	Total	Male	Female	Total	Male	Female	Total	Male	Female	Total	Male	Female
2020	89.9	90.4	89.3	94.6	94.7	94.6	96.3	96.3	96.3	94.7	93.9	95.4	96.3	98.1	96.5
2019	86.4	84.6	88.4	93.0	93.3	94.3	96.3	96.2	96.4	91.4	89.3	93.4	96.7	96.2	97.2
2018	85.2	83.4	87.2	92.9	91.7	94.1	95.6	94.9	96.2	92.2	90.8	93.4	97.5	97.6	97.5
2017	82.7	80.7	84.8	92.3	91.2	93.5	95.6	94.8	96.3	91.8	90.9	92.6	96.9	97.9	95.9
2016	80.6	78.3	83.2	91.7	90.7	92.7	95.2	94.9	95.6	90.7	91.0	90.5	96.7	96.2	97.2
2015	77.1	75.7	78.6	90.8	90.0	91.6	95.4	95.2	95.6	92.2	91.5	92.8	95.5	95.8	95.1
2014	74.7	72.4	77.4	90.8	89.9	91.7	95.6	95.4	95.9	89.1	88.9	89.3	96.3	96.3	97.4
2013	75.8	73.1	78.8	89.6	88.1	91.1	94.2	93.4	95.0	89.5	87.0	91.7	94.9	94.0	95.9
2012	75.0	73.3	76.9	89.6	88.2	91.0	94.6	93.8	95.4	88.4	86.8	89.8	95.5	96.1	94.8
2011	71.5	69.2	74.3	88.9	87.1	90.8	94.4	93.3	95.5	87.9	87.6	88.3	94.7	92.8	96.5
2010	69.4	65.7	74.1	88.5	87.3	89.8	94.4	94.5	94.3	89.9	86.5	91.0	93.1	92.3	93.9
2009	68.9	66.2	72.5	88.4	87.0	89.9	94.5	94.4	94.6	88.8	88.5	89.1	95.1	95.7	94.6
2008	68.3	65.6	71.9	87.6	85.5	89.8	93.7	92.6	94.8	87.7	85.6	89.4	95.7	95.5	95.9
2007	65.0	60.5	70.7	86.5	84.2	88.8	93.4	92.7	94.1	87.4	87.0	87.8	96.3	95.8	96.8
2006	63.3	60.6	66.7	86.0	83.9	88.2	93.3	92.2	94.5	85.6	83.2	87.7	96.0	96.4	95.7
2005	63.3	63.2	63.4	85.6	84.2	87.0	92.8	91.7	93.8	86.6	86.4	86.7	95.5	96.7	94.4
2004	62.4	60.1	65.2	85.9	83.9	87.9	93.2	92.1	94.4	87.8	89.9	86.2	95.7	97.0	94.5
2003	61.7	59.6	64.2	85.7	83.9	87.6	93.6	92.8	94.4	87.4	86.4	88.5	97.2	97.5	97.0
2002	62.4	60.2	65.0	NA	NA	NA	NA	NA	NA	NA	NA	NA	NA	NA	NA
2001	62.4	58.3	67.3	NA	NA	NA	NA	NA	NA	NA	NA	NA	NA	NA	NA
2000	62.8	59.2	66.4	NA	NA	NA	NA	NA	NA	NA	NA	NA	NA	NA	NA
1999	61.6	57.4	66.0	NA	NA	NA	NA	NA	NA	NA	NA	NA	NA	NA	NA
1998	62.8	59.9	66.3	NA	NA	NA	NA	NA	NA	NA	NA	NA	NA	NA	NA
1997	61.8	59.2	64.9	NA	NA	NA	NA	NA	NA	NA	NA	NA	NA	NA	NA
1996	61.1	59.7	62.9	NA	NA	NA	NA	NA	NA	NA	NA	NA	NA	NA	NA
1995	57.1	55.7	58.7	NA	NA	NA	NA	NA	NA	NA	NA	NA	NA	NA	NA
1994	60.3	58.0	63.0	NA	NA	NA	NA	NA	NA	NA	NA	NA	NA	NA	NA
1993	60.9	58.3	64.0	NA	NA	NA	NA	NA	NA	NA	NA	NA	NA	NA	NA
1992	60.9	61.1	60.6	NA	NA	NA	NA	NA	NA	NA	NA	NA	NA	NA	NA
1991	56.7	56.4	57.1	NA	NA	NA	NA	NA	NA	NA	NA	NA	NA	NA	NA
1990	58.2	56.6	59.9	NA	NA	NA	NA	NA	NA	NA	NA	NA	NA	NA	NA
1989	61.0	61.0	61.0	NA	NA	NA	NA	NA	NA	NA	NA	NA	NA	NA	NA
1988	62.0	59.4	65.0	NA	NA	NA	NA	NA	NA	NA	NA	NA	NA	NA	NA
1987	59.8	58.6	61.0	NA	NA	NA	NA	NA	NA	NA	NA	NA	NA	NA	NA

Note: Starting in 2001, data are from the expanded CPS sample.

NA = Not available

[1]Data in the column labeled "Black" include Black and other races from 1940 to 1962: from 1963 to 2003, data are for the Black population only.

[2]Starting in 2012, data were calculated using population controls based on the 2010 Census.

[3]Starting in 2003, respondents could choose more than one race. The race data in this table for White, non-Hispanic White, Black, and Asian from 2003 onward represent those respondents who indicated only one racial identity. Prior to 2003, Asians were grouped with Pacific Islanders.

[4]Starting in 2001, data were calculated using population controls based on Census 2000.

[5]Begining with data for 1992, a new question results in different categories than for earlier years. Data shown as 'Completed 4 Years of High School or more' is now collected in the category 'High School Graduate.' Data shown as 'College 1 to 3 years' is now collected in the 'Some college' and the two 'Associate degree' categories. Data shown as 'Completed 4 Years of College or more', is now collected in the categories, 'Bachelor's degree,' 'Master's degree,' 'Doctorate degree,' and 'Professional degree'. Due to the change in question format, median years of schooling cannot be derived.

Table A-32. Percent of People 25 Years Old and Over Who Have Completed High School or College, by Race, Hispanic Origin, and Sex, Selected Years, 1940–2020—*Continued*

(Percent; civilian noninstitutionalized population.)

Age and Year	All races			White			Non-Hispanic White			Black[1]			Asian		
	Total	Male	Female	Total	Male	Female	Total	Male	Female	Total	Male	Female	Total	Male	Female
1986	86.1	85.9	86.4	86.5	85.6	87.4	NA	NA	NA	83.4	86.5	80.6	NA	NA	NA
1985	86.1	85.9	86.4	86.8	86.4	87.3	NA	NA	NA	80.6	80.8	80.4	NA	NA	NA
1984	85.9	85.6	86.3	86.9	86.8	87.0	NA	NA	NA	78.9	75.9	81.5	NA	NA	NA
1983	86.0	86.0	86.0	86.9	86.9	86.9	NA	NA	NA	79.4	78.9	79.8	NA	NA	NA
1982	86.2	86.3	86.1	86.9	87.0	86.8	NA	NA	NA	80.9	80.5	81.3	NA	NA	NA
1981	86.3	86.5	86.1	87.6	87.6	87.6	NA	NA	NA	77.3	78.4	76.4	NA	NA	NA
1980	85.4	85.4	85.5	86.9	86.8	87.0	NA	NA	NA	76.6	74.8	78.1	NA	NA	NA
1979	85.6	86.3	84.9	87.0	87.7	86.4	NA	NA	NA	74.8	73.9	75.4	NA	NA	NA
1978	85.3	86.0	84.6	86.3	86.8	85.8	NA	NA	NA	77.3	78.5	76.3	NA	NA	NA
1977	85.4	86.6	84.2	86.8	87.6	86.0	NA	NA	NA	74.4	77.5	72.0	NA	NA	NA
1976	84.7	86.0	83.5	85.9	87.3	84.6	NA	NA	NA	73.8	72.5	74.9	NA	NA	NA
1975	83.1	84.5	81.8	84.4	85.7	83.2	NA	NA	NA	71.0	72.2	70.1	NA	NA	NA
1974	81.9	83.1	80.8	83.4	84.1	82.7	NA	NA	NA	68.2	71.1	66.0	NA	NA	NA
1973	80.2	80.6	79.8	82.0	82.4	81.6	NA	NA	NA	64.2	63.1	64.9	NA	NA	NA
1972	79.8	80.5	79.2	81.5	82.3	80.8	NA	NA	NA	64.1	61.8	66.2	NA	NA	NA
1971	77.2	78.1	76.4	79.5	80.8	78.3	NA	NA	NA	57.5	54.1	60.7	NA	NA	NA
1970	75.4	76.6	74.2	77.8	79.2	76.4	NA	NA	NA	56.2	54.5	57.9	NA	NA	NA
1969	74.7	75.6	73.8	77.0	77.5	76.6	NA	NA	NA	55.8	59.8	52.3	NA	NA	NA
1968	73.2	73.7	72.7	75.3	75.5	75.0	NA	NA	NA	55.8	58.1	53.6	NA	NA	NA
1967	72.5	72.1	72.9	74.8	74.3	75.3	NA	NA	NA	53.4	51.7	55.0	NA	NA	NA
1966	71.0	70.9	71.2	73.8	73.2	74.4	NA	NA	NA	47.9	48.9	47.0	NA	NA	NA
1965	70.3	70.5	70.1	72.8	72.7	72.8	NA	NA	NA	50.3	50.3	50.4	NA	NA	NA
1964	69.2	68.8	69.5	72.1	71.8	72.4	NA	NA	NA	45.0	41.6	47.9	NA	NA	NA
1962	65.9	65.8	66.1	69.2	69.2	69.3	NA	NA	NA	41.6	38.9	43.8	NA	NA	NA
1959	63.9	63.9	64.0	67.2	66.9	67.4	NA	NA	NA	39.5	40.6	38.6	NA	NA	NA
1957	60.2	57.9	62.4	63.3	60.7	65.7	NA	NA	NA	31.6	27.4	35.2	NA	NA	NA
1952	57.1	55.3	58.7	NA	NA	NA	NA	NA	NA	28.1	27.9	28.3	NA	NA	NA
1950	52.8	50.6	55.0	NA	NA	NA	NA	NA	NA	23.6	21.3	25.5	NA	NA	NA
1947	51.4	49.4	53.3	54.9	52.9	56.8	NA	NA	NA	22.3	19.6	24.7	NA	NA	NA
1940	38.1	36.0	40.1	41.2	38.9	43.4	NA	NA	NA	12.3	10.6	13.6	NA	NA	NA
Completed 4 Years of College or More															
2020	39.2	34.7	43.8	39.1	34.6	43.9	44.6	39.2	50.1	27.9	23.3	32.3	71.0	68.4	73.5
2019	38.7	35.7	41.8	38.6	34.7	42.7	44.9	40.8	49.2	29.0	28.4	29.5	70.1	69.5	70.6
2018	37.0	33.2	40.8	37.9	33.6	42.4	43.5	38.8	48.4	22.3	18.6	25.7	69.5	68.3	70.8
2017	35.7	32.0	39.3	36.4	32.2	40.7	42.1	37.7	46.5	22.2	20.4	23.9	61.9	58.1	65.9
2016	36.1	32.7	39.5	37.0	33.6	40.5	42.9	39.5	46.3	22.7	20.2	25.0	64.7	60.3	68.8
2015	35.6	32.4	38.9	36.7	33.2	40.3	43.0	39.5	46.6	20.5	16.5	24.2	65.0	62.8	67.2
2014	34.0	30.9	37.2	34.8	31.6	38.2	40.8	37.7	43.9	21.5	19.5	23.4	61.7	56.3	66.5
2013	33.6	30.2	37.0	34.3	30.8	37.9	40.4	37.1	43.8	20.1	16.8	23.1	59.0	54.3	63.2
2012	33.5	29.8	37.2	33.7	29.9	37.6	39.8	36.0	43.6	22.7	18.5	26.2	60.8	56.8	64.5
2011	32.2	28.4	36.1	33.1	29.2	37.4	39.2	35.5	43.0	19.6	16.1	22.8	56.2	51.5	60.6
2010	31.7	27.8	35.7	32.7	28.8	37.0	38.6	34.8	42.4	19.0	14.8	22.9	55.4	52.0	58.6
2009	30.6	26.6	34.8	31.3	27.0	36.0	37.2	32.6	42.0	19.0	15.2	22.4	59.3	58.0	60.6
2008	30.8	26.8	34.9	31.1	26.7	35.9	37.1	32.6	41.7	20.6	18.7	22.3	59.4	55.1	63.5
2007	29.6	26.3	33.0	29.8	25.8	34.0	35.5	31.9	39.2	18.9	17.9	19.9	60.9	59.8	62.0
2006	28.4	25.3	31.6	28.3	25.0	31.7	34.3	31.4	37.2	18.6	14.9	21.6	60.9	59.8	61.9
2005	28.8	25.5	32.2	28.9	25.3	32.7	34.5	30.7	38.2	17.4	14.1	20.1	61.6	60.5	62.5
2004	28.7	26.1	31.4	28.9	25.8	32.1	34.5	31.4	37.5	16.9	13.4	19.7	61.4	62.0	60.9
2003	28.4	26.0	30.9	28.3	25.3	31.5	34.2	31.4	37.1	17.2	17.5	17.0	61.6	60.9	62.3
2002	29.3	26.9	31.8	29.7	26.5	33.1	35.9	32.6	39.2	17.5	17.4	17.7	NA	NA	NA
2001	28.4	25.5	31.3	28.5	25.1	32.1	33.7	30.4	36.9	16.8	15.6	17.9	NA	NA	NA
2000	29.1	27.9	30.1	29.6	27.8	31.3	34.0	32.3	35.8	17.5	18.1	17.0	NA	NA	NA
1999	28.2	26.8	29.5	29.3	27.6	30.9	33.6	32.0	35.1	15.0	13.1	16.5	NA	NA	NA
1998	27.3	25.6	29.0	28.4	26.5	30.4	32.3	30.5	34.2	15.8	14.2	17.0	NA	NA	NA
1997	27.8	26.3	29.3	28.9	27.2	30.7	32.6	31.2	34.1	14.4	12.1	16.4	NA	NA	NA
1996	27.1	26.1	28.2	28.1	27.2	29.1	31.6	30.9	32.3	14.6	12.4	16.4	NA	NA	NA
1995	24.7	24.5	24.9	26.0	25.4	26.6	28.8	28.4	29.2	15.3	17.2	13.6	NA	NA	NA

Note: Starting in 2001, data are from the expanded CPS sample.
NA = Not available
[1]Data in the column labeled "Black" include Black and other races from 1940 to 1962: from 1963 to 2003, data are for the Black population only.
[2]Starting in 2012, data were calculated using population controls based on the 2010 Census.
[3]Starting in 2003, respondents could choose more than one race. The race data in this table for White, non-Hispanic White, Black, and Asian from 2003 onward represent those respondents who indicated only one racial identity. Prior to 2003, Asians were grouped with Pacific Islanders.
[4]Starting in 2001, data were calculated using population controls based on Census 2000.
[5]Begining with data for 1992, a new question results in different categories than for earlier years: Data shown as 'Completed 4 Years of High School or more' is now collected in the category 'High School Graduate.' Data shown as 'College 1 to 3 years' is now collected in the 'Some college' and the two 'Associate degree' categories. Data shown as 'Completed 4 Years of College or more', is now collected in the categories, 'Bachelor's degree,' 'Master's degree,' 'Doctorate degree,' and 'Professional degree'. Due to the change in question format, median years of schooling cannot be derived.

Table A-32. Percent of People 25 Years Old and Over Who Have Completed High School or College, by Race, Hispanic Origin, and Sex, Selected Years, 1940–2020—*Continued*

(Percent; civilian noninstitutionalized population.)

Age and Year	Hispanic (of any race)			White alone or in combination			Non-Hispanic White alone or in combination			Black alone or in combination			Asian alone or in combination		
	Total	Male	Female	Total	Male	Female	Total	Male	Female	Total	Male	Female	Total	Male	Female
1986	59.1	58.2	60.0	NA	NA	NA	NA	NA	NA	NA	NA	NA	NA	NA	NA
1985	60.9	58.6	63.1	NA	NA	NA	NA	NA	NA	NA	NA	NA	NA	NA	NA
1984	58.6	56.8	60.2	NA	NA	NA	NA	NA	NA	NA	NA	NA	NA	NA	NA
1983	58.3	57.8	58.9	NA	NA	NA	NA	NA	NA	NA	NA	NA	NA	NA	NA
1982	60.9	60.7	61.2	NA	NA	NA	NA	NA	NA	NA	NA	NA	NA	NA	NA
1981	59.8	59.1	60.4	NA	NA	NA	NA	NA	NA	NA	NA	NA	NA	NA	NA
1980	58.6	58.3	58.8	NA	NA	NA	NA	NA	NA	NA	NA	NA	NA	NA	NA
1979	57.0	55.5	58.5	NA	NA	NA	NA	NA	NA	NA	NA	NA	NA	NA	NA
1978	56.6	58.5	54.7	NA	NA	NA	NA	NA	NA	NA	NA	NA	NA	NA	NA
1977	58.1	62.1	54.8	NA	NA	NA	NA	NA	NA	NA	NA	NA	NA	NA	NA
1976	58.1	57.6	58.4	NA	NA	NA	NA	NA	NA	NA	NA	NA	NA	NA	NA
1975	51.7	51.1	52.1	NA	NA	NA	NA	NA	NA	NA	NA	NA	NA	NA	NA
1974	52.5	55.1	49.9	NA	NA	NA	NA	NA	NA	NA	NA	NA	NA	NA	NA
1973	NA	NA	NA	NA	NA	NA	NA	NA	NA	NA	NA	NA	NA	NA	NA
1972	NA	NA	NA	NA	NA	NA	NA	NA	NA	NA	NA	NA	NA	NA	NA
1971	NA	NA	NA	NA	NA	NA	NA	NA	NA	NA	NA	NA	NA	NA	NA
1970	NA	NA	NA	NA	NA	NA	NA	NA	NA	NA	NA	NA	NA	NA	NA
1969	NA	NA	NA	NA	NA	NA	NA	NA	NA	NA	NA	NA	NA	NA	NA
1968	NA	NA	NA	NA	NA	NA	NA	NA	NA	NA	NA	NA	NA	NA	NA
1967	NA	NA	NA	NA	NA	NA	NA	NA	NA	NA	NA	NA	NA	NA	NA
1966	NA	NA	NA	NA	NA	NA	NA	NA	NA	NA	NA	NA	NA	NA	NA
1965	NA	NA	NA	NA	NA	NA	NA	NA	NA	NA	NA	NA	NA	NA	NA
1964	NA	NA	NA	NA	NA	NA	NA	NA	NA	NA	NA	NA	NA	NA	NA
1962	NA	NA	NA	NA	NA	NA	NA	NA	NA	NA	NA	NA	NA	NA	NA
1959	NA	NA	NA	NA	NA	NA	NA	NA	NA	NA	NA	NA	NA	NA	NA
1957	NA	NA	NA	NA	NA	NA	NA	NA	NA	NA	NA	NA	NA	NA	NA
1952	NA	NA	NA	NA	NA	NA	NA	NA	NA	NA	NA	NA	NA	NA	NA
1950	NA	NA	NA	NA	NA	NA	NA	NA	NA	NA	NA	NA	NA	NA	NA
1947	NA	NA	NA	NA	NA	NA	NA	NA	NA	NA	NA	NA	NA	NA	NA
1940	NA	NA	NA	NA	NA	NA	NA	NA	NA	NA	NA	NA	NA	NA	NA
Completed 4 Years of College or More															
2020	24.9	22.9	27.0	38.9	34.2	43.9	44.1	38.6	49.8	28.2	23.0	33.1	68.3	64.3	72.4
2019	20.6	18.2	23.1	38.3	34.6	42.2	44.6	40.7	48.7	29.1	28.3	29.8	67.8	67.4	68.3
2018	20.7	18.4	23.2	37.5	33.2	42.0	43.1	38.4	47.9	22.0	18.0	25.5	67.5	66.3	68.7
2017	18.5	15.0	22.4	36.2	32.1	40.4	41.8	37.5	46.3	22.4	20.6	24.1	61.2	56.9	65.7
2016	18.7	16.2	21.5	36.7	33.2	40.4	42.5	38.9	46.1	22.9	20.1	25.4	63.2	58.3	67.8
2015	16.4	14.5	18.5	36.4	33.0	40.0	42.6	39.1	46.3	20.7	17.0	24.1	63.5	60.6	66.3
2014	15.1	12.4	18.3	34.5	31.2	38.0	40.6	37.4	43.8	21.4	18.7	23.9	60.0	54.4	65.3
2013	15.7	13.1	18.6	34.1	30.6	37.7	40.1	36.8	43.5	19.8	16.6	22.8	58.1	53.7	62.2
2012	14.8	12.5	17.4	33.5	29.8	37.4	39.6	35.9	43.4	22.8	18.1	27.0	59.6	55.7	63.4
2011	12.8	9.6	16.8	33.0	29.0	37.1	39.0	35.4	42.7	19.8	16.3	22.9	55.7	52.0	59.1
2010	13.5	10.8	16.0	32.6	28.6	36.8	38.4	34.6	42.3	19.3	14.8	23.5	53.7	49.6	57.6
2009	12.2	11.0	13.8	31.1	26.8	35.9	37.1	32.4	41.9	19.0	15.0	22.6	58.0	56.7	59.3
2008	12.4	10.0	15.5	31.0	26.6	35.8	36.9	32.4	41.5	20.9	19.3	22.3	57.4	52.9	61.8
2007	11.6	8.6	15.4	29.7	25.7	33.8	35.3	31.7	39.0	19.1	18.1	19.9	59.0	57.8	60.1
2006	9.5	6.9	12.8	28.1	24.8	31.6	34.1	31.2	37.0	18.9	15.0	22.3	59.4	58.4	60.5
2005	11.2	10.2	12.4	28.8	25.3	32.5	34.3	30.6	38.1	17.6	14.6	20.3	60.3	59.0	61.5
2004	10.9	9.6	12.4	28.7	25.7	31.8	34.2	31.2	37.2	16.8	13.4	19.5	59.9	61.1	58.9
2003	10.0	8.4	12.0	28.2	25.2	31.4	34.0	31.2	36.9	17.3	17.4	17.3	60.3	58.8	61.7
2002	8.9	8.3	9.7	NA	NA	NA	NA	NA	NA	NA	NA	NA	NA	NA	NA
2001	10.5	8.2	13.3	NA	NA	NA	NA	NA	NA	NA	NA	NA	NA	NA	NA
2000	9.7	8.3	11.0	NA	NA	NA	NA	NA	NA	NA	NA	NA	NA	NA	NA
1999	8.0	7.5	10.4	NA	NA	NA	NA	NA	NA	NA	NA	NA	NA	NA	NA
1998	10.4	9.5	11.3	NA	NA	NA	NA	NA	NA	NA	NA	NA	NA	NA	NA
1997	11.0	9.6	10.1	NA	NA	NA	NA	NA	NA	NA	NA	NA	NA	NA	NA
1996	10.0	10.2	9.8	NA	NA	NA	NA	NA	NA	NA	NA	NA	NA	NA	NA
1995	8.9	7.8	10.1	NA	NA	NA	NA	NA	NA	NA	NA	NA	NA	NA	NA

Note: Starting in 2001, data are from the expanded CPS sample.

NA = Not available

[1]Data in the column labeled "Black" include Black and other races from 1940 to 1962; from 1963 to 2003, data are for the Black population only.

[2]Starting in 2012, data were calculated using population controls based on the 2010 Census.

[3]Starting in 2003, respondents could choose more than one race. The race data in this table for White, non-Hispanic White, Black, and Asian from 2003 onward represent those respondents who indicated only one racial identity. Prior to 2003, Asians were grouped with Pacific Islanders.

[4]Starting in 2001, data were calculated using population controls based on Census 2000.

[5]Begining with data for 1992, a new question results in different categories than for earlier years: Data shown as 'Completed 4 Years of High School or more' is now collected in the category 'High School Graduate.' Data shown as 'College 1 to 3 years' is now collected in the 'Some college' and the two 'Associate degree' categories. Data shown as 'Completed 4 Years of College or more', is now collected in the categories, 'Bachelor's degree,' 'Master's degree,' 'Doctorate degree,' and 'Professional degree'. Due to the change in question format, median years of schooling cannot be derived.

Table A-32. Percent of People 25 Years Old and Over Who Have Completed High School or College, by Race, Hispanic Origin, and Sex, Selected Years, 1940–2020—*Continued*

(Percent; civilian noninstitutionalized population.)

Age and Year	All races			White			Non-Hispanic White			Black[1]			Asian		
	Total	Male	Female	Total	Male	Female	Total	Male	Female	Total	Male	Female	Total	Male	Female
1994	23.3	22.5	24.0	24.2	23.6	24.8	27.1	26.8	27.4	13.7	11.7	15.4	NA	NA	NA
1993	23.7	23.4	23.9	24.7	24.4	25.1	27.2	27.2	27.1	13.2	12.6	13.8	NA	NA	NA
1992	23.6	23.2	24.0	25.0	24.2	25.7	NA	NA	NA	11.3	12.0	10.6	NA	NA	NA
1991	23.2	23.0	23.4	24.6	24.1	25.0	NA	NA	NA	11.0	11.5	10.6	NA	NA	NA
1990	23.2	23.7	22.8	24.2	24.2	24.3	NA	NA	NA	13.4	15.1	11.9	NA	NA	NA
1989	23.4	23.9	22.9	24.4	24.8	24.0	NA	NA	NA	12.7	12.0	13.3	NA	NA	NA
1988	22.5	23.2	21.9	23.5	24.0	22.9	NA	NA	NA	12.2	12.6	11.9	NA	NA	NA
1987	22.0	22.3	21.7	23.0	23.3	22.8	NA	NA	NA	11.4	11.6	11.1	NA	NA	NA
1986	22.4	22.9	21.9	23.5	24.1	22.9	NA	NA	NA	11.8	10.1	13.3	NA	NA	NA
1985	22.2	23.1	21.3	23.2	24.2	22.2	NA	NA	NA	11.5	10.3	12.6	NA	NA	NA
1984	21.9	23.2	20.7	23.1	24.3	21.9	NA	NA	NA	11.6	12.9	10.5	NA	NA	NA
1983	22.5	23.9	21.1	23.4	25.0	21.8	NA	NA	NA	12.9	13.1	12.8	NA	NA	NA
1982	21.7	23.3	20.2	22.7	24.5	20.9	NA	NA	NA	12.6	11.8	13.2	NA	NA	NA
1981	21.3	23.1	19.6	22.4	24.3	20.5	NA	NA	NA	11.6	12.1	11.1	NA	NA	NA
1980	22.5	24.0	21.0	23.7	25.5	22.0	NA	NA	NA	11.6	10.5	12.5	NA	NA	NA
1979	23.1	25.6	20.5	24.3	27.1	21.5	NA	NA	NA	12.4	13.3	11.7	NA	NA	NA
1978	23.3	26.0	20.6	24.5	27.6	21.4	NA	NA	NA	11.8	10.7	12.6	NA	NA	NA
1977	24.0	27.0	21.1	25.3	28.5	22.1	NA	NA	NA	12.6	12.8	12.4	NA	NA	NA
1976	23.7	27.5	20.1	24.6	28.7	20.6	NA	NA	NA	13.0	12.0	13.6	NA	NA	NA
1975	21.9	25.1	18.7	22.8	26.3	19.4	NA	NA	NA	10.7	11.4	10.1	NA	NA	NA
1974	20.7	23.9	17.6	22.0	25.3	18.8	NA	NA	NA	7.9	8.8	7.2	NA	NA	NA
1973	19.0	21.6	16.4	19.9	22.8	17.0	NA	NA	NA	8.1	7.1	8.8	NA	NA	NA
1972	19.0	22.0	16.0	19.9	23.1	16.7	NA	NA	NA	8.3	7.1	9.4	NA	NA	NA
1971	16.9	20.1	13.8	17.9	21.3	14.6	NA	NA	NA	6.4	6.4	6.5	NA	NA	NA
1970	16.4	20.0	12.9	17.3	21.3	13.3	NA	NA	NA	7.3	6.7	8.0	NA	NA	NA
1969	16.0	19.4	12.8	17.0	20.6	13.4	NA	NA	NA	6.7	8.1	5.5	NA	NA	NA
1968	14.7	18.0	11.6	15.6	19.1	12.3	NA	NA	NA	5.3	5.3	5.3	NA	NA	NA
1967	14.6	17.2	12.1	15.5	18.3	12.7	NA	NA	NA	5.4	4.2	6.3	NA	NA	NA
1966	14.0	16.8	11.3	14.7	17.9	11.8	NA	NA	NA	5.9	5.4	6.4	NA	NA	NA
1965	12.4	15.6	9.5	13.0	16.4	9.8	NA	NA	NA	6.8	7.3	6.8	NA	NA	NA
1964	12.8	16.6	9.2	13.6	17.5	9.9	NA	NA	NA	5.5	7.5	3.9	NA	NA	NA
1962	13.1	17.2	9.2	14.3	18.7	10.0	NA	NA	NA	4.2	5.7	3.0	NA	NA	NA
1959	11.1	14.8	7.6	11.9	15.9	8.1	NA	NA	NA	4.6	5.6	3.7	NA	NA	NA
1957	10.4	13.5	7.5	11.1	14.5	7.8	NA	NA	NA	4.1	3.3	5.0	NA	NA	NA
1952	10.1	13.8	6.7	NA	NA	NA	NA	NA	NA	4.6	3.2	5.8	NA	NA	NA
1950	7.7	9.6	5.9	NA	NA	NA	NA	NA	NA	2.9	2.4	3.2	NA	NA	NA
1947	5.6	5.8	5.4	5.9	6.2	5.7	NA	NA	NA	2.8	2.6	2.9	NA	NA	NA
1940	5.9	6.9	4.9	6.4	7.5	5.3	NA	NA	NA	1.6	1.5	1.7	NA	NA	NA

Note: Starting in 2001, data are from the expanded CPS sample.
NA = Not available
[1]Data in the column labeled "Black" include Black and other races from 1940 to 1962: from 1963 to 2003, data are for the Black population only.
[2]Starting in 2012, data were calculated using population controls based on the 2010 Census.
[3]Starting in 2003, respondents could choose more than one race. The race data in this table for White, non-Hispanic White, Black, and Asian from 2003 onward represent those respondents who indicated only one racial identity. Prior to 2003, Asians were grouped with Pacific Islanders.
[4]Starting in 2001, data were calculated using population controls based on Census 2000.
[5]Begining with data for 1992, a new question results in different categories than for earlier years: Data shown as 'Completed 4 Years of High School or more' is now collected in the category 'High School Graduate.' Data shown as 'College 1 to 3 years' is now collected in the 'Some college' and the two 'Associate degree' categories. Data shown as 'Completed 4 Years of College or more', is now collected in the categories, 'Bachelor's degree,' 'Master's degree,' 'Doctorate degree,' and 'Professional degree'. Due to the change in question format, median years of schooling cannot be derived.

Table A-32. Percent of People 25 Years Old and Over Who Have Completed High School or College, by Race, Hispanic Origin, and Sex, Selected Years, 1940–2020—*Continued*

(Percent; civilian noninstitutionalized population.)

Age and Year	Hispanic (of any race)			White alone or in combination			Non-Hispanic White alone or in combination			Black alone or in combination			Asian alone or in combination		
	Total	Male	Female	Total	Male	Female	Total	Male	Female	Total	Male	Female	Total	Male	Female
1994	8.0	6.6	9.8	NA	NA	NA	NA	NA	NA	NA	NA	NA	NA	NA	NA
1993	8.3	7.1	9.8	NA	NA	NA	NA	NA	NA	NA	NA	NA	NA	NA	NA
1992	9.5	8.8	10.3	NA	NA	NA	NA	NA	NA	NA	NA	NA	NA	NA	NA
1991	9.2	8.1	10.4	NA	NA	NA	NA	NA	NA	NA	NA	NA	NA	NA	NA
1990	8.1	7.3	9.1	NA	NA	NA	NA	NA	NA	NA	NA	NA	NA	NA	NA
1989	10.1	9.6	10.6	NA	NA	NA	NA	NA	NA	NA	NA	NA	NA	NA	NA
1988	11.4	12.1	10.6	NA	NA	NA	NA	NA	NA	NA	NA	NA	NA	NA	NA
1987	8.7	9.2	8.2	NA	NA	NA	NA	NA	NA	NA	NA	NA	NA	NA	NA
1986	9.0	8.9	9.1	NA	NA	NA	NA	NA	NA	NA	NA	NA	NA	NA	NA
1985	11.1	10.9	11.2	NA	NA	NA	NA	NA	NA	NA	NA	NA	NA	NA	NA
1984	10.6	9.6	11.6	NA	NA	NA	NA	NA	NA	NA	NA	NA	NA	NA	NA
1983	10.4	9.6	11.1	NA	NA	NA	NA	NA	NA	NA	NA	NA	NA	NA	NA
1982	9.7	10.7	8.7	NA	NA	NA	NA	NA	NA	NA	NA	NA	NA	NA	NA
1981	7.5	8.6	6.5	NA	NA	NA	NA	NA	NA	NA	NA	NA	NA	NA	NA
1980	7.7	8.4	6.9	NA	NA	NA	NA	NA	NA	NA	NA	NA	NA	NA	NA
1979	7.3	7.9	6.8	NA	NA	NA	NA	NA	NA	NA	NA	NA	NA	NA	NA
1978	9.6	9.6	9.7	NA	NA	NA	NA	NA	NA	NA	NA	NA	NA	NA	NA
1977	6.7	7.2	6.4	NA	NA	NA	NA	NA	NA	NA	NA	NA	NA	NA	NA
1976	7.4	10.3	4.8	NA	NA	NA	NA	NA	NA	NA	NA	NA	NA	NA	NA
1975	8.8	10.0	7.3	NA	NA	NA	NA	NA	NA	NA	NA	NA	NA	NA	NA
1974	5.7	7.2	4.6	NA	NA	NA	NA	NA	NA	NA	NA	NA	NA	NA	NA
1973	NA	NA	NA	NA	NA	NA	NA	NA	NA	NA	NA	NA	NA	NA	NA
1972	NA	NA	NA	NA	NA	NA	NA	NA	NA	NA	NA	NA	NA	NA	NA
1971	NA	NA	NA	NA	NA	NA	NA	NA	NA	NA	NA	NA	NA	NA	NA
1970	NA	NA	NA	NA	NA	NA	NA	NA	NA	NA	NA	NA	NA	NA	NA
1969	NA	NA	NA	NA	NA	NA	NA	NA	NA	NA	NA	NA	NA	NA	NA
1968	NA	NA	NA	NA	NA	NA	NA	NA	NA	NA	NA	NA	NA	NA	NA
1967	NA	NA	NA	NA	NA	NA	NA	NA	NA	NA	NA	NA	NA	NA	NA
1966	NA	NA	NA	NA	NA	NA	NA	NA	NA	NA	NA	NA	NA	NA	NA
1965	NA	NA	NA	NA	NA	NA	NA	NA	NA	NA	NA	NA	NA	NA	NA
1964	NA	NA	NA	NA	NA	NA	NA	NA	NA	NA	NA	NA	NA	NA	NA
1962	NA	NA	NA	NA	NA	NA	NA	NA	NA	NA	NA	NA	NA	NA	NA
1959	NA	NA	NA	NA	NA	NA	NA	NA	NA	NA	NA	NA	NA	NA	NA
1957	NA	NA	NA	NA	NA	NA	NA	NA	NA	NA	NA	NA	NA	NA	NA
1952	NA	NA	NA	NA	NA	NA	NA	NA	NA	NA	NA	NA	NA	NA	NA
1950	NA	NA	NA	NA	NA	NA	NA	NA	NA	NA	NA	NA	NA	NA	NA
1947	NA	NA	NA	NA	NA	NA	NA	NA	NA	NA	NA	NA	NA	NA	NA
1940	NA	NA	NA	NA	NA	NA	NA	NA	NA	NA	NA	NA	NA	NA	NA

Note: Starting in 2001, data are from the expanded CPS sample.

NA = Not available

[1]Data in the column labeled "Black" include Black and other races from 1940 to 1962: from 1963 to 2003, data are for the Black population only.

[2]Starting in 2012, data were calculated using population controls based on the 2010 Census.

[3]Starting in 2003, respondents could choose more than one race. The race data in this table for White, non-Hispanic White, Black, and Asian from 2003 onward represent those respondents who indicated only one racial identity. Prior to 2003, Asians were grouped with Pacific Islanders.

[4]Starting in 2001, data were calculated using population controls based on Census 2000.

[5]Begining with data for 1992, a new question results in different categories than for earlier years: Data shown as 'Completed 4 Years of High School or more' is now collected in the category 'High School Graduate.' Data shown as 'College 1 to 3 years' is now collected in the 'Some college' and the two 'Associate degree' categories. Data shown as 'Completed 4 Years of College or more', is now collected in the categories, 'Bachelor's degree,' 'Master's degree,' 'Doctorate degree,' and 'Professional degree'. Due to the change in question format, median years of schooling cannot be derived.

Table A-33. Years of School Completed by People 25 Years Old and Over, by Age and Sex, Selected Years, 1940–2020

(Numbers in thousands; civilian noninstitutionalized population, except where noted.)

Year, sex, and age	Total	Elementary 0 to 4 years	Elementary 5 to 8 years	High school 1 to 3 years	High school 4 years	College 1 to 3 years	College 4 years or more	Median years
25 YEARS OLD AND OVER								
Both Sexes								
2020	223,058	2,106	5,788	12,313	61,597	57,552	83,701	NA
2019	221,478	2,181	6,422	13,372	62,259	57,428	79,816	NA
2018	219,830	2,129	6,600	13,682	62,685	57,810	76,924	NA
2017	216,921	2,208	6,600	13,734	62,512	57,765	74,103	NA
2016	215,015	2,414	7,078	13,961	62,002	57,660	71,900	NA
2015	212,132	2,601	7,295	14,686	62,575	56,031	68,945	NA
2014	209,287	2,525	7,388	14,545	62,240	55,709	66,879	NA
2013	206,899	2,344	7,578	14,595	61,704	55,173	65,506	NA
2012	204,579	2,484	7,800	14,993	62,113	53,900	63,291	NA
2011	201,543	2,589	7,688	14,763	61,911	53,249	61,343	NA
2010	199,928	2,615	7,836	15,260	62,456	51,920	59,840	NA
2009	198,285	2,785	8,043	15,587	61,626	51,670	58,574	NA
2008	196,305	2,599	8,226	15,516	61,183	50,994	57,787	NA
2007	194,318	2,830	8,462	16,451	61,490	49,243	55,842	NA
2006	191,884	2,951	8,791	16,154	60,898	49,371	53,720	NA
2005	189,367	2,983	8,935	16,099	60,893	48,076	52,381	NA
2004	186,876	2,858	8,888	15,999	59,811	47,571	51,749	NA
2003	185,183	2,915	9,361	16,323	59,292	46,910	50,383	NA
2002	182,142	2,902	9,668	16,378	58,456	46,042	48,696	NA
2001	180,389	2,810	9,518	16,279	58,272	46,281	47,228	NA
2000	175,230	2,742	9,438	15,674	58,086	44,445	44,845	NA
1999	173,754	2,742	9,655	16,443	57,935	43,176	43,803	NA
1998	172,211	2,834	9,948	16,776	58,174	42,506	41,973	NA
1997	170,581	2,840	10,472	17,211	57,586	41,774	40,697	NA
1996	168,323	3,027	10,595	17,102	56,559	41,372	39,668	NA
1995	166,438	3,074	10,873	16,566	56,450	41,249	38,226	NA
1994	164,512	3,156	11,359	16,925	56,515	40,014	36,544	NA
1993	162,826	3,380	11,747	17,067	57,589	37,451	35,590	NA
1992	160,827	3,449	11,989	17,672	57,860	35,520	34,337	NA
1991	158,694	3,803	13,046	17,379	61,272	29,170	34,026	12.7
1990	156,538	3,833	13,758	17,461	60,119	28,075	33,291	12.7
1989	154,155	3,861	14,061	17,719	59,336	26,614	32,565	12.7
1988	151,635	3,714	14,550	17,847	58,940	25,799	30,787	12.7
1987	149,144	3,640	15,301	17,417	57,669	25,479	29,637	12.7
1986	146,606	3,894	15,672	17,484	56,338	24,729	28,489	12.6
1985	143,524	3,873	16,020	17,553	54,866	23,405	27,808	12.6
1984	140,794	3,884	16,258	17,433	54,073	22,281	26,862	12.6
1983	138,020	4,119	16,714	17,681	52,060	21,531	25,915	12.6
1982	135,526	4,119	17,232	18,006	51,426	20,692	24,050	12.6
1981	132,899	4,358	17,868	18,041	49,915	20,042	22,674	12.5
1980	130,409	4,390	18,426	18,086	47,934	19,379	22,193	12.5
1979	125,295	4,324	18,504	17,579	45,915	18,393	20,579	12.5
1978	123,019	4,445	19,309	18,175	44,381	17,379	19,332	12.4
1977	120,870	4,509	19,567	18,318	43,602	16,247	18,627	12.4
1976	118,848	4,601	19,912	18,204	43,157	15,477	17,496	12.4
1975	116,897	4,912	20,633	18,237	42,353	14,518	16,244	12.3
1974	115,005	5,106	21,200	18,274	41,460	13,665	15,300	12.3
1973	112,866	5,100	21,838	18,420	40,448	12,831	14,228	12.3
1972	111,133	5,124	22,503	18,855	39,171	12,117	13,364	12.2
1971	110,627	5,574	24,029	18,601	38,029	11,782	12,612	12.2
1970	109,310	5,747	24,519	18,682	37,134	11,164	12,062	12.2
1969	107,750	6,014	24,976	18,527	36,133	10,564	11,535	12.1
1968	106,469	6,248	25,467	18,724	34,603	10,254	11,171	12.1
1967	104,864	6,400	26,178	18,647	33,173	9,914	10,550	12.0
1966	103,876	6,705	26,478	18,859	32,391	9,235	10,212	12.0
1965	103,245	6,982	27,063	18,617	31,703	9,139	9,742	11.8
1964	102,421	7,295	27,551	18,419	30,728	9,085	9,345	11.7
1962	100,664	7,826	28,438	17,751	28,477	9,170	9,002	11.4
1960	99,465	8,303	31,218	19,140	24,440	8,747	7,617	10.6
1959	97,478	7,816	28,490	17,520	26,219	7,888	7,734	11.0

Note: Starting in 2012, data were created using population controls based on 2010 Census data. Starting in 2001, data were created using population controls based on Census 2000 data. Also starting in 2001, data are from the expanded CPS sample. Begining with data for 1992, a new question results in different categories than for earlier years. Data shown as 'High School, 4 years' are now collected in the category 'High School Graduate.' Data shown as 'College 1 to 3 years' are now collected in the 'Some college' and the two 'Associate degree' categories. Data shown as 'College 4 years or more,' are now collected in the categories, 'Bachelor's degree,' 'Master's degree,' 'Doctorate degree,' and 'Professional degree.' Due to the change in question format, median years of schooling cannot be derived. Total includes persons who did not report on years of school completed.
NA = Not available.

Table A-33. Years of School Completed by People 25 Years Old and Over, by Age and Sex, Selected Years, 1940–2020—*Continued*

(Numbers in thousands; civilian noninstitutionalized population, except where noted.)

Year, sex, and age	Total	Elementary		High school		College		Median years
		0 to 4 years	5 to 8 years	1 to 3 years	4 years	1 to 3 years	4 years or more	
1957	95,630	8,561	29,316	16,951	24,832	6,985	7,172	10.6
1952	88,358	8,004	30,274	15,228	21,074	6,714	6,118	10.1
1950	87,484	9,491	31,617	14,817	17,625	6,246	5,272	9.3
1947	82,578	8,611	32,308	13,487	16,926	5,533	4,424	9.0
1940	74,776	10,105	34,413	11,182	10,552	4,075	3,407	8.6
Male								
2020	107,517	1,053	2,854	6,250	31,355	26,580	39,426	NA
2019	106,695	1,082	3,230	6,792	31,257	26,527	37,807	NA
2018	105,862	973	3,284	6,939	31,325	26,668	36,674	NA
2017	104,324	1,090	3,312	6,934	31,296	26,581	35,112	NA
2016	103,372	1,183	3,513	7,144	30,780	26,468	34,283	NA
2015	101,887	1,243	3,669	7,278	30,997	25,778	32,923	NA
2014	100,592	1,184	3,761	7,403	30,718	25,430	32,095	NA
2013	99,305	1,127	3,836	7,314	30,014	25,283	31,731	NA
2012	98,119	1,237	3,879	7,388	30,216	24,632	30,766	NA
2011	97,220	1,234	3,883	7,443	30,370	24,319	29,971	NA
2010	96,325	1,279	3,931	7,705	30,682	23,570	29,158	NA
2009	95,518	1,372	4,027	7,754	30,025	23,634	28,706	NA
2008	94,470	1,310	4,136	7,853	29,491	23,247	28,433	NA
2007	93,421	1,458	4,249	8,294	29,604	22,219	27,596	NA
2006	92,233	1,472	4,395	7,940	29,380	22,136	26,910	NA
2005	90,899	1,505	4,402	7,787	29,151	21,794	26,259	NA
2004	89,558	1,496	4,308	7,766	27,889	21,763	26,336	NA
2003	88,597	1,482	4,566	8,026	27,356	21,568	25,598	NA
2002	86,906	1,457	4,743	7,894	26,947	21,127	24,828	NA
2001	86,096	1,419	4,673	7,615	26,956	21,120	24,313	NA
2000	83,611	1,341	4,577	7,298	26,651	20,493	23,252	NA
1999	82,917	1,339	4,651	7,736	26,368	20,043	22,782	NA
1998	82,376	1,431	4,727	8,017	26,575	19,792	21,832	NA
1997	81,620	1,454	5,023	8,212	26,226	19,332	21,374	NA
1996	80,339	1,537	5,067	7,930	25,649	19,301	20,854	NA
1995	79,463	1,598	5,231	7,691	25,378	18,933	20,631	NA
1994	78,539	1,669	5,427	7,789	25,404	18,544	19,705	NA
1993	77,644	1,709	5,594	7,821	25,766	17,521	19,234	NA
1992	76,579	1,737	5,726	8,085	25,774	16,631	18,627	NA
1991	75,487	2,018	6,299	7,887	27,189	13,720	18,373	12.8
1990	74,421	2,004	6,557	8,000	26,426	13,271	18,164	12.8
1989	73,225	1,956	6,659	8,076	25,897	12,725	17,913	12.8
1988	71,911	1,852	6,849	8,247	25,638	12,057	17,268	12.7
1987	70,677	1,794	7,259	7,909	24,998	12,062	16,654	12.7
1986	69,503	1,978	7,446	7,872	24,260	11,856	16,091	12.7
1985	67,756	1,947	7,629	7,783	23,552	11,164	15,682	12.7
1984	66,350	1,945	7,680	7,837	22,990	10,678	15,211	12.7
1983	65,004	2,103	7,750	7,867	22,048	10,310	14,926	12.7
1982	63,764	2,074	7,987	7,960	21,749	10,020	13,974	12.6
1981	62,509	2,141	8,322	8,084	21,019	9,734	13,208	12.6
1980	61,389	2,212	8,627	8,046	20,080	9,593	12,832	12.6
1979	58,986	2,190	8,785	7,636	19,250	9,100	12,025	12.6
1978	57,922	2,230	9,195	7,821	18,620	8,657	11,398	12.5
1977	56,917	2,296	9,330	7,969	18,290	8,104	10,926	12.5
1976	55,902	2,371	9,463	7,923	18,048	7,699	10,397	12.5
1975	55,036	2,568	9,760	7,985	17,769	7,274	9,679	12.4
1974	54,167	2,637	10,186	7,966	17,188	6,756	9,135	12.4
1973	53,067	2,598	10,488	8,120	17,011	6,376	8,473	12.3
1972	52,351	2,634	10,854	8,413	16,424	5,972	8,055	12.3
1971	52,357	2,933	11,703	8,264	16,008	5,798	7,653	12.2
1970	51,784	3,031	11,925	8,355	15,571	5,580	7,321	12.2
1969	51,031	3,095	12,182	8,398	15,177	5,263	6,917	12.1
1968	50,510	3,261	12,407	8,564	14,613	4,945	6,721	12.1
1967	49,756	3,417	12,736	8,463	14,015	4,755	6,372	12.0
1966	49,410	3,614	12,992	8,611	13,672	4,342	6,180	11.8
1965	49,242	3,774	13,308	8,529	13,334	4,370	5,923	11.7

Note: Starting in 2012, data were created using population controls based on 2010 Census data. Starting in 2001, data were created using population controls based on Census 2000 data. Also starting in 2001, data are from the expanded CPS sample. Begining with data for 1992, a new question results in different categories than for earlier years. Data shown as 'High School, 4 years' are now collected in the category 'High School Graduate.' Data shown as 'College 1 to 3 years' are now collected in the 'Some college' and the two 'Associate degree' categories. Data shown as 'College 4 years or more,' are now collected in the categories, 'Bachelor's degree,' 'Master's degree,' 'Doctorate degree,' and 'Professional degree.' Due to the change in question format, median years of schooling cannot be derived. Total includes persons who did not report on years of school completed.

NA = Not available

Table A-33. Years of School Completed by People 25 Years Old and Over, by Age and Sex, Selected Years, 1940–2020—*Continued*

(Numbers in thousands; civilian noninstitutionalized population, except where noted.)

Year, sex, and age	Total	Years of school completed						Median years
		Elementary		High school		College		
		0 to 4 years	5 to 8 years	1 to 3 years	4 years	1 to 3 years	4 years or more	
1964	48,975	3,959	13,467	8,537	12,902	4,394	5,714	11.5
1962	48,283	4,213	13,927	8,399	11,932	4,315	5,497	11.1
1960	47,997	4,522	15,562	8,988	10,175	4,127	4,626	10.3
1959	47,041	4,257	14,039	8,326	10,870	3,801	4,765	10.7
1957	46,208	4,610	14,634	8,003	10,230	3,347	4,359	10.3
1952	42,368	4,396	14,876	7,048	8,760	3,164	3,480	9.7
1950	42,627	5,074	15,852	6,974	7,511	2,888	3,008	9.0
1947	40,483	4,615	16,086	6,535	7,353	2,625	2,478	8.9
1940	37,463	5,550	17,639	5,333	4,507	1,824	2,021	8.6
Female								
2020	115540	1,053	2,935	6,063	30,243	30,972	44,275	NA
2019	114783	1,098	3,192	6,580	31,002	30,902	42,009	NA
2018	113,969	1,156	3,316	6,743	31,360	31,142	40,251	NA
2017	112,597	1,117	3,288	6,799	31,216	31,185	38,991	NA
2016	111,643	1,231	3,565	6,817	31,221	31,192	37,617	NA
2015	110,245	1,358	3,626	7,408	31,578	30,253	36,021	NA
2014	108,695	1,341	3,627	7,142	31,522	30,279	34,784	NA
2013	107,594	1,217	3,741	7,282	31,690	29,890	33,775	NA
2012	106,460	1,246	3,920	7,604	31,898	29,267	32,524	NA
2011	104,323	1,355	3,806	7,320	31,541	28,930	31,372	NA
2010	103,603	1,336	3,904	7,555	31,774	28,350	30,683	NA
2009	102,767	1,413	4,016	7,833	31,601	28,036	29,868	NA
2008	101,835	1,289	4,090	7,663	31,692	27,747	29,354	NA
2007	100,897	1,371	4,213	8,157	31,887	27,024	28,245	NA
2006	99,651	1,479	4,395	8,215	31,518	27,234	26,810	NA
2005	98,467	1,477	4,532	8,311	31,742	26,283	26,122	NA
2004	97,319	1,363	4,580	8,233	31,921	25,808	25,413	NA
2003	96,586	1,433	4,795	8,297	31,936	25,342	24,784	NA
2002	95,146	1,445	4,926	8,484	31,509	24,915	23,868	NA
2001	94,293	1,392	4,845	8,664	31,316	25,161	22,915	NA
2000	91,620	1,400	4,861	8,378	31,435	23,953	21,594	NA
1999	90,837	1,404	5,004	8,707	31,566	23,133	21,021	NA
1998	89,835	1,403	5,220	8,758	31,599	22,714	20,142	NA
1997	88,961	1,387	5,450	8,999	31,360	22,442	19,323	NA
1996	87,984	1,491	5,528	9,171	30,911	22,071	18,813	NA
1995	86,975	1,476	5,642	8,874	31,072	22,317	17,594	NA
1994	85,973	1,487	5,932	9,135	31,111	21,470	16,838	NA
1993	85,181	1,672	6,154	9,246	31,823	19,930	16,357	NA
1992	84,248	1,712	6,263	9,587	32,086	18,889	15,709	NA
1991	83,207	1,784	6,747	9,491	34,083	15,449	15,652	12.7
1990	82,116	1,829	7,200	9,462	33,693	14,806	15,126	12.7
1989	80,930	1,904	7,402	9,643	33,440	13,888	14,652	12.6
1988	79,724	1,862	7,700	9,599	33,303	13,741	13,519	12.6
1987	78,467	1,846	8,042	9,508	32,671	13,417	12,983	12.6
1986	77,102	1,916	8,226	9,612	32,078	12,874	12,399	12.6
1985	75,768	1,926	8,390	9,770	31,314	12,242	12,126	12.6
1984	74,444	1,939	8,571	9,596	31,083	11,603	11,651	12.6
1983	73,016	2,015	8,964	9,814	30,012	11,220	10,990	12.5
1982	71,762	2,045	9,245	10,046	29,677	10,673	10,076	12.5
1981	70,390	2,217	9,545	9,957	28,896	10,309	9,466	12.5
1980	69,020	2,178	9,800	10,040	27,854	9,786	9,362	12.4
1979	66,309	2,133	9,720	9,945	26,665	9,293	8,554	12.4
1978	65,097	2,214	10,114	10,353	25,761	8,721	7,934	12.4
1977	63,953	2,213	10,236	10,349	25,312	8,142	7,701	12.4
1976	62,946	2,230	10,449	10,281	25,109	7,779	7,098	12.3
1975	61,861	2,344	10,871	10,252	24,584	7,243	6,565	12.3
1974	60,838	2,469	11,015	10,308	23,972	6,910	6,165	12.3
1973	59,799	2,502	11,350	10,300	23,437	6,454	5,755	12.2
1972	58,782	2,490	11,649	10,442	22,746	6,145	5,309	12.2
1971	58,270	2,641	12,327	10,339	22,021	5,984	4,959	12.2
1970	57,527	2,716	12,595	10,327	21,563	5,584	4,743	12.1
1969	56,719	2,919	12,796	10,131	20,955	5,301	4,619	12.1

Note: Starting in 2012, data were created using population controls based on 2010 Census data. Starting in 2001, data were created using population controls based on Census 2000 data. Also starting in 2001, data are from the expanded CPS sample. Begining with data for 1992, a new question results in different categories than for earlier years. Data shown as 'High School, 4 years' are now collected in the category 'High School Graduate.' Data shown as 'College 1 to 3 years' are now collected in the 'Some college' and the two 'Associate degree' categories. Data shown as 'College 4 years or more,' are now collected in the categories, 'Bachelor's degree,' 'Master's degree,' 'Doctorate degree,' and 'Professional degree.' Due to the change in question format, median years of schooling cannot be derived. Total includes persons who did not report on years of school completed.
NA = Not available.

Table A-33. Years of School Completed by People 25 Years Old and Over, by Age and Sex, Selected Years, 1940–2020—*Continued*

(Numbers in thousands; civilian noninstitutionalized population, except where noted.)

| Year, sex, and age | Total | Elementary | | High school | | College | | Median years |
		0 to 4 years	5 to 8 years	1 to 3 years	4 years	1 to 3 years	4 years or more	
1968	55,959	2,987	13,060	10,160	19,991	5,309	4,450	12.1
1967	55,107	2,985	13,439	10,185	19,157	5,162	4,178	12.0
1966	54,467	3,090	13,488	10,246	18,719	4,892	4,032	12.0
1965	54,004	3,207	13,753	10,085	18,369	4,767	3,820	12.0
1964	53,447	3,333	14,086	9,881	17,825	4,686	3,629	11.8
1962	52,381	3,613	14,511	9,352	16,545	4,855	3,505	11.6
1960	51,468	3,781	15,656	10,151	14,267	4,620	2,991	10.9
1959	50,437	3,559	14,451	9,194	15,349	4,087	2,969	11.2
1957	49,422	3,951	14,682	8,948	14,602	3,638	2,813	10.9
1952	45,990	3,608	15,398	8,180	12,314	3,550	2,638	10.4
1950	44,857	4,417	15,824	7,843	10,114	3,358	2,264	9.6
1947	42,095	3,996	16,222	6,952	9,573	2,908	1,946	8.9
1940	37,313	4,554	16,773	5,849	6,044	2,251	1,386	8.7
25 TO 34 YEARS								
Both Sexes								
2020	45,260	168	557	1,968	11,797	12,178	18,592	NA
2019	45,208	232	679	2,353	11,639	12,269	18,037	NA
2018	44,854	182	776	2,435	11,460	12,501	17,501	NA
2017	44,250	218	732	2,532	11,494	12,792	16,482	NA
2016	43,763	210	858	2,656	11,224	12,609	16,207	NA
2015	43,006	292	863	2,938	10,965	12,420	15,528	NA
2014	42,466	286	946	3,018	11,040	12,178	14,997	NA
2013	41,797	260	1,035	3,116	10,950	11,955	14,481	NA
2012	41,219	273	1,063	3,079	10,974	11,765	14,065	NA
2011	41,584	318	1,140	3,098	11,250	12,046	13,731	NA
2010	41,085	323	1,169	3,271	11,186	11,655	13,480	NA
2009	40,520	321	1,226	3,202	11,351	11,409	13,010	NA
2008	40,146	282	1,189	3,296	11,297	11,113	12,969	NA
2007	39,868	380	1,283	3,462	11,408	10,961	12,375	NA
2006	39,481	359	1,410	3,375	11,302	11,229	11,806	NA
2005	39,310	414	1,375	3,422	11,269	10,865	11,965	NA
2004	39,201	430	1,399	3,239	11,244	11,044	11,844	NA
2003	39,242	370	1,370	3,336	11,392	10,986	11,791	NA
2002	38,670	433	1,393	3,245	10,988	10,776	11,834	NA
2001	38,865	380	1,317	3,202	11,294	11,146	11,526	NA
2000	37,786	287	1,135	3,052	11,546	10,700	11,066	NA
1999	38,474	280	1,142	3,296	11,826	10,893	11,040	NA
1998	39,354	319	1,207	3,228	12,569	11,220	10,811	NA
1997	40,256	334	1,163	3,624	12,710	11,524	10,892	NA
1996	40,919	418	1,169	3,780	13,087	11,624	10,841	NA
1995	41,388	394	1,264	3,667	14,061	11,659	10,342	NA
1994	41,946	367	1,297	4,057	14,483	11,913	9,829	NA
1993	41,864	382	1,223	3,894	15,036	11,361	9,968	NA
1992	42,493	433	1,250	4,071	16,021	10,860	9,861	NA
1991	42,905	465	1,322	4,178	17,503	9,283	10,153	12.9
1990	43,240	505	1,413	4,041	17,635	9,320	10,326	12.9
1989	43,240	446	1,352	4,013	17,901	9,072	10,454	12.9
1988	42,953	430	1,308	4,095	17,887	9,076	10,155	12.9
1987	42,635	390	1,360	3,995	17,539	9,157	10,196	12.9
1986	42,053	387	1,359	3,797	17,311	9,104	10,094	12.9
1985	40,858	362	1,328	3,703	16,748	8,980	9,737	12.9
1984	40,173	404	1,371	3,638	16,431	8,555	9,771	12.9
1983	39,342	376	1,324	3,664	15,804	8,567	9,605	12.9
1982	38,703	337	1,371	3,598	15,893	8,304	9,200	12.9
1981	37,828	337	1,428	3,665	15,419	8,198	8,782	12.9
1980	36,615	362	1,424	3,571	14,481	7,942	8,836	12.9
1979	34,053	370	1,381	3,452	13,338	7,415	8,096	12.9
1978	33,120	325	1,459	3,515	12,993	7,008	7,821	12.9
1977	32,284	269	1,383	3,715	12,845	6,398	7,676	12.8
1976	31,148	247	1,508	3,619	12,920	5,813	7,041	12.8
1975	30,092	313	1,644	3,743	12,544	5,403	6,443	12.7

Note: Starting in 2012, data were created using population controls based on 2010 Census data. Starting in 2001, data were created using population controls based on Census 2000 data. Also starting in 2001, data are from the expanded CPS sample. Begining with data for 1992, a new question results in different categories than for earlier years. Data shown as 'High School, 4 years' are now collected in the category 'High School Graduate.' Data shown as 'College 1 to 3 years' are now collected in the 'Some college' and the two 'Associate degree' categories. Data shown as 'College 4 years or more,' are now collected in the categories, 'Bachelor's degree,' Master's degree,' 'Doctorate degree,' and 'Professional degree.' Due to the change in question format, median years of schooling cannot be derived. Total includes persons who did not report on years of school completed.
NA = Not available.

Table A-33. Years of School Completed by People 25 Years Old and Over, by Age and Sex, Selected Years, 1940–2020—*Continued*

(Numbers in thousands; civilian noninstitutionalized population, except where noted.)

Year, sex, and age	Total	Years of school completed						Median years
		Elementary		High school		College		
		0 to 4 years	5 to 8 years	1 to 3 years	4 years	1 to 3 years	4 years or more	
1974	28,972	352	1,654	3,763	12,362	5,056	5,785	12.7
1973	27,793	333	1,850	3,915	12,194	4,454	5,047	12.6
1972	26,517	285	1,791	3,981	11,635	4,090	4,734	12.6
1971	25,545	327	2,011	3,986	11,232	3,822	4,169	12.6
1970	24,865	329	1,937	4,251	10,929	3,491	3,926	12.5
1969	24,072	359	2,086	4,140	10,592	3,202	3,693	12.5
1968	23,285	350	2,246	4,129	10,157	2,989	3,413	12.5
1967	22,388	319	2,293	4,017	9,645	2,946	3,169	12.5
1966	22,023	430	2,208	4,158	9,546	2,647	3,037	12.4
1965	21,980	543	2,437	4,058	9,500	2,561	2,880	12.4
1964	21,997	502	2,591	4,176	9,370	2,529	2,830	12.4
1962	22,130	597	2,936	4,371	8,815	2,552	2,859	12.4
1960	22,821	709	3,738	5,135	8,166	2,572	2,499	12.4
1959	22,922	761	3,348	4,741	8,979	2,398	2,480	12.3
1957	23,437	750	3,971	4,965	8,927	2,275	2,351	12.2
1952	23,138	844	4,362	4,898	8,620	2,220	2,052	12.2
1950	23,626	1,147	5,308	5,050	7,660	2,198	1,252	11.9
1947	22,627	1,015	5,523	4,997	7,630	1,908	1,378	11.9
1940	21,339	1,377	7,676	4,553	4,702	1,554	1,288	10.0
Male								
2020	22,783	94	285	1,064	6,897	6,092	8,352	NA
2019	22,726	147	379	1,303	6,593	5,939	8,365	NA
2018	22,490	95	432	1,431	6,530	6,047	7,955	NA
2017	22,121	135	390	1,410	6,456	6,267	7,464	NA
2016	21,845	116	468	1,427	6,386	6,015	7,432	NA
2015	21,427	166	488	1,584	6,198	5,920	7,071	NA
2014	21,217	151	512	1,611	6,323	5,910	6,710	NA
2013	20,816	161	582	1,747	6,058	5,749	6,519	NA
2012	20,464	161	579	1,707	6,127	5,619	6,270	NA
2011	20,985	190	657	1,791	6,444	5,750	6,151	NA
2010	20,689	186	641	1,866	6,458	5,587	5,951	NA
2009	20,440	184	695	1,806	6,495	5,508	5,752	NA
2008	20,210	172	714	1,874	6,356	5,277	5,816	NA
2007	20,024	246	757	1,930	6,361	5,137	5,593	NA
2006	19,827	218	834	1,835	6,233	5,336	5,371	NA
2005	19,677	241	769	1,827	6,216	5,198	5,426	NA
2004	19,598	280	793	1,723	6,020	5,286	5,495	NA
2003	19,564	216	771	1,831	6,028	5,252	5,466	NA
2002	19,234	280	809	1,782	5,751	5,131	5,480	NA
2001	19,330	233	748	1,677	6,099	5,161	5,411	NA
2000	18,563	155	593	1,637	5,989	4,870	5,318	NA
1999	18,294	157	616	1,724	6,114	5,052	5,260	NA
1998	19,526	190	654	1,735	6,592	5,233	5,125	NA
1997	20,039	193	629	2,007	6,482	5,477	5,249	NA
1996	20,390	225	601	2,055	6,701	5,536	5,274	NA
1995	20,589	229	708	1,930	7,176	5,373	5,174	NA
1994	20,873	230	716	2,134	7,408	5,510	4,873	NA
1993	20,856	237	679	1,986	7,604	5,308	5,041	NA
1992	21,125	231	682	2,057	8,113	5,116	4,927	NA
1991	21,319	270	694	2,095	8,810	4,441	5,009	12.9
1990	21,462	295	759	2,153	8,649	4,392	5,215	12.9
1989	21,461	251	698	2,129	8,659	4,391	5,335	12.9
1988	21,277	237	651	2,227	8,569	4,273	5,319	12.9
1987	21,142	223	698	2,030	8,544	4,384	5,263	12.9
1986	20,956	227	715	1,887	8,359	4,488	5,279	12.9
1985	20,184	194	700	1,823	7,955	4,433	5,080	12.9
1984	19,876	231	721	1,739	7,798	4,238	5,150	12.9
1983	19,438	213	659	1,724	7,351	4,284	5,207	13.0
1982	19,090	182	659	1,654	7,380	4,162	5,053	13.0
1981	18,625	176	733	1,679	6,991	4,185	4,863	13.0
1980	18,051	198	699	1,639	6,393	4,166	4,957	13.0
1979	16,719	197	695	1,476	5,852	3,862	4,637	13.0

Note: Starting in 2012, data were created using population controls based on 2010 Census data. Starting in 2001, data were created using population controls based on Census 2000 data. Also starting in 2001, data are from the expanded CPS sample. Begining with data for 1992, a new question results in different categories than for earlier years. Data shown as 'High School, 4 years' are now collected in the category 'High School Graduate.' Data shown as 'College 1 to 3 years' are now collected in the 'Some college' and the two 'Associate degree' categories. Data shown as 'College 4 years or more,' are now collected in the categories, 'Bachelor's degree,' 'Master's degree,' 'Doctorate degree,' and 'Professional degree.' Due to the change in question format, median years of schooling cannot be derived. Total includes persons who did not report on years of school completed.
NA = Not available.

Table A-33. Years of School Completed by People 25 Years Old and Over, by Age and Sex, Selected Years, 1940–2020—*Continued*

(Numbers in thousands; civilian noninstitutionalized population, except where noted.)

Year, sex, and age	Total	Years of school completed						Median years
		Elementary		High school		College		
		0 to 4 years	5 to 8 years	1 to 3 years	4 years	1 to 3 years	4 years or more	
1978	16,263	154	717	1,526	5,701	3,698	4,471	13.1
1977	15,863	134	672	1,625	5,634	3,403	4,396	13.0
1976	15,266	134	724	1,566	5,672	3,085	4,087	12.9
1975	14,776	177	815	1,605	5,508	2,915	3,757	12.9
1974	14,222	211	859	1,617	5,491	2,672	3,372	12.8
1973	13,638	204	966	1,760	5,363	2,416	2,927	12.7
1972	13,030	157	927	1,796	5,150	2,191	2,809	12.7
1971	12,596	170	1,092	1,771	5,049	2,005	2,506	12.6
1970	12,236	189	1,063	1,896	4,833	1,842	2,412	12.6
1969	11,788	204	1,121	1,849	4,652	1,719	2,241	12.6
1968	11,381	193	1,192	1,880	4,473	1,505	2,136	12.5
1967	10,876	170	1,209	1,814	4,187	1,522	1,973	12.5
1966	10,701	241	1,162	1,839	4,191	1,374	1,894	12.5
1965	10,693	325	1,240	1,802	4,188	1,316	1,822	12.5
1964	10,729	297	1,344	1,962	4,008	1,306	1,812	12.4
1962	10,762	334	1,569	2,008	3,700	1,309	1,842	12.4
1960	11,184	420	2,026	2,441	3,356	1,316	1,624	12.2
1959	11,226	416	1,822	2,238	3,682	1,256	1,658	12.3
1957	11,368	423	2,097	2,446	3,542	1,181	1,556	12.2
1952	10,936	502	2,202	2,268	3,450	1,118	1,268	12.1
1950	11,454	631	2,705	2,426	3,250	1,117	1,037	11.5
1947	10,894	544	2,665	2,494	3,337	993	738	11.7
1940	10,521	779	3,932	2,220	2,049	692	744	9.7
Female								
2020	22,477	74	272	904	4,900	6,087	10,240	NA
2019	22,482	84	300	1,051	5,045	6,330	9,671	NA
2018	22,364	87	344	1,004	4,930	6,454	9,547	NA
2017	22,129	84	342	1,122	5,037	6,526	9,018	NA
2016	21,918	93	390	1,229	4,838	6,594	8,774	NA
2015	21,579	126	375	1,354	4,767	6,500	8,457	NA
2014	21,248	135	435	1,407	4,717	6,267	8,287	NA
2013	20,981	99	454	1,369	4,892	6,205	7,962	NA
2012	20,755	112	484	1,372	4,847	6,145	7,795	NA
2011	20,599	128	483	1,307	4,806	6,296	7,580	NA
2010	20,396	137	527	1,405	4,728	6,068	7,530	NA
2009	20,079	137	531	1,395	4,856	5,901	7,258	NA
2008	19,937	111	475	1,421	4,941	5,836	7,153	NA
2007	19,843	134	527	1,532	5,047	5,824	6,781	NA
2006	19,654	140	577	1,538	5,069	5,894	6,435	NA
2005	19,633	173	607	1,594	5,053	5,667	6,539	NA
2004	19,603	150	606	1,516	5,224	5,758	6,349	NA
2003	19,679	153	598	1,503	5,364	5,734	6,325	NA
2002	19,436	153	584	1,463	5,237	5,645	6,353	NA
2001	19,536	147	569	1,525	5,195	5,985	6,115	NA
2000	19,222	130	542	1,415	5,557	5,831	5,750	NA
1999	19,551	122	525	1,572	5,712	5,842	5,779	NA
1998	19,828	130	553	1,493	5,977	5,986	5,688	NA
1997	20,217	149	533	1,615	6,227	6,047	5,643	NA
1996	20,528	195	569	1,734	6,386	6,090	5,568	NA
1995	20,800	165	556	1,738	6,885	6,286	5,170	NA
1994	21,073	138	581	1,923	7,075	6,404	4,953	NA
1993	21,007	143	543	1,907	7,432	6,054	4,928	NA
1992	21,368	203	567	2,014	7,908	6,711	4,933	NA
1991	21,586	195	629	2,005	8,693	4,841	5,143	12.9
1990	21,779	209	653	1,889	8,986	4,927	5,112	12.9
1989	21,777	195	654	1,885	9,242	4,681	5,119	12.9
1988	21,675	193	657	1,869	9,319	4,801	4,836	12.9
1987	21,494	168	662	1,965	8,995	4,772	4,932	12.9
1986	21,097	160	644	1,910	8,952	4,616	4,813	12.9
1985	20,673	168	627	1,880	8,794	4,547	4,657	12.9
1984	20,297	173	649	1,904	8,634	4,319	4,621	12.9
1983	19,903	161	665	1,941	8,452	4,285	4,398	12.9

Note: Starting in 2012, data were created using population controls based on 2010 Census data. Starting in 2001, data were created using population controls based on Census 2000 data. Also starting in 2001, data are from the expanded CPS sample. Begining with data for 1992, a new question results in different categories than for earlier years. Data shown as 'High School, 4 years' are now collected in the category 'High School Graduate.' Data shown as 'College 1 to 3 years' are now collected in the 'Some college' and the two 'Associate degree' categories. Data shown as 'College 4 years or more,' are now collected in the categories, 'Bachelor's degree,' 'Master's degree,' 'Doctorate degree,' and 'Professional degree.' Due to the change in question format, median years of schooling cannot be derived. Total includes persons who did not report on years of school completed.

NA = Not available.

Table A-33. Years of School Completed by People 25 Years Old and Over, by Age and Sex, Selected Years, 1940–2020—*Continued*

(Numbers in thousands; civilian noninstitutionalized population, except where noted.)

Year, sex, and age	Total	Elementary 0 to 4 years	Elementary 5 to 8 years	High school 1 to 3 years	High school 4 years	College 1 to 3 years	College 4 years or more	Median years
1982	19,614	155	713	1,942	8,512	4,140	4,148	12.8
1981	19,203	161	698	1,986	8,427	4,013	3,918	12.8
1980	18,565	164	725	1,932	8,087	3,777	3,879	12.8
1979	17,334	173	685	1,977	7,486	3,553	3,460	12.8
1978	16,857	172	742	1,989	7,292	3,311	3,351	12.6
1977	16,421	136	710	2,088	7,212	2,995	3,280	12.7
1976	15,882	112	784	2,054	7,248	2,731	2,954	12.7
1975	15,316	135	833	2,139	7,037	2,489	2,686	12.6
1974	14,750	142	796	2,145	6,871	2,383	2,413	12.6
1973	14,155	129	884	2,154	6,830	2,037	2,121	12.6
1972	13,487	128	862	2,184	6,485	1,899	1,926	12.5
1971	12,950	156	919	2,212	6,183	1,816	1,663	12.5
1970	12,629	140	876	2,355	6,096	1,648	1,512	12.5
1969	12,285	155	965	2,291	5,941	1,481	1,451	12.4
1968	11,904	157	1,053	2,246	5,684	1,484	1,278	12.4
1967	11,512	149	1,084	2,200	5,458	1,426	1,195	12.4
1966	11,322	186	1,047	2,319	5,355	1,273	1,134	12.4
1965	11,284	218	1,197	2,256	5,310	1,244	1,060	12.4
1964	11,269	202	1,248	2,216	5,362	1,221	1,018	12.4
1962	11,368	263	1,367	2,363	5,115	1,243	1,017	12.3
1960	11,637	289	1,712	2,694	4,810	1,256	875	12.2
1959	11,696	345	1,526	2,503	5,297	1,142	822	12.3
1957	12,069	327	1,874	2,519	5,385	1,094	795	12.2
1952	12,202	342	2,160	2,630	5,162	1,102	784	12.2
1950	12,172	516	2,603	2,624	4,410	1,081	714	12.1
1947	11,733	471	2,858	2,503	4,293	915	640	12.0
1940	10,818	598	3,744	2,333	2,653	862	544	10.3
35 TO 54 YEARS								
Both Sexes								
2020	80,999	685	2,133	4,364	20,261	20,302	33,254	NA
2019	81,727	716	2,309	4,957	21,303	20,572	31,869	NA
2018	82,196	690	2,289	4,974	21,680	21,340	31,223	NA
2017	82,072	709	2,403	5,059	22,103	21,621	30,176	NA
2016	82,571	799	2,636	5,296	22,298	22,070	29,473	NA
2015	82,715	862	2,742	5,471	23,153	21,826	28,660	NA
2014	82,687	875	2,612	5,433	23,238	22,472	28,057	NA
2013	83,324	778	2,611	5,437	23,708	22,831	27,959	NA
2012	83,883	863	2,762	5,569	24,608	22,792	27,288	NA
2011	83,796	899	2,474	5,682	25,039	22,796	26,907	NA
2010	84,834	852	2,549	5,937	26,145	22,911	26,440	NA
2009	85,688	909	2,716	6,046	26,121	23,384	26,513	NA
2008	86,067	905	2,742	5,882	26,108	23,504	26,926	NA
2007	86,224	874	2,720	6,310	26,675	22,777	26,869	NA
2006	85,918	965	2,769	6,274	26,636	23,317	25,958	NA
2005	85,311	954	2,757	5,892	27,232	23,129	25,347	NA
2004	84,642	963	2,582	5,938	26,649	23,093	25,417	NA
2003	84,308	957	2,620	6,112	26,346	23,039	25,234	NA
2002	83,829	941	2,636	5,874	26,740	23,148	24,489	NA
2001	83,286	886	2,612	5,899	26,356	23,271	24,262	NA
2000	81,435	932	2,521	5,702	26,481	22,618	23,183	NA
1999	79,976	872	2,535	6,052	26,367	21,561	22,589	NA
1998	78,520	890	2,613	6,164	26,079	21,267	21,506	NA
1997	76,973	867	2,686	6,045	26,054	20,684	20,635	NA
1996	74,661	968	2,710	5,803	24,924	20,105	20,152	NA
1995	73,028	927	2,561	5,664	24,070	19,926	19,878	NA
1994	71,049	987	2,680	5,415	23,804	19,210	18,956	NA
1993	68,845	942	2,486	5,538	23,927	17,984	17,970	NA
1992	66,594	899	2,608	5,845	23,442	16,658	17,144	NA
1991	64,351	995	3,057	5,522	24,815	13,348	16,614	12.9
1990	62,499	980	3,104	5,529	24,434	12,553	15,899	12.9
1989	60,494	999	3,315	5,800	23,334	11,627	15,417	12.9

Note: Starting in 2012, data were created using population controls based on 2010 Census data. Starting in 2001, data were created using population controls based on Census 2000 data. Also starting in 2001, data are from the expanded CPS sample. Begining with data for 1992, a new question results in different categories than for earlier years. Data shown as 'High School, 4 years' are now collected in the category 'High School Graduate.' Data shown as 'College 1 to 3 years' are now collected in the 'Some college' and the two 'Associate degree' categories. Data shown as 'College 4 years or more,' are now collected in the categories, 'Bachelor's degree,' 'Master's degree,' 'Doctorate degree,' and 'Professional degree.' Due to the change in question format, median years of schooling cannot be derived. Total includes persons who did not report on years of school completed.
NA = Not available.

Table A-33. Years of School Completed by People 25 Years Old and Over, by Age and Sex, Selected Years, 1940–2020—*Continued*

(Numbers in thousands; civilian noninstitutionalized population, except where noted.)

| Year, sex, and age | Total | Elementary | | High school | | College | | Median years |
		0 to 4 years	5 to 8 years	1 to 3 years	4 years	1 to 3 years	4 years or more	
1988	58,555	958	3,272	5,889	23,049	11,017	14,369	12.8
1987	56,650	842	3,398	5,656	22,820	10,523	13,409	12.8
1986	55,170	896	3,614	5,769	22,151	10,110	12,629	12.8
1985	53,697	899	3,639	5,978	21,600	9,217	12,363	12.8
1984	52,297	893	3,754	6,158	21,290	8,702	11,500	12.7
1983	50,956	973	4,044	6,313	20,788	8,045	10,795	12.7
1982	49,722	963	4,320	6,657	20,445	7,580	9,756	12.6
1981	48,680	1,038	4,531	6,773	20,032	7,115	9,181	12.6
1980	48,124	1,034	4,676	7,063	19,584	6,943	8,822	12.6
1979	47,437	1,030	4,895	7,132	19,488	6,655	8,237	12.5
1978	46,921	1,107	5,262	7,590	19,012	6,286	7,667	12.5
1977	46,409	1,192	5,445	7,781	18,781	6,013	7,196	12.5
1976	46,271	1,245	5,729	7,671	18,893	5,957	6,776	12.5
1975	46,193	1,296	5,942	7,765	19,010	5,673	6,506	12.4
1974	46,217	1,293	6,244	7,896	19,038	5,375	6,372	12.4
1973	45,910	1,344	6,519	8,001	18,651	5,318	6,076	12.4
1972	45,956	1,367	7,004	8,521	18,400	5,074	5,589	12.3
1971	46,294	1,439	7,588	8,393	18,334	5,082	5,460	12.3
1970	46,319	1,461	7,935	8,555	18,200	4,875	5,294	12.3
1969	46,255	1,644	8,313	8,586	17,773	4,749	5,190	12.3
1968	46,396	1,654	8,698	8,838	17,362	4,642	5,200	12.2
1967	46,321	1,771	9,036	9,138	16,906	4,525	4,947	12.2
1966	46,313	1,837	9,528	9,309	16,605	4,230	4,805	12.1
1965	46,296	1,827	9,812	9,266	16,359	4,384	4,647	12.1
1964	46,089	1,905	10,259	9,289	15,760	4,397	4,482	12.1
1962	45,287	2,181	10,795	8,938	14,668	4,452	4,253	12.0
1960	44,742	2,424	12,536	9,502	12,517	4,123	3,639	11.3
1959	43,989	2,303	11,657	8,719	13,244	3,715	3,709	11.8
1957	42,645	2,658	12,349	8,384	12,041	3,248	3,360	11.3
1952	39,014	2,606	13,274	7,348	9,374	3,148	2,802	10.5
1950	38,432	3,404	14,420	6,976	7,262	2,878	2,516	9.7
1947	36,717	3,203	15,184	6,311	6,715	2,622	2,221	9.0
1940	33,845	4,549	16,270	4,972	4,217	1,836	1,540	8.6
Male								
2020	39,591	393	1,110	2,385	11,048	9,479	15,176	NA
2019	40,180	388	1,202	2,690	11,688	9,863	14,348	NA
2018	40,411	356	1,182	2,657	11,753	9,991	14,472	NA
2017	40,303	395	1,305	2,711	12,032	10,026	13,834	NA
2016	40,539	443	1,336	2,903	12,021	10,217	13,620	NA
2015	40,565	469	1,416	2,987	12,401	9,996	13,296	NA
2014	40,525	489	1,459	2,992	12,246	10,199	13,139	NA
2013	40,868	409	1,464	2,962	12,417	10,473	13,142	NA
2012	41,167	462	1,525	2,927	12,869	10,439	12,944	NA
2011	41,209	447	1,292	3,027	13,250	10,339	12,854	NA
2010	41,858	446	1,367	3,227	13,824	10,311	12,682	NA
2009	42,263	500	1,458	3,278	13,644	10,670	12,713	NA
2008	42,419	507	1,490	3,228	13,625	10,711	12,858	NA
2007	42,476	491	1,433	3,480	13,737	10,359	12,976	NA
2006	42,344	549	1,472	3,356	13,660	10,608	12,701	NA
2005	42,024	547	1,476	3,063	14,017	10,429	12,491	NA
2004	41,612	577	1,323	3,157	13,238	10,636	12,682	NA
2003	41,340	538	1,372	3,282	12,903	10,622	12,622	NA
2002	41,154	513	1,333	3,063	13,133	10,739	12,373	NA
2001	40,858	488	1,368	2,974	12,784	10,827	12,417	NA
2000	40,024	479	1,288	2,845	12,845	10,716	11,854	NA
1999	39,300	470	1,290	3,101	12,544	10,233	11,664	NA
1998	38,654	486	1,333	3,284	12,239	10,098	11,214	NA
1997	37,912	486	1,370	3,143	12,326	9,713	10,870	NA
1996	36,596	520	1,319	2,877	11,749	9,514	10,526	NA
1995	35,994	529	1,368	2,781	11,223	9,305	10,784	NA
1994	34,998	545	1,383	2,621	11,009	9,073	10,369	NA
1993	33,751	478	1,316	2,660	10,983	8,624	9,687	NA

Note: Starting in 2012, data were created using population controls based on 2010 Census data. Starting in 2001, data were created using population controls based on Census 2000 data. Also starting in 2001, data are from the expanded CPS sample. Begining with data for 1992, a new question results in different categories than for earlier years. Data shown as 'High School, 4 years' are now collected in the category 'High School Graduate.' Data shown as 'College 1 to 3 years' are now collected in the 'Some college' and the two 'Associate degree' categories. Data shown as 'College 4 years or more,' are now collected in the categories, 'Bachelor's degree,' 'Master's degree,' 'Doctorate degree,' and 'Professional degree.' Due to the change in question format, median years of schooling cannot be derived. Total includes persons who did not report on years of school completed.

NA = Not available.

Table A-33. Years of School Completed by People 25 Years Old and Over, by Age and Sex, Selected Years, 1940–2020—*Continued*

(Numbers in thousands; civilian noninstitutionalized population, except where noted.)

Year, sex, and age	Total	Elementary		High school		College		Median years
		0 to 4 years	5 to 8 years	1 to 3 years	4 years	1 to 3 years	4 years or more	
1992	32,619	472	1,368	2,750	10,670	7,968	9,389	NA
1991	31,460	530	1,624	2,612	11,092	6,430	9,169	13.0
1990	30,623	527	1,658	2,573	10,790	6,169	8,905	13.0
1989	29,597	504	1,762	2,628	10,235	5,719	8,749	13.0
1988	28,645	498	1,725	2,654	10,100	5,327	8,340	12.9
1987	27,680	412	1,801	2,617	9,781	5,173	7,895	12.9
1986	26,925	475	1,919	2,699	9,393	5,013	7,426	12.9
1985	26,181	501	1,928	2,726	9,210	4,502	7,314	12.9
1984	25,460	506	2,014	2,831	8,926	4,257	6,929	12.8
1983	24,796	548	2,108	2,862	8,795	3,884	6,601	12.8
1982	24,164	530	2,302	2,989	8,609	3,757	5,977	12.7
1981	23,646	572	2,425	3,112	8,431	3,519	5,588	12.7
1980	23,373	590	2,492	3,202	8,278	3,442	5,370	12.7
1979	22,976	545	2,612	3,194	8,232	3,306	5,090	12.6
1978	22,719	609	2,779	3,377	8,001	3,136	4,817	12.6
1977	22,445	661	2,889	3,554	7,822	3,000	4,520	12.5
1976	22,403	730	3,004	3,473	7,904	2,969	4,323	12.5
1975	22,358	763	3,100	3,510	7,952	2,879	4,153	12.5
1974	22,367	733	3,286	3,532	8,004	2,730	4,081	12.6
1973	22,166	716	3,413	3,586	7,836	2,714	3,901	12.4
1972	22,200	749	3,674	3,917	7,663	2,564	3,631	12.4
1971	22,474	849	3,985	3,823	7,674	2,578	3,567	12.3
1970	22,475	834	4,208	3,876	7,612	2,555	3,390	12.3
1969	22,420	889	4,359	4,012	7,427	2,456	3,277	12.3
1968	22,521	931	4,487	4,160	7,324	2,364	3,257	12.2
1967	22,482	1,000	4,700	4,270	7,143	2,244	3,128	12.2
1966	22,508	1,085	4,886	4,455	6,990	2,029	3,063	12.1
1965	22,534	1,081	5,076	4,462	6,815	2,161	2,937	12.1
1964	22,457	1,158	5,226	4,416	6,657	2,212	2,789	12.2
1962	22,081	1,235	5,545	4,359	6,202	2,142	2,598	11.9
1960	21,919	1,397	6,415	4,579	5,364	1,957	2,206	11.1
1959	21,511	1,350	5,781	4,329	5,604	1,827	2,250	11.5
1957	20,873	1,491	6,293	3,987	5,195	1,558	1,972	11.0
1952	18,888	1,466	6,512	3,462	4,040	1,518	1,576	10.3
1950	18,896	1,834	7,338	3,339	3,151	1,271	1,403	9.6
1947	18,165	1,678	7,765	3,102	2,907	1,168	1,258	8.6
1940	17,127	2,480	8,458	2,388	1,798	819	917	8.5
Female								
2020	41,408	292	1,022	1,980	9,214	10,823	18,077	NA
2019	41,547	327	1,107	2,267	9,616	10,709	17,521	NA
2018	41,785	334	1,107	2,317	9,927	11,349	16,751	NA
2017	41,769	314	1,098	2,348	10,072	11,595	16,342	NA
2016	42,031	356	1,300	2,393	10,276	11,853	15,853	NA
2015	42,150	394	1,326	2,484	10,752	11,830	15,364	NA
2014	42,163	385	1,153	2,440	10,993	12,273	14,919	NA
2013	42,456	369	1,147	2,475	11,290	12,358	14,817	NA
2012	42,716	400	1,237	2,642	11,739	12,352	14,345	NA
2011	42,587	452	1,183	2,654	11,789	12,457	14,053	NA
2010	42,976	406	1,181	2,710	12,321	12,600	13,758	NA
2009	43,424	409	1,258	2,768	12,476	12,713	13,800	NA
2008	43,648	398	1,253	2,654	12,483	12,792	14,067	NA
2007	43,748	382	1,288	2,830	12,938	12,419	13,892	NA
2006	43,573	417	1,298	2,915	12,976	12,710	13,255	NA
2005	43,287	407	1,280	2,829	13,215	12,700	12,856	NA
2004	43,030	386	1,259	2,781	13,411	12,458	12,736	NA
2003	42,968	419	1,248	2,830	13,443	12,417	12,611	NA
2002	42,675	428	1,303	2,811	13,607	12,410	12,116	NA
2001	42,428	398	1,244	2,926	13,572	12,444	11,844	NA
2000	41,411	452	1,235	2,858	13,635	11,905	11,330	NA
1999	40,676	402	1,248	2,950	13,825	11,326	10,925	NA
1998	39,866	403	1,279	2,879	13,841	11,168	10,293	NA
1997	39,061	381	1,319	2,902	13,726	10,969	9,766	NA

Note: Starting in 2012, data were created using population controls based on 2010 Census data. Starting in 2001, data were created using population controls based on Census 2000 data. Also starting in 2001, data are from the expanded CPS sample. Begining with data for 1992, a new question results in different categories than for earlier years. Data shown as 'High School, 4 years' are now collected in the category 'High School Graduate.' Data shown as 'College 1 to 3 years' are now collected in the 'Some college' and the two 'Associate degree' categories. Data shown as 'College 4 years or more,' are now collected in the categories, 'Bachelor's degree,' 'Master's degree,' 'Doctorate degree,' and 'Professional degree.' Due to the change in question format, median years of schooling cannot be derived. Total includes persons who did not report on years of school completed.
NA = Not available.

Table A-33. Years of School Completed by People 25 Years Old and Over, by Age and Sex, Selected Years, 1940–2020—*Continued*

(Numbers in thousands; civilian noninstitutionalized population, except where noted.)

Year, sex, and age	Total	Years of school completed						Median years
		Elementary		High school		College		
		0 to 4 years	5 to 8 years	1 to 3 years	4 years	1 to 3 years	4 years or more	
1996	38,065	449	1,301	2,924	13,174	10,592	9,623	NA
1995	37,034	396	1,192	2,881	12,846	10,623	9,096	NA
1994	36,051	443	1,298	2,792	12,795	10,140	8,587	NA
1993	35,093	462	1,169	2,877	12,944	9,358	8,283	NA
1992	33,975	427	1,240	3,096	12,770	8,687	7,756	NA
1991	32,891	464	1,431	2,910	13,723	6,919	7,443	12.8
1990	31,876	454	1,448	2,955	13,643	6,383	6,997	12.8
1989	30,898	498	1,552	3,171	13,099	5,908	6,669	12.8
1988	29,908	462	1,547	3,234	12,949	5,689	6,029	12.7
1987	28,969	430	1,598	3,039	13,038	5,349	5,513	12.7
1986	28,244	420	1,694	3,071	12,759	5,098	5,202	12.7
1985	27,516	398	1,710	3,252	12,391	4,715	5,049	12.7
1984	26,838	389	1,740	3,331	12,364	4,444	4,570	12.6
1983	26,161	427	1,935	3,450	11,993	4,161	4,193	12.6
1982	25,555	433	2,017	3,666	11,833	3,827	3,778	12.6
1981	25,034	467	2,105	3,661	11,599	3,605	3,595	12.5
1980	24,751	444	2,186	3,862	11,307	3,501	3,452	12.5
1979	24,461	486	2,282	3,935	11,258	3,353	3,147	12.5
1978	24,202	497	2,483	4,212	11,012	3,149	2,849	12.5
1977	23,964	534	2,557	4,227	10,959	3,014	2,678	12.4
1976	23,868	517	2,721	4,198	10,989	2,988	2,455	12.4
1975	23,835	533	2,842	4,256	11,058	2,793	2,352	12.4
1974	23,850	559	2,956	4,364	11,033	2,647	2,290	12.4
1973	23,744	628	3,106	4,415	10,815	2,603	2,174	12.3
1972	23,756	618	3,330	4,604	10,736	2,509	1,958	12.3
1971	23,821	590	3,604	4,570	10,660	2,505	1,894	12.3
1970	23,845	629	3,728	4,679	10,588	2,318	1,903	12.3
1969	23,834	755	3,953	4,575	10,349	2,293	1,913	12.3
1968	23,874	725	4,212	4,676	10,038	2,281	1,943	12.2
1967	23,839	773	4,334	4,868	9,762	2,282	1,819	12.2
1966	23,806	752	4,644	4,853	9,615	2,200	1,741	12.2
1965	23,765	746	4,735	4,803	9,545	2,223	1,712	12.2
1964	23,632	748	5,033	4,871	9,103	2,183	1,691	12.1
1962	23,206	946	5,250	4,579	8,466	2,310	1,655	12.1
1960	22,823	1,027	6,121	4,923	7,153	2,166	1,433	11.6
1959	22,478	953	5,876	4,390	7,640	1,888	1,459	12.0
1957	21,772	1,167	6,056	4,397	6,846	1,690	1,388	11.5
1952	20,126	1,140	6,762	3,886	5,334	1,630	1,226	10.7
1950	19,536	1,570	7,082	3,637	4,111	1,607	1,113	9.7
1947	18,552	1,525	7,419	3,209	3,808	1,454	963	9.3
1940	16,718	2,070	7,812	2,584	2,419	1,017	623	8.7
55 YEARS AND OLDER								
Both Sexes								
2020	96,798	1,253	3,099	5,981	29,539	25,071	31,856	NA
2019	94,543	1,233	3,434	6,062	29,317	24,587	29,910	NA
2018	92,780	1,258	3,535	6,273	29,545	23,970	28,200	NA
2017	90,599	1,280	3,465	6,143	28,916	23,351	27,444	NA
2016	88,682	1,406	3,584	6,009	28,481	22,981	26,221	NA
2015	86,411	1,447	3,690	6,276	28,457	21,785	24,756	NA
2014	84,134	1,365	3,829	6,094	27,962	21,059	23,825	NA
2013	81,778	1,306	3,931	6,043	27,046	20,387	23,066	NA
2012	79,478	1,348	3,974	6,344	26,531	19,343	21,937	NA
2011	76,163	1,372	4,073	5,983	25,622	18,408	20,705	NA
2010	74,008	1,440	4,118	6,051	25,125	17,354	19,920	NA
2009	72,077	1,555	4,101	6,338	24,154	16,877	19,051	NA
2008	70,092	1,411	4,294	6,338	23,779	16,378	17,892	NA
2007	68,226	1,576	4,458	6,680	23,408	15,505	16,599	NA
2006	66,485	1,628	4,610	6,508	22,961	14,824	15,956	NA
2005	64,745	1,614	4,803	6,704	22,392	14,083	15,069	NA
2004	63,034	1,465	4,907	6,821	21,918	13,434	14,488	NA
2003	61,633	1,680	5,372	6,870	21,554	12,884	13,358	NA

Note: Starting in 2012, data were created using population controls based on 2010 Census data. Starting in 2001, data were created using population controls based on Census 2000 data. Also starting in 2001, data are from the expanded CPS sample. Begining with data for 1992, a new question results in different categories than for earlier years. Data shown as 'High School, 4 years' are now collected in the category 'High School Graduate.' Data shown as 'College 1 to 3 years' are now collected in the 'Some college' and the two 'Associate degree' categories. Data shown as 'College 4 years or more,' are now collected in the categories, 'Bachelor's degree,' 'Master's degree,' 'Doctorate degree,' and 'Professional degree.' Due to the change in question format, median years of schooling cannot be derived. Total includes persons who did not report on years of school completed.
NA = Not available.

Table A-33. Years of School Completed by People 25 Years Old and Over, by Age and Sex, Selected Years, 1940–2020—*Continued*

(Numbers in thousands; civilian noninstitutionalized population, except where noted.)

Year, sex, and age	Total	Elementary 0 to 4 years	Elementary 5 to 8 years	High school 1 to 3 years	High school 4 years	College 1 to 3 years	College 4 years or more	Median years
2002	59,644	1,528	5,639	7,258	20,728	12,117	12,374	NA
2001	58,238	1,544	5,589	7,178	20,622	11,864	11,440	NA
2000	56,008	1,524	5,780	6,921	20,059	11,126	10,598	NA
1999	55,303	1,589	5,978	7,096	19,742	10,722	10,174	NA
1998	54,337	1,624	6,126	7,385	19,526	10,022	9,654	NA
1997	53,352	1,628	6,622	7,543	18,823	9,565	9,169	NA
1996	52,742	1,642	6,716	7,520	18,549	9,642	8,677	NA
1995	52,022	1,755	7,048	7,232	18,320	9,662	8,005	NA
1994	51,516	1,802	7,382	7,454	18,228	8,890	7,761	NA
1993	52,117	2,058	8,038	7,637	18,626	8,106	7,652	NA
1992	51,740	2,118	8,133	7,756	18,397	8,005	7,332	NA
1991	51,439	2,341	8,668	7,675	18,954	6,540	7,258	12.6
1990	50,798	2,349	9,239	7,893	18,050	6,202	7,064	12.3
1989	50,421	2,412	9,395	7,907	18,102	5,914	6,693	12.3
1988	50,128	2,325	9,969	7,860	18,004	5,705	6,263	12.3
1987	49,858	2,408	10,544	7,766	17,310	5,799	6,033	12.2
1986	49,383	2,611	10,699	7,917	16,876	5,515	5,767	12.2
1985	48,969	2,612	11,052	7,872	16,516	5,208	5,708	12.2
1984	48,324	2,584	11,131	7,636	16,353	5,026	5,593	12.2
1983	47,723	2,769	11,348	7,703	15,470	4,915	5,514	12.1
1982	47,102	2,818	11,541	7,751	15,091	4,807	5,095	12.1
1981	46,391	2,983	11,909	7,600	14,464	4,721	4,711	12.0
1980	45,670	2,994	12,326	7,451	13,869	4,494	4,535	12.0
1979	43,806	2,924	12,230	6,999	13,088	4,321	4,245	12.0
1978	42,977	3,013	12,593	7,069	12,376	4,086	3,843	11.6
1977	42,176	3,047	12,740	6,823	11,977	3,835	3,754	11.3
1976	41,429	3,107	12,674	6,915	11,346	3,709	3,677	11.1
1975	40,613	3,303	13,045	6,730	10,798	3,442	3,295	10.8
1974	39,817	3,461	13,302	6,615	10,060	3,233	3,145	10.4
1973	39,163	3,424	13,467	6,504	9,604	3,060	3,105	10.2
1972	38,659	3,471	13,706	6,351	9,136	2,952	3,042	10.0
1971	38,787	3,808	14,430	6,225	8,463	2,878	2,982	9.6
1970	38,126	3,957	14,647	5,877	8,005	2,797	2,843	9.2
1969	37,424	4,012	14,576	5,801	7,768	2,615	2,653	9.1
1968	36,789	4,244	14,522	5,760	7,085	2,624	2,558	8.9
1967	36,155	4,310	14,849	5,495	6,622	2,443	2,434	8.7
1966	35,540	4,438	14,742	5,392	6,240	2,358	2,370	8.6
1965	34,969	4,612	14,814	5,293	5,844	2,194	2,215	8.5
1964	34,335	4,888	14,701	4,954	5,598	2,159	2,033	8.3
1962	33,247	5,048	14,707	4,442	4,994	2,166	1,890	8.1
1960	31,902	5,169	14,944	4,503	3,757	2,051	1,479	8.5
1959	30,567	4,752	13,485	4,060	3,996	1,775	1,545	8.1
1957	29,548	5,153	12,996	3,602	3,864	1,462	1,461	8.0
1952	26,206	4,554	12,638	2,982	3,080	1,346	1,264	7.7
1950	25,427	4,940	11,947	2,791	2,704	1,170	1,005	8.3
1947	23,234	4,393	11,601	2,179	2,581	1,003	825	7.5
1940	19,592	4,178	10,467	1,656	1,633	685	579	8.2
Male								
2020	45,143	566	1,459	2,802	13,410	11,009	15,897	NA
2019	43,789	547	1,649	2,800	12,976	10,724	15,093	NA
2018	42,961	522	1,670	2,851	13,041	10,630	14,247	NA
2017	41,901	561	1,617	2,813	12,808	10,288	13,814	NA
2016	40,988	624	1,708	2,814	12,374	10,236	13,231	NA
2015	39,895	608	1,765	2,707	12,398	9,863	12,556	NA
2014	38,850	544	1,790	2,800	12,150	9,320	12,246	NA
2013	37,621	557	1,790	2,605	11,539	9,060	12,070	NA
2012	36,489	614	1,775	2,754	11,220	8,574	11,552	NA
2011	35,027	597	1,934	2,625	10,676	8,230	10,966	NA
2010	33,778	647	1,923	2,611	10,399	7,672	10,525	NA
2009	32,814	689	1,874	2,669	9,886	7,456	10,241	NA
2008	31,841	631	1,932	2,751	9,510	7,259	9,759	NA
2007	30,920	721	2,060	2,884	9,505	6,723	9,026	NA

Note: Starting in 2012, data were created using population controls based on 2010 Census data. Starting in 2001, data were created using population controls based on Census 2000 data. Also starting in 2001, data are from the expanded CPS sample. Begining with data for 1992, a new question results in different categories than for earlier years. Data shown as 'High School, 4 years' are now collected in the category 'High School Graduate.' Data shown as 'College 1 to 3 years' are now collected in the 'Some college' and the two 'Associate degree' categories. Data shown as 'College 4 years or more,' are now collected in the categories, 'Bachelor's degree,' 'Master's degree,' 'Doctorate degree,' and 'Professional degree.' Due to the change in question format, median years of schooling cannot be derived. Total includes persons who did not report on years of school completed.
NA = Not available.

Table A-33. Years of School Completed by People 25 Years Old and Over, by Age and Sex, Selected Years, 1940–2020—*Continued*

(Numbers in thousands; civilian noninstitutionalized population, except where noted.)

| Year, sex, and age | Total | Elementary | | High school | | College | | Median years |
		0 to 4 years	5 to 8 years	1 to 3 years	4 years	1 to 3 years	4 years or more	
2006	30,060	705	2,090	2,784	9,488	6,193	8,837	NA
2005	29,198	717	2,157	2,896	8,918	6,167	8,341	NA
2004	28,347	639	2,192	2,885	8,631	5,841	8,159	NA
2003	27,694	729	2,423	2,912	8,425	5,694	7,510	NA
2002	26,608	664	2,601	3,048	8,063	5,257	6,975	NA
2001	25,908	697	2,558	2,964	8,073	5,131	6,485	NA
2000	25,023	706	2,696	2,817	7,816	4,906	6,079	NA
1999	24,694	712	2,746	2,911	7,712	4,756	5,856	NA
1998	24,197	755	2,740	3,000	7,745	4,461	5,496	NA
1997	23,668	773	3,026	3,060	7,417	4,139	5,255	NA
1996	23,352	795	3,058	2,998	7,198	4,254	5,055	NA
1995	22,881	839	3,153	2,980	6,980	4,254	4,675	NA
1994	22,669	894	3,327	3,037	6,987	3,962	4,462	NA
1993	23,038	992	3,595	3,174	7,178	3,587	4,508	NA
1992	22,836	1,033	3,676	3,277	6,991	3,549	4,312	NA
1991	22,708	1,217	3,980	3,183	7,287	2,850	4,193	12.4
1990	22,337	1,182	4,141	3,274	6,986	2,707	4,046	12.4
1989	22,167	1,202	4,198	3,317	7,003	2,616	3,829	12.3
1988	21,989	1,117	4,471	3,366	6,968	2,455	3,609	12.3
1987	21,855	1,160	4,762	3,261	6,673	2,504	3,496	12.3
1986	21,622	1,275	4,813	3,286	6,509	2,355	3,385	12.2
1985	21,391	1,252	5,001	3,234	6,387	2,229	3,289	12.2
1984	21,014	1,209	4,951	3,270	6,265	2,185	3,132	12.2
1983	20,769	1,343	4,986	3,282	5,906	2,141	3,117	12.1
1982	20,508	1,362	5,026	3,313	5,759	2,102	2,946	12.1
1981	20,237	1,394	5,165	3,292	5,597	2,032	2,758	12.0
1980	19,967	1,424	5,436	3,206	5,409	1,986	2,506	11.9
1979	19,292	1,446	5,479	2,964	5,167	1,935	2,301	11.8
1978	18,939	1,467	5,701	2,919	4,919	1,824	2,110	11.4
1977	18,608	1,502	5,770	2,787	4,835	1,700	2,011	11.2
1976	18,233	1,507	5,733	2,884	4,473	1,646	1,989	11.0
1975	17,903	1,628	5,845	2,871	4,308	1,480	1,768	10.5
1974	17,579	1,693	6,042	2,817	3,993	1,356	1,682	10.1
1973	17,263	1,678	6,111	2,774	3,811	1,245	1,645	9.9
1972	17,120	1,728	6,252	2,698	3,612	1,215	1,614	9.6
1971	17,288	1,913	6,629	2,668	3,285	1,214	1,579	9.1
1970	17,074	2,011	6,655	2,583	3,127	1,182	1,516	9.0
1969	16,822	2,003	6,701	2,536	3,099	1,086	1,397	8.8
1968	16,609	2,137	6,728	2,523	2,816	1,078	1,328	8.7
1967	16,398	2,247	6,827	2,379	2,685	989	1,271	8.5
1966	16,201	2,288	6,944	2,317	2,491	939	1,223	8.3
1965	16,015	2,368	6,992	2,265	2,331	893	1,164	8.2
1964	15,789	2,504	6,897	2,159	2,237	876	1,113	8.1
1962	15,440	2,644	6,813	2,032	2,030	864	1,057	8.0
1960	14,895	2,704	7,121	1,969	1,453	853	796	8.4
1959	14,304	2,491	6,436	1,759	1,584	718	857	7.9
1957	13,967	2,696	6,244	1,570	1,493	608	831	7.7
1952	12,544	2,428	6,162	1,318	1,262	528	636	7.5
1950	12,277	2,609	5,808	1,209	1,111	500	569	8.2
1947	11,424	2,393	5,656	939	1,109	464	482	7.3
1940	9,815	2,293	5,249	724	660	313	361	8.1
Female								
2020	51,656	687	1,640	3,179	16,120	14,062	15,958	NA
2019	50,755	687	1,786	3,262	16,341	13,862	14,817	NA
2018	49,819	736	1,865	3,422	16,504	13,340	13,953	NA
2017	48,698	719	1,849	3,329	16,107	13,063	13,630	NA
2016	47,694	782	1,875	3,195	16,107	12,745	12,990	NA
2015	46,516	839	1,925	3,570	16,059	11,922	12,201	NA
2014	45,284	821	2,039	3,295	15,812	11,739	11,578	NA
2013	44,158	749	2,141	3,438	15,507	11,327	10,996	NA
2012	42,989	734	2,199	3,590	15,311	10,769	10,384	NA
2011	41,136	775	2,140	3,358	14,946	10,178	9,739	NA

Note: Starting in 2012, data were created using population controls based on 2010 Census data. Starting in 2001, data were created using population controls based on Census 2000 data. Also starting in 2001, data are from the expanded CPS sample. Begining with data for 1992, a new question results in different categories than for earlier years. Data shown as 'High School, 4 years' are now collected in the category 'High School Graduate.' Data shown as 'College 1 to 3 years' are now collected in the 'Some college' and the two 'Associate degree' categories. Data shown as 'College 4 years or more,' are now collected in the categories, 'Bachelor's degree,' 'Master's degree,' 'Doctorate degree,' and 'Professional degree.' Due to the change in question format, median years of schooling cannot be derived. Total includes persons who did not report on years of school completed.
NA – Not available.

Table A-33. Years of School Completed by People 25 Years Old and Over, by Age and Sex, Selected Years, 1940–2020—*Continued*

(Numbers in thousands; civilian noninstitutionalized population, except where noted.)

Year, sex, and age	Total	Years of school completed						Median years
		Elementary		High school		College		
		0 to 4 years	5 to 8 years	1 to 3 years	4 years	1 to 3 years	4 years or more	
2010	40,230	793	2,195	3,440	14,725	9,682	9,395	NA
2009	39,263	867	2,228	3,669	14,268	9,421	8,810	NA
2008	38,251	780	2,362	3,588	14,269	9,119	8,133	NA
2007	37,306	855	2,398	3,796	13,902	8,781	7,573	NA
2006	36,425	922	2,521	3,761	13,472	8,630	7,119	NA
2005	35,547	897	2,645	3,887	13,474	7,916	6,728	NA
2004	34,687	826	2,715	3,936	13,287	7,593	6,329	NA
2003	33,939	860	2,949	3,964	13,129	7,190	5,848	NA
2002	33,035	864	3,038	4,210	12,664	6,860	5,399	NA
2001	32,329	847	3,032	4,213	12,549	6,733	4,956	NA
2000	30,985	817	3,085	4,105	12,243	6,218	4,517	NA
1999	30,609	879	3,232	4,186	12,031	5,965	4,319	NA
1998	30,140	868	3,386	4,386	11,780	5,560	4,160	NA
1997	29,684	855	3,596	4,483	11,407	5,427	3,916	NA
1996	29,390	848	3,659	4,523	11,350	5,387	3,623	NA
1995	29,142	915	3,894	4,255	11,340	5,410	3,330	NA
1994	28,848	909	4,054	4,419	11,242	4,926	3,298	NA
1993	29,080	1,066	4,442	4,462	11,447	4,519	3,149	NA
1992	28,904	1,084	4,456	4,478	11,409	4,455	3,021	NA
1991	28,729	1,125	4,687	4,495	11,667	3,690	3,066	12.3
1990	28,461	1,167	5,098	4,619	11,063	3,495	3,019	12.3
1989	28,255	1,211	5,195	4,587	11,099	3,300	2,863	12.3
1988	28,139	1,208	5,498	4,495	11,034	3,250	2,655	12.3
1987	28,004	1,248	5,782	4,504	10,637	3,294	2,539	12.2
1986	27,762	1,336	5,886	4,630	10,367	3,160	2,382	12.2
1985	27,578	1,360	6,052	4,638	10,129	2,979	2,420	12.2
1984	27,309	1,377	6,183	4,363	10,086	2,843	2,459	12.2
1983	26,954	1,428	6,364	4,423	9,567	2,774	2,398	12.1
1982	26,593	1,458	6,511	4,435	9,330	2,705	2,150	12.1
1981	26,152	1,589	6,742	4,308	8,868	2,690	1,954	12.0
1980	25,703	1,571	6,889	4,245	8,460	2,509	2,030	12.0
1979	24,514	1,474	6,750	4,034	7,920	2,389	1,944	12.0
1978	24,038	1,545	6,889	4,149	7,457	2,263	1,733	11.6
1977	23,568	1,546	6,972	4,034	7,141	2,135	1,742	11.0
1976	23,196	1,602	6,942	4,029	6,871	2,063	1,690	11.0
1975	22,710	1,675	7,198	3,858	6,490	1,962	1,527	10.9
1974	22,238	1,762	7,261	3,799	6,068	1,880	1,463	10.7
1973	21,900	1,746	7,359	3,729	5,790	1,814	1,461	10.5
1972	21,539	1,743	7,455	3,654	5,526	1,737	1,425	10.3
1971	21,500	1,896	7,805	3,556	5,179	1,665	1,402	9.9
1970	21,052	1,946	7,993	3,292	4,879	1,615	1,327	9.5
1969	20,601	2,009	7,878	3,264	4,669	1,526	1,255	9.4
1968	20,180	2,106	7,795	3,237	4,269	1,544	1,229	9.2
1967	19,756	2,063	8,021	3,117	3,937	1,454	1,164	8.9
1966	19,339	2,152	7,797	3,074	3,749	1,419	1,147	8.9
1965	18,955	2,243	7,821	3,026	3,514	1,300	1,048	8.7
1964	18,546	2,383	7,805	2,794	3,360	1,282	920	8.5
1962	17,807	2,404	7,894	2,410	2,964	1,302	833	8.3
1960	17,007	2,465	7,823	2,534	2,304	1,198	683	8.6
1959	16,263	2,261	7,049	2,301	2,412	1,057	688	8.3
1957	15,581	2,457	6,752	2,032	2,371	854	630	8.2
1952	13,662	2,126	6,476	1,664	1,818	818	628	7.9
1950	13,150	2,331	6,139	1,582	1,593	670	436	8.4
1947	11,810	2,000	5,945	1,240	1,472	539	343	7.6
1940	9,777	1,886	5,217	932	973	372	219	8.3

Note: Starting in 2012, data were created using population controls based on 2010 Census data. Starting in 2001, data were created using population controls based on Census 2000 data. Also starting in 2001, data are from the expanded CPS sample. Begining with data for 1992, a new question results in different categories than for earlier years. Data shown as 'High School, 4 years' are now collected in the category 'High School Graduate.' Data shown as 'College 1 to 3 years' are now collected in the 'Some college' and the two 'Associate degree' categories. Data shown as 'College 4 years or more,' are now collected in the categories, 'Bachelor's degree,' 'Master's degree,' 'Doctorate degree,' and 'Professional degree.' Due to the change in question format, median years of schooling cannot be derived. Total includes persons who did not report on years of school completed.
NA = Not available.

This page is intentionally left blank

Table A-34. Mean Earnings of Workers 18 Years Old and Over, by Educational Attainment, Race, Hispanic Origin, and Sex, 1975–2019

(Dollars except as noted.)

Race, sex, year, and Hispanic origin	Total		Not a high school graduate		High school graduate	
	Mean earnings	Number of workers (thousands)	Mean earnings	Number of workers (thousands)	Mean earnings	Number of workers (thousands)
ALL RACES						
Both Sexes						
2019..............................	58,544	167,215	29,278	11,413	39,371	42,598
2018..............................	55,619	165,179	27,037	12,058	38,936	42,882
2017..............................	53,536	163,871	26,832	12,240	38,145	42,816
2016..............................	51,893	162,218	27,800	12,281	36,702	42,897
2015..............................	49,994	161,074	25,315	13,159	35,615	42,404
2014..............................	47,653	158,000	25,236	13,197	34,099	42,529
2013..............................	46,187	156,031	23,755	12,961	32,881	42,433
2012..............................	45,598	155,148	21,622	13,030	32,630	41,915
2011[2]..........................	44,729	152,711	21,107	13,594	32,493	42,129
2010..............................	42,956	151,747	20,935	13,540	30,999	42,650
2009..............................	42,469	152,707	20,241	14,083	30,627	44,396
2008..............................	42,588	155,989	21,023	15,217	31,283	45,182
2007..............................	42,064	155,738	21,484	15,330	31,286	45,393
2006..............................	41,412	154,438	20,873	16,652	31,071	45,936
2005..............................	39,579	152,215	19,915	16,317	29,448	45,652
2004..............................	37,899	150,096	19,169	16,373	28,645	45,545
2003[3]..........................	37,046	148,660	18,734	16,282	27,915	45,064
2002..............................	36,308	148,492	18,826	16,931	27,280	45,407
2001..............................	35,805	147,829	18,793	17,293	26,795	45,641
2000[4]..........................	34,514	147,966	17,738	17,425	25,692	45,977
1999..............................	32,359	146,212	16,127	17,224	24,551	46,531
1998..............................	30,928	142,053	16,053	16,742	23,594	45,987
1997..............................	29,514	140,367	16,124	16,962	22,895	45,976
1996..............................	28,106	138,703	15,011	17,075	22,154	45,908
1995..............................	26,792	136,221	14,013	16,990	21,431	44,546
1994..............................	25,852	135,096	13,697	16,479	20,248	44,614
1993..............................	24,674	133,119	12,820	16,575	19,422	44,779
1992..............................	23,036	131,891	12,685	17,055	18,637	45,600
1991..............................	22,332	130,371	12,613	17,553	18,261	46,508
1990..............................	21,793	130,080	12,582	18,698	17,820	51,977
1989..............................	21,414	129,094	12,242	19,137	17,594	51,846
1988..............................	20,060	127,564	11,889	19,635	16,750	51,297
1987..............................	19,016	124,874	11,824	19,748	15,939	50,815
1986..............................	18,149	122,757	11,203	19,665	15,120	50,104
1985..............................	17,181	120,651	10,726	19,692	14,457	49,674
1984..............................	16,083	118,183	10,384	20,206	13,893	48,452
1983..............................	15,137	115,095	9,853	20,020	13,044	47,560
1982..............................	14,351	113,451	9,387	20,789	12,560	46,584
1981..............................	13,624	113,301	9,357	22,296	12,109	47,332
1980..............................	12,665	111,919	8,845	23,028	11,314	46,795
1979..............................	11,795	110,826	8,420	23,783	10,624	45,497
1978..............................	10,812	106,436	7,759	23,787	9,834	43,510
1977..............................	9,887	103,119	7,066	24,854	9,013	41,696
1976..............................	9,180	100,510	6,720	25,035	8,393	40,570
1975..............................	8,552	97,881	6,198	24,916	7,843	39,827
Male						
2019..............................	67,784	87,767	33,824	7,073	45,188	24,980
2018..............................	65,058	86,913	31,846	7,520	45,259	24,992
2017..............................	62,662	86,872	31,688	7,597	44,466	25,137
2016..............................	61,232	85,718	32,463	7,695	43,534	24,908
2015..............................	58,944	85,263	30,230	8,210	41,942	24,647
2014..............................	56,701	83,402	29,618	8,256	39,874	24,468
2013..............................	54,658	82,576	27,586	8,286	37,763	24,327
2012..............................	54,118	81,979	24,955	8,183	38,454	23,783
2011[2]..........................	52,273	80,502	25,155	8,359	38,679	23,800
2010..............................	50,855	79,949	24,560	8,428	36,281	24,076
2009..............................	50,186	80,799	23,036	8,851	35,468	25,143
2008..............................	51,148	82,727	24,831	9,596	36,753	25,290
2007..............................	50,110	82,932	24,985	9,780	36,839	25,396
2006..............................	49,647	82,310	24,072	10,541	37,356	25,489

[1]For data prior to 1991, "Some college/Associate degree" equals 1 to 3 years of college completed; "Bachelor's degree" equals 4 years of college; "Advanced degree" equals 5 or more years of college completed.
[2]Starting in 2011, earnings data were created using population controls based on Census 2010 data.
[3]Starting in 2003, respondents could choose more than one race. The race data in this table from 2003 onward represent respondents who indicated only one race.
[4]Beginning in 2000, earnings data are from the expanded Current Population Survey (CPS) sample and were calculated using population controls based on Census 2000.
[5]May be of any race.
... = Not available.

Table A-34. Mean Earnings of Workers 18 Years Old and Over, by Educational Attainment, Race, Hispanic Origin, and Sex, 1975–2019—*Continued*

(Dollars except as noted.)

Race, sex, year, and Hispanic origin	Some college or associate's degree[1]		Bachelor's degree[1]		Advanced degree[1]	
	Mean earnings	Number of workers (thousands)	Mean earnings	Number of workers (thousands)	Mean earnings	Number of workers (thousands)
ALL RACES						
Both Sexes						
2019	45,091	46,885	73,163	42,153	106,766	24,164
2018	43,053	46,887	71,155	40,231	99,919	23,118
2017	41,507	47,382	67,763	39,153	98,369	22,277
2016	40,201	48,128	67,267	37,272	95,203	21,639
2015	38,943	47,961	65,482	36,348	92,525	21,199
2014	37,945	47,023	62,466	35,305	88,056	19,944
2013	36,428	46,952	59,661	34,422	90,304	19,261
2012	35,943	47,469	60,159	33,948	89,253	18,783
2011[2]	35,585	45,999	59,415	33,188	87,981	17,800
2010	34,469	45,604	57,619	32,371	83,930	17,582
2009	34,773	45,239	56,665	32,127	85,818	16,860
2008	34,808	46,663	58,613	31,890	83,144	17,035
2007	35,138	46,577	57,181	31,832	80,977	16,604
2006	34,650	45,073	56,788	31,006	82,320	15,769
2005	33,496	45,434	54,689	29,658	79,946	15,152
2004	32,012	44,381	51,554	29,050	78,093	14,746
2003[3]	31,498	44,048	51,206	28,672	74,602	14,592
2002	31,046	43,776	51,194	28,257	72,824	14,119
2001	30,782	43,214	50,623	27,980	72,869	13,700
2000[4]	29,939	43,874	49,595	27,488	71,194	13,200
1999	28,469	43,019	45,644	26,490	67,756	12,949
1998	27,566	41,412	43,782	25,818	63,473	12,095
1997	26,235	40,802	40,478	25,035	63,229	11,591
1996	25,181	40,410	38,112	24,028	61,317	11,281
1995	23,862	40,142	36,980	23,285	56,667	11,258
1994	22,226	40,135	37,224	22,712	56,105	11,155
1993	21,539	39,429	35,121	21,815	55,789	10,521
1992	20,680	37,730	32,525	21,080	48,548	10,426
1991	20,551	35,732	31,323	20,475	46,038	10,103
1990	20,694	28,993	31,112	18,128	41,458	12,285
1989	20,255	28,078	30,736	17,767	41,019	12,265
1988	19,066	27,217	28,344	17,308	37,724	12,109
1987	18,054	26,404	26,919	16,497	35,968	11,411
1986	17,073	26,113	26,511	15,788	34,787	11,087
1985	16,349	25,402	24,877	15,373	32,909	10,510
1984	14,936	24,463	23,072	14,653	30,192	10,410
1983	14,245	23,208	21,532	13,929	28,333	10,377
1982	13,503	22,602	20,272	13,425	26,915	10,051
1981	13,176	21,759	19,006	12,579	25,281	9,336
1980	12,409	21,384	18,075	12,175	23,308	8,535
1979	11,377	21,174	16,514	11,751	21,874	8,621
1978	10,357	20,121	15,291	11,001	20,173	8,017
1977	9,607	18,905	14,207	10,357	19,077	7,309
1976	8,813	17,786	13,033	10,132	17,911	6,985
1975	8,388	16,917	12,332	9,764	16,725	6,457
Male						
2019	54,044	23,341	87,398	20,828	129,882	11,543
2018	52,460	23,286	84,803	20,083	123,215	11,029
2017	50,012	23,606	81,607	19,657	119,590	10,871
2016	48,123	23,891	82,089	18,627	116,617	10,595
2015	46,154	23,578	79,927	18,287	113,279	10,539
2014	46,137	23,057	76,109	17,725	110,645	9,895
2013	43,841	23,112	72,124	17,203	115,282	9,647
2012	43,593	23,267	72,546	17,175	110,501	9,570
2011[2]	43,239	22,469	71,162	16,769	109,063	9,102
2010	41,214	21,978	69,764	16,486	103,488	8,980
2009	41,773	21,895	69,479	16,226	105,636	8,683
2008	42,221	22,830	72,868	16,100	103,980	8,909
2007	41,709	22,916	70,898	16,109	100,550	8,730
2006	41,521	21,952	69,818	15,769	101,441	8,556

[1]For data prior to 1991, "Some college/Associate degree" equals 1 to 3 years of college completed, "Bachelor's degree" equals 4 years of college; "Advanced degree" equals 5 or more years of college completed.
[2]Starting in 2011, earnings data were created using population controls based on Census 2010 data.
[3]Starting in 2003, respondents could choose more than one race. The race data in this table from 2003 onward represent respondents who indicated only one race.
[4]Beginning in 2000, earnings data are from the expanded Current Population Survey (CPS) sample and were calculated using population controls based on Census 2000.
[5]May be of any race.
… = Not available.

Table A-34. Mean Earnings of Workers 18 Years Old and Over, by Educational Attainment, Race, Hispanic Origin, and Sex, 1975–2019—*Continued*

(Dollars except as noted.)

Race, sex, year, and Hispanic origin	Total		Not a high school graduate		High school graduate	
	Mean earnings	Number of workers (thousands)	Mean earnings	Number of workers (thousands)	Mean earnings	Number of workers (thousands)
2005............................	48,034	81,258	23,222	10,273	35,248	25,348
2004............................	45,989	79,776	22,512	10,191	34,054	25,186
2003[3].........................	44,726	78,869	21,447	10,173	33,266	24,292
2002............................	44,310	78,757	22,091	10,526	32,673	24,174
2001............................	43,648	78,342	21,508	10,572	32,363	24,239
2000[4]	42,772	78,319	21,007	10,535	31,446	24,439
1999............................	40,222	77,118	18,769	10,294	30,363	24,456
1998............................	38,134	75,213	19,155	10,085	28,742	24,155
1997............................	36,556	74,596	19,575	10,348	28,307	24,152
1996............................	34,705	73,955	17,826	10,583	27,642	23,966
1995............................	33,251	72,634	16,748	10,312	26,333	23,473
1994............................	32,087	72,246	16,633	9,981	25,038	23,418
1993............................	30,568	71,183	14,946	10,151	23,973	23,388
1992............................	28,148	71,138	14,747	10,661	22,811	23,816
1991............................	27,494	70,145	15,056	10,679	22,663	24,110
1990............................	27,164	70,218	14,991	11,412	22,378	26,753
1989............................	27,025	69,798	14,727	11,774	22,508	26,469
1988............................	25,344	69,006	14,551	11,993	21,481	26,080
1987............................	24,015	67,951	14,544	12,117	20,364	25,981
1986............................	23,057	67,189	13,703	12,208	19,453	25,562
1985............................	21,823	66,439	13,124	12,137	18,575	25,496
1984............................	20,452	65,005	12,775	12,325	18,016	24,827
1983............................	19,175	63,816	12,052	12,376	16,728	24,449
1982............................	18,244	63,489	11,513	12,868	16,160	24,059
1981............................	17,542	63,547	11,668	13,701	15,900	24,435
1980............................	16,382	62,825	11,042	14,273	15,002	24,023
1979............................	15,430	62,464	10,628	14,711	14,317	23,318
1978............................	14,154	60,586	9,894	14,550	13,188	22,650
1977............................	12,888	59,441	8,939	15,369	12,092	21,846
1976............................	11,923	58,419	8,522	15,634	11,189	21,499
1975............................	11,091	57,297	7,843	15,613	10,475	21,347
Female						
2019............................	48,336	79,447	21,869	4,340	31,123	17,618
2018............................	45,136	78,265	19,068	4,537	30,103	17,889
2017............................	43,240	76,999	18,885	4,643	29,158	17,679
2016............................	41,429	76,500	19,974	4,586	27,242	17,988
2015............................	39,929	75,811	17,162	4,949	26,832	17,756
2014............................	37,538	74,597	17,915	4,941	26,275	18,060
2013............................	36,664	73,454	16,964	4,675	26,322	18,106
2012............................	36,052	73,169	15,995	4,847	24,991	18,132
2011[2]..........................	35,205	72,209	14,643	5,234	24,460	18,328
2010............................	34,160	71,799	14,959	5,112	24,153	18,574
2009............................	33,797	71,907	15,514	5,232	24,304	19,253
2008............................	32,922	73,262	14,521	5,621	24,329	19,892
2007............................	32,899	72,805	15,315	5,550	24,234	19,997
2006............................	32,015	72,128	15,352	6,110	23,236	20,447
2005............................	29,897	70,956	14,294	6,044	22,208	20,304
2004............................	28,722	70,320	13,658	6,182	21,954	20,359
2003[3]	28,367	69,790	14,214	6,108	21,659	20,772
2002............................	27,271	69,735	13,459	6,404	21,141	21,233
2001............................	26,962	69,487	14,524	6,720	20,489	21,402
2000[4]	25,228	69,647	12,739	6,890	19,162	21,538
1999............................	23,584	69,094	12,203	6,929	18,112	22,075
1998............................	22,818	66,840	11,353	6,657	17,898	21,832
1997............................	21,528	65,771	10,725	6,614	16,906	21,824
1996............................	20,570	64,748	10,421	6,492	16,161	21,942
1995............................	19,414	63,587	9,790	6,678	15,970	21,073
1994............................	18,684	62,850	9,189	6,498	14,955	21,195
1993............................	17,900	61,937	9,462	6,425	14,446	21,391
1992............................	17,050	60,753	9,248	6,394	14,073	21,783
1991............................	16,320	60,226	8,818	6,875	13,523	22,398
1990............................	15,493	59,862	8,808	7,286	12,986	25,224
1989............................	14,809	59,296	8,268	7,363	12,468	25,377

[1]For data prior to 1991, "Some college/Associate degree" equals 1 to 3 years of college completed; "Bachelor's degree" equals 4 years of college; "Advanced degree" equals 5 or more years of college completed.
[2]Starting in 2011, earnings data were created using population controls based on Census 2010 data.
[3]Starting in 2003, respondents could choose more than one race. The race data in this table from 2003 onward represent respondents who indicated only one race.
[4]Beginning in 2000, earnings data are from the expanded Current Population Survey (CPS) sample and were calculated using population controls based on Census 2000.
[5]May be of any race.
... = Not available.

Table A-34. Mean Earnings of Workers 18 Years Old and Over, by Educational Attainment, Race, Hispanic Origin, and Sex, 1975–2019—*Continued*

(Dollars except as noted.)

Race, sex, year, and Hispanic origin	Some college or associate's degree[1]		Bachelor's degree[1]		Advanced degree[1]	
	Mean earnings	Number of workers (thousands)	Mean earnings	Number of workers (thousands)	Mean earnings	Number of workers (thousands)
2005............................	40,995	22,173	67,980	15,217	100,379	8,245
2004............................	39,488	21,477	63,697	14,877	97,702	8,044
2003[3]........................	38,451	21,534	63,084	14,849	91,831	8,019
2002............................	38,377	21,599	63,503	14,667	90,761	7,788
2001............................	37,429	21,390	63,354	14,507	90,130	7,631
2000[4]........................	37,372	21,526	62,609	14,375	88,077	7,442
1999............................	35,455	21,211	57,669	13,810	84,065	7,347
1998............................	34,179	20,545	55,057	13,486	77,217	6,942
1997............................	32,641	20,359	50,056	13,008	78,032	6,728
1996............................	31,426	20,208	46,702	12,562	74,406	6,636
1995............................	29,851	19,918	46,111	12,251	69,588	6,679
1994............................	27,636	19,859	46,278	12,324	67,032	6,663
1993............................	26,614	19,532	43,499	11,810	68,221	6,302
1992............................	25,366	19,009	39,912	11,340	58,166	6,312
1991............................	25,345	18,075	38,484	11,126	54,448	6,154
1990............................	26,120	14,844	38,901	9,807	49,768	7,402
1989............................	25,555	14,384	38,692	9,737	50,144	7,434
1988............................	23,827	14,019	35,906	9,466	45,677	7,449
1987............................	22,781	13,433	33,677	9,286	43,140	7,134
1986............................	21,784	13,502	33,376	8,908	41,836	7,009
1985............................	20,698	13,385	31,433	8,794	39,768	6,627
1984............................	18,863	12,818	29,203	8,387	35,804	6,648
1983............................	18,052	12,261	27,239	8,010	33,635	6,719
1982............................	17,108	12,103	25,758	7,865	32,109	6,594
1981............................	16,870	11,784	24,353	7,393	30,072	6,235
1980............................	15,871	11,663	23,340	7,132	27,846	5,733
1979............................	14,716	11,781	21,482	6,889	26,411	5,765
1978............................	13,382	11,352	19,861	6,611	24,274	5,422
1977............................	12,393	10,848	18,187	6,341	22,786	5,038
1976............................	11,376	10,282	16,714	6,135	21,202	4,868
1975............................	10,805	9,851	15,758	5,960	19,672	4,526
Female						
2019............................	36,214	23,543	59,259	21,325	85,623	12,620
2018............................	33,771	23,600	57,551	20,148	78,664	12,088
2017............................	33,063	23,775	53,804	19,495	78,142	11,405
2016............................	32,391	24,236	52,461	18,645	74,656	11,043
2015............................	31,970	24,382	50,056	18,061	72,006	10,660
2014............................	30,064	23,966	48,650	17,580	65,814	10,049
2013............................	29,242	23,840	47,209	17,218	65,242	9,614
2012............................	28,588	24,202	47,477	16,773	67,182	9,213
2011[2]........................	28,275	23,529	47,418	16,419	65,915	8,697
2010............................	28,195	23,626	45,015	15,885	63,515	8,602
2009............................	28,207	23,344	43,589	15,900	64,771	8,176
2008............................	27,708	23,833	44,078	15,789	60,301	8,126
2007............................	28,773	23,660	43,127	15,722	59,273	7,873
2006............................	28,126	23,121	43,302	15,237	59,636	7,213
2005............................	26,348	23,260	40,684	14,440	55,553	6,906
2004............................	25,003	22,904	38,806	14,173	54,559	6,702
2003[3]........................	24,848	22,514	38,447	13,823	53,579	6,572
2002............................	23,905	22,176	37,909	13,589	50,756	6,330
2001............................	24,268	21,824	36,913	13,472	51,160	6,068
2000[4]........................	22,779	22,348	35,328	13,113	49,368	5,757
1999............................	21,675	21,808	32,547	12,680	46,369	5,602
1998............................	21,056	20,867	31,452	12,332	44,954	5,153
1997............................	19,856	20,442	30,119	12,027	42,744	4,863
1996............................	18,933	20,202	28,701	11,466	42,625	4,646
1995............................	17,962	20,224	26,841	11,034	37,813	4,578
1994............................	16,928	20,276	26,483	10,388	39,905	4,493
1993............................	16,555	19,897	25,232	10,005	37,212	4,218
1992............................	15,922	18,721	23,926	9,741	33,791	4,114
1991............................	15,643	17,657	22,800	9,349	32,932	3,949
1990............................	15,002	14,149	21,933	8,321	28,862	4,883
1989............................	14,688	13,694	21,089	8,030	26,977	4,831

[1]For data prior to 1991, "Some college/Associate degree" equals 1 to 3 years of college completed; "Bachelor's degree" equals 4 years of college; "Advanced degree" equals 5 or more years of college completed.
[2]Starting in 2011, earnings data were created using population controls based on Census 2010 data.
[3]Starting in 2003, respondents could choose more than one race. The race data in this table from 2003 onward represent respondents who indicated only one race.
[4]Beginning in 2000, earnings data are from the expanded Current Population Survey (CPS) sample and were calculated using population controls based on Census 2000.
[5]May be of any race.
… = Not available.

Table A-34. Mean Earnings of Workers 18 Years Old and Over, by Educational Attainment, Race, Hispanic Origin, and Sex, 1975–2019—*Continued*

(Dollars except as noted.)

Race, sex, year, and Hispanic origin	Total		Not a high school graduate		High school graduate	
	Mean earnings	Number of workers (thousands)	Mean earnings	Number of workers (thousands)	Mean earnings	Number of workers (thousands)
1988	13,833	58,558	7,711	7,642	11,857	25,217
1987	13,049	56,923	7,504	7,631	11,309	24,834
1986	12,214	55,568	7,109	7,457	10,606	24,542
1985	11,493	54,212	6,874	7,555	10,115	24,178
1984	10,742	53,178	6,644	7,881	9,561	23,625
1983	10,111	51,279	6,292	7,644	9,147	23,111
1982	9,403	49,962	5,932	7,921	8,715	22,525
1981	8,619	49,754	5,673	8,595	8,063	22,897
1980	7,909	49,094	5,263	8,755	7,423	22,772
1979	7,099	48,362	4,840	9,072	6,741	22,179
1978	6,396	45,850	4,397	9,237	6,192	20,860
1977	5,804	43,678	4,032	9,485	5,624	19,850
1976	5,373	42,091	3,723	9,401	5,240	19,071
1975	4,968	40,584	3,438	9,303	4,802	18,480

WHITE

Both Sexes

Race, sex, year, and Hispanic origin	Total		Not a high school graduate		High school graduate	
2019	59,739	129,846	29,207	9,001	40,941	32,891
2018	57,035	128,742	27,675	9,470	40,744	33,256
2017	54,838	128,070	27,220	9,696	39,781	33,308
2016	53,178	127,241	28,489	9,615	38,326	33,491
2015	51,183	127,291	26,441	10,404	37,106	33,342
2014	48,971	125,227	26,065	10,553	35,528	33,616
2013	47,452	124,663	24,363	10,220	34,192	33,746
2012	46,844	124,316	22,048	10,491	33,928	33,498
2011[2]	46,053	123,044	21,704	10,891	33,719	33,803
2010	44,257	122,556	21,540	10,753	32,132	34,288
2009	43,337	125,151	20,457	11,507	31,429	36,125
2008	43,666	127,552	21,590	12,379	32,126	36,819
2007	43,139	127,413	22,289	12,363	32,223	37,058
2006	42,395	126,570	21,464	13,582	32,083	37,362
2005	40,717	124,870	20,264	13,157	30,569	37,122
2004	38,946	123,452	19,367	13,290	29,605	37,115
2003[3]	38,053	122,599	19,110	13,094	28,708	36,951
2002	37,376	122,699	19,264	13,740	28,145	37,380
2001	36,844	122,930	19,120	14,012	27,700	37,969
2000[4]	35,527	123,039	18,285	14,172	26,444	38,133
1999	33,342	121,518	16,651	13,912	25,267	38,622
1998	32,057	119,201	16,474	13,531	24,409	38,397
1997	30,515	117,985	16,596	13,780	23,618	38,409
1996	28,844	117,230	15,358	13,972	22,782	38,463
1995	27,556	115,636	14,234	13,869	22,154	37,802
1994	26,696	114,586	13,941	13,119	20,911	37,562
1993	25,440	113,342	13,171	13,480	19,918	37,826
1992	23,739	112,406	13,046	13,863	19,171	38,704
1991	22,998	111,842	12,914	14,041	18,766	39,769
1990	22,401	111,972	12,773	15,191	18,257	44,635
1989	22,035	111,243	12,654	15,628	18,011	44,726
1988	20,616	110,159	12,236	16,042	17,183	44,399
1987	19,599	108,407	12,502	16,165	16,339	44,235
1986	18,698	106,384	11,605	16,094	15,514	43,593
1985	17,709	104,818	11,115	16,149	14,815	43,347
1984	16,546	103,022	10,732	16,559	14,274	42,547
1983	15,556	101,035	10,239	16,568	13,357	42,007
1982	14,767	99,488	9,719	17,132	12,854	41,157
1981	14,027	99,510	9,737	18,298	12,355	42,080
1980	13,040	98,358	9,743	18,925	11,524	41,600
1979	12,155	97,544	8,827	19,504	10,431	40,458
1978	11,135	94,002	8,135	19,516	10,020	38,915
1977	10,191	91,254	7,415	20,492	9,173	37,521
1976	9,469	89,099	7,018	20,625	8,559	36,523
1975	8,815	86,894	6,438	20,696	8,005	35,799

[1]For data prior to 1991, "Some college/Associate degree" equals 1 to 3 years of college completed; "Bachelor's degree" equals 4 years of college; "Advanced degree" equals 5 or more years of college completed.
[2]Starting in 2011, earnings data were created using population controls based on Census 2010 data.
[3]Starting in 2003, respondents could choose more than one race. The race data in this table from 2003 onward represent respondents who indicated only one race.
[4]Beginning in 2000, earnings data are from the expanded Current Population Survey (CPS) sample and were calculated using population controls based on Census 2000.
[5]May be of any race.
… = Not available.

Table A-34. Mean Earnings of Workers 18 Years Old and Over, by Educational Attainment, Race, Hispanic Origin, and Sex, 1975–2019—*Continued*

(Dollars except as noted.)

Race, sex, year, and Hispanic origin	Some college or associate's degree[1]		Bachelor's degree[1]		Advanced degree[1]	
	Mean earnings	Number of workers (thousands)	Mean earnings	Number of workers (thousands)	Mean earnings	Number of workers (thousands)
1988............................	14,009	13,198	19,216	7,842	25,010	4,660
1987............................	13,158	12,971	18,217	7,211	24,004	4,277
1986............................	12,029	12,611	17,623	6,880	22,672	4,078
1985............................	11,504	12,017	16,114	6,579	21,202	3,883
1984............................	10,614	11,645	14,865	6,266	20,275	3,762
1983............................	9,981	10,947	13,808	5,919	18,593	3,658
1982............................	9,348	10,499	12,511	5,560	17,009	3,457
1981............................	8,811	9,975	11,384	5,186	15,647	3,101
1980............................	8,256	9,721	10,628	5,043	14,022	2,802
1979............................	7,190	9,393	9,474	4,862	12,717	2,856
1978............................	6,441	8,769	8,408	4,390	11,603	2,595
1977............................	5,856	8,057	7,923	4,016	10,848	2,271
1976............................	5,301	7,504	7,383	3,997	10,345	2,117
1975............................	5,019	7,066	6,963	3,804	9,818	1,931

WHITE

Both Sexes

2019............................	46,879	36,653	74,966	32,947	106,753	18,352
2018............................	44,379	36,543	73,348	31,770	100,195	17,702
2017............................	42,859	36,748	69,284	31,127	99,044	17,190
2016............................	41,583	37,481	68,538	29,950	95,647	16,701
2015............................	39,959	37,686	66,926	29,216	92,640	16,640
2014............................	39,590	36,920	63,422	28,313	88,835	15,823
2013............................	37,528	37,388	60,962	27,869	91,369	15,439
2012............................	36,943	37,706	61,527	27,651	90,948	14,967
2011[2].........................	36,204	36,861	61,253	27,096	90,060	14,391
2010............................	36,330	36,009	59,285	26,579	85,255	14,326
2009............................	35,634	37,035	57,762	26,595	86,188	13,887
2008............................	35,622	37,891	59,866	26,487	84,739	13,973
2007............................	35,685	37,988	58,652	26,310	82,384	13,692
2006............................	35,338	36,878	57,932	25,763	83,185	12,983
2005............................	34,326	37,409	55,785	24,652	81,697	12,527
2004............................	32,764	36,551	52,877	24,061	78,963	12,435
2003[3].........................	32,346	36,318	52,259	24,010	75,638	12,226
2002............................	31,878	36,023	52,479	23,638	73,870	11,916
2001............................	31,482	35,722	51,631	23,531	74,398	11,694
2000[4].........................	30,638	36,334	50,969	23,110	71,903	11,288
1999............................	29,225	35,575	46,914	22,382	68,418	11,027
1998............................	28,318	34,540	44,852	22,266	65,379	10,467
1997............................	26,906	34,274	41,439	21,528	65,058	9,994
1996............................	25,511	34,087	38,936	20,846	61,779	9,861
1995............................	24,349	33,850	37,711	20,203	57,054	9,914
1994............................	22,648	34,006	37,996	19,917	56,475	9,981
1993............................	21,924	33,728	35,846	18,922	56,964	9,386
1992............................	21,178	32,164	33,007	18,422	49,315	9,254
1991............................	21,013	30,977	31,837	18,035	46,496	9,019
1990............................	21,095	25,105	31,626	15,993	41,908	11,049
1989............................	20,678	24,212	31,266	15,723	41,610	10,952
1988............................	19,384	23,643	28,886	15,221	38,129	10,854
1987............................	18,265	23,083	27,741	14,624	36,175	10,300
1986............................	17,371	22,653	27,061	14,055	35,265	9,987
1985............................	16,701	22,131	25,376	13,670	33,401	9,522
1984............................	15,197	21,451	23,472	13,056	30,515	9,409
1983............................	14,486	20,452	21,914	12,577	28,532	9,430
1982............................	13,799	19,967	20,760	12,103	27,040	9,127
1981............................	13,424	19,102	19,389	11,450	25,564	8,582
1980............................	12,677	18,888	18,434	11,067	23,466	7,876
1979............................	11,574	18,835	16,758	10,807	22,085	7,940
1978............................	10,504	18,022	15,463	10,171	20,531	7,376
1977............................	9,771	16,968	14,462	9,534	19,337	6,739
1976............................	8,958	16,127	13,279	9,325	18,153	6,498
1975............................	8,525	15,423	12,597	8,955	16,920	6,021

[1]For data prior to 1991, "Some college/Associate degree" equals 1 to 3 years of college completed; "Bachelor's degree" equals 4 years of college, "Advanced degree" equals 5 or more years of college completed.
[2]Starting in 2011, earnings data were created using population controls based on Census 2010 data.
[3]Starting in 2003, respondents could choose more than one race. The race data in this table from 2003 onward represent respondents who indicated only one race.
[4]Beginning in 2000, earnings data are from the expanded Current Population Survey (CPS) sample and were calculated using population controls based on Census 2000.
[5]May be of any race.
... = Not available.

Table A-34. Mean Earnings of Workers 18 Years Old and Over, by Educational Attainment, Race, Hispanic Origin, and Sex, 1975–2019—*Continued*

(Dollars except as noted.)

Race, sex, year, and Hispanic origin	Total		Not a high school graduate		High school graduate	
	Mean earnings	Number of workers (thousands)	Mean earnings	Number of workers (thousands)	Mean earnings	Number of workers (thousands)
Male						
2019.............................	69,554	69,489	33,880	5,742	47,041	19,766
2018.............................	66,977	69,057	32,458	6,098	47,199	19,815
2017.............................	64,266	69,222	32,096	6,277	46,284	19,933
2016.............................	62,680	68,496	33,153	6,255	45,390	19,941
2015.............................	60,652	68,610	31,336	6,755	43,711	19,807
2014.............................	58,387	67,466	30,342	6,858	41,492	19,815
2013.............................	56,215	67,148	28,253	6,773	39,191	19,796
2012.............................	55,802	66,906	25,725	6,809	40,070	19,390
2011[2]...........................	55,013	66,151	25,819	6,917	40,247	19,524
2010.............................	52,646	65,828	25,311	6,896	37,684	19,685
2009.............................	51,287	67,464	23,353	7,426	36,418	20,855
2008.............................	52,672	68,816	25,386	8,113	37,852	20,899
2007.............................	51,781	69,099	25,886	8,170	38,214	21,129
2006.............................	51,013	68,752	24,579	8,932	38,833	21,090
2005.............................	49,611	67,874	23,556	8,582	36,753	20,914
2004.............................	47,389	66,714	22,596	8,592	35,362	20,761
2003[3]...........................	46,114	66,199	21,791	8,500	34,224	20,238
2002.............................	45,793	66,202	22,539	8,841	33,920	20,156
2001.............................	45,071	66,216	22,006	8,833	33,545	20,465
2000[4]...........................	44,181	66,222	21,561	8,859	32,528	20,553
1999.............................	41,622	65,134	19,279	8,549	31,289	20,579
1998.............................	39,638	64,181	19,632	8,430	29,782	20,388
1997.............................	37,933	63,738	20,071	8,670	29,298	20,426
1996.............................	35,821	63,532	18,246	8,899	28,591	20,329
1995.............................	34,276	62,520	17,032	8,660	27,467	19,982
1994.............................	33,292	62,029	16,835	8,133	26,125	19,833
1993.............................	31,719	61,356	15,295	8,430	24,781	19,835
1992.............................	29,201	61,270	15,180	8,776	23,677	20,333
1991.............................	28,516	60,770	15,499	8,720	23,475	20,765
1990.............................	28,105	60,676	15,319	9,476	23,135	23,088
1989.............................	28,013	60,877	15,217	9,805	23,291	23,029
1988.............................	26,184	60,221	14,943	10,008	22,216	22,707
1987.............................	24,898	59,468	15,303	10,132	21,012	22,682
1986.............................	23,892	58,932	14,168	10,239	20,128	22,392
1985.............................	22,604	58,385	13,579	10,163	19,203	22,357
1984.............................	21,174	57,362	13,248	10,280	18,681	21,989
1983.............................	19,812	56,641	12,573	10,387	17,281	21,733
1982.............................	18,859	56,364	11,952	10,816	16,662	21,436
1981.............................	18,141	56,397	12,094	11,523	16,352	21,809
1980.............................	16,945	55,772	11,539	11,937	15,382	21,453
1979.............................	15,971	55,556	11,127	12,291	13,916	20,834
1978.............................	14,627	54,113	10,358	12,141	13,534	20,328
1977.............................	13,329	53,174	9,366	12,903	12,377	19,773
1976.............................	12,342	52,312	8,867	13,117	11,497	19,446
1975.............................	11,448	51,510	8,110	13,191	10,726	19,361
Female						
2019.............................	48,440	60,356	20,973	3,258	31,754	13,124
2018.............................	45,531	59,684	19,024	3,371	31,228	13,441
2017.............................	43,749	58,847	18,270	3,419	30,089	13,374
2016.............................	42,098	58,744	19,807	3,360	27,929	13,549
2015.............................	40,112	58,680	17,379	3,649	27,440	13,535
2014.............................	37,971	57,761	18,129	3,695	26,965	13,800
2013.............................	37,222	57,515	16,718	3,446	27,097	13,949
2012.............................	36,404	57,409	15,250	3,682	25,487	14,107
2011[2]...........................	35,635	56,892	14,541	3,974	24,793	14,279
2010.............................	34,521	56,728	14,799	3,857	24,648	14,603
2009.............................	34,040	57,687	15,187	4,080	24,615	15,270
2008.............................	33,115	58,735	14,370	4,265	24,610	15,919
2007.............................	32,899	58,313	15,278	4,192	24,276	15,929
2006.............................	32,148	57,818	15,483	4,650	23,334	16,272
2005.............................	30,125	56,995	14,086	4,575	22,590	16,208
2004.............................	29,018	56,738	13,461	4,698	22,296	16,354

[1]For data prior to 1991, "Some college/Associate degree" equals 1 to 3 years of college completed; "Bachelor's degree" equals 4 years of college; "Advanced degree" equals 5 or more years of college completed.
[2]Starting in 2011, earnings data were created using population controls based on Census 2010 data.
[3]Starting in 2003, respondents could choose more than one race. The race data in this table from 2003 onward represent respondents who indicated only one race.
[4]Beginning in 2000, earnings data are from the expanded Current Population Survey (CPS) sample and were calculated using population controls based on Census 2000.
[5]May be of any race.
… = Not available.

Table A-34. Mean Earnings of Workers 18 Years Old and Over, by Educational Attainment, Race, Hispanic Origin, and Sex, 1975–2019—*Continued*

(Dollars except as noted.)

Race, sex, year, and Hispanic origin	Some college or associate's degree[1]		Bachelor's degree[1]		Advanced degree[1]	
	Mean earnings	Number of workers (thousands)	Mean earnings	Number of workers (thousands)	Mean earnings	Number of workers (thousands)
Male						
2019.............................	56,511	18,621	90,516	16,530	131,420	8,828
2018.............................	54,482	18,546	87,842	16,080	125,533	8,516
2017.............................	51,974	18,724	83,478	15,913	122,160	8,373
2016.............................	50,063	18,951	84,069	15,136	116,854	8,211
2015.............................	47,900	18,905	82,495	14,884	115,094	8,257
2014.............................	48,405	18,518	78,348	14,409	112,351	7,864
2013.............................	45,403	18,729	74,018	14,113	117,959	7,735
2012.............................	45,049	18,825	74,594	14,268	114,150	7,612
2011[2]	44,155	18,279	73,630	13,978	112,515	7,451
2010.............................	42,479	18,019	72,241	13,845	106,142	7,383
2009.............................	42,884	18,273	71,286	13,740	106,571	7,168
2008.............................	43,463	18,849	75,053	13,596	107,099	7,356
2007.............................	42,903	18,995	73,477	13,577	103,293	7,227
2006.............................	42,684	18,340	71,735	13,326	103,340	7,063
2005.............................	42,206	18,583	69,852	12,900	103,144	6,893
2004.............................	40,617	18,005	65,583	12,582	99,899	6,774
2003[3]	39,594	18,060	65,264	12,665	94,017	6,734
2002.............................	39,605	18,068	65,439	12,512	92,733	6,623
2001.............................	38,501	17,957	65,046	12,396	92,304	6,562
2000[4]	38,476	18,179	64,831	12,271	89,812	6,359
1999.............................	36,757	17,031	59,672	11,869	85,405	6,307
1998.............................	35,277	17,407	56,620	11,874	79,734	6,083
1997.............................	33,691	17,423	51,678	11,340	80,322	5,879
1996.............................	32,238	17,418	48,014	11,065	75,481	5,821
1995.............................	30,529	17,136	47,016	10,851	70,155	5,891
1994.............................	28,240	17,091	47,575	10,992	67,629	5,979
1993.............................	27,297	16,959	44,505	10,452	70,000	5,680
1992.............................	26,095	16,468	40,802	10,040	59,297	5,651
1991.............................	26,090	15,873	39,547	9,893	55,256	5,519
1990.............................	26,841	13,003	39,780	8,770	50,385	6,731
1989.............................	26,260	12,582	39,654	8,750	51,031	6,710
1988.............................	24,462	12,277	36,637	8,467	46,181	6,762
1987.............................	23,310	11,771	34,865	8,384	43,440	6,499
1986.............................	22,303	11,846	34,273	8,041	42,480	6,413
1985.............................	21,240	11,831	32,165	7,970	40,358	6,064
1984.............................	19,344	11,387	29,781	7,624	36,219	6,081
1983.............................	18,388	10,974	27,726	7,379	33,981	6,168
1982.............................	17,571	10,822	26,404	7,242	32,266	6,047
1981.............................	17,303	10,448	24,943	6,824	30,396	5,794
1980.............................	16,313	10,400	23,803	6,618	27,991	5,363
1979.............................	15,043	10,572	21,785	6,464	26,645	5,395
1978.............................	13,589	10,350	20,085	6,205	24,635	5,088
1977.............................	12,657	9,853	18,521	5,941	23,093	4,704
1976.............................	11,616	9,394	16,995	5,765	21,490	4,589
1975.............................	11,028	9,096	16,079	5,587	19,858	4,275
Female						
2019.............................	36,933	18,032	59,309	16,417	83,885	9,523
2018.............................	33,968	17,996	58,494	15,690	76,703	9,185
2017.............................	33,390	18,023	54,436	15,213	77,089	8,816
2016.............................	32,911	18,530	52,669	14,814	75,138	8,490
2015.............................	31,966	18,781	50,759	14,332	70,520	8,382
2014.............................	30,718	18,401	47,954	13,904	65,599	7,959
2013.............................	29,622	18,658	47,565	13,755	64,670	7,704
2012.............................	28,861	18,881	47,596	13,383	66,034	7,355
2011[2]	28,383	18,501	48,064	13,117	65,952	6,940
2010.............................	28,400	18,590	45,200	12,735	63,046	6,943
2009.............................	28,573	16,762	43,309	12,855	64,441	6,718
2008.............................	27,859	19,041	43,848	12,891	59,877	6,616
2007.............................	28,466	18,993	42,846	12,733	59,006	6,464
2006.............................	28,069	18,537	43,142	12,437	59,141	5,920
2005.............................	26,547	18,825	40,344	11,751	55,461	5,634
2004.............................	25,140	18,546	38,950	11,479	53,910	5,661

[1]For data prior to 1991, "Some college/Associate degree" equals 1 to 3 years of college completed; "Bachelor's degree" equals 4 years of college; "Advanced degree" equals 5 or more years of college completed.
[2]Starting in 2011, earnings data were created using population controls based on Census 2010 data.
[3]Starting in 2003, respondents could choose more than one race. The race data in this table from 2003 onward represent respondents who indicated only one race.
[4]Beginning in 2000, earnings data are from the expanded Current Population Survey (CPS) sample and were calculated using population controls based on Census 2000.
[5]May be of any race.
... = Not available.

Table A-34. Mean Earnings of Workers 18 Years Old and Over, by Educational Attainment, Race, Hispanic Origin, and Sex, 1975–2019—*Continued*

(Dollars except as noted.)

Race, sex, year, and Hispanic origin	Total		Not a high school graduate		High school graduate	
	Mean earnings	Number of workers (thousands)	Mean earnings	Number of workers (thousands)	Mean earnings	Number of workers (thousands)
2003[3]	28,591	56,400	14,149	4,593	22,028	16,712
2002	27,512	56,496	13,354	4,898	21,388	17,224
2001	27,240	56,714	14,197	5,178	20,866	17,503
2000[4]	25,441	56,816	12,823	5,313	19,330	17,579
1999	23,778	56,385	12,463	5,364	18,400	18,044
1998	23,213	55,020	11,255	5,102	18,327	18,009
1997	21,779	54,247	10,700	5,111	17,166	17,983
1996	20,590	53,697	10,290	5,073	16,270	18,134
1995	19,647	53,117	9,582	5,208	16,196	17,820
1994	18,912	52,557	9,220	4,987	15,078	17,729
1993	18,028	51,986	9,624	5,050	14,557	17,991
1992	17,194	51,137	9,363	5,087	14,184	18,370
1991	16,431	51,072	8,677	5,321	13,621	19,004
1990	15,559	50,905	8,725	5,715	13,031	21,547
1989	14,810	50,366	8,338	5,823	12,406	21,697
1988	13,902	49,938	7,747	6,034	11,915	21,692
1987	13,161	48,939	7,798	6,033	11,421	21,553
1986	12,247	47,452	7,123	5,855	10,641	21,201
1985	11,555	46,433	6,931	5,986	10,142	20,990
1984	10,732	45,660	6,614	6,279	9,561	20,558
1983	10,126	44,394	6,317	6,181	9,150	20,274
1982	9,419	43,124	5,896	6,316	8,714	19,721
1981	8,646	43,113	5,727	6,775	8,054	20,271
1980	7,926	42,586	6,675	6,988	7,415	20,147
1979	7,105	41,988	4,909	7,213	6,731	19,624
1978	6,398	39,889	4,476	7,375	6,176	18,587
1977	5,808	38,080	4,097	7,589	5,604	17,748
1976	5,383	36,787	3,788	7,508	5,214	17,077
1975	4,982	35,384	3,500	7,505	4,800	16,438
NON-HISPANIC WHITE						
Both Sexes						
2019	64,433	103,533	30,069	3,494	42,902	24,523
2018	61,057	103,357	27,707	3,784	42,466	25,039
2017	58,601	103,373	27,145	4,032	41,289	25,484
2016	56,574	103,334	27,014	3,981	39,265	25,971
2015	54,352	103,957	26,974	4,394	38,588	25,921
2014	52,171	102,756	29,080	4,344	36,826	26,583
2013	50,604	102,814	26,750	4,136	35,595	27,119
2012	49,981	102,974	23,126	4,503	35,399	26,822
2011[2]	49,147	102,365	22,642	4,849	35,365	27,313
2010	47,033	102,462	22,584	4,822	33,360	28,045
2009	45,939	105,137	21,229	5,216	32,562	29,860
2008	46,179	107,294	21,765	5,798	33,159	30,598
2007	45,542	107,434	23,015	5,908	33,094	30,855
2006	44,813	106,828	22,206	6,876	32,931	31,345
2005	42,963	106,337	21,134	6,603	31,445	31,484
2004	40,943	105,506	19,742	6,755	30,197	31,793
2003[3]	40,094	105,214	19,769	6,768	29,571	31,831
2002	39,220	105,706	19,423	7,380	28,756	32,365
2001	38,711	106,384	19,659	7,812	28,426	33,050
2000[4]	37,346	106,709	19,147	7,957	27,122	33,231
1999	35,010	106,139	17,098	8,171	25,924	33,983
1998	33,336	105,523	16,837	8,488	24,801	34,344
Male						
2019	75,888	54,723	34,672	2,235	49,578	14,670
2018	72,737	54,698	33,657	2,360	49,509	14,761
2017	69,548	55,091	32,263	2,530	48,476	15,170
2016	67,180	54,893	31,668	2,543	46,416	15,315
2015	65,206	55,185	33,263	2,799	45,748	15,274
2014	63,100	54,432	35,105	2,752	43,312	15,583
2013	60,804	54,529	32,329	2,717	40,991	15,819

[1]For data prior to 1991, "Some college/Associate degree" equals 1 to 3 years of college completed; "Bachelor's degree" equals 4 years of college; "Advanced degree" equals 5 or more years of college completed.
[2]Starting in 2011, earnings data were created using population controls based on Census 2010 data.
[3]Starting in 2003, respondents could choose more than one race. The race data in this table from 2003 onward represent respondents who indicated only one race.
[4]Beginning in 2000, earnings data are from the expanded Current Population Survey (CPS) sample and were calculated using population controls based on Census 2000.
[5]May be of any race.
... = Not available.

Table A-34. Mean Earnings of Workers 18 Years Old and Over, by Educational Attainment, Race, Hispanic Origin, and Sex, 1975–2019—*Continued*

(Dollars except as noted.)

Race, sex, year, and Hispanic origin	Some college or associate's degree[1]		Bachelor's degree[1]		Advanced degree[1]	
	Mean earnings	Number of workers (thousands)	Mean earnings	Number of workers (thousands)	Mean earnings	Number of workers (thousands)
2003[3]	25,177	18,258	37,739	11,344	53,102	5,492
2002	24,101	17,954	37,903	11,126	50,270	5,293
2001	24,387	17,764	36,698	11,135	51,499	5,131
2000[4]	22,790	18,155	35,273	10,838	48,982	4,929
1999	21,655	17,744	32,510	10,513	45,722	4,720
1998	21,246	17,132	31,406	10,393	45,462	4,384
1997	19,892	16,852	30,041	10,188	43,236	4,114
1996	18,482	16,669	28,667	9,781	42,049	4,041
1995	18,011	16,714	26,916	9,352	37,864	4,022
1994	16,998	16,915	26,198	8,925	39,816	4,002
1993	16,490	16,769	25,161	8,470	36,988	3,705
1992	16,018	15,695	23,670	8,382	33,655	3,602
1991	15,677	15,104	22,469	8,143	32,685	3,501
1990	14,922	12,102	21,725	7,223	28,694	4,318
1989	14,640	11,630	20,741	6,973	26,709	4,242
1988	13,898	11,366	19,169	6,754	24,824	4,092
1987	13,015	11,312	18,170	6,240	23,753	3,801
1986	11,964	10,807	17,418	6,014	22,320	3,574
1985	11,488	10,300	15,883	5,700	21,202	3,458
1984	10,504	10,064	14,617	5,432	20,092	3,328
1983	9,969	9,478	13,664	5,198	18,230	3,262
1982	9,336	9,145	12,352	4,061	16,779	3,080
1981	8,740	8,654	11,196	4,626	15,523	2,788
1980	8,221	8,488	10,447	4,449	13,809	2,513
1979	7,135	8,263	9,275	4,343	12,420	2,545
1978	6,342	7,672	8,231	3,966	11,404	2,288
1977	5,774	7,115	7,750	3,593	10,655	2,035
1976	5,250	6,733	7,262	3,560	10,131	1,909
1975	4,926	6,327	6,822	3,368	9,728	1,746
NON-HISPANIC WHITE						
Both Sexes						
2019	48,628	29,687	77,313	29,097	108,813	16,731
2018	45,772	29,939	74,950	28,312	101,350	16,281
2017	43,996	30,141	71,054	27,773	100,150	15,941
2016	42,932	30,953	70,220	26,916	96,689	15,510
2015	40,812	31,693	67,636	26,508	93,599	15,438
2014	40,487	31,236	64,462	25,783	89,735	14,808
2013	38,371	31,688	61,913	25,437	92,569	14,432
2012	37,942	32,362	62,537	25,246	91,627	14,039
2011[2]	36,992	31,780	62,389	24,891	90,659	13,529
2010	36,079	31,698	60,257	24,425	86,040	13,473
2009	36,249	32,430	58,487	24,533	86,770	13,095
2008	36,158	33,221	60,866	24,445	85,017	13,230
2007	36,290	33,431	59,727	24,366	82,900	12,871
2006	35,872	32,403	58,917	23,855	83,785	12,347
2005	34,866	33,355	56,462	23,013	82,205	11,879
2004	33,217	32,560	53,411	22,545	79,355	11,853
2003[3]	32,825	32,460	52,856	22,474	76,200	11,680
2002	32,318	32,344	53,185	22,221	74,122	11,395
2001	31,905	32,118	52,300	22,204	74,932	11,198
2000[4]	31,217	32,836	51,351	21,824	72,356	10,859
1999	29,765	32,155	47,480	21,261	68,946	10,569
1998	23,897	31,459	45,342	21,175	65,461	10,059
Male						
2019	58,996	15,056	93,400	14,709	134,870	8,051
2018	56,700	15,278	90,455	14,407	126,583	7,890
2017	53,779	15,353	85,885	14,239	123,866	7,797
2016	51,782	15,718	86,312	13,676	118,068	7,639
2015	49,241	15,920	83,548	13,498	116,321	7,692
2014	49,712	15,606	80,075	13,117	113,515	7,372
2013	46,713	15,873	75,345	12,910	120,004	7,208

[1]For data prior to 1991, "Some college/Associate degree" equals 1 to 3 years of college completed; "Bachelor's degree" equals 4 years of college; "Advanced degree" equals 5 or more years of college completed.
[2]Starting in 2011, earnings data were created using population controls based on Census 2010 data.
[3]Starting in 2003, respondents could choose more than one race. The race data in this table from 2003 onward represent respondents who indicated only one race.
[4]Beginning in 2000, earnings data are from the expanded Current Population Survey (CPS) sample and were calculated using population controls based on Census 2000.
[5]May be of any race.
… = Not available.

Table A-34. Mean Earnings of Workers 18 Years Old and Over, by Educational Attainment, Race, Hispanic Origin, and Sex, 1975–2019—*Continued*

(Dollars except as noted.)

Race, sex, year, and Hispanic origin	Total		Not a high school graduate		High school graduate	
	Mean earnings	Number of workers (thousands)	Mean earnings	Number of workers (thousands)	Mean earnings	Number of workers (thousands)
2012............................	60,396	54,569	28,026	2,784	42,157	15,388
2011[2]	59,584	54,244	27,872	2,978	42,772	15,644
2010............................	56,719	54,268	27,427	2,989	39,449	15,938
2009............................	55,318	55,638	25,695	3,187	38,160	17,015
2008............................	56,538	56,822	26,479	3,654	39,405	17,206
2007............................	55,662	57,080	27,874	3,716	39,764	17,309
2006............................	54,843	56,843	26,100	4,289	40,180	17,470
2005............................	53,263	56,675	25,511	4,127	38,134	17,507
2004............................	50,597	55,930	23,590	4,204	36,324	17,568
2003[3]	49,386	55,774	22,957	4,224	35,589	17,225
2002............................	48,817	55,994	23,250	4,580	34,909	17,218
2001............................	47,973	56,528	23,096	4,749	34,627	17,672
2000[4]	47,084	56,675	23,296	4,763	33,669	17,733
1999............................	44,403	56,071	20,502	4,787	32,532	17,844
1998............................	41,612	56,246	20,781	5,152	30,429	18,048
Female						
2019............................	51,591	48,810	21,892	1,258	32,961	9,852
2018............................	47,928	48,659	17,849	1,424	32,350	10,277
2017............................	46,110	48,282	18,522	1,502	30,718	10,313
2016............................	44,556	48,441	18,777	1,437	28,989	10,656
2015............................	42,070	48,771	15,942	1,595	28,315	10,646
2014............................	39,860	48,324	18,662	1,591	27,637	10,999
2013............................	39,084	48,284	16,062	1,418	28,041	11,300
2012............................	38,240	48,405	15,189	1,718	26,303	11,433
2011[2]	37,382	48,120	14,314	1,870	25,435	11,669
2010............................	36,125	48,194	14,687	1,833	25,343	12,107
2009............................	35,396	49,498	14,216	2,029	25,147	12,845
2008............................	34,517	50,471	13,730	2,144	25,133	13,391
2007............................	34,069	50,353	14,779	2,192	24,570	13,546
2006............................	33,407	49,984	15,751	2,857	23,805	13,875
2005............................	31,208	49,661	13,837	2,476	23,004	13,977
2004............................	30,051	49,576	13,401	2,551	22,631	14,225
2003[3]	29,613	49,439	14,475	2,543	22,473	14,605
2002............................	28,410	49,712	13,163	2,800	21,762	15,146
2001............................	28,210	49,856	14,328	3,062	21,301	15,378
2000[4]	26,315	50,034	12,962	3,194	19,631	15,498
1999............................	24,492	50,068	12,283	3,384	18,618	16,139
1998............................	23,891	49,277	10,746	3,336	18,568	16,295
BLACK						
Both Sexes						
2019............................	46,007	20,774	26,661	1,337	33,518	6,434
2018............................	42,382	20,439	23,817	1,466	31,675	6,338
2017............................	41,570	20,112	23,690	1,329	31,889	6,293
2016............................	40,767	19,755	24,054	1,496	30,131	6,150
2015............................	39,394	19,150	19,783	1,582	29,211	6,015
2014............................	37,012	18,657	22,353	1,420	28,439	5,905
2013............................	35,817	18,023	21,403	1,590	26,670	5,689
2012............................	34,800	17,838	18,889	1,486	26,625	5,639
2011[2]	34,755	17,295	17,488	1,613	27,562	5,539
2010............................	32,900	17,016	17,849	1,643	25,781	5,557
2009............................	33,362	16,744	18,936	1,618	26,970	5,803
2008............................	32,874	17,509	18,123	1,748	27,265	6,060
2007............................	33,333	17,453	17,439	1,854	27,179	5,996
2006............................	32,443	17,234	17,823	1,943	26,368	6,159
2005............................	30,472	17,000	17,216	2,025	23,904	6,101
2004............................	29,096	16,632	17,827	2,044	23,498	6,139
2003[3]	28,838	16,389	16,201	2,095	23,777	5,941
2002............................	28,179	16,352	16,516	2,148	22,823	5,822
2001............................	27,031	16,683	17,248	2,382	21,743	5,729
2000[4]	26,204	16,756	15,201	2,434	21,789	6,020
1999............................	24,930	17,107	13,505	2,451	21,008	6,188

[1]For data prior to 1991, "Some college/Associate degree" equals 1 to 3 years of college completed; "Bachelor's degree" equals 4 years of college; "Advanced degree" equals 5 or more years of college completed.
[2]Starting in 2011, earnings data were created using population controls based on Census 2010 data.
[3]Starting in 2003, respondents could choose more than one race. The race data in this table from 2003 onward represent respondents who indicated only one race.
[4]Beginning in 2000, earnings data are from the expanded Current Population Survey (CPS) sample and were calculated using population controls based on Census 2000.
[5]May be of any race.
... = Not available.

Table A-34. Mean Earnings of Workers 18 Years Old and Over, by Educational Attainment, Race, Hispanic Origin, and Sex, 1975–2019—*Continued*

(Dollars except as noted.)

Race, sex, year, and Hispanic origin	Some college or associate's degree[1]		Bachelor's degree[1]		Advanced degree[1]	
	Mean earnings	Number of workers (thousands)	Mean earnings	Number of workers (thousands)	Mean earnings	Number of workers (thousands)
2012.............................	46,477	16,175	75,826	13,080	115,598	7,139
2011[2]............................	45,443	15,675	75,168	12,900	113,244	7,045
2010.............................	43,567	15,564	73,425	12,791	107,361	6,987
2009.............................	43,802	15,981	72,305	12,708	107,872	6,746
2008.............................	44,237	16,439	76,613	12,562	107,498	6,960
2007.............................	43,835	16,684	75,214	12,597	104,317	6,772
2006.............................	43,589	16,024	73,376	12,321	104,031	6,738
2005.............................	43,137	16,456	70,932	12,048	104,107	6,535
2004.............................	41,467	15,952	66,527	11,739	100,533	6,467
2003[3]............................	40,316	16,048	66,390	11,849	95,029	6,427
2002.............................	40,368	16,121	66,638	11,764	93,686	6,309
2001.............................	39,133	16,114	66,196	11,692	92,954	6,299
2000[4]............................	39,379	16,435	65,459	11,594	90,150	6,149
1999.............................	37,651	16,087	60,564	11,283	86,004	6,070
1998.............................	29,555	15,849	57,346	11,335	79,524	5,862
Female						
2019.............................	37,958	14,631	60,867	14,387	84,645	8,680
2018.............................	34,384	14,661	58,885	13,904	77,623	8,391
2017.............................	33,840	14,788	55,450	13,533	77,446	8,144
2016.............................	33,801	15,235	53,598	13,240	75,942	7,871
2015.............................	32,304	15,772	51,126	13,009	71,035	7,746
2014.............................	31,276	15,630	48,291	12,665	66,161	7,436
2013.............................	29,999	15,815	48,070	12,526	65,190	7,223
2012.............................	29,413	16,187	48,247	12,165	66,824	6,900
2011[2]............................	28,766	16,105	48,640	11,990	66,120	6,484
2010.............................	28,856	16,134	45,779	11,634	63,074	6,486
2009.............................	28,911	16,448	43,636	11,825	64,351	6,349
2008.............................	28,244	16,781	44,220	11,883	60,063	6,270
2007.............................	28,772	16,746	43,150	11,769	59,121	6,099
2006.............................	28,322	16,379	43,473	11,534	59,458	5,608
2005.............................	26,812	16,899	40,562	10,964	55,422	5,344
2004.............................	25,294	16,609	39,161	10,805	53,927	5,386
2003[3]............................	25,499	16,411	37,761	10,624	53,164	5,253
2002.............................	24,318	16,222	38,049	10,457	49,845	5,085
2001.............................	24,628	16,004	36,844	10,512	51,756	4,898
2000[4]............................	23,038	16,401	35,362	10,230	49,126	4,710
1999.............................	21,869	16,067	32,687	9,979	45,934	4,499
1998.............................	18,198	15,610	31,516	9,840	45,805	4,196
BLACK						
Both Sexes						
2019.............................	37,994	6,615	60,580	4,189	90,712	2,196
2018.............................	38,299	6,651	54,959	3,837	76,871	2,145
2017.............................	36,777	6,816	53,938	3,740	78,350	1,932
2016.............................	34,740	6,841	57,409	3,394	80,903	1,873
2015.............................	34,653	6,606	55,506	3,220	80,976	1,725
2014.............................	32,074	6,605	51,983	3,084	72,257	1,642
2013.............................	32,137	6,228	49,904	2,997	72,496	1,517
2012.............................	31,730	6,398	48,972	2,854	60,329	1,459
2011[2]............................	32,891	5,964	45,477	2,796	70,140	1,380
2010.............................	30,592	5,969	44,502	2,593	71,127	1,255
2009.............................	30,520	5,577	47,799	2,583	66,923	1,162
2008.............................	30,248	5,933	46,527	2,550	66,198	1,216
2007.............................	32,787	5,813	46,502	2,682	64,247	1,107
2006.............................	31,234	5,581	47,903	2,503	64,834	1,045
2005.............................	28,848	5,390	47,101	2,412	63,664	1,071
2004.............................	27,779	5,192	42,342	2,348	65,538	909
2003[3]............................	27,187	5,119	42,968	2,321	64,164	911
2002.............................	27,626	5,255	42,285	2,275	59,944	851
2001.............................	26,907	5,481	40,165	2,212	55,771	877
2000[4]............................	26,324	5,431	41,513	2,060	52,373	809
1999.............................	25,169	5,437	37,362	2,155	52,516	876,836

[1]For data prior to 1991, "Some college/Associate degree" equals 1 to 3 years of college completed; "Bachelor's degree" equals 4 years of college; "Advanced degree" equals 5 or more years of college completed.
[2]Starting in 2011, earnings data were created using population controls based on Census 2010 data.
[3]Starting in 2003, respondents could choose more than one race. The race data in this table from 2003 onward represent respondents who indicated only one race.
[4]Beginning in 2000, earnings data are from the expanded Current Population Survey (CPS) sample and were calculated using population controls based on Census 2000.
[5]May be of any race.
... = Not available.

Table A-34. Mean Earnings of Workers 18 Years Old and Over, by Educational Attainment, Race, Hispanic Origin, and Sex, 1975–2019—*Continued*

(Dollars except as noted.)

Race, sex, year, and Hispanic origin	Total		Not a high school graduate		High school graduate	
	Mean earnings	Number of workers (thousands)	Mean earnings	Number of workers (thousands)	Mean earnings	Number of workers (thousands)
1998.............................	22,829	16,201	13,672	2,402	19,236	6,053
1997.............................	21,909	15,873	13,185	2,437	18,980	5,964
1996.............................	21,978	15,255	13,110	2,383	18,722	5,844
1995.............................	20,537	14,847	12,956	2,389	17,072	5,453
1994.............................	19,772	14,754	12,705	2,290	16,446	5,596
1993.............................	18,614	14,315	11,065	2,352	16,122	5,521
1992.............................	17,397	14,087	11,091	2,444	15,230	5,498
1991.............................	16,809	13,865	11,248	2,860	15,060	5,512
1990.............................	16,627	13,731	11,184	2,853	14,794	6,049
1989.............................	16,072	13,600	10,066	2,883	14,613	5,894
1988.............................	15,318	13,356	10,202	2,970	13,835	5,760
1987.............................	14,136	13,023	9,976	3,015	12,862	5,699
1986.............................	13,494	12,729	9,365	3,028	12,276	5,470
1985.............................	12,926	12,427	9,116	3,009	11,791	5,223
1984.............................	12,002	11,948	8,725	3,127	10,882	4,927
1983.............................	11,299	11,296	7,867	3,035	10,557	4,692
1982.............................	10,612	11,081	7,799	3,188	10,287	4,591
1981.............................	10,117	11,088	7,520	3,514	9,994	4,388
1980.............................	11,085	5,576	8,421	2,054	11,563	2,119
1979.............................	8,720	10,856	6,424	3,776	8,723	4,267
1978.............................	7,981	10,420	5,918	3,841	8,152	3,944
1977.............................	7,271	10,014	5,406	3,946	7,553	3,604
1976.............................	6,716	9,744	5,304	4,008	6,805	3,515
1975.............................	6,190	9,368	4,989	3,922	6,281	3,495
Male						
2019.............................	49,652	9,668	30,322	714	36,777	3,426
2018.............................	46,402	9,484	28,044	754	36,716	3,358
2017.............................	46,085	9,427	27,150	656	36,451	3,406
2016.............................	46,686	9,231	26,919	769	34,968	3,235
2015.............................	43,781	8,979	23,846	796	33,881	3,158
2014.............................	42,454	8,645	25,516	746	32,836	3,036
2013.............................	40,785	8,348	26,346	843	29,893	2,887
2012.............................	38,244	8,293	19,497	800	30,276	2,891
2011[2]	38,633	7,951	21,035	812	31,219	2,811
2010.............................	35,828	7,801	19,893	884	29,560	2,888
2009.............................	37,553	7,657	21,828	861	30,723	2,996
2008.............................	36,057	8,116	22,344	866	30,985	3,166
2007.............................	35,668	8,088	19,705	985	29,640	2,994
2006.............................	36,045	7,932	21,294	982	30,122	3,067
2005.............................	34,165	7,836	19,890	1,056	27,360	3,050
2004.............................	33,020	7,669	22,796	1,030	26,608	3,120
2003[3]	32,545	7,469	17,915	1,039	28,102	2,910
2002.............................	31,790	7,483	19,294	1,072	25,582	2,832
2001.............................	30,502	7,727	18,543	1,210	25,037	2,759
2000[4]	30,109	7,700	17,992	1,235	25,219	2,942
1999.............................	28,533	8,032	16,109	1,258	25,680	3,024
1998.............................	26,090	7,488	16,013	1,190	22,698	2,974
1997.............................	25,080	7,370	15,423	1,304	22,440	2,862
1996.............................	25,067	7,125	15,461	1,290	22,267	2,836
1995.............................	23,876	7,090	14,877	1,280	19,514	2,812
1994.............................	22,614	7,009	15,984	1,191	18,527	2,818
1993.............................	21,108	6,833	13,074	1,305	18,668	2,775
1992.............................	19,317	6,922	12,748	1,439	16,963	2,744
1991.............................	18,607	6,830	12,845	1,624	17,352	2,731
1990.............................	18,859	6,781	13,031	1,563	17,046	3,013
1989.............................	18,108	6,654	11,827	1,614	16,658	2,848
1988.............................	17,782	6,593	12,439	1,671	16,345	2,795
1987.............................	16,171	6,505	11,899	1,711	14,800	2,769
1986.............................	15,441	6,326	11,248	1,691	14,214	2,666
1985.............................	14,932	6,237	10,802	1,716	13,721	2,572
1984.............................	13,560	5,899	10,216	1,780	12,382	2,339
1983.............................	12,789	5,707	9,094	1,768	11,956	2,312
1982.............................	12,203	5,535	9,153	1,798	11,952	2,213

[1]For data prior to 1991, "Some college/Associate degree" equals 1 to 3 years of college completed; "Bachelor's degree" equals 4 years of college; "Advanced degree" equals 5 or more years of college completed.
[2]Starting in 2011, earnings data were created using population controls based on Census 2010 data.
[3]Starting in 2003, respondents could choose more than one race. The race data in this table from 2003 onward represent respondents who indicated only one race.
[4]Beginning in 2000, earnings data are from the expanded Current Population Survey (CPS) sample and were calculated using population controls based on Census 2000.
[5]May be of any race.
... = Not available.

Table A-34. Mean Earnings of Workers 18 Years Old and Over, by Educational Attainment, Race, Hispanic Origin, and Sex, 1975–2019—*Continued*

(Dollars except as noted.)

Race, sex, year, and Hispanic origin	Some college or associate's degree[1]		Bachelor's degree[1]		Advanced degree[1]	
	Mean earnings	Number of workers (thousands)	Mean earnings	Number of workers (thousands)	Mean earnings	Number of workers (thousands)
1998	23,927	4,559	36,373	1,897	44,760	764
1997	22,899	4,902	32,062	1,846	42,791	724
1996	23,628	4,783	31,955	1,655	48,731	590
1995	21,824	4,727	29,666	1,684	46,654	595
1994	19,631	4,610	30,938	1,679	48,653	579
1993	18,867	4,279	29,953	1,638	41,221	525
1992	17,702	4,151	27,365	1,463	39,014	530
1991	17,598	3,581	25,630	1,383	36,735	528
1990	18,209	3,004	26,448	1,217	32,962	607
1989	17,385	3,008	25,357	1,121	32,740	694
1988	16,760	2,802	23,689	1,204	30,802	621
1987	15,491	2,617	20,805	1,097	29,163	596
1986	14,743	2,662	21,403	1,004	27,503	564
1985	13,805	2,615	20,533	1,046	26,246	535
1984	12,890	2,396	19,330	937	24,072	561
1983	12,426	2,206	17,207	828	23,506	535
1982	11,119	2,067	15,152	747	22,959	488
1981	11,456	2,078	14,587	708	19,463	398
1980	12,393	964	15,616	283	19,960	353
1979	9,895	1,826	13,473	622	18,182	366
1978	9,026	1,689	12,870	557	15,076	389
1977	8,321	1,578	11,088	532	14,749	354
1976	7,331	1,370	10,331	547	15,013	305
1975	7,212	1,193	9,473	517	12,333	241
Male						
2019	42,898	2,911	67,135	1,863	109,444	752
2018	44,903	2,887	58,970	1,740	85,193	743
2017	41,410	3,002	61,434	1,628	92,812	733
2016	39,407	3,004	70,026	1,531	103,465	691
2015	39,459	2,874	63,477	1,466	88,699	683
2014	37,116	2,831	60,458	1,376	91,652	653
2013	38,126	2,696	57,304	1,312	88,641	608
2012	36,043	2,804	53,983	1,210	81,253	585
2011[2]	38,029	2,654	49,390	1,155	85,528	518
2010	34,405	2,479	40,560	1,067	81,674	483
2009	35,889	2,301	55,655	1,030	78,574	467
2008	34,209	2,505	51,691	1,059	73,940	518
2007	34,035	2,492	53,029	1,155	74,351	459
2006	34,750	2,334	52,569	1,086	74,507	460
2005	33,544	2,273	52,070	1,011	77,210	444
2004	32,367	2,176	47,746	957	79,168	387
2003[3]	31,556	2,156	45,635	966	76,871	397
2002	32,764	2,283	47,018	974	75,050	321
2001	31,084	2,457	46,511	943	67,007	356
2000[4]	30,966	2,291	49,270	880	60,207	349
1999	28,278	2,388	42,170	993 347	59,255	368 292
1998	26,586	2,215	42,539	792	51,198	318
1997	27,215	2,108	35,792	818	49,940	278
1996	26,365	2,047	35,558	700	65,981	253
1995	26,846	2,047	36,026	659	57,186	293
1994	23,748	1,959	34,073	758	52,829	281
1993	21,734	1,804	35,147	721	47,372	228
1992	20,550	1,835	30,920	657	43,795	246
1991	19,974	1,571	26,075	650	41,313	255
1990	21,152	1,372	29,471	564	39,104	269
1989	20,253	1,352	27,493	515	38,166	326
1988	19,265	1,311	28,506	533	36,452	283
1987	18,081	1,250	23,345	482	34,073	294
1986	17,419	1,226	23,412	480	31,054	263
1985	16,415	1,230	23,818	477	31,947	243
1984	14,960	1,106	21,986	424	27,893	250
1983	15,113	996	20,370	363	25,466	268
1982	12,926	953	17,658	319	26,452	253

[1]For data prior to 1991, "Some college/Associate degree" equals 1 to 3 years of college completed; "Bachelor's degree" equals 4 years of college; "Advanced degree" equals 5 or more years of college completed.
[2]Starting in 2011, earnings data were created using population controls based on Census 2010 data.
[3]Starting in 2003, respondents could choose more than one race. The race data in this table from 2003 onward represent respondents who indicated only one race.
[4]Beginning in 2000, earnings data are from the expanded Current Population Survey (CPS) sample and were calculated using population controls based on Census 2000.
[5]May be of any race.
… = Not available.

Table A-34. Mean Earnings of Workers 18 Years Old and Over, by Educational Attainment, Race, Hispanic Origin, and Sex, 1975–2019—*Continued*

(Dollars except as noted.)

Race, sex, year, and Hispanic origin	Total		Not a high school graduate		High school graduate	
	Mean earnings	Number of workers (thousands)	Mean earnings	Number of workers (thousands)	Mean earnings	Number of workers (thousands)
1981..............................	11,937	5,651	9,266	1,925	11,905	2,191
1980..............................	11,085	5,576	8,421	2,054	11,563	2,119
1979..............................	10,403	5,581	7,938	2,138	10,662	2,087
1978..............................	9,651	5,350	7,423	2,156	9,869	1,982
1977..............................	8,710	5,220	6,648	2,230	9,332	1,770
1976..............................	7,991	5,156	6,670	2,289	8,056	1,766
1975..............................	7,541	4,864	6,364	2,247	7,847	1,684
Female						
2019..............................	42,835	11,106	22,460	622	29,807	3,008
2018..............................	38,901	10,954	19,333	711	25,994	2,980
2017..............................	37,585	10,684	20,316	672	26,507	2,886
2016..............................	35,576	10,524	21,023	727	24,763	2,915
2015..............................	35,521	10,170	15,665	786	24,047	2,856
2014..............................	32,313	10,012	18,852	674	23,785	2,868
2013..............................	31,531	9,675	15,831	747	23,349	2,801
2012..............................	31,808	9,544	18,178	685	22,783	2,747
2011[2]	31,455	9,343	13,893	801	23,795	2,728
2010..............................	30,421	9,216	15,467	759	21,690	2,668
2009..............................	29,831	9,087	15,644	756	22,964	2,806
2008..............................	29,734	9,392	13,976	881	23,195	2,893
2007..............................	31,317	9,365	14,869	868	24,724	3,001
2006..............................	29,371	9,302	14,277	961	22,643	3,092
2005..............................	27,314	9,163	14,300	968	20,449	3,051
2004..............................	25,738	8,963	12,785	1,015	20,284	3,019
2003[3]	25,735	8,919	14,513	1,056	19,623	3,030
2002..............................	25,131	8,868	13,748	1,075	20,209	2,989
2001..............................	24,036	8,956	15,912	1,172	18,683	2,970
2000[4]	22,884	9,056	12,321	1,198	18,510	3,078
1999..............................	21,742	9,076	10,762	1,194	16,541	3,163
1998..............................	20,026	8,713	11,372	1,212	15,892	3,078
1997..............................	19,161	8,503	10,607	1,132	15,789	3,102
1996..............................	19,271	8,129	10,337	1,094	15,379	3,008
1995..............................	17,485	7,757	10,739	1,108	14,473	2,641
1994..............................	17,200	7,745	9,150	1,099	14,333	2,777
1993..............................	16,336	7,481	8,562	1,048	13,550	2,746
1992..............................	15,542	7,165	8,719	1,005	13,504	2,754
1991..............................	15,064	7,035	9,151	1,237	12,810	2,781
1990..............................	14,449	6,950	8,946	1,290	12,560	3,036
1989..............................	14,122	6,946	7,827	1,269	12,701	3,046
1988..............................	12,916	6,763	7,325	1,299	11,469	2,965
1987..............................	12,106	6,518	7,452	1,304	11,030	2,930
1986..............................	11,571	6,403	6,984	1,337	10,434	2,804
1985..............................	10,904	6,190	6,879	1,293	9,918	2,651
1984..............................	10,482	6,049	6,754	1,347	9,527	2,588
1983..............................	9,778	5,589	6,154	1,267	9,197	2,380
1982..............................	9,024	5,546	6,047	1,390	8,737	2,378
1981..............................	8,225	5,437	5,404	1,589	8,088	2,197
1980..............................	7,684	(NA)	4,685	(NA)	7,508	(NA)
1979..............................	6,940	5,275	4,448	1,638	6,866	2,180
ASIAN						
Both Sexes						
2019..............................	75,205	10,793	31,016	562	37,327	1,554
2018..............................	71,116	10,421	25,219	532	34,610	1,605
2017..............................	67,599	10,215	29,306	568	35,164	1,639
2016..............................	63,650	9,941	28,588	536	32,548	1,758
2015..............................	61,603	9,439	23,418	571	34,215	1,533
2014..............................	57,351	9,170	21,969	577	29,809	1,571
2013..............................	54,752	8,732	24,616	588	30,996	1,616
2012..............................	55,151	8,469	23,994	521	30,149	1,445
2011[2]	51,500	8,014	21,640	563	28,302	1,478
2010..............................	49,263	8,028	20,747	595	28,490	1,520

[1]For data prior to 1991, "Some college/Associate degree" equals 1 to 3 years of college completed; "Bachelor's degree" equals 4 years of college; "Advanced degree" equals 5 or more years of college completed.
[2]Starting in 2011, earnings data were created using population controls based on Census 2010 data.
[3]Starting in 2003, respondents could choose more than one race. The race data in this table from 2003 onward represent respondents who indicated only one race.
[4]Beginning in 2000, earnings data are from the expanded Current Population Survey (CPS) sample and were calculated using population controls based on Census 2000.
[5]May be of any race.
... = Not available.

Table A-34. Mean Earnings of Workers 18 Years Old and Over, by Educational Attainment, Race, Hispanic Origin, and Sex, 1975–2019—*Continued*

(Dollars except as noted.)

Race, sex, year, and Hispanic origin	Some college or associate's degree[1]		Bachelor's degree[1]		Advanced degree[1]	
	Mean earnings	Number of workers (thousands)	Mean earnings	Number of workers (thousands)	Mean earnings	Number of workers (thousands)
1981...............................	13,740	1,002	16,624	327	21,082	205
1980...............................	12,393	964	15,616	283	23,346	156
1979...............................	11,971	931	16,161	259	21,092	166
1978...............................	11,197	770	16,009	260	18,083	181
1977...............................	10,023	799	12,978	234	16,385	188
1976...............................	8,688	726	12,246	233	17,859	143
1975...............................	8,505	599	11,318	213	13,720	121
Female						
2019...............................	34,140	3,704	55,329	2,326	80,946	1,444
2018...............................	33,234	3,764	51,630	2,097	72,456	1,401
2017...............................	33,131	3,814	48,158	2,111	69,498	1,199
2016...............................	31,087	3,837	47,036	1,862	67,707	1,182
2015...............................	30,951	3,732	48,842	1,753	75,911	1,041
2014...............................	28,290	3,773	45,149	1,707	59,429	988
2013...............................	27,564	3,531	44,139	1,684	61,698	909
2012...............................	28,363	3,593	45,282	1,644	59,675	874
2011[2]............................	28,771	3,310	42,721	1,640	60,889	862
2010...............................	27,884	3,491	41,665	1,526	64,532	772
2009...............................	26,748	3,276	42,587	1,552	59,073	694
2008...............................	27,354	3,428	42,858	1,491	60,430	697
2007...............................	31,850	3,320	41,560	1,526	57,070	647
2006...............................	28,706	3,246	44,326	1,417	57,206	584
2005...............................	25,422	3,116	43,516	1,401	54,044	626
2004...............................	24,468	3,015	38,626	1,391	55,436	522
2003[3]............................	24,007	2,963	41,066	1,355	54,346	514
2002...............................	23,679	2,972	38,741	1,301	50,766	529
2001...............................	23,511	3,023	35,448	1,269	48,080	521
2000[4]............................	22,937	3,140	35,719	1,179	46,416	459
1999...............................	22,733	3,049	33,251	1,162	47,635	509
1998...............................	20,371	2,870	31,952	1,105	40,214	448
1997...............................	19,643	2,794	29,091	1,027	38,392	448
1996...............................	21,581	2,736	29,311	954	35,785	337
1995...............................	17,985	2,679	25,577	1,025	36,585	304
1994...............................	16,589	2,651	28,356	921	44,618	297
1993...............................	16,778	2,475	25,865	917	36,485	296
1992...............................	15,445	2,316	24,465	806	34,880	285
1991...............................	15,742	2,011	25,235	733	32,470	273
1990...............................	15,734	1,632	23,837	653	28,074	338
1989...............................	15,044	1,656	23,541	606	27,933	368
1988...............................	14,557	1,491	19,862	671	26,072	338
1987...............................	13,123	1,367	18,815	615	24,383	302
1986...............................	12,459	1,436	19,562	524	24,400	301
1985...............................	11,488	1,385	17,779	569	21,502	292
1984...............................	11,115	1,290	17,134	513	21,000	311
1983...............................	10,215	1,210	14,738	465	21,539	267
1982...............................	9,574	1,114	13,284	428	19,198	235
1981...............................	9,329	1,076	12,839	381	17,743	193
1980...............................	8,544	(NA)	12,389	(NA)	17,278	(NA)
1979...............................	7,735	895	11,555	363	15,766	200
ASIAN						
Both Sexes						
2019...............................	42,493	1,679	75,200	3,846	119,211	3,151
2018...............................	41,595	1,826	72,857	3,660	117,834	2,795
2017...............................	38,302	1,894	71,845	3,353	109,714	2,759
2016...............................	37,793	1,996	68,610	3,022	105,557	2,627
2015...............................	36,914	1,847	65,558	3,056	101,667	2,429
2014...............................	32,524	1,792	64,864	3,106	97,309	2,123
2013...............................	34,638	1,767	57,841	2,755	96,266	2,003
2012...............................	33,239	1,744	59,507	2,717	93,772	2,040
2011[2]............................	35,034	1,582	57,150	2,645	87,205	1,743
2010...............................	30,519	1,629	56,689	2,576	84,369	1,707

[1]For data prior to 1991, "Some college/Associate degree" equals 1 to 3 years of college completed; "Bachelor's degree" equals 4 years of college; "Advanced degree" equals 5 or more years of college completed.
[2]Starting in 2011, earnings data were created using population controls based on Census 2010 data.
[3]Starting in 2003, respondents could choose more than one race. The race data in this table from 2003 onward represent respondents who indicated only one race.
[4]Beginning in 2000, earnings data are from the expanded Current Population Survey (CPS) sample and were calculated using population controls based on Census 2000.
[5]May be of any race.
… = Not available.

Table A-34. Mean Earnings of Workers 18 Years Old and Over, by Educational Attainment, Race, Hispanic Origin, and Sex, 1975–2019—*Continued*

(Dollars except as noted.)

Race, sex, year, and Hispanic origin	Total		Not a high school graduate		High school graduate	
	Mean earnings	Number of workers (thousands)	Mean earnings	Number of workers (thousands)	Mean earnings	Number of workers (thousands)
2009.............................	53,419	7,158	20,461	487	29,312	1,367
2008.............................	51,063	7,118	21,200	540	29,390	1,213
2007.............................	49,571	7,137	21,305	512	28,773	1,241
2006.............................	50,940	7,073	20,573	599	29,426	1,301
2005.............................	45,751	6,684	22,909	598	27,082	1,304
2004.............................	44,361	6,369	19,684	497	28,289	1,192
2003[3].............................	42,163	6,190	19,558	539	25,704	1,162
2002.............................	40,793	6,086	16,746	536	24,900	1,138
Male						
2019.............................	85,813	5,706	34,015	318	43,907	820
2018.............................	82,771	5,528	28,683	283	40,718	866
2017.............................	79,440	5,452	35,303	283	41,576	913
2016.............................	75,610	5,258	36,311	267	37,255	933
2015.............................	71,362	5,014	26,616	303	39,038	814
2014.............................	66,326	4,817	26,516	279	33,374	823
2013.............................	64,019	4,690	24,897	288	35,882	881
2012.............................	64,502	4,455	24,256	251	32,794	748
2011[2].............................	60,397	4,195	25,534	298	32,500	754
2010.............................	57,180	4,196	24,064	315	31,683	766
2009.............................	62,328	3,811	21,167	255	33,080	695
2008.............................	60,007	3,776	23,814	279	34,904	606
2007.............................	57,890	3,731	24,213	244	33,607	630
2006.............................	60,516	3,757	23,311	298	32,528	710
2005.............................	54,257	3,564	28,150	307	30,547	721
2004.............................	52,544	3,440	20,691	235	31,710	676
2003[3].............................	48,890	3,333	23,745	291	28,522	582
2002.............................	48,934	3,272	17,659	298	29,547	578
Female						
2019.............................	63,307	5,087	27,108	244	29,959	733
2018.............................	57,945	4,892	21,264	248	27,444	739
2017.............................	54,045	4,763	23,370	285	27,099	725
2016.............................	50,220	4,683	20,875	268	27,217	824
2015.............................	50,544	4,424	19,791	267	28,748	718
2014.............................	47,419	4,353	17,691	297	25,886	748
2013.............................	43,995	4,041	24,346	300	25,129	734
2012.............................	44,770	4,013	23,751	270	27,308	697
2011[2].............................	41,727	3,819	17,263	265	23,926	723
2010.............................	40,595	3,832	17,016	280	25,246	754
2009.............................	43,270	3,346	19,684	232	25,420	672
2008.............................	40,954	3,341	18,395	260	23,886	607
2007.............................	40,455	3,405	18,643	267	23,785	611
2006.............................	40,089	3,315	17,855	300	25,696	590
2005.............................	36,033	3,119	17,383	291	22,789	582
2004.............................	34,748	2,929	18,780	262	23,802	516
2003[3].............................	34,315	2,857	14,614	247	22,876	580
2002.............................	31,328	2,814	15,595	237	20,094	559
HISPANIC[5]						
Both Sexes						
2019.............................	41,353	29,534	29,080	6,043	34,876	9,335
2018.............................	40,613	28,535	28,024	6,288	35,105	9,172
2017.............................	38,816	27,827	27,291	6,237	34,472	8,807
2016.............................	38,276	26,936	29,264	6,260	34,751	8,477
2015.............................	37,083	26,263	25,697	6,630	31,647	8,240
2014.............................	33,944	25,254	23,747	6,819	30,329	7,869
2013.............................	32,368	24,393	22,431	6,704	28,415	7,313
2012.............................	31,596	23,811	21,087	6,545	28,097	7,462
2011[2].............................	30,739	23,027	20,953	6,583	26,681	7,176
2010.............................	29,971	22,326	20,625	6,469	26,314	6,981
2009.............................	29,565	21,551	19,816	6,667	25,998	6,753
2008.............................	30,291	21,853	21,310	6,972	27,020	6,702

[1]For data prior to 1991, "Some college/Associate degree" equals 1 to 3 years of college completed; "Bachelor's degree" equals 4 years of college; "Advanced degree" equals 5 or more years of college completed.
[2]Starting in 2011, earnings data were created using population controls based on Census 2010 data.
[3]Starting in 2003, respondents could choose more than one race. The race data in this table from 2003 onward represent respondents who indicated only one race.
[4]Beginning in 2000, earnings data are from the expanded Current Population Survey (CPS) sample and were calculated using population controls based on Census 2000.
[5]May be of any race.
... = Not available.

Table A-34. Mean Earnings of Workers 18 Years Old and Over, by Educational Attainment, Race, Hispanic Origin, and Sex, 1975–2019—*Continued*

(Dollars except as noted.)

Race, sex, year, and Hispanic origin	Some college or associate's degree[1]		Bachelor's degree[1]		Advanced degree[1]	
	Mean earnings	Number of workers (thousands)	Mean earnings	Number of workers (thousands)	Mean earnings	Number of workers (thousands)
2009	32,958	1,356	55,730	2,376	98,871	1,569
2008	32,671	1,466	58,524	2,298	83,721	1,600
2007	34,423	1,456	54,451	2,354	81,943	1,572
2006	33,238	1,350	56,197	2,268	88,408	1,553
2005	31,460	1,337	51,064	2,108	80,145	1,335
2004	29,524	1,364	47,912	2,119	81,259	1,196
2003[3]	27,209	1,355	48,333	1,878	74,046	1,254
2002	27,340	1,325	46,628	1,911	72,852	1,174
Male						
2019	47,902	856	86,639	1,917	131,411	1,793
2018	46,021	967	87,714	1,823	132,138	1,587
2017	45,422	964	86,369	1,694	122,087	1,597
2016	44,013	1,022	78,528	1,520	124,668	1,513
2015	39,272	894	74,452	1,587	116,397	1,414
2014	36,790	903	71,685	1,581	112,262	1,229
2013	37,731	936	66,653	1,417	112,837	1,166
2012	38,417	871	69,657	1,361	105,017	1,222
2011[2]	42,378	810	65,740	1,316	98,812	1,015
2010	34,428	837	64,963	1,285	96,506	992
2009	37,691	722	62,561	1,198	113,711	940
2008	37,283	773	67,088	1,186	97,060	931
2007	41,876	773	60,356	1,156	93,604	926
2006	37,263	658	67,144	1,150	101,676	939
2005	35,401	675	60,739	1,048	92,552	811
2004	33,798	680	56,998	1,079	90,870	770
2003[3]	31,775	673	52,508	992	83,098	793
2002	32,750	664	55,198	971	82,170	758
Female						
2019	36,864	823	63,824	1,928	103,104	1,358
2018	36,608	859	58,117	1,837	99,047	1,208
2017	30,923	930	57,009	1,658	92,705	1,162
2016	31,258	973	58,567	1,501	79,613	1,114
2015	34,704	953	55,956	1,469	81,135	1,015
2014	28,185	888	57,793	1,525	76,741	893
2013	31,154	831	48,505	1,337	73,159	836
2012	28,077	873	49,308	1,355	76,942	817
2011[2]	27,328	772	48,647	1,329	71,001	727
2010	26,383	791	48,453	1,291	67,541	715
2009	27,574	634	48,783	1,178	76,637	628
2008	27,528	693	49,380	1,111	65,148	669
2007	25,992	683	48,748	1,197	65,206	645
2006	29,415	692	44,932	1,118	68,084	613
2005	27,439	662	41,494	1,059	60,934	524
2004	25,280	684	38,488	1,040	63,894	426
2003[3]	22,703	682	43,655	885	58,489	461
2002	21,912	661	37,766	939	55,851	415
HISPANIC[5]						
Both Sexes						
2019	39,084	7,876	56,698	4,408	86,723	1,870
2018	37,847	7,523	59,364	3,910	87,619	1,641
2017	37,370	7,587	54,190	3,767	83,067	1,428
2016	35,288	7,404	53,283	3,421	79,831	1,073
2015	36,780	6,887	58,152	3,096	82,499	1,409
2014	33,822	6,541	52,143	2,852	73,952	1,171
2013	32,153	6,524	50,673	2,759	74,926	1,090
2012	30,694	6,042	50,592	2,707	77,985	1,054
2011[2]	31,423	5,773	47,873	2,528	78,606	966
2010	30,826	5,551	47,753	2,390	71,403	935
2009	31,004	5,036	49,017	2,256	74,675	837
2008	31,644	5,149	48,081	2,225	77,630	802

[1]For data prior to 1991, "Some college/Associate degree" equals 1 to 3 years of college completed; "Bachelor's degree" equals 4 years of college; "Advanced degree" equals 5 or more years of college completed.
[2]Starting in 2011, earnings data were created using population controls based on Census 2010 data.
[3]Starting in 2003, respondents could choose more than one race. The race data in this table from 2003 onward represent respondents who indicated only one race.
[4]Beginning in 2000, earnings data are from the expanded Current Population Survey (CPS) sample and were calculated using population controls based on Census 2000.
[5]May be of any race.
… = Not available.

Table A-34. Mean Earnings of Workers 18 Years Old and Over, by Educational Attainment, Race, Hispanic Origin, and Sex, 1975–2019—*Continued*

(Dollars except as noted.)

Race, sex, year, and Hispanic origin	Total		Not a high school graduate		High school graduate	
	Mean earnings	Number of workers (thousands)	Mean earnings	Number of workers (thousands)	Mean earnings	Number of workers (thousands)
2007............................	29,910	21,561	21,303	6,888	27,604	6,682
2006............................	29,155	21,209	20,581	7,134	27,508	6,495
2005............................	27,760	20,025	19,294	6,995	25,659	6,080
2004............................	27,263	19,343	19,025	6,935	25,823	5,741
2003[3].........................	25,810	18,786	18,349	6,767	23,472	5,517
2002............................	25,824	18,409	18,981	6,748	24,163	5,499
2001............................	24,786	17,575	18,334	6,533	22,866	5,265
2000[4].........................	23,855	17,161	17,156	6,428	22,009	5,145
1999............................	21,809	16,275	15,991	6,021	20,443	4,907
1998............................	22,117	14,372	15,832	5,281	20,978	4,219
1997............................	20,766	13,972	15,069	5,238	19,558	4,082
1996............................	19,439	13,365	13,287	5,062	18,528	3,783
1995............................	18,262	12,434	13,068	4,784	18,333	3,594
1994............................	18,568	12,035	13,733	4,686	17,323	3,444
1993............................	17,102	11,644	11,852	4,425	16,591	3,367
1992............................	16,501	11,350	11,674	4,426	16,438	3,349
1991............................	16,300	10,006	11,335	3,906	16,142	3,045
1990............................	15,943	9,729	10,368	3,929	15,417	3,282
1989............................	15,714	9,570	11,500	3,985	14,901	3,188
1988............................	15,007	9,226	11,045	3,824	14,667	2,953
1987............................	14,695	8,817	10,961	3,457	13,958	2,982
1986............................	13,558	8,393	9,896	3,379	13,389	2,835
1985............................	13,120	7,840	9,956	3,223	13,044	2,661
1984............................	12,583	7,349	9,671	3,129	12,858	2,457
1983............................	11,901	6,222	9,473	2,674	12,077	2,030
1982............................	11,307	5,914	8,498	2,583	11,539	1,967
1981............................	10,872	5,930	8,645	2,648	11,046	1,966
1980............................	10,062	5,723	8,119	2,649	10,182	1,824
1979............................	9,248	5,545	7,683	2,533	9,338	1,812
1978............................	8,460	4,898	7,138	2,345	8,512	1,554
1977............................	7,761	4,752	6,547	2,306	8,079	1,461
1976............................	7,081	4,303	5,984	2,107	7,580	1,309
1975............................	6,567	4,078	5,462	2,028	6,759	1,293
Male						
2019............................	45,995	16,414	33,770	3,828	39,349	5,637
2018............................	44,851	16,016	32,348	4,122	40,028	5,594
2017............................	43,300	15,759	31,968	4,104	38,865	5,328
2016............................	44,237	15,189	33,701	4,124	41,541	5,136
2015............................	41,556	14,962	29,719	4,327	36,549	4,982
2014............................	38,152	14,478	27,032	4,478	34,347	4,686
2013............................	35,990	13,980	25,151	4,475	32,070	4,366
2012............................	35,423	13,622	24,012	4,379	32,313	4,460
2011[2].........................	34,135	13,134	24,189	4,277	29,872	4,272
2010............................	33,274	12,773	23,709	4,263	29,768	4,188
2009............................	32,279	12,643	21,588	4,486	28,908	4,109
2008............................	34,240	12,857	24,340	4,720	30,618	3,990
2007............................	33,040	12,885	23,923	4,726	30,932	4,111
2006............................	32,532	12,711	23,060	4,920	32,148	3,884
2005............................	31,008	12,015	21,623	4,744	29,471	3,667
2004............................	30,828	11,562	21,606	4,633	29,694	3,440
2003[3].........................	28,806	11,195	20,637	4,556	26,652	3,234
2002............................	29,084	10,979	21,611	4,506	27,992	3,205
2001............................	27,964	10,258	20,614	4,289	26,745	2,985
2000[4].........................	27,253	9,996	19,501	4,236	25,629	2,940
1999............................	24,381	9,576	17,713	3,944	23,196	2,875
1998............................	25,534	8,288	17,756	3,428	24,739	2,413
1997............................	23,520	8,261	17,447	3,444	22,253	2,391
1996............................	21,870	7,975	14,986	3,382	21,593	2,116
1995............................	20,312	7,337	14,774	3,140	20,882	2,039
1994............................	21,288	7,117	16,355	3,111	19,667	1,937
1993............................	19,460	6,957	13,572	2,928	18,765	1,954
1992............................	18,318	6,811	13,041	2,981	18,884	1,888
1991............................	18,516	5,932	13,134	2,548	18,582	1,705

[1]For data prior to 1991, "Some college/Associate degree" equals 1 to 3 years of college completed; "Bachelor's degree" equals 4 years of college; "Advanced degree" equals 5 or more years of college completed.
[2]Starting in 2011, earnings data were created using population controls based on Census 2010 data.
[3]Starting in 2003, respondents could choose more than one race. The race data in this table from 2003 onward represent respondents who indicated only one race.
[4]Beginning in 2000, earnings data are from the expanded Current Population Survey (CPS) sample and were calculated using population controls based on Census 2000.
[5]May be of any race.
… = Not available.

Table A-34. Mean Earnings of Workers 18 Years Old and Over, by Educational Attainment, Race, Hispanic Origin, and Sex, 1975–2019—*Continued*

(Dollars except as noted.)

Race, sex, year, and Hispanic origin	Some college or associate's degree[1]		Bachelor's degree[1]		Advanced degree[1]	
	Mean earnings	Number of workers (thousands)	Mean earnings	Number of workers (thousands)	Mean earnings	Number of workers (thousands)
2007	31,040	5,000	44,696	2,114	73,111	874
2006	31,380	4,863	45,371	2,038	70,432	678
2005	29,836	4,467	45,933	1,775	70,916	705
2004	29,260	4,369	45,166	1,669	69,839	629
2003[3]	28,494	4,235	43,676	1,663	62,794	603
2002	27,757	4,024	40,949	1,568	67,679	569
2001	27,523	3,842	40,586	1,416	62,194	517
2000[4]	25,276	3,737	44,661	1,395	63,908	455
1999	24,207	3,662	35,704	1,194	55,097	491
1998	23,091	3,289	35,014	1,156	62,583	425
1997	22,001	3,075	33,465	1,140	58,571	437
1996	22,209	3,096	32,955	1,027	49,873	398
1995	19,923	2,856	30,602	866	45,612	334
1994	21,041	2,723	29,165	844	51,898	337
1993	19,043	2,728	30,359	799	45,034	325
1992	18,769	2,515	27,944	767	40,741	293
1991	19,075	2,080	26,623	665	39,609	311
1990	19,206	1,534	25,703	601	38,075	382
1989	18,707	1,513	28,157	535	39,273	349
1988	18,101	1,511	23,745	596	33,843	340
1987	16,899	1,400	23,105	644	34,413	335
1986	16,523	1,411	22,707	471	28,316	295
1985	15,310	1,226	20,878	458	28,357	273
1984	14,359	1,116	19,924	381	26,327	265
1983	13,371	976	17,972	320	24,352	222
1982	13,108	873	18,186	303	28,167	186
1981	12,971	834	16,114	320	24,082	161
1980	11,891	808	15,676	283	21,910	157
1979	10,181	768	14,940	240	18,273	190
1978	9,575	661	13,985	213	17,333	125
1977	8,172	656	12,572	210	16,660	118
1976	7,252	592	11,242	177	14,000	118
1975	7,154	474	10,573	173	15,756	111
Male						
2019	45,400	3,973	66,080	2,101	96,873	873
2018	43,825	3,716	64,478	1,892	110,367	689
2017	43,481	3,834	62,469	1,845	95,960	646
2016	42,172	3,652	62,670	1,643	98,834	633
2015	40,672	3,426	69,600	1,570	95,226	655
2014	40,192	3,331	59,791	1,439	92,887	542
2013	37,245	3,222	59,368	1,360	89,624	555
2012	36,238	2,949	60,552	1,308	89,780	525
2011[2]	36,660	2,928	54,936	1,200	96,359	456
2010	35,925	2,756	56,924	1,147	83,343	420
2009	36,071	2,485	58,570	1,122	84,368	439
2008	37,864	2,615	56,980	1,109	96,976	422
2007	35,861	2,510	50,805	1,057	87,195	478
2006	36,217	2,500	51,336	1,066	87,835	340
2005	34,754	2,326	54,700	896	84,033	380
2004	34,447	2,241	53,567	916	84,152	332
2003[3]	34,157	2,193	49,298	867	71,446	344
2002	32,935	2,112	46,115	815	73,836	338
2001	32,595	1,962	45,445	748	75,746	272
2000[4]	30,155	1,873	55,050	722	81,447	223
1999	28,621	1,873	41,740	623	66,191	262
1998	26,483	1,652	40,889	569	83,754	226
1997	25,923	1,598	37,963	557	68,097	272
1996	26,682	1,687	38,130	531	49,307	259
1995	22,171	1,475	35,109	466	50,802	215
1994	24,517	1,410	33,797	450	60,858	210
1993	22,417	1,444	37,554	438	52,441	194
1992	21,266	1,353	32,859	415	45,065	173
1991	21,086	1,132	31,699	356	45,107	192

[1]For data prior to 1991, "Some college/Associate degree" equals 1 to 3 years of college completed; "Bachelor's degree" equals 4 years of college; "Advanced degree" equals 5 or more years of college completed.
[2]Starting in 2011, earnings data were created using population controls based on Census 2010 data.
[3]Starting in 2003, respondents could choose more than one race. The race data in this table from 2003 onward represent respondents who indicated only one race.
[4]Beginning in 2000, earnings data are from the expanded Current Population Survey (CPS) sample and were calculated using population controls based on Census 2000.
[5]May be of any race.
… = Not available.

Table A-34. Mean Earnings of Workers 18 Years Old and Over, by Educational Attainment, Race, Hispanic Origin, and Sex, 1975–2019—*Continued*

(Dollars except as noted.)

Race, sex, year, and Hispanic origin	Total		Not a high school graduate		High school graduate	
	Mean earnings	Number of workers (thousands)	Mean earnings	Number of workers (thousands)	Mean earnings	Number of workers (thousands)
1990	18,320	5,745	13,182	2,562	18,100	1,812
1989	18,087	5,641	13,167	2,632	17,579	1,711
1988	17,357	5,477	12,836	2,517	17,446	1,621
1987	17,048	5,248	12,823	2,281	16,774	1,616
1986	15,624	5,037	11,262	2,262	15,948	1,546
1985	15,293	4,702	11,671	2,111	15,602	1,491
1984	14,957	4,344	11,441	2,022	15,763	1,319
1983	14,265	3,577	11,353	1,678	14,584	1,074
1982	13,484	3,480	10,108	1,622	13,883	1,083
1981	13,052	3,504	10,447	1,686	13,513	1,037
1980	12,310	3,401	9,825	1,707	13,108	961
1979	11,332	3,269	9,393	1,615	11,714	952
1978	10,473	2,915	8,836	1,498	10,940	815
1977	9,655	2,833	8,192	1,460	10,386	776
1976	8,787	2,571	7,440	1,321	9,640	712
1975	8,162	2,456	6,745	1,287	8,546	691
Female						
2019	35,546	13,120	20,976	2,215	28,057	3,698
2018	35,190	12,519	19,793	2,165	27,405	3,577
2017	32,961	12,067	18,292	2,132	27,743	3,478
2016	30,569	11,747	20,694	2,135	24,313	3,340
2015	31,160	11,301	18,138	2,302	24,151	3,258
2014	28,291	10,775	17,461	2,340	24,412	3,183
2013	27,504	10,412	16,971	2,229	22,999	2,946
2012	26,479	10,189	15,174	2,166	21,832	3,001
2011[2]	26,230	9,892	14,949	2,305	21,988	2,904
2010	25,554	9,553	14,667	2,206	21,136	2,793
2009	25,713	8,907	16,170	2,180	21,473	2,644
2008	24,646	8,995	14,960	2,552	21,725	2,712
2007	25,262	8,676	15,574	2,162	22,283	2,570
2006	24,104	8,497	15,072	2,214	20,608	2,611
2005	22,887	8,009	14,365	2,250	19,864	2,413
2004	21,967	7,781	13,830	2,302	20,037	2,301
2003[3]	21,391	7,591	13,632	2,210	18,967	2,283
2002	21,008	7,430	13,694	2,241	18,810	2,293
2001	20,330	7,316	13,976	2,243	17,786	2,279
2000[4]	19,115	7,164	12,622	2,191	17,180	2,204
1999	18,132	6,699	12,722	2,077	16,548	2,032
1998	17,461	6,804	12,273	1,854	15,952	1,806
1997	16,781	5,711	10,503	1,794	15,747	1,691
1996	15,841	5,390	9,867	1,680	14,635	1,667
1995	15,310	5,096	9,809	1,644	14,989	1,555
1994	14,631	4,918	8,559	1,576	14,313	1,508
1993	13,602	4,687	8,489	1,498	13,584	1,413
1992	13,774	4,539	8,854	1,445	13,277	1,461
1991	13,073	4,074	7,960	1,358	13,037	1,339
1990	12,516	3,984	5,093	1,367	12,109	1,470
1989	12,307	3,929	8,256	1,353	11,799	1,477
1988	11,573	3,749	7,597	1,307	11,284	1,332
1987	11,234	3,569	7,350	1,176	10,627	1,366
1986	10,457	3,356	7,130	1,117	10,319	1,289
1985	9,865	3,138	6,699	1,112	9,784	1,170
1984	9,150	3,005	6,438	1,107	9,492	1,138
1983	8,704	2,645	6,305	996	9,261	956
1982	8,195	2,434	5,781	961	8,668	884
1981	7,723	2,426	5,486	962	8,292	929
1980	6,770	2,322	5,028	942	6,923	863
1979	6,255	2,276	4,675	918	6,708	860
1978	5,501	1,983	4,135	847	5,834	739
1977	4,964	1,919	3,707	846	5,466	685
1976	4,548	1,732	3,537	786	5,124	597
1975	4,152	1,622	3,233	741	4,708	602

[1]For data prior to 1991, "Some college/Associate degree" equals 1 to 3 years of college completed; "Bachelor's degree" equals 4 years of college; "Advanced degree" equals 5 or more years of college completed.
[2]Starting in 2011, earnings data were created using population controls based on Census 2010 data.
[3]Starting in 2003, respondents could choose more than one race. The race data in this table from 2003 onward represent respondents who indicated only one race.
[4]Beginning in 2000, earnings data are from the expanded Current Population Survey (CPS) sample and were calculated using population controls based on Census 2000.
[5]May be of any race.
… = Not available.

Table A-34. Mean Earnings of Workers 18 Years Old and Over, by Educational Attainment, Race, Hispanic Origin, and Sex, 1975–2019—*Continued*

(Dollars except as noted.)

Race, sex, year, and Hispanic origin	Some college or associate's degree[1]		Bachelor's degree[1]		Advanced degree[1]	
	Mean earnings	Number of workers (thousands)	Mean earnings	Number of workers (thousands)	Mean earnings	Number of workers (thousands)
1990	22,376	852	31,485	314	47,479	205
1989	22,374	810	32,767	292	49,088	196
1988	21,631	811	26,935	333	40,916	194
1987	19,414	758	26,581	383	39,014	211
1986	19,675	778	27,427	274	32,538	176
1985	18,168	678	24,723	267	32,831	155
1984	17,261	611	23,835	223	30,727	168
1983	16,626	514	21,911	170	28,680	141
1982	15,560	495	22,565	153	34,474	125
1981	15,432	489	19,201	177	27,619	114
1980	14,331	451	19,224	167	24,642	114
1979	12,489	441	18,923	142	21,299	118
1978	11,545	393	16,898	127	20,702	82
1977	9,924	391	15,189	120	19,025	85
1976	8,843	342	13,650	114	16,184	81
1975	8,807	279	12,881	113	17,991	86
Female						
2019	32,653	3,902	48,151	2,306	77,841	997
2010	32,013	3,807	54,567	2,018	71,121	951
2017	31,127	3,753	46,237	1,921	72,396	781
2016	28,587	3,752	44,608	1,778	63,592	740
2015	30,937	3,460	46,372	1,525	71,443	754
2014	27,210	3,209	44,347	1,412	57,642	629
2013	27,184	3,302	42,216	1,398	59,686	535
2012	25,408	3,093	41,277	1,398	66,273	528
2011[2]	26,032	2,844	41,483	1,327	62,746	510
2010	25,797	2,795	39,292	1,243	61,673	515
2009	26,065	2,550	39,566	1,134	64,405	398
2008	25,226	2,534	39,231	1,115	56,175	380
2007	26,179	2,489	38,584	1,057	56,129	396
2006	26,260	2,362	38,825	971	52,896	337
2005	24,493	2,141	37,003	879	55,554	324
2004	23,796	2,128	34,949	753	53,887	298
2003[3]	22,411	2,042	37,550	795	51,294	258
2002	22,035	1,911	35,357	753	58,623	230
2001	22,229	1,879	35,142	668	47,176	245
2000[4]	20,372	1,864	33,489	672	47,057	232
1999	19,588	1,789	29,108	570	42,463	230
1998	20,460	1,639	29,317	587	38,422	200
1997	17,759	1,477	29,173	584	43,051	165
1996	16,856	1,409	27,407	495	50,960	139
1995	17,521	1,380	25,338	399	36,255	118
1994	17,309	1,313	23,867	393	37,269	127
1993	15,250	1,284	21,627	361	34,001	131
1992	15,858	1,162	22,144	352	34,457	119
1991	15,720	948	20,791	309	30,713	119
1990	15,245	682	19,378	287	27,184	177
1989	14,482	703	22,617	243	26,700	153
1988	14,012	700	19,707	263	24,444	146
1987	13,929	642	18,003	261	26,584	124
1986	12,648	633	16,142	197	22,071	119
1985	11,791	548	15,503	191	22,480	118
1984	10,848	505	14,404	158	18,706	97
1983	9,750	462	13,507	150	16,817	81
1982	9,896	378	13,719	150	15,244	61
1981	9,483	345	12,292	143	15,503	47
1980	8,808	357	10,568	116	14,668	43
1979	7,069	327	9,168	98	13,313	72
1978	6,686	268	9,684	86	10,908	43
1977	5,588	265	9,082	90	10,569	33
1976	5,075	250	6,884	63	9,218	37
1975	4,790	195	6,226	60	8,067	25

[1]For data prior to 1991, "Some college/Associate degree" equals 1 to 3 years of college completed; "Bachelor's degree" equals 4 years of college; "Advanced degree" equals 5 or more years of college completed.
[2]Starting in 2011, earnings data were created using population controls based on Census 2010 data.
[3]Starting in 2003, respondents could choose more than one race. The race data in this table from 2003 onward represent respondents who indicated only one race.
[4]Beginning in 2000, earnings data are from the expanded Current Population Survey (CPS) sample and were calculated using population controls based on Census 2000.
[5]May be of any race.
... – Not available.

Table A-34. Mean Earnings of Workers 18 Years Old and Over, by Educational Attainment, Race, Hispanic Origin, and Sex, 1975–2019—*Continued*

(Dollars except as noted.)

Race, sex, year, and Hispanic origin	Total		Not a high school graduate		High school graduate	
	Mean earnings	Number of workers (thousands)	Mean earnings	Number of workers (thousands)	Mean earnings	Number of workers (thousands)
WHITE ALONE OR IN COMBINATION						
Both Sexes						
2019	59,471	132,975	29,623	9,258	40,726	33,763
2018	56,743	131,740	27,594	9,782	40,561	34,044
2017	54,535	130,955	27,180	10,024	39,663	34,025
2016	52,885	129,984	28,492	9,901	38,170	34,183
2015	50,981	129,762	26,268	10,609	36,948	33,995
2014	48,772	127,557	25,894	10,790	35,354	34,216
2013	47,280	127,029	24,264	10,470	34,101	34,391
2012	46,650	126,527	22,019	10,696	33,803	34,058
2011[2]	45,898	125,256	21,648	11,080	33,584	34,425
2010	44,103	124,707	21,427	10,993	32,023	34,908
2009	43,213	127,001	20,468	11,708	31,351	36,656
2008	43,550	129,419	21,483	12,630	32,072	37,299
2007	43,000	129,203	22,245	12,568	32,126	37,570
2006	42,249	128,366	21,389	13,800	31,998	37,915
2005	40,592	126,882	20,225	13,424	30,494	37,723
2004	38,855	125,388	19,365	13,540	29,595	37,639
2003[3]	37,958	124,456	18,734	16,282	27,915	45,064
2002	37,290	124,337	19,278	13,957	28,107	37,863
Male						
2019	69,210	70,994	34,298	5,873	46,842	20,261
2018	66,592	70,514	32,386	6,295	47,055	20,239
2017	63,878	70,702	32,027	6,487	46,168	20,339
2016	62,320	69,912	33,197	6,429	45,231	20,309
2015	60,364	69,837	31,168	6,866	43,502	20,177
2014	58,148	68,611	30,224	6,989	41,291	20,145
2013	55,973	68,402	28,083	6,948	39,102	20,165
2012	55,544	68,068	25,701	6,940	39,910	19,715
2011[2]	54,835	67,254	25,719	7,030	40,105	19,864
2010	52,457	66,903	25,205	7,032	37,540	20,047
2009	51,133	68,426	23,327	7,561	36,321	21,162
2008	52,502	69,829	25,254	8,263	37,740	21,192
2007	51,599	70,073	25,848	8,305	38,072	21,436
2006	50,826	69,702	24,524	9,055	38,699	21,401
2005	49,437	68,987	23,526	8,740	36,608	21,289
2004	47,275	67,758	22,576	8,751	35,348	21,074
2003[3]	45,989	67,198	21,787	8,682	34,225	20,534
2002	45,682	67,082	22,601	8,977	33,846	20,430
Female						
2019	48,317	61,981	21,512	3,385	31,548	13,502
2018	45,400	61,226	18,941	3,486	31,039	13,805
2017	43,571	60,252	18,290	3,537	29,995	13,686
2016	41,905	60,071	19,780	3,472	27,833	13,873
2015	40,046	59,924	17,281	3,743	27,376	13,817
2014	37,859	58,945	17,930	3,801	26,854	14,070
2013	37,138	58,627	16,731	3,522	27,011	14,226
2012	36,293	58,458	15,217	3,756	25,408	14,343
2011[2]	35,534	58,001	14,581	4,050	24,687	14,561
2010	34,434	57,804	14,718	3,960	24,581	14,861
2009	33,961	58,574	15,254	4,146	24,561	15,494
2008	33,060	59,590	14,345	4,366	24,615	16,107
2007	32,810	59,130	15,226	4,263	24,226	16,134
2006	32,059	58,663	15,408	4,745	23,313	16,514
2005	30,053	57,895	14,066	4,684	22,574	16,434
2004	28,954	57,630	13,498	4,788	22,277	16,566
2003[3]	28,532	57,257	14,086	4,684	22,029	16,926
2002	27,457	57,254	13,286	4,979	21,381	17,433

[1]For data prior to 1991, "Some college/Associate degree" equals 1 to 3 years of college completed; "Bachelor's degree" equals 4 years of college; "Advanced degree" equals 5 or more years of college completed.
[2]Starting in 2011, earnings data were created using population controls based on Census 2010 data.
[3]Starting in 2003, respondents could choose more than one race. The race data in this table from 2003 onward represent respondents who indicated only one race.
[4]Beginning in 2000, earnings data are from the expanded Current Population Survey (CPS) sample and were calculated using population controls based on Census 2000.
[5]May be of any race.
… = Not available.

Table A-34. Mean Earnings of Workers 18 Years Old and Over, by Educational Attainment, Race, Hispanic Origin, and Sex, 1975–2019—*Continued*

(Dollars except as noted.)

Race, sex, year, and Hispanic origin	Some college or associate's degree[1]		Bachelor's degree[1]		Advanced degree[1]	
	Mean earnings	Number of workers (thousands)	Mean earnings	Number of workers (thousands)	Mean earnings	Number of workers (thousands)
WHITE ALONE OR IN COMBINATION						
Both Sexes						
2019..............................	46,542	37,662	74,677	33,652	106,928	18,637
2018..............................	44,105	37,541	73,115	32,347	100,070	18,024
2017..............................	42,587	37,794	69,035	31,680	98,853	17,429
2016..............................	41,339	38,480	68,292	30,471	95,331	16,947
2015..............................	39,835	38,596	66,733	29,682	92,570	16,877
2014..............................	39,403	37,756	63,404	28,754	88,614	16,039
2013..............................	37,330	38,164	60,859	28,374	91,349	15,627
2012..............................	36,751	38,544	61,399	28,072	90,761	15,154
2011[2]	36,139	37,718	61,173	27,455	89,895	14,575
2010..............................	35,295	37,355	59,122	26,941	85,131	14,511
2009..............................	35,540	37,684	57,662	26,920	86,067	14,031
2008..............................	35,528	38,593	59,824	26,784	84,687	14,111
2007..............................	35,565	38,664	58,565	26,583	82,309	13,816
2006..............................	35,276	37,530	57,807	26,035	83,002	13,084
2005..............................	34,279	38,149	55,758	24,919	81,437	12,665
2004..............................	32,736	37,287	52,790	24,361	78,747	12,560
2003[3]	31,498	44,048	51,206	28,672	74,601	14,592
2002..............................	31,767	36,639	52,509	23,865	73,773	12,011
Male						
2019..............................	56,095	19,119	90,075	16,818	131,766	8,921
2018..............................	54,167	19,000	87,522	16,344	125,050	8,634
2017..............................	51,639	19,232	83,192	16,168	121,690	8,475
2016..............................	49,685	19,464	83,750	15,397	116,488	8,312
2015..............................	47,616	19,353	82,230	15,086	115,139	8,353
2014..............................	48,193	18,921	78,225	14,611	112,251	7,943
2013..............................	45,088	19,129	73,958	14,346	117,941	7,813
2012..............................	44,814	19,246	74,396	14,465	113,877	7,700
2011[2]	44,135	18,674	73,557	14,163	112,265	7,521
2010..............................	42,500	18,359	72,047	14,004	105,955	7,461
2009..............................	42,760	18,567	71,166	13,886	106,451	7,248
2008..............................	43,307	19,210	75,024	13,734	107,065	7,428
2007..............................	42,760	19,343	73,390	13,697	103,214	7,291
2006..............................	42,605	18,686	71,602	13,443	103,097	7,116
2005..............................	47,139	18,954	69,821	13,045	102,904	6,957
2004..............................	40,627	18,362	65,498	12,728	99,543	6,843
2003[3]	39,555	18,421	65,237	12,774	93,792	6,785
2002..............................	39,439	18,377	65,548	12,621	92,575	6,675
Female						
2019..............................	36,692	18,542	59,294	16,834	84,123	9,716
2018..............................	33,793	18,541	58,401	16,002	77,099	9,390
2017..............................	33,208	18,562	54,279	15,511	77,240	8,954
2016..............................	32,797	19,015	52,505	15,074	74,966	8,635
2015..............................	32,010	19,243	50,716	14,596	70,453	8,523
2014..............................	30,572	18,835	48,092	14,143	65,422	8,095
2013..............................	29,534	19,035	47,464	14,028	64,762	7,814
2012..............................	28,709	19,298	47,584	13,607	66,881	7,454
2011[2]	28,299	19,044	47,976	13,292	66,041	7,053
2010..............................	28,332	18,995	45,130	12,937	63,092	7,050
2009..............................	28,528	19,116	43,275	13,034	64,283	6,782
2008..............................	27,819	19,383	43,826	13,060	50,814	6,603
2007..............................	28,362	19,321	42,807	12,886	58,951	6,525
2006..............................	28,008	18,844	43,078	12,591	59,042	5,968
2005..............................	25,518	19,194	40,306	11,873	55,273	5,707
2004..............................	25,079	18,925	38,886	11,633	53,859	5,718
2003[3]	25,093	18,616	37,750	11,476	53,021	5,552
2002..............................	24,046	18,261	37,872	11,243	50,255	5,336

[1]For data prior to 1991, "Some college/Associate degree" equals 1 to 3 years of college completed; "Bachelor's degree" equals 4 years of college; "Advanced degree" equals 5 or more years of college completed.
[2]Starting in 2011, earnings data were created using population controls based on Census 2010 data.
[3]Starting in 2003, respondents could choose more than one race. The race data in this table from 2003 onward represent respondents who indicated only one race.
[4]Beginning in 2000, earnings data are from the expanded Current Population Survey (CPS) sample and were calculated using population controls based on Census 2000.
[5]May be of any race.
... = Not available.

Table A-34. Mean Earnings of Workers 18 Years Old and Over, by Educational Attainment, Race, Hispanic Origin, and Sex, 1975–2019—*Continued*

(Dollars except as noted.)

Race, sex, year, and Hispanic origin	Total		Not a high school graduate		High school graduate	
	Mean earnings	Number of workers (thousands)	Mean earnings	Number of workers (thousands)	Mean earnings	Number of workers (thousands)
NON-HISPANIC WHITE ALONE OR IN COMBINATION						
Both Sexes						
2019	64,081	105,915	30,150	3,635	42,632	25,160
2018	60,731	105,563	27,347	3,940	42,274	25,586
2017	58,297	105,469	26,904	4,157	41,142	26,003
2016	56,249	105,396	27,150	4,117	39,070	26,546
2015	54,138	105,849	26,738	4,515	38,446	26,400
2014	51,984	104,543	28,791	4,447	36,673	27,032
2013	50,424	104,642	26,562	4,238	35,470	27,636
2012	49,757	104,714	23,002	4,588	35,260	27,261
2011[2]	48,950	104,217	22,468	4,960	35,205	27,811
2010	46,894	104,136	22,408	4,940	33,268	28,501
2009	45,813	106,618	21,241	5,331	32,478	30,276
2008	46,050	108,823	21,579	5,959	33,105	30,982
2007	45,393	108,929	22,945	6,040	32,992	31,288
2006	44,652	108,297	22,094	6,995	32,844	31,802
2005	42,839	107,945	21,088	6,744	31,367	31,951
2004	40,847	107,086	19,667	6,893	30,195	32,217
2003[3]	39,989	106,658	19,764	6,906	29,561	32,225
2002	39,135	107,050	19,491	7,516	28,714	32,758
Male						
2019	75,443	55,836	34,757	2,302	49,310	15,031
2018	72,324	55,743	33,159	2,457	49,347	15,067
2017	69,152	56,133	31,964	2,602	48,321	15,471
2016	66,808	55,923	32,056	2,622	46,245	15,570
2015	64,884	56,124	33,003	2,862	45,533	15,559
2014	62,883	55,277	34,929	2,799	43,134	15,831
2013	60,564	55,448	32,072	2,770	40,829	16,130
2012	60,103	55,462	27,899	2,824	41,984	15,644
2011[2]	59,346	55,152	27,620	3,049	42,612	15,908
2010	56,546	55,081	27,242	3,050	39,332	16,198
2009	55,161	56,390	25,612	3,262	38,049	17,253
2008	56,357	57,636	26,226	3,743	39,288	17,435
2007	55,457	57,886	27,810	3,800	39,602	17,567
2006	54,624	57,615	25,996	4,358	40,034	17,723
2005	53,084	57,553	25,469	4,213	38,034	17,787
2004	50,488	56,762	23,520	4,288	36,323	17,817
2003[3]	49,227	56,549	22,947	4,313	35,550	17,549
2002	48,700	56,714	23,426	4,663	34,830	17,446
Female						
2019	51,413	50,078	22,191	1,332	32,721	10,129
2018	47,760	49,819	17,716	1,482	32,142	10,518
2017	45,948	49,335	18,429	1,554	30,597	10,532
2016	44,314	49,473	18,546	1,495	28,808	10,886
2015	42,009	49,725	15,893	1,653	28,275	10,840
2014	39,755	49,266	18,362	1,647	27,542	11,201
2013	38,994	49,193	16,163	1,468	27,957	11,505
2012	38,106	49,251	15,161	1,763	26,205	11,617
2011[2]	37,264	49,065	14,246	1,910	25,304	11,902
2010	34,434	57,804	14,718	3,960	24,581	14,861
2009	35,318	50,227	14,347	2,068	25,096	13,022
2008	34,445	51,187	13,726	2,215	25,148	13,547
2007	33,979	51,043	14,690	2,239	24,530	13,721
2006	33,316	50,682	15,642	2,636	23,794	14,079
2005	31,139	50,391	13,793	2,530	22,994	14,163
2004	28,954	57,630	13,498	4,788	22,277	16,566
2003[3]	29,564	50,108	14,469	2,592	22,479	14,765
2002	28,359	50,335	13,060	2,853	21,745	15,312

[1]For data prior to 1991, "Some college/Associate degree" equals 1 to 3 years of college completed; "Bachelor's degree" equals 4 years of college; "Advanced degree" equals 5 or more years of college completed.
[2]Starting in 2011, earnings data were created using population controls based on Census 2010 data.
[3]Starting in 2003, respondents could choose more than one race. The race data in this table from 2003 onward represent respondents who indicated only one race.
[4]Beginning in 2000, earnings data are from the expanded Current Population Survey (CPS) sample and were calculated using population controls based on Census 2000.
[5]May be of any race.
... = Not available.

Table A-34. Mean Earnings of Workers 18 Years Old and Over, by Educational Attainment, Race, Hispanic Origin, and Sex, 1975–2019—*Continued*

(Dollars except as noted.)

Race, sex, year, and Hispanic origin	Some college or associate's degree[1]		Bachelor's degree[1]		Advanced degree[1]	
	Mean earnings	Number of workers (thousands)	Mean earnings	Number of workers (thousands)	Mean earnings	Number of workers (thousands)
NON-HISPANIC WHITE ALONE OR IN COMBINATION						
Both Sexes						
2019	48,264	30,487	77,020	29,686	108,996	16,945
2018	45,464	30,696	74,740	28,795	101,172	16,544
2017	43,712	30,929	70,848	28,240	100,016	16,138
2016	42,644	31,746	69,962	27,347	96,379	15,729
2015	40,705	32,404	67,469	26,896	93,459	15,633
2014	40,306	31,919	64,462	26,162	89,586	14,981
2013	38,177	32,311	61,814	25,858	92,592	14,598
2012	37,725	33,054	62,395	25,607	91,442	14,202
2011[2]	36,916	32,528	62,300	25,217	90,442	13,699
2010	36,046	32,321	60,111	24,730	85,960	13,644
2009	36,163	32,964	58,398	24,814	86,674	13,231
2008	36,042	33,806	60,818	24,717	84,996	13,350
2007	36,176	33,994	59,637	24,622	82,840	12,983
2006	35,795	32,962	58,785	24,103	83,629	12,433
2005	34,824	33,991	56,441	23,253	81,944	12,003
2004	33,192	33,201	53,335	22,815	79,166	11,961
2003[3]	32,732	33,062	52,823	22,686	76,029	11,777
2002	32,210	32,876	53,244	22,415	74,011	11,482
Male						
2019	58,579	15,447	93,002	14,931	135,123	8,123
2018	56,378	15,607	90,190	14,618	126,140	7,993
2017	53,400	15,721	85,654	14,456	123,474	7,881
2016	51,344	16,121	86,032	13,879	117,742	7,730
2015	48,967	16,271	83,328	13,664	116,296	7,766
2014	49,537	15,922	80,000	13,283	113,429	7,439
2013	46,426	16,176	75,330	13,088	119,984	7,282
2012	46,207	16,520	75,609	13,257	115,320	7,215
2011[2]	45,417	16,018	75,075	13,067	112,884	7,108
2010	43,587	15,845	73,245	12,929	107,217	7,058
2009	43,680	16,218	72,222	12,834	107,782	6,821
2008	44,075	16,739	76,560	12,692	107,540	7,025
2007	43,707	16,973	75,109	12,715	104,236	6,830
2006	43,491	16,320	73,244	12,424	103,794	6,787
2005	43,083	16,769	70,891	12,187	103,850	6,593
2004	41,490	16,260	66,467	11,870	100,220	6,527
2003[3]	40,196	16,358	66,368	11,946	94,830	6,471
2002	40,195	16,390	66,776	11,859	100,412	6,510
Female						
2019	37,668	15,039	60,847	14,755	84,939	8,822
2018	34,175	15,089	58,810	14,177	77,832	8,551
2017	33,698	15,208	55,319	13,783	77,626	8,257
2016	33,667	15,625	53,401	13,468	75,732	7,998
2015	32,372	16,132	51,092	13,232	70,913	7,866
2014	31,118	15,997	48,436	12,879	66,065	7,541
2013	29,907	16,135	47,960	12,769	65,324	7,315
2012	29,250	16,534	48,210	12,349	66,783	6,986
2011[2]	28,668	16,510	48,561	12,150	66,241	6,591
2010	28,332	18,995	45,130	12,937	63,092	7,050
2009	28,882	16,745	43,589	11,980	64,211	6,409
2008	28,163	17,007	44,203	12,025	59,983	6,332
2007	28,665	17,020	43,115	11,907	59,092	6,153
2006	28,248	16,641	43,402	11,678	59,389	5,646
2005	26,782	17,222	40,527	11,065	55,242	5,409
2004	25,079	18,925	38,886	11,633	53,859	5,718
2003[3]	25,422	16,704	37,757	10,739	53,102	5,306
2002	24,271	16,485	38,042	10,556	49,827	5,127

[1]For data prior to 1991, "Some college/Associate degree" equals 1 to 3 years of college completed; "Bachelor's degree" equals 4 years of college; "Advanced degree" equals 5 or more years of college completed.
[2]Starting in 2011, earnings data were created using population controls based on Census 2010 data.
[3]Starting in 2003, respondents could choose more than one race. The race data in this table from 2003 onward represent respondents who indicated only one race.
[4]Beginning in 2000, earnings data are from the expanded Current Population Survey (CPS) sample and were calculated using population controls based on Census 2000.
[5]May be of any race.
... = Not available.

Table A-34. Mean Earnings of Workers 18 Years Old and Over, by Educational Attainment, Race, Hispanic Origin, and Sex, 1975–2019—*Continued*

(Dollars except as noted.)

Race, sex, year, and Hispanic origin	Total		Not a high school graduate		High school graduate	
	Mean earnings	Number of workers (thousands)	Mean earnings	Number of workers (thousands)	Mean earnings	Number of workers (thousands)
BLACK ALONE OR IN COMBINATION						
Both Sexes						
2019...............	46,417	22,366	29,324	1,455	33,267	6,883
2018...............	42,214	21,858	23,705	1,591	31,505	6,738
2017...............	41,274	21,401	23,937	1,484	31,926	6,656
2016...............	40,580	20,976	24,895	1,638	30,186	6,459
2015...............	39,326	20,228	19,655	1,677	29,060	6,260
2014...............	36,922	19,750	22,204	1,514	28,241	6,204
2013...............	35,571	19,045	20,951	1,726	26,594	5,960
2012...............	34,798	18,798	18,964	1,599	26,408	5,885
2011[2]	34,640	18,098	17,330	1,701	27,323	5,766
2010...............	33,050	17,838	17,525	1,747	25,842	5,786
2009...............	33,294	17,389	18,841	1,691	26,805	5,972
2008...............	32,878	18,157	18,049	1,826	27,123	6,220
2007...............	33,318	18,023	17,555	1,903	27,096	6,149
2006...............	32,384	17,721	17,842	1,995	26,290	6,305
2005...............	30,521	17,540	17,264	2,097	23,810	6,246
2004...............	29,031	17,110	17,821	2,085	23,458	6,299
2003[3]	28,854	16,871	16,238	2,177	23,956	6,082
2002...............	28,255	16,833	17,114	2,217	22,762	5,940
Male						
2019...............	50,103	10,469	33,728	778	36,641	3,681
2018...............	46,264	10,127	27,788	833	36,822	3,544
2017...............	45,864	10,030	27,639	747	36,658	3,602
2016...............	46,496	9,842	28,803	868	35,148	3,389
2015...............	43,773	9,472	23,797	848	33,581	3,287
2014...............	42,302	9,139	25,531	802	32,701	3,179
2013...............	40,318	8,860	25,377	934	29,742	3,044
2012...............	38,147	8,772	19,877	869	29,982	3,033
2011[2]	38,722	8,350	20,704	861	31,081	2,927
2010...............	36,190	8,193	19,428	944	29,801	3,003
2009...............	37,500	7,963	21,585	912	30,541	3,087
2008...............	36,386	8,442	21,894	913	30,690	3,263
2007...............	35,669	8,405	19,932	1,019	29,508	3,083
2006...............	36,026	8,170	21,361	1,006	29,973	3,146
2005...............	34,258	8,127	19,996	1,093	27,189	3,142
2004...............	32,919	7,885	22,755	1,050	26,575	3,202
2003[3]	32,574	7,689	17,982	1,088	28,323	2,981
2002...............	31,967	7,734	20,537	1,114	25,510	2,902
Female						
2019...............	43,173	11,896	24,253	676	29,387	3,202
2018...............	38,718	11,731	19,221	758	25,604	3,193
2017...............	37,224	11,370	20,184	737	26,345	3,054
2016...............	35,351	11,134	20,483	769	24,709	3,069
2015...............	35,411	10,756	15,420	829	24,060	2,972
2014...............	32,288	10,611	18,457	712	23,553	3,025
2013...............	31,442	10,185	15,723	791	23,309	2,916
2012...............	31,867	10,026	17,876	730	22,606	2,851
2011[2]	31,144	9,748	13,869	840	23,449	2,839
2010...............	30,383	9,646	15,292	804	21,570	2,783
2009...............	29,740	9,426	15,631	779	22,805	2,884
2008...............	29,829	9,715	14,204	913	23,187	2,957
2007...............	31,263	9,618	14,816	884	24,669	3,065
2006...............	29,268	9,551	14,257	988	22,622	3,159
2005...............	27,295	9,413	14,289	1,003	20,389	3,104
2004...............	25,707	9,225	12,818	1,035	20,236	3,097
2003[3]	25,739	9,182	14,495	1,089	19,765	3,100
2002...............	25,099	9,098	13,656	1,103	20,137	3,038

[1]For data prior to 1991, "Some college/Associate degree" equals 1 to 3 years of college completed; "Bachelor's degree" equals 4 years of college; "Advanced degree" equals 5 or more years of college completed.
[2]Starting in 2011, earnings data were created using population controls based on Census 2010 data.
[3]Starting in 2003, respondents could choose more than one race. The race data in this table from 2003 onward represent respondents who indicated only one race.
[4]Beginning in 2000, earnings data are from the expanded Current Population Survey (CPS) sample and were calculated using population controls based on Census 2000.
[5]May be of any race.
... = Not available.

Table A-34. Mean Earnings of Workers 18 Years Old and Over, by Educational Attainment, Race, Hispanic Origin, and Sex, 1975–2019—*Continued*

(Dollars except as noted.)

Race, sex, year, and Hispanic origin	Some college or associate's degree[1]		Bachelor's degree[1]		Advanced degree[1]	
	Mean earnings	Number of workers (thousands)	Mean earnings	Number of workers (thousands)	Mean earnings	Number of workers (thousands)
BLACK ALONE OR IN COMBINATION						
Both Sexes						
2019	37,945	7,162	61,222	4,523	93,008	2,341
2018	38,025	7,120	54,482	4,122	77,599	2,285
2017	36,242	7,272	53,964	3,948	77,781	2,039
2016	34,166	7,299	57,751	3,598	79,881	1,981
2015	34,345	7,059	55,584	3,393	81,381	1,837
2014	31,932	7,047	52,652	3,257	71,738	1,725
2013	31,867	6,541	49,351	3,229	72,413	1,587
2012	31,438	6,743	49,385	3,021	69,209	1,548
2011[2]	32,580	6,274	45,809	2,922	70,880	1,433
2010	30,901	6,262	44,743	2,730	71,409	1,313
2009	30,451	5,823	47,773	2,696	67,075	1,205
2008	30,266	6,207	46,983	2,654	66,247	1,248
2007	32,580	6,056	46,555	2,761	64,714	1,152
2006	31,175	5,759	47,740	2,580	64,563	1,080
2005	28,817	5,576	47,641	2,501	63,065	1,118
2004	27,801	5,370	42,131	2,415	64,545	942
2003[3]	27,095	5,296	42,991	2,374	63,966	940
2002	27,682	5,441	42,099	2,348	60,458	884
Male						
2019	42,712	3,200	67,176	1,998	114,049	810
2018	44,706	3,105	58,203	1,860	86,444	783
2017	40,854	3,197	61,668	1,708	92,018	775
2016	38,631	3,230	70,663	1,626	101,400	727
2015	39,238	3,084	63,992	1,537	90,477	714
2014	37,034	3,034	60,583	1,446	91,907	675
2013	37,568	2,852	56,800	1,387	88,936	640
2012	35,733	2,973	54,483	1,270	81,457	625
2011[2]	37,776	2,799	50,163	1,218	87,635	543
2010	35,132	2,618	48,948	1,113	82,022	514
2009	35,842	2,409	55,824	1,068	79,551	485
2008	34,159	2,631	52,773	1,103	73,362	530
2007	33,845	2,621	52,951	1,200	75,355	480
2006	34,784	2,417	52,382	1,124	74,769	475
2005	33,449	2,380	53,556	1,049	76,407	462
2004	32,466	2,258	47,448	976	77,648	398
2003[3]	31,591	2,233	45,705	982	76,954	402
2002	32,696	2,375	46,942	1,009	76,003	332
Female						
2019	34,093	3,961	56,510	2,525	81,864	1,530
2018	32,056	4,014	51,423	2,261	72,984	1,502
2017	32,623	4,074	48,089	2,240	69,040	1,263
2016	30,622	4,069	47,094	1,971	67,406	1,254
2015	30,548	3,974	48,620	1,855	75,598	1,123
2014	28,073	4,013	46,315	1,810	58,757	1,050
2013	27,457	3,688	43,738	1,841	61,233	946
2012	28,051	3,769	45,688	1,751	60,912	923
2011[2]	28,395	3,475	42,696	1,704	60,632	889
2010	27,861	3,644	41,846	1,616	64,577	799
2009	26,646	3,414	42,487	1,627	58,664	719
2008	27,399	3,675	42,861	1,550	60,996	718
2007	31,614	3,435	41,636	1,561	57,105	672
2006	28,565	3,342	44,157	1,456	56,541	605
2005	25,366	3,195	43,369	1,452	53,669	656
2004	24,415	3,111	38,522	1,438	54,931	543
2003[3]	23,816	3,063	41,073	1,391	54,265	538
2002	23,621	3,066	38,447	1,339	51,101	552

[1] For data prior to 1991, "Some college/Associate degree" equals 1 to 3 years of college completed; "Bachelor's degree" equals 4 years of college; "Advanced degree" equals 5 or more years of college completed.
[2] Starting in 2011, earnings data were created using population controls based on Census 2010 data.
[3] Starting in 2003, respondents could choose more than one race. The race data in this table from 2003 onward represent respondents who indicated only one race.
[4] Beginning in 2000, earnings data are from the expanded Current Population Survey (CPS) sample and were calculated using population controls based on Census 2000.
[5] May be of any race.
… = Not available.

Table A-34. Mean Earnings of Workers 18 Years Old and Over, by Educational Attainment, Race, Hispanic Origin, and Sex, 1975–2019—*Continued*

(Dollars except as noted.)

Race, sex, year, and Hispanic origin	Total		Not a high school graduate		High school graduate	
	Mean earnings	Number of workers (thousands)	Mean earnings	Number of workers (thousands)	Mean earnings	Number of workers (thousands)
ASIAN ALONE OR IN COMBINATION						
Both Sexes						
2019	73,685	11,705	31,329	627	37,394	1,735
2018	69,591	11,270	25,065	569	35,222	1,738
2017	66,240	10,932	29,126	602	35,168	1,758
2016	62,413	10,599	27,996	567	32,276	1,866
2015	60,892	10,057	23,340	591	33,847	1,652
2014	56,577	9,805	21,960	610	29,376	1,703
2013	54,320	9,367	24,499	613	31,088	1,726
2012	54,277	9,067	23,974	543	30,241	1,555
2011[2]	50,943	8,587	21,649	592	28,304	1,609
2010	48,480	8,563	20,592	620	28,452	1,629
2009	61,575	4,022	20,995	267	32,985	747
2008	50,622	7,553	21,195	569	29,163	1,300
2007	48,865	7,563	21,399	530	28,524	1,331
2006	50,094	7,501	20,142	631	29,502	1,413
2005	45,269	7,131	22,330	629	27,059	1,413
2004	43,856	6,771	19,536	525	27,946	1,292
2003[3]	41,563	6,560	19,548	564	25,554	1,256
2002	40,323	6,424	16,969	559	25,038	1,221
Male						
2019	83,815	6,086	34,418	341	43,570	931
2018	80,618	5,954	28,661	309	40,956	946
2017	77,742	5,821	34,659	300	41,564	981
2016	74,131	5,602	34,904	289	37,283	984
2015	70,202	5,322	26,205	315	38,246	886
2014	65,545	5,124	26,738	294	32,798	887
2013	63,189	5,032	24,585	302	36,133	951
2012	63,269	4,759	24,720	262	32,762	819
2011[2]	59,326	4,489	25,638	318	32,392	828
2010	56,115	4,461	23,836	330	31,685	820
2009	61,575	4,022	20,995	267	32,985	747
2008	59,565	4,007	23,204	297	34,568	655
2007	56,990	3,945	24,261	254	33,105	685
2006	59,328	3,980	22,631	318	32,716	783
2005	53,761	3,797	27,107	328	30,490	790
2004	52,032	3,634	20,799	252	31,194	730
2003[3]	48,062	3,522	23,122	308	28,514	635
2002	48,128	3,469	18,101	312	29,493	633
Female						
2019	62,710	5,618	27,651	286	30,229	803
2018	57,238	5,315	20,784	259	28,375	792
2017	53,139	5,111	23,640	302	27,100	777
2016	49,273	4,996	20,803	277	26,695	882
2015	50,426	4,734	20,074	276	28,752	765
2014	46,761	4,681	17,496	315	25,652	815
2013	44,026	4,335	24,416	311	24,895	775
2012	44,342	4,307	23,277	280	27,432	735
2011[2]	41,759	4,097	17,012	274	23,973	781
2010	40,177	4,102	16,895	290	25,175	809
2009	42,848	3,561	20,121	239	25,448	713
2008	40,518	3,546	18,999	272	23,665	644
2007	40,002	3,617	18,753	275	23,660	645
2006	39,652	3,520	17,610	313	25,508	630
2005	35,593	3,333	17,122	301	22,703	622
2004	34,387	3,137	18,375	273	23,721	562
2003[3]	34,031	3,038	15,233	255	22,530	621
2002	31,157	2,954	15,536	247	20,242	588

[1]For data prior to 1991, "Some college/Associate degree" equals 1 to 3 years of college completed; "Bachelor's degree" equals 4 years of college; "Advanced degree" equals 5 or more years of college completed.
[2]Starting in 2011, earnings data were created using population controls based on Census 2010 data.
[3]Starting in 2003, respondents could choose more than one race. The race data in this table from 2003 onward represent respondents who indicated only one race.
[4]Beginning in 2000, earnings data are from the expanded Current Population Survey (CPS) sample and were calculated using population controls based on Census 2000.
[5]May be of any race.
… = Not available.

Table A-34. Mean Earnings of Workers 18 Years Old and Over, by Educational Attainment, Race, Hispanic Origin, and Sex, 1975–2019—*Continued*

(Dollars except as noted.)

Race, sex, year, and Hispanic origin	Some college or associate's degree[1]		Bachelor's degree[1]		Advanced degree[1]	
	Mean earnings	Number of workers (thousands)	Mean earnings	Number of workers (thousands)	Mean earnings	Number of workers (thousands)
ASIAN ALONE OR IN COMBINATION						
Both Sexes						
2019	40,969	1,941	75,118	4,128	118,641	3,273
2018	40,026	2,111	72,079	3,902	116,324	2,948
2017	37,559	2,149	70,857	3,573	109,132	2,848
2016	37,279	2,246	67,706	3,189	104,680	2,729
2015	38,217	2,051	64,314	3,259	101,782	2,501
2014	32,506	1,974	64,665	3,294	96,335	2,222
2013	33,613	1,984	58,218	2,948	96,346	2,094
2012	32,728	1,989	58,891	2,865	93,791	2,113
2011[2]	34,825	1,796	57,118	2,784	87,273	1,804
2010	30,190	1,832	55,988	2,713	84,095	1,770
2009	37,106	793	62,504	1,237	113,267	976
2008	32,577	1,630	58,179	2,403	84,523	1,649
2007	33,846	1,630	54,204	2,454	81,694	1,615
2006	33,050	1,495	55,827	2,375	87,887	1,585
2005	31,332	1,504	51,750	2,204	79,229	1,379
2004	29,377	1,491	47,711	2,226	81,310	1,237
2003[3]	27,083	1,495	47,945	1,948	73,812	1,295
2002	27,146	1,456	46,218	1,984	72,943	1,202
Male						
2019	46,576	986	85,918	2,011	131,655	1,815
2018	44,559	1,110	86,473	1,939	130,513	1,649
2017	43,886	1,100	85,215	1,806	121,921	1,633
2016	43,483	1,171	77,744	1,604	124,132	1,554
2015	39,357	1,004	73,370	1,671	117,211	1,444
2014	37,109	998	71,395	1,677	112,206	1,266
2013	36,128	1,060	67,355	1,521	113,152	1,196
2012	37,917	981	68,713	1,439	104,757	1,256
2011[2]	41,887	918	65,569	1,392	98,425	1,032
2010	34,074	935	64,038	1,365	96,127	1,012
2009	37,106	793	62,504	1,237	113,267	976
2008	37,228	865	66,800	1,228	98,718	959
2007	40,965	875	60,606	1,187	93,566	942
2006	37,104	736	66,740	1,191	101,474	950
2005	35,583	758	62,247	1,097	92,170	823
2004	34,237	736	56,581	1,127	91,406	789
2003[3]	31,430	746	52,179	1,024	83,131	807
2002	32,427	744	54,683	1,006	82,134	772
Female						
2019	35,173	954	64,859	2,117	102,424	1,457
2018	34,996	1,000	57,864	1,963	98,312	1,299
2017	30,923	1,049	56,176	1,766	91,932	1,214
2016	30,524	1,075	57,544	1,584	78,963	1,175
2015	37,124	1,046	54,785	1,588	80,694	1,056
2014	27,803	976	57,684	1,617	75,320	956
2013	30,727	924	48,470	1,426	73,960	898
2012	27,683	1,008	48,971	1,425	77,697	856
2011[2]	27,441	878	48,660	1,391	72,373	772
2010	26,144	897	47,839	1,348	68,048	759
2009	27,565	717	48,655	1,241	76,052	650
2008	27,315	764	49,076	1,174	64,802	690
2007	25,597	765	48,200	1,266	65,098	673
2006	29,116	759	44,846	1,183	67,514	634
2005	27,007	745	41,350	1,107	60,077	556
2004	24,634	754	38,618	1,099	63,553	448
2003[3]	22,750	748	43,252	924	58,391	487
2002	21,615	711	37,507	978	56,417	429

[1]For data prior to 1991, "Some college/Associate degree" equals 1 to 3 years of college completed; "Bachelor's degree" equals 4 years of college; "Advanced degree" equals 5 or more years of college completed.
[2]Starting in 2011, earnings data were created using population controls based on Census 2010 data.
[3]Starting in 2003, respondents could choose more than one race. The race data in this table from 2003 onward represent respondents who indicated only one race.
[4]Beginning in 2000, earnings data are from the expanded Current Population Survey (CPS) sample and were calculated using population controls based on Census 2000.
[5]May be of any race.
… = Not available.

Table A-35. Median Income of People 25 Years Old and Over, by Highest Level of Educational Attainment and Sex, 1991–2020

(Dollars except as noted; people 25 years old and over as of March of the following year; income in current and 2020 CPI-U-RS adjusted dollars.)

	Total			Elementary/secondary					
				Less than 9th Grade			9th to 12th grade (no diploma)		
		Median income			Median income			Median income	
Sex and year	Number of persons with income (thousands)	Current dollars	2020 dollars	Number of persons with income (thousands)	Current dollars	2020 dollars	Number of persons with income (thousands)	Current dollars	2020 dollars
Male									
2020	103,527	48,917	48,917	3,714	23,358	23,358	5,578	25,102	25,102
2019	103,016	49,647	49,647	3,609	24,420	24,420	5,595	25,598	25,598
2018	101,876	46,680	46,680	3,935	22,678	22,678	6,080	23,649	23,649
2017[1]	101,067	45,399	46,506	3,939	21,393	21,914	6,315	24,293	24,885
2017	101,040	45,256	46,359	3,903	21,899	22,433	6,249	24,085	24,672
2016	99,369	42,747	44,731	4,021	21,263	22,250	6,172	23,165	24,240
2015	98,367	41,886	44,395	4,328	20,877	22,128	6,420	22,214	23,545
2014	96,753	40,846	43,367	4,467	19,553	20,760	6,445	21,701	23,041
2013[2]	95,921	40,328	43,542	4,682	18,503	19,978	6,120	20,021	21,617
2013[3]	95,253	39,602	42,759	4,464	19,701	21,271	6,557	21,417	23,124
2012	94,263	38,428	42,106	4,510	18,002	19,725	6,418	19,780	21,673
2011	93,141	37,653	42,130	4,633	17,505	19,587	6,650	20,437	22,867
2010	92,242	36,852	42,534	4,757	16,384	18,910	6,625	19,356	22,340
2009	91,745	36,801	43,176	4,736	16,473	19,327	6,948	19,720	23,136
2008	91,653	37,463	43,800	4,973	17,043	19,926	7,158	20,845	24,371
2007	90,647	37,828	45,925	5,036	16,625	20,184	7,200	20,643	25,062
2006	89,816	36,847	46,003	5,283	17,169	21,435	7,684	21,184	26,448
2005	88,804	35,758	46,090	5,475	16,321	21,037	7,276	20,934	26,983
2004	87,570	34,823	46,406	5,520	16,171	21,550	7,254	19,593	26,110
2003	86,532	33,517	45,872	5,405	15,461	21,160	7,245	18,990	25,990
2002	85,668	32,471	45,450	5,705	15,130	21,177	7,488	19,802	27,717
2001	84,389	32,494	46,199	5,809	14,594	20,749	7,421	19,434	27,631
2000	83,860	32,155	47,018	5,724	14,131	20,663	7,226	18,915	27,658
1999	82,795	31,545	47,692	5,728	13,529	20,454	7,085	17,653	26,689
1998	80,869	30,654	47,331	5,641	12,571	19,410	7,366	17,462	26,962
1997	80,263	28,919	45,257	5,839	12,157	19,025	7,601	16,818	26,319
1996	79,423	27,248	43,564	6,139	12,174	19,464	7,671	16,058	25,673
1995	78,264	26,346	43,243	6,277	11,723	19,242	7,490	15,791	25,919
1994	77,546	25,465	42,804	6,507	11,324	19,035	7,286	14,584	24,514
1993	76,419	24,605	42,222	6,734	10,895	18,696	7,377	14,550	24,968
1992	75,872	23,894	42,036	7,000	10,374	18,251	7,524	14,218	25,013
1991	75,137	23,686	42,706	7,143	10,319	18,605	7,759	14,736	26,569
Female									
2020	106,128	31,663	31,663	2,877	13,468	13,468	4,654	15,177	15,177
2019	105,587	31,773	31,773	2,903	13,129	13,129	4,960	15,694	15,694
2018	103,733	30,137	30,137	3,082	12,735	12,735	5,201	14,176	14,176
2017[1]	103,240	28,391	29,083	3,270	12,282	12,581	5,433	14,037	14,379
2017	103,352	27,709	28,384	3,294	12,365	12,666	5,471	13,801	14,137
2016	101,906	27,259	28,524	3,212	12,045	12,604	5,471	13,666	14,300
2015	101,006	26,282	27,856	3,569	11,863	12,574	5,508	12,768	13,533
2014	99,193	25,071	26,619	3,644	11,558	12,271	5,934	12,364	13,127
2013[2]	98,670	24,773	26,748	3,664	11,249	12,146	5,692	11,840	12,784
2013[3]	96,915	24,756	26,729	3,633	11,395	12,303	5,677	11,869	12,815
2012	96,256	23,946	26,238	3,674	10,841	11,879	5,898	11,981	13,128
2011	95,404	23,395	26,177	3,839	11,113	12,434	6,235	12,193	13,643
2010	94,679	22,934	26,470	3,897	10,680	12,327	6,003	12,075	13,937
2009	93,426	23,159	27,171	4,036	10,516	12,338	6,175	12,278	14,405
2008	93,143	22,944	26,825	4,201	10,625	12,422	6,413	11,904	13,917
2007	92,075	23,052	27,986	4,070	10,539	12,795	6,286	11,982	14,547
2006	91,315	21,900	27,342	4,257	10,451	13,048	6,750	11,914	14,874
2005	90,762	20,806	26,818	4,579	9,496	12,240	6,812	11,136	14,354
2004	89,794	20,147	26,848	4,742	9,576	12,761	6,982	10,751	14,327
2003	89,118	19,679	26,933	4,734	9,296	12,723	6,965	10,786	14,762
2002	88,903	18,965	26,545	5,015	8,965	12,548	7,103	10,613	14,855
2001	88,075	18,549	26,372	5,196	8,846	12,577	7,376	10,330	14,687
2000	87,619	18,032	26,367	5,195	8,546	12,496	7,565	10,063	14,715
1999	87,229	17,022	25,735	5,397	8,261	12,489	7,525	9,632	14,562
1998	84,819	16,258	25,103	5,419	7,914	12,220	7,559	9,582	14,795
1997	83,821	15,573	24,371	5,647	7,505	11,745	7,661	8,861	13,867
1996	83,056	14,682	23,473	5,775	7,276	11,633	7,929	8,544	13,660
1995	82,457	13,821	22,685	6,020	7,096	11,647	8,122	8,057	13,224
1994	81,829	12,766	21,458	6,183	6,865	11,539	7,943	7,618	12,805
1993	80,898	12,234	20,994	6,423	6,480	11,120	8,152	7,187	12,333
1992	79,854	11,922	20,974	6,921	6,337	11,149	8,248	7,293	12,830
1991	79,383	11,580	20,879	7,065	6,268	11,301	8,561	7,055	12,720

100,000+ = The medians were topcoded. Beginning with 2009 income data, the Census Bureau expanded the upper income interval used to calculate medians and Gini indexes from $100,000 to $250,000.
X = Not available.
[1]Implementation of an updated CPS ASEC processing system.
[2]The 2014 CPS ASEC included redesigned questions for income and health insurance coverage. All of the approximately 98,000 addresses were eligible to receive the redesigned set of health insurance coverage questions. The redesigned income questions were implemented to a subsample of the 98,000 addresses using a probability split panel design. Approximately 68,000 addresses were eligible to receive a set of income questions similar to those used in the 2013 CPS ASEC and the remaining 30,000 addresses were eligible to receive the redesigned income questions. The source of these 2013 estimates is the portion of the CPS ASEC sample which received the redesigned income questions, approximately 30,000 addresses.
[3]The source of these 2013 estimates is the portion of the CPS ASEC sample which received the income questions consistent with the 2013 CPS ASEC, approximately 68,000 addresses.

Table A-35. Median Income of People 25 Years Old and Over, by Highest Level of Educational Attainment and Sex, 1991–2020—*Continued*

(Dollars except as noted; people 25 years old and over as of March of the following year; income in current and 2020 CPI-U-RS adjusted dollars.)

	Elementary/secondary			College					
	High school graduate (includes equivalency)			Some college, no degree			Associate degree		
	Number of persons with income (thousands)	Median income		Number of persons with income (thousands)	Median income		Number of persons with income (thousands)	Median income	
Sex and year		Current dollars	2020 dollars		Current dollars	2020 dollars		Current dollars	2020 dollars
Male									
2020	29,803	36,271	36,271	15,672	42,920	42,920	9,961	51,436	51,436
2019	29,598	37,144	37,144	15,715	45,639	45,639	10,089	51,250	51,250
2018	29,311	36,476	36,476	16,034	42,379	42,379	9,647	50,034	50,034
2017[1]	29,321	35,143	36,000	16,234	40,718	41,711	9,356	46,852	47,994
2017	29,381	35,276	36,136	16,300	40,912	41,909	9,401	46,518	47,652
2016	29,326	33,516	35,071	16,171	40,232	42,099	9,355	45,987	48,121
2015	28,760	32,307	34,242	16,218	39,823	42,208	9,171	43,785	46,408
2014	28,988	32,080	34,060	15,963	37,865	40,202	8,728	43,871	46,579
2013[2]	29,036	31,188	33,674	16,248	37,741	40,749	8,509	42,717	46,122
2013[3]	28,677	31,288	33,782	15,615	37,424	40,407	8,654	42,176	45,538
2012	28,115	31,064	34,037	15,752	37,062	40,609	8,499	41,731	45,725
2011	28,295	30,616	34,257	15,301	36,552	40,898	8,286	41,916	46,900
2010	28,307	30,250	34,914	15,395	36,226	41,811	7,924	40,974	47,291
2009	28,946	30,303	35,552	15,184	36,693	43,049	7,399	42,163	49,467
2008	28,450	30,879	36,102	15,523	37,297	43,606	7,375	42,608	49,815
2007	27,988	31,337	38,045	15,321	37,447	45,463	7,244	43,006	52,211
2006	28,253	31,009	38,714	14,526	37,271	46,532	6,973	41,807	52,195
2005	28,077	30,134	38,841	14,505	36,930	47,601	7,000	41,903	54,011
2004	27,799	29,332	39,088	14,405	36,162	48,190	6,782	39,765	52,991
2003	26,800	28,763	39,365	14,586	35,073	48,001	6,618	39,015	53,397
2002	26,298	27,526	38,528	14,747	35,023	49,022	6,274	37,970	53,147
2001	25,954	28,343	40,297	14,340	33,777	48,023	6,352	38,870	55,264
2000	26,175	27,480	40,182	14,433	33,319	48,720	6,272	38,026	55,603
1999	26,278	27,188	41,104	14,440	32,575	49,249	5,939	36,558	55,270
1998	26,636	26,542	40,982	13,935	31,627	48,834	5,766	35,962	55,527
1997	25,777	25,453	39,833	13,892	30,536	47,788	5,591	32,930	51,534
1996	25,510	24,814	39,672	13,756	29,160	46,621	5,210	33,065	52,864
1995	24,909	23,365	38,351	13,715	28,004	45,965	5,230	31,027	50,927
1994	24,704	22,387	37,631	13,573	26,768	44,995	5,046	30,643	51,508
1993	24,682	21,782	37,378	13,247	26,323	45,171	4,901	29,736	51,027
1992	25,143	21,645	38,080	12,728	26,318	46,301	4,540	28,791	50,651
1991	25,297	21,546	38,848	12,366	26,591	47,944	4,083	29,358	52,933
Female									
2020	27,091	21,835	21,835	15,858	28,182	28,182	12,360	31,858	31,858
2019	26,755	22,052	22,052	16,314	28,653	28,653	12,478	31,652	31,652
2018	27,264	21,133	21,133	16,616	26,498	26,498	11,924	30,957	30,957
2017[1]	27,595	20,342	20,838	16,915	25,625	26,250	11,935	30,567	31,312
2017	27,672	20,199	20,691	16,919	25,161	25,774	11,905	30,406	31,147
2016	27,483	19,904	20,828	17,033	25,433	26,613	11,870	29,538	30,909
2015	27,607	19,810	20,997	17,437	24,512	25,980	11,409	28,664	30,381
2014	27,688	19,208	20,394	16,851	23,504	24,955	11,069	27,122	28,796
2013[2]	27,640	20,060	21,659	16,776	22,301	24,079	11,265	27,340	29,519
2013[3]	27,482	18,325	19,786	16,805	22,814	24,632	10,887	27,340	29,519
2012	27,717	18,213	19,956	16,625	22,469	24,619	10,757	27,159	29,758
2011	28,051	17,887	20,014	16,427	22,490	25,174	10,353	27,180	30,412
2010	28,314	17,826	20,574	16,661	22,808	26,325	10,197	28,147	32,487
2009	28,154	18,340	21,517	16,208	23,107	27,110	9,936	27,027	31,709
2008	28,217	18,293	21,387	16,329	23,252	27,185	9,662	27,715	32,403
2007	28,134	18,162	22,050	16,600	23,532	28,569	9,166	27,668	33,590
2006	28,538	17,546	21,906	16,099	22,709	28,352	9,043	26,295	32,829
2005	28,409	16,695	21,519	16,402	21,545	27,770	9,070	26,074	33,608
2004	28,561	16,165	21,542	15,791	21,159	28,197	8,861	25,199	33,581
2003	28,976	15,962	21,846	15,691	21,007	28,751	8,523	24,808	33,953
2002	29,161	15,972	22,356	15,616	20,602	28,837	8,323	23,766	33,265
2001	28,945	15,665	22,272	16,420	20,101	28,579	8,177	22,638	32,186
2000	28,968	15,153	22,157	15,825	20,166	29,487	8,108	23,124	33,813
1999	29,798	14,652	22,152	15,693	19,599	29,631	7,482	21,916	33,134
1998	29,330	13,786	21,286	15,173	18,445	28,480	6,931	21,290	32,873
1997	29,332	13,407	20,981	14,677	17,153	26,844	6,914	21,073	32,978
1996	29,212	12,702	20,308	14,528	16,255	25,988	6,839	20,460	32,711
1995	28,785	12,046	19,772	14,619	15,552	25,527	6,642	19,450	31,925
1994	29,110	11,390	19,146	14,911	14,585	24,516	6,573	17,954	30,179
1993	29,171	11,089	19,029	14,390	14,489	24,863	6,282	18,346	31,482
1992	29,596	10,901	19,178	13,615	14,401	25,335	5,539	17,331	30,490
1991	30,149	10,818	19,505	13,013	13,963	25,176	5,236	17,364	31,308

100,000+ = The medians were topcoded. Beginning with 2009 income data, the Census Bureau expanded the upper income interval used to calculate medians and Gini indexes from $100,000 to $250,000.

X = Not available.

[1] Implementation of an updated CPS ASEC processing system.

[2] The 2014 CPS ASEC included redesigned questions for income and health insurance coverage. All of the approximately 98,000 addresses were eligible to receive the redesigned set of health insurance coverage questions. The redesigned income questions were implemented to a subsample of the 98,000 addresses using a probability split panel design. Approximately 68,000 addresses were eligible to receive a set of income questions similar to those used in the 2013 CPS ASEC and the remaining 30,000 addresses were eligible to receive the redesigned income questions. The source of these 2013 estimates is the portion of the CPS ASEC sample which received the redesigned income questions, approximately 30,000 addresses.

[3] The source of these 2013 estimates is the portion of the CPS ASEC sample which received the income questions consistent with the 2013 CPS ASEC, approximately 68,000 addresses.

Table A-35. Median Income of People 25 Years Old and Over, by Highest Level of Educational Attainment and Sex, 1991–2020—Continued

(Dollars except as noted; people 25 years old and over as of March of the following year; income in current and 2020 CPI-U-RS adjusted dollars.)

	College								
	Bachelor's or higher degree								
	Total			Bachelor's degree			Master's degree		
	Number of persons with income (thousands)	Median income		Number of persons with income (thousands)	Median income		Number of persons with income (thousands)	Median income	
Sex and year		Current dollars	2020 dollars		Current dollars	2020 dollars		Current dollars	2020 dollars
Male									
2020	38,799	77,224	77,224	24,164	70,653	70,653	10,115	87,172	87,172
2019	38,411	77,326	77,326	23,885	69,505	69,505	10,038	88,280	88,280
2018	36,869	74,161	74,161	23,087	65,981	65,981	9,430	85,600	85,600
2017[1]	35,902	72,335	74,098	22,516	64,396	65,966	9,098	82,469	84,479
2017	35,807	72,315	74,078	22,462	65,325	66,917	9,059	82,722	84,738
2016	34,324	70,853	74,141	21,342	63,269	66,205	8,880	80,083	83,799
2015	33,470	70,437	74,656	20,772	62,304	66,036	8,594	78,222	82,908
2014	32,162	67,367	71,525	20,147	60,933	64,694	7,992	76,386	81,101
2013[2]	31,326	69,639	75,190	19,388	60,808	65,655	7,867	75,525	81,545
2013[3]	31,285	65,526	70,749	19,513	58,170	62,807	7,705	75,407	81,418
2012	30,969	63,272	69,327	19,320	56,656	62,078	7,652	71,364	78,194
2011	29,976	62,282	69,688	18,859	56,404	63,111	7,238	71,537	80,044
2010	29,234	61,522	71,008	18,378	55,225	63,740	7,100	69,576	80,303
2009	28,532	61,280	71,895	18,205	54,091	63,461	6,728	69,825	81,920
2008	28,174	63,277	73,980	17,726	57,278	66,966	6,896	70,973	82,978
2007	27,857	62,421	75,782	17,654	56,826	68,990	6,759	71,097	86,315
2006	27,097	61,168	76,367	17,129	54,403	67,921	6,350	67,425	84,179
2005	26,470	58,114	74,906	16,764	51,700	66,639	6,137	64,468	83,096
2004	25,810	56,434	75,205	16,302	51,081	68,071	6,059	63,260	84,301
2003	25,879	55,751	76,302	16,295	50,916	69,684	6,076	61,698	84,441
2002	25,155	55,188	77,246	16,057	50,600	70,825	5,768	60,830	85,144
2001	24,512	54,069	76,873	15,723	49,985	71,067	5,522	61,960	88,092
2000	24,028	53,488	78,212	15,452	49,080	71,767	5,346	59,732	87,342
1999	23,325	52,246	78,988	14,922	47,289	71,494	5,178	59,189	89,485
1998	22,525	50,272	77,622	14,614	45,749	70,639	4,772	55,784	86,133
1997	21,563	47,126	73,750	13,900	41,949	65,648	4,583	52,530	82,207
1996	21,136	44,161	70,604	13,510	39,624	63,350	4,709	50,003	79,944
1995	20,644	43,322	71,107	13,065	39,040	64,079	4,774	49,076	80,552
1994	20,429	42,027	70,644	12,997	38,701	65,053	4,558	46,635	78,389
1993	19,479	41,649	71,470	12,360	37,474	64,306	4,320	45,597	78,245
1992	18,937	40,557	71,351	11,938	36,745	64,645	4,308	44,293	77,924
1991	18,490	39,803	71,766	11,657	36,067	65,030	4,356	43,125	77,755
Female									
2020	43,288	52,212	52,212	26,453	46,686	46,686	13,340	60,999	60,999
2019	42,177	51,766	51,766	26,057	45,942	45,942	12,774	60,601	60,601
2018	39,645	50,385	50,385	24,458	43,951	43,951	12,023	56,545	56,545
2017[1]	38,092	49,395	50,599	23,578	42,174	43,202	11,341	56,945	58,333
2017	38,092	48,223	49,399	23,562	41,827	42,847	11,379	56,806	58,191
2016	36,837	46,788	48,959	22,865	41,045	42,950	11,009	54,571	57,103
2015	35,477	45,170	47,876	22,045	40,115	42,518	10,558	51,494	54,579
2014	34,007	43,330	46,005	21,336	40,033	42,504	9,876	50,255	53,357
2013[2]	33,633	42,063	45,416	21,508	37,424	40,407	9,661	49,731	53,695
2013[3]	32,432	43,115	46,552	20,430	39,201	42,326	9,397	50,507	54,533
2012	31,585	42,027	46,049	20,125	37,285	40,853	9,124	49,703	54,460
2011	30,498	41,338	46,254	19,629	36,812	41,189	8,650	48,738	54,533
2010	29,606	41,112	47,451	18,909	36,359	41,965	8,507	48,488	55,964
2009	28,917	40,766	47,828	18,844	35,972	42,203	7,945	50,576	59,337
2008	28,321	40,801	47,702	18,381	36,294	42,433	7,801	48,000	56,119
2007	27,820	40,712	49,426	18,347	36,167	43,909	7,590	48,077	58,368
2006	26,626	39,450	49,253	17,931	35,094	43,814	6,876	46,250	57,742
2005	25,490	37,055	47,762	17,090	32,668	42,107	6,560	44,385	57,210
2004	24,857	35,726	47,609	16,668	31,585	42,091	6,464	42,243	56,294
2003	24,229	35,125	48,073	16,198	31,309	42,850	6,268	41,334	56,570
2002	23,686	34,292	47,998	16,003	30,788	43,094	6,073	40,939	57,302
2001	22,961	33,842	48,115	15,660	30,973	44,036	5,749	40,744	57,928
2000	21,958	33,148	48,470	15,102	30,418	44,478	5,421	40,619	59,395
1999	21,334	31,604	47,781	14,690	28,520	43,118	5,220	39,712	60,039
1998	20,409	30,692	47,390	14,218	27,415	42,330	4,837	36,888	56,957
1997	19,590	29,781	46,606	13,787	26,401	41,317	4,488	35,882	56,154
1996	18,775	27,556	44,056	13,247	25,192	40,277	4,285	33,302	53,243
1995	18,269	26,843	44,059	12,875	24,065	39,499	4,205	33,509	55,001
1994	17,109	26,237	44,102	11,773	23,405	39,342	4,166	32,069	53,905
1993	16,480	25,246	43,322	11,447	22,452	38,528	4,003	31,389	53,864
1992	15,933	25,093	44,146	11,133	22,383	39,378	3,873	30,169	53,076
1991	15,359	23,627	42,600	10,721	20,967	37,804	3,745	29,747	53,635

100,000+ = The medians were topcoded. Beginning with 2009 income data, the Census Bureau expanded the upper income interval used to calculate medians and Gini indexes from $100,000 to $250,000.
X = Not available.
[1]Implementation of an updated CPS ASEC processing system.
[2]The 2014 CPS ASEC included redesigned questions for income and health insurance coverage. All of the approximately 98,000 addresses were eligible to receive the redesigned set of health insurance coverage questions. The redesigned income questions were implemented to a subsample of the 98,000 addresses using a probability split panel design. Approximately 68,000 addresses were eligible to receive a set of income questions similar to those used in the 2013 CPS ASEC and the remaining 30,000 addresses were eligible to receive the redesigned income questions. The source of these 2013 estimates is the portion of the CPS ASEC sample which received the redesigned income questions, approximately 30,000 addresses.
[3]The source of these 2013 estimates is the portion of the CPS ASEC sample which received the income questions consistent with the 2013 CPS ASEC, approximately 68,000 addresses.

Table A-35. Median Income of People 25 Years Old and Over, by Highest Level of Educational Attainment and Sex, 1991–2020—*Continued*

(Dollars except as noted; people 25 years old and over as of March of the following year; income in current and 2020 CPI-U-RS adjusted dollars.)

Sex and year	College					
	Bachelor's or higher degree					
	Professional degree			Doctorate degree		
	Number of persons with income (thousands)	Median income		Number of persons with income (thousands)	Median income	
		Current dollars	2020 dollars		Current dollars	2020 dollars
Male						
2020	1,952	110,937	110,937	2,567	112,912	112,912
2019	1,898	127,625	127,625	2,590	106,472	106,472
2018	1,796	120,030	120,030	2,556	100,658	100,658
2017[1]	1,725	121,925	124,897	2,562	104,946	107,504
2017	1,724	110,651	113,348	2,561	102,423	104,920
2016	1,735	107,506	112,495	2,367	101,591	106,305
2015	1,824	111,881	118,583	2,281	91,604	97,091
2014	1,940	107,050	113,658	2,082	91,770	97,435
2013[2]	1,762	102,353	110,511	2,309	101,336	109,413
2013[3]	1,802	101,504	109,595	2,265	93,712	101,182
2012	1,847	100,064	109,640	2,150	91,742	100,522
2011	1,903	98,883	110,641	1,976	82,376	92,171
2010	1,856	96,212	111,046	1,900	86,200	99,491
2009	1,844	102,398	120,136	1,755	89,845	105,408
2008	1,930	100,000+	(X)	1,622	90,575	105,895
2007	1,843	100,000+	(X)	1,601	86,171	104,616
2006	1,969	96,926	121,010	1,649	90,511	113,001
2005	1,912	90,878	117,137	1,656	76,937	99,168
2004	1,876	90,210	120,215	1,573	80,033	106,653
2003	1,901	88,530	121,164	1,606	73,853	101,076
2002	1,816	88,216	123,476	1,514	76,147	106,583
2001	1,779	81,602	116,019	1,488	72,642	103,200
2000	1,711	83,701	122,391	1,520	71,271	104,215
1999	1,774	81,545	123,284	1,451	70,461	106,527
1998	1,695	76,362	117,907	1,443	65,319	100,856
1997	1,741	72,274	113,106	1,338	68,643	107,424
1996	1,702	71,869	114,903	1,215	62,255	99,533
1995	1,657	66,257	108,752	1,149	57,356	94,142
1994	1,691	61,739	103,778	1,183	57,478	96,615
1993	1,650	69,678	119,568	1,149	55,751	95,669
1992	1,639	68,429	120,386	1,053	51,681	90,921
1991	1,547	63,741	114,926	929	51,845	93,478
Female						
2020	1,422	82,015	82,015	2,073	82,316	82,316
2019	1,364	82,093	82,093	1,901	86,047	86,047
2018	1,275	77,868	77,868	1,889	77,412	77,412
2017[1]	1,345	78,121	80,025	1,827	80,081	82,033
2017	1,335	77,090	78,969	1,817	77,766	79,662
2016	1,333	76,523	80,074	1,629	72,018	75,360
2015	1,278	65,012	68,906	1,595	68,887	73,014
2014	1,319	63,353	67,264	1,475	62,388	66,230
2013[2]	1,224	61,224	66,104	1,241	65,673	70,908
2013[3]	1,294	68,826	74,312	1,310	64,001	69,102
2012	1,126	67,428	73,881	1,210	67,057	73,475
2011	1,098	61,206	68,484	1,121	63,913	71,513
2010	1,053	60,477	69,801	1,136	70,417	81,274
2009	1,142	60,259	70,697	987	65,587	76,948
2008	1,197	58,364	68,236	942	60,619	70,872
2007	1,060	61,875	75,119	823	61,554	74,730
2006	1,037	60,463	75,487	782	61,091	76,271
2005	1,090	59,934	77,252	749	56,820	73,238
2004	991	50,311	67,045	734	55,996	74,621
2003	990	48,536	66,427	773	53,003	72,541
2002	940	44,748	62,634	663	52,336	73,255
2001	899	46,635	66,304	653	52,181	74,189
2000	852	46,084	67,386	584	51,460	75,247
1999	824	45,432	68,687	600	46,511	70,318
1998	788	43,490	67,151	567	46,275	71,451
1997	807	45,199	70,735	508	46,545	72,841
1996	715	42,059	67,243	527	42,431	67,838
1995	732	38,588	63,337	457	39,821	65,361
1994	709	35,806	60,187	462	40,793	68,569
1993	583	32,742	56,186	447	42,737	73,337
1992	569	36,640	64,460	358	39,322	69,178
1991	556	34,064	61,418	337	37,242	67,148

100,000+ = The medians were topcoded. Beginning with 2009 income data, the Census Bureau expanded the upper income interval used to calculate medians and Gini indexes from $100,000 to $250,000.

X = Not available.

[1]Implementation of an updated CPS ASEC processing system.

[2]The 2014 CPS ASEC included redesigned questions for income and health insurance coverage. All of the approximately 98,000 addresses were eligible to receive the redesigned set of health insurance coverage questions. The redesigned income questions were implemented to a subsample of the 98,000 addresses using a probability split panel design. Approximately 68,000 addresses were eligible to receive a set of income questions similar to those used in the 2013 CPS ASEC and the remaining 30,000 addresses were eligible to receive the redesigned income questions. The source of these 2013 estimates is the portion of the CPS ASEC sample which received the redesigned income questions, approximately 30,000 addresses.

[3]The source of these 2013 estimates is the portion of the CPS ASEC sample which received the income questions consistent with the 2013 CPS ASEC, approximately 68,000 addresses.

Table A-36. Unemployment Rates of Persons 16 to 64 Years Old, by Age Group and Highest Level of Educational Attainment, Selected Years 1975–2020

(Number; percent.)

Year	16 to 19 years old				20 to 24 years old				
	Unemployment rate for all education levels	Less than high school completion	High school completion	At least some college	Unemployment rate for all education levels	Less than high school completion	High school completion	At least some college	Bachelor's or higher degree
2020..............................	17.4	18.6	17.9	13.4	9.8	20.6	12.1	8.4	5.1
2019..............................	14.5	16.7	14.5	11.1	7.5	15.9	8.8	6.7	3.3
2018..............................	15.4	16.3	16.7	9.5	8.7	19.5	11.1	5.3	5.3
2017..............................	14.8	21.7	12.6	9.2	8.1	16.0	9.7	6.4	4.7
2016..............................	20.2	21.6	22.0	11.8	10.5	17.3	12.2	9.9	4.9
2015..............................	22.5	25.6	23.3	13.2	12.3	19.9	15.8	9.6	5.1
2014..............................	22.9	22.9	25.0	15.1	14.9	25.3	18.9	12.2	6.7
2013..............................	29.4	36.3	29.2	16.2	15.2	29.2	17.5	12.2	7.0
2012..............................	30.6	41.1	28.7	19.6	15.5	27.6	18.3	12.7	6.0
2011..............................	28.8	35.1	28.9	16.2	18.1	30.1	21.6	14.0	8.7
2010..............................	31.9	41.7	29.6	18.1	18.8	32.3	22.3	14.2	7.9
2009..............................	30.3	38.9	29.1	18.1	17.0	29.0	20.3	12.1	7.9
2008..............................	20.9	30.8	17.2	11.3	10.7	19.2	13.0	6.8	4.5
2007..............................	19.5	28.6	15.1	8.9	9.3	18.6	9.4	7.2	3.4
2006..............................	20.6	25.8	17.6	17.7	9.3	15.7	10.4	7.1	3.9
2005..............................	22.8	30.3	19.1	15.8	10.9	18.9	12.0	7.3	5.4
2000..............................	17.2	21.4	15.3	‡	9.2	16.6	10.0	5.2	5.0
1995..............................	21.0	30.3	15.1	12.4	10.7	19.5	12.0	7.3	4.1
1990..............................	17.0	26.2	11.7	‡	8.2	17.4	7.8	4.8	3.1
1985..............................	NA	NA	NA	NA	NA	NA	NA	NA	NA
1980..............................	NA	NA	NA	NA	NA	NA	NA	NA	NA
1975..............................	NA	NA	NA	NA	NA	NA	NA	NA	NA

NA = Not available.
‡ = Reporting standards not met.

Table A-36. Unemployment Rates of Persons 16 to 64 Years Old, by Age Group and Highest Level of Educational Attainment, Selected Years 1975–2020—*Continued*

(Number; percent.)

Year	25 to 34 years old					35 to 44 years old				
	Unemployment rate for all education levels	Less than high school completion	High school completion	At least some college	Bachelor's or higher degree	Unemployment rate for all education levels	Less than high school completion	High school completion	At least some college	Bachelor's or higher degree
2020	5.5	8.7	8.8	5.8	3.1	4.4	9.4	5.8	4.9	2.7
2019	4.1	9.6	5.6	4.7	2.1	2.9	5.7	4.3	3.1	1.4
2018	4.3	9.1	6.4	4.7	2.0	3.3	5.5	4.9	3.2	2.1
2017	4.9	13.2	7.2	4.4	2.5	4.0	6.9	5.7	4.4	2.3
2016	5.6	13.1	8.6	5.6	2.4	4.1	6.2	6.6	4.5	2.0
2015	5.9	12.5	8.9	6.5	2.4	4.4	8.4	6.3	4.5	2.1
2014	7.4	13.7	10.5	7.8	3.7	5.7	11.5	7.4	6.1	2.8
2013	8.0	15.1	12.1	8.0	3.6	6.4	11.5	8.5	6.7	3.6
2012	9.2	16.8	12.8	10.1	4.1	7.1	14.1	9.1	7.4	3.6
2011	10.0	19.7	14.3	10.1	4.3	8.2	15.9	11.3	7.5	4.6
2010	10.8	20.3	15.9	10.6	4.5	9.2	17.8	11.9	9.2	4.6
2009	10.1	19.9	14.1	9.8	4.5	7.9	15.3	10.6	7.2	4.2
2008	5.9	14.2	8.5	5.0	2.2	4.3	9.1	6.0	3.8	1.9
2007	4.9	10.3	6.2	4.6	2.2	3.7	9.3	4.8	3.0	1.5
2006	5.5	11.0	6.5	5.3	2.8	4.1	8.6	5.1	3.7	2.0
2005	5.8	11.6	7.7	5.4	2.6	4.2	8.7	5.2	3.9	2.0
2000	4.0	10.3	4.8	3.6	1.6	3.5	8.4	3.9	3.1	1.8
1995	5.8	12.9	6.8	5.0	2.7	4.6	10.5	5.1	4.7	2.2
1990	4.8	12.0	5.1	3.8	1.9	3.3	8.3	3.7	2.8	1.6
1985	7.3	15.5	9.1	5.4	2.8	5.6	12.4	6.1	4.8	2.2
1980	6.8	13.7	7.9	6.0	2.5	4.3	9.0	4.2	3.1	1.6
1975	8.6	17.2	9.4	6.7	2.9	6.4	11.2	5.7	4.6	2.3

NA = Not available.
‡ = Reporting standards not met.

Table A-36. Unemployment Rates of Persons 16 to 64 Years Old, by Age Group and Highest Level of Educational Attainment, Selected Years 1975–2020—*Continued*

(Number; percent.)

Year	45 to 54 years old					55 to 64 years old				
	Unemployment rate for all education levels	Less than high school completion	High school completion	At least some college	Bachelor's or higher degree	Unemployment rate for all education levels	Less than high school completion	High school completion	At least some college	Bachelor's or higher degree
2020	4.0	8.3	4.6	4.0	3.0	3.7	6.6	4.3	3.7	2.7
2019	3.0	5.5	3.3	3.3	2.1	2.6	5.6	2.6	2.6	2.0
2018	3.2	6.5	3.5	3.3	2.2	3.3	5.6	4.0	3.2	2.2
2017	3.3	6.9	4.3	2.9	2.1	3.2	6.0	3.6	3.2	2.4
2016	3.7	6.6	5.0	3.4	2.3	3.9	6.5	4.1	4.1	3.2
2015	4.1	8.6	5.2	4.1	2.2	4.2	6.9	4.4	4.3	3.3
2014	4.9	8.0	6.1	4.8	3.2	5.2	8.2	5.6	5.5	4.0
2013	6.0	12.3	7.8	5.2	3.8	5.7	11.2	6.4	5.8	4.2
2012	6.8	13.5	7.8	6.9	3.9	6.6	11.5	7.1	7.1	4.8
2011	7.5	16.3	9.3	7.1	4.0	6.9	10.0	8.4	7.3	4.9
2010	8.4	15.6	11.0	7.6	4.8	7.3	10.1	9.3	7.7	5.0
2009	7.4	13.6	8.8	7.5	4.3	6.7	12.7	7.8	7.0	4.3
2008	3.9	8.9	4.7	4.0	1.9	3.3	5.6	3.4	3.7	2.4
2007	3.5	7.3	4.0	3.7	1.8	3.1	5.3	3.7	3.5	1.8
2006	3.4	5.9	3.9	3.4	2.3	2.9	6.0	2.9	3.1	2.0
2005	3.9	7.0	4.6	3.7	2.5	3.7	7.5	4.3	3.5	2.3
2000	2.4	6.1	2.7	2.4	1.3	2.8	5.2	3.1	2.8	1.4
1995	3.9	7.9	4.0	3.9	2.4	3.9	6.7	3.4	3.2	3.3
1990	2.5	4.7	2.3	2.6	1.4	2.8	3.9	3.0	2.2	1.8
1985	5.4	10.2	5.4	3.2	2.1	4.6	7.1	4.5	3.0	2.2
1980	3.9	6.6	3.4	3.0	1.3	3.2	5.2	2.7	2.0	‡
1975	5.9	8.5	5.6	4.7	2.0	5.5	7.1	5.1	4.1	1.5

NA = Not available.
‡ = Reporting standards not met.

Table A-37. Degrees Conferred by Post-Secondary Institutions, by Level of Degree and Sex of Student, 1970–71 through 2018–19

(Number.)

Degree conferred, level of degree, and sex of student (when available)	1970-71	1971-72	1972-73	1973-74	1974-75	1975-76	1976-77	1977-78
Agriculture and Natural Resources								
Bachelor's degrees, total	12,672	13,516	14,756	16,253	17,528	19,402	21,467	22,650
Male	12,136	12,779	13,661	14,684	15,061	15,845	16,690	17,069
Female	536	737	1,095	1,569	2,467	3,557	4,777	5,581
Master's degrees, total	2,457	2,680	2,807	2,928	3,067	3,340	3,724	4,023
Male	2,313	2,490	2,588	2,640	2,703	2,862	3,177	3,268
Female	144	190	219	288	364	478	547	755
Doctor's degrees, total	1,086	971	1,059	930	991	928	893	971
Male	1,055	945	1,031	897	958	867	831	909
Female	31	26	28	33	33	61	62	62
Biological and Biomedical Sciences								
Bachelor's degrees, total	35,705	37,269	42,207	48,244	51,609	54,154	53,464	51,360
Male	25,319	26,314	29,625	33,217	34,580	35,498	34,178	31,673
Female	10,386	10,955	12,582	15,027	17,029	18,656	19,286	19,687
Master's degrees, total	5,625	5,989	6,156	6,408	6,429	6,457	6,953	6,651
Male	3,782	4,056	4,317	4,512	4,554	4,466	4,670	4,353
Female	1,843	1,933	1,839	1,896	1,875	1,991	2,283	2,298
Doctor's degrees, total	3,603	3,587	3,583	3,358	3,334	3,347	3,335	3,255
Male	3,018	2,981	2,892	2,684	2,612	2,631	2,627	2,481
Female	585	606	691	674	722	716	708	774
Business								
Bachelor's degrees, total	115,396	121,917	126,717	132,304	133,639	143,171	152,010	160,775
Male	104,936	110,331	113,337	115,363	111,983	114,986	116,394	117,103
Female	10,460	11,586	13,380	16,941	21,656	28,185	35,616	43,672
Master's degrees, total	26,490	30,509	31,208	32,691	36,315	42,592	46,505	48,347
Male	25,458	29,317	29,689	30,557	33,274	37,654	39,852	40,224
Female	1,032	1,192	1,519	2,134	3,041	4,938	6,653	8,123
Doctor's degrees, total	774	876	917	922	939	906	839	834
Male	753	857	864	873	900	856	785	760
Female	21	19	53	49	39	50	54	74
Computer and Information Sciences								
Bachelor's degrees, total	2,388	3,402	4,304	4,756	5,033	5,652	6,407	7,201
Male	2,064	2,941	3,664	3,976	4,080	4,534	4,876	5,349
Female	324	461	640	780	953	1,118	1,531	1,852
Master's degrees, total	1,588	1,977	2,113	2,276	2,299	2,603	2,798	3,038
Male	1,424	1,752	1,888	1,983	1,961	2,226	2,332	2,471
Female	164	225	225	293	338	377	466	567
Doctor's degrees, total	128	167	196	198	213	244	216	196
Male	125	155	181	189	199	221	197	181
Female	3	12	15	9	14	23	19	15
Education								
Bachelor's degrees, total	176,307	190,880	193,984	184,907	166,758	154,437	143,234	135,821
Male	44,896	49,344	51,300	48,997	44,463	42,004	39,867	37,410
Female	131,411	141,536	142,684	135,910	122,295	112,433	103,367	98,411
Master's degrees, total	87,666	96,668	103,777	110,402	117,841	126,061	124,267	116,916
Male	38,365	41,141	43,298	44,112	44,430	44,831	42,308	37,662
Female	49,301	55,527	60,479	66,290	73,411	81,230	81,959	79,254
Doctor's degrees, total	6,041	6,648	6,857	6,757	6,975	7,202	7,338	7,018
Male	4,771	5,104	5,191	4,974	4,856	4,826	4,832	4,281
Female	1,270	1,544	1,666	1,783	2,119	2,376	2,506	2,737
Engineering and Engineering Technologies								
Bachelor's degrees, total	50,182	51,258	51,384	50,412	47,131	46,676	49,482	56,150
Male	49,775	50,726	50,766	49,611	46,105	45,184	47,238	52,353
Female	407	532	618	801	1,026	1,492	2,244	3,797
Master's degrees, total	16,947	17,299	16,988	15,851	15,837	16,800	16,659	16,887
Male	16,734	17,009	16,694	15,470	15,426	16,174	15,891	15,940
Female	213	290	294	381	411	626	768	947
Doctor's degrees, total	3,688	3,708	3,513	3,374	3,181	2,874	2,622	2,483
Male	3,663	3,685	3,459	3,318	3,113	2,805	2,547	2,424
Female	25	23	54	56	68	69	75	59
Chemical, Civil, Electrical, and Mechanical Engineering Chemical engineering								
Bachelor's degree	3,579	3,625	3,578	3,399	3,070	3,140	3,524	4,569
Master's degree	1,100	1,154	1,051	1,044	990	1,031	1,086	1,235

NOTE: Data are for postsecondary institutions participating in Title IV federal financial aid programs.
NA – Not available.
[1]Includes geology/earth science, general; geochemistry; geophysics; paleontology; hydrology; oceanography; and geological and earth sciences, other.
[2]Includes physics, general; atomic/molecular physics; elementary particle physics; nuclear physics; optics; acoustics; theoretical physics; and physics, other.

Table A-37. Degrees Conferred by Post-Secondary Institutions, by Level of Degree and Sex of Student, 1970–71 through 2018–19—*Continued*

(Number.)

Degree conferred, level of degree, and sex of student (when available)	1978-79	1979-80	1980-81	1981-82	1982-83	1983-84	1984-85	1985-86
Agriculture and Natural Resources								
Bachelor's degrees, total	23,134	22,802	21,886	21,029	20,909	19,317	18,107	16,823
Male	16,854	16,045	15,154	14,443	14,085	13,206	12,477	11,544
Female	6,280	6,757	6,732	6,586	6,824	6,111	5,630	5,279
Master's degrees, total	3,994	3,976	4,003	4,163	4,254	4,178	3,928	3,801
Male	3,187	3,082	3,061	3,114	3,129	2,989	2,846	2,701
Female	807	894	942	1,049	1,125	1,189	1,082	1,100
Doctor's degrees, total	950	991	1,067	1,079	1,149	1,172	1,213	1,158
Male	877	879	940	925	1,004	1,001	1,036	966
Female	73	112	127	154	145	171	177	192
Biological and Biomedical Sciences								
Bachelor's degrees, total	48,713	46,254	43,078	41,501	39,924	38,593	38,354	38,395
Male	29,173	26,797	24,124	22,722	21,572	20,565	20,071	20,000
Female	19,540	19,457	18,954	18,779	18,352	18,028	18,283	18,395
Master's degrees, total	6,638	6,339	5,766	5,679	5,711	5,489	5,109	5,064
Male	4,198	4,042	3,602	3,384	3,298	3,123	2,775	2,733
Female	2,440	2,297	2,164	2,295	2,413	2,366	2,334	2,331
Doctor's degrees, total	3,459	3,568	3,640	3,662	3,386	3,496	3,465	3,405
Male	2,593	2,651	2,620	2,611	2,306	2,416	2,335	2,273
Female	866	917	1,020	1,051	1,080	1,080	1,130	1,132
Business								
Bachelor's degrees, total	172,392	186,264	200,521	215,190	226,442	229,013	232,282	236,700
Male	119,765	123,639	126,798	130,693	131,451	129,296	127,467	128,415
Female	52,627	62,625	73,723	84,497	94,991	99,717	104,815	108,285
Master's degrees, total	50,397	55,008	57,888	61,251	64,741	66,129	66,981	66,676
Male	40,766	42,744	43,411	44,230	45,987	46,167	46,199	45,927
Female	9,631	12,264	14,477	17,021	18,754	19,962	20,782	20,749
Doctor's degrees, total	852	767	808	826	770	926	827	923
Male	752	650	686	676	638	727	685	720
Female	100	117	122	150	132	199	142	203
Computer and Information Sciences								
Bachelor's degrees, total	8,719	11,154	15,121	20,267	24,565	32,439	39,121	42,337
Male	6,272	7,782	10,202	13,218	15,641	20,416	24,737	27,208
Female	2,447	3,372	4,919	7,049	8,924	12,023	14,384	15,129
Master's degrees, total	3,055	3,647	4,218	4,935	5,321	6,190	7,101	8,070
Male	2,480	2,883	3,247	3,625	3,813	4,379	5,064	5,658
Female	575	764	971	1,310	1,508	1,811	2,037	2,412
Doctor's degrees, total	236	240	252	251	262	251	248	344
Male	206	213	227	230	228	225	223	299
Female	30	27	25	21	34	26	25	45
Education								
Bachelor's degrees, total	125,873	118,038	108,074	100,932	97,908	92,310	88,078	87,147
Male	33,743	30,901	27,039	24,380	23,651	22,200	21,254	20,982
Female	92,130	87,137	81,035	76,552	74,257	70,110	66,824	66,165
Master's degrees, total	109,866	101,819	96,713	91,601	83,254	75,700	74,667	74,816
Male	34,410	30,300	27,548	25,339	22,824	21,164	20,539	20,302
Female	75,456	71,519	69,165	66,262	60,430	54,536	54,128	54,514
Doctor's degrees, total	7,170	7,314	7,279	6,999	7,063	6,914	6,614	6,610
Male	4,174	4,100	3,843	3,612	3,550	3,448	3,174	3,088
Female	2,996	3,214	3,436	3,387	3,513	3,466	3,440	3,522
Engineering and Engineering Technologies								
Bachelor's degrees, total	62,898	69,387	75,355	80,632	89,811	95,295	97,099	97,122
Male	57,603	62,877	67,573	71,305	78,673	82,841	83,991	84,050
Female	5,295	6,510	7,782	9,327	11,138	12,454	13,108	13,072
Master's degrees, total	16,012	16,765	17,216	18,475	19,949	21,197	22,124	22,146
Male	14,971	15,535	15,761	16,747	18,038	18,916	19,688	19,545
Female	1,041	1,230	1,455	1,728	1,911	2,281	2,436	2,601
Doctor's degrees, total	2,545	2,546	2,608	2,676	2,871	3,032	3,269	3,456
Male	2,459	2,447	2,499	2,532	2,742	2,864	3,055	3,220
Female	86	99	109	144	129	168	214	236
Chemical, Civil, Electrical, and Mechanical Engineering Chemical engineering								
Bachelor's degree	5,568	6,320	6,527	6,740	7,185	7,475	7,146	5,877

NOTE: Data are for postsecondary institutions participating in Title IV federal financial aid programs.

NA = Not available.

[1]Includes geology/earth science, general; geochemistry; geophysics; paleontology; hydrology; oceanography; and geological and earth sciences, other.

[2]Includes physics, general; atomic/molecular physics; elementary particle physics; nuclear physics; optics; acoustics; theoretical physics; and physics, other.

Table A-37. Degrees Conferred by Post-Secondary Institutions, by Level of Degree and Sex of Student, 1970–71 through 2018–19—*Continued*

(Number.)

Degree conferred, level of degree, and sex of student (when available)	1986-87	1987-88	1988-89	1989-90	1990-91	1991-92	1992-93	1993-94
Agriculture and Natural Resources								
Bachelor's degrees, total	14,991	14,222	13,492	12,900	13,124	15,113	16,769	18,056
Male	10,314	9,744	9,298	8,822	8,832	9,867	11,079	11,746
Female	4,677	4,478	4,194	4,078	4,292	5,246	5,690	6,310
Master's degrees, total	3,522	3,479	3,245	3,382	3,295	3,730	3,959	4,110
Male	2,460	2,427	2,231	2,239	2,160	2,409	2,474	2,512
Female	1,062	1,052	1,014	1,143	1,135	1,321	1,485	1,598
Doctor's degrees, total	1,049	1,142	1,183	1,295	1,185	1,205	1,159	1,262
Male	871	926	950	1,038	953	955	869	969
Female	178	216	233	257	232	250	290	293
Biological and Biomedical Sciences								
Bachelor's degrees, total	38,074	36,688	36,068	37,304	39,482	42,892	47,009	51,296
Male	19,684	18,267	17,998	18,363	19,418	20,816	22,870	25,071
Female	18,390	18,421	18,070	18,941	20,064	22,076	24,139	26,225
Master's degrees, total	4,995	4,871	5,034	4,941	4,834	4,862	5,026	5,462
Male	2,646	2,530	2,598	2,509	2,417	2,437	2,540	2,681
Female	2,349	2,341	2,436	2,432	2,417	2,425	2,486	2,781
Doctor's degrees, total	3,469	3,688	3,617	3,922	4,152	4,442	4,749	4,891
Male	2,268	2,389	2,299	2,478	2,618	2,749	2,866	2,910
Female	1,201	1,299	1,318	1,444	1,534	1,693	1,883	1,981
Business								
Bachelor's degrees, total	240,346	242,859	246,262	248,568	249,165	256,208	256,473	246,265
Male	128,506	129,467	131,098	132,284	131,557	135,263	135,368	128,946
Female	111,840	113,392	115,164	116,284	117,608	121,035	121,105	117,319
Master's degrees, total	67,093	69,230	73,065	76,676	78,255	84,517	89,425	93,285
Male	44,913	45,980	48,540	50,585	50,883	54,609	57,504	59,223
Female	22,180	23,250	24,525	26,091	27,372	29,908	31,921	34,062
Doctor's degrees, total	1,062	1,063	1,100	1,003	1,105	1,242	1,346	1,364
Male	808	810	800	818	876	953	969	980
Female	254	253	300	275	309	289	377	384
Computer and Information Sciences								
Bachelor's degrees, total	39,767	34,651	30,560	27,347	25,159	24,821	24,519	24,527
Male	25,962	23,414	21,143	19,159	17,771	17,685	17,606	17,528
Female	13,805	11,237	9,417	8,188	7,388	7,136	6,913	6,999
Master's degrees, total	8,481	9,197	9,414	9,677	9,324	9,655	10,353	10,568
Male	5,985	6,726	6,775	6,960	6,563	6,980	7,557	7,836
Female	2,496	2,471	2,639	2,717	2,761	2,675	2,796	2,732
Doctor's degrees, total	374	428	551	627	676	772	805	810
Male	322	380	466	534	584	669	689	685
Female	52	48	85	93	92	103	116	125
Education								
Bachelor's degrees, total	86,788	90,928	96,740	105,112	110,807	107,836	107,578	107,440
Male	20,705	20,947	21,643	23,007	23,417	22,655	23,199	24,424
Female	66,083	69,981	75,097	82,105	87,390	85,181	84,379	83,016
Master's degrees, total	72,619	75,270	79,793	84,890	87,352	91,225	94,497	97,427
Male	18,955	18,777	19,616	20,469	20,448	20,897	21,857	22,656
Female	53,664	56,493	60,177	64,421	66,904	70,328	72,640	74,771
Doctor's degrees, total	5,905	5,568	5,884	6,503	6,189	6,423	6,581	6,450
Male	2,745	2,530	2,522	2,776	2,614	2,652	2,712	2,555
Female	3,160	3,038	3,362	3,727	3,575	3,771	3,869	3,895
Engineering and Engineering Technologies								
Bachelor's degrees, total	93,560	89,406	85,982	82,480	79,751	78,036	78,619	78,580
Male	80,543	76,886	74,020	70,859	68,482	67,086	67,214	66,867
Female	13,017	12,520	11,962	11,621	11,269	10,950	11,405	11,713
Master's degrees, total	23,101	23,839	25,066	25,294	25,450	26,373	29,103	30,102
Male	20,137	20,815	21,731	21,753	21,780	22,397	24,721	25,394
Female	2,964	3,024	3,335	3,541	3,670	3,976	4,382	4,708
Doctor's degrees, total	3,854	4,237	4,572	5,030	5,330	5,499	5,870	5,954
Male	3,585	3,941	4,160	4,576	4,834	4,967	5,300	5,288
Female	269	296	412	454	496	532	570	666
Chemical, Civil, Electrical, and Mechanical Engineering Chemical engineering								
Bachelor's degree	4,991	3,917	3,663	3,430	3,444	3,754	4,459	5,163

NOTE: Data are for postsecondary institutions participating in Title IV federal financial aid programs.
NA – Not available.
[1]Includes geology/earth science, general; geochemistry; geophysics; paleontology; hydrology; oceanography; and geological and earth sciences, other.
[2]Includes physics, general; atomic/molecular physics; elementary particle physics; nuclear physics; optics; acoustics; theoretical physics; and physics, other.

Table A-37. Degrees Conferred by Post-Secondary Institutions, by Level of Degree and Sex of Student, 1970–71 through 2018–19—*Continued*

(Number.)

Degree conferred, level of degree, and sex of student (when available)	1994-95	1995-96	1996-97	1997-98	1998-99	1999-2000	2000-01	2001-02
Agriculture and Natural Resources								
Bachelor's degrees, total	19,832	21,425	22,597	23,276	24,179	24,238	23,370	23,331
Male	12,686	13,531	13,791	13,806	14,045	13,843	12,840	12,630
Female	7,146	7,894	8,806	9,470	10,134	10,395	10,530	10,701
Master's degrees, total	4,234	4,551	4,505	4,464	4,376	4,360	4,272	4,503
Male	2,541	2,642	2,601	2,545	2,360	2,356	2,251	2,340
Female	1,693	1,909	1,904	1,919	2,016	2,004	2,021	2,163
Doctor's degrees, total	1,256	1,259	1,202	1,290	1,249	1,168	1,127	1,148
Male	955	926	875	924	869	803	741	760
Female	301	333	327	366	380	365	386	388
Biological and Biomedical Sciences								
Bachelor's degrees, total	55,983	61,014	63,973	65,917	65,310	63,630	60,576	60,309
Male	26,734	28,921	29,562	29,663	28,507	26,579	24,600	23,694
Female	29,249	32,093	34,411	36,254	36,803	37,051	35,976	36,615
Master's degrees, total	5,873	6,593	6,986	6,848	6,966	6,850	7,017	7,011
Male	2,920	3,212	3,419	3,336	3,279	3,171	3,075	3,033
Female	2,953	3,381	3,567	3,512	3,687	3,679	3,942	3,978
Doctor's degrees, total	5,069	5,250	5,313	5,474	5,250	5,463	5,225	5,104
Male	3,012	3,062	3,014	3,123	3,010	3,068	2,923	2,836
Female	2,057	2,188	2,299	2,351	2,240	2,395	2,302	2,268
Business								
Bachelor's degrees, total	233,895	226,623	225,934	232,079	239,924	256,070	263,515	278,217
Male	121,663	116,545	116,023	119,379	121,741	128,521	132,275	138,343
Female	112,232	110,078	109,911	112,700	118,183	127,549	131,240	139,874
Master's degrees, total	93,540	93,554	97,204	101,652	106,830	111,532	115,602	119,725
Male	58,931	58,400	59,333	62,357	64,271	67,078	68,471	70,463
Female	34,609	35,154	37,871	39,295	42,559	44,454	47,131	49,262
Doctor's degrees, total	1,391	1,366	1,336	1,290	1,216	1,194	1,180	1,156
Male	1,011	972	947	885	848	812	783	746
Female	380	394	389	405	368	382	397	410
Computer and Information Sciences								
Bachelor's degrees, total	24,737	24,506	25,422	27,829	30,552	37,788	44,142	50,365
Male	17,684	17,757	18,527	20,372	22,289	27,185	31,923	36,462
Female	7,053	6,749	6,895	7,457	8,263	10,603	12,219	13,903
Master's degrees, total	10,595	10,579	10,513	11,765	12,843	14,990	16,911	17,173
Male	7,805	7,729	7,526	8,343	8,866	9,978	11,195	11,447
Female	2,790	2,850	2,987	3,422	3,977	5,012	5,716	5,726
Doctor's degrees, total	887	869	857	858	806	779	768	752
Male	726	743	721	718	656	648	632	581
Female	161	126	136	140	150	131	136	171
Education								
Bachelor's degrees, total	105,929	105,384	105,116	105,833	107,372	108,034	105,458	106,295
Male	25,619	26,214	26,242	26,285	26,321	26,103	24,580	24,049
Female	80,310	79,170	78,874	79,548	81,051	81,931	80,878	82,246
Master's degrees, total	99,835	104,936	108,720	113,374	118,226	123,045	127,829	135,189
Male	23,511	24,955	25,518	26,814	28,077	29,081	29,997	31,907
Female	76,324	79,981	83,202	86,560	90,149	93,964	97,832	103,282
Doctor's degrees, total	6,475	6,246	6,297	6,261	6,471	6,409	6,284	6,549
Male	2,490	2,404	2,367	2,334	2,297	2,295	2,237	2,211
Female	3,985	3,842	3,930	3,927	4,174	4,114	4,047	4,338
Engineering and Engineering Technologies								
Bachelor's degrees, total	78,483	77,997	75,659	74,557	72,796	73,323	72,869	74,588
Male	66,157	65,362	62,994	61,880	59,859	59,668	59,489	60,417
Female	12,326	12,635	12,665	12,677	12,937	13,655	13,380	14,171
Master's degrees, total	29,949	28,843	27,016	27,244	26,689	26,648	27,187	26,987
Male	25,028	23,840	22,047	21,800	21,348	21,047	21,341	21,212
Female	4,921	5,003	4,969	5,444	5,341	5,601	5,846	5,775
Doctor's degrees, total	6,108	6,354	6,166	5,966	5,413	5,367	5,547	5,181
Male	5,378	5,559	5,408	5,230	4,643	4,539	4,630	4,285
Female	730	795	758	736	770	828	917	896
Chemical, Civil, Electrical, and Mechanical Engineering Chemical engineering								
Bachelor's degree	5,901	6,319	6,564	6,319	6,038	5,807	5,611	5,462
Master's degree	1,085	1,176	1,131	1,128	1,130	1,078	1,083	973

NOTE: Data are for postsecondary institutions participating in Title IV federal financial aid programs.
NA = Not available.
[1]Includes geology/earth science, general; geochemistry; geophysics; paleontology; hydrology; oceanography; and geological and earth sciences, other.
[2]Includes physics, general; atomic/molecular physics; elementary particle physics; nuclear physics; optics; acoustics; theoretical physics; and physics, other.

Table A-37. Degrees Conferred by Post-Secondary Institutions, by Level of Degree and Sex of Student, 1970–71 through 2018–19—*Continued*

(Number.)

Degree conferred, level of degree, and sex of student (when available)	2002-03	2003-04	2004-05	2005-06	2006-07	2007-08	2008-09	2009-10
Agriculture and Natural Resources								
Bachelor's degrees, total	23,348	22,835	23,002	23,053	23,133	24,113	24,982	26,343
Male	12,343	11,889	11,987	12,063	12,309	12,634	13,096	13,524
Female	11,005	10,946	11,015	10,990	10,824	11,479	11,886	12,819
Master's degrees, total	4,492	4,783	4,746	4,640	4,623	4,684	4,878	5,215
Male	2,232	2,306	2,288	2,280	2,174	2,180	2,328	2,512
Female	2,260	2,477	2,458	2,360	2,449	2,504	2,550	2,703
Doctor's degrees, total	1,229	1,185	1,173	1,194	1,272	1,257	1,328	1,149
Male	790	758	763	710	768	742	741	626
Female	439	427	410	484	504	515	587	523
Biological and Biomedical Sciences								
Bachelor's degrees, total	61,294	62,624	65,915	70,607	76,832	79,829	82,828	86,391
Male	23,356	23,691	25,104	27,183	30,600	32,401	33,707	35,866
Female	37,938	38,933	40,811	43,424	46,232	47,428	49,121	50,525
Master's degrees, total	7,050	7,732	8,284	8,781	8,898	9,689	10,018	10,730
Male	3,015	3,271	3,361	3,709	3,639	4,094	4,250	4,612
Female	4,035	4,461	4,923	5,072	5,259	5,595	5,768	6,118
Doctor's degrees, total	5,268	5,538	5,935	6,162	6,764	7,400	7,499	7,672
Male	2,866	2,975	3,025	3,138	3,440	3,645	3,549	3,603
Female	2,402	2,563	2,910	3,024	3,324	3,755	3,950	4,069
Business								
Bachelor's degrees, total	293,391	307,149	311,574	318,042	327,531	335,254	348,056	358,119
Male	145,075	152,513	155,940	159,683	166,350	170,978	177,924	183,272
Female	148,316	154,636	155,634	158,359	161,181	164,276	170,132	174,847
Master's degrees, total	127,685	139,347	142,617	146,406	150,211	155,637	168,404	177,748
Male	75,239	80,858	82,151	83,550	84,115	86,258	91,991	96,742
Female	52,446	58,489	60,466	62,856	66,096	69,379	76,413	81,006
Doctor's degrees, total	1,252	1,481	1,498	1,711	2,029	2,084	2,123	2,249
Male	820	960	901	1,049	1,188	1,250	1,302	1,338
Female	432	521	597	662	841	834	821	911
Computer and Information Sciences								
Bachelor's degrees, total	57,433	59,488	54,111	47,480	42,170	38,476	37,992	39,593
Male	41,950	44,585	42,125	37,705	34,342	31,694	31,213	32,414
Female	15,483	14,903	11,986	9,775	7,828	6,782	6,779	7,179
Master's degrees, total	19,509	20,143	18,416	17,055	16,232	17,087	17,907	17,955
Male	13,267	13,868	13,136	12,470	11,985	12,513	13,063	13,019
Female	6,242	6,275	5,280	4,585	4,247	4,574	4,844	4,936
Doctor's degrees, total	816	909	1,119	1,416	1,595	1,698	1,580	1,599
Male	648	709	905	1,109	1,267	1,323	1,226	1,250
Female	168	200	214	307	328	375	354	349
Education								
Bachelor's degrees, total	105,845	106,278	105,451	107,238	105,641	102,582	101,716	101,287
Male	22,604	22,802	22,513	22,448	22,516	21,828	21,163	20,739
Female	83,241	83,476	82,938	84,790	83,125	80,754	80,553	80,548
Master's degrees, total	147,883	162,345	167,490	174,620	176,572	175,880	178,538	182,165
Male	34,033	37,843	38,863	40,700	40,164	40,055	40,312	41,284
Female	113,850	124,502	128,627	133,920	136,408	135,825	138,226	140,881
Doctor's degrees, total	6,832	7,088	7,681	7,584	8,261	8,491	9,028	9,237
Male	2,314	2,403	2,557	2,664	2,681	2,773	2,956	3,023
Female	4,518	4,685	5,124	4,920	5,580	5,718	6,072	6,214
Engineering and Engineering Technologies								
Bachelor's degrees, total	77,231	78,079	79,544	81,406	81,854	83,608	84,404	88,735
Male	62,821	63,401	65,033	66,866	68,081	69,540	70,504	73,838
Female	14,410	14,678	14,511	14,540	13,773	14,068	13,900	14,897
Master's degrees, total	30,583	35,053	34,988	33,389	31,989	34,430	38,008	39,391
Male	24,097	27,561	27,049	25,568	24,746	26,461	29,458	30,554
Female	6,486	7,492	7,939	7,821	7,243	7,969	8,550	8,837
Doctor's degrees, total	5,252	5,859	6,467	7,318	7,928	7,977	7,803	7,773
Male	4,353	4,821	5,263	5,848	6,285	6,263	6,123	5,986
Female	899	1,038	1,204	1,470	1,643	1,714	1,680	1,787
Chemical, Civil, Electrical, and Mechanical Engineering Chemical engineering								
Bachelor's degree	5,109	4,742	4,397	4,326	4,492	4,795	5,036	5,740
Master's degree	1,065	1,165	1,183	1,116	957	933	994	1,043

NOTE: Data are for postsecondary institutions participating in Title IV federal financial aid programs.
NA = Not available.
[1]Includes geology/earth science, general; geochemistry; geophysics; paleontology; hydrology; oceanography; and geological and earth sciences, other.
[2]Includes physics, general; atomic/molecular physics; elementary particle physics; nuclear physics; optics; acoustics; theoretical physics; and physics, other.

Table A-37. Degrees Conferred by Post-Secondary Institutions, by Level of Degree and Sex of Student, 1970–71 through 2018–19—*Continued*

(Number.)

Degree conferred, level of degree, and sex of student (when available)	2010-11	2011-12	2012-13	2013-14	2014-15	2015-16	2016-17	2017-18	2018-19
Agriculture and Natural Resources									
Bachelor's degrees, total	28,630	30,972	33,592	35,125	36,278	36,995	37,734	39,314	40,458
Male	14,678	15,485	16,618	17,254	17,585	17,617	17,823	18,202	18,208
Female	13,952	15,487	16,974	17,871	18,693	19,378	19,911	21,112	22,250
Master's degrees, total	5,766	6,390	6,336	6,544	6,426	6,702	6,843	6,967	7,288
Male	2,746	3,026	2,912	2,966	2,904	2,965	3,037	2,997	3,080
Female	3,020	3,364	3,424	3,578	3,522	3,737	3,806	3,970	4,208
Doctor's degrees, total	1,246	1,333	1,411	1,407	1,561	1,526	1,561	1,496	1,613
Male	675	721	767	739	811	827	805	798	837
Female	571	612	644	668	750	699	756	698	776
Biological and Biomedical Sciences									
Bachelor's degrees, total	89,984	95,850	100,397	104,657	109,904	113,794	116,768	118,663	121,191
Male	36,888	39,542	41,556	43,440	45,104	45,613	45,514	44,852	44,624
Female	53,096	56,308	58,841	61,217	64,800	68,181	71,254	73,811	76,567
Master's degrees, total	11,324	12,419	13,300	13,964	14,655	15,717	16,282	17,180	18,090
Male	4,869	5,378	5,783	6,073	6,252	6,707	6,839	7,028	7,337
Female	6,455	7,041	7,517	7,891	8,403	9,010	9,443	10,152	10,753
Doctor's degrees, total	7,693	7,935	7,939	8,302	8,053	7,939	8,087	8,222	7,978
Male	3,648	3,708	3,689	3,884	3,763	3,733	3,852	3,829	3,829
Female	4,045	4,227	4,250	4,418	4,290	4,206	4,235	4,393	4,149
Business									
Bachelor's degrees, total	365,133	367,235	360,887	358,132	363,741	371,690	381,109	386,201	390,564
Male	187,116	190,180	187,843	188,468	191,288	196,309	201,724	204,839	208,098
Female	178,017	177,055	173,044	169,664	172,453	175,381	179,385	181,362	182,466
Master's degrees, total	187,178	191,606	188,617	189,364	185,236	186,835	187,412	192,184	197,089
Male	101,440	103,250	101,599	101,061	98,593	99,488	98,775	99,860	101,515
Female	85,738	88,356	87,018	88,303	86,643	87,347	88,637	92,324	95,574
Doctor's degrees, total	2,286	2,538	2,828	3,039	3,116	3,325	3,328	3,338	3,636
Male	1,357	1,461	1,605	1,722	1,716	1,933	1,853	1,926	1,986
Female	929	1,077	1,223	1,317	1,400	1,392	1,475	1,412	1,650
Computer and Information Sciences									
Bachelor's degrees, total	43,066	47,406	50,961	55,271	59,586	64,402	71,416	79,598	88,633
Male	35,477	38,796	41,874	45,320	48,844	52,330	57,763	63,704	70,319
Female	7,589	8,610	9,087	9,951	10,742	12,072	13,653	15,894	18,314
Master's degrees, total	19,516	20,925	22,782	24,514	31,475	40,130	46,553	46,468	45,667
Male	14,010	15,132	16,539	17,472	21,893	27,788	32,172	31,397	30,670
Female	5,506	5,793	6,243	7,042	9,582	12,342	14,381	15,071	14,997
Doctor's degrees, total	1,588	1,698	1,834	1,982	1,998	1,989	1,982	2,017	2,224
Male	1,267	1,332	1,480	1,566	1,548	1,591	1,538	1,580	1,716
Female	321	366	354	416	450	398	444	437	508
Education									
Bachelor's degrees, total	104,008	105,656	104,698	98,838	91,596	87,221	85,130	82,621	83,946
Male	21,206	21,714	21,824	20,357	18,467	17,429	16,067	15,167	15,069
Female	82,802	83,942	82,874	78,481	73,129	69,792	69,063	67,454	68,877
Master's degrees, total	185,127	179,047	164,652	154,655	146,581	145,792	145,624	146,367	146,432
Male	42,043	41,364	37,816	35,974	33,963	33,791	33,163	32,871	32,105
Female	143,084	137,683	126,836	118,681	112,618	112,001	112,461	113,496	114,327
Doctor's degrees, total	9,642	10,118	10,572	10,929	11,772	11,838	12,692	12,780	13,020
Male	3,070	3,262	3,418	3,464	3,838	3,693	4,015	4,112	4,135
Female	6,572	6,856	7,154	7,465	7,934	8,145	8,677	8,668	8,885
Engineering and Engineering Technologies									
Bachelor's degrees, total	93,097	98,654	102,997	108,976	115,105	123,948	133,790	140,683	146,307
Male	77,080	81,364	84,645	88,941	93,541	99,568	106,559	111,171	114,886
Female	16,017	17,290	18,352	20,035	21,564	24,380	27,231	29,512	31,421
Master's degrees, total	43,179	45,116	45,328	47,343	51,441	57,713	60,229	58,968	55,922
Male	33,372	34,712	34,496	35,791	38,453	43,198	45,206	43,627	41,092
Female	9,807	10,404	10,832	11,552	12,988	14,515	15,023	15,341	14,830
Doctor's degrees, total	8,425	8,856	9,467	10,117	10,362	10,398	10,523	11,029	11,350
Male	6,548	6,838	7,305	7,820	7,958	7,960	8,027	8,331	8,565
Female	1,877	2,018	2,162	2,297	2,404	2,438	2,496	2,698	2,785
Chemical, Civil, Electrical, and Mechanical Engineering **Chemical engineering**									
Bachelor's degrees, total	6,311	7,027	7,529	8,104	8,980	9,917	10,915	11,542	11,267
Master's degree	1,283	1,389	1,450	1,518	1,626	1,699	1,797	1,920	1,816

NOTE: Data are for postsecondary institutions participating in Title IV federal financial aid programs.

NA = Not available.

[1]Includes geology/earth science, general; geochemistry; geophysics; paleontology; hydrology; oceanography; and geological and earth sciences, other.

[2]Includes physics, general; atomic/molecular physics; elementary particle physics; nuclear physics; optics; acoustics; theoretical physics; and physics, other.

Table A-37. Degrees Conferred by Post-Secondary Institutions, by Level of Degree and Sex of Student, 1970–71 through 2018–19—*Continued*

(Number.)

Degree conferred, level of degree, and sex of student (when available)	1970-71	1971-72	1972-73	1973-74	1974-75	1975-76	1976-77	1977-78
Doctor's degree	406	394	397	400	346	308	291	259
Civil engineering								
Bachelor's degree	6,526	6,803	7,390	8,017	7,651	7,923	8,228	9,135
Master's degree	2,425	2,487	2,627	2,652	2,769	2,999	2,964	2,685
Doctor's degree	446	415	397	368	356	370	309	277
Electrical, Electronics, and Communications Engineering								
Bachelor's degree	12,198	12,101	12,313	11,316	10,161	9,791	9,936	11,133
Master's degree	4,282	4,206	3,895	3,499	3,469	3,774	3,788	3,740
Doctor's degree	879	824	791	705	701	649	566	503
Mechanical engineering								
Bachelor's degree	8,858	8,530	8,523	7,677	6,890	6,800	7,703	8,875
Master's degree	2,237	2,282	2,141	1,843	1,858	1,907	1,952	1,942
Doctor's degree	438	411	370	385	340	305	283	279
Health Professions and Related Programs								
Bachelor's degrees, total	25,223	28,611	33,562	41,421	49,002	53,885	57,222	59,445
Male	5,785	7,005	7,752	9,347	10,844	11,386	11,896	11,600
Female	19,438	21,606	25,810	32,074	38,158	42,499	45,326	47,845
Master's degrees, total	5,330	6,011	7,978	9,232	10,277	12,164	12,627	14,027
Male	2,165	2,749	3,189	3,444	3,686	3,837	3,865	3,972
Female	3,165	4,062	4,789	5,788	6,591	8,327	8,762	10,055
Doctor's degrees, total	15,988	16,538	18,215	20,094	22,191	25,267	24,972	26,516
Male	14,863	15,373	16,870	18,287	19,808	21,980	21,022	21,622
Female	1,125	1,165	1,345	1,807	2,383	3,287	3,950	4,894
Mathematics and Statistics								
Bachelor's degrees, total	24,801	23,713	23,067	21,635	18,181	15,984	14,196	12,569
Male	15,369	14,454	13,796	12,791	10,586	9,475	8,303	7,398
Female	9,432	9,259	9,271	8,844	7,595	6,509	5,893	5,171
Master's degrees, total	5,191	5,198	5,028	4,834	4,327	3,857	3,695	3,373
Male	3,673	3,655	3,525	3,337	2,905	2,547	2,396	2,228
Female	1,518	1,543	1,503	1,497	1,422	1,310	1,299	1,145
Doctor's degrees, total	1,199	1,128	1,068	1,031	975	856	823	805
Male	1,106	1,039	966	931	865	762	714	681
Female	93	89	102	100	110	94	109	124
Chemistry, Geology and Earth Science, and Physics								
Chemistry								
Bachelor's degree	11,061	10,588	10,124	10,430	10,541	11,015	11,200	11,304
Master's degree	2,244	2,229	2,198	2,082	1,961	1,745	1,717	1,832
Doctor's degree	2,093	1,943	1,827	1,755	1,773	1,578	1,522	1,461
Geology and Earth Science[1]								
Bachelor's degree	3,312	3,766	4,117	4,526	4,566	4,677	5,280	5,648
Master's degree	1,074	1,233	1,296	1,479	1,320	1,384	1,446	1,633
Doctor's degree	408	433	430	416	433	445	480	419
Physics[2]								
Bachelor's degree	5,071	4,634	4,259	3,952	3,706	3,544	3,420	3,330
Master's degree	2,188	2,033	1,747	1,655	1,574	1,451	1,319	1,294
Doctor's degree	1,482	1,344	1,338	1,115	1,080	997	945	873
Psychology								
Bachelor's degrees, total	38,187	43,433	47,940	52,139	51,245	50,278	47,861	44,879
Male	21,227	23,352	25,117	25,868	24,284	22,898	20,627	18,422
Female	16,960	20,081	22,823	26,271	26,961	27,380	27,234	26,457
Master's degrees, total	5,717	6,764	7,619	8,796	9,394	10,167	10,859	10,282
Male	3,395	3,934	4,325	4,983	5,035	5,136	5,293	4,670
Female	2,322	2,830	3,294	3,813	4,359	5,031	5,566	5,612
Doctor's degrees, total	2,144	2,277	2,550	2,872	2,913	3,157	3,386	3,164
Male	1,629	1,694	1,797	1,987	1,979	2,115	2,127	1,974
Female	515	583	753	885	934	1,042	1,259	1,190
Economics, History, Political Science and Government, and Sociology Economics								
Bachelor's degree	15,758	15,231	14,770	14,285	14,046	14,741	15,296	15,661
Master's degree	1,995	2,224	2,225	2,141	2,127	2,087	2,158	1,995
Doctor's degree	721	794	845	788	815	763	758	706

NOTE: Data are for postsecondary institutions participating in Title IV federal financial aid programs.
NA = Not available.
[1] Includes geology/earth science, general; geochemistry; geophysics; paleontology; hydrology; oceanography; and geological and earth sciences, other.
[2] Includes physics, general; atomic/molecular physics; elementary particle physics; nuclear physics; optics; acoustics; theoretical physics; and physics, other.

Table A-37. Degrees Conferred by Post-Secondary Institutions, by Level of Degree and Sex of Student, 1970–71 through 2018–19—*Continued*

(Number.)

Degree conferred, level of degree, and sex of student (when available)	1978-79	1979-80	1980-81	1981-82	1982-83	1983-84	1984-85	1985-86
Master's degree...............................	1,149	1,270	1,267	1,285	1,368	1,514	1,544	1,361
Doctor's degree...............................	304	284	300	311	319	330	418	446
Civil engineering								
Bachelor's degree...........................	9,809	10,326	10,678	10,524	9,989	9,693	9,162	8,679
Master's degree...............................	2,646	2,683	2,891	2,995	3,074	3,146	3,172	2,926
Doctor's degree...............................	253	270	325	329	340	369	377	395
Electrical, Electronics, and Communications Engineering								
Bachelor's degree...........................	12,338	13,821	14,938	16,455	18,049	19,943	21,691	23,742
Master's degree...............................	3,591	3,836	3,901	4,462	4,531	5,078	5,153	5,534
Doctor's degree...............................	586	525	535	526	550	585	660	722
Mechanical engineering								
Bachelor's degree...........................	10,107	11,808	13,329	13,922	15,675	16,629	16,794	16,194
Master's degree...............................	1,877	2,060	2,291	2,399	2,511	2,797	3,053	3,075
Doctor's degree...............................	271	281	276	333	299	319	409	426
Health Professions and Related Programs								
Bachelor's degrees, total	62,095	63,848	63,665	63,660	65,642	65,305	65,331	65,309
Male...	11,214	11,330	10,531	10,110	10,247	10,068	9,741	9,629
Female	50,881	52,518	53,134	53,550	55,395	55,237	55,590	55,680
Master's degrees, total	15,110	15,374	16,176	16,212	16,941	17,351	17,442	18,603
Male...	4,155	4,060	4,024	3,743	4,138	4,124	4,046	4,355
Female	10,955	11,314	12,152	12,469	12,803	13,227	13,396	14,248
Doctor's degrees, total	27,766	28,190	29,595	30,096	30,800	31,655	31,493	31,922
Male...	22,194	22,157	22,792	22,968	22,920	22,851	22,045	22,069
Female	5,572	6,033	6,803	7,128	7,880	8,804	9,448	9,853
Mathematics and Statistics								
Bachelor's degrees, total	11,806	11,378	11,078	11,599	12,294	13,087	15,009	16,122
Male...	6,899	6,562	6,342	6,593	6,888	7,290	8,080	8,623
Female	4,907	4,816	4,736	5,006	5,406	5,797	6,929	7,499
Master's degrees, total	3,036	2,860	2,567	2,727	2,810	2,723	2,859	3,131
Male...	1,985	1,828	1,692	1,821	1,838	1,773	1,858	2,028
Female	1,051	1,032	875	906	972	950	1,001	1,103
Doctor's degrees, total	730	724	728	681	697	695	699	742
Male...	608	624	614	587	581	569	590	618
Female	122	100	114	94	116	126	109	124
Chemistry, Geology and Earth Science, and Physics								
Chemistry								
Bachelor's degree...........................	11,499	11,229	11,331	11,058	10,789	10,698	10,472	10,110
Master's degree...............................	1,724	1,671	1,616	1,683	1,582	1,632	1,675	1,712
Doctor's degree...............................	1,475	1,500	1,586	1,682	1,691	1,707	1,735	1,878
Geology and Earth Science[1]								
Bachelor's degree...........................	5,753	5,785	6,332	6,650	6,981	7,524	7,194	5,760
Master's degree...............................	1,596	1,623	1,702	1,848	1,784	1,747	1,927	2,036
Doctor's degree...............................	414	440	404	452	406	408	401	395
Physics[2]								
Bachelor's degree...........................	3,337	3,396	3,441	3,472	3,793	3,907	4,097	4,180
Master's degree...............................	1,319	1,192	1,294	1,284	1,369	1,532	1,523	1,501
Doctor's degree...............................	918	830	866	873	873	953	951	1,010
Psychology								
Bachelor's degrees, total	42,697	42,093	41,068	41,212	40,460	39,955	39,900	40,628
Male...	16,540	15,440	14,332	13,645	13,131	12,812	12,706	12,605
Female	26,157	26,653	26,736	27,567	27,329	27,143	27,194	28,023
Master's degrees, total	10,132	9,938	10,223	9,947	9,981	9,525	9,891	9,845
Male...	4,405	4,096	4,066	3,823	3,647	3,400	3,452	3,347
Female	5,727	5,842	6,157	6,124	6,334	6,125	6,439	6,498
Doctor's degrees, total	3,228	3,395	3,576	3,461	3,602	3,535	3,447	3,593
Male...	1,895	1,921	2,002	1,856	1,838	1,774	1,739	1,724
Female	1,333	1,474	1,574	1,605	1,764	1,761	1,708	1,869
Economics, History, Political Science and Government, and Sociology Economics								
Bachelor's degree...........................	16,409	17,863	18,753	19,876	20,517	20,719	20,711	21,602
Master's degree...............................	1,955	1,821	1,911	1,964	1,972	1,891	1,992	1,937
Doctor's degree...............................	712	677	727	677	734	729	749	789

NOTE: Data are for postsecondary institutions participating in Title IV federal financial aid programs.
NA = Not available.
[1]Includes geology/earth science, general; geochemistry; geophysics; paleontology; hydrology; oceanography; and geological and earth sciences, other.
[2]Includes physics, general; atomic/molecular physics; elementary particle physics; nuclear physics; optics; acoustics; theoretical physics; and physics, other.

Table A-37. Degrees Conferred by Post-Secondary Institutions, by Level of Degree and Sex of Student, 1970–71 through 2018–19—*Continued*

(Number.)

Degree conferred, level of degree, and sex of student (when available)	1986-87	1987-88	1988-89	1989-90	1990-91	1991-92	1992-93	1993-94
Master's degree	1,184	1,088	1,093	1,035	903	956	990	1,032
Doctor's degree	497	579	602	562	611	590	595	604
Civil engineering								
Bachelor's degree	8,147	7,488	7,312	7,252	7,314	8,034	8,868	9,479
Master's degree	2,901	2,836	2,903	2,812	2,927	3,113	3,610	3,873
Doctor's degree	451	481	505	516	536	540	577	651
Electrical, Electronics, and Communications Engineering								
Bachelor's degree	24,547	23,597	21,908	20,711	19,320	17,958	17,281	15,823
Master's degree	6,183	6,688	7,028	7,225	7,095	7,360	7,870	7,791
Doctor's degree	724	860	998	1,162	1,220	1,282	1,413	1,470
Mechanical engineering								
Bachelor's degree	15,450	14,900	14,843	14,336	13,977	14,067	14,464	15,030
Master's degree	3,198	3,329	3,498	3,424	3,516	3,653	3,982	4,099
Doctor's degree	528	596	633	742	757	851	871	887
Health Professions and Related Programs								
Bachelor's degrees, total	63,963	61,614	59,850	58,983	59,875	62,779	68,434	75,890
Male	9,137	8,955	8,878	9,075	9,619	10,330	11,605	13,377
Female	54,826	52,659	50,972	49,908	50,256	52,449	56,829	62,513
Master's degrees, total	18,442	18,774	19,493	20,406	21,354	23,671	26,190	28,442
Male	3,818	4,004	4,197	4,486	4,423	4,794	5,249	5,813
Female	14,624	14,770	15,296	15,920	16,931	18,877	20,941	22,629
Doctor's degrees, total	29,500	30,060	30,546	30,101	29,842	31,479	31,089	30,959
Male	19,686	19,853	19,893	19,118	18,492	19,362	18,446	17,988
Female	9,814	10,207	10,653	10,983	11,350	12,117	12,643	12,971
Mathematics and Statistics								
Bachelor's degrees, total	16,257	15,712	15,017	14,276	14,393	14,468	14,384	14,171
Male	8,673	8,408	8,081	7,674	7,580	7,668	7,566	7,594
Female	7,584	7,304	6,936	6,602	6,813	6,800	6,818	6,577
Master's degrees, total	3,283	3,413	3,405	3,624	3,549	3,558	3,644	3,682
Male	1,995	2,052	2,061	2,172	2,096	2,151	2,151	2,237
Female	1,288	1,361	1,344	1,452	1,453	1,407	1,493	1,445
Doctor's degrees, total	723	750	866	917	978	1,048	1,138	1,125
Male	598	625	700	754	790	825	867	880
Female	125	125	166	163	188	223	271	245
Chemistry, Geology and Earth Science, and Physics **Chemistry**								
Bachelor's degree	9,660	9,043	8,618	8,122	8,311	8,629	8,903	9,417
Master's degree	1,695	1,671	1,742	1,643	1,637	1,746	1,822	1,968
Doctor's degree	1,932	1,944	1,974	2,135	2,196	2,233	2,216	2,298
Geology and Earth Science[1]								
Bachelor's degree	3,943	3,204	2,847	2,372	2,367	2,784	3,123	3,456
Master's degree	1,835	1,722	1,609	1,399	1,336	1,245	1,195	1,221
Doctor's degree	399	462	492	562	600	549	626	577
Physics[2]								
Bachelor's degree	4,318	4,100	4,352	4,155	4,236	4,098	4,063	4,001
Master's degree	1,543	1,675	1,736	1,831	1,725	1,834	1,777	1,945
Doctor's degree	1,074	1,093	1,112	1,192	1,209	1,337	1,277	1,465
Psychology								
Bachelor's degrees, total	43,152	45,371	49,083	53,952	58,655	63,683	66,931	69,419
Male	13,395	13,579	14,265	15,336	16,067	17,062	17,942	18,668
Female	29,757	31,792	34,818	38,616	42,588	46,621	48,080	50,751
Master's degrees, total	11,000	10,400	11,329	10,730	11,349	11,659	12,518	13,723
Male	3,516	3,256	3,465	3,377	3,329	3,335	3,380	3,763
Female	7,484	7,232	7,864	7,353	8,020	8,324	9,138	9,960
Doctor's degrees, total	4,062	3,973	4,143	3,811	3,932	3,814	4,100	4,021
Male	1,801	1,783	1,773	1,566	1,520	1,490	1,570	1,497
Female	2,261	2,190	2,370	2,245	2,412	2,324	2,530	2,524
Economics, History, Political Science and Government, and Sociology Economics								
Bachelor's degree	22,378	22,911	23,454	23,923	23,488	23,423	21,321	19,496
Master's degree	1,855	1,847	1,886	1,950	1,951	2,106	2,292	2,521
Doctor's degree	750	770	827	806	802	866	879	869

NOTE: Data are for postsecondary institutions participating in Title IV federal financial aid programs.
NA = Not available.
[1]Includes geology/earth science, general; geochemistry; geophysics; paleontology; hydrology; oceanography; and geological and earth sciences, other.
[2]Includes physics, general; atomic/molecular physics; elementary particle physics; nuclear physics; optics; acoustics; theoretical physics; and physics, other.

Table A-37. Degrees Conferred by Post-Secondary Institutions, by Level of Degree and Sex of Student, 1970–71 through 2018–19—Continued

(Number.)

Degree conferred, level of degree, and sex of student (when available)	1994-95	1995-96	1996-97	1997-98	1998-99	1999-2000	2000-01	2001-02
Doctor's degree	571	670	650	652	575	590	610	605
Civil engineering								
Bachelor's degree	9,927	10,607	10,437	9,926	9,178	8,136	7,588	7,665
Master's degree	4,077	3,905	3,833	3,795	3,656	3,433	3,310	3,295
Doctor's degree	625	616	640	610	534	543	571	574
Electrical, Electronics, and Communications Engineering								
Bachelor's degree	14,929	13,900	13,336	12,995	12,606	12,930	13,091	13,056
Master's degree	7,693	7,103	6,393	6,737	6,708	6,926	6,815	6,587
Doctor's degree	1,543	1,591	1,512	1,458	1,309	1,392	1,417	1,235
Mechanical engineering								
Bachelor's degree	14,794	14,177	13,493	13,071	12,753	12,807	12,817	13,058
Master's degree	4,213	3,881	3,608	3,441	3,268	3,273	3,371	3,391
Doctor's degree	890	940	913	933	788	776	849	772
Health Professions and Related Programs								
Bachelor's degrees, total	81,596	86,087	87,997	86,843	84,989	80,863	75,933	72,887
Male	14,812	15,942	16,440	15,700	15,191	13,342	12,514	10,869
Female	66,784	70,145	71,557	71,143	69,798	67,521	63,419	62,018
Master's degrees, total	31,770	33,920	36,162	39,567	40,628	42,593	43,623	43,560
Male	6,718	7,017	7,536	8,644	9,152	9,500	9,711	9,588
Female	25,052	26,903	28,626	30,923	31,476	33,093	33,912	33,972
Doctor's degrees, total	32,124	32,678	34,971	35,369	35,939	37,829	39,019	39,435
Male	18,463	18,495	19,619	19,370	19,673	19,984	20,260	19,760
Female	13,661	14,183	15,352	15,999	16,266	17,845	18,759	19,675
Mathematics and Statistics								
Bachelor's degrees, total	13,494	12,713	12,401	11,795	12,011	11,418	11,171	11,950
Male	7,154	6,847	6,649	6,247	6,206	5,955	5,791	6,333
Female	6,340	5,866	5,752	5,548	5,805	5,463	5,380	5,617
Master's degrees, total	3,820	3,651	3,504	3,409	3,304	3,208	3,209	3,350
Male	2,289	2,178	2,055	1,985	1,912	1,749	1,857	1,913
Female	1,531	1,473	1,449	1,424	1,392	1,459	1,352	1,437
Doctor's degrees, total	1,181	1,158	1,134	1,215	1,107	1,075	997	923
Male	919	919	861	903	812	803	715	658
Female	262	239	273	312	295	272	282	265
Chemistry, Geology and Earth Science, and Physics								
Chemistry								
Bachelor's degree	9,706	10,395	10,609	10,528	10,109	9,989	9,466	9,084
Master's degree	2,062	2,214	2,203	2,108	2,019	1,857	1,952	1,823
Doctor's degree	2,211	2,228	2,202	2,291	2,175	2,028	2,056	1,984
Geology and Earth Science[1]								
Bachelor's degree	4,032	4,019	4,023	3,866	3,570	3,516	3,495	3,449
Master's degree	1,280	1,288	1,258	1,227	1,196	1,186	1,220	1,263
Doctor's degree	539	555	564	588	533	492	472	494
Physics[2]								
Bachelor's degree	3,823	3,679	3,376	3,441	3,200	3,342	3,418	3,627
Master's degree	1,817	1,678	1,496	1,371	1,326	1,232	1,365	1,344
Doctor's degree	1,424	1,462	1,410	1,393	1,257	1,208	1,169	1,096
Psychology								
Bachelor's degrees, total	72,233	73,416	74,308	74,107	73,747	74,194	73,645	76,775
Male	19,570	19,836	19,408	18,976	18,376	17,451	16,585	17,284
Female	52,663	53,580	54,900	55,131	55,371	56,743	57,060	59,491
Master's degrees, total	15,378	15,152	15,769	15,142	15,560	15,740	16,539	16,357
Male	4,210	4,090	4,155	3,978	3,959	3,821	3,892	3,814
Female	11,168	11,062	11,614	11,164	11,601	11,919	12,647	12,543
Doctor's degrees, total	4,252	4,141	4,507	4,541	4,678	4,731	5,091	4,759
Male	1,562	1,380	1,495	1,470	1,528	1,529	1,598	1,503
Female	2,690	2,761	3,012	3,071	3,150	3,202	3,493	3,256
Economics, History, Political Science and Government, and Sociology Economics								
Bachelor's degree	17,673	16,674	16,539	17,074	17,577	18,441	19,437	20,927
Master's degree	2,400	2,533	2,433	2,435	2,332	2,168	2,139	2,330
Doctor's degree	910	916	968	928	819	851	851	826

NOTE: Data are for postsecondary institutions participating in Title IV federal financial aid programs.
NA = Not available.
[1]Includes geology/earth science, general; geochemistry; geophysics; paleontology; hydrology; oceanography; and geological and earth sciences, other.
[2]Includes physics, general; atomic/molecular physics; elementary particle physics; nuclear physics; optics; acoustics; theoretical physics; and physics, other.

Table A-37. Degrees Conferred by Post-Secondary Institutions, by Level of Degree and Sex of Student, 1970–71 through 2018–19—*Continued*

(Number.)

Degree conferred, level of degree, and sex of student (when available)	2002-03	2003-04	2004-05	2005-06	2006-07	2007-08	2008-09	2009-10
Doctor's degree	542	623	773	819	835	853	789	830
Civil engineering								
Bachelor's degree	7,836	7,827	8,186	9,090	9,671	10,455	10,785	11,335
Master's degree	3,596	3,790	3,834	3,768	3,482	3,595	3,794	4,079
Doctor's degree	599	636	713	750	805	752	763	717
Electrical, Electronics, and Communications Engineering								
Bachelor's degree	13,627	14,123	14,171	13,966	13,089	12,375	11,620	11,450
Master's degree	7,621	9,511	9,054	8,123	7,777	8,631	9,178	9,052
Doctor's degree	1,256	1,440	1,566	1,860	2,042	1,996	1,812	1,869
Mechanical engineering								
Bachelor's degree	13,693	14,050	14,609	15,850	16,601	17,367	17,352	18,498
Master's degree	3,695	4,420	4,637	4,443	4,294	4,497	4,620	4,818
Doctor's degree	747	787	915	1,096	1,106	1,109	1,142	996
Health Professions and Related Programs								
Bachelor's degrees, total	71,261	73,934	80,685	91,973	101,810	111,478	120,420	129,623
Male	10,096	10,017	10,858	12,914	14,325	16,286	17,776	19,309
Female	61,165	63,917	69,827	79,059	87,485	95,192	102,644	110,314
Master's degrees, total	42,748	44,939	46,703	51,380	54,531	58,120	62,642	69,112
Male	9,280	9,670	9,816	10,630	10,636	11,010	11,848	12,874
Female	33,468	35,269	36,887	40,750	43,895	47,110	50,794	56,238
Doctor's degrees, total	39,799	41,861	44,201	45,677	48,943	51,675	54,846	57,750
Male	19,493	19,587	19,697	19,640	20,522	21,616	22,678	23,946
Female	20,306	22,274	24,504	26,037	28,421	30,059	32,168	33,804
Mathematics and Statistics								
Bachelor's degrees, total	12,505	13,327	14,351	14,770	14,954	15,192	15,507	16,029
Male	6,784	7,203	7,937	8,115	8,360	8,490	8,801	9,087
Female	5,721	6,124	6,414	6,655	6,594	6,702	6,706	6,942
Master's degrees, total	3,620	4,191	4,477	4,730	4,884	4,980	5,211	5,639
Male	1,996	2,302	2,525	2,712	2,859	2,860	3,064	3,378
Female	1,624	1,889	1,952	2,018	2,025	2,120	2,147	2,261
Doctor's degrees, total	1,007	1,060	1,176	1,293	1,351	1,360	1,535	1,596
Male	734	762	841	911	949	938	1,059	1,118
Female	273	298	335	382	402	422	476	478
Chemistry, Geology and Earth Science, and Physics								
Chemistry								
Bachelor's degree	9,013	9,016	9,664	10,606	10,994	11,568	11,852	12,107
Master's degree	1,777	2,009	1,879	2,044	2,097	2,194	2,085	2,123
Doctor's degree	2,092	2,033	2,148	2,403	2,514	2,410	2,556	2,470
Geology and Earth Science[1]								
Bachelor's degree	3,381	3,312	3,276	3,322	3,319	3,561	3,809	4,093
Master's degree	1,323	1,389	1,420	1,476	1,437	1,350	1,352	1,447
Doctor's degree	466	463	476	505	640	577	614	613
Physics[2]								
Bachelor's degree	3,900	4,118	4,182	4,541	4,043	4,062	4,024	4,904
Master's degree	1,438	1,625	1,785	1,846	1,777	1,791	1,653	1,793
Doctor's degree	1,089	1,119	1,254	1,341	1,442	1,507	1,580	1,571
Psychology								
Bachelor's degrees, total	78,650	82,098	85,614	88,134	90,039	92,587	94,273	97,215
Male	17,514	18,193	19,000	19,865	20,343	21,202	21,490	22,262
Female	61,136	63,905	66,614	68,269	69,696	71,385	72,783	74,953
Master's degrees, total	17,161	17,808	18,830	19,770	21,037	21,431	23,415	23,763
Male	3,839	3,789	3,900	4,079	4,265	4,356	4,789	4,799
Female	13,322	14,109	14,930	15,691	16,772	17,075	18,626	18,964
Doctor's degrees, total	4,835	4,827	5,106	4,921	5,153	5,296	5,477	5,540
Male	1,483	1,496	1,466	1,347	1,382	1,440	1,478	1,478
Female	3,352	3,331	3,640	3,574	3,771	3,856	3,999	4,062
Economics, History, Political Science and Government, and Sociology Economics								
Bachelor's degree	23,007	24,069	24,217	23,807	23,916	25,278	26,301	27,623
Master's degree	2,582	2,824	3,092	2,941	2,962	3,187	3,233	3,358
Doctor's degree	836	849	973	930	941	1,025	1,015	983

NOTE: Data are for postsecondary institutions participating in Title IV federal financial aid programs.
NA = Not available.
[1]Includes geology/earth science, general; geochemistry; geophysics; paleontology; hydrology; oceanography; and geological and earth sciences, other.
[2]Includes physics, general; atomic/molecular physics; elementary particle physics; nuclear physics; optics; acoustics; theoretical physics; and physics, other.

Table A-37. Degrees Conferred by Post-Secondary Institutions, by Level of Degree and Sex of Student, 1970–71 through 2018–19—*Continued*

(Number.)

Degree conferred, level of degree, and sex of student (when available)	2010-11	2011-12	2012-13	2013-14	2014-15	2015-16	2016-17	2017-18	2018-19
Doctor's degree..	831	823	835	992	1,015	1,009	989	1,010	1,066
Civil engineering									
Bachelor's degree..	12,557	12,808	13,262	12,995	12,673	13,244	13,596	14,039	14,671
Master's degree..	4,860	5,359	5,353	5,501	5,365	5,626	5,677	5,796	5,578
Doctor's degree..	751	787	868	972	1,031	1,015	1,077	1,056	1,224
Electrical, Electronics, and Communications Engineering									
Bachelor's degree..	11,575	12,110	12,835	13,856	14,599	15,680	16,921	16,901	17,584
Master's degree..	9,691	9,696	9,485	9,829	11,917	13,782	12,792	11,514	10,385
Doctor's degree..	2,037	2,119	2,118	2,301	2,320	2,258	2,290	2,327	2,296
Mechanical engineering									
Bachelor's degree..	19,171	20,541	21,990	24,301	26,394	29,216	32,308	35,182	36,817
Master's degree..	5,802	5,840	5,872	6,182	6,841	7,558	8,278	8,150	7,819
Doctor's degree..	1,106	1,213	1,321	1,387	1,526	1,470	1,450	1,586	1,633
Health Professions and Related Programs									
Bachelor's degrees, total	143,463	163,675	181,149	198,777	216,228	228,907	237,979	244,909	251,355
Male	21,540	24,905	28,208	30,932	33,658	36,262	37,746	38,022	39,433
Female	121,923	138,770	152,941	167,845	182,570	192,645	200,233	206,887	211,922
Master's degrees, total................................	75,571	84,355	90,933	97,416	103,052	110,350	119,242	125,216	131,569
Male	14,034	15,675	16,747	17,751	18,793	20,424	21,984	22,768	23,652
Female	61,537	68,680	74,186	79,665	84,259	89,926	97,258	102,448	107,917
Doctor's degrees, total	60,221	62,097	64,192	67,447	71,004	73,687	77,693	80,305	82,895
Male	25,386	26,074	26,852	28,082	29,427	30,387	31,845	32,494	32,942
Female	34,835	36,023	37,340	39,365	41,577	43,300	45,848	47,811	49,953
Mathematics and Statistics									
Bachelor's degrees, total	17,182	18,841	20,449	20,987	21,854	22,778	24,075	25,256	26,146
Male	9,782	10,722	11,599	11,970	12,462	13,090	14,003	14,541	15,037
Female	7,400	8,119	8,850	9,017	9,392	9,688	10,072	10,715	11,109
Master's degrees, total................................	5,866	6,246	6,957	7,273	7,589	8,451	9,082	10,443	11,380
Male	3,459	3,695	4,178	4,256	4,508	4,924	5,113	5,959	6,599
Female	2,407	2,551	2,779	3,017	3,081	3,527	3,969	4,484	4,781
Doctor's degrees, total	1,586	1,669	1,823	1,863	1,801	1,855	1,925	2,010	2,003
Male	1,132	1,198	1,292	1,325	1,298	1,324	1,403	1,448	1,410
Female	454	471	531	538	503	531	522	562	593
Chemistry, Geology and Earth Science, and Physics									
Chemistry									
Bachelor's degree..	12,656	13,473	13,814	14,443	14,447	14,483	14,954	14,737	14,420
Master's degree..	2,272	2,435	2,396	2,357	2,425	2,455	2,489	2,388	2,355
Doctor's degree..	2,599	2,537	2,617	2,796	2,792	2,894	2,887	2,951	3,044
Geology and Earth Science[1]									
Bachelor's degree..	4,611	5,111	5,539	5,959	6,405	6,552	6,616	6,702	6,343
Master's degree..	1,568	1,807	1,845	1,933	1,955	1,912	1,940	1,813	1,869
Doctor's degree..	567	612	657	735	681	771	737	759	807
Physics[2]									
Bachelor's degree..	5,199	5,531	6,082	6,263	6,658	6,948	7,112	7,515	7,678
Master's degree..	1,769	1,873	1,975	1,866	1,926	1,956	1,849	2,149	1,961
Doctor's degree..	1,670	1,752	1,740	1,768	1,840	1,845	1,826	1,879	1,873
Psychology									
Bachelor's degrees, total	100,906	109,099	114,446	117,312	117,573	117,447	116,859	116,432	116,536
Male	23,230	25,420	26,814	27,306	26,803	26,277	25,520	24,578	24,313
Female	77,676	83,679	87,632	90,006	90,770	91,170	91,339	91,854	92,223
Master's degrees, total................................	25,062	27,052	27,787	27,926	26,772	27,645	27,539	27,841	29,135
Male	5,127	5,482	5,715	5,729	5,538	5,571	5,586	5,526	5,600
Female	19,935	21,570	22,072	22,197	21,234	22,074	21,953	22,315	23,535
Doctor's degrees, total	5,851	5,936	6,326	6,634	6,583	6,540	6,702	6,275	6,214
Male	1,481	1,525	1,628	1,680	1,624	1,658	1,691	1,649	1,596
Female	4,370	4,411	4,698	4,954	4,959	4,882	5,011	4,626	4,618
Economics, History, Political Science and Government, and Sociology Economics									
Bachelor's degree..	28,517	27,994	28,449	29,999	32,683	33,474	34,056	35,327	35,184
Master's degree..	3,731	3,890	3,872	4,115	3,993	3,953	4,044	4,098	4,366
Doctor's degree..	1,018	1,130	1,076	1,059	1,128	1,162	1,150	1,195	1,223

NOTE: Data are for postsecondary institutions participating in Title IV federal financial aid programs.
NA = Not available.
[1]Includes geology/earth science, general; geochemistry; geophysics; paleontology; hydrology; oceanography; and geological and earth sciences, other.
[2]Includes physics, general; atomic/molecular physics; elementary particle physics; nuclear physics; optics; acoustics; theoretical physics; and physics, other.

Table A-37. Degrees Conferred by Post-Secondary Institutions, by Level of Degree and Sex of Student, 1970–71 through 2018–19—*Continued*

(Number.)

Degree conferred, level of degree, and sex of student (when available)	1970-71	1971-72	1972-73	1973-74	1974-75	1975-76	1976-77	1977-78
History								
Bachelor's degree	44,663	43,695	40,943	37,049	31,470	28,400	25,433	23,004
Master's degree	5,157	5,217	5,030	4,533	4,226	3,658	3,393	3,033
Doctor's degree	991	1,133	1,140	1,114	1,117	1,014	921	813
Political Science and Government								
Bachelor's degree	27,482	28,135	30,100	30,744	29,126	28,302	26,411	26,069
Master's degree	2,318	2,451	2,398	2,448	2,333	2,191	2,222	2,069
Doctor's degree	700	758	747	766	680	723	641	636
Sociology								
Bachelor's degree	33,263	35,216	35,436	35,491	31,488	27,634	24,713	22,750
Master's degree	1,808	1,944	1,923	2,196	2,112	2,009	1,830	1,611
Doctor's degree	574	636	583	632	693	729	714	599
Visual and Performing Arts								
Bachelor's degrees, total	30,394	33,831	36,017	39,730	40,782	42,138	41,793	40,951
Male	12,256	13,580	14,267	15,821	15,532	16,491	16,166	15,572
Female	18,138	20,251	21,750	23,909	25,250	25,647	25,627	25,379
Master's degrees, total	6,675	7,537	7,254	8,001	8,362	8,817	8,636	9,036
Male	3,510	4,049	4,005	4,325	4,448	4,507	4,211	4,327
Female	3,165	3,488	3,249	3,676	3,914	4,310	4,425	4,709
Doctor's degrees, total	621	572	616	585	649	620	662	708
Male	483	428	449	440	446	447	447	448
Female	138	144	167	145	203	173	215	260

NOTE: Data are for postsecondary institutions participating in Title IV federal financial aid programs.
NA = Not available.
[1]Includes geology/earth science, general; geochemistry; geophysics; paleontology; hydrology; oceanography; and geological and earth sciences, other.
[2]Includes physics, general; atomic/molecular physics; elementary particle physics; nuclear physics; optics; acoustics; theoretical physics; and physics, other.

Table A-37. Degrees Conferred by Post-Secondary Institutions, by Level of Degree and Sex of Student, 1970–71 through 2018–19—*Continued*

(Number.)

Degree conferred, level of degree, and sex of student (when available)	1978-79	1979-80	1980-81	1981-82	1982-83	1983-84	1984-85	1985-86
History								
Bachelor's degree	21,019	19,301	18,301	17,146	16,467	16,643	16,049	16,415
Master's degree	2,536	2,367	2,237	2,210	2,041	1,940	1,921	1,961
Doctor's degree	756	712	643	636	575	561	468	497
Political Science and Government								
Bachelor's degree	25,628	25,457	24,977	25,658	25,791	25,719	25,834	26,439
Master's degree	2,037	1,938	1,875	1,954	1,829	1,769	1,500	1,704
Doctor's degree	563	535	484	513	435	457	441	439
Sociology								
Bachelor's degree	20,285	18,881	17,272	16,042	14,105	13,145	11,968	12,271
Master's degree	1,415	1,341	1,240	1,145	1,112	1,008	1,022	965
Doctor's degree	612	583	610	558	522	520	480	504
Visual and Performing Arts								
Bachelor's degrees, total	40,969	40,892	40,479	40,422	39,804	40,131	38,285	37,241
Male	15,380	15,065	14,798	14,819	14,695	15,089	14,518	14,236
Female	25,589	25,827	25,681	25,603	25,109	25,042	23,767	23,005
Master's degrees, total	8,524	8,708	8,629	8,746	8,763	8,526	8,720	8,420
Male	3,933	4,067	4,056	3,866	4,013	3,897	3,896	3,775
Female	4,591	4,641	4,573	4,880	4,750	4,629	4,824	4,645
Doctor's degrees, total	700	655	654	670	692	730	696	722
Male	454	413	396	380	404	406	407	396
Female	246	242	258	290	288	324	289	326

NOTE: Data are for postsecondary institutions participating in Title IV federal financial aid programs.
NA = Not available.
[1]Includes geology/earth science, general; geochemistry; geophysics; paleontology; hydrology; oceanography; and geological and earth sciences, other.
[2]Includes physics, general; atomic/molecular physics; elementary particle physics; nuclear physics; optics; acoustics; theoretical physics; and physics, other.

Table A-37. Degrees Conferred by Post-Secondary Institutions, by Level of Degree and Sex of Student, 1970–71 through 2018–19—*Continued*

(Number.)

Degree conferred, level of degree, and sex of student (when available)	1986-87	1987-88	1988-89	1989-90	1990-91	1991-92	1992-93	1993-94
History								
Bachelor's degree	18,997	18,207	20,139	22,470	24,341	26,900	27,774	27,503
Master's degree	2,021	2,093	2,121	2,369	2,591	2,754	2,952	3,009
Doctor's degree	534	517	487	570	606	644	690	752
Political Science and Government								
Bachelor's degree	26,817	27,207	30,450	33,560	35,737	37,805	37,931	36,097
Master's degree	1,618	1,579	1,598	1,580	1,772	1,908	1,943	2,147
Doctor's degree	435	391	452	480	468	535	529	616
Sociology								
Bachelor's degree	12,239	13,024	14,435	16,035	17,550	19,568	20,896	22,368
Master's degree	950	984	1,135	1,198	1,260	1,347	1,521	1,639
Doctor's degree	451	452	451	432	465	501	536	530
Visual and Performing Arts								
Bachelor's degrees, total	36,873	37,150	38,420	39,934	42,186	46,522	47,761	49,053
Male	13,980	14,225	14,698	15,189	15,761	17,616	18,610	19,538
Female	22,893	22,925	23,722	24,745	26,425	28,906	29,151	29,515
Master's degrees, total	8,508	7,939	8,267	8,481	8,657	9,353	9,440	9,925
Male	3,756	3,442	3,611	3,706	3,830	4,078	4,099	4,229
Female	4,752	4,497	4,656	4,775	4,827	5,275	5,341	5,696
Doctor's degrees, total	793	727	753	849	838	906	882	1,054
Male	447	424	446	472	466	504	478	585
Female	346	303	307	377	372	402	404	469

NOTE: Data are for postsecondary institutions participating in Title IV federal financial aid programs.
NA = Not available.
[1]Includes geology/earth science, general; geochemistry; geophysics; paleontology; hydrology; oceanography; and geological and earth sciences, other.
[2]Includes physics, general; atomic/molecular physics; elementary particle physics; nuclear physics; optics; acoustics; theoretical physics; and physics, other.

Table A-37. Degrees Conferred by Post-Secondary Institutions, by Level of Degree and Sex of Student, 1970–71 through 2018–19—*Continued*

(Number.)

Degree conferred, level of degree, and sex of student (when available)	1994-95	1995-96	1996-97	1997-98	1998-99	1999-2000	2000-01	2001-02
History								
Bachelor's degree...	26,598	26,005	25,214	25,726	24,742	25,247	25,090	26,001
Master's degree..	3,091	2,898	2,901	2,895	2,618	2,573	2,365	2,420
Doctor's degree..	816	805	873	937	931	984	931	924
Political Science and Government								
Bachelor's degree...	33,013	30,775	28,969	28,044	27,476	27,635	27,792	29,354
Master's degree..	2,019	2,024	1,909	1,957	1,667	1,627	1,596	1,641
Doctor's degree..	637	634	686	705	694	693	688	625
Sociology								
Bachelor's degree...	22,886	24,071	24,672	24,806	24,979	25,598	25,268	25,202
Master's degree..	1,748	1,772	1,731	1,737	1,940	1,996	1,845	1,928
Doctor's degree..	546	527	591	596	521	595	546	534
Visual and Performing Arts								
Bachelor's degrees, total...	48,690	49,296	50,083	52,077	54,446	58,791	61,148	66,773
Male...	19,781	20,126	20,729	21,483	22,270	24,003	24,967	27,130
Female...	28,909	29,170	29,354	30,594	32,176	34,788	36,181	39,643
Master's degrees, total...	10,277	10,280	10,627	11,145	10,762	10,918	11,404	11,595
Male...	4,374	4,361	4,470	4,596	4,544	4,672	4,788	4,912
Female...	5,903	5,919	6,157	6,549	6,218	6,246	6,616	6,683
Doctor's degrees, total...	1,080	1,067	1,060	1,163	1,117	1,127	1,167	1,114
Male...	545	524	525	566	567	537	568	490
Female...	535	543	535	597	550	590	599	624

NOTE: Data are for postsecondary institutions participating in Title IV federal financial aid programs.
NA = Not available.
[1]Includes geology/earth science, general; geochemistry; geophysics; paleontology; hydrology; oceanography; and geological and earth sciences, other.
[2]Includes physics, general; atomic/molecular physics; elementary particle physics; nuclear physics; optics; acoustics; theoretical physics; and physics, other.

Table A-37. Degrees Conferred by Post-Secondary Institutions, by Level of Degree and Sex of Student, 1970–71 through 2018–19—*Continued*

(Number.)

Degree conferred, level of degree, and sex of student (when available)	2002-03	2003-04	2004-05	2005-06	2006-07	2007-08	2008-09	2009-10
History								
Bachelor's degree	27,757	29,808	31,398	33,153	34,446	34,441	34,713	35,191
Master's degree	2,521	2,522	2,893	2,992	3,144	3,403	3,543	3,858
Doctor's degree	861	855	819	852	807	860	918	888
Political Science and Government								
Bachelor's degree	33,205	35,581	38,107	39,409	39,899	40,259	39,202	39,462
Master's degree	1,664	1,869	1,983	2,054	2,102	2,156	2,171	2,252
Doctor's degree	671	618	636	649	614	639	709	745
Sociology								
Bachelor's degree	26,095	26,939	28,473	28,467	28,960	28,815	28,735	28,650
Master's degree	1,897	2,009	1,499	1,547	1,545	1,560	1,580	1,428
Doctor's degree	591	558	527	562	569	585	628	603
Visual and Performing Arts								
Bachelor's degrees, total	71,482	77,181	80,955	83,297	85,186	87,703	89,143	91,798
Male	27,922	30,037	31,355	32,117	32,729	33,862	35,055	35,768
Female	43,560	47,144	49,600	51,180	52,457	53,841	54,088	56,030
Master's degrees, total	11,982	12,906	13,183	13,530	13,767	14,164	14,918	15,562
Male	4,975	5,531	5,646	5,801	5,910	5,998	6,325	6,531
Female	7,007	7,375	7,537	7,729	7,857	8,166	8,593	9,031
Doctor's degrees, total	1,293	1,282	1,278	1,383	1,364	1,453	1,569	1,599
Male	613	572	594	639	625	675	726	700
Female	680	710	684	744	739	778	843	899

NOTE: Data are for postsecondary institutions participating in Title IV federal financial aid programs.

NA = Not available.

[1]Includes geology/earth science, general; geochemistry; geophysics; paleontology; hydrology; oceanography; and geological and earth sciences, other.

[2]Includes physics, general; atomic/molecular physics; elementary particle physics; nuclear physics; optics; acoustics; theoretical physics; and physics, other.

Table A-37. Degrees Conferred by Post-Secondary Institutions, by Level of Degree and Sex of Student, 1970–71 through 2018–19—*Continued*

(Number.)

Degree conferred, level of degree, and sex of student (when available)	2010-11	2011-12	2012-13	2013-14	2014-15	2015-16	2016-17	2017-18	2018-19
History									
Bachelor's degree	35,008	35,122	34,188	31,122	28,038	25,589	24,054	23,382	23,169
Master's degree	4,003	4,155	4,083	3,955	3,703	3,465	3,435	3,272	3,340
Doctor's degree	908	969	1,003	1,040	986	980	925	911	840
Political Science and Government									
Bachelor's degree	40,133	39,792	38,466	37,360	35,442	33,955	34,196	34,968	36,715
Master's degree	2,488	2,510	2,332	2,294	2,082	1,983	1,842	1,854	1,964
Doctor's degree	722	746	821	792	844	793	796	789	772
Sociology									
Bachelor's degree	29,281	30,136	30,531	30,070	29,000	28,001	27,433	27,294	26,702
Master's degree	1,559	1,696	1,603	1,611	1,447	1,363	1,391	1,411	1,439
Doctor's degree	656	626	615	674	722	646	682	687	622
Visual and Performing Arts									
Bachelor's degrees, total	93,939	95,806	97,799	97,414	95,840	92,979	91,291	88,582	89,730
Male	36,342	37,164	38,063	38,177	38,024	36,712	35,304	34,202	33,922
Female	57,597	58,642	59,736	59,237	57,816	56,267	55,987	54,380	55,808
Master's degrees, total	16,277	17,307	17,869	17,869	17,756	18,052	17,516	17,686	17,113
Male	6,881	7,320	7,610	7,712	7,643	7,679	7,561	7,399	7,086
Female	9,396	9,987	10,259	10,157	10,113	10,373	9,955	10,287	10,027
Doctor's degrees, total	1,646	1,728	1,814	1,778	1,793	1,809	1,774	1,759	1,845
Male	770	790	850	869	837	853	812	852	911
Female	876	938	964	909	956	956	962	907	934

NOTE: Data are for postsecondary institutions participating in Title IV federal financial aid programs.

NA = Not available.

[1]Includes geology/earth science, general; geochemistry; geophysics; paleontology; hydrology; oceanography; and geological and earth sciences, other.

[2]Includes physics, general; atomic/molecular physics; elementary particle physics; nuclear physics; optics; acoustics; theoretical physics; and physics, other.

NOTES AND DEFINITIONS: NATIONAL EDUCATION STATISTICS

ENROLLMENT TABLES A-1 through A-8 and A-10 THROUGH A-17

Source: U.S. Census Bureau. School Enrollment in the United States. *Current Population Survey (CPS) Report.* https://www.census.gov/data/tables/2020/demo/school-enrollment/2020-cps.html and https://www.census.gov/data/tables/time-series/demo/school-enrollment/cps-historical-time-series.html

ENROLLMENT TABLES A-9 and A-18 THROUGH A-23

Source: U.S. Department of Education, National Center for Education Statistics, Institute of Education Sciences, *Digest of Education Statistics, 2019 and 2020.* https://nces.ed.gov/programs/digest/current_tables.asp

ATTAINMENT TABLES A-24 THROUGH A-34

Source: U.S. Census Bureau. Educational Attainment in the United States. *Current Population Survey (CPS) Report.* https://www.census.gov/data/tables/2020/demo/educational-attainment/cps-detailed-tables.html and https://www.census.gov/data/tables/time-series/demo/educational-attainment/cps-historical-time-series.html

ATTAINMENT TABLE A-35

Source: U.S. Census Bureau. Historical Income Tables: People. Table P-16. *Current Population Survey (CPS) Report.* https://www.census.gov/data/tables/time-series/demo/income-poverty/historical-income-people.html

ATTAINMENT TABLES A-36 AND A-37

Source: U.S. Department of Education, National Center for Education Statistics, Institute of Education Sciences, *Digest of Education Statistics, 2019 and 2020.* https://nces.ed.gov/programs/digest/current_tables.asp

SCHOOL ENROLLMENT AND EDUCATIONAL ATTAINMENT TABLES

The School Enrollment and Educational Attainment tables in Part A are derived from the Current Population Survey (CPS). The Census Bureau disseminated comparable tables in the P-20 series of *Current Population Reports* (CPR) for most years between 1947 and 1994. Since then, these tables have not been available in printed form. However, they can be found on the Census Bureau website at www.census.gov. In the historical series, data before 1992 are not strictly comparable to data after 1992. Before 1992, the CPS did not ask questions about degrees received; educational attainment was gauged only by years of school completed.

Age. Age classification is based on the age of the person at his or her last birthday.

Citizenship status. There are five categories of citizenship status: (1) born in the United States; (2) born in Puerto Rico or another outlying area of the United States; (3) born abroad to U.S. citizen parents; (4) naturalized citizens; and (5) non-citizens. Place of birth was asked for every household member and for the parents of every household member in the CPS sample. People born in the United States or its outlying areas, or whose parents were born in the United States or its outlying areas, were not asked citizenship questions. Citizenship statuses (1), (2), and (3) were assigned during the editing phase of data preparation, based on the place of birth of the household member or the place of birth of the household member's parents. People born outside the United States and its outlying areas, whose parents were born outside the United States and its outlying areas, were asked, "Are you a citizen of the United States?" 'Yes' answers were assigned to the "naturalized citizen" category (4), and 'No' answers were assigned to the "not a citizen" category (5) during the editing process. People for whom no birthplace was provided were also assigned a citizenship status during the editing process; for example, the citizenship status of a child might have been assigned based on the citizenship status of the child's mother.

Dropouts. See School, Dropout rate, annual high school.

Earnings. See Income.

Educational attainment. Data on educational attainment are derived from a single question that asks, "What is the highest grade of school ... completed, or the highest degree ... received?"

The single educational attainment question now in use was introduced into the CPS in January 1992. It is similar to the question used in the 1990 Decennial Census of Population and Housing. Consequently, data on educational attainment from the 1992 CPS are not directly comparable to CPS data from earlier years. The new question replaces the previous two-part question used in the CPS, which asked respondents to report the highest grade they attended and whether or not they completed that grade.

The question concerning educational attainment applies only to progress in "regular" schools. Such schools include graded public, private, and parochial elementary and high schools (both junior and senior high schools), colleges, universities, and professional schools, and both day schools and night schools. Thus, regular schooling is that which may advance a person toward an elementary school certificate, a high school diploma, or a college, university, or professional school degree. Non-regular schooling was counted only if the credits obtained were regarded as transferable to a school within the regular school system.

Family. A family is a group of two people or more residing together (including the householder) related by birth, marriage, or adoption; all such people (including related subfamily members) are considered members of one family. Beginning with the 1980 Current Population Survey, unrelated subfamilies (formerly referred to as secondary families) are no longer included in the count of families, nor are members of unrelated subfamilies included in the count of family members. The number of families is equal to the number of family households; however, the count of family members differs from the count of family household members, as family household members include any non-relatives living in the household.

Family household. A family household is a household maintained by a householder within a family (as defined above). It includes any unrelated people (unrelated subfamily members and/or secondary individuals) residing in the household. The number of family households is equal to the number of families; however, the count of family household members differs from the count of family members. Family household members include all people living in the household, whereas family members include only the householder and his or her relatives. (See Family for more information.)

Hispanic origin. People of Hispanic origin were identified by a question that asked respondents to self-identify their origin or descent. Respondents were asked to select their origin (and the origin of other household members) from a "flash card" listing different ethnicities. People of Hispanic origin were those who indicated that their descent was of Mexican, Puerto Rican, Cuban, Central or South American, or some other Hispanic origin. It should be noted that people of Hispanic origin may be of any race.

People who were of non-Hispanic White origin were identified by crossing the responses to two self-identification questions: (1) origin or descent; and (2) race. Respondents were asked to select their race (and the race of other household members) from a "flash card" listing racial groups. There are six racial categories CPS respondents can select from: White; Black; American Indian or Alaska Native; Asian; Native Hawaiian or Pacific Islander; and Other. The Other category includes any race other than the six indicated races. Respondents who reported more than one race are included in the Two or More Races category. Respondents who identified their race as White and did not select one of the Hispanic origin subgroups (Mexican, Puerto Rican, Cuban, Central or South American) were classified as non-Hispanic White.

Household. A household consists of all the people who occupy a housing unit. A house, apartment, group of rooms, or single room is regarded as a housing unit when it is occupied or intended for occupancy as separate living quarters (meaning that occupants do not live and eat with any other persons in the structure and have direct access to their dwelling from outside or through a common hall). A household includes related family members and all unrelated people—such as lodgers, foster children, wards, or employees—who share the housing unit. A person living alone in a housing unit, or a group of unrelated people sharing a dwelling (such as partners or roomers), are also counted as a household. The count of households excludes group quarters. There are two major categories of households: "family" and "nonfamily." (See Family household and Nonfamily household for more information.)

Householder. The householder is the person (or one of the people) in whose name the housing unit is owned or rented (maintained). If there is no such person, any adult member of the household—excluding roomers, boarders, and paid employees—can be counted as the householder. If a married couple jointly owns or rents the housing unit, the householder may be either the husband or the wife. The person designated as the householder is the "reference person" to whom the relationship of all other household members, if any, is recorded.

The number of householders is equal to the number of households. The number of family householders is also equal to the number of families.

INCOME. Definitions of income and the types of income are found below.

Income, Official definition of. For each person age 15 years and over in the sample, the CPS asks questions about the amount of money income received during the preceding calendar year from each of the following sources: earnings; unemployment compensation; workers' compensation; Social Security; Supplemental Security Income; public assistance or welfare payments; veterans' payments; survivor benefits; disability benefits; pension or retirement income; interest, dividends, rents, royalties, and estates and trusts; educational assistance; child support; alimony; financial assistance from outside the household; and other income.

Although the income statistics refer to receipts during the preceding calendar year, demographic characteristics such as age, labor force status, and family or household composition are as of the survey date. The income of the family/household does not include amounts received by members who were members of the family/household during all or part of the income year if these people no longer resided in the family/household at the time of interview. However, the CPS collects income data for people who are current residents, but who did not reside in the household during the income year.

Data on consumer income collected in the CPS by the Census Bureau cover money income (exclusive of certain money receipts, such as capital gains) received before payments for personal income taxes, Social Security, union dues, Medicare deductions, and so on. Therefore, money income does not reflect the fact that some families receive part of their income in the form of noncash benefits, such as food stamps, health benefits, rent-free housing, and goods produced and consumed on the farm. Money income also does not reflect the fact that noncash benefits are also received by some nonfarm residents. These benefits often take the form of the use of business transportation and facilities, full or partial payments by business for retirement programs, medical and educational expenses, and so on. Data users should consider these elements when comparing income levels. Moreover, readers should be aware that respondents in household surveys tend to underreport their income for many different reasons. Based on an analysis of independently derived income estimates, the Census Bureau determined that respondents report income earned from wages or salaries much more accurately than income earned from other sources of income, and that the reported wage and salary income is nearly equal to independent estimates of aggregate income.

The Census Bureau collects data for the following income sources:

Alimony. Alimony includes all periodic payments received from ex-spouses. It excludes one-time property settlements.

Child support. Child support includes all periodic payments received from an absent parent for the support of his or her children, even if these payments are made through a state or local government office.

Disability benefits. Disability benefits include payments people received due to a health problem or disability (other than those received from Social Security). Respondents can report payments from 10 sources, including workers' compensation, companies or unions, federal government (civil service), military, state or local governments, railroad retirement, accident or disability insurance, Black Lung payments, state temporary sickness, or other disability payments.

Dividends. Dividends include income received from stock holdings and mutual fund shares. The CPS does not include capital gains from the sale of stock holdings as income.

Earnings. The Census Bureau classifies earnings from respondents' longest job (or self-employment) and other employment earnings into three types:

- Money wage or salary income, is the total income people receive for work performed as an employee during the income year. This category includes wages, salary, armed forces pay, commissions, tips, piece-rate payments, and cash bonuses earned, before deductions are made for items such as taxes, bonds, pensions, and union dues.

- Net income from nonfarm self-employment is the net money income (gross receipts minus expenses) from a respondent's own business, professional enterprise, or partnership. Gross receipts include the value of all goods sold and all services rendered. Expenses include items such as the costs of goods purchased; rent, heat, power, and depreciation charges; wages and salaries paid; and business taxes (but not personal income taxes). In general, the Census Bureau considers inventory changes in determining net income from nonfarm self-employment; replies based on income tax returns or other official records reflect inventory changes. However, when respondents do not report values of inventory changes, interviewers will accept net income figures exclusive of inventory changes. The Census Bureau does not include the value of saleable merchandise consumed by the proprietors of retail stores as part of net income.

- Net income from farm self-employment is the net money income (gross receipts minus operating expenses) from the operation of a farm by a person acting on their own account as owner, renter, or sharecropper. Gross receipts include the value of all products sold, payments from government farm programs, money received from renting farm equipment to others, rent received from farm property if payment is based on the percentage of crops produced, and incidental receipts from the sale of items such as wood, sand, and gravel.

- Operating expenses include items such as the cost of feed, fertilizer, seed, and other farming supplies; cash wages paid to farmhands; depreciation charges; cash rent; interest on farm mortgages; farm building repairs; and farm taxes (not state and federal personal income taxes). The Census Bureau does not include the value of fuel, food, or other farm products used for family living as part of net income, and only considers inventory changes in determining net income when they are accounted for in income tax returns or other official records. Otherwise, the Census Bureau does not take inventory changes into account.

Educational assistance. Educational assistance includes Pell Grants, other government educational assistance, scholarships or grants, and any financial assistance received from employers, friends, or relatives not residing in the student's household.

Financial assistance from outside the household. Financial assistance from outside the household includes periodic payments received from nonhousehold members. This type of assistance excludes gifts and sporadic assistance.

Government transfers. Government transfers include payments received from the following sources: unemployment compensation, state workers' compensation, Social Security, Supplemental Security Income (SSI), public assistance, veterans' payments, government survivor benefits, government disability benefits, government pensions, and government educational assistance.

Interest income. Interest income includes payments received or credited to accounts from bonds, treasury notes, individual retirement accounts (IRAs), certificates of deposit, interest-bearing savings and checking accounts, and all other interest-paying investments.

Other income. Other income includes any other unclassified payments received regularly. Some examples are state programs such as foster child payments, military family allotments, and income received from foreign government pensions.

Pension or retirement income. Pension or retirement income includes payments received from eight sources, including companies or unions; federal government (civil service); military; state or local governments; railroad retirement; annuities or paid-up insurance policies; IRAs, Keogh, or 401(k) payments; or other retirement income.

Public assistance or welfare payments. Public assistance or welfare payments include cash payments to low-income persons, including payments given under programs such as Aid to Families with Dependent Children (AFDC, ADC) and Temporary Assistance to Needy Families (TANF), emergency assistance, and other general assistance.

Rents, royalties, and estates and trusts. Rents, royalties, and estates and trusts include net income received from the rental of a house, a store, or other property; receipts from boarders or lodgers; net royalty income; and periodic payments from estate or trust funds.

Social Security. Social Security includes pensions, survivors' benefits, and permanent disability insurance payments made by the Social Security Administration prior to medical insurance deductions. The Census Bureau does not include Medicare reimbursements for health services as Social Security benefits.

Supplemental Security Income. Supplemental Security Income includes federal, state, and local welfare agency payments to low-income people age 65 years and over and to blind or disabled people of any age.

Survivor benefits. Survivor benefits include payments received from survivors' or widows' pensions, estates, trusts, annuities, or any other types of survivors' benefits. Respondents can report payments from 10 different sources, including private companies or unions, federal government (civil service), military, state or local governments, railroad retirement, workers' compensation, Black Lung payments, estates and trusts, annuities or paid-up insurance policies, and other survivor payments.

Unemployment compensation. Unemployment compensation includes payments made to the respondent from government unemployment agencies or private companies during periods of unemployment. It also accounts for any strike benefits the respondent received from union funds.

Veterans' payments. Veterans' payments include periodic payments from the Department of Veterans Affairs to disabled members of the armed forces or survivors of deceased veterans for education and on-the-job training. These payments also include means-tested assistance to veterans.

Workers' compensation. Workers' compensation includes periodic payments from public or private insurance companies for work-related injuries.

The Census Bureau does not count the following receipts as income: (1) capital gains (or losses) from the sale of property, including stocks, bonds, houses, or cars (unless the person was engaged in the business of selling such property, in which case the CPS counts the net proceeds as income from self-employment); (2) withdrawals of bank deposits; (3) money borrowed; (4) tax refunds; (5) gifts; and (6) lump-sum inheritances or insurance payments.

The Census Bureau combines all sources of income into two major types:

Total money earnings. Total money earnings is the algebraic sum of money wages, salary, and net income from farm and nonfarm self-employment.

Income other than earnings. Income other than earnings is the algebraic sum of all sources of money income, except wages and salaries and income from self-employment.

Mean (average) income. Mean (average) income is the amount obtained by dividing the total aggregate income of a group by the number of units in that group. The means for households, families, and unrelated individuals are based respectively on all households, all families, and all unrelated individuals. The means (averages) for people are based on people age 15 years and over with income.

Median income. Median income is the amount that divides the income distribution into two equal groups. Half of all people have incomes above the median, and half of all people have incomes below the median. The medians for households, families, and unrelated individuals are respectively based on all households, all families, and all unrelated individuals. The medians for people are based on people age 15 years and over with income.

LABOR FORCE STATUS. Definitions of labor force characteristics are found below:

Civilian labor force. Consists of people classified as employed or unemployed. Excluded are institutionalized people and people on active duty in the United States Armed Forces. The entire labor force consists of people classified as employed or unemployed and people in the armed forces.

Current job (basic data). A worker's current job is the job held during the reference week (the week before the survey). A person holding two or more jobs is classified as being in the job at which he or she spent the most hours during the reference week. The unemployed are classified according to their most recent full-time job of two weeks or more, or by the job (either the full-time or part-time job) from which they were laid off. The occupation/industry classification system for the 1990 Decennial Census of Population was first used to code CPS data for the January 1992 file. The occupation/industry classification system for the 2000 Decennial Census of Population was first used to code CPS data for the January 2003 file.

Employed. Employed persons include all civilians who, during the survey week, did any work at all (for at least one hour) as paid employees or in their own business or profession, or on their own farm, or who worked 15 hours or more as unpaid workers on a farm or a business operated by a member of the family; and all people who had jobs but were not working due to illness, bad weather, vacation, labor-management dispute, or personal reasons, whether or not they were seeking other jobs. Each employed person is counted only once. People who held two or more jobs are counted as working in the job at which they worked the greatest number of hours during the survey week. If a person worked an equal number of hours at two or more jobs, he or she is counted as working at the job that they have held the longest.

Labor force. Workers are classified as being in the labor force if they are employed, unemployed, or in the armed forces during the survey week. The "civilian labor force" includes all civilians classified as employed or unemployed. The file includes labor force data for civilians age 15 years and over. However, the official definition of the civilian labor force consists of workers age 16 years and over.

Not in labor force. All civilians age 15 years and over who are not classified as employed or unemployed are considered not to be in the labor force. These people are further classified as being engaged in a major activity such as keeping house, going to school, unable to work because of long-term physical or mental illness, and "other," which is mostly composed of retired persons. Those who report doing unpaid work on a family-owned farm or in a family-owned business for less than 15 hours are also classified as not in the labor force.

For persons not in the labor force, questions about previous work experience, intentions to seek work again, current desire for a job, and reasons for not seeking work are only asked of households in the fourth and eighth months of the sample. These are the "outgoing" groups—those that were in the sample for three previous months and would not be in it for the subsequent month.

Finally, it should be noted that the unemployment rate represents the number of unemployed persons as a percentage of the civilian labor force age 16 years and over. This measure can be computed for groups within the labor force by sex, age, marital status, race, and so on. The job loser, job leaver, reentrant, and new entrant rates are each calculated as a percentage of the civilian labor force age 16 years and over; the sum of the rates for the four groups thus equals the total unemployment rate.

Unemployed. Unemployed persons are civilians who, during the survey week, had no employment but were available for work and had engaged in any specific job-seeking activity within the past four previous weeks, such as registering at a public or private employment office, meeting with prospective employers, checking with friends or relatives, placing and answering advertisements, writing letters of application, or being on a union or professional register. Others in this category were waiting to be called back to a job from which they had been laid off or were within 30 days of starting a new wage or salary job. This category consists of job leavers, job losers, new job entrants, and job reentrants.

Work experience. A person with work experience is one who did any work for pay or profit or worked without pay on a family-operated farm or business at any time during the preceding calendar year, on a part-time or full-time basis. A full-time worker is a worker who worked 35 hours or more per week during a majority of the weeks in the preceding calendar year. A year-round worker is a worker who worked for 50 weeks or more during the preceding calendar year. A full-time, year-round worker is a person who worked full-time (35 or more hours per week) for 50 or more weeks during the previous calendar year.

Level of school completed. The statistics on level of school completed indicate the number of persons enrolled at each of five levels: nursery school, kindergarten, elementary school (first to eighth grades), high school (ninth to twelfth grades), and college or professional school. The last group includes graduate students at colleges and universities. Those enrolled in elementary school, middle school, intermediate school, or junior high through eighth grade are classified as being in elementary school. All persons enrolled in ninth through twelfth grade are classified as being in high school.

Modal grade. See School, Modal grade.

Nativity. There are two major categories of nativity, native born and foreign born. A person who is native is a citizen at birth. All people with the following citizenship status are native born: (1) born in the United States; (2) born in Puerto Rico or an outlying area of the United States; and (3) born abroad of American parents. (See Citizenship status for more information.) All other people are classified as foreign born.

Nonfamily household. A nonfamily household consists of a householder living alone (a one-person household) or a household shared exclusively by unrelated people.

Population coverage. The sample for the CPS includes the civilian noninstitutional population of the United States, along with members of the armed forces in the United States living off post or with their families on post. It excludes all other members of the armed forces. The information on the Hispanic population from the CPS was collected in the 50 states and the District of Columbia and does not include residents of outlying areas or of U.S. territories such as Guam, Puerto Rico, and the U.S. Virgin Islands.

Race. The race of individuals was identified through a question requiring self-identification of the person's race. Respondents were asked to select their race from a "flash card" listing racial groups. Since March 1989, the population has been divided into five groups on the basis of race: White; Black; American Indian, Eskimo or Aleut; Asian or Pacific Islander; and Other races. The last category includes any other race except the five mentioned. In most of the published tables, "Other races" are included in the total population data line but are not shown individually.

Reference person. The reference person serves as the central point for determining relationships within the household. The household reference person is the person listed as the householder. (See Householder for more information.) The subfamily reference person is either the single parent or the husband or wife in a married-couple situation.

Rounding. Percentages are rounded to the nearest 10th of a percent; therefore, the percentages in a distribution do not always sum to exactly 100 percent.

School, Dropout rate, annual high school. The annual high school dropout rate is an estimate of the proportion of students who drop out of school in a single year. This section briefly explains how the annual dropout rate is calculated; for further explanation and details of its derivation, see *Current Population Report (Series P-20, No. 413): "School Enrollment—Social and Economic Characteristics of Students: October 1983."*

Annual dropout rates for a single grade (X) are estimated as the ratio between the number of people enrolled in grade (X) in the year preceding the survey who did not complete grade (X) and are not currently enrolled in grade (X) at the start of the year preceding this survey. People reported as enrolled last year but not currently enrolled are presented by the highest grade completed in Table 8 of the *Current Population Report* on school enrollment. They are presumed to have dropped out of the succeeding grade (except for those who graduated this year). Thus, individuals counted as 10th grade dropouts are those whose highest grade completed is the 9th grade, but who are not currently enrolled in school. (The dropout classification also includes those people who finished the 9th grade in the spring preceding the survey and were not enrolled on the survey date.) These estimates form the numerator of the annual grade-specific dropout rate.

People currently enrolled in high school are presumed to have been enrolled in and have successfully completed the preceding grade during the preceding year. For example, those who have successfully completed the 10th grade would be enrolled in the 11th grade. Along with the people who dropped out of that grade, they comprise the denominator of the estimate of the annual grade-specific dropout rate:

$$\text{Dropout from Grade n} = \frac{\text{Not enrolled and highest grade completed} = n-1}{\left(\begin{array}{c}\text{Enrolled in } n+1 + \text{Not enrolled and} \\ \text{highest grade completed} = n-1\end{array}\right)}$$

It cannot be presumed that all 12th grade graduates will enroll in college. The estimate of the number of people enrolled in the 12th grade one year before the survey is constructed as the sum of the number of people reported to have graduated from high school "this year" (whether or not they are currently enrolled in college) and those not currently enrolled who were enrolled last year and whose highest grade completed is the 11th grade (dropouts). The annual dropout rate for all grades during one year can be obtained by summing the components of the rates for the individual grades—the sum of all people previously enrolled in the 10th, 11th, or 12th grade last year, but who are not currently enrolled and do not have a high school diploma.

In addition to the annual rate, two other estimates of dropouts are frequently used. The annual dropout rate is different from a "pool" (or status) measure, such as the proportion of high school dropouts within an age group. A third measure of dropouts is the "cohort measure," most commonly from a longitudinal study, in which the proportion of a specific group of people enrolled in a specific year is calculated. These people did not receive diplomas (and are no longer in school) some years later. For example, the proportion of a cohort enrolled in 9th grade in year X, who were not enrolled and had not received a diploma by year X equals 4.

School enrollment. The school enrollment statistics from the CPS are based on replies to inquiries concerning current regular school enrollment. Those counted as enrolled had attended a public, parochial, or other private school in the regular school system at any time during the current or previous school year. Such schools include nursery schools, kindergartens, elementary schools, high schools, colleges, universities, and professional schools. Attendance could have been on either a full-time or part-time basis during the day or night. Regular schooling is that which advances a person toward an elementary or high school diploma or toward a college, university, or professional school degree. Children enrolled in nursery schools and kindergarten are included in the enrollment figures for regular schools and are shown separately.

Enrollment in schools not in the regular school system, such as trade schools, business colleges, and schools for the mentally handicapped is not included, as these schools do not advance students toward regular school degrees.

People enrolled in classes not requiring their physical presence in school, such as correspondence courses or other courses of independent study, and those enrolled in training courses given directly on the job, are also excluded from the count of those enrolled in school, unless such courses are being counted for credit at a regular school.

School enrollment in the year preceding current survey. All respondents were asked to state their school enrollment status as of October of the preceding year. Before 1988, this question was only asked of people not currently attending regular school and people who were enrolled in college. In the tabulations of previous year's secondary school enrollment, those currently enrolled in high school were assumed to have been enrolled the previous year.

Comparability of enrollment data in previous years. Changes in the edit and tabulation packages used to process the October CPS school enrollment supplement caused some minor revisions to the estimates. The current edit and tabulation package began with 1987 data. The 1986 data published in the *Current Population Report (Series P-20 No. 429)* were reprocessed with the rewritten programs in order to clarify comparability. Time series tables usually show only the revised estimates for 1986. The previous edit and tabulation package was used from 1967 to 1986.

Major changes in the data caused by the 1987 edit revisions were: (1) Among 14- and 15-year-olds, an edit improvement allowed people with unreported enrollment data, who were previously imputed as "not enrolled," to be enrolled; (2) Revisions in the tabulation of enrollment in the previous year simplified the calculation of an annual high school dropout rate; (3) Edit improvements caused increases in college enrollment estimates, most notably above the age of 24. This age group was largely ignored in earlier edits; (4) Type of college is fully allocated (discussed earlier in the section); (5) Tabulations of type of college (2-year and 4-year colleges) were made available by race; (6) Dependent family members became consistently defined; (7) New tabulations of employment status, vocational course enrollment, college retention and reentry, and families with children enrolled in public and private school became available beginning in 1987.

In the series of reports on school enrollment for 1987 to 1992, race and Hispanic origin were erroneously tabulated for a small percentage of children age 3 to 14 years. Race and Hispanic origin of an adult in the household were attributed to the child, rather than using the child's reported characteristics. In the vast majority of cases, these characteristics were the same for family members, but for a small percentage of children, they were different. The correction made the following proportional changes in the numbers of children in each group: White (-0.5 percent), Black (+3.1 percent), and Hispanic (-4.6 percent).

Published data on enrollment from the October CPS for 1981 to 1993 used population controls based on the 1980 census. Beginning in 1994, estimates used 1990 census–based population controls, including adjustment for undercount. Time series tables show two sets of data for 1993; the data labeled "1993r" were processed using population controls based on the 1990 census with adjustments for undercount. The change in 1994 from a paper-and-pencil survey to a computer-assisted survey had some affect on the data. Most notably, the enrollment question for children age 3 to 5 years was different from the question for older children—it included a reference to nursery school. In 1994, reported nursery school enrollment was significantly higher than in earlier years.

Attendance, full-time and part-time. College students are classified according to their attendance status. A student is categorized as attending college full-time if he or she was taking 12 or more hours of classes during the average school week, and part-time if he or she was taking less than 12 hours of classes per average school week.

College enrollment. The college enrollment statistics are based on reports of school enrollment, including the grade in which the respondent was enrolled. Students enrolled in college at any time during the current term or school year were counted as enrolled, except those who had left for the remainder of the term. Thus, regular college enrollment includes those attending two-year or four-year colleges, universities, or professional schools (such as medical or law schools) in courses that advance students toward a recognized college or university degree (such as a B.A. or an M.A.). Attendance may be full-time or part-time during the day or night. The college student need not be working toward a degree, but he or she must be enrolled in a class for which credit would be applied toward a degree. (See school enrollment for more information.) Students are classified by year of college, based on the academic year (not calendar year). The undergraduate years are the first through fourth year, or freshman through senior years. Graduate or professional school years include the fifth year and higher.

Two-year and four-year colleges. College students were asked if their school was a two-year college (junior or community college) or a four-year college or university. Students enrolled in the first four years of college (undergraduates) were classified by the type of school that they attended. Graduate students are shown as a separate group.

Vocational school enrollment. Vocational school enrollment includes enrollment in business, vocational, technical, secretarial, trade, or correspondence courses that are not counted as regular school enrollment. This category excludes recreation or adult education classes. Courses that counted as college enrollment are also excluded.

School, Modal grade. Enrolled people are classified according to their relative progress in school and whether the grade or year in which they were enrolled was below, at, or above the modal (or typical) grade for students of their age at the time of the survey. The modal grade is the year of school in which the largest proportion of students of a given age were enrolled.

School, Nursery. A nursery school is defined as a group or class that has been organized to provide educational experiences for children during the year or years preceding kindergarten. It includes instruction as an important and integral phase of its childcare program. Private homes, in which essentially custodial care is provided, are not considered nursery schools. Children attending nursery school are classified as attending for part of the day or for the full day. Part-day attendance refers to those who attend either in the morning or in the afternoon. Full-day attendance refers to those who attend in the morning and in the afternoon. Children enrolled in Head Start programs or similar local agency-sponsored programs that provide preschool education to young children are counted as being enrolled in nursery school.

School, Public or private. A public school is defined as any educational institution operated by publicly elected or appointed school officials and supported by public funds. Private schools include educational institutions established and operated by religious bodies, as well as those that are under other private controls. In cases in which a school or college was both publicly and privately controlled or supported, enrollment was counted according to whether the school was primarily public or private.

Undocumented immigrants or illegal aliens. Since all residents of the United States living in households are represented in the sample of households interviewed by the CPS, undocumented immigrants or illegal aliens are probably included in CPS data. Because the CPS makes no attempt to ascertain the legal status of any person interviewed, these individuals cannot be identified from CPS data.

POSTSECONDARY EDUCATION TABLES

Tables A-9 and A-18 through A-23 were adapted from the most current published tables from the National Center for Education Statistics' *Digest of Education Statistics.*

Consumer Price Index. This price index measures the average change in the cost of a fixed market basket of goods and services purchased by consumers.

Control of institution describes whether an institution is operated by publicly elected or appointed officials (public control) or by privately elected or appointed officials and derives its major source of funds from private sources (private not-for-profit or private for-profit control). There are nine institutional categories resulting from dividing the universe according to control and level. Control categories are public, private not-for-profit, and private for-profit. Level categories are 4-year and higher (4 year), 2-but-less-than 4-year (2 year), and less than

2-year. For example: Public, 4-year is one of the institution sectors.

Fall enrollment. IPEDS collects data on the number of students enrolled in the fall at postsecondary institutions. Students reported are those enrolled in courses creditable toward a degree or other formal award; students enrolled in courses that are part of a vocational or occupational program, including those enrolled in off-campus or extension centers; and high school students taking regular college courses for credit. Institutions report annually the number of full- and part-time students, by gender, race/ethnicity, and level (undergraduate, graduate, first-professional); the total number of undergraduate entering students (first-time, full- and part-time students, transfer-ins, and nondegree students); and retention rates. In even-numbered years, data are collected for state of residence of first-time students and for the number of those students who graduated from high school or received high school equivalent certificates in the past 12 months. Also in even-numbered years, 4-year institutions are required to provide enrollment data by gender, race/ethnicity, and level for selected fields of study. In odd-numbered years, data are collected for enrollment by age category by student level and gender.

Data through 1995 are for institutions of higher education, while later data are for degree-granting institutions. Degree-granting institutions grant associate's or higher degrees and participate in Title IV federal financial aid programs. The degree-granting classification is very similar to the earlier higher education classification, but it includes more 2-year colleges and excludes a few higher education institutions that did not grant degrees.

Nonresident alien is a person who is not a citizen or national of the United States and who is in this country on a visa or temporary basis and does not have the right to remain indefinitely.

A **Postbaccalaureate student** is a student with a bachelor's degree who is enrolled in graduate-level or first-professional courses.

Price of attendance includes tuition and required fees, books and supplies, room and board charges, and other expenses. Amounts are institutional averages as reported by the institution, not average amounts paid by students (for example, charges are not weighted by enrollment). Out-of-state average tuition and required fees were used for private institutions that reported varying tuitions by residency. The 2,578 institutions with academic calendars that differ by program or allow continuous enrollment are not included. U.S. service academies are not included. All amounts from 2011–2012 were converted to 2013–2014 dollars using the average Consumer Price Index values for the 12-month periods ending in October 2011 and October 2013. On-campus average price is based on those institutions that offer on-campus housing and/or meal service. Off-campus average price is based on those institutions that do not require full-time, first-time students to live on campus. For public institutions, "in district" refers to the charges paid by a student who lives in the locality surrounding the institution, such as a county.

Race/ethnicity categories were developed in 1997 by the Office of Management and Budget (OMB) and are used to describe groups to which individuals belong, identify with, or belong in the eyes of the community. The categories do not denote scientific definitions of anthropological origins. The designations are used to categorize U.S. citizens, resident aliens, and other eligible non-citizens. Individuals are asked to first designate ethnicity as Hispanic/Latino or not Hispanic/Latino. Hispanic/Latino refers to a person of Cuban, Mexican, Puerto Rican, South or Central American, or other Spanish culture or origin, regardless of race. Second, individuals are asked to indicate all races that apply among the following:

American Indian or Alaska Native—A person having origins in any of the original peoples of North and South America (including Central America) who maintains cultural identification through tribal affiliation or community attachment.

Asian—A person having origins in any of the original peoples of the Far East, Southeast Asia, or the Indian Subcontinent, including, for example, Cambodia, China, India, Japan, Korea, Malaysia, Pakistan, the Philippine Islands, Thailand, and Vietnam.

Black or African American—A person having origins in any of the black racial groups of Africa.

Native Hawaiian or Other Pacific Islander— A person having origins in any of the original peoples of Hawaii, Guam, Samoa, or other Pacific Islands.

White—A person having origins in any of the original peoples of Europe, the Middle East, or North Africa.

Before 1997, slightly different race/ethnicity categories were used, and persons could identify with only one racial category.

Tuition and required fees is the amount of tuition and required fees covering a full academic year most frequently charged to students. These values represent what a typical student would be charged and may not be the same for all students at an institution. If tuition is charged on a per-credit-hour basis, the average full-time credit hour load for an entire academic year is used to estimate average tuition. Required fees include all fixed sum charges that are required of such a large proportion of all students that the student who does not pay the charges is an exception.

PART B
REGION AND STATE EDUCATION STATISTICS

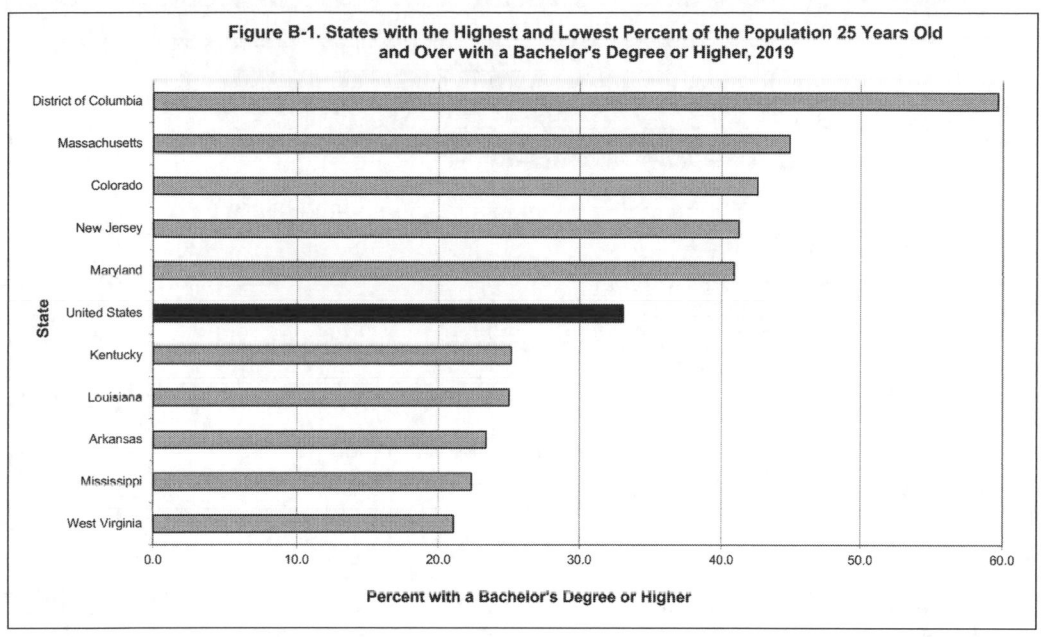

Figure B-1. States with the Highest and Lowest Percent of the Population 25 Years Old and Over with a Bachelor's Degree or Higher, 2019

The proportion of the U.S. population with a bachelor's degree or more was 33.1 percent for the population age 25 and over in 2019. In the District of Columbia, 59.7 percent of residents held a bachelor's degree or more, the highest rate in the nation. Among the states, 14 had proportions of college graduates exceeding 35 percent. West Virginia had the lowest college attainment level of 21.1 percent. The Northeast region had the highest college attainment rate (37.9 percent), followed by the West (34.4 percent), the Midwest (31.6 percent), and the South (30.9 percent). (Table B-2)

Among people age 25 years old and older in 2019, people who self-identified as Asian had the highest college attainment (55.6 percent), followed by White (34.4 percent), Black (22.5 percent), and Hispanic (17.6 percent) individuals. The District of Columbia had the highest percent of White, Asian, and Hispanic individuals with bachelor's degrees or more (89.3 percent, 80.3 percent, and 52.0 percent respectively). Wyoming was the state with the highest percent of Black individuals with bachelor's degrees or more (46.5 percent). (Table B-2)

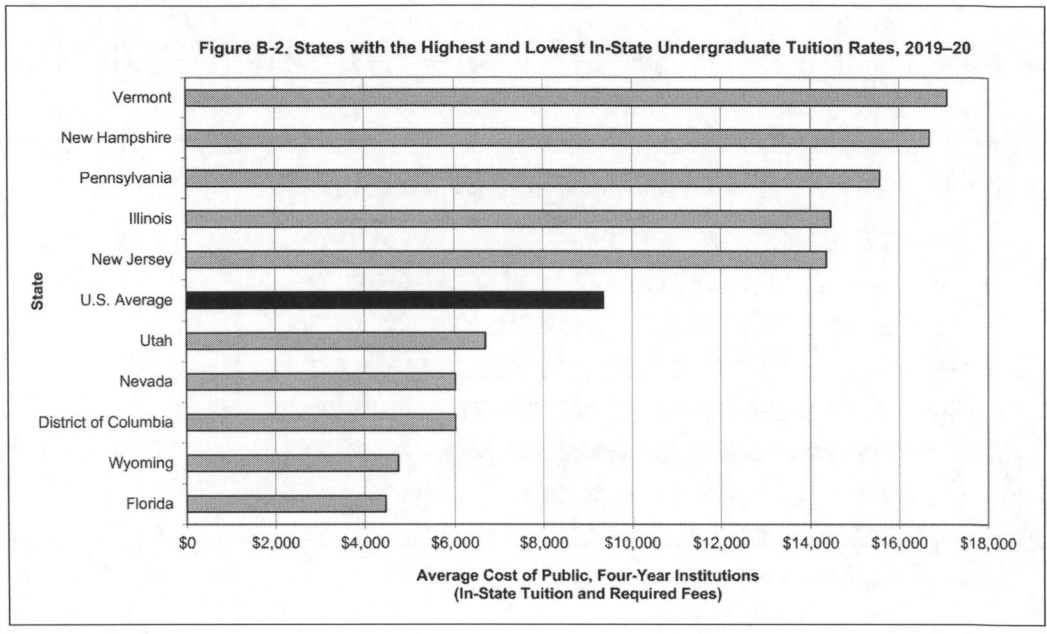

Figure B-2. States with the Highest and Lowest In-State Undergraduate Tuition Rates, 2019–20

The average cost of in-state tuition and fees at public, 4-year colleges during the 2019–20 school year was $9,349. Out-of-state tuition at public, 4-year colleges averaged $27,023, and the average tuition and fees at private, 4-year colleges was $32,769. Vermont was the state with the highest in-state tuition and fees ($17,083), and Florida was the state with the lowest average in-state tuition and fees ($4,463). Vermont also had the most expensive out-of-state tuition and fees at a cost of $41,057 per year. The District of Columbia had the lowest out-of-state cost with a tuition rate of $12,704 for non-residents. South Dakota had the smallest margin between in-state and out-of-state tuition, with its out-of-state tuition rate ($12,866) being just $3,888 more than the in-state rate ($8,978). (Table B-15)

There are several ways to measure high school dropouts. "Event dropout rates" provide the state's estimate of students who have left their schools with no documented reason (for example, transfer, move, or illness). In 2019, 5.1 percent of the population 16 to 24 years old were estimated to have dropped out of school before graduation because they are no longer enrolled in school and are not high school graduates. The District of Columbia had the lowest percentage of dropouts (2.2 percent) and New Mexico had the highest percentage of dropouts (8.1 percent). (Table B-11)

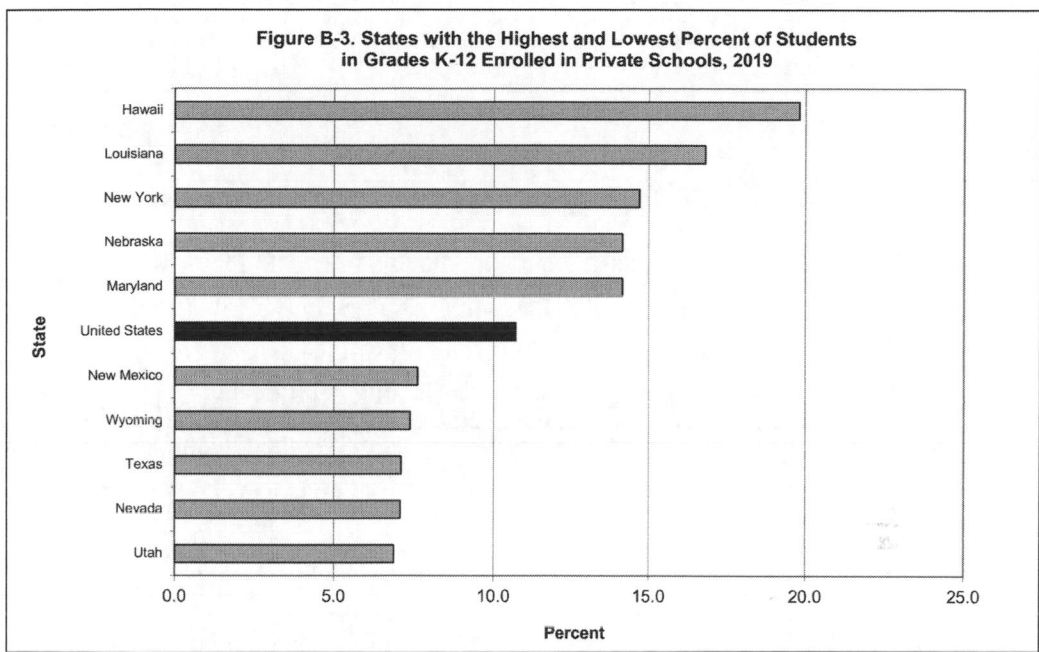

Figure B-3. States with the Highest and Lowest Percent of Students in Grades K-12 Enrolled in Private Schools, 2019

Hawaii was the state with the highest percent of students in grades K-12 enrolled in private school in 2019 (19.8 percent). In that state, there were a particularly large number of high-school students enrolled in private school (23.3 percent, compared to 10.2 percent of high-schoolers nationwide enrolled in private school). The state with the lowest percent of private school students in grades K-12 was Utah, where just 6.9 percent of students were enrolled in private school. Nevada had the lowest percent of high schoolers enrolled in private school in 2019 (5.9 percent). Rhode Island had the largest percent of undergraduates among the population 3 years and over enrolled in school (29.4 percent). The District of Columbia had the largest proportion of graduate students among the population age 3 and over enrolled in school (14.2 percent). (Table B-5)

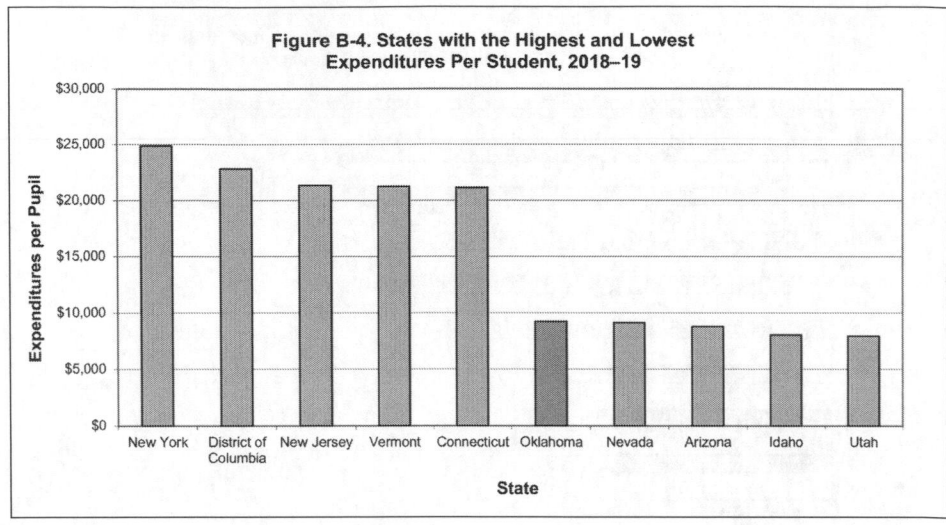

Figure B-4. States with the Highest and Lowest Expenditures Per Student, 2018–19

Nationally, education expenditures for 2018–19 were 52.4 percent for instruction, 30.9 percent for support services, and 16.7 percent for non-instruction related expenses. New York had the highest proportion of instruction-related expenditures, with 62.3 percent of the state's total expenditures for elementary and secondary programs used for this purpose. The District of Columbia had the lowest, with 38.1 percent of expenditures going toward instruction. The state with the largest expenditure per student was New York, where the expenditure per pupil was $24,882. Utah, the state with the smallest expenditure per student, spent $7,950 per pupil. (Table B-10)

Schools can be divided into four types: regular, special education, career and technical, and alternative education. Minnesota was the state with the highest percent of special education schools (13.0 percent) and alternative education schools (18.5 percent) in 2019–20. Arizona had highest percent of career and technical schools (11.7 percent). Louisiana had the highest proportion of Title I schoolwide schools (86.9 percent), and New Hampshire had the lowest proportion of Title I schools (19.2 percent). (Table B-4)

Nationally, the student-teacher ratio was 15.9 in Fall 2019. Arizona had the highest student-teacher ratio, with an average of 23.6 students per teacher. Vermont had the lowest student-teacher ratio (10.8 students per teacher). (Table B-9)

During the 2018–19 school year, 52.3 percent of students nationwide were eligible for free or reduced-price lunch. The District of Columbia had the highest percent of students eligible for free or reduced-price lunch (76.4 percent), followed by Mississippi (74.0 percent), and New Mexico (72.3 percent). The states with the highest percent of students with IEPs during the 2019–20 school year were New York (19.9 percent), Pennsylvania (19.8 percent), and Maine (19.7 percent). (Table B-7)

Table B-1. Educational Attainment of the Population 18 Years and Over, by Region, Age, and Sex, 2019

(Number; percent.)

Characteristic	United States		Northeast		Midwest		South		West	
	Number	Percent	Number	Percent	Number	Percent	Number	Percent	Number	Percent
Total.......................................	255,271,738	100.0	44,491,642	100.0	53,001,257	100.0	97,129,283	100.0	60,649,556	100.0
18 to 24 years................................	30,373,170	11.9	5,097,235	11.5	6,386,198	12.0	11,633,544	12.0	7,256,193	12.0
Less than 9th grade....................	430,596	1.4	68,674	1.3	95,777	1.5	175,026	1.5	91,119	1.3
9th to 12th grade, no diploma.....	3,231,484	10.6	460,408	9.0	670,804	10.5	1,353,533	11.6	746,739	10.3
High school graduate (includes equivalency)............................	9,921,331	32.7	1,539,374	30.2	2,067,788	32.4	3,923,225	33.7	2,390,944	33.0
Some college, no degree.............	11,482,480	37.8	1,922,255	37.7	2,426,118	38.0	4,307,240	37.0	2,826,867	39.0
Associate's degree	1,685,800	5.6	245,721	4.8	352,812	5.5	670,518	5.8	416,749	5.7
Bachelor's degree.......................	3,352,406	11.0	788,028	15.5	720,358	11.3	1,112,264	9.6	731,756	10.1
Graduate or professional degree.	269,073	0.9	72,775	1.4	52,541	0.8	91,738	0.8	52,019	0.7
25 to 34 years................................	45,578,475	17.9	7,715,613	17.3	9,075,588	17.1	17,125,244	17.6	11,662,030	19.2
Less than 9th grade....................	1,182,302	2.6	188,140	2.4	193,117	2.1	478,917	2.8	322,128	2.8
9th to 12th grade, no diploma.....	2,606,207	5.7	338,012	4.4	433,702	4.8	1,124,671	6.6	709,822	6.1
High school graduate (includes equivalency)............................	11,140,748	24.4	1,730,258	22.4	2,206,394	24.3	4,504,294	26.3	2,699,802	23.2
Some college, no degree.............	9,778,564	21.5	1,292,468	16.8	1,987,736	21.9	3,782,456	22.1	2,715,904	23.3
Associate's degree	4,033,109	8.8	624,977	8.1	895,463	9.9	1,535,067	9.0	977,020	8.4
Bachelor's degree.......................	11,770,702	25.8	2,342,621	30.4	2,379,751	26.2	3,999,686	23.4	3,048,644	26.1
Graduate or professional degree.	5,066,843	11.1	1,199,137	15.5	979,425	10.8	1,700,153	9.9	1,188,128	10.2
35 to 44 years................................	41,914,845	16.4	6,878,858	15.5	8,446,830	15.9	16,149,341	16.6	10,439,816	17.2
Less than 9th grade....................	1,878,547	4.5	253,559	3.7	267,071	3.2	773,308	4.8	584,609	5.6
9th to 12th grade, no diploma.....	2,725,778	6.5	352,805	5.1	445,304	5.3	1,173,505	7.3	754,164	7.2
High school graduate (includes equivalency)............................	9,731,105	23.2	1,576,498	22.9	1,991,710	23.6	4,007,078	24.8	2,155,819	20.6
Some college, no degree.............	7,975,203	19.0	1,054,256	15.3	1,679,695	19.9	3,139,845	19.4	2,101,407	20.1
Associate's degree	3,915,980	9.3	595,521	8.7	913,415	10.8	1,494,633	9.3	912,411	8.7
Bachelor's degree.......................	9,374,311	22.4	1,700,843	24.7	1,928,014	22.8	3,344,446	20.7	2,401,008	23.0
Graduate or professional degree.	6,313,921	15.1	1,345,376	19.6	1,221,621	14.5	2,216,526	13.7	1,530,398	14.7
45 to 64 years................................	83,331,220	32.6	14,987,869	33.7	17,535,679	33.1	31,675,473	32.6	19,132,199	31.5
Less than 9th grade....................	4,043,215	4.9	604,042	4.0	509,874	2.9	1,508,115	4.8	1,421,184	7.4
9th to 12th grade, no diploma.....	5,467,719	6.6	843,809	5.6	964,421	5.5	2,373,434	7.5	1,286,055	6.7
High school graduate (includes equivalency)............................	23,030,202	27.6	4,430,715	29.6	5,281,239	30.1	9,075,875	28.7	4,242,373	22.2
Some college, no degree.............	16,521,361	19.8	2,359,869	15.7	3,673,476	20.9	6,306,385	19.9	4,181,631	21.9
Associate's degree	7,745,212	9.3	1,371,936	9.2	1,815,936	10.4	2,835,229	9.0	1,722,111	9.0
Bachelor's degree.......................	16,093,480	19.3	3,100,219	20.7	3,314,558	18.9	5,845,519	18.5	3,033,184	20.0
Graduate or professional degree.	10,430,031	12.5	2,277,279	15.2	1,976,175	11.3	3,730,916	11.8	2,445,661	12.8
65 years and over	54,074,028	21.2	9,812,067	22.1	11,556,962	21.8	20,545,681	21.2	12,159,318	20.0
Less than 9th grade....................	3,770,621	7.0	701,495	7.1	507,372	4.4	1,538,094	7.5	1,023,660	8.4
9th to 12th grade, no diploma.....	3,944,152	7.3	720,650	7.3	790,183	6.8	1,733,528	8.4	699,791	5.8
High school graduate (includes equivalency)............................	16,580,298	30.7	3,310,264	33.7	4,209,402	36.4	6,291,606	30.6	2,769,026	22.8
Some college, no degree.............	10,638,958	19.7	1,466,756	14.9	2,356,464	20.4	4,054,364	19.7	2,761,374	22.7
Associate's degree	3,687,636	6.8	636,918	6.5	755,511	6.5	1,335,813	6.5	959,394	7.9
Bachelor's degree.......................	8,491,986	15.7	1,505,999	15.3	1,649,801	14.3	3,108,326	15.1	2,227,860	18.3
Graduate or professional degree.	6,960,377	12.9	1,469,985	15.0	1,288,229	11.1	2,483,950	12.1	1,718,213	14.1
Male	124,267,346	48.7	21,426,582	48.2	25,870,856	48.8	46,946,758	48.3	30,023,150	49.5
18 to 24 years................................	15,556,254	12.5	2,574,089	12.0	3,263,180	12.6	5,966,720	12.7	3,752,265	12.5
Less than 9th grade....................	253,626	1.6	40,027	1.6	52,019	1.6	108,456	1.8	53,124	1.4
9th to 12th grade, no diploma.....	1,873,139	12.0	265,702	10.3	383,847	11.8	786,516	13.2	437,074	11.6
High school graduate (includes equivalency)............................	5,613,801	36.1	863,864	33.6	1,174,413	36.0	2,229,606	37.4	1,345,918	35.9
Some college, no degree.............	5,543,981	35.6	926,530	36.0	1,164,656	35.7	2,053,207	34.4	1,399,588	37.3
Associate's degree	754,294	4.8	110,788	4.3	165,746	5.1	291,758	4.9	186,002	5.0
Bachelor's degree.......................	1,416,531	9.1	342,314	13.3	302,092	9.3	463,547	7.8	308,570	8.2
Graduate or professional degree.	100,882	0.6	24,864	1.0	20,407	0.6	33,630	0.6	21,981	0.6
25 to 34 years................................	23,099,299	18.6	3,900,264	18.2	4,600,279	17.8	8,578,806	18.3	6,019,950	20.1
Less than 9th grade....................	682,687	3.0	107,320	2.8	103,942	2.3	282,332	3.3	189,093	3.1
9th to 12th grade, no diploma.....	1,499,692	6.5	189,751	4.9	256,318	5.6	643,403	7.5	410,220	6.8
High school graduate (includes equivalency)............................	6,464,769	28.0	1,013,042	26.0	1,301,637	28.3	2,576,187	30.0	1,573,903	26.1
Some college, no degree.............	4,994,460	21.6	683,601	17.5	1,007,867	21.9	1,888,722	22.0	1,414,270	23.5
Associate's degree	1,857,056	8.0	295,580	7.6	415,951	9.0	678,032	7.9	467,493	7.8
Bachelor's degree.......................	5,520,794	23.9	1,134,543	29.1	1,120,386	24.4	1,822,889	21.2	1,442,976	24.0
Graduate or professional degree.	2,079,841	9.0	476,427	12.2	394,178	8.6	687,241	8.0	521,995	8.7
35 to 44 years................................	20,920,715	16.8	3,408,611	15.9	4,231,629	16.4	7,985,711	17.0	5,294,764	17.6
Less than 9th grade....................	1,015,410	4.9	138,228	4.1	139,411	3.3	429,465	5.4	308,306	5.8
9th to 12th grade, no diploma.....	1,546,874	7.4	198,906	5.8	257,382	6.1	670,393	8.4	420,193	7.9
High school graduate (includes equivalency)............................	5,573,933	26.6	898,862	26.4	1,184,740	28.0	2,275,189	28.5	1,215,142	22.9

Table B-1. Educational Attainment of the Population 18 Years and Over, by Region, Age, and Sex, 2019—*Continued*

(Number; percent.)

Characteristic	United States Number	United States Percent	Northeast Number	Northeast Percent	Midwest Number	Midwest Percent	South Number	South Percent	West Number	West Percent
Some college, no degree.............	4,000,639	19.1	542,318	15.9	840,812	19.9	1,532,664	19.2	1,084,845	20.5
Associate's degree	1,732,527	8.3	267,493	7.8	398,260	9.4	640,877	8.0	425,897	8.0
Bachelor's degree........................	4,350,263	20.8	800,536	23.5	897,071	21.2	1,512,747	18.9	1,139,909	21.5
Graduate or professional degree .	2,701,069	12.9	562,268	16.5	513,953	12.1	924,376	11.6	700,472	13.2
45 to 64 years..............................	40,646,797	32.7	7,267,421	33.9	8,627,366	33.3	15,311,600	32.6	9,440,410	31.4
Less than 9th grade	2,088,875	5.1	309,345	4.3	267,749	3.1	811,681	5.3	700,100	7.4
9th to 12th grade, no diploma.....	2,981,479	7.3	452,220	6.2	539,105	6.2	1,289,898	8.4	700,256	7.4
High school graduate (includes equivalency)...............................	12,002,869	29.5	2,310,913	31.8	2,801,461	32.5	4,671,654	30.5	2,218,841	23.5
Some college, no degree.............	7,890,025	19.4	1,146,132	15.8	1,781,468	20.6	2,946,611	19.2	2,015,814	21.4
Associate's degree	3,227,173	7.9	549,395	7.6	763,140	8.8	1,157,835	7.6	756,803	8.0
Bachelor's degree........................	7,519,558	18.5	1,452,981	20.0	1,548,304	17.9	2,684,911	17.5	1,833,362	19.4
Graduate or professional degree .	4,936,818	12.1	1,046,435	14.4	926,139	10.7	1,749,010	11.4	1,215,234	12.9
65 years and over	24,044,281	19.3	4,276,197	20.0	5,148,402	19.9	9,103,921	19.4	5,515,761	18.4
Less than 9th grade	1,614,697	6.7	289,146	6.8	226,838	4.4	684,108	7.5	414,605	7.5
9th to 12th grade, no diploma.....	1,657,216	6.9	307,890	7.2	340,015	6.6	719,020	7.9	290,291	5.3
High school graduate (includes equivalency)...............................	6,510,243	27.1	1,272,791	29.8	1,695,794	32.9	2,446,393	26.9	1,095,265	19.9
Some college, no degree.............	4,693,401	19.5	652,440	15.3	1,054,807	20.5	1,763,070	19.4	1,223,084	22.2
Associate's degree	1,574,653	6.5	256,990	6.0	320,523	6.2	563,129	6.2	434,011	7.9
Bachelor's degree........................	4,255,044	17.7	744,277	17.4	826,674	16.1	1,587,631	17.4	1,096,462	19.9
Graduate or professional degree .	3,739,027	15.6	752,663	17.6	683,751	13.3	1,340,570	14.7	962,043	17.4
Female	131,004,392	51.3	23,065,060	51.8	27,130,401	51.2	50,182,525	51.7	30,626,406	50.5
18 to 24 years..............................	14,816,916	11.3	2,523,146	10.9	3,123,018	11.5	5,666,824	11.3	3,503,928	11.4
Less than 9th grade	176,970	1.2	28,647	1.1	43,758	1.4	66,570	1.2	37,995	1.1
9th to 12th grade, no diploma.....	1,358,345	9.2	194,706	7.7	286,957	9.2	567,017	10.0	309,665	8.8
High school graduate (includes equivalency)...............................	4,307,530	29.1	675,510	26.8	893,375	28.6	1,693,619	29.9	1,045,026	29.8
Some college, no degree.............	5,938,499	40.1	995,725	39.5	1,261,462	40.4	2,254,033	39.8	1,427,279	40.7
Associate's degree	931,506	6.3	134,933	5.3	187,066	6.0	378,760	6.7	230,747	6.6
Bachelor's degree........................	1,935,875	13.1	445,714	17.7	418,266	13.4	648,717	11.4	423,178	12.1
Graduate or professional degree .	168,191	1.1	47,911	1.9	32,134	1.0	58,108	1.0	30,038	0.9
25 to 34 years..............................	22,479,176	17.2	3,815,349	16.5	4,475,309	16.5	8,546,438	17.0	5,642,080	18.4
Less than 9th grade	499,615	2.2	80,820	2.1	89,175	2.0	196,585	2.3	133,035	2.4
9th to 12th grade, no diploma.....	1,106,515	4.9	148,261	3.9	177,384	4.0	481,268	5.6	299,602	5.3
High school graduate (includes equivalency)...............................	4,675,979	20.8	717,216	18.8	904,757	20.2	1,928,107	22.6	1,125,899	20.0
Some college, no degree.............	4,784,104	21.3	608,867	16.0	979,869	21.9	1,893,734	22.2	1,301,634	23.1
Associate's degree	2,176,053	9.7	329,397	8.6	479,512	10.7	857,035	10.0	510,109	9.0
Bachelor's degree........................	6,249,908	27.8	1,208,078	31.7	1,259,365	28.1	2,176,797	25.5	1,605,668	28.5
Graduate or professional degree .	2,987,002	13.3	722,710	18.9	585,247	13.1	1,012,912	11.9	666,133	11.8
35 to 44 years..............................	20,994,130	16.0	3,470,247	15.0	4,215,201	15.5	8,163,630	16.3	5,145,052	16.8
Less than 9th grade	863,137	4.1	115,331	3.3	127,660	3.0	343,843	4.2	276,303	5.4
9th to 12th grade, no diploma.....	1,178,904	5.6	153,899	4.4	187,922	4.5	503,112	6.2	333,971	6.5
High school graduate (includes equivalency)...............................	4,157,172	19.8	677,636	19.5	806,970	19.1	1,731,889	21.2	940,677	18.3
Some college, no degree.............	3,974,564	18.9	511,938	14.8	838,883	19.9	1,607,181	19.7	1,016,562	19.8
Associate's degree	2,183,453	10.4	328,028	9.5	515,155	12.2	853,756	10.5	486,514	9.5
Bachelor's degree........................	5,024,048	23.9	900,307	25.9	1,030,943	24.5	1,831,699	22.4	1,261,099	24.5
Graduate or professional degree .	3,612,852	17.2	783,108	22.6	707,668	16.8	1,292,150	15.8	829,926	16.1
45 to 64 years..............................	42,684,423	32.6	7,720,448	33.5	8,908,313	32.8	16,363,873	32.6	9,691,789	31.6
Less than 9th grade	1,954,340	4.6	294,697	3.8	242,125	2.7	696,434	4.3	721,084	7.4
9th to 12th grade, no diploma.....	2,486,240	5.8	391,589	5.1	425,316	4.8	1,083,536	6.6	585,799	6.0
High school graduate (includes equivalency)...............................	11,027,333	25.8	2,119,802	27.5	2,479,778	27.8	4,404,221	26.9	2,023,532	20.9
Some college, no degree.............	8,631,336	20.2	1,213,737	15.7	1,892,008	21.2	3,359,774	20.5	2,165,817	22.3
Associate's degree	4,518,039	10.6	822,541	10.7	1,052,796	11.8	1,677,394	10.3	965,308	10.0
Bachelor's degree........................	8,573,922	20.1	1,647,238	21.3	1,766,254	19.8	3,160,608	19.3	1,999,822	20.6
Graduate or professional degree .	5,493,213	12.9	1,230,844	15.9	1,050,036	11.8	1,981,906	12.1	1,230,427	12.7
65 years and over	30,029,747	22.9	5,535,870	24.0	6,408,560	23.6	11,441,760	22.8	6,643,557	21.7
Less than 9th grade	2,155,924	7.2	412,349	7.4	280,534	4.4	853,986	7.5	609,055	9.2
9th to 12th grade, no diploma.....	2,286,936	7.6	412,760	7.5	450,168	7.0	1,014,508	8.9	409,500	6.2
High school graduate (includes equivalency)...............................	10,070,055	33.5	2,037,473	36.8	2,513,608	39.2	3,845,213	33.6	1,673,761	25.2
Some college, no degree.............	5,945,557	19.8	814,316	14.7	1,301,657	20.3	2,291,294	20.0	1,538,290	23.2
Associate's degree	2,112,983	7.0	379,928	6.9	434,988	6.8	772,684	6.8	525,383	7.9
Bachelor's degree........................	4,236,942	14.1	761,722	13.8	823,127	12.8	1,520,695	13.3	1,131,398	17.0
Graduate or professional degree .	3,221,350	10.7	717,322	13.0	604,478	9.4	1,143,380	10.0	756,170	11.4

Table B-2. Educational Attainment of the Population 25 Years Old and Over, by Sex, Race, Hispanic Origin, and Region or State, 2019

(Number; percent.)

Region or State	Population	Total, age 25 years and over								
		Less than 9th grade	9th to 12th grade, no diploma	High school graduate (includes equivalency)	Some college, no degree	Associate degree	Bachelor's degree	Graduate or professional degree	High school graduate or higher (percent)	Bachelor's degree or higher (percent)
United States	224,898,568	10,874,685	14,743,856	60,482,353	44,914,086	19,381,937	45,730,479	28,771,172	88.6	33.1
Northeast Region	39,394,407	1,747,236	2,255,276	11,047,735	6,173,349	3,229,352	8,649,682	6,291,777	89.8	37.9
Midwest Region	46,615,059	1,477,434	2,633,610	13,688,745	9,697,371	4,380,325	9,272,124	5,465,450	91.2	31.6
South Region	85,495,739	4,298,434	6,405,138	23,878,853	17,283,050	7,200,742	16,297,977	10,131,545	87.5	30.9
West Region	53,393,363	3,351,581	3,449,832	11,867,020	11,760,316	4,571,518	11,510,696	6,882,400	87.3	34.4
Alabama	3,360,058	130,320	302,753	1,039,241	700,473	301,914	547,975	337,382	87.1	26.3
Alaska	484,050	10,424	20,666	139,156	124,261	43,394	89,583	56,574	93.6	30.2
Arizona	4,944,540	252,459	360,539	1,170,685	1,236,845	431,854	931,038	561,120	87.6	30.2
Arkansas	2,036,456	94,376	160,617	710,306	444,052	151,738	307,185	168,182	87.5	23.3
California......................	26,937,822	2,346,235	1,955,278	5,546,711	5,542,372	2,118,792	5,889,724	3,538,760	84.0	35.0
Colorado	3,974,943	127,702	174,518	836,590	805,570	334,961	1,057,825	637,777	92.4	42.7
Connecticut..................	2,496,420	99,132	132,707	668,361	410,972	190,700	549,166	445,382	90.7	39.8
Delaware	687,311	23,925	42,597	207,642	128,063	56,885	134,287	93,912	90.3	33.2
District of Columbia	505,145	16,459	24,709	79,881	65,745	16,922	129,825	171,604	91.9	59.7
Florida.........................	15,484,502	712,764	1,081,871	4,396,122	3,001,381	1,538,727	2,982,643	1,770,994	88.4	30.7
Georgia	7,080,222	319,929	536,096	1,939,945	1,414,554	568,130	1,410,395	891,173	87.9	32.5
Hawaii	906,668	36,278	39,700	273,421	205,964	106,096	219,979	115,230	92.4	33.6
Idaho...........................	1,170,997	34,969	64,937	306,274	304,578	124,584	220,189	116,466	91.5	28.7
Illinois	8,694,694	388,348	494,289	2,255,611	1,737,416	710,058	1,886,240	1,222,732	89.8	35.8
Indiana	4,502,015	162,057	306,026	1,526,825	896,654	397,627	777,771	435,055	89.6	26.9
Iowa............................	2,123,004	57,894	98,587	658,822	433,870	251,578	420,199	202,054	92.6	29.3
Kansas	1,918,081	63,799	93,958	504,035	430,549	173,251	414,851	237,638	91.8	34.0
Kentucky	3,048,442	154,759	235,894	1,012,643	619,035	260,188	453,040	312,883	87.2	25.1
Louisiana	3,140,201	138,644	302,200	1,066,026	646,746	202,310	503,947	280,328	86.0	25.0
Maine..........................	991,152	20,783	46,531	311,108	184,723	99,008	205,722	123,277	93.2	33.2
Maryland......................	4,183,858	168,321	233,831	1,030,636	753,547	287,293	911,781	798,449	90.4	40.9
Massachusetts	4,850,576	203,412	217,529	1,158,066	729,016	360,810	1,197,208	984,535	91.3	45.0
Michigan	6,894,627	186,035	410,252	2,005,981	1,572,770	648,794	1,252,685	818,110	91.4	30.0
Minnesota	3,847,212	103,730	141,960	939,997	785,721	442,578	942,830	490,396	93.6	37.3
Mississippi...................	1,979,664	91,377	199,540	598,609	440,939	207,448	270,712	171,039	85.3	22.3
Missouri.......................	4,206,162	122,379	269,436	1,308,859	900,486	333,721	775,808	495,473	90.7	30.2
Montana.......................	741,950	12,087	30,595	211,079	169,641	69,400	171,309	77,839	94.2	33.6
Nebraska......................	1,271,770	43,627	57,645	326,389	280,333	141,189	277,159	145,428	92.0	33.2
Nevada.........................	2,136,466	109,903	171,012	593,417	525,746	187,469	355,837	193,082	86.9	25.7
New Hampshire..............	979,750	19,331	46,341	275,105	174,078	96,658	224,636	143,601	93.3	37.6
New Jersey	6,191,229	287,999	311,620	1,666,321	974,540	398,984	1,555,781	995,984	90.3	41.2
New Mexico	1,425,988	82,436	118,892	376,390	324,141	129,531	221,281	173,317	85.9	27.7
New York......................	13,664,734	795,539	898,691	3,524,192	2,075,506	1,204,588	2,898,440	2,267,778	87.6	37.8
North Carolina...............	7,187,077	299,154	519,770	1,839,042	1,480,044	727,882	1,471,420	849,765	88.6	32.3
North Dakota.................	504,375	13,284	19,735	134,432	112,811	70,716	108,527	44,870	93.5	30.4
Ohio.............................	8,049,805	221,017	519,830	2,627,758	1,622,014	702,601	1,464,945	891,640	90.8	29.3
Oklahoma.....................	2,619,244	100,954	202,312	825,284	596,289	207,896	447,888	238,621	88.4	26.2
Oregon.........................	2,988,118	98,217	160,182	687,243	741,058	269,102	627,911	404,405	91.4	34.5
Pennsylvania.................	9,028,036	273,775	538,057	3,103,046	1,420,062	775,694	1,761,627	1,155,775	91.0	32.3
Rhode Island.................	746,952	37,697	42,510	212,282	129,984	64,204	156,087	104,188	89.3	34.8
South Carolina	3,563,204	132,646	283,032	1,015,260	725,158	352,549	656,496	398,063	88.3	29.6
South Dakota	588,029	16,462	29,832	176,644	120,476	69,831	121,231	53,553	92.1	29.7
Tennessee	4,693,962	202,493	360,324	1,400,753	953,282	348,886	845,100	503,124	88.0	28.7
Texas...........................	18,772,550	1,436,483	1,445,905	4,734,422	3,976,607	1,402,600	3,750,797	2,025,736	84.6	30.8
Utah	1,911,592	46,767	86,293	442,206	486,888	184,777	448,109	216,552	93.0	34.8
Vermont........................	445,558	9,568	21,290	129,254	74,468	38,706	101,015	71,257	93.1	38.7
Virginia.........................	5,872,757	222,224	362,488	1,387,610	1,107,258	468,107	1,312,800	1,012,270	90.0	39.6
Washington...................	5,290,324	187,558	252,516	1,167,347	1,199,747	527,524	1,204,728	750,904	91.7	37.0
West Virginia.................	1,281,086	53,606	111,199	515,431	229,877	101,267	161,686	108,020	87.1	21.1
Wisconsin.....................	4,015,285	98,802	192,060	1,223,392	804,271	438,381	829,878	428,501	92.8	31.3
Wyoming	389,847	6,546	14,704	117,501	93,505	44,034	73,183	40,374	94.5	29.1

[1]May be of any race.
… = Not available

Table B-2. Educational Attainment of the Population 25 Years Old and Over, by Sex, Race, Hispanic Origin, and Region or State, 2019—*Continued*

(Number; percent.)

Region or State	Male, age 25 years and over									
	Population	Less than 9th grade	9th to 12th grade, no diploma	High school graduate (includes equivalency)	Some college, no degree	Associate degree	Bachelor's degree	Graduate or professional degree	High school graduate or higher (percent)	Bachelor's degree or higher (percent)
United States	108,711,092	5,401,669	7,685,261	30,551,814	21,578,525	8,391,409	21,645,659	13,456,755	88.0	32.3
Northeast Region	18,852,493	844,039	1,148,767	5,495,608	3,024,491	1,369,458	4,132,337	2,837,793	89.4	37.0
Midwest Region	22,607,676	737,940	1,392,820	6,983,632	4,684,954	1,897,874	4,392,435	2,518,021	90.6	30.6
South Region	40,980,038	2,207,586	3,322,714	11,969,423	8,131,067	3,039,873	7,608,178	4,701,197	86.5	30.0
West Region.................	26,270,885	1,612,104	1,820,960	6,103,151	5,738,013	2,084,204	5,512,709	3,399,744	86.9	33.9
Alabama......................	1,586,206	71,215	152,700	512,181	319,537	124,955	255,317	150,301	85.9	25.6
Alaska	248,666	5,845	10,642	78,101	66,261	21,997	40,480	25,340	93.4	26.5
Arizona.......................	2,423,466	125,602	188,217	593,553	592,821	199,184	446,041	278,048	87.1	29.9
Arkansas	975,517	49,841	81,100	362,841	209,719	56,732	138,501	76,783	86.6	22.1
California.....................	13,208,824	1,111,415	1,030,198	2,845,945	2,709,335	951,967	2,806,332	1,753,632	83.8	34.5
Colorado.....................	1,982,756	66,925	90,936	438,996	406,110	150,857	519,763	309,169	92.0	41.8
Connecticut..................	1,195,271	50,027	70,183	329,406	198,237	80,368	261,219	205,831	89.9	39.1
Delaware	325,736	11,488	24,067	98,750	61,608	23,579	62,719	43,525	89.1	32.6
District of Columbia	236,952	8,124	13,386	36,627	26,972	8,169	62,428	81,246	90.9	60.6
Florida........................	7,435,836	349,619	571,380	2,167,938	1,429,199	649,865	1,410,262	857,573	87.6	30.5
Georgia	3,352,785	168,720	277,058	967,909	653,765	244,460	654,577	386,296	86.7	31.0
Hawaii	488,577	14,584	17,956	145,966	105,146	52,976	99,134	52,815	93.3	31.1
Idaho..........................	579,656	17,143	35,945	162,883	141,396	57,615	102,458	62,216	90.8	28.4
Illinois........................	4,192,414	189,100	263,650	1,133,810	830,315	310,574	900,767	564,198	89.2	34.9
Indiana	2,174,011	83,764	157,183	777,020	417,779	168,165	370,748	199,352	88.9	26.2
Iowa...........................	1,040,234	30,675	52,520	347,951	210,828	109,952	194,498	93,810	92.0	27.7
Kansas	935,211	32,307	49,880	260,089	207,452	79,778	195,407	110,304	91.2	32.7
Kentucky	1,468,976	82,751	124,901	525,573	288,595	97,986	220,641	128,529	85.9	23.8
Louisiana	1,491,097	78,344	157,650	536,578	297,354	80,509	222,046	118,616	84.2	22.8
Maine	475,676	10,868	25,626	162,607	87,021	44,415	92,083	53,056	92.3	30.5
Maryland.....................	1,979,022	88,195	118,798	516,202	354,630	115,779	417,359	368,059	89.5	39.7
Massachusetts	2,312,900	99,740	107,288	590,020	348,014	145,579	572,590	449,669	91.0	44.2
Michigan	3,338,285	90,930	213,705	1,009,979	771,368	270,111	596,013	386,179	90.9	29.4
Minnesota	1,893,200	47,551	78,903	497,978	386,797	205,669	451,563	224,739	93.3	35.7
Mississippi..................	928,666	50,314	104,916	305,725	200,942	81,174	117,492	68,103	83.3	20.0
Missouri......................	2,021,577	63,474	138,581	667,680	425,150	138,553	368,603	219,536	90.0	29.1
Montana......................	367,446	6,666	16,809	109,837	83,427	30,358	82,825	37,524	93.6	32.8
Nebraska.....................	624,305	22,385	31,517	167,659	134,082	71,378	130,034	67,250	91.4	31.6
Nevada........................	1,061,616	53,331	86,608	303,515	267,456	87,320	167,519	95,867	86.8	24.8
New Hampshire.............	479,211	9,928	27,571	144,178	83,519	42,564	107,286	64,165	92.2	35.8
New Jersey	2,966,074	140,880	158,039	804,887	483,983	164,457	726,690	487,138	89.9	40.9
New Mexico	691,222	38,868	61,306	196,679	154,835	59,854	101,314	78,366	85.5	26.0
New York.....................	6,500,808	370,237	451,796	1,748,881	1,035,209	520,358	1,395,801	978,526	87.4	36.5
North Carolina..............	3,398,408	158,893	279,143	927,213	686,315	295,114	674,417	377,313	87.1	30.9
North Dakota................	254,515	6,525	11,648	72,697	60,565	34,542	48,572	19,966	92.9	26.9
Ohio	3,870,968	112,360	268,705	1,324,274	785,690	274,437	693,201	412,301	90.2	28.6
Oklahoma....................	1,269,169	51,961	102,749	419,818	283,759	91,780	207,982	111,120	87.8	25.1
Oregon	1,459,257	51,478	89,416	346,700	353,440	129,143	298,995	190,085	90.3	33.5
Pennsylvania................	4,346,893	138,184	274,609	1,539,562	689,364	327,733	854,109	523,332	90.5	31.7
Rhode Island................	357,935	19,346	20,242	105,478	63,923	26,856	75,811	46,279	88.9	34.1
South Carolina	1,678,161	71,741	148,500	496,169	328,559	150,629	313,518	169,045	86.9	28.8
South Dakota	293,272	9,316	16,728	93,409	57,884	32,441	59,698	23,796	91.1	28.5
Tennessee	2,238,460	104,982	189,922	735,374	451,148	144,599	387,959	224,476	86.8	27.4
Texas..........................	9,165,437	724,394	733,467	2,382,325	1,903,611	637,094	1,781,441	1,003,105	84.1	30.4
Utah...........................	949,043	24,164	44,780	216,579	232,133	81,110	222,158	128,119	92.7	36.9
Vermont......................	217,725	4,829	13,413	70,589	35,221	17,128	46,748	29,797	91.6	35.2
Virginia.......................	2,825,457	108,758	187,372	708,896	527,730	197,146	606,292	489,263	89.5	38.8
Washington..................	2,612,977	92,016	140,490	598,117	581,291	241,293	591,069	368,701	91.1	36.7
West Virginia................	624,153	28,246	55,605	269,304	107,624	40,303	75,227	47,844	86.6	19.7
Wisconsin	1,969,678	49,553	109,800	631,086	397,044	202,274	383,331	196,590	91.9	29.4
Wyoming	197,379	4,067	7,657	66,280	44,362	20,530	34,621	19,862	94.1	27.6

[1]May be of any race.
... = Not available

Table B-2. Educational Attainment of the Population 25 Years Old and Over, by Sex, Race, Hispanic Origin, and Region or State, 2019—*Continued*

(Number; percent.)

Region or State	Population	Less than 9th grade	9th to 12th grade, no diploma	High school graduate (includes equivalency)	Some college, no degree	Associate degree	Bachelor's degree	Graduate or professional degree	High school graduate or higher (percent)	Bachelor's degree or higher (percent)
				Female, age 25 years and over						
United States	116,187,476	5,473,016	7,058,595	29,930,539	23,335,561	10,990,528	24,084,820	15,314,417	89.2	33.9
Northeast Region	20,541,914	903,197	1,106,509	5,552,127	3,148,858	1,859,894	4,517,345	3,453,984	90.2	38.8
Midwest Region	24,007,383	739,494	1,240,790	6,705,113	5,012,417	2,482,451	4,879,689	2,947,429	91.8	32.6
South Region	44,515,701	2,090,848	3,082,424	11,909,430	9,151,983	4,160,869	8,689,799	5,430,348	88.4	31.7
West Region	27,122,478	1,739,477	1,628,872	5,763,869	6,022,303	2,487,314	5,997,987	3,482,656	87.6	35.0
Alabama	1,773,852	59,105	150,053	527,060	380,936	176,959	292,658	187,081	88.2	27.0
Alaska	235,392	4,579	10,024	61,055	58,000	21,397	49,103	31,234	93.8	34.1
Arizona	2,521,074	126,857	172,322	577,132	644,024	232,670	484,997	283,072	88.1	30.5
Arkansas	1,060,939	44,535	79,517	347,465	234,333	95,006	168,684	91,399	88.3	24.5
California	13,729,048	1,234,820	925,080	2,700,766	2,833,037	1,166,825	3,083,392	1,785,128	84.3	35.5
Colorado	1,992,187	60,777	83,582	307,594	399,460	184,104	538,062	328,608	92.8	43.5
Connecticut	1,301,149	49,105	62,524	338,955	212,735	110,332	287,947	239,551	91.4	40.5
Delaware	361,575	12,437	18,530	108,892	66,455	33,306	71,568	50,387	91.4	33.7
District of Columbia	268,193	8,335	11,323	43,254	38,773	8,753	67,397	90,358	92.7	58.8
Florida	8,048,666	363,145	510,491	2,228,184	1,572,182	888,862	1,572,381	913,421	89.1	30.9
Georgia	3,727,437	151,209	259,038	972,036	760,789	323,670	755,818	504,877	89.0	33.8
Hawaii	508,091	21,694	21,744	127,455	100,818	53,120	120,845	62,415	91.5	36.1
Idaho	591,341	17,826	28,992	142,391	163,182	66,969	117,731	54,250	92.1	29.1
Illinois	4,502,280	199,248	230,639	1,121,801	907,101	399,484	985,473	658,534	90.5	36.5
Indiana	2,328,004	78,293	148,843	749,805	478,875	229,462	407,023	235,703	90.2	27.6
Iowa	1,082,770	27,219	46,067	310,871	223,042	141,626	225,701	108,244	93.2	30.8
Kansas	982,864	31,492	44,078	243,946	223,097	93,473	219,444	127,334	92.3	35.3
Kentucky	1,579,466	72,008	110,993	487,070	330,440	162,202	232,399	184,354	88.4	26.4
Louisiana	1,649,104	60,300	144,550	529,448	349,392	121,801	281,901	161,712	87.6	26.9
Maine	515,476	9,915	20,905	148,501	97,702	54,593	113,639	70,221	94.0	35.7
Maryland	2,204,836	80,126	115,033	514,434	398,917	171,514	494,422	430,390	91.1	41.9
Massachusetts	2,537,676	103,672	110,241	568,046	381,002	215,231	624,618	534,866	91.6	45.7
Michigan	3,556,342	95,105	196,547	996,002	801,402	378,683	656,672	431,931	91.8	30.6
Minnesota	1,954,012	56,179	63,057	442,019	398,924	236,909	491,267	265,657	93.9	38.7
Mississippi	1,050,998	41,063	94,624	292,084	239,997	126,274	153,220	102,936	87.1	24.4
Missouri	2,184,585	58,905	130,855	641,179	475,336	195,168	407,205	275,937	91.3	31.3
Montana	374,504	5,421	13,786	101,242	86,214	39,042	88,484	40,315	94.9	34.4
Nebraska	647,465	21,242	26,128	158,730	146,251	69,811	147,125	78,178	92.7	34.8
Nevada	1,074,850	56,572	84,404	289,902	258,290	100,149	188,318	97,215	86.9	26.6
New Hampshire	500,539	9,403	18,770	130,927	90,559	54,094	117,350	79,436	94.4	39.3
New Jersey	3,225,155	147,119	153,581	861,434	490,557	234,527	829,091	508,846	90.7	41.5
New Mexico	734,766	43,568	57,586	179,711	169,306	69,677	119,967	94,951	86.2	29.2
New York	7,163,926	425,302	446,895	1,775,311	1,040,297	684,230	1,502,639	1,289,252	87.8	39.0
North Carolina	3,788,669	140,261	240,627	911,829	793,729	432,768	797,003	472,452	89.9	33.5
North Dakota	249,860	6,759	8,087	61,735	52,246	36,174	59,955	24,904	94.1	34.0
Ohio	4,178,837	108,657	251,125	1,303,484	836,324	428,164	771,744	479,339	91.4	29.9
Oklahoma	1,350,075	48,993	99,563	405,466	312,530	116,116	239,906	127,501	89.0	27.2
Oregon	1,528,861	46,739	70,766	340,543	387,618	139,959	328,916	214,320	92.3	35.5
Pennsylvania	4,681,143	135,591	263,448	1,563,484	730,698	447,961	907,518	632,443	91.5	32.9
Rhode Island	389,017	18,351	22,268	106,804	66,061	37,348	80,276	57,909	89.6	35.5
South Carolina	1,885,043	60,905	134,532	519,091	396,599	201,920	342,978	229,018	89.6	30.3
South Dakota	294,757	7,146	13,104	83,235	62,592	37,390	61,533	29,757	93.1	31.0
Tennessee	2,455,502	97,511	170,402	745,379	502,134	204,287	457,141	278,648	89.1	30.0
Texas	8,607,113	712,009	712,438	2,352,097	2,072,996	765,506	1,969,356	1,022,631	85.2	31.1
Utah	962,549	22,603	41,513	225,627	254,755	103,667	225,951	88,433	93.3	32.7
Vermont	227,833	4,739	7,877	58,665	39,247	21,578	54,267	41,460	94.5	42.0
Virginia	3,047,300	113,466	175,116	678,714	579,528	270,961	706,508	523,007	90.5	40.3
Washington	2,677,347	95,542	112,026	569,230	618,456	286,231	613,659	382,203	92.2	37.2
West Virginia	656,933	25,360	55,594	246,127	122,253	60,964	86,459	60,176	87.7	22.3
Wisconsin	2,045,607	49,249	82,260	592,306	407,227	236,107	446,547	231,911	93.6	33.2
Wyoming	192,468	2,479	7,047	51,221	49,143	23,504	38,562	20,512	95.1	30.7

[1]May be of any race.
… = Not available

Table B-2. Educational Attainment of the Population 25 Years Old and Over, by Sex, Race, Hispanic Origin, and Region or State, 2019—*Continued*

(Number; percent.)

Region or State	Population	White alone, age 25 years and over					
		Less than a high school diploma	High school graduate (includes equivalency)	Some college or associate's degree	Bachelor's degree or higher	High school graduate or higher (percent)	Bachelor's degree or higher (percent)
United States	167,334,031	16,059,994	45,168,415	48,491,383	57,614,239	90.4	34.4
Northeast Region	38,601,748	2,896,840	11,465,389	11,687,362	12,552,157	92.5	32.5
Midwest Region	29,349,798	2,236,666	8,283,638	7,097,576	11,731,918	92.4	40.0
South Region	61,935,787	7,028,785	17,092,273	17,718,528	20,096,201	88.7	32.4
West Region	37,446,698	3,897,703	8,327,115	11,987,917	13,233,963	89.6	35.3
Alabama	2,363,674	272,567	703,265	713,276	674,566	88.5	28.5
Alaska	336,103	13,623	81,493	120,929	120,058	95.9	35.7
Arizona	4,002,380	448,909	941,141	1,365,801	1,246,529	88.8	31.1
Arkansas	1,625,302	186,131	568,025	475,900	395,246	88.5	24.3
California	16,461,029	2,238,619	3,397,327	4,968,577	5,856,506	86.4	35.6
Colorado	3,406,342	225,301	696,900	974,174	1,509,967	93.4	44.3
Connecticut	1,939,577	138,595	502,622	471,592	826,768	92.9	42.6
Delaware	490,907	45,086	141,737	133,986	170,098	90.8	34.6
District of Columbia	230,095	4,171	5,954	14,441	205,529	98.2	89.3
Florida	12,023,439	1,226,998	3,351,605	3,535,800	3,909,036	89.8	32.5
Georgia	4,279,288	454,537	1,143,892	1,163,492	1,517,367	89.4	35.5
Hawaii	259,996	8,020	54,114	82,106	115,756	96.9	44.5
Idaho	1,066,998	76,803	278,728	400,381	311,086	92.8	29.2
Illinois	6,414,127	521,595	1,696,106	1,806,561	2,389,865	91.9	37.3
Indiana	3,843,248	361,425	1,320,287	1,110,926	1,050,610	90.6	27.3
Iowa	1,950,864	124,635	613,165	636,931	576,133	93.6	29.5
Kansas	1,653,103	112,454	432,480	524,360	583,809	93.2	35.3
Kentucky	2,705,849	340,994	912,080	771,660	681,115	87.4	25.2
Louisiana	2,036,883	240,316	673,801	545,036	577,730	88.2	28.4
Maine	944,133	61,368	299,158	271,270	312,337	93.5	33.1
Maryland	2,385,477	170,392	560,188	569,372	1,085,525	92.9	45.5
Massachusetts	3,865,466	253,367	929,572	885,108	1,797,419	93.4	46.5
Michigan	5,564,561	429,437	1,621,596	1,795,493	1,718,035	92.3	30.9
Minnesota	3,298,386	146,084	810,479	1,072,726	1,269,097	95.6	38.5
Mississippi	1,217,710	142,140	352,718	408,637	314,215	88.3	25.8
Missouri	3,537,955	306,371	1,096,454	1,036,719	1,098,411	91.3	31.0
Montana	672,576	34,911	191,045	215,758	230,862	94.8	34.3
Nebraska	1,130,659	73,333	288,192	381,342	387,792	93.5	34.3
Nevada	1,444,872	157,059	404,891	494,792	388,130	89.1	26.9
New Hampshire	919,746	59,123	261,232	258,655	340,736	93.6	37.0
New Jersey	4,294,038	344,820	1,177,377	967,461	1,804,380	92.0	42.0
New Mexico	1,081,586	135,725	275,119	338,636	332,106	87.5	30.7
New York	8,910,770	736,141	2,220,857	2,180,692	3,773,080	91.7	42.3
North Carolina	5,103,713	473,626	1,260,967	1,578,199	1,790,921	90.7	35.1
North Dakota	446,532	25,686	119,472	160,036	141,338	94.2	31.7
Ohio	6,706,983	552,138	2,233,581	1,892,540	2,028,724	91.8	30.2
Oklahoma	1,999,360	209,490	628,435	605,729	555,706	89.5	27.8
Oregon	2,568,427	190,706	596,786	890,928	890,007	92.6	34.7
Pennsylvania	7,439,802	560,718	2,594,017	1,797,244	2,487,823	92.5	33.4
Rhode Island	613,613	56,378	174,628	157,371	225,236	90.8	36.7
South Carolina	2,483,427	226,996	644,376	768,318	843,737	90.9	34.0
South Dakota	516,050	31,260	152,996	169,427	162,367	93.9	31.5
Tennessee	3,744,336	423,484	1,192,130	1,015,133	1,113,589	88.7	29.7
Texas	13,971,984	2,122,808	3,520,467	4,028,221	4,300,488	84.8	30.8
Utah	1,694,118	93,524	386,159	608,502	605,933	94.5	35.8
Vermont	422,653	26,156	124,175	108,183	164,139	93.8	38.8
Virginia	4,069,698	331,618	943,952	1,084,707	1,709,421	91.9	42.0
Washington	4,090,653	255,875	918,040	1,397,625	1,519,113	93.7	37.1
West Virginia	1,204,645	157,431	488,681	306,621	251,912	86.9	20.9
Wisconsin	3,539,280	212,422	1,080,581	1,100,301	1,145,976	94.0	32.4
Wyoming	361,618	18,628	105,372	129,708	107,910	94.8	29.8

[1] May be of any race.

... = Not available

Table B-2. Educational Attainment of the Population 25 Years Old and Over, by Sex, Race, Hispanic Origin, and Region or State, 2019—*Continued*

(Number; percent.)

Region or State	Black or African American alone, age 25 years and over						
	Population	Less than a high school diploma	High school graduate (includes equivalency)	Some college or associate's degree	Bachelor's degree or higher	High school graduate or higher (percent)	Bachelor's degree or higher (percent)
United States	27,336,967	3,537,086	8,732,838	8,902,977	6,164,066	87.1	22.5
Northeast Region	4,533,097	600,591	1,465,877	1,583,761	882,868	86.8	19.5
Midwest Region	4,531,148	611,562	1,522,838	1,312,078	1,084,670	86.5	23.9
South Region	15,792,403	2,090,887	5,117,279	5,040,528	3,543,709	86.8	22.4
West Region.................	2,480,319	234,046	626,844	966,610	652,819	90.6	26.3
Alabama......................	855,485	127,765	308,132	255,223	164,365	85.1	19.2
Alaska	15,832	1,672	5,155	5,478	3,527	89.4	22.3
Arizona.......................	214,990	21,719	47,591	87,000	58,680	89.9	27.3
Arkansas.....................	292,048	38,272	109,869	94,224	49,683	86.9	17.0
California.....................	1,573,950	148,975	390,803	607,546	426,626	90.5	27.1
Colorado.....................	155,881	11,920	41,503	59,301	43,077	92.4	27.6
Connecticut..................	257,234	35,115	89,391	76,819	55,909	86.3	21.7
Delaware	145,150	13,656	54,418	41,415	35,661	90.6	24.6
District of Columbia	220,748	29,868	67,667	61,193	62,020	86.5	28.1
Florida.........................	2,216,463	347,859	753,382	687,258	427,964	84.3	19.3
Georgia	2,186,956	264,883	681,361	698,653	542,059	87.9	24.8
Hawaii.........................	18,397	301	2,900	9,486	5,710	98.4	31.0
Idaho..........................	5,607	399	1,587	2,872	749	92.9	13.4
Illinois........................	1,177,578	158,421	335,514	416,955	266,688	86.5	22.6
Indiana	395,797	48,698	145,196	125,408	76,495	87.7	19.3
Iowa...........................	72,382	12,304	24,106	25,208	10,764	83.0	14.9
Kansas	101,769	12,844	31,364	36,299	21,262	87.4	20.9
Kentucky	232,582	27,500	76,855	83,355	44,872	88.2	19.3
Louisiana	948,531	169,833	350,550	266,370	161,778	82.1	17.1
Maine..........................	11,899	1,487	2,891	2,990	4,531	87.5	38.1
Maryland......................	1,241,353	118,381	366,446	374,099	382,427	90.5	30.8
Massachusetts	350,938	50,202	98,502	104,131	98,103	85.7	28.0
Michigan	889,006	107,297	296,454	324,928	160,327	87.9	18.0
Minnesota	207,288	37,079	58,214	66,928	45,067	82.1	21.7
Mississippi..................	702,026	134,501	231,659	223,889	111,977	80.8	16.0
Missouri......................	450,283	55,057	162,033	145,379	87,814	87.8	19.5
Montana......................	2,977	462	525	729	1,261	84.5	42.4
Nebraska.....................	54,590	8,006	17,309	17,451	11,824	85.3	21.7
Nevada........................	192,799	18,597	60,059	79,129	35,014	90.4	18.2
New Hampshire.............	13,726	1,929	4,118	2,608	5,071	85.9	36.9
New Jersey	813,816	91,364	274,402	241,873	206,177	88.8	25.3
New Mexico	29,349	3,803	5,690	11,528	8,328	87.0	28.4
New York......................	2,097,135	313,601	675,424	594,039	514,071	85.0	24.5
North Carolina..............	1,486,857	201,584	453,900	498,246	333,127	86.4	22.4
North Dakota................	13,471	915	4,246	5,380	2,930	93.2	21.8
Ohio	939,875	123,826	310,698	341,268	164,083	86.8	17.5
Oklahoma....................	180,859	19,076	60,497	65,552	35,734	89.5	19.8
Oregon........................	51,503	4,929	13,336	17,545	15,693	90.4	30.5
Pennsylvania................	931,454	112,507	359,066	272,083	187,798	87.9	20.2
Rhode Island................	49,190	4,375	17,398	15,919	11,498	91.1	23.4
South Carolina	899,954	144,896	330,356	267,131	157,571	83.9	17.5
South Dakota	11,679	2,670	2,743	4,060	2,206	77.1	18.9
Tennessee	737,044	94,424	244,728	237,845	160,047	87.2	21.7
Texas..........................	2,280,400	201,619	677,732	822,016	588,132	91.2	25.7
Utah	19,937	2,741	4,856	8,863	3,477	86.3	17.4
Vermont.......................	5,756	982	1,646	1,616	1,512	82.9	26.3
Virginia	1,110,132	153,100	329,908	347,254	279,870	86.2	25.2
Washington	195,806	18,489	52,064	76,107	49,146	90.6	25.1
West Virginia................	46,716	3,670	19,819	16,805	6,422	92.1	13.7
Wisconsin	219,379	33,474	78,000	74,497	33,408	84.7	15.2
Wyoming	3,291	39	775	946	1,531	98.8	46.5

[1]May be of any race.
... = Not available

Table B-2. Educational Attainment of the Population 25 Years Old and Over, by Sex, Race, Hispanic Origin, and Region or State, 2019—*Continued*

(Number; percent.)

Region or State	Population	Less than a high school diploma	High school graduate (includes equivalency)	Some college or associate's degree	Bachelor's degree or higher	High school graduate or higher (percent)	Bachelor's degree or higher (percent)
			Asian alone, age 25 years and over				
United States	13,381,406	1,634,327	1,931,625	2,380,606	7,434,848	87.8	55.6
Northeast Region.............	1,540,588	196,028	203,814	230,224	910,522	87.3	59.1
Midwest Region..............	2,646,189	394,903	395,484	340,941	1,514,861	85.1	57.2
South Region..................	3,112,253	360,094	443,740	501,878	1,806,541	88.4	58.0
West Region....................	6,082,376	683,302	888,587	1,307,563	3,202,924	88.8	52.7
Alabama.........................	47,226	5,856	6,987	8,005	26,378	87.6	55.9
Alaska	30,918	2,063	10,169	9,851	8,835	93.3	28.6
Arizona..........................	172,708	19,271	21,063	29,535	102,839	88.8	59.5
Arkansas........................	29,658	2,792	6,308	4,045	16,513	90.6	55.7
California.......................	4,363,485	499,622	588,567	904,888	2,370,408	88.5	54.3
Colorado	134,942	13,429	22,524	26,952	72,037	90.0	53.4
Connecticut....................	114,306	10,713	15,012	13,985	74,596	90.6	65.3
Delaware	25,875	1,443	3,037	4,337	17,058	94.4	65.9
District of Columbia........	22,230	1,031	1,940	1,414	17,845	95.4	80.3
Florida...........................	441,665	56,578	80,337	81,402	223,348	87.2	50.6
Georgia	302,385	40,051	45,576	43,402	173,356	86.8	57.3
Hawaii	434,234	45,903	106,929	129,323	152,079	89.4	35.0
Idaho.............................	18,301	2,476	3,440	3,600	8,785	86.5	48.0
Illinois...........................	513,285	48,798	56,928	73,922	333,637	90.5	65.0
Indiana..........................	101,424	15,659	13,889	11,969	59,907	84.6	59.1
Iowa..............................	48,872	9,893	6,790	7,255	24,934	79.8	51.0
Kansas...........................	56,876	8,319	10,704	9,506	28,347	85.4	49.8
Kentucky	47,711	6,633	6,791	6,969	27,318	86.1	57.3
Louisiana	54,463	9,041	11,847	8,623	24,952	83.4	45.8
Maine............................	10,990	2,005	2,257	1,699	5,029	81.8	45.8
Maryland........................	277,535	29,587	33,792	38,559	175,597	89.3	63.3
Massachusetts................	326,204	44,719	41,762	33,450	206,273	86.3	63.2
Michigan........................	218,309	22,170	25,327	29,441	141,371	89.8	64.8
Minnesota......................	180,643	33,366	28,560	35,435	83,282	81.5	46.1
Mississippi.....................	20,681	3,283	3,806	5,034	8,558	84.1	41.4
Missouri.........................	87,803	9,380	10,779	13,796	53,848	89.3	61.3
Montana.........................	6,867	471	1,092	2,011	3,293	93.1	48.0
Nebraska........................	30,283	6,814	4,145	5,047	14,277	77.5	47.1
Nevada..........................	198,870	18,475	37,640	57,344	85,411	90.7	42.9
New Hampshire...............	25,955	2,180	4,148	2,908	16,719	91.6	64.4
New Jersey	613,693	43,574	62,969	67,794	439,356	92.9	71.6
New Mexico	27,650	3,007	4,977	5,948	13,718	89.1	49.6
New York........................	1,213,907	240,608	221,328	172,013	579,958	80.2	47.8
North Carolina................	213,997	27,313	26,504	34,954	125,226	87.2	58.5
North Dakota..................	7,164	1,368	871	2,019	2,906	80.9	40.6
Ohio	185,785	24,537	24,447	20,655	116,146	86.8	62.5
Oklahoma.......................	58,425	10,829	11,184	11,197	25,215	81.5	43.2
Oregon...........................	136,123	16,383	17,305	28,945	73,490	88.0	54.0
Pennsylvania...................	309,518	46,918	42,608	43,509	176,483	84.8	57.0
Rhode Island...................	25,461	3,146	4,597	4,307	13,411	87.6	52.7
South Carolina	58,659	7,112	9,852	11,559	30,136	87.9	51.4
South Dakota	7,098	1,341	1,421	1,307	3,029	81.1	42.7
Tennessee	87,030	12,267	13,988	15,337	45,438	85.9	52.2
Texas.............................	1,008,252	106,876	132,693	157,980	610,703	89.4	60.6
Utah	52,276	5,075	8,388	10,077	28,736	90.3	55.0
Vermont.........................	6,155	1,040	803	1,276	3,036	83.1	49.3
Virginia..........................	405,441	38,101	48,109	67,628	251,603	90.6	62.1
Washington....................	502,312	57,058	65,319	98,361	281,574	88.6	56.1
West Virginia..................	11,020	1,301	989	1,433	7,297	88.2	66.2
Wisconsin	103,046	14,383	19,953	19,872	48,838	86.0	47.4
Wyoming	3,690	69	1,174	728	1,719	98.1	46.6

[1]May be of any race.

... = Not available

Table B-2. Educational Attainment of the Population 25 Years Old and Over, by Sex, Race, Hispanic Origin, and Region or State, 2019—*Continued*

(Number; percent.)

Region or State	Hispanic or Latino[1], age 25 years and over						
	Population	Less than a high school diploma	High school graduate (includes equivalency)	Some college or associate's degree	Bachelor's degree or higher	High school graduate or higher (percent)	Bachelor's degree or higher (percent)
United States	34,949,077	10,325,431	9,853,963	8,605,585	6,164,098	70.5	17.6
Northeast Region	2,942,446	824,597	876,321	723,116	518,412	72.0	17.6
Midwest Region	5,018,519	1,330,243	1,530,638	1,140,200	1,017,438	73.5	20.3
South Region	13,370,478	3,873,183	3,721,131	3,156,543	2,619,621	71.0	19.6
West Region...............	13,617,634	4,297,408	3,725,873	3,585,726	2,008,627	68.4	14.8
Alabama	104,045	40,287	24,236	22,443	17,079	61.3	16.4
Alaska	28,365	3,964	6,647	12,113	5,641	86.0	19.9
Arizona.......................	1,292,262	373,731	363,031	376,059	179,441	71.1	13.9
Arkansas	117,900	48,702	39,034	18,558	11,606	58.7	9.8
California....................	9,150,608	3,074,068	2,419,795	2,340,965	1,315,780	66.4	14.4
Colorado	712,267	176,630	218,631	185,275	131,731	75.2	18.5
Connecticut.................	347,589	90,070	117,998	76,961	61,954	73.9	17.8
Delaware	49,372	18,634	13,470	10,396	6,872	62.3	13.9
District of Columbia	50,141	9,642	6,734	7,701	26,064	80.8	52.0
Florida........................	3,773,205	770,993	1,064,287	968,352	969,573	79.6	25.7
Georgia	546,665	194,898	138,200	108,632	104,935	64.3	19.2
Hawaii	77,881	6,875	25,901	27,175	17,930	91.2	23.0
Idaho..........................	115,826	36,180	33,709	31,262	14,675	68.8	12.7
Illinois	1,256,316	360,905	385,576	298,932	210,903	71.3	16.8
Indiana........................	247,337	74,430	79,467	54,829	38,611	69.9	15.6
Iowa...........................	94,822	30,787	27,233	23,705	13,097	67.5	13.8
Kansas	177,719	56,166	51,450	45,017	25,086	68.4	14.1
Kentucky	84,517	25,124	24,454	18,249	16,690	70.3	19.7
Louisiana	145,024	38,258	47,126	34,386	25,254	73.6	17.4
Maine	13,580	1,367	3,380	3,694	5,139	89.9	37.8
Maryland.....................	358,740	117,737	96,019	66,228	78,756	67.2	22.0
Massachusetts	486,528	130,369	144,111	110,814	101,234	73.2	20.8
Michigan	273,449	66,817	78,141	69,482	59,009	75.6	21.6
Minnesota	158,254	39,548	41,971	40,678	36,057	75.0	22.8
Mississippi..................	46,120	14,857	14,605	11,205	5,453	67.8	11.8
Missouri......................	138,178	30,709	36,010	39,864	31,595	77.8	22.9
Montana......................	22,102	3,388	5,602	7,189	5,923	84.7	26.8
Nebraska.....................	106,780	39,253	30,335	22,848	14,344	63.2	13.4
Nevada	512,330	168,839	164,850	124,168	54,473	67.0	10.6
New Hampshire...........	29,638	6,320	8,226	7,696	7,396	78.7	25.0
New Jersey	1,134,354	279,191	365,774	250,526	238,863	75.4	21.1
New Mexico	630,721	138,751	197,711	190,338	103,921	78.0	16.5
New York	2,359,532	645,991	677,529	538,927	497,085	72.6	21.1
North Carolina.............	513,662	190,987	128,902	106,515	87,258	62.8	17.0
North Dakota...............	15,357	2,444	5,659	4,593	2,661	84.1	17.3
Ohio	247,310	59,143	73,630	64,487	50,050	76.1	20.2
Oklahoma....................	215,930	79,509	83,753	46,687	25,981	63.2	12.0
Oregon........................	301,623	93,795	77,826	81,871	48,131	68.9	16.0
Pennsylvania...............	544,225	147,380	180,810	126,097	89,938	72.9	16.5
Rhode Island...............	97,435	28,307	31,756	23,387	13,985	70.9	14.4
South Carolina	157,206	53,773	39,975	35,132	28,326	65.8	18.0
South Dakota	16,720	3,211	4,524	4,714	4,271	80.8	25.5
Tennessee	188,951	69,768	49,533	34,661	34,989	63.1	18.5
Texas..........................	6,538,918	2,073,793	1,856,044	1,553,994	1,055,087	68.3	16.1
Utah	233,666	58,972	69,971	68,166	36,557	74.8	15.6
Vermont......................	5,638	642	1,054	2,098	1,844	88.6	32.7
Virginia.......................	465,976	124,310	110,526	108,622	122,518	73.3	26.3
Washington.................	509,771	156,560	130,605	131,600	91,006	69.3	17.9
West Virginia...............	14,106	1,911	4,233	4,782	3,180	86.5	22.5
Wisconsin	210,204	61,184	62,325	53,967	32,728	70.9	15.6
Wyoming	30,212	5,655	11,594	9,545	3,418	81.3	11.3

[1]May be of any race.
... = Not available

Table B-3. Number of Virtual Schools and Virtual School Enrollment, by State, 2019–20

(Number; percent.)

| State | Number of Virtual Schools | | Enrollment | | | | |
| | Fully Virtual | Not Fully Virtual | Total State Enrollment | Virtual School Enrollment | | Virtual School Enrollment as a Percent of Total Enrollment | |
				Fully Virtual	Not Fully Virtual	Fully Virtual	Not Fully Virtual
UNITED STATES	691	8,673	50,453,111	293,717	4,751,775	0.6	9.4
Alabama.............................	7	-	744,235	7,633	-	1.0	-
Alaska................................	1	202	132,017	6	49,946	-	37.8
Arizona..............................	70	-	1,147,415	18,212	-	1.6	-
Arkansas...........................	7	497	496,927	4,298	252,991	0.9	50.9
California...........................	47	1,264	6,147,545	28,496	987,680	0.5	16.1
Colorado	24	24	912,959	11,203	10,527	1.2	1.2
Connecticut.......................	-	-	510,658	-	-	-	-
Delaware	-	-	139,930	-	-	-	-
District of Columbia	1	-	89,524	196	-	0.2	-
Florida...............................	222	-	2,858,325	16,403	-	0.6	-
Georgia	7	-	1,769,657	15,158	-	0.9	-
Hawaii...............................	-	1	181,088	-	585	-	0.3
Idaho.................................	14	4	310,800	7,010	1,298	2.3	0.4
Illinois	2	-	1,942,839	522	-	-	-
Indiana..............................	10	-	1,051,086	10,922	-	1.0	-
Iowa..................................	5	416	509,007	1,220	163,929	0.2	32.2
Kansas	18	-	492,160	8,381	-	1.7	-
Kentucky	12	444	691,868	846	261,536	0.1	37.8
Louisiana	7	-	710,439	6,035	-	0.8	-
Maine................................	2	-	175,126	806	-	0.5	-
Maryland............................	-	2	909,404	-	1,162	-	0.1
Massachusetts....................	2	-	948,445	2,846	-	0.3	-
Michigan	68	166	1,448,303	17,293	87,413	1.2	6.0
Minnesota..........................	25	10	891,477	7,029	515	0.8	0.1
Mississippi.........................	-	13	466,002	-	8,155	-	1.7
Missouri.............................	2	-	904,926	-	-	-	-
Montana.............................	-	206	148,598	-	31,912	-	21.5
Nebraska............................	4	-	330,018	153	-	-	-
Nevada	2	-	500,855	1,502	-	0.3	-
New Hampshire...................	2	-	176,054	349	-	0.2	-
New Jersey	-	-	1,375,288	-	-	-	-
New Mexico	3	3	330,381	2,467	442	0.7	0.1
New York............................	-	-	2,658,992	-	-	-	-
North Carolina.....................	5	333	1,560,350	5,184	209,736	0.3	13.4
North Dakota.......................	-	154	116,042	-	35,553	-	30.6
Ohio..................................	14	-	1,688,434	25,962	-	1.5	-
Oklahoma...........................	-	14	702,729	-	21,532	-	3.1
Oregon	11	427	574,674	7,250	220,700	1.3	38.4
Pennsylvania.......................	15	-	1,711,137	35,808	-	2.1	-
Rhode Island.......................	-	1	141,792	-	225	-	0.2
South Carolina	5	1,260	786,817	11,085	775,732	1.4	98.6
South Dakota	6	159	139,483	177	30,585	0.1	21.9
Tennessee	16	167	1,014,744	3,916	131,835	0.4	13.0
Texas.................................	9	-	5,495,398	20,099	-	0.4	-
Utah..................................	1	17	684,475	667	12,973	0.1	1.9
Vermont.............................	-	89	83,314	-	31,756	-	38.1
Virginia..............................	-	371	1,296,941	-	402,086	-	31.0
Washington.........................	11	410	1,142,073	6,579	235,460	0.6	20.6
West Virginia.......................	-	-	263,486	-	-	-	-
Wisconsin...........................	34	2,019	854,258	8,004	785,511	0.9	92.0
Wyoming	-	-	94,616	-	-	-	-

- = Zero or rounds to zero.

Table B-4. Number of Operating Public Elementary and Secondary Schools, by School Type, Charter, Magnet, Title I, Title I Schoolwide Status, and State, 2019–20

(Number.)

State	Number of Operating Schools	School Type				Charter	Magnet	Title[2]	Title I schoolwide[2]
		Regular	Special Education	Career and Technical	Alternative Education				
UNITED STATES[1]	98,507	89,842	1,933	1,495	5,237	7,550	3,497	70,386	57,740
Alabama..	1,533	1,322	81	68	62	4	34	938	919
Alaska	506	478	4	3	21	29	32	384	362
Arizona...	2,326	1,865	29	271	161	558	*	1,765	1,319
Arkansas......................................	1,076	1,048	2	23	3	83	32	967	913
California......................................	10,378	9,099	157	69	1,053	1,321	533	7,598	6,303
Colorado	1,920	1,795	5	7	113	261	27	739	619
Connecticut..................................	1,004	982	2	17	3	22	103	608	329
Delaware	222	192	19	6	5	22	3	148	148
District of Columbia	230	222	2	0	6	114	NA	184	182
Florida..	4,192	3,611	158	36	387	675	590	3,074	2,902
Georgia	2,304	2,261	12	0	31	89	14	1,626	1,578
Hawaii	293	291	1	0	1	37	NA	181	181
Idaho..	751	654	10	13	74	68	22	544	540
Illinois..	4,351	3,993	217	0	141	141	146	3,161	2,277
Indiana...	1,912	1,854	21	30	7	101	25	1,501	1,167
Iowa...	1,310	1,291	2	0	17	2	NA	1,084	643
Kansas	1,311	1,306	4	0	1	9	37	1,125	846
Kentucky	1,535	1,211	10	126	188	0	59	1,112	1,085
Louisiana	1,363	1,318	29	10	6	140	41	1,209	1,185
Maine	594	566	1	27	0	12	2	500	362
Maryland.......................................	1,420	1,312	36	26	46	46	102	713	666
Massachusetts	1,847	1,776	11	36	24	81	0	1,136	765
Michigan.......................................	3,552	2,958	188	46	360	371	351	2,294	1,627
Minnesota.....................................	2,545	1,736	331	7	471	245	82	2,206	1,221
Mississippi....................................	1,047	885	2	92	68	6	14	838	838
Missouri..	2,431	2,261	48	62	60	71	30	1,847	1,566
Montana..	826	822	2	0	2	NA	NA	754	459
Nebraska.......................................	1,082	1,004	27	0	51	NA	NA	449	352
Nevada..	726	663	13	0	50	78	48	468	444
New Hampshire..............................	496	496	0	0	0	40	1	416	95
New Jersey	2,565	2,364	61	70	70	88	NA	1,668	693
New Mexico	884	830	9	0	45	97	34	767	757
New York.......................................	4,819	4,596	135	49	39	316	111	3,632	3,100
North Carolina...............................	2,664	2,555	25	8	76	196	221	2,151	1,991
North Dakota.................................	485	485	0	0	0	NA	NA	255	151
Ohio	3,536	3,450	13	73	0	313	*	2,703	2,044
Oklahoma......................................	1,794	1,785	4	0	5	64	NA	1,266	1,187
Oregon..	1,255	1,219	1	0	35	133	NA	560	519
Pennsylvania.................................	2,958	2,864	4	84	6	179	54	2,396	1,806
Rhode Island.................................	316	302	1	10	3	37	NA	239	155
South Carolina	1,265	1,198	8	44	15	80	127	619	618
South Dakota	700	656	13	1	30	NA	NA	574	333
Tennessee	1,878	1,830	16	11	21	118	123	1,511	1,465
Texas..	8,991	8,109	12	0	870	906	267	7,384	7,046
Utah	1,071	976	60	7	28	132	22	336	239
Vermont	308	292	0	15	1	NA	2	241	204
Virginia...	2,122	1,871	40	89	122	8	144	769	682
Washington....................................	2,473	2,045	89	20	319	10	54	1,635	1,424
West Virginia.................................	725	655	2	34	34	NA	0	340	337
Wisconsin......................................	2,255	2,140	13	5	97	236	10	1,556	954
Wyoming	360	348	3	0	9	5	NA	215	142

[1]Reporting states. A reporting state's total is shown if data for any item in the table were not available for some, but not more than 15 percent, of all schools in the United States.

[2]Schools eligible for Title I schoolwide programs are also included in the count of all Title I eligible schools. A Title I eligible school is one in which the percentage of children from low-income families is at least 35 percent of children from low-income families served by the LEA as a whole. A schoolwide Title I eligible school has a percentage of low-income students that is at least 40 percent. For the complete definitions, refer to the glossary available in the CCD Reference Library, document #7 (https://nces.ed.gov/ccd/reference_library.asp).

* = Not available.

NA = Not applicable. Some states/jurisdictions do not have charter school authorization and some states/jurisdictions do not designate magnet schools.

Table B-5. Population 3 Years and Over Enrolled in Public or Private School, by Selected Grade Levels and Region or State, 2019

(Number; percent.)

Region or State	Total enrolled population	Nursery school			Kindergarten		
		Total enrolled	Percent in public school	Percent in private school	Total enrolled	Percent in public school	Percent in private school
UNITED STATES	80,465,620	5,044,389	59.7	40.3	4,011,764	87.6	12.4
Northeast Region..................................	13,228,363	860,223	56.7	43.3	635,168	86.1	13.9
Midwest Region....................................	16,589,013	1,080,657	63.3	36.7	841,504	86.4	13.6
South Region..	30,869,765	1,924,186	60.1	39.9	1,549,252	88.0	12.0
West Region..	19,778,479	1,179,323	58.0	42.0	985,840	89.1	10.9
Alabama..	1,164,195	65,500	64.4	35.6	60,362	86.7	13.3
Alaska...	180,074	11,471	63.1	36.9	11,916	92.6	7.4
Arizona..	1,773,809	91,621	65.4	34.6	85,086	89.3	10.7
Arkansas...	738,272	50,302	72.6	27.4	38,926	90.2	9.8
California...	10,305,759	604,513	58.5	41.5	501,476	89.9	10.1
Colorado	1,406,414	94,038	61.0	39.0	69,622	93.0	7.0
Connecticut...	882,104	52,328	57.3	42.7	42,818	94.8	5.2
Delaware...	227,551	14,393	55.9	44.1	10,699	86.6	13.4
District of Columbia	169,418	17,354	75.5	24.5	9,221	90.8	9.2
Florida...	4,795,224	314,700	54.4	45.6	221,192	84.8	15.2
Georgia	2,771,807	181,271	62.8	37.2	142,208	90.2	9.8
Hawaii...	317,419	24,827	35.4	64.6	16,663	80.9	19.1
Idaho...	457,955	23,531	48.5	51.5	25,700	86.6	13.4
Illinois...	3,123,418	220,385	60.0	40.0	143,711	84.5	15.5
Indiana..	1,646,376	97,833	61.7	38.3	79,674	86.8	13.2
Iowa..	783,468	54,923	72.6	27.4	43,862	89.6	10.4
Kansas..	753,423	51,104	67.4	32.6	39,216	86.8	13.2
Kentucky...	1,025,269	63,759	65.4	34.6	51,113	87.9	12.1
Louisiana	1,149,360	80,394	64.6	35.4	62,180	81.9	18.1
Maine	275,036	16,400	61.0	39.0	12,779	86.7	13.3
Maryland..	1,509,619	100,085	50.9	49.1	67,143	84.1	15.9
Massachusetts.......................................	1,691,491	104,969	50.6	49.4	75,037	89.6	10.4
Michigan..	2,387,441	144,796	66.2	33.8	118,974	87.4	12.6
Minnesota..	1,386,106	98,330	67.3	32.7	70,167	89.9	10.1
Mississippi...	754,558	52,404	63.6	36.4	38,624	86.4	13.6
Missouri...	1,444,801	96,538	58.6	41.4	74,263	85.8	14.2
Montana...	242,758	12,710	54.4	45.6	12,297	89.1	10.9
Nebraska...	507,156	33,488	61.8	38.2	26,660	81.0	19.0
Nevada..	707,075	37,463	67.2	32.8	34,608	92.3	7.7
New Hampshire......................................	298,926	20,615	49.7	50.3	13,508	90.6	9.4
New Jersey	2,192,217	166,380	58.0	42.0	117,651	87.2	12.8
New Mexico..	516,495	27,671	68.6	31.4	24,362	88.4	11.6
New York..	4,594,259	293,750	61.2	38.8	220,364	82.7	17.3
North Carolina..	2,556,961	152,450	51.8	48.2	120,219	88.8	11.2
North Dakota..	187,040	9,991	73.2	26.8	8,251	94.8	5.2
Ohio..	2,771,284	184,171	59.9	40.1	141,535	84.6	15.4
Oklahoma..	999,896	64,349	76.1	23.9	55,802	90.0	10.0
Oregon..	947,627	58,703	50.0	50.0	48,408	84.1	15.9
Pennsylvania...	2,896,469	182,378	51.3	48.7	135,543	84.5	15.5
Rhode Island...	253,795	14,013	57.7	42.3	11,170	92.7	7.3
South Carolina	1,180,396	59,581	59.6	40.4	62,015	86.0	14.0
South Dakota	214,461	15,523	64.6	35.4	13,452	92.6	7.4
Tennessee	1,572,331	88,895	58.0	42.0	82,161	86.6	13.4
Texas	7,763,174	466,305	64.3	35.7	414,867	90.7	9.3
Utah	1,012,792	62,386	58.4	41.6	53,254	89.0	11.0
Vermont...	144,066	9,390	71.3	28.7	6,298	92.1	7.9
Virginia..	2,118,036	132,600	47.8	52.2	93,308	85.7	14.3
Washington..	1,764,122	122,229	51.4	48.6	95,733	85.1	14.9
West Virginia..	373,698	19,844	78.8	21.2	19,212	96.7	3.3
Wisconsin..	1,384,039	73,575	68.4	31.6	81,739	86.6	13.4
Wyoming	146,180	8,160	71.8	28.2	6,715	91.2	8.8

Table B-5. Population 3 Years and Over Enrolled in Public or Private School, by Selected Grade Levels and Region or State, 2019—*Continued*

(Number; percent.)

Region or State	Elementary: grades 1-4			Elementary: grades 5-8			High school: grades 9-12		
	Total enrolled	Percent in public school	Percent in private school	Total enrolled	Percent in public school	Percent in private school	Total enrolled	Percent in public school	Percent in private school
UNITED STATES	15,728,625	89.4	10.6	16,918,899	89.2	10.8	16,932,635	89.8	10.2
Northeast Region	2,441,779	88.0	12.0	2,653,119	88.0	12.0	2,746,045	86.8	13.2
Midwest Region	3,293,995	87.8	12.2	3,522,079	88.2	11.8	3,535,649	90.0	10.0
South Region	6,191,696	89.7	10.3	6,672,733	89.0	11.0	6,512,212	89.8	10.2
West Region	3,801,155	91.2	8.8	4,070,968	91.4	8.6	4,138,729	91.8	8.2
Alabama	236,267	89.9	10.1	252,866	87.6	12.4	248,164	86.9	13.1
Alaska	40,280	91.0	9.0	37,128	92.8	7.2	37,219	91.1	8.9
Arizona	354,299	90.9	9.1	390,888	91.9	8.1	386,787	92.8	7.2
Arkansas	157,360	90.5	9.5	155,462	92.7	7.3	159,614	92.9	7.1
California	1,895,898	91.9	8.1	2,026,836	91.5	8.5	2,133,603	91.6	8.4
Colorado	272,713	92.0	8.0	294,975	91.3	8.7	290,150	91.4	8.6
Connecticut	159,068	91.5	8.5	167,795	90.7	9.3	194,410	88.8	11.2
Delaware	44,633	87.6	12.4	45,858	86.6	13.4	49,508	89.9	10.1
District of Columbia	28,171	89.1	10.9	24,894	84.1	15.9	19,289	83.5	16.5
Florida	912,157	86.1	13.9	1,006,115	85.8	14.2	993,773	88.1	11.9
Georgia	551,927	91.9	8.1	592,959	89.1	10.9	584,349	90.1	9.9
Hawaii	62,403	82.6	17.4	63,415	81.2	18.8	64,938	76.7	23.3
Idaho	93,130	86.6	13.4	103,563	91.1	8.9	103,810	90.8	9.2
Illinois	603,415	89.1	10.9	657,517	88.4	11.6	665,932	90.7	9.3
Indiana	331,380	87.4	12.6	370,786	87.6	12.4	357,591	90.2	9.8
Iowa	159,087	89.5	10.5	161,203	91.2	8.8	158,248	92.1	7.9
Kansas	154,320	88.8	11.2	161,322	90.1	9.9	157,106	90.1	9.9
Kentucky	202,152	89.4	10.6	234,784	87.4	12.6	219,823	87.0	13.0
Louisiana	241,830	83.0	17.0	250,964	83.2	16.8	242,881	83.8	16.2
Maine	52,633	89.2	10.8	56,952	90.7	9.3	60,658	86.3	13.7
Maryland	288,002	87.5	12.5	312,651	85.4	14.6	305,148	85.1	14.9
Massachusetts	286,604	92.5	7.5	312,906	91.0	9.0	336,422	88.4	11.6
Michigan	454,261	89.0	11.0	487,248	89.5	10.5	522,075	90.8	9.2
Minnesota	286,475	89.0	11.0	294,778	90.5	9.5	297,824	92.8	7.2
Mississippi	158,750	90.2	9.8	164,833	86.9	13.1	155,686	86.8	13.2
Missouri	299,032	86.6	13.4	313,618	86.6	13.4	307,608	88.4	11.6
Montana	50,610	86.9	13.1	50,974	89.0	11.0	52,301	89.4	10.6
Nebraska	102,276	84.2	15.8	106,058	86.9	13.1	103,156	87.7	12.3
Nevada	148,317	91.6	8.4	161,318	93.1	6.9	158,269	94.1	5.9
New Hampshire	52,642	91.5	8.5	62,669	90.5	9.5	63,598	89.1	10.9
New Jersey	417,139	89.8	10.2	452,205	90.2	9.8	455,654	87.7	12.3
New Mexico	105,805	93.0	7.0	118,347	91.9	8.1	106,957	93.3	6.7
New York	846,114	85.7	14.3	916,532	85.7	14.3	944,207	85.2	14.8
North Carolina	494,853	89.3	10.7	543,387	87.9	12.1	540,099	90.9	9.1
North Dakota	37,767	90.0	10.0	39,491	91.9	8.1	35,207	91.1	8.9
Ohio	550,585	86.4	13.6	585,566	86.6	13.4	589,542	87.4	12.6
Oklahoma	214,627	90.3	9.7	223,196	90.9	9.1	209,546	89.7	10.3
Oregon	186,728	88.9	11.1	199,267	90.9	9.1	194,947	90.7	9.3
Pennsylvania	562,342	86.2	13.8	609,802	86.8	13.2	614,072	86.5	13.5
Rhode Island	40,148	89.6	10.4	49,617	89.9	10.1	48,449	89.9	10.1
South Carolina	248,733	90.0	10.0	264,830	88.9	11.1	253,806	91.1	8.9
South Dakota	45,213	90.0	10.0	49,641	88.2	11.8	43,382	88.6	11.4
Tennessee	321,487	86.0	14.0	356,534	86.7	13.3	342,101	86.1	13.9
Texas	1,605,125	92.9	7.1	1,735,884	93.0	7.0	1,668,907	93.4	6.6
Utah	206,069	92.4	7.6	215,431	94.0	6.0	210,717	94.0	6.0
Vermont	25,089	93.1	6.9	24,641	94.9	5.1	28,575	89.2	10.8
Virginia	409,466	89.9	10.1	425,920	89.3	10.7	435,600	89.6	10.4
Washington	351,490	89.7	10.3	377,519	89.7	10.3	370,024	92.9	7.1
West Virginia	76,156	92.7	7.3	81,596	90.9	9.1	83,918	91.8	8.2
Wisconsin	270,184	85.4	14.6	294,851	85.7	14.3	297,978	90.4	9.6
Wyoming	33,413	92.9	7.1	31,307	92.8	7.2	29,007	92.4	7.6

Table B-5. Population 3 Years and Over Enrolled in Public or Private School, by Selected Grade Levels and Region or State, 2019—*Continued*

(Number; percent.)

Region or State	College, undergraduate			Graduate, professional school		
	Total enrolled	Percent in public school	Percent in private school	Total enrolled	Percent in public school	Percent in private school
UNITED STATES	17,507,427	78.9	21.1	4,321,881	60.0	40.0
Northeast Region	3,031,096	63.1	36.9	860,933	42.1	57.9
Midwest Region	3,448,619	78.8	21.2	866,510	64.7	35.3
South Region	6,436,449	82.3	17.7	1,583,237	65.7	34.3
West Region..	4,591,263	84.7	15.3	1,011,201	62.4	37.6
Alabama...	245,959	87.5	12.5	55,077	78.1	21.9
Alaska...	32,585	83.1	16.9	9,475	75.7	24.3
Arizona..	379,433	86.6	13.4	85,695	66.5	33.5
Arkansas...	144,756	82.6	17.4	31,852	81.2	18.8
California...	2,602,279	85.6	14.4	541,154	56.9	43.1
Colorado..	300,591	86.9	13.1	84,325	68.0	32.0
Connecticut..	208,462	68.5	31.5	57,223	50.7	49.3
Delaware..	49,071	84.2	15.8	13,389	64.6	35.4
District of Columbia	46,376	25.2	74.8	24,113	30.4	69.6
Florida...	1,092,451	80.2	19.8	254,836	60.6	39.4
Georgia..	570,395	82.7	17.3	148,698	65.8	34.2
Hawaii..	68,224	80.0	20.0	16,949	63.0	37.0
Idaho...	90,843	73.7	26.3	17,378	70.8	29.2
Illinois...	640,069	72.6	27.4	192,389	51.0	49.0
Indiana..	336,963	78.6	21.4	72,149	70.7	29.3
Iowa..	167,931	77.0	23.0	38,214	60.9	39.1
Kansas...	154,872	85.0	15.0	35,483	78.6	21.4
Kentucky..	204,507	82.3	17.7	49,131	70.1	29.9
Louisiana	222,438	84.2	15.8	48,673	66.6	33.4
Maine...	62,332	69.8	30.2	13,282	61.2	38.8
Maryland..	321,720	81.6	18.4	114,870	57.1	42.9
Massachusetts..	430,747	52.5	47.5	144,806	30.4	69.6
Michigan..	535,091	85.7	14.3	124,996	77.9	22.1
Minnesota	266,465	78.0	22.0	72,067	63.6	36.4
Mississippi...	154,486	89.1	10.9	29,775	71.1	28.9
Missouri...	273,925	74.0	26.0	79,817	59.4	40.6
Montana...	50,132	90.8	9.2	13,734	77.1	22.9
Nebraska..	104,516	80.8	19.2	31,002	68.5	31.5
Nevada...	134,114	81.6	18.4	32,986	66.2	33.8
New Hampshire..	69,266	65.5	34.5	16,628	46.7	53.3
New Jersey	451,251	73.2	26.8	131,937	48.9	51.1
New Mexico	105,715	88.9	11.1	27,638	83.7	16.3
New York..	1,071,424	62.6	37.4	301,868	40.1	59.9
North Carolina..	578,192	80.9	19.1	127,761	63.5	36.5
North Dakota..	46,309	91.5	8.5	10,024	75.9	24.1
Ohio..	581,547	76.9	23.1	138,538	68.0	32.0
Oklahoma...	192,580	86.9	13.1	39,796	75.2	24.8
Oregon...	209,253	82.8	17.2	50,321	65.2	34.8
Pennsylvania..	621,464	61.5	38.5	170,868	44.6	55.4
Rhode Island..	74,656	57.8	42.2	15,742	44.5	55.5
South Carolina..	236,545	80.0	20.0	54,886	67.8	32.2
South Dakota..	39,996	86.5	13.5	7,254	70.9	29.1
Tennessee..	303,160	76.9	23.1	77,993	61.3	38.7
Texas...	1,522,926	85.7	14.3	349,160	71.9	28.1
Utah..	223,677	73.6	26.4	41,258	70.5	29.5
Vermont...	41,494	70.3	29.7	8,579	59.0	41.0
Virginia..	476,758	79.6	20.4	144,384	59.6	40.4
Washington...	364,428	84.9	15.1	82,699	66.4	33.6
West Virginia..	74,129	87.0	13.0	18,843	81.7	18.3
Wisconsin...	300,935	82.4	17.6	64,777	65.2	34.8
Wyoming	29,989	92.3	7.7	7,589	79.0	21.0

Table B-6. Number of Operating Public Schools and Districts, Student Membership, Teachers, and Pupil/Teacher Ratio, by State, 2019–20

(Number; percent.)

Region or state	Number of operating schools	Number of operating school districts	Student membership	Number of teachers	Pupil/Teacher ratio
UNITED STATES	98,507	19,247	50,710,441	3,198,170	15.9
Alabama..	1,533	179	744,235	42,022	17.7
Alaska..	506	54	132017	7,484	17.6
Arizona...	2,326	696	1,152,586	48,912	23.6
Arkansas.......................................	1,076	293	496,927	38,629	12.9
California.......................................	10,378	2,140	6,163,001	271,805	22.7
Colorado.......................................	1920	271	913,223	53,901	16.9
Connecticut....................................	1004	206	523,690	42,386	12.4
Delaware.......................................	222	44	139930	9,747	14.4
District of Columbia	230	64	89878	7,409	12.1
Florida..	4,192	76	2,858,461	166,002	17.2
Georgia	2304	234	1,769,657	117,837	15.0
Hawaii..	293	1	181,088	12,221	14.8
Idaho...	751	171	311096	17,207	18.1
Illinois..	4351	1056	1943117	132,815	14.6
Indiana...	1912	429	1,051,411	61,712	17.0
Iowa..	1310	336	517,324	35,737	14.5
Kansas...	1311	332	497,963	36,603	13.6
Kentucky.......................................	1535	185	691,996	42,223	16.4
Louisiana	1363	193	710,439	38,589	18.4
Maine	594	275	180,291	14,826	12.2
Maryland.......................................	1420	25	909404	61,485	14.8
Massachusetts	1847	429	959394	75,152	12.8
Michigan.......................................	3552	891	1,495,925	84,838	17.6
Minnesota......................................	2545	569	893,203	55,630	16.1
Mississippi.....................................	1047	154	466,002	31,578	14.8
Missouri..	2431	565	910,466	69,145	13.2
Montana..	826	485	149917	10,675	14.0
Nebraska.......................................	1082	279	330,018	24,028	13.7
Nevada...	726	21	496934	25,509	19.5
New Hampshire................................	496	309	177,351	14,695	12.1
New Jersey	2565	702	1411917	117,060	12.1
New Mexico	884	145	331206	21,850	15.2
New York.......................................	4819	1046	2692589	217,398	12.4
North Carolina.................................	2664	342	1,560,350	100,777	15.5
North Dakota...................................	485	224	116185	9,284	12.5
Ohio	3536	1,037	1,689,867	105,998	15.9
Oklahoma......................................	1794	596	703,719	43,315	16.2
Oregon...	1255	222	610648	30,238	20.2
Pennsylvania...................................	2958	788	1,732,449	124,294	13.9
Rhode Island...................................	316	64	143,557	10,704	13.4
South Carolina	1265	101	786,879	53,556	14.7
South Dakota	700	166	139,949	9,930	14.1
Tennessee......................................	1,878	147	1014744	64,784	15.7
Texas...	8991	1227	5495398	364,478	15.1
Utah..	1071	159	684,694	30,256	22.6
Vermont..	308	187	86759	8,042	10.8
Virginia...	2122	215	1,297,012	87,147	14.9
Washington.....................................	2473	334	1,142,073	62,212	18.4
West Virginia...................................	725	60	263486	18,854	14.0
Wisconsin	2255	462	855400	59,801	14.3
Wyoming	360	61	94,616	7,391	12.8

Table B-7. Participation in Public School Services, by State

(Number; percent.)

State	Enrollment in public elementary and secondary schools (2018-19)	Percent of students eligible for free or reduced-price lunch (2018-19)	Percent of students served under IDEA, Part B (2019-20)	Percent English language learner students (Fall 2018)
UNITED STATES	50,138,019	52.3	14.4	10.2
Alabama........................	738,485	55.2	13.1	3.8
Alaska..........................	130,905	48.0	14.6	11.5
Arizona.........................	994,358	53.7	13.3	7.3
Arkansas.......................	491,696	63.9	15.4	8.1
California.......................	6,171,073	59.4	12.0	19.4
Colorado	911,339	40.8	11.9	11.4
Connecticut....................	514,690	41.7	16.4	7.9
Delaware.......................	138,397	31.4	19.0	9.7
District of Columbia	87,686	76.4	16.6	11.3
Florida..........................	2,846,142	55.1	14.7	10.1
Georgia.........................	1,767,145	60.3	12.8	7.0
Hawaii..........................	181,278	45.9	11.2	9.2
Idaho...........................	308,816	38.5	11.7	6.3
Illinois..........................	1,956,231	48.9	15.1	12.1
Indiana.........................	1,055,086	48.9	17.3	5.9
Iowa............................	506,308	42.5	13.6	6.5
Kansas.........................	491,423	46.8	15.7	9.3
Kentucky.......................	677,718	56.8	16.0	4.2
Louisiana.......................	710,797	53.5	12.6	3.7
Maine...........................	175,230	44.1	19.7	3.4
Maryland.......................	896,811	46.3	12.6	9.7
Massachusetts.................	951,400	39.9	18.7	10.3
Michigan.......................	1,456,140	50.0	13.4	6.6
Minnesota......................	888,786	36.4	16.3	8.5
Mississippi.....................	471,298	74.0	15.1	3.2
Missouri........................	908,255	50.2	14.5	3.9
Montana........................	147,375	39.0	13.0	2.4
Nebraska.......................	326,081	45.2	16.1	7.2
Nevada.........................	492,353	61.3	12.8	15.2
New Hampshire................	177,355	27.0	17.2	2.9
New Jersey	1,365,233	37.6	17.7	6.3
New Mexico	333,526	72.3	16.5	15.8
New York.......................	2,673,904	53.9	19.9	9.1
North Carolina.................	1,552,472	56.0	13.2	7.5
North Dakota...................	111,651	30.3	14.5	3.7
Ohio	1,692,789	45.3	16.4	3.4
Oklahoma.......................	698,683	60.3	16.7	8.3
Oregon..........................	551,871	48.9	14.9	8.6
Pennsylvania...................	1,709,334	50.9	19.8	4.0
Rhode Island...................	141,742	47.4	17.2	8.9
South Carolina.................	780,529	62.0	13.9	6.0
South Dakota...................	138,402	36.9	15.8	4.4
Tennessee......................	1,006,267	58.8	13.2	4.6
Texas...........................	5,430,433	60.6	10.8	18.7
Utah............................	674,355	32.9	12.9	7.6
Vermont........................	83,642	36.4	18.0	2.2
Virginia.........................	1,282,643	44.4	13.9	8.5
Washington.....................	1,118,916	43.0	13.5	11.8
West Virginia...................	267,968	50.4	17.8	0.8
Wisconsin	858,766	39.5	14.2	6.4
Wyoming	94,236	36.4	17.0	2.9

Table B-8. Number of Private Schools, Students, Full-time Equivalent (FTE) Teachers, and 2018–19 High School Graduates, by State, 2019–20

(Number)

State	Number of private schools	Students	FTE Teachers	Number of 2018-19 High School Graduates
UNITED STATES	30,492	4,652,904	481,200	340,609
Alabama..	403	64,810	6,362	5,003
Alaska	43	3,058	387	*
Arizona..	402	59,171	5,631	4,152
Arkansas..	171	24,234	2,662	1,684
California..	3,222	541,646	51,344	38,851
Colorado..	358	45,900	5,100	3,206
Connecticut..	315	53,047	7,309	6,920
Delaware..	139	20,199	2,120	1,300
District of Columbia	72	14,752	1,929	1,387
Florida...	2,506	395,043	37,480	27,085
Georgia	858	145,135	17,031	11,096
Hawaii	165	41,191	3,756	3,305
Idaho	155	15,084	1,423	878
Illinois	1,282	191,454	17,905	12,649
Indiana	869	115,421	9,580	6,849
Iowa	217	42,573	4,096	2,713
Kansas	216	41,014	3,669	2,575
Kentucky..	409	72,565	7,160	5,417
Louisiana	406	117,465	11,050	10,196
Maine...	152	18,357	2,084	2,998
Maryland..	705	129,476	14,424	10,551
Massachusetts..	657	104,405	15,217	11,303
Michigan..	798	125,206	11,093	8,664
Minnesota..	521	71,734	6,556	5,120
Mississippi...	183	37,015	3,651	2,978
Missouri...	642	94,062	9,502	6,681
Montana...	121	8,350	949	414
Nebraska..	194	35,456	2,804	2,473
Nevada...	130	20,626	1776	1,424
New Hampshire...	209	17,934	2,573	2,174
New Jersey	1,068	162,354	19014	13,432
New Mexico	174	18,201	1,956	1,194
New York..	1,656	355,784	40,008	26,890
North Carolina..	757	121,525	13,358	8,252
North Dakota..	57	9,552	904	*
Ohio	1,290	195,894	18,809	12,640
Oklahoma...	177	32,650	3,421	2,239
Oregon...	375	45,487	4,415	3,440
Pennsylvania...	2,458	245,171	25,276	18,130
Rhode Island..	112	16,071	1,825	1,606
South Carolina	427	50,367	5,597	3,401
South Dakota..	80	11,563	1,007	763
Tennessee..	566	99,832	11,547	8,336
Texas...	1,738	246,706	28,563	16,788
Utah	169	16,223	1,790	1,388
Vermont..	112	9,142	1205	952
Virginia..	1,024	111,427	13,116	7,560
Washington...	672	94,937	9,682	5,552
West Virginia..	130	12,530	1,373	838
Wisconsin...	890	128,987	11,412	6,549
Wyoming	40	2,120	301	*

* = Reporting standards not met.

Table B-9. Staff Employed by Public Elementary and Secondary School Systems, Fall 2019

(Number; percent.)

State	Total staff	Student/ Teacher Ratio	Student/ Staff Ratio	Principals and assistant principals		Teachers		Instructional aides		Guidance counselors		Librarians	
				Number	Percent	Number	Percent	Number	Percent	Number	Percent	Number	Percent
UNITED STATES	6,683,302	15.9	7.6	193,734	2.9	3,198,170	47.9	883,071	13.2	119,539	1.8	39,447	0.6
Alabama..........................	76,456	17.7	9.7	3,993	5.2	42,022	55.0	6,740	8.8	1,757	2.3	1,305	1.7
Alaska	16,980	17.6	7.8	670	3.9	7,484	44.1	2,731	16.1	305	1.8	135	0.8
Arizona...........................	106,835	23.6	10.8	2,546	2.4	48,912	45.8	16,767	15.7	1,359	1.3	419	0.4
Arkansas.........................	77,034	12.9	6.5	1,946	2.5	38,629	50.1	9,111	11.8	1,351	1.8	924	1.2
California.........................	613,096	23.0	10.2	18,050	2.9	271,805	44.3	87,748	14.3	10,254	1.7	87	0.0
Colorado	117,692	16.9	7.8	3,798	3.2	53,901	45.8	18,255	15.5	3,098	2.6	512	0.4
Connecticut.....................	96,886	12.4	5.4	2,259	2.3	42,386	43.7	16,879	17.4	1,449	1.5	730	0.8
Delaware.........................	17,133	14.4	8.2	536	3.1	9,747	56.9	2,585	15.1	360	2.1	109	0.6
District of Columbia	16,578	12.1	5.4	919	5.5	7,409	44.7	2,353	14.2	235	1.4	110	0.7
Florida............................	344,008	17.2	8.3	9,067	2.6	166,002	48.3	36,380	10.6	6,371	1.9	1,991	0.6
Georgia	237,311	15.0	7.5	6,850	2.9	117,837	49.7	27,299	11.5	4,094	1.7	2,061	0.9
Hawaii.............................	23,336	14.8	7.8	740	3.2	12,221	52.4	2,565	11.0	660	2.8	126	0.5
Idaho...............................	29,943	18.1	10.4	749	2.5	17,207	57.5	3,425	11.4	598	2.0	34	0.1
Illinois.............................	257,248	14.6	7.6	8,876	3.5	132,815	51.6	35,299	13.7	3,281	1.3	1,400	0.5
Indiana............................	148,730	17.0	7.1	3,521	2.4	61,712	41.5	17,878	12.0	2,165	1.5	597	0.4
Iowa................................	77,460	14.5	6.7	1,744	2.3	35,737	46.1	14,163	18.3	1,347	1.7	380	0.5
Kansas............................	72,548	13.6	6.9	2,028	2.8	36,603	50.5	10,333	14.2	1,189	1.6	618	0.9
Kentucky	98,882	16.4	7.0	3,592	3.6	42,223	42.7	13,074	13.2	1,729	1.7	1,024	1.0
Louisiana	79,255	18.4	9.0	3,308	4.2	38,589	48.7	11,510	14.5	1,623	2.0	957	1.2
Maine..............................	36,567	12.2	4.9	982	2.7	14,826	40.5	6,601	18.1	583	1.6	187	0.5
Maryland..........................	121,158	14.8	7.5	3,669	3.0	61,485	50.7	11,950	9.9	2,554	2.1	1,150	0.9
Massachusetts..................	137,602	12.8	7.0	5,532	4.0	75,152	54.6	26,923	19.6	2,463	1.8	616	0.4
Michigan	191,891	17.6	7.8	6,983	3.6	84,838	44.2	21,160	11.0	2,231	1.2	509	0.3
Minnesota	122,018	16.1	7.3	2,612	2.1	55,630	45.6	20,764	17.0	1,419	1.2	483	0.4
Mississippi.......................	67,226	14.8	6.9	2,119	3.2	31,578	47.0	8,397	12.5	1,104	1.6	744	1.1
Missouri...........................	125,333	13.2	7.3	3,526	2.8	69,145	55.2	14,888	11.9	2,706	2.2	1,334	1.1
Montana..........................	21,734	14.0	6.9	550	2.5	10,675	49.1	2,954	13.6	494	2.3	373	1.7
Nebraska.........................	48,202	13.7	6.8	1,114	2.3	24,028	49.8	7,074	14.7	887	1.8	535	1.1
Nevada............................	48,718	19.5	10.2	858	1.8	25,509	52.4	6,847	14	1,041	2.1	278	0.6
New Hampshire.................	32,018	12.1	5.5	540	1.7	14,695	45.9	6,293	19.7	828	2.6	333	1.0
New Jersey	242,254	12.1	5.8	5,316	2.2	117,060	48.3	41,241	17.0	4,058	1.7	1,255	0.5
New Mexico	38,221	15.2	8.7	1,221	3.2	21,850	57.2	6,201	16.2	702	1.8	211	0.6
New York..........................	426,192	12.4	6.3	9,976	2.3	217,398	51.0	78,629	18.4	7,465	1.8	539	0.1
North Carolina..................	194,618	15.5	8.0	6,086	3.1	100,777	51.8	22,102	11.4	4,474	2.3	2,025	1.0
North Dakota....................	19,133	12.5	6.1	513	2.7	9,284	48.5	3,217	16.8	386	2.0	177	0.9
Ohio................................	340,436	15.9	5.0	5,930	1.7	105,998	31.1	26,714	7.8	4,134	1.2	803	0.2
Oklahoma........................	88,901	16.2	7.9	2,373	2.7	43,315	48.7	11,287	12.7	1,714	1.9	890	1.0
Oregon............................	70,069	20.2	8.7	1,843	2.6	30,238	43.2	11,985	17.1	1,360	1.9	151	0.2
Pennsylvania....................	252,559	13.9	6.9	5,545	2.2	124,294	49.2	33,802	13.4	4,817	1.9	1,589	0.6
Rhode Island....................	20,519	13.4	7.0	591	2.9	10,704	52.2	2,752	13.4	348	1.7	184	0.9
South Carolina	98,587	14.7	8.0	3,494	3.5	53,556	54.3	13,144	13.3	2,270	2.3	1,099	1.1
South Dakota	20,168	14.1	6.9	446	2.2	9,930	49.2	2,985	14.8	380	1.9	70	0.3
Tennessee	135,257	15.7	7.5	3,885	2.9	64,784	47.9	16,855	12.5	3,368	2.5	1,526	1.1
Texas..............................	738,419	15.1	7.4	28,339	3.8	364,478	49.4	78,377	10.6	13,345	1.8	4,563	0.6
Utah................................	61,023	22.6	11.2	1,674	2.7	30,256	49.6	10,308	16.9	1,251	2.1	228	0.4
Vermont...........................	18,695	10.8	4.6	555	3.0	8,042	43.0	3,935	21.0	431	2.3	205	1.1
Virginia............................	186,269	14.9	7.0	4,398	2.4	87,147	46.8	20,166	10.8	3,867	2.1	1,814	1.0
Washington......................	103,507	18.4	11.0	3,594	3.5	62,212	60.1	13,804	13.3	2,454	2.4	849	0.8
West Virginia....................	37,262	14.0	7.1	1,139	3.1	18,854	50.6	3,650	9.8	763	2.0	209	0.6
Wisconsin	114,709	14.3	7.5	2,748	2.4	59,801	52.1	10,444	9.1	2,122	1.9	917	0.8
Wyoming	16,626	12.8	5.7	393	2.4	7,391	44.5	2,527	15.2	295	1.8	83	0.5

- = Zero or rounds to zero.
NA = Not available.

Table B-9. Staff Employed by Public Elementary and Secondary School Systems, Fall 2019—*Continued*

(Number; percent.)

State	School staff		School district staff						Student support staff		Other support services staff	
	School and library support staff		Officials and administrators		Instruction coordinators		Administrative support staff					
	Number	Percent	Number	Percent	Number	Percent	Number	Percent	Number	Percent	Number	Percent
UNITED STATES	281,179	4.2	77,875	1.2	104,603	1.6	192,642	2.9	392,699	5.9	1,200,343	18.0
Alabama..............................	2,394	3.1	1,115	1.5	53	0.069	2093.86	2.7	2,004	2.6	12,981	17.0
Alaska	1,192	7.0	718	4.2	0	0	785.69	4.6	703	4.1	2,258	13.3
Arizona...............................	3,936	3.7	1,484	1.4	624	0.584	4098.74	3.8	12,311	11.5	14,379	13.5
Arkansas	3,230	4.2	656	0.9	1,172	1.5	2,605	3.4	7,304	9.5	10,106	13.1
California.............................	35,273	5.8	4,041	0.7	25,130	4.1	21,835	3.6	21,263	3.5	117,610	19.2
Colorado	6,060	5.1	1,339	1.1	3,723	3.2	4,757	4.0	8,284	7.0	13,967	11.9
Connecticut........................	3,371	3.5	2,098	2.2	2,748	2.8	1,575	1.6	5,473	5.6	17,918	18.5
Delaware	390	2.3	121	0.7	359	2.1	116	0.7	880	5.1	1,931	11.3
District of Columbia	609	3.7	331	2.0	201	1.2	1,094	6.6	2,187	13.2	1,131	6.8
Florida................................	18,666	5.4	2,237	0.7	2,523	0.7	6,494	1.9	31,600	9.2	62,676	18.2
Georgia	10,566	4.5	3,059	1.3	4,118	1.7	2,772	1.2	9,266	3.9	49,390	20.8
Hawaii	1,005	4.3	353	1.5	617	2.6	744	3.2	1,728	7.4	2,578	11.0
Idaho..................................	1,284	4.3	156	0.5	375	1.3	723	2.4	597	2.0	4,793	16.0
Illinois	8,958	3.5	6,079	2.4	1,432	0.6	5,630	2.2	27,557	10.7	25,921	10.1
Indiana...............................	8,035	5.4	658	0.4	5,335	3.6	726	0.5	9,596	6.5	38,508	25.9
Iowa...................................	2,658	3.4	1,928	2.5	2,563	3.3	1,891	2.4	4,842	6.3	10,206	13.2
Kansas	2,022	3.9	469	0.6	1,228	1.7	1,461	2.0	4,755	6.6	11,042	15.2
Kentucky............................	5,603	5.7	992	1.0	1,776	1.8	2,347	2.4	3,459	3.5	23,064	23.3
Louisiana	3,555	4.5	100	0.1	1,778	2.2	458	0.6	3,511	4.4	13,866	17.5
Maine	1,634	4.5	677	1.9	625	1.7	700	1.9	4,370	11.9	5,383	14.7
Maryland............................	5,918	4.9	4,100	3.4	2,167	1.8	1,919	1.6	6,827	5.6	19,419	16.0
Massachusetts	6,672	4.8	2,757	2.0	533	0.4	2,986	2.2	11,802	8.6	2,166	1.6
Michigan	12,566	6.5	4,424	2.3	1,300	0.7	1,129	0.6	16,534	8.6	40,218	21.0
Minnesota	4,534	3.7	2,558	2.1	2,991	2.5	2,231	1.8	15,221	12.5	13,575	11.1
Mississippi.........................	2,617	3.9	985	1.5	724	1.1	2,094	3.1	3,384	5.0	13,480	20.1
Missouri.............................	333	0.3	904	0.7	1,525	1.2	5,491	4.4	5,905	4.7	19,577	15.6
Montana.............................	0	0.0	486	2.2	200	0.9	25	0.1	750	3.5	5,225	24.0
Nebraska............................	1,976	4.1	686	1.4	746	1.5	1,238	2.6	1,745	3.6	8,172	17.0
Nevada...............................	2,807	5.8	54	0.1	1,773	4	1,504	3	694	1.4	7,354	15.1
New Hampshire...................	1,463	4.6	743	2.3	283	0.9	723	2.3	1,484	4.6	4,634	14.5
New Jersey	9,568	3.9	1,448	0.6	4,058	1.7	5,477	2.3	13,932	5.8	38,840	16.0
New Mexico	2,135	5.6	244	0.6	274	0.7	30	0.1	1,556	4.1	3,796	9.9
New York............................	3,906	0.9	4,248	1.0	6,386	1.5	23,902	5.6	15,970	3.7	57,774	13.6
North Carolina....................	7,190	3.7	1,748	0.9	1,146	0.6	5,703	2.9	11,826	6.1	31,540	16.2
North Dakota......................	774	4.0	526	2.8	220	1.1	305	1.6	984	5.1	2,747	14.4
Ohio...................................	14,389	4.2	2,700	0.8	2,316	0.7	15,254	4.5	30,272	8.9	131,927	38.8
Oklahoma...........................	4,426	5.0	819	0.9	375	0.4	3,086	3.5	5,609	6.3	15,006	16.9
Oregon	4,661	6.7	472	0.7	497	0.7	2,566	3.7	3,136	4.5	13,161	18.8
Pennsylvania......................	11,361	4.5	2,684	1.1	1,885	0.7	7,560	3.0	10,300	4.1	48,722	19.3
Rhode Island......................	736	3.6	312	1.5	237	1.2	618	2.5	2,153	10.5	1,986	9.7
South Carolina	3,981	4.0	957	1.0	1,533	1.6	3,730	3.8	3,044	3.1	11,779	11.9
South Dakota	616	3.1	745	3.7	140	0.7	347	1.7	1,144	5.7	3,366	16.7
Tennessee	4,770	3.5	403	0.3	1,773	1.3	2,653	2.0	5,251	3.9	29,989	22.2
Texas.................................	29,677	4.0	7,773	1.1	4,488	0.6	24,427	3.3	28,610	3.9	154,341	20.9
Utah...................................	2,776	4.5	431	0.7	2,399	3.9	1,712	2.8	1,364	2.2	8,624	14.1
Vermont.............................	856	4.6	173	0.9	474	2.5	574	3.1	1,586	8.5	1,865	10.0
Virginia..............................	8,358	4.5	1,994	1.1	1,831	1.0	4,601	2.5	13,858	7.4	38,234	20.5
Washington	5,064	4.0	1,423	1.4	4,040	3.9	3,398	3.3	4,042	3.9	2,618	2.5
West Virginia......................	455	1.2	876	2.4	383	1.0	1,325	3.6	1,283	3.4	8,326	22.3
Wisconsin	4,433	3.9	1,198	1.0	1,290	1.1	2,774	2.4	9,817	8.6	19,154	16.7
Wyoming	921	5.5	389	2.3	222	1.3	456	2.7	926	5.6	3,025	18.2

- = Zero or rounds to zero.
NA = Not available.

Table B-10. Revenues and Expenditures for Public Elementary and Secondary Schools, by State, 2018–19

(Dollars in thousands except as noted; percent.)

State	Total revenue (thousands of dollars)	Percent from: Federal government	Percent from: State government	Percent from: Local government	Total current expenditures (thousands of dollars)	Current expenditure per pupil (dollars)	Percent for: Instruction	Percent for: Support services	Percent for: Non-instruction
UNITED STATES	764,716,225	7.9	46.7	45.4	769,038,919	13,187	52.4	30.9	16.7
Alabama	8,444,012	10.8	55.8	33.4	8,350,629	10,107	50.8	32.8	16.4
Alaska	2,560,774	15.4	62.5	22.1	2,571,459	18,393	49.9	40.4	9.7
Arizona	11,646,059	12.1	49.1	38.9	11,859,149	8,773	45.1	33.5	21.3
Arkansas	5,811,290	11.0	51.1	37.9	6,080,406	10,412	47.5	32.8	19.7
California	100,451,374	8.0	58.0	34.0	100,092,748	13,641	50.9	31.4	17.7
Colorado	12,361,826	5.9	42.7	51.4	12,609,433	11,072	44.2	32.9	22.9
Connecticut	11,952,708	4.5	39.8	55.7	12,172,308	21,140	56.5	32.4	11.1
Delaware	2,286,338	8.3	62.0	29.6	2,360,866	15,929	57.6	32.2	10.2
District of Columbia	2,576,906	8.0	†	92.0	2,664,763	22,831	38.1	35.1	26.8
Florida	31,631,952	11.2	38.6	50.2	32,216,750	9,986	54.0	29.9	16.1
Georgia	22,560,817	8.8	45.9	45.3	22,214,682	11,203	53.8	30.5	15.6
Hawaii	3,124,747	9.6	88.3	2.1	3,214,009	16,132	52.9	33.6	13.5
Idaho	2,909,800	9.5	66.3	24.2	2,900,116	8,043	51.2	31.0	17.8
Illinois	31,156,018	7.5	26.6	65.9	36,424,722	16,281	54.3	31.9	13.8
Indiana	13,518,860	7.6	62.2	30.2	12,608,077	10,252	48.6	33.2	18.2
Iowa	7,272,669	7.2	52.7	40.1	7,221,197	11,933	50.9	30.4	18.7
Kansas	6,937,265	8.2	63.8	27.9	6,913,154	11,328	48.2	29.7	22.2
Kentucky	8,651,926	11.0	55.3	33.6	8,698,153	11,280	51.3	30.9	17.8
Louisiana	9,422,978	12.6	43.7	43.8	9,171,373	11,920	51.6	36.0	12.4
Maine	3,025,712	6.4	39.1	54.5	3,118,144	15,686	53.1	34.1	12.7
Maryland	16,180,904	5.6	43.0	51.4	15,800,061	15,576	56.0	30.0	14.1
Massachusetts	18,991,990	4.7	39.3	56.1	19,326,043	19,196	60.8	31.9	7.3
Michigan	21,540,678	8.3	59.7	32.0	20,996,066	12,052	49.1	34.2	16.7
Minnesota	14,404,670	5.4	65.9	28.7	14,933,697	13,297	51.2	24.5	24.3
Mississippi	4,899,797	13.9	49.7	36.3	4,779,070	9,253	51.7	34.2	14.1
Missouri	12,145,801	7.8	32.4	59.8	11,935,056	11,349	48.8	34.1	17.1
Montana	2,045,107	13.1	42.8	44.1	2,172,689	11,984	48.2	30.2	21.6
Nebraska	4,659,503	7.4	32.2	60.4	4,765,792	12,746	54.2	29.4	16.4
Nevada	5,428,429	9.0	34.3	56.8	5,580,753	9,126	47.1	30.3	22.6
New Hampshire	3,275,053	5.1	30.8	64.2	3,306,651	17,457	58.5	31.4	10.0
New Jersey	33,054,506	4.1	44.5	51.3	32,229,687	21,331	54.9	35.0	10.1
New Mexico	4,121,959	13.1	68.8	18.1	3,977,268	10,466	50.0	33.5	16.5
New York	75,411,423	4.9	39.4	55.7	72,395,151	24,882	62.3	26.5	11.2
North Carolina	15,988,930	10.5	62.8	26.7	16,647,814	9,799	57.1	29.8	13.1
North Dakota	1,862,138	10.5	54.8	34.6	1,869,274	14,033	51.3	27.7	20.9
Ohio	25,791,960	7.5	41.3	51.2	26,109,229	13,433	51.8	32.7	15.5
Oklahoma	7,326,279	10.6	49.1	40.2	7,361,192	9,203	49.3	32.2	18.5
Oregon	8,903,669	6.5	51.6	41.8	9,339,749	12,457	45.2	29.9	25.0
Pennsylvania	33,512,607	7.0	37.8	55.3	33,037,839	16,892	54.6	30.6	14.8
Rhode Island	2,686,747	7.6	42.8	49.6	2,742,160	17,539	55.2	34.0	10.8
South Carolina	11,052,179	8.3	49.3	42.4	10,542,408	10,994	44.6	32.6	22.8
South Dakota	1,704,964	13.9	34.2	51.9	1,661,534	10,325	51.1	30.4	18.5
Tennessee	10,963,858	10.8	46.6	42.7	11,231,507	9,941	53.8	30.7	15.5
Texas	66,946,288	10.9	36.6	52.5	67,728,086	9,868	46.0	28.8	25.2
Utah	6,548,369	7.0	55.2	37.8	6,634,115	7,950	51.2	26.3	22.5
Vermont	1,812,788	6.3	90.3	3.4	1,926,771	21,217	59.8	33.3	6.8
Virginia	17,613,494	6.6	40.1	53.2	17,955,756	12,642	55.1	32.2	12.7
Washington	19,405,697	5.5	69.4	25.1	20,393,826	14,342	47.2	29.1	23.7
West Virginia	3,618,442	11.3	55.8	32.9	3,581,478	12,269	52.7	33.4	13.9
Wisconsin	12,708,122	6.7	49.5	43.8	12,897,721	12,690	49.6	31.9	18.5
Wyoming	1,805,845	7.3	53.4	39.3	1,718,339	16,228	53.0	33.3	13.7

NA = Not available.

Table B-11. Percentage of High School Dropouts Among Persons 16 to 24 Years Old, by Race/ Ethnicity and State, 2019

(Percent.)

State	Total	White	Black	Hispanic	Asian	Pacific Islander	American Indian/ Alaska Native	Two or more races
UNITED STATES	5.1	4.1	5.6	7.7	1.8	8.0	9.6	5.1
Alabama..................................	5.9	5.7	5.5	12.2	NA	NA	NA	3.8
Alaska....................................	7.2	4.3	NA	NA	NA	NA	12.1	NA
Arizona..................................	6.8	4.2	4.4	9.6	2.3	NA	12.7	4.5
Arkansas	5.5	6.0	4.5	3.6	NA	NA	NA	6.5
California...............................	4.1	2.5	4.8	5.8	1.2	5.3	7.1	2.5
Colorado	5.4	3.5	7.5	9.9	NA	NA	NA	2.4
Connecticut............................	3.9	2.8	2.3	7.9	NA	NA	NA	NA
Delaware	4.8	5.5	4.1	5.4	NA	NA	NA	NA
District of Columbia	2.2	NA	4.2	NA	NA	NA	NA	NA
Florida...................................	6.0	5.4	6.6	7.0	1.6	NA	NA	5.7
Georgia	6.5	6.0	6.1	10.2	3.3	NA	NA	6.7
Hawaii...................................	3.5	NA	NA	3.7	2.3	10.6	NA	4.2
Idaho.....................................	5.6	4.4	NA	12.5	NA	NA	NA	NA
Illinois...................................	4.8	3.7	6.5	6.6	0.8	NA	NA	7.4
Indiana..................................	6.1	6.3	6.8	4.6	2.1	NA	NA	7.1
Iowa......................................	4.0	3.4	5.1	7.8	NA	NA	NA	NA
Kansas	5.0	3.7	9.8	9.5	NA	NA	NA	NA
Kentucky	5.9	5.9	2.7	8.9	NA	NA	NA	12.4
Louisiana...............................	7.2	6.8	7.7	10.7	NA	NA	NA	NA
Maine....................................	4.9	5.0	NA	NA	NA	NA	NA	NA
Maryland................................	5.0	3.0	5.0	13.8	NA	NA	NA	5.1
Massachusetts.......................	3.3	2.4	3.8	7.2	NA	NA	NA	NA
Michigan	5.4	4.7	7.3	8.9	2.3	NA	NA	7.4
Minnesota..............................	4.2	3.0	7.5	6.7	3.7	NA	28.1	6.3
Mississippi.............................	7.5	5.4	9.0	17.7	NA	NA	NA	NA
Missouri.................................	4.9	4.7	4.5	9.1	NA	NA	NA	5.9
Montana................................	5.6	5.2	NA	NA	NA	NA	10.8	NA
Nebraska...............................	3.0	2.1	NA	6.4	NA	NA	NA	NA
Nevada..................................	7.5	4.8	11.3	9.7	3.0	NA	NA	6.6
New Hampshire......................	4.5	3.9	NA	17.5	NA	NA	NA	NA
New Jersey	2.9	2.1	3.0	5.4	NA	NA	NA	2.5
New Mexico	8.1	5.1	NA	8.7	NA	NA	9.6	NA
New York................................	4.7	3.1	6.0	8.3	2.1	NA	NA	4.5
North Carolina........................	5.1	3.5	5.1	11.3	4.3	NA	7.2	5.5
North Dakota..........................	7.0	4.9	NA	NA	NA	NA	15.5	NA
Ohio......................................	5.4	5.4	5.6	5.3	NA	NA	NA	7.7
Oklahoma...............................	6.4	5.3	7.7	8.9	NA	NA	9.3	6.7
Oregon	6.0	5.7	NA	8.4	NA	NA	NA	6.8
Pennsylvania..........................	4.6	4.7	3.6	8.4	1.4	NA	NA	1.7
Rhode Island..........................	4.7	2.3	10.5	8.4	NA	NA	NA	18.8
South Carolina	5.5	5.3	5.0	9.5	NA	NA	NA	4.0
South Dakota	5.4	2.7	NA	NA	NA	NA	20.5	NA
Tennessee..............................	4.4	3.9	3.2	10.3	3.5	NA	NA	5.6
Texas....................................	5.9	3.3	5.1	8.5	1.5	NA	NA	4.9
Utah	3.9	3.1	NA	5.7	NA	NA	14.0	NA
Vermont.................................	3.9	2.5	NA	NA	NA	NA	NA	NA
Virginia..................................	3.4	2.7	3.2	8.0	2.2	NA	NA	1.7
Washington............................	5.8	4.8	4.2	9.8	2.8	9.7	7.3	7.1
West Virginia..........................	5.2	5.1	6.3	NA	NA	NA	NA	NA
Wisconsin	4.0	3.0	8.6	8.4	NA	NA	NA	NA
Wyoming	4.3	3.5	NA	NA	NA	NA	NA	NA

NA = Not available. Reporting standards not met.
NOTE: Status dropouts are 16- to 24-year-olds who are not enrolled in school and who have not completed a high school program, regardless of when they left school. People who have received equivalency credentials, such as the GED, are counted as high school completers. Data are based on sample surveys of the entire population residing within the United States, including both noninstitutionalized persons (e.g., those living in households, college housing, or military housing located within the United States) and institutionalized persons (e.g., those living in prisons, nursing facilities, or other healthcare facilities). Totals include other racial/ethnic groups not separately shown. Race categories exclude persons of Hispanic ethnicity.

Table B-12. Total Fall Enrollment in Degree-Granting Postsecondary Institutions, by Level and Control of School, and State, 2019

(Number.)

State	Public				Private							
	Undergraduate			Post-baccalaureate	Undergraduate					Postbaccalaureate		
	Total	4-year	2-year		Total	Nonprofit 4-year	For-profit 4-year	Nonprofit 2-year	For-profit 2-year	Total	Nonprofit 4-year	For-profit 4-year
UNITED STATES ...	13,001,543	7,603,444	5,398,099	1,499,514	3,563,523	2,760,234	602,344	44,644	156,301	1,572,919	1,340,385	232,534
Alabama	216,326	136,404	79,922	38,477	36,888	20,225	16,126	NA	537	11,339	5,322	6,017
Alaska	20,428	20,428	NA	1,900	833	377	NA	95	361	192	192	NA
Arizona	340,111	159,598	180,513	37,537	165,055	5,909	148,920	36	10,190	66,441	5,835	60,606
Arkansas	123,897	78,838	45,059	18,053	14,351	12,981	404	914	52	2,286	2,194	92
California	2,127,557	900,505	1,227,052	119,671	282,437	169,010	86,815	1,547	25,065	185,420	154,933	30,487
Colorado	243,282	221,800	21,482	40,273	61,867	20,065	32,175	72	9,555	22,701	13,290	9,411
Connecticut	97,384	52,236	45,148	13,281	59,211	49,482	9,729	NA	NA	23,810	22,897	913
Delaware	37,653	37,653	NA	4,583	11,555	11,068	352	135	NA	6,192	6,140	52
District of Columbia	3,828	3,828	NA	624	49,494	40,760	8,363	NA	371	44,963	40,811	4,152
Florida	726,217	703,813	22,404	71,735	215,087	130,662	48,624	19,866	15,935	53,744	49,567	4,177
Georgia	387,725	265,796	121,929	57,068	82,152	58,903	15,910	2,103	5,236	26,810	21,663	5,147
Hawaii	44,564	21,490	23,074	5,413	9,293	8,479	188	NA	626	1,164	1,099	65
Idaho	70,920	53,677	17,243	7,904	42,438	41,984	NA	NA	454	702	702	NA
Illinois	402,219	130,883	271,336	50,245	162,996	127,429	31,849	364	3,354	103,044	85,734	17,310
Indiana	281,340	208,651	72,689	51,310	72,191	68,861	338	386	2,606	18,065	17,993	72
Iowa	149,552	60,729	88,823	14,360	40,268	37,528	2,686	NA	54	13,853	13,334	519
Kansas	154,578	77,475	77,103	22,642	25,669	18,245	6,507	NA	917	5,649	4,462	1,187
Kentucky	175,993	97,647	78,346	23,621	36,848	29,792	5,831	NA	1,225	30,045	29,333	712
Louisiana	185,195	119,313	65,882	27,765	22,947	19,142	208	506	3,091	7,843	7,843	NA
Maine	44,152	26,825	17,327	4,155	18,144	17,700	390	54	NA	5,207	5,207	NA
Maryland	253,636	140,337	113,299	41,153	29,858	25,674	2,684	NA	1,500	30,266	29,726	540
Massachusetts	175,438	96,411	79,027	27,355	173,634	171,875	609	1,050	100	116,070	116,070	NA
Michigan	392,201	252,183	140,018	62,747	54,979	52,912	338	NA	1,729	15,564	15,564	NA
Minnesota	217,689	103,234	114,455	24,063	71,630	49,682	21,733	121	94	89,347	20,453	68,894
Mississippi	134,425	63,293	71,132	13,935	12,515	11,612	561	NA	342	6,094	6,030	64
Missouri	199,643	117,043	82,600	26,367	87,998	84,164	2,450	184	1,200	48,900	48,686	214
Montana	39,054	31,386	7,668	5,362	3,272	2,851	NA	366	55	378	378	NA
Nebraska	85,229	45,010	40,219	14,273	24,890	24,791	40	16	43	11,117	11,117	NA
Nevada	101,467	101,467	NA	9,093	6,223	1,035	1,217	NA	3,971	2,988	2,932	56
New Hampshire	33,058	21,870	11,188	4,163	105,419	105,312	NA	107	NA	26,698	26,698	NA
New Jersey	288,336	150,770	137,566	38,871	61,281	50,630	6,013	200	4,438	24,687	24,309	378
New Mexico	106,283	42,265	64,018	11,833	2,282	648	502	NA	1,132	1,418	764	654
New York	608,044	331,923	276,121	70,348	379,442	340,607	29,684	3,306	5,845	177,978	175,047	2,931
North Carolina	414,621	192,108	222,513	48,349	77,999	67,933	8,237	556	1,273	27,594	26,470	1,124
North Dakota	39,318	32,061	7,257	6,272	5,213	4,569	644	NA	NA	1,551	1,542	9
Ohio	453,332	308,545	144,787	58,526	116,435	101,063	4,871	1,052	9,449	28,152	28,077	75
Oklahoma	147,322	93,378	53,944	20,627	20,015	16,888	673	671	1,783	4,692	4,692	NA
Oregon	171,341	84,727	86,614	18,560	22,242	20,264	1,212	33	733	13,573	13,330	243
Pennsylvania	339,033	220,552	118,481	50,265	209,677	192,176	3,560	5,055	8,886	94,365	94,030	335
Rhode Island	35,755	20,980	14,775	4,008	32,896	32,896	NA	NA	NA	7,418	7,418	NA
South Carolina	176,284	106,508	69,776	21,525	37,337	32,219	3,195	NA	1,923	6,426	5,133	1,293
South Dakota	38,121	31,018	7,103	5,347	7,025	5,380	1,645	NA	NA	1,448	1,340	108
Tennessee	201,279	113,442	87,837	25,067	72,017	58,232	7,791	779	5,215	24,723	23,369	1,354
Texas	1,329,575	691,479	638,096	150,574	135,223	98,701	16,689	1,711	18,122	42,319	41,215	1,104
Utah	175,517	146,000	29,517	13,834	149,537	143,341	3,693	1,994	509	42,395	41,352	1,043
Vermont	22,295	17,191	5,104	2,836	12,931	12,873	58	NA	NA	3,124	3,124	NA
Virginia	335,242	174,794	160,448	49,151	113,796	85,751	24,065	372	3,608	58,874	56,001	2,873
Washington	289,892	259,983	29,909	25,760	35,831	29,403	3,755	993	1,680	11,536	11,385	151
West Virginia	70,462	53,754	16,708	11,333	47,811	6,305	38,906	NA	2,600	9,553	1,434	8,119
Wisconsin	249,677	156,961	92,716	24,840	44,138	41,845	2,104	NA	189	14,201	14,148	53
Wyoming	29,678	9,807	19,871	2,442	253	NA	NA	NA	253	NA	NA	NA

NA = Not applicable.
NOTE: Degree-granting institutions grant associate's or higher degrees and participate in Title IV federal financial aid programs.

Table B-13. Degrees Conferred by Institutions of Higher Education, by State, 2018–2019

(Number.)

State	Total degrees	Associate's degrees				Bachelor's degrees			
		Total	Public	Private not-for-profit	Private for-profit	Total	Public	Private not-for-profit	Private for-profit
UNITED STATES	4,070,790	1,036,662	915,011	54,432	67,219	2,012,854	1,340,147	575,586	07,121
Alabama.......................................	62,371	13,198	10,759	220	2,219	33,068	25,928	3,688	3,452
Alaska..	3,772	1,197	1,149	12	36	1,922	1,863	59	0
Arizona.......................................	120,649	26,875	19,275	149	7,451	60,301	33,258	907	26,136
Arkansas....................................	33,632	10,060	9,619	412	29	16,746	14,188	2,540	18
California....................................	519,889	197,152	185,168	1,660	10,324	219,511	164,747	40,163	14,601
Colorado	68,202	12,961	10,014	428	2,519	36,814	27,777	3,902	5,135
Connecticut................................	43,916	6,614	5,388	943	283	23,785	11,854	10,910	1,021
Delaware	13,249	2,037	1,945	79	13	7,274	5,021	2,222	31
District of Columbia	27,620	759	195	226	338	10,220	386	9,151	683
Florida..	246,438	94,671	76,670	12,305	5,696	108,197	78,990	22,463	6,744
Georgia	97,580	18,553	16,470	898	1,185	54,036	41,025	10,631	2,380
Hawaii..	12,171	4,015	3,755	204	56	6,365	4,681	1,562	122
Idaho..	20,542	5,193	3,479	1,585	129	12,955	6,895	6,060	0
Illinois..	160,311	35,642	32,914	829	1,899	72,735	32,455	30,641	9,639
Indiana.......................................	88,852	14,656	12,714	1,486	456	51,271	36,911	14,243	117
Iowa...	44,161	11,293	10,750	344	199	24,153	14,319	9,130	704
Kansas.......................................	40,576	10,958	9,902	276	780	20,359	16,008	3,679	672
Kentucky....................................	51,290	12,049	10,547	281	1,221	24,522	18,985	4,875	662
Louisiana	40,978	6,804	5,956	300	548	23,093	19,532	3,561	0
Maine...	12,820	2,572	2,344	115	113	7,337	4,127	3,210	0
Maryland.....................................	75,468	16,890	16,624	21	245	34,586	28,545	5,752	289
Massachusetts............................	124,565	12,198	10,819	1,275	104	61,699	21,838	39,755	106
Michigan.....................................	111,861	25,444	23,480	1,766	198	59,782	47,805	11,848	129
Minnesota...................................	86,022	17,088	14,982	782	1,324	37,024	21,456	10,786	4,782
Mississippi.................................	36,987	13,632	13,566	55	11	16,608	14,274	2,321	13
Missouri......................................	80,854	15,322	12,306	2,640	376	40,610	23,036	17,149	425
Montana......................................	10,480	2,409	2,336	54	19	6,242	5,438	804	0
Nebraska....................................	26,621	5,007	4,807	164	36	14,445	9,134	5,290	21
Nevada.......................................	19,280	6,209	5,759	0	450	9,702	8,943	503	256
New Hampshire...........................	33,553	4,566	2,097	2,469	0	19,005	5,397	13,608	0
New Jersey	87,911	22,647	20,773	241	1,633	44,690	33,705	10,057	928
New Mexico	22,254	9,670	9,491	0	179	8,560	8,284	174	102
New York.....................................	299,217	64,521	51,197	7,239	6,085	143,790	68,457	71,868	3,465
North Carolina............................	116,110	34,326	32,925	853	548	56,892	41,884	14,474	534
North Dakota..............................	11,435	2,323	1,970	164	189	6,623	5,926	687	10
Ohio...	134,058	31,330	25,982	3,025	2,323	72,250	50,892	20,974	384
Oklahoma...................................	41,125	11,240	10,708	191	341	21,574	17,752	3,791	31
Oregon.......................................	48,009	13,538	13,181	29	328	24,107	18,720	5,380	7
Pennsylvania..............................	164,242	23,031	17,214	3,234	2,583	91,190	48,358	42,295	537
Rhode Island..............................	19,761	3,311	1,988	1,323	0	12,345	4,808	7,537	0
South Carolina	45,686	10,322	9,689	329	304	26,761	20,178	6,301	282
South Dakota	11,090	2,433	2,167	34	232	6,170	4,734	1,077	359
Tennessee	65,208	14,090	11,949	938	1,203	34,960	22,388	12,171	401
Texas...	304,221	97,018	91,062	1,469	4,487	141,280	118,027	21,333	1,920
Utah...	80,752	13,939	12,007	1,261	671	46,121	17,697	28,080	344
Vermont......................................	10,139	941	796	122	23	6,481	3,605	2,842	34
Virginia.......................................	113,788	23,251	18,129	1,458	3,664	59,752	38,997	17,466	3,289
Washington.................................	79,712	30,855	30,197	147	511	35,690	28,308	7,099	283
West Virginia...............................	30,635	6,718	3,382	141	3,195	16,841	9,470	1,358	6,013
Wisconsin	61,464	12,459	11,740	256	463	36,626	27,357	9,209	60
Wyoming.....................................	5,625	2,675	2,675	0	0	2,228	2,228	0	0

[1]Includes Ph.D., Ed.D., and comparable degrees at the doctoral level. Includes most degrees formerly classified as first-professional prior to 2010–11, such as M.D., D.D.S., and law degrees.
NOTE: Data are for postsecondary institutions participating in Title IV federal financial aid programs.

Table B-13. Degrees Conferred by Institutions of Higher Education, by State, 2018–2019— *Continued*

(Number.)

State	Master's degrees				Doctoral degrees[1]			
	Total	Public	Private not-for-profit	Private for-profit	Total	Public	Private not-for-profit	Private for-profit
UNITED STATES	833,706	386,166	380,885	66,655	187,568	94,563	85,706	7,299
Alabama................................	13,418	10,467	865	2,086	2,687	1,973	690	24
Alaska..................................	605	558	47	0	48	43	5	0
Arizona.................................	29,583	10,497	675	18,411	3,890	2,171	862	857
Arkansas...............................	5,766	5,253	495	18	1,060	971	89	0
California...............................	83,342	33,317	41,245	8,780	19,884	7,198	10,920	1,766
Colorado	15,447	9,343	3,866	2,238	2,980	1,906	563	511
Connecticut............................	11,322	3,318	7,716	288	2,195	779	1,416	0
Delaware	3,480	1,118	2,350	12	458	331	127	0
District of Columbia	13,226	133	12,035	1,058	3,415	65	3,350	0
Florida..................................	34,375	18,582	13,929	1,864	9,195	5,179	3,941	75
Georgia	20,136	12,676	5,193	2,267	4,855	2,686	1,890	279
Hawaii	1,312	868	407	37	479	479	0	0
Idaho	2,008	1,782	226	0	386	372	14	0
Illinois..................................	42,953	12,706	25,112	5,135	8,981	3,131	5,563	287
Indiana.................................	18,865	13,400	5,429	36	4,060	2,844	1,216	0
Iowa	5,865	2,859	2,848	158	2,850	1,443	1,407	0
Kansas	7,570	5,658	1,406	506	1,689	1,495	194	0
Kentucky	12,207	5,511	6,418	278	2,512	1,821	607	84
Louisiana	8,645	6,410	2,235	0	2,436	1,627	809	0
Maine...................................	2,195	811	1,384	0	716	156	560	0
Maryland...............................	21,045	11,258	9,535	252	2,947	2,109	838	0
Massachusetts........................	42,146	6,871	35,275	0	8,522	920	7,602	0
Michigan...............................	20,919	17,063	3,856	0	5,716	4,650	1,066	0
Minnesota.............................	26,203	5,514	5,822	14,867	5,707	1,816	1,165	2,726
Mississippi............................	5,216	3,399	1,808	9	1,531	1,199	332	0
Missouri................................	19,721	6,614	13,023	84	5,201	1,768	3,433	0
Montana................................	1,309	1,166	143	0	520	520	0	0
Nebraska	5,390	2,970	2,420	0	1,779	890	889	0
Nevada	2,296	1,804	445	47	1,073	564	509	0
New Hampshire.......................	9,465	1,100	8,365	0	517	170	347	0
New Jersey	17,236	9,992	7,111	133	3,338	2,348	990	0
New Mexico	3,341	3,037	281	23	683	682	1	0
New York...............................	76,229	19,747	55,067	1,415	14,677	3,204	11,472	1
North Carolina........................	19,722	12,550	6,785	387	5,170	2,872	2,283	15
North Dakota..........................	1,876	1,421	454	1	613	494	119	0
Ohio	24,153	15,639	8,446	68	6,325	4,750	1,575	0
Oklahoma..............................	6,671	5,213	1,458	0	1,640	1,352	288	0
Oregon.................................	8,152	4,400	3,680	72	2,292	1,074	1,218	0
Pennsylvania..........................	39,367	13,123	26,098	146	10,654	3,432	7,222	0
Rhode Island..........................	3,328	869	2,459	0	777	262	515	0
South Carolina	6,516	5,038	1,248	230	2,087	1,642	212	233
South Dakota	2,024	1,388	393	243	463	407	16	40
Tennessee	11,974	5,697	6,003	274	4,184	1,916	2,103	165
Texas...................................	54,215	42,640	11,086	489	11,708	8,956	2,722	30
Utah	19,343	4,035	15,192	116	1,349	953	230	166
Vermont................................	2,335	645	1,690	0	382	262	120	0
Virginia.................................	24,971	11,803	11,420	1,748	5,814	3,448	2,333	33
Washington............................	10,282	6,642	3,582	58	2,885	2,101	777	7
West Virginia..........................	5,937	2,737	391	2,809	1,139	1,009	130	0
Wisconsin	9,518	6,038	3,468	12	2,861	1,885	976	0
Wyoming	484	484	0	0	238	238	0	0

[1]Includes Ph.D., Ed.D., and comparable degrees at the doctoral level. Includes most degrees formerly classified as first-professional prior to 2010–11, such as M.D., D.D.S., and law degrees.
NOTE: Data are for postsecondary institutions participating in Title IV federal financial aid programs.

Table B-14. Race/Ethnicity and U.S. Residency Status of Students Enrolled in Institutions of Higher Education, Fall 2019

(Number; percent.)

State	Total enrolled	Percent of U.S. resident students							Nonresident alien total
		White (percent)	Black (percent)	Hispanic (may be of any race) (percent)	Asian (percent)	Pacific Islander (percent)	American Indian/ Alaska Native (percent)	Two or more races (percent)	
UNITED STATES	19,637,499	54.3	13.3	20.3	7.1	0.3	0.7	4.1	974,083
Alabama	303,030	64.0	26.1	4.2	2.1	0.1	0.6	2.8	9,107
Alaska	23,353	58.7	3.1	8.8	5.4	2.2	10.7	11.2	459
Arizona	609,144	49.4	13.0	26.4	4.1	0.5	2.3	4.3	17,481
Arkansas	158,587	69.5	15.9	7.5	2.0	0.1	0.7	4.2	4,774
California	2,715,085	27.7	6.5	44.5	15.6	0.5	0.4	4.8	146,854
Colorado	368,123	62.7	8.0	19.2	4.0	0.3	1.0	4.9	11,657
Connecticut	193,686	58.3	13.8	17.3	6.2	0.1	0.3	4.1	11,289
Delaware	59,983	58.4	22.6	10.5	4.0	0.1	0.4	4.1	4,182
District of Columbia	98,909	48.5	27.4	11.4	8.0	0.2	0.4	4.1	11,539
Florida	1,066,783	44.0	18.3	29.6	3.9	0.2	0.3	3.6	46,425
Georgia	553,755	49.0	31.6	9.4	6.2	0.1	0.3	3.3	25,790
Hawaii	60,434	17.0	1.9	13.5	32.2	6.9	0.3	28.3	3,798
Idaho	121,964	79.2	1.2	11.0	1.8	0.4	0.8	5.6	6,924
Illinois	718,504	54.8	12.7	21.3	7.8	0.1	0.2	3.0	41,317
Indiana	422,906	72.6	10.9	8.3	3.8	0.1	0.3	4.0	24,235
Iowa	218,033	79.2	6.1	8.1	3.3	0.2	0.5	2.8	10,431
Kansas	208,538	70.4	8.3	11.8	3.2	0.2	1.3	4.8	13,011
Kentucky	266,507	79.7	9.1	4.7	2.6	0.1	0.2	3.5	15,872
Louisiana	243,750	55.2	31.7	6.0	2.7	0.6	0.7	3.2	7,254
Maine	71,658	84.9	4.5	3.6	2.9	0.1	0.9	3.1	1,588
Maryland	354,913	46.1	29.5	10.8	8.5	0.2	0.3	4.6	21,927
Massachusetts	492,497	62.2	10.0	13.8	9.9	0.1	0.2	3.8	61,858
Michigan	525,491	72.1	11.9	6.2	4.9	0.1	0.6	4.2	27,826
Minnesota	402,729	66.9	15.6	6.8	6.1	0.2	0.7	3.7	14,733
Mississippi	166,969	56.8	36.1	2.8	1.7	0.1	0.5	2.0	3,082
Missouri	362,908	73.6	11.8	6.3	3.8	0.2	0.5	3.9	16,326
Montana	48,066	81.1	0.9	4.4	2.2	0.2	7.0	4.2	1,199
Nebraska	135,509	75.2	5.6	11.6	3.4	0.2	0.7	3.3	5,111
Nevada	119,771	41.2	7.9	30.4	11.5	1.0	0.7	7.4	2,107
New Hampshire	169,338	70.7	13.3	9.7	2.8	0.3	0.6	2.6	4,182
New Jersey	413,175	48.0	14.5	23.7	10.6	0.2	0.2	2.8	22,090
New Mexico	121,816	31.7	2.8	50.6	2.2	0.2	9.9	2.5	3,111
New York	1,235,812	50.4	14.6	20.3	11.2	0.2	0.4	3.0	109,322
North Carolina	568,563	59.1	22.5	9.6	3.9	0.1	1.1	3.6	19,684
North Dakota	52,354	82.6	3.5	4.0	1.5	0.1	4.3	3.9	2,285
Ohio	656,445	75.1	12.0	5.2	3.4	0.1	0.3	4.0	29,905
Oklahoma	192,656	59.7	8.4	10.9	3.3	0.2	7.4	10.1	8,569
Oregon	225,716	66.2	3.2	15.6	6.6	0.7	1.1	6.7	10,115
Pennsylvania	693,340	69.5	11.4	8.6	6.6	0.1	0.2	3.7	46,103
Rhode Island	80,077	66.9	8.0	15.2	5.4	0.1	0.3	4.1	4,543
South Carolina	241,572	64.5	23.7	5.8	2.0	0.1	0.4	3.6	5,351
South Dakota	51,941	83.0	3.4	3.8	1.4	0.1	5.5	2.7	1,715
Tennessee	323,086	69.0	18.7	5.6	3.0	0.1	0.3	3.3	8,064
Texas	1,657,691	35.7	12.6	41.5	6.7	0.1	0.3	2.9	63,516
Utah	381,283	75.1	5.3	11.4	3.0	0.7	0.7	3.9	7,401
Vermont	41,186	83.1	3.8	5.9	3.0	0.1	0.3	3.8	1,575
Virginia	557,063	57.8	19.9	9.8	7.3	0.2	0.3	4.6	19,266
Washington	363,019	58.6	5.0	15.3	10.9	0.7	1.1	8.6	22,142
West Virginia	139,159	76.3	10.1	7.2	1.9	0.4	0.5	3.6	3,697
Wisconsin	332,856	77.6	5.6	8.4	4.4	0.1	0.7	3.2	12,208
Wyoming	32,373	82.7	1.3	9.8	1.0	0.2	1.6	3.5	871

[1]NOTE: Includes special education, vocational/technical education, and alternative schools. Tabulation includes schools that offer kindergarten or higher grade. Includes enrollment of students in prekindergarten through grade 12 in schools that offer kindergarten or higher grade. Detail may not sum to totals because of rounding.

Table B-15. Average Undergraduate Tuition, Fees, and Room and Board Rates for Full-Time College Students, by State, 2019–20

(Dollars.)

State	Public 4-year					Private 4-year				Public 2-year, tuition and required fees	
	In-state				Out-of-state tuition and required fees						
	Total	Tuition and required fees	Room	Board		Total	Tuition and required fees	Room	Board	In-state	Out-of-state
UNITED STATES	21,035	9,349	6,655	5,031	27,023	45,932	32,769	7,401	5,761	3,377	8,126
Alabama.........................	20,497	10,323	5,703	4,471	26,517	27,086	16,743	5,198	5,146	4,854	9,707
Alaska	19,619	8,297	5,843	5,479	26,767	27,774	19,682	4,102	3,989	NA	NA
Arizona..........................	24,016	11,072	7,610	5,334	27,417	22,652	12,895	5,339	4,418	2,151	7,642
Arkansas	18,223	8,689	5,486	4,049	21,460	32,388	23,875	4,370	4,143	3,398	4,688
California.......................	23,037	8,192	8,426	6,419	32,177	51,750	37,009	8,180	6,561	1,270	8,194
Colorado	22,185	9,144	6,541	6,499	30,773	37,020	23,791	7,813	5,416	3,355	7,103
Connecticut...................	27,564	13,886	7,491	6,186	35,197	58,574	43,242	8,873	6,459	4,516	13,490
Delaware	24,358	11,091	7,906	5,361	31,582	27,406	14,858	6,184	6,364	NA	NA
District of Columbia	NA	6,020	NA	NA	12,704	60,830	44,134	11,197	5,499	NA	NA
Florida...........................	15,237	4,463	6,330	4,444	18,514	39,850	27,381	7,137	5,332	2,506	9,111
Georgia	18,554	7,457	6,745	4,352	23,167	42,802	29,752	7,314	5,736	3,156	8,398
Hawaii	21,854	10,109	5,785	5,960	31,774	32,126	17,977	6,414	7,734	3,225	8,391
Idaho.............................	16,338	7,518	4,268	4,552	24,845	14,380	6,429	2,602	5,349	3,335	8,295
Illinois...........................	25,806	14,455	6,143	5,208	29,515	49,076	35,570	7,704	5,802	4,035	11,450
Indiana	19,985	9,268	5,634	5,083	29,533	46,504	34,263	6,363	5,878	4,500	8,661
Iowa..............................	19,809	9,373	5,842	4,593	27,346	44,850	35,019	4,880	4,952	5,306	6,664
Kansas	19,101	9,088	5,260	4,753	23,745	33,811	24,179	4,699	4,933	3,542	4,695
Kentucky	21,799	10,888	6,156	4,755	26,048	36,281	26,928	4,563	4,790	4,395	14,826
Louisiana	19,498	9,571	5,865	4,062	22,128	53,025	39,482	7,414	6,129	4,166	8,282
Maine............................	20,458	10,103	5,323	5,032	28,523	54,375	40,353	7,028	6,994	3,778	6,642
Maryland........................	22,504	9,714	7,305	5,485	27,984	58,737	44,048	8,410	6,279	4,330	10,308
Massachusetts.................	27,618	13,729	8,587	5,302	31,894	64,196	47,980	9,463	6,754	5,336	10,690
Michigan	24,086	13,315	5,341	5,430	36,832	39,785	29,405	5,335	5,046	3,703	6,564
Minnesota	21,611	11,748	5,579	4,284	24,442	45,198	34,321	5,813	5,064	5,566	6,151
Mississippi.....................	19,080	8,604	6,250	4,226	19,402	27,219	18,612	4,493	4,114	3,432	5,835
Missouri.........................	18,734	8,992	5,759	3,983	20,877	37,083	26,377	6,284	4,422	3,545	6,797
Montana.........................	16,732	6,967	4,457	5,308	25,239	41,541	31,724	4,795	5,022	3,871	8,596
Nebraska........................	19,520	8,582	5,982	4,957	22,152	35,110	25,313	5,663	4,134	3,103	3,969
Nevada...........................	17,987	6,023	6,358	5,606	21,678	40,471	26,284	6,946	7,241	NA	NA
New Hampshire................	28,734	16,679	7,480	4,575	30,594	47,517	33,446	8,842	5,228	7,130	15,335
New Jersey	28,372	14,360	9,052	4,960	29,435	52,632	38,652	8,189	5,791	4,779	8,092
New Mexico	16,193	7,152	4,887	4,154	19,181	36,962	25,363	6,686	4,913	1,724	6,624
New York........................	23,875	8,467	10,180	5,228	22,669	56,958	41,404	9,331	6,224	5,476	9,228
North Carolina.................	17,569	7,228	5,816	4,525	23,357	48,007	35,379	6,556	6,072	2,494	8,658
North Dakota...................	17,449	8,628	3,930	4,892	13,936	23,702	15,732	3,316	4,655	5,073	6,031
Ohio	22,388	9,902	6,869	5,617	24,830	45,869	34,009	6,141	5,720	4,330	7,528
Oklahoma.......................	16,960	8,009	4,816	4,134	21,695	39,275	29,429	4,882	4,965	4,150	9,484
Oregon...........................	23,582	10,813	7,573	5,196	32,068	55,132	42,202	6,754	6,176	4,881	8,640
Pennsylvania...................	27,403	15,565	7,127	4,711	30,222	56,756	42,812	7,668	6,277	5,348	13,480
Rhode Island...................	25,592	13,105	7,858	4,629	30,871	59,321	43,919	9,293	6,108	4,700	12,544
South Carolina	22,790	12,497	6,399	3,894	32,853	36,235	26,270	4,967	4,998	4,916	10,206
South Dakota	17,298	8,978	4,092	4,228	12,866	33,606	25,353	4,019	4,233	6,469	6,043
Tennessee	20,360	10,164	5,365	4,831	24,786	40,037	29,200	6,108	4,730	4,379	16,937
Texas.............................	18,711	8,598	5,360	4,752	24,889	48,032	36,014	6,718	5,300	2,380	6,373
Utah	14,619	6,700	3,671	4,248	21,273	15,707	7,600	4,092	4,015	3,929	12,460
Vermont..........................	29,665	17,083	7,980	4,602	41,057	61,021	46,445	8,073	6,503	6,654	13,398
Virginia..........................	25,074	13,655	6,390	5,028	35,831	34,748	23,493	6,009	5,246	5,237	11,529
Washington.....................	19,846	7,168	6,725	5,953	30,155	52,333	39,791	6,531	6,011	4,468	6,500
West Virginia...................	19,034	8,195	5,786	5,053	22,242	22,446	12,673	4,679	5,094	4,344	9,976
Wisconsin	17,784	8,764	5,497	3,523	25,522	46,798	35,554	6,495	4,749	4,476	6,499
Wyoming	14,901	4,747	4,493	5,661	14,803	NA	NA	NA	NA	4,136	10,101

NA = Not applicable.

NOTES AND DEFINITIONS: REGION AND STATE EDUCATION STATISTICS

TABLES B-1 AND B-2

Source: U.S. Census Bureau. *American Community Survey, 2019.* Tables B15001, C15002, C15002A, C15002B, C15002D, C15002I, S0901, and C14002. (ACS 1-Year Estimates) http://data.census.gov.

Tables B-1 and B-2 are from the American Community Survey (ACS), the sample survey that has replaced the long form of the decennial census. The sample data are estimates of the actual figures that would have been obtained from a complete count. Estimates derived from a sample are expected to be different from the 100-percent figures because they are subject to sampling and nonsampling errors. Sampling error in data arises from the selection of people and housing units included in the sample. Nonsampling error affects both sample and 100-percent data. It is introduced as a result of errors that may occur during the data collection and processing phases of the census. Conclusions should not be based on small numbers or small differences and users should consult the ACS website to determine the appropriate margins of error. The ACS is ongoing and data are released on an annual basis for all regions and states.

Due to the impact of the COVID-19 pandemic on data collection for the ACS, the U.S. Census Bureau will not be releasing 2020 1-Year Estimates.

For additional information about the American Community Survey, see https://www.census.gov/programs-surveys/acs.

Educational Attainment. In the ACS, respondents are classified according to the highest degree or the highest level of school completed. Statistics for educational attainment only include persons 25 years old and over. The question includes instructions for people currently enrolled in school to report the level of the previous grade attended or the highest degree received.

High school graduate or higher. This category includes persons who have received a high school diploma or its equivalent (for example, GED), and those who reported any level higher than a high school diploma.

Bachelor's degree or higher. This category includes persons who have received bachelor's degrees, master's degrees, professional school degrees (such as law school or medical school degrees), and doctoral degrees.

Geographic Definitions

Data are presented for the four major regions of the United States. These groups of states are as follows:

Northeast: Connecticut, Maine, Massachusetts, New Hampshire, New Jersey, New York, Pennsylvania, Rhode Island, and Vermont

Midwest: Illinois, Indiana, Iowa, Kansas, Michigan, Minnesota, Missouri, Nebraska, North Dakota, Ohio, South Dakota, and Wisconsin

South: Alabama, Arkansas, Delaware, District of Columbia, Florida, Georgia, Kentucky, Louisiana, Maryland, Mississippi, North Carolina, Oklahoma, South Carolina, Tennessee, Texas, Virginia, and West Virginia

West: Alaska, Arizona, California, Colorado, Hawaii, Idaho, Montana, Nevada, New Mexico, Oregon, Utah, Washington, and Wyoming

Income and Poverty. The Census Bureau reports income from several major household surveys and programs. The Census Bureau recommends using the ACS for single-year estimates of income and poverty at the state level.

330 THE ALMANAC OF AMERICAN EDUCATION

Total income is the sum of the amounts reported separately for wages, salary, commissions, bonuses, or tips; self-employment income from own nonfarm or farm businesses, including proprietorships and partnerships; interest, dividends, net rental income, royalty income, or income from estates and trusts; Social Security or Railroad Retirement income; Supplemental Security Income (SSI); any public assistance or welfare payments from the state or local welfare office; retirement, survivor, or disability pensions; and any other sources of income received regularly such as Veterans' (VA) payments, unemployment compensation, child support, or alimony. Receipts not counted as income include various "lump sum" payments, such as capital gains or inheritances. The total represents the amount of income received before deductions for personal income taxes, Social Security, bond purchases, union dues, Medicare deductions, and the like.

Poverty status is based on the definition prescribed by the U.S. Office of Management and Budget as the standard to be used by federal agencies for statistical purposes.

School enrollment is enrollment in a regular school, either public or private, including nursery schools, kindergarten, and elementary schools, as well as schooling that leads to a high school diploma or college degree. Schools supported and controlled primarily by the federal, state, or local government are defined as public schools (including tribal schools). Schools primarily supported and controlled by religious organizations or other private groups are considered private schools.

TABLES B-3 THROUGH B-15

Sources: U.S. Department of Education, National Center for Education Statistics, Institute of Education Sciences, *Digest of Education Statistics, 2019 and 2020.* https://nces.ed.gov/programs/digest/current_tables.asp

U.S. Department of Education, National Center for Education Statistics (NCES), Common Core of Data (CCD), Tables 2 and 3. https://nces.ed.gov/ccd/tables/201920_summary_2.asp; https://nces.ed.gov/ccd/tables/201920_summary_3.asp

U.S. Department of Education, National Center for Education Statistics (NCES), Common Core of Data (CCD), Virtual Schools, Counts, and Enrollment, Table 3. https://nces.ed.gov/ccd/tables/201920_Virtual_Schools_table_3.asp

A **charter school** is a school that provides free public elementary and/or secondary education to eligible students under a specific charter granted by the state legislature or other appropriate authority; the school must have also been designated as a charter school by these authorities. Charter schools can be administered by regular school districts, State Education Agencies (SEAs), or chartering organizations.

A **Title I eligible** school is a school designated under appropriate state and federal regulations as being high poverty and eligible for participation in programs (such as remedial reading or remedial math) authorized by Title I of P.L. 107–110. A Title I school is one in which the percentage of children from low-income families is at least as high as the percentage of children from low-income families served by the LEA as a whole, or a school designated by the LEA as Title I eligible because 35 percent or more of the children are from low-income families. A Title I schoolwide school is a school in which all the students are designated under appropriate state and federal regulations as eligible for participation in Title I programs authorized by Title I of P.L. 107–110. The number of students who received Title I services is from the Public School Data File of the Schools and Staffing Survey.

STUDENTS WHO ARE ELIGIBLE FOR FREE OR REDUCED-PRICE LUNCH

The Free and Reduced-Price Lunch Program is a program under the National School

Lunch Act that provides cash subsidies for free or reduced-price meals to students based on family size and income criteria. Participation in the Free and Reduced-Price Lunch Program depends on income, and eligibility is often used to estimate student needs.

STUDENTS WITH INDIVIDUAL EDUCATION PROGRAM

An Individualized Education Program (IEP) is a written instructional plan for students with disabilities who are designated as special education students under IDEA (Individuals with Disabilities Education Act). An IEP includes a statement of present levels of educational performance of a child; a statement of annual goals, including short-term instructional objectives; a statement of specific educational services to be provided and the extent to which the child will be able to participate in regular educational programs; a projected date for initiation and the anticipated duration of services; appropriate objectives, criteria, and evaluation procedures; and schedules for determining, on at least an annual basis, whether instructional objectives are being achieved.

STUDENTS WHO ARE ENGLISH-LANGUAGE LEARNERS

This category includes the number of students who are served in appropriate programs of language assistance (e.g., English as a Second Language, High Intensity Language Training, and bilingual education). This designation changed from Limited-English Proficient (LEP) to English Language Learners (ELL) in the 2001–2002 school year.

PRIVATE SCHOOLS

Since 1989, the Census Bureau has conducted the biennial Private School Universe Survey (PSS) for NCES. The PSS is designed to generate biennial data on the total number of private schools, students, and teachers and to build a universe of private schools in all of the states and the District of Columbia to serve as a sampling frame of private schools for NCES sample surveys. The target population for the PSS is every school in all of the states and the District of Columbia that are not primarily supported by public funds, provide instruction for one or more grades between kindergarten and grade 12 (or comparable ungraded levels), and have one or more teachers. Organizations or institutions that provide support for home schooling, but do not provide classroom instruction, are not included. Although the PSS has begun to collect limited data on the many private schools for which kindergarten is the highest grade, the data in this volume are for (traditional) schools that include at least one grade between grades 1 and 12.

A private school is controlled by an individual or agency other than a state, a subdivision of a state, or the federal government; is usually supported primarily by nonpublic funds; and the operation of its program does not rest with publicly elected or appointed officials. Private schools include both nonprofit and proprietary institutions.

Data for private schools in Arkansas, Colorado, Washington, D.C., Idaho, Indiana, and Nebraska, should be interpreted with caution. The coefficient of variation for these estimates is larger than 25 percent.

PUBLIC SCHOOL STAFF

The number of teachers represents full-time equivalent teachers employed within the state. Instructional aides directly assist teachers in providing instruction. Instructional coordinators help teachers through curriculum development and in-service training. Support staff includes those involved with food, health, library, maintenance, transportation, security, and other services in public schools. School administrators are principals and assistant principals. School district administrators include the Local Education Agency (LEA) superintendents, deputies, assistant superintendents, and other persons with district-wide responsibilities.

REVENUES

The state data include adjustments made by NCES. Values that were missing and not reported elsewhere in the survey were imputed based on corresponding proportions in reporting states. Other adjustments were made when a single value was reported that included two or more categories. NCES distributed portions of the single reported value to the missing items. In Nebraska and Wyoming, the fiscal data do not include prekindergarten. In Illinois and Wisconsin, revenues for charter schools are not included. In addition to these adjustments, the NPEFS may also include state-run education programs. Consequently, these numbers may differ from the state totals in Table C, which are derived from a different survey.

Revenues from federal sources include direct grants-in-aid from the federal government, federal grants-in-aid through the state or an intermediate agency, and other revenue in lieu of taxes to compensate a school district for nontaxable federal institutions within a district's boundaries.

State revenues include revenues that can be used without restriction, revenues for categorical purposes, and revenues in lieu of taxation. Also included are revenues from payments made by a state for the benefit of the Local Education Agency (LEA) or contributions of equipment or supplies. Such revenues include the payment of a pension fund by the state on behalf of an LEA employee for services rendered and contributions of fixed assets (property, plant, or equipment), such as school buses and textbooks.

Revenues from local sources include local property and non-property tax revenues, taxes levied or assessed by an LEA, revenues from a local government to the LEA, tuition received, transportation fees, earnings on investments from LEA holdings, net revenues from food services (gross receipts less gross expenditures), net revenues from student activities (gross receipts less gross expenditures), and other revenues (textbook sales, donations, and property rentals). Intermediate revenues were included in local revenue totals. Intermediate revenues are derived from sources other than Local or State Education Agencies; these sources operate at an intermediate level between Local and State Education Agencies and possess independent fundraising capabilities (such as county or municipal agencies).

EXPENDITURES

The state data include adjustments made by NCES. Values that were missing and not reported elsewhere in the survey were imputed based on proportions in reporting states. Other adjustments were made when a single value was reported that included two or more categories. NCES distributed portions of the single reported value to the missing items. In Nebraska and Wyoming, the fiscal data do not include prekindergarten. In Illinois and Wisconsin, expenditures for charter schools are not included. In addition to these adjustments, the NPEFS may include state-run education programs. Consequently, these numbers may differ from the state totals in Table C, which come from a different survey.

Current expenditures consist of expenditures for the categories of instruction, support services, and non-instructional services for salaries; employee benefits; purchased services and supplies; and payments by the state made for or on behalf of school systems. These expenditures do not include expenditures for debt service, capital outlay, and property (e.g., equipment), or direct costs (e.g., Head Start, adult education, community colleges, etc.) and community services expenditures.

Instruction and instruction-related expenses comprise current expenditures for activities that deal directly with the interaction between students and teachers. These expenditures include teacher salaries and benefits, supplies (such as textbooks), instructional staff support (for example, salaries for librarians and instructional specialists), and purchased instructional services.

Support services expenditures consist of current expenditures for activities supporting instruction. These services include operation and maintenance of buildings, school administration, student support services (e.g., nurses, therapists, and guidance counselors), student transportation, school district administration, business services, research, and data processing.

Non-instruction expenditures are mostly for food service, but also consist of expenditures for enterprise operations, such as bookstores and interscholastic athletics.

DROPOUTS

Status dropouts are 16- to 24-year-olds who are not enrolled in school and who have not completed a high school program, regardless of when they left school. People who have received GED credentials are counted as high school completers. Data are based on sample surveys of the entire population in the given age range residing within the United States, including both noninstitutionalized persons (e.g., those living in households, college housing, or military housing located within the United States) and institutionalized persons (e.g., those living in prisons, nursing facilities, or other healthcare facilities). Totals include other racial/ethnic groups not separately shown. Race categories exclude persons of Hispanic ethnicity.

HIGHER EDUCATION

The Integrated Postsecondary Education Data System (IPEDS) surveys approximately 10,000 postsecondary institutions, including universities, colleges, and institutions offering technical and vocational education beyond the high school level. This survey, which began in 1986, replaced the Higher Education General Information Survey (HEGIS). IPEDS is made up of eight integrated components that obtain information on who provides postsecondary education (institutions), who participates in it and completes it (students), what programs are offered and which ones are completed, and the specific human and financial resources involved in the provision of institutionally based postsecondary education. These components are organized into the following categories: Institutional Characteristics, including instructional activity; Fall Enrollment, including age and residence; Enrollment in Occupationally Specific Programs; Completions; Finance; Staff; Salaries of Full-Time Instructional Faculty; and Academic Libraries.

Institutions of higher education include those with courses leading to an associate's degree or higher, or those with courses accepted for credit toward such degrees. A public institution is controlled and operated by publicly elected or appointed officials and derives its primary support from public funds. A private institution is controlled by an individual or agency other than a state, a subdivision of a state, or the federal government; it is usually primarily supported by nonpublic funds, and the operation of its program does not rest with publicly elected or appointed officials. Private institutions comprise both not-for-profit and proprietary institutions.

Full-time students include undergraduate students enrolled for 12 or more semester credits, 12 or more quarter credits, or 24 or more contact hours a week each term; graduate students enrolled for 9 or more semester credits or 9 or more quarter credits, or students involved in thesis or dissertation preparation who are considered full time students by the institution; and first-professional students (as defined by the institution).

Types of institutions include the following:

Degree-granting institutions, which offer associate's, bachelor's, master's, doctoral and/or first-professional degrees.

Level categories include four-year and higher (four-year) institutions, at least two but less than four-year (two-year) institutions, and less than two-year institutions.

A four-year institution is a postsecondary institution that offers programs of at least four years' duration or programs at or above the baccalaureate level. This category includes schools that only offer post-baccalaureate certificates and those that only offer graduate programs. Also included are freestanding medical, law, and other first-professional schools.

A two-year institution is a postsecondary institution that offers programs of at least two years' duration but less than four years' duration. This category includes occupational and vocational schools with programs of at least 1,800 hours and academic institutions with programs of less than four years' duration. It does not include bachelor's degree–granting institutions where the baccalaureate program can be completed in three years.

Control categories are public, private not-for-profit, and private for-profit.

Undergraduate students are registered at an institution of higher education and are working in a program leading to a baccalaureate degree or other formal award below the baccalaureate, such as an associate degree.

Postbaccalaureate students are working towards master's or doctor's degree or are enrolled in graduate-level classes, but not enrolled in degree programs.

Race/ethnicity categories are categories used to describe groups to which individuals belong, identify with, or belong to in the eyes of the community. A person may be counted in only one group. Classification is based on self-identification. Race categories exclude persons of Hispanic ethnicity.

A nonresident alien is a person who is not a citizen or national of the United States, and who is in this country on a visa or temporary basis; a nonresident alien does not have the right to remain in the United States indefinitely.

Migration refers to the movement of students from their home state of residence to another state to attend a postsecondary institution. The percentages in columns 123 and 124 refer to all first-time postsecondary students enrolled in degree granting institutions in fall 2012.

An associate's degree is a degree granted for the successful completion of a sub-baccalaureate program of studies, and usually requires at least two years (or the equivalent) of full-time college-level study. This category also includes degrees granted in a cooperative or work-study program.

A bachelor's degree is a degree granted for the successful completion of a baccalaureate program of studies, and usually requires at least four years (or the equivalent) of full-time college-level study. This category includes degrees granted in a cooperative or work-study program.

A master's degree is awarded for successful completion of a program generally requiring 1 or 2 years of full-time, college-level study beyond the bachelor's degree. One type of master's degree, including the master of arts degree (M.A.), and the master of science degree (M.S.), is awarded in the liberal arts and sciences for advanced scholarship in a subject field or discipline and demonstrated ability to perform scholarly research. A second type of master's degree is awarded for the completion of a professionally oriented program. These include master's degrees in education (M.Ed.), business administration (M.B.A.), fine arts (M.F.A.), music (M.M.), social work (M.S.W.), and public administration (M.P.A.) A third type of master's degree is awarded in professional fields for study beyond the first-professional degree, such as the master of laws (LL.M.) and the masters of science in various medical specializations. Some master's degrees—such as divinity degrees (M.Div. or M.H.L./Rav), which were formerly classified as "first-professional"— may require more than 2 years of full-time study beyond the bachelor's degree.

A doctor's degree is an earned degree that generally carries the title of Doctor. The Doctor of Philosophy degree (Ph.D.) is the highest academic degree and requires mastery within a field of knowledge and demonstrated ability to perform scholarly research. Other doctor's degrees are awarded for fulfilling specialized requirements in professional fields, such as education (Ed.D.), musical arts (D.M.A.), business administration (D.B.A.), and engineering (D.Eng. or D.E.S.). Many doctor's degrees in academic and professional fields require an earned master's degree as a prerequisite. The doctor's degree classification includes most degrees that NCES formerly classified as first-professional degrees. Such degrees are awarded in the fields of dentistry (D.D.S. or D.M.D.), medicine (M.D.), optometry (O.D.), osteopathic medicine (D.O.), pharmacy (Pharm.D.), podiatry (D.P.M., Pod.D., or D.P.), veterinary medicine (D.V.M.), chiropractic (D.C. or D.C.M.), and law (L.L.B. or J.D.).

Tuition and required fees are payments or charges for instruction or compensation for services, privileges, or the use of equipment, books, or other goods. Data are for the entire academic year and are average charges. In-state tuition and fees were weighted by the number of full-time-equivalent undergraduates but were not adjusted to reflect student residency. Out-of-state tuition and fees were weighted by the number of first-time freshmen attending the institution in fall 2018 from out of state.

PART C

COUNTY EDUCATION STATISTICS

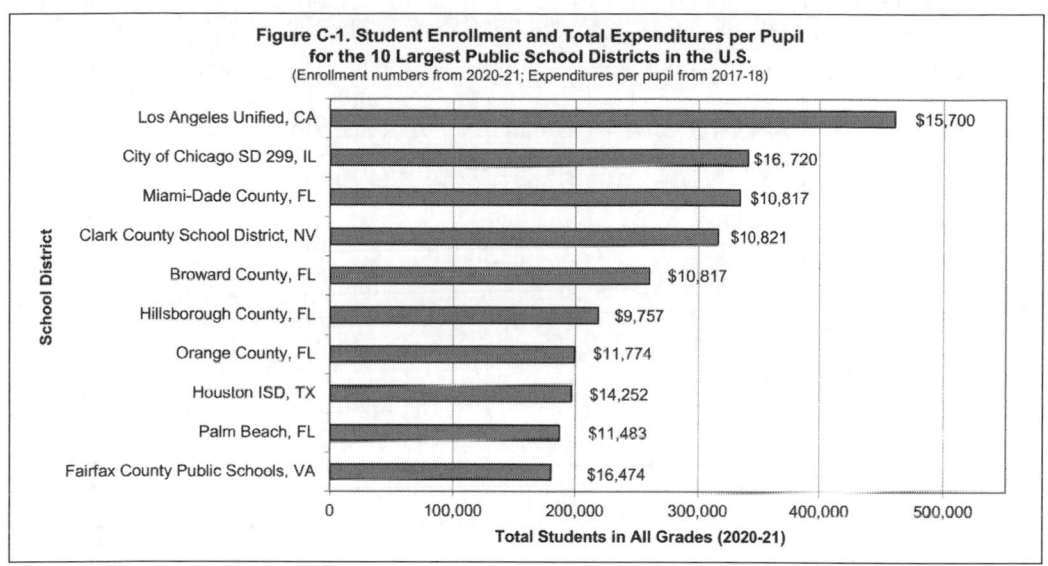

Figure C-1. Student Enrollment and Total Expenditures per Pupil for the 10 Largest Public School Districts in the U.S. (Enrollment numbers from 2020-21; Expenditures per pupil from 2017-18)

In 2020-21, the largest school district in the country was the Los Angeles Unified School District in California, which enrolled 460,633 students in all grades. The next largest school districts were the City of Chicago School District 299 in Illinois, with 341,382 students, and Miami-Dade County School District in Florida, which had 334,261 students enrolled. (Table C-1)

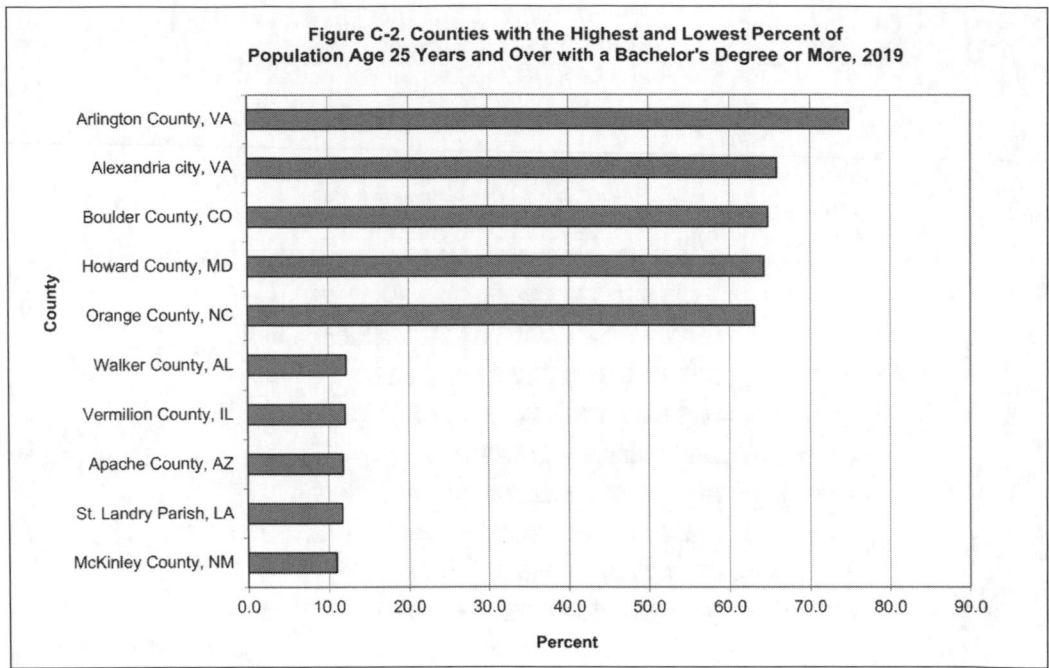

Figure C-2. Counties with the Highest and Lowest Percent of Population Age 25 Years and Over with a Bachelor's Degree or More, 2019

In 2019, there were 6 counties where more than 97 percent of the population age 25 years old and over had graduated from high school. The highest proportion was 98.5 percent of the population in Ozaukee County, Wisconsin. Four U.S. counties had high school attainment levels of less than 70 percent: Merced County, California; Cameron County, Texas; Hidalgo County, Texas; and Webb County, Texas. (Table C-2)

In 2019, 11 counties had 60 percent or more of the population with a bachelor's degree or more. Arlington County, Virginia (which is near Washington, DC), led the way with 74.9 percent of population age 25 years and over having bachelor's degrees or more. Five of the top ten counties were in the Washington, DC, metropolitan area. The others were Boulder County, Colorado (64.8 percent with bachelor's degrees or higher), Orange County, North Carolina (63.1 percent), Hamilton County, Indiana (63.0 percent), New York County, New York (62.0 percent), and Williamson County, Tennessee (61.8 percent). McKinley County, New Mexico, had the lowest college attainment rate, with 11.0 percent of the population having a bachelor's degree or more. (Table C-2)

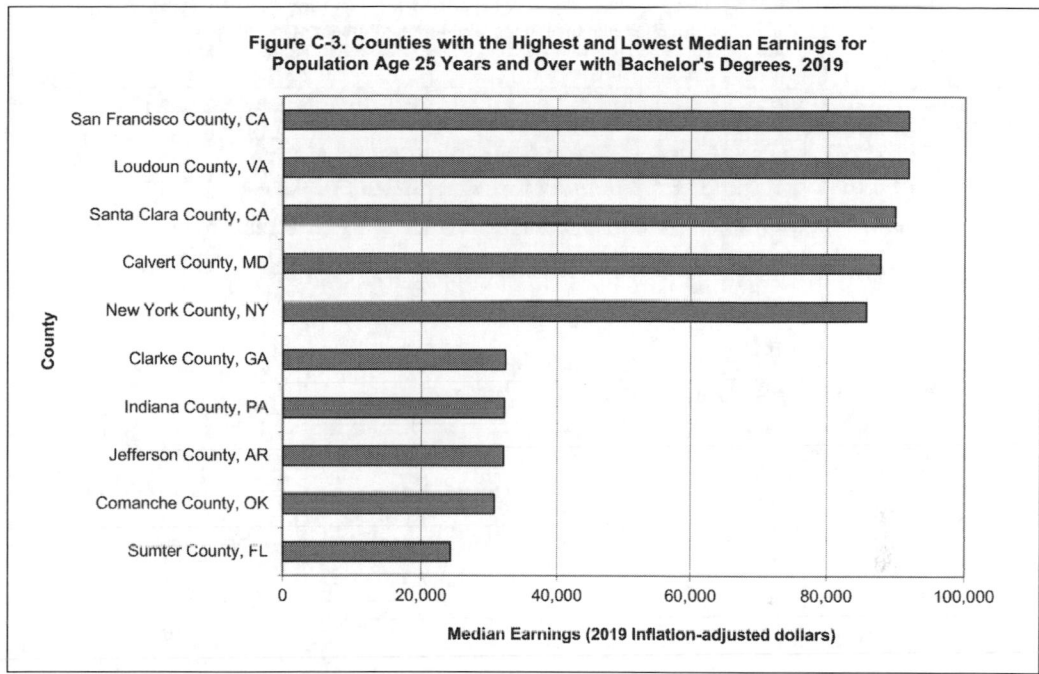

Figure C-3. Counties with the Highest and Lowest Median Earnings for Population Age 25 Years and Over with Bachelor's Degrees, 2019

Arlington County, Virginia, was the county with the highest median earnings for 2019 at $80,929. Six counties had median earnings over $70,000. Sumter County, Florida, had the lowest median earnings: $23,864. Fourteen counties had median earnings less than $30,000. (Table C-2)

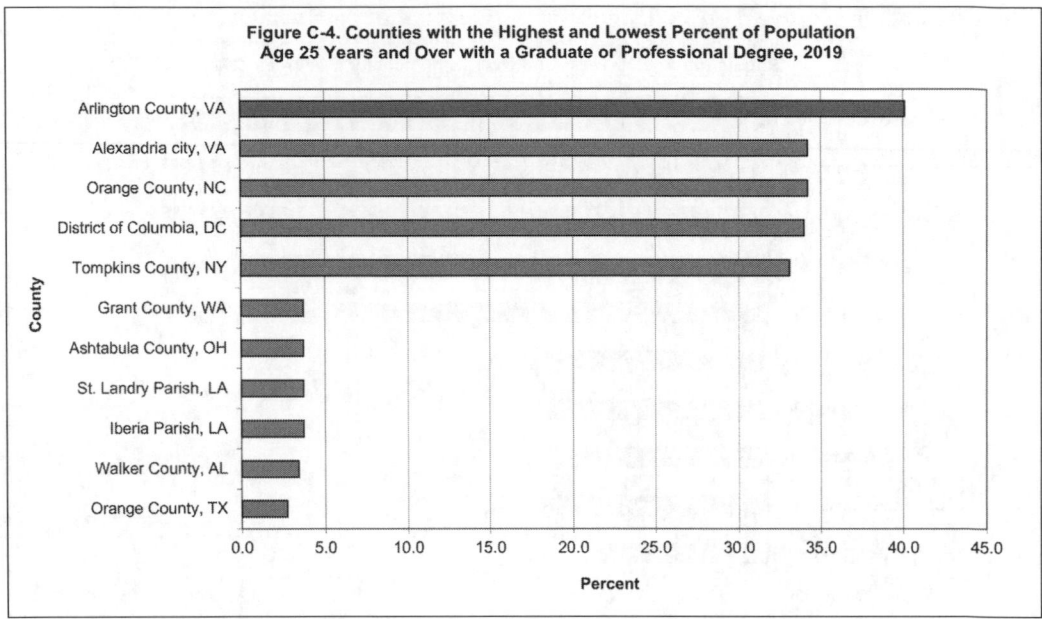

Figure C-4. Counties with the Highest and Lowest Percent of Population Age 25 Years and Over with a Graduate or Professional Degree, 2019

Arlington County, Virginia, also had the highest percent of people with graduate or professional degrees (40.1 percent) in the country, followed by Alexandria city, Virginia (34.2 percent). Orange County, Texas, was the county with the smallest proportion of the population holding a graduate or professional degree (2.7 percent), followed by Walker County, Alabama (3.4 percent). (Table C-2)

Table C-1. Characteristics of the 20 Largest Public School Districts in Each State

(Number; dollars.)

State/School District	County Name	Number of Operational Schools (2020-21)	Total Students in All Grades (2020-21)	Full-Time Equivalent Teachers (2020-21)	Pupil/ Teacher Ratio (2020-21)	Total Revenue per Pupil (2017-18)	Total Expenditures per Pupil (2017-18)
ALABAMA							
Auburn City	Lee County	13	8,971	501.5	17.9	$14,506	$13,042
Autauga County	Autauga County	15	8,955	470.5	19.0	$8,896	$8,801
Baldwin County	Baldwin County	46	30,210	1,895.4	15.9	$11,710	$10,670
Birmingham City	Jefferson County	51	21,597	1,208.4	17.9	$12,052	$11,696
Cullman County	Cullman County	28	9,312	524.1	17.8	$10,306	$10,112
Decatur City	Morgan County	20	8,781	543.5	16.2	$12,100	$15,507
Elmore County	Elmore County	16	11,519	592.0	19.5	$9,327	$9,007
Hoover City	Jefferson County	18	13,640	979.9	13.9	$12,798	$12,728
Huntsville City	Madison County	46	23,514	1,447.6	16.2	$11,991	$11,737
Jefferson County	Jefferson County	58	35,336	1,993.3	17.7	$10,440	$10,145
Lee County	Lee County	14	9,310	565.7	16.5	$10,376	$10,664
Limestone County	Limestone County	17	13,041	478.7	27.3	$9,685	$9,404
Madison City	Madison County	11	11,804	711.0	16.6	$11,089	$10,795
Madison County	Madison County	30	19,142	1,019.9	18.8	$10,002	$9,858
Mobile County	Mobile County	91	52,460	2,960.8	17.7	$10,284	$10,109
Montgomery County	Montgomery County	52	27,399	1,436.0	19.1	$10,423	$9,995
Shelby County	Shelby County	31	20,438	1,227.0	16.7	$10,910	$10,858
St Clair County	St. Clair County	20	9,407	539.2	17.5	$9,474	$9,168
Tuscaloosa City	Tuscaloosa County	20	10,744	664.7	16.2	$12,832	$20,168
Tuscaloosa County	Tuscaloosa County	35	18,766	1,069.6	17.6	$10,255	$11,753
ALASKA							
Anchorage School District	Anchorage Municipality	97	41,856	2,624.9	16.0	$15,586	$15,936
Bering Strait School District	Nome Census Area	15	1,839	170.0	10.8	$36,975	$33,989
Chugach School District	Anchorage Municipality	4	694	18.2	38.2	$15,561	$16,482
Craig City School District	Prince of Wales-Hyder Census Area	4	867	30.3	28.6	$16,496	$16,911
Delta/Greely School Dictrict	Southeast Fairbanks Census Area	5	775	43.9	17.7	$16,167	$15,988
Denali Borough School District	Denali Borough	4	1,206	30.9	39.0	$11,436	$10,466
Fairbanks North Star Borough School District	Fairbanks North Star Borough	36	11,386	714.2	15.9	$17,856	$17,176
Galena City School District	Yukon-Koyukuk Census Area	4	9,366	77.9	120.2	$7,601	$7,578
Juneau Borough School District	Juneau City and Borough	15	4,124	286.5	14.4	$19,347	$17,948
Kenai Peninsula Borough School District	Kenai Peninsula Borough	42	7,962	548.4	14.5	$17,836	$17,799
Ketchikan Gateway Borough School District	Ketchikan Gateway Borough	9	2,161	160.6	13.5	$18,560	$17,913
Kodiak Island Borough School District	Kodiak Island Borough	12	2,294	162.0	14.2	$22,436	$22,028
Lower Kuskokwim School District	Bethel Census Area	29	4,082	274.1	14.9	$39,461	$39,652
Lower Yukon School District	Kusilvak Census Area	11	2,103	122.3	17.2	$29,349	$33,246
Matanuska-Susitna Borough School District	Matanuska-Susitna Borough	47	18,220	1,009.3	18.1	$15,884	$15,252
Nenana City School District	Yukon-Koyukuk Census Area	2	1,909	23.4	81.6	$9,424	$9,317
North Slope Borough School District	North Slope Borough	12	2,138	172.5	12.4	$34,936	$36,620
Northwest Arctic Borough School District	Northwest Arctic Borough	13	2,050	138.5	14.8	$31,834	$35,814
Sitka School District	Sitka City and Borough	6	1,151	97.8	11.8	$21,883	$21,135
Yukon-Koyukuk School District	Fairbanks North Star Borough	10	4,331	62.9	68.9	$18,503	$18,977
ARIZONA							
Cartwright Elementary District	Maricopa County	21	15,177	780.2	19.5	$8,532	$8,386
Chandler Unified District #80	Maricopa County	44	43,790	2,491.5	17.6	$8,961	$8,934
Deer Valley Unified District	Maricopa County	40	32,061	1,928.6	16.6	$9,220	$8,730
Dysart Unified District	Maricopa County	26	23,011	1,201.1	19.2	$8,744	$7,978
Gilbert Unified District	Maricopa County	39	32,661	1,931.5	16.0	$8,543	$8,205
Glendale Union High School District	Maricopa County	11	16,462	734.4	22.4	$10,694	$9,951
Higley Unified School District	Maricopa County	16	12,679	729.7	17.4	$9,292	$8,311
Kyrene Elementary District	Maricopa County	26	15,632	949.9	16.5	$9,378	$9,492
Marana Unified District	Pima County	20	12,395	751.4	16.5	$9,350	$9,569
Mesa Unified District	Maricopa County	78	57,956	3,321.3	17.5	$9,158	$8,982
Paradise Valley Unified District	Maricopa County	44	29,109	1,008.1	16.1	$10,186	$9,813
Peoria Unified School District	Maricopa County	44	35,329	1,959.6	18.0	$8,622	$8,183
Phoenix Union High School District	Maricopa County	19	27,037	1,479.8	18.3	$13,027	$13,141
Scottsdale Unified District	Maricopa County	30	21,496	1,272.1	16.9	$10,572	$10,516
Sunnyside Unified District	Pima County	22	14,942	767.4	19.5	$8,346	$7,989
Tempe Union High School District	Maricopa County	8	12,868	620.1	20.8	$9,960	$8,591
Tolleson Union High School District	Maricopa County	8	12,442	567.2	21.9	$9,050	$7,506
Tucson Unified District	Pima County	90	41,898	2,742.4	15.3	$9,640	$9,856

NA = Not available.
X = Not applicable.

Table C-1. Characteristics of the 20 Largest Public School Districts in Each State—*Continued*

(Number; dollars.)

State/School District	County Name	Number of Operational Schools (2020-21)	Total Students in All Grades (2020-21)	Full-Time Equivalent Teachers (2020-21)	Pupil/ Teacher Ratio (2020-21)	Total Revenue per Pupil (2017-18)	Total Expenditures per Pupil (2017-18)
ARIZONA—*(Continued)*							
Vail Unified District	Pima County	23	13,642	669.8	20.4	$8,928	$8,844
Washington Elementary School District	Maricopa County	32	20,511	1,308.4	15.7	$9,504	$9,544
ARKANSAS							
Benton School District	Saline County	7	5,485	361.5	15.2	$9,904	$9,353
Bentonville School District	Benton County	23	17,970	1,193.1	15.1	$12,400	$11,934
Bryant School District	Saline County	12	9,353	610.7	15.3	$10,361	$12,232
Cabot School District	Lonoke County	16	10,471	669.9	15.6	$9,623	$9,173
Conway School District	Faulkner County	17	10,035	624.2	16.1	$10,601	$10,894
El Dorado School District	Union County	6	4,150	305.9	13.6	$10,560	$9,308
Fayetteville School District	Washington County	16	10,233	705.8	14.5	$12,967	$12,165
Fort Smith School District	Sebastian County	26	14,361	1,033.8	13.9	$11,523	$11,208
Jonesboro School District	Craighead County	11	6,616	444.4	14.9	$11,467	$11,691
Lake Hamilton School District	Garland County	6	4,342	249.8	17.4	$10,444	$10,094
Little Rock School District	Pulaski County	43	21,612	1,609.5	13.4	$14,989	$14,861
North Little Rock School District	Pulaski County	14	7,930	587.3	13.5	$12,415	$12,369
Pulaski County Special School District	Pulaski County	24	11,742	876.4	13.4	$14,594	$16,831
Rogers School District	Benton County	23	15,545	1,182.0	13.2	$11,184	$10,852
Russellville School District	Pope County	10	5,361	452.2	11.9	$11,868	$12,098
Sheridan School District	Grant County	7	4,183	259.4	16.1	$10,459	$12,744
Siloam Springs School District	Benton County	6	4,294	291.6	14.7	$10,509	$10,246
Springdale School District	Washington County	29	22,663	1,653.2	13.7	$11,019	$10,487
Van Buren School District	Crawford County	11	5,506	425.3	13.0	$10,622	$10,535
West Memphis School District	Crittenden County	10	5,150	437.1	11.8	$11,171	$12,044
CALIFORNIA							
Capistrano Unified	Orange County	59	43,719	1,728.4	25.3	$10,795	$10,472
Clovis Unified	Fresno County	49	42,790	1,800.6	23.8	$13,170	$12,356
Corona-Norco Unified	Riverside County	53	51,318	2,063.0	24.9	$13,011	$13,808
Elk Grove Unified	Sacramento County	66	63,157	2,722.2	23.2	$12,614	$12,937
Fresno Unified	Fresno County	100	70,088	2,159.3	32.5	$15,231	$14,843
Garden Grove Unified	Orange County	66	40,124	1,688.9	23.8	$14,695	$16,663
Irvine Unified	Orange County	43	35,660	1,379.9	25.8	$14,791	$15,285
Kern High	Kern County	24	42,370	1,727.1	24.5	$14,913	$14,470
Long Beach Unified	Los Angeles County	84	69,413	2,808.8	24.7	$15,667	$16,603
Los Angeles Unified	Los Angeles County	782	460,633	21,873.0	21.1	$16,416	$15,700
Poway Unified	San Diego County	38	35,663	1,527.2	23.4	$13,500	$12,610
Riverside Unified	Riverside County	49	39,443	1,634.8	24.1	$13,455	$13,296
Sacramento City Unified	Sacramento County	73	40,711	1,765.3	23.1	$14,288	$14,258
San Bernardino City Unified	San Bernardino County	75	46,693	2,070.0	22.6	$14,610	$14,702
San Diego Unified	San Diego County	176	97,968	4,266.9	23.0	$15,137	$15,100
San Francisco Unified	San Francisco County	114	51,790	2,501.6	20.7	$17,373	$16,807
San Juan Unified	Sacramento County	68	39,218	1,711.0	22.9	$13,068	$13,050
Santa Ana Unified	Orange County	54	44,271	1,836.5	24.1	$15,125	$14,067
Stockton Unified	San Joaquin County	55	36,190	1,585.0	22.8	$13,565	$13,628
Sweetwater Union High	San Diego County	28	37,060	1,576.9	23.5	$14,231	$14,742
COLORADO							
Academy School District No. 20	El Paso County	40	25,711	1,606.8	16.0	$10,866	$12,161
Adams 12 Five Star Schools	Adams County	53	36,654	2,053.7	17.9	$11,657	$12,625
Aurora Joint District No. 28	Arapahoe County	64	37,907	2,403.1	15.8	$13,011	$12,507
Boulder Valley School District	Boulder County	56	29,240	1,717.1	17.0	$14,866	$18,019
Cherry Creek School District No. 5	Arapahoe County	70	54,184	3,367.9	16.1	$12,483	$14,076
Colorado Springs School District No. 11	El Paso County	56	23,885	1,518.8	15.7	$12,762	$11,308
Douglas County School District	Douglas County	90	62,979	3,664.7	17.2	$10,593	$10,187
El Paso County Colorado School District 49	El Paso County	31	23,984	1,210.6	19.8	$10,027	$11,194
GreeleySchool District No. 6	Weld County	33	21,903	1,223.6	17.9	$11,459	$11,167
Harrison School District No. 2	El Paso County	27	11,177	739.3	15.1	$10,600	$10,389
Jefferson County School District	Jefferson County	165	80,099	4,700.9	17.0	$11,007	$10,865
Littleton School District No. 6	Arapahoe County	24	14,132	848.8	16.7	$11,841	$11,822
Mesa County Valley School District No. 51	Mesa County	47	21,084	1,325.9	15.9	$11,425	$11,251
Poudre School District	Larimer County	51	29,418	1,866.1	15.8	$12,016	$10,687
Pueblo School District No. 60	Pueblo County	35	15,219	920.9	16.5	$10,588	$9,814
School District 27J	Adams County	28	19,203	959.5	20.0	$10,464	$13,358
School District No. 1	Denver County	205	89,081	6,120.7	14.6	$15,482	$16,346
St. Vrain Valley School District	Boulder County	53	31,312	1,918.4	16.3	$12,445	$14,346
State Charter School Institute	Denver County	43	20,749	1,087.4	19.1	$9,374	$9,352
Thompson School District	Larimer County	33	14,965	913.0	16.4	$10,511	$10,333
CONNECTICUT							
Bridgeport School District	Fairfield County	36	19,276	1,377.7	14.0	$21,223	$21,526
Bristol School District	Hartford County	13	7,611	550.0	13.8	$19,403	$19,400

NA = Not available.
X = Not applicable.

Table C-1. Characteristics of the 20 Largest Public School Districts in Each State—*Continued*

(Number; dollars.)

State/School District	County Name	Number of Operational Schools (2020-21)	Total Students in All Grades (2020-21)	Full-Time Equivalent Teachers (2020-21)	Pupil/ Teacher Ratio (2020-21)	Total Revenue per Pupil (2017-18)	Total Expenditures per Pupil (2017-18)
CONNECTICUT—*(Continued)*							
Capitol Region Education Council	Hartford County	16	8,792	762.0	11.5	X	X
Connecticut Technical Education and Career System	Hartford County	17	11,331	1,011.8	11.2	$0	X
Danbury School District	Fairfield County	18	11,813	845.7	14.0	$16,081	$15,876
East Hartford School District	Hartford County	12	6,546	519.4	12.6	$21,358	$21,358
Fairfield School District	Fairfield County	16	9,387	830.6	11.3	$23,626	$22,527
Greenwich School District	Fairfield County	15	8,773	732.5	12.0	$26,512	$27,204
Hartford School District	Hartford County	39	17,054	1,284.2	13.3	$26,917	$26,832
Manchester School District	Hartford County	10	6,044	582.7	10.4	$24,465	$27,207
Meriden School District	New Haven County	12	8,072	529.2	15.3	$20,950	$20,525
New Britain School District	Hartford County	14	9,616	713.7	13.5	$19,221	$19,453
New Haven School District	New Haven County	39	19,827	1,532.8	12.9	$21,955	$21,676
Norwalk School District	Fairfield County	21	11,509	875.4	13.2	$23,311	$22,438
Southington School District	Hartford County	12	6,152	497.8	12.4	$18,951	$18,238
Stamford School District	Fairfield County	21	16,157	1,341.2	12.1	$23,984	$23,291
Stratford School District	Fairfield County	13	6,632	500.4	13.3	$20,873	$22,762
Trumbull School District	Fairfield County	9	6,719	496.6	13.5	$20,458	$19,860
Waterbury School District	New Haven County	29	18,374	1,373.1	13.4	$18,671	$18,489
West Hartford School District	Hartford County	16	9,117	740.4	12.3	$21,223	$21,002
DELAWARE							
Appoquinimink School District	New Castle County	18	11,914	776.6	15.3	$17,349	$14,448
Brandywine School District	New Castle County	17	10,405	760.3	13.7	$18,799	$17,494
Caesar Rodney School District	Kent County	13	7,960	543.7	14.6	$19,060	$16,326
Cape Henlopen School District	Sussex County	9	5,892	469.0	12.6	$27,725	$25,855
Capital School District	Kent County	13	6,332	500.6	12.7	$17,162	$16,669
Christina School District	New Castle County	28	12,963	1,106.4	11.7	$22,481	$22,779
Colonial School District	New Castle County	15	9,795	685.0	14.3	$17,507	$15,579
Delmar School District	Sussex County	3	1,365	72.0	19.0	$11,599	$12,108
Indian River School District	Sussex County	16	10,592	761.5	13.9	$15,450	$14,717
Lake Forest School District	Kent County	7	3,505	250.5	14.0	$13,496	$14,294
Laurel School District	Sussex County	4	2,546	170.6	14.9	$12,637	$19,829
Milford School District	Sussex County	6	4,214	279.0	15.1	$14,263	$12,873
MOT Charter School	New Castle County	1	1,383	82.0	16.9	$12,040	$12,076
New Castle County Vocational-Technical School District	New Castle County	4	4,644	349.0	13.3	$21,849	$25,118
Newark Charter School	New Castle County	1	2,436	140.6	17.3	$12,785	$12,678
Odyssey Charter School	New Castle County	1	1,926	147.0	13.1	$12,622	$12,564
Red Clay Consolidated School District	New Castle County	28	15,057	1,082.8	13.9	$18,630	$17,500
Seaford School District	Sussex County	7	3,224	230.5	14.0	$15,413	$15,474
Smyrna School District	Kent County	8	5,883	395.0	14.9	$13,437	$12,940
Woodbridge School District	Sussex County	4	2,478	173.0	14.3	$15,281	$14,855
DISTRICT OF COLUMBIA							
BASIS DC PCS	District of Columbia	1	664	49.1	13.5	$19,356	$14,798
Capital City PCS	District of Columbia	3	1,018	110.1	9.3	$26,472	$22,982
Center City PCS	District of Columbia	6	1,452	137.0	10.6	$23,186	$21,430
DC Prep PCS	District of Columbia	6	2,168	174.0	12.5	$24,163	$22,606
DC Scholars PCS	District of Columbia	1	608	39.0	15.6	$26,286	$24,081
District of Columbia International School	District of Columbia	1	1,452	136.0	10.7	$26,821	$34,281
District of Columbia Public Schools	District of Columbia	115	49,896	4,335.1	11.5	$31,280	$32,098
E.L. Haynes PCS	District of Columbia	3	1,199	100.7	11.9	$27,729	$24,562
Eagle Academy PCS	District of Columbia	2	706	55.0	12.8	$28,618	$23,714
Elsie Whitlow Stokes Community Freedom PCS	District of Columbia	2	585	57.0	10.3	$31,692	$25,838
Friendship PCS	District of Columbia	15	4,565	359.0	12.7	$24,541	$21,566
Ingenuity Prep PCS	District of Columbia	1	761	75.5	10.1	$27,131	$24,575
KIPP DC PCS	District of Columbia	18	7,000	540.8	12.9	$25,100	$22,522
Meridian PCS	District of Columbia	1	605	62.0	9.8	$24,357	$20,695
Mundo Verde Bilingual PCS	District of Columbia	2	955	62.0	15.4	$23,596	$21,665
Paul PCS	District of Columbia	2	726	77.0	9.4	$25,713	$24,690
Rocketship Education DC PCS	District of Columbia	3	1,525	86.1	17.7	$52,529	$31,008
Two Rivers PCS	District of Columbia	3	985	79.7	12.4	$25,308	$23,053
Washington Latin PCS	District of Columbia	2	734	71.2	10.3	$21,843	$18,782
Washington Yu Ying PCS	District of Columbia	1	580	54.0	10.7	$23,309	$18,810
FLORIDA							
Brevard	Brevard County	114	70,996	4,397.1	16.2	$10,322	$10,186
Broward	Broward County	331	260,235	13,737.5	18.9	$10,263	$10,600
Collier	Collier County	73	46,329	2,713.8	17.1	$13,387	$12,683
Duval	Duval County	204	126,815	6,539.0	19.4	$9,697	$9,640
Hillsborough	Hillsborough County	303	218,943	13,711.0	16.0	$10,023	$9,757
Lake	Lake County	64	43,706	2,620.7	16.7	$9,791	$9,022

NA – Not available.
X = Not applicable.

Table C-1. Characteristics of the 20 Largest Public School Districts in Each State—*Continued*

(Number; dollars.)

State/School District	County Name	Number of Operational Schools (2020-21)	Total Students in All Grades (2020-21)	Full-Time Equivalent Teachers (2020-21)	Pupil/ Teacher Ratio (2020-21)	Total Revenue per Pupil (2017-18)	Total Expenditures per Pupil (2017-18)
FLORIDA—*(Continued)*							
Lee	Lee County	119	94,927	5,156.2	18.4	$10,732	$11,171
Manatee	Manatee County	80	49,181	2,856.8	17.2	$11,085	$11,857
Miami-Dade	Miami-Dade County	516	334,261	16,758.0	20.0	$10,760	$10,817
Orange	Orange County	264	199,089	11,757.0	16.9	$12,262	$11,774
Osceola	Osceola County	85	68,640	3,925.9	17.5	$10,554	$10,153
Palm Beach	Palm Beach County	236	187,057	11,696.5	16.0	$12,278	$11,483
Pasco	Pasco County	103	77,125	4,790.2	16.1	$9,990	$9,935
Pinellas	Pinellas County	157	96,068	6,829.4	14.1	$10,567	$10,933
Polk	Polk County	164	100,495	5,865.0	17.1	$10,295	$10,030
Sarasota	Sarasota County	62	42,618	2,793.0	15.3	$13,656	$13,400
Seminole	Seminole County	77	66,226	3,307.2	20.0	$9,520	$9,585
St. John's	St. Johns County	52	44,550	2,445.8	18.2	$10,765	$10,639
St. Lucie	St. Lucie County	52	41,779	2,252.8	18.6	$10,594	$10,125
Volusia	Volusia County	92	61,088	3,664.9	16.7	$10,331	$9,920
GEORGIA							
Atlanta Public Schools	Fulton County	87	51,012	4,099.2	12.4	$20,510	$17,283
Bibb County	Bibb County	34	21,373	1,484.1	14.4	$12,896	$12,483
Cherokee County	Cherokee County	36	41,373	2,769.1	14.9	$11,514	$10,795
Clayton County	Clayton County	67	52,149	3,292.6	15.8	$10,888	$11,275
Cobb County	Cobb County	109	107,379	7,347.7	14.6	$12,003	$11,669
Columbia County	Columbia County	31	28,266	1,758.2	16.1	$10,300	$10,557
Coweta County	Coweta County	28	22,241	1,508.2	14.8	$10,964	$10,670
DeKalb County	DeKalb County	131	93,470	7,108.9	13.2	$13,089	$13,221
Douglas County	Douglas County	35	25,884	1,690.7	15.3	$11,482	$11,036
Fayette County	Fayette County	24	19,912	1,452.2	13.7	$13,076	$13,526
Forsyth County	Forsyth County	39	51,152	3,157.3	16.2	$11,073	$11,063
Fulton County	Fulton County	107	90,300	6,261.2	14.4	$13,632	$12,797
Gwinnett County	Gwinnett County	139	177,401	11,361.3	15.6	$11,583	$11,257
Hall County	Hall County	37	26,914	1,804.3	14.9	$11,065	$11,685
Henry County	Henry County	50	42,388	2,683.4	15.8	$11,579	$13,018
Houston County	Houston County	37	29,681	1,974.0	15.0	$11,115	$10,806
Muscogee County	Muscogee County	53	30,757	2,025.4	15.2	$11,389	$12,119
Paulding County	Paulding County	33	29,966	1,892.6	15.8	$10,439	$10,199
Richmond County	Richmond County	54	29,093	1,988.9	14.6	$11,214	$11,795
Savannah-Chatham County	Chatham County	58	36,502	2,660.8	13.7	$14,310	$12,947
HAWAII							
Hawaii Department of Education	Honolulu County	294	176,441	12,145.4	14.5	$18,095	$16,981
IDAHO							
Boise Independent District	Ada County	49	23,703	1,538.3	15.4	$10,317	$11,324
Bonneville Joint District	Bonneville County	24	13,230	649.2	20.4	$7,777	$7,256
Caldwell District	Canyon County	11	5,584	338.4	16.5	$8,366	$7,853
Cassia County Joint District	Cassia County	17	5,391	319.5	16.9	$8,029	$7,628
Coeur D'Alene District	Kootenai County	19	10,011	575.7	17.4	$8,603	$8,729
Idaho Falls District	Bonneville County	22	9,813	514.7	19.1	$7,926	$7,079
Jefferson County Joint District	Jefferson County	12	6,287	311.1	20.2	$6,720	$5,941
Jerome Joint District	Jerome County	7	4,072	218.3	18.7	$7,892	$7,206
Joint School District No. 2	Ada County	60	37,989	2,097.9	18.1	$8,333	$7,317
Kuna Joint District	Ada County	11	5,416	291.5	18.6	$8,402	$7,665
Lakeland District	Kootenai County	11	4,290	230.4	18.6	$9,629	$8,715
Lewiston Independent District	Nez Perce County	13	4,578	285.9	16.0	$10,880	$10,103
Madison District	Madison County	10	5,370	267.8	20.1	$8,281	$7,224
Minidoka County Joint District	Minidoka County	12	4,253	277.7	15.3	$8,386	$7,981
Nampa School District	Canyon County	27	14,899	878.5	17.0	$8,518	$7,709
Oneida County District	Oneida County	5	7,809	367.2	21.3	$6,258	$6,109
Pocatello District	Bannock County	24	11,885	630.5	18.9	$7,725	$7,494
Post Falls District	Kootenai County	12	5,813	296.4	19.6	$7,713	$7,312
Twin Falls District	Twin Falls County	18	9,126	498.8	18.3	$8,806	$8,170
Vallivue School Distrct	Canyon County	13	8,916	486.0	18.4	$8,444	$7,995
ILLINOIS							
Aurora East USD 131	Kane County	20	13,224	NA	NA	$17,243	$17,315
City of Chicago SD 299	Cook County	649	341,382	NA	NA	$17,425	$16,720
CUSD 200	DuPage County	20	11,903	NA	NA	$20,519	$19,053
CUSD 300	McHenry County	28	20,216	NA	NA	$17,658	$15,944
CUSD 308	Kendall County	22	17,169	NA	NA	$22,332	$21,539
Indian Prairie CUSD 204	DuPage County	33	26,091	NA	NA	$16,164	$14,959
McLean County USD 5	McLean County	26	12,536	NA	NA	$15,568	$14,269

NA = Not available.
X = Not applicable.

Table C-1. Characteristics of the 20 Largest Public School Districts in Each State—*Continued*

(Number; dollars.)

State/School District	County Name	Number of Operational Schools (2020-21)	Total Students in All Grades (2020-21)	Full-Time Equivalent Teachers (2020-21)	Pupil/ Teacher Ratio (2020-21)	Total Revenue per Pupil (2017-18)	Total Expenditures per Pupil (2017-18)
ILLINOIS—*(Continued)*							
Naperville CUSD 203	DuPage County	22	16,289	NA	NA	$20,402	$10,212
Palatine CCSD 15	Cook County	20	11,540	NA	NA	$18,137	$18,408
Peoria SD 150	Peoria County	32	12,515	NA	NA	$17,385	$16,988
Plainfield SD 202	Will County	30	25,085	NA	NA	$14,051	$12,612
Rockford SD 205	Winnebago County	46	26,739	NA	NA	$18,489	$18,751
Schaumburg CCSD 54	Cook County	28	15,292	NA	NA	$16,848	$17,203
SD U-46	Kane County	58	36,476	NA	NA	$16,568	$14,896
Springfield SD 186	Sangamon County	35	13,483	NA	NA	$16,650	$15,714
St Charles CUSD 303	Kane County	17	11,896	NA	NA	$19,132	$18,614
Township HSD 211	Cook County	7	11,968	NA	NA	$28,327	$28,920
Township HSD 214	Cook County	11	12,061	NA	NA	$28,586	$28,026
Valley View CUSD 365U	Will County	20	15,521	NA	NA	$21,210	$19,592
Waukegan CUSD 60	Lake County	22	14,455	NA	NA	$18,314	$16,580
INDIANA							
Bartholomew Consolidated School Corp	Bartholomew County	17	11,474	608.9	18.8	$13,283	$12,346
Carmel Clay Schools	Hamilton County	15	16,395	892.3	18.4	$12,831	$11,448
Elkhart Community Schools	Elkhart County	20	11,939	962.0	12.4	$13,278	$11,832
Evansville Vanderburgh School Corp	Vanderburgh County	39	22,191	2,030.3	10.9	$13,576	$13,150
Fort Wayne Community Schools	Allen County	49	28,460	1,602.9	17.8	$13,007	$13,055
Franklin Township Community School Corp	Marion County	11	10,587	580.0	18.3	$11,809	$10,352
Hamilton Southeastern Schools	Hamilton County	23	21,760	1,154.9	18.8	$12,349	$11,404
Indianapolis Public Schools	Marion County	54	22,928	2,233.4	10.3	$17,638	$17,492
MSD Lawrence Township	Marion County	17	15,683	768.2	20.4	$13,379	$13,181
MSD Pike Township	Marion County	13	10,919	783.9	13.9	$13,919	$13,516
MSD Warren Township	Marion County	15	11,612	1,019.2	11.4	$12,959	$12,281
MSD Washington Township	Marion County	14	10,888	650.7	16.7	$14,388	$12,826
MSD Wayne Township	Marion County	18	16,473	1,512.1	10.9	$14,999	$13,644
New Albany-Floyd County Consolidated School Corp	Floyd County	16	11,524	587.2	19.6	$12,964	$11,884
Penn-Harris-Madison School Corp	St. Joseph County	15	11,488	548.2	21.0	$10,616	$9,964
Perry Township Schools	Marion County	17	16,835	898.8	18.7	$12,483	$12,157
School City of Hammond	Lake County	19	12,303	683.0	18.0	$13,257	$12,032
South Bend Community School Corp	St. Joseph County	33	16,297	1,027.3	15.9	$14,715	$12,887
Tippecanoe School Corp	Tippecanoe County	20	13,464	765.4	17.6	$11,721	$10,559
Vigo County School Corp	Vigo County	28	13,674	962.3	14.2	$11,955	$11,524
IOWA							
Ankeny Community School District	Polk County	17	12,188	768.0	15.9	$13,179	$11,560
Bettendorf Community School District	Scott County	7	4,719	310.9	15.2	$13,595	$13,705
Cedar Falls Community School District	Black Hawk County	10	5,808	419.8	13.8	$14,032	$16,507
Cedar Rapids Community School District	Linn County	32	15,786	1,101.6	14.3	$14,402	$13,076
College Community School District	Linn County	10	5,669	372.7	15.2	$15,262	$17,640
Council Bluffs Community School District	Pottawattamie County	15	8,910	596.3	14.9	$14,414	$13,384
Davenport Community School District	Scott County	30	14,609	1,086.1	13.5	$14,096	$13,196
Des Moines Independent Community School District	Polk County	60	31,720	2,236.8	14.2	$14,686	$14,321
Dubuque Community School District	Dubuque County	18	10,746	837.8	12.8	$13,902	$13,750
Iowa City Community School District	Johnson County	28	14,428	1,012.7	14.3	$13,828	$15,615
Johnston Community School District	Polk County	8	7,408	444.2	16.7	$14,605	$14,937
Linn-Mar Community School District	Linn County	12	7,762	499.5	15.5	$13,464	$12,205
Marshalltown Community School District	Marshall County	9	5,076	373.9	13.6	$12,984	$12,503
Muscatine Community School District	Muscatine County	9	4,778	345.8	13.8	$12,827	$11,835
Pleasant Valley Community School District	Scott County	7	5,331	323.2	16.5	$12,103	$13,757
Sioux City Community School District	Woodbury County	20	14,941	935.3	16.0	$12,859	$12,269
Southeast Polk Community School District	Polk County	11	7,139	451.7	15.8	$14,161	$12,029
Waterloo Community School District	Black Hawk County	19	10,741	792.4	13.6	$13,352	$12,040
Waukee Community School District	Dallas County	14	11,781	776.7	15.2	$14,098	$12,635
West Des Moines Community School District	Polk County	14	9,248	603.9	15.3	$14,887	$14,847
KANSAS							
Andover	Butler County	11	8,737	355.3	24.6	$8,267	$8,890
Auburn Washburn	Shawnee County	9	6,016	505.4	11.9	$11,269	$10,633
Blue Valley	Johnson County	35	22,148	1,573.7	14.1	$15,223	$13,732
De Soto	Johnson County	12	7,112	496.3	14.3	$12,531	$13,007
Derby	Sedgwick County	12	7,255	516.6	14.0	$11,371	$10,654
Dodge City	Ford County	12	7,124	423.3	16.8	$13,489	$13,021
Garden City	Finney County	17	7,370	571.5	12.9	$13,819	$11,683
Gardner Edgerton	Johnson County	11	5,831	473.5	12.3	$13,420	$12,727
Geary County Schools	Geary County	16	7,041	649.3	10.8	$13,213	$12,319

NA = Not available.
X = Not applicable.

Table C-1. Characteristics of the 20 Largest Public School Districts in Each State—*Continued*

(Number; dollars.)

State/School District	County Name	Number of Operational Schools (2020-21)	Total Students in All Grades (2020-21)	Full-Time Equivalent Teachers (2020-21)	Pupil/ Teacher Ratio (2020-21)	Total Revenue per Pupil (2017-18)	Total Expenditures per Pupil (2017-18)
KANSAS—*(Continued)*							
Goddard	Sedgwick County	11	6,167	380.7	16.2	$11,681	$11,773
Kansas City	Wyandotte County	43	22,140	1,569.4	14.1	$14,008	$14,887
Lawrence	Douglas County	21	11,427	887.6	12.9	$12,832	$13,878
Maize	Sedgwick County	10	7,798	448.6	17.4	$11,218	$12,711
Manhattan-Ogden	Riley County	12	6,675	546.8	12.2	$13,000	$12,177
Olathe	Johnson County	51	29,128	2,306.3	12.6	$14,844	$12,362
Salina	Saline County	12	6,898	552.1	12.5	$16,856	$16,081
Shawnee Mission Pub Sch	Johnson County	44	26,117	1,828.9	14.3	$12,456	$13,269
Spring Hill	Miami County	9	5,836	329.8	17.7	$11,960	$23,310
Topeka Public Schools	Shawnee County	27	12,436	1,126.9	11.0	$14,205	$15,343
Wichita	Sedgwick County	89	46,908	4,584.2	10.2	$13,420	$12,674
KENTUCKY							
Boone County	Boone County	25	20,280	1,353.2	15.0	$12,126	$12,425
Bullitt County	Bullitt County	25	12,725	768.2	16.6	$10,877	$11,184
Christian County	Christian County	18	8,219	506.6	16.2	$11,102	$10,769
Daviess County	Daviess County	23	11,102	689.0	16.1	$11,416	$10,852
Fayette County	Fayette County	79	41,203	2,968.2	13.9	$14,190	$14,072
Hardin County	Hardin County	27	14,655	906.8	16.2	$11,382	$11,297
Henderson County	Henderson County	13	7,044	454.9	15.5	$11,349	$12,200
Hopkins County	Hopkins County	19	6,498	417.0	15.6	$11,573	$10,586
Jefferson County	Jefferson County	172	95,911	6,236.4	15.4	$14,844	$15,238
Jessamine County	Jessamine County	14	8,207	562.2	14.6	$11,642	$11,146
Kenton County	Kenton County	22	14,021	780.0	18.0	$11,452	$11,292
Laurel County	Laurel County	19	8,850	546.0	16.2	$10,690	$10,690
Madison County	Madison County	20	11,045	693.8	15.9	$11,117	$11,493
McCracken County	McCracken County	14	6,905	415.6	16.6	$11,411	$10,801
Oldham County	Oldham County	22	12,416	796.9	15.6	$11,458	$10,950
Pike County	Pike County	19	8,094	508.0	15.9	$12,876	$13,342
Pulaski County	Pulaski County	14	8,294	495.0	16.8	$11,280	$10,734
Scott County	Scott County	17	9,440	592.8	15.9	$11,614	$13,070
Shelby County	Shelby County	14	6,961	436.2	16.0	$12,538	$12,548
Warren County	Warren County	34	16,860	1,015.6	16.6	$10,822	$12,074
LOUISIANA							
Acadia Parish	Acadia Parish	27	9,603	509.2	18.9	$9,955	$9,697
Ascension Parish	Ascension Parish	30	23,154	1,304.5	17.8	$13,235	$13,828
Bossier Parish	Bossier Parish	34	22,431	1,239.5	18.1	$11,787	$12,544
Caddo Parish	Caddo Parish	59	36,153	1,560.9	23.2	$12,491	$12,562
Calcasieu Parish	Calcasieu Parish	58	27,932	1,802.2	15.5	$14,439	$13,109
East Baton Rouge Parish	East Baton Rouge Parish	81	40,283	2,199.2	18.3	$15,496	$15,813
Iberia Parish	Iberia Parish	23	11,822	644.5	18.3	$11,255	$11,234
Jefferson Parish	Jefferson Parish	81	48,160	2,302.7	20.9	$12,341	$12,339
Lafayette Parish	Lafayette Parish	46	30,878	1,629.0	19.0	$11,925	$12,641
Lafourche Parish	Lafourche Parish	31	14,393	742.5	19.4	$11,523	$11,516
Livingston Parish	Livingston Parish	44	25,687	1,287.9	19.9	$10,959	$10,989
Ouachita Parish	Ouachita Parish	36	18,355	1,025.5	17.9	$11,527	$10,954
Rapides Parish	Rapides Parish	47	22,297	1,322.8	16.9	$11,317	$10,973
St. Charles Parish	St. Charles Parish	15	9,460	647.0	14.6	$18,340	$19,290
St. Landry Parish	St. Landry Parish	34	12,527	781.0	16.0	$10,351	$10,472
St. Tammany Parish	St. Tammany Parish	56	36,820	2,060.4	17.9	$13,232	$13,048
Tangipahoa Parish	Tangipahoa Parish	33	19,549	1,057.5	18.5	$10,270	$10,498
Terrebonne Parish	Terrebonne Parish	32	16,563	880.1	18.8	$10,705	$10,924
Vermilion Parish	Vermilion Parish	20	9,516	547.9	17.4	$9,902	$9,932
Vernon Parish	Vernon Parish	18	8,125	464.5	17.5	$11,014	$10,744
MAINE							
Auburn Public Schools	Androscoggin County	8	3,383	297.6	11.4	$13,382	$12,804
Bangor Public Schools	Penobscot County	10	3,468	281.5	12.3	$14,363	$14,122
Biddeford Public Schools	York County	6	2,346	198.7	11.8	$16,771	$15,521
Brunswick Public Schools	Cumberland County	4	2,375	218.1	10.9	$16,842	$16,761
Gorham Public Schools	Cumberland County	5	2,742	215.5	12.7	$15,370	$14,397
Lewiston Public Schools	Androscoggin County	8	5,184	453.1	11.4	$15,990	$15,263
Portland Public Schools	Cumberland County	17	6,523	605.7	10.8	$17,625	$19,163
RSU 06/MSAD 06	York County	8	3,429	274.6	12.5	$15,007	$14,382
RSU 14	Cumberland County	6	3,139	249.2	12.6	$15,880	$15,314
RSU 17/MSAD 17	Oxford County	10	3,192	274.5	11.6	$13,541	$13,212
RSU 18	Kennebec County	8	2,714	199.2	13.6	$14,247	$13,930
RSU 21	York County	6	2,494	200.1	12.5	$18,769	$24,036
RSU 57/MSAD 57	York County	7	2,752	230.0	12.0	$14,935	$14,000
RSU 60/MSAD 60	York County	7	2,931	262.6	11.2	$14,677	$14,009

NA = Not available.
X = Not applicable.

Table C-1. Characteristics of the 20 Largest Public School Districts in Each State—*Continued*

(Number; dollars.)

State/School District	County Name	Number of Operational Schools (2020-21)	Total Students in All Grades (2020-21)	Full-Time Equivalent Teachers (2020-21)	Pupil/ Teacher Ratio (2020-21)	Total Revenue per Pupil (2017-18)	Total Expenditures per Pupil (2017-18)
MAINE—*(Continued)*							
RSU 75/MSAD 75	Sagadahoc County	7	2,408	209.0	11.5	$18,170	$10,000
Saco Public Schools	York County	5	2,782	168.3	16.5	$14,121	$14,219
Sanford Public Schools	York County	6	3,107	253.7	12.3	$15,952	$29,320
Scarborough Public Schools	Cumberland County	6	2,872	258.9	11.1	$16,931	$16,313
South Portland Public Schools	Cumberland County	8	2,913	260.4	11.2	$18,220	$17,505
Westbrook Public Schools	Cumberland County	6	2,369	216.6	10.9	$16,922	$20,030
MARYLAND							
Allegany County Public Schools	Allegany County	22	8,075	604.5	13.4	$18,475	$18,267
Anne Arundel County Public Schools	Anne Arundel County	125	83,044	5,957.5	13.9	$15,991	$16,789
Baltimore City Public Schools	Baltimore city	159	77,856	5,063.1	15.4	$19,063	$18,784
Baltimore County Public Schools	Baltimore County	178	111,084	7,821.4	14.2	$17,146	$16,864
Calvert County Public Schools	Calvert County	25	15,292	992.6	15.4	$17,079	$16,721
Caroline County Public Schools	Caroline County	10	5,553	418.0	13.3	$14,956	$14,745
Carroll County Public Schools	Carroll County	44	24,568	1,774.8	13.8	$14,968	$14,706
Cecil County Public Schools	Cecil County	29	14,718	1,118.0	13.2	$15,761	$15,269
Charles County Public Schools	Charles County	39	26,768	1,853.0	14.5	$16,940	$17,103
Dorchester County Public Schools	Dorchester County	13	4,662	370.0	12.6	$20,291	$20,018
Frederick County Public Schools	Frederick County	68	43,221	2,801.2	15.4	$16,867	$16,205
Harford County Public Schools	Harford County	54	37,333	2,496.1	15.0	$15,267	$14,781
Howard County Public Schools	Howard County	77	57,293	4,241.0	13.5	$17,833	$17,424
Montgomery County Public Schools	Montgomery County	209	160,564	11,510.6	14.0	$21,203	$18,233
Prince George's County Public Schools	Prince George's County	209	131,646	9,368.2	14.1	$17,878	$17,060
Queen Anne's County Public Schools	Queen Anne's County	14	7,395	508.5	14.5	$14,213	$14,216
St. Mary's County Public Schools	St. Mary's County	28	17,246	1,088.8	15.8	$13,967	$13,678
Washington County Public Schools	Washington County	44	21,939	1,490.3	14.7	$14,544	$14,400
Wicomico County Public Schools	Wicomico County	25	14,354	1,171.2	12.3	$16,959	$17,151
Worcester County Public Schools	Worcester County	14	6,711	583.0	11.5	$18,507	$18,511
MASSACHUSETTS							
Boston	Suffolk County	115	48,112	4,595.5	10.5	$30,604	$30,762
Brockton	Plymouth County	23	15,384	986.2	15.6	$16,954	$16,530
Brookline	Norfolk County	13	6,891	674.6	10.2	$30,216	$29,816
Chicopee	Hampden County	15	6,850	586.6	11.7	$17,425	$17,199
Everett	Middlesex County	10	6,883	561.7	12.3	$18,717	$18,186
Fall River	Bristol County	16	9,998	769.6	13.0	$19,366	$18,846
Framingham	Middlesex County	14	8,733	733.2	11.9	$22,625	$22,461
Haverhill	Essex County	16	7,771	594.3	13.1	$17,588	$16,870
Lawrence	Essex County	26	12,842	1,123.3	11.4	$19,067	$18,343
Lexington	Middlesex County	10	6,901	621.4	11.1	$22,766	$25,728
Lowell	Middlesex County	27	14,023	1,092.0	12.8	$18,091	$18,171
Lynn	Essex County	25	15,587	1,152.1	13.5	$17,680	$16,955
New Bedford	Bristol County	25	12,565	991.2	12.7	$21,506	$18,205
Newton	Middlesex County	22	12,024	1,091.0	11.0	$22,523	$23,193
Plymouth	Plymouth County	13	7,085	633.7	11.2	$22,935	$22,994
Quincy	Norfolk County	19	9,480	737.2	12.9	$18,811	$22,065
Revere	Suffolk County	11	7,166	561.1	12.8	$17,678	$17,723
Springfield	Hampden County	65	24,239	2,096.7	11.6	$21,029	$20,289
Taunton	Bristol County	12	7,735	531.2	14.6	$18,377	$15,844
Worcester	Worcester County	45	23,986	1,840.6	13.0	$18,826	$17,994
MICHIGAN							
Ann Arbor Public Schools	Washtenaw County	32	17,451	1,244.9	14.0	$17,283	$17,314
Chippewa Valley Schools	Macomb County	20	14,855	754.1	19.7	$12,013	$10,962
Dearborn City School District	Wayne County	36	20,417	1,278.8	16.0	$13,450	$12,764
Detroit Public Schools Community District	Wayne County	107	48,782	3,074.5	15.9	$14,558	$13,252
Farmington Public School District	Oakland County	16	9,108	590.6	16.4	$15,904	$18,288
Forest Hills Public Schools	Kent County	18	9,365	502.9	18.6	$14,104	$12,592
Grand Rapids Public Schools	Kent County	51	14,034	914.6	15.3	$16,798	$18,461
Kalamazoo Public Schools	Kalamazoo County	31	12,581	686.0	18.3	$14,150	$14,008
Kentwood Public Schools	Kent County	16	9,228	525.6	17.6	$13,276	$13,468
L'Anse Creuse Public Schools	Macomb County	19	9,881	521.2	19.0	$12,468	$12,424
Lansing School District	Ingham County	29	9,989	636.5	15.7	$15,854	$17,133
Livonia Public Schools School District	Wayne County	26	13,457	828.9	16.2	$14,552	$15,130
Plymouth-Canton Community Schools	Wayne County	23	16,632	923.6	18.0	$12,221	$11,443
Rochester Community School District	Oakland County	21	15,092	791.8	19.1	$13,416	$14,706
Traverse City Area Public Schools	Grand Traverse County	16	9,007	461.1	19.5	$12,654	$12,902
Troy School District	Oakland County	21	12,815	760.1	16.9	$14,228	$13,958
Utica Community Schools	Macomb County	38	25,701	1,357.4	18.9	$11,655	$11,286
Walled Lake Consolidated Schools	Oakland County	20	12,622	663.5	19.0	$13,520	$12,595

NA = Not available.
X = Not applicable.

Table C-1. Characteristics of the 20 Largest Public School Districts in Each State—*Continued*

(Number; dollars.)

State/School District	County Name	Number of Operational Schools (2020-21)	Total Students in All Grades (2020-21)	Full-Time Equivalent Teachers (2020-21)	Pupil/ Teacher Ratio (2020-21)	Total Revenue per Pupil (2017-18)	Total Expenditures per Pupil (2017-18)
MICHIGAN—*(Continued)*							
Warren Consolidated Schools	Macomb County	23	12,947	700.4	18.5	$13,741	$15,624
Wayne-Westland Community School District	Wayne County	17	9,652	582.3	16.6	$13,361	$12,477
MINNESOTA							
Anoka-Hennepin Public School District	Anoka County	51	37,719	2,177.9	17.3	$14,173	$14,280
Bloomington Public School District	Hennepin County	22	10,139	528.0	19.2	$16,805	$18,165
Eastern Carver County Public School	Carver County	21	9,485	556.3	17.1	$15,465	$16,959
Elk River School District	Sherburne County	29	13,464	607.6	22.2	$13,848	$14,111
Lakeville Public School District	Dakota County	16	11,275	684.7	16.5	$14,534	$14,304
Mankato Public School District	Blue Earth County	23	8,693	573.2	15.2	$13,560	$13,976
Minneapolis Public School District	Hennepin County	96	32,722	2,155.8	15.2	$19,721	$21,645
Minnetonka Public School District	Hennepin County	12	11,106	714.1	15.6	$14,816	$14,919
Mounds View Public School District	Ramsey County	28	11,806	715.6	16.5	$15,416	$14,719
North St. Paul-Maplewood Oakdale	Ramsey County	23	10,352	553.7	18.7	$17,004	$15,541
Osseo Public School District	Hennepin County	35	20,672	1,156.3	17.9	$16,076	$16,925
Prior Lake-Savage Area Schools	Scott County	12	8,892	437.2	20.3	$13,478	$13,487
Robbinsdale Public School District	Hennepin County	30	11,692	583.3	20.1	$16,384	$17,306
Rochester Public School District	Olmsted County	42	17,474	803.5	21.8	$14,454	$14,456
Rosemount-Apple Valley-Eagan	Dakota County	38	29,156	1,825.1	16.0	$14,073	$15,419
South Washington County School District	Washington County	27	19,001	882.3	21.5	$14,816	$17,303
St. Cloud Public School District	Stearns County	20	9,628	631.4	15.3	$16,142	$20,665
St. Paul Public School District	Ramsey County	100	34,928	2,309.8	15.1	$18,772	$21,953
Wayzata Public School District	Hennepin County	19	12,013	734.7	16.4	$15,653	$15,865
White Bear Lake School District	Ramsey County	22	8,705	544.7	16.0	$15,126	$14,495
MISSISSIPPI							
Biloxi Public School District	Harrison County	10	5,952	421.7	14.1	$11,076	$11,975
Clinton Public School District	Hinds County	9	5,250	301.9	17.4	$9,216	$9,492
Desoto Co School District	DeSoto County	41	34,067	2,161.9	15.8	$8,425	$7,946
Gulfport School District	Harrison County	11	6,367	386.3	16.5	$10,402	$10,828
Harrison Co School District	Harrison County	22	13,666	854.0	16.0	$9,928	$9,083
Hinds Co School District	Hinds County	11	5,364	355.2	15.1	$10,868	$11,407
Jackson Co School District	Jackson County	14	8,765	580.0	15.1	$9,548	$9,466
Jackson Public School District	Hinds County	55	20,401	1,497.6	13.6	$10,679	$10,002
Jones Co School District	Jones County	11	8,073	573.1	14.1	$9,212	$8,375
Lamar County School District	Lamar County	19	10,298	734.7	14.0	$9,340	$8,871
Lauderdale Co School District	Lauderdale County	11	5,680	425.6	13.4	$8,879	$8,687
Lee County School District	Lee County	14	6,389	464.1	13.8	$9,222	$8,718
Lowndes Co School District	Lowndes County	10	5,173	375.4	13.8	$10,329	$12,821
Madison Co School District	Madison County	23	12,988	970.8	13.4	$11,230	$10,700
Meridian Public Schools	Lauderdale County	12	4,940	372.4	13.3	$10,701	$10,336
Ocean Springs School District	Jackson County	7	5,739	409.1	14.0	$9,056	$8,603
Pascagoula-Gautier School District	Jackson County	19	6,508	513.9	12.7	$13,711	$13,410
Rankin Co School District	Rankin County	28	18,384	1,313.6	14.0	$9,867	$9,917
Tupelo Public School District	Lee County	14	7,005	515.7	13.6	$11,257	$12,054
Vicksburg Warren School District	Warren County	16	7,236	523.9	13.8	$10,552	$9,894
MISSOURI							
Blue Springs R-IV	Jackson County	22	14,687	905.8	16.2	$12,365	$10,900
Columbia 93	Boone County	35	18,145	1,444.6	12.6	$14,692	$14,450
Ferguson-Florissant R-II	St. Louis County	23	9,313	683.7	13.6	$12,377	$13,042
Fox C-6	Jefferson County	18	11,022	777.9	14.2	$11,429	$10,827
Francis Howell R-III	St. Charles County	23	16,936	1,185.2	14.3	$12,915	$11,898
Ft. Zumwalt R-II	St. Charles County	27	17,310	1,406.3	12.3	$13,320	$12,718
Hazelwood	St. Louis County	33	16,473	1,149.1	14.3	$12,510	$11,295
Independence 30	Jackson County	31	14,240	948.0	15.0	$12,591	$13,805
Kansas City 33	Jackson County	35	14,113	1,121.6	12.6	$16,083	$15,152
Lee's Summit R-VII	Jackson County	27	17,790	1,217.0	14.6	$13,496	$12,369
Liberty 53	Clay County	20	12,632	853.4	14.8	$13,141	$11,787
Mehlville R-IX	St. Louis County	18	9,969	713.4	14.0	$11,428	$10,268
North Kansas City 74	Clay County	34	19,673	1,461.7	13.5	$13,783	$15,570
Park Hill	Platte County	20	11,992	872.8	13.7	$14,059	$14,054
Parkway C-2	St. Louis County	28	17,132	1,197.4	14.3	$14,920	$14,857
Rockwood R-VI	St. Louis County	31	19,822	1,457.6	13.6	$13,650	$13,288
Springfield R-XII	Greene County	54	23,731	1,467.3	16.2	$12,344	$10,737
St. Joseph	Buchanan County	24	10,643	684.3	15.6	$10,742	$10,804
St. Louis City	St. Louis city	74	19,299	1,682.9	11.5	$17,492	$15,753
Wentzville R-IV	St. Charles County	19	17,400	1,235.9	14.1	$13,436	$11,793
MONTANA							
Belgrade Elem	Gallatin County	4	2,297	155.8	14.7	$10,283	$9,938
Billings Elem	Yellowstone County	28	10,980	744.2	14.8	$10,909	$10,588

NA = Not available.
X = Not applicable.

Table C-1. Characteristics of the 20 Largest Public School Districts in Each State—*Continued*

(Number; dollars.)

State/School District	County Name	Number of Operational Schools (2020-21)	Total Students in All Grades (2020-21)	Full-Time Equivalent Teachers (2020-21)	Pupil/ Teacher Ratio (2020-21)	Total Revenue per Pupil (2017-18)	Total Expenditures per Pupil (2017-18)
MONTANA—(*Continued*)							
Billings H S	Yellowstone County	3	5,550	337.4	16.5	$12,082	$12,076
Bozeman Elem	Gallatin County	10	4,464	297.2	15.0	$11,864	$11,575
Bozeman H S	Gallatin County	2	2,389	148.9	16.0	$14,552	$19,351
Browning Elem	Glacier County	7	1,392	112.3	12.4	$19,628	$17,080
Butte Elem	Silver Bow County	7	2,948	190.2	15.5	$10,372	$10,469
Columbia Falls Elem	Flathead County	3	1,430	101.1	14.2	$11,477	$11,008
East Helena K-12	Lewis and Clark County	5	1,505	96.4	15.6	X	X
Flathead H S	Flathead County	2	2,952	192.7	15.3	$13,099	$13,358
Frenchtown K-12 Schools	Missoula County	4	1,345	93.6	14.4	$12,244	$11,009
Great Falls Elem	Cascade County	17	7,026	465.8	15.1	$10,293	$11,923
Great Falls H S	Cascade County	2	2,981	191.7	15.6	$11,681	$15,908
Hamilton K-12 Schools	Ravalli County	4	1,498	104.4	14.4	$11,576	$11,562
Helena Elem	Lewis and Clark County	13	5,123	342.2	15.0	$12,154	$17,276
Helena H S	Lewis and Clark County	2	2,620	182.0	14.4	$11,456	$11,330
Hellgate Elem	Missoula County	4	1,473	99.3	14.8	$12,179	$20,144
Kalispell Elem	Flathead County	7	2,883	207.1	13.9	$11,807	$15,741
Missoula Elem	Missoula County	12	5,264	392.1	13.4	$11,903	$18,028
Missoula H S	Missoula County	4	3,717	259.8	14.3	$15,651	$20,016
NEBRASKA							
Bellevue Public Schools	Sarpy County	21	9,386	656.5	14.3	$11,850	$12,518
Bennington Public Schools	Douglas County	6	3,589	225.2	16.0	$12,422	$13,365
Columbus Public Schools	Platte County	9	4,159	258.2	16.1	$12,929	$12,814
Elkhorn Public Schools	Douglas County	19	10,642	688.0	15.5	$12,239	$12,995
Fremont Public Schools	Dodge County	14	4,868	310.3	15.7	$12,305	$11,942
Grand Island Public Schools	Hall County	23	9,920	716.8	13.8	$12,351	$13,963
Gretna Public Schools	Sarpy County	9	6,023	379.7	15.9	$12,187	$12,391
Hastings Public Schools	Adams County	7	3,672	264.4	13.9	$12,468	$12,944
Kearney Public Schools	Buffalo County	14	6,055	375.9	16.1	$12,272	$12,346
Lexington Public Schools	Dawson County	8	3,104	213.5	14.5	$12,908	$12,980
Lincoln Public Schools	Lancaster County	73	41,674	3,131.8	13.3	$12,640	$12,341
Millard Public Schools	Douglas County	36	23,633	1,501.2	15.7	$11,062	$11,306
Norfolk Public Schools	Madison County	12	4,444	289.3	15.4	$12,110	$11,813
North Platte Public Schools	Lincoln County	12	3,919	261.9	15.0	$11,913	$11,593
Omaha Public Schools	Douglas County	111	51,914	3,259.9	15.9	$13,650	$16,123
Papillion La Vista Community Schools	Sarpy County	22	11,831	800.7	14.8	$11,656	$10,870
Ralston Public Schools	Douglas County	8	3,210	228.7	14.0	$12,630	$11,485
Scottsbluff Public Schools	Scotts Bluff County	8	3,452	217.2	15.9	$13,241	$13,632
South Sioux City Community Schs	Dakota County	8	3,734	287.5	13.0	$12,429	$12,623
Westside Community Schools	Douglas County	14	6,091	422.2	14.4	$14,303	$16,768
NEVADA							
Carson City School District	Carson City	13	7,787	509.0	15.3	$11,918	$12,734
Churchill County School District	Churchill County	7	3,200	175.0	18.3	$12,413	$11,854
Clark County School District	Clark County	374	315,646	14,395.0	21.9	$10,655	$10,821
Correctional School District	Elko County	1	38	–	–	X	X
Davidson Academy School District	Washoe County	1	234	36.0	6.5	$22,267	$23,791
Douglas County School District	Douglas County	16	5,385	410.0	13.1	$12,986	$12,105
Elko County School District	Elko County	34	9,608	529.0	18.2	$13,449	$12,651
Esmeralda County School District	Esmeralda County	4	101	7.0	14.4	$36,890	$34,575
Eureka County School District	Eureka County	3	324	74.0	4.4	$37,254	$34,522
Humboldt County School District	Humboldt County	15	3,267	245.0	13.3	$13,376	$12,606
Lander County School District	Lander County	5	1,027	53.0	19.4	$20,476	$11,507
Lincoln County School District	Lincoln County	11	881	91.0	9.7	$14,481	$13,690
Lyon County School District	Lyon County	20	8,817	500.0	17.6	$11,293	$11,099
Mineral County School District	Mineral County	5	572	32.0	17.9	$16,375	$19,915
Nye County School District	Nye County	28	6,363	325.0	16.5	$13,239	$12,848
Pershing County School District	Pershing County	5	637	68.0	9.4	$20,966	$23,240
State-Sponsored Charter Schools	Carson City	69	53,223	2,216.0	24.0	$7,660	$9,928
Storey County School District	Storey County	4	448	44.0	10.2	$19,725	$15,149
Washoe County School District	Washoe County	111	64,584	3,994.0	16.2	$11,003	$11,312
White Pine County School District	White Pine County	10	1,216	43.0	28.3	$10,828	$9,798
NEW HAMPSHIRE							
Bedford School District	Hillsborough County	6	4,266	316.6	13.5	$14,681	$14,769
Concord School District	Merrimack County	7	4,093	319.2	12.8	$18,680	$18,735
Derry School District	Rockingham County	8	3,133	248.4	12.6	$25,051	$24,100
Dover School District	Strafford County	5	3,846	284.5	13.5	$15,258	$25,427
Exeter Region Coop School District	Rockingham County	2	2,633	213.0	12.4	$18,704	$18,197
Goffstown School District	Hillsborough County	5	2,767	215.2	12.9	$15,165	$14,862
Hudson School District	Hillsborough County	6	3,053	243.5	12.5	$15,156	$15,027
Keene School District	Cheshire County	7	3,120	265.8	11.7	$19,731	$18,698

NA = Not available.
X = Not applicable.

Table C-1. Characteristics of the 20 Largest Public School Districts in Each State—*Continued*

(Number; dollars.)

State/School District	County Name	Number of Operational Schools (2020-21)	Total Students in All Grades (2020-21)	Full-Time Equivalent Teachers (2020-21)	Pupil/ Teacher Ratio (2020-21)	Total Revenue per Pupil (2017-18)	Total Expenditures per Pupil (2017-18)
NEW HAMPSHIRE—*(Continued)*							
Londonderry School District	Rockingham County	6	4,093	330.0	12.4	$17,591	$17,130
Manchester School District	Hillsborough County	22	12,410	1,031.6	12.0	$14,113	$13,431
Merrimack School District	Hillsborough County	6	3,582	298.3	12.0	$18,927	$18,736
Merrimack Valley School District	Merrimack County	7	2,224	195.4	11.4	$16,255	$16,225
Milford School District	Hillsborough County	5	2,155	170.1	12.7	$17,391	$17,013
Nashua School District	Hillsborough County	19	10,239	870.4	11.8	$15,480	$14,737
Pinkerton Academy School District	Rockingham County	1	3,160	236.0	13.4	$0	X
Portsmouth School District	Rockingham County	6	2,531	237.5	10.7	$19,609	$19,237
Rochester School District	Strafford County	11	4,098	342.4	12.0	$15,226	$15,116
Salem School District	Rockingham County	8	3,519	281.9	12.5	$20,420	$23,418
Timberlane Regional School District	Rockingham County	7	3,278	295.6	11.1	$19,401	$18,988
Windham School District	Rockingham County	4	2,958	209.6	14.1	$15,696	$19,787
NEW JERSEY							
Bayonne School District	Hudson County	13	10,059	763.0	13.2	$17,189	$16,239
Cherry Hill School District	Camden County	19	10,596	887.6	11.9	$20,586	$19,711
Clifton Public School District	Passaic County	18	10,514	870.5	12.1	$19,045	$18,398
Edison Township School District	Middlesex County	19	16,632	1,226.6	13.6	$17,341	$17,517
Elizabeth Public Schools	Union County	37	28,090	2,173.5	12.9	$20,623	$20,526
Freehold Regional High School District	Monmouth County	6	10,519	687.5	15.3	$20,348	$20,116
Hamilton Township Public School District	Mercer County	23	11,678	952.9	12.3	$20,428	$20,586
Jersey City Public Schools	Hudson County	39	26,782	2,183.0	12.3	$25,048	$24,928
New Brunswick School District	Middlesex County	12	9,961	757.9	13.1	$21,535	$21,226
Newark Public School District	Essex County	63	40,423	2,886.5	14.0	$29,512	$28,858
Passaic City School District	Passaic County	17	13,494	1,066.0	12.7	$23,394	$24,414
Paterson Public School District	Passaic County	50	25,937	1,916.0	13.5	$21,915	$21,924
Perth Amboy Public School District	Middlesex County	12	10,786	898.7	12.0	$22,879	$23,658
Plainfield Public School District	Union County	13	9,744	601.5	16.2	$21,928	$22,204
Toms River Regional School District	Ocean County	18	14,618	1,102.9	13.3	$17,609	$17,245
Trenton Public Schools	Mercer County	21	14,708	967.7	15.2	$24,010	$23,600
Union City School District	Hudson County	14	13,101	837.0	15.7	$20,307	$21,768
Vineland Public School District	Cumberland County	14	10,266	731.9	14.0	$20,188	$22,304
West Windsor-Plainsboro Regional School District	Mercer County	10	9,386	773.2	12.1	$20,437	$19,002
Woodbridge Township School District	Middlesex County	25	13,860	1,153.1	12.0	$18,677	$18,429
NEW MEXICO							
Alamogordo Public Schools	Otero County	15	5,572	322.4	17.3	$9,826	$9,126
Albuquerque Public Schools	Bernalillo County	174	83,031	6,050.4	13.7	$11,481	$11,343
Artesia Public Schools	Eddy County	10	3,741	239.7	15.6	$12,570	$12,492
Belen Consolidated Schools	Valencia County	11	3,667	234.8	15.6	$11,787	$11,041
Carlsbad Municipal Schools	Eddy County	15	8,847	442.0	20.0	$14,284	$11,545
Central Consolidated Schools	San Juan County	17	5,173	385.5	13.4	$13,958	$13,654
Clovis Municipal Schools	Curry County	18	7,765	460.6	16.9	$10,206	$10,073
Deming Public Schools	Luna County	13	5,115	374.3	13.7	$10,715	$11,809
Farmington Municipal Schools	San Juan County	20	10,768	683.6	15.8	$9,897	$9,879
Gadsden Independent Schools	DoÃ±a Ana County	28	12,844	910.2	14.1	$11,341	$10,668
Gallup-Mckinley Cty Schools	McKinley County	33	12,281	746.9	16.4	$12,756	$12,461
Grants-Cibola County Schools	Cibola County	12	3,206	263.0	12.2	$12,551	$11,443
Hobbs Municipal Schools	Lea County	18	9,776	553.4	17.7	$10,314	$9,037
Las Cruces Public Schools	DoÃ±a Ana County	40	23,711	1,496.0	15.9	$10,761	$10,388
Los Alamos Public Schools	Los Alamos County	8	3,539	248.1	14.3	$13,307	$11,617
Los Lunas Public Schools	Valencia County	16	8,050	451.7	17.8	$9,820	$9,903
Lovington Municipal Schools	Lea County	10	3,502	208.5	16.8	$11,643	$9,971
Rio Rancho Public Schools	Sandoval County	20	16,807	1,115.4	15.1	$9,938	$9,459
Roswell Independent Schools	Chaves County	22	9,801	580.5	16.9	$10,163	$9,527
Santa Fe Public Schools	Santa Fe County	30	12,403	868.4	14.3	$14,434	$13,639
NEW YORK							
Buffalo City School District	Erie County	60	31,428	2,730.9	11.5	$30,513	$29,923
New York City Geographic District # 2	New York County	118	60,446	4,496.6	13.4	X	X
New York City Geographic District # 8	Bronx County	52	25,994	2,096.0	12.4	X	X
New York City Geographic District # 9	Bronx County	69	31,384	2,522.9	12.4	X	X
New York City Geographic District #10	Bronx County	84	51,467	4,058.6	12.7	X	X
New York City Geographic District #11	Bronx County	62	36,296	3,040.5	11.9	X	X
New York City Geographic District #15	Kings County	48	30,388	2,562.6	11.9	X	X
New York City Geographic District #20	Kings County	45	50,119	3,391.5	14.8	X	X
New York City Geographic District #21	Kings County	40	34,525	2,591.5	13.3	X	X
New York City Geographic District #22	Kings County	40	33,200	2,248.9	14.8	X	X
New York City Geographic District #24	Queens County	56	54,293	4,182.1	13.0	X	X

NA = Not available.
X = Not applicable.

Table C-1. Characteristics of the 20 Largest Public School Districts in Each State—*Continued*

(Number; dollars.)

State/School District	County Name	Number of Operational Schools (2020-21)	Total Students in All Grades (2020-21)	Full-Time Equivalent Teachers (2020-21)	Pupil/ Teacher Ratio (2020-21)	Total Revenue per Pupil (2017-18)	Total Expenditures per Pupil (2017-18)
NEW YORK —*(Continued)*							
New York City Geographic District #25	Queens County	46	36,061	2,612.7	13.8	X	X
New York City Geographic District #26	Queens County	34	31,351	2,470.6	12.7	X	X
New York City Geographic District #27	Queens County	63	43,540	3,095.9	14.1	X	X
New York City Geographic District #28	Queens County	50	40,347	2,685.8	15.0	X	X
New York City Geographic District #29	Queens County	46	24,957	1,749.9	14.3	X	X
New York City Geographic District #30	Queens County	50	37,841	2,574.2	14.7	X	X
New York City Geographic District #31	Richmond County	72	62,857	4,668.6	13.5	X	X
Rochester City School District	Monroe County	47	24,898	2,194.7	11.3	$31,334	$35,874
Yonkers City School District	Westchester County	40	25,488	1,429.0	17.8	$23,672	$23,713
NORTH CAROLINA							
Alamance-Burlington Schools	Alamance County	36	21,931	1,502.2	14.6	$9,220	$9,122
Buncombe County Schools	Buncombe County	44	22,298	1,622.2	13.8	$11,146	$11,405
Cabarrus County Schools	Cabarrus County	42	32,810	2,081.4	15.8	$10,452	$10,570
Charlotte-Mecklenburg Schools	Mecklenburg County	176	142,733	9,284.4	15.4	$10,150	$11,361
Cumberland County Schools	Cumberland County	89	49,278	3,434.3	14.4	$9,290	$9,467
Davidson County Schools	Davidson County	36	17,964	1,152.6	15.6	$8,674	$8,986
Durham Public Schools	Durham County	54	32,005	2,380.7	13.4	$11,889	$11,615
Gaston County Schools	Gaston County	55	29,777	1,910.5	15.6	$9,526	$9,644
Guilford County Schools	Guilford County	126	70,047	4,770.1	14.7	$10,024	$10,378
Harnett County Schools	Harnett County	28	19,470	1,250.9	15.6	$8,607	$8,883
Iredell-Statesville Schools	Iredell County	37	20,163	1,275.2	15.8	$9,680	$9,070
Johnston County Public Schools	Johnston County	46	36,422	2,411.4	15.1	$9,250	$9,815
New Hanover County Schools	New Hanover County	43	24,841	1,696.1	14.7	$10,185	$11,584
Onslow County Schools	Onslow County	37	26,269	1,659.3	15.8	$9,251	$9,723
Pitt County Schools	Pitt County	38	23,312	1,612.2	14.5	$9,371	$9,885
Public Schools of Robeson County	Robeson County	36	21,083	1,355.1	15.6	$10,107	$10,234
Rowan-Salisbury Schools	Rowan County	35	18,205	1,254.9	14.5	$9,580	$9,650
Union County Public Schools	Union County	52	40,207	2,425.8	16.6	$9,306	$9,477
Wake County Schools	Wake County	192	159,802	10,515.9	15.2	$9,218	$11,184
Winston Salem / Forsyth County Schools	Forsyth County	79	51,843	3,635.2	14.3	$9,647	$10,377
NORTH DAKOTA							
Belcourt 7	Rolette County	4	1,594	123.8	12.9	$17,273	$17,259
Beulah 27	Mercer County	3	719	55.9	12.9	$12,718	$13,222
Bismarck 1	Burleigh County	24	13,433	888.9	15.1	$14,380	$15,639
Central Cass 17	Cass County	3	953	65.1	14.7	$14,343	$32,202
Devils Lake 1	Ramsey County	5	1,666	129.1	12.9	$13,941	$13,689
Dickinson 1	Stark County	10	3,810	260.9	14.6	$15,052	$15,672
Fargo 1	Cass County	22	11,304	899.5	12.6	$15,608	$15,226
Grafton 3	Walsh County	3	909	92.5	9.8	$14,470	$12,551
Grand Forks 1	Grand Forks County	19	7,567	649.0	11.7	$14,241	$14,427
Jamestown 1	Stutsman County	7	2,206	176.8	12.5	$14,505	$14,257
Kindred 2	Cass County	2	841	67.8	12.4	$14,480	$12,523
Mandan 1	Morton County	9	4,095	263.6	15.5	$13,755	$14,044
Mckenzie Co 1	McKenzie County	5	1,836	144.1	12.7	$18,482	$14,422
Minot 1	Ward County	19	7,672	542.4	14.1	$15,044	$14,213
New Town 1	Mountrail County	3	944	87.9	10.7	$24,771	$19,351
Valley City 2	Barnes County	4	1,060	68.4	15.5	$13,008	$13,840
Wahpeton 37	Richland County	4	1,215	82.7	14.7	$15,019	$12,769
West Fargo 6	Cass County	21	11,561	942.6	12.3	$14,879	$16,797
Williams County 8	Williams County	3	779	46.2	15.8	$26,088	$43,002
Williston 1	Williams County	10	4,297	325.3	13.2	$12,765	$12,435
OHIO							
Akron City	Summit County	47	20,563	1,494.4	13.8	$17,753	$19,526
Cincinnati Public Schools	Hamilton County	64	34,635	2,322.9	14.0	$19,727	$10,790
Cleveland Municipal	Cuyahoga County	95	34,941	2,456.0	14.2	$21,259	$26,096
Columbus City School District	Franklin County	116	46,657	3,097.2	15.1	$18,715	$20,590
Dayton City	Montgomery County	27	11,721	822.3	14.3	$20,733	$22,140
Dublin City	Franklin County	22	16,254	838.5	19.4	$15,294	$13,575
Fairfield City	Butler County	10	9,708	483.2	20.1	$10,874	$11,720
Hamilton City	Butler County	12	9,415	484.8	19.4	$12,433	$11,785
Hilliard City	Franklin County	23	16,027	1,079.8	14.8	$14,371	$14,856
Lakota Local	Butler County	20	16,415	691.8	23.7	$12,468	$11,780
Mason City	Warren County	4	10,267	487.5	21.1	$13,700	$12,450
Northwest Local	Hamilton County	11	8,541	459.8	18.6	$11,757	$18,120
Ohio Virtual Academy	Lucas County	1	21,049	413.0	51.0	$8,494	$8,375
Olentangy Local	Delaware County	26	22,089	1,153.9	19.1	$13,525	$13,931
Parma City	Cuyahoga County	15	9,318	519.1	18.0	$15,250	$15,844

NA = Not available.
X = Not applicable.

Table C-1. Characteristics of the 20 Largest Public School Districts in Each State—*Continued*

(Number; dollars.)

State/School District	County Name	Number of Operational Schools (2020-21)	Total Students in All Grades (2020-21)	Full-Time Equivalent Teachers (2020-21)	Pupil/ Teacher Ratio (2020-21)	Total Revenue per Pupil (2017-18)	Total Expenditures per Pupil (2017-18)
OHIO—*(Continued)*							
Pickerington Local	Fairfield County	15	10,454	515.7	20.3	$13,397	$13,007
South-Western City	Franklin County	34	21,654	1,231.8	17.6	$13,365	$12,158
Toledo City	Lucas County	55	22,312	1,623.5	13.7	$16,691	$18,906
Westerville City	Franklin County	22	14,576	806.4	18.1	$13,841	$12,126
Worthington City	Franklin County	18	10,530	615.3	17.1	$14,978	$14,000
OKLAHOMA							
Bartlesville	Washington County	9	5,828	359.7	16.2	$9,078	$7,817
Bixby	Tulsa County	10	6,560	394.1	16.7	$9,291	$9,885
Broken Arrow	Tulsa County	27	18,619	1,036.9	18.0	$8,862	$8,430
Deer Creek	Oklahoma County	9	6,741	382.4	17.6	$9,226	$9,040
Edmond	Oklahoma County	26	23,496	1,383.3	17.0	$9,134	$9,110
Enid	Garfield County	16	7,390	444.7	16.6	$9,067	$8,792
Epic Blended Learning Charter	Oklahoma County	6	23,714	572.0	41.5	$4,535	$3,583
Epic One On One Charter School	Oklahoma County	3	35,731	792.6	45.1	$5,581	$6,782
Jenks	Tulsa County	8	11,979	720.1	16.6	$10,010	$10,505
Lawton	Comanche County	25	12,897	893.0	14.4	$9,067	$9,444
Midwest City-Del City	Oklahoma County	21	11,044	861.5	12.8	$8,292	$8,730
Moore	Cleveland County	34	23,390	1,403.9	16.7	$8,552	$8,595
Mustang	Canadian County	16	11,868	731.0	16.2	$8,183	$7,771
Norman	Cleveland County	25	14,419	967.2	14.9	$9,096	$9,739
Oklahoma City	Oklahoma County	59	31,026	2,193.4	14.2	$9,604	$9,596
Owasso	Tulsa County	13	9,035	528.2	17.1	$8,413	$7,858
Putnam City	Oklahoma County	26	17,829	1,245.5	14.3	$9,166	$9,110
Tulsa	Tulsa County	69	32,569	2,102.0	15.5	$10,981	$11,090
Union	Tulsa County	17	14,959	866.9	17.3	$11,221	$9,876
Yukon	Canadian County	12	8,158	529.4	15.4	$8,674	$8,565
OREGON							
Beaverton SD 48J	Washington County	55	39,594	2,126.1	18.6	$13,727	$15,593
Bend-LaPine Administrative SD 1	Deschutes County	35	17,543	883.3	19.9	$13,066	$12,792
Corvallis SD 509J	Benton County	13	6,462	345.3	18.7	$12,926	$11,741
David Douglas SD 40	Multnomah County	14	9,299	492.8	18.9	$15,462	$14,851
Eugene SD 4J	Lane County	37	16,683	847.1	19.7	$13,980	$13,564
Greater Albany Public SD 8J	Linn County	20	8,990	464.5	19.4	$12,458	$13,971
Gresham-Barlow SD 10J	Multnomah County	21	11,661	554.8	21.0	$12,944	$14,622
Hillsboro SD 1J	Washington County	35	19,407	870.6	22.3	$13,490	$13,335
Klamath County SD	Klamath County	21	6,784	361.6	18.8	$13,325	$12,856
Lake Oswego SD 7J	Clackamas County	11	6,860	391.2	17.5	$15,404	$14,637
Medford SD 549C	Jackson County	25	13,962	734.6	19.0	$12,002	$11,552
North Clackamas SD 12	Clackamas County	30	16,458	848.6	19.4	$13,898	$17,979
Oregon City SD 62	Clackamas County	14	7,420	384.7	19.3	$12,536	$11,914
Portland SD 1J	Multnomah County	86	46,965	2,815.5	16.7	$17,010	$17,685
Redmond SD 2J	Deschutes County	13	7,070	357.0	19.8	$12,583	$11,706
Reynolds SD 7	Multnomah County	19	10,560	580.4	18.2	$13,880	$21,347
Salem-Keizer SD 24J	Marion County	65	39,906	2,042.2	19.5	$13,255	$12,897
Springfield SD 19	Lane County	21	9,779	527.6	18.5	$12,532	$14,405
Tigard-Tualatin SD 23J	Washington County	17	11,860	651.5	18.2	$14,252	$15,539
West Linn-Wilsonville SD 3J	Clackamas County	17	9,302	525.0	17.7	$13,767	$14,785
PENNSYLVANIA							
Allentown City SD	Lehigh County	21	16,231	1,064.0	15.3	$19,168	$19,656
Bethlehem Area SD	Northampton County	22	13,005	924.7	14.1	$20,444	$19,980
Central Bucks SD	Bucks County	23	17,571	1,256.5	14.0	$18,396	$17,292
Central Dauphin SD	Dauphin County	19	11,894	837.1	14.2	$16,992	$17,259
Commonwealth Charter Academy CS	Dauphin County	1	16,419	525.0	31.3	$15,097	$14,594
Council Rock SD	Bucks County	14	10,494	751.1	14.0	$21,953	$24,389
Cumberland Valley SD	Cumberland County	11	9,403	572.5	16.4	$15,527	$19,909
Downingtown Area SD	Chester County	16	12,909	928.6	13.9	$18,042	$16,714
Erie City SD	Erie County	15	10,310	762.3	13.5	$19,329	$17,236
Hazleton Area SD	Luzerne County	11	11,551	689.0	16.8	$13,512	$13,265
Lancaster SD	Lancaster County	19	10,384	861.3	12.1	$20,094	$19,329
North Penn SD	Montgomery County	17	12,603	931.6	13.5	$20,555	$20,000
Parkland SD	Lehigh County	12	9,541	635.0	15.0	$18,732	$18,303
Pennsbury SD	Bucks County	15	9,544	809.3	11.8	$20,572	$21,185
Pennsylvania Cyber CS	Beaver County	1	10,917	408.0	26.8	$15,596	$13,699
Philadelphia City SD	Philadelphia County	217	124,111	7,855.7	15.8	$26,037	$25,287
Pittsburgh SD	Allegheny County	56	21,407	1,925.8	11.1	$30,470	$30,523
Reading SD	Berks County	19	17,659	1,097.0	16.1	$15,716	$14,710
Upper Darby SD	Delaware County	14	12,420	821.6	15.1	$15,937	$15,613
West Chester Area SD	Chester County	16	11,972	878.4	13.6	$20,630	$19,877

NA = Not available.
X = Not applicable.

Table C-1. Characteristics of the 20 Largest Public School Districts in Each State—*Continued*

(Number; dollars.)

State/School District	County Name	Number of Operational Schools (2020-21)	Total Students in All Grades (2020-21)	Full-Time Equivalent Teachers (2020-21)	Pupil/ Teacher Ratio (2020-21)	Total Revenue per Pupil (2017-18)	Total Expenditures per Pupil (2017-18)
RHODE ISLAND							
Barrington	Bristol County	6	3,388	230.1	14.7	$16,258	$16,653
Bristol Warren	Bristol County	6	3,061	228.4	13.4	$19,449	$19,081
Central Falls	Providence County	6	2,780	189.7	14.7	$21,178	$20,933
Chariho	Washington County	8	3,143	260.7	12.1	$19,700	$20,396
Coventry	Kent County	8	4,390	348.9	12.6	$16,499	$16,322
Cranston	Providence County	24	10,403	789.1	13.2	$17,103	$16,880
Cumberland	Providence County	9	4,602	332.2	13.9	$16,019	$15,451
East Greenwich	Kent County	6	2,532	174.8	14.5	$16,948	$16,992
East Providence	Providence County	13	5,041	395.2	12.8	$18,268	$18,023
Johnston	Providence County	8	3,110	242.6	12.8	$19,645	$19,522
Lincoln	Providence County	6	3,213	220.9	14.6	$19,512	$19,458
North Kingstown	Washington County	8	3,923	323.8	12.1	$18,049	$18,273
North Providence	Providence County	8	3,525	260.9	13.5	$17,252	$17,500
Pawtucket	Providence County	16	8,450	583.6	14.5	$16,988	$18,181
Providence	Providence County	41	22,440	1,655.6	13.6	$19,460	$18,818
South Kingstown	Washington County	7	2,750	223.8	12.3	$21,463	$21,251
Warwick	Kent County	19	8,140	672.4	12.1	$20,361	$21,269
West Warwick	Kent County	6	3,551	279.2	12.7	$17,974	$17,503
Westerly	Washington County	6	2,433	217.8	11.2	$22,879	$22,645
Woonsocket	Providence County	10	5,742	399.3	14.4	$16,631	$17,266
SOUTH CAROLINA							
Aiken 01	Aiken County	42	22,538	1,529.6	14.7	$12,026	$11,712
Anderson 05	Anderson County	20	12,771	866.9	14.7	$12,332	$11,627
Beaufort 01	Beaufort County	32	21,219	1,698.6	12.5	$15,323	$14,465
Berkeley 01	Berkeley County	46	36,575	2,287.0	16.0	$12,295	$12,612
Charleston 01	Charleston County	81	48,330	3,586.6	13.5	$17,867	$16,320
Charter Institute at Erskine	Richland County	22	23,750	886.5	26.8	X	X
Dorchester 02	Dorchester County	24	24,684	1,594.8	15.5	$10,514	$10,862
Florence 01	Florence County	24	15,186	1,164.6	13.0	$11,962	$11,801
Greenville 01	Greenville County	91	74,094	4,990.4	14.9	$12,051	$11,261
Horry 01	Horry County	57	44,479	3,109.0	14.3	$13,432	$14,148
Lancaster 01	Lancaster County	22	13,940	900.5	15.5	$12,708	$15,707
Lexington 01	Lexington County	31	27,072	1,953.2	13.9	$14,091	$13,309
Lexington 05	Richland County	22	16,780	1,324.0	12.7	$14,475	$13,885
Pickens 01	Pickens County	24	15,689	1,003.8	15.6	$11,200	$10,216
Richland 01	Richland County	48	22,202	1,921.2	11.6	$18,450	$18,152
Richland 02	Richland County	33	27,761	1,964.0	14.1	$14,209	$12,659
SC Public Charter School District	Richland County	33	15,773	1,097.6	14.4	$19,544	$19,457
Sumter 01	Sumter County	25	15,586	965.0	16.2	$11,194	$10,492
York 03	York County	28	16,652	1,266.1	13.2	$12,445	$15,009
York 04	York County	19	16,883	1,214.8	13.9	$13,738	$15,714
SOUTH DAKOTA							
Aberdeen School District 06-1	Brown County	10	4,485	300.4	14.9	$10,603	$9,899
Belle Fourche School District 09-1	Butte County	5	1,380	96.2	14.3	$10,584	$11,520
Brandon Valley School District 49-2	Minnehaha County	7	4,721	255.1	18.5	$10,280	$9,607
Brookings School District 05-1	Brookings County	6	3,346	236.9	14.1	$10,773	$10,093
Dakota Valley School District 61-8	Union County	4	1,377	89.3	15.4	$11,812	$10,221
Douglas School District 51-1	Pennington County	5	2,755	180.0	15.3	$10,601	$9,160
Harrisburg School District 41-2	Lincoln County	9	5,457	386.1	14.1	$11,787	$10,589
Huron School District 02-2	Beadle County	9	2,766	171.5	16.1	$11,741	$11,115
Meade School District 46-1	Meade County	12	3,006	207.7	14.5	$10,530	$14,932
Mitchell School District 17-2	Davison County	9	2,775	185.0	15.0	$10,691	$10,242
Oglala Lakota County 65-1	Oglala Lakota County	6	1,807	116.8	15.5	$25,805	$44,533
Pierre School District 32-2	Hughes County	5	2,771	171.5	16.2	$10,705	$9,773
Rapid City Area School District 51-4	Pennington County	26	12,814	855.7	15.0	$10,473	$10,269
Sioux Falls School District 49-5	Minnehaha County	43	24,868	1,595.2	15.6	$10,592	$10,244
Spearfish School District 40-2	Lawrence County	8	2,345	169.5	13.8	$10,103	$9,260
Tea Area School District 41-5	Lincoln County	5	2,061	124.2	16.6	$10,317	$9,826
Todd County School District 66-1	Todd County	13	2,158	160.8	13.4	$17,112	$14,872
Watertown School District 14-4	Codington County	9	3,953	249.0	15.9	$10,069	$10,072
West Central School District 49-7	Minnehaha County	6	1,384	91.3	15.2	$10,500	$9,720
Yankton School District 63-3	Yankton County	6	2,955	170.5	17.3	$9,923	$10,373
TENNESSEE							
Achievement School District	Davidson County	27	9,027	474.7	19.0	$12,202	$12,046
Blount County	Blount County	22	10,399	679.5	15.3	$10,154	$10,181
Bradley County	Bradley County	17	9,701	648.9	15.0	$9,009	$9,118
Collierville	Shelby County	9	9,043	553.7	16.3	$13,605	$15,786

NA = Not available.
X = Not applicable.

Table C-1. Characteristics of the 20 Largest Public School Districts in Each State—*Continued*

(Number; dollars.)

State/School District	County Name	Number of Operational Schools (2020-21)	Total Students in All Grades (2020-21)	Full-Time Equivalent Teachers (2020-21)	Pupil/ Teacher Ratio (2020-21)	Total Revenue per Pupil (2017-18)	Total Expenditures per Pupil (2017-18)
TENNESSEE—*(Continued)*							
Davidson County	Davidson County	162	80,494	5,245.5	15.4	$13,120	$14,722
Hamblen County	Hamblen County	18	10,210	667.7	15.3	$9,450	$9,353
Hamilton County	Hamilton County	79	44,100	3,085.9	14.3	$10,416	$10,050
Knox County	Knox County	91	59,169	3,931.4	15.1	$9,271	$9,191
Madison County	Madison County	23	12,378	833.7	14.9	$9,808	$10,303
Maury County	Maury County	24	12,734	850.8	15.0	$9,078	$9,616
Montgomery County	Montgomery County	39	36,426	2,184.0	16.7	$9,156	$9,434
Putnam County	Putnam County	22	11,609	744.6	15.6	$9,216	$9,678
Robertson County	Robertson County	25	13,960	735.0	19.0	$9,594	$9,586
Rutherford County	Rutherford County	50	47,186	3,008.1	15.7	$9,452	$12,251
Sevier County	Sevier County	32	14,140	999.3	14.2	$11,473	$11,589
Shelby County	Shelby County	221	110,780	6,546.1	16.9	$12,535	$12,427
Sumner County	Sumner County	49	29,588	2,001.5	14.8	$9,499	$9,237
Tipton County	Tipton County	14	10,393	610.5	17.0	$8,772	$8,494
Williamson County	Williamson County	49	39,817	2,553.6	15.6	$12,365	$12,027
Wilson County	Wilson County	24	18,444	1,244.1	14.8	$9,060	$11,786
TEXAS							
Aldine ISD	Harris County	78	63,302	4,243.8	14.9	$11,123	$16,268
Arlington ISD	Tarrant County	78	56,840	4,114.7	13.8	$11,087	$12,109
Austin ISD	Travis County	126	74,871	5,508.2	13.6	$18,950	$19,469
Conroe ISD	Montgomery County	61	64,563	4,110.6	15.7	$10,257	$11,849
Cypress-Fairbanks ISD	Harris County	90	114,881	7,659.4	15.0	$10,711	$11,355
Dallas ISD	Dallas County	233	145,113	10,265.9	14.1	$12,676	$12,499
El Paso ISD	El Paso County	85	50,661	3,730.5	13.6	$10,598	$11,191
Fort Bend ISD	Fort Bend County	82	76,735	5,054.4	15.2	$10,943	$11,940
Fort Worth ISD	Tarrant County	146	76,858	5,488.2	14.0	$11,523	$12,036
Frisco ISD	Collin County	74	63,493	4,388.9	14.5	$11,394	$10,457
Garland ISD	Dallas County	73	53,921	3,609.3	14.9	$11,335	$12,462
Houston ISD	Harris County	276	196,943	11,750.1	16.8	$12,507	$14,252
Idea Public Schools	Hidalgo County	111	62,158	2,892.3	21.5	$12,034	$9,399
Katy ISD	Fort Bend County	73	84,176	5,881.8	14.3	$11,774	$13,543
Klein ISD	Harris County	52	52,824	3,617.1	14.6	$11,082	$12,078
Lewisville ISD	Denton County	64	49,361	3,691.7	13.4	$12,242	$12,127
North East ISD	Bexar County	75	60,483	4,224.6	14.3	$11,384	$11,904
Northside ISD	Bexar County	121	103,151	6,844.9	15.1	$11,146	$11,131
Pasadena ISD	Harris County	67	50,614	3,752.3	13.5	$12,297	$12,020
Plano ISD	Collin County	79	50,154	3,786.9	13.2	$15,417	$15,563
UTAH							
Alpine District	Utah County	91	82,800	NA	NA	$8,259	$8,529
American Preparatory Academy	Salt Lake County	6	5,329	NA	NA	$8,019	$8,897
Box Elder District	Box Elder County	24	12,062	NA	NA	$8,985	$9,100
Cache District	Cache County	26	19,214	NA	NA	$8,910	$9,261
Canyons District	Salt Lake County	51	34,383	NA	NA	$9,690	$10,136
Davis District	Davis County	95	72,082	NA	NA	$8,683	$9,435
Granite District	Salt Lake County	92	63,430	NA	NA	$8,819	$8,766
Iron District	Iron County	18	11,091	NA	NA	$8,838	$8,140
Jordan District	Salt Lake County	65	57,267	NA	NA	$8,027	$9,059
Logan City District	Cache County	11	5,704	NA	NA	$10,485	$9,544
Murray District	Salt Lake County	12	6,175	NA	NA	$9,218	$8,547
Nebo District	Utah County	46	35,912	NA	NA	$8,898	$8,172
Ogden City District	Weber County	25	10,710	NA	NA	$10,604	$9,588
Provo District	Utah County	23	13,575	NA	NA	$9,471	$11,295
Salt Lake District	Salt Lake County	43	20,798	NA	NA	$11,529	$10,911
Tooele District	Tooele County	26	21,535	NA	NA	$8,460	$8,182
Uintah District	Uintah County	13	6,787	NA	NA	$10,882	$8,630
Wasatch District	Wasatch County	9	9,251	NA	NA	$11,158	$11,580
Washington District	Washington County	54	36,992	NA	NA	$8,675	$9,435
Weber District	Weber County	48	32,423	NA	NA	$8,271	$8,359
VERMONT							
Addison Central Unified School District	Addison County	9	1,742	136.2	12.8	$20,263	$21,214
Barre Unified Union School District #97	Washington County	4	2,169	220.8	9.8	X	X
Burlington School District	Chittenden County	10	3,591	307.0	11.7	$22,650	$21,765
Champlain Valley Unified School District	Chittenden County	5	4,150	286.5	14.5	$19,464	$22,778
Colchester School District	Chittenden County	5	2,361	171.9	13.7	$18,158	$18,146
Essex-Westford Educational Community Unified School District	Chittenden County	10	3,831	340.7	11.2	$23,182	$22,316
Hartford School District	Windsor County	6	1,441	167.8	8.6	$26,192	$25,911
Harwood Unified School District	Washington County	7	1,813	173.2	10.5	$21,883	$22,432

NA = Not available.
X = Not applicable.

Table C-1. Characteristics of the 20 Largest Public School Districts in Each State—*Continued*

(Number; dollars.)

State/School District	County Name	Number of Operational Schools (2020-21)	Total Students in All Grades (2020-21)	Full-Time Equivalent Teachers (2020-21)	Pupil/ Teacher Ratio (2020-21)	Total Revenue per Pupil (2017-18)	Total Expenditures per Pupil (2017-18)
VERMONT—(*Continued*)							
Kingdom East Unified Union School District........	Caledonia County	7	1,631	130.2	12.5	X	X
Lamoille South Unified Union School District #90.	Lamoille County	7	1,581	117.9	13.4	X	X
Maple Run Unified School District	Franklin County	5	2,597	219.3	11.8	$20,690	$21,118
Milton Incorporated School District	Chittenden County	3	1,534	133.3	11.5	$18,802	$18,813
Missisquoi Valley School District #89	Franklin County	4	1,784	170.5	10.5	X	X
Mount Anthony UHSD #14.................................	Bennington County	2	1,468	94.0	15.6	$17,483	$17,713
Mount Mansfield Unified Union School District #401.	Chittenden County	8	2,569	169.9	15.1	X	X
Rutland City School District	Rutland County	6	2,012	165.0	12.2	$24,685	$24,119
South Burlington School District.........................	Chittenden County	5	2,688	216.4	12.4	$19,350	$19,351
Taconic and Green Regional School District........	Bennington County	5	1,611	78.5	20.5	X	X
Washington Central Unified Union School District #92	Washington County	6	1,473	129.0	11.4	X	X
Windham Southeast Unified Union School District #96	Windham County	9	2,353	208.8	11.3	X	X
VIRGINIA							
Alexandria City Public Schools..........................	Alexandria city	19	15,775	1,106.8	14.3	$17,478	$18,239
Arlington County Public Schools.........................	Arlington County	41	26,831	1,856.5	14.5	$22,685	$23,970
Chesapeake City Public Schools	Chesapeake city	48	39,673	2,766.1	14.3	$12,339	$12,675
Chesterfield Co Public Schools	Chesterfield County	69	60,840	4,212.1	14.4	$11,198	$11,402
Fairfax County Public Schools	Fairfax County	222	100,020	13,149.8	13.7	$15,562	$16,474
Frederick County Public Schools........................	Winchester city	19	13,521	985.8	13.7	$13,927	$13,246
Hampton City Public Schools.............................	Hampton city	33	19,223	1,368.3	14.1	$11,740	$11,863
Hanover County Public Schools	Hanover County	25	16,519	773.8	21.4	$10,567	$11,112
Henrico County Public Schools..........................	Henrico County	81	50,191	2,938.9	17.1	$11,860	$11,421
Loudoun County Public Schools	Loudoun County	96	81,066	6,114.6	13.3	$14,959	$15,604
Newport News City Public Schools	Newport News city	45	27,113	1,776.9	15.3	$12,858	$12,424
Norfolk City Public Schools	Norfolk city	51	27,955	2,185.2	12.8	$12,186	$12,109
Prince William County Public Schools	Prince William County	95	89,548	5,650.4	15.9	$13,422	$13,368
Richmond City Public Schools...........................	Richmond city	54	28,225	1,525.3	18.5	$15,262	$15,038
Roanoke City Public Schools	Roanoke city	26	13,853	906.5	15.3	$14,716	$14,020
Roanoke County Public Schools	Roanoke County	29	13,690	1,002.9	13.7	$11,668	$11,003
Spotsylvania County Public Schools	Spotsylvania County	34	23,025	1,451.7	15.9	$12,223	$12,143
Stafford County Public Schools	Stafford County	34	29,372	1,843.9	15.9	$10,588	$10,979
Suffolk City Public Schools	Suffolk city	22	13,869	900.2	14.2	$13,873	$13,048
Virginia Beach City Public Schools.....................	Virginia Beach city	87	65,612	4,354.7	15.1	$12,305	$13,041
WASHINGTON							
Auburn School District......................................	King County	25	17,007	1,005.6	16.9	$15,867	$15,308
Bellevue School District	King County	31	20,191	1,157.6	17.4	$18,845	$23,068
Bethel School District.......................................	Pierce County	32	20,076	1,148.8	17.5	$14,432	$13,282
Edmonds School District...................................	Snohomish County	38	20,851	1,151.8	18.1	$16,576	$19,187
Everett School District......................................	Snohomish County	33	20,226	1,103.5	18.3	$16,017	$15,733
Evergreen School District (Clark).......................	Clark County	39	23,564	1,450.2	16.3	$14,392	$14,219
Federal Way School District	King County	46	21,765	1,240.4	17.6	$15,212	$15,351
Highline School District	King County	42	18,635	1,016.1	18.3	$16,361	$17,262
Issaquah School District	King County	28	20,164	1,120.4	18.0	$15,555	$19,701
Kennewick School District	Benton County	32	18,396	1,048.1	17.6	$15,232	$15,636
Kent School District	King County	44	25,720	1,444.3	17.8	$13,922	$14,354
Lake Washington School District	King County	57	30,964	1,760.3	17.6	$15,408	$19,157
Northshore School District................................	Snohomish County	39	23,310	1,298.4	18.0	$14,879	$14,362
Pasco School District.......................................	Franklin County	28	18,614	1,024.3	18.2	$13,543	$13,492
Puyallup School District....................................	Pierce County	37	22,398	1,200.6	18.7	$14,308	$16,100
Seattle School District No. 1	King County	109	53,973	3,377.6	16.0	$19,107	$18,240
Spokane School District....................................	Spokane County	64	28,280	1,743.6	16.2	$15,301	$15,030
Tacoma School District.....................................	Pierce County	67	28,688	1,625.4	17.7	$17,102	$17,693
Vancouver School District.................................	Clark County	41	21,897	1,270.7	17.2	$13,670	$14,223
Yakima School District......................................	Yakima County	29	15,858	873.6	18.2	$13,710	$13,888
WEST VIRGINIA							
Berkeley County Schools	Berkeley County	32	19,278	1,309.5	14.7	$11,444	$11,651
Cabell County Schools	Cabell County	26	11,875	849.8	14.0	$12,503	$11,899
Fayette County Schools....................................	Fayette County	13	5,688	427.5	13.3	$12,418	$11,882
Greenbrier County Schools	Greenbrier County	14	4,719	335.0	14.1	$13,075	$12,371
Harrison County Schools	Harrison County	27	10,111	790.3	12.8	$13,150	$13,673
Jackson County Schools	Jackson County	13	4,266	322.7	13.2	$12,470	$12,307
Jefferson County Schools	Jefferson County	16	8,506	580.5	14.7	$12,813	$12,037
Kanawha County Schools..................................	Kanawha County	69	24,721	1,757.6	14.1	$12,464	$12,099
Logan County Schools......................................	Logan County	18	5,229	383.7	13.6	$12,811	$12,839

NA = Not available.
X – Not applicable.

Table C-1. Characteristics of the 20 Largest Public School Districts in Each State—*Continued*

(Number; dollars.)

State/School District	County Name	Number of Operational Schools (2020-21)	Total Students in All Grades (2020-21)	Full-Time Equivalent Teachers (2020-21)	Pupil/ Teacher Ratio (2020-21)	Total Revenue per Pupil (2017-18)	Total Expenditures per Pupil (2017-18)
WEST VIRGINIA—(*Continued*)							
Marion County Schools	Marion County	22	7,658	551.5	13.9	$11,971	$11,933
Marshall County Schools	Marshall County	14	4,320	366.0	11.8	$16,800	$15,487
Mercer County Schools	Mercer County	25	8,465	611.5	13.8	$12,034	$11,385
Mineral County Schools	Mineral County	14	4,001	296.0	13.5	$12,324	$12,062
Monongalia County Schools	Monongalia County	18	11,113	783.0	14.2	$13,039	$12,964
Ohio County Schools	Ohio County	13	5,064	398.0	12.7	$14,166	$13,265
Preston County Schools	Preston County	10	4,210	297.0	14.2	$10,681	$9,877
Putnam County Schools	Putnam County	23	9,147	671.5	13.6	$12,211	$12,001
Raleigh County Schools	Raleigh County	27	10,869	799.0	13.6	$13,417	$13,091
Wayne County Schools	Wayne County	18	6,461	478.0	13.5	$11,409	$11,486
Wood County Schools	Wood County	26	11,864	855.0	13.9	$12,144	$11,624
WISCONSIN							
Appleton Area School District	Outagamie County	38	15,745	1,016.7	15.5	$12,359	$11,905
Eau Claire Area School District	Eau Claire County	24	11,008	746.7	14.7	$13,704	$14,018
Elmbrook School District	Waukesha County	10	7,280	491.6	14.8	$14,532	$13,506
Fond du Lac School District	Fond du Lac County	16	6,678	495.6	13.5	$13,768	$12,719
Green Bay Area Public School District	Brown County	43	19,171	1,497.1	12.8	$15,458	$15,124
Janesville School District	Rock County	23	9,574	799.8	12.0	$13,214	$13,298
Kenosha School District	Kenosha County	43	19,244	1,391.8	13.8	$13,767	$14,201
Madison Metropolitan School District	Dane County	54	26,151	2,158.9	12.1	$16,117	$15,965
Middleton-Cross Plains Area School District	Dane County	12	7,410	562.2	13.2	$13,341	$12,681
Milwaukee School District	Milwaukee County	158	71,510	4,345.2	16.5	$16,278	$16,803
Neenah Joint School District	Winnebago County	14	6,572	407.1	16.1	$12,017	$12,004
Oshkosh Area School District	Winnebago County	22	9,191	772.6	11.9	$13,325	$13,476
Racine Unified School District	Racine County	29	16,254	1,323.8	12.3	$16,565	$17,109
Sheboygan Area School District	Sheboygan County	25	9,663	709.9	13.6	$14,119	$14,736
Stevens Point Area Public School District	Portage County	17	6,938	471.9	14.7	$13,102	$13,243
Sun Prairie Area School District	Dane County	15	8,366	653.9	12.8	$14,783	$19,833
Waukesha School District	Waukesha County	28	12,344	829.7	14.9	$12,744	$12,516
Wausau School District	Marathon County	20	7,786	591.1	13.2	$14,913	$14,662
Wauwatosa School District	Milwaukee County	17	6,917	486.3	14.2	$12,716	$12,702
West Allis-West Milwaukee School District	Milwaukee County	18	7,418	549.7	13.5	$14,209	$14,104
WYOMING							
Albany County School District #1	Albany County	17	3,917	365.9	10.7	$17,566	$17,078
Big Horn County School District #1	Big Horn County	6	1,837	94.0	19.5	$17,384	$17,039
Campbell County School District #1	Campbell County	23	8,567	659.3	13.0	$20,136	$19,126
Carbon County School District #1	Carbon County	5	1,680	150.9	11.1	$20,553	$21,532
Converse County School District #1	Converse County	9	1,643	150.0	11.0	$20,386	$19,748
Fremont County School District #1	Fremont County	6	1,705	135.6	12.6	$18,458	$17,384
Fremont County School District #25	Fremont County	8	2,311	181.2	12.8	$18,796	$18,686
Goshen County School District #1	Goshen County	12	1,606	147.1	10.9	$20,539	$19,410
Laramie County School District #1	Laramie County	38	13,994	1,047.6	13.4	$16,957	$16,188
Lincoln County School District #2	Lincoln County	9	2,924	204.1	14.3	$16,991	$16,640
Natrona County School District #1	Natrona County	28	13,110	927.0	14.1	$18,477	$17,498
Niobrara County School District #1	Niobrara County	4	1,397	90.2	15.5	$16,227	$16,115
Park County School District # 1	Park County	7	1,797	135.7	13.2	$16,397	$16,133
Park County School District # 6	Park County	8	1,974	171.0	11.5	$17,239	$16,936
Sheridan County School District #1	Sheridan County	8	1,203	88.2	13.6	$18,545	$17,500
Sheridan County School District #2	Sheridan County	10	3,519	262.5	13.4	$15,745	$14,986
Sweetwater County School District #1	Sweetwater County	17	5,141	405.9	12.7	$19,296	$16,719
Sweetwater County School District #2	Sweetwater County	10	2,359	192.3	12.3	$19,787	$18,191
Teton County School District #1	Teton County	10	2,749	249.1	11.0	$26,598	$25,975
Uinta County School District #1	Uinta County	8	2,645	209.7	12.6	$18,152	$17,401

NA = Not available.
X = Not applicable.

This page is intentionally left blank

Table C-2. Educational Attainment of the Population, by Selected Counties, 2019

(Number; percent; dollars.)

State/County	Population 18 to 24 years				
	Total	Less than high school graduate (percent)	High school graduate (includes equivalency) (percent)	Some college or associate's degree (percent)	Bachelor's degree or higher (percent)
UNITED STATES	30,373,170	12.1	32.7	43.4	11.9
ALABAMA	457,530	12.3	34.7	45.3	7.6
Baldwin County, Alabama...	16,614	13.9	44.5	32.2	9.3
Calhoun County, Alabama	10,047	8.9	20.9	64.8	5.4
Cullman County, Alabama	6,160	11.9	30.4	50.5	7.3
DeKalb County, Alabama	7,072	17.5	34.5	44.1	3.8
Elmore County, Alabama	5,605	18.8	34.4	38.9	7.9
Etowah County, Alabama..	8,535	14.3	24.9	58.4	2.4
Houston County, Alabama..	8,142	11.8	46.5	39.2	2.5
Jefferson County, Alabama	57,373	10.9	33.2	42.2	13.8
Lauderdale County, Alabama......................................	10,176	9.3	27.5	54.9	8.3
Lee County, Alabama..	28,496	5.4	25.4	59.4	9.7
Limestone County, Alabama.......................................	8,067	12.1	43.9	34.5	9.5
Madison County, Alabama..	35,057	9.6	29.8	49.3	11.3
Marshall County, Alabama..	7,683	20.7	38.5	35.5	5.2
Mobile County, Alabama	36,415	15.2	36.5	42.0	6.3
Montgomery County, Alabama	22,175	8.9	32.6	48.4	10.1
Morgan County, Alabama	10,235	12.1	50.9	35.0	2.0
St. Clair County, Alabama...	6,475	19.3	30.6	39.3	10.9
Shelby County, Alabama	18,232	10.9	32.4	42.4	14.3
Talladega County, Alabama..	7,442	7.5	51.2	41.3	0.0
Tuscaloosa County, Alabama......................................	33,771	9.5	32.0	51.1	7.3
Walker County, Alabama	4,753	17.1	44.3	35.6	3.0
ALASKA..	67,738	12.5	40.1	42.8	4.6
Anchorage Municipality, Alaska..................................	28,342	9.0	41.8	43.7	5.5
Fairbanks North Star Borough, Alaska	12,565	6.6	22.6	66.1	4.6
Matanuska-Susitna Borough, Alaska..........................	9,305	19.7	42.8	34.2	3.3
ARIZONA	694,529	14.5	35.5	39.9	10.1
Apache County, Arizona	6,532	16.1	32.6	48.8	2.5
Cochise County, Arizona	10,486	20.9	29.6	48.8	0.7
Coconino County, Arizona	30,789	4.2	27.9	61.6	6.3
Maricopa County, Arizona	415,899	14.1	36.0	37.4	12.4
Mohave County, Arizona	13,365	20.8	46.5	29.0	3.7
Navajo County, Arizona	8,316	22.4	44.8	30.8	2.0
Pima County, Arizona...	121,224	12.3	33.5	44.2	10.0
Pinal County, Arizona...	36,198	25.4	40.4	29.2	5.0
Yavapai County, Arizona...	15,991	20.8	31.2	45.8	2.2
Yuma County, Arizona..	23,129	13.9	32.0	50.6	3.6
ARKANSAS...	282,336	11.8	34.5	44.7	9.0
Benton County, Arkansas	22,680	10.8	32.3	39.8	17.1
Craighead County, Arkansas	12,383	5.3	23.0	64.3	7.4
Faulkner County, Arkansas...	20,754	6.3	16.3	65.6	11.8
Garland County, Arkansas..	7,282	4.1	64.3	26.7	4.9
Jefferson County, Arkansas..	6,583	6.8	42.2	44.1	6.9
Lonoke County, Arkansas...	5,391	8.6	54.3	27.5	9.6
Pulaski County, Arkansas...	32,978	11.5	30.9	36.9	20.7
Saline County, Arkansas...	9,376	23.3	39.5	32.6	4.6
Sebastian County, Arkansas.......................................	11,776	13.4	31.5	50.5	4.6
Washington County, Arkansas	35,778	9.4	27.2	55.3	8.1
White County, Arkansas	9,032	16.1	26.5	50.7	6.8
CALIFORNIA	3,683,287	10.0	31.3	47.2	11.6
Alameda County, California...	136,124	8.7	27.4	46.8	17.1
Butte County, California..	30,915	9.1	23.7	56.7	10.5
Contra Costa County, California	91,955	11.2	32.6	43.2	13.1
El Dorado County, California	12,404	9.9	43.4	35.8	10.8
Fresno County, California	96,278	11.3	35.1	46.6	7.1
Humboldt County, California	16,845	6.6	26.7	61.7	5.0
Imperial County, California...	17,862	17.6	28.1	50.8	3.5
Kern County, California...	89,126	18.2	39.6	37.9	4.3
Kings County, California..	16,514	13.4	41.2	41.3	4.0
Lake County, California	3,768	32.9	25.2	41.9	0.0
Los Angeles County, California...................................	932,944	10.6	27.8	48.6	13.0
Madera County, California..	14,795	24.0	29.4	43.2	3.4
Marin County, California..	18,717	9.9	34.7	38.7	16.7

N = Data for this geographic area cannot be displayed because the number of sample cases is too small.

Table C-2. Educational Attainment of the Population, by Selected Counties, 2019—*Continued*

(Number; percent; dollars.)

State/County	Population 25 years and over							
	Total	Less than 9th grade (percent)	9th to 12th grade, no diploma (percent)	High school graduate (includes equivalency) (percent)	Some college, no degree (percent)	Associate's degree (percent)	Bachelor's degree (percent)	Graduate or professional degree (percent)
UNITED STATES	224,898,568	4.8	6.6	26.9	20.0	8.6	20.3	12.8
ALABAMA	3,360,058	3.9	9.0	30.9	20.8	9.0	16.3	10.0
Baldwin County, Alabama..............................	159,717	1.9	7.6	26.2	21.9	10.1	20.5	11.7
Calhoun County, Alabama..............................	79,084	4.2	11.2	34.5	21.8	9.0	11.5	7.8
Cullman County, Alabama..............................	58,795	4.5	14.2	30.5	23.5	11.5	10.1	5.6
DeKalb County, Alabama...............................	47,007	9.9	11.4	38.0	18.4	9.4	7.9	4.9
Elmore County, Alabama...............................	57,553	3.6	6.7	34.7	20.0	10.1	16.4	8.5
Etowah County, Alabama...............................	71,744	3.8	12.0	32.1	25.5	9.3	10.5	6.8
Houston County, Alabama..............................	73,454	5.1	9.9	30.4	22.6	9.4	14.2	8.5
Jefferson County, Alabama	451,818	2.2	6.6	26.9	21.0	8.6	20.4	14.3
Lauderdale County, Alabama..........................	64,267	4.8	10.2	34.2	20.8	7.7	13.2	9.0
Lee County, Alabama...................................	101,326	3.0	5.0	22.0	19.0	9.5	21.0	20.4
Limestone County, Alabama...........................	68,441	3.1	9.5	33.5	18.9	9.5	18.6	7.0
Madison County, Alabama..............................	257,136	2.2	4.9	19.5	20.3	9.0	26.6	17.4
Marshall County, Alabama.............................	64,756	6.8	11.1	32.8	20.2	9.0	15.0	5.1
Mobile County, Alabama	280,453	3.3	9.3	36.1	20.3	8.2	14.9	8.0
Montgomery County, Alabama.........................	151,310	3.2	7.3	24.9	21.3	8.0	20.2	15.2
Morgan County, Alabama..............................	82,462	5.8	8.3	35.2	19.5	7.8	15.4	8.0
St. Clair County, Alabama.............................	62,861	5.3	9.2	35.7	24.1	12.2	8.7	4.9
Shelby County, Alabama...............................	149,221	2.6	3.9	20.1	21.0	7.9	29.2	15.3
Talladega County, Alabama...........................	55,521	5.2	14.5	35.3	21.0	8.7	9.1	6.3
Tuscaloosa County, Alabama..........................	131,589	2.9	8.0	30.7	19.2	7.6	19.1	12.5
Walker County, Alabama	44,577	4.6	13.1	35.3	24.3	10.6	8.8	3.4
ALASKA...	484,058	2.2	4.3	28.7	25.7	9.0	18.5	11.7
Anchorage Municipality, Alaska.......................	190,461	1.7	3.2	25.2	24.2	9.3	22.2	14.1
Fairbanks North Star Borough, Alaska	61,280	2.3	2.1	20.8	33.0	8.7	16.7	16.6
Matanuska-Susitna Borough, Alaska..................	70,425	1.7	4.3	33.4	25.6	10.7	17.1	7.3
ARIZONA	4,944,540	5.1	7.3	23.7	25.0	8.7	18.8	11.3
Apache County, Arizona	46,255	9.0	9.3	31.3	29.8	8.9	6.1	5.7
Cochise County, Arizona	88,433	4.5	6.8	26.8	25.2	11.6	15.1	9.9
Coconino County, Arizona	84,682	2.3	4.3	20.4	25.1	8.4	22.0	17.6
Maricopa County, Arizona	3,017,076	5.2	6.6	22.3	23.6	8.8	21.3	12.3
Mohave County, Arizona	163,211	2.5	10.5	33.8	30.7	8.9	8.6	4.9
Navajo County, Arizona	73,486	4.9	11.5	28.5	33.1	8.8	7.1	6.1
Pima County, Arizona..................................	710,449	4.7	7.2	22.0	25.3	8.2	18.9	13.7
Pinal County, Arizona..................................	324,018	4.9	8.3	30.0	28.7	8.6	14.0	5.4
Yavapai County, Arizona	181,941	1.6	6.6	26.0	29.0	8.3	15.6	12.9
Yuma County, Arizona.................................	137,087	13.8	12.0	26.0	25.5	8.5	9.1	5.1
ARKANSAS...	2,036,456	4.6	7.9	34.9	21.8	7.5	15.1	8.3
Benton County, Arkansas	183,203	5.0	5.5	29.0	18.7	6.8	22.5	12.5
Craighead County, Arkansas..........................	71,813	4.8	5.8	32.9	22.1	8.9	15.6	9.8
Faulkner County, Arkansas............................	76,684	2.5	3.7	32.5	22.6	9.3	20.9	8.5
Garland County, Arkansas.............................	72,565	2.9	5.9	28.8	25.5	8.3	18.4	10.1
Jefferson County, Arkansas...........................	45,719	3.4	9.8	39.4	22.2	6.8	12.0	6.4
Lonoke County, Arkansas..............................	49,301	3.8	7.1	40.8	20.3	8.9	12.5	6.5
Pulaski County, Arkansas..............................	268,684	2.8	5.6	26.2	22.4	8.2	20.9	14.0
Saline County, Arkansas...............................	84,730	1.8	8.6	34.6	20.3	8.2	17.7	8.9
Sebastian County, Arkansas...........................	85,379	4.9	10.6	28.6	23.9	6.9	16.6	8.5
Washington County, Arkansas	145,660	7.4	8.3	27.3	19.1	6.0	19.2	12.7
White County, Arkansas...............................	51,446	5.7	12.9	42.7	12.6	9.8	10.0	6.4
CALIFORNIA	26,937,872	8.7	7.3	20.6	20.6	7.9	21.9	13.1
Alameda County, California............................	1,195,107	5.2	5.2	17.3	15.5	6.2	29.3	21.3
Butte County, California................................	143,815	3.7	7.9	21.7	26.5	9.8	20.6	9.8
Contra Costa County, California	802,187	5.2	5.7	17.9	20.1	8.1	25.8	17.2
El Dorado County, California	142,068	2.8	4.2	22.3	24.3	11.1	24.6	10.8
Fresno County, California..............................	621,440	12.7	10.6	22.0	23.2	9.4	14.7	7.3
Humboldt County, California	93,098	2.1	7.0	20.7	28.0	11.8	20.5	9.9
Imperial County, California	111,755	12.0	16.4	23.3	23.6	6.4	13.9	4.5
Kern County, California................................	551,956	13.0	10.6	28.1	22.7	8.4	11.7	5.3
Kings County, California...............................	95,083	13.5	15.0	22.6	24.6	6.7	12.0	5.6
Lake County, California................................	47,186	4.6	9.5	30.4	32.0	8.1	9.9	5.5
Los Angeles County, California........................	6,961,614	11.8	8.4	20.7	18.5	6.9	22.3	11.5
Madera County, California.............................	99,392	15.1	12.0	25.2	25.6	8.0	10.2	3.9
Marin County, California...............................	188,509	4.5	3.0	11.2	15.8	5.9	36.3	23.4

N = Data for this geographic area cannot be displayed because the number of sample cases is too small.

Table C-2. Educational Attainment of the Population, by Selected Counties, 2019—*Continued*

(Number; percent; dollars.)

State/County		Population 18 to 24 years			
	Total	Less than high school graduate (percent)	High school graduate (includes equivalency) (percent)	Some college or associate's degree (percent)	Bachelor's degree or higher (percent)
CALIFORNIA—*(Continued)*					
Mendocino County, California	6,869	13.8	34.6	48.5	3.1
Merced County, California	29,440	10.5	28.4	57.4	3.7
Monterey County, California	42,946	14.1	28.3	52.2	5.4
Napa County, California	12,155	5.4	44.5	42.9	7.2
Nevada County, California	5,916	10.0	56.7	29.5	3.8
Orange County, California	285,538	9.3	28.6	48.0	14.2
Placer County, California	28,650	10.5	31.2	44.6	13.7
Riverside County, California	235,474	9.9	37.5	46.1	6.6
Sacramento County, California	130,401	9.3	36.6	44.9	9.3
San Bernardino County, California	219,659	10.8	37.6	44.4	7.3
San Diego County, California	336,060	7.4	33.3	47.9	11.3
San Francisco County, California	62,024	3.7	20.2	42.1	34.0
San Joaquin County, California	73,677	11.2	39.3	44.0	5.5
San Luis Obispo County, California	42,827	3.2	25.1	60.6	11.1
San Mateo County, California	55,801	9.3	29.6	35.3	25.8
Santa Barbara County, California	69,881	8.0	24.0	57.4	10.6
Santa Clara County, California	161,254	9.0	24.2	45.8	21.1
Santa Cruz County, California	40,243	7.0	27.5	51.5	14.1
Shasta County, California	13,758	11.6	43.1	36.2	9.2
Solano County, California	38,051	12.6	29.7	50.8	7.0
Sonoma County, California	39,735	11.1	32.9	45.9	10.2
Stanislaus County, California	53,308	9.7	40.4	45.8	4.0
Sutter County, California	9,110	12.3	30.5	50.0	7.2
Tehama County, California	3,906	27.7	38.5	29.2	4.6
Tulare County, California	46,486	11.8	40.8	44.4	2.9
Ventura County, California	78,461	8.7	32.5	49.6	9.2
Yolo County, California	44,853	4.4	25.2	55.6	14.8
Yuba County, California	6,314	15.1	30.3	48.6	6.1
COLORADO	527,473	12.4	31.8	42.0	13.7
Adams County, Colorado	45,363	20.1	42.0	29.8	8.1
Arapahoe County, Colorado	52,627	16.4	34.5	32.0	17.1
Boulder County, Colorado	46,943	6.3	23.5	53.6	16.6
Broomfield County, Colorado	5,380	12.9	32.8	36.8	17.5
Denver County, Colorado	58,044	12.0	29.0	35.4	23.6
Douglas County, Colorado	27,202	8.5	35.9	39.8	15.8
El Paso County, Colorado	77,821	10.3	32.0	48.8	8.9
Jefferson County, Colorado	43,778	10.8	31.9	42.0	15.4
Larimer County, Colorado	49,663	4.4	24.2	53.5	18.0
Mesa County, Colorado	14,127	15.7	33.4	44.6	6.4
Pueblo County, Colorado	14,633	18.6	27.2	48.6	5.6
Weld County, Colorado	29,580	15.6	36.3	40.6	7.5
CONNECTICUT	341,435	10.3	29.9	43.2	16.5
Fairfield County, Connecticut	86,006	11.0	25.9	42.2	20.9
Hartford County, Connecticut	79,746	10.6	29.2	40.7	19.5
Litchfield County, Connecticut	12,655	19.8	36.7	29.2	14.3
Middlesex County, Connecticut	14,818	8.4	24.5	42.2	24.9
New Haven County, Connecticut	83,454	10.3	35.7	41.3	12.7
New London County, Connecticut	26,131	9.7	37.1	39.1	14.1
Tolland County, Connecticut	26,424	1.5	22.4	67.9	8.1
Windham County, Connecticut	12,201	15.9	24.4	52.0	7.6
DELAWARE	82,507	11.2	32.6	46.3	10.0
Kent County, Delaware	17,628	11.6	29.8	48.1	10.5
New Castle County, Delaware	50,741	9.7	33.6	46.8	9.9
Sussex County, Delaware	14,138	15.9	32.2	42.1	9.8
DISTRICT OF COLUMBIA	72,703	4.4	26.2	46.3	23.1
District of Columbia, District of Columbia	72,703	4.4	26.2	46.3	23.1
FLORIDA	1,761,280	14.3	32.1	42.9	10.6
Alachua County, Florida	54,783	6.0	20.2	55.4	18.4
Bay County, Florida	12,727	11.4	45.3	28.3	15.0
Brevard County, Florida	41,797	19.4	33.5	40.7	6.4
Broward County, Florida	150,776	16.1	31.8	41.9	10.3
Charlotte County, Florida	7,969	18.1	44.6	29.6	7.7
Citrus County, Florida	7,713	24.0	37.7	36.3	2.0

N = Data for this geographic area cannot be displayed because the number of sample cases is too small.

Table C-2. Educational Attainment of the Population, by Selected Counties, 2019—*Continued*

(Number; percent; dollars.)

State/County	Total	Less than 9th grade (percent)	9th to 12th grade, no diploma (percent)	High school graduate (includes equivalency) (percent)	Some college, no degree (percent)	Associate's degree (percent)	Bachelor's degree (percent)	Graduate or professional degree (percent)
CALIFORNIA—*(Continued)*								
Mendocino County, California	61,561	7.2	9.2	22.4	28.7	9.2	14.6	8.7
Merced County, California	167,460	19.1	11.8	24.3	23.0	7.4	10.2	4.3
Monterey County, California	277,924	19.6	8.3	20.5	17.3	8.6	15.0	10.7
Napa County, California	97,666	8.0	6.5	18.4	22.6	8.3	22.1	14.1
Nevada County, California	77,008	1.7	3.0	22.2	26.6	10.7	22.5	13.3
Orange County, California	2,200,478	7.3	6.6	17.8	19.6	7.7	25.8	15.2
Placer County, California	281,521	2.5	3.4	18.0	23.2	11.0	27.8	14.1
Riverside County, California	1,620,917	8.6	8.3	26.3	25.1	8.3	15.0	8.5
Sacramento County, California	1,058,536	5.2	5.9	23.3	24.7	9.7	20.8	10.4
San Bernardino County, California	1,390,788	8.2	11.0	25.8	24.4	8.1	14.6	7.9
San Diego County, California	2,287,472	6.3	5.7	18.2	21.8	8.3	24.5	15.4
San Francisco County, California	701,279	6.8	4.8	11.9	12.4	4.9	35.1	24.1
San Joaquin County, California	484,712	11.7	8.7	29.1	22.1	8.4	14.1	5.9
San Luis Obispo County, California	191,183	3.4	5.8	19.4	24.9	9.2	22.8	14.4
San Mateo County, California	555,980	5.6	3.9	15.3	15.4	7.4	28.8	23.6
Santa Barbara County, California	278,334	12.6	6.1	18.2	20.9	7.7	20.6	13.9
Santa Clara County, California	1,350,681	6.5	4.5	13.8	14.7	6.9	28.0	25.7
Santa Cruz County, California	181,121	8.6	3.9	15.4	19.6	8.6	25.3	18.5
Shasta County, California	127,504	1.4	5.4	24.9	33.1	13.5	15.3	6.5
Solano County, California	310,707	5.5	5.3	23.6	26.6	10.1	19.1	9.8
Sonoma County, California	359,124	5.4	4.9	19.0	23.8	9.5	23.4	14.1
Stanislaus County, California	340,670	11.4	8.2	30.6	25.3	7.1	12.4	4.9
Sutter County, California	62,991	10.4	10.1	23.1	25.1	10.3	12.4	8.6
Tehama County, California	45,751	5.7	11.1	32.4	24.7	9.8	9.7	6.6
Tulare County, California	277,457	16.2	9.7	25.6	24.3	10.6	9.1	4.6
Ventura County, California	577,254	8.4	5.2	20.9	21.5	9.2	21.9	12.9
Yolo County, California	131,248	6.4	4.9	20.0	19.2	9.7	22.2	17.7
Yuba County, California	50,675	6.7	12.4	25.6	27.6	10.0	13.1	4.8
COLORADO	3,974,943	3.2	4.4	21.0	20.3	8.4	26.6	16.0
Adams County, Colorado	336,931	6.1	9.0	29.8	21.0	8.6	17.1	8.3
Arapahoe County, Colorado	451,535	3.4	4.0	19.9	20.2	8.6	26.9	16.9
Boulder County, Colorado	217,746	2.9	2.7	10.1	13.2	6.3	35.6	29.2
Broomfield County, Colorado	49,543	1.7	2.0	13.4	17.0	9.0	33.0	23.9
Denver County, Colorado	530,543	4.2	4.6	17.0	16.0	5.0	32.6	20.5
Douglas County, Colorado	235,325	0.5	1.6	12.5	19.4	7.9	36.2	21.9
El Paso County, Colorado	471,313	1.9	3.1	20.8	23.4	11.7	24.5	14.5
Jefferson County, Colorado	425,906	2.0	3.4	19.9	19.4	7.7	30.9	16.8
Larimer County, Colorado	238,189	0.8	2.7	18.0	20.1	9.3	30.1	18.9
Mesa County, Colorado	107,348	2.5	6.4	27.5	25.7	8.2	19.7	10.1
Pueblo County, Colorado	116,378	2.9	5.8	29.2	26.3	12.4	15.4	8.0
Weld County, Colorado	210,630	6.6	5.7	25.0	22.6	10.1	18.2	11.6
CONNECTICUT	2,496,420	4.0	5.3	26.8	16.5	7.6	22.0	17.8
Fairfield County, Connecticut	647,664	5.4	4.4	21.9	12.7	6.5	27.5	21.5
Hartford County, Connecticut	625,639	4.1	5.7	25.6	17.2	8.5	21.2	17.8
Litchfield County, Connecticut	135,306	1.8	4.4	30.7	17.1	9.8	21.3	14.7
Middlesex County, Connecticut	119,565	1.5	5.1	26.7	15.9	8.1	24.1	18.7
New Haven County, Connecticut	600,678	4.4	6.2	30.6	16.8	6.9	18.7	16.5
New London County, Connecticut	188,179	2.0	4.7	28.4	23.5	8.1	18.1	15.2
Tolland County, Connecticut	97,922	1.8	4.0	27.5	16.8	9.0	22.8	18.0
Windham County, Connecticut	81,467	2.8	8.1	35.2	21.2	9.0	14.8	8.9
DELAWARE	687,311	3.5	6.2	30.2	18.6	8.3	10.5	13.7
Kent County, Delaware	121,055	3.8	7.5	31.9	22.0	9.4	15.7	8.8
New Castle County, Delaware	388,655	3.0	5.5	29.7	17.6	7.4	21.5	15.3
Sussex County, Delaware	176,801	4.3	6.8	30.1	17.9	9.5	17.9	13.4
DISTRICT OF COLUMBIA	505,145	3.3	4.9	15.8	13.0	3.3	25.7	34.0
District of Columbia, District of Columbia	505,145	3.3	4.9	15.8	13.0	3.3	25.7	34.0
FLORIDA	15,484,502	4.6	7.0	28.4	19.4	9.9	19.3	11.4
Alachua County, Florida	165,792	1.8	4.4	19.9	16.3	11.7	23.4	22.5
Bay County, Florida	126,060	2.2	6.8	28.6	25.0	11.0	16.2	10.2
Brevard County, Florida	450,772	1.7	5.8	27.8	21.7	12.6	18.8	11.6
Broward County, Florida	1,392,064	4.7	5.9	28.3	18.3	9.8	20.7	12.2
Charlotte County, Florida	158,584	2.6	6.9	35.6	23.6	9.3	14.0	8.1
Citrus County, Florida	120,131	2.8	9.3	31.3	24.8	9.3	12.7	9.9

N = Data for this geographic area cannot be displayed because the number of sample cases is too small.

Table C-2. Educational Attainment of the Population, by Selected Counties, 2019—*Continued*

(Number; percent; dollars.)

State/County	Total	Population 18 to 24 years			
		Less than high school graduate (percent)	High school graduate (includes equivalency) (percent)	Some college or associate's degree (percent)	Bachelor's degree or higher (percent)
FLORIDA—(*Continued*)					
Clay County, Florida	17,678	11.2	54.5	29.2	5.1
Collier County, Florida	26,653	16.2	34.4	40.8	8.7
Columbia County, Florida	7,673	25.2	46.9	25.6	2.3
Duval County, Florida	83,390	11.2	40.8	40.0	8.0
Escambia County, Florida	35,160	9.2	30.3	43.6	16.8
Flagler County, Florida	7,620	18.5	46.1	29.5	5.9
Hernando County, Florida	13,468	16.7	39.6	38.2	5.5
Highlands County, Florida	7,281	16.6	57.1	20.4	5.9
Hillsborough County, Florida	129,467	12.9	31.2	43.9	12.0
Indian River County, Florida	9,503	26.6	37.9	28.6	7.0
Lake County, Florida	24,350	18.0	47.5	26.5	8.0
Lee County, Florida	52,353	17.5	32.5	41.1	8.9
Leon County, Florida	63,034	8.8	17.7	59.0	14.4
Manatee County, Florida	28,040	26.0	29.9	36.0	8.1
Marion County, Florida	24,472	16.8	42.7	37.0	3.5
Martin County, Florida	9,905	8.9	31.3	51.0	8.8
Miami-Dade County, Florida	225,335	12.7	28.6	47.2	11.6
Monroe County, Florida	5,342	17.1	36.8	39.7	6.4
Nassau County, Florida	4,305	9.2	48.5	28.2	14.1
Okaloosa County, Florida	18,815	16.8	31.9	33.7	17.6
Orange County, Florida	143,238	10.9	27.6	48.6	12.9
Osceola County, Florida	36,545	8.3	28.4	54.8	8.4
Palm Beach County, Florida	111,830	17.3	26.0	42.2	14.5
Pasco County, Florida	39,792	13.7	36.0	41.0	9.4
Pinellas County, Florida	64,853	12.5	35.2	43.2	9.1
Polk County, Florida	61,355	18.0	39.1	36.3	6.5
Putnam County, Florida	5,139	25.8	46.1	27.1	1.0
St. Johns County, Florida	20,086	15.8	32.8	39.0	12.4
St. Lucie County, Florida	23,944	17.3	40.7	36.5	5.5
Santa Rosa County, Florida	14,991	12.1	36.1	36.8	14.9
Sarasota County, Florida	26,246	17.7	36.5	38.4	7.4
Seminole County, Florida	38,569	9.9	20.9	52.9	16.3
Sumter County, Florida	4,934	28.9	51.6	11.0	8.5
Volusia County, Florida	43,681	14.5	32.0	45.2	8.2
Walton County, Florida	4,362	5.9	31.0	56.6	6.5
GEORGIA	1,034,172	15.0	34.4	40.6	10.0
Barrow County, Georgia	6,369	19.1	35.0	35.0	10.9
Bartow County, Georgia	9,942	13.9	49.4	31.4	5.3
Bibb County, Georgia	15,624	13.7	27.3	53.8	5.2
Bulloch County, Georgia	20,043	5.0	17.0	73.7	4.3
Carroll County, Georgia	14,244	12.4	37.0	49.2	1.4
Catoosa County, Georgia	5,434	17.2	39.8	40.3	2.7
Chatham County, Georgia	31,835	13.4	34.3	33.8	18.4
Cherokee County, Georgia	20,126	21.3	30.6	35.9	12.2
Clarke County, Georgia	34,556	1.9	21.0	66.3	10.8
Clayton County, Georgia	29,946	23.9	35.7	34.5	5.8
Cobb County, Georgia	67,654	12.1	29.0	43.2	15.7
Columbia County, Georgia	13,754	15.3	28.2	44.7	11.8
Coweta County, Georgia	11,311	9.9	28.4	49.0	12.8
DeKalb County, Georgia	63,632	10.5	32.6	38.8	18.1
Dougherty County, Georgia	11,541	20.4	44.1	30.8	4.8
Douglas County, Georgia	16,508	22.7	35.4	33.3	8.7
Fayette County, Georgia	8,114	6.7	47.5	32.0	13.8
Floyd County, Georgia	9,726	10.9	36.0	46.9	6.2
Forsyth County, Georgia	18,402	16.7	35.9	35.3	12.1
Fulton County, Georgia	107,102	13.4	22.5	44.3	19.8
Glynn County, Georgia	6,820	18.0	44.4	33.8	3.8
Gwinnett County, Georgia	85,632	14.0	34.2	41.3	10.5
Hall County, Georgia	18,735	26.5	30.4	34.2	8.9
Henry County, Georgia	22,707	23.7	24.9	39.3	12.1
Houston County, Georgia	16,227	9.7	26.8	58.6	5.0
Jackson County, Georgia	4,140	20.7	37.4	36.0	5.9
Lowndes County, Georgia	19,256	15.6	31.8	39.7	12.8
Muscogee County, Georgia	19,872	15.1	35.2	44.1	5.6
Newton County, Georgia	10,655	19.9	41.9	32.7	5.6
Paulding County, Georgia	14,406	13.3	41.1	38.9	6.8
Richmond County, Georgia	22,867	16.2	45.8	33.5	4.4

N = Data for this geographic area cannot be displayed because the number of sample cases is too small.

Table C-2. Educational Attainment of the Population, by Selected Counties, 2019—*Continued*

(Number; percent; dollars.)

State/County	Total	Less than 9th grade (percent)	9th to 12th grade, no diploma (percent)	High school graduate (includes equivalency) (percent)	Some college, no degree (percent)	Associate's degree (percent)	Bachelor's degree (percent)	Graduate or professional degree (percent)
FLORIDA—*(Continued)*								
Clay County, Florida	151,268	1.8	3.4	27.9	24.1	14.3	18.7	9.9
Collier County, Florida	293,211	5.7	5.3	27.1	17.3	8.7	20.8	14.9
Columbia County, Florida	48,523	2.5	10.9	42.2	21.8	7.2	10.2	5.2
Duval County, Florida	658,820	3.2	6.5	28.6	21.1	10.1	20.3	10.3
Escambia County, Florida	216,927	3.4	7.9	30.0	24.1	10.7	14.8	9.1
Flagler County, Florida	88,396	2.6	6.2	35.0	21.4	8.4	17.6	9.0
Hernando County, Florida	144,676	2.8	8.2	33.1	25.9	10.2	13.2	6.5
Highlands County, Florida	80,665	4.8	10.0	35.8	23.7	8.9	11.1	5.6
Hillsborough County, Florida	1,017,078	5.0	6.3	26.9	17.4	9.7	21.7	13.0
Indian River County, Florida	124,448	3.5	5.6	29.0	21.0	9.7	20.7	10.6
Lake County, Florida	273,207	3.6	7.0	30.0	22.7	11.3	15.8	9.5
Lee County, Florida	584,326	4.7	6.2	31.0	19.6	9.4	18.1	10.9
Leon County, Florida	175,914	2.2	5.4	18.2	19.4	8.0	25.8	21.0
Manatee County, Florida	302,893	3.1	6.6	29.9	20.1	9.7	18.3	12.4
Marion County, Florida	273,855	3.2	7.9	36.6	21.2	10.6	12.6	8.0
Martin County, Florida	125,010	2.4	6.4	24.6	22.4	8.7	21.5	14.0
Miami-Dade County, Florida	1,941,926	9.5	10.1	26.1	14.6	8.9	19.3	11.4
Monroe County, Florida	58,378	3.3	3.7	27.5	20.7	10.4	20.8	13.7
Nassau County, Florida	66,706	4.3	7.1	30.6	20.6	7.8	18.8	10.8
Okaloosa County, Florida	144,638	1.9	5.3	27.7	23.3	10.2	20.6	11.0
Orange County, Florida	944,200	4.5	7.2	25.1	17.5	10.4	23.3	11.9
Osceola County, Florida	248,607	5.6	8.8	29.3	20.2	11.8	15.9	8.4
Palm Beach County, Florida	1,101,068	5.9	5.1	23.7	18.3	9.3	22.7	15.0
Pasco County, Florida	402,199	2.8	6.9	33.0	21.0	10.9	16.8	8.6
Pinellas County, Florida	754,705	2.8	6.2	27.4	20.7	9.9	21.6	11.4
Polk County, Florida	504,283	4.8	8.6	34.2	21.2	10.5	13.7	7.0
Putnam County, Florida	53,584	4.4	13.2	39.0	21.6	9.4	7.6	4.8
St. Johns County, Florida	187,354	1.2	3.2	22.2	19.0	8.5	28.6	17.4
St. Lucie County, Florida	240,303	4.6	8.7	33.1	21.5	10.4	14.0	7.6
Santa Rosa County, Florida	129,127	2.7	6.3	28.3	24.6	11.3	17.9	8.8
Sarasota County, Florida	346,738	2.2	4.1	28.0	20.2	9.2	20.7	15.7
Seminole County, Florida	334,286	2.3	4.1	21.4	19.2	11.9	26.6	14.6
Sumter County, Florida	118,386	1.2	4.3	31.9	20.8	8.6	20.6	12.6
Volusia County, Florida	412,871	2.9	5.9	33.1	21.8	12.2	15.2	8.8
Walton County, Florida	54,627	1.9	7.5	28.0	21.9	10.9	21.0	8.9
GEORGIA	7,080,222	4.5	7.6	27.4	20.0	8.0	19.9	12.6
Barrow County, Georgia	55,286	4.3	10.9	31.6	21.3	8.8	15.0	8.1
Bartow County, Georgia	72,076	5.5	10.7	34.9	25.0	6.2	13.0	4.8
Bibb County, Georgia	100,417	4.0	9.0	30.6	24.3	7.1	13.6	11.3
Bulloch County, Georgia	44,070	1.1	9.0	31.7	21.7	9.8	16.0	10.7
Carroll County, Georgia	77,477	4.6	12.4	35.5	22.3	6.3	11.3	7.6
Catoosa County, Georgia	46,682	1.7	8.0	32.4	24.0	10.5	16.6	6.8
Chatham County, Georgia	197,156	3.0	7.4	24.7	25.4	5.5	21.3	12.8
Cherokee County, Georgia	176,477	3.8	5.4	23.0	21.8	7.8	26.7	11.4
Clarke County, Georgia	71,774	2.2	6.6	16.1	17.2	9.8	24.4	23.7
Clayton County, Georgia	181,688	6.3	10.0	35.4	20.8	8.7	12.6	6.2
Cobb County, Georgia	515,943	4.6	3.3	18.1	18.6	7.3	30.4	17.6
Columbia County, Georgia	103,621	2.0	4.8	21.6	19.3	11.4	26.5	14.3
Coweta County, Georgia	101,159	4.1	6.3	26.8	25.5	10.6	16.7	10.1
DeKalb County, Georgia	521,555	4.0	6.0	21.4	16.0	7.7	25.5	19.4
Dougherty County, Georgia	56,078	4.6	13.1	28.0	23.8	10.0	9.4	11.0
Douglas County, Georgia	92,396	3.6	5.7	31.2	19.6	8.1	19.9	11.9
Fayette County, Georgia	79,987	1.2	2.8	21.1	20.1	9.7	29.7	15.3
Floyd County, Georgia	66,042	6.1	8.4	37.2	18.1	7.3	11.9	10.9
Forsyth County, Georgia	160,296	2.8	3.7	14.3	16.4	6.8	36.3	19.7
Fulton County, Georgia	729,041	1.8	4.3	15.4	15.1	5.8	33.7	23.9
Glynn County, Georgia	60,245	3.3	6.7	28.0	25.4	8.5	14.4	13.8
Gwinnett County, Georgia	601,285	6.2	5.9	21.1	17.8	9.7	25.6	13.6
Hall County, Georgia	135,110	11.8	8.6	26.9	19.9	7.3	15.5	9.9
Henry County, Georgia	152,577	3.1	5.3	33.9	22.7	8.8	18.0	8.3
Houston County, Georgia	101,387	2.6	4.6	31.2	19.8	13.9	16.3	11.6
Jackson County, Georgia	50,045	5.4	9.5	33.4	16.9	9.8	18.5	6.5
Lowndes County, Georgia	69,672	3.2	6.2	32.4	21.3	11.8	17.5	7.7
Muscogee County, Georgia	127,592	3.8	7.4	26.3	26.8	11.0	13.0	11.7
Newton County, Georgia	72,226	4.5	9.7	34.1	26.5	7.4	10.5	7.4
Paulding County, Georgia	110,398	3.3	8.9	30.8	27.1	7.9	13.8	8.3
Richmond County, Georgia	133,688	4.2	9.0	35.1	23.1	8.6	12.3	7.7

N = Data for this geographic area cannot be displayed because the number of sample cases is too small.

Table C-2. Educational Attainment of the Population, by Selected Counties, 2019—*Continued*

(Number; percent; dollars.)

State/County	Population 18 to 24 years				
	Total	Less than high school graduate (percent)	High school graduate (includes equivalency) (percent)	Some college or associate's degree (percent)	Bachelor's degree or higher (percent)
GEORGIA—*(Continued)*					
Rockdale County, Georgia	8,709	12.0	39.0	37.4	11.6
Spalding County, Georgia	5,582	20.5	47.7	29.1	2.7
Troup County, Georgia	6,524	18.2	42.3	39.1	0.4
Walker County, Georgia	5,616	16.8	48.3	31.1	3.8
Walton County, Georgia	6,376	9.0	65.0	21.5	4.5
Whitfield County, Georgia	10,170	14.7	34.0	48.7	2.7
HAWAII	119,017	7.4	43.2	41.2	8.2
Hawaii County, Hawaii	14,257	10.4	38.2	45.4	6.0
Honolulu County, Hawaii	88,983	6.5	43.9	40.8	8.7
Kauai County, Hawaii	5,120	10.2	45.0	42.4	2.3
Maui County, Hawaii	10,657	9.3	43.3	37.8	9.6
IDAHO	166,713	12.0	37.5	42.8	7.7
Ada County, Idaho	40,520	9.9	27.8	50.5	11.8
Bannock County, Idaho	8,882	7.5	39.1	47.6	5.9
Bonneville County, Idaho	9,920	17.8	36.8	35.8	9.7
Canyon County, Idaho	21,875	12.5	45.7	34.4	7.5
Kootenai County, Idaho	12,319	22.1	37.9	37.5	2.5
Twin Falls County, Idaho	7,764	10.2	57.5	31.2	1.2
ILLINOIS	1,162,448	11.7	29.5	44.1	14.7
Adams County, Illinois	4,856	7.2	29.7	32.8	30.3
Champaign County, Illinois	48,517	8.0	16.4	52.8	22.8
Cook County, Illinois	447,152	11.9	27.6	42.3	18.2
DeKalb County, Illinois	20,898	3.2	15.2	68.2	13.4
DuPage County, Illinois	78,374	10.4	24.0	44.1	21.5
Kane County, Illinois	47,937	13.2	32.0	42.8	12.0
Kankakee County, Illinois	13,308	11.0	44.0	38.4	6.7
Kendall County, Illinois	10,050	5.9	38.4	43.4	12.3
Lake County, Illinois	70,627	9.8	37.7	40.6	11.9
LaSalle County, Illinois	8,113	12.3	32.2	49.7	5.9
McHenry County, Illinois	25,468	10.1	36.1	41.7	12.2
McLean County, Illinois	30,523	8.7	16.6	64.7	10.0
Macon County, Illinois	8,759	18.7	35.5	40.8	4.9
Madison County, Illinois	20,971	8.7	27.0	55.9	8.4
Peoria County, Illinois	16,208	11.6	26.2	49.6	12.6
Rock Island County, Illinois	12,718	8.9	43.7	38.4	9.1
St. Clair County, Illinois	20,514	14.8	36.0	41.5	7.7
Sangamon County, Illinois	15,163	16.2	27.6	45.4	10.8
Tazewell County, Illinois	9,284	14.1	32.6	41.4	12.0
Vermilion County, Illinois	6,163	20.2	45.3	31.8	2.7
Will County, Illinois	62,635	11.9	31.8	41.5	14.8
Williamson County, Illinois	4,787	16.0	30.9	46.8	6.4
Winnebago County, Illinois	24,017	19.6	34.8	37.1	8.4
INDIANA	662,783	14.2	35.5	39.6	10.7
Allen County, Indiana	34,496	14.4	31.9	40.8	12.9
Bartholomew County, Indiana	6,370	11.1	43.1	26.9	18.9
Boone County, Indiana	5,001	5.9	40.5	20.1	33.5
Clark County, Indiana	9,807	20.9	43.9	30.1	5.0
Delaware County, Indiana	22,034	4.1	21.4	68.3	6.2
Elkhart County, Indiana	18,595	22.4	35.0	31.8	10.8
Floyd County, Indiana	6,740	24.0	24.1	31.3	20.6
Grant County, Indiana	8,322	6.8	32.4	52.9	7.9
Hamilton County, Indiana	26,361	14.4	34.3	24.9	26.4
Hancock County, Indiana	6,229	28.3	29.8	41.4	0.5
Hendricks County, Indiana	13,017	17.6	26.2	43.3	12.9
Howard County, Indiana	5,873	10.9	31.3	52.5	5.3
Johnson County, Indiana	14,008	22.9	35.0	31.1	11.0
Kosciusko County, Indiana	6,632	13.0	38.2	40.4	8.3
Lake County, Indiana	41,143	17.5	43.5	29.1	9.9
LaPorte County, Indiana	9,195	14.8	54.1	24.4	6.7
Madison County, Indiana	11,059	16.3	43.6	30.6	9.4
Marion County, Indiana	90,395	13.4	36.7	35.9	14.0
Monroe County, Indiana	40,630	3.1	21.1	64.2	11.6
Morgan County, Indiana	5,680	28.3	39.8	25.5	6.5
Porter County, Indiana	16,196	14.1	42.7	34.8	8.4

N = Data for this geographic area cannot be displayed because the number of sample cases is too small.

Table C-2. Educational Attainment of the Population, by Selected Counties, 2019—*Continued*

(Number; percent; dollars.)

State/County	Total	Less than 9th grade (percent)	9th to 12th grade, no diploma (percent)	High school graduate (includes equivalency) (percent)	Some college, no degree (percent)	Associate's degree (percent)	Bachelor's degree (percent)	Graduate or professional degree (percent)
GEORGIA—*(Continued)*								
Rockdale County, Georgia	60,224	3.1	8.9	29.2	26.1	9.2	15.8	7.8
Spalding County, Georgia	45,479	4.7	10.5	42.3	15.5	9.3	10.3	7.4
Troup County, Georgia	46,785	3.8	7.3	40.3	20.8	8.1	13.4	6.4
Walker County, Georgia	49,130	6.7	13.0	35.4	21.7	6.4	10.3	6.4
Walton County, Georgia	65,348	3.6	10.7	32.2	23.5	6.5	15.4	8.1
Whitfield County, Georgia	67,441	16.9	11.3	29.4	19.0	6.9	9.7	6.8
HAWAII	996,668	3.6	4.0	27.4	20.7	10.6	22.1	11.6
Hawaii County, Hawaii	143,872	3.7	3.7	31.1	22.2	9.3	19.7	10.3
Honolulu County, Hawaii	680,706	3.5	3.9	25.8	19.9	11.0	23.4	12.4
Kauai County, Hawaii	51,455	3.3	3.9	30.4	21.3	12.6	18.7	9.9
Maui County, Hawaii	120,620	4.7	4.7	30.7	22.8	9.4	18.9	8.8
IDAHO	1,170,997	3.0	5.5	26.1	26.0	10.6	18.8	9.9
Ada County, Idaho	329,339	1.4	3.8	19.8	24.9	10.4	25.4	14.3
Bannock County, Idaho	56,426	1.3	4.7	24.6	32.2	7.7	19.8	9.7
Bonneville County, Idaho	72,956	2.9	4.1	25.8	23.4	11.1	22.9	9.8
Canyon County, Idaho	143,774	6.3	6.8	30.0	25.9	10.6	14.6	5.9
Kootenai County, Idaho	115,561	1.2	5.2	25.6	30.9	12.5	15.5	9.1
Twin Falls County, Idaho	54,509	7.3	7.2	26.7	28.1	9.3	12.4	9.0
ILLINOIS	8,694,694	4.5	5.7	25.9	20.0	8.2	21.7	14.1
Adams County, Illinois	46,146	1.9	7.0	37.2	20.8	9.2	15.9	8.0
Champaign County, Illinois	121,881	2.7	3.9	22.8	15.6	8.8	20.4	25.9
Cook County, Illinois	3,590,364	6.1	6.0	22.8	17.9	6.7	23.8	16.8
DeKalb County, Illinois	61,531	2.8	4.5	24.0	23.1	9.7	23.3	12.6
DuPage County, Illinois	636,969	3.0	3.1	18.8	17.5	6.9	30.5	20.2
Kane County, Illinois	351,487	7.0	7.1	24.1	20.8	7.9	21.7	11.4
Kankakee County, Illinois	72,229	3.5	6.1	37.7	23.4	9.7	11.9	7.7
Kendall County, Illinois	82,912	3.7	3.6	21.8	19.0	12.5	22.6	16.9
Lake County, Illinois	459,783	5.0	4.7	20.3	18.7	6.3	27.1	17.9
LaSalle County, Illinois	77,631	2.4	8.2	37.4	24.9	10.9	10.6	5.7
McHenry County, Illinois	210,880	2.5	4.0	26.8	21.9	9.8	24.0	10.9
McLean County, Illinois	104,545	2.0	3.5	22.2	18.3	8.2	30.7	15.1
Macon County, Illinois	72,287	1.7	4.9	39.8	24.9	7.1	14.4	7.2
Madison County, Illinois	184,866	1.4	5.2	28.7	23.4	11.0	18.9	11.3
Peoria County, Illinois	120,735	1.7	5.1	29.8	21.5	9.5	19.4	13.0
Rock Island County, Illinois	97,621	3.8	7.6	30.3	23.9	10.4	14.3	9.7
St. Clair County, Illinois	178,605	2.6	5.9	27.3	26.3	10.4	16.1	11.5
Sangamon County, Illinois	136,578	2.1	4.9	28.0	22.2	8.7	21.9	12.2
Tazewell County, Illinois	92,059	1.5	4.2	32.4	23.9	10.7	19.2	8.1
Vermilion County, Illinois	51,836	2.4	8.0	44.5	21.8	11.2	7.9	4.2
Will County, Illinois	459,279	3.8	4.8	27.4	20.2	8.6	22.8	12.4
Williamson County, Illinois	47,356	2.1	4.6	30.7	22.8	10.4	18.8	10.6
Winnebago County, Illinois	192,880	4.0	7.2	30.5	23.4	10.1	16.0	8.8
INDIANA	4,502,015	3.6	6.8	33.9	19.9	8.8	17.3	9.7
Allen County, Indiana	247,992	4.4	6.1	27.5	21.6	11.4	19.6	9.3
Bartholomew County, Indiana	57,421	4.5	4.6	29.3	17.2	8.0	21.6	14.9
Boone County, Indiana	45,007	2.5	5.2	16.8	19.4	9.6	27.9	18.6
Clark County, Indiana	82,101	1.6	7.6	33.8	22.4	12.2	15.1	7.3
Delaware County, Indiana	71,731	0.6	7.2	36.6	20.7	12.2	11.7	10.9
Elkhart County, Indiana	131,077	9.1	8.4	37.2	18.9	6.4	14.0	5.9
Floyd County, Indiana	53,589	1.2	6.8	32.3	21.9	9.2	18.1	10.8
Grant County, Indiana	43,982	4.7	6.5	39.0	21.6	7.0	12.8	8.4
Hamilton County, Indiana	221,657	0.9	1.9	13.6	13.8	6.7	38.6	24.4
Hancock County, Indiana	54,474	3.4	7.1	30.3	21.1	8.8	21.0	8.4
Hendricks County, Indiana	115,132	1.2	3.6	29.6	20.1	8.5	25.6	11.4
Howard County, Indiana	57,393	4.4	5.8	34.4	28.7	8.6	11.9	6.3
Johnson County, Indiana	105,736	2.7	4.8	32.5	20.5	8.3	21.8	9.4
Kosciusko County, Indiana	53,973	4.8	8.7	34.9	17.9	6.6	17.0	10.2
Lake County, Indiana	331,902	4.3	6.0	36.1	23.1	7.9	14.9	7.7
LaPorte County, Indiana	77,292	2.4	9.0	39.3	20.4	10.9	12.4	5.5
Madison County, Indiana	90,782	3.4	8.1	38.7	21.7	9.5	12.1	6.5
Marion County, Indiana	637,578	4.2	8.6	29.8	18.5	7.8	20.0	11.1
Monroe County, Indiana	84,605	1.2	3.5	24.4	18.2	6.5	23.6	22.6
Morgan County, Indiana	49,000	2.2	7.3	38.5	26.6	8.0	11.7	5.6
Porter County, Indiana	117,121	1.7	3.4	38.0	19.4	9.9	17.7	10.0

N = Data for this geographic area cannot be displayed because the number of sample cases is too small.

Table C-2. Educational Attainment of the Population, by Selected Counties, 2019—*Continued*

(Number; percent; dollars.)

State/County		Population 18 to 24 years			
	Total	Less than high school graduate (percent)	High school graduate (includes equivalency) (percent)	Some college or associate's degree (percent)	Bachelor's degree or higher (percent)
INDIANA—*(Continued)*					
St. Joseph County, Indiana	29,865	7.7	31.3	48.3	12.7
Tippecanoe County, Indiana	46,802	4.4	33.8	50.6	11.2
Vanderburgh County, Indiana	17,988	11.2	38.9	40.3	9.7
Vigo County, Indiana	15,921	7.7	28.3	56.4	7.6
Wayne County, Indiana	5,896	18.6	52.6	25.1	3.7
IOWA	310,236	10.4	29.4	50.1	10.1
Black Hawk County, Iowa	19,233	9.5	22.3	61.7	6.6
Dallas County, Iowa	7,378	6.2	32.9	42.0	18.9
Dubuque County, Iowa	10,173	8.2	23.5	56.3	11.9
Johnson County, Iowa	31,976	10.5	18.2	53.2	18.2
Linn County, Iowa	20,497	7.6	27.6	52.7	12.1
Polk County, Iowa	42,390	12.4	31.4	42.5	13.7
Pottawattamie County, Iowa	7,667	8.8	54.0	32.9	4.2
Scott County, Iowa	14,050	13.7	34.3	40.2	11.8
Story County, Iowa	26,940	0.9	14.8	77.6	6.7
Woodbury County, Iowa	9,512	7.3	30.1	54.9	7.6
KANSAS	294,932	11.5	31.3	46.5	10.7
Butler County, Kansas	5,452	9.1	42.5	40.4	8.1
Douglas County, Kansas	27,168	1.4	23.1	59.4	16.1
Johnson County, Kansas	48,150	9.8	29.8	41.1	19.4
Leavenworth County, Kansas	7,904	7.8	46.0	44.4	1.7
Riley County, Kansas	25,117	3.1	20.9	68.1	7.9
Sedgwick County, Kansas	47,005	12.8	36.5	42.8	7.9
Shawnee County, Kansas	15,421	11.2	39.4	35.3	14.1
Wyandotte County, Kansas	14,053	19.4	38.3	27.7	14.7
KENTUCKY	417,406	12.2	37.0	41.2	9.7
Boone County, Kentucky	11,637	15.6	34.6	37.5	12.2
Bullitt County, Kentucky	6,166	6.7	50.4	40.6	2.3
Campbell County, Kentucky	9,342	2.7	37.8	41.9	17.6
Christian County, Kentucky	10,208	12.9	42.8	41.6	2.7
Daviess County, Kentucky	7,872	8.8	36.4	44.5	10.3
Fayette County, Kentucky	44,233	6.0	21.2	54.8	18.0
Hardin County, Kentucky	9,527	17.3	48.7	28.7	5.3
Jefferson County, Kentucky	65,212	11.1	36.5	36.9	15.5
Kenton County, Kentucky	14,456	8.8	45.2	30.0	16.0
McCracken County, Kentucky	5,124	5.3	41.6	48.3	4.8
Madison County, Kentucky	16,684	8.0	30.5	52.2	9.3
Oldham County, Kentucky	5,387	14.9	26.7	46.4	11.9
Warren County, Kentucky	21,372	6.6	30.7	52.1	10.6
LOUISIANA	423,707	15.8	35.1	40.6	8.5
Ascension Parish, Louisiana	10,303	14.6	45.2	33.4	6.8
Bossier Parish, Louisiana	10,876	17.7	32.5	44.0	5.7
Caddo Parish, Louisiana	20,748	20.1	29.7	39.3	10.8
Calcasieu Parish, Louisiana	17,854	20.7	28.6	45.8	4.8
East Baton Rouge Parish, Louisiana	58,609	9.6	25.8	51.5	13.0
Iberia Parish, Louisiana	5,462	25.1	41.6	31.8	1.6
Jefferson Parish, Louisiana	32,164	16.0	36.0	34.3	13.7
Lafayette Parish, Louisiana	22,852	9.6	29.6	49.3	11.5
Lafourche Parish, Louisiana	8,422	17.2	44.8	35.4	2.6
Livingston Parish, Louisiana	12,009	12.5	40.2	37.8	9.5
Orleans Parish, Louisiana	33,605	12.8	25.6	51.6	10.0
Ouachita Parish, Louisiana	14,638	16.7	19.8	50.3	13.2
Rapides Parish, Louisiana	11,271	12.4	46.5	37.9	3.2
St. Landry Parish, Louisiana	6,754	29.1	49.7	18.4	2.9
St. Tammany Parish, Louisiana	19,550	21.7	39.3	31.7	7.3
Tangipahoa Parish, Louisiana	14,685	19.3	26.8	50.0	4.0
Terrebonne Parish, Louisiana	7,724	11.0	34.4	33.9	20.7
MAINE	106,707	10.8	34.6	41.7	12.8
Androscoggin County, Maine	9,169	6.2	38.1	39.4	16.2
Aroostook County, Maine	4,632	16.2	38.8	42.4	2.6
Cumberland County, Maine	25,058	9.0	27.9	38.8	24.3
Kennebec County, Maine	10,046	11.7	31.6	45.6	11.2

N = Data for this geographic area cannot be displayed because the number of sample cases is too small.

Table C-2. Educational Attainment of the Population, by Selected Counties, 2019—*Continued*

(Number; percent; dollars.)

State/County	Population 25 years and over							
	Total	Less than 9th grade (percent)	9th to 12th grade, no diploma (percent)	High school graduate (includes equivalency) (percent)	Some college, no degree (percent)	Associate's degree (percent)	Bachelor's degree (percent)	Graduate or professional degree (percent)
INDIANA—*(Continued)*								
St. Joseph County, Indiana	178,476	2.4	7.3	32.1	19.6	8.4	18.0	12.1
Tippecanoe County, Indiana	108,603	3.2	6.2	27.2	16.8	7.2	21.3	18.1
Vanderburgh County, Indiana	124,267	2.2	7.1	34.3	19.4	9.5	19.0	8.6
Vigo County, Indiana	69,630	1.6	6.2	34.4	22.5	9.5	14.9	10.8
Wayne County, Indiana	45,134	4.4	7.6	35.9	23.1	11.3	10.8	7.0
IOWA	2,123,004	2.7	4.6	31.0	20.4	11.9	19.8	9.5
Black Hawk County, Iowa	83,655	2.2	4.9	32.7	19.4	10.5	19.9	10.3
Dallas County, Iowa	61,134	1.4	1.8	17.1	13.9	11.6	38.2	15.9
Dubuque County, Iowa	65,072	1.9	3.7	34.4	15.7	11.6	21.8	10.8
Johnson County, Iowa	89,161	2.3	3.5	15.9	16.4	8.1	28.6	25.3
Linn County, Iowa	153,872	1.8	4.1	28.0	19.2	13.9	22.6	10.4
Polk County, Iowa	326,674	3.7	4.1	23.9	21.1	9.7	26.4	11.1
Pottawattamie County, Iowa	63,895	2.8	6.2	31.7	23.3	12.8	16.3	6.9
Scott County, Iowa	118,176	2.4	4.8	27.7	21.8	11.4	20.0	11.9
Story County, Iowa	54,858	0.9	1.7	16.9	18.7	10.4	29.1	22.4
Woodbury County, Iowa	66,887	7.5	6.5	32.6	21.9	9.7	14.6	7.2
KANSAS	1,918,081	3.3	4.9	26.3	22.4	9.0	21.6	12.4
Butler County, Kansas	44,092	1.7	5.2	26.5	27.3	8.3	19.5	11.4
Douglas County, Kansas	72,338	1.6	3.3	20.9	18.1	8.9	29.7	17.4
Johnson County, Kansas	409,324	1.6	2.3	15.0	17.9	7.2	34.6	21.4
Leavenworth County, Kansas	54,599	2.7	4.6	28.5	24.8	7.6	19.9	11.8
Riley County, Kansas	37,327	0.7	2.4	17.8	25.2	8.8	25.1	20.0
Sedgwick County, Kansas	337,752	3.6	6.1	26.4	23.8	8.7	20.3	11.1
Shawnee County, Kansas	120,718	1.8	4.5	30.6	23.5	8.2	20.6	10.7
Wyandotte County, Kansas	105,645	9.8	9.6	33.3	19.1	8.4	12.5	7.4
KENTUCKY	3,048,442	5.1	7.7	33.2	20.3	8.5	14.9	10.3
Boone County, Kentucky	87,428	3.5	4.3	26.5	24.2	9.6	20.8	11.1
Bullitt County, Kentucky	57,989	3.2	8.4	40.4	21.5	11.0	10.8	4.8
Campbell County, Kentucky	64,791	3.2	5.3	26.8	17.5	7.1	26.2	13.9
Christian County, Kentucky	41,216	6.1	8.6	28.3	24.2	11.8	15.4	5.5
Daviess County, Kentucky	68,986	5.0	7.9	31.1	21.1	10.1	15.3	9.5
Fayette County, Kentucky	211,577	3.1	4.4	21.2	19.2	7.1	24.7	20.3
Hardin County, Kentucky	74,583	2.3	6.1	31.1	24.6	12.1	15.0	8.8
Jefferson County, Kentucky	532,991	2.7	5.8	26.7	21.5	8.2	21.1	14.0
Kenton County, Kentucky	113,122	3.5	5.5	29.1	19.8	9.3	20.2	12.6
McCracken County, Kentucky	45,495	3.4	7.3	33.3	22.3	9.1	14.3	10.3
Madison County, Kentucky	57,084	2.4	6.5	30.5	19.8	7.9	18.7	14.1
Oldham County, Kentucky	44,929	1.4	4.8	23.7	20.8	8.1	26.0	15.3
Warren County, Kentucky	81,148	6.0	4.5	25.7	18.9	9.5	21.3	14.1
LOUISIANA	3,140,201	4.4	9.6	33.9	20.6	6.4	16.0	8.9
Ascension Parish, Louisiana	82,678	1.5	6.3	34.2	22.3	10.1	17.1	8.6
Bossier Parish, Louisiana	84,723	4.2	5.2	33.3	26.7	8.3	13.8	8.5
Caddo Parish, Louisiana	163,212	3.0	10.4	34.1	21.9	6.9	14.5	9.2
Calcasieu Parish, Louisiana	134,238	3.5	10.4	35.4	19.2	8.5	14.5	8.4
East Baton Rouge Parish, Louisiana	281,377	2.4	6.6	28.2	22.3	5.6	22.0	12.9
Iberia Parish, Louisiana	46,888	6.3	9.2	47.5	13.3	7.5	12.4	3.7
Jefferson Parish, Louisiana	305,032	4.9	7.5	30.4	22.3	6.9	18.0	9.9
Lafayette Parish, Louisiana	163,888	4.1	5.9	29.3	20.1	5.7	24.6	10.3
Lafourche Parish, Louisiana	66,430	8.7	13.1	40.0	16.4	5.1	11.4	5.2
Livingston Parish, Louisiana	92,898	4.2	13.6	35.6	19.1	6.1	16.8	4.5
Orleans Parish, Louisiana	279,405	2.0	9.4	23.1	21.0	3.9	21.7	18.0
Ouachita Parish, Louisiana	100,705	3.5	9.6	32.5	22.3	6.1	16.6	9.4
Rapides Parish, Louisiana	86,467	4.2	9.7	36.4	23.3	7.0	13.5	5.9
St. Landry Parish, Louisiana	54,195	8.4	14.6	42.8	17.3	5.1	8.0	3.7
St. Tammany Parish, Louisiana	179,016	2.5	6.3	26.9	23.1	5.1	23.0	13.1
Tangipahoa Parish, Louisiana	87,255	6.3	9.1	35.7	18.2	6.0	15.5	9.3
Terrebonne Parish, Louisiana	75,048	7.7	11.6	38.7	18.5	7.6	10.2	5.7
MAINE	991,152	2.1	4.7	31.4	18.6	10.0	20.8	12.4
Androscoggin County, Maine	75,037	3.3	5.6	34.1	18.1	13.8	16.7	8.4
Aroostook County, Maine	50,069	4.2	4.8	40.5	19.2	12.4	12.5	6.5
Cumberland County, Maine	216,410	1.8	3.4	21.2	15.8	7.7	31.4	18.7
Kennebec County, Maine	89,536	2.3	4.4	32.9	21.9	9.7	16.7	12.1

N – Data for this geographic area cannot be displayed because the number of sample cases is too small.

Table C-2. Educational Attainment of the Population, by Selected Counties, 2019—*Continued*

(Number; percent; dollars.)

State/County	Population 18 to 24 years				
	Total	Less than high school graduate (percent)	High school graduate (includes equivalency) (percent)	Some college or associate's degree (percent)	Bachelor's degree or higher (percent)
MAINE—(*Continued*)					
Penobscot County, Maine	16,023	7.6	33.0	51.9	7.6
York County, Maine	14,929	12.3	45.3	32.5	9.9
MARYLAND	529,535	11.8	30.6	41.5	16.0
Allegany County, Maryland	8,929	12.2	39.0	46.5	2.4
Anne Arundel County, Maryland	50,545	9.8	33.5	38.1	18.6
Baltimore County, Maryland	72,386	10.3	33.2	43.6	12.9
Calvert County, Maryland	6,844	5.4	42.0	31.6	21.0
Carroll County, Maryland	14,844	5.4	31.7	44.4	18.4
Cecil County, Maryland	8,783	10.9	31.9	51.9	5.3
Charles County, Maryland	14,201	7.6	42.6	37.4	12.4
Frederick County, Maryland	21,625	19.0	28.7	38.3	14.1
Harford County, Maryland	19,961	12.6	32.2	40.4	14.8
Howard County, Maryland	26,063	10.4	26.3	37.7	25.6
Montgomery County, Maryland	81,523	14.9	25.0	33.4	26.7
Prince George's County, Maryland	85,570	11.3	30.9	46.2	11.5
St. Mary's County, Maryland	11,408	9.3	40.6	37.1	12.9
Washington County, Maryland	12,084	19.0	37.2	34.6	9.2
Wicomico County, Maryland	15,490	11.7	20.1	61.3	6.9
Baltimore city, Maryland	56,373	12.7	28.3	42.0	17.1
MASSACHUSETTS	690,150	9.2	27.1	44.2	19.5
Barnstable County, Massachusetts	13,751	15.0	29.0	38.0	18.0
Berkshire County, Massachusetts	11,852	10.7	28.6	54.6	6.1
Bristol County, Massachusetts	50,198	10.7	37.0	38.3	14.0
Essex County, Massachusetts	70,580	13.5	31.4	38.5	16.7
Franklin County, Massachusetts	4,967	3.7	46.5	38.8	11.0
Hampden County, Massachusetts	46,744	11.7	33.6	44.9	9.8
Hampshire County, Massachusetts	37,056	3.8	10.5	77.9	7.9
Middlesex County, Massachusetts	158,706	7.9	24.6	40.2	27.2
Norfolk County, Massachusetts	61,868	6.7	27.8	36.6	28.9
Plymouth County, Massachusetts	44,446	10.9	35.2	40.5	13.4
Suffolk County, Massachusetts	108,552	7.2	17.4	51.3	24.1
Worcester County, Massachusetts	79,818	10.3	31.9	43.7	14.0
MICHIGAN	949,408	12.7	32.4	43.3	11.6
Allegan County, Michigan	8,826	14.8	52.2	25.0	8.0
Bay County, Michigan	7,594	19.5	26.6	43.1	10.8
Berrien County, Michigan	12,858	18.8	30.6	45.1	5.4
Calhoun County, Michigan	12,265	12.7	40.4	40.4	6.6
Clinton County, Michigan	7,070	10.5	35.0	46.0	8.6
Eaton County, Michigan	9,651	12.8	28.0	50.3	8.9
Genesee County, Michigan	34,308	14.6	37.6	40.8	7.0
Grand Traverse County, Michigan	7,166	13.1	31.1	41.1	14.8
Ingham County, Michigan	55,276	6.0	25.1	58.5	10.5
Isabella County, Michigan	17,764	4.6	28.9	59.5	7.0
Jackson County, Michigan	13,533	16.5	31.6	49.4	2.5
Kalamazoo County, Michigan	41,971	9.4	27.4	48.4	14.8
Kent County, Michigan	61,729	11.7	34.3	39.6	14.4
Lapeer County, Michigan	7,521	27.2	33.3	35.4	4.0
Lenawee County, Michigan	8,841	14.9	43.3	37.8	4.0
Livingston County, Michigan	15,176	16.9	32.1	37.4	13.5
Macomb County, Michigan	69,918	9.8	35.5	41.7	13.0
Marquette County, Michigan	9,961	12.3	27.1	48.5	12.2
Midland County, Michigan	6,432	9.3	21.6	50.4	18.8
Monroe County, Michigan	11,835	15.7	33.7	43.9	6.7
Muskegon County, Michigan	15,363	14.6	39.8	40.3	5.3
Oakland County, Michigan	101,508	11.2	29.0	40.9	19.0
Ottawa County, Michigan	38,783	11.0	30.9	48.4	9.8
Saginaw County, Michigan	17,361	18.0	34.2	41.2	6.7
St. Clair County, Michigan	13,034	15.9	44.3	30.9	9.0
Shiawassee County, Michigan	5,449	14.5	42.1	40.1	3.3
Van Buren County, Michigan	5,501	11.6	32.9	50.0	5.4
Washtenaw County, Michigan	67,177	7.3	14.1	57.4	21.2
Wayne County, Michigan	149,384	15.0	36.2	38.1	10.7
MINNESOTA	489,751	12.1	29.6	43.2	15.1
Anoka County, Minnesota	26,767	12.7	33.7	41.9	11.7
Blue Earth County, Minnesota	14,968	2.5	27.4	60.3	9.7

N = Data for this geographic area cannot be displayed because the number of sample cases is too small.

Table C-2. Educational Attainment of the Population, by Selected Counties, 2019—*Continued*

(Number; percent; dollars.)

State/County	Total	Population 25 years and over						
		Less than 9th grade (percent)	9th to 12th grade, no diploma (percent)	High school graduate (includes equivalency) (percent)	Some college, no degree (percent)	Associate's degree (percent)	Bachelor's degree (percent)	Graduate or professional degree (percent)
MAINE—*(Continued)*								
Penobscot County, Maine	109,291	2.4	4.5	32.8	20.1	10.7	19.5	10.0
York County, Maine	154,666	1.3	5.1	30.8	19.3	10.9	19.6	13.0
MARYLAND	4,183,858	4.0	5.6	24.6	18.0	6.9	21.8	19.1
Allegany County, Maryland	49,440	2.6	7.5	43.2	16.1	9.6	13.3	7.9
Anne Arundel County, Maryland	400,105	2.1	4.9	23.4	18.5	7.2	24.7	19.2
Baltimore County, Maryland	575,977	2.7	5.2	25.5	18.2	7.6	23.3	17.5
Calvert County, Maryland	64,371	0.9	3.3	32.0	23.1	9.0	16.2	15.4
Carroll County, Maryland	117,243	1.4	3.8	28.5	18.9	10.2	21.6	15.6
Cecil County, Maryland	71,592	1.3	7.6	35.6	20.7	9.6	16.3	8.8
Charles County, Maryland	110,194	3.2	4.0	31.9	24.3	8.0	16.7	12.0
Frederick County, Maryland	177,932	4.2	3.4	24.2	18.9	7.4	23.6	18.3
Harford County, Maryland	179,036	2.3	3.9	25.2	22.1	9.5	21.0	16.0
Howard County, Maryland	220,678	1.7	3.1	13.3	12.5	4.9	32.1	32.2
Montgomery County, Maryland	727,128	5.7	4.1	14.4	12.7	5.4	26.4	31.4
Prince George's County, Maryland	622,295	7.2	6.2	25.9	20.5	6.7	19.2	14.4
St. Mary's County, Maryland	75,021	3.0	6.6	33.6	15.9	10.1	19.0	11.6
Washington County, Maryland	106,200	3.5	8.6	37.2	21.9	6.3	12.4	10.1
Wicomico County, Maryland	65,728	5.7	8.9	31.5	17.7	5.9	16.6	13.6
Baltimore city, Maryland	417,550	4.5	9.8	28.3	19.3	4.8	17.6	15.7
MASSACHUSETTS	4,850,576	4.2	4.5	23.9	15.0	7.4	24.7	20.3
Barnstable County, Massachusetts	167,562	1.1	2.4	20.2	19.4	9.8	26.2	20.9
Berkshire County, Massachusetts	92,243	2.2	5.6	29.6	18.4	10.4	17.5	16.4
Bristol County, Massachusetts	399,297	7.4	6.3	30.0	17.5	8.8	20.0	10.0
Essex County, Massachusetts	552,144	5.6	5.1	24.3	15.0	7.8	24.6	16.8
Franklin County, Massachusetts	53,376	2.3	5.6	27.2	16.1	11.5	20.4	16.9
Hampden County, Massachusetts	319,983	5.3	7.9	33.4	16.7	8.8	16.7	11.2
Hampshire County, Massachusetts	100,574	1.4	3.8	18.6	15.2	8.4	25.4	27.3
Middlesex County, Massachusetts	1,137,894	2.9	3.2	19.0	11.9	5.8	28.2	29.0
Norfolk County, Massachusetts	497,759	2.9	3.2	18.8	13.1	6.8	28.7	26.4
Plymouth County, Massachusetts	366,337	3.6	3.4	28.4	17.7	8.7	24.5	13.7
Suffolk County, Massachusetts	564,188	7.3	4.8	21.5	13.1	5.2	25.7	22.4
Worcester County, Massachusetts	577,452	2.9	5.2	28.2	17.8	9.0	22.0	15.0
MICHIGAN	6,894,627	2.7	6.0	29.1	22.8	9.4	18.2	11.9
Allegan County, Michigan	81,159	2.2	5.6	41.5	19.5	7.4	17.6	6.1
Bay County, Michigan	74,917	1.5	5.6	34.3	25.9	11.1	14.8	6.8
Berrien County, Michigan	107,341	2.1	7.6	27.2	25.4	10.7	15.9	11.1
Calhoun County, Michigan	91,740	2.2	7.2	37.6	22.9	9.9	13.2	7.1
Clinton County, Michigan	54,934	2.3	2.6	26.5	24.2	10.6	19.8	14.1
Eaton County, Michigan	77,708	1.4	3.3	29.0	25.5	11.4	18.9	10.5
Genesee County, Michigan	280,937	2.2	7.4	30.7	27.4	10.8	13.5	8.0
Grand Traverse County, Michigan	67,821	1.0	4.2	22.3	24.6	8.7	25.1	14.0
Ingham County, Michigan	179,605	2.8	3.5	21.3	23.3	8.6	22.5	18.0
Isabella County, Michigan	39,906	3.0	5.9	33.8	22.1	8.1	14.1	13.0
Jackson County, Michigan	111,444	3.0	6.8	35.8	22.5	9.0	15.3	7.7
Kalamazoo County, Michigan	166,083	3.1	4.5	22.9	22.7	8.6	22.8	15.5
Kent County, Michigan	438,160	3.8	4.6	23.7	22.9	8.8	23.8	12.4
Lapeer County, Michigan	62,672	2.1	6.5	34.7	28.2	9.3	12.8	6.4
Lenawee County, Michigan	69,088	2.5	7.3	35.4	23.2	10.4	13.7	7.6
Livingston County, Michigan	136,805	1.0	4.1	26.8	22.9	9.5	24.0	11.7
Macomb County, Michigan	622,199	3.6	5.7	30.5	24.1	10.7	16.0	9.3
Marquette County, Michigan	44,541	1.2	3.6	30.4	20.2	9.4	24.1	11.1
Midland County, Michigan	58,581	1.7	4.0	28.8	18.3	10.9	22.0	14.3
Monroe County, Michigan	107,063	2.3	6.8	32.1	22.5	11.8	16.5	8.0
Muskegon County, Michigan	118,945	2.6	5.3	34.2	24.4	12.7	14.2	6.6
Oakland County, Michigan	896,196	1.8	3.3	18.9	19.2	8.0	27.8	21.1
Ottawa County, Michigan	183,870	2.4	4.8	28.0	20.3	8.9	23.9	11.7
Saginaw County, Michigan	132,466	2.6	7.7	33.1	23.6	11.2	14.0	7.9
St. Clair County, Michigan	113,904	1.6	6.8	31.8	25.8	12.4	14.1	7.6
Shiawassee County, Michigan	48,493	2.2	6.0	39.6	24.0	10.2	12.4	5.6
Van Buren County, Michigan	52,769	4.8	6.9	31.7	23.5	10.0	14.4	8.7
Washtenaw County, Michigan	232,925	1.2	3.4	14.2	18.0	7.2	25.8	30.0
Wayne County, Michigan	1,187,569	3.6	8.7	31.3	23.3	8.2	14.6	10.4
MINNESOTA	3,847,212	2.7	3.7	24.4	20.4	11.5	24.5	12.7
Anoka County, Minnesota	245,395	1.9	3.8	27.1	22.2	12.7	23.8	8.5
Blue Earth County, Minnesota	39,211	0.9	2.9	26.5	22.3	10.8	25.2	11.3

N = Data for this geographic area cannot be displayed because the number of sample cases is too small.

Table C-2. Educational Attainment of the Population, by Selected Counties, 2019—*Continued*

(Number; percent; dollars.)

State/County	Population 18 to 24 years				
	Total	Less than high school graduate (percent)	High school graduate (includes equivalency) (percent)	Some college or associate's degree (percent)	Bachelor's degree or higher (percent)
MINNESOTA—(*Continued*)					
Carver County, Minnesota	8,211	11.4	25.0	48.5	15.1
Crow Wing County, Minnesota	3,967	15.2	32.8	44.6	7.3
Dakota County, Minnesota	34,406	13.6	31.9	38.5	16.0
Hennepin County, Minnesota	107,423	10.1	26.8	37.9	25.2
Olmsted County, Minnesota	11,356	16.4	40.5	23.4	19.7
Ramsey County, Minnesota	52,342	12.8	25.7	45.9	15.6
Rice County, Minnesota	10,237	10.3	14.8	70.2	4.7
St. Louis County, Minnesota	23,689	6.1	25.5	51.5	16.9
Scott County, Minnesota	11,463	20.2	25.6	31.7	22.6
Sherburne County, Minnesota	8,093	19.3	30.2	44.2	6.2
Stearns County, Minnesota	23,597	7.4	25.8	58.3	8.4
Washington County, Minnesota	19,589	11.2	31.6	39.3	17.9
Wright County, Minnesota	9,704	13.7	35.3	37.0	14.0
MISSISSIPPI	298,065	15.0	28.4	49.8	6.8
DeSoto County, Mississippi	16,284	20.2	28.2	45.4	6.2
Forrest County, Mississippi	10,834	8.0	16.6	68.4	7.1
Harrison County, Mississippi	21,929	11.7	27.3	55.0	6.0
Hinds County, Mississippi	25,474	11.4	31.1	49.5	8.0
Jackson County, Mississippi	11,464	11.3	41.0	38.5	9.3
Jones County, Mississippi	6,443	16.8	26.7	48.0	8.5
Lauderdale County, Mississippi	5,803	14.3	37.9	44.4	3.4
Lee County, Mississippi	8,540	19.2	11.3	59.8	9.7
Madison County, Mississippi	9,332	6.1	19.2	60.0	14.8
Rankin County, Mississippi	12,672	15.8	27.4	39.8	17.0
MISSOURI	558,571	11.3	33.8	43.2	11.7
Boone County, Missouri	34,590	2.3	17.3	69.9	10.5
Buchanan County, Missouri	7,459	17.1	21.2	49.5	12.2
Cape Girardeau County, Missouri	10,698	2.1	31.1	57.9	8.9
Cass County, Missouri	8,225	9.8	50.8	30.3	9.1
Christian County, Missouri	6,347	9.8	25.9	55.7	8.6
Clay County, Missouri	20,496	11.4	34.1	46.2	8.2
Cole County, Missouri	5,461	5.0	39.4	26.2	29.4
Franklin County, Missouri	7,676	21.6	28.6	42.2	7.6
Greene County, Missouri	40,298	11.2	21.7	53.4	13.6
Jackson County, Missouri	58,068	12.8	39.6	34.2	13.4
Jasper County, Missouri	11,462	20.1	33.2	38.2	8.5
Jefferson County, Missouri	16,627	11.2	41.8	40.0	7.1
Platte County, Missouri	8,062	16.4	26.4	39.5	17.7
St. Charles County, Missouri	33,272	11.4	27.7	48.0	12.8
St. Francois County, Missouri	5,033	11.8	32.9	55.3	0.0
St. Louis County, Missouri	83,082	9.4	33.2	38.5	19.0
St. Louis city, Missouri	26,301	5.5	28.5	42.4	23.6
MONTANA	100,304	14.0	35.2	41.3	9.5
Cascade County, Montana	8,510	7.1	39.8	47.0	6.1
Flathead County, Montana	6,724	11.3	47.9	36.5	4.4
Gallatin County, Montana	18,919	9.6	23.4	51.5	15.5
Lewis and Clark County, Montana	6,192	22.3	33.5	36.1	8.1
Missoula County, Montana	15,418	5.4	30.3	50.7	13.6
Yellowstone County, Montana	11,908	11.1	44.7	37.8	6.5
NEBRASKA	187,542	9.2	29.1	47.4	14.4
Douglas County, Nebraska	51,616	7.6	31.1	44.0	17.2
Lancaster County, Nebraska	48,453	6.0	19.7	58.0	16.3
Sarpy County, Nebraska	15,585	6.2	29.7	47.2	16.8
NEVADA	252,953	13.6	42.2	37.7	6.5
Clark County, Nevada	184,971	14.3	44.2	35.5	6.1
Washoe County, Nevada	42,837	8.9	33.1	48.9	9.1
NEW HAMPSHIRE	123,941	11.3	32.1	44.2	12.5
Cheshire County, New Hampshire	8,565	2.3	26.0	66.0	5.6
Grafton County, New Hampshire	11,242	5.8	25.3	60.1	8.9
Hillsborough County, New Hampshire	35,154	13.3	33.3	38.2	15.2
Merrimack County, New Hampshire	13,842	20.7	33.0	39.4	6.9

N = Data for this geographic area cannot be displayed because the number of sample cases is too small.

Table C-2. Educational Attainment of the Population, by Selected Counties, 2019—*Continued*

(Number; percent; dollars.)

State/County	Total	Population 25 years and over						
		Less than 9th grade (percent)	9th to 12th grade, no diploma (percent)	High school graduate (includes equivalency) (percent)	Some college, no degree (percent)	Associate's degree (percent)	Bachelor's degree (percent)	Graduate or professional degree (percent)
MINNESOTA—(*Continued*)								
Carver County, Minnesota	69,175	3.0	3.2	15.1	17.3	9.4	35.9	16.1
Crow Wing County, Minnesota	46,894	0.5	4.4	30.4	24.8	14.5	16.0	9.4
Dakota County, Minnesota	290,701	2.0	2.4	21.2	20.3	11.4	28.7	13.9
Hennepin County, Minnesota	882,398	3.1	2.8	16.5	18.0	8.9	32.4	18.4
Olmsted County, Minnesota	108,246	3.3	2.0	20.7	15.4	11.5	24.5	22.5
Ramsey County, Minnesota	370,025	4.5	4.2	21.8	17.5	8.8	26.9	16.3
Rice County, Minnesota	42,197	1.4	5.0	30.7	18.4	12.9	18.9	12.7
St. Louis County, Minnesota	137,764	1.6	3.5	26.4	25.5	13.0	19.5	10.5
Scott County, Minnesota	97,194	1.8	3.9	20.6	19.6	12.6	28.9	12.5
Sherburne County, Minnesota	63,742	1.4	3.6	30.7	24.7	13.0	18.8	7.8
Stearns County, Minnesota	100,173	5.8	3.7	29.3	21.8	12.3	18.9	8.3
Washington County, Minnesota	179,294	1.3	2.3	21.1	19.9	9.7	29.3	16.6
Wright County, Minnesota	90,127	1.2	2.5	29.1	21.2	12.2	22.8	11.0
MISSISSIPPI	1,979,664	4.6	10.1	30.2	22.3	10.5	13.7	8.6
DeSoto County, Mississippi	121,767	2.3	7.5	27.8	23.8	10.4	17.2	10.9
Forrest County, Mississippi	47,190	3.1	8.1	29.6	22.5	11.6	15.1	9.9
Harrison County, Mississippi	136,815	3.1	7.5	30.3	24.5	11.1	15.1	8.2
Hinds County, Mississippi	151,101	3.7	8.2	24.5	26.2	8.4	16.4	12.5
Jackson County, Mississippi	98,981	3.1	6.8	30.1	25.3	10.9	16.2	7.6
Jones County, Mississippi	44,623	5.6	8.1	35.2	19.9	12.5	11.5	7.2
Lauderdale County, Mississippi	51,061	4.6	14.7	25.0	23.1	13.8	12.4	6.3
Lee County, Mississippi	55,589	4.5	11.9	26.7	20.6	11.2	16.7	8.5
Madison County, Mississippi	70,657	3.2	5.5	20.4	15.6	6.5	31.0	17.7
Rankin County, Mississippi	107,148	2.6	7.6	25.5	23.2	10.8	20.2	9.9
MISSOURI	4,206,162	2.9	6.4	31.1	21.4	7.9	18.4	11.8
Boone County, Missouri	109,405	2.5	3.9	20.1	19.2	7.3	25.7	21.2
Buchanan County, Missouri	60,706	4.4	6.0	42.4	21.0	6.6	14.5	5.1
Cape Girardeau County, Missouri	51,517	2.1	7.0	28.8	22.5	5.4	21.2	13.2
Cass County, Missouri	72,252	2.0	4.4	37.8	22.9	7.1	15.8	9.9
Christian County, Missouri	59,930	2.4	7.3	28.7	22.5	9.9	18.6	10.6
Clay County, Missouri	169,514	2.2	3.6	29.2	23.1	9.6	22.5	9.7
Cole County, Missouri	54,710	2.4	5.6	29.0	20.6	9.5	21.8	11.1
Franklin County, Missouri	72,871	4.0	6.6	32.7	25.3	11.7	13.0	6.8
Greene County, Missouri	192,520	3.5	4.9	29.0	25.4	7.0	19.4	10.8
Jackson County, Missouri	480,715	2.4	6.1	29.6	22.1	7.3	20.4	12.2
Jasper County, Missouri	79,894	5.5	9.2	32.8	23.4	5.4	16.8	6.9
Jefferson County, Missouri	157,026	2.5	7.9	32.1	24.1	13.6	12.6	7.1
Platte County, Missouri	71,879	1.4	2.6	23.7	20.0	8.2	27.0	17.1
St. Charles County, Missouri	276,339	1.5	4.2	23.4	21.5	9.0	25.8	14.6
St. Francois County, Missouri	48,484	4.8	8.7	36.9	27.7	7.8	6.5	7.7
St. Louis County, Missouri	693,434	1.5	4.5	21.4	19.8	7.2	25.4	20.2
St. Louis city, Missouri	218,004	3.4	7.1	24.7	20.8	5.5	20.4	18.1
MONTANA	741,950	1.6	4.1	28.4	22.9	9.4	23.1	10.5
Cascade County, Montana	54,619	2.4	4.8	33.7	24.6	8.8	17.6	8.0
Flathead County, Montana	74,553	0.8	3.2	27.6	23.0	9.8	26.3	9.3
Gallatin County, Montana	73,589	0.9	1.3	18.0	20.3	6.8	35.2	17.5
Lewis and Clark County, Montana	49,458	0.6	2.7	23.6	19.5	9.1	28.3	16.3
Missoula County, Montana	81,796	1.4	2.8	22.1	20.1	9.1	30.0	14.4
Yellowstone County, Montana	112,005	1.8	4.6	31.2	21.0	8.5	22.1	10.9
NEBRASKA	1,271,770	3.4	4.5	25.7	22.0	11.1	21.8	11.4
Douglas County, Nebraska	374,023	4.1	4.4	21.6	20.9	7.4	26.5	15.0
Lancaster County, Nebraska	198,449	2.8	4.1	20.4	19.7	12.8	25.6	14.7
Sarpy County, Nebraska	120,539	1.4	2.1	23.3	22.9	10.9	26.2	13.1
NEVADA	2,136,466	5.1	8.0	27.8	24.6	8.8	16.7	9.0
Clark County, Nevada	1,560,947	5.5	8.2	28.2	24.0	8.5	16.8	8.8
Washoe County, Nevada	328,153	4.7	6.6	22.5	25.3	9.3	19.3	12.2
NEW HAMPSHIRE	979,750	2.0	4.7	28.1	17.8	9.9	22.9	14.7
Cheshire County, New Hampshire	53,697	2.7	3.1	30.6	20.7	9.0	21.1	12.8
Grafton County, New Hampshire	64,180	2.3	6.4	23.8	17.3	8.8	20.3	21.1
Hillsborough County, New Hampshire	297,602	2.7	5.0	26.3	18.1	10.1	24.4	13.4
Merrimack County, New Hampshire	108,510	2.0	6.0	29.1	16.9	10.3	21.3	14.4

N = Data for this geographic area cannot be displayed because the number of sample cases is too small.

Table C-2. Educational Attainment of the Population, by Selected Counties, 2019—*Continued*

(Number; percent; dollars.)

State/County	Population 18 to 24 years				
	Total	Less than high school graduate (percent)	High school graduate (includes equivalency) (percent)	Some college or associate's degree (percent)	Bachelor's degree or higher (percent)
NEW HAMPSHIRE—*(Continued)*					
Rockingham County, New Hampshire................	22,217	9.3	40.6	30.1	19.9
Strafford County, New Hampshire......................	20,533	5.2	20.6	61.3	13.0
NEW JERSEY	752,937	9.5	29.3	42.5	18.7
Atlantic County, New Jersey................................	24,683	10.9	28.6	45.9	14.6
Bergen County, New Jersey	74,163	8.1	23.9	41.8	26.1
Burlington County, New Jersey	36,899	9.1	35.5	37.6	17.7
Camden County, New Jersey...............................	41,040	12.6	33.2	39.5	14.7
Cape May County, New Jersey	6,132	8.1	47.3	33.1	11.5
Cumberland County, New Jersey	11,270	17.1	38.8	34.1	9.9
Essex County, New Jersey	69,333	11.6	34.6	39.9	13.9
Gloucester County, New Jersey..........................	25,981	3.6	29.3	51.7	15.3
Hudson County, New Jersey	52,068	9.5	25.8	41.6	23.1
Hunterdon County, New Jersey...........................	9,882	10.2	35.1	29.2	25.5
Mercer County, New Jersey................................	41,153	8.6	23.1	58.9	9.4
Middlesex County, New Jersey............................	76,973	8.6	25.9	50.0	15.5
Monmouth County, New Jersey	49,925	8.0	26.5	40.4	25.1
Morris County, New Jersey	41,892	9.4	26.7	36.6	27.2
Ocean County, New Jersey.................................	43,993	6.4	30.0	43.2	20.4
Passaic County, New Jersey...............................	48,205	13.4	40.6	32.1	13.8
Salem County, New Jersey.................................	5,015	4.2	28.2	53.0	14.5
Somerset County, New Jersey	27,734	10.4	23.5	39.1	27.1
Sussex County, New Jersey	11,404	10.4	31.6	43.9	14.1
Union County, New Jersey	46,439	10.2	27.4	45.3	17.1
Warren County, New Jersey	8,753	6.7	27.7	44.5	21.1
NEW MEXICO	196,991	15.5	36.5	40.4	7.7
Bernalillo County, New Mexico............................	60,061	11.9	33.5	43.4	11.2
Chaves County, New Mexico...............................	5,918	11.1	66.8	22.1	0.0
Doña Ana County, New Mexico	30,938	10.7	29.2	51.2	8.9
Lea County, New Mexico....................................	7,453	25.7	34.5	32.2	7.6
McKinley County, New Mexico............................	6,572	22.1	34.8	42.9	0.2
Otero County, New Mexico.................................	6,601	16.0	38.0	39.9	6.1
Sandoval County, New Mexico............................	11,127	11.4	36.2	47.0	5.4
San Juan County, New Mexico............................	10,423	25.9	28.6	44.4	1.1
Santa Fe County, New Mexico	11,288	17.2	42.8	33.1	6.8
Valencia County, New Mexico	9,341	18.8	42.8	27.8	10.6
NEW YORK	1,766,731	10.3	28.2	43.2	18.4
Albany County, New York....................................	43,901	4.8	33.6	41.2	20.5
Bronx County, New York	137,331	19.4	27.3	42.5	10.8
Broome County, New York	27,051	6.2	33.6	44.6	15.6
Cattaraugus County, New York............................	6,604	13.7	37.2	42.5	6.6
Cayuga County, New York	5,798	20.7	28.6	41.7	9.0
Chautauqua County, New York	12,402	15.8	36.1	43.7	4.4
Chemung County, New York................................	6,596	16.6	33.6	44.7	5.1
Clinton County, New York	10,675	4.5	30.6	57.8	7.1
Dutchess County, New York................................	31,325	11.7	29.0	49.2	10.1
Erie County, New York.......................................	83,447	7.6	31.0	45.3	16.1
Jefferson County, New York	13,874	8.7	53.1	32.3	5.9
Kings County, New York.....................................	202,230	11.1	30.1	38.2	20.6
Livingston County, New York	9,687	7.1	31.7	56.4	4.8
Madison County, New York.................................	9,235	5.8	26.7	61.6	5.9
Monroe County, New York	71,906	7.6	28.4	48.3	15.7
Nassau County, New York..................................	116,989	8.8	24.8	41.8	24.7
New York County, New York...............................	145,284	7.1	20.1	38.7	34.1
Niagara County, New York..................................	16,439	9.7	30.0	42.2	18.2
Oneida County, New York...................................	21,322	12.7	28.5	46.6	12.2
Onondaga County, New York...............................	47,488	7.9	25.0	48.8	18.3
Ontario County, New York	9,967	3.1	40.1	34.8	22.0
Orange County, New York	40,814	10.7	34.8	41.3	13.2
Oswego County, New York	12,628	10.0	27.8	55.2	7.0
Putnam County, New York..................................	7,290	7.3	24.5	48.1	20.1
Queens County, New York..................................	168,832	10.3	26.2	45.3	18.2
Rensselaer County, New York	16,456	7.7	39.2	37.4	15.6
Richmond County, New York...............................	38,961	10.2	26.5	41.7	21.6
Rockland County, New York................................	29,647	16.3	29.3	33.1	21.4
St. Lawrence County, New York	14,624	9.4	25.4	60.8	4.4

N = Data for this geographic area cannot be displayed because the number of sample cases is too small.

Table C-2. Educational Attainment of the Population, by Selected Counties, 2019—*Continued*

(Number; percent; dollars.)

State/County	Total	Population 25 years and over						
		Less than 9th grade (percent)	9th to 12th grade, no diploma (percent)	High school graduate (includes equivalency) (percent)	Some college, no degree (percent)	Associate's degree (percent)	Bachelor's degree (percent)	Graduate or professional degree (percent)
NEW HAMPSHIRE—(*Continued*)								
Rockingham County, New Hampshire	227,909	1.1	2.9	27.8	16.8	8.8	25.8	16.7
Strafford County, New Hampshire	86,617	1.9	4.4	27.1	19.4	11.1	21.1	15 0
NEW JERSEY	6,191,229	4.7	5.0	26.9	15.7	6.4	25.1	16.1
Atlantic County, New Jersey	183,492	4.8	7.5	33.8	19.2	6.4	19.1	9.1
Bergen County, New Jersey	661,729	3.6	3.5	20.9	14.0	6.0	31.7	20.3
Burlington County, New Jersey	316,291	1.8	4.1	27.3	18.8	8.4	25.0	14.6
Camden County, New Jersey	351,426	4.6	5.8	30.0	18.4	7.7	21.2	12.4
Cape May County, New Jersey	69,957	2.4	4.1	34.9	19.3	7.2	18.2	13.9
Cumberland County, New Jersey	102,701	6.1	12.7	40.4	17.6	7.1	10.4	5.7
Essex County, New Jersey	540,264	6.7	6.5	29.8	16.0	5.2	21.9	13.8
Gloucester County, New Jersey	202,556	2.5	4.5	32.0	18.2	8.8	22.2	11.7
Hudson County, New Jersey	483,796	9.0	5.3	23.2	12.4	4.9	26.8	18.5
Hunterdon County, New Jersey	90,777	1.8	4.0	19.2	15.0	6.0	32.0	22.1
Mercer County, New Jersey	248,215	4.7	6.5	23.3	14.2	6.8	23 0	21.5
Middlesex County, New Jersey	569,641	4.9	6.2	24.5	14.8	5.7	26.0	17.9
Monmouth County, New Jersey	439,267	1.8	3.5	22.9	16.1	7.6	29.1	19.1
Morris County, New Jersey	347,474	2.5	2.7	19.5	13.2	5.6	33.7	22.8
Ocean County, New Jersey	416,503	2.3	4.8	34.6	18.2	7.8	21.4	10.9
Passaic County, New Jersey	334,603	8.9	5.8	35.5	15.4	5.3	19.6	9.5
Salem County, New Jersey	44,241	4.4	7.9	37.5	19.4	10.8	12 0	8.1
Somerset County, New Jersey	230,443	3.3	2.2	20.5	12.1	6.0	31.2	24.8
Sussex County, New Jersey	101,838	1.6	4.0	26.8	20.5	8.9	23.9	14.2
Union County, New Jersey	379,853	8.3	5.4	29.0	14.9	5.3	22.9	14.3
Warren County, New Jersey	76,162	1.6	5.0	29.8	21.7	8.0	25.1	8.8
NEW MEXICO	1,425,988	5.8	8.3	26.4	22.7	9.1	15.5	12.2
Bernalillo County, New Mexico	473,995	3.8	7.3	23.9	20.8	9.1	19.5	15.6
Chaves County, New Mexico	41,909	10.1	13.3	25.2	26.2	7.7	11.0	6.4
Doña Ana County, New Mexico	134,579	13.6	8.4	20.8	20.2	9.7	15.3	11.9
Lea County, New Mexico	42,477	11.7	12.6	27.8	24.4	10.4	7.3	5.7
McKinley County, New Mexico	44,710	6.8	14.3	36.9	24.8	6.2	5.6	5.4
Otero County, New Mexico	45,409	8.4	6.7	32.3	29.5	8.9	8.6	5.7
Sandoval County, New Mexico	102,218	2.7	4.5	26.4	22.8	10.7	19.0	13.9
San Juan County, New Mexico	81,169	3.4	10.9	30.4	25.2	15.6	8.2	6.2
Santa Fe County, New Mexico	112,842	5.8	6.0	19.3	21.6	7.1	21.5	18.6
Valencia County, New Mexico	50,276	4.0	8.8	32.8	24.5	10.0	9.8	10.0
NEW YORK	13,664,734	5.8	6.6	25.8	15.2	8.8	21.2	16.6
Albany County, New York	205,840	2.7	5.3	21.3	14.6	12.5	23.3	20.3
Bronx County, New York	932,813	11.5	14.1	29.1	17.1	7.8	12.7	7.7
Broome County, New York	126,674	3.0	6.6	30.9	18.9	13.4	13.8	13.4
Cattaraugus County, New York	52,903	3.3	6.1	39.1	18.1	12.2	11.4	9.9
Cayuga County, New York	56,060	4.5	8 3	33.3	18.7	12.1	14.8	8.4
Chautauqua County, New York	89,055	3.5	6.6	33.5	16.9	13.4	14.6	11 3
Chemung County, New York	59,575	1.6	6.3	32.2	20.7	14.0	13.7	11.6
Clinton County, New York	56,005	4.3	8.5	35.9	15.7	10.1	14.3	11.2
Dutchess County, New York	208,001	2.8	5.0	27.5	18.7	10.8	19.1	16.1
Erie County, New York	649,982	2.5	4.5	28.0	18.4	12.7	19.2	14.7
Jefferson County, New York	70,019	2.7	6.6	36.2	20.5	11.7	13.5	8.9
Kings County, New York	1,777,543	8.5	7.8	26.6	12.2	5.8	23.6	15.6
Livingston County, New York	41,954	2.6	6.1	34.6	16.8	14.6	13.5	11.7
Madison County, New York	48,107	1.1	5.4	37.6	16.7	15.0	13.7	10.5
Monroe County, New York	516,914	3.3	6.0	22.1	16.2	11 7	23.0	17.7
Nassau County, New York	948,980	4.7	3 4	21.9	15.0	7.9	26.3	20.9
New York County, New York	1,251,551	6.4	5.9	12.7	9.6	3.4	32.2	29.8
Niagara County, New York	151,144	2.1	6.1	31.1	19.7	12.9	17.4	10.7
Oneida County, New York	158,832	4.0	7.3	30.3	18.5	11.6	16 0	12.2
Onondaga County, New York	315,947	3.1	5.4	26.2	16.9	12.0	20.0	16.4
Ontario County, New York	78,035	2.4	4.0	26.5	15.1	12.6	20.9	18.5
Orange County, New York	246,320	3.6	6.8	27.6	20.0	10.5	17.2	14.4
Oswego County, New York	79,882	2.9	8.5	35.7	18.6	12.2	13.0	9.2
Putnam County, New York	72,210	3.2	4.6	26.4	20.8	7.0	21.1	17.0
Queens County, New York	1,633,699	10.1	6.9	27.3	14.5	8.0	20.5	12.7
Rensselaer County, New York	111,620	2.5	5.9	28.3	14.7	13.5	18.7	16.3
Richmond County, New York	333,496	4.9	6.1	29.2	16.3	7.3	21.6	14.7
Rockland County, New York	203,574	4.7	6.4	21.3	17.1	8.2	22.8	19.4
St. Lawrence County, New York	72,234	5.1	7 7	35.4	16.7	12.4	12.0	10.7

N = Data for this geographic area cannot be displayed because the number of sample cases is too small.

Table C-2. Educational Attainment of the Population, by Selected Counties, 2019—*Continued*

(Number; percent; dollars.)

	Population 18 to 24 years				
State/County	Total	Less than high school graduate (percent)	High school graduate (includes equivalency) (percent)	Some college or associate's degree (percent)	Bachelor's degree or higher (percent)
NEW YORK —(*Continued*)					
Saratoga County, New York	18,930	9.7	28.1	44.7	17.5
Schenectady County, New York	12,868	5.8	41.3	40.6	12.3
Steuben County, New York	7,294	20.6	33.6	34.3	11.4
Suffolk County, New York	131,886	9.8	28.0	43.2	19.0
Sullivan County, New York	5,226	8.3	37.2	42.4	12.1
Tompkins County, New York	28,029	0.7	10.0	65.8	23.5
Ulster County, New York	16,616	10.5	22.2	50.4	16.9
Warren County, New York	4,425	8.7	23.3	51.4	16.6
Wayne County, New York	6,304	13.0	36.9	39.7	10.3
Westchester County, New York	83,974	9.1	24.9	42.0	24.0
NORTH CAROLINA	1,007,035	12.0	31.8	45.3	10.8
Alamance County, North Carolina	18,021	12.5	29.1	53.7	4.7
Brunswick County, North Carolina	7,258	7.1	36.8	48.4	7.7
Buncombe County, North Carolina	19,693	13.2	42.0	36.2	8.6
Burke County, North Carolina	6,680	11.6	44.0	34.8	9.6
Cabarrus County, North Carolina	18,508	10.7	43.1	34.5	11.7
Caldwell County, North Carolina	6,499	19.3	49.0	25.2	6.5
Carteret County, North Carolina	5,242	16.3	30.4	49.3	4.0
Catawba County, North Carolina	13,464	8.3	33.8	47.7	10.2
Chatham County, North Carolina	4,618	18.0	34.2	37.9	9.9
Cleveland County, North Carolina	10,263	8.3	29.7	56.4	5.6
Craven County, North Carolina	12,507	7.4	60.4	26.8	5.4
Cumberland County, North Carolina	43,859	9.9	37.3	47.5	5.3
Davidson County, North Carolina	11,780	13.3	27.3	48.6	10.8
Durham County, North Carolina	32,206	10.2	20.1	50.7	19.0
Forsyth County, North Carolina	37,025	17.7	31.8	40.2	10.3
Franklin County, North Carolina	5,782	19.5	32.2	42.5	5.8
Gaston County, North Carolina	17,531	13.4	35.9	38.9	11.8
Guilford County, North Carolina	58,963	10.0	22.5	56.8	10.7
Harnett County, North Carolina	13,194	12.4	48.4	29.3	9.8
Henderson County, North Carolina	6,743	12.8	28.1	57.2	2.0
Iredell County, North Carolina	14,648	12.4	47.5	30.5	9.5
Johnston County, North Carolina	17,708	17.6	29.6	48.8	4.0
Lincoln County, North Carolina	5,876	7.9	42.3	39.6	10.2
Mecklenburg County, North Carolina	100,094	12.2	23.2	47.8	16.8
Moore County, North Carolina	6,051	11.8	33.3	44.9	10.1
Nash County, North Carolina	8,576	27.3	27.9	35.8	9.0
New Hanover County, North Carolina	29,481	8.7	22.2	54.5	14.6
Onslow County, North Carolina	40,952	6.5	49.8	40.9	2.8
Orange County, North Carolina	26,283	4.1	17.0	59.1	19.7
Pitt County, North Carolina	30,208	6.9	31.6	47.8	13.7
Randolph County, North Carolina	11,780	18.2	36.6	40.0	5.2
Robeson County, North Carolina	13,369	16.6	34.5	45.3	3.5
Rockingham County, North Carolina	6,620	18.4	28.1	49.5	4.1
Rowan County, North Carolina	12,648	11.1	26.7	49.1	13.2
Rutherford County, North Carolina	5,210	10.7	38.5	36.6	14.2
Surry County, North Carolina	5,751	16.1	31.3	47.2	5.4
Union County, North Carolina	22,433	18.4	35.3	40.4	5.8
Wake County, North Carolina	101,240	8.8	26.1	44.2	20.8
Wayne County, North Carolina	13,622	14.2	31.9	48.6	5.3
Wilkes County, North Carolina	6,020	3.4	59.8	36.8	0.0
Wilson County, North Carolina	7,245	23.6	38.9	27.2	10.3
NORTH DAKOTA	80,981	9.2	26.5	51.5	12.8
Burleigh County, North Dakota	9,671	6.5	41.0	43.7	8.8
Cass County, North Dakota	24,132	6.4	17.6	56.1	19.9
Grand Forks County, North Dakota	13,533	7.0	14.8	65.1	13.0
Ward County, North Dakota	8,848	7.5	37.0	48.2	7.3
OHIO	1,064,448	12.8	35.7	41.4	10.1
Allen County, Ohio	9,673	12.9	41.6	40.0	5.5
Ashtabula County, Ohio	7,656	15.6	51.7	29.2	3.5
Athens County, Ohio	17,953	5.2	20.6	66.2	7.9
Belmont County, Ohio	5,116	24.2	52.1	23.2	0.5
Butler County, Ohio	48,126	9.9	42.7	41.0	6.4
Clark County, Ohio	12,491	11.2	41.5	41.9	5.5
Clermont County, Ohio	15,793	11.4	45.7	29.7	13.2

N = Data for this geographic area cannot be displayed because the number of sample cases is too small.

Table C-2. Educational Attainment of the Population, by Selected Counties, 2019—*Continued*

(Number; percent; dollars.)

State/County	Total	Population 25 years and over						
		Less than 9th grade (percent)	9th to 12th grade, no diploma (percent)	High school graduate (includes equivalency) (percent)	Some college, no degree (percent)	Associate's degree (percent)	Bachelor's degree (percent)	Graduate or professional degree (percent)
NEW YORK —(*Continued*)								
Saratoga County, New York	165,720	1.3	4.9	24.6	15.6	11.0	24.2	18.3
Schenectady County, New York	108,994	2.6	4.6	28.8	16.7	12.2	20.8	14.3
Steuben County, New York	67,762	2.7	5.9	36.3	17.1	13.6	11.9	12.5
Suffolk County, New York	1,035,815	4.1	5.0	26.2	16.5	9.8	20.7	17.6
Sullivan County, New York	54,336	5.5	6.8	35.2	18.1	8.5	14.8	11.0
Tompkins County, New York	59,698	1.9	2.7	17.1	12.3	9.2	23.8	33.1
Ulster County, New York	129,942	3.0	6.2	28.6	17.2	12.1	16.5	16.4
Warren County, New York	48,358	4.4	4.9	27.6	16.6	13.0	18.7	14.8
Wayne County, New York	64,603	2.9	7.3	33.6	19.2	13.0	13.9	10.0
Westchester County, New York	673,174	5.0	5.1	19.2	13.0	6.3	25.4	25.9
NORTH CAROLINA	7,187,077	4.2	7.2	25.6	20.6	10.1	20.5	11.8
Alamance County, North Carolina	114,122	5.2	7.5	30.3	20.6	11.0	17.8	7.5
Brunswick County, North Carolina	114,779	1.7	5.0	26.4	22.1	11.9	21.0	12.0
Buncombe County, North Carolina	193,633	3.2	4.8	23.8	17.1	10.7	24.9	15.6
Burke County, North Carolina	67,177	7.3	10.4	32.9	18.6	12.2	10.7	7.8
Cabarrus County, North Carolina	142,955	3.5	5.6	26.2	20.6	9.8	22.6	11.8
Caldwell County, North Carolina	59,342	6.4	14.8	29.1	21.2	11.7	12.8	4.1
Carteret County, North Carolina	52,454	2.0	7.1	26.3	25.9	8.1	18.3	12.4
Catawba County, North Carolina	111,167	4.6	8.9	28.8	21.6	12.7	16.8	6.8
Chatham County, North Carolina	55,042	6.4	6.4	21.5	13.4	8.3	21.6	22.4
Cleveland County, North Carolina	66,240	6.0	9.0	35.5	18.8	11.8	12.2	6.6
Craven County, North Carolina	67,879	3.2	6.6	27.3	25.5	15.6	13.5	8.4
Cumberland County, North Carolina	208,611	2.7	6.3	27.1	28.2	10.9	15.8	9.1
Davidson County, North Carolina	120,125	5.8	8.6	35.3	22.1	9.3	13.1	5.8
Durham County, North Carolina	223,247	6.8	4.9	18.6	14.6	6.7	24.1	25.2
Forsyth County, North Carolina	258,434	4.6	6.6	26.4	20.2	9.0	20.3	12.9
Franklin County, North Carolina	48,608	2.9	7.7	30.7	22.3	14.3	16.5	5.6
Gaston County, North Carolina	157,145	4.3	10.4	29.7	22.9	9.2	16.6	6.9
Guilford County, North Carolina	359,317	4.1	7.5	22.5	19.3	9.6	23.9	13.2
Harnett County, North Carolina	87,796	3.2	7.8	30.4	22.2	12.3	16.7	7.5
Henderson County, North Carolina	88,613	2.8	6.7	24.3	25.3	10.9	18.8	11.2
Iredell County, North Carolina	126,121	2.8	7.0	27.9	20.8	10.6	21.2	9.7
Johnston County, North Carolina	138,897	4.8	7.7	24.9	22.3	16.3	18.1	5.9
Lincoln County, North Carolina	62,105	2.1	5.8	32.5	21.3	12.3	17.2	8.8
Mecklenburg County, North Carolina	752,114	4.9	4.7	16.2	19.9	8.6	29.8	15.9
Moore County, North Carolina	73,523	3.8	5.0	21.5	20.9	9.5	25.8	13.4
Nash County, North Carolina	65,190	4.4	9.7	37.3	20.2	10.7	13.8	4.0
New Hanover County, North Carolina	162,287	2.1	4.9	19.1	20.9	9.9	28.0	15.0
Onslow County, North Carolina	108,676	2.4	5.9	29.7	24.5	12.8	17.5	7.1
Orange County, North Carolina	93,642	1.8	3.7	13.1	12.2	6.0	28.9	34.2
Pitt County, North Carolina	112,043	3.6	8.1	25.6	17.8	12.8	19.3	12.8
Randolph County, North Carolina	100,084	6.5	12.0	34.7	21.3	10.6	10.1	4.9
Robeson County, North Carolina	85,215	6.4	15.5	34.6	18.8	9.9	10.0	4.9
Rockingham County, North Carolina	66,036	4.7	12.6	41.3	18.6	8.6	9.6	4.7
Rowan County, North Carolina	98,238	5.3	8.4	30.5	24.6	12.9	11.4	6.9
Rutherford County, North Carolina	48,325	3.5	9.5	31.4	26.3	9.5	14.7	5.0
Surry County, North Carolina	51,205	6.2	11.6	27.1	23.0	13.9	13.2	5.1
Union County, North Carolina	154,095	3.5	5.7	23.5	21.3	8.6	25.4	12.1
Wake County, North Carolina	747,815	2.7	4.0	15.2	16.3	7.7	32.9	21.2
Wayne County, North Carolina	80,491	7.8	6.5	31.9	21.8	13.9	11.8	6.3
Wilkes County, North Carolina	49,347	5.9	11.5	35.3	21.0	9.6	13.0	3.8
Wilson County, North Carolina	55,881	7.2	11.3	32.2	20.5	9.8	12.6	6.4
NORTH DAKOTA	504,375	2.6	3.9	26.7	22.4	14.0	21.5	8.9
Burleigh County, North Dakota	64,200	3.2	2.5	24.0	19.2	15.2	25.4	10.5
Cass County, North Dakota	117,528	2.0	2.7	22.1	20.7	11.0	28.3	13.2
Grand Forks County, North Dakota	41,481	1.2	2.4	19.3	23.0	16.4	21.5	16.1
Ward County, North Dakota	43,064	0.9	2.5	28.9	22.8	16.0	20.3	8.5
OHIO	8,049,805	2.7	6.6	32.6	20.1	8.7	18.2	11.1
Allen County, Ohio	69,051	1.9	7.2	41.9	21.7	7.9	13.3	6.1
Ashtabula County, Ohio	68,336	3.8	8.1	45.5	21.7	7.2	10.0	3.7
Athens County, Ohio	37,297	2.0	5.2	31.0	16.4	9.1	17.2	19.0
Belmont County, Ohio	49,321	2.7	6.7	45.7	16.7	11.4	11.0	5.9
Butler County, Ohio	245,864	1.8	6.6	33.8	17.6	8.1	21.0	11.1
Clark County, Ohio	91,882	1.7	7.9	41.8	22.5	9.9	9.3	6.9
Clermont County, Ohio	143,749	2.5	6.8	32.0	21.7	7.8	19.8	9.4

N = Data for this geographic area cannot be displayed because the number of sample cases is too small.

Table C-2. Educational Attainment of the Population, by Selected Counties, 2019—*Continued*

(Number; percent; dollars.)

State/County	Population 18 to 24 years				
	Total	Less than high school graduate (percent)	High school graduate (includes equivalency) (percent)	Some college or associate's degree (percent)	Bachelor's degree or higher (percent)
OHIO—*(Continued)*					
Columbiana County, Ohio	7,424	14.2	47.8	31.8	6.1
Cuyahoga County, Ohio	106,237	12.1	31.7	41.4	14.8
Delaware County, Ohio	16,386	10.8	33.5	43.0	12.7
Erie County, Ohio	5,376	9.1	48.6	38.4	4.0
Fairfield County, Ohio	12,530	11.7	41.5	37.8	9.0
Franklin County, Ohio	127,248	12.1	29.8	42.7	15.3
Geauga County, Ohio	7,883	26.5	28.0	32.4	13.1
Greene County, Ohio	19,824	5.8	23.9	56.4	14.0
Hamilton County, Ohio	76,960	9.5	36.2	39.5	14.8
Hancock County, Ohio	6,732	4.1	36.8	44.6	14.5
Jefferson County, Ohio	6,177	10.0	40.7	42.8	6.5
Lake County, Ohio	18,153	14.2	33.6	41.2	11.0
Licking County, Ohio	16,699	13.3	33.2	46.4	7.1
Lorain County, Ohio	25,896	16.6	32.3	44.1	7.1
Lucas County, Ohio	36,854	15.2	33.7	41.5	9.6
Mahoning County, Ohio	21,149	17.5	33.6	39.7	9.2
Marion County, Ohio	4,782	8.4	54.7	32.2	4.7
Medina County, Ohio	12,867	16.8	34.1	40.8	8.3
Miami County, Ohio	8,275	12.6	46.7	39.3	1.4
Montgomery County, Ohio	49,533	11.0	32.3	47.3	9.3
Muskingum County, Ohio	8,510	11.2	47.3	38.6	2.9
Portage County, Ohio	26,304	5.8	22.6	61.7	9.9
Richland County, Ohio	9,656	18.8	35.6	40.7	4.9
Ross County, Ohio	5,654	10.1	67.2	15.7	7.0
Scioto County, Ohio	6,314	15.0	38.0	38.9	8.1
Stark County, Ohio	30,785	10.8	42.5	39.1	7.6
Summit County, Ohio	46,046	11.1	33.9	42.3	12.8
Trumbull County, Ohio	15,393	21.0	42.4	30.5	6.2
Tuscarawas County, Ohio	7,019	15.6	41.7	35.6	7.1
Warren County, Ohio	18,029	14.7	38.4	36.4	10.5
Wayne County, Ohio	12,186	21.5	37.8	34.5	6.3
Wood County, Ohio	22,799	4.0	23.5	63.0	9.5
OKLAHOMA	385,498	14.4	35.4	41.7	8.5
Canadian County, Oklahoma	12,512	16.3	40.6	36.3	6.8
Cleveland County, Oklahoma	43,395	8.1	19.3	60.0	12.6
Comanche County, Oklahoma	14,845	10.4	45.4	39.5	4.7
Creek County, Oklahoma	5,627	20.6	53.1	22.1	4.2
Muskogee County, Oklahoma	5,871	23.7	38.2	30.6	7.6
Oklahoma County, Oklahoma	72,124	12.9	33.9	41.9	11.3
Payne County, Oklahoma	21,055	5.3	22.6	65.1	7.0
Pottawatomie County, Oklahoma	7,239	22.4	28.2	43.6	5.7
Rogers County, Oklahoma	7,958	15.7	38.4	39.4	6.5
Tulsa County, Oklahoma	57,477	13.7	34.1	41.7	10.5
Wagoner County, Oklahoma	6,299	14.6	44.4	32.8	8.3
OREGON	366,803	13.3	31.2	44.8	10.7
Benton County, Oregon	21,018	1.7	17.2	66.0	15.0
Clackamas County, Oregon	31,689	12.9	38.0	39.2	10.0
Deschutes County, Oregon	13,603	15.1	37.7	42.8	4.4
Douglas County, Oregon	7,075	21.2	36.0	39.4	3.5
Jackson County, Oregon	16,827	11.1	39.4	45.5	4.0
Josephine County, Oregon	5,297	30.0	26.1	40.9	3.0
Klamath County, Oregon	5,070	8.1	27.6	53.1	11.1
Lane County, Oregon	47,635	9.5	27.0	50.7	12.8
Linn County, Oregon	10,238	16.8	31.0	45.9	6.3
Marion County, Oregon	32,246	15.8	35.6	40.5	8.1
Multnomah County, Oregon	63,723	12.1	22.7	49.8	15.4
Polk County, Oregon	11,384	5.1	34.1	48.6	12.2
Umatilla County, Oregon	6,415	21.0	47.2	25.9	5.9
Washington County, Oregon	49,155	15.5	28.4	41.0	15.2
Yamhill County, Oregon	10,515	7.5	37.5	48.8	6.2
PENNSYLVANIA	1,141,628	12.0	34.9	39.7	13.5
Adams County, Pennsylvania	10,239	6.5	48.7	37.1	7.7
Allegheny County, Pennsylvania	105,078	8.9	29.8	41.0	20.3
Armstrong County, Pennsylvania	4,227	8.4	55.6	24.9	11.0
Beaver County, Pennsylvania	11,457	10.2	36.9	44.1	8.7

N = Data for this geographic area cannot be displayed because the number of sample cases is too small.

Table C-2. Educational Attainment of the Population, by Selected Counties, 2019—*Continued*

(Number; percent; dollars.)

State/County	Total	Less than 9th grade (percent)	9th to 12th grade, no diploma (percent)	High school graduate (includes equivalency) (percent)	Some college, no degree (percent)	Associate's degree (percent)	Bachelor's degree (percent)	Graduate or professional degree (percent)
OHIO—*(Continued)*								
Columbiana County, Ohio	73,872	2.6	5.7	46.4	19.4	10.4	10.4	5.2
Cuyahoga County, Ohio	874,679	3.0	6.7	26.9	21.4	8.3	19.8	13.9
Delaware County, Ohio	138,636	0.5	3.1	18.4	19.0	6.8	31.5	20.6
Erie County, Ohio	53,808	2.0	5.5	37.0	21.1	10.1	15.4	8.8
Fairfield County, Ohio	107,394	1.8	4.5	33.6	22.0	8.7	19.7	9.7
Franklin County, Ohio	884,103	3.1	5.6	23.5	19.3	6.7	26.2	15.6
Geauga County, Ohio	64,228	7.8	3.1	26.3	17.4	9.5	23.1	13.0
Greene County, Ohio	114,206	0.8	3.9	23.5	22.7	8.2	23.5	17.5
Hamilton County, Ohio	553,480	2.2	5.9	25.9	17.2	8.4	23.6	16.8
Hancock County, Ohio	52,463	2.0	6.2	34.9	21.7	8.5	14.3	12.4
Jefferson County, Ohio	46,725	1.6	5.3	45.4	17.7	11.0	12.6	6.4
Lake County, Ohio	166,562	2.0	5.7	31.0	24.7	10.4	17.6	8.7
Licking County, Ohio	119,819	1.7	7.0	33.2	20.4	10.7	17.7	9.2
Lorain County, Ohio	216,161	2.6	7.9	31.5	21.6	11.5	15.1	9.8
Lucas County, Ohio	293,502	2.8	8.1	29.1	22.9	10.2	16.8	10.2
Mahoning County, Ohio	161,985	2.5	6.9	36.2	21.2	7.8	16.8	8.7
Marion County, Ohio	46,591	1.9	9.4	43.4	24.4	7.4	8.3	5.2
Medina County, Ohio	127,164	0.5	4.1	30.4	21.0	9.2	22.2	12.5
Miami County, Ohio	74,110	2.6	5.8	36.5	23.1	10.2	12.8	9.0
Montgomery County, Ohio	365,816	2.7	7.0	26.9	25.4	9.4	17.4	11.1
Muskingum County, Ohio	59,137	3.1	10.2	41.4	18.2	8.7	10.7	7.7
Portage County, Ohio	106,424	2.5	5.6	38.3	17.6	7.4	17.2	11.5
Richland County, Ohio	85,392	3.6	7.7	40.2	18.4	11.3	11.2	7.6
Ross County, Ohio	54,460	2.7	7.0	45.7	19.9	8.9	11.0	4.9
Scioto County, Ohio	52,701	4.0	10.6	37.9	19.0	9.2	13.0	6.3
Stark County, Ohio	260,893	2.0	6.5	39.8	19.9	9.8	14.7	7.3
Summit County, Ohio	382,817	2.2	5.3	30.5	21.6	7.7	20.8	11.8
Trumbull County, Ohio	142,450	3.4	8.0	42.7	18.7	7.8	13.2	6.3
Tuscarawas County, Ohio	64,032	6.6	9.0	44.2	15.1	6.9	13.1	5.3
Warren County, Ohio	159,843	1.1	3.7	27.3	16.0	7.0	27.5	17.4
Wayne County, Ohio	75,847	9.5	5.3	37.5	18.8	6.8	13.1	9.1
Wood County, Ohio	81,457	1.3	3.6	30.0	18.1	10.0	22.8	14.2
OKLAHOMA	2,619,244	3.9	7.7	31.5	22.8	7.9	17.1	9.1
Canadian County, Oklahoma	97,242	3.4	8.1	31.8	21.8	7.5	18.8	8.6
Cleveland County, Oklahoma	180,400	2.7	4.9	24.0	24.2	8.5	21.9	13.7
Comanche County, Oklahoma	77,989	1.8	7.4	34.1	28.6	7.3	12.4	8.4
Creek County, Oklahoma	49,128	2.2	9.3	40.2	22.1	8.6	12.5	5.1
Muskogee County, Oklahoma	45,522	4.2	9.5	30.9	22.5	11.5	15.3	6.1
Oklahoma County, Oklahoma	522,715	5.1	7.1	26.0	22.3	7.0	20.2	12.4
Payne County, Oklahoma	45,198	1.9	4.2	27.8	20.0	6.9	21.0	18.1
Pottawatomie County, Oklahoma	48,262	2.4	8.9	37.0	23.2	8.5	13.3	6.7
Rogers County, Oklahoma	63,129	3.0	6.1	30.4	25.0	11.8	16.7	7.0
Tulsa County, Oklahoma	430,396	3.6	6.6	25.2	22.2	8.8	22.2	11.3
Wagoner County, Oklahoma	55,510	3.2	5.7	33.2	25.6	9.5	16.0	6.9
OREGON	2,988,118	3.3	5.4	23.0	24.8	9.0	21.0	13.5
Benton County, Oregon	57,153	0.9	1.8	13.0	18.0	8.5	30.6	27.3
Clackamas County, Oregon	298,137	1.8	4.6	22.4	24.9	9.2	23.9	13.2
Deschutes County, Oregon	145,040	2.2	4.6	18.9	24.4	11.1	23.6	15.1
Douglas County, Oregon	82,538	1.4	6.3	34.3	32.6	9.7	9.5	6.2
Jackson County, Oregon	159,402	2.8	6.6	28.3	26.0	8.7	16.0	11.6
Josephine County, Oregon	65,400	0.8	10.0	33.2	30.5	8.7	10.7	6.1
Klamath County, Oregon	48,479	3.4	6.7	33.1	24.4	10.8	13.3	0.4
Lane County, Oregon	264,861	2.0	5.2	23.2	28.5	8.8	19.2	13.1
Linn County, Oregon	90,726	3.3	9.0	26.7	32.6	9.5	12.2	6.6
Marion County, Oregon	230,945	7.0	6.7	24.2	26.2	9.7	16.8	8.5
Multnomah County, Oregon	599,465	3.7	4.3	17.0	20.0	7.2	28.5	19.3
Polk County, Oregon	55,301	2.6	4.0	22.1	28.2	10.8	19.6	12.6
Umatilla County, Oregon	52,110	3.8	9.6	29.0	27.0	11.7	11.8	7.1
Washington County, Oregon	417,283	3.4	3.0	19.3	21.7	8.5	26.2	17.9
Yamhill County, Oregon	73,372	3.4	8.6	24.1	29.0	9.9	16.2	8.8
PENNSYLVANIA	9,028,036	3.0	6.0	34.4	15.7	8.6	19.5	12.8
Adams County, Pennsylvania	72,723	3.6	7.3	42.6	17.1	7.9	12.0	9.6
Allegheny County, Pennsylvania	884,569	1.5	3.2	26.2	16.1	10.0	24.8	18.1
Armstrong County, Pennsylvania	48,151	2.7	5.0	51.7	16.1	8.9	11.0	4.6
Beaver County, Pennsylvania	121,056	1.7	5.8	33.0	20.3	12.4	17.5	9.4

N = Data for this geographic area cannot be displayed because the number of sample cases is too small.

Table C-2. Educational Attainment of the Population, by Selected Counties, 2019—*Continued*

(Number; percent; dollars.)

State/County	Population 18 to 24 years				
	Total	Less than high school graduate (percent)	High school graduate (includes equivalency) (percent)	Some college or associate's degree (percent)	Bachelor's degree or higher (percent)
PENNSYLVANIA—(*Continued*)					
Berks County, Pennsylvania	40,120	14.2	37.7	38.1	10.0
Blair County, Pennsylvania	9,208	14.7	44.2	29.3	11.9
Bucks County, Pennsylvania	47,973	11.5	30.5	35.3	22.7
Butler County, Pennsylvania	15,765	7.2	37.7	40.5	14.7
Cambria County, Pennsylvania	11,522	6.7	37.6	49.5	6.2
Carbon County, Pennsylvania	4,099	22.3	44.6	23.8	9.3
Centre County, Pennsylvania	38,136	4.1	28.6	56.9	10.4
Chester County, Pennsylvania	47,846	13.0	27.2	38.3	21.5
Clearfield County, Pennsylvania	5,404	17.0	54.6	23.9	4.5
Columbia County, Pennsylvania	9,367	8.6	29.7	55.9	5.8
Crawford County, Pennsylvania	7,796	20.4	33.8	38.7	7.0
Cumberland County, Pennsylvania	24,151	11.0	25.8	52.8	10.4
Dauphin County, Pennsylvania	22,009	13.3	45.0	30.6	11.1
Delaware County, Pennsylvania	55,825	10.0	34.7	40.9	14.4
Erie County, Pennsylvania	26,112	12.5	36.9	38.8	11.8
Fayette County, Pennsylvania	9,230	6.7	57.4	22.3	13.6
Franklin County, Pennsylvania	11,303	21.3	43.6	30.8	4.3
Indiana County, Pennsylvania	12,104	11.5	23.6	59.8	5.0
Lackawanna County, Pennsylvania	16,800	8.2	25.8	49.5	16.5
Lancaster County, Pennsylvania	48,229	24.7	35.5	29.1	10.7
Lawrence County, Pennsylvania	6,895	11.3	42.4	39.7	6.6
Lebanon County, Pennsylvania	12,055	9.5	55.7	25.3	9.5
Lehigh County, Pennsylvania	33,469	11.6	33.2	45.3	9.9
Luzerne County, Pennsylvania	27,113	13.1	32.6	47.4	6.9
Lycoming County, Pennsylvania	9,590	9.3	43.8	40.6	6.2
Mercer County, Pennsylvania	10,393	10.6	48.1	33.0	8.3
Monroe County, Pennsylvania	17,910	15.2	37.5	36.5	10.9
Montgomery County, Pennsylvania	65,786	9.5	28.9	42.3	19.3
Northampton County, Pennsylvania	30,181	12.1	30.2	46.2	11.5
Northumberland County, Pennsylvania	6,155	23.6	49.5	22.0	4.8
Philadelphia County, Pennsylvania	153,369	10.7	33.2	39.0	17.1
Schuylkill County, Pennsylvania	9,510	21.7	42.7	31.9	3.7
Somerset County, Pennsylvania	4,951	17.0	52.0	22.3	8.8
Washington County, Pennsylvania	17,848	8.8	37.8	41.9	11.5
Westmoreland County, Pennsylvania	25,559	8.3	32.6	46.3	12.8
York County, Pennsylvania	35,896	12.6	38.4	39.1	9.9
RHODE ISLAND	108,834	9.3	32.3	45.9	12.5
Kent County, Rhode Island	11,848	11.5	37.2	34.4	16.9
Newport County, Rhode Island	8,005	9.8	26.1	40.6	23.6
Providence County, Rhode Island	66,343	10.8	32.9	47.8	8.4
Washington County, Rhode Island	16,461	4.1	32.3	47.2	16.5
SOUTH CAROLINA	473,210	12.6	35.1	42.8	9.4
Aiken County, South Carolina	14,017	11.8	32.9	51.0	4.3
Anderson County, South Carolina	17,417	15.1	46.6	32.2	6.1
Beaufort County, South Carolina	18,116	17.9	48.3	30.2	3.7
Berkeley County, South Carolina	20,731	13.6	38.6	36.9	10.8
Charleston County, South Carolina	36,300	11.0	20.5	47.4	21.2
Darlington County, South Carolina	6,867	22.2	29.0	34.9	14.0
Dorchester County, South Carolina	12,118	12.5	52.0	31.9	3.6
Florence County, South Carolina	11,923	14.6	37.9	35.0	12.5
Greenville County, South Carolina	44,869	13.9	35.8	36.8	13.5
Greenwood County, South Carolina	6,358	3.0	30.2	57.7	9.1
Horry County, South Carolina	25,310	7.1	39.8	48.6	4.5
Kershaw County, South Carolina	4,674	17.6	48.4	26.5	7.5
Lancaster County, South Carolina	6,464	12.0	37.0	40.2	10.8
Laurens County, South Carolina	5,797	18.4	35.5	40.8	5.4
Lexington County, South Carolina	22,500	13.0	35.8	40.6	10.6
Oconee County, South Carolina	5,437	19.3	43.0	24.6	13.0
Orangeburg County, South Carolina	8,499	8.8	31.1	54.0	6.1
Pickens County, South Carolina	22,818	6.7	24.5	52.4	16.3
Richland County, South Carolina	63,170	8.4	29.8	53.7	8.0
Spartanburg County, South Carolina	28,942	9.3	38.7	42.2	9.8
Sumter County, South Carolina	10,188	17.2	32.0	41.9	8.9
York County, South Carolina	22,146	12.6	32.6	48.3	6.5
SOUTH DAKOTA	81,361	13.8	34.3	41.5	10.5
Minnehaha County, South Dakota	15,832	13.9	29.9	41.8	14.4
Pennington County, South Dakota	9,274	11.7	42.5	38.5	7.2

N = Data for this geographic area cannot be displayed because the number of sample cases is too small.

Table C-2. Educational Attainment of the Population, by Selected Counties, 2019—*Continued*

(Number; percent; dollars.)

State/County	Total	Population 25 years and over						
		Less than 9th grade (percent)	9th to 12th grade, no diploma (percent)	High school graduate (includes equivalency) (percent)	Some college, no degree (percent)	Associate's degree (percent)	Bachelor's degree (percent)	Graduate or professional degree (percent)
PENNSYLVANIA—*(Continued)*								
Berks County, Pennsylvania	287,425	5.2	7.6	37.4	15.4	8.9	16.3	9.1
Blair County, Pennsylvania	88,001	2.6	5.8	44.1	15.0	9.3	14.9	8.2
Bucks County, Pennsylvania	453,452	2.0	4.0	27.2	16.1	8.4	24.9	17.3
Butler County, Pennsylvania	134,990	0.7	3.8	32.0	15.7	10.3	24.4	13.1
Cambria County, Pennsylvania	93,957	1.4	4.7	46.4	14.8	12.0	13.2	7.4
Carbon County, Pennsylvania	48,384	3.3	7.2	46.3	15.4	9.3	11.8	6.7
Centre County, Pennsylvania	100,886	2.0	4.9	28.4	14.1	6.7	21.6	22.2
Chester County, Pennsylvania	359,177	2.8	3.3	20.3	12.6	6.4	32.0	22.7
Clearfield County, Pennsylvania	59,496	3.2	8.7	51.0	12.3	8.7	10.4	5.8
Columbia County, Pennsylvania	44,205	2.5	7.0	42.1	13.7	9.9	15.8	9.1
Crawford County, Pennsylvania	59,674	5.1	6.0	45.6	14.7	7.1	13.5	8.0
Cumberland County, Pennsylvania	177,952	2.6	5.0	30.5	15.0	8.5	23.6	14.7
Dauphin County, Pennsylvania	193,460	3.0	6.7	33.8	14.3	10.2	19.6	11.8
Delaware County, Pennsylvania	386,376	1.9	5.1	29.2	16.1	7.0	23.6	17.1
Erie County, Pennsylvania	186,755	2.4	6.8	36.5	14.8	10.0	18.7	10.8
Fayette County, Pennsylvania	95,435	2.4	9.7	46.8	15.0	8.3	11.7	6.1
Franklin County, Pennsylvania	109,489	3.6	8.3	44.3	14.4	7.4	13.3	8.7
Indiana County, Pennsylvania	56,900	3.5	5.8	43.4	16.2	7.7	14.0	9.4
Lackawanna County, Pennsylvania	149,972	2.6	6.0	37.8	15.6	8.8	18.2	10.9
Lancaster County, Pennsylvania	369,623	7.0	7.3	34.8	14.6	8.0	18.4	9.8
Lawrence County, Pennsylvania	61,638	1.8	5.7	44.5	14.9	10.3	14.6	8.3
Lebanon County, Pennsylvania	90,178	4.8	8.5	44.2	13.9	7.7	13.7	7.2
Lehigh County, Pennsylvania	252,649	4.1	5.9	35.2	16.4	8.8	18.7	10.8
Luzerne County, Pennsylvania	227,307	3.0	5.6	39.9	19.9	10.1	12.8	8.9
Lycoming County, Pennsylvania	80,491	2.7	7.7	39.5	15.8	10.2	15.4	8.9
Mercer County, Pennsylvania	78,317	3.7	7.1	41.7	13.5	10.6	14.6	8.8
Monroe County, Pennsylvania	119,245	2.1	6.7	35.2	20.7	9.3	17.0	9.0
Montgomery County, Pennsylvania	586,787	1.8	3.3	22.8	14.3	7.8	28.5	21.6
Northampton County, Pennsylvania	215,118	2.9	5.7	35.2	16.1	9.2	19.3	11.5
Northumberland County, Pennsylvania	66,938	3.4	8.0	51.9	14.3	6.4	11.4	4.7
Philadelphia County, Pennsylvania	1,088,441	5.0	9.0	32.5	16.5	5.9	18.0	13.0
Schuylkill County, Pennsylvania	104,188	2.1	7.4	47.0	16.9	9.9	11.5	5.1
Somerset County, Pennsylvania	54,894	3.7	7.6	48.0	13.2	9.8	11.5	6.2
Washington County, Pennsylvania	148,862	2.2	4.9	34.7	17.0	10.3	20.3	10.7
Westmoreland County, Pennsylvania	259,586	1.5	4.0	37.1	16.7	11.4	19.1	10.2
York County, Pennsylvania	314,523	3.0	7.0	38.0	16.1	9.5	17.3	9.1
RHODE ISLAND	746,952	5.0	5.7	28.4	17.4	8.6	20.9	13.9
Kent County, Rhode Island	122,379	2.4	5.7	29.2	20.4	9.8	20.8	11.7
Newport County, Rhode Island	61,095	2.0	3.9	23.7	15.2	7.7	27.4	20.0
Providence County, Rhode Island	441,579	7.2	6.6	30.0	17.8	8.6	18.3	11.5
Washington County, Rhode Island	88,728	1.0	3.6	23.8	14.1	8.6	28.4	20.4
SOUTH CAROLINA	3,563,204	3.7	7.9	28.5	20.4	9.9	18.4	11.2
Aiken County, South Carolina	119,990	3.2	6.7	30.9	20.2	9.8	19.4	9.9
Anderson County, South Carolina	130,650	2.9	9.7	31.7	19.2	11.7	15.7	9.0
Beaufort County, South Carolina	138,686	2.7	4.4	21.4	21.7	8.8	23.5	17.5
Berkeley County, South Carolina	153,104	3.1	6.6	29.9	22.4	10.5	17.2	10.3
Charleston County, South Carolina	294,309	2.6	5.4	20.4	17.0	8.4	28.4	17.8
Darlington County, South Carolina	45,089	5.1	11.6	36.7	17.7	9.2	12.8	7.0
Dorchester County, South Carolina	111,372	4.0	7.6	25.3	24.1	10.9	19.4	8.8
Florence County, South Carolina	94,107	3.7	8.1	34.5	20.9	8.0	14.9	9.8
Greenville County, South Carolina	358,605	3.6	7.9	22.9	19.2	10.0	23.5	13.0
Greenwood County, South Carolina	48,788	3.4	7.4	31.1	20.4	12.0	16.4	10.3
Horry County, South Carolina	265,998	3.9	7.1	32.5	21.6	10.5	15.3	9.0
Kershaw County, South Carolina	46,523	2.8	9.3	32.0	21.4	10.3	15.5	8.5
Lancaster County, South Carolina	70,463	5.9	7.3	27.9	22.4	13.5	15.5	7.4
Laurens County, South Carolina	46,889	4.5	10.2	34.2	20.3	11.1	12.9	6.8
Lexington County, South Carolina	207,409	3.9	7.7	26.4	21.1	10.9	19.3	10.7
Oconee County, South Carolina	57,928	5.8	9.1	31.0	18.1	9.5	14.9	11.6
Orangeburg County, South Carolina	58,454	3.1	11.2	31.8	21.1	11.8	10.8	10.1
Pickens County, South Carolina	80,497	3.5	9.2	29.5	19.8	11.3	14.9	11.8
Richland County, South Carolina	263,496	2.3	6.5	21.5	19.2	8.2	24.8	17.5
Spartanburg County, South Carolina	217,131	4.2	9.2	28.6	22.0	9.8	15.9	10.4
Sumter County, South Carolina	71,171	4.7	7.2	30.2	24.9	11.3	13.7	8.0
York County, South Carolina	191,318	2.3	4.9	23.9	23.8	10.1	22.5	12.6
SOUTH DAKOTA	588,029	2.8	5.1	30.0	20.5	11.9	20.6	9.1
Minnehaha County, South Dakota	128,596	3.8	3.8	25.2	20.3	11.7	25.5	9.7
Pennington County, South Dakota	78,460	0.9	5.2	27.4	24.6	10.2	20.9	10.9

N = Data for this geographic area cannot be displayed because the number of sample cases is too small.

Table C-2. Educational Attainment of the Population, by Selected Counties, 2019—*Continued*

(Number; percent; dollars.)

State/County	Population 18 to 24 years				
	Total	Less than high school graduate (percent)	High school graduate (includes equivalency) (percent)	Some college or associate's degree (percent)	Bachelor's degree or higher (percent)
TENNESSEE	624,460	10.9	34.7	43.0	11.4
Anderson County, Tennessee	5,639	2.6	67.1	29.3	1.0
Blount County, Tennessee	10,095	11.0	39.8	43.5	5.7
Bradley County, Tennessee..................................	9,103	14.7	26.8	51.1	7.3
Davidson County, Tennessee................................	67,195	6.4	27.3	43.8	22.6
Greene County, Tennessee	5,390	3.0	45.3	49.3	2.4
Hamilton County, Tennessee	32,173	10.0	26.3	54.0	9.8
Knox County, Tennessee	54,893	6.6	27.6	48.1	17.7
Madison County, Tennessee................................	10,727	10.0	34.0	52.1	3.9
Maury County, Tennessee	7,196	7.7	51.2	36.3	4.8
Montgomery County, Tennessee	23,296	10.5	34.3	48.2	6.9
Putnam County, Tennessee	10,968	6.4	20.6	64.3	8.8
Robertson County, Tennessee..............................	5,214	11.7	51.6	31.6	5.1
Rutherford County, Tennessee.............................	42,577	10.7	30.0	47.7	11.6
Sevier County, Tennessee...................................	7,605	9.6	35.8	43.9	10.7
Shelby County, Tennessee..................................	84,794	11.4	30.9	44.6	13.1
Sullivan County, Tennessee................................	11,998	6.6	45.6	39.0	8.8
Sumner County, Tennessee.................................	14,940	7.0	32.4	49.9	10.7
Washington County, Tennessee............................	16,288	5.7	39.2	36.6	18.5
Williamson County, Tennessee.............................	18,518	16.6	32.5	26.7	24.1
Wilson County, Tennessee	10,259	18.2	35.0	36.3	10.5
TEXAS..	2,826,700	13.9	34.6	42.1	9.5
Angelina County, Texas	7,540	15.8	48.1	32.9	3.2
Bastrop County, Texas.......................................	9,554	5.5	58.8	29.3	6.4
Bell County, Texas	40,652	12.0	42.7	38.2	7.1
Bexar County, Texas	204,553	15.3	37.1	40.4	7.2
Bowie County, Texas	8,256	21.0	23.1	49.3	6.6
Brazoria County, Texas......................................	30,953	12.2	35.8	38.7	13.3
Brazos County, Texas	57,845	2.9	20.5	62.1	14.5
Cameron County, Texas......................................	44,882	18.1	38.0	40.6	3.3
Collin County, Texas	85,315	10.3	33.5	42.5	13.7
Comal County, Texas	11,978	12.5	46.1	35.7	5.7
Coryell County, Texas..	10,051	6.6	56.5	35.3	1.6
Dallas County, Texas	250,631	14.9	32.4	39.3	13.3
Denton County, Texas..	82,498	8.7	26.7	49.3	15.2
Ector County, Texas..	15,216	19.5	38.9	35.8	5.8
Ellis County, Texas	17,072	17.2	38.4	40.1	4.3
El Paso County, Texas	94,688	11.1	35.3	45.8	7.8
Fort Bend County, Texas....................................	67,050	13.5	29.8	42.9	13.9
Galveston County, Texas....................................	28,711	11.2	36.6	45.5	6.7
Grayson County, Texas......................................	12,387	21.4	39.0	36.8	2.7
Gregg County, Texas	10,916	6.9	40.3	47.4	5.3
Guadalupe County, Texas	14,454	9.1	52.9	32.2	5.8
Harris County, Texas	434,396	15.5	34.1	40.2	10.2
Harrison County, Texas	5,558	14.7	46.3	31.3	7.6
Hays County, Texas	38,047	9.1	31.9	50.1	8.8
Henderson County, Texas...................................	6,607	13.1	49.3	32.9	4.7
Hidalgo County, Texas.......................................	96,873	16.5	29.3	49.2	5.0
Hunt County, Texas	9,831	8.5	36.4	48.1	7.0
Jefferson County, Texas	23,505	14.8	33.1	45.4	6.6
Johnson County, Texas......................................	15,458	15.7	50.2	27.6	6.6
Kaufman County, Texas.....................................	12,386	20.8	34.5	32.6	12.1
Liberty County, Texas	7,089	17.4	48.0	32.3	2.3
Lubbock County, Texas......................................	51,251	7.8	27.2	52.7	12.3
McLennan County, Texas	37,096	10.6	30.5	52.8	6.1
Midland County, Texas	14,543	21.5	27.7	39.8	11.0
Montgomery County, Texas.................................	50,337	14.7	31.9	43.0	10.5
Nacogdoches County, Texas................................	11,219	9.3	26.1	53.7	10.9
Nueces County, Texas.......................................	35,532	14.6	34.9	46.6	3.9
Orange County, Texas.......................................	6,117	10.3	46.2	37.3	6.2
Parker County, Texas..	11,521	15.6	37.2	41.1	6.1
Potter County, Texas	11,076	12.3	50.3	33.0	4.5
Randall County, Texas.......................................	14,100	7.9	31.9	45.2	15.0
Rockwall County, Texas.....................................	7,662	7.0	34.8	47.4	10.9
San Patricio County, Texas.................................	6,090	25.9	36.0	27.5	10.6
Smith County, Texas...	23,428	6.2	32.9	55.8	5.1
Tarrant County, Texas.......................................	197,127	12.6	34.9	42.4	10.1

N = Data for this geographic area cannot be displayed because the number of sample cases is too small.

Table C-2. Educational Attainment of the Population, by Selected Counties, 2019—*Continued*

(Number; percent; dollars.)

State/County	Population 25 years and over							
	Total	Less than 9th grade (percent)	9th to 12th grade, no diploma (percent)	High school graduate (includes equivalency) (percent)	Some college, no degree (percent)	Associate's degree (percent)	Bachelor's degree (percent)	Graduate or professional degree (percent)
TENNESSEE	4,693,962	4.3	7.7	31.5	20.3	7.4	18.0	10.7
Anderson County, Tennessee	55,758	3.3	7.9	36.5	21.0	10.1	12.3	9.0
Blount County, Tennessee	96,046	4.3	7.6	36.3	22.6	6.0	14.7	8.6
Bradley County, Tennessee	75,366	5.2	10.3	33.6	21.3	7.1	16.3	6.3
Davidson County, Tennessee	483,895	4.1	6.4	19.8	17.8	6.3	28.3	17.3
Greene County, Tennessee	50,371	6.0	9.6	41.6	17.4	6.3	11.2	7.8
Hamilton County, Tennessee	259,208	3.8	6.9	24.1	21.1	9.0	22.4	12.7
Knox County, Tennessee	316,983	2.9	5.4	25.5	19.7	8.8	22.4	15.2
Madison County, Tennessee	65,367	3.1	7.2	34.0	21.4	7.1	16.8	10.3
Maury County, Tennessee	66,799	3.3	7.6	34.0	19.6	10.4	18.1	7.0
Montgomery County, Tennessee	129,477	1.9	4.4	27.3	22.5	13.1	19.1	11.7
Putnam County, Tennessee	52,987	6.6	6.3	32.6	20.3	5.9	18.9	9.5
Robertson County, Tennessee	49,004	5.6	9.6	36.0	22.0	5.6	16.2	5.0
Rutherford County, Tennessee	208,175	2.7	4.9	27.3	25.5	8.8	20.5	10.3
Sevier County, Tennessee	70,573	5.2	10.2	38.0	20.8	6.9	13.8	5.2
Shelby County, Tennessee	620,000	3.8	7.9	28.1	22.6	6.0	18.9	12.8
Sullivan County, Tennessee	116,476	4.1	7.3	33.3	21.0	7.9	16.3	10.1
Sumner County, Tennessee	131,695	4.1	6.1	30.7	20.3	8.2	20.8	9.8
Washington County, Tennessee	89,010	3.1	7.5	30.8	18.2	8.6	18.0	13.8
Williamson County, Tennessee	155,962	1.3	3.3	13.5	14.4	5.8	38.9	22.9
Wilson County, Tennessee	100,464	2.7	4.3	29.6	20.4	7.9	22.8	12.2
TEXAS	18,772,550	7.7	7.7	25.2	21.2	7.5	20.0	10.8
Angelina County, Texas	57,118	6.7	7.1	32.5	28.9	6.1	10.5	8.0
Bastrop County, Texas	56,957	9.5	8.5	35.3	25.4	4.8	10.6	5.8
Bell County, Texas	222,526	2.9	6.6	25.7	27.9	11.6	15.4	9.9
Bexar County, Texas	1,292,560	7.4	7.9	25.6	22.6	8.3	17.8	10.3
Bowie County, Texas	62,896	4.9	8.6	33.2	27.5	6.7	12.1	7.0
Brazoria County, Texas	245,811	4.9	6.5	27.3	24.3	7.6	20.0	9.4
Brazos County, Texas	124,081	4.9	6.7	21.9	19.4	4.7	23.8	18.6
Cameron County, Texas	251,660	18.2	13.5	26.2	17.6	7.4	11.8	5.4
Collin County, Texas	684,124	3.3	2.6	16.2	17.9	7.5	32.5	20.1
Comal County, Texas	109,243	2.5	4.1	23.5	20.6	9.5	25.9	13.9
Coryell County, Texas	48,826	3.3	8.7	29.1	30.9	11.0	11.4	5.6
Dallas County, Texas	1,704,727	10.4	8.8	23.6	19.1	5.6	20.2	12.2
Denton County, Texas	589,252	2.7	4.9	17.5	21.5	7.2	30.6	15.5
Ector County, Texas	100,671	10.6	13.2	30.1	23.5	7.5	10.0	5.2
Ellis County, Texas	119,062	4.7	7.4	27.8	25.7	8.4	17.7	8.4
El Paso County, Texas	520,251	11.4	8.8	25.5	21.4	9.6	16.4	6.9
Fort Bend County, Texas	522,896	5.1	4.1	17.6	19.1	7.8	27.9	18.3
Galveston County, Texas	231,134	4.0	5.4	26.3	24.5	9.1	19.8	10.8
Grayson County, Texas	91,846	4.8	5.5	31.1	26.6	10.3	14.5	7.3
Gregg County, Texas	81,223	4.7	8.6	27.9	26.4	10.3	15.0	7.1
Guadalupe County, Texas	111,089	3.2	7.9	29.3	19.6	10.7	19.5	9.8
Harris County, Texas	3,033,489	9.7	8.1	23.7	19.0	7.4	20.4	11.8
Harrison County, Texas	44,410	4.7	9.7	31.7	26.9	7.3	13.2	6.5
Hays County, Texas	139,245	3.1	6.3	25.6	21.8	6.7	24.7	11.8
Henderson County, Texas	59,318	4.4	14.0	35.0	23.2	7.7	10.8	5.0
Hidalgo County, Texas	493,247	19.5	13.0	24.5	18.8	5.2	13.5	5.5
Hunt County, Texas	65,064	6.5	9.4	34.0	24.7	5.3	12.5	7.7
Jefferson County, Texas	167,653	7.4	8.5	30.3	24.1	8.7	13.9	7.0
Johnson County, Texas	114,824	4.8	9.5	39.8	21.0	6.0	13.5	5.4
Kaufman County, Texas	85,762	4.6	10.1	31.5	26.4	8.5	14.0	5.0
Liberty County, Texas	57,272	8.8	11.4	36.4	24.8	6.2	8.4	3.0
Lubbock County, Texas	185,987	6.6	6.7	25.3	24.0	5.3	19.4	12.6
McLennan County, Texas	156,625	5.0	8.2	26.4	22.5	12.1	16.4	9.4
Midland County, Texas	110,966	6.5	7.7	22.9	26.5	7.1	19.9	9.4
Montgomery County, Texas	398,614	5.0	6.8	23.2	24.4	6.7	23.0	10.9
Nacogdoches County, Texas	38,985	7.7	7.5	31.2	25.1	4.9	14.6	9.0
Nueces County, Texas	238,820	6.7	8.8	31.1	21.6	8.1	14.8	8.8
Orange County, Texas	56,626	4.3	8.3	31.1	24.6	12.9	16.1	2.7
Parker County, Texas	95,222	4.1	8.1	27.6	21.7	13.5	16.6	8.4
Potter County, Texas	74,335	9.9	13.1	31.5	23.4	8.8	9.0	4.4
Randall County, Texas	90,495	3.0	3.6	24.8	24.6	8.8	23.5	11.7
Rockwall County, Texas	69,312	3.3	2.5	17.7	24.5	11.9	23.6	16.5
San Patricio County, Texas	42,954	10.4	7.9	36.3	24.0	6.2	11.2	4.0
Smith County, Texas	152,733	6.1	6.7	23.8	26.4	9.7	18.4	9.0
Tarrant County, Texas	1,358,155	5.9	6.8	24.4	21.1	7.6	23.1	11.0

N = Data for this geographic area cannot be displayed because the number of sample cases is too small.

Table C-2. Educational Attainment of the Population, by Selected Counties, 2019—*Continued*

(Number; percent; dollars.)

State/County	Population 18 to 24 years				
	Total	Less than high school graduate (percent)	High school graduate (includes equivalency) (percent)	Some college or associate's degree (percent)	Bachelor's degree or higher (percent)
TEXAS—*(Continued)*					
Taylor County, Texas	18,911	7.0	38.4	44.1	10.5
Tom Green County, Texas	14,727	8.1	33.3	47.0	11.6
Travis County, Texas	115,382	9.1	26.8	46.4	17.7
Victoria County, Texas	9,799	17.2	46.4	32.4	4.0
Walker County, Texas	15,514	6.2	13.8	68.4	11.7
Webb County, Texas	31,528	17.3	30.7	46.9	5.1
Wichita County, Texas	17,556	8.0	39.0	45.1	7.9
Williamson County, Texas	46,552	12.2	37.3	40.4	10.1
Wise County, Texas	5,717	15.1	49.7	32.7	2.5
UTAH	364,058	10.7	33.0	49.3	7.0
Cache County, Utah	23,066	8.4	19.2	64.0	8.4
Davis County, Utah	33,522	13.5	39.7	43.3	3.5
Salt Lake County, Utah	110,813	11.8	35.6	42.7	9.9
Tooele County, Utah	5,838	11.5	41.4	44.0	3.0
Utah County, Utah	106,163	6.9	27.3	58.7	7.1
Washington County, Utah	16,483	9.3	40.2	44.7	5.8
Weber County, Utah	25,530	12.5	37.7	46.7	3.1
VERMONT	64,872	8.0	32.8	47.2	12.1
Chittenden County, Vermont	24,391	4.4	22.3	55.9	17.4
VIRGINIA	805,157	9.7	34.0	43.1	13.1
Albemarle County, Virginia	13,700	9.0	32.0	44.1	14.8
Arlington County, Virginia	18,825	4.7	11.8	23.9	59.6
Augusta County, Virginia	5,279	8.4	51.3	20.8	19.5
Bedford County, Virginia	6,531	6.2	46.0	38.6	9.1
Chesterfield County, Virginia	30,727	13.2	37.0	42.1	7.7
Fairfax County, Virginia	95,471	12.7	25.5	37.9	23.9
Fauquier County, Virginia	5,446	7.1	35.1	51.2	6.7
Frederick County, Virginia	6,326	17.7	35.6	33.0	13.7
Hanover County, Virginia	9,612	14.7	40.0	33.8	11.5
Henrico County, Virginia	25,069	15.7	40.3	35.4	8.6
James City County, Virginia	4,830	10.5	24.3	46.5	18.7
Loudoun County, Virginia	31,476	16.3	20.7	40.3	22.7
Montgomery County, Virginia	28,014	1.9	21.1	67.4	9.6
Prince William County, Virginia	41,188	9.9	31.0	51.3	7.8
Roanoke County, Virginia	7,673	17.9	43.3	31.7	7.1
Rockingham County, Virginia	7,246	6.9	36.4	48.0	8.8
Spotsylvania County, Virginia	11,577	12.0	48.2	33.5	6.3
Stafford County, Virginia	14,635	7.0	48.3	36.7	8.0
York County, Virginia	5,654	4.1	41.7	43.0	11.2
Alexandria city, Virginia	8,200	8.8	36.3	29.7	25.2
Chesapeake city, Virginia	20,919	16.3	32.2	40.8	10.7
Hampton city, Virginia	15,223	5.7	25.6	62.6	6.2
Lynchburg city, Virginia	19,573	4.8	27.8	50.9	16.5
Newport News city, Virginia	20,261	9.8	43.7	41.3	5.1
Norfolk city, Virginia	43,719	5.5	48.4	40.4	5.7
Portsmouth city, Virginia	9,302	16.5	27.3	49.4	6.8
Richmond city, Virginia	27,817	5.6	29.0	44.8	20.6
Roanoke city, Virginia	8,704	8.3	48.7	30.6	12.4
Suffolk city, Virginia	7,177	13.3	34.0	49.5	3.1
Virginia Beach city, Virginia	40,495	6.5	37.6	44.6	11.3
WASHINGTON	661,604	14.2	32.8	41.3	11.7
Benton County, Washington	16,907	20.6	32.3	36.7	10.4
Chelan County, Washington	5,946	23.6	38.4	37.0	1.1
Clallam County, Washington	4,142	15.6	39.0	40.7	4.7
Clark County, Washington	39,877	17.8	38.4	35.0	8.8
Cowlitz County, Washington	7,921	15.7	41.1	40.7	2.4
Franklin County, Washington	9,062	26.4	26.3	40.9	6.3
Grant County, Washington	8,751	24.8	45.9	22.4	7.0
Grays Harbor County, Washington	4,855	25.6	41.4	30.2	2.8
Island County, Washington	8,139	18.2	35.4	42.3	4.1
King County, Washington	180,726	11.4	23.7	41.5	23.4
Kitsap County, Washington	25,718	12.9	37.2	41.5	8.4
Lewis County, Washington	5,918	19.3	41.6	35.9	3.2

N = Data for this geographic area cannot be displayed because the number of sample cases is too small.

Table C-2. Educational Attainment of the Population, by Selected Counties, 2019—*Continued*

(Number; percent; dollars.)

State/County	Total	Less than 9th grade (percent)	9th to 12th grade, no diploma (percent)	High school graduate (includes equivalency) (percent)	Some college, no degree (percent)	Associate's degree (percent)	Bachelor's degree (percent)	Graduate or professional degree (percent)
TEXAS—(*Continued*)								
Taylor County, Texas	84,874	3.4	5.3	31.1	25.1	8.4	17.4	9.4
Tom Green County, Texas	76,497	6.0	6.6	29.8	27.2	6.4	13.6	10.5
Travis County, Texas	888,630	5.9	4.2	15.8	15.7	5.7	32.6	20.0
Victoria County, Texas	59,261	6.8	8.3	31.7	22.8	11.3	12.0	7.1
Walker County, Texas	46,727	6.4	7.0	40.1	19.9	7.1	13.1	6.3
Webb County, Texas	156,048	18.3	15.7	19.8	17.9	8.1	15.0	5.2
Wichita County, Texas	85,011	3.5	8.5	34.9	23.2	7.7	13.2	9.1
Williamson County, Texas	394,429	3.1	3.3	21.1	22.5	8.4	28.4	13.3
Wise County, Texas	46,688	6.8	7.5	36.4	25.6	6.4	12.8	4.5
UTAH	1,911,592	2.4	4.5	23.1	25.5	9.7	23.4	11.3
Cache County, Utah	66,833	1.8	5.7	21.6	28.0	6.6	23.1	13.2
Davis County, Utah	209,151	1.3	2.4	20.9	27.9	11.0	25.1	11.4
Salt Lake County, Utah	740,478	3.2	5.2	22.7	22.7	8.9	24.5	12.8
Tooele County, Utah	43,188	0.5	5.6	32.7	29.3	9.0	16.2	6.7
Utah County, Utah	320,787	1.7	2.6	17.8	26.6	10.2	29.0	12.1
Washington County, Utah	116,046	1.7	4.6	21.9	31.0	13.5	16.8	10.5
Weber County, Utah	162,187	2.8	5.3	28.8	26.3	9.7	19.5	7.6
VERMONT	445,558	2.1	4.8	29.0	16.7	8.7	22.7	16.0
Chittenden County, Vermont	110,844	3.1	3.6	18.5	14.9	8.5	29.2	22.2
VIRGINIA	5,872,757	3.8	6.2	23.6	18.9	8.0	22.4	17.2
Albemarle County, Virginia	74,077	2.1	2.7	15.3	15.2	4.1	30.1	30.4
Arlington County, Virginia	175,033	3.3	2.2	7.2	7.8	4.6	34.8	40.1
Augusta County, Virginia	57,274	4.0	8.5	40.3	20.9	7.0	13.8	5.5
Bedford County, Virginia	56,485	3.9	6.6	25.6	25.1	7.2	19.2	12.5
Chesterfield County, Virginia	238,956	2.9	4.7	24.1	20.0	8.1	24.9	15.4
Fairfax County, Virginia	785,130	4.2	3.1	12.0	12.2	6.1	31.5	30.9
Fauquier County, Virginia	49,325	3.0	5.4	25.9	22.0	8.3	22.5	13.0
Frederick County, Virginia	62,677	3.6	7.2	32.3	20.6	8.4	15.6	12.3
Hanover County, Virginia	74,806	1.5	4.7	26.1	19.7	7.7	24.7	15.6
Henrico County, Virginia	231,548	2.6	5.9	21.9	20.2	6.7	25.2	17.6
James City County, Virginia	56,634	2.0	2.5	19.1	16.7	7.8	26.3	25.5
Loudoun County, Virginia	266,796	2.7	2.9	12.2	13.6	6.3	36.9	25.4
Montgomery County, Virginia	56,445	1.8	2.9	27.2	17.2	5.3	21.5	24.1
Prince William County, Virginia	302,837	6.6	4.7	18.1	19.4	8.2	25.6	17.4
Roanoke County, Virginia	67,995	1.4	7.1	24.5	17.7	10.9	24.3	14.1
Rockingham County, Virginia	56,875	6.3	9.4	35.3	16.3	6.5	15.0	11.3
Spotsylvania County, Virginia	90,746	3.2	5.4	28.6	21.6	9.5	20.0	11.6
Stafford County, Virginia	98,469	3.3	3.4	25.1	21.0	7.2	24.3	15.6
York County, Virginia	46,576	2.8	2.8	18.5	17.0	7.8	26.4	24.7
Alexandria city, Virginia	122,536	3.1	3.9	10.4	11.1	5.5	31.7	34.2
Chesapeake city, Virginia	164,745	2.2	7.0	24.7	23.2	10.9	19.6	12.5
Hampton city, Virginia	91,041	2.2	6.1	30.1	25.5	9.8	15.9	10.3
Lynchburg city, Virginia	46,645	2.5	10.0	23.4	20.7	6.2	23.1	14.1
Newport News city, Virginia	117,211	2.4	6.7	30.4	22.6	11.7	15.5	10.8
Norfolk city, Virginia	152,165	3.3	8.4	25.9	23.2	8.6	18.9	11.7
Portsmouth city, Virginia	63,624	2.2	10.0	29.3	27.2	9.8	14.2	7.3
Richmond city, Virginia	163,388	4.8	10.6	21.7	18.8	4.8	23.7	15.6
Roanoke city, Virginia	68,745	4.7	7.1	35.5	20.3	8.6	13.8	10.0
Suffolk city, Virginia	62,892	2.3	6.6	25.1	25.1	10.1	19.5	11.4
Virginia Beach city, Virginia	310,431	1.7	4.2	18.7	24.9	12.2	22.9	15.3
WASHINGTON	5,290,324	3.5	4.8	22.1	22.7	10.0	22.8	14.2
Benton County, Washington	133,790	5.2	4.2	24.0	23.2	11.3	20.3	11.8
Chelan County, Washington	52,950	8.2	9.3	25.0	21.1	11.0	17.7	7.6
Clallam County, Washington	60,272	1.3	6.9	26.4	26.9	10.0	15.3	13.2
Clark County, Washington	333,679	1.8	4.7	26.3	25.1	10.6	20.7	10.8
Cowlitz County, Washington	77,474	3.3	6.8	29.4	32.8	12.4	10.3	5.0
Franklin County, Washington	54,970	16.0	11.4	27.4	18.0	10.2	11.5	5.5
Grant County, Washington	60,165	12.0	10.7	29.5	18.2	11.6	14.3	3.7
Grays Harbor County, Washington	54,932	3.6	4.4	36.8	23.9	11.9	11.5	7.9
Island County, Washington	61,817	1.1	3.8	20.1	27.8	12.6	20.1	14.5
King County, Washington	1,620,440	3.5	3.4	14.4	17.2	7.3	31.7	22.4
Kitsap County, Washington	190,817	1.4	2.4	22.2	28.7	10.5	23.0	11.8
Lewis County, Washington	57,583	3.5	10.4	28.1	28.2	10.9	12.1	6.9

N = Data for this geographic area cannot be displayed because the number of sample cases is too small.

Table C-2. Educational Attainment of the Population, by Selected Counties, 2019—*Continued*

(Number; percent; dollars.)

State/County	Population 18 to 24 years				
	Total	Less than high school graduate (percent)	High school graduate (includes equivalency) (percent)	Some college or associate's degree (percent)	Bachelor's degree or higher (percent)
WASHINGTON—(*Continued*)					
Mason County, Washington	4,580	22.5	61.9	15.6	0.0
Pierce County, Washington	81,962	13.4	38.4	40.7	7.4
Skagit County, Washington	9,455	11.9	41.1	43.2	3.7
Snohomish County, Washington	62,348	16.4	36.5	37.9	9.2
Spokane County, Washington	49,080	11.1	34.1	46.6	8.2
Thurston County, Washington	23,714	15.6	38.8	37.8	7.9
Whatcom County, Washington	32,247	9.2	28.6	52.6	9.6
Yakima County, Washington	23,383	18.1	45.1	31.7	5.1
WEST VIRGINIA	152,243	12.3	39.0	38.8	10.0
Berkeley County, West Virginia	8,992	15.7	33.3	32.3	18.7
Cabell County, West Virginia	11,702	11.1	35.7	39.8	13.4
Harrison County, West Virginia	4,761	26.6	39.4	26.2	7.8
Kanawha County, West Virginia	11,934	16.0	42.1	33.7	8.3
Monongalia County, West Virginia	21,545	3.5	19.9	59.6	17.0
Raleigh County, West Virginia	5,577	2.0	41.1	34.7	22.2
Wood County, West Virginia	6,358	15.0	56.3	20.2	8.6
WISCONSIN	543,737	10.3	33.4	44.5	11.8
Brown County, Wisconsin	24,513	10.5	29.8	43.7	16.0
Dane County, Wisconsin	72,512	4.0	22.3	48.8	25.0
Dodge County, Wisconsin	5,929	10.5	45.4	35.3	8.8
Eau Claire County, Wisconsin	16,829	6.7	29.5	56.5	7.3
Fond du Lac County, Wisconsin	9,486	8.2	31.5	54.8	5.4
Jefferson County, Wisconsin	7,384	6.9	42.6	48.6	1.9
Kenosha County, Wisconsin	16,485	14.0	41.9	38.8	5.3
La Crosse County, Wisconsin	18,096	2.3	25.4	63.7	8.6
Manitowoc County, Wisconsin	5,662	5.8	51.0	33.8	9.4
Marathon County, Wisconsin	9,837	13.1	40.6	39.2	7.1
Milwaukee County, Wisconsin	89,483	14.3	30.8	43.4	11.5
Outagamie County, Wisconsin	15,310	10.2	36.4	41.2	12.2
Ozaukee County, Wisconsin	7,502	4.8	28.6	40.5	26.2
Portage County, Wisconsin	11,604	8.6	33.4	52.3	5.7
Racine County, Wisconsin	16,508	16.0	43.2	31.3	9.5
Rock County, Wisconsin	15,018	11.1	38.4	46.6	4.0
St. Croix County, Wisconsin	6,647	4.4	54.5	30.9	10.2
Sheboygan County, Wisconsin	9,473	6.4	45.6	34.4	13.5
Walworth County, Wisconsin	13,256	9.4	29.8	52.7	8.2
Washington County, Wisconsin	9,861	6.9	33.3	45.7	14.1
Waukesha County, Wisconsin	31,054	12.5	34.2	38.2	15.2
Winnebago County, Wisconsin	18,999	7.9	33.1	48.9	10.2
Wood County, Wisconsin	4,689	10.2	41.0	37.7	11.2
WYOMING	54,723	11.4	33.7	46.0	8.9
Laramie County, Wyoming	8,742	10.5	50.7	30.5	8.3
Natrona County, Wyoming	6,222	6.5	27.5	59.2	6.8

N = Data for this geographic area cannot be displayed because the number of sample cases is too small.

Table C-2. Educational Attainment of the Population, by Selected Counties, 2019—*Continued*

(Number; percent; dollars.)

State/County	Population 25 years and over							
	Total	Less than 9th grade (percent)	9th to 12th grade, no diploma (percent)	High school graduate (includes equivalency) (percent)	Some college, no degree (percent)	Associate's degree (percent)	Bachelor's degree (percent)	Graduate or professional degree (percent)
WASHINGTON—(*Continued*)								
Mason County, Washington	49,157	3.4	6.0	30.0	28.7	11.0	12.4	8.6
Pierce County, Washington	612,563	2.6	5.4	27.8	24.5	11.6	18.6	9.5
Skagit County, Washington	91,972	3.7	6.2	25.4	27.8	9.9	17.6	9.4
Snohomish County, Washington	575,484	2.9	4.3	23.2	25.4	11.2	21.9	11.1
Spokane County, Washington	358,868	1.7	4.6	22.6	26.9	13.3	19.5	11.5
Thurston County, Washington	205,115	1.8	4.8	22.6	25.5	10.9	20.0	14.3
Whatcom County, Washington	152,930	1.3	4.5	24.0	23.5	10.9	22.6	13.2
Yakima County, Washington	153,801	16.0	9.4	27.8	21.3	8.2	11.1	6.2
WEST VIRGINIA	1,281,086	4.2	8.7	40.2	17.9	7.9	12.6	8.4
Berkeley County, West Virginia	82,743	3.4	8.6	37.8	18.7	8.4	14.2	9.0
Cabell County, West Virginia	62,154	4.7	9.0	33.0	16.2	7.9	17.9	11.2
Harrison County, West Virginia	48,151	1.7	8.1	39.7	15.3	9.6	16.0	9.7
Kanawha County, West Virginia	130,020	2.7	7.1	38.6	18.7	7.2	14.9	10.9
Monongalia County, West Virginia	66,795	2.4	6.6	23.6	15.3	7.3	20.2	24.6
Raleigh County, West Virginia	52,700	5.3	6.2	40.7	21.5	6.7	11.7	7.9
Wood County, West Virginia	59,703	3.0	8.2	33.1	24.3	11.1	12.8	7.6
WISCONSIN	4,015,285	2.5	4.8	30.5	20.0	10.9	20.7	10.7
Brown County, Wisconsin	177,809	4.0	3.7	30.1	19.9	12.1	21.6	8.7
Dane County, Wisconsin	363,916	1.3	2.7	16.7	15.8	9.4	31.9	22.2
Dodge County, Wisconsin	63,466	2.8	7.5	39.5	20.5	12.2	13.5	4.0
Eau Claire County, Wisconsin	66,896	1.7	2.7	25.7	21.8	15.3	20.9	12.0
Fond du Lac County, Wisconsin	72,712	1.7	5.3	36.1	20.8	12.5	15.4	8.2
Jefferson County, Wisconsin	59,478	2.8	4.3	34.3	19.3	12.3	19.2	7.8
Kenosha County, Wisconsin	114,483	2.9	5.6	28.9	22.3	10.6	17.9	11.7
La Crosse County, Wisconsin	76,786	1.7	2.5	27.2	20.5	13.0	22.3	12.8
Manitowoc County, Wisconsin	57,164	1.8	4.5	39.0	21.1	11.8	14.7	7.2
Marathon County, Wisconsin	94,762	2.5	5.2	34.9	19.9	12.8	17.0	7.6
Milwaukee County, Wisconsin	630,822	4.4	6.5	28.9	20.1	8.4	20.7	11.0
Outagamie County, Wisconsin	128,752	1.7	4.2	31.9	20.1	12.1	20.9	9.0
Ozaukee County, Wisconsin	62,768	0.4	1.0	23.1	17.5	9.7	30.6	17.6
Portage County, Wisconsin	45,971	1.5	3.6	33.6	15.6	10.2	24.8	10.7
Racine County, Wisconsin	134,721	2.1	8.3	30.3	22.6	10.7	17.0	9.1
Rock County, Wisconsin	110,935	2.0	6.2	37.3	20.4	11.0	15.5	7.7
St. Croix County, Wisconsin	61,770	0.8	3.8	24.6	19.1	13.2	26.9	11.6
Sheboygan County, Wisconsin	80,744	1.6	3.5	34.8	20.9	11.3	20.5	7.4
Walworth County, Wisconsin	69,576	2.5	5.9	31.2	21.8	7.7	20.5	10.3
Washington County, Wisconsin	97,023	0.6	4.4	30.3	21.3	12.3	23.1	8.0
Waukesha County, Wisconsin	287,092	1.3	2.3	21.4	19.5	9.6	30.2	15.9
Winnebago County, Wisconsin	117,903	2.1	5.6	32.3	18.8	10.1	22.2	8.9
Wood County, Wisconsin	52,656	2.8	6.1	39.0	19.6	12.8	12.7	7.0
WYOMING	389,847	1.7	3.8	30.1	24.0	11.3	18.8	10.4
Laramie County, Wyoming	67,775	2.4	3.2	28.0	24.9	11.5	17.8	12.3
Natrona County, Wyoming	54,280	1.5	5.6	34.4	25.9	12.1	14.1	6.6

N = Data for this geographic area cannot be displayed because the number of sample cases is too small.

Table C-2. Educational Attainment of the Population, by Selected Counties, 2019—*Continued*

(Number; percent; dollars.)

State/County	Population 25 to 34 years			Population 35 to 44 years		
	Total	High school graduate or more (percent)	Bachelor's degree or more (percent)	Total	High school graduate or more (percent)	Bachelor's degree or more (percent)
UNITED STATES	45,578,475	91.7	36.9	41,914,845	89.0	37.4
ALABAMA	637,403	89.3	27.5	605,739	87.8	29.6
Baldwin County, Alabama.............................	24,401	90.3	27.0	28,477	90.6	39.6
Calhoun County, Alabama.............................	14,981	88.7	13.7	14,394	83.9	21.9
Cullman County, Alabama.............................	10,588	88.0	16.9	10,281	85.4	24.8
DeKalb County, Alabama..............................	8,436	83.5	15.9	9,017	69.1	16.8
Elmore County, Alabama..............................	13,121	89.2	22.6	10,084	97.0	24.3
Etowah County, Alabama..............................	12,286	83.2	8.9	11,934	85.0	28.8
Houston County, Alabama.............................	13,868	87.9	19.3	13,214	87.1	23.7
Jefferson County, Alabama	95,477	93.9	40.8	84,192	88.8	40.0
Lauderdale County, Alabama........................	10,833	87.8	19.8	10,597	83.5	18.9
Lee County, Alabama...................................	22,519	92.1	47.8	22,401	94.4	45.0
Limestone County, Alabama..........................	12,286	86.0	26.6	13,100	90.9	28.9
Madison County, Alabama............................	52,680	91.1	45.3	46,056	92.7	42.9
Marshall County, Alabama............................	12,099	78.9	21.1	11,407	80.9	17.8
Mobile County, Alabama	58,515	90.5	23.1	49,290	88.7	25.4
Montgomery County, Alabama.......................	32,904	92.8	35.0	28,653	89.1	36.5
Morgan County, Alabama.............................	11,759	90.3	14.0	15,336	84.1	27.4
St. Clair County, Alabama............................	12,436	86.1	12.2	11,304	85.3	20.0
Shelby County, Alabama	27,287	93.1	42.2	29,919	96.3	49.1
Talladega County, Alabama..........................	9,499	76.4	8.3	9,636	81.7	16.1
Tuscaloosa County, Alabama........................	30,237	94.8	37.2	25,141	87.8	32.9
Walker County, Alabama	7,059	78.6	4.4	7,176	87.6	14.0
ALASKA...	117,978	92.4	25.9	93,035	95.1	35.0
Anchorage Municipality, Alaska....................	49,731	93.0	34.0	37,828	96.8	42.7
Fairbanks North Star Borough, Alaska	16,186	98.4	24.8	12,659	97.1	39.2
Matanuska-Susitna Borough, Alaska............	14,699	93.3	17.6	14,137	91.6	25.6
ARIZONA	1,001,594	88.7	28.2	898,533	86.6	32.2
Apache County, Arizona	9,316	86.1	9.2	7,153	93.4	11.2
Cochise County, Arizona	15,467	86.9	23.5	14,188	86.2	24.7
Coconino County, Arizona	19,997	95.9	38.7	15,283	93.1	45.6
Maricopa County, Arizona	658,682	89.9	32.7	583,814	86.0	34.8
Mohave County, Arizona	20,109	82.0	7.3	19,281	90.1	18.9
Navajo County, Arizona...............................	12,793	81.5	4.3	13,028	85.4	21.2
Pima County, Arizona..................................	135,885	88.5	27.5	120,304	87.9	36.2
Pinal County, Arizona..................................	60,718	83.2	9.3	60,986	89.0	18.8
Yavapai County, Arizona..............................	19,717	89.3	16.9	20,965	90.9	21.2
Yuma County, Arizona.................................	30,027	80.8	9.4	22,967	81.2	19.9
ARKANSAS..	386,602	91.0	25.6	377,184	89.3	27.3
Benton County, Arkansas	41,123	92.7	42.5	40,324	91.8	38.4
Craighead County, Arkansas	16,407	84.2	23.9	15,686	91.0	26.6
Faulkner County, Arkansas..........................	16,493	96.4	31.3	16,977	99.0	35.6
Garland County, Arkansas...........................	10,991	94.6	18.3	11,839	88.5	35.1
Jefferson County, Arkansas.........................	8,910	94.3	17.3	7,692	90.0	9.6
Lonoke County, Arkansas............................	10,179	92.7	18.3	10,433	93.8	21.1
Pulaski County, Arkansas............................	57,542	92.6	35.2	50,979	90.2	40.0
Saline County, Arkansas..............................	14,903	92.0	34.3	16,077	92.9	30.9
Sebastian County, Arkansas........................	17,072	86.0	30.8	15,520	85.8	27.8
Washington County, Arkansas	33,619	85.4	38.7	32,640	83.6	33.2
White County, Arkansas	9,766	84.5	23.8	8,721	88.8	16.7
CALIFORNIA	6,036,052	90.4	38.2	5,298,911	84.5	38.2
Alameda County, California	278,792	94.1	58.5	255,680	91.3	58.6
Butte County, California...............................	29,152	92.0	24.2	24,949	84.4	31.3
Contra Costa County, California	146,499	89.8	35.0	156,803	86.7	46.9
El Dorado County, California	19,605	90.2	29.1	23,073	94.0	41.3
Fresno County, California.............................	154,601	84.9	22.9	129,486	75.1	22.7
Humboldt County, California	18,419	93.9	23.6	17,407	88.8	30.1
Imperial County, California...........................	27,562	77.3	17.3	22,000	81.2	33.7
Kern County, California................................	141,225	84.6	18.0	115,848	76.4	17.8
Kings County, California...............................	26,301	79.1	15.2	20,966	71.9	17.2
Lake County, California	7,711	89.2	11.8	7,634	79.7	16.8
Los Angeles County, California.....................	1,636,784	89.8	40.0	1,375,634	81.8	37.1
Madera County, California............................	21,339	78.4	14.4	20,918	70.7	12.7
Marin County, California...............................	21,341	86.8	52.5	28,975	88.0	61.2

N = Data for this geographic area cannot be displayed because the number of sample cases is too small.

Table C-2. Educational Attainment of the Population, by Selected Counties, 2019—*Continued*

(Number; percent; dollars.)

State/County	Population 45 to 64 years			Population 65 years and over		
	Total	High school graduate or more (percent)	Bachelor's degree or more (percent)	Total	High school graduate or more (percent)	Bachelor's degree or more (percent)
UNITED STATES	83,331,220	88.6	31.8	54,074,028	85.7	28.6
ALABAMA	1,262,604	87.9	26.4	854,312	83.8	23.2
Baldwin County, Alabama...........................	59,151	91.3	31.8	47,688	89.6	31.0
Calhoun County, Alabama...........................	29,153	85.6	18.9	20,556	80.5	22.1
Cullman County, Alabama	22,503	80.9	13.1	15,423	74.4	12.7
DeKalb County, Alabama	17,616	82.0	10.3	11,938	77.5	11.1
Elmore County, Alabama	21,587	88.6	25.8	12,761	86.3	26.1
Etowah County, Alabama...........................	27,530	86.1	17.4	19,994	81.5	15.3
Houston County, Alabama...........................	27,351	85.2	23.5	19,021	81.2	23.3
Jefferson County, Alabama	163,853	92.6	32.3	108,296	88.6	28.4
Lauderdale County, Alabama...........................	23,613	86.3	24.8	19,224	82.6	22.3
Lee County, Alabama...........................	35,661	93.1	37.2	20,745	87.2	37.9
Limestone County, Alabama	26,775	88.0	24.4	16,280	84.7	23.9
Madison County, Alabama...........................	100,510	94.4	45.8	57,890	92.1	40.7
Marshall County, Alabama...........................	24,513	83.8	22.2	16,737	82.7	17.8
Mobile County, Alabama...........................	104,639	87.1	23.2	68,009	84.6	20.5
Montgomery County, Alabama...........................	54,147	89.1	38.5	35,606	87.5	30.1
Morgan County, Alabama...........................	33,691	86.7	27.5	21,676	83.4	19.3
St. Clair County, Alabama...........................	24,702	86.1	11.4	14,419	84.4	13.4
Shelby County, Alabama	56,777	93.8	47.4	35,238	90.9	37.7
Talladega County, Alabama...........................	21,775	80.7	18.8	14,611	81.3	14.2
Tuscaloosa County, Alabama...........................	47,358	88.3	30.8	28,863	86.7	25.0
Walker County, Alabama	18,330	84.0	15.4	12,012	78.8	10.7
ALASKA...........................	182,457	94.1	30.2	90,588	92.5	30.8
Anchorage Municipality, Alaska...........................	70,086	95.6	35.1	32,816	95.1	35.1
Fairbanks North Star Borough, Alaska	21,485	96.7	36.2	10,950	87.9	33.2
Matanuska-Susitna Borough, Alaska....................	27,992	94.5	26.8	13,597	96.6	25.1
ARIZONA	1,737,172	87.0	29.6	1,307,241	88.3	31.0
Apache County, Arizona	18,183	85.0	11.7	11,603	65.9	14.5
Cochise County, Arizona	29,839	89.5	22.3	28,939	89.9	28.7
Coconino County, Arizona	30,816	94.3	35.2	18,586	89.9	42.9
Maricopa County, Arizona	1,078,113	87.4	33.1	696,467	89.4	33.8
Mohave County, Arizona	57,994	89.0	13.7	65,827	85.8	13.5
Navajo County, Arizona	27,105	83.8	11.5	20,560	83.2	15.7
Pima County, Arizona	241,664	87.0	30.3	212,596	89.3	36.6
Pinal County, Arizona	106,648	85.9	19.9	95,666	88.6	25.8
Yavapai County, Arizona...........................	64,129	91.1	30.9	77,130	93.3	31.5
Yuma County, Arizona	43,285	69.3	14.5	40,808	70.7	14.1
ARKANSAS...........................	748,433	87.7	22.2	524,237	83.3	20.5
Benton County, Arkansas	63,571	87.2	31.3	38,185	87.3	29.4
Craighead County, Arkansas	24,839	92.3	27.8	14,881	88.6	22.0
Faulkner County, Arkansas	27,104	92.5	25.3	16,110	87.7	27.8
Garland County, Arkansas	25,936	92.6	29.8	23,799	89.6	28.8
Jefferson County, Arkansas...........................	17,103	87.7	22.3	12,014	77.9	19.2
Lonoke County, Arkansas	18,286	86.3	20.1	10,403	85.6	15.7
Pulaski County, Arkansas	96,189	93.6	32.7	63,974	89.0	33.9
Saline County, Arkansas...........................	31,152	89.9	20.7	22,598	85.5	26.3
Sebastian County, Arkansas...........................	31,118	86.7	21.3	21,669	79.3	24.0
Washington County, Arkansas	50,243	84.6	30.7	29,158	83.1	24.7
White County, Arkansas	19,744	82.2	12.6	13,215	73.1	16.1
CALIFORNIA	9,767,911	81.6	32.9	5,034,990	81.1	32.3
Alameda County, California	422,358	89.6	47.2	238,277	82.6	38.9
Butte County, California...........................	49,155	88.3	32.0	40,559	88.6	32.6
Contra Costa County, California	311,991	89.1	44.3	186,894	90.4	43.7
El Dorado County, California	57,301	94.4	39.6	42,089	91.7	29.0
Fresno County, California	211,617	73.0	20.5	125,736	74.0	22.8
Humboldt County, California	32,246	91.2	28.9	25,026	89.6	37.5
Imperial County, California...........................	38,510	67.9	15.0	23,683	62.5	10.9
Kern County, California...........................	193,223	71.0	14.8	101,660	75.1	19.3
Kings County, California...........................	31,709	67.2	20.1	16,107	67.3	17.2
Lake County, California	17,475	83.7	15.4	14,366	90.2	16.7
Los Angeles County, California...........................	2,535,441	76.0	30.4	1,413,755	73.2	29.4
Madera County, California...........................	34,288	67.0	12.1	22,847	78.9	18.2
Marin County, California...........................	78,635	93.5	62.1	59,558	95.5	58.3

N = Data for this geographic area cannot be displayed because the number of sample cases is too small.

Table C-2. Educational Attainment of the Population, by Selected Counties, 2019—*Continued*

(Number; percent; dollars.)

	Population 25 to 34 years			Population 35 to 44 years		
State/County	Total	High school graduate or more (percent)	Bachelor's degree or more (percent)	Total	High school graduate or more (percent)	Bachelor's degree or more (percent)
CALIFORNIA—(*Continued*)						
Mendocino County, California	8,430	77.3	29.8	10,799	84.4	16.3
Merced County, California	41,053	79.7	15.0	36,588	74.3	16.0
Monterey County, California	61,159	78.3	22.5	57,771	63.7	19.3
Napa County, California	17,125	90.5	33.4	16,887	86.3	34.9
Nevada County, California	10,144	97.9	28.4	11,883	99.2	38.5
Orange County, California	457,902	92.3	45.5	410,729	85.5	46.0
Placer County, California	42,356	91.2	42.7	53,144	95.2	49.8
Riverside County, California	345,381	89.5	21.8	320,798	83.4	23.9
Sacramento County, California	244,536	91.9	33.4	211,156	90.4	31.5
San Bernardino County, California	336,303	88.0	24.2	283,746	80.7	25.0
San Diego County, California	549,118	93.8	40.9	452,635	90.0	45.1
San Francisco County, California	204,061	97.2	79.8	141,927	94.0	65.4
San Joaquin County, California	106,728	84.7	18.1	101,242	77.9	22.4
San Luis Obispo County, California	31,779	93.3	33.9	32,080	87.2	36.8
San Mateo County, California	114,318	93.7	59.5	111,071	91.1	63.1
Santa Barbara County, California	59,846	83.6	35.9	50,654	73.5	29.5
Santa Clara County, California	315,114	94.7	63.1	278,958	90.2	59.7
Santa Cruz County, California	33,165	89.8	42.9	31,799	86.9	41.3
Shasta County, California	22,996	93.7	21.0	20,956	97.2	28.2
Solano County, California	65,438	91.3	26.8	57,782	87.5	28.2
Sonoma County, California	61,535	92.6	31.7	61,553	83.6	32.5
Stanislaus County, California	78,774	88.4	16.7	70,383	83.4	19.4
Sutter County, California	12,894	81.8	16.2	11,722	73.3	24.0
Tehama County, California	8,096	86.9	13.6	9,099	74.7	18.1
Tulare County, California	66,710	86.3	12.0	59,012	73.4	14.0
Ventura County, California	113,309	90.0	29.0	104,866	85.7	34.7
Yolo County, California	29,946	93.5	44.0	27,437	86.1	39.0
Yuba County, California	13,130	88.6	19.4	9,176	80.8	21.2
COLORADO	907,627	93.8	44.4	805,306	91.3	45.7
Adams County, Colorado	85,655	87.9	28.0	76,461	83.1	31.0
Arapahoe County, Colorado	104,474	93.5	43.1	95,130	92.2	45.7
Boulder County, Colorado	46,369	95.6	64.3	40,746	92.2	74.7
Broomfield County, Colorado	10,735	98.1	61.0	10,405	96.3	59.1
Denver County, Colorado	172,142	95.2	62.0	117,716	91.8	54.9
Douglas County, Colorado	39,301	97.1	54.1	51,904	96.8	63.2
El Paso County, Colorado	116,485	96.1	34.2	92,583	93.4	41.4
Jefferson County, Colorado	88,288	94.4	52.3	82,233	95.9	55.5
Larimer County, Colorado	53,029	98.8	49.5	44,701	92.9	49.2
Mesa County, Colorado	19,179	93.8	27.9	19,894	90.7	28.1
Pueblo County, Colorado	21,977	90.1	20.6	20,773	91.1	22.0
Weld County, Colorado	49,494	91.5	31.8	44,463	86.5	31.0
CONNECTICUT	444,509	93.4	44.4	426,967	91.5	45.2
Fairfield County, Connecticut	108,198	92.1	52.3	117,338	90.8	52.4
Hartford County, Connecticut	119,057	92.8	44.3	111,539	90.7	46.3
Litchfield County, Connecticut	20,500	97.3	46.7	18,662	94.3	35.2
Middlesex County, Connecticut	17,810	94.5	48.1	17,894	91.5	55.1
New Haven County, Connecticut	114,713	93.8	41.3	101,405	90.5	40.9
New London County, Connecticut	33,911	94.0	33.9	30,493	95.3	31.1
Tolland County, Connecticut	16,002	95.8	47.7	16,105	97.4	52.3
Windham County, Connecticut	14,318	93.6	25.4	13,531	93.7	28.7
DELAWARE	128,412	91.2	32.8	113,704	87.6	37.8
Kent County, Delaware	24,919	90.9	25.8	20,856	91.9	36.9
New Castle County, Delaware	81,002	91.5	37.4	69,737	88.7	39.4
Sussex County, Delaware	22,491	90.5	24.1	23,111	80.6	33.6
DISTRICT OF COLUMBIA	164,375	95.1	73.4	108,905	93.0	66.0
District of Columbia, District of Columbia	164,375	95.1	73.4	108,905	93.0	66.0
FLORIDA	2,768,060	90.7	31.0	2,612,250	88.9	33.9
Alachua County, Florida	40,540	94.9	48.2	30,979	92.5	51.4
Bay County, Florida	23,211	93.1	27.7	21,012	92.1	35.3
Brevard County, Florida	70,135	92.9	30.3	63,155	96.0	33.6
Broward County, Florida	261,831	93.0	34.0	260,809	91.1	35.7
Charlotte County, Florida	14,987	86.9	14.9	14,661	84.8	16.7
Citrus County, Florida	12,271	79.0	12.6	11,902	86.9	24.4
Clay County, Florida	25,534	97.0	27.4	28,635	96.9	27.7
Collier County, Florida	34,396	90.0	23.9	36,537	84.8	30.2

N = Data for this geographic area cannot be displayed because the number of sample cases is too small.

Table C-2. Educational Attainment of the Population, by Selected Counties, 2019—*Continued*

(Number; percent; dollars.)

State/County	Population 45 to 64 years			Population 65 years and over		
	Total	High school graduate or more (percent)	Bachelor's degree or more (percent)	Total	High school graduate or more (percent)	Bachelor's degree or more (percent)
CALIFORNIA—*(Continued)*						
Mendocino County, California	22,031	81.3	16.5	20,301	88.3	31.8
Merced County, California	58,109	59.7	11.9	31,710	66.3	16.5
Monterey County, California	98,327	69.1	26.1	60,667	78.7	34.4
Napa County, California	36,628	78.5	37.2	27,026	91.2	37.4
Nevada County, California	27,255	92.0	36.5	27,726	95.9	36.7
Orange County, California	846,551	83.9	38.6	485,296	84.7	36.9
Placer County, California	106,876	95.8	42.1	79,145	92.7	35.9
Riverside County, California	588,523	80.1	22.2	366,215	81.6	26.9
Sacramento County, California	378,915	87.7	30.7	223,929	86.4	29.6
San Bernardino County, California	509,927	77.5	21.0	260,812	77.7	20.4
San Diego County, California	801,247	85.3	38.0	484,472	84.5	37.1
San Francisco County, California	213,827	85.0	48.6	141,464	75.2	39.3
San Joaquin County, California	177,332	79.5	19.9	99,410	76.0	19.7
San Luis Obispo County, California	67,700	88.2	35.3	59,624	94.2	41.3
San Mateo County, California	203,955	90.9	49.9	126,636	86.7	40.4
Santa Barbara County, California	97,504	78.9	33.0	70,330	88.1	39.1
Santa Clara County, California	489,784	87.8	49.9	266,825	83.1	43.4
Santa Cruz County, California	68,074	84.6	43.7	48,083	90.3	46.4
Shasta County, California	45,557	92.0	20.7	37,995	92.4	20.1
Solano County, California	114,873	89.3	28.6	72,614	88.6	32.0
Sonoma County, California	133,934	89.6	38.0	102,102	91.6	43.1
Stanislaus County, California	126,027	77.3	16.2	73,595	73.9	18.0
Sutter County, California	23,253	82.4	22.4	15,122	77.9	20.5
Tehama County, California	15,303	86.7	16.2	13,253	82.9	16.7
Tulare County, California	97,954	69.1	13.5	53,781	68.9	15.6
Ventura County, California	222,456	85.5	36.5	136,623	85.8	37.1
Yolo County, California	45,370	88.4	36.0	28,495	86.8	42.5
Yuba County, California	18,094	75.1	16.3	10,275	81.8	15.7
COLORADO	1,416,632	92.5	41.9	845,378	91.8	39.2
Adams County, Colorado	119,191	83.4	21.1	55,624	85.7	23.0
Arapahoe County, Colorado	163,562	92.3	43.0	88,369	92.1	44.0
Boulder County, Colorado	83,085	94.4	63.9	47,546	95.2	58.4
Broomfield County, Colorado	18,728	94.9	57.7	9,675	96.9	48.3
Denver County, Colorado	153,933	89.3	46.7	86,752	85.9	44.4
Douglas County, Colorado	99,929	98.5	60.6	44,191	98.5	50.0
El Paso County, Colorado	166,917	95.5	41.3	95,328	94.3	38.8
Jefferson County, Colorado	156,296	94.6	46.4	99,089	93.7	38.8
Larimer County, Colorado	82,630	96.9	50.0	57,829	96.4	47.0
Mesa County, Colorado	37,153	89.8	29.9	31,122	91.3	31.9
Pueblo County, Colorado	41,949	92.8	25.1	31,679	90.3	24.1
Weld County, Colorado	75,818	86.8	29.2	40,855	85.8	27.6
CONNECTICUT	995,912	91.6	39.0	629,032	86.8	34.2
Fairfield County, Connecticut	268,330	91.6	51.4	153,798	85.8	40.2
Hartford County, Connecticut	239,527	91.8	38.1	155,516	85.6	31.0
Litchfield County, Connecticut	56,471	93.6	33.7	39,673	91.8	34.4
Middlesex County, Connecticut	50,164	95.3	36.5	33,697	91.0	42.8
New Haven County, Connecticut	231,846	89.6	31.7	152,714	85.2	31.9
New London County, Connecticut	74,005	94.5	34.6	49,770	90.1	32.2
Tolland County, Connecticut	41,261	94.1	39.0	24,554	91.1	32.1
Windham County, Connecticut	34,308	87.6	20.8	19,310	85.2	24.1
DELAWARE	255,557	91.5	33.9	189,638	89.7	29.7
Kent County, Delaware	44,087	87.4	22.6	31,993	86.6	18.0
New Castle County, Delaware	148,067	93.4	38.0	80,840	90.6	32.1
Sussex County, Delaware	63,403	90.1	32.2	67,796	90.1	32.1
DISTRICT OF COLUMBIA	144,328	90.8	47.8	87,537	86.0	45.5
District of Columbia, District of Columbia	144,328	90.8	47.8	87,537	86.0	45.5
FLORIDA	5,605,994	89.0	30.2	4,498,198	86.0	29.2
Alachua County, Florida	54,909	94.8	46.3	39,364	92.3	38.6
Bay County, Florida	49,552	91.0	23.4	32,285	89.0	24.2
Brevard County, Florida	171,708	92.4	30.8	145,774	90.8	28.5
Broward County, Florida	534,818	89.8	33.8	334,606	84.3	28.7
Charlotte County, Florida	51,021	91.1	23.3	77,915	92.0	23.7
Citrus County, Florida	40,568	89.6	22.5	55,390	88.9	24.5
Clay County, Florida	61,642	94.4	29.3	35,457	92.4	29.1
Collier County, Florida	95,751	88.9	31.4	126,527	89.9	43.9

N = Data for this geographic area cannot be displayed because the number of sample cases is too small.

Table C-2. Educational Attainment of the Population, by Selected Counties, 2019—*Continued*

(Number; percent; dollars.)

State/County	Population 25 to 34 years			Population 35 to 44 years		
	Total	High school graduate or more (percent)	Bachelor's degree or more (percent)	Total	High school graduate or more (percent)	Bachelor's degree or more (percent)
FLORIDA—*(Continued)*						
Columbia County, Florida	8,068	78.5	12.0	7,876	89.9	26.2
Duval County, Florida	157,115	91.7	29.6	124,092	91.0	34.3
Escambia County, Florida	48,724	90.9	27.3	34,710	87.8	23.9
Flagler County, Florida	10,247	91.0	25.3	11,208	93.4	21.4
Hernando County, Florida	19,730	89.0	16.9	19,739	94.2	21.9
Highlands County, Florida	7,347	81.9	12.1	9,707	92.5	21.9
Hillsborough County, Florida	225,612	90.6	38.7	203,737	89.7	39.2
Indian River County, Florida	15,260	91.0	25.8	14,865	86.1	26.4
Lake County, Florida	39,087	89.7	23.9	40,964	91.1	33.6
Lee County, Florida	82,852	87.2	25.7	80,572	86.6	25.5
Leon County, Florida	41,652	94.7	51.4	31,772	93.3	54.1
Manatee County, Florida	41,082	89.5	26.2	41,161	88.0	31.3
Marion County, Florida	39,613	90.1	14.5	36,615	86.1	22.1
Martin County, Florida	15,650	92.7	20.9	13,484	90.2	43.8
Miami-Dade County, Florida	383,209	90.4	35.8	369,126	85.5	36.1
Monroe County, Florida	9,103	91.5	34.7	8,660	90.1	33.5
Nassau County, Florida	10,988	91.2	18.8	9,136	89.2	27.2
Okaloosa County, Florida	33,147	94.0	30.4	25,965	89.2	30.8
Orange County, Florida	234,299	90.8	38.3	200,209	89.2	38.4
Osceola County, Florida	52,744	88.5	26.6	57,948	89.0	27.0
Palm Beach County, Florida	177,743	88.5	32.2	171,872	86.4	40.9
Pasco County, Florida	60,791	91.3	22.8	69,910	92.7	35.5
Pinellas County, Florida	116,999	92.4	36.5	107,171	91.7	37.6
Polk County, Florida	95,470	89.7	17.3	86,569	84.3	21.5
Putnam County, Florida	7,138	84.4	8.2	8,097	81.2	5.6
St. Johns County, Florida	23,330	93.5	35.9	34,893	98.2	55.8
St. Lucie County, Florida	36,644	89.6	23.9	38,835	82.1	24.1
Santa Rosa County, Florida	24,795	89.9	21.3	23,082	94.6	33.6
Sarasota County, Florida	35,235	96.1	26.0	35,800	90.3	34.1
Seminole County, Florida	68,314	94.9	43.1	65,968	94.3	44.9
Sumter County, Florida	6,013	85.1	8.7	8,714	84.8	20.9
Volusia County, Florida	65,058	92.9	20.9	58,550	89.9	24.1
Walton County, Florida	8,817	93.4	25.5	10,036	95.1	34.5
GEORGIA	1,458,596	90.6	34.7	1,401,934	87.5	35.6
Barrow County, Georgia	12,111	88.0	23.2	12,425	85.1	30.0
Bartow County, Georgia	13,990	90.1	20.8	13,537	85.0	18.9
Bibb County, Georgia	21,039	88.8	26.0	17,841	88.7	24.1
Bulloch County, Georgia	11,379	97.5	26.2	7,938	86.7	24.8
Carroll County, Georgia	16,176	89.7	21.1	17,267	75.2	11.3
Catoosa County, Georgia	8,421	98.1	9.3	8,046	87.5	29.7
Chatham County, Georgia	47,343	92.7	37.5	35,838	86.1	39.3
Cherokee County, Georgia	32,323	92.9	39.9	36,436	94.2	43.0
Clarke County, Georgia	19,852	93.0	54.9	12,251	93.9	52.5
Clayton County, Georgia	44,728	88.6	21.8	39,843	79.3	19.1
Cobb County, Georgia	112,173	94.9	49.0	106,681	89.6	51.4
Columbia County, Georgia	20,936	90.6	41.6	22,083	94.5	29.9
Coweta County, Georgia	19,247	91.0	26.1	19,050	85.9	36.8
DeKalb County, Georgia	127,742	90.1	48.1	108,290	89.2	49.2
Dougherty County, Georgia	10,740	89.3	23.5	10,335	85.5	18.2
Douglas County, Georgia	15,786	94.9	44.6	20,488	89.1	37.2
Fayette County, Georgia	10,407	93.2	33.2	14,764	97.6	55.8
Floyd County, Georgia	12,670	83.8	20.4	10,601	87.8	32.8
Forsyth County, Georgia	22,546	92.5	55.7	39,945	90.8	64.2
Fulton County, Georgia	183,771	96.5	62.4	150,614	93.9	63.0
Glynn County, Georgia	10,859	87.2	18.8	9,650	87.6	29.0
Gwinnett County, Georgia	123,579	88.9	42.0	133,177	87.2	38.2
Hall County, Georgia	25,534	81.6	22.3	24,598	71.0	22.7
Henry County, Georgia	28,384	96.0	31.9	30,816	92.2	28.6
Houston County, Georgia	21,061	90.4	30.0	20,865	94.9	29.1
Jackson County, Georgia	10,529	89.3	27.9	10,027	82.8	24.3
Lowndes County, Georgia	18,698	92.5	17.8	14,121	91.9	31.7
Muscogee County, Georgia	29,951	93.8	25.0	25,336	91.1	23.1
Newton County, Georgia	15,216	90.8	15.4	13,838	86.4	19.2
Paulding County, Georgia	20,199	90.2	26.7	26,085	83.4	26.0
Richmond County, Georgia	32,969	90.6	22.9	23,274	86.8	25.3
Rockdale County, Georgia	10,012	84.7	21.5	11,748	87.0	24.1
Spalding County, Georgia	7,968	96.8	11.9	7,166	82.2	16.8
Troup County, Georgia	11,580	93.2	14.4	7,949	82.1	20.1
Walker County, Georgia	8,305	86.4	15.7	8,988	82.1	25.4

N = Data for this geographic area cannot be displayed because the number of sample cases is too small.

Table C-2. Educational Attainment of the Population, by Selected Counties, 2019—*Continued*

(Number; percent; dollars.)

State/County	Population 45 to 64 years			Population 65 years and over		
	Total	High school graduate or more (percent)	Bachelor's degree or more (percent)	Total	High school graduate or more (percent)	Bachelor's degree or more (percent)
FLORIDA—*(Continued)*						
Columbia County, Florida	19,283	85.6	11.9	13,296	90.7	16.1
Duval County, Florida	239,237	90.9	30.2	138,376	87.3	29.0
Escambia County, Florida	78,934	88.5	21.3	54,559	87.8	24.8
Flagler County, Florida	31,117	92.6	27.6	35,824	89.5	27.6
Hernando County, Florida	51,939	90.3	19.9	53,268	85.9	19.8
Highlands County, Florida	26,089	80.7	12.9	37,522	86.9	18.9
Hillsborough County, Florida	373,654	89.0	34.0	214,075	85.2	27.7
Indian River County, Florida	39,596	90.8	30.2	54,727	92.2	35.0
Lake County, Florida	94,252	89.5	22.0	98,904	88.5	25.7
Lee County, Florida	196,239	89.0	27.9	224,663	90.5	32.4
Leon County, Florida	61,821	89.5	41.5	40,669	93.7	44.7
Manatee County, Florida	106,680	90.4	27.1	113,970	91.5	35.4
Marion County, Florida	90,677	89.3	21.2	106,950	89.3	21.8
Martin County, Florida	44,441	91.9	38.3	51,435	90.4	35.3
Miami-Dade County, Florida	737,544	82.1	30.5	452,047	64.8	22.0
Monroe County, Florida	22,991	95.2	31.1	17,624	92.3	39.3
Nassau County, Florida	25,885	86.6	28.1	20,697	89.5	38.1
Okaloosa County, Florida	51,116	94.2	31.5	34,410	92.6	33.5
Orange County, Florida	338,695	88.7	34.6	170,997	82.8	28.5
Osceola County, Florida	87,134	87.1	23.4	50,781	76.5	20.5
Palm Beach County, Florida	386,894	89.7	38.1	364,559	89.7	38.4
Pasco County, Florida	146,092	90.6	26.1	125,406	88.2	20.2
Pinellas County, Florida	282,899	91.8	33.8	247,636	89.1	28.4
Polk County, Florida	173,219	88.4	20.1	149,025	84.0	23.3
Putnam County, Florida	20,854	83.0	12.4	17,495	81.4	17.2
St. Johns County, Florida	73,889	95.3	44.7	55,242	95.4	45.5
St. Lucie County, Florida	83,691	89.8	18.3	81,133	84.2	22.5
Santa Rosa County, Florida	50,002	93.1	26.3	31,248	85.9	26.7
Sarasota County, Florida	114,109	93.0	33.4	161,594	94.5	41.3
Seminole County, Florida	124,889	93.6	41.2	75,115	92.1	36.3
Sumter County, Florida	24,875	95.6	26.8	78,784	95.9	38.4
Volusia County, Florida	152,067	92.0	24.1	137,196	89.9	25.5
Walton County, Florida	20,845	94.0	27.7	14,929	81.3	32.5
GEORGIA	2,696,500	88.6	32.9	1,523,192	84.4	26.8
Barrow County, Georgia	20,372	85.2	21.9	10,378	80.1	17.0
Bartow County, Georgia	28,338	85.1	19.7	16,211	75.4	10.6
Bibb County, Georgia	37,051	88.5	24.7	24,486	81.7	24.9
Bulloch County, Georgia	15,698	87.6	31.5	9,055	87.0	20.4
Carroll County, Georgia	27,419	85.9	23.0	16,615	79.6	17.8
Catoosa County, Georgia	18,321	89.5	31.1	11,894	87.8	17.2
Chatham County, Georgia	67,395	90.0	31.5	46,580	88.7	30.2
Cherokee County, Georgia	69,371	90.3	40.9	38,347	86.7	27.1
Clarke County, Georgia	25,192	87.2	38.6	14,479	93.1	51.5
Clayton County, Georgia	69,058	85.4	18.2	28,059	78.1	15.2
Cobb County, Georgia	200,672	92.0	49.3	96,417	91.5	40.4
Columbia County, Georgia	38,532	95.9	48.9	22,070	89.7	37.1
Coweta County, Georgia	41,296	91.5	25.5	21,566	88.1	20.9
DeKalb County, Georgia	187,824	91.3	43.0	97,699	88.5	39.7
Dougherty County, Georgia	20,306	81.3	20.5	14,697	76.1	19.6
Douglas County, Georgia	38,563	92.6	31.0	17,559	85.0	16.1
Fayette County, Georgia	32,903	96.2	50.7	21,913	96.0	35.0
Floyd County, Georgia	25,758	83.9	17.6	17,013	87.9	26.5
Forsyth County, Georgia	67,330	95.4	57.5	30,475	93.6	42.2
Fulton County, Georgia	266,900	93.9	56.5	127,756	90.1	46.4
Glynn County, Georgia	21,890	89.3	28.8	17,846	94.0	32.6
Gwinnett County, Georgia	246,085	88.6	41.3	98,444	85.5	31.6
Hall County, Georgia	53,916	81.2	25.0	31,062	81.9	30.6
Henry County, Georgia	65,367	92.1	26.5	28,010	85.4	17.1
Houston County, Georgia	39,263	95.6	27.5	20,198	87.7	25.1
Jackson County, Georgia	18,628	84.6	23.7	10,861	84.0	24.8
Lowndes County, Georgia	22,176	91.8	29.7	14,677	85.4	21.9
Muscogee County, Georgia	45,506	88.3	25.1	26,799	82.1	25.2
Newton County, Georgia	28,465	86.7	21.5	14,707	78.3	12.2
Paulding County, Georgia	46,231	90.3	21.6	17,883	85.3	12.7
Richmond County, Georgia	47,743	88.3	17.3	29,702	80.3	16.7
Rockdale County, Georgia	24,663	92.5	25.4	13,801	83.5	21.6
Spalding County, Georgia	18,021	82.3	18.0	12,324	82.2	21.6
Troup County, Georgia	16,609	88.5	22.3	10,647	90.0	21.2
Walker County, Georgia	18,853	77.5	13.1	12,984	79.3	16.4

N = Data for this geographic area cannot be displayed because the number of sample cases is too small.

Table C-2. Educational Attainment of the Population, by Selected Counties, 2019—*Continued*

(Number; percent; dollars.)

State/County	Population 25 to 34 years			Population 35 to 44 years		
	Total	High school graduate or more (percent)	Bachelor's degree or more (percent)	Total	High school graduate or more (percent)	Bachelor's degree or more (percent)
GEORGIA—(*Continued*)						
Walton County, Georgia	13,431	87.5	23.8	11,122	88.0	32.7
Whitfield County, Georgia	12,745	90.7	17.4	15,106	60.6	12.3
HAWAII	195,781	96.2	33.3	185,133	94.8	38.2
Hawaii County, Hawaii	21,122	95.7	23.3	25,683	92.5	32.2
Honolulu County, Hawaii	146,382	96.5	36.5	125,615	96.3	42.9
Kauai County, Hawaii	8,035	94.5	25.2	9,940	93.3	26.8
Maui County, Hawaii	20,242	95.2	24.2	23,890	89.7	25.1
IDAHO	234,800	92.7	27.5	225,804	91.6	33.1
Ada County, Idaho	70,119	94.2	37.9	68,200	95.5	44.3
Bannock County, Idaho	13,297	96.9	30.6	11,003	95.9	39.2
Bonneville County, Idaho	17,084	95.0	36.0	14,791	95.1	40.6
Canyon County, Idaho	31,419	88.5	15.4	28,987	85.0	26.7
Kootenai County, Idaho	20,618	97.3	17.6	20,385	90.8	18.1
Twin Falls County, Idaho	11,422	81.3	19.3	10,528	91.0	23.9
ILLINOIS	1,748,323	93.3	43.1	1,641,179	90.2	41.9
Adams County, Illinois	7,879	90.5	25.8	8,160	92.5	34.3
Champaign County, Illinois	28,867	93.0	56.1	22,799	93.6	50.3
Cook County, Illinois	841,725	93.7	51.8	700,021	89.7	46.6
DeKalb County, Illinois	12,550	94.0	46.8	11,822	94.2	36.2
DuPage County, Illinois	116,204	95.8	54.2	120,994	93.6	55.5
Kane County, Illinois	63,003	91.3	36.2	70,405	80.2	35.4
Kankakee County, Illinois	12,314	88.0	28.1	13,231	93.6	20.7
Kendall County, Illinois	17,166	95.7	38.8	19,095	95.4	52.0
Lake County, Illinois	78,325	92.7	38.8	87,089	87.8	50.0
LaSalle County, Illinois	13,300	89.5	13.4	13,463	88.6	22.8
McHenry County, Illinois	35,131	94.4	37.6	39,177	94.5	38.6
McLean County, Illinois	21,096	95.2	49.5	21,561	94.6	56.5
Macon County, Illinois	13,199	96.3	24.3	12,029	91.7	20.4
Madison County, Illinois	34,824	94.3	32.7	31,619	92.9	44.3
Peoria County, Illinois	23,609	95.6	39.5	21,694	93.1	41.9
Rock Island County, Illinois	16,552	91.5	23.9	17,204	84.0	26.3
St. Clair County, Illinois	34,978	94.5	22.9	32,573	94.0	34.5
Sangamon County, Illinois	24,672	91.2	33.2	23,985	93.5	40.2
Tazewell County, Illinois	15,173	94.4	33.0	16,838	93.9	31.3
Vermilion County, Illinois	9,020	89.5	11.9	8,435	87.8	11.9
Will County, Illinois	82,925	93.6	35.5	92,931	89.1	42.3
Williamson County, Illinois	8,654	95.2	31.1	8,901	96.7	35.3
Winnebago County, Illinois	34,366	88.3	24.8	34,265	85.9	27.5
INDIANA	886,319	90.6	30.8	825,768	89.6	31.9
Allen County, Indiana	52,113	91.9	32.6	48,086	89.0	32.0
Bartholomew County, Indiana	12,579	85.3	49.8	10,847	93.6	44.5
Boone County, Indiana	7,606	91.4	42.5	10,105	86.7	47.3
Clark County, Indiana	15,720	97.9	28.3	16,730	83.9	19.1
Delaware County, Indiana	12,949	95.4	24.2	10,993	91.9	20.6
Elkhart County, Indiana	26,657	85.7	16.2	23,446	75.9	24.6
Floyd County, Indiana	9,820	95.0	35.2	9,861	93.0	31.5
Grant County, Indiana	7,845	93.4	23.4	6,327	92.2	21.7
Hamilton County, Indiana	38,248	98.7	68.9	50,345	97.4	71.0
Hancock County, Indiana	10,368	98.6	29.7	9,516	98.0	46.8
Hendricks County, Indiana	22,787	94.9	33.3	23,510	93.9	47.8
Howard County, Indiana	10,446	89.5	12.3	9,369	86.2	18.9
Johnson County, Indiana	20,453	94.7	34.6	20,217	93.6	43.0
Kosciusko County, Indiana	10,870	89.4	36.6	8,899	93.5	26.2
Lake County, Indiana	60,112	91.8	22.4	61,329	91.9	26.8
LaPorte County, Indiana	13,758	84.7	19.5	13,416	84.0	19.2
Madison County, Indiana	16,463	83.5	21.2	15,102	91.9	23.8
Marion County, Indiana	164,580	87.7	37.3	124,692	88.8	33.6
Monroe County, Indiana	19,957	97.3	49.1	15,701	96.8	60.3
Morgan County, Indiana	7,958	95.5	10.4	8,707	91.6	14.4
Porter County, Indiana	20,423	94.2	25.7	22,705	95.8	31.9
St. Joseph County, Indiana	36,641	92.1	35.7	30,967	89.3	38.1
Tippecanoe County, Indiana	27,971	91.3	48.0	20,848	88.7	40.9
Vanderburgh County, Indiana	25,155	90.1	31.4	22,247	91.3	32.7
Vigo County, Indiana	14,001	89.3	24.7	11,703	91.9	30.2
Wayne County, Indiana	7,374	90.3	19.4	7,587	90.5	19.7

N = Data for this geographic area cannot be displayed because the number of sample cases is too small.

Table C-2. Educational Attainment of the Population, by Selected Counties, 2019—*Continued*

(Number; percent; dollars.)

State/County	Population 45 to 64 years			Population 65 years and over		
	Total	High school graduate or more (percent)	Bachelor's degree or more (percent)	Total	High school graduate or more (percent)	Bachelor's degree or more (percent)
GEORGIA—(*Continued*)						
Walton County, Georgia	25,685	88.2	23.5	15,110	78.2	16.4
Whitfield County, Georgia	24,640	68.8	13.4	14,950	72.0	25.5
HAWAII	346,284	93.3	32.8	269,470	86.8	31.8
Hawaii County, Hawaii	53,042	93.6	27.7	44,025	90.0	34.7
Honolulu County, Hawaii	230,853	93.4	35.6	177,856	85.8	30.7
Kauai County, Hawaii	18,213	95.2	31.0	15,267	88.7	28.7
Maui County, Hawaii	44,168	91.6	25.5	32,320	87.2	34.8
IDAHO	421,776	90.8	27.6	288,617	91.3	28.0
Ada County, Idaho	119,486	94.3	40.2	71,534	95.2	36.3
Bannock County, Idaho	19,792	91.6	23.7	12,334	93.3	29.0
Bonneville County, Idaho	25,488	89.3	27.4	15,593	94.8	30.4
Canyon County, Idaho	50,716	86.5	19.7	32,652	87.6	21.0
Kootenai County, Idaho	42,476	94.4	26.7	32,082	91.7	30.2
Twin Falls County, Idaho	18,565	86.2	20.1	13,994	83.8	22.8
ILLINOIS	3,259,831	89.7	33.9	2,045,361	86.8	27.5
Adams County, Illinois	16,795	91.7	21.3	13,312	89.9	19.6
Champaign County, Illinois	42,330	93.7	42.7	27,885	93.4	38.0
Cook County, Illinois	1,272,487	86.5	36.3	776,131	82.2	29.8
DeKalb County, Illinois	23,460	91.2	34.6	13,699	93.1	28.2
DuPage County, Illinois	250,875	93.9	51.8	148,896	92.6	42.2
Kane County, Illinois	142,139	86.4	32.4	75,940	86.1	29.9
Kankakee County, Illinois	27,968	92.9	18.2	18,716	85.9	15.1
Kendall County, Illinois	31,914	92.6	38.3	14,737	86.0	26.8
Lake County, Illinois	191,042	91.0	47.4	103,327	89.5	41.1
LaSalle County, Illinois	29,586	88.1	15.7	21,282	91.4	14.7
McHenry County, Illinois	89,925	94.3	36.7	46,647	90.5	26.4
McLean County, Illinois	38,444	95.2	44.2	23,444	92.5	35.2
Macon County, Illinois	25,884	94.0	21.4	21,175	91.8	20.6
Madison County, Illinois	72,024	93.5	29.0	46,399	93.0	20.7
Peoria County, Illinois	43,812	93.8	30.5	31,620	90.7	23.4
Rock Island County, Illinois	36,224	88.6	22.8	27,641	89.6	24.0
St. Clair County, Illinois	69,052	90.8	30.1	42,002	88.4	21.9
Sangamon County, Illinois	51,870	94.4	33.1	36,051	91.9	32.2
Tazewell County, Illinois	33,996	94.3	25.4	26,052	94.5	24.1
Vermilion County, Illinois	19,774	89.3	11.7	14,607	91.4	13.0
Will County, Illinois	189,970	92.1	36.0	93,453	90.3	26.2
Williamson County, Illinois	16,623	93.6	29.6	13,178	89.2	23.8
Winnebago County, Illinois	73,618	90.7	23.0	50,631	88.5	25.5
INDIANA	1,705,456	90.1	25.8	1,084,472	88.0	21.7
Allen County, Indiana	91,031	87.3	28.1	56,762	91.3	24.2
Bartholomew County, Indiana	20,069	92.0	31.5	13,926	92.6	25.3
Boone County, Indiana	17,880	94.4	52.4	9,416	95.1	37.7
Clark County, Indiana	30,050	92.2	24.7	19,601	88.4	16.8
Delaware County, Indiana	27,484	91.0	21.4	20,305	92.1	24.3
Elkhart County, Indiana	49,488	83.1	19.0	31,486	83.4	21.0
Floyd County, Indiana	20,945	91.9	29.6	12,963	89.2	19.9
Grant County, Indiana	17,197	89.0	26.2	12,613	84.1	12.9
Hamilton County, Indiana	88,414	97.8	64.0	44,650	94.6	47.3
Hancock County, Indiana	21,263	87.7	31.7	13,327	79.2	13.0
Hendricks County, Indiana	44,356	96.7	38.4	24,479	93.9	27.3
Howard County, Indiana	21,881	89.7	17.1	15,697	92.4	23.2
Johnson County, Indiana	41,346	91.9	29.5	23,720	90.7	21.0
Kosciusko County, Indiana	20,681	83.4	22.6	13,523	84.5	27.0
Lake County, Indiana	128,067	90.5	22.5	82,394	85.4	19.8
LaPorte County, Indiana	30,430	92.0	15.9	19,688	89.1	19.2
Madison County, Indiana	34,608	89.8	16.6	24,609	88.0	16.4
Marion County, Indiana	224,265	86.3	28.2	124,041	86.4	25.2
Monroe County, Indiana	29,166	95.1	39.7	19,781	92.3	41.7
Morgan County, Indiana	20,390	90.3	21.0	11,945	86.6	17.9
Porter County, Indiana	45,512	96.7	29.9	28,481	92.0	22.3
St. Joseph County, Indiana	67,423	90.2	26.0	43,445	89.7	26.4
Tippecanoe County, Indiana	37,314	90.2	35.7	22,470	92.2	33.3
Vanderburgh County, Indiana	45,451	92.9	27.1	31,414	87.6	21.6
Vigo County, Indiana	28,013	93.9	22.8	17,913	92.1	28.0
Wayne County, Indiana	17,452	87.8	17.2	12,721	85.4	16.4

N = Data for this geographic area cannot be displayed because the number of sample cases is too small.

Table C-2. Educational Attainment of the Population, by Selected Counties, 2019—*Continued*

(Number; percent; dollars.)

State/County	Population 25 to 34 years			Population 35 to 44 years		
	Total	High school graduate or more (percent)	Bachelor's degree or more (percent)	Total	High school graduate or more (percent)	Bachelor's degree or more (percent)
IOWA..................	400,299	94.3	36.1	392,097	92.3	35.1
Black Hawk County, Iowa	16,730	94.4	35.7	15,205	93.5	47.6
Dallas County, Iowa...........................	13,700	98.7	65.3	15,777	97.0	66.0
Dubuque County, Iowa.........................	11,724	97.7	46.6	10,739	96.2	39.3
Johnson County, Iowa...........................	21,757	94.6	63.4	18,323	95.6	56.6
Linn County, Iowa	31,159	95.9	37.2	28,206	96.1	36.3
Polk County, Iowa..............................	74,289	95.1	46.5	69,208	91.2	40.3
Pottawattamie County, Iowa..................	10,881	94.9	24.4	11,729	91.3	28.9
Scott County, Iowa.............................	22,407	94.9	34.1	22,621	96.2	38.5
Story County, Iowa.............................	15,877	98.9	57.9	9,638	97.0	58.2
Woodbury County, Iowa........................	13,711	88.7	16.8	13,577	74.7	21.5
KANSAS	377,373	93.0	37.3	362,905	90.2	37.7
Butler County, Kansas.........................	7,131	92.8	38.6	9,689	90.5	35.5
Douglas County, Kansas	17,335	97.4	47.7	14,236	92.7	51.5
Johnson County, Kansas......................	82,070	95.7	58.5	85,318	95.5	60.7
Leavenworth County, Kansas	10,301	95.1	22.2	11,014	94.0	46.2
Riley County, Kansas..........................	12,610	98.7	49.7	7,011	97.2	52.4
Sedgwick County, Kansas	73,745	92.0	34.3	64,319	89.2	33.4
Shawnee County, Kansas	21,735	96.5	33.5	20,383	87.9	29.3
Wyandotte County, Kansas	25,313	86.9	28.8	22,197	73.9	18.7
KENTUCKY	576,692	91.8	30.1	556,896	89.7	29.3
Boone County, Kentucky	15,520	95.2	34.9	18,609	91.0	42.1
Bullitt County, Kentucky.......................	10,543	100.0	23.4	11,319	93.4	25.1
Campbell County, Kentucky...................	13,347	96.0	59.2	11,450	92.2	41.0
Christian County, Kentucky	12,527	90.4	16.5	6,883	87.9	25.1
Daviess County, Kentucky	12,949	86.2	30.6	13,095	87.1	33.9
Fayette County, Kentucky.....................	49,777	93.4	48.3	43,578	92.2	48.4
Hardin County, Kentucky......................	15,126	95.4	22.3	14,568	91.4	29.4
Jefferson County, Kentucky...................	113,270	96.1	45.9	96,390	91.0	38.4
Kenton County, Kentucky......................	24,473	89.0	40.6	21,679	93.6	39.4
McCracken County, Kentucky.................	7,255	86.9	18.0	7,801	88.9	36.0
Madison County, Kentucky....................	11,633	89.7	43.9	11,145	92.8	37.6
Oldham County, Kentucky.....................	6,720	89.9	36.9	9,100	96.3	45.8
Warren County, Kentucky.....................	17,869	91.4	39.9	16,961	85.5	28.1
LOUISIANA.........................	643,422	87.8	28.3	606,785	87.2	27.9
Ascension Parish, Louisiana	18,463	90.9	27.2	18,336	97.8	30.0
Bossier Parish, Louisiana.....................	17,804	91.5	19.0	18,176	83.9	22.9
Caddo Parish, Louisiana	32,347	85.1	21.8	29,268	87.1	22.3
Calcasieu Parish, Louisiana..................	28,579	80.8	16.9	26,020	89.0	27.6
East Baton Rouge Parish, Louisiana	64,420	91.5	41.3	54,403	88.6	37.3
Iberia Parish, Louisiana.......................	9,388	85.3	18.1	8,403	91.1	19.8
Jefferson Parish, Louisiana...................	61,606	91.8	32.6	54,288	90.2	31.0
Lafayette Parish, Louisiana	38,773	94.0	45.3	33,205	90.3	35.5
Lafourche Parish, Louisiana..................	14,110	81.8	23.3	11,587	89.5	16.7
Livingston Parish, Louisiana	20,688	79.3	27.8	19,528	81.1	30.7
Orleans Parish, Louisiana	66,383	91.2	47.1	55,768	88.7	43.7
Ouachita Parish, Louisiana...................	21,516	88.7	29.1	19,275	90.3	29.0
Rapides Parish, Louisiana....................	16,419	87.6	17.5	16,324	82.2	19.9
St. Landry Parish, Louisiana	10,354	74.4	8.9	9,484	79.8	14.3
St. Tammany Parish, Louisiana..............	28,744	91.1	42.3	34,802	90.7	45.2
Tangipahoa Parish, Louisiana................	17,356	89.4	21.5	17,294	85.6	31.4
Terrebonne Parish, Louisiana................	17,381	88.1	23.8	13,885	80.9	11.7
MAINE	164,231	94.9	35.5	153,615	96.3	37.4
Androscoggin County, Maine	12,846	98.7	25.8	13,432	92.3	30.5
Aroostook County, Maine......................	6,660	97.0	20.9	7,042	98.3	21.1
Cumberland County, Maine...................	41,032	96.0	55.6	36,867	98.1	58.2
Kennebec County, Maine......................	14,652	93.2	30.8	13,543	98.0	32.3
Penobscot County, Maine	20,402	93.9	38.6	16,739	96.0	31.3
York County, Maine.............................	26,507	94.6	29.3	23,414	96.1	36.0
MARYLAND	820,575	93.2	43.3	786,924	89.8	45.4
Allegany County, Maryland....................	8,474	91.3	21.1	8,040	91.0	22.8
Anne Arundel County, Maryland.............	80,901	94.4	45.2	78,156	92.9	50.4
Baltimore County, Maryland..................	112,414	96.1	41.6	102,514	91.4	47.5
Calvert County, Maryland	10,840	96.0	21.9	12,128	97.9	45.0
Carroll County, Maryland......................	18,775	96.8	37.0	19,097	97.3	55.1

N = Data for this geographic area cannot be displayed because the number of sample cases is too small.

Table C-2. Educational Attainment of the Population, by Selected Counties, 2019—*Continued*

(Number; percent; dollars.)

State/County	Population 45 to 64 years			Population 65 years and over		
	Total	High school graduate or more (percent)	Bachelor's degree or more (percent)	Total	High school graduate or more (percent)	Bachelor's degree or more (percent)
IOWA.............................	777,033	93.1	27.0	553,575	91.0	23.6
Black Hawk County, Iowa...........................	29,510	91.1	20.7	22,210	93.7	27.0
Dallas County, Iowa.................................	20,348	95.6	46.7	11,309	96.1	37.5
Dubuque County, Iowa..............................	24,788	95.3	28.7	17,821	89.7	24.9
Johnson County, Iowa..............................	30,698	93.5	48.6	18,383	93.7	48.5
Linn County, Iowa	57,978	94.6	34.4	36,529	90.3	24.7
Polk County, Iowa	116,484	91.6	33.2	66,693	91.1	32.2
Pottawattamie County, Iowa.......................	24,567	89.3	23.2	16,718	90.5	18.6
Scott County, Iowa..................................	44,743	93.4	30.5	28,405	87.4	27.1
Story County, Iowa..................................	16,888	97.7	48.6	12,455	95.4	41.9
Woodbury County, Iowa............................	24,138	89.4	25.7	15,461	88.0	20.4
KANSAS	699,807	91.9	33.0	477,996	91.7	30.1
Butler County, Kansas..............................	16,541	95.2	30.1	10,731	92.3	23.0
Douglas County, Kansas	24,651	96.0	47.7	16,116	93.0	41.6
Johnson County, Kansas...........................	151,458	96.6	57.9	90,478	96.3	46.2
Leavenworth County, Kansas	21,286	90.8	28.0	11,998	92.7	33.0
Riley County, Kansas...............................	10,556	95.7	33.8	7,150	95.2	46.7
Sedgwick County, Kansas	122,810	89.9	30.0	76,878	90.3	29.0
Shawnee County, Kansas	45,331	93.2	30.5	33,269	96.2	32.3
Wyandotte County, Kansas	37,466	82.1	16.6	20,669	77.3	15.9
KENTUCKY	1,160,295	87.5	23.5	754,559	81.4	20.8
Boone County, Kentucky	34,819	91.7	28.5	18,480	92.0	25.5
Bullitt County, Kentucky	22,532	89.4	12.8	13,595	73.8	6.3
Campbell County, Kentucky........................	24,555	94.7	36.4	15,439	81.9	28.6
Christian County, Kentucky	12,534	79.6	16.1	9,272	83.8	30.5
Daviess County, Kentucky..........................	25,496	88.7	20.1	17,446	85.5	20.3
Fayette County, Kentucky..........................	73,996	92.6	43.3	44,226	91.3	40.6
Hardin County, Kentucky...........................	28,500	92.0	23.2	16,389	87.7	21.3
Jefferson County, Kentucky........................	195,467	90.6	31.7	127,864	89.1	28.2
Kenton County, Kentucky	42,201	92.2	29.5	24,769	88.8	24.8
McCracken County, Kentucky......................	17,755	91.1	27.4	12,684	88.3	17.5
Madison County, Kentucky.........................	21,151	93.4	28.7	13,155	87.0	25.8
Oldham County, Kentucky..........................	19,088	96.5	41.9	10,021	89.3	39.0
Warren County, Kentucky..........................	29,455	90.0	36.5	16,863	90.8	35.9
LOUISIANA	1,147,800	86.3	23.1	742,194	82.9	22.7
Ascension Parish, Louisiana	29,479	91.8	27.8	16,400	88.2	15.3
Bossier Parish, Louisiana	30,230	92.5	26.0	18,513	93.4	18.8
Caddo Parish, Louisiana	58,647	87.0	22.8	42,950	86.9	27.4
Calcasieu Parish, Louisiana........................	48,780	89.3	24.4	30,859	83.7	22.4
East Baton Rouge Parish, Louisiana	98,906	92.0	31.8	63,648	90.9	31.0
Iberia Parish, Louisiana............................	17,944	82.6	14.8	11,153	81.7	13.8
Jefferson Parish, Louisiana........................	112,047	86.3	25.9	77,091	84.2	24.8
Lafayette Parish, Louisiana........................	50,733	90.1	30.7	33,177	84.5	29.4
Lafourche Parish, Louisiana........................	24,554	78.3	14.9	16,179	66.7	13.5
Livingston Parish, Louisiana........................	33,745	83.9	16.9	18,937	83.3	12.3
Orleans Parish, Louisiana	96,670	86.8	35.1	60,584	83.9	35.0
Ouachita Parish, Louisiana.........................	36,374	85.4	21.4	23,540	84.4	27.6
Rapides Parish, Louisiana..........................	32,109	88.9	17.6	21,615	83.6	22.9
St. Landry Parish, Louisiana	20,464	85.8	12.7	13,893	63.8	10.4
St. Tammany Parish, Louisiana....................	70,421	92.0	32.2	45,049	90.3	31.3
Tangipahoa Parish, Louisiana......................	32,509	85.4	21.5	20,096	78.4	27.1
Terrebonne Parish, Louisiana......................	27,262	81.8	16.8	16,520	71.2	9.7
MAINE	387,328	94.0	31.4	285,978	89.6	32.0
Androscoggin County, Maine	30,038	92.3	25.1	19,521	83.6	21.0
Aroostook County, Maine	19,629	93.5	21.7	16,738	82.5	14.0
Cumberland County, Maine........................	82,154	95.2	49.4	56,357	91.4	42.0
Kennebec County, Maine...........................	36,144	92.9	28.4	25,197	91.4	26.4
Penobscot County, Maine	42,724	95.4	27.2	29,426	87.2	25.2
York County, Maine	60,900	94.3	29.6	43,845	90.5	36.9
MARYLAND	1,616,472	91.6	40.5	959,887	86.5	35.7
Allegany County, Maryland.........................	18,386	94.6	22.7	14,540	82.6	18.2
Anne Arundel County, Maryland...................	154,221	94.3	44.7	86,827	89.3	35.5
Baltimore County, Maryland.......................	216,090	94.0	41.4	144,959	86.5	34.5
Calvert County, Maryland..........................	27,226	95.1	31.4	14,177	94.9	28.3
Carroll County, Maryland...........................	50,193	95.9	35.8	29,178	89.9	28.0

N = Data for this geographic area cannot be displayed because the number of sample cases is too small.

Table C-2. Educational Attainment of the Population, by Selected Counties, 2019—*Continued*

(Number; percent; dollars.)

State/County	Population 25 to 34 years			Population 35 to 44 years		
	Total	High school graduate or more (percent)	Bachelor's degree or more (percent)	Total	High school graduate or more (percent)	Bachelor's degree or more (percent)
MARYLAND—*(Continued)*						
Cecil County, Maryland	13,039	94.0	30.7	12,196	95.1	36.6
Charles County, Maryland	20,003	94.7	28.8	21,957	94.1	32.5
Frederick County, Maryland	32,755	95.0	46.6	36,349	88.8	47.3
Harford County, Maryland	31,957	95.0	40.4	32,228	94.6	46.1
Howard County, Maryland	39,117	96.7	66.6	46,325	94.9	67.1
Montgomery County, Maryland	131,637	91.4	53.4	144,468	88.4	58.2
Prince George's County, Maryland	132,059	90.3	38.0	121,793	82.6	34.0
St. Mary's County, Maryland	14,973	94.8	34.2	14,409	92.4	30.0
Washington County, Maryland	19,772	91.8	27.5	19,253	87.5	25.4
Wicomico County, Maryland	11,366	87.4	33.2	12,370	89.2	30.0
Baltimore city, Maryland	112,273	92.5	47.5	77,086	88.1	38.0
MASSACHUSETTS	992,607	94.4	54.3	849,654	93.0	51.2
Barnstable County, Massachusetts	19,619	97.0	39.6	19,425	91.5	44.0
Berkshire County, Massachusetts	12,954	95.2	35.3	13,456	89.9	42.8
Bristol County, Massachusetts	73,643	93.0	38.5	69,349	90.7	33.0
Essex County, Massachusetts	99,576	92.3	40.5	95,478	88.3	45.8
Franklin County, Massachusetts	8,158	91.9	44.2	8,560	93.7	40.6
Hampden County, Massachusetts	62,850	86.2	29.1	55,090	90.7	31.6
Hampshire County, Massachusetts	16,201	96.6	62.4	15,192	95.6	58.4
Middlesex County, Massachusetts	250,181	96.5	67.4	214,315	95.8	66.0
Norfolk County, Massachusetts	91,608	96.3	66.8	89,756	94.3	64.5
Plymouth County, Massachusetts	57,432	94.8	38.9	58,999	94.2	45.0
Suffolk County, Massachusetts	188,441	95.1	66.7	104,922	91.1	52.1
Worcester County, Massachusetts	108,696	94.0	42.8	100,582	94.0	41.7
MICHIGAN	1,302,017	92.8	34.0	1,174,029	91.4	34.9
Allegan County, Michigan	14,433	95.3	27.2	14,604	91.4	23.2
Bay County, Michigan	12,189	94.9	23.9	12,164	91.7	28.4
Berrien County, Michigan	18,354	91.8	26.3	17,242	93.0	27.1
Calhoun County, Michigan	16,572	91.5	21.8	16,100	88.5	21.9
Clinton County, Michigan	9,518	95.5	37.7	9,411	96.6	44.7
Eaton County, Michigan	14,496	94.4	35.3	12,675	95.0	30.3
Genesee County, Michigan	50,664	92.3	22.5	46,993	89.7	24.2
Grand Traverse County, Michigan	12,064	99.1	46.1	10,647	91.8	38.4
Ingham County, Michigan	41,508	95.3	44.7	34,268	91.5	44.5
Isabella County, Michigan	9,127	91.4	26.8	6,870	90.0	30.2
Jackson County, Michigan	20,163	92.7	29.8	18,814	91.4	24.3
Kalamazoo County, Michigan	34,127	93.7	41.0	32,551	91.6	43.5
Kent County, Michigan	104,524	93.2	41.9	83,776	92.4	38.9
Lapeer County, Michigan	9,677	91.9	22.5	9,567	87.5	23.3
Lenawee County, Michigan	10,879	90.3	14.8	12,184	87.7	25.9
Livingston County, Michigan	21,397	97.7	38.1	22,589	95.1	49.0
Macomb County, Michigan	119,593	92.2	30.4	104,359	91.8	29.3
Marquette County, Michigan	7,623	96.7	41.8	7,554	97.3	39.4
Midland County, Michigan	10,131	96.1	47.3	10,533	96.1	41.7
Monroe County, Michigan	17,660	92.5	24.0	17,673	96.3	29.7
Muskegon County, Michigan	22,270	91.5	17.8	20,035	95.1	25.3
Oakland County, Michigan	168,474	97.1	56.4	156,835	95.9	57.9
Ottawa County, Michigan	34,465	96.5	41.8	36,769	90.8	38.3
Saginaw County, Michigan	24,168	86.0	24.4	20,400	90.0	32.8
St. Clair County, Michigan	18,212	94.7	23.6	17,156	91.4	31.0
Shiawassee County, Michigan	8,055	88.8	19.5	7,782	91.3	28.5
Van Buren County, Michigan	8,817	94.6	24.5	8,639	82.2	26.3
Washtenaw County, Michigan	52,674	96.9	62.6	44,329	94.6	59.0
Wayne County, Michigan	253,346	90.0	26.6	204,189	87.7	28.2
MINNESOTA	765,578	94.7	43.1	730,399	94.1	43.4
Anoka County, Minnesota	47,577	96.1	39.1	49,136	94.2	37.7
Blue Earth County, Minnesota	8,801	96.7	39.1	7,506	97.4	48.9
Carver County, Minnesota	11,399	93.9	53.9	15,204	94.5	59.7
Crow Wing County, Minnesota	7,054	96.8	24.0	7,312	96.5	28.5
Dakota County, Minnesota	54,344	94.9	44.3	59,586	94.3	47.5
Hennepin County, Minnesota	213,168	95.4	58.3	175,820	94.1	56.7
Olmsted County, Minnesota	24,136	93.9	56.6	19,132	98.1	62.7
Ramsey County, Minnesota	92,000	94.6	47.9	70,355	91.2	46.2
Rice County, Minnesota	7,375	98.9	30.7	7,906	86.7	30.5
St. Louis County, Minnesota	23,225	95.5	33.7	23,528	96.7	34.5
Scott County, Minnesota	18,603	95.5	35.5	22,386	94.8	51.7
Sherburne County, Minnesota	12,520	95.6	20.2	14,026	94.8	28.6

N = Data for this geographic area cannot be displayed because the number of sample cases is too small.

Table C-2. Educational Attainment of the Population, by Selected Counties, 2019—*Continued*

(Number; percent; dollars.)

State/County	Population 45 to 64 years			Population 65 years and over		
	Total	High school graduate or more (percent)	Bachelor's degree or more (percent)	Total	High school graduate or more (percent)	Bachelor's degree or more (percent)
MARYLAND—*(Continued)*						
Cecil County, Maryland	29,704	91.1	20.0	16,653	85.8	21.4
Charles County, Maryland	47,629	93.4	28.8	20,605	88.2	24.4
Frederick County, Maryland	69,534	95.3	41.7	39,294	88.3	33.2
Harford County, Maryland	72,565	96.0	35.2	42,286	88.3	30.5
Howard County, Maryland	88,608	95.9	65.3	46,628	92.6	58.1
Montgomery County, Maryland	281,979	91.0	59.6	169,044	89.7	57.7
Prince George's County, Maryland	242,190	88.0	33.7	126,253	83.8	28.3
St. Mary's County, Maryland	30,259	90.9	33.2	15,380	82.9	22.8
Washington County, Maryland	40,805	89.0	21.9	26,370	83.5	17.5
Wicomico County, Maryland	25,266	82.2	30.3	16,726	86.0	28.2
Baltimore city, Maryland	141,926	85.4	25.3	86,265	75.3	23.7
MASSACHUSETTS	1,836,022	91.7	43.2	1,172,293	86.9	35.4
Barnstable County, Massachusetts	61,357	97.2	47.0	67,161	97.2	50.3
Berkshire County, Massachusetts	35,760	92.8	30.6	30,073	91.3	33.2
Bristol County, Massachusetts	158,247	87.4	30.1	98,058	76.4	21.6
Essex County, Massachusetts	218,388	89.9	43.9	138,702	86.9	35.0
Franklin County, Massachusetts	20,350	92.4	30.9	16,308	90.9	40.0
Hampden County, Massachusetts	120,977	88.6	30.0	81,066	81.9	21.2
Hampshire County, Massachusetts	39,819	96.9	51.5	29,362	90.7	45.9
Middlesex County, Massachusetts	420,714	94.1	54.7	252,684	89.5	43.9
Norfolk County, Massachusetts	194,431	94.9	54.8	121,964	90.0	39.9
Plymouth County, Massachusetts	152,625	92.9	38.0	97,281	91.3	33.9
Suffolk County, Massachusetts	171,842	84.4	35.9	98,983	76.8	30.1
Worcester County, Massachusetts	234,361	93.0	36.9	133,813	86.8	28.7
MICHIGAN	2,652,172	92.1	29.0	1,766,409	89.1	25.5
Allegan County, Michigan	31,855	91.1	24.1	20,267	92.0	20.9
Bay County, Michigan	29,177	94.6	17.1	21,387	90.3	22.5
Berrien County, Michigan	40,781	90.5	25.1	30,964	87.9	29.9
Calhoun County, Michigan	34,574	92.9	20.8	24,494	88.1	17.3
Clinton County, Michigan	22,044	95.1	33.6	13,961	93.9	24.3
Eaton County, Michigan	29,179	96.6	30.2	21,358	94.5	23.9
Genesee County, Michigan	110,071	91.9	22.8	73,209	87.2	17.2
Grand Traverse County, Michigan	25,616	96.3	36.5	19,494	91.8	38.6
Ingham County, Michigan	63,382	94.9	36.4	40,447	92.0	39.0
Isabella County, Michigan	14,693	90.1	26.2	9,296	93.3	26.7
Jackson County, Michigan	43,340	90.2	19.5	29,127	87.8	22.5
Kalamazoo County, Michigan	58,972	92.6	36.3	40,433	91.8	34.5
Kent County, Michigan	157,154	91.8	34.1	92,706	88.7	31.3
Lapeer County, Michigan	26,996	92.8	19.1	16,432	91.0	15.1
Lenawee County, Michigan	26,734	91.1	21.0	19,291	90.5	22.4
Livingston County, Michigan	58,484	96.5	35.1	34,335	90.2	26.5
Macomb County, Michigan	245,938	90.9	25.5	152,309	88.3	18.3
Marquette County, Michigan	16,267	93.4	30.8	13,097	95.4	34.3
Midland County, Michigan	22,448	93.9	36.5	15,469	92.5	25.3
Monroe County, Michigan	43,353	92.4	26.6	28,377	84.5	18.6
Muskegon County, Michigan	46,249	92.1	19.7	30,391	90.6	21.9
Oakland County, Michigan	353,397	95.6	47.5	217,490	91.3	38.8
Ottawa County, Michigan	67,106	94.1	36.4	45,530	89.9	27.6
Saginaw County, Michigan	50,744	92.6	19.7	37,154	88.2	17.0
St. Clair County, Michigan	47,544	90.3	17.8	30,992	92.0	21.3
Shiawassee County, Michigan	19,595	94.0	16.7	13,061	90.4	12.7
Van Buren County, Michigan	20,838	90.2	21.6	14,475	85.2	22.4
Washtenaw County, Michigan	82,670	96.4	53.8	53,252	92.7	49.8
Wayne County, Michigan	453,398	88.6	26.2	276,606	84.3	21.0
MINNESOTA	1,429,744	94.2	35.8	921,491	91.4	29.8
Anoka County, Minnesota	96,952	95.2	32.6	51,730	91.0	20.1
Blue Earth County, Minnesota	13,321	95.9	32.6	9,583	95.0	29.9
Carver County, Minnesota	29,692	95.2	53.4	12,880	90.0	37.7
Crow Wing County, Minnesota	17,551	94.7	24.5	14,977	94.0	25.5
Dakota County, Minnesota	113,626	96.6	42.6	63,145	95.3	36.7
Hennepin County, Minnesota	309,675	93.6	47.1	183,735	93.5	42.6
Olmsted County, Minnesota	39,348	95.2	41.0	25,630	92.3	35.8
Ramsey County, Minnesota	125,718	89.4	41.2	81,952	90.5	38.0
Rice County, Minnesota	16,301	93.4	32.1	10,615	95.4	32.4
St. Louis County, Minnesota	51,086	95.3	28.8	39,925	92.8	26.6
Scott County, Minnesota	39,470	95.6	44.4	16,735	88.9	27.1
Sherburne County, Minnesota	25,875	96.0	27.9	11,321	92.5	28.5

N = Data for this geographic area cannot be displayed because the number of sample cases is too small.

Table C-2. Educational Attainment of the Population, by Selected Counties, 2019—*Continued*

(Number; percent; dollars.)

State/County	Population 25 to 34 years			Population 35 to 44 years		
	Total	High school graduate or more (percent)	Bachelor's degree or more (percent)	Total	High school graduate or more (percent)	Bachelor's degree or more (percent)
MINNESOTA—*(Continued)*						
Stearns County, Minnesota	18,913	93.5	31.3	18,991	92.6	30.8
Washington County, Minnesota	30,151	97.3	45.5	36,438	97.0	52.2
Wright County, Minnesota	16,380	98.1	38.9	19,461	97.0	46.2
MISSISSIPPI	368,227	88.5	22.8	379,610	87.5	23.3
DeSoto County, Mississippi	24,222	92.7	30.9	26,139	90.5	33.3
Forrest County, Mississippi	10,535	94.9	25.2	9,217	81.4	18.6
Harrison County, Mississippi	26,102	93.7	22.9	26,382	92.4	18.2
Hinds County, Mississippi	33,303	92.4	34.8	27,897	87.3	28.5
Jackson County, Mississippi	17,585	91.9	23.0	18,809	92.9	25.4
Jones County, Mississippi	8,846	86.7	12.8	8,300	81.2	17.5
Lauderdale County, Mississippi	9,931	75.5	26.8	8,985	81.0	16.4
Lee County, Mississippi	9,246	87.7	29.3	12,116	85.9	34.2
Madison County, Mississippi	13,136	93.0	54.3	15,858	89.8	47.6
Rankin County, Mississippi	22,437	89.9	21.5	21,975	86.7	37.4
MISSOURI	823,722	93.2	35.5	756,709	92.0	35.5
Boone County, Missouri	27,796	94.0	50.3	21,286	97.9	49.1
Buchanan County, Missouri	12,193	89.9	19.5	10,851	92.4	22.7
Cape Girardeau County, Missouri	10,191	96.8	39.0	8,496	89.5	43.3
Cass County, Missouri	13,075	93.2	28.8	13,138	90.8	26.2
Christian County, Missouri	11,900	94.4	27.6	12,347	86.6	36.3
Clay County, Missouri	35,481	96.2	35.0	34,011	94.4	35.8
Cole County, Missouri	10,130	92.1	32.6	10,040	87.3	34.9
Franklin County, Missouri	12,523	92.8	19.3	11,998	93.8	20.6
Greene County, Missouri	41,705	92.7	31.2	33,812	91.5	35.2
Jackson County, Missouri	109,697	92.8	39.4	89,807	92.1	37.0
Jasper County, Missouri	17,395	92.3	24.2	14,992	86.0	30.7
Jefferson County, Missouri	27,721	93.9	26.1	30,441	93.9	24.1
Platte County, Missouri	13,579	99.3	46.6	14,708	95.6	48.5
St. Charles County, Missouri	51,308	96.8	51.2	54,927	93.5	47.2
St. Francois County, Missouri	10,799	92.1	12.5	9,383	84.4	15.8
St. Louis County, Missouri	128,856	96.5	48.5	120,691	95.9	53.1
St. Louis city, Missouri	61,329	94.8	54.6	39,963	93.4	47.3
MONTANA	133,119	94.1	37.5	132,472	95.1	39.5
Cascade County, Montana	10,975	93.8	27.3	9,443	95.3	38.4
Flathead County, Montana	12,378	94.5	51.9	13,517	97.0	40.0
Gallatin County, Montana	19,041	97.9	55.5	14,983	96.7	57.3
Lewis and Clark County, Montana	8,716	98.5	43.0	8,300	96.3	54.5
Missoula County, Montana	18,717	95.7	38.5	16,379	90.3	51.3
Yellowstone County, Montana	21,717	91.9	39.4	21,738	98.6	33.9
NEBRASKA	257,931	93.4	39.4	243,052	92.4	41.5
Douglas County, Nebraska	87,633	92.4	46.5	77,929	90.6	50.4
Lancaster County, Nebraska	43,126	96.7	48.2	40,761	92.0	45.1
Sarpy County, Nebraska	27,109	98.0	37.7	25,989	97.5	50.8
NEVADA	449,055	88.7	24.2	410,321	84.3	26.9
Clark County, Nevada	337,397	88.5	23.8	313,092	84.1	26.6
Washoe County, Nevada	70,847	91.1	31.5	59,214	83.5	34.0
NEW HAMPSHIRE	170,730	94.9	40.4	158,985	94.4	44.5
Cheshire County, New Hampshire	9,137	92.4	34.2	7,739	95.3	38.2
Grafton County, New Hampshire	11,119	94.1	48.3	9,754	96.9	45.0
Hillsborough County, New Hampshire	57,502	93.6	41.2	52,499	93.4	46.5
Merrimack County, New Hampshire	18,504	95.2	38.1	17,547	93.6	46.7
Rockingham County, New Hampshire	37,790	96.5	49.1	36,416	97.4	50.0
Strafford County, New Hampshire	16,863	96.9	39.5	15,395	95.6	38.5
NEW JERSEY	1,148,458	94.0	47.8	1,144,104	90.8	48.3
Atlantic County, New Jersey	30,123	91.9	30.3	31,483	88.3	31.3
Bergen County, New Jersey	108,207	95.3	59.1	123,814	94.3	63.3
Burlington County, New Jersey	56,063	96.2	45.0	55,312	94.1	46.7
Camden County, New Jersey	70,845	94.8	39.5	64,658	92.7	39.0
Cape May County, New Jersey	9,238	97.2	28.0	8,845	91.7	29.9
Cumberland County, New Jersey	22,023	82.9	11.8	19,775	78.0	15.2
Essex County, New Jersey	110,494	92.3	37.2	110,820	87.9	40.8
Gloucester County, New Jersey	34,872	97.7	43.4	37,169	94.5	42.2
Hudson County, New Jersey	141,570	95.9	66.5	107,686	89.3	53.4

N = Data for this geographic area cannot be displayed because the number of sample cases is too small.

Table C-2. Educational Attainment of the Population, by Selected Counties, 2019—*Continued*

(Number; percent; dollars.)

State/County	Population 45 to 64 years			Population 65 years and over		
	Total	High school graduate or more (percent)	Bachelor's degree or more (percent)	Total	High school graduate or more (percent)	Bachelor's degree or more (percent)
MINNESOTA—(*Continued*)						
Stearns County, Minnesota	36,553	92.6	27.9	25,716	83.9	20.5
Washington County, Minnesota	72,565	96.6	47.1	40,140	94.9	37.8
Wright County, Minnesota	35,763	96.0	30.1	18,523	94.7	23.3
MISSISSIPPI	745,023	86.4	22.1	486,804	79.5	21.6
DeSoto County, Mississippi	46,998	90.0	27.9	24,408	87.7	20.4
Forrest County, Mississippi	16,971	90.9	26.9	10,467	85.4	27.2
Harrison County, Mississippi	52,503	87.5	26.5	31,828	86.2	22.9
Hinds County, Mississippi	55,788	91.8	25.5	34,113	78.4	29.1
Jackson County, Mississippi	38,445	90.8	22.1	24,142	85.7	25.9
Jones County, Mississippi	15,146	88.1	22.7	12,331	87.2	18.8
Lauderdale County, Mississippi	19,230	82.7	17.9	12,915	81.3	15.3
Lee County, Mississippi	21,281	82.4	19.4	12,946	80.7	23.4
Madison County, Mississippi	27,244	95.3	49.3	14,419	84.0	44.0
Rankin County, Mississippi	38,415	92.8	30.9	24,321	87.5	30.5
MISSOURI	1,567,788	90.8	29.1	1,057,943	87.6	24.0
Boone County, Missouri	37,948	92.0	45.1	22,375	91.6	43.8
Buchanan County, Missouri	23,475	88.9	21.2	14,187	88.5	14.5
Cape Girardeau County, Missouri	19,801	91.4	32.0	13,029	86.9	28.4
Cass County, Missouri	27,873	94.6	25.8	18,166	94.2	23.0
Christian County, Missouri	21,891	91.1	33.7	13,792	88.9	17.1
Clay County, Missouri	63,952	95.4	32.3	36,070	89.5	26.0
Cole County, Missouri	20,908	95.7	34.9	13,632	89.7	28.7
Franklin County, Missouri	29,760	89.2	21.6	18,590	84.6	16.7
Greene County, Missouri	68,211	91.9	29.4	48,792	90.3	26.7
Jackson County, Missouri	173,239	91.0	29.5	107,972	90.5	26.7
Jasper County, Missouri	28,182	84.2	23.2	19,325	80.3	18.5
Jefferson County, Missouri	64,352	89.7	18.1	34,512	82.2	14.1
Platte County, Missouri	28,121	94.2	44.1	15,471	96.5	37.6
St. Charles County, Missouri	106,797	94.5	38.4	63,307	92.5	28.9
St. Francois County, Missouri	17,027	85.1	15.2	11,275	85.2	12.8
St. Louis County, Missouri	259,512	93.5	46.5	184,375	91.7	37.3
St. Louis city, Missouri	73,444	87.9	27.3	43,268	81.4	26.9
MONTANA	268,450	95.3	31.3	207,909	92.4	30.2
Cascade County, Montana	18,823	92.7	21.2	15,378	90.4	21.8
Flathead County, Montana	27,730	98.2	27.5	20,928	93.2	33.7
Gallatin County, Montana	24,064	99.3	49.3	15,501	96.4	50.3
Lewis and Clark County, Montana	18,750	96.7	43.4	13,692	95.9	41.1
Missoula County, Montana	27,182	98.5	45.8	19,518	96.3	42.5
Yellowstone County, Montana	40,157	93.9	31.8	28,393	90.8	28.7
NEBRASKA	458,492	91.4	30.7	312,295	91.5	25.4
Douglas County, Nebraska	131,607	90.9	38.4	76,854	92.8	32.3
Lancaster County, Nebraska	69,089	91.8	37.1	45,473	92.9	33.2
Sarpy County, Nebraska	44,702	96.0	40.7	22,739	94.3	26.7
NEVADA	778,871	86.0	24.9	498,219	88.5	27.3
Clark County, Nevada	567,799	85.4	25.0	342,659	87.8	27.6
Washoe County, Nevada	118,529	88.4	29.8	79,563	90.9	32.1
NEW HAMPSHIRE	396,888	93.6	35.4	253,147	90.9	34.7
Cheshire County, New Hampshire	21,062	96.1	31.5	15,759	92.2	35.0
Grafton County, New Hampshire	24,395	91.1	38.7	18,912	87.1	39.0
Hillsborough County, New Hampshire	120,458	92.4	35.1	67,143	90.1	32.9
Merrimack County, New Hampshire	44,363	91.6	33.3	28,096	89.4	30.6
Rockingham County, New Hampshire	95,969	96.3	40.1	57,734	94.2	37.5
Strafford County, New Hampshire	33,764	94.6	35.9	20,595	88.0	32.0
NEW JERSEY	2,423,592	91.3	40.2	1,475,075	85.5	32.2
Atlantic County, New Jersey	72,771	89.3	29.2	49,115	82.1	23.6
Bergen County, New Jersey	265,097	94.5	51.6	164,611	87.9	39.4
Burlington County, New Jersey	127,552	95.2	39.4	77,364	90.8	30.7
Camden County, New Jersey	134,264	88.4	31.5	81,659	84.9	27.8
Cape May County, New Jersey	27,053	93.8	35.0	24,821	92.5	31.3
Cumberland County, New Jersey	37,399	83.9	15.7	23,504	78.2	21.5
Essex County, New Jersey	207,875	87.9	34.5	111,075	78.3	31.6
Gloucester County, New Jersey	83,191	93.3	32.4	47,324	87.8	23.3
Hudson County, New Jersey	152,380	83.9	32.2	82,160	66.9	22.1

N = Data for this geographic area cannot be displayed because the number of sample cases is too small.

Table C-2. Educational Attainment of the Population, by Selected Counties, 2019—*Continued*

(Number; percent; dollars.)

State/County	Population 25 to 34 years			Population 35 to 44 years		
	Total	High school graduate or more (percent)	Bachelor's degree or more (percent)	Total	High school graduate or more (percent)	Bachelor's degree or more (percent)
NEW JERSEY—(*Continued*)						
Hunterdon County, New Jersey	12,105	91.6	58.2	14,168	91.1	59.7
Mercer County, New Jersey	45,746	90.2	48.5	46,358	90.3	50.2
Middlesex County, New Jersey	109,141	94.0	51.3	113,602	89.1	52.7
Monmouth County, New Jersey	68,193	96.8	51.9	71,431	92.5	57.2
Morris County, New Jersey	54,285	97.9	63.5	59,988	92.6	63.9
Ocean County, New Jersey	66,955	94.5	41.3	61,538	94.7	38.2
Passaic County, New Jersey	67,982	89.0	33.2	62,606	86.0	31.5
Salem County, New Jersey	6,725	92.9	17.8	7,624	86.3	23.7
Somerset County, New Jersey	35,806	95.4	60.4	42,156	96.6	65.8
Sussex County, New Jersey	15,139	93.9	40.9	16,800	95.0	49.9
Union County, New Jersey	70,617	91.3	39.5	76,781	85.6	42.4
Warren County, New Jersey	12,329	96.3	40.6	11,490	96.5	38.8
NEW MEXICO	278,627	89.1	24.1	261,847	85.0	26.9
Bernalillo County, New Mexico	100,450	89.8	31.8	91,043	88.8	37.3
Chaves County, New Mexico	8,545	76.9	16.7	7,892	74.5	17.6
Doña Ana County, New Mexico	29,722	93.3	31.0	23,907	74.7	22.5
Lea County, New Mexico	8,418	86.3	13.7	10,222	82.9	15.8
McKinley County, New Mexico	11,163	84.9	14.4	8,185	88.2	10.1
Otero County, New Mexico	9,017	90.3	8.9	8,522	77.2	13.5
Sandoval County, New Mexico	18,580	96.9	24.6	18,641	87.0	36.5
San Juan County, New Mexico	16,896	85.9	6.5	15,231	85.2	14.6
Santa Fe County, New Mexico	16,860	89.0	23.5	17,160	85.4	28.8
Valencia County, New Mexico	7,445	85.0	11.1	9,039	85.6	18.7
NEW YORK	2,865,401	92.3	47.2	2,430,106	89.4	43.9
Albany County, New York	40,729	92.3	48.9	35,917	93.2	50.5
Bronx County, New York	227,113	83.7	25.5	180,518	77.8	22.3
Broome County, New York	21,728	94.1	36.4	20,066	87.1	30.3
Cattaraugus County, New York	8,514	92.3	18.2	8,235	90.5	26.1
Cayuga County, New York	8,981	90.4	29.1	9,510	82.5	19.0
Chautauqua County, New York	14,645	89.7	22.3	13,667	88.5	39.9
Chemung County, New York	10,759	89.3	33.2	9,182	90.7	22.5
Clinton County, New York	10,240	92.3	28.0	9,973	89.9	33.2
Dutchess County, New York	34,121	93.3	37.5	35,168	96.8	35.9
Erie County, New York	131,885	94.9	42.7	105,466	94.3	42.2
Jefferson County, New York	18,457	93.1	25.7	12,724	91.7	29.3
Kings County, New York	470,688	91.4	53.1	357,558	89.0	48.1
Livingston County, New York	6,470	93.2	29.3	6,810	94.2	30.1
Madison County, New York	7,364	94.9	17.5	7,342	98.0	26.5
Monroe County, New York	105,912	92.9	47.5	85,563	90.6	45.6
Nassau County, New York	159,711	94.2	54.0	163,814	93.1	55.7
New York County, New York	361,731	96.8	77.0	234,018	93.2	69.5
Niagara County, New York	27,332	92.7	37.9	23,192	95.3	31.7
Oneida County, New York	29,204	91.2	34.3	25,337	88.7	37.6
Onondaga County, New York	60,866	93.3	42.7	52,852	89.9	39.7
Ontario County, New York	12,951	93.7	40.5	11,578	94.3	51.4
Orange County, New York	45,085	95.1	33.6	45,637	91.4	37.9
Oswego County, New York	14,422	85.0	27.0	12,664	93.0	28.6
Putnam County, New York	12,458	91.6	39.1	11,648	89.5	43.3
Queens County, New York	360,026	92.7	47.0	306,325	86.1	38.1
Rensselaer County, New York	22,532	94.8	47.1	18,651	86.7	45.8
Richmond County, New York	63,991	93.4	47.4	59,901	91.2	43.4
Rockland County, New York	37,319	87.8	32.9	37,240	85.9	38.4
St. Lawrence County, New York	12,736	85.0	26.0	11,678	87.1	27.8
Saratoga County, New York	27,893	95.3	43.3	28,041	95.4	56.3
Schenectady County, New York	22,283	94.7	32.7	19,194	92.3	44.4
Steuben County, New York	11,362	90.3	27.1	11,010	95.0	29.7
Suffolk County, New York	177,876	93.0	44.0	172,326	87.9	40.4
Sullivan County, New York	8,817	95.9	25.8	7,751	90.6	27.0
Tompkins County, New York	12,901	97.1	74.0	10,239	97.7	61.4
Ulster County, New York	21,170	90.1	32.2	21,518	91.8	37.9
Warren County, New York	7,884	92.1	36.6	6,593	93.6	38.2
Wayne County, New York	10,441	93.2	29.1	9,890	95.8	26.6
Westchester County, New York	112,485	91.7	50.9	123,477	89.8	57.7
NORTH CAROLINA	1,401,663	90.5	35.6	1,312,661	88.2	36.6
Alamance County, North Carolina	21,436	87.6	29.1	20,590	88.4	24.8
Brunswick County, North Carolina	14,711	82.8	24.2	13,978	94.7	31.0
Buncombe County, North Carolina	37,500	92.9	42.8	34,448	92.7	46.5

N = Data for this geographic area cannot be displayed because the number of sample cases is too small.

Table C-2. Educational Attainment of the Population, by Selected Counties, 2019—*Continued*

(Number; percent; dollars.)

State/County	Population 45 to 64 years			Population 65 years and over		
	Total	High school graduate or more (percent)	Bachelor's degree or more (percent)	Total	High school graduate or more (percent)	Bachelor's degree or more (percent)
NEW JERSEY—*(Continued)*						
Hunterdon County, New Jersey	40,195	96.4	56.6	24,309	93.8	44.5
Mercer County, New Jersey	98,624	88.5	43.4	57,487	86.7	38.6
Middlesex County, New Jersey	219,136	89.0	41.7	127,762	84.1	33.2
Monmouth County, New Jersey	187,259	96.8	49.4	112,384	91.5	38.0
Morris County, New Jersey	146,989	95.6	56.8	86,212	93.1	46.5
Ocean County, New Jersey	149,681	93.3	31.1	138,329	91.0	26.7
Passaic County, New Jersey	128,836	87.1	28.9	75,179	78.5	24.0
Salem County, New Jersey	17,543	89.1	20.0	12,349	83.8	19.1
Somerset County, New Jersey	99,294	94.6	56.7	53,187	91.9	43.9
Sussex County, New Jersey	45,280	95.2	37.0	24,619	92.8	30.5
Union County, New Jersey	150,692	88.8	37.1	81,763	78.0	30.4
Warren County, New Jersey	32,481	94.2	37.2	19,862	88.4	21.6
NEW MEXICO	507,784	86.3	27.1	377,730	83.5	31.6
Bernalillo County, New Mexico	167,601	89.6	34.4	114,901	87.3	37.4
Chaves County, New Mexico	15,153	74.7	17.4	10,319	80.8	18.1
Doña Ana County, New Mexico	45,776	77.6	26.9	35,174	67.6	27.7
Lea County, New Mexico	16,141	70.9	13.0	7,696	64.1	8.7
McKinley County, New Mexico	15,287	79.0	7.0	10,075	64.4	14.0
Otero County, New Mexico	16,065	85.8	16.7	11,805	85.2	15.6
Sandoval County, New Mexico	37,946	93.6	32.1	27,051	93.0	37.4
San Juan County, New Mexico	29,789	89.9	16.6	19,253	79.2	18.0
Santa Fe County, New Mexico	40,886	85.4	40.9	37,936	92.1	51.9
Valencia County, New Mexico	19,695	94.9	23.9	14,097	78.5	19.5
NEW YORK	5,073,259	87.7	34.7	3,295,968	82.1	30.0
Albany County, New York	75,697	92.2	41.9	53,497	90.8	37.5
Bronx County, New York	335,730	73.3	18.0	189,452	62.1	16.7
Broome County, New York	47,834	88.0	24.4	37,046	93.1	23.4
Cattaraugus County, New York	20,692	90.0	21.5	15,462	90.7	20.2
Cayuga County, New York	22,526	88.4	25.1	15,043	86.6	19.3
Chautauqua County, New York	34,728	90.0	23.6	26,015	90.4	23.8
Chemung County, New York	23,619	93.7	24.3	16,015	92.5	22.9
Clinton County, New York	21,739	86.3	22.0	14,053	82.9	23.5
Dutchess County, New York	85,817	93.0	36.5	52,895	87.1	31.2
Erie County, New York	243,624	94.0	31.2	160,007	89.4	25.8
Jefferson County, New York	23,213	92.2	17.6	15,625	85.1	19.8
Kings County, New York	581,919	81.3	31.1	367,378	72.6	25.6
Livingston County, New York	17,072	92.0	25.2	11,602	87.4	20.1
Madison County, New York	19,866	93.1	25.3	13,535	90.8	24.8
Monroe County, New York	192,916	91.9	40.2	132,523	87.5	32.9
Nassau County, New York	378,787	92.4	47.2	246,668	88.9	37.3
New York County, New York	379,199	84.4	52.9	276,603	76.0	48.4
Niagara County, New York	59,543	92.4	26.5	41,077	88.6	21.9
Oneida County, New York	60,586	88.6	25.5	43,705	87.0	22.5
Onondaga County, New York	122,147	92.0	35.3	80,082	90.6	31.0
Ontario County, New York	30,968	93.6	36.8	22,538	93.1	35.9
Orange County, New York	100,304	90.5	31.0	55,294	82.0	25.8
Oswego County, New York	33,190	89.9	20.2	19,606	86.5	17.8
Putnam County, New York	30,819	95.1	41.2	17,285	89.3	28.3
Queens County, New York	598,888	82.2	28.5	368,460	72.2	23.2
Rensselaer County, New York	42,253	93.6	30.9	28,184	89.3	24.5
Richmond County, New York	130,303	90.1	33.3	79,301	82.0	26.7
Rockland County, New York	77,246	91.0	47.6	51,769	88.5	43.7
St. Lawrence County, New York	28,298	91.0	21.8	19,522	83.2	18.9
Saratoga County, New York	66,782	93.8	43.6	43,004	91.6	31.4
Schenectady County, New York	40,168	92.3	34.6	27,349	92.3	31.0
Steuben County, New York	26,382	92.3	23.7	19,008	88.8	20.7
Suffolk County, New York	429,856	91.9	38.0	255,757	89.6	33.3
Sullivan County, New York	23,030	83.3	23.0	14,738	87.9	29.6
Tompkins County, New York	21,169	94.7	51.8	15,389	93.7	46.5
Ulster County, New York	51,278	93.6	31.1	35,976	86.5	32.8
Warren County, New York	18,454	90.8	28.6	15,427	88.6	35.8
Wayne County, New York	26,782	89.6	21.9	17,490	84.8	22.4
Westchester County, New York	268,813	92.3	54.0	168,399	84.8	42.6
NORTH CAROLINA	2,721,818	89.5	31.9	1,750,935	86.0	27.2
Alamance County, North Carolina	43,036	87.3	26.0	29,060	86.2	22.1
Brunswick County, North Carolina	39,355	93.8	29.4	46,735	95.8	30.3
Buncombe County, North Carolina	67,569	92.0	30.4	54,116	90.8	37.5

N = Data for this geographic area cannot be displayed because the number of sample cases is too small.

Table C-2. Educational Attainment of the Population, by Selected Counties, 2019—*Continued*

(Number; percent; dollars.)

State/County	Population 25 to 34 years			Population 35 to 44 years		
	Total	High school graduate or more (percent)	Bachelor's degree or more (percent)	Total	High school graduate or more (percent)	Bachelor's degree or more (percent)
NORTH CAROLINA—(*Continued*)						
Burke County, North Carolina	10,655	87.2	17.3	10,696	71.9	14.9
Cabarrus County, North Carolina	29,190	97.1	43.1	28,102	92.3	41.3
Caldwell County, North Carolina	9,521	88.1	18.4	8,132	83.0	25.3
Carteret County, North Carolina	6,321	90.2	42.4	7,298	89.2	26.2
Catawba County, North Carolina	19,700	94.5	25.6	17,994	90.7	25.3
Chatham County, North Carolina	8,219	85.9	41.8	7,343	77.0	41.9
Cleveland County, North Carolina	10,348	87.5	17.4	11,710	82.4	19.1
Craven County, North Carolina	13,653	92.5	18.8	10,440	87.8	18.2
Cumberland County, North Carolina	56,877	92.8	22.3	40,268	92.7	28.7
Davidson County, North Carolina	20,577	94.9	18.5	16,947	88.3	28.6
Durham County, North Carolina	58,885	91.8	57.5	45,968	83.9	49.8
Forsyth County, North Carolina	50,895	89.6	33.6	46,024	86.2	35.7
Franklin County, North Carolina	8,303	91.9	26.0	8,957	89.3	22.5
Gaston County, North Carolina	30,771	89.4	27.0	27,731	92.7	27.6
Guilford County, North Carolina	74,284	89.4	38.9	64,923	86.8	40.5
Harnett County, North Carolina	20,277	91.8	30.7	17,116	89.6	25.9
Henderson County, North Carolina	12,295	92.6	24.4	13,516	86.6	23.5
Iredell County, North Carolina	21,523	91.7	35.9	22,956	91.1	39.2
Johnston County, North Carolina	24,528	90.6	30.9	29,156	84.3	30.0
Lincoln County, North Carolina	9,722	91.3	20.2	10,177	91.1	38.2
Mecklenburg County, North Carolina	190,917	92.1	50.6	163,146	89.3	50.5
Moore County, North Carolina	12,885	92.8	48.0	11,363	87.4	37.9
Nash County, North Carolina	11,231	84.1	18.2	10,682	91.6	19.9
New Hanover County, North Carolina	31,268	92.2	44.3	30,060	91.8	41.0
Onslow County, North Carolina	34,669	92.9	24.6	21,798	92.2	29.6
Orange County, North Carolina	19,193	95.6	66.4	16,654	95.9	67.9
Pitt County, North Carolina	25,655	88.4	31.7	20,706	87.2	42.9
Randolph County, North Carolina	17,664	89.3	14.4	16,377	76.7	12.5
Robeson County, North Carolina	16,593	83.3	12.3	15,493	71.8	11.5
Rockingham County, North Carolina	9,496	82.0	17.8	10,584	90.3	18.0
Rowan County, North Carolina	17,290	88.4	16.6	16,904	86.9	22.8
Rutherford County, North Carolina	7,488	95.4	11.9	6,718	88.8	18.1
Surry County, North Carolina	8,136	86.7	23.0	7,659	89.6	18.5
Union County, North Carolina	22,847	90.3	33.9	33,879	86.8	46.4
Wake County, North Carolina	163,904	93.3	59.0	165,078	93.2	59.4
Wayne County, North Carolina	15,139	85.4	17.5	13,128	82.7	20.5
Wilkes County, North Carolina	6,621	82.0	13.8	8,315	84.1	16.9
Wilson County, North Carolina	8,102	71.8	15.7	11,302	84.2	19.4
NORTH DAKOTA	117,574	94.6	33.4	96,037	95.3	38.1
Burleigh County, North Dakota	12,696	98.6	41.9	12,564	96.6	37.3
Cass County, North Dakota	32,569	96.0	44.5	24,795	94.5	51.5
Grand Forks County, North Dakota	11,639	95.6	34.2	7,039	95.0	48.1
Ward County, North Dakota	11,984	98.3	30.5	8,446	95.9	38.6
OHIO	1,544,717	92.6	34.2	1,404,148	91.9	34.7
Allen County, Ohio	12,641	88.4	20.1	12,730	89.4	27.1
Ashtabula County, Ohio	11,691	91.0	14.2	10,771	88.6	17.9
Athens County, Ohio	8,239	96.4	50.3	6,609	94.6	35.8
Belmont County, Ohio	7,979	90.8	17.1	8,595	96.3	19.6
Butler County, Ohio	43,989	94.5	35.3	46,862	90.3	38.2
Clark County, Ohio	15,030	90.1	11.6	14,679	89.3	18.3
Clermont County, Ohio	25,812	90.5	27.4	25,161	94.9	42.2
Columbiana County, Ohio	11,341	95.7	19.9	11,233	94.1	22.2
Cuyahoga County, Ohio	177,166	92.5	40.6	143,793	92.4	40.1
Delaware County, Ohio	20,062	98.2	49.6	32,356	98.5	68.4
Erie County, Ohio	9,220	94.9	32.1	7,364	89.2	22.9
Fairfield County, Ohio	17,255	97.9	29.9	22,351	94.5	40.6
Franklin County, Ohio	240,165	94.8	50.0	178,176	91.4	44.2
Geauga County, Ohio	8,296	81.3	29.3	9,653	90.1	36.4
Greene County, Ohio	23,944	96.5	45.8	19,005	97.0	40.5
Hamilton County, Ohio	124,750	94.3	46.7	98,687	94.3	47.1
Hancock County, Ohio	10,590	92.8	38.0	8,723	91.6	28.3
Jefferson County, Ohio	7,355	92.6	26.2	6,489	96.5	27.6
Lake County, Ohio	27,947	96.2	30.4	26,400	91.7	28.2
Licking County, Ohio	19,189	93.1	25.5	22,245	94.4	32.8
Lorain County, Ohio	34,305	91.6	25.6	38,196	88.3	26.4
Lucas County, Ohio	62,740	89.9	31.8	48,757	90.7	27.5
Mahoning County, Ohio	26,018	91.9	29.5	25,619	92.3	32.2
Marion County, Ohio	8,332	91.3	15.0	8,037	89.3	21.4

N = Data for this geographic area cannot be displayed because the number of sample cases is too small.

Table C-2. Educational Attainment of the Population, by Selected Counties, 2019—*Continued*

(Number; percent; dollars.)

State/County	Population 45 to 64 years			Population 65 years and over		
	Total	High school graduate or more (percent)	Bachelor's degree or more (percent)	Total	High school graduate or more (percent)	Bachelor's degree or more (percent)
NORTH CAROLINA—(*Continued*)						
Burke County, North Carolina	27,117	81.8	20.0	18,709	86.1	19.4
Cabarrus County, North Carolina	55,144	89.8	35.4	30,519	85.8	18.0
Caldwell County, North Carolina	25,419	74.4	13.9	16,270	78.3	16.2
Carteret County, North Carolina	20,969	90.5	29.5	17,866	92.5	29.9
Catawba County, North Carolina	44,165	83.5	22.3	29,308	83.1	22.4
Chatham County, North Carolina	20,572	89.6	48.3	18,908	89.2	41.1
Cleveland County, North Carolina	25,575	87.2	19.6	18,607	82.1	18.3
Craven County, North Carolina	23,664	91.7	22.7	20,122	88.4	25.1
Cumberland County, North Carolina	70,818	91.4	25.4	40,648	86.3	23.7
Davidson County, North Carolina	51,234	85.0	18.1	31,367	79.1	15.4
Durham County, North Carolina	73,664	90.7	47.3	44,730	88.9	41.2
Forsyth County, North Carolina	99,921	89.1	34.5	61,594	89.5	29.1
Franklin County, North Carolina	19,552	88.8	22.0	11,796	89.0	19.5
Gaston County, North Carolina	60,898	83.9	22.9	37,745	78.7	18.3
Guilford County, North Carolina	137,178	90.0	38.3	82,932	86.2	30.6
Harnett County, North Carolina	33,268	91.0	24.8	17,135	81.6	13.5
Henderson County, North Carolina	31,877	89.1	29.6	30,925	92.7	35.4
Iredell County, North Carolina	53,088	90.6	30.7	28,554	87.7	20.8
Johnston County, North Carolina	57,550	88.3	22.5	27,663	86.5	15.1
Lincoln County, North Carolina	27,139	92.3	24.3	15,067	93.1	24.4
Mecklenburg County, North Carolina	270,759	90.7	44.3	127,292	88.0	35.1
Moore County, North Carolina	24,636	92.6	35.8	24,639	90.7	38.5
Nash County, North Carolina	25,499	88.4	16.2	17,778	80.2	18.6
New Hanover County, North Carolina	58,527	96.3	46.7	42,432	90.1	38.7
Onslow County, North Carolina	33,473	92.1	23.7	18,736	88.1	20.5
Orange County, North Carolina	35,868	93.8	63.0	21,927	93.4	56.7
Pitt County, North Carolina	40,960	89.7	30.0	24,722	87.0	26.9
Randolph County, North Carolina	39,242	83.1	13.0	26,801	76.9	19.6
Robeson County, North Carolina	32,636	81.9	16.3	20,493	72.7	17.1
Rockingham County, North Carolina	27,217	83.8	10.5	18,739	77.4	15.8
Rowan County, North Carolina	38,865	88.7	19.5	25,179	80.7	14.7
Rutherford County, North Carolina	18,665	83.8	22.9	15,454	85.9	20.3
Surry County, North Carolina	20,108	81.9	18.5	15,302	76.6	15.1
Union County, North Carolina	66,716	93.8	38.9	30,653	89.1	27.3
Wake County, North Carolina	285,169	94.6	54.2	133,664	90.9	41.2
Wayne County, North Carolina	31,425	85.7	16.9	20,799	88.1	18.9
Wilkes County, North Carolina	18,962	84.6	16.2	15,449	79.7	18.7
Wilson County, North Carolina	21,410	85.9	20.1	15,067	78.5	18.9
NORTH DAKOTA	170,587	95.5	28.7	120,177	88.0	23.8
Burleigh County, North Dakota	22,784	97.5	35.9	16,156	84.5	30.1
Cass County, North Dakota	37,440	96.0	37.1	22,724	94.0	33.6
Grand Forks County, North Dakota	13,419	98.4	38.1	9,384	95.5	33.5
Ward County, North Dakota	13,992	95.7	26.7	8,642	96.3	20.3
OHIO	3,057,392	91.7	28.1	2,043,548	87.4	23.6
Allen County, Ohio	25,316	93.3	15.4	18,364	90.4	19.0
Ashtabula County, Ohio	26,640	90.7	14.3	19,234	82.4	9.9
Athens County, Ohio	13,640	89.8	30.1	8,809	92.3	33.0
Belmont County, Ohio	18,679	91.5	14.6	14,068	85.9	18.2
Butler County, Ohio	97,874	93.8	32.5	57,139	86.3	23.6
Clark County, Ohio	36,096	91.5	16.4	26,077	89.8	17.5
Clermont County, Ohio	58,303	93.3	29.3	34,473	83.3	21.0
Columbiana County, Ohio	29,548	92.0	13.9	21,750	87.9	12.0
Cuyahoga County, Ohio	323,660	90.3	31.4	230,060	87.1	27.4
Delaware County, Ohio	56,854	96.1	52.0	29,364	93.2	36.3
Erie County, Ohio	21,186	93.1	23.6	16,038	91.6	20.9
Fairfield County, Ohio	42,445	94.6	29.1	25,343	88.8	19.8
Franklin County, Ohio	303,036	91.0	38.6	162,726	86.6	33.0
Geauga County, Ohio	26,782	89.5	43.7	19,497	91.7	28.2
Greene County, Ohio	41,302	96.3	43.6	29,955	91.8	33.6
Hamilton County, Ohio	200,995	92.0	37.9	129,048	87.5	32.7
Hancock County, Ohio	19,720	91.8	26.3	13,430	91.1	17.4
Jefferson County, Ohio	18,340	95.0	17.3	14,541	89.3	13.6
Lake County, Ohio	64,743	93.2	27.3	47,472	89.4	21.4
Licking County, Ohio	49,176	90.4	28.5	29,209	89.4	20.8
Lorain County, Ohio	84,439	91.3	24.5	59,221	86.6	24.2
Lucas County, Ohio	110,620	88.9	25.6	71,385	87.5	24.3
Mahoning County, Ohio	61,591	91.1	24.0	48,757	88.6	21.7
Marion County, Ohio	18,512	90.4	10.8	11,710	83.7	11.1

N – Data for this geographic area cannot be displayed because the number of sample cases is too small.

Table C-2. Educational Attainment of the Population, by Selected Counties, 2019—*Continued*

(Number; percent; dollars.)

State/County	Population 25 to 34 years			Population 35 to 44 years		
	Total	High school graduate or more (percent)	Bachelor's degree or more (percent)	Total	High school graduate or more (percent)	Bachelor's degree or more (percent)
OHIO—(*Continued*)						
Medina County, Ohio	19,731	96.7	33.4	22,623	95.2	45.0
Miami County, Ohio	12,081	95.0	22.0	13,447	89.6	26.6
Montgomery County, Ohio	73,220	92.8	30.5	60,958	89.9	27.0
Muskingum County, Ohio	9,782	83.2	18.0	9,643	87.6	21.8
Portage County, Ohio	19,221	94.5	33.6	17,097	93.5	35.5
Richland County, Ohio	15,873	89.7	19.4	13,312	92.7	22.3
Ross County, Ohio	10,008	91.8	14.3	9,893	94.8	24.0
Scioto County, Ohio	10,036	87.0	15.0	8,706	91.5	25.3
Stark County, Ohio	43,780	93.5	23.0	43,452	92.4	23.7
Summit County, Ohio	72,374	93.6	33.5	63,979	93.1	38.1
Trumbull County, Ohio	22,668	88.2	22.6	21,655	89.1	23.7
Tuscarawas County, Ohio	10,624	76.6	17.7	10,777	87.2	20.3
Warren County, Ohio	27,007	94.4	43.3	31,861	97.9	51.3
Wayne County, Ohio	13,182	85.1	25.8	12,652	83.4	29.1
Wood County, Ohio	16,444	95.3	43.4	13,648	97.0	41.8
OKLAHOMA	536,999	89.9	25.7	501,516	87.9	29.2
Canadian County, Oklahoma	20,645	93.2	29.7	22,759	82.0	30.1
Cleveland County, Oklahoma	40,032	94.5	40.7	36,695	92.9	40.5
Comanche County, Oklahoma	20,938	90.1	16.5	15,568	94.6	19.8
Creek County, Oklahoma	8,441	90.0	17.4	8,365	86.1	23.2
Muskogee County, Oklahoma	8,885	88.3	16.4	8,638	86.1	22.0
Oklahoma County, Oklahoma	123,419	89.4	34.2	104,521	86.0	36.3
Payne County, Oklahoma	11,731	96.7	43.9	8,248	95.6	43.7
Pottawatomie County, Oklahoma	8,639	94.1	17.8	9,580	87.0	27.1
Rogers County, Oklahoma	11,665	90.4	23.4	11,135	90.7	22.8
Tulsa County, Oklahoma	95,358	90.6	30.3	84,832	88.1	36.3
Wagoner County, Oklahoma	10,497	93.9	19.8	10,693	91.3	24.8
OREGON	594,585	92.8	35.1	578,846	90.2	39.9
Benton County, Oregon	11,360	99.6	43.7	11,142	94.4	61.1
Clackamas County, Oregon	49,935	95.2	34.2	58,826	92.8	43.5
Deschutes County, Oregon	24,463	98.2	36.3	26,366	87.3	36.7
Douglas County, Oregon	12,133	98.3	15.2	12,297	86.5	25.1
Jackson County, Oregon	25,544	89.8	22.2	26,685	86.7	31.3
Josephine County, Oregon	9,990	86.1	9.9	9,196	92.5	15.3
Klamath County, Oregon	8,672	84.9	19.0	7,826	91.2	31.7
Lane County, Oregon	49,618	92.4	31.1	48,154	93.8	36.4
Linn County, Oregon	17,570	89.3	28.1	15,406	85.2	15.7
Marion County, Oregon	48,617	88.6	21.7	44,447	81.0	29.0
Multnomah County, Oregon	152,197	94.4	50.1	136,684	93.1	53.7
Polk County, Oregon	9,448	98.2	28.7	10,173	95.6	39.1
Umatilla County, Oregon	12,317	85.6	14.1	9,081	93.5	17.4
Washington County, Oregon	95,084	95.6	46.1	90,676	91.9	48.2
Yamhill County, Oregon	14,868	78.4	19.1	13,431	90.4	33.8
PENNSYLVANIA	1,704,848	93.1	40.0	1,520,179	92.2	38.9
Adams County, Pennsylvania	11,030	90.8	24.0	10,892	89.1	27.2
Allegheny County, Pennsylvania	188,156	95.7	56.8	147,350	96.4	53.8
Armstrong County, Pennsylvania	7,240	91.9	19.7	7,068	94.7	26.7
Beaver County, Pennsylvania	20,386	95.5	33.0	18,177	95.4	38.8
Berks County, Pennsylvania	52,567	91.1	25.7	48,799	87.3	28.5
Blair County, Pennsylvania	15,336	91.7	26.0	13,637	92.4	37.3
Bucks County, Pennsylvania	69,604	95.5	50.0	76,973	94.8	47.2
Butler County, Pennsylvania	21,837	97.3	42.1	21,579	97.9	53.4
Cambria County, Pennsylvania	13,387	95.3	26.0	13,821	98.1	30.0
Carbon County, Pennsylvania	7,286	95.7	18.7	7,214	95.1	23.1
Centre County, Pennsylvania	22,280	92.8	57.5	17,174	94.0	47.5
Chester County, Pennsylvania	60,414	93.5	56.8	65,560	92.1	61.9
Clearfield County, Pennsylvania	9,695	85.3	25.1	9,466	90.2	18.9
Columbia County, Pennsylvania	6,999	96.3	38.5	7,014	92.9	19.5
Crawford County, Pennsylvania	9,290	87.3	28.3	8,936	87.2	28.0
Cumberland County, Pennsylvania	32,580	90.5	42.4	30,555	93.7	42.2
Dauphin County, Pennsylvania	38,363	92.4	39.8	33,120	88.7	35.2
Delaware County, Pennsylvania	73,056	95.6	43.7	69,595	90.5	48.8
Erie County, Pennsylvania	34,675	94.1	39.1	31,593	91.3	32.8
Fayette County, Pennsylvania	15,846	92.0	18.3	14,213	88.9	25.8
Franklin County, Pennsylvania	17,790	90.2	24.3	19,379	89.4	27.9
Indiana County, Pennsylvania	10,635	89.8	30.3	8,356	92.8	34.4
Lackawanna County, Pennsylvania	26,980	92.5	35.3	24,589	92.7	29.5

N = Data for this geographic area cannot be displayed because the number of sample cases is too small.

Table C-2. Educational Attainment of the Population, by Selected Counties, 2019—*Continued*

(Number; percent; dollars.)

State/County	Population 45 to 64 years			Population 65 years and over		
	Total	High school graduate or more (percent)	Bachelor's degree or more (percent)	Total	High school graduate or more (percent)	Bachelor's degree or more (percent)
OHIO—*(Continued)*						
Medina County, Ohio	51,623	96.9	37.9	33,187	92.2	23.7
Miami County, Ohio	27,814	95.3	21.1	20,768	86.0	19.5
Montgomery County, Ohio	134,016	91.3	29.3	97,622	87.1	27.0
Muskingum County, Ohio	23,850	89.3	19.4	15,862	84.6	15.3
Portage County, Ohio	42,192	91.1	26.3	27,914	90.7	24.8
Richland County, Ohio	32,678	88.7	16.6	23,529	85.7	19.4
Ross County, Ohio	21,628	87.7	13.3	12,931	90.2	15.0
Scioto County, Ohio	20,113	88.2	20.5	13,846	76.7	17.1
Stark County, Ohio	100,255	92.7	22.4	73,406	88.2	19.8
Summit County, Ohio	146,557	92.8	32.5	99,907	90.8	28.7
Trumbull County, Ohio	54,643	90.7	19.7	43,484	86.0	15.5
Tuscarawas County, Ohio	23,975	86.7	19.3	18,656	84.5	16.3
Warren County, Ohio	66,332	96.6	46.7	34,643	90.5	36.6
Wayne County, Ohio	28,717	87.0	19.8	21,296	83.9	19.0
Wood County, Ohio	31,180	96.4	35.9	20,185	91.7	30.3
OKLAHOMA	945,507	88.7	25.8	635,222	87.2	24.8
Canadian County, Oklahoma	34,100	90.8	26.7	19,738	87.1	23.1
Cleveland County, Oklahoma	64,176	93.6	33.4	39,497	87.7	29.4
Comanche County, Oklahoma	26,805	93.1	20.5	14,678	83.4	28.5
Creek County, Oklahoma	19,086	90.3	17.8	13,236	86.5	13.9
Muskogee County, Oklahoma	16,424	87.5	20.5	11,575	83.2	26.2
Oklahoma County, Oklahoma	182,812	86.8	30.0	111,963	89.6	31.8
Payne County, Oklahoma	13,875	90.3	35.6	11,344	94.1	35.3
Pottawatomie County, Oklahoma	18,109	87.5	20.5	11,934	88.0	15.2
Rogers County, Oklahoma	24,857	92.9	25.2	15,472	87.9	21.7
Tulsa County, Oklahoma	153,754	90.2	34.8	96,452	89.5	32.3
Wagoner County, Oklahoma	20,682	90.2	24.2	13,638	90.3	21.8
OREGON	1,047,191	90.6	32.8	767,496	92.1	32.5
Benton County, Oregon	19,646	97.2	65.0	15,005	98.2	57.2
Clackamas County, Oregon	110,965	93.2	36.6	78,411	93.7	34.9
Deschutes County, Oregon	53,541	93.6	41.1	40,670	93.4	38.4
Douglas County, Oregon	28,619	92.5	13.9	29,489	92.1	13.8
Jackson County, Oregon	55,719	91.1	26.5	51,454	92.6	29.7
Josephine County, Oregon	23,202	86.6	17.4	23,012	91.9	19.8
Klamath County, Oregon	17,211	93.4	20.7	14,770	88.0	19.0
Lane County, Oregon	91,057	91.0	28.9	76,032	94.5	34.6
Linn County, Oregon	32,911	89.4	14.4	24,839	86.0	20.0
Marion County, Oregon	81,513	83.7	23.8	56,368	88.7	27.4
Multnomah County, Oregon	197,449	89.3	44.1	113,135	91.7	44.2
Polk County, Oregon	19,949	92.8	33.2	15,731	89.6	28.5
Umatilla County, Oregon	18,123	87.1	21.8	12,589	82.1	20.6
Washington County, Oregon	147,952	92.6	41.7	83,571	94.6	41.5
Yamhill County, Oregon	26,272	88.6	23.2	18,801	92.9	25.7
PENNSYLVANIA	3,414,791	91.7	30.5	2,388,218	87.8	25.2
Adams County, Pennsylvania	29,103	89.4	18.5	21,698	87.8	21.6
Allegheny County, Pennsylvania	313,579	96.2	38.8	235,484	92.9	30.5
Armstrong County, Pennsylvania	19,192	93.9	13.3	14,651	89.2	11.3
Beaver County, Pennsylvania	46,234	92.2	24.0	36,259	89.8	21.2
Berks County, Pennsylvania	111,846	87.0	26.0	74,213	84.7	22.1
Blair County, Pennsylvania	33,051	94.3	20.4	25,977	87.7	17.5
Bucks County, Pennsylvania	186,217	95.5	41.4	120,658	90.3	35.7
Butler County, Pennsylvania	55,433	95.8	36.8	36,141	92.3	26.2
Cambria County, Pennsylvania	36,334	95.0	19.9	30,415	90.0	14.9
Carbon County, Pennsylvania	20,005	90.0	21.1	13,879	82.9	12.6
Centre County, Pennsylvania	37,236	92.8	41.7	24,196	93.1	31.8
Chester County, Pennsylvania	145,849	95.7	57.3	87,354	92.9	43.5
Clearfield County, Pennsylvania	23,473	89.9	16.1	16,862	86.0	9.4
Columbia County, Pennsylvania	17,199	89.2	27.6	12,993	87.7	16.8
Crawford County, Pennsylvania	23,388	92.6	21.9	18,060	85.9	14.2
Cumberland County, Pennsylvania	67,067	94.8	40.0	47,750	89.7	30.7
Dauphin County, Pennsylvania	73,908	89.6	30.9	48,078	88.7	23.2
Delaware County, Pennsylvania	149,108	94.2	39.5	94,617	91.0	34.3
Erie County, Pennsylvania	70,692	90.3	27.0	49,795	89.0	24.2
Fayette County, Pennsylvania	37,754	89.2	16.9	27,622	83.4	14.6
Franklin County, Pennsylvania	41,109	87.1	20.1	31,211	87.6	19.6
Indiana County, Pennsylvania	21,240	94.3	19.7	16,669	85.7	18.1
Lackawanna County, Pennsylvania	55,694	91.9	30.4	42,709	89.2	23.4

N = Data for this geographic area cannot be displayed because the number of sample cases is too small.

Table C-2. Educational Attainment of the Population, by Selected Counties, 2019—*Continued*

(Number; percent; dollars.)

State/County	Population 25 to 34 years			Population 35 to 44 years		
	Total	High school graduate or more (percent)	Bachelor's degree or more (percent)	Total	High school graduate or more (percent)	Bachelor's degree or more (percent)
PENNSYLVANIA—(*Continued*)						
Lancaster County, Pennsylvania	72,220	85.0	31.9	63,869	87.9	35.6
Lawrence County, Pennsylvania	9,614	92.7	23.8	9,121	94.5	31.7
Lebanon County, Pennsylvania	17,218	85.3	28.1	16,213	91.4	29.4
Lehigh County, Pennsylvania	48,117	95.2	31.8	47,166	93.1	35.9
Luzerne County, Pennsylvania	40,091	93.0	19.0	37,911	91.6	25.3
Lycoming County, Pennsylvania	14,697	92.1	25.8	13,223	87.9	27.3
Mercer County, Pennsylvania	11,679	89.4	25.4	11,128	91.7	30.1
Monroe County, Pennsylvania	19,507	91.7	28.5	18,500	93.1	20.6
Montgomery County, Pennsylvania	103,927	97.9	56.5	106,310	95.1	57.4
Northampton County, Pennsylvania	37,466	97.1	39.8	35,066	94.6	35.9
Northumberland County, Pennsylvania	12,302	88.7	18.8	9,948	92.2	25.4
Philadelphia County, Pennsylvania	304,816	92.2	44.8	201,727	88.6	35.0
Schuylkill County, Pennsylvania	17,007	93.2	22.9	17,006	90.3	19.3
Somerset County, Pennsylvania	8,211	94.8	22.2	8,234	90.7	25.2
Washington County, Pennsylvania	22,788	96.3	37.4	24,053	95.3	45.0
Westmoreland County, Pennsylvania	37,573	94.1	35.9	38,213	95.4	36.2
York County, Pennsylvania	56,108	92.0	32.7	54,456	91.9	32.7
RHODE ISLAND	148,180	92.8	42.6	124,433	92.1	38.3
Kent County, Rhode Island	21,669	94.7	42.6	19,328	93.7	36.3
Newport County, Rhode Island	10,494	98.2	54.9	8,771	94.6	58.6
Providence County, Rhode Island	99,832	91.1	39.6	79,149	90.3	32.0
Washington County, Rhode Island	12,383	97.3	54.1	11,843	95.9	53.8
SOUTH CAROLINA	670,757	90.2	31.8	628,604	89.3	32.4
Aiken County, South Carolina	22,696	92.2	33.5	19,546	89.8	26.4
Anderson County, South Carolina	24,362	93.7	28.3	24,418	84.4	27.3
Beaufort County, South Carolina	20,499	92.4	28.1	17,757	91.7	30.9
Berkeley County, South Carolina	34,458	90.0	32.5	29,628	90.2	25.6
Charleston County, South Carolina	67,794	92.3	51.9	55,864	94.8	56.5
Darlington County, South Carolina	7,604	90.1	20.5	6,945	87.6	18.7
Dorchester County, South Carolina	22,772	86.1	25.1	23,370	87.1	40.8
Florence County, South Carolina	18,393	94.5	27.8	16,258	92.3	26.6
Greenville County, South Carolina	73,809	88.4	40.4	66,973	89.1	40.8
Greenwood County, South Carolina	9,287	94.3	25.5	8,853	93.4	18.0
Horry County, South Carolina	39,591	87.4	20.6	39,068	84.1	25.1
Kershaw County, South Carolina	7,488	88.3	25.1	8,544	92.2	28.8
Lancaster County, South Carolina	10,855	89.7	22.9	13,290	90.1	28.6
Laurens County, South Carolina	8,483	90.8	21.7	7,562	88.9	21.7
Lexington County, South Carolina	39,983	90.3	36.6	38,586	87.1	29.3
Oconee County, South Carolina	9,374	90.0	35.1	7,323	82.9	26.7
Orangeburg County, South Carolina	10,013	85.9	17.6	8,714	89.9	17.8
Pickens County, South Carolina	15,649	89.1	30.0	13,058	95.5	29.4
Richland County, South Carolina	60,812	91.7	43.6	51,893	90.8	46.5
Spartanburg County, South Carolina	43,317	91.4	25.7	39,336	87.8	24.6
Sumter County, South Carolina	14,734	95.4	17.2	12,785	88.7	26.3
York County, South Carolina	35,852	92.9	36.5	39,348	93.0	40.6
SOUTH DAKOTA	114,420	92.3	35.0	106,071	93.2	32.6
Minnehaha County, South Dakota	28,841	94.7	41.6	25,716	95.8	38.3
Pennington County, South Dakota	14,411	92.0	30.6	12,788	93.3	35.0
TENNESSEE	934,878	92.3	33.6	849,159	89.4	32.8
Anderson County, Tennessee	9,459	92.9	19.5	8,540	91.1	19.1
Blount County, Tennessee	16,319	87.4	22.4	14,374	91.0	29.4
Bradley County, Tennessee	14,674	87.2	26.4	13,963	90.5	27.8
Davidson County, Tennessee	143,001	93.5	59.2	95,473	89.0	48.6
Greene County, Tennessee	7,719	93.0	20.7	8,099	79.2	19.2
Hamilton County, Tennessee	53,464	94.3	39.3	46,304	87.2	42.1
Knox County, Tennessee	65,315	93.5	37.4	59,474	92.7	42.3
Madison County, Tennessee	11,330	89.7	28.5	11,361	94.5	29.5
Maury County, Tennessee	13,831	88.3	30.1	11,305	92.1	29.0
Montgomery County, Tennessee	37,377	95.9	28.9	29,751	95.2	37.3
Putnam County, Tennessee	10,602	92.3	22.5	9,119	91.7	45.2
Robertson County, Tennessee	9,629	90.7	28.0	9,414	90.6	24.8
Rutherford County, Tennessee	46,301	95.7	34.8	46,709	93.7	32.7
Sevier County, Tennessee	11,866	95.1	18.3	11,096	87.1	25.0
Shelby County, Tennessee	141,059	91.0	32.1	116,569	87.4	34.7
Sullivan County, Tennessee	18,855	97.1	31.4	17,429	90.2	25.7
Sumner County, Tennessee	23,312	92.4	30.3	25,727	86.9	34.9

N = Data for this geographic area cannot be displayed because the number of sample cases is too small.

Table C-2. Educational Attainment of the Population, by Selected Counties, 2019—*Continued*

(Number; percent; dollars.)

State/County	Population 45 to 64 years			Population 65 years and over		
	Total	High school graduate or more (percent)	Bachelor's degree or more (percent)	Total	High school graduate or more (percent)	Bachelor's degree or more (percent)
PENNSYLVANIA—(*Continued*)						
Lancaster County, Pennsylvania	133,188	87.0	26.7	100,346	83.0	23.0
Lawrence County, Pennsylvania	23,834	93.3	21.3	19,069	90.5	20.2
Lebanon County, Pennsylvania	37,402	86.2	18.4	27,345	85.5	14.9
Lehigh County, Pennsylvania	94,368	89.9	29.5	62,998	83.8	23.3
Luzerne County, Pennsylvania	86,411	92.3	23.7	62,864	89.4	18.1
Lycoming County, Pennsylvania	29,886	91.1	22.5	22,685	87.2	23.9
Mercer County, Pennsylvania	30,764	90.0	23.8	24,746	86.8	18.7
Monroe County, Pennsylvania	51,296	90.6	28.7	29,942	90.8	23.1
Montgomery County, Pennsylvania	225,519	95.3	50.8	151,031	92.2	39.4
Northampton County, Pennsylvania	82,831	92.3	29.8	59,755	84.3	23.5
Northumberland County, Pennsylvania	25,119	90.8	14.5	19,569	84.1	11.7
Philadelphia County, Pennsylvania	360,548	83.8	22.6	221,350	78.2	22.2
Schuylkill County, Pennsylvania	40,761	92.3	15.4	29,414	86.4	12.9
Somerset County, Pennsylvania	21,583	91.3	18.1	16,866	81.3	11.3
Washington County, Pennsylvania	58,359	92.6	25.8	43,662	89.9	26.7
Westmoreland County, Pennsylvania	102,746	95.7	28.5	81,054	92.6	24.1
York County, Pennsylvania	123,001	91.4	24.1	80,958	85.3	21.2
RHODE ISLAND	287,184	89.4	33.0	187,155	84.4	29.4
Kent County, Rhode Island	49,649	93.6	31.6	31,733	86.1	24.7
Newport County, Rhode Island	22,960	95.5	45.3	18,870	89.9	40.6
Providence County, Rhode Island	162,894	84.9	26.5	99,704	80.0	23.5
Washington County, Rhode Island	37,566	96.2	48.5	26,936	92.9	44.6
SOUTH CAROLINA	1,328,305	88.9	28.2	935,538	85.6	28.1
Aiken County, South Carolina	44,266	92.1	26.5	33,482	86.5	31.5
Anderson County, South Carolina	53,418	87.2	23.6	37,352	85.4	22.3
Beaufort County, South Carolina	46,664	91.5	37.9	53,766	94.6	51.8
Berkeley County, South Carolina	57,216	91.2	25.5	31,802	89.1	27.3
Charleston County, South Carolina	101,377	92.3	40.9	69,274	89.2	40.4
Darlington County, South Carolina	17,550	88.0	20.9	12,990	71.0	18.6
Dorchester County, South Carolina	41,336	91.1	25.7	23,894	87.2	23.0
Florence County, South Carolina	35,405	89.2	23.0	24,051	78.8	23.6
Greenville County, South Carolina	133,481	89.6	34.2	84,342	86.4	33.2
Greenwood County, South Carolina	16,377	85.8	27.4	14,271	87.3	28.8
Horry County, South Carolina	98,851	90.3	23.1	88,488	90.3	27.1
Kershaw County, South Carolina	18,053	88.4	23.1	12,438	83.6	21.5
Lancaster County, South Carolina	25,564	84.6	19.0	20,754	85.6	24.1
Laurens County, South Carolina	18,374	83.7	17.8	12,470	82.0	20.0
Lexington County, South Carolina	80,503	90.0	31.6	48,337	85.1	22.4
Oconee County, South Carolina	22,226	80.3	23.9	19,005	89.2	25.2
Orangeburg County, South Carolina	22,401	88.2	21.9	17,326	80.2	22.9
Pickens County, South Carolina	30,118	84.1	25.7	21,672	85.5	24.0
Richland County, South Carolina	95,148	92.2	41.9	55,643	89.1	37.6
Spartanburg County, South Carolina	82,590	87.7	28.6	51,888	80.1	24.5
Sumter County, South Carolina	25,472	88.7	23.4	18,180	81.0	19.6
York County, South Carolina	74,061	93.3	35.2	42,057	91.6	28.6
SOUTH DAKOTA	213,739	92.9	29.0	153,799	90.1	24.8
Minnehaha County, South Dakota	47,755	90.4	33.1	26,284	90.4	29.0
Pennington County, South Dakota	29,529	94.4	29.9	21,732	94.8	33.2
TENNESSEE	1,770,960	88.3	27.8	1,138,965	82.9	23.1
Anderson County, Tennessee	21,623	86.8	20.7	16,136	88.0	24.5
Blount County, Tennessee	37,293	89.9	23.4	28,060	84.7	20.4
Bradley County, Tennessee	28,190	82.4	20.7	18,539	81.3	18.3
Davidson County, Tennessee	150,522	87.5	37.8	86,899	87.2	34.4
Greene County, Tennessee	19,504	85.1	22.9	15,049	81.5	13.1
Hamilton County, Tennessee	93,920	91.5	33.5	65,520	83.6	29.1
Knox County, Tennessee	116,419	91.7	38.6	75,775	89.1	32.9
Madison County, Tennessee	25,420	91.3	28.7	17,256	83.9	22.5
Maury County, Tennessee	25,893	89.6	21.6	15,770	86.7	23.8
Montgomery County, Tennessee	42,142	93.1	29.6	20,207	89.1	27.5
Putnam County, Tennessee	19,674	87.7	29.4	13,592	79.3	20.1
Robertson County, Tennessee	19,559	86.6	22.2	11,202	71.9	10.4
Rutherford County, Tennessee	79,410	92.7	30.5	35,755	86.0	23.7
Sevier County, Tennessee	27,613	82.8	15.9	19,998	79.5	20.3
Shelby County, Tennessee	231,219	89.5	32.5	131,153	84.4	27.3
Sullivan County, Tennessee	45,131	86.5	23.4	35,061	85.7	27.7
Sumner County, Tennessee	51,817	92.3	33.3	30,839	86.1	22.6

N = Data for this geographic area cannot be displayed because the number of sample cases is too small.

Table C-2. Educational Attainment of the Population, by Selected Counties, 2019—*Continued*

(Number; percent; dollars.)

State/County	Population 25 to 34 years			Population 35 to 44 years		
	Total	High school graduate or more (percent)	Bachelor's degree or more (percent)	Total	High school graduate or more (percent)	Bachelor's degree or more (percent)
TENNESSEE—(*Continued*)						
Washington County, Tennessee	17,525	94.4	39.9	13,831	90.3	35.2
Williamson County, Tennessee	20,472	98.2	66.4	37,607	93.1	62.4
Wilson County, Tennessee	18,189	95.0	46.2	20,583	92.1	40.8
TEXAS	4,242,661	89.6	32.8	3,959,419	85.0	33.5
Angelina County, Texas	11,218	93.6	20.3	11,724	87.6	12.3
Bastrop County, Texas	10,768	81.9	8.0	10,852	75.7	18.0
Bell County, Texas	60,395	92.1	22.5	47,895	91.2	28.3
Bexar County, Texas	320,679	90.8	27.7	275,076	86.0	32.4
Bowie County, Texas	11,935	84.9	13.1	10,722	86.7	15.3
Brazoria County, Texas	50,522	92.5	29.0	56,179	92.2	40.5
Brazos County, Texas	34,708	90.8	48.8	27,245	92.2	41.5
Cameron County, Texas	53,297	83.0	17.2	50,695	73.2	18.8
Collin County, Texas	132,326	95.1	50.5	164,365	93.4	60.0
Comal County, Texas	18,346	95.4	34.5	18,684	96.0	51.8
Coryell County, Texas	14,311	90.7	17.4	10,017	84.3	10.8
Dallas County, Texas	438,125	87.5	38.4	360,295	78.1	32.0
Denton County, Texas	131,152	94.6	46.7	135,797	90.8	51.8
Ector County, Texas	28,829	87.5	20.5	22,636	84.8	15.5
Ellis County, Texas	22,799	93.6	25.9	25,009	87.3	31.0
El Paso County, Texas	127,347	91.7	27.0	103,617	88.3	25.9
Fort Bend County, Texas	95,950	93.6	42.1	123,841	94.4	56.0
Galveston County, Texas	46,730	91.8	34.5	43,763	91.0	33.4
Grayson County, Texas	15,013	92.9	18.2	17,245	87.6	14.8
Gregg County, Texas	17,275	87.5	16.5	16,068	85.5	21.9
Guadalupe County, Texas	21,605	90.2	24.0	24,010	90.1	33.1
Harris County, Texas	753,587	87.9	35.7	675,273	81.3	33.1
Harrison County, Texas	8,111	81.3	12.0	7,707	95.2	31.5
Hays County, Texas	31,916	91.2	36.4	31,874	88.1	37.7
Henderson County, Texas	9,972	66.5	12.5	8,585	87.9	13.1
Hidalgo County, Texas	116,661	85.1	22.3	108,441	73.4	21.0
Hunt County, Texas	11,527	91.2	26.7	11,735	79.8	16.1
Jefferson County, Texas	36,064	88.4	26.1	32,516	78.2	20.3
Johnson County, Texas	22,064	91.0	19.0	22,980	82.7	17.5
Kaufman County, Texas	17,474	86.8	21.1	20,348	87.9	25.1
Liberty County, Texas	13,088	92.1	13.6	11,441	79.3	15.0
Lubbock County, Texas	46,036	93.3	36.8	37,173	89.1	38.3
McLennan County, Texas	32,274	91.8	26.2	30,589	85.3	26.8
Midland County, Texas	30,621	88.8	30.8	26,628	90.7	31.2
Montgomery County, Texas	75,709	91.1	31.0	85,303	83.4	35.3
Nacogdoches County, Texas	8,211	87.4	14.3	7,123	90.4	38.9
Nueces County, Texas	52,031	90.8	24.7	47,815	84.5	20.4
Orange County, Texas	12,198	90.5	16.8	9,397	91.8	17.4
Parker County, Texas	15,643	85.0	23.9	18,265	90.7	25.2
Potter County, Texas	16,904	76.4	9.6	15,425	76.7	14.3
Randall County, Texas	18,919	94.8	36.8	19,038	94.7	37.7
Rockwall County, Texas	11,625	96.1	39.0	16,699	90.1	40.1
San Patricio County, Texas	8,090	95.6	5.6	9,162	85.5	19.2
Smith County, Texas	32,324	92.3	24.4	27,463	84.7	23.7
Tarrant County, Texas	313,443	90.6	35.3	289,070	87.1	35.8
Taylor County, Texas	20,023	93.6	24.8	16,682	90.3	27.5
Tom Green County, Texas	17,037	95.6	23.4	15,341	95.0	26.0
Travis County, Texas	257,251	93.6	58.6	205,707	87.6	52.7
Victoria County, Texas	10,941	94.3	21.7	11,077	87.5	16.1
Walker County, Texas	8,488	92.2	22.5	9,505	92.6	15.8
Webb County, Texas	38,011	79.0	21.2	35,438	69.8	27.0
Wichita County, Texas	19,284	93.4	18.5	15,371	88.9	25.5
Williamson County, Texas	82,727	96.2	40.0	97,023	94.7	46.7
Wise County, Texas	8,433	96.2	19.1	9,156	82.4	27.9
UTAH	472,153	94.2	35.0	443,692	93.8	38.1
Cache County, Utah	18,773	96.1	32.4	15,531	95.5	44.9
Davis County, Utah	49,580	98.5	37.4	53,145	95.8	40.8
Salt Lake County, Utah	191,572	92.8	38.6	172,233	93.6	39.8
Tooele County, Utah	10,788	95.3	17.1	10,122	95.1	25.3
Utah County, Utah	92,775	97.0	41.0	80,685	94.9	44.7
Washington County, Utah	20,411	93.7	26.6	20,474	90.5	26.5
Weber County, Utah	40,417	91.5	26.4	36,595	93.4	30.3
VERMONT	76,649	93.7	42.2	70,815	93.9	44.5
Chittenden County, Vermont	24,324	94.0	56.2	20,094	92.7	62.4

N = Data for this geographic area cannot be displayed because the number of sample cases is too small.

Table C-2. Educational Attainment of the Population, by Selected Counties, 2019—*Continued*

(Number; percent; dollars.)

State/County	Population 45 to 64 years			Population 65 years and over		
	Total	High school graduate or more (percent)	Bachelor's degree or more (percent)	Total	High school graduate or more (percent)	Bachelor's degree or more (percent)
TENNESSEE—(*Continued*)						
Washington County, Tennessee.....	34,112	93.1	30.8	23,542	79.5	24.9
Williamson County, Tennessee....	65,675	97.2	65.4	32,208	92.8	50.6
Wilson County, Tennessee	38,454	94.3	32.0	23,238	89.9	26.3
TEXAS....	6,831,743	83.6	29.8	3,738,727	80.5	27.4
Angelina County, Texas	19,356	85.4	21.2	14,820	80.5	18.9
Bastrop County, Texas....	21,493	87.4	17.8	13,844	78.8	19.6
Bell County, Texas	73,886	91.0	26.0	40,350	86.5	24.8
Bexar County, Texas....	448,977	83.0	27.1	247,828	78.3	25.7
Bowie County, Texas....	24,556	86.2	19.8	15,683	88.2	24.9
Brazoria County, Texas	94,403	86.6	27.1	44,707	84.2	20.9
Brazos County, Texas	40,476	84.2	37.0	21,652	87.3	43.2
Cameron County, Texas....	88,970	67.9	16.9	58,698	51.4	16.1
Collin County, Texas....	270,858	95.3	53.0	116,575	91.2	43.3
Comal County, Texas....	43,939	93.5	39.7	28,274	90.0	35.6
Coryell County, Texas	16,401	85.8	19.2	8,097	92.2	19.6
Dallas County, Texas	614,563	77.7	29.0	291,744	80.4	31.0
Denton County, Texas....	228,227	93.1	46.1	94,076	89.8	37.2
Ector County, Texas....	33,337	64.9	12.2	15,069	67.1	10.9
Ellis County, Texas	47,985	86.7	26.2	23,269	85.7	20.9
El Paso County, Texas	183,950	79.1	24.1	105,337	58.2	15.0
Fort Bend County, Texas....	208,906	89.4	46.2	94,199	86.0	37.9
Galveston County, Texas	89,459	91.4	29.5	51,182	87.5	26.0
Grayson County, Texas....	34,351	89.5	22.9	25,237	89.6	26.9
Gregg County, Texas....	28,146	83.6	25.9	19,734	91.5	22.0
Guadalupe County, Texas	42,292	90.1	32.2	23,182	84.4	25.1
Harris County, Texas	1,090,713	80.4	30.0	513,916	79.3	30.6
Harrison County, Texas	16,562	81.5	15.7	12,030	87.9	23.0
Hays County, Texas	49,798	91.0	37.1	25,657	92.3	33.9
Henderson County, Texas	21,192	82.0	17.5	19,569	86.2	16.7
Hidalgo County, Texas	169,365	62.5	17.7	98,780	48.9	15.4
Hunt County, Texas	26,489	83.5	18.4	15,313	83.2	21.3
Jefferson County, Texas	62,731	83.1	18.6	36,342	86.7	20.2
Johnson County, Texas	44,773	84.0	17.1	25,007	86.8	23.5
Kaufman County, Texas	31,096	84.5	17.1	16,844	82.2	13.0
Liberty County, Texas	20,162	75.6	11.4	12,581	74.2	10.2
Lubbock County, Texas	63,943	84.0	27.5	38,835	81.1	27.7
McLennan County, Texas	55,919	85.8	24.1	37,843	85.2	27.5
Midland County, Texas	35,418	84.9	27.2	18,299	75.5	28.0
Montgomery County, Texas....	156,291	90.0	37.4	81,311	87.0	28.2
Nacogdoches County, Texas....	13,990	79.9	23.1	9,661	85.4	20.8
Nueces County, Texas	84,616	86.0	26.2	54,358	75.9	21.3
Orange County, Texas	21,512	86.5	21.6	13,519	83.0	17.3
Parker County, Texas....	38,875	88.0	25.4	22,439	87.1	25.2
Potter County, Texas....	26,234	75.9	13.7	15,772	80.0	16.0
Randall County, Texas....	30,795	92.1	31.0	21,743	93.1	37.8
Rockwall County, Texas....	28,134	95.1	41.2	12,854	95.9	38.4
San Patricio County, Texas....	15,382	82.9	19.4	10,320	65.4	12.9
Smith County, Texas....	53,728	85.1	28.4	39,218	88.0	31.0
Tarrant County, Texas....	510,964	86.0	33.2	244,678	85.7	32.1
Taylor County, Texas....	27,766	91.4	28.0	20,403	90.2	26.2
Tom Green County, Texas....	25,837	82.2	23.2	18,282	80.9	24.6
Travis County, Texas....	296,234	88.6	50.2	129,438	88.8	45.9
Victoria County, Texas....	22,329	85.0	18.8	14,914	76.2	20.0
Walker County, Texas....	18,900	80.5	18.1	9,834	87.5	22.6
Webb County, Texas....	55,372	63.4	17.5	27,227	48.6	15.8
Wichita County, Texas........	30,030	86.7	20.6	19,720	84.5	26.3
Williamson County, Texas....	141,466	93.1	40.0	73,213	90.5	40.4
Wise County, Texas....	19,133	82.8	12.3	9,966	85.8	15.9
UTAH....	630,549	91.6	33.8	365,198	93.0	32.1
Cache County, Utah....	19,980	88.8	38.0	12,549	89.3	28.6
Davis County, Utah....	69,835	94.8	35.1	36,591	96.8	31.7
Salt Lake County, Utah....	246,070	89.1	35.7	130,603	91.8	35.1
Tooele County, Utah....	15,603	94.0	24.7	6,675	89.9	24.2
Utah County, Utah....	97,042	95.6	40.7	50,285	94.7	36.3
Washington County, Utah....	35,926	94.1	25.3	39,235	95.0	29.8
Weber County, Utah....	54,680	91.0	26.2	30,495	92.2	25.4
VERMONT	172,893	93.4	36.7	125,201	91.7	35.9
Chittenden County, Vermont	40,201	94.3	49.1	26,225	91.6	42.2

N = Data for this geographic area cannot be displayed because the number of sample cases is too small.

Table C-2. Educational Attainment of the Population, by Selected Counties, 2019—*Continued*

(Number; percent; dollars.)

State/County	Population 25 to 34 years			Population 35 to 44 years		
	Total	High school graduate or more (percent)	Bachelor's degree or more (percent)	Total	High school graduate or more (percent)	Bachelor's degree or more (percent)
VIRGINIA	1,174,655	93.4	42.4	1,128,152	91.3	44.7
Albemarle County, Virginia..................	13,401	96.3	58.3	12,398	96.0	65.1
Arlington County, Virginia	56,528	98.6	84.9	39,677	93.2	75.2
Augusta County, Virginia.....................	8,941	93.4	17.4	9,843	84.7	28.3
Bedford County, Virginia	7,784	91.5	31.6	8,256	93.1	52.3
Chesterfield County, Virginia................	42,956	94.7	32.6	47,669	90.4	43.5
Fairfax County, Virginia......................	151,762	94.6	63.7	165,764	92.0	66.4
Fauquier County, Virginia....................	8,262	85.0	28.2	8,749	93.4	45.0
Frederick County, Virginia...................	11,018	89.2	33.7	10,261	90.6	37.7
Hanover County, Virginia....................	10,583	94.9	40.1	13,850	94.3	56.0
Henrico County, Virginia	48,370	94.6	46.4	44,321	92.1	44.8
James City County, Virginia	8,287	91.2	39.5	8,518	98.8	41.7
Loudoun County, Virginia....................	47,142	95.5	58.0	70,394	94.1	70.5
Montgomery County, Virginia................	13,116	98.0	51.9	10,228	97.0	43.2
Prince William County, Virginia.............	62,432	92.1	38.5	70,935	88.7	46.9
Roanoke County, Virginia....................	10,676	85.6	36.4	11,341	97.5	40.5
Rockingham County, Virginia................	9,441	94.6	34.9	9,779	77.1	28.7
Spotsylvania County, Virginia...............	15,613	92.6	36.6	18,973	91.6	38.5
Stafford County, Virginia....................	18,846	93.1	38.3	23,614	91.6	37.9
York County, Virginia........................	7,500	100.0	44.6	9,085	94.3	56.0
Alexandria city, Virginia.....................	34,911	95.7	65.9	30,343	91.9	70.9
Chesapeake city, Virginia...................	31,442	91.2	29.0	35,640	91.8	35.0
Hampton city, Virginia.......................	21,901	94.6	31.0	15,773	87.9	21.7
Lynchburg city, Virginia.....................	13,066	97.8	49.7	7,447	89.8	28.7
Newport News city, Virginia.................	31,523	91.1	27.1	21,751	95.7	28.5
Norfolk city, Virginia.........................	45,947	93.1	34.0	28,126	90.6	34.3
Portsmouth city, Virginia....................	14,669	96.5	34.8	12,699	93.1	21.3
Richmond city, Virginia......................	50,970	91.9	48.3	28,750	82.4	41.9
Roanoke city, Virginia.......................	14,690	92.9	30.8	12,317	92.5	25.5
Suffolk city, Virginia.........................	12,232	96.1	34.3	12,290	93.1	28.7
Virginia Beach city, Virginia................	72,683	95.2	38.0	61,209	95.1	41.0
WASHINGTON	1,164,010	92.9	39.8	1,032,245	90.8	40.2
Benton County, Washington.................	27,601	91.8	29.1	28,218	88.8	32.3
Chelan County, Washington.................	9,356	86.0	27.2	9,843	79.2	26.3
Clallam County, Washington	8,469	87.9	23.7	8,196	90.9	25.6
Clark County, Washington...................	65,991	92.6	31.1	64,122	92.0	29.6
Cowlitz County, Washington.................	14,615	88.5	15.8	13,288	81.1	15.1
Franklin County, Washington	13,711	73.1	18.5	13,317	72.1	19.8
Grant County, Washington	13,459	81.0	20.1	11,788	74.5	12.4
Grays Harbor County, Washington........	8,591	94.8	15.8	8,168	94.3	21.0
Island County, Washington	11,414	97.1	23.3	9,419	93.0	30.2
King County, Washington....................	416,655	95.9	61.3	342,732	92.9	59.7
Kitsap County, Washington.................	39,866	96.4	23.2	34,074	96.2	36.9
Lewis County, Washington..................	10,043	82.2	15.1	9,216	85.5	20.1
Mason County, Washington.................	8,025	89.9	10.8	7,766	83.6	10.7
Pierce County, Washington	141,209	91.3	25.8	121,601	91.8	30.3
Skagit County, Washington	16,558	88.9	22.0	15,537	87.0	32.7
Snohomish County, Washington............	123,322	94.6	35.9	119,234	91.0	37.4
Spokane County, Washington..............	78,107	93.2	30.7	65,597	94.3	31.8
Thurston County, Washington..............	39,829	92.1	29.6	39,598	94.8	34.8
Whatcom County, Washington..............	29,325	95.3	31.6	28,365	91.1	37.4
Yakima County, Washington................	35,135	79.2	15.4	29,453	71.3	20.4
WEST VIRGINIA	211,267	91.8	24.5	219,899	91.3	27.0
Berkeley County, West Virginia	16,432	92.8	19.8	16,258	89.6	24.8
Cabell County, West Virginia	11,420	90.9	38.3	10,836	95.0	40.0
Harrison County, West Virginia	7,739	90.6	24.9	8,802	93.2	35.0
Kanawha County, West Virginia............	23,198	96.3	30.1	21,672	89.3	29.1
Monongalia County, West Virginia	17,087	86.1	49.7	13,777	97.4	53.5
Raleigh County, West Virginia..............	8,701	94.6	21.5	9,364	97.8	28.0
Wood County, West Virginia	9,068	88.6	20.6	10,127	89.3	28.2
WISCONSIN..........................	737,315	94.6	37.2	714,436	92.9	37.6
Brown County, Wisconsin	34,724	95.8	36.6	33,391	91.5	33.8
Dane County, Wisconsin	85,318	97.1	64.7	74,512	96.1	63.0
Dodge County, Wisconsin...................	10,482	96.7	20.9	10,754	89.6	20.0
Eau Claire County, Wisconsin..............	14,385	96.0	39.3	12,007	96.0	36.8
Fond du Lac County, Wisconsin...........	11,896	95.7	29.5	12,214	88.7	33.3
Jefferson County, Wisconsin...............	9,802	94.8	27.6	10,786	96.2	39.0
Kenosha County, Wisconsin................	22,812	93.6	27.7	21,965	90.7	39.5

N = Data for this geographic area cannot be displayed because the number of sample cases is too small.

Table C-2. Educational Attainment of the Population, by Selected Counties, 2019—*Continued*

(Number; percent; dollars.)

State/County	Population 45 to 64 years			Population 65 years and over		
	Total	High school graduate or more (percent)	Bachelor's degree or more (percent)	Total	High school graduate or more (percent)	Bachelor's degree or more (percent)
VIRGINIA	2,211,014	90.4	39.5	1,358,336	85.6	33.2
Albemarle County, Virginia	27,267	94.4	62.6	21,011	95.1	56.6
Arlington County, Virginia	52,806	93.1	71.2	26,022	90.6	60.1
Augusta County, Virginia	21,653	88.0	16.1	16,837	85.4	19.4
Bedford County, Virginia	23,230	93.0	31.6	17,215	82.3	22.0
Chesterfield County, Virginia	94,104	93.0	44.3	54,227	91.5	36.4
Fairfax County, Virginia	306,975	92.8	62.4	160,629	91.4	57.0
Fauquier County, Virginia	20,259	93.9	37.5	12,055	90.9	30.0
Frederick County, Virginia	25,433	90.7	21.9	15,965	85.7	27.0
Hanover County, Virginia	30,863	94.5	42.4	19,510	91.6	25.9
Henrico County, Virginia	85,073	90.2	41.9	53,784	90.6	39.3
James City County, Virginia	19,812	97.8	53.5	20,017	93.4	59.3
Loudoun County, Virginia	109,110	95.8	64.8	40,150	90.1	46.5
Montgomery County, Virginia	20,283	95.5	47.5	12,818	91.0	38.0
Prince William County, Virginia	120,728	87.8	43.9	48,742	86.9	40.5
Roanoke County, Virginia	25,159	95.2	44.8	20,819	86.8	30.6
Rockingham County, Virginia	21,629	87.0	22.6	16,026	79.1	24.5
Spotsylvania County, Virginia	36,260	92.3	30.7	19,900	88.4	22.7
Stafford County, Virginia	39,694	95.6	42.8	16,315	90.4	37.8
York County, Virginia	18,933	93.9	59.2	11,058	91.5	37.4
Alexandria city, Virginia	38,964	90.5	63.9	18,318	94.2	62.0
Chesapeake city, Virginia	64,149	92.0	34.5	33,514	87.4	27.5
Hampton city, Virginia	32,083	95.2	27.6	21,284	86.3	22.6
Lynchburg city, Virginia	14,377	82.2	35.0	11,755	81.3	31.5
Newport News city, Virginia	39,705	90.4	24.3	24,232	87.0	26.3
Norfolk city, Virginia	49,838	85.9	27.8	28,254	82.4	26.6
Portsmouth city, Virginia	21,968	85.9	14.9	14,288	77.1	18.6
Richmond city, Virginia	52,012	83.6	33.4	31,856	76.6	32.3
Roanoke city, Virginia	25,081	86.5	20.6	16,657	83.2	21.0
Suffolk city, Virginia	24,552	91.8	31.8	13,818	83.6	28.3
Virginia Beach city, Virginia	110,280	93.3	38.5	66,259	93.4	35.3
WASHINGTON	1,886,384	91.6	35.1	1,207,685	91.5	34.4
Benton County, Washington	46,948	90.8	33.1	31,023	91.1	33.3
Chelan County, Washington	19,108	76.7	19.2	14,643	90.1	31.4
Clallam County, Washington	20,008	91.4	26.2	23,599	93.7	33.0
Clark County, Washington	125,192	94.3	32.8	78,374	94.0	31.4
Cowlitz County, Washington	28,559	93.5	13.1	21,012	91.5	18.0
Franklin County, Washington	19,122	70.7	11.7	8,820	76.3	21.9
Grant County, Washington	21,490	74.8	19.6	13,428	80.1	18.2
Grays Harbor County, Washington	21,313	91.5	19.3	16,860	90.2	20.6
Island County, Washington	20,404	92.1	31.8	20,580	98.0	45.9
King County, Washington	556,995	92.5	50.0	304,058	90.4	45.6
Kitsap County, Washington	66,970	97.3	39.5	49,907	94.6	36.2
Lewis County, Washington	21,017	86.6	16.6	17,307	88.2	23.4
Mason County, Washington	17,493	87.7	25.5	15,873	97.9	26.3
Pierce County, Washington	221,502	92.5	27.8	128,251	92.1	29.3
Skagit County, Washington	31,960	90.3	21.9	27,917	92.3	32.6
Snohomish County, Washington	218,361	93.3	31.7	114,567	91.8	27.8
Spokane County, Washington	128,644	93.7	28.8	86,520	93.7	33.5
Thurston County, Washington	74,437	93.6	35.7	51,251	93.0	35.8
Whatcom County, Washington	53,344	95.1	36.4	41,896	94.1	36.7
Yakima County, Washington	53,818	70.6	16.9	35,395	78.7	16.9
WEST VIRGINIA	482,520	88.0	19.6	367,400	80.8	17.4
Berkeley County, West Virginia	32,257	87.4	24.9	17,796	83.5	21.5
Cabell County, West Virginia	22,421	85.5	24.9	17,477	78.9	21.8
Harrison County, West Virginia	18,458	91.7	24.1	13,152	85.8	22.1
Kanawha County, West Virginia	48,193	92.1	24.5	37,757	84.7	22.8
Monongalia County, West Virginia	21,678	96.2	41.5	14,253	82.7	35.5
Raleigh County, West Virginia	19,034	91.2	18.3	15,601	76.4	15.2
Wood County, West Virginia	23,247	88.4	18.0	17,261	89.2	19.0
WISCONSIN	1,543,638	93.1	29.7	1,019,896	90.9	25.3
Brown County, Wisconsin	68,291	91.8	29.7	41,403	91.1	23.1
Dane County, Wisconsin	126,701	95.5	47.6	77,385	95.8	44.6
Dodge County, Wisconsin	25,906	89.5	17.3	16,324	85.5	14.4
Eau Claire County, Wisconsin	23,863	97.2	33.5	18,641	92.9	23.6
Fond du Lac County, Wisconsin	29,024	95.3	22.3	19,578	90.7	15.9
Jefferson County, Wisconsin	23,902	92.7	24.1	14,988	89.4	22.5
Kenosha County, Wisconsin	45,070	93.8	32.4	24,636	86.1	17.5

N = Data for this geographic area cannot be displayed because the number of sample cases is too small.

Table C-2. Educational Attainment of the Population, by Selected Counties, 2019—*Continued*

(Number; percent; dollars.)

State/County	Population 25 to 34 years			Population 35 to 44 years		
	Total	High school graduate or more (percent)	Bachelor's degree or more (percent)	Total	High school graduate or more (percent)	Bachelor's degree or more (percent)
WISCONSIN—*(Continued)*						
La Crosse County, Wisconsin...............................	15,455	95.5	36.2	13,937	99.6	47.1
Manitowoc County, Wisconsin............................	8,655	94.4	27.0	8,615	96.2	17.2
Marathon County, Wisconsin	15,971	94.9	29.4	16,961	91.6	29.2
Milwaukee County, Wisconsin............................	155,678	93.6	38.9	122,128	89.2	34.6
Outagamie County, Wisconsin	26,655	93.1	33.7	24,969	95.3	34.9
Ozaukee County, Wisconsin	9,052	99.3	43.1	9,949	99.1	57.9
Portage County, Wisconsin................................	8,092	97.4	44.9	8,042	93.4	42.6
Racine County, Wisconsin..................................	22,020	86.4	26.2	24,650	86.2	26.5
Rock County, Wisconsin	19,554	92.9	27.5	19,454	92.3	28.1
St. Croix County, Wisconsin...............................	10,059	98.6	45.9	13,233	92.5	37.3
Sheboygan County, Wisconsin...........................	14,438	95.0	35.2	13,052	95.0	32.4
Walworth County, Wisconsin	10,395	92.2	27.5	11,595	91.4	33.9
Washington County, Wisconsin	13,999	99.5	38.0	16,624	96.7	36.5
Waukesha County, Wisconsin	42,515	96.7	48.8	50,118	97.9	64.5
Winnebago County, Wisconsin	23,601	92.6	31.0	21,014	90.3	36.9
Wood County, Wisconsin....................................	8,354	98.4	19.4	8,096	92.1	26.6
WYOMING...	76,649	93.8	26.4	73,671	94.9	33.5
Laramie County, Wyoming.................................	14,095	95.5	26.2	12,167	94.3	33.9
Natrona County, Wyoming.................................	11,124	91.0	15.1	11,009	93.6	26.5

N = Data for this geographic area cannot be displayed because the number of sample cases is too small.

Table C-2. Educational Attainment of the Population, by Selected Counties, 2019—*Continued*

(Number; percent; dollars.)

State/County	Population 45 to 64 years			Population 65 years and over		
	Total	High school graduate or more (percent)	Bachelor's degree or more (percent)	Total	High school graduate or more (percent)	Bachelor's degree or more (percent)
WISCONSIN—*(Continued)*						
La Crosse County, Wisconsin	27,090	96.9	32.5	20,304	92.0	29.4
Manitowoc County, Wisconsin	22,924	94.5	23.5	16,970	91.0	19.4
Marathon County, Wisconsin	37,025	93.9	23.3	24,805	88.7	20.5
Milwaukee County, Wisconsin	220,768	87.5	27.4	132,248	86.2	27.6
Outagamie County, Wisconsin	48,626	96.3	30.0	28,502	90.2	21.9
Ozaukee County, Wisconsin	25,908	99.0	53.7	17,859	97.3	37.6
Portage County, Wisconsin	17,659	94.6	31.8	12,178	94.6	29.9
Racine County, Wisconsin	54,472	91.1	26.8	33,579	92.0	24.5
Rock County, Wisconsin	44,457	91.1	22.6	27,470	92.1	17.7
St. Croix County, Wisconsin	25,181	97.3	37.0	13,297	92.4	37.2
Sheboygan County, Wisconsin	32,222	96.7	26.3	21,032	92.0	22.4
Walworth County, Wisconsin	28,347	90.4	28.2	19,239	92.9	34.5
Washington County, Wisconsin	40,668	94.8	32.2	25,732	91.6	22.1
Waukesha County, Wisconsin	116,614	96.2	46.1	77,845	95.7	32.4
Winnebago County, Wisconsin	44,294	94.2	33.8	28,994	90.8	23.0
Wood County, Wisconsin	20,717	90.0	18.8	15,489	88.0	17.4
WYOMING	140,738	95.2	26.9	98,789	94.0	31.2
Laramie County, Wyoming	24,692	96.4	29.4	16,821	90.7	31.5
Natrona County, Wyoming	19,474	94.3	17.5	12,673	92.1	25.3

N = Data for this geographic area cannot be displayed because the number of sample cases is too small.

Table C-2. Educational Attainment of the Population, by Selected Counties, 2019—*Continued*

(Number; percent; dollars.)

State/County	Educational attainment by race/ethnicity, 25 years and over								
	White alone			White alone, not Hispanic			Black alone		
	Total	High school graduate or more (percent)	Bachelor's degree or more (percent)	Total	High school graduate or more (percent)	Bachelor's degree or more (percent)	Total	High school graduate or more (percent)	Bachelor's degree or more (percent)
UNITED STATES	167,334,031	90.4	34.4	144,203,068	93.3	36.9	27,336,967	87.1	22.5
ALABAMA	2,363,674	88.5	28.5	2,299,781	89.1	28.8	855,485	85.1	19.2
Baldwin County, Alabama	138,720	92.2	33.1	136,823	92.2	33.1	12,416	83.0	31.4
Calhoun County, Alabama	59,838	86.3	21.2	58,922	86.7	21.4	15,807	86.1	15.3
Cullman County, Alabama	56,181	81.2	15.3	54,705	81.5	14.9	N	N	N
DeKalb County, Alabama	42,647	82.9	13.2	41,434	83.4	13.4	N	N	N
Elmore County, Alabama	44,102	90.6	26.2	42,835	91.6	26.8	12,100	86.8	16.5
Etowah County, Alabama	58,563	86.0	18.4	57,912	85.9	18.3	10,262	79.9	9.3
Houston County, Alabama	52,019	89.0	26.6	50,363	90.3	27.0	18,892	75.0	11.5
Jefferson County, Alabama	245,394	92.9	43.8	237,302	93.7	44.7	187,778	89.8	22.0
Lauderdale County, Alabama	56,566	85.6	22.3	55,952	85.6	22.5	6,498	87.6	25.6
Lee County, Alabama	70,441	92.4	42.4	68,498	93.0	42.9	23,399	90.9	29.6
Limestone County, Alabama	55,187	88.6	26.9	54,279	88.8	27.2	9,815	82.7	16.4
Madison County, Alabama	182,039	94.9	46.3	175,158	95.5	46.5	58,456	88.4	35.4
Marshall County, Alabama	60,689	82.4	19.9	55,808	85.6	21.1	N	N	N
Mobile County, Alabama	172,134	88.0	25.6	167,606	88.3	25.7	95,432	88.8	17.3
Montgomery County, Alabama	58,347	95.0	46.4	56,067	96.2	47.0	84,797	85.8	26.0
Morgan County, Alabama	69,641	86.3	26.4	65,834	88.8	27.4	9,636	82.6	6.9
St. Clair County, Alabama	55,115	86.4	14.3	54,592	86.4	14.4	6,643	78.3	6.2
Shelby County, Alabama	122,844	95.2	46.4	119,199	95.6	46.5	18,139	87.3	31.9
Talladega County, Alabama	36,989	83.1	18.0	36,718	83.4	18.0	17,289	76.3	10.8
Tuscaloosa County, Alabama	86,959	90.6	37.0	84,076	91.2	37.6	41,397	86.6	20.5
Walker County, Alabama	40,840	81.6	12.6	40,542	82.0	12.7	N	N	N
ALASKA	336,103	95.9	35.7	316,918	96.5	36.7	15,832	89.4	22.3
Anchorage Municipality, Alaska	130,180	96.8	43.0	120,340	97.4	45.1	10,906	90.9	22.9
Fairbanks North Star Borough, Alaska	48,559	96.8	34.2	45,291	96.7	35.5	N	N	N
Matanuska-Susitna Borough, Alaska	60,697	94.9	25.3	58,608	95.1	25.0	N	N	N
ARIZONA	4,002,380	88.8	31.1	3,010,564	94.6	36.6	214,990	89.9	27.3
Apache County, Arizona	11,619	88.6	18.0	10,128	91.9	20.0	N	N	N
Cochise County, Arizona	77,300	89.0	25.1	54,097	94.1	29.5	3,383	97.4	38.0
Coconino County, Arizona	55,879	97.6	52.4	49,360	98.2	54.5	N	N	N
Maricopa County, Arizona	2,454,787	88.9	33.8	1,847,462	95.2	40.1	163,517	90.1	28.7
Mohave County, Arizona	148,684	87.4	13.4	132,505	89.0	14.6	N	N	N
Navajo County, Arizona	37,327	91.9	19.8	34,297	94.3	21.4	N	N	N
Pima County, Arizona	564,919	90.6	35.4	414,154	95.6	41.4	24,397	84.2	23.8
Pinal County, Arizona	265,817	87.7	20.7	201,967	92.8	23.9	14,625	94.6	14.7
Yavapai County, Arizona	166,082	93.2	28.8	154,171	94.3	29.6	N	N	N
Yuma County, Arizona	121,701	74.2	14.1	51,661	91.6	20.6	N	N	N
ARKANSAS	1,625,302	88.5	24.3	1,550,578	89.9	24.9	292,048	86.9	17.0
Benton County, Arkansas	162,642	89.9	33.3	141,585	93.4	36.6	2,722	94.3	55.9
Craighead County, Arkansas	61,026	89.0	25.9	57,644	92.8	26.6	8,013	93.0	18.6
Faulkner County, Arkansas	66,806	94.0	29.6	65,284	94.1	29.9	8,238	91.7	28.2
Garland County, Arkansas	63,966	92.1	30.5	62,089	92.9	31.0	5,699	91.8	11.5
Jefferson County, Arkansas	20,525	84.7	14.8	20,465	85.0	14.8	23,672	87.8	21.8
Lonoke County, Arkansas	44,628	90.4	20.4	42,849	91.3	20.4	3,166	75.4	4.8
Pulaski County, Arkansas	160,700	92.9	39.3	152,977	94.2	40.5	92,739	90.1	25.2
Saline County, Arkansas	76,299	89.6	27.4	73,922	90.4	28.1	5,599	92.9	17.1
Sebastian County, Arkansas	66,627	88.0	26.5	63,688	88.4	26.8	5,488	79.0	22.6
Washington County, Arkansas	122,132	88.4	34.7	110,842	93.0	37.7	4,341	84.1	16.5
White County, Arkansas	47,961	81.6	16.4	46,918	81.8	16.8	N	N	N
CALIFORNIA	16,461,029	86.4	35.6	11,075,547	95.3	45.3	1,573,950	90.5	27.1
Alameda County, California	489,465	94.0	55.8	402,674	96.4	61.1	128,093	92.8	30.6
Butte County, California	120,306	90.2	32.5	108,903	92.1	34.0	2,553	87.0	17.0
Contra Costa County, California	448,337	93.1	46.7	377,291	96.6	50.9	70,180	94.9	33.0
El Dorado County, California	125,356	93.6	34.8	114,212	94.9	36.3	N	N	N
Fresno County, California	404,313	78.9	23.7	215,743	91.8	33.9	29,298	89.9	20.1
Humboldt County, California	76,827	92.7	32.8	73,784	92.9	32.6	N	N	N
Imperial County, California	74,480	75.9	18.1	14,194	95.0	28.5	N	N	N
Kern County, California	399,382	78.0	17.0	216,434	90.2	23.7	28,074	88.9	15.6
Kings County, California	69,985	71.7	17.2	34,548	91.2	27.2	7,175	80.4	24.0

N = Data for this geographic area cannot be displayed because the number of sample cases is too small.

Table C-2. Educational Attainment of the Population, by Selected Counties, 2019—*Continued*

(Number; percent; dollars.)

State/County	American Indian or Alaska Native alone			Asian alone			Native Hawaiian or Other Pacific Islander alone		
	Total	High school graduate or more (percent)	Bachelor's degree or more (percent)	Total	High school graduate or more (percent)	Bachelor's degree or more (percent)	Total	High school graduate or more (percent)	Bachelor's degree or more (percent)
UNITED STATES	1,802,438	81.5	16.1	13,381,406	87.8	55.6	395,310	86.3	18.1
ALABAMA	16,782	78.9	18.7	47,226	87.6	55.9	N	N	N
Baldwin County, Alabama...........................	N	N	N	N	N	N	N	N	N
Calhoun County, Alabama...........................	N	N	N	N	N	N	N	N	N
Cullman County, Alabama...........................	N	N	N	N	N	N	N	N	N
DeKalb County, Alabama............................	N	N	N	N	N	N	N	N	N
Elmore County, Alabama............................	N	N	N	N	N	N	N	N	N
Etowah County, Alabama...........................	N	N	N	N	N	N	N	N	N
Houston County, Alabama..........................	N	N	N	662	71.3	36.4	N	N	N
Jefferson County, Alabama.........................	N	N	N	8,220	89.1	61.5	N	N	N
Lauderdale County, Alabama......................	N	N	N	N	N	N	N	N	N
Lee County, Alabama...............................	N	N	N	N	N	N	N	N	N
Limestone County, Alabama.......................	N	N	N	N	N	N	N	N	N
Madison County, Alabama.........................	N	N	N	7,658	97.6	64.8	N	N	N
Marshall County, Alabama.........................	N	N	N	N	N	N	N	N	N
Mobile County, Alabama............................	N	N	N	5,172	68.4	36.9	N	N	N
Montgomery County, Alabama....................	N	N	N	5,158	94.5	64.4	N	N	N
Morgan County, Alabama...........................	N	N	N	N	N	N	N	N	N
St. Clair County, Alabama..........................	N	N	N	N	N	N	N	N	N
Shelby County, Alabama...........................	N	N	N	N	N	N	N	N	N
Talladega County, Alabama.......................	N	N	N	N	N	N	N	N	N
Tuscaloosa County, Alabama......................	N	N	N	2,173	81.9	30.6	N	N	N
Walker County, Alabama	N	N	N	N	N	N	N	N	N
ALASKA..................................	66,228	83.5	9.0	30,918	93.3	28.6	N	N	N
Anchorage Municipality, Alaska..................	15,468	85.0	10.8	17,343	97.0	28.8	N	N	N
Fairbanks North Star Borough, Alaska	4,575	90.5	33.8	N	N	N	N	N	N
Matanuska-Susitna Borough, Alaska..................	4,450	82.9	9.5	N	N	N	N	N	N
ARIZONA	198,701	79.5	11.2	172,708	88.8	59.5	9,550	87.7	10.2
Apache County, Arizona	32,395	80.2	8.8	N	N	N	N	N	N
Cochise County, Arizona.............................	N	N	N	N	N	N	N	N	N
Coconino County, Arizona...........................	21,423	82.3	8.2	N	N	N	N	N	N
Maricopa County, Arizona...........................	56,284	84.3	19.2	136,878	90.0	62.6	6,573	85.2	13.0
Mohave County, Arizona.............................	2,756	84.7	8.9	N	N	N	N	N	N
Navajo County, Arizona	30,397	75.1	6.2	N	N	N	N	N	N
Pima County, Arizona.................................	23,309	71.9	9.4	20,859	87.5	54.1	N	N	N
Pinal County, Arizona.................................	15,087	77.7	7.0	5,122	76.1	31.3	N	N	N
Yavapai County, Arizona.............................	3,300	75.5	21.6	N	N	N	N	N	N
Yuma County, Arizona................................	2,014	59.9	16.5	N	N	N	N	N	N
ARKANSAS................................	12,770	83.3	15.3	29,658	90.6	55.7	4,386	44.3	11.8
Benton County, Arkansas	2,926	81.7	12.0	7,890	96.4	78.4	N	N	N
Craighead County, Arkansas	N	N	N	N	N	N	N	N	N
Faulkner County, Arkansas.........................	N	N	N	N	N	N	N	N	N
Garland County, Arkansas..........................	N	N	N	N	N	N	N	N	N
Jefferson County, Arkansas........................	N	N	N	N	N	N	N	N	N
Lonoke County, Arkansas...........................	N	N	N	N	N	N	N	N	N
Pulaski County, Arkansas...........................	N	N	N	6,224	98.2	71.4	N	N	N
Saline County, Arkansas............................	N	N	N	N	N	N	N	N	N
Sebastian County, Arkansas.......................	N	N	N	3,538	89.7	44.7	N	N	N
Washington County, Arkansas	N	N	N	3,196	79.5	46.4	N	N	N
White County, Arkansas.............................	N	N	N	N	N	N	N	N	N
CALIFORNIA	218,013	78.4	16.8	4,363,485	88.5	54.3	106,486	86.5	20.7
Alameda County, California.........................	8,131	81.7	27.0	387,062	88.6	61.5	9,799	89.3	22.5
Butte County, California..............................	N	N	N	5,766	88.1	33.4	N	N	N
Contra Costa County, California	4,473	76.1	20.5	150,242	91.1	59.0	N	N	N
El Dorado County, California.......................	N	N	N	7,619	94.0	50.0	N	N	N
Fresno County, California	8,850	83.6	8.2	69,077	79.9	30.8	N	N	N
Humboldt County, California........................	4,065	87.6	11.4	N	N	N	N	N	N
Imperial County, California..........................	N	N	N	1,866	79.4	44.2	N	N	N
Kern County, California	6,193	68.5	4.7	30,367	83.3	43.4	N	N	N
Kings County, California..............................	N	N	N	4,078	94.0	37.1	N	N	N

N = Data for this geographic area cannot be displayed because the number of sample cases is too small.

Table C-2. Educational Attainment of the Population, by Selected Counties, 2019—*Continued*

(Number; percent; dollars.)

State/County	White alone			White alone, not Hispanic			Black alone		
	Total	High school graduate or more (percent)	Bachelor's degree or more (percent)	Total	High school graduate or more (percent)	Bachelor's degree or more (percent)	Total	High school graduate or more (percent)	Bachelor's degree or more (percent)
CALIFORNIA—(*Continued*)									
Lake County, California	38,241	88.0	16.0	35,079	91.4	17.0	N	N	N
Los Angeles County, California	3,710,088	81.5	36.1	2,062,021	95.4	52.9	581,836	90.1	27.9
Madera County, California	69,646	81.0	16.5	40,600	93.7	21.2	3,111	82.7	4.6
Marin County, California	155,734	95.6	64.0	143,270	97.9	66.7	3,760	87.2	20.1
Mendocino County, California	54,423	85.8	24.1	44,372	91.6	26.9	N	N	N
Merced County, California	92,120	77.0	17.2	53,972	87.9	23.1	6,484	84.1	13.0
Monterey County, California	141,048	86.5	38.4	100,127	95.9	47.4	8,766	90.1	18.7
Napa County, California	74,245	89.2	39.9	57,548	96.0	47.3	N	N	N
Nevada County, California	72,777	96.0	35.1	68,089	97.0	36.3	N	N	N
Orange County, California	1,342,307	89.8	40.8	974,398	96.8	49.2	38,360	92.3	33.6
Placer County, California	238,360	94.5	40.4	211,515	96.2	42.3	5,344	99.3	46.5
Riverside County, California	1,028,768	86.5	24.7	650,253	94.7	31.1	109,723	92.0	24.8
Sacramento County, California	625,484	92.2	32.2	516,330	95.0	34.7	98,867	92.0	24.8
San Bernardino County, California	886,106	81.2	20.7	444,396	92.5	29.0	115,703	88.5	24.5
San Diego County, California	1,653,225	88.4	40.2	1,134,118	96.2	49.9	108,728	91.4	25.4
San Francisco County, California	332,778	96.9	74.9	297,090	98.5	78.5	35,155	85.3	35.0
San Joaquin County, California	285,583	80.4	18.1	174,975	92.6	24.3	35,953	86.7	16.7
San Luis Obispo County, California	167,684	92.0	38.6	139,836	95.5	42.2	3,195	90.5	6.5
San Mateo County, California	286,281	93.1	54.9	229,266	97.3	61.4	13,724	95.1	37.5
Santa Barbara County, California	219,017	82.7	35.6	141,498	97.0	48.9	6,806	88.5	39.1
Santa Clara County, California	624,654	90.6	51.6	454,730	97.1	62.3	33,240	91.7	38.7
Santa Cruz County, California	146,553	90.6	46.9	115,677	97.8	53.8	N	N	N
Shasta County, California	112,754	93.7	21.9	105,803	94.3	21.9	N	N	N
Solano County, California	172,413	89.7	27.9	129,137	95.2	31.6	44,030	92.8	26.1
Sonoma County, California	280,178	94.4	42.2	248,671	96.5	44.6	5,793	84.8	27.5
Stanislaus County, California	282,823	80.7	16.2	164,814	90.6	20.9	8,616	83.0	12.6
Sutter County, California	44,105	81.6	20.4	31,920	92.2	25.2	N	N	N
Tehama County, California	39,649	84.2	17.1	32,929	90.4	20.6	N	N	N
Tulare County, California	187,119	77.0	15.3	95,595	91.2	23.9	3,482	92.7	24.4
Ventura County, California	469,448	86.4	34.0	291,180	97.1	45.6	10,854	95.4	40.2
Yolo County, California	99,532	88.9	37.8	68,360	95.9	48.0	3,370	94.7	25.3
Yuba County, California	40,810	80.3	17.3	29,981	88.4	18.5	N	N	N
COLORADO	3,406,342	93.4	44.3	2,877,914	96.8	49.0	155,881	92.4	27.6
Adams County, Colorado	274,908	86.1	26.1	188,011	94.8	33.7	10,871	93.2	23.7
Arapahoe County, Colorado	334,982	94.3	47.8	292,549	97.0	51.7	47,670	95.6	29.3
Boulder County, Colorado	198,162	95.2	65.8	177,031	98.3	70.1	N	N	N
Broomfield County, Colorado	43,216	97.8	58.3	39,176	99.1	60.7	N	N	N
Denver County, Colorado	421,739	92.1	57.4	325,238	97.9	67.9	43,287	89.6	26.6
Douglas County, Colorado	209,457	98.1	58.6	195,387	98.3	59.3	3,866	89.5	34.0
El Paso County, Colorado	387,839	96.1	41.2	345,451	97.2	43.6	28,532	97.3	29.4
Jefferson County, Colorado	390,228	94.8	48.0	345,195	96.9	51.3	4,278	82.5	47.1
Larimer County, Colorado	221,645	96.8	49.2	203,904	97.3	50.6	N	N	N
Mesa County, Colorado	102,008	91.4	30.3	91,340	92.4	32.9	N	N	N
Pueblo County, Colorado	97,095	93.2	25.1	66,396	96.3	29.5	N	N	N
Weld County, Colorado	188,251	89.3	30.9	148,702	95.6	36.0	2,223	81.4	9.2
CONNECTICUT	1,939,577	92.9	42.6	1,748,083	94.6	44.9	257,234	86.3	21.7
Fairfield County, Connecticut	482,513	93.3	54.7	415,114	96.1	59.6	74,730	83.1	22.1
Hartford County, Connecticut	451,295	92.9	42.3	403,824	94.5	44.7	81,380	88.7	22.6
Litchfield County, Connecticut	126,914	94.0	35.7	120,984	94.9	35.7	N	N	N
Middlesex County, Connecticut	105,819	94.7	43.8	103,161	94.7	43.6	6,176	80.9	34.0
New Haven County, Connecticut	452,916	91.2	37.7	401,579	93.4	40.5	77,215	87.0	20.3
New London County, Connecticut	156,675	94.7	35.3	148,644	95.7	36.2	10,529	89.3	15.6
Tolland County, Connecticut	87,471	94.4	40.6	83,809	95.3	40.9	N	N	N
Windham County, Connecticut	75,974	89.9	24.7	70,968	90.4	25.6	N	N	N
DELAWARE	490,907	90.8	34.6	457,913	93.0	36.1	145,150	90.6	24.6
Kent County, Delaware	85,086	88.2	25.4	79,163	89.0	26.3	29,995	89.1	23.6
New Castle County, Delaware	255,419	92.0	38.5	235,157	94.7	40.4	96,651	92.8	26.8
Sussex County, Delaware	150,402	90.3	33.3	143,593	92.3	34.3	18,504	81.2	14.5
DISTRICT OF COLUMBIA	230,095	98.2	89.3	204,162	99.5	92.1	220,748	86.5	28.1
District of Columbia, District of Columbia	230,095	98.2	89.3	204,162	99.5	92.1	220,748	86.5	28.1

N = Data for this geographic area cannot be displayed because the number of sample cases is too small.

Table C-2. Educational Attainment of the Population, by Selected Counties, 2019—*Continued*

(Number; percent; dollars.)

| | Educational attainment by race/ethnicity, 25 years and over | | | | | | | | |
| | American Indian or Alaska Native alone | | | Asian alone | | | Native Hawaiian or Other Pacific Islander alone | | |
State/County	Total	High school graduate or more (percent)	Bachelor's degree or more (percent)	Total	High school graduate or more (percent)	Bachelor's degree or more (percent)	Total	High school graduate or more (percent)	Bachelor's degree or more (percent)
CALIFORNIA—(*Continued*)									
Lake County, California	N	N	N	N	N	N	N	N	N
Los Angeles County, California	56,226	68.5	15.9	1,142,812	89.1	53.6	18,109	87.6	22.9
Madera County, California	N	N	N	3,005	54.8	16.7	N	N	N
Marin County, California	N	N	N	12,554	92.7	60.3	N	N	N
Mendocino County, California	2,205	65.3	6.9	N	N	N	N	N	N
Merced County, California	1,957	94.1	8.9	13,532	82.5	34.7	N	N	N
Monterey County, California	N	N	N	20,321	89.3	36.7	N	N	N
Napa County, California	N	N	N	7,606	87.2	37.8	N	N	N
Nevada County, California	N	N	N	N	N	N	N	N	N
Orange County, California	8,987	80.0	28.0	495,753	89.1	56.4	6,563	90.9	26.0
Placer County, California	N	N	N	22,536	92.5	67.6	N	N	N
Riverside County, California	14,067	85.1	19.2	121,797	89.2	47.1	5,807	85.3	21.0
Sacramento County, California	6,839	87.8	18.9	176,710	84.3	41.9	13,042	79.8	13.9
San Bernardino County, California	10,667	85.6	14.3	115,812	92.6	56.6	5,816	92.0	12.5
San Diego County, California	16,619	88.6	15.2	298,565	90.1	52.4	9,429	87.2	30.6
San Francisco County, California	N	N	N	252,800	79.3	48.8	N	N	N
San Joaquin County, California	3,424	76.1	16.8	82,367	81.7	35.5	3,636	94.9	25.0
San Luis Obispo County, California	2,483	76.3	31.4	6,733	84.8	52.2	N	N	N
San Mateo County, California	2,703	71.3	20.7	178,711	93.4	60.9	6,169	77.7	18.6
Santa Barbara County, California	3,201	77.9	20.5	14,547	92.3	55.5	N	N	N
Santa Clara County, California	5,442	76.4	18.3	536,745	90.9	65.6	4,661	97.3	14.4
Santa Cruz County, California	N	N	N	8,034	96.7	54.3	N	N	N
Shasta County, California	N	N	N	3,940	88.5	41.6	N	N	N
Solano County, California	N	N	N	53,144	91.1	40.2	2,843	88.1	14.0
Sonoma County, California	N	N	N	15,083	86.8	46.7	N	N	N
Stanislaus County, California	2,432	87.7	29.9	22,160	83.3	37.9	N	N	N
Sutter County, California	N	N	N	10,839	66.6	25.5	N	N	N
Tehama County, California	N	N	N	N	N	N	N	N	N
Tulare County, California	5,690	78.7	22.8	11,383	71.5	27.7	N	N	N
Ventura County, California	3,295	65.5	9.0	48,430	95.8	57.4	N	N	N
Yolo County, California	N	N	N	15,798	92.2	64.5	N	N	N
Yuba County, California	N	N	N	2,718	77.9	21.7	N	N	N
COLORADO	38,549	84.1	22.0	134,942	90.0	53.4	5,685	60.5	16.9
Adams County, Colorado	3,426	67.1	18.6	14,213	84.0	35.6	N	N	N
Arapahoe County, Colorado	3,609	81.9	16.4	29,326	86.2	50.0	N	N	N
Boulder County, Colorado	N	N	N	10,233	95.7	70.3	N	N	N
Broomfield County, Colorado	N	N	N	3,618	92.1	59.2	N	N	N
Denver County, Colorado	3,466	97.5	31.2	21,027	88.8	60.2	N	N	N
Douglas County, Colorado	N	N	N	12,831	97.1	69.8	N	N	N
El Paso County, Colorado	4,921	79.3	26.1	14,216	92.5	42.9	N	N	N
Jefferson County, Colorado	3,074	100.0	29.9	12,172	91.6	50.5	N	N	N
Larimer County, Colorado	N	N	N	4,385	90.9	61.8	N	N	N
Mesa County, Colorado	N	N	N	N	N	N	N	N	N
Pueblo County, Colorado	4,250	70.4	9.6	N	N	N	N	N	N
Weld County, Colorado	N	N	N	3,407	93.8	51.3	N	N	N
CONNECTICUT	5,100	90.3	24.7	114,306	90.6	65.3	N	N	N
Fairfield County, Connecticut	N	N	N	36,479	91.1	68.4	N	N	N
Hartford County, Connecticut	N	N	N	35,336	90.6	70.0	N	N	N
Litchfield County, Connecticut	N	N	N	2,734	91.9	53.8	N	N	N
Middlesex County, Connecticut	N	N	N	3,687	86.8	41.2	N	N	N
New Haven County, Connecticut	N	N	N	23,443	91.1	65.6	N	N	N
New London County, Connecticut	N	N	N	7,919	88.2	46.4	N	N	N
Tolland County, Connecticut	N	N	N	N	N	N	N	N	N
Windham County, Connecticut	N	N	N	N	N	N	N	N	N
DELAWARE	3,160	83.2	11.8	25,875	94.4	66.0	N	N	N
Kent County, Delaware	N	N	N	2,401	99.2	25.2	N	N	N
New Castle County, Delaware	N	N	N	21,266	94.0	70.5	N	N	N
Sussex County, Delaware	N	N	N	N	N	N	N	N	N
DISTRICT OF COLUMBIA	N	N	N	22,230	95.4	80.3	N	N	N
District of Columbia, District of Columbia	N	N	N	22,230	95.4	80.3	N	N	N

N = Data for this geographic area cannot be displayed because the number of sample cases is too small.

Table C-2. Educational Attainment of the Population, by Selected Counties, 2019—*Continued*

(Number; percent; dollars.)

State/County	Educational attainment by race/ethnicity, 25 years and over								
	White alone			White alone, not Hispanic			Black alone		
	Total	High school graduate or more (percent)	Bachelor's degree or more (percent)	Total	High school graduate or more (percent)	Bachelor's degree or more (percent)	Total	High school graduate or more (percent)	Bachelor's degree or more (percent)
FLORIDA..	12,023,439	89.8	32.5	8,887,273	93.1	34.5	2,216,463	84.3	19.3
Alachua County, Florida................................	116,724	95.3	50.8	105,617	95.6	49.8	31,765	88.9	21.4
Bay County, Florida	105,268	92.0	28.1	99,625	92.0	28.2	11,866	89.0	12.1
Brevard County, Florida................................	380,949	93.0	31.2	348,481	93.1	31.2	38,487	86.9	20.9
Broward County, Florida................................	889,455	91.3	37.5	536,155	94.0	40.2	366,215	87.0	21.5
Charlotte County, Florida................................	142,991	91.9	22.7	136,326	92.6	23.1	8,105	71.3	9.8
Citrus County, Florida................................	112,031	88.0	21.9	107,162	88.2	22.3	3,229	75.8	12.4
Clay County, Florida	121,563	95.5	28.2	113,350	95.4	28.4	16,938	91.1	32.2
Collier County, Florida................................	269,097	90.6	37.2	205,100	95.4	43.3	15,627	71.4	16.2
Columbia County, Florida	38,751	86.2	16.6	37,143	86.3	15.2	7,797	88.4	5.2
Duval County, Florida................................	411,812	91.7	35.0	370,917	92.7	35.8	179,621	87.6	18.7
Escambia County, Florida................................	154,716	90.6	27.2	147,302	91.2	27.1	43,830	82.2	10.8
Flagler County, Florida................................	75,232	90.8	26.2	68,995	91.3	27.4	7,463	95.0	15.9
Hernando County, Florida................................	131,142	90.5	20.6	116,316	91.3	21.0	6,627	76.8	7.6
Highlands County, Florida................................	69,994	87.3	17.6	58,610	88.8	17.7	7,285	78.7	9.2
Hillsborough County, Florida................................	737,540	90.4	36.7	524,197	93.3	41.2	158,830	88.0	23.1
Indian River County, Florida................................	112,357	92.4	32.4	100,092	94.6	34.6	8,789	78.7	17.3
Lake County, Florida................................	230,763	90.4	25.6	198,890	91.8	26.7	25,237	84.7	27.6
Lee County, Florida	507,946	90.5	30.2	422,602	94.1	33.3	40,114	85.7	15.1
Leon County, Florida................................	113,695	95.3	52.3	106,950	96.0	53.8	50,062	85.2	30.9
Manatee County, Florida................................	268,603	91.2	31.4	234,076	94.6	34.4	20,857	89.7	17.9
Marion County, Florida................................	232,354	90.0	21.7	203,366	91.1	21.5	30,583	84.6	12.2
Martin County, Florida................................	113,894	92.4	36.6	103,741	93.8	38.1	5,614	72.5	21.2
Miami-Dade County, Florida................................	1,501,054	80.4	33.1	242,940	94.7	52.8	303,913	80.0	17.4
Monroe County, Florida................................	51,082	92.7	36.1	40,438	97.8	41.1	4,512	98.4	18.3
Nassau County, Florida................................	60,234	88.3	30.5	58,816	89.0	31.0	4,577	93.0	24.7
Okaloosa County, Florida................................	116,567	94.4	34.0	111,532	94.6	34.2	12,172	87.9	17.3
Orange County, Florida................................	623,508	91.1	37.9	398,863	94.8	44.9	186,981	83.0	24.9
Osceola County, Florida................................	181,052	88.1	26.2	83,116	91.1	28.8	29,577	79.8	15.4
Palm Beach County, Florida................................	835,371	91.8	42.0	649,778	95.8	46.3	182,483	81.0	19.3
Pasco County, Florida	354,923	90.6	24.0	308,089	91.4	24.5	21,714	89.0	33.1
Pinellas County, Florida................................	636,600	91.7	34.2	588,280	92.3	34.6	66,468	88.1	17.3
Polk County, Florida................................	392,948	88.4	21.7	315,307	90.7	22.9	69,973	82.3	13.4
Putnam County, Florida................................	44,006	82.2	12.9	40,470	86.4	13.9	7,959	86.0	11.6
St. Johns County, Florida................................	169,361	96.1	46.9	158,620	96.3	47.1	9,630	91.0	26.4
St. Lucie County, Florida................................	182,106	88.4	21.9	148,838	90.6	22.1	42,145	81.4	15.0
Santa Rosa County, Florida................................	113,457	92.4	27.6	108,920	92.3	27.7	6,973	84.1	14.7
Sarasota County, Florida................................	321,591	94.2	37.1	300,770	94.8	37.8	12,041	89.7	16.7
Seminole County, Florida................................	248,475	95.4	43.3	207,011	96.6	46.3	38,420	89.1	23.2
Sumter County, Florida................................	107,602	95.2	33.6	103,609	95.8	33.9	7,155	85.2	15.3
Volusia County, Florida................................	339,418	92.1	25.2	311,105	92.9	25.9	37,348	89.7	17.2
Walton County, Florida................................	48,591	91.0	30.9	47,024	91.3	31.2	N	N	N
GEORGIA	4,279,288	89.4	35.5	3,947,682	91.2	36.5	2,186,956	87.9	24.8
Barrow County, Georgia.............................	44,249	85.9	23.1	40,286	86.7	23.0	6,562	81.1	20.2
Bartow County, Georgia	62,129	83.7	19.5	58,851	85.0	19.7	6,945	88.9	1.1
Bibb County, Georgia.............................	43,954	90.8	36.4	42,345	91.8	37.1	51,744	84.3	13.5
Bulloch County, Georgia.............................	30,778	90.3	30.6	29,963	90.0	29.6	11,969	92.2	17.1
Carroll County, Georgia.............................	59,599	84.0	21.5	56,739	86.2	21.6	14,125	85.2	9.0
Catoosa County, Georgia.............................	44,909	90.5	23.8	43,396	90.4	24.6	N	N	N
Chatham County, Georgia.............................	110,132	94.6	41.8	104,199	95.0	42.3	74,272	85.0	24.4
Cherokee County, Georgia.............................	152,500	92.2	38.3	141,689	94.0	39.6	12,136	92.6	33.9
Clarke County, Georgia.............................	45,125	96.3	60.2	40,176	96.6	64.3	21,318	82.4	20.4
Clayton County, Georgia.............................	32,234	75.1	12.5	21,370	80.0	12.5	129,706	88.6	20.7
Cobb County, Georgia.............................	305,657	94.0	53.0	283,623	95.6	54.8	139,766	96.1	40.3
Columbia County, Georgia.............................	78,207	93.1	43.3	72,802	94.8	43.8	18,665	95.3	27.8
Coweta County, Georgia.............................	78,089	91.7	28.5	73,457	92.5	29.5	17,679	84.9	22.7
DeKalb County, Georgia.............................	188,911	94.1	68.8	169,667	98.0	73.1	277,415	89.9	28.7
Dougherty County, Georgia.............................	16,869	86.6	31.4	16,330	86.1	30.2	37,909	80.6	15.5
Douglas County, Georgia.............................	46,018	89.0	23.8	40,460	91.7	25.6	41,512	94.9	41.3
Fayette County, Georgia.............................	53,401	97.1	48.9	49,660	97.6	50.6	19,759	92.6	31.8
Floyd County, Georgia.............................	52,551	87.9	24.7	49,465	89.4	26.0	9,212	83.4	17.8
Forsyth County, Georgia.............................	121,333	95.4	51.4	113,853	96.7	52.2	7,018	95.6	64.3
Fulton County, Georgia.............................	341,131	97.5	74.1	312,101	98.3	75.7	309,945	90.3	35.4
Glynn County, Georgia.............................	42,772	93.9	33.3	41,352	93.8	33.6	14,509	84.4	13.9

N = Data for this geographic area cannot be displayed because the number of sample cases is too small.

Table C-2. Educational Attainment of the Population, by Selected Counties, 2019—*Continued*

(Number; percent; dollars.)

State/County	American Indian or Alaska Native alone — Total	High school graduate or more (percent)	Bachelor's degree or more (percent)	Asian alone — Total	High school graduate or more (percent)	Bachelor's degree or more (percent)	Native Hawaiian or Other Pacific Islander alone — Total	High school graduate or more (percent)	Bachelor's degree or more (percent)
FLORIDA..	41,021	81.3	23.9	441,665	87.2	50.6	9,935	80.8	33.3
Alachua County, Florida..	N	N	N	9,632	94.4	72.9	N	N	N
Bay County, Florida..	N	N	N	2,809	75.0	23.6	N	N	N
Brevard County, Florida...	N	N	N	11,488	90.9	44.0	N	N	N
Broward County, Florida..	3,382	82.4	33.0	53,960	85.9	48.6	N	N	N
Charlotte County, Florida...	N	N	N	2,172	74.4	30.3	N	N	N
Citrus County, Florida..	N	N	N	N	N	N	N	N	N
Clay County, Florida..	N	N	N	5,324	92.5	31.8	N	N	N
Collier County, Florida...	N	N	N	3,700	62.2	39.9	N	N	N
Columbia County, Florida..	N	N	N	N	N	N	N	N	N
Duval County, Florida..	N	N	N	32,463	94.0	43.6	N	N	N
Escambia County, Florida..	N	N	N	6,328	86.7	32.5	N	N	N
Flagler County, Florida..	N	N	N	N	N	N	N	N	N
Hernando County, Florida..	N	N	N	N	N	N	N	N	N
Highlands County, Florida..	N	N	N	N	N	N	N	N	N
Hillsborough County, Florida....................................	N	N	N	43,953	84.9	62.2	N	N	N
Indian River County, Florida....................................	N	N	N	N	N	N	N	N	N
Lake County, Florida..	N	N	N	5,502	93.6	24.4	N	N	N
Lee County, Florida	N	N	N	9,671	90.8	49.7	N	N	N
Leon County, Florida..	N	N	N	N	N	N	N	N	N
Manatee County, Florida..	N	N	N	7,018	73.1	48.8	N	N	N
Marion County, Florida...	N	N	N	3,361	82.8	23.2	N	N	N
Martin County, Florida...	N	N	N	N	N	N	N	N	N
Miami-Dade County, Florida.....................................	N	N	N	32,711	91.5	58.7	N	N	N
Monroe County, Florida..	N	N	N	N	N	N	N	N	N
Nassau County, Florida..	N	N	N	N	N	N	N	N	N
Okaloosa County, Florida...	N	N	N	4,442	90.3	32.1	N	N	N
Orange County, Florida..	N	N	N	55,368	85.9	50.6	N	N	N
Osceola County, Florida...	N	N	N	6,816	90.7	49.7	N	N	N
Palm Beach County, Florida	N	N	N	31,586	89.1	51.6	N	N	N
Pasco County, Florida	N	N	N	10,794	91.6	55.0	N	N	N
Pinellas County, Florida...	N	N	N	25,718	82.5	42.7	N	N	N
Polk County, Florida...	N	N	N	9,912	79.0	42.6	N	N	N
Putnam County, Florida..	N	N	N	N	N	N	N	N	N
St. Johns County, Florida...	N	N	N	4,797	97.4	63.0	N	N	N
St. Lucie County, Florida..	N	N	N	5,645	70.2	44.7	N	N	N
Santa Rosa County, Florida	N	N	N	N	N	N	N	N	N
Sarasota County, Florida	N	N	N	5,162	84.5	54.2	N	N	N
Seminole County, Florida...	N	N	N	16,392	90.0	69.3	N	N	N
Sumter County, Florida	N	N	N	N	N	N	N	N	N
Volusia County, Florida..	N	N	N	7,710	88.6	33.6	N	N	N
Walton County, Florida..	N	N	N	N	N	N	N	N	N
GEORGIA	24,821	67.3	13.8	302,385	86.8	57.3	3,675	85.0	31.8
Barrow County, Georgia	N	N	N	N	N	N	N	N	N
Bartow County, Georgia	N	N	N	N	N	N	N	N	N
Bibb County, Georgia	N	N	N	2,288	78.8	60.6	N	N	N
Bulloch County, Georgia...	N	N	N	N	N	N	N	N	N
Carroll County, Georgia..	N	N	N	N	N	N	N	N	N
Catoosa County, Georgia...	N	N	N	N	N	N	N	N	N
Chatham County, Georgia...	N	N	N	5,932	64.2	21.1	N	N	N
Cherokee County, Georgia..	N	N	N	N	N	N	N	N	N
Clarke County, Georgia..	N	N	N	N	N	N	N	N	N
Clayton County, Georgia..	N	N	N	9,552	67.2	19.8	N	N	N
Cobb County, Georgia	N	N	N	29,254	93.1	69.3	N	N	N
Columbia County, Georgia..	N	N	N	3,827	87.2	52.1	N	N	N
Coweta County, Georgia...	N	N	N	N	N	N	N	N	N
DeKalb County, Georgia...	5,957	64.8	6.8	32,532	81.0	56.2	N	N	N
Dougherty County, Georgia.......................................	N	N	N	N	N	N	N	N	N
Douglas County, Georgia..	N	N	N	N	N	N	N	N	N
Fayette County, Georgia...	N	N	N	N	N	N	N	N	N
Floyd County, Georgia..	N	N	N	N	N	N	N	N	N
Forsyth County, Georgia...	N	N	N	23,311	95.0	80.5	N	N	N
Fulton County, Georgia...	N	N	N	53,697	96.8	85.9	N	N	N
Glynn County, Georgia	N	N	N	N	N	N	N	N	N

N = Data for this geographic area cannot be displayed because the number of sample cases is too small.

Table C-2. Educational Attainment of the Population, by Selected Counties, 2019—*Continued*

(Number; percent; dollars.)

State/County	Educational attainment by race/ethnicity, 25 years and over								
	White alone			White alone, not Hispanic			Black alone		
	Total	High school graduate or more (percent)	Bachelor's degree or more (percent)	Total	High school graduate or more (percent)	Bachelor's degree or more (percent)	Total	High school graduate or more (percent)	Bachelor's degree or more (percent)
GEORGIA—*(Continued)*									
Gwinnett County, Georgia	291,085	90.4	42.4	237,645	95.2	46.9	165,471	94.5	39.3
Hall County, Georgia	118,239	79.4	26.2	91,122	88.6	30.4	9,993	90.9	21.7
Henry County, Georgia	72,763	89.3	21.3	66,483	93.3	22.1	71,969	95.5	31.5
Houston County, Georgia	64,284	94.2	28.8	61,258	94.9	29.2	30,080	92.1	25.4
Jackson County, Georgia	42,848	86.8	26.2	40,447	87.6	25.8	4,007	85.8	19.9
Lowndes County, Georgia	41,028	94.2	31.9	39,563	95.3	32.7	24,771	85.7	12.1
Muscogee County, Georgia	57,911	90.3	30.7	54,685	90.2	31.0	59,575	88.2	18.8
Newton County, Georgia	38,259	81.9	17.9	34,770	86.2	19.6	33,342	90.1	17.9
Paulding County, Georgia	84,856	86.2	20.9	78,946	87.7	21.2	21,097	94.7	26.9
Richmond County, Georgia	51,272	86.2	26.9	49,059	86.0	26.3	73,615	86.6	12.6
Rockdale County, Georgia	24,712	85.7	17.9	20,804	87.0	19.6	31,488	91.3	28.3
Spalding County, Georgia	29,690	85.3	19.2	27,728	86.6	19.5	15,090	83.2	14.9
Troup County, Georgia	28,103	91.7	28.1	27,350	91.8	28.7	16,343	86.3	3.8
Walker County, Georgia	45,629	80.3	16.5	45,408	80.2	16.5	N	N	N
Walton County, Georgia	50,895	88.9	25.0	48,783	88.9	25.0	12,050	71.3	14.6
Whitfield County, Georgia	60,736	71.8	16.5	43,750	83.9	21.5	2,891	91.3	21.3
HAWAII	259,996	96.9	44.5	237,027	97.3	46.3	18,397	98.4	31.0
Hawaii County, Hawaii	55,759	97.0	41.6	51,790	97.4	43.9	N	N	N
Honolulu County, Hawaii	138,786	97.6	48.6	125,726	97.8	49.9	16,895	98.8	29.7
Kauai County, Hawaii	18,129	96.8	40.1	17,239	97.1	40.5	N	N	N
Maui County, Hawaii	47,317	94.9	37.6	42,272	96.0	40.6	N	N	N
IDAHO	1,066,998	92.8	29.2	998,524	94.2	30.1	5,607	92.9	13.4
Ada County, Idaho	301,205	95.3	39.6	285,028	96.1	40.5	N	N	N
Bannock County, Idaho	50,031	95.3	28.8	48,218	95.2	28.8	N	N	N
Bonneville County, Idaho	67,028	93.9	33.3	62,584	95.3	34.2	N	N	N
Canyon County, Idaho	118,379	91.9	22.2	108,803	93.2	23.2	N	N	N
Kootenai County, Idaho	110,242	94.0	24.6	106,894	94.0	25.1	N	N	N
Twin Falls County, Idaho	52,351	85.4	21.3	46,005	90.2	23.2	N	N	N
ILLINOIS	6,414,127	91.9	37.3	5,640,997	94.6	39.9	1,177,578	86.5	22.6
Adams County, Illinois	43,399	91.3	24.1	42,787	91.1	23.7	N	N	N
Champaign County, Illinois	92,924	95.1	46.9	88,714	96.4	47.5	14,313	82.9	16.0
Cook County, Illinois	2,121,092	90.4	47.2	1,661,656	95.1	55.1	812,165	87.1	23.7
DeKalb County, Illinois	53,726	93.3	34.0	51,325	94.5	34.4	N	N	N
DuPage County, Illinois	497,249	95.1	49.8	444,385	97.1	53.0	28,250	89.3	33.4
Kane County, Illinois	273,150	89.0	36.0	220,923	96.3	41.5	19,425	90.7	23.5
Kankakee County, Illinois	60,432	91.5	20.1	55,659	93.3	20.9	9,479	85.6	10.4
Kendall County, Illinois	68,358	93.8	39.6	58,606	96.4	42.4	6,171	92.6	40.3
Lake County, Illinois	353,407	92.0	47.1	302,496	96.6	52.8	28,756	87.4	20.3
LaSalle County, Illinois	71,979	90.9	17.0	67,982	92.1	17.6	N	N	N
McHenry County, Illinois	196,680	94.3	34.6	177,300	96.3	36.4	3,012	95.6	49.5
McLean County, Illinois	90,167	95.6	45.6	86,804	95.8	46.0	7,253	88.3	29.1
Macon County, Illinois	58,620	94.5	23.5	57,978	94.6	23.4	11,179	88.4	10.4
Madison County, Illinois	165,749	94.6	31.1	162,240	94.9	31.1	14,046	80.6	21.1
Peoria County, Illinois	93,516	95.1	33.4	90,987	95.3	33.7	19,121	87.4	15.2
Rock Island County, Illinois	81,247	91.0	25.7	75,569	92.6	26.7	9,083	74.1	6.3
St. Clair County, Illinois	121,006	93.4	30.4	116,736	93.7	30.5	50,435	88.1	19.9
Sangamon County, Illinois	117,117	94.4	35.5	114,600	94.6	35.8	14,162	83.3	17.7
Tazewell County, Illinois	89,539	94.6	27.5	88,067	94.6	27.0	N	N	N
Vermilion County, Illinois	44,376	91.2	13.4	43,040	92.5	13.3	6,128	82.4	2.0
Will County, Illinois	346,975	93.0	35.6	305,833	95.7	38.5	52,321	92.1	31.7
Williamson County, Illinois	43,758	93.4	30.0	43,438	93.6	30.3	N	N	N
Winnebago County, Illinois	159,606	89.8	25.2	143,908	93.0	27.0	22,265	85.7	13.5
INDIANA	3,843,248	90.6	27.3	3,692,360	91.3	27.7	395,797	87.7	19.3
Allen County, Indiana	201,712	92.4	30.7	192,723	93.6	31.4	26,346	88.0	18.4
Bartholomew County, Indiana	49,686	90.9	32.1	47,210	91.7	31.7	N	N	N
Boone County, Indiana	42,238	92.9	47.2	40,935	92.7	46.2	N	N	N
Clark County, Indiana	73,848	90.8	21.6	71,018	92.5	21.2	N	N	N
Delaware County, Indiana	65,076	93.1	22.9	63,717	93.0	23.4	4,775	80.0	5.7
Elkhart County, Indiana	113,189	83.9	21.0	105,225	85.3	21.8	6,939	83.2	13.1
Floyd County, Indiana	50,058	92.4	29.6	49,042	93.3	30.1	2,169	92.6	6.7
Grant County, Indiana	39,252	88.8	22.2	38,240	88.7	22.3	2,455	91.2	9.7

N = Data for this geographic area cannot be displayed because the number of sample cases is too small.

Table C-2. Educational Attainment of the Population, by Selected Counties, 2019—*Continued*

(Number; percent; dollars.)

| | Educational attainment by race/ethnicity, 25 years and over | | | | | | | | |
| | American Indian or Alaska Native alone | | | Asian alone | | | Native Hawaiian or Other Pacific Islander alone | | |
State/County	Total	High school graduate or more (percent)	Bachelor's degree or more (percent)	Total	High school graduate or more (percent)	Bachelor's degree or more (percent)	Total	High school graduate or more (percent)	Bachelor's degree or more (percent)
GEORGIA—*(Continued)*									
Gwinnett County, Georgia	N	N	N	79,887	84.6	44.8	N	N	N
Hall County, Georgia	N	N	N	2,434	66.7	24.6	N	N	N
Henry County, Georgia	N	N	N	5,308	73.7	22.7	N	N	N
Houston County, Georgia	N	N	N	N	N	N	N	N	N
Jackson County, Georgia	N	N	N	N	N	N	N	N	N
Lowndes County, Georgia	N	N	N	N	N	N	N	N	N
Muscogee County, Georgia	N	N	N	3,730	88.1	32.0	N	N	N
Newton County, Georgia	N	N	N	N	N	N	N	N	N
Paulding County, Georgia	N	N	N	N	N	N	N	N	N
Richmond County, Georgia	N	N	N	2,074	71.8	34.7	N	N	N
Rockdale County, Georgia	N	N	N	N	N	N	N	N	N
Spalding County, Georgia	N	N	N	N	N	N	N	N	N
Troup County, Georgia	N	N	N	N	N	N	N	N	N
Walker County, Georgia	N	N	N	N	N	N	N	N	N
Walton County, Georgia	N	N	N	N	N	N	N	N	N
Whitfield County, Georgia	N	N	N	1,201	90.1	36.8	N	N	N
HAWAII	3,815	70.0	28.6	434,234	89.4	35.0	98,477	89.1	12.2
Hawaii County, Hawaii	N	N	N	37,978	90.9	32.6	15,750	89.1	10.4
Honolulu County, Hawaii	N	N	N	339,406	89.7	36.9	65,315	90.0	13.2
Kauai County, Hawaii	N	N	N	17,840	89.5	27.7	5,322	86.5	9.2
Maui County, Hawaii	N	N	N	39,008	85.6	24.8	12,082	85.6	10.0
IDAHO	14,880	82.3	19.9	18,301	86.5	48.0	N	N	N
Ada County, Idaho	2,615	87.1	29.7	9,073	85.6	49.2	N	N	N
Bannock County, Idaho	N	N	N	N	N	N	N	N	N
Bonneville County, Idaho	N	N	N	N	N	N	N	N	N
Canyon County, Idaho	N	N	N	N	N	N	N	N	N
Kootenai County, Idaho	N	N	N	N	N	N	N	N	N
Twin Falls County, Idaho	N	N	N	N	N	N	N	N	N
ILLINOIS	20,287	74.0	23.6	513,285	90.5	65.0	2,792	93.4	34.1
Adams County, Illinois	N	N	N	N	N	N	N	N	N
Champaign County, Illinois	N	N	N	10,617	93.0	77.8	N	N	N
Cook County, Illinois	10,328	71.1	24.9	292,621	89.5	63.1	N	N	N
DeKalb County, Illinois	N	N	N	N	N	N	N	N	N
DuPage County, Illinois	N	N	N	80,606	93.6	73.4	N	N	N
Kane County, Illinois	N	N	N	15,047	85.0	53.0	N	N	N
Kankakee County, Illinois	N	N	N	N	N	N	N	N	N
Kendall County, Illinois	N	N	N	N	N	N	N	N	N
Lake County, Illinois	N	N	N	39,009	96.7	75.4	N	N	N
LaSalle County, Illinois	N	N	N	N	N	N	N	N	N
McHenry County, Illinois	N	N	N	6,244	78.9	49.0	N	N	N
McLean County, Illinois	N	N	N	5,160	86.6	74.7	N	N	N
Macon County, Illinois	N	N	N	N	N	N	N	N	N
Madison County, Illinois	N	N	N	1,967	89.4	37.0	N	N	N
Peoria County, Illinois	N	N	N	N	N	N	N	N	N
Rock Island County, Illinois	N	N	N	1,644	88.2	61.8	N	N	N
St. Clair County, Illinois	N	N	N	2,614	79.0	33.3	N	N	N
Sangamon County, Illinois	N	N	N	N	N	N	N	N	N
Tazewell County, Illinois	N	N	N	N	N	N	N	N	N
Vermilion County, Illinois	N	N	N	N	N	N	N	N	N
Will County, Illinois	N	N	N	27,967	92.1	58.0	N	N	N
Williamson County, Illinois	N	N	N	N	N	N	N	N	N
Winnebago County, Illinois	N	N	N	5,204	84.3	63.5	N	N	N
INDIANA	13,195	81.2	11.0	101,424	84.6	59.1	N	N	N
Allen County, Indiana	N	N	N	9,297	49.2	32.5	N	N	N
Bartholomew County, Indiana	N	N	N	N	N	N	N	N	N
Boone County, Indiana	N	N	N	N	N	N	N	N	N
Clark County, Indiana	N	N	N	N	N	N	N	N	N
Delaware County, Indiana	N	N	N	N	N	N	N	N	N
Elkhart County, Indiana	N	N	N	N	N	N	N	N	N
Floyd County, Indiana	N	N	N	N	N	N	N	N	N
Grant County, Indiana	N	N	N	N	N	N	N	N	N

N = Data for this geographic area cannot be displayed because the number of sample cases is too small.

Table C-2. Educational Attainment of the Population, by Selected Counties, 2019—*Continued*

(Number; percent; dollars.)

| | Educational attainment by race/ethnicity, 25 years and over | | | | | | | | |
| | White alone | | | White alone, not Hispanic | | | Black alone | | |
State/County	Total	High school graduate or more (percent)	Bachelor's degree or more (percent)	Total	High school graduate or more (percent)	Bachelor's degree or more (percent)	Total	High school graduate or more (percent)	Bachelor's degree or more (percent)
INDIANA—(*Continued*)									
Hamilton County, Indiana	194,341	97.9	62.8	187,931	98.2	63.5	10,072	100.0	59.6
Hancock County, Indiana	50,511	90.2	29.3	50,121	90.2	29.3	N	N	N
Hendricks County, Indiana	99,651	95.1	36.0	96,959	95.0	36.2	8,133	99.5	40.4
Howard County, Indiana	50,893	90.2	19.0	50,329	90.3	19.2	5,225	84.1	11.3
Johnson County, Indiana	96,996	93.8	31.9	95,019	94.0	32.5	N	N	N
Kosciusko County, Indiana	50,091	86.4	27.0	48,317	88.2	27.5	N	N	N
Lake County, Indiana	221,501	92.6	25.8	193,950	93.8	27.3	73,100	88.1	15.3
LaPorte County, Indiana	67,179	90.0	19.3	64,140	90.8	20.0	7,787	76.9	7.7
Madison County, Indiana	81,336	88.9	18.6	79,371	89.5	18.2	7,183	86.4	14.1
Marion County, Indiana	415,725	89.0	35.1	383,033	90.8	36.6	169,458	87.3	20.4
Monroe County, Indiana	75,962	95.1	44.2	74,865	95.2	44.5	N	N	N
Morgan County, Indiana	47,744	90.9	17.7	47,453	90.9	17.7	N	N	N
Porter County, Indiana	108,846	95.0	27.6	100,406	95.3	27.8	3,848	94.5	11.0
St. Joseph County, Indiana	144,639	91.6	31.7	137,287	92.6	31.6	19,583	86.1	17.0
Tippecanoe County, Indiana	92,129	92.4	38.1	87,365	92.7	38.7	5,248	93.2	34.1
Vanderburgh County, Indiana	109,364	91.3	28.7	108,179	91.4	28.8	9,559	84.3	13.3
Vigo County, Indiana	61,357	92.6	25.8	60,512	92.8	25.6	4,938	90.6	18.3
Wayne County, Indiana	41,309	88.5	17.4	41,125	88.5	17.5	N	N	N
IOWA	1,950,864	93.6	29.5	1,877,984	94.6	30.2	72,382	83.0	14.9
Black Hawk County, Iowa	72,602	93.6	31.0	70,794	93.7	31.2	7,135	86.5	17.9
Dallas County, Iowa	55,483	97.3	53.6	53,024	97.9	54.2	N	N	N
Dubuque County, Iowa	61,354	95.3	33.3	61,033	95.3	33.1	N	N	N
Johnson County, Iowa	75,631	95.3	56.1	73,280	95.6	56.6	N	N	N
Linn County, Iowa	139,066	95.5	33.2	135,887	95.7	33.5	6,961	74.2	10.9
Polk County, Iowa	284,275	94.5	39.3	268,257	96.3	41.0	19,926	84.1	20.1
Pottawattamie County, Iowa	60,348	91.6	23.5	57,731	92.5	23.4	N	N	N
Scott County, Iowa	104,425	94.3	33.3	99,028	94.6	33.7	7,925	86.4	9.4
Story County, Iowa	44,962	97.7	49.7	44,809	97.7	49.6	N	N	N
Woodbury County, Iowa	58,747	88.8	23.9	51,485	94.4	26.7	N	N	N
KANSAS	1,653,103	93.2	35.3	1,530,789	95.1	36.9	101,769	87.4	20.9
Butler County, Kansas	41,264	93.4	31.1	40,009	93.7	31.0	N	N	N
Douglas County, Kansas	61,552	95.7	48.8	58,840	96.2	48.9	N	N	N
Johnson County, Kansas	354,763	96.8	57.0	337,396	98.0	58.6	17,439	91.6	39.1
Leavenworth County, Kansas	47,626	94.7	33.1	45,261	94.8	34.4	4,151	82.4	23.8
Riley County, Kansas	31,297	97.0	46.3	29,775	98.0	47.8	N	N	N
Sedgwick County, Kansas	273,842	92.0	34.0	246,914	94.7	35.8	27,753	88.7	16.8
Shawnee County, Kansas	101,268	95.7	34.4	95,261	96.2	35.9	9,340	81.7	8.6
Wyandotte County, Kansas	63,709	83.8	21.7	49,685	91.3	25.9	23,362	85.1	15.8
KENTUCKY	2,705,849	87.4	25.2	2,648,824	87.7	25.2	232,582	88.2	19.3
Boone County, Kentucky	81,940	93.4	31.9	78,870	94.7	33.0	N	N	N
Bullitt County, Kentucky	55,770	88.9	15.6	55,047	88.8	15.8	N	N	N
Campbell County, Kentucky	62,098	92.0	40.6	61,344	92.0	40.5	N	N	N
Christian County, Kentucky	29,666	83.1	22.7	28,158	83.8	23.5	9,238	91.7	12.6
Daviess County, Kentucky	63,145	88.9	25.3	62,274	89.0	25.4	1,595	93.0	42.0
Fayette County, Kentucky	162,526	94.1	48.8	157,326	95.3	49.8	29,208	89.5	23.1
Hardin County, Kentucky	60,226	91.4	21.9	57,950	91.2	21.4	9,127	91.3	26.3
Jefferson County, Kentucky	399,770	92.3	37.3	378,915	92.9	37.8	107,576	88.6	21.6
Kenton County, Kentucky	105,182	91.8	33.5	103,746	92.2	33.4	4,417	84.5	15.2
McCracken County, Kentucky	40,088	89.9	25.6	39,849	90.1	25.5	4,111	81.8	9.4
Madison County, Kentucky	53,361	91.2	32.3	52,706	91.4	32.2	N	N	N
Oldham County, Kentucky	40,882	94.3	41.8	39,583	94.4	42.2	3,050	86.1	39.0
Warren County, Kentucky	67,989	92.1	36.9	65,887	92.8	37.2	7,089	82.6	18.4
LOUISIANA	2,036,883	88.2	28.4	1,938,051	88.9	28.9	948,531	82.1	17.1
Ascension Parish, Louisiana	59,802	93.9	28.7	58,095	93.8	28.9	19,041	90.9	16.0
Bossier Parish, Louisiana	62,764	90.9	26.0	58,749	93.6	27.5	18,001	89.0	9.3
Caddo Parish, Louisiana	81,640	91.1	31.6	79,724	91.2	31.9	75,742	81.7	15.4
Calcasieu Parish, Louisiana	97,989	87.9	24.5	94,751	88.8	24.7	30,816	80.4	15.5
East Baton Rouge Parish, Louisiana	139,443	95.6	46.3	134,728	95.8	46.7	123,220	86.9	21.7
Iberia Parish, Louisiana	30,198	87.8	20.3	29,664	88.3	20.4	13,750	76.9	6.4
Jefferson Parish, Louisiana	203,006	89.2	30.1	172,440	90.8	32.8	75,032	86.5	20.8
Lafayette Parish, Louisiana	118,902	91.6	38.7	113,903	93.0	39.9	39,311	85.7	21.6

N = Data for this geographic area cannot be displayed because the number of sample cases is too small.

Table C-2. Educational Attainment of the Population, by Selected Counties, 2019—*Continued*

(Number; percent; dollars.)

	Educational attainment by race/ethnicity, 25 years and over								
	American Indian or Alaska Native alone			Asian alone			Native Hawaiian or Other Pacific Islander alone		
State/County	Total	High school graduate or more (percent)	Bachelor's degree or more (percent)	Total	High school graduate or more (percent)	Bachelor's degree or more (percent)	Total	High school graduate or more (percent)	Bachelor's degree or more (percent)
INDIANA—(*Continued*)									
Hamilton County, Indiana	N	N	N	13,552	89.2	74.5	N	N	N
Hancock County, Indiana	N	N	N	N	N	N	N	N	N
Hendricks County, Indiana	N	N	N	N	N	N	N	N	N
Howard County, Indiana	N	N	N	N	N	N	N	N	N
Johnson County, Indiana	N	N	N	3,291	59.4	37.5	N	N	N
Kosciusko County, Indiana	N	N	N	N	N	N	N	N	N
Lake County, Indiana	N	N	N	6,021	85.1	50.3	N	N	N
LaPorte County, Indiana	N	N	N	N	N	N	N	N	N
Madison County, Indiana	N	N	N	N	N	N	N	N	N
Marion County, Indiana	N	N	N	22,741	82.8	53.7	N	N	N
Monroe County, Indiana	N	N	N	N	N	N	N	N	N
Morgan County, Indiana	N	N	N	N	N	N	N	N	N
Porter County, Indiana	N	N	N	N	N	N	N	N	N
St. Joseph County, Indiana	N	N	N	4,336	95.2	67.9	N	N	N
Tippecanoe County, Indiana	N	N	N	6,845	95.0	74.5	N	N	N
Vanderburgh County, Indiana	N	N	N	N	N	N	N	N	N
Vigo County, Indiana	N	N	N	N	N	N	N	N	N
Wayne County, Indiana	N	N	N	N	N	N	N	N	N
IOWA	7,678	82.0	8.3	48,872	79.8	51.0	N	N	N
Black Hawk County, Iowa	N	N	N	N	N	N	N	N	N
Dallas County, Iowa	N	N	N	N	N	N	N	N	N
Dubuque County, Iowa	N	N	N	N	N	N	N	N	N
Johnson County, Iowa	N	N	N	N	N	N	N	N	N
Linn County, Iowa	N	N	N	N	N	N	N	N	N
Polk County, Iowa	N	N	N	14,889	68.5	35.1	N	N	N
Pottawattamie County, Iowa	N	N	N	N	N	N	N	N	N
Scott County, Iowa	N	N	N	3,706	68.9	45.7	N	N	N
Story County, Iowa	N	N	N	N	N	N	N	N	N
Woodbury County, Iowa	N	N	N	1,955	68.7	2.6	N	N	N
KANSAS	16,317	86.9	14.8	56,876	85.4	49.8	N	N	N
Butler County, Kansas	N	N	N	N	N	N	N	N	N
Douglas County, Kansas	N	N	N	N	N	N	N	N	N
Johnson County, Kansas	N	N	N	21,822	93.9	69.0	N	N	N
Leavenworth County, Kansas	N	N	N	N	N	N	N	N	N
Riley County, Kansas	N	N	N	N	N	N	N	N	N
Sedgwick County, Kansas	N	N	N	15,022	79.1	28.3	N	N	N
Shawnee County, Kansas	N	N	N	N	N	N	N	N	N
Wyandotte County, Kansas	N	N	N	5,511	65.4	30.8	N	N	N
KENTUCKY	5,539	76.0	17.0	47,711	86.1	57.3	N	N	N
Boone County, Kentucky	N	N	N	2,369	67.1	27.2	N	N	N
Bullitt County, Kentucky	N	N	N	N	N	N	N	N	N
Campbell County, Kentucky	N	N	N	N	N	N	N	N	N
Christian County, Kentucky	N	N	N	N	N	N	N	N	N
Daviess County, Kentucky	N	N	N	N	N	N	N	N	N
Fayette County, Kentucky	N	N	N	9,263	93.6	72.8	N	N	N
Hardin County, Kentucky	N	N	N	N	N	N	N	N	N
Jefferson County, Kentucky	N	N	N	15,482	91.9	71.9	N	N	N
Kenton County, Kentucky	N	N	N	N	N	N	N	N	N
McCracken County, Kentucky	N	N	N	N	N	N	N	N	N
Madison County, Kentucky	N	N	N	N	N	N	N	N	N
Oldham County, Kentucky	N	N	N	724	100.0	32.5	N	N	N
Warren County, Kentucky	N	N	N	N	N	N	N	N	N
LOUISIANA	18,751	78.7	16.6	54,463	83.4	45.8	N	N	N
Ascension Parish, Louisiana	N	N	N	N	N	N	N	N	N
Bossier Parish, Louisiana	N	N	N	N	N	N	N	N	N
Caddo Parish, Louisiana	N	N	N	N	N	N	N	N	N
Calcasieu Parish, Louisiana	N	N	N	2,016	86.1	57.8	N	N	N
East Baton Rouge Parish, Louisiana	N	N	N	9,312	86.1	44.9	N	N	N
Iberia Parish, Louisiana	N	N	N	N	N	N	N	N	N
Jefferson Parish, Louisiana	N	N	N	13,120	79.1	43.5	N	N	N
Lafayette Parish, Louisiana	N	N	N	2,354	85.5	52.5	N	N	N

N = Data for this geographic area cannot be displayed because the number of sample cases is too small.

Table C-2. Educational Attainment of the Population, by Selected Counties, 2019—*Continued*

(Number; percent; dollars.)

State/County	Educational attainment by race/ethnicity, 25 years and over								
	White alone			White alone, not Hispanic			Black alone		
	Total	High school graduate or more (percent)	Bachelor's degree or more (percent)	Total	High school graduate or more (percent)	Bachelor's degree or more (percent)	Total	High school graduate or more (percent)	Bachelor's degree or more (percent)
LOUISIANA—*(Continued)*									
Lafourche Parish, Louisiana	56,204	78.3	17.2	54,053	78.8	17.8	7,366	79.7	16.5
Livingston Parish, Louisiana	84,587	83.4	19.3	83,289	83.6	19.3	5,429	81.1	51.4
Orleans Parish, Louisiana	104,672	95.6	64.7	96,147	96.9	66.2	157,313	82.5	22.7
Ouachita Parish, Louisiana	62,465	88.9	31.9	61,917	88.8	32.0	34,209	84.5	15.4
Rapides Parish, Louisiana	57,519	90.3	22.1	55,983	91.3	21.7	25,305	77.6	13.2
St. Landry Parish, Louisiana	32,249	80.3	15.4	31,014	80.2	16.0	21,257	71.5	6.3
St. Tammany Parish, Louisiana	151,829	92.9	38.0	143,997	93.4	38.1	20,617	81.9	22.0
Tangipahoa Parish, Louisiana	62,867	85.6	25.3	60,321	86.6	26.1	22,621	80.7	22.3
Terrebonne Parish, Louisiana	54,536	80.3	16.5	52,318	80.3	17.2	13,456	79.6	10.0
MAINE	944,133	93.5	33.1	935,086	93.5	33.0	11,899	87.5	38.1
Androscoggin County, Maine	71,572	92.1	24.6	70,984	92.3	24.8	N	N	N
Aroostook County, Maine	47,915	90.9	18.0	47,641	91.1	18.1	N	N	N
Cumberland County, Maine	201,763	95.6	50.9	199,053	95.6	50.8	5,716	91.7	36.9
Kennebec County, Maine	85,845	93.4	27.7	85,161	93.3	27.4	N	N	N
Penobscot County, Maine	104,150	93.3	29.1	103,148	93.5	29.2	N	N	N
York County, Maine	148,236	93.7	32.7	146,750	93.6	32.6	N	N	N
MARYLAND	2,385,477	92.9	45.5	2,223,960	94.1	46.5	1,241,353	90.5	30.8
Allegany County, Maryland	44,161	90.5	21.9	43,871	90.8	22.0	N	N	N
Anne Arundel County, Maryland	296,490	93.8	44.7	279,471	94.4	45.4	68,576	91.7	40.8
Baltimore County, Maryland	357,976	92.9	43.4	345,288	93.4	43.8	160,997	92.2	33.3
Calvert County, Maryland	52,554	96.3	34.3	50,674	96.4	34.4	9,002	94.1	15.2
Carroll County, Maryland	109,129	94.9	36.9	106,511	95.0	37.1	3,827	94.5	29.2
Cecil County, Maryland	64,151	91.1	24.6	62,736	91.2	24.4	5,717	89.9	26.5
Charles County, Maryland	48,443	92.4	30.2	45,123	92.9	30.9	53,993	93.9	27.2
Frederick County, Maryland	145,945	92.6	42.8	134,411	95.3	44.4	16,706	97.2	31.0
Harford County, Maryland	144,496	94.1	37.9	139,391	94.4	38.2	23,838	91.5	26.6
Howard County, Maryland	127,155	96.0	65.8	118,802	97.4	67.4	42,185	95.6	52.9
Montgomery County, Maryland	390,858	94.7	67.6	336,070	97.8	72.9	130,457	92.3	42.1
Prince George's County, Maryland	103,617	87.4	41.7	82,695	93.4	47.5	401,366	93.2	34.9
St. Mary's County, Maryland	59,968	91.1	33.0	57,431	91.5	33.9	10,174	84.2	13.2
Washington County, Maryland	89,202	88.5	22.5	86,434	88.9	23.1	11,709	85.1	11.5
Wicomico County, Maryland	44,967	87.6	34.7	43,154	88.7	35.6	16,367	88.0	18.7
Baltimore city, Maryland	137,930	91.2	60.3	128,143	92.0	60.8	254,060	83.1	17.0
MASSACHUSETTS	3,865,466	93.4	46.5	3,601,315	94.8	48.2	350,938	85.7	28.0
Barnstable County, Massachusetts	156,082	96.7	48.6	152,320	97.8	49.2	4,412	97.9	26.2
Berkshire County, Massachusetts	85,466	93.1	34.3	84,633	93.1	34.4	2,265	89.8	21.3
Bristol County, Massachusetts	347,162	87.2	30.1	336,613	87.3	30.4	17,600	82.4	24.8
Essex County, Massachusetts	446,558	93.1	45.5	406,589	95.3	48.0	21,766	85.2	32.3
Franklin County, Massachusetts	50,312	92.2	36.3	49,503	92.4	36.3	N	N	N
Hampden County, Massachusetts	264,426	87.5	28.5	216,672	91.9	32.5	26,884	89.4	24.2
Hampshire County, Massachusetts	90,807	94.9	51.7	88,492	95.5	51.8	N	N	N
Middlesex County, Massachusetts	883,783	95.6	57.6	838,642	96.3	58.6	55,729	89.6	36.1
Norfolk County, Massachusetts	388,015	96.7	56.9	376,633	96.8	56.9	34,266	89.1	36.7
Plymouth County, Massachusetts	309,340	96.0	41.0	303,354	96.5	41.4	37,128	76.2	19.2
Suffolk County, Massachusetts	328,341	92.6	60.1	274,476	96.0	67.5	119,200	84.1	22.7
Worcester County, Massachusetts	496,764	92.7	36.2	455,386	94.5	38.1	26,243	90.3	36.7
MICHIGAN	5,564,561	92.3	30.9	5,377,567	92.8	31.1	889,006	87.9	18.0
Allegan County, Michigan	76,977	92.4	23.7	73,674	93.8	24.4	N	N	N
Bay County, Michigan	71,553	92.8	21.3	68,929	93.2	21.8	N	N	N
Berrien County, Michigan	89,527	91.7	28.9	85,861	92.1	28.8	12,721	79.8	11.1
Calhoun County, Michigan	76,835	91.4	21.6	74,146	91.5	22.1	8,625	85.4	9.7
Clinton County, Michigan	52,172	95.1	33.9	50,922	95.6	34.1	N	N	N
Eaton County, Michigan	68,849	95.5	28.3	66,291	95.5	28.6	4,551	94.2	36.5
Genesee County, Michigan	218,107	91.2	23.1	213,201	91.3	23.1	52,133	88.4	13.2
Grand Traverse County, Michigan	64,975	94.9	39.2	63,843	94.8	39.2	N	N	N
Ingham County, Michigan	141,587	94.9	39.2	132,016	95.5	40.3	20,749	89.0	34.8
Isabella County, Michigan	35,882	91.8	25.7	34,719	91.6	25.2	N	N	N
Jackson County, Michigan	99,390	91.2	24.2	97,254	91.3	24.1	8,056	82.4	9.8
Kalamazoo County, Michigan	139,399	94.2	39.6	136,523	94.2	39.4	15,932	80.2	25.1
Kent County, Michigan	364,366	93.5	38.8	344,094	95.3	39.9	37,292	90.2	15.9
Lapeer County, Michigan	60,483	92.2	19.3	58,946	93.0	19.8	N	N	N

N = Data for this geographic area cannot be displayed because the number of sample cases is too small.

Table C-2. Educational Attainment of the Population, by Selected Counties, 2019—*Continued*

(Number; percent; dollars.)

State/County	American Indian or Alaska Native alone			Asian alone			Native Hawaiian or Other Pacific Islander alone		
	Total	High school graduate or more (percent)	Bachelor's degree or more (percent)	Total	High school graduate or more (percent)	Bachelor's degree or more (percent)	Total	High school graduate or more (percent)	Bachelor's degree or more (percent)
LOUISIANA—*(Continued)*									
Lafourche Parish, Louisiana	N	N	N	N	N	N	N	N	N
Livingston Parish, Louisiana	N	N	N	N	N	N	N	N	N
Orleans Parish, Louisiana	N	N	N	8,207	84.6	53.7	N	N	N
Ouachita Parish, Louisiana	N	N	N	N	N	N	N	N	N
Rapides Parish, Louisiana	N	N	N	N	N	N	N	N	N
St. Landry Parish, Louisiana	N	N	N	N	N	N	N	N	N
St. Tammany Parish, Louisiana	N	N	N	N	N	N	N	N	N
Tangipahoa Parish, Louisiana	N	N	N	N	N	N	N	N	N
Terrebonne Parish, Louisiana	N	N	N	N	N	N	N	N	N
MAINE	6,426	94.1	24.8	10,990	81.8	45.8	N	N	N
Androscoggin County, Maine	N	N	N	N	N	N	N	N	N
Aroostook County, Maine	N	N	N	N	N	N	N	N	N
Cumberland County, Maine	N	N	N	4,808	78.8	46.0	N	N	N
Kennebec County, Maine	N	N	N	N	N	N	N	N	N
Penobscot County, Maine	986	96.7	41.5	N	N	N	N	N	N
York County, Maine	N	N	N	N	N	N	N	N	N
MARYLAND	14,328	79.2	26.1	277,535	89.3	63.3	N	N	N
Allegany County, Maryland	N	N	N	N	N	N	N	N	N
Anne Arundel County, Maryland	N	N	N	15,556	88.2	50.0	N	N	N
Baltimore County, Maryland	N	N	N	34,746	86.0	54.5	N	N	N
Calvert County, Maryland	N	N	N	N	N	N	N	N	N
Carroll County, Maryland	N	N	N	2,140	87.6	50.7	N	N	N
Cecil County, Maryland	N	N	N	N	N	N	N	N	N
Charles County, Maryland	N	N	N	3,820	88.3	44.0	N	N	N
Frederick County, Maryland	N	N	N	8,820	90.8	58.6	N	N	N
Harford County, Maryland	N	N	N	5,511	91.2	64.1	N	N	N
Howard County, Maryland	N	N	N	41,754	93.3	74.0	N	N	N
Montgomery County, Maryland	N	N	N	117,968	89.7	66.9	N	N	N
Prince George's County, Maryland	N	N	N	27,146	86.0	54.3	N	N	N
St. Mary's County, Maryland	N	N	N	N	N	N	N	N	N
Washington County, Maryland	N	N	N	N	N	N	N	N	N
Wicomico County, Maryland	N	N	N	N	N	N	N	N	N
Baltimore city, Maryland	N	N	N	10,629	91.2	68.2	N	N	N
MASSACHUSETTS	12,808	73.1	20.4	326,204	86.3	63.2	N	N	N
Barnstable County, Massachusetts	N	N	N	N	N	N	N	N	N
Berkshire County, Massachusetts	N	N	N	N	N	N	N	N	N
Bristol County, Massachusetts	N	N	N	8,758	89.8	70.7	N	N	N
Essex County, Massachusetts	N	N	N	19,389	79.8	46.7	N	N	N
Franklin County, Massachusetts	N	N	N	N	N	N	N	N	N
Hampden County, Massachusetts	N	N	N	8,144	76.9	40.1	N	N	N
Hampshire County, Massachusetts	N	N	N	N	N	N	N	N	N
Middlesex County, Massachusetts	N	N	N	139,701	92.1	73.1	N	N	N
Norfolk County, Massachusetts	N	N	N	57,877	79.0	54.7	N	N	N
Plymouth County, Massachusetts	N	N	N	5,656	84.2	47.8	N	N	N
Suffolk County, Massachusetts	N	N	N	50,666	81.6	55.8	N	N	N
Worcester County, Massachusetts	N	N	N	29,282	85.2	63.2	N	N	N
MICHIGAN	38,741	87.6	11.7	218,309	89.8	64.8	N	N	N
Allegan County, Michigan	N	N	N	N	N	N	N	N	N
Bay County, Michigan	N	N	N	N	N	N	N	N	N
Berrien County, Michigan	N	N	N	N	N	N	N	N	N
Calhoun County, Michigan	N	N	N	N	N	N	N	N	N
Clinton County, Michigan	N	N	N	N	N	N	N	N	N
Eaton County, Michigan	N	N	N	N	N	N	N	N	N
Genesee County, Michigan	N	N	N	2,777	75.5	60.2	N	N	N
Grand Traverse County, Michigan	N	N	N	N	N	N	N	N	N
Ingham County, Michigan	N	N	N	11,125	88.8	70.6	N	N	N
Isabella County, Michigan	1,430	73.1	17.0	N	N	N	N	N	N
Jackson County, Michigan	N	N	N	N	N	N	N	N	N
Kalamazoo County, Michigan	N	N	N	3,988	83.5	52.2	N	N	N
Kent County, Michigan	N	N	N	13,323	77.0	49.9	N	N	N
Lapeer County, Michigan	N	N	N	N	N	N	N	N	N

N = Data for this geographic area cannot be displayed because the number of sample cases is too small.

Table C-2. Educational Attainment of the Population, by Selected Counties, 2019—*Continued*

(Number; percent; dollars.)

| | Educational attainment by race/ethnicity, 25 years and over | | | | | | | | |
| | White alone | | | White alone, not Hispanic | | | Black alone | | |
State/County	Total	High school graduate or more (percent)	Bachelor's degree or more (percent)	Total	High school graduate or more (percent)	Bachelor's degree or more (percent)	Total	High school graduate or more (percent)	Bachelor's degree or more (percent)
MICHIGAN—(*Continued*)									
Lenawee County, Michigan	65,503	90.1	21.8	61,402	91.6	22.1	N	N	N
Livingston County, Michigan	132,280	95.3	35.7	129,727	95.3	35.6	N	N	N
Macomb County, Michigan	514,205	91.1	25.5	504,390	91.4	25.7	66,977	91.2	16.6
Marquette County, Michigan	41,887	95.4	35.8	41,569	95.5	36.1	N	N	N
Midland County, Michigan	55,188	94.5	35.1	54,526	94.5	35.0	N	N	N
Monroe County, Michigan	101,992	90.7	24.3	99,541	90.5	24.1	N	N	N
Muskegon County, Michigan	100,687	93.7	22.8	96,758	94.4	23.2	13,640	84.9	7.0
Oakland County, Michigan	684,014	95.0	48.4	660,458	95.2	48.6	119,331	94.1	33.7
Ottawa County, Michigan	168,558	94.8	37.4	159,962	95.9	38.6	N	N	N
Saginaw County, Michigan	104,311	90.9	24.1	97,070	91.8	24.1	22,056	84.5	10.1
St. Clair County, Michigan	108,152	91.8	21.6	106,221	92.2	21.7	N	N	N
Shiawassee County, Michigan	47,273	91.9	18.4	46,019	91.9	18.1	N	N	N
Van Buren County, Michigan	48,184	88.3	24.1	44,680	90.2	25.5	N	N	N
Washtenaw County, Michigan	178,638	96.0	57.3	171,194	96.3	58.0	27,074	89.2	28.3
Wayne County, Michigan	659,129	89.6	30.3	626,612	90.6	30.9	442,805	86.5	14.8
MINNESOTA	3,298,386	95.6	38.5	3,208,417	96.0	38.8	207,288	82.1	21.7
Anoka County, Minnesota	210,697	95.5	33.1	205,975	95.9	33.3	13,706	91.7	27.7
Blue Earth County, Minnesota	36,625	96.1	35.2	36,108	96.3	35.5	N	N	N
Carver County, Minnesota	64,038	95.4	52.5	62,365	96.7	53.5	N	N	N
Crow Wing County, Minnesota	45,268	95.0	25.3	45,016	95.0	25.3	N	N	N
Dakota County, Minnesota	246,925	97.6	44.1	237,504	98.1	44.9	16,530	90.2	27.9
Hennepin County, Minnesota	678,281	97.6	56.4	657,463	98.1	56.8	96,210	79.7	17.4
Olmsted County, Minnesota	93,056	96.4	47.2	89,309	97.3	48.0	5,030	70.4	23.3
Ramsey County, Minnesota	268,511	95.7	48.0	254,253	96.5	49.4	38,952	86.9	26.0
Rice County, Minnesota	37,893	95.6	34.5	36,673	96.1	34.8	N	N	N
St. Louis County, Minnesota	128,715	95.7	30.6	127,533	95.9	30.5	N	N	N
Scott County, Minnesota	83,486	95.2	42.2	80,461	95.6	41.9	N	N	N
Sherburne County, Minnesota	59,679	96.1	26.9	59,144	96.2	27.1	1,626	78.8	23.6
Stearns County, Minnesota	90,564	94.3	28.7	89,406	94.6	28.9	N	N	N
Washington County, Minnesota	154,527	97.3	46.7	151,088	97.6	46.8	8,176	90.7	23.6
Wright County, Minnesota	84,860	96.3	33.4	83,872	96.4	33.8	N	N	N
MISSISSIPPI	1,217,710	88.3	25.8	1,190,544	88.7	26.1	702,026	80.8	16.0
DeSoto County, Mississippi	82,889	90.6	27.1	79,807	90.8	27.4	34,528	89.1	28.6
Forrest County, Mississippi	29,545	92.2	34.6	28,389	92.7	35.7	16,930	82.2	6.5
Harrison County, Mississippi	98,455	90.4	26.0	93,745	90.4	26.5	30,307	89.2	15.3
Hinds County, Mississippi	41,941	93.1	44.9	41,188	93.8	45.5	106,460	86.2	22.5
Jackson County, Mississippi	73,662	91.3	25.3	69,824	91.8	25.8	19,643	90.1	14.8
Jones County, Mississippi	31,497	87.7	23.0	30,162	90.4	23.9	12,707	82.7	8.7
Lauderdale County, Mississippi	29,081	90.3	27.8	28,305	90.8	28.6	21,437	67.8	6.5
Lee County, Mississippi	38,930	86.7	29.1	38,447	86.7	29.0	14,942	77.8	14.5
Madison County, Mississippi	42,182	96.7	60.7	41,325	97.5	61.6	25,455	84.7	31.2
Rankin County, Mississippi	81,895	92.2	28.9	80,881	92.7	29.1	21,442	84.3	32.2
MISSOURI	3,537,955	91.3	31.0	3,449,298	91.6	31.2	450,283	87.8	19.5
Boone County, Missouri	91,725	93.7	47.8	89,644	93.7	48.2	8,213	90.7	29.4
Buchanan County, Missouri	53,109	91.3	20.8	51,473	91.1	20.7	3,451	93.0	8.9
Cape Girardeau County, Missouri	46,333	91.1	34.0	45,663	91.0	34.3	3,269	86.4	9.5
Cass County, Missouri	66,910	93.4	25.3	65,171	93.3	25.0	3,857	93.6	24.8
Christian County, Missouri	57,880	90.0	28.4	56,530	91.3	29.0	N	N	N
Clay County, Missouri	146,810	95.1	33.8	141,997	95.4	34.2	9,754	91.6	20.9
Cole County, Missouri	46,424	93.8	34.4	45,281	93.9	34.4	6,331	85.7	27.0
Franklin County, Missouri	70,110	89.5	20.0	69,813	89.5	20.1	N	N	N
Greene County, Missouri	175,813	92.4	30.5	172,764	92.4	30.4	5,437	76.0	17.1
Jackson County, Missouri	342,744	93.0	37.1	322,972	93.9	37.9	102,781	90.0	18.4
Jasper County, Missouri	74,241	84.9	23.5	70,266	87.3	24.5	N	N	N
Jefferson County, Missouri	152,141	89.6	20.0	149,617	89.7	20.3	N	N	N
Platte County, Missouri	62,530	96.7	45.4	59,441	96.8	45.1	4,643	89.7	40.0
St. Charles County, Missouri	249,681	94.6	39.6	244,705	94.5	39.6	14,049	94.9	47.2
St. Francois County, Missouri	44,431	87.0	14.6	43,970	87.5	14.7	N	N	N
St. Louis County, Missouri	488,998	95.7	51.9	479,339	95.7	51.8	154,279	89.2	20.3
St. Louis city, Missouri	113,110	94.4	54.7	108,102	95.3	54.9	90,905	84.4	16.5

N = Data for this geographic area cannot be displayed because the number of sample cases is too small.

Table C-2. Educational Attainment of the Population, by Selected Counties, 2019—*Continued*

(Number; percent; dollars.)

| | Educational attainment by race/ethnicity, 25 years and over | | | | | | | | |
| | American Indian or Alaska Native alone | | | Asian alone | | | Native Hawaiian or Other Pacific Islander alone | | |
State/County	Total	High school graduate or more (percent)	Bachelor's degree or more (percent)	Total	High school graduate or more (percent)	Bachelor's degree or more (percent)	Total	High school graduate or more (percent)	Bachelor's degree or more (percent)
MICHIGAN—*(Continued)*									
Lenawee County, Michigan	N	N	N	N	N	N	N	N	N
Livingston County, Michigan	N	N	N	1,486	84.3	33.0	N	N	N
Macomb County, Michigan	N	N	N	25,461	84.6	44.5	N	N	N
Marquette County, Michigan	N	N	N	N	N	N	N	N	N
Midland County, Michigan	N	N	N	N	N	N	N	N	N
Monroe County, Michigan	N	N	N	N	N	N	N	N	N
Muskegon County, Michigan	N	N	N	N	N	N	N	N	N
Oakland County, Michigan	2,267	88.4	12.7	71,796	95.8	79.6	N	N	N
Ottawa County, Michigan	N	N	N	5,297	73.4	18.5	N	N	N
Saginaw County, Michigan	N	N	N	N	N	N	N	N	N
St. Clair County, Michigan	N	N	N	N	N	N	N	N	N
Shiawassee County, Michigan	N	N	N	N	N	N	N	N	N
Van Buren County, Michigan	N	N	N	N	N	N	N	N	N
Washtenaw County, Michigan	N	N	N	19,756	97.5	84.8	N	N	N
Wayne County, Michigan	4,148	87.5	11.5	41,182	86.7	58.4	N	N	N
MINNESOTA	34,650	83.6	14.8	100,643	81.5	46.1	N	N	N
Anoka County, Minnesota	N	N	N	11,349	86.6	31.9	N	N	N
Blue Earth County, Minnesota	N	N	N	N	N	N	N	N	N
Carver County, Minnesota	N	N	N	3,591	67.9	45.1	N	N	N
Crow Wing County, Minnesota	N	N	N	N	N	N	N	N	N
Dakota County, Minnesota	N	N	N	14,824	89.3	53.5	N	N	N
Hennepin County, Minnesota	4,864	85.0	24.6	61,732	88.3	58.1	N	N	N
Olmsted County, Minnesota	N	N	N	7,164	87.2	66.2	N	N	N
Ramsey County, Minnesota	1,893	78.5	29.1	47,208	70.9	32.9	N	N	N
Rice County, Minnesota	N	N	N	N	N	N	N	N	N
St. Louis County, Minnesota	2,620	72.4	16.5	N	N	N	N	N	N
Scott County, Minnesota	N	N	N	5,543	84.9	45.4	N	N	N
Sherburne County, Minnesota	N	N	N	N	N	N	N	N	N
Stearns County, Minnesota	N	N	N	N	N	N	N	N	N
Washington County, Minnesota	N	N	N	10,535	90.8	58.6	N	N	N
Wright County, Minnesota	N	N	N	N	N	N	N	N	N
MISSISSIPPI	8,424	75.8	9.2	20,681	84.1	41.4	N	N	N
DeSoto County, Mississippi	N	N	N	N	N	N	N	N	N
Forrest County, Mississippi	N	N	N	N	N	N	N	N	N
Harrison County, Mississippi	N	N	N	3,643	67.1	21.1	N	N	N
Hinds County, Mississippi	N	N	N	N	N	N	N	N	N
Jackson County, Mississippi	N	N	N	2,542	75.0	41.1	N	N	N
Jones County, Mississippi	N	N	N	N	N	N	N	N	N
Lauderdale County, Mississippi	N	N	N	N	N	N	N	N	N
Lee County, Mississippi	N	N	N	N	N	N	N	N	N
Madison County, Mississippi	N	N	N	2,180	86.7	32.4	N	N	N
Rankin County, Mississippi	N	N	N	N	N	N	N	N	N
MISSOURI	18,101	88.3	15.4	87,803	89.3	61.3	4,114	79.2	16.9
Boone County, Missouri	N	N	N	N	N	N	N	N	N
Buchanan County, Missouri	N	N	N	N	N	N	N	N	N
Cape Girardeau County, Missouri	N	N	N	N	N	N	N	N	N
Cass County, Missouri	N	N	N	N	N	N	N	N	N
Christian County, Missouri	N	N	N	N	N	N	N	N	N
Clay County, Missouri	N	N	N	3,489	85.4	44.4	N	N	N
Cole County, Missouri	N	N	N	N	N	N	N	N	N
Franklin County, Missouri	N	N	N	N	N	N	N	N	N
Greene County, Missouri	N	N	N	N	N	N	N	N	N
Jackson County, Missouri	1,695	87.3	33.3	8,847	85.0	49.1	N	N	N
Jasper County, Missouri	N	N	N	N	N	N	N	N	N
Jefferson County, Missouri	N	N	N	N	N	N	N	N	N
Platte County, Missouri	N	N	N	N	N	N	N	N	N
St. Charles County, Missouri	N	N	N	7,547	82.5	51.8	N	N	N
St. Francois County, Missouri	N	N	N	N	N	N	N	N	N
St. Louis County, Missouri	N	N	N	31,359	96.0	78.1	N	N	N
St. Louis city, Missouri	N	N	N	7,500	81.2	59.7	N	N	N

N = Data for this geographic area cannot be displayed because the number of sample cases is too small.

Table C-2. Educational Attainment of the Population, by Selected Counties, 2019—*Continued*

(Number; percent; dollars.)

| | Educational attainment by race/ethnicity, 25 years and over | | | | | | | | |
| | White alone | | | White alone, not Hispanic | | | Black alone | | |
State/County	Total	High school graduate or more (percent)	Bachelor's degree or more (percent)	Total	High school graduate or more (percent)	Bachelor's degree or more (percent)	Total	High school graduate or more (percent)	Bachelor's degree or more (percent)
MONTANA	672,576	94.8	34.3	658,762	95.0	34.5	2,977	84.5	42.4
Cascade County, Montana	50,305	93.0	25.4	49,352	93.1	25.4	N	N	N
Flathead County, Montana	70,342	96.2	34.8	69,777	96.2	34.9	N	N	N
Gallatin County, Montana	69,405	98.5	53.5	68,401	98.5	54.1	N	N	N
Lewis and Clark County, Montana	46,264	97.5	44.2	45,672	97.5	44.3	N	N	N
Missoula County, Montana	75,615	95.6	45.1	73,880	95.8	44.6	N	N	N
Yellowstone County, Montana	102,859	93.6	33.8	99,641	94.2	34.4	N	N	N
NEBRASKA	1,130,659	93.5	34.3	1,055,888	95.7	35.7	54,590	85.3	21.7
Douglas County, Nebraska	307,695	93.2	43.9	279,647	96.5	47.0	37,206	84.5	21.2
Lancaster County, Nebraska	176,064	94.9	41.9	168,316	96.5	43.0	7,082	85.9	20.5
Sarpy County, Nebraska	107,178	97.3	41.4	100,533	98.2	42.4	4,243	92.0	23.0
NEVADA	1,444,872	89.1	26.9	1,148,711	94.2	30.7	192,799	90.4	18.2
Clark County, Nevada	974,939	88.3	26.9	736,197	94.3	31.7	181,932	90.6	17.8
Washoe County, Nevada...............................	259,281	92.3	33.1	225,038	95.9	36.1	6,849	92.8	29.0
NEW HAMPSHIRE	919,746	93.6	37.0	897,818	93.9	37.3	13,726	85.9	36.9
Cheshire County, New Hampshire	52,122	94.8	34.0	51,619	94.8	34.0	N	N	N
Grafton County, New Hampshire	59,954	91.3	40.0	59,090	91.2	39.7	N	N	N
Hillsborough County, New Hampshire	269,875	92.9	37.3	257,549	94.2	38.5	6,801	78.0	29.4
Merrimack County, New Hampshire.............	103,286	92.0	34.9	102,411	92.1	35.0	N	N	N
Rockingham County, New Hampshire	217,518	96.0	42.1	212,422	96.1	41.9	2,101	93.8	35.2
Strafford County, New Hampshire................	80,983	94.0	35.7	79,499	93.9	35.8	N	N	N
NEW JERSEY	4,294,038	92.0	42.0	3,577,879	94.8	45.8	813,816	88.8	25.3
Atlantic County, New Jersey........................	125,763	90.9	31.5	112,954	93.3	33.2	23,540	84.9	12.4
Bergen County, New Jersey	476,078	93.2	49.7	376,322	95.6	53.7	37,821	91.8	45.4
Burlington County, New Jersey	233,720	95.0	41.0	219,431	95.5	42.2	52,177	91.5	30.5
Camden County, New Jersey........................	235,502	93.1	37.5	212,882	94.9	39.4	64,502	89.8	21.0
Cape May County, New Jersey	65,010	94.7	33.6	61,621	95.0	34.6	2,690	76.0	9.2
Cumberland County, New Jersey	70,451	83.4	19.7	52,840	93.1	23.0	20,381	80.6	8.5
Essex County, New Jersey...........................	246,698	88.8	46.2	176,034	94.2	57.7	213,736	87.1	21.7
Gloucester County, New Jersey...................	169,251	93.8	33.3	163,370	94.7	33.5	21,069	90.6	33.8
Hudson County, New Jersey	281,098	85.5	42.7	152,458	93.6	59.1	57,670	86.2	30.4
Hunterdon County, New Jersey	82,438	95.9	53.8	78,403	97.0	54.9	N	N	N
Mercer County, New Jersey.........................	155,999	91.4	47.3	130,090	95.3	52.3	49,779	84.5	18.7
Middlesex County, New Jersey	330,778	89.2	36.3	261,364	92.2	41.1	57,544	91.7	31.2
Monmouth County, New Jersey	369,000	95.6	49.8	341,740	96.5	51.6	32,144	92.6	24.6
Morris County, New Jersey	286,606	95.5	55.5	252,306	97.4	58.5	12,159	95.3	37.4
Ocean County, New Jersey..........................	384,892	93.2	32.1	359,422	93.7	33.1	13,043	93.9	27.7
Passaic County, New Jersey........................	230,099	86.8	33.3	148,201	93.9	42.1	37,329	89.0	16.3
Salem County, New Jersey..........................	36,224	89.4	21.6	34,361	89.6	22.4	5,665	81.0	8.5
Somerset County, New Jersey	148,299	95.2	53.9	133,381	97.3	56.9	22,475	93.9	39.8
Sussex County, New Jersey	95,716	94.5	37.2	88,793	95.2	37.6	N	N	N
Union County, New Jersey	201,938	89.7	44.8	158,476	93.5	50.8	82,879	90.8	26.5
Warren County, New Jersey	68,478	93.8	33.2	63,430	94.0	33.5	3,359	95.1	31.0
NEW MEXICO	1,081,586	87.5	30.7	606,478	94.4	41.2	29,349	87.0	28.4
Bernalillo County, New Mexico....................	361,788	90.7	38.2	207,510	96.4	49.8	12,801	86.1	34.8
Chaves County, New Mexico	37,466	76.6	17.9	18,737	88.1	23.3	N	N	N
Doña Ana County, New Mexico	108,752	78.8	27.3	42,840	94.2	45.0	N	N	N
Lea County, New Mexico.............................	38,041	76.0	12.5	17,373	87.9	17.5	1,556	87.8	2.4
McKinley County, New Mexico.....................	6,613	92.8	35.5	4,848	92.7	41.3	N	N	N
Otero County, New Mexico..........................	36,630	85.6	15.1	24,352	92.7	18.9	N	N	N
Sandoval County, New Mexico....................	76,240	94.9	36.5	49,190	96.7	41.5	N	N	N
San Juan County, New Mexico....................	44,787	89.0	19.5	34,662	90.5	21.9	N	N	N
Santa Fe County, New Mexico	95,930	89.2	43.5	56,415	97.7	62.5	N	N	N
Valencia County, New Mexico	43,127	86.9	20.5	19,292	90.9	27.6	N	N	N
NEW YORK	8,910,770	91.7	42.3	7,894,691	93.7	44.5	2,097,135	85.0	24.5
Albany County, New York............................	162,395	94.9	45.6	156,059	95.3	46.0	21,291	83.0	29.6
Bronx County, New York	227,750	74.2	24.9	94,201	84.8	39.2	359,027	78.9	19.5
Broome County, New York	112,851	91.6	28.0	111,248	91.7	28.1	6,311	85.8	14.7
Cattaraugus County, New York....................	49,306	90.9	21.6	48,947	90.9	21.6	N	N	N

N = Data for this geographic area cannot be displayed because the number of sample cases is too small.

Table C-2. Educational Attainment of the Population, by Selected Counties, 2019—*Continued*

(Number; percent; dollars.)

| | Educational attainment by race/ethnicity, 25 years and over | | | | | | | | |
| | American Indian or Alaska Native alone | | | Asian alone | | | Native Hawaiian or Other Pacific Islander alone | | |
State/County	Total	High school graduate or more (percent)	Bachelor's degree or more (percent)	Total	High school graduate or more (percent)	Bachelor's degree or more (percent)	Total	High school graduate or more (percent)	Bachelor's degree or more (percent)
MONTANA	37,153	87.5	15.2	6,867	93.1	48.0	N	N	N
Cascade County, Montana	N	N	N	N	N	N	N	N	N
Flathead County, Montana	N	N	N	N	N	N	N	N	N
Gallatin County, Montana	N	N	N	N	N	N	N	N	N
Lewis and Clark County, Montana	N	N	N	N	N	N	N	N	N
Missoula County, Montana	N	N	N	N	N	N	N	N	N
Yellowstone County, Montana	4,607	95.9	14.8	N	N	N	N	N	N
NEBRASKA	10,910	83.4	10.6	30,283	77.5	47.1	N	N	N
Douglas County, Nebraska	2,424	77.1	6.0	14,618	79.0	57.9	N	N	N
Lancaster County, Nebraska	N	N	N	8,794	73.3	38.8	N	N	N
Sarpy County, Nebraska	N	N	N	3,259	86.7	32.8	N	N	N
NEVADA	28,056	75.8	14.8	198,870	90.7	42.9	14,368	88.0	19.6
Clark County, Nevada	14,528	66.7	15.9	173,741	90.2	42.3	11,411	87.9	19.0
Washoe County, Nevada	4,966	84.3	17.2	18,760	94.9	52.4	N	N	N
NEW HAMPSHIRE	N	N	N	25,955	91.6	64.4	N	N	N
Cheshire County, New Hampshire	N	N	N	N	N	N	N	N	N
Grafton County, New Hampshire	N	N	N	N	N	N	N	N	N
Hillsborough County, New Hampshire	N	N	N	12,070	89.1	59.6	N	N	N
Merrimack County, New Hampshire	N	N	N	N	N	N	N	N	N
Rockingham County, New Hampshire	N	N	N	5,144	95.9	59.6	N	N	N
Strafford County, New Hampshire	N	N	N	N	N	N	N	N	N
NEW JERSEY	12,055	75.7	28.4	613,693	92.9	71.6	N	N	N
Atlantic County, New Jersey	N	N	N	14,228	81.1	36.2	N	N	N
Bergen County, New Jersey	N	N	N	113,462	95.7	70.3	N	N	N
Burlington County, New Jersey	N	N	N	15,819	88.1	56.4	N	N	N
Camden County, New Jersey	N	N	N	20,701	83.5	60.0	N	N	N
Cape May County, New Jersey	N	N	N	N	N	N	N	N	N
Cumberland County, New Jersey	N	N	N	1,491	93.6	35.8	N	N	N
Essex County, New Jersey	N	N	N	32,122	95.6	72.4	N	N	N
Gloucester County, New Jersey	N	N	N	5,985	92.8	61.9	N	N	N
Hudson County, New Jersey	N	N	N	82,498	94.2	78.4	N	N	N
Hunterdon County, New Jersey	N	N	N	N	N	N	N	N	N
Mercer County, New Jersey	N	N	N	28,679	93.8	83.7	N	N	N
Middlesex County, New Jersey	N	N	N	137,340	91.1	73.9	N	N	N
Monmouth County, New Jersey	N	N	N	24,093	91.3	68.6	N	N	N
Morris County, New Jersey	N	N	N	37,438	93.5	75.5	N	N	N
Ocean County, New Jersey	N	N	N	8,288	90.3	56.7	N	N	N
Passaic County, New Jersey	N	N	N	18,273	91.1	47.8	N	N	N
Salem County, New Jersey	N	N	N	N	N	N	N	N	N
Somerset County, New Jersey	N	N	N	42,036	95.8	84.1	N	N	N
Sussex County, New Jersey	N	N	N	2,231	100.0	53.0	N	N	N
Union County, New Jersey	N	N	N	22,118	95.4	70.7	N	N	N
Warren County, New Jersey	N	N	N	N	N	N	N	N	N
NEW MEXICO	125,785	81.8	11.8	27,650	89.1	49.6	N	N	N
Bernalillo County, New Mexico	22,745	91.6	26.8	14,159	85.7	46.0	N	N	N
Chaves County, New Mexico	N	N	N	672	81.5	38.2	N	N	N
Doña Ana County, New Mexico	N	N	N	N	N	N	N	N	N
Lea County, New Mexico	N	N	N	N	N	N	N	N	N
McKinley County, New Mexico	33,253	75.1	5.0	N	N	N	N	N	N
Otero County, New Mexico	3,196	82.2	12.3	N	N	N	N	N	N
Sandoval County, New Mexico	11,391	81.9	14.4	N	N	N	N	N	N
San Juan County, New Mexico	31,164	80.5	6.9	N	N	N	N	N	N
Santa Fe County, New Mexico	3,896	90.5	8.5	N	N	N	N	N	N
Valencia County, New Mexico	N	N	N	N	N	N	N	N	N
NEW YORK	50,556	76.0	18.5	1,213,907	80.2	47.8	5,020	82.3	18.9
Albany County, New York	N	N	N	12,606	84.5	56.9	N	N	N
Bronx County, New York	5,868	75.3	10.5	38,188	78.8	40.1	N	N	N
Broome County, New York	N	N	N	3,732	70.4	32.0	N	N	N
Cattaraugus County, New York	1,637	90.9	10.5	N	N	N	N	N	N

N = Data for this geographic area cannot be displayed because the number of sample cases is too small.

Table C-2. Educational Attainment of the Population, by Selected Counties, 2019—*Continued*

(Number; percent; dollars.)

State/County	Educational attainment by race/ethnicity, 25 years and over								
	White alone			White alone, not Hispanic			Black alone		
	Total	High school graduate or more (percent)	Bachelor's degree or more (percent)	Total	High school graduate or more (percent)	Bachelor's degree or more (percent)	Total	High school graduate or more (percent)	Bachelor's degree or more (percent)
NEW YORK—(*Continued*)									
Cayuga County, New York	51,536	89.0	24.5	50,892	89.5	24.4	N	N	N
Chautauqua County, New York	83,145	91.3	26.1	80,613	91.4	26.0	N	N	N
Chemung County, New York	53,528	93.2	26.1	52,234	93.7	25.6	3,746	79.5	10.1
Clinton County, New York	51,693	88.2	26.3	50,729	88.2	26.6	N	N	N
Dutchess County, New York	165,478	93.1	37.5	153,747	93.6	38.4	22,381	91.8	20.0
Erie County, New York	527,571	95.1	36.2	515,388	95.3	36.4	77,194	86.5	17.7
Jefferson County, New York	62,861	91.0	22.4	60,035	91.0	22.5	3,103	90.5	21.8
Kings County, New York	783,732	90.2	55.2	659,773	93.0	61.0	574,467	86.3	24.2
Livingston County, New York	39,416	92.2	25.9	39,095	92.3	26.0	N	N	N
Madison County, New York	46,700	93.9	24.3	46,268	93.9	24.4	N	N	N
Monroe County, New York	409,987	93.6	44.6	387,435	94.9	45.9	70,855	81.1	18.2
Nassau County, New York	656,805	93.8	50.0	580,032	95.9	52.3	109,459	92.7	33.7
New York County, New York	732,236	94.6	77.4	618,310	98.0	84.0	170,988	83.8	31.0
Niagara County, New York	134,853	92.1	28.6	133,201	92.0	28.5	8,486	88.9	19.2
Oneida County, New York	140,513	91.2	29.9	136,245	91.9	30.5	7,974	68.0	10.3
Onondaga County, New York	263,608	94.6	38.6	257,713	94.9	38.6	30,477	82.0	21.2
Ontario County, New York	73,292	94.1	40.3	71,933	94.3	40.8	N	N	N
Orange County, New York	188,906	91.0	33.4	161,850	92.4	34.3	27,037	88.6	24.8
Oswego County, New York	77,695	88.6	21.9	77,048	88.8	21.8	N	N	N
Putnam County, New York	63,050	93.3	38.8	56,539	94.0	39.0	N	N	N
Queens County, New York	620,068	87.4	39.1	434,282	92.1	47.0	297,663	87.5	25.7
Rensselaer County, New York	99,411	92.8	36.1	97,110	92.8	36.2	7,054	80.4	10.8
Richmond County, New York	249,372	90.4	36.6	210,270	93.2	39.3	30,478	90.3	27.2
Rockland County, New York	141,057	92.7	46.4	126,423	92.9	47.7	26,787	82.8	25.8
St. Lawrence County, New York	67,429	88.2	23.0	66,936	88.5	23.1	N	N	N
Saratoga County, New York	155,605	93.8	41.3	152,342	94.0	41.3	N	N	N
Schenectady County, New York	85,465	94.6	37.6	82,915	95.1	38.1	10,377	93.3	18.9
Steuben County, New York	64,436	91.6	23.5	64,154	91.7	23.5	1,409	94.5	20.6
Suffolk County, New York	849,278	92.8	39.9	732,730	95.1	43.2	74,835	87.1	29.2
Sullivan County, New York	42,250	92.9	28.0	40,103	93.3	28.6	3,870	83.8	22.4
Tompkins County, New York	51,825	96.2	56.7	50,493	96.2	55.9	N	N	N
Ulster County, New York	113,413	91.8	34.4	106,699	92.4	34.9	7,201	85.7	16.2
Warren County, New York	46,010	91.6	33.1	45,285	92.8	33.4	N	N	N
Wayne County, New York	60,341	90.9	24.8	59,120	91.5	25.4	N	N	N
Westchester County, New York	441,300	92.8	57.9	373,262	95.3	61.9	103,448	87.8	34.5
NORTH CAROLINA	5,103,713	90.7	35.1	4,805,279	92.2	36.0	1,486,857	86.4	22.4
Alamance County, North Carolina	82,533	88.3	27.6	77,050	91.3	28.7	23,449	88.8	16.6
Brunswick County, North Carolina	99,868	93.1	34.2	97,628	93.7	34.8	8,900	92.0	23.6
Buncombe County, North Carolina	175,276	92.6	42.1	168,012	93.5	43.1	11,717	90.7	18.4
Burke County, North Carolina	57,475	86.3	21.0	56,771	86.4	21.3	2,848	84.8	3.8
Cabarrus County, North Carolina	104,276	92.9	34.9	97,893	93.8	34.8	25,671	88.0	25.2
Caldwell County, North Carolina	54,250	78.9	17.5	53,435	79.1	17.5	N	N	N
Carteret County, North Carolina	48,502	91.3	31.0	47,282	91.4	30.9	2,327	82.9	20.9
Catawba County, North Carolina	93,123	88.1	24.2	89,048	89.2	24.5	8,935	83.4	16.0
Chatham County, North Carolina	43,804	89.0	45.2	41,276	89.7	46.9	6,172	94.7	53.7
Cleveland County, North Carolina	51,181	86.5	21.0	50,320	86.8	20.9	13,009	83.4	12.7
Craven County, North Carolina	50,582	92.6	25.8	47,692	93.3	26.9	14,340	87.7	8.9
Cumberland County, North Carolina	105,954	92.3	26.8	93,633	93.4	27.7	78,666	90.3	22.2
Davidson County, North Carolina	104,453	86.9	19.8	98,362	87.3	20.0	11,733	87.4	13.3
Durham County, North Carolina	124,835	89.9	56.0	108,280	97.1	62.5	77,037	90.0	35.3
Forsyth County, North Carolina	176,854	91.0	37.0	160,460	94.6	39.1	65,687	86.6	21.6
Franklin County, North Carolina	34,119	91.6	25.9	31,909	94.3	27.3	11,957	86.3	13.7
Gaston County, North Carolina	123,461	85.6	23.2	117,254	85.7	23.7	25,309	84.8	22.5
Guilford County, North Carolina	208,431	92.1	44.3	196,173	93.2	45.1	115,237	85.8	24.8
Harnett County, North Carolina	62,554	90.7	25.6	57,864	91.9	25.3	19,097	88.6	18.8
Henderson County, North Carolina	82,569	91.0	30.7	76,876	92.3	32.3	2,961	87.7	13.9
Iredell County, North Carolina	103,091	92.2	32.4	99,321	92.8	33.0	13,682	82.6	15.3
Johnston County, North Carolina	107,932	89.5	24.9	99,962	91.9	26.1	22,125	90.6	25.1
Lincoln County, North Carolina	57,201	92.2	26.9	53,864	93.5	27.2	3,902	89.6	10.1
Mecklenburg County, North Carolina	418,619	93.9	55.7	379,872	96.7	58.6	231,274	91.6	31.4
Moore County, North Carolina	60,822	95.0	40.9	58,928	94.9	40.7	8,562	76.4	31.5
Nash County, North Carolina	34,824	91.4	23.2	34,544	91.6	23.2	26,074	84.7	12.6
New Hanover County, North Carolina	134,928	94.9	46.9	130,493	95.3	47.4	19,357	84.9	19.9
Onslow County, North Carolina	83,575	93.2	24.1	74,684	94.3	24.6	16,980	85.1	25.0

N = Data for this geographic area cannot be displayed because the number of sample cases is too small.

Table C-2. Educational Attainment of the Population, by Selected Counties, 2019—*Continued*

(Number; percent; dollars.)

State/County	American Indian or Alaska Native alone			Asian alone			Native Hawaiian or Other Pacific Islander alone		
	Total	High school graduate or more (percent)	Bachelor's degree or more (percent)	Total	High school graduate or more (percent)	Bachelor's degree or more (percent)	Total	High school graduate or more (percent)	Bachelor's degree or more (percent)
NEW YORK—(*Continued*)									
Cayuga County, New York	N	N	N	N	N	N	N	N	N
Chautauqua County, New York	N	N	N	N	N	N	N	N	N
Chemung County, New York	N	N	N	N	N	N	N	N	N
Clinton County, New York	N	N	N	N	N	N	N	N	N
Dutchess County, New York	N	N	N	6,500	91.2	52.8	N	N	N
Erie County, New York	3,757	89.0	18.4	19,942	80.9	50.3	N	N	N
Jefferson County, New York	N	N	N	N	N	N	N	N	N
Kings County, New York	4,556	66.1	25.9	222,754	69.2	36.0	N	N	N
Livingston County, New York	N	N	N	N	N	N	N	N	N
Madison County, New York	N	N	N	N	N	N	N	N	N
Monroe County, New York	N	N	N	16,297	77.0	55.8	N	N	N
Nassau County, New York	N	N	N	98,194	93.2	64.5	N	N	N
New York County, New York	N	N	N	161,631	81.5	67.4	N	N	N
Niagara County, New York	N	N	N	N	N	N	N	N	N
Oneida County, New York	N	N	N	4,634	53.0	24.1	N	N	N
Onondaga County, New York	N	N	N	8,484	68.0	46.3	N	N	N
Ontario County, New York	N	N	N	N	N	N	N	N	N
Orange County, New York	N	N	N	7,319	90.6	54.6	N	N	N
Oswego County, New York	N	N	N	N	N	N	N	N	N
Putnam County, New York	N	N	N	N	N	N	N	N	N
Queens County, New York	8,536	74.5	17.7	440,933	79.2	38.4	N	N	N
Rensselaer County, New York	N	N	N	N	N	N	N	N	N
Richmond County, New York	N	N	N	37,222	82.2	44.1	N	N	N
Rockland County, New York	N	N	N	14,166	92.8	70.0	N	N	N
St. Lawrence County, New York	N	N	N	N	N	N	N	N	N
Saratoga County, New York	N	N	N	N	N	N	N	N	N
Schenectady County, New York	N	N	N	5,354	87.1	46.1	N	N	N
Steuben County, New York	N	N	N	N	N	N	N	N	N
Suffolk County, New York	3,755	72.9	9.2	39,634	89.2	57.5	N	N	N
Sullivan County, New York	N	N	N	N	N	N	N	N	N
Tompkins County, New York	N	N	N	N	N	N	N	N	N
Ulster County, New York	N	N	N	1,922	85.3	49.0	N	N	N
Warren County, New York	N	N	N	N	N	N	N	N	N
Wayne County, New York	N	N	N	N	N	N	N	N	N
Westchester County, New York	2,254	86.0	26.0	43,827	94.1	74.5	N	N	N
NORTH CAROLINA	81,694	77.4	14.7	213,997	87.2	58.5	4,374	88.7	34.3
Alamance County, North Carolina	N	N	N	N	N	N	N	N	N
Brunswick County, North Carolina	N	N	N	N	N	N	N	N	N
Buncombe County, North Carolina	N	N	N	N	N	N	N	N	N
Burke County, North Carolina	N	N	N	2,096	66.3	7.0	N	N	N
Cabarrus County, North Carolina	N	N	N	5,974	94.8	64.8	N	N	N
Caldwell County, North Carolina	N	N	N	N	N	N	N	N	N
Carteret County, North Carolina	N	N	N	N	N	N	N	N	N
Catawba County, North Carolina	N	N	N	4,083	88.3	34.1	N	N	N
Chatham County, North Carolina	N	N	N	N	N	N	N	N	N
Cleveland County, North Carolina	N	N	N	N	N	N	N	N	N
Craven County, North Carolina	N	N	N	N	N	N	N	N	N
Cumberland County, North Carolina	3,134	82.9	4.4	6,507	85.0	37.6	N	N	N
Davidson County, North Carolina	N	N	N	N	N	N	N	N	N
Durham County, North Carolina	N	N	N	10,615	86.5	74.1	N	N	N
Forsyth County, North Carolina	N	N	N	6,168	92.1	72.8	N	N	N
Franklin County, North Carolina	N	N	N	N	N	N	N	N	N
Gaston County, North Carolina	N	N	N	N	N	N	N	N	N
Guilford County, North Carolina	N	N	N	17,861	75.0	46.4	N	N	N
Harnett County, North Carolina	N	N	N	N	N	N	N	N	N
Henderson County, North Carolina	N	N	N	N	N	N	N	N	N
Iredell County, North Carolina	N	N	N	3,558	93.9	55.3	N	N	N
Johnston County, North Carolina	N	N	N	N	N	N	N	N	N
Lincoln County, North Carolina	N	N	N	N	N	N	N	N	N
Mecklenburg County, North Carolina	N	N	N	41,060	88.1	60.0	N	N	N
Moore County, North Carolina	N	N	N	N	N	N	N	N	N
Nash County, North Carolina	N	N	N	N	N	N	N	N	N
New Hanover County, North Carolina	N	N	N	N	N	N	N	N	N
Onslow County, North Carolina	N	N	N	2,547	80.2	21.1	N	N	N

N – Data for this geographic area cannot be displayed because the number of sample cases is too small.

Table C-2. Educational Attainment of the Population, by Selected Counties, 2019—*Continued*

(Number; percent; dollars.)

State/County	White alone			White alone, not Hispanic			Black alone		
	Total	High school graduate or more (percent)	Bachelor's degree or more (percent)	Total	High school graduate or more (percent)	Bachelor's degree or more (percent)	Total	High school graduate or more (percent)	Bachelor's degree or more (percent)
NORTH CAROLINA—(*Continued*)									
Orange County, North Carolina	72,735	96.0	68.6	67,127	96.8	69.7	11,836	86.5	29.1
Pitt County, North Carolina	63,658	94.6	42.1	62,563	95.2	42.6	39,228	79.7	17.1
Randolph County, North Carolina	87,945	82.5	14.2	83,349	85.0	14.8	5,534	84.0	18.4
Robeson County, North Carolina	25,531	83.2	18.0	24,269	85.0	18.7	19,905	80.0	12.7
Rockingham County, North Carolina	50,715	85.4	14.3	49,563	85.5	14.7	12,906	74.2	10.9
Rowan County, North Carolina	78,969	87.6	18.6	74,899	89.3	18.5	13,966	87.5	18.7
Rutherford County, North Carolina	42,437	87.8	21.2	41,487	88.9	20.8	4,829	81.0	5.5
Surry County, North Carolina	47,510	82.2	18.4	44,745	83.8	19.2	N	N	N
Union County, North Carolina	125,272	91.5	38.4	115,078	94.1	40.2	17,649	92.4	28.3
Wake County, North Carolina	501,390	96.5	59.7	471,820	97.7	61.8	149,263	90.1	34.8
Wayne County, North Carolina	52,793	86.1	20.3	47,033	92.3	21.3	24,658	88.1	11.1
Wilkes County, North Carolina	45,470	83.8	17.6	43,444	85.1	18.0	N	N	N
Wilson County, North Carolina	29,956	86.9	27.3	28,859	87.5	27.2	21,754	81.9	9.9
NORTH DAKOTA	446,532	94.2	31.7	438,065	94.5	31.7	13,471	93.2	21.8
Burleigh County, North Dakota	59,771	94.7	36.2	59,189	94.7	36.5	N	N	N
Cass County, North Dakota	102,519	96.8	45.0	101,194	96.8	45.0	6,896	94.3	17.5
Grand Forks County, North Dakota	36,350	96.2	36.6	35,614	96.2	36.4	N	N	N
Ward County, North Dakota	38,093	97.5	29.6	37,234	97.5	29.9	N	N	N
OHIO	6,706,983	91.8	30.2	6,552,807	92.1	30.4	939,875	86.8	17.5
Allen County, Ohio	58,791	92.2	20.2	57,640	92.2	20.2	7,372	89.1	12.5
Ashtabula County, Ohio	64,210	87.7	14.3	62,553	87.6	13.7	N	N	N
Athens County, Ohio	35,049	92.4	33.9	34,606	92.5	34.1	N	N	N
Belmont County, Ohio	46,727	91.0	17.4	46,458	91.0	17.5	N	N	N
Butler County, Ohio	211,463	92.4	31.6	205,102	93.3	31.8	20,886	90.6	29.9
Clark County, Ohio	81,639	90.7	16.5	80,179	90.9	16.3	7,740	91.1	10.1
Clermont County, Ohio	137,546	90.9	29.4	135,639	91.0	29.3	N	N	N
Columbiana County, Ohio	70,566	91.6	16.0	70,045	91.7	16.1	N	N	N
Cuyahoga County, Ohio	573,660	92.9	41.0	548,470	93.7	42.0	242,929	85.8	14.3
Delaware County, Ohio	120,543	96.6	50.4	118,295	96.6	50.4	4,774	88.3	30.8
Erie County, Ohio	47,601	93.5	25.7	46,244	93.9	26.3	4,323	86.8	8.1
Fairfield County, Ohio	94,724	94.2	29.2	93,667	94.2	29.3	7,899	91.1	31.7
Franklin County, Ohio	611,985	93.2	46.8	590,286	93.8	47.3	185,059	88.3	22.3
Geauga County, Ohio	62,717	89.1	36.7	62,365	89.0	36.4	N	N	N
Greene County, Ohio	100,876	95.3	39.9	99,148	95.2	40.0	6,440	96.6	48.8
Hamilton County, Ohio	390,342	93.8	47.0	381,291	94.4	47.4	133,644	86.5	18.2
Hancock County, Ohio	48,940	92.5	25.8	47,570	93.0	26.2	N	N	N
Jefferson County, Ohio	43,273	93.0	18.7	43,097	93.1	18.5	2,431	95.6	18.3
Lake County, Ohio	155,163	92.9	26.9	150,616	93.6	27.3	6,775	91.3	11.2
Licking County, Ohio	111,209	91.8	27.1	109,804	91.8	27.2	4,817	89.2	28.5
Lorain County, Ohio	190,472	90.5	26.0	176,870	91.9	27.3	14,717	80.9	12.4
Lucas County, Ohio	223,255	91.9	30.1	214,477	92.1	30.6	51,264	80.6	10.6
Mahoning County, Ohio	135,278	92.2	27.6	129,509	93.4	28.3	20,770	84.9	12.1
Marion County, Ohio	41,849	89.5	13.4	41,284	89.7	13.6	N	N	N
Medina County, Ohio	121,632	95.3	35.0	119,998	95.5	35.1	N	N	N
Miami County, Ohio	70,638	92.0	21.5	69,790	92.5	21.5	N	N	N
Montgomery County, Ohio	273,654	91.2	29.7	269,496	91.5	29.9	70,888	88.2	21.4
Muskingum County, Ohio	54,901	87.4	18.1	54,901	87.4	18.1	N	N	N
Portage County, Ohio	99,383	91.9	29.2	97,880	91.9	29.2	3,844	90.9	18.0
Richland County, Ohio	74,889	89.7	20.1	74,122	89.5	20.3	7,969	78.8	6.3
Ross County, Ohio	49,656	90.7	16.6	49,278	90.7	16.4	3,181	81.7	4.6
Scioto County, Ohio	49,764	85.8	19.2	49,556	85.7	18.9	N	N	N
Stark County, Ohio	234,159	92.1	23.0	231,839	92.2	22.9	18,568	88.7	7.7
Summit County, Ohio	311,433	94.4	35.5	306,395	94.5	35.5	50,265	90.6	15.0
Trumbull County, Ohio	128,630	88.3	19.5	127,086	88.2	19.5	11,585	91.9	16.5
Tuscarawas County, Ohio	62,185	85.0	18.7	61,240	85.0	18.3	N	N	N
Warren County, Ohio	139,774	95.5	42.4	137,652	95.4	42.7	6,502	89.2	34.8
Wayne County, Ohio	73,238	85.7	22.5	72,755	85.7	22.6	N	N	N
Wood County, Ohio	77,034	95.7	36.4	74,161	96.2	36.7	N	N	N
OKLAHOMA	1,999,360	89.5	27.8	1,851,190	91.6	29.0	180,859	89.5	19.8
Canadian County, Oklahoma	83,222	90.4	28.6	77,674	93.1	29.3	N	N	N
Cleveland County, Oklahoma	147,677	92.9	36.6	137,361	94.0	37.4	7,309	89.6	34.4
Comanche County, Oklahoma	51,212	92.1	24.1	46,669	91.7	24.3	12,147	93.6	18.0
Creek County, Oklahoma	40,645	88.7	17.9	39,168	89.2	18.4	N	N	N

N = Data for this geographic area cannot be displayed because the number of sample cases is too small.

Table C-2. Educational Attainment of the Population, by Selected Counties, 2019—*Continued*

(Number; percent; dollars.)

	Educational attainment by race/ethnicity, 25 years and over								
	American Indian or Alaska Native alone			Asian alone			Native Hawaiian or Other Pacific Islander alone		
State/County	Total	High school graduate or more (percent)	Bachelor's degree or more (percent)	Total	High school graduate or more (percent)	Bachelor's degree or more (percent)	Total	High school graduate or more (percent)	Bachelor's degree or more (percent)
NORTH CAROLINA—(*Continued*)									
Orange County, North Carolina	N	N	N	7,228	91.9	62.6	N	N	N
Pitt County, North Carolina	N	N	N	N	N	N	N	N	N
Randolph County, North Carolina	N	N	N	N	N	N	N	N	N
Robeson County, North Carolina	34,413	76.6	14.0	N	N	N	N	N	N
Rockingham County, North Carolina	N	N	N	N	N	N	N	N	N
Rowan County, North Carolina	N	N	N	N	N	N	N	N	N
Rutherford County, North Carolina	N	N	N	N	N	N	N	N	N
Surry County, North Carolina	N	N	N	N	N	N	N	N	N
Union County, North Carolina	N	N	N	5,186	93.6	65.1	N	N	N
Wake County, North Carolina	N	N	N	56,986	93.1	74.7	N	N	N
Wayne County, North Carolina	N	N	N	N	N	N	N	N	N
Wilkes County, North Carolina	N	N	N	N	N	N	N	N	N
Wilson County, North Carolina	N	N	N	N	N	N	N	N	N
NORTH DAKOTA	21,476	84.5	17.6	7,164	80.9	40.6	N	N	N
Burleigh County, North Dakota	N	N	N	N	N	N	N	N	N
Cass County, North Dakota	N	N	N	N	N	N	N	N	N
Grand Forks County, North Dakota	N	N	N	N	N	N	N	N	N
Ward County, North Dakota	N	N	N	N	N	N	N	N	N
OHIO	15,473	79.2	17.7	185,785	86.8	62.5	3,809	70.8	38.9
Allen County, Ohio	N	N	N	N	N	N	N	N	N
Ashtabula County, Ohio	N	N	N	N	N	N	N	N	N
Athens County, Ohio	N	N	N	N	N	N	N	N	N
Belmont County, Ohio	N	N	N	N	N	N	N	N	N
Butler County, Ohio	N	N	N	8,314	76.3	51.1	N	N	N
Clark County, Ohio	N	N	N	N	N	N	N	N	N
Clermont County, Ohio	N	N	N	N	N	N	N	N	N
Columbiana County, Ohio	N	N	N	N	N	N	N	N	N
Cuyahoga County, Ohio	2,372	61.9	14.5	29,151	85.6	63.3	N	N	N
Delaware County, Ohio	N	N	N	10,425	96.0	81.4	N	N	N
Erie County, Ohio	N	N	N	N	N	N	N	N	N
Fairfield County, Ohio	N	N	N	2,087	80.5	35.8	N	N	N
Franklin County, Ohio	N	N	N	48,523	87.3	63.0	N	N	N
Geauga County, Ohio	N	N	N	N	N	N	N	N	N
Greene County, Ohio	N	N	N	N	N	N	N	N	N
Hamilton County, Ohio	N	N	N	15,379	91.7	70.5	N	N	N
Hancock County, Ohio	N	N	N	N	N	N	N	N	N
Jefferson County, Ohio	N	N	N	N	N	N	N	N	N
Lake County, Ohio	N	N	N	2,144	85.5	36.9	N	N	N
Licking County, Ohio	N	N	N	N	N	N	N	N	N
Lorain County, Ohio	N	N	N	2,711	85.5	38.3	N	N	N
Lucas County, Ohio	N	N	N	5,781	90.6	65.9	N	N	N
Mahoning County, Ohio	N	N	N	N	N	N	N	N	N
Marion County, Ohio	N	N	N	N	N	N	N	N	N
Medina County, Ohio	N	N	N	N	N	N	N	N	N
Miami County, Ohio	N	N	N	N	N	N	N	N	N
Montgomery County, Ohio	N	N	N	7,768	92.8	75.5	N	N	N
Muskingum County, Ohio	N	N	N	N	N	N	N	N	N
Portage County, Ohio	N	N	N	N	N	N	N	N	N
Richland County, Ohio	N	N	N	N	N	N	N	N	N
Ross County, Ohio	N	N	N	N	N	N	N	N	N
Scioto County, Ohio	N	N	N	N	N	N	N	N	N
Stark County, Ohio	N	N	N	2,877	89.1	51.9	N	N	N
Summit County, Ohio	N	N	N	12,258	60.7	38.5	N	N	N
Trumbull County, Ohio	N	N	N	N	N	N	N	N	N
Tuscarawas County, Ohio	N	N	N	N	N	N	N	N	N
Warren County, Ohio	N	N	N	10,665	96.8	78.4	N	N	N
Wayne County, Ohio	N	N	N	N	N	N	N	N	N
Wood County, Ohio	N	N	N	N	N	N	N	N	N
OKLAHOMA	187,385	86.4	17.6	58,425	81.5	43.2	2,691	82.3	10.6
Canadian County, Oklahoma	3,643	83.5	28.2	3,005	62.9	28.8	N	N	N
Cleveland County, Oklahoma	7,467	90.9	15.3	7,110	87.8	45.5	N	N	N
Comanche County, Oklahoma	3,595	92.9	14.8	2,707	85.6	29.1	N	N	N
Creek County, Oklahoma	5,181	89.2	17.2	N	N	N	N	N	N

N = Data for this geographic area cannot be displayed because the number of sample cases is too small.

Table C-2. Educational Attainment of the Population, by Selected Counties, 2019—*Continued*

(Number; percent; dollars.)

	Educational attainment by race/ethnicity, 25 years and over								
	White alone			White alone, not Hispanic			Black alone		
State/County	Total	High school graduate or more (percent)	Bachelor's degree or more (percent)	Total	High school graduate or more (percent)	Bachelor's degree or more (percent)	Total	High school graduate or more (percent)	Bachelor's degree or more (percent)
OKLAHOMA—(*Continued*)									
Muskogee County, Oklahoma	29,240	86.9	22.1	28,356	86.7	22.7	4,504	92.7	18.5
Oklahoma County, Oklahoma	376,046	88.7	35.6	324,029	94.1	39.2	75,697	89.9	20.6
Payne County, Oklahoma	36,633	94.3	40.1	35,943	94.6	40.2	N	N	N
Pottawatomie County, Oklahoma	38,741	89.3	21.2	37,393	89.8	21.7	1,453	88.9	22.3
Rogers County, Oklahoma	49,657	91.4	25.1	48,029	92.3	25.5	N	N	N
Tulsa County, Oklahoma	320,263	91.4	36.3	290,880	93.8	38.7	40,082	89.9	21.0
Wagoner County, Oklahoma	43,923	91.6	23.9	42,102	92.4	24.7	1,969	99.3	27.9
OREGON	2,568,427	92.6	34.7	2,376,419	94.4	36.1	51,503	90.4	30.5
Benton County, Oregon	49,407	98.3	58.1	47,994	98.6	58.5	N	N	N
Clackamas County, Oregon	263,913	94.1	36.3	252,089	95.3	37.2	3,227	91.4	36.1
Deschutes County, Oregon	135,619	93.5	39.8	129,998	94.0	41.0	N	N	N
Douglas County, Oregon	77,381	92.5	16.1	74,065	92.9	16.3	N	N	N
Jackson County, Oregon	146,607	90.8	27.5	134,737	93.2	28.2	N	N	N
Josephine County, Oregon	61,022	89.3	17.2	57,869	90.2	17.5	N	N	N
Klamath County, Oregon	43,136	90.2	20.6	39,321	91.3	21.3	N	N	N
Lane County, Oregon	235,930	93.4	32.6	226,876	93.7	32.8	2,912	100.0	37.2
Linn County, Oregon	82,747	88.8	18.7	79,741	89.4	18.8	N	N	N
Marion County, Oregon	193,423	88.9	26.5	166,986	92.5	29.0	N	N	N
Multnomah County, Oregon	480,767	94.2	50.9	441,000	96.5	53.3	28,744	88.8	24.9
Polk County, Oregon	50,078	93.6	32.3	46,168	95.5	32.7	N	N	N
Umatilla County, Oregon	44,552	88.7	19.6	36,807	91.5	20.7	N	N	N
Washington County, Oregon	321,458	95.0	43.0	289,226	97.2	46.2	8,374	92.4	45.1
Yamhill County, Oregon	65,275	91.0	25.7	59,203	93.6	26.8	N	N	N
PENNSYLVANIA	7,439,802	92.5	33.4	7,155,025	93.0	33.9	931,454	87.9	20.2
Adams County, Pennsylvania	69,477	89.8	22.1	67,125	90.4	22.8	N	N	N
Allegheny County, Pennsylvania	731,811	96.3	44.6	720,819	96.3	44.5	101,419	91.8	23.1
Armstrong County, Pennsylvania	47,073	92.2	15.8	46,944	92.3	15.8	N	N	N
Beaver County, Pennsylvania	111,814	92.9	27.3	110,546	93.3	27.4	7,210	85.9	15.6
Berks County, Pennsylvania	243,448	89.2	26.4	220,730	90.6	27.5	15,090	82.9	14.9
Blair County, Pennsylvania	85,180	91.5	22.7	84,556	91.8	22.8	N	N	N
Bucks County, Pennsylvania	399,402	94.9	42.2	387,426	95.3	42.8	16,545	95.7	28.6
Butler County, Pennsylvania	131,070	95.5	36.9	129,095	95.5	36.9	N	N	N
Cambria County, Pennsylvania	89,646	93.9	21.2	88,600	93.9	21.3	2,776	93.5	7.5
Carbon County, Pennsylvania	45,362	91.0	18.9	44,276	91.0	18.6	N	N	N
Centre County, Pennsylvania	90,893	93.9	43.1	88,871	94.0	42.5	3,917	68.1	14.8
Chester County, Pennsylvania	305,090	95.4	55.5	294,426	96.2	56.0	18,672	91.9	31.9
Clearfield County, Pennsylvania	55,233	89.9	16.3	54,620	90.1	16.5	N	N	N
Columbia County, Pennsylvania	42,586	90.6	24.2	41,632	90.5	24.8	N	N	N
Crawford County, Pennsylvania	57,618	89.1	21.4	57,338	89.1	21.4	N	N	N
Cumberland County, Pennsylvania	159,120	93.0	38.3	154,986	93.2	38.7	5,962	80.7	20.4
Dauphin County, Pennsylvania	142,034	92.7	32.7	136,425	93.0	32.9	32,999	88.4	26.7
Delaware County, Pennsylvania	276,158	94.6	44.0	269,581	94.7	44.3	76,843	90.6	25.0
Erie County, Pennsylvania	166,612	92.7	30.6	164,180	92.8	30.6	11,107	81.8	14.1
Fayette County, Pennsylvania	89,136	88.4	18.5	88,830	88.5	18.5	3,882	78.1	2.1
Franklin County, Pennsylvania	102,383	88.5	22.3	99,011	88.4	22.5	N	N	N
Indiana County, Pennsylvania	54,691	90.8	23.0	54,325	90.8	23.0	N	N	N
Lackawanna County, Pennsylvania	137,425	92.2	29.3	130,973	92.7	30.0	4,183	88.6	25.6
Lancaster County, Pennsylvania	330,685	86.7	29.1	313,244	87.4	29.9	14,687	85.6	20.0
Lawrence County, Pennsylvania	58,315	93.1	22.9	57,994	93.1	22.8	N	N	N
Lebanon County, Pennsylvania	86,723	88.6	22.1	83,516	89.1	22.3	N	N	N
Lehigh County, Pennsylvania	212,453	91.4	31.2	174,136	93.7	35.1	17,154	84.4	12.9
Luzerne County, Pennsylvania	200,222	93.0	22.6	193,058	94.0	22.9	11,972	87.8	10.9
Lycoming County, Pennsylvania	75,738	89.5	24.4	74,472	89.4	24.2	3,618	91.8	11.7
Mercer County, Pennsylvania	72,741	89.7	23.7	72,067	90.0	24.0	4,278	78.2	11.2
Monroe County, Pennsylvania	95,623	91.3	25.5	82,216	92.6	26.4	16,088	92.5	27.3
Montgomery County, Pennsylvania	475,563	95.9	50.4	456,742	96.5	51.1	52,579	90.3	34.1
Northampton County, Pennsylvania	186,094	92.7	31.2	171,857	93.2	32.7	11,192	89.2	23.2
Northumberland County, Pennsylvania	64,312	88.9	15.9	62,506	89.7	16.4	N	N	N
Philadelphia County, Pennsylvania	467,047	91.1	45.5	422,814	92.7	48.0	432,647	86.9	17.6
Schuylkill County, Pennsylvania	97,897	90.9	16.9	95,227	91.7	17.1	N	N	N
Somerset County, Pennsylvania	52,543	89.0	17.9	52,154	89.2	18.0	N	N	N
Washington County, Pennsylvania	141,696	93.0	31.3	140,041	93.2	31.4	4,245	90.3	17.1
Westmoreland County, Pennsylvania	248,823	94.8	29.3	247,108	94.8	29.2	5,714	88.0	10.6
York County, Pennsylvania	282,021	91.1	27.5	271,667	92.1	28.3	16,387	87.0	12.7

N = Data for this geographic area cannot be displayed because the number of sample cases is too small.

Table C-2. Educational Attainment of the Population, by Selected Counties, 2019—*Continued*

(Number; percent; dollars.)

	Educational attainment by race/ethnicity, 25 years and over								
	American Indian or Alaska Native alone			Asian alone			Native Hawaiian or Other Pacific Islander alone		
State/County	Total	High school graduate or more (percent)	Bachelor's degree or more (percent)	Total	High school graduate or more (percent)	Bachelor's degree or more (percent)	Total	High school graduate or more (percent)	Bachelor's degree or more (percent)
OKLAHOMA—(*Continued*)									
Muskogee County, Oklahoma	6,999	85.7	19.5	N	N	N	N	N	N
Oklahoma County, Oklahoma	16,877	86.6	22.8	19,791	83.9	48.6	N	N	N
Payne County, Oklahoma	1,564	85.6	18.3	N	N	N	N	N	N
Pottawatomie County, Oklahoma	6,164	83.4	12.3	N	N	N	N	N	N
Rogers County, Oklahoma	6,781	88.5	16.9	N	N	N	N	N	N
Tulsa County, Oklahoma	22,731	86.4	26.3	14,757	81.2	40.6	N	N	N
Wagoner County, Oklahoma	4,839	87.6	15.6	571	69.2	6.5	N	N	N
OREGON	34,708	85.9	20.2	136,123	88.0	54.0	8,893	93.1	20.3
Benton County, Oregon	N	N	N	N	N	N	N	N	N
Clackamas County, Oregon	N	N	N	14,218	94.0	64.2	N	N	N
Deschutes County, Oregon	N	N	N	N	N	N	N	N	N
Douglas County, Oregon	N	N	N	N	N	N	N	N	N
Jackson County, Oregon	N	N	N	2,353	89.4	39.3	N	N	N
Josephine County, Oregon	N	N	N	N	N	N	N	N	N
Klamath County, Oregon	N	N	N	N	N	N	N	N	N
Lane County, Oregon	2,823	88.1	16.0	5,501	92.1	45.7	N	N	N
Linn County, Oregon	N	N	N	N	N	N	N	N	N
Marion County, Oregon	3,684	68.6	6.7	6,417	91.0	33.2	N	N	N
Multnomah County, Oregon	4,502	84.2	39.3	44,954	77.0	43.0	4,213	94.5	17.3
Polk County, Oregon	N	N	N	N	N	N	N	N	N
Umatilla County, Oregon	1,503	86.7	12.9	N	N	N	N	N	N
Washington County, Oregon	N	N	N	49,833	94.3	66.5	N	N	N
Yamhill County, Oregon	N	N	N	N	N	N	N	N	N
PENNSYLVANIA	17,215	77.5	20.5	309,518	84.8	57.0	2,139	78.1	33.0
Adams County, Pennsylvania	N	N	N	608	100.0	42.9	N	N	N
Allegheny County, Pennsylvania	N	N	N	31,307	87.6	70.9	N	N	N
Armstrong County, Pennsylvania	N	N	N	N	N	N	N	N	N
Beaver County, Pennsylvania	N	N	N	N	N	N	N	N	N
Berks County, Pennsylvania	N	N	N	4,332	89.5	49.1	N	N	N
Blair County, Pennsylvania	N	N	N	N	N	N	N	N	N
Bucks County, Pennsylvania	N	N	N	23,534	90.6	65.2	N	N	N
Butler County, Pennsylvania	N	N	N	N	N	N	N	N	N
Cambria County, Pennsylvania	N	N	N	N	N	N	N	N	N
Carbon County, Pennsylvania	N	N	N	N	N	N	N	N	N
Centre County, Pennsylvania	N	N	N	N	N	N	N	N	N
Chester County, Pennsylvania	N	N	N	20,833	93.3	80.0	N	N	N
Clearfield County, Pennsylvania	N	N	N	N	N	N	N	N	N
Columbia County, Pennsylvania	N	N	N	N	N	N	N	N	N
Crawford County, Pennsylvania	N	N	N	N	N	N	N	N	N
Cumberland County, Pennsylvania	N	N	N	7,247	90.7	68.4	N	N	N
Dauphin County, Pennsylvania	N	N	N	9,705	65.6	42.8	N	N	N
Delaware County, Pennsylvania	N	N	N	22,569	87.8	59.5	N	N	N
Erie County, Pennsylvania	N	N	N	2,474	72.9	53.3	N	N	N
Fayette County, Pennsylvania	N	N	N	N	N	N	N	N	N
Franklin County, Pennsylvania	N	N	N	N	N	N	N	N	N
Indiana County, Pennsylvania	N	N	N	N	N	N	N	N	N
Lackawanna County, Pennsylvania	N	N	N	4,583	85.3	46.3	N	N	N
Lancaster County, Pennsylvania	N	N	N	7,659	74.5	37.8	N	N	N
Lawrence County, Pennsylvania	N	N	N	N	N	N	N	N	N
Lebanon County, Pennsylvania	N	N	N	N	N	N	N	N	N
Lehigh County, Pennsylvania	N	N	N	8,304	82.3	47.6	N	N	N
Luzerne County, Pennsylvania	N	N	N	2,288	89.2	48.1	N	N	N
Lycoming County, Pennsylvania	N	N	N	N	N	N	N	N	N
Mercer County, Pennsylvania	N	N	N	N	N	N	N	N	N
Monroe County, Pennsylvania	N	N	N	2,424	91.5	33.9	N	N	N
Montgomery County, Pennsylvania	N	N	N	45,512	92.3	69.3	N	N	N
Northampton County, Pennsylvania	N	N	N	5,814	93.3	54.9	N	N	N
Northumberland County, Pennsylvania	N	N	N	N	N	N	N	N	N
Philadelphia County, Pennsylvania	3,945	71.8	9.9	83,466	75.8	42.3	N	N	N
Schuylkill County, Pennsylvania	N	N	N	N	N	N	N	N	N
Somerset County, Pennsylvania	N	N	N	N	N	N	N	N	N
Washington County, Pennsylvania	N	N	N	1,396	83.3	54.9	N	N	N
Westmoreland County, Pennsylvania	N	N	N	N	N	N	N	N	N
York County, Pennsylvania	N	N	N	4,711	80.3	41.5	N	N	N

N = Data for this geographic area cannot be displayed because the number of sample cases is too small.

Table C-2. Educational Attainment of the Population, by Selected Counties, 2019—*Continued*

(Number; percent; dollars.)

State/County	Educational attainment by race/ethnicity, 25 years and over								
	White alone			White alone, not Hispanic			Black alone		
	Total	High school graduate or more (percent)	Bachelor's degree or more (percent)	Total	High school graduate or more (percent)	Bachelor's degree or more (percent)	Total	High school graduate or more (percent)	Bachelor's degree or more (percent)
RHODE ISLAND................................	613,613	90.8	36.7	565,077	92.3	38.5	49,190	91.1	23.4
Kent County, Rhode Island............................	110,960	92.4	32.4	108,829	92.5	32.5	2,852	84.6	36.5
Newport County, Rhode Island....................	56,664	94.3	47.5	54,139	94.0	48.7	N	N	N
Providence County, Rhode Island	331,498	87.9	32.1	289,880	90.6	34.7	43,362	91.8	21.6
Washington County, Rhode Island	83,068	95.7	48.5	81,501	95.7	48.6	N	N	N
SOUTH CAROLINA	2,483,427	90.9	34.0	2,396,696	91.5	34.4	899,954	83.9	17.5
Aiken County, South Carolina......................	88,278	92.6	31.5	84,312	93.1	32.4	28,874	83.2	20.2
Anderson County, South Carolina	113,598	88.8	27.7	111,800	89.2	27.9	20,321	83.2	7.8
Beaufort County, South Carolina................	109,888	95.7	48.4	103,990	96.9	49.9	20,292	84.8	8.9
Berkeley County, South Carolina................	102,204	92.2	31.8	100,216	92.3	32.1	36,349	88.3	19.5
Charleston County, South Carolina..............	206,605	96.6	56.3	202,084	96.8	56.6	70,743	83.3	18.4
Darlington County, South Carolina..............	27,598	89.4	27.9	26,711	90.4	28.8	16,795	74.0	6.2
Dorchester County, South Carolina.............	76,702	92.2	30.7	74,256	92.7	30.4	26,396	86.2	24.7
Florence County, South Carolina	52,736	90.0	30.8	51,605	90.8	31.3	38,594	85.7	15.5
Greenville County, South Carolina..............	270,325	91.6	42.1	255,974	92.1	43.1	60,050	82.9	14.6
Greenwood County, South Carolina	32,514	90.0	31.5	30,913	90.1	30.2	15,727	87.7	12.6
Horry County, South Carolina	225,972	91.0	26.2	218,020	92.1	26.5	30,035	81.4	9.2
Kershaw County, South Carolina.................	33,072	87.8	26.0	32,806	88.0	25.8	12,041	86.8	14.9
Lancaster County, South Carolina...............	54,364	90.1	25.5	51,691	91.3	26.7	14,548	75.0	10.6
Laurens County, South Carolina.................	33,086	85.5	18.9	32,373	85.8	18.4	10,968	85.7	20.3
Lexington County, South Carolina...............	167,799	89.2	30.8	161,222	90.6	31.7	29,068	87.4	24.8
Oconee County, South Carolina..................	52,156	86.8	27.7	50,538	87.0	27.5	4,180	81.7	13.9
Orangeburg County, South Carolina............	22,035	86.4	21.2	21,746	86.8	21.5	35,235	85.6	21.0
Pickens County, South Carolina..................	71,401	87.4	27.1	70,149	87.5	26.9	5,843	81.4	10.8
Richland County, South Carolina.................	120,366	94.4	52.1	115,822	94.9	52.4	125,840	89.8	32.5
Spartanburg County, South Carolina...........	163,046	88.7	29.5	154,779	90.2	30.2	42,796	79.9	16.3
Sumter County, South Carolina..................	34,858	91.6	26.3	33,799	92.1	27.1	32,408	84.7	18.0
York County, South Carolina	146,234	93.8	36.9	139,091	94.3	37.5	34,141	90.2	23.6
SOUTH DAKOTA	516,050	93.9	31.5	505,241	94.2	31.6	11,679	77.1	18.9
Minnehaha County, South Dakota..............	115,022	94.6	37.7	110,586	95.1	38.0	6,231	71.4	13.7
Pennington County, South Dakota	68,725	94.5	33.9	67,240	94.9	34.3	N	N	N
TENNESSEE	3,744,336	88.7	29.7	3,613,025	89.6	30.1	737,044	87.2	21.7
Anderson County, Tennessee	50,566	89.4	20.9	49,952	89.8	20.9	N	N	N
Blount County, Tennessee...........................	91,712	88.6	23.5	89,082	89.7	24.1	N	N	N
Bradley County, Tennessee.........................	67,149	86.8	23.9	65,600	86.9	23.9	4,186	79.1	14.4
Davidson County, Tennessee......................	323,611	91.1	52.1	297,060	94.5	55.3	120,156	88.7	29.6
Greene County, Tennessee	48,069	84.6	19.3	47,634	84.9	19.4	N	N	N
Hamilton County, Tennessee	201,513	91.0	38.4	194,179	92.0	38.9	44,937	84.6	16.9
Knox County, Tennessee	277,336	92.0	38.7	268,405	92.9	39.2	23,888	93.2	21.1
Madison County, Tennessee........................	40,627	92.1	32.8	39,823	92.5	33.2	21,779	86.7	18.3
Maury County, Tennessee...........................	57,836	89.1	24.9	54,765	92.1	26.2	7,488	88.8	27.4
Montgomery County, Tennessee..................	92,889	94.4	31.6	85,813	94.3	32.0	25,143	93.9	25.7
Putnam County, Tennessee	49,290	86.2	28.4	47,391	87.4	27.9	N	N	N
Robertson County, Tennessee.....................	43,674	85.7	21.9	42,363	86.1	21.9	3,906	78.5	14.4
Rutherford County, Tennessee	163,192	92.9	31.5	153,742	94.0	31.5	30,778	94.4	33.3
Sevier County, Tennessee...........................	67,334	84.3	18.8	65,190	85.2	19.3	N	N	N
Shelby County, Tennessee..........................	261,651	92.7	45.4	244,870	94.9	47.5	321,714	86.7	19.9
Sullivan County, Tennessee........................	111,165	89.0	26.4	110,241	89.0	26.4	2,394	90.6	14.7
Sumner County, Tennessee.........................	115,565	91.0	29.7	113,262	91.4	29.7	9,378	93.1	43.8
Washington County, Tennessee...................	82,776	89.4	31.5	81,039	89.2	31.8	3,432	100.0	37.0
Williamson County, Tennessee....................	138,724	95.3	60.8	133,015	95.5	62.3	6,713	95.9	53.3
Wilson County, Tennessee	88,604	93.0	34.5	86,300	94.1	34.7	7,603	94.3	41.2
TEXAS...	13,971,984	84.8	30.8	8,669,915	94.4	39.4	2,289,499	91.2	25.7
Angelina County, Texas	47,380	85.5	20.6	37,454	92.2	21.7	8,611	92.9	7.9
Bastrop County, Texas................................	41,449	86.1	21.5	34,539	90.3	21.8	N	N	N
Bell County, Texas......................................	144,030	91.1	27.7	109,523	94.7	29.0	54,025	89.6	19.9
Bexar County, Texas...................................	1,012,592	84.5	27.9	394,623	96.5	43.1	98,128	93.4	28.4
Bowie County, Texas	45,412	86.6	23.9	42,456	88.3	25.2	14,650	84.9	5.4
Brazoria County, Texas...............................	179,384	88.2	26.4	121,481	93.3	31.8	36,507	96.4	35.0
Brazos County, Texas	98,185	87.6	44.1	70,652	95.2	55.5	14,497	89.9	17.1
Cameron County, Texas...............................	235,383	68.7	17.4	29,303	88.7	34.7	N	N	N

N = Data for this geographic area cannot be displayed because the number of sample cases is too small.

Table C-2. Educational Attainment of the Population, by Selected Counties, 2019—*Continued*

(Number; percent; dollars.)

| | Educational attainment by race/ethnicity, 25 years and over | | | | | | | | |
| | American Indian or Alaska Native alone | | | Asian alone | | | Native Hawaiian or Other Pacific Islander alone | | |
State/County	Total	High school graduate or more (percent)	Bachelor's degree or more (percent)	Total	High school graduate or more (percent)	Bachelor's degree or more (percent)	Total	High school graduate or more (percent)	Bachelor's degree or more (percent)
RHODE ISLAND..	N	N	N	25,461	87.6	52.7	N	N	N
Kent County, Rhode Island...................................	N	N	N	N	N	N	N	N	N
Newport County, Rhode Island............................	N	N	N	N	N	N	N	N	N
Providence County, Rhode Island	N	N	N	18,050	84.3	47.7	N	N	N
Washington County, Rhode Island	N	N	N	N	N	N	N	N	N
SOUTH CAROLINA	13,884	77.3	18.9	58,659	87.9	51.4	N	N	N
Aiken County, South Carolina...............................	N	N	N	N	N	N	N	N	N
Anderson County, South Carolina	N	N	N	N	N	N	N	N	N
Beaufort County, South Carolina	N	N	N	N	N	N	N	N	N
Berkeley County, South Carolina	N	N	N	4,077	86.8	22.1	N	N	N
Charleston County, South Carolina	N	N	N	N	N	N	N	N	N
Darlington County, South Carolina	N	N	N	N	N	N	N	N	N
Dorchester County, South Carolina......................	N	N	N	N	N	N	N	N	N
Florence County, South Carolina.........................	N	N	N	N	N	N	N	N	N
Greenville County, South Carolina........................	N	N	N	9,307	88.7	51.4	N	N	N
Greenwood County, South Carolina	N	N	N	N	N	N	N	N	N
Horry County, South Carolina..............................	N	N	N	3,174	88.0	47.4	N	N	N
Kershaw County, South Carolina..........................	N	N	N	N	N	N	N	N	N
Lancaster County, South Carolina	N	N	N	N	N	N	N	N	N
Laurens County, South Carolina..........................	N	N	N	N	N	N	N	N	N
Lexington County, South Carolina........................	N	N	N	4,419	89.2	61.3	N	N	N
Oconee County, South Carolina...........................	N	N	N	N	N	N	N	N	N
Orangeburg County, South Carolina.....................	N	N	N	N	N	N	N	N	N
Pickens County, South Carolina	N	N	N	N	N	N	N	N	N
Richland County, South Carolina..........................	N	N	N	7,558	84.9	68.6	N	N	N
Spartanburg County, South Carolina.....................	N	N	N	5,628	86.5	20.3	N	N	N
Sumter County, South Carolina............................	N	N	N	N	N	N	N	N	N
York County, South Carolina	1,629	83.9	10.0	5,026	90.6	71.9	N	N	N
SOUTH DAKOTA	38,100	80.0	8.8	7,098	81.1	42.7	N	N	N
Minnehaha County, South Dakota	N	N	N	2,652	67.0	17.5	N	N	N
Pennington County, South Dakota	4,890	85.4	6.5	N	N	N	N	N	N
TENNESSEE	14,977	78.0	15.5	87,030	85.9	52.2	N	N	N
Anderson County, Tennessee	N	N	N	N	N	N	N	N	N
Blount County, Tennessee	N	N	N	N	N	N	N	N	N
Bradley County, Tennessee..................................	N	N	N	N	N	N	N	N	N
Davidson County, Tennessee...............................	N	N	N	18,256	83.4	55.8	N	N	N
Greene County, Tennessee	N	N	N	N	N	N	N	N	N
Hamilton County, Tennessee................................	N	N	N	N	N	N	N	N	N
Knox County, Tennessee	N	N	N	7,615	87.0	64.9	N	N	N
Madison County, Tennessee.................................	N	N	N	N	N	N	N	N	N
Maury County, Tennessee	N	N	N	N	N	N	N	N	N
Montgomery County, Tennessee...........................	N	N	N	N	N	N	N	N	N
Putnam County, Tennessee	N	N	N	N	N	N	N	N	N
Robertson County, Tennessee..............................	N	N	N	N	N	N	N	N	N
Rutherford County, Tennessee	N	N	N	8,213	84.5	15.6	N	N	N
Sevier County, Tennessee....................................	N	N	N	N	N	N	N	N	N
Shelby County, Tennessee...................................	N	N	N	17,848	81.5	52.2	N	N	N
Sullivan County, Tennessee	N	N	N	N	N	N	N	N	N
Sumner County, Tennessee..................................	N	N	N	2,477	72.2	44.0	N	N	N
Washington County, Tennessee............................	N	N	N	N	N	N	N	N	N
Williamson County, Tennessee.............................	N	N	N	N	N	N	N	N	N
Wilson County, Tennessee	N	N	N	N	N	N	N	N	N
TEXAS..	98,802	84.3	24.0	1,008,252	89.4	60.6	16,349	88.9	22.2
Angelina County, Texas	N	N	N	N	N	N	N	N	N
Bastrop County, Texas...	N	N	N	N	N	N	N	N	N
Bell County, Texas	N	N	N	8,175	85.9	29.2	N	N	N
Bexar County, Texas..	11,492	81.9	16.7	42,011	92.2	54.3	N	N	N
Bowie County, Texas	N	N	N	N	N	N	N	N	N
Brazoria County, Texas..	N	N	N	18,516	89.0	60.1	N	N	N
Brazos County, Texas	N	N	N	7,458	94.0	73.2	N	N	N
Cameron County, Texas.......................................	N	N	N	N	N	N	N	N	N

N = Data for this geographic area cannot be displayed because the number of sample cases is too small.

Table C-2. Educational Attainment of the Population, by Selected Counties, 2019—*Continued*

(Number; percent; dollars.)

	Educational attainment by race/ethnicity, 25 years and over								
	White alone			White alone, not Hispanic			Black alone		
State/County	Total	High school graduate or more (percent)	Bachelor's degree or more (percent)	Total	High school graduate or more (percent)	Bachelor's degree or more (percent)	Total	High school graduate or more (percent)	Bachelor's degree or more (percent)
TEXAS—*(Continued)*									
Collin County, Texas	473,818	94.1	48.6	400,079	97.6	52.6	68,389	95.9	46.0
Comal County, Texas	100,384	93.6	40.3	77,327	95.6	40.6	N	N	N
Coryell County, Texas	36,800	88.9	18.0	29,851	91.8	18.8	5,970	86.3	14.2
Dallas County, Texas	1,036,971	78.7	33.8	581,608	95.4	51.3	393,341	90.9	25.8
Denton County, Texas	445,177	92.8	44.1	363,596	96.7	47.4	58,608	93.9	43.8
Ector County, Texas	79,457	76.6	15.4	36,119	90.0	22.8	6,610	90.6	16.5
Ellis County, Texas	97,873	88.8	26.0	76,686	94.0	30.6	12,482	93.6	29.6
El Paso County, Texas	420,109	80.5	24.4	67,844	94.5	41.0	18,611	98.3	28.1
Fort Bend County, Texas	269,878	90.1	44.2	178,607	97.2	52.9	107,005	96.1	42.7
Galveston County, Texas	186,057	91.3	30.5	140,809	95.7	35.6	28,111	89.3	27.4
Grayson County, Texas	81,460	90.4	22.7	73,833	93.8	24.2	4,661	89.8	1.3
Gregg County, Texas	61,974	86.1	24.5	50,700	91.2	27.8	15,907	87.9	11.6
Guadalupe County, Texas	92,520	89.1	30.4	58,738	96.6	37.4	9,800	96.9	28.9
Harris County, Texas	1,871,684	81.7	33.9	1,003,744	96.2	49.7	580,351	91.6	26.0
Harrison County, Texas	33,589	87.3	21.8	30,012	90.3	24.1	7,692	83.4	13.1
Hays County, Texas	125,447	90.6	37.7	80,299	97.3	48.9	4,692	90.9	12.7
Henderson County, Texas	53,457	83.6	16.4	48,222	86.3	17.6	N	N	N
Hidalgo County, Texas	411,078	69.3	18.9	38,545	92.4	35.6	3,608	78.8	28.8
Hunt County, Texas	55,092	86.3	21.9	49,808	90.1	23.4	5,539	79.9	16.2
Jefferson County, Texas	101,373	83.6	23.8	74,532	93.9	30.5	54,112	89.2	13.4
Johnson County, Texas	104,937	85.7	18.2	86,470	90.4	20.5	4,704	91.1	20.6
Kaufman County, Texas	69,478	85.0	18.6	56,757	89.1	20.0	11,853	93.4	18.7
Liberty County, Texas	46,701	80.8	12.4	37,780	86.2	13.8	5,617	92.0	16.8
Lubbock County, Texas	150,397	87.6	34.1	104,496	94.5	42.6	13,269	90.3	16.0
McLennan County, Texas	128,259	87.2	27.3	95,963	93.8	32.9	20,460	87.6	12.3
Midland County, Texas	81,810	88.1	31.9	54,946	95.1	40.3	8,109	91.0	22.1
Montgomery County, Texas	348,537	87.9	33.0	277,338	94.1	36.8	20,175	92.3	29.5
Nacogdoches County, Texas	30,099	85.0	27.1	24,812	92.0	30.6	7,649	84.4	8.1
Nueces County, Texas	215,292	83.7	22.6	77,778	94.0	31.9	9,133	90.1	16.1
Orange County, Texas	49,507	87.4	18.5	46,526	88.3	18.4	5,353	87.9	17.7
Parker County, Texas	90,416	88.5	24.6	82,862	90.7	25.4	N	N	N
Potter County, Texas	59,549	80.5	15.4	37,579	89.9	20.8	7,979	75.6	2.2
Randall County, Texas	82,266	93.4	34.5	68,430	95.9	36.8	N	N	N
Rockwall County, Texas	57,961	95.5	42.7	49,638	96.7	45.0	5,530	98.9	26.1
San Patricio County, Texas	39,649	82.2	15.5	18,003	95.3	22.8	N	N	N
Smith County, Texas	119,402	87.0	29.2	99,817	93.8	33.2	25,486	91.7	21.4
Tarrant County, Texas	926,680	88.9	35.9	692,576	95.2	41.5	224,439	92.5	29.5
Taylor County, Texas	70,790	91.6	27.6	57,177	94.3	30.2	6,888	97.6	19.5
Tom Green County, Texas	68,630	88.2	23.9	43,902	94.7	29.9	N	N	N
Travis County, Texas	664,211	91.9	56.6	478,444	98.1	66.3	72,632	91.4	29.1
Victoria County, Texas	52,308	84.7	20.1	29,940	94.8	27.6	4,617	95.1	11.8
Walker County, Texas	34,600	87.0	19.6	28,303	94.6	23.5	10,712	84.4	19.3
Webb County, Texas	148,439	65.1	19.2	7,136	88.5	39.8	N	N	N
Wichita County, Texas	70,978	89.8	24.0	59,152	93.4	26.7	8,227	82.3	4.6
Williamson County, Texas	318,872	93.5	40.3	245,142	96.8	45.1	26,594	98.6	29.6
Wise County, Texas	44,865	85.5	17.1	38,024	92.1	18.8	N	N	N
UTAH	1,694,118	94.5	35.8	1,540,298	96.1	37.6	19,937	86.3	17.4
Cache County, Utah	61,157	94.9	37.4	55,932	96.7	39.9	N	N	N
Davis County, Utah	191,739	96.5	37.0	178,195	97.7	38.7	N	N	N
Salt Lake County, Utah	612,072	94.0	39.2	551,237	95.6	41.3	12,337	84.9	18.8
Tooele County, Utah	40,685	93.9	23.9	35,891	94.9	25.4	N	N	N
Utah County, Utah	295,622	95.9	41.4	266,376	97.6	43.7	N	N	N
Washington County, Utah	108,503	94.8	27.7	101,671	95.6	28.7	N	N	N
Weber County, Utah	149,448	92.5	27.6	129,084	95.2	29.7	N	N	N
VERMONT	422,653	93.8	38.8	418,747	93.8	38.9	5,756	82.9	26.3
Chittenden County, Vermont	100,159	95.9	52.9	98,481	95.8	53.1	2,953	85.0	30.3
VIRGINIA	4,069,698	91.9	42.0	3,782,506	93.0	43.0	1,110,132	86.2	25.2
Albemarle County, Virginia	62,997	95.5	62.6	60,291	96.2	63.5	6,081	90.5	27.3
Arlington County, Virginia	128,545	95.5	80.5	110,399	99.0	86.2	16,165	93.7	50.4
Augusta County, Virginia	52,952	88.0	20.3	51,192	89.3	20.5	3,428	76.3	4.4
Bedford County, Virginia	52,029	91.5	32.7	51,361	91.7	32.8	3,029	62.5	7.6
Chesterfield County, Virginia	162,019	93.7	43.4	154,505	94.6	44.4	51,939	94.0	34.3

N = Data for this geographic area cannot be displayed because the number of sample cases is too small.

Table C-2. Educational Attainment of the Population, by Selected Counties, 2019—*Continued*

(Number; percent; dollars.)

State/County	American Indian or Alaska Native alone			Asian alone			Native Hawaiian or Other Pacific Islander alone		
	Total	High school graduate or more (percent)	Bachelor's degree or more (percent)	Total	High school graduate or more (percent)	Bachelor's degree or more (percent)	Total	High school graduate or more (percent)	Bachelor's degree or more (percent)
TEXAS—(*Continued*)									
Collin County, Texas	2,249	90.6	42.4	112,941	94.6	76.6	N	N	N
Comal County, Texas	N	N	N	N	N	N	N	N	N
Coryell County, Texas	N	N	N	N	N	N	N	N	N
Dallas County, Texas	8,119	80.0	16.2	121,268	89.7	62.0	N	N	N
Denton County, Texas	N	N	N	57,481	93.5	71.7	N	N	N
Ector County, Texas	N	N	N	N	N	N	N	N	N
Ellis County, Texas	N	N	N	N	N	N	N	N	N
El Paso County, Texas	3,455	89.3	16.8	6,687	85.5	42.5	N	N	N
Fort Bend County, Texas	N	N	N	112,532	92.4	60.4	N	N	N
Galveston County, Texas	N	N	N	9,042	87.5	50.0	N	N	N
Grayson County, Texas	N	N	N	N	N	N	N	N	N
Gregg County, Texas	N	N	N	N	N	N	N	N	N
Guadalupe County, Texas	N	N	N	N	N	N	N	N	N
Harris County, Texas	14,016	81.0	23.1	242,381	86.5	54.0	N	N	N
Harrison County, Texas	N	N	N	N	N	N	N	N	N
Hays County, Texas	N	N	N	N	N	N	N	N	N
Henderson County, Texas	N	N	N	N	N	N	N	N	N
Hidalgo County, Texas	N	N	N	5,586	79.5	55.3	N	N	N
Hunt County, Texas	N	N	N	N	N	N	N	N	N
Jefferson County, Texas	N	N	N	6,484	69.2	39.5	N	N	N
Johnson County, Texas	N	N	N	N	N	N	N	N	N
Kaufman County, Texas	N	N	N	N	N	N	N	N	N
Liberty County, Texas	N	N	N	N	N	N	N	N	N
Lubbock County, Texas	N	N	N	4,596	92.4	68.4	N	N	N
McLennan County, Texas	N	N	N	N	N	N	N	N	N
Midland County, Texas	N	N	N	N	N	N	N	N	N
Montgomery County, Texas	N	N	N	13,169	97.9	67.6	N	N	N
Nacogdoches County, Texas	N	N	N	N	N	N	N	N	N
Nueces County, Texas	N	N	N	N	N	N	N	N	N
Orange County, Texas	N	N	N	N	N	N	N	N	N
Parker County, Texas	N	N	N	N	N	N	N	N	N
Potter County, Texas	N	N	N	N	N	N	N	N	N
Randall County, Texas	N	N	N	N	N	N	N	N	N
Rockwall County, Texas	N	N	N	2,633	86.9	41.4	N	N	N
San Patricio County, Texas	N	N	N	N	N	N	N	N	N
Smith County, Texas	N	N	N	N	N	N	N	N	N
Tarrant County, Texas	7,468	85.2	33.3	81,340	86.3	52.8	N	N	N
Taylor County, Texas	N	N	N	N	N	N	N	N	N
Tom Green County, Texas	N	N	N	N	N	N	N	N	N
Travis County, Texas	7,529	82.0	42.0	62,967	91.5	76.5	N	N	N
Victoria County, Texas	N	N	N	N	N	N	N	N	N
Walker County, Texas	N	N	N	N	N	N	N	N	N
Webb County, Texas	N	N	N	N	N	N	N	N	N
Wichita County, Texas	N	N	N	1,824	85.5	52.4	N	N	N
Williamson County, Texas	N	N	N	30,843	92.1	71.6	N	N	N
Wise County, Texas	N	N	N	N	N	N	N	N	N
UTAH	20,630	81.9	11.7	52,276	90.3	55.0	16,930	90.9	15.4
Cache County, Utah	N	N	N	2,080	80.3	42.1	N	N	N
Davis County, Utah	N	N	N	4,897	93.4	46.7	N	N	N
Salt Lake County, Utah	6,129	89.4	19.4	34,599	89.4	59.4	10,016	88.1	10.2
Tooele County, Utah	N	N	N	N	N	N	N	N	N
Utah County, Utah	N	N	N	4,814	90.8	62.0	2,961	94.7	29.6
Washington County, Utah	N	N	N	N	N	N	N	N	N
Weber County, Utah	N	N	N	2,771	96.9	41.2	N	N	N
VERMONT	2,033	71.9	15.5	6,155	83.1	49.3	N	N	N
Chittenden County, Vermont	N	N	N	3,388	69.3	41.3	N	N	N
VIRGINIA	15,850	82.8	29.9	405,441	90.6	62.1	3,029	93.5	30.2
Albemarle County, Virginia	N	N	N	N	N	N	N	N	N
Arlington County, Virginia	N	N	N	17,844	94.0	70.5	N	N	N
Augusta County, Virginia	N	N	N	N	N	N	N	N	N
Bedford County, Virginia	N	N	N	N	N	N	N	N	N
Chesterfield County, Virginia	N	N	N	9,236	91.4	60.2	N	N	N

N = Data for this geographic area cannot be displayed because the number of sample cases is too small.

Table C-2. Educational Attainment of the Population, by Selected Counties, 2019—*Continued*

(Number; percent; dollars.)

| | Educational attainment by race/ethnicity, 25 years and over | | | | | | | | |
| | White alone | | | White alone, not Hispanic | | | Black alone | | |
State/County	Total	High school graduate or more (percent)	Bachelor's degree or more (percent)	Total	High school graduate or more (percent)	Bachelor's degree or more (percent)	Total	High school graduate or more (percent)	Bachelor's degree or more (percent)
VIRGINIA—(*Continued*)									
Fairfax County, Virginia	482,723	94.8	67.0	413,083	98.0	73.0	76,656	94.9	50.1
Fauquier County, Virginia	43,192	92.4	36.5	40,105	95.3	38.4	4,190	86.2	25.4
Frederick County, Virginia	57,487	88.6	28.7	53,448	89.8	30.4	N	N	N
Hanover County, Virginia	64,739	95.6	41.2	63,666	95.6	41.3	7,130	81.3	30.3
Henrico County, Virginia	133,192	94.8	50.5	128,198	94.9	50.7	68,144	88.2	20.2
James City County, Virginia	46,905	96.5	55.8	44,191	97.4	56.3	6,810	85.9	21.0
Loudoun County, Virginia	171,118	96.7	62.9	151,642	97.9	66.1	21,063	93.2	46.3
Montgomery County, Virginia	49,652	95.1	44.0	49,123	95.1	43.9	N	N	N
Prince William County, Virginia	177,908	90.4	45.0	135,788	96.3	52.0	64,896	95.1	42.8
Roanoke County, Virginia	61,443	91.3	37.7	59,807	91.6	37.8	N	N	N
Rockingham County, Virginia	53,455	85.5	27.4	51,461	86.6	27.9	N	N	N
Spotsylvania County, Virginia	66,486	93.9	33.9	63,994	94.5	34.0	14,931	93.3	18.6
Stafford County, Virginia	66,492	95.1	42.3	61,552	95.7	43.3	19,584	96.7	38.0
York County, Virginia	34,482	94.9	50.7	33,534	94.8	50.8	7,180	96.2	49.8
Alexandria city, Virginia	78,749	94.9	75.6	67,513	97.8	79.5	25,648	91.5	44.1
Chesapeake city, Virginia	102,317	94.7	34.1	97,674	94.8	33.5	48,994	84.6	26.7
Hampton city, Virginia	39,734	93.1	25.8	37,291	93.7	27.0	45,195	92.1	27.3
Lynchburg city, Virginia	30,328	90.1	43.6	29,562	90.0	43.1	13,877	82.3	16.9
Newport News city, Virginia	59,299	92.0	30.8	53,563	93.7	32.8	47,189	89.4	19.6
Norfolk city, Virginia	76,323	92.7	39.6	72,056	93.3	40.1	61,985	83.0	18.4
Portsmouth city, Virginia	27,529	90.3	22.9	26,361	90.2	23.1	33,781	85.9	20.4
Richmond city, Virginia	79,665	93.1	64.9	76,190	94.7	66.3	70,843	78.6	12.9
Roanoke city, Virginia	45,988	88.9	26.3	44,181	89.2	26.9	19,346	85.2	9.9
Suffolk city, Virginia	33,881	95.9	36.4	32,777	96.4	36.9	25,058	84.3	22.4
Virginia Beach city, Virginia	211,504	96.4	41.5	199,124	96.5	42.0	55,967	91.5	30.4
WASHINGTON	4,090,653	93.7	37.1	3,821,704	95.2	38.2	195,806	90.6	25.1
Benton County, Washington	113,729	94.2	33.4	100,832	95.6	35.6	N	N	N
Chelan County, Washington	43,334	90.0	29.2	40,245	91.7	30.2	N	N	N
Clallam County, Washington	54,574	92.5	29.3	52,235	92.7	29.4	N	N	N
Clark County, Washington	288,385	94.8	31.6	272,404	95.7	32.3	6,833	93.9	30.2
Cowlitz County, Washington	69,798	89.8	15.9	67,319	90.6	16.0	N	N	N
Franklin County, Washington	39,786	80.3	19.8	26,831	94.4	26.0	N	N	N
Grant County, Washington	45,580	82.9	21.2	37,536	91.1	22.8	N	N	N
Grays Harbor County, Washington	49,436	91.9	18.8	45,967	93.4	20.0	N	N	N
Island County, Washington	53,741	95.6	36.8	51,745	95.4	37.0	N	N	N
King County, Washington	1,063,074	96.4	57.1	1,005,529	97.3	58.2	97,278	86.6	27.4
Kitsap County, Washington	159,463	96.8	36.2	152,662	97.2	36.9	5,249	98.6	23.1
Lewis County, Washington	52,085	88.4	20.4	50,075	89.7	20.9	N	N	N
Mason County, Washington	43,465	92.5	21.1	41,803	93.1	21.8	N	N	N
Pierce County, Washington	460,774	93.2	29.3	433,465	93.9	29.7	41,819	95.4	23.0
Skagit County, Washington	79,190	91.8	28.6	74,100	94.5	29.8	N	N	N
Snohomish County, Washington	437,984	94.3	31.6	414,541	95.1	31.8	17,926	91.0	20.8
Spokane County, Washington	324,551	94.1	31.3	313,782	94.3	31.5	5,927	93.9	12.6
Thurston County, Washington	172,205	94.4	34.9	160,954	95.4	35.5	6,464	94.5	32.2
Whatcom County, Washington	131,828	95.0	36.7	126,970	95.7	36.7	N	N	N
Yakima County, Washington	119,433	78.0	18.5	79,979	92.2	25.1	N	N	N
WEST VIRGINIA	1,204,645	86.9	20.9	1,194,674	86.9	20.9	46,716	92.1	13.7
Berkeley County, West Virginia	73,323	88.2	24.6	71,059	88.4	24.8	6,689	86.5	10.8
Cabell County, West Virginia	57,320	85.7	28.1	56,803	85.8	28.1	3,104	90.4	24.6
Harrison County, West Virginia	45,877	90.6	25.7	45,711	90.5	25.8	N	N	N
Kanawha County, West Virginia	117,144	90.1	25.5	116,086	90.0	25.4	9,299	91.3	16.5
Monongalia County, West Virginia	60,681	91.0	44.1	59,884	90.8	43.8	2,313	100.0	25.4
Raleigh County, West Virginia	47,391	87.4	19.3	46,677	87.5	18.9	3,989	98.2	11.1
Wood County, West Virginia	58,036	88.7	20.7	57,758	88.7	20.8	N	N	N
WISCONSIN	3,539,280	94.0	32.4	3,408,152	94.8	33.0	219,379	84.7	15.2
Brown County, Wisconsin	157,698	94.2	30.9	152,212	95.3	31.7	3,854	77.4	22.1
Dane County, Wisconsin	316,898	97.0	54.8	303,587	97.9	55.9	16,334	91.0	34.5
Dodge County, Wisconsin	60,794	89.6	18.2	58,517	90.3	18.6	N	N	N
Eau Claire County, Wisconsin	62,882	95.7	33.4	61,686	96.2	33.6	N	N	N
Fond du Lac County, Wisconsin	68,611	93.1	22.6	67,058	93.8	22.9	N	N	N
Jefferson County, Wisconsin	56,495	93.1	27.6	54,920	93.6	27.7	N	N	N
Kenosha County, Wisconsin	102,694	92.0	30.0	93,042	92.8	31.7	6,892	87.9	23.5

N = Data for this geographic area cannot be displayed because the number of sample cases is too small.

Table C-2. Educational Attainment of the Population, by Selected Counties, 2019—*Continued*

(Number; percent; dollars.)

	Educational attainment by race/ethnicity, 25 years and over								
	American Indian or Alaska Native alone			Asian alone			Native Hawaiian or Other Pacific Islander alone		
State/County	Total	High school graduate or more (percent)	Bachelor's degree or more (percent)	Total	High school graduate or more (percent)	Bachelor's degree or more (percent)	Total	High school graduate or more (percent)	Bachelor's degree or more (percent)
VIRGINIA—*(Continued)*									
Fairfax County, Virginia	N	N	N	164,313	91.4	64.3	N	N	N
Fauquier County, Virginia	N	N	N	N	N	N	N	N	N
Frederick County, Virginia	N	N	N	N	N	N	N	N	N
Hanover County, Virginia	N	N	N	N	N	N	N	N	N
Henrico County, Virginia	N	N	N	19,806	87.2	73.9	N	N	N
James City County, Virginia	N	N	N	N	N	N	N	N	N
Loudoun County, Virginia	1,238	77.1	37.6	55,413	94.2	76.0	N	N	N
Montgomery County, Virginia	N	N	N	N	N	N	N	N	N
Prince William County, Virginia	N	N	N	29,701	87.3	52.9	N	N	N
Roanoke County, Virginia	N	N	N	N	N	N	N	N	N
Rockingham County, Virginia	N	N	N	N	N	N	N	N	N
Spotsylvania County, Virginia	N	N	N	2,390	91.1	55.7	N	N	N
Stafford County, Virginia	N	N	N	3,749	89.1	46.9	N	N	N
York County, Virginia	N	N	N	3,137	84.0	60.9	N	N	N
Alexandria city, Virginia	N	N	N	8,603	91.4	70.1	N	N	N
Chesapeake city, Virginia	N	N	N	7,577	87.3	46.3	N	N	N
Hampton city, Virginia	N	N	N	2,436	67.4	32.8	N	N	N
Lynchburg city, Virginia	N	N	N	N	N	N	N	N	N
Newport News city, Virginia	N	N	N	4,898	94.6	46.4	N	N	N
Norfolk city, Virginia	N	N	N	6,198	92.4	52.9	N	N	N
Portsmouth city, Virginia	N	N	N	N	N	N	N	N	N
Richmond city, Virginia	N	N	N	N	N	N	N	N	N
Roanoke city, Virginia	N	N	N	N	N	N	N	N	N
Suffolk city, Virginia	N	N	N	N	N	N	N	N	N
Virginia Beach city, Virginia	N	N	N	25,248	85.7	38.2	N	N	N
WASHINGTON	66,153	82.3	15.7	502,312	88.6	56.1	31,931	88.0	10.5
Benton County, Washington	N	N	N	3,402	80.0	65.3	N	N	N
Chelan County, Washington	N	N	N	N	N	N	N	N	N
Clallam County, Washington	2,817	84.2	14.6	N	N	N	N	N	N
Clark County, Washington	1,890	90.8	31.3	16,261	90.1	43.4	2,253	76.3	22.2
Cowlitz County, Washington	N	N	N	N	N	N	N	N	N
Franklin County, Washington	N	N	N	N	N	N	N	N	N
Grant County, Washington	N	N	N	N	N	N	N	N	N
Grays Harbor County, Washington	N	N	N	N	N	N	N	N	N
Island County, Washington	N	N	N	2,966	82.1	22.3	N	N	N
King County, Washington	10,074	79.8	27.4	313,217	89.4	63.6	10,939	84.6	10.8
Kitsap County, Washington	2,526	89.0	19.2	10,864	91.8	36.6	N	N	N
Lewis County, Washington	N	N	N	N	N	N	N	N	N
Mason County, Washington	1,258	75.7	20.5	N	N	N	N	N	N
Pierce County, Washington	7,578	82.6	14.0	43,081	87.0	33.9	7,767	87.0	7.7
Skagit County, Washington	2,378	80.7	8.6	1,921	80.1	36.5	N	N	N
Snohomish County, Washington	5,911	84.2	18.1	71,049	88.8	50.6	N	N	N
Spokane County, Washington	4,969	83.2	13.8	7,805	82.1	43.5	N	N	N
Thurston County, Washington	N	N	N	11,751	85.0	39.6	N	N	N
Whatcom County, Washington	3,427	91.1	19.1	5,479	90.1	53.5	N	N	N
Yakima County, Washington	6,275	70.3	2.3	2,093	86.5	50.7	N	N	N
WEST VIRGINIA	2,261	84.4	20.4	11,020	88.2	66.2	N	N	N
Berkeley County, West Virginia	N	N	N	N	N	N	N	N	N
Cabell County, West Virginia	N	N	N	N	N	N	N	N	N
Harrison County, West Virginia	N	N	N	N	N	N	N	N	N
Kanawha County, West Virginia	N	N	N	N	N	N	N	N	N
Monongalia County, West Virginia	N	N	N	N	N	N	N	N	N
Raleigh County, West Virginia	N	N	N	N	N	N	N	N	N
Wood County, West Virginia	N	N	N	N	N	N	N	N	N
WISCONSIN	34,006	90.8	14.5	103,046	86.0	47.4	N	N	N
Brown County, Wisconsin	3,909	90.9	8.6	5,477	88.4	55.0	N	N	N
Dane County, Wisconsin	N	N	N	19,944	91.4	67.5	N	N	N
Dodge County, Wisconsin	N	N	N	N	N	N	N	N	N
Eau Claire County, Wisconsin	N	N	N	N	N	N	N	N	N
Fond du Lac County, Wisconsin	N	N	N	N	N	N	N	N	N
Jefferson County, Wisconsin	N	N	N	N	N	N	N	N	N
Kenosha County, Wisconsin	N	N	N	N	N	N	N	N	N

N = Data for this geographic area cannot be displayed because the number of sample cases is too small.

Table C-2. Educational Attainment of the Population, by Selected Counties, 2019—*Continued*

(Number; percent; dollars.)

| | Educational attainment by race/ethnicity, 25 years and over | | | | | | | | |
| | White alone | | | White alone, not Hispanic | | | Black alone | | |
State/County	Total	High school graduate or more (percent)	Bachelor's degree or more (percent)	Total	High school graduate or more (percent)	Bachelor's degree or more (percent)	Total	High school graduate or more (percent)	Bachelor's degree or more (percent)
WISCONSIN—(*Continued*)									
La Crosse County, Wisconsin......................	71,020	96.1	35.1	70,312	96.3	35.1	N	N	N
Manitowoc County, Wisconsin.....................	54,195	94.3	22.2	53,201	94.6	22.2	N	N	N
Marathon County, Wisconsin	88,030	92.9	24.6	86,921	93.4	24.8	N	N	N
Milwaukee County, Wisconsin.....................	409,132	92.7	39.3	366,060	95.4	42.2	147,046	84.7	13.1
Outagamie County, Wisconsin	118,124	95.3	30.5	115,836	95.5	30.6	N	N	N
Ozaukee County, Wisconsin	59,230	98.6	48.7	58,060	98.6	48.8	N	N	N
Portage County, Wisconsin.........................	43,583	95.7	34.8	43,078	95.8	35.0	N	N	N
Racine County, Wisconsin...........................	113,883	92.0	29.0	104,480	94.1	30.4	12,921	74.8	6.2
Rock County, Wisconsin	99,667	93.3	24.0	97,802	93.4	24.0	4,691	92.5	13.2
St. Croix County, Wisconsin........................	59,882	95.6	38.0	58,808	96.4	38.4	N	N	N
Sheboygan County, Wisconsin.....................	73,143	95.5	28.2	71,155	96.1	28.4	N	N	N
Walworth County, Wisconsin	65,671	92.3	31.7	61,885	94.7	33.1	N	N	N
Washington County, Wisconsin	92,752	95.0	31.1	91,442	95.3	31.2	N	N	N
Waukesha County, Wisconsin	268,121	96.9	45.5	259,704	97.5	46.2	3,765	92	31
Winnebago County, Wisconsin	108,489	95.0	32.5	106,166	95.2	33.0	2,211	68	7
Wood County, Wisconsin.............................	50,416	92.1	19.5	49,257	92.2	19.7	N	N	N
WYOMING.....................................	361,618	94.8	29.8	340,863	95.7	30.8	3,291	99	47
Laramie County, Wyoming..........................	60,989	94.6	31.7	55,827	96.0	33.4	N	N	N
Natrona County, Wyoming	51,454	93.0	21.2	48,479	94.7	22.1	N	N	N

N = Data for this geographic area cannot be displayed because the number of sample cases is too small.

Table C-2. Educational Attainment of the Population, by Selected Counties, 2019—*Continued*

(Number; percent; dollars.)

| | Educational attainment by race/ethnicity, 25 years and over | | | | | | | | |
| | American Indian or Alaska Native alone | | | Asian alone | | | Native Hawaiian or Other Pacific Islander alone | | |
State/County	Total	High school graduate or more (percent)	Bachelor's degree or more (percent)	Total	High school graduate or more (percent)	Bachelor's degree or more (percent)	Total	High school graduate or more (percent)	Bachelor's degree or more (percent)
WISCONSIN—*(Continued)*									
La Crosse County, Wisconsin	N	N	N	3,232	89.0	34.5	N	N	N
Manitowoc County, Wisconsin	N	N	N	N	N	N	N	N	N
Marathon County, Wisconsin	N	N	N	4,364	92.7	36.6	N	N	N
Milwaukee County, Wisconsin	3,423	94.1	20.0	25,802	77.9	37.9	N	N	N
Outagamie County, Wisconsin	1,914	90.1	13.0	3,949	80.9	31.5	N	N	N
Ozaukee County, Wisconsin	N	N	N	N	N	N	N	N	N
Portage County, Wisconsin	N	N	N	N	N	N	N	N	N
Racine County, Wisconsin	N	N	N	1,725	81.1	25.8	N	N	N
Rock County, Wisconsin	N	N	N	N	N	N	N	N	N
St. Croix County, Wisconsin	N	N	N	N	N	N	N	N	N
Sheboygan County, Wisconsin	N	N	N	4,124	83.7	28.6	N	N	N
Walworth County, Wisconsin	N	N	N	N	N	N	N	N	N
Washington County, Wisconsin	N	N	N	N	N	N	N	N	N
Waukesha County, Wisconsin	N	N	N	10,408	96	70	N	N	N
Winnebago County, Wisconsin	N	N	N	3,301	77	29	N	N	N
Wood County, Wisconsin	N	N	N	N	N	N	N	N	N
WYOMING	8,656	92	11	3,690	98	47	N	N	N
Laramie County, Wyoming	N	N	N	N	N	N	N	N	N
Natrona County, Wyoming	N	N	N	N	N	N	N	N	N

N = Data for this geographic area cannot be displayed because the number of sample cases is too small.

Table C-2. Educational Attainment of the Population, by Selected Counties, 2019—*Continued*

(Number; percent; dollars.)

State/County	Educational attainment by race/ethnicity, 25 years and over								
	Some other race alone			Two or more races			Hispanic or Latino (of any race)		
	Total	High school graduate or more (percent)	Bachelor's degree or more (percent)	Total	High school graduate or more (percent)	Bachelor's degree or more (percent)	Total	High school graduate or more (percent)	Bachelor's degree or more (percent)
UNITED STATES	9,752,522	64.4	13.3	4,895,894	89.2	33.4	34,949,077	70.5	17.6
ALABAMA	36,540	51.7	10.8	39,473	86.2	32.8	104,045	61.3	16.4
Baldwin County, Alabama..................................	N	N	N	N	N	N	5,145	82.0	24.5
Calhoun County, Alabama..................................	N	N	N	N	N	N	N	N	N
Cullman County, Alabama..................................	N	N	N	N	N	N	N	N	N
DeKalb County, Alabama..................................	N	N	N	N	N	N	4,516	33.4	1.4
Elmore County, Alabama..................................	N	N	N	N	N	N	N	N	N
Etowah County, Alabama..................................	N	N	N	N	N	N	N	N	N
Houston County, Alabama.................................	N	N	N	686	78.9	24.8	1,984	53.9	14.0
Jefferson County, Alabama	4,361	61.7	16.9	4,569	94.3	37.1	12,770	66.8	14.6
Lauderdale County, Alabama.............................	N	N	N	N	N	N	N	N	N
Lee County, Alabama.......................................	N	N	N	N	N	N	N	N	N
Limestone County, Alabama.............................	N	N	N	N	N	N	N	N	N
Madison County, Alabama................................	N	N	N	4,488	89.1	52.3	9,836	71.8	34.3
Marshall County, Alabama................................	N	N	N	N	N	N	5,595	48.3	6.3
Mobile County, Alabama	N	N	N	4,071	80.9	30.8	7,365	70.1	16.4
Montgomery County, Alabama..........................	N	N	N	N	N	N	3,490	64.4	27.0
Morgan County, Alabama.................................	N	N	N	N	N	N	4,743	46.6	7.5
St. Clair County, Alabama................................	N	N	N	N	N	N	N	N	N
Shelby County, Alabama	N	N	N	N	N	N	6,009	74.6	32.1
Talladega County, Alabama..............................	N	N	N	N	N	N	N	N	N
Tuscaloosa County, Alabama............................	N	N	N	N	N	N	3,162	70.7	19.4
Walker County, Alabama	N	N	N	N	N	N	N	N	N
ALASKA...	6,790	84.4	17.3	22,413	96.2	29.2	28,365	86.0	19.9
Anchorage Municipality, Alaska........................	2,880	85.8	22.4	8,985	97.6	38.5	14,289	88.6	20.2
Fairbanks North Star Borough, Alaska	N	N	N	N	N	N	N	N	N
Matanuska-Susitna Borough, Alaska...................	N	N	N	2,896	93.2	21.5	2,938	88.9	28.1
ARIZONA	223,940	70.1	11.2	122,271	88.4	29.3	1,292,262	71.1	13.9
Apache County, Arizona	N	N	N	N	N	N	N	N	N
Cochise County, Arizona	N	N	N	3,143	90.2	22.2	26,825	76.5	15.2
Coconino County, Arizona	N	N	N	2,399	100.0	27.9	10,087	92.6	30.8
Maricopa County, Arizona	128,517	68.2	12.4	70,520	91.4	32.4	771,974	69.9	14.0
Mohave County, Arizona	4,518	58.5	3.3	3,968	100.0	13.9	21,617	71.4	5.7
Navajo County, Arizona....................................	3,131	70.7	0.3	N	N	N	8,096	69.0	0.9
Pima County, Arizona.......................................	50,754	73.4	11.4	25,316	80.7	26.2	225,759	75.1	16.5
Pinal County, Arizona.......................................	14,306	78.1	7.4	7,924	81.6	24.5	83,208	72.2	9.7
Yavapai County, Arizona..................................	6,900	72.8	5.0	N	N	N	19,297	75.1	14.1
Yuma County, Arizona......................................	5,919	67.6	8.3	3,154	81.0	16.5	78,069	62.5	9.6
ARKANSAS..	38,425	52.1	7.5	33,858	85.7	25.3	117,900	58.7	9.8
Benton County, Arkansas	3,112	62.2	8.9	3,291	98.4	49.3	24,903	66.6	11.6
Craighead County, Arkansas	N	N	N	N	N	N	N	N	N
Faulkner County, Arkansas...............................	N	N	N	N	N	N	N	N	N
Garland County, Arkansas................................	N	N	N	N	N	N	2,436	67.4	11.3
Jefferson County, Arkansas..............................	N	N	N	N	N	N	N	N	N
Lonoke County, Arkansas.................................	N	N	N	N	N	N	N	N	N
Pulaski County, Arkansas.................................	N	N	N	3,416	89.8	46.0	12,597	68.8	16.8
Saline County, Arkansas..................................	N	N	N	N	N	N	2,893	66.4	10.5
Sebastian County, Arkansas.............................	N	N	N	N	N	N	9,442	55.2	10.4
Washington County, Arkansas	8,566	38.9	5.6	N	N	N	19,950	39.9	4.4
White County, Arkansas	N	N	N	N	N	N	N	N	N
CALIFORNIA	3,279,489	61.9	11.5	935,420	89.1	36.4	9,150,608	66.4	14.4
Alameda County, California...............................	119,770	71.0	18.2	52,787	92.6	53.8	225,685	77.0	24.5
Butte County, California....................................	6,429	60.4	4.4	6,525	91.4	29.9	19,864	67.6	12.8
Contra Costa County, California	90,966	61.3	10.0	34,103	90.2	37.3	175,906	68.7	16.1
El Dorado County, California	2,626	52.6	16.2	2,746	94.4	43.0	15,142	75.9	19.1
Fresno County, California	91,393	58.2	9.4	16,556	80.5	25.4	294,209	63.0	11.3
Humboldt County, California	N	N	N	4,677	94.5	23.1	7,714	80.6	24.7
Imperial County, California...............................	27,384	57.2	17.4	2,615	90.1	28.9	90,978	67.7	16.8
Kern County, California	70,495	56.9	7.7	16,919	87.6	17.8	262,914	62.4	8.6
Kings County, California....................................	9,258	50.3	6.1	N	N	N	46,738	53.2	7.5
Lake County, California	N	N	N	N	N	N	8,056	63.0	4.4

N = Data for this geographic area cannot be displayed because the number of sample cases is too small.

Table C-2. Educational Attainment of the Population, by Selected Counties, 2019—*Continued*

(Number; percent; dollars.)

State/County	Median earnings in the past 12 months (2019 inflation-adjusted dollars)					
	Population 25 years and over with earnings					
	Total	Less than high school graduate	High school graduate (includes equivalency)	Some college or associate's degree	Bachelor's degree	Graduate or professional degree
UNITED STATES	41,801	25,876	31,956	38,125	56,344	75,495
ALABAMA	37,217	22,395	30,845	35,107	50,643	60,922
Baldwin County, Alabama.............................	39,627	20,711	30,500	37,139	42,839	57,366
Calhoun County, Alabama.............................	35,441	20,589	30,086	35,269	45,331	57,117
Cullman County, Alabama.............................	32,905	28,829	31,475	31,382	43,046	50,848
DeKalb County, Alabama.............................	31,528	21,683	31,694	35,365	40,858	46,667
Elmore County, Alabama.............................	37,103	30,395	30,994	39,240	44,428	68,117
Etowah County, Alabama.............................	30,599	21,492	26,228	31,654	38,125	78,270
Houston County, Alabama.............................	35,563	25,898	30,033	31,862	54,427	54,674
Jefferson County, Alabama	40,400	21,560	30,479	32,427	52,963	65,627
Lauderdale County, Alabama.........................	36,531	21,810	34,040	39,218	38,671	55,773
Lee County, Alabama.................................	40,537	10,696	33,650	34,332	42,033	58,852
Limestone County, Alabama..........................	41,336	15,945	29,960	40,111	56,830	61,614
Madison County, Alabama............................	45,347	20,278	32,492	36,548	55,967	85,150
Marshall County, Alabama............................	32,180	22,021	30,702	32,363	51,977	52,097
Mobile County, Alabama	36,324	24,479	31,210	34,003	47,645	55,361
Montgomery County, Alabama........................	35,900	21,504	26,676	31,225	45,522	59,526
Morgan County, Alabama.............................	36,950	20,384	32,124	37,261	53,394	75,768
St. Clair County, Alabama.............................	41,308	22,425	37,499	41,286	58,782	67,643
Shelby County, Alabama.............................	51,047	29,220	36,765	45,041	62,167	64,390
Talladega County, Alabama..........................	34,399	21,111	31,129	33,235	52,733	51,920
Tuscaloosa County, Alabama.........................	37,660	24,566	30,852	31,993	51,321	54,425
Walker County, Alabama	38,318	36,181	32,297	36,461	60,434	65,661
ALASKA...	47,809	23,264	36,522	47,878	53,033	71,947
Anchorage Municipality, Alaska......................	50,012	23,602	36,048	50,156	54,890	75,795
Fairbanks North Star Borough, Alaska	55,940	26,449	44,595	55,651	42,178	70,742
Matanuska-Susitna Borough, Alaska..................	49,859	25,387	40,355	48,724	61,264	70,790
ARIZONA	39,956	25,701	31,371	37,016	52,077	69,902
Apache County, Arizona	35,292	22,319	30,949	35,598	37,844	55,496
Cochise County, Arizona	35,373	24,518	24,627	35,071	49,681	80,634
Coconino County, Arizona	38,699	23,734	32,312	35,530	42,903	60,201
Maricopa County, Arizona	41,740	26,707	31,955	39,876	55,942	73,588
Mohave County, Arizona	31,097	22,939	30,906	29,827	47,912	52,108
Navajo County, Arizona	30,478	24,020	23,258	30,724	42,582	60,719
Pima County, Arizona.................................	35,198	22,273	29,299	32,336	47,053	62,202
Pinal County, Arizona.................................	39,148	26,156	36,561	40,162	45,664	52,243
Yavapai County, Arizona..............................	31,322	23,616	27,459	29,168	39,668	60,438
Yuma County, Arizona.................................	30,075	19,517	27,129	32,077	41,924	70,396
ARKANSAS	35,215	25,695	30,057	31,778	46,964	62,027
Benton County, Arkansas	41,914	30,014	34,203	39,074	56,930	80,000
Craighead County, Arkansas	36,222	24,225	30,203	33,132	50,157	63,538
Faulkner County, Arkansas	40,734	24,827	34,563	35,297	51,552	56,370
Garland County, Arkansas............................	27,470	23,111	20,936	25,470	47,057	60,269
Jefferson County, Arkansas...........................	30,454	19,543	25,922	26,006	32,022	48,250
Lonoke County, Arkansas.............................	40,376	38,386	32,752	40,685	50,130	64,554
Pulaski County, Arkansas.............................	37,106	22,065	30,229	31,720	48,167	61,033
Saline County, Arkansas..............................	44,047	29,409	35,858	39,036	54,410	69,589
Sebastian County, Arkansas..........................	31,041	26,388	24,613	30,233	46,168	70,585
Washington County, Arkansas	35,900	24,781	31,052	34,434	46,521	64,567
White County, Arkansas	32,574	19,930	31,099	27,195	45,870	54,389
CALIFORNIA	45,095	25,949	33,494	41,090	65,078	92,334
Alameda County, California	61,748	30,469	42,417	50,583	78,633	101,945
Butte County, California...............................	38,191	29,059	31,269	32,742	48,789	81,437
Contra Costa County, California	57,962	29,960	41,682	50,188	78,426	101,368
El Dorado County, California..........................	50,688	26,253	39,151	48,282	66,633	93,268
Fresno County, California	36,279	23,458	31,243	36,649	54,504	80,299
Humboldt County, California	36,069	36,108	26,250	35,268	41,719	56,356
Imperial County, California	32,476	17,322	36,205	32,315	44,681	65,855
Kern County, California	35,265	22,748	27,865	38,141	61,372	90,536
Kings County, California...............................	36,783	22,616	37,399	39,022	60,251	92,095
Lake County, California	31,630	26,006	30,526	31,815	59,462	31,233

N = Data for this geographic area cannot be displayed because the number of sample cases is too small.

Table C-2. Educational Attainment of the Population, by Selected Counties, 2019—*Continued*

(Number; percent; dollars.)

	Educational attainment by race/ethnicity, 25 years and over								
	Some other race alone			Two or more races			Hispanic or Latino (of any race)		
State/County	Total	High school graduate or more (percent)	Bachelor's degree or more (percent)	Total	High school graduate or more (percent)	Bachelor's degree or more (percent)	Total	High school graduate or more (percent)	Bachelor's degree or more (percent)
CALIFORNIA—*(Continued)*									
Los Angeles County, California	1,239,114	60.6	11.2	213,429	87.4	39.6	3,021,478	63.0	13.6
Madera County, California	19,634	44.4	5.5	2,496	80.1	8.5	50,007	56.1	8.2
Marin County, California	10,277	45.2	16.5	5,445	98.4	52.2	24,146	60.1	24.9
Mendocino County, California	N	N	N	N	N	N	12,353	58.7	11.3
Merced County, California	49,451	47.0	4.1	3,882	77.0	15.2	90,187	54.0	6.4
Monterey County, California	96,937	44.5	5.3	8,358	91.3	34.9	142,746	51.2	8.9
Napa County, California	9,470	52.9	9.6	3,746	90.0	39.3	27,738	62.3	12.9
Nevada County, California	N	N	N	N	N	N	5,143	82.3	19.3
Orange County, California	245,863	58.1	11.9	62,645	90.3	45.7	637,379	66.3	16.4
Placer County, California	4,044	79.8	22.1	8,932	92.1	27.7	33,620	81.9	25.3
Riverside County, California	296,277	64.6	9.2	44,478	89.6	26.2	707,430	69.7	11.9
Sacramento County, California	81,293	69.4	13.7	56,301	92.1	29.2	208,400	76.2	18.1
San Bernardino County, California	205,589	65.2	9.8	51,095	87.0	25.6	679,754	69.0	11.8
San Diego County, California	116,734	72.5	20.2	84,172	92.9	40.7	674,835	72.5	19.4
San Francisco County, California	49,602	77.5	23.4	26,308	95.0	67.6	94,366	80.4	32.6
San Joaquin County, California	34,109	63.7	9.0	39,640	75.2	13.0	174,695	63.4	8.7
San Luis Obispo County, California	6,895	68.5	13.5	3,986	98.8	21.1	35,999	73.0	19.9
San Mateo County, California	50,927	67.4	17.8	17,465	91.4	51.3	114,643	72.6	24.6
Santa Barbara County, California	27,176	59.4	13.0	7,324	92.0	43.6	110,034	58.2	11.6
Santa Clara County, California	100,478	65.1	14.7	45,461	94.5	47.6	285,423	71.1	20.0
Santa Cruz County, California	16,331	52.4	16.3	6,153	97.0	49.3	50,521	61.7	20.0
Shasta County, California	2,687	93.0	18.9	3,905	91.2	14.2	10,396	88.2	19.7
Solano County, California	20,805	68.8	16.2	15,446	94.2	29.4	69,969	72.8	16.3
Sonoma County, California	39,937	59.7	7.4	13,413	87.5	28.5	77,534	68.1	15.4
Stanislaus County, California	18,854	66.2	9.5	12,291	85.4	19.8	142,839	67.4	9.8
Sutter County, California	2,861	69.7	12.4	3,098	93.8	10.7	16,616	60.4	7.5
Tehama County, California	N	N	N	N	N	N	9,834	62.2	5.3
Tulare County, California	58,909	63.7	3.9	10,460	74.4	14.6	161,362	63.2	6.0
Ventura County, California	27,326	67.5	11.0	16,976	90.0	35.0	214,781	69.0	14.8
Yolo County, California	5,602	77.0	15.3	4,424	90.1	58.9	38,184	74.2	16.9
Yuba County, California	N	N	N	3,362	83.7	25.6	12,161	59.1	13.1
COLORADO	128,870	73.4	16.0	104,674	91.5	38.7	712,267	75.2	18.5
Adams County, Colorado	19,143	72.7	12.2	13,925	75.2	22.9	115,568	68.1	10.3
Arapahoe County, Colorado	21,693	73.4	14.9	12,814	91.8	38.4	70,699	75.1	18.4
Boulder County, Colorado	N	N	N	4,714	85.9	56.5	24,032	68.8	28.0
Broomfield County, Colorado	N	N	N	N	N	N	5,451	78.5	30.2
Denver County, Colorado	23,538	78.4	21.8	17,201	94.2	54.0	126,448	74.2	22.5
Douglas County, Colorado	4,068	94.2	27.7	N	N	N	19,074	95.1	43.5
El Paso County, Colorado	17,493	74.9	15.2	16,963	95.6	31.5	68,183	84.3	20.2
Jefferson County, Colorado	6,564	89.5	20.7	9,442	96.0	50.8	55,422	80.9	24.1
Larimer County, Colorado	3,066	83.8	14.6	4,340	94.0	57.9	22,435	90.6	32.2
Mesa County, Colorado	N	N	N	N	N	N	11,989	80.7	9.9
Pueblo County, Colorado	7,121	76.6	10.0	3,756	92.8	26.3	44,478	83.6	14.5
Weld County, Colorado	9,543	56.0	14.8	4,824	84.6	17.2	52,790	64.4	12.3
CONNECTICUT	121,383	69.2	14.3	58,085	83.7	31.0	347,589	73.9	17.8
Fairfield County, Connecticut	38,882	64.1	14.4	14,233	89.7	43.0	116,112	72.1	20.2
Hartford County, Connecticut	39,730	68.7	13.3	16,560	76.9	23.9	96,294	73.2	15.7
Litchfield County, Connecticut	N	N	N	N	N	N	7,889	77.5	32.5
Middlesex County, Connecticut	N	N	N	N	N	N	5,843	84.6	29.2
New Haven County, Connecticut	30,889	71.0	14.2	15,232	85.2	30.0	92,479	73.7	15.3
New London County, Connecticut	5,504	85.8	15.2	5,603	74.6	15.3	16,124	80.8	15.4
Tolland County, Connecticut	N	N	N	N	N	N	5,618	80.5	31.5
Windham County, Connecticut	N	N	N	N	N	N	7,230	81.0	9.1
DELAWARE	12,058	59.4	13.5	9,900	90.7	34.1	49,372	62.3	13.9
Kent County, Delaware	N	N	N	N	N	N	7,342	80.6	12.2
New Castle County, Delaware	7,786	54.8	14.2	5,987	86.6	39.7	31,851	61.2	14.8
Sussex County, Delaware	3,149	59.3	10.4	1,792	93.5	38.8	10,179	52.3	12.5
DISTRICT OF COLUMBIA	17,430	69.3	33.9	13,127	94.3	74.9	50,141	80.8	52.0
District of Columbia, District of Columbia	17,430	69.3	33.9	13,127	94.3	74.9	50,141	80.8	52.0
FLORIDA	468,004	75.0	19.7	283,975	87.2	31.0	3,773,205	79.6	25.7
Alachua County, Florida	N	N	N	3,807	85.9	43.9	15,081	88.6	54.7
Bay County, Florida	N	N	N	N	N	N	6,898	88.6	26.8

N = Data for this geographic area cannot be displayed because the number of sample cases is too small.

Table C-2. Educational Attainment of the Population, by Selected Counties, 2019—*Continued*

(Number; percent; dollars.)

State/County	Median earnings in the past 12 months (2019 inflation-adjusted dollars)					
	Population 25 years and over with earnings					
	Total	Less than high school graduate	High school graduate (includes equivalency)	Some college or associate's degree	Bachelor's degree	Graduate or professional degree
CALIFORNIA—(*Continued*)						
Los Angeles County, California	40,677	25,043	31,705	38,782	60,216	81,800
Madera County, California	29,746	22,631	32,069	26,098	48,202	56,300
Marin County, California	63,972	26,135	41,677	49,122	76,824	126,720
Mendocino County, California	35,887	18,150	43,032	33,785	47,812	42,614
Merced County, California	33,675	29,593	31,659	37,726	47,344	70,650
Monterey County, California	35,726	24,061	31,494	40,698	59,846	85,392
Napa County, California	50,622	27,402	41,000	43,695	76,863	90,405
Nevada County, California	39,216	19,292	35,709	35,432	60,089	54,911
Orange County, California	49,152	26,393	32,231	43,740	66,608	91,837
Placer County, California	59,365	26,581	37,255	48,805	80,951	97,961
Riverside County, California	40,364	26,443	33,903	41,081	52,262	78,518
Sacramento County, California	43,744	27,743	33,839	40,646	60,744	85,029
San Bernardino County, California	39,246	26,664	32,295	38,974	54,230	75,805
San Diego County, California	46,395	26,200	31,552	40,417	62,806	89,813
San Francisco County, California	74,175	25,309	34,872	47,112	91,809	121,346
San Joaquin County, California	40,462	29,968	35,753	41,455	57,071	80,754
San Luis Obispo County, California	41,806	29,334	35,707	39,270	55,404	75,351
San Mateo County, California	67,707	30,977	38,774	51,234	82,635	131,461
Santa Barbara County, California	40,820	25,481	31,732	41,682	61,180	86,061
Santa Clara County, California	69,611	32,006	39,851	49,640	89,859	131,480
Santa Cruz County, California	45,945	26,373	36,192	40,535	65,443	84,758
Shasta County, California	38,650	35,600	31,209	33,471	60,729	66,044
Solano County, California	49,777	31,055	41,739	49,042	64,080	72,903
Sonoma County, California	46,272	29,779	36,612	46,351	61,631	70,952
Stanislaus County, California	40,814	30,057	34,432	42,469	62,802	86,962
Sutter County, California	35,512	17,955	33,331	40,289	45,023	67,196
Tehama County, California	35,827	26,661	30,670	34,574	58,915	56,950
Tulare County, California	32,217	22,063	31,625	33,752	60,196	83,816
Ventura County, California	45,349	25,970	32,470	44,676	62,685	92,472
Yolo County, California	47,377	27,424	39,923	46,925	50,243	85,477
Yuba County, California	40,281	25,371	35,701	43,963	60,433	66,880
COLORADO	46,887	30,968	35,537	40,819	58,229	71,616
Adams County, Colorado	41,871	32,479	34,880	41,844	58,852	66,229
Arapahoe County, Colorado	47,988	31,687	36,780	43,249	60,409	69,083
Boulder County, Colorado	51,446	31,213	35,446	37,760	57,394	75,887
Broomfield County, Colorado	65,381	36,832	46,503	46,496	75,007	83,802
Denver County, Colorado	51,532	31,345	31,889	43,521	61,887	75,214
Douglas County, Colorado	66,061	46,747	38,879	49,030	76,366	86,486
El Paso County, Colorado	42,343	27,652	35,662	36,453	51,965	76,070
Jefferson County, Colorado	52,590	33,837	38,867	43,417	66,412	75,597
Larimer County, Colorado	46,348	16,864	32,392	41,331	51,327	65,254
Mesa County, Colorado	35,020	21,760	32,514	31,478	46,402	46,997
Pueblo County, Colorado	35,972	17,500	28,516	34,601	49,229	55,266
Weld County, Colorado	44,686	36,576	39,935	42,063	54,687	66,343
CONNECTICUT	50,788	24,426	37,017	42,884	64,143	85,175
Fairfield County, Connecticut	55,628	24,146	35,274	42,688	71,493	100,982
Hartford County, Connecticut	51,156	23,444	35,532	45,721	65,129	82,399
Litchfield County, Connecticut	48,268	26,304	45,228	41,255	57,496	66,918
Middlesex County, Connecticut	52,355	11,389	39,699	43,584	66,967	77,364
New Haven County, Connecticut	47,066	25,127	36,292	42,451	60,008	77,755
New London County, Connecticut	45,611	31,856	38,275	38,994	51,632	81,359
Tolland County, Connecticut	60,956	28,537	47,074	51,303	67,253	90,122
Windham County, Connecticut	41,797	27,879	37,253	42,942	51,403	64,894
DELAWARE	43,164	31,024	33,671	38,048	56,603	70,579
Kent County, Delaware	37,174	28,333	32,918	35,140	44,175	66,535
New Castle County, Delaware	48,948	30,547	36,245	41,865	61,801	74,775
Sussex County, Delaware	37,978	32,355	30,006	35,437	53,313	61,640
DISTRICT OF COLUMBIA	71,361	30,883	31,768	44,248	75,222	101,956
District of Columbia, District of Columbia	71,361	30,883	31,768	44,248	75,222	101,956
FLORIDA	36,021	23,292	30,064	34,752	47,810	62,425
Alachua County, Florida	40,906	14,830	31,937	35,874	46,871	61,175
Bay County, Florida	35,540	24,127	27,745	36,666	41,027	81,305

N – Data for this geographic area cannot be displayed because the number of sample cases is too small.

Table C-2. Educational Attainment of the Population, by Selected Counties, 2019—*Continued*

(Number; percent; dollars.)

State/County	Educational attainment by race/ethnicity, 25 years and over								
	Some other race alone			Two or more races			Hispanic or Latino (of any race)		
	Total	High school graduate or more (percent)	Bachelor's degree or more (percent)	Total	High school graduate or more (percent)	Bachelor's degree or more (percent)	Total	High school graduate or more (percent)	Bachelor's degree or more (percent)
FLORIDA—*(Continued)*									
Brevard County, Florida	7,154	91.5	17.4	10,895	96.6	26.1	41,962	90.4	28.7
Broward County, Florida	43,356	80.0	19.0	34,532	82.0	30.1	417,459	86.0	31.3
Charlotte County, Florida	N	N	N	N	N	N	10,177	83.6	15.0
Citrus County, Florida	N	N	N	N	N	N	6,013	84.2	15.2
Clay County, Florida	N	N	N	N	N	N	13,526	95.6	26.4
Collier County, Florida	2,775	62.5	1.0	N	N	N	67,575	75.0	17.7
Columbia County, Florida	N	N	N	N	N	N	2,248	76.5	45.9
Duval County, Florida	17,345	83.8	28.2	14,782	84.3	25.0	61,043	82.4	25.8
Escambia County, Florida	N	N	N	7,943	96.6	24.1	11,164	76.3	22.9
Flagler County, Florida	N	N	N	N	N	N	7,796	83.0	11.7
Hernando County, Florida	N	N	N	N	N	N	18,391	83.8	16.6
Highlands County, Florida	N	N	N	N	N	N	13,650	73.9	14.1
Hillsborough County, Florida	46,513	67.9	18.0	27,060	90.3	35.1	276,482	80.4	24.7
Indian River County, Florida	N	N	N	N	N	N	13,185	75.2	14.3
Lake County, Florida	7,141	77.5	14.6	N	N	N	38,665	82.9	20.4
Lee County, Florida	19,272	57.3	13.7	5,521	87.5	39.1	106,564	69.7	14.8
Leon County, Florida	N	N	N	N	N	N	9,237	87.4	30.6
Manatee County, Florida	N	N	N	2,874	94.4	27.5	38,290	67.7	11.0
Marion County, Florida	N	N	N	3,376	79.1	28.1	32,853	81.5	22.1
Martin County, Florida	N	N	N	N	N	N	12,469	76.9	18.2
Miami-Dade County, Florida	70,114	73.0	22.6	30,874	85.9	29.5	1,377,363	77.4	28.7
Monroe County, Florida	N	N	N	N	N	N	12,778	76.8	16.6
Nassau County, Florida	N	N	N	N	N	N	2,445	70.3	5.8
Okaloosa County, Florida	4,880	66.9	11.9	5,840	95.2	28.3	11,902	80.1	22.1
Orange County, Florida	50,705	75.3	21.2	24,039	88.6	43.5	291,498	82.7	25.4
Osceola County, Florida	24,059	72.9	14.5	6,821	85.6	22.8	131,843	82.2	21.5
Palm Beach County, Florida	29,699	64.5	20.1	17,755	88.7	34.8	225,343	75.0	25.9
Pasco County, Florida	6,559	75.2	14.3	6,642	89.3	41.2	57,066	84.7	20.2
Pinellas County, Florida	9,658	89.3	36.5	14,133	89.0	34.2	64,065	85.6	29.6
Polk County, Florida	23,197	75.4	15.6	6,523	79.6	34.0	103,924	78.2	16.1
Putnam County, Florida	N	N	N	N	N	N	3,950	35.8	0.7
St. Johns County, Florida	N	N	N	N	N	N	12,591	92.9	42.5
St. Lucie County, Florida	N	N	N	N	N	N	41,716	80.2	21.4
Santa Rosa County, Florida	N	N	N	2,875	85.5	33.5	6,894	90.6	18.0
Sarasota County, Florida	2,831	81.2	20.8	4,776	91.9	31.9	25,531	86.4	24.9
Seminole County, Florida	23,785	87.3	32.0	5,864	91.0	36.4	69,291	88.0	27.9
Sumter County, Florida	N	N	N	N	N	N	5,260	79.4	26.0
Volusia County, Florida	21,473	80.9	12.6	5,985	85.7	24.9	52,105	82.3	15.9
Walton County, Florida	N	N	N	N	N	N	2,458	86.0	26.8
GEORGIA	174,770	57.6	14.1	108,327	87.2	36.5	546,665	64.3	19.2
Barrow County, Georgia	N	N	N	N	N	N	5,915	72.6	21.1
Bartow County, Georgia	N	N	N	N	N	N	N	N	N
Bibb County, Georgia	N	N	N	N	N	N	2,718	60.9	10.1
Bulloch County, Georgia	N	N	N	N	N	N	N	N	N
Carroll County, Georgia	N	N	N	N	N	N	N	N	N
Catoosa County, Georgia	N	N	N	N	N	N	N	N	N
Chatham County, Georgia	N	N	N	2,049	79.2	48.5	10,502	85.6	22.8
Cherokee County, Georgia	N	N	N	N	N	N	15,694	63.5	18.0
Clarke County, Georgia	N	N	N	N	N	N	6,453	93.9	33.6
Clayton County, Georgia	6,120	57.0	6.1	N	N	N	18,154	64.1	9.9
Cobb County, Georgia	27,955	51.5	12.8	10,445	95.0	50.6	53,492	61.3	20.1
Columbia County, Georgia	N	N	N	N	N	N	6,356	72.9	34.6
Coweta County, Georgia	N	N	N	N	N	N	6,505	69.0	11.2
DeKalb County, Georgia	7,786	62.0	13.0	8,770	83.7	54.8	32,973	57.5	22.9
Dougherty County, Georgia	N	N	N	N	N	N	N	N	N
Douglas County, Georgia	N	N	N	N	N	N	7,513	65.4	13.5
Fayette County, Georgia	N	N	N	N	N	N	5,360	92.9	23.9
Floyd County, Georgia	N	N	N	N	N	N	5,608	56.5	5.0
Forsyth County, Georgia	5,013	45.8	21.1	N	N	N	12,854	60.1	29.0
Fulton County, Georgia	11,131	67.8	30.8	11,261	94.4	62.3	43,744	83.8	47.7
Glynn County, Georgia	N	N	N	N	N	N	N	N	N
Gwinnett County, Georgia	48,275	55.6	11.6	14,516	85.6	36.7	108,404	63.6	17.6
Hall County, Georgia	N	N	N	N	N	N	30,123	48.8	12.0
Henry County, Georgia	N	N	N	N	N	N	8,705	57.4	20.1
Houston County, Georgia	N	N	N	N	N	N	4,811	78.8	15.5

N = Data for this geographic area cannot be displayed because the number of sample cases is too small.

Table C-2. Educational Attainment of the Population, by Selected Counties, 2019—*Continued*

(Number; percent; dollars.)

| State/County | Median earnings in the past 12 months (2019 inflation-adjusted dollars) | | | | | |
| | Population 25 years and over with earnings | | | | | |
	Total	Less than high school graduate	High school graduate (includes equivalency)	Some college or associate's degree	Bachelor's degree	Graduate or professional degree
FLORIDA—(*Continued*)						
Brevard County, Florida	36,790	20,816	28,019	34,815	50,218	70,727
Broward County, Florida	37,078	21,938	31,397	36,083	48,139	71,146
Charlotte County, Florida	31,326	24,588	25,344	31,015	45,580	61,774
Citrus County, Florida	31,077	25,804	28,173	29,542	45,623	48,217
Clay County, Florida	39,148	26,197	32,256	36,751	42,992	69,835
Collier County, Florida	36,057	22,483	31,255	37,184	51,407	64,551
Columbia County, Florida	31,947	30,142	25,861	31,025	52,783	57,272
Duval County, Florida	38,125	22,451	31,273	34,999	54,386	70,053
Escambia County, Florida	35,049	20,071	28,890	35,293	46,548	50,774
Flagler County, Florida	36,162	13,981	29,272	36,377	54,424	50,661
Hernando County, Florida	32,322	19,310	30,338	31,257	41,646	62,021
Highlands County, Florida	30,464	20,426	26,854	30,852	42,086	51,280
Hillsborough County, Florida	39,378	24,773	30,330	36,893	51,289	72,048
Indian River County, Florida	31,562	22,753	28,390	31,318	44,552	71,814
Lake County, Florida	32,661	21,947	27,418	32,486	46,957	51,373
Lee County, Florida	35,354	26,831	31,312	33,389	45,790	55,494
Leon County, Florida	39,146	24,397	25,763	31,612	47,353	55,701
Manatee County, Florida	35,508	25,382	26,936	35,287	53,152	67,299
Marion County, Florida	32,368	28,914	30,543	30,229	41,447	61,995
Martin County, Florida	38,791	22,027	25,255	35,362	62,734	63,158
Miami-Dade County, Florida	32,598	22,589	27,662	32,830	45,195	61,161
Monroe County, Florida	37,400	26,327	31,067	34,417	51,096	60,898
Nassau County, Florida	38,519	30,934	36,856	39,146	41,475	57,581
Okaloosa County, Florida	36,172	17,057	27,230	38,395	40,259	76,406
Orange County, Florida	35,941	22,048	27,120	32,546	46,477	61,141
Osceola County, Florida	31,562	25,421	25,943	32,056	39,964	51,533
Palm Beach County, Florida	37,485	23,792	27,874	35,757	50,076	66,795
Pasco County, Florida	39,682	26,141	31,555	38,217	52,652	62,913
Pinellas County, Florida	39,006	22,931	30,406	36,241	49,771	63,089
Polk County, Florida	31,855	22,106	30,123	31,978	42,719	51,613
Putnam County, Florida	31,115	25,933	27,096	32,186	41,342	46,624
St. Johns County, Florida	48,349	23,887	34,957	40,514	60,796	70,481
St. Lucie County, Florida	33,767	24,446	30,913	35,200	44,306	47,172
Santa Rosa County, Florida	37,758	23,488	26,969	38,644	42,104	67,411
Sarasota County, Florida	36,080	20,865	32,799	32,752	43,502	61,225
Seminole County, Florida	41,402	24,400	31,039	33,968	52,905	66,751
Sumter County, Florida	23,864	18,855	22,112	35,491	24,263	14,548
Volusia County, Florida	32,403	30,128	30,696	31,869	41,946	52,241
Walton County, Florida	35,617	29,728	26,415	35,489	45,193	67,156
GEORGIA	40,312	25,479	31,184	35,846	53,662	70,027
Barrow County, Georgia	41,298	29,199	36,346	41,421	47,404	61,662
Bartow County, Georgia	40,536	35,195	36,359	40,075	47,362	65,642
Bibb County, Georgia	32,809	20,826	30,675	32,161	42,143	58,533
Bulloch County, Georgia	34,291	30,115	36,038	23,127	35,480	56,000
Carroll County, Georgia	37,840	27,248	29,039	37,375	43,966	58,563
Catoosa County, Georgia	39,630	32,232	31,157	37,072	48,842	60,635
Chatham County, Georgia	35,287	23,101	31,309	29,132	46,491	61,680
Cherokee County, Georgia	50,008	25,279	35,944	45,141	62,055	76,244
Clarke County, Georgia	31,118	32,891	25,044	23,169	32,296	47,468
Clayton County, Georgia	33,223	27,870	30,046	37,325	36,908	44,015
Cobb County, Georgia	47,929	26,292	32,996	40,403	60,822	75,646
Columbia County, Georgia	50,925	27,068	36,010	44,368	61,418	71,208
Coweta County, Georgia	45,924	34,426	41,439	43,350	51,609	65,531
DeKalb County, Georgia	41,673	21,911	28,213	34,988	55,615	79,814
Dougherty County, Georgia	32,122	22,081	27,141	31,178	40,897	47,469
Douglas County, Georgia	40,948	30,251	32,992	38,474	47,408	59,662
Fayette County, Georgia	51,973	25,047	41,105	42,038	73,500	65,502
Floyd County, Georgia	31,397	17,727	27,194	30,761	41,444	62,075
Forsyth County, Georgia	61,098	25,941	41,091	42,274	77,336	87,233
Fulton County, Georgia	54,376	21,710	29,628	36,148	66,932	86,548
Glynn County, Georgia	36,915	25,702	31,668	37,059	51,316	63,056
Gwinnett County, Georgia	41,209	27,193	31,552	37,311	52,162	66,561
Hall County, Georgia	36,258	23,485	34,458	40,357	55,859	62,076
Henry County, Georgia	43,036	31,481	33,909	49,677	49,973	66,094
Houston County, Georgia	41,088	32,162	36,477	38,287	60,405	71,949

N – Data for this geographic area cannot be displayed because the number of sample cases is too small.

Table C-2. Educational Attainment of the Population, by Selected Counties, 2019—*Continued*

(Number; percent; dollars.)

| | Educational attainment by race/ethnicity, 25 years and over | | | | | | | | |
| | Some other race alone | | | Two or more races | | | Hispanic or Latino (of any race) | | |
State/County	Total	High school graduate or more (percent)	Bachelor's degree or more (percent)	Total	High school graduate or more (percent)	Bachelor's degree or more (percent)	Total	High school graduate or more (percent)	Bachelor's degree or more (percent)
GEORGIA—*(Continued)*									
Jackson County, Georgia	N	N	N	N	N	N	N	N	N
Lowndes County, Georgia	N	N	N	N	N	N	2,944	69.8	12.7
Muscogee County, Georgia	N	N	N	N	N	N	7,752	82.5	23.4
Newton County, Georgia	N	N	N	N	N	N	N	N	N
Paulding County, Georgia	N	N	N	N	N	N	6,760	61.8	15.0
Richmond County, Georgia	N	N	N	N	N	N	5,359	90.0	28.0
Rockdale County, Georgia	N	N	N	N	N	N	4,984	75.1	10.0
Spalding County, Georgia	N	N	N	N	N	N	N	N	N
Troup County, Georgia	N	N	N	N	N	N	N	N	N
Walker County, Georgia	N	N	N	N	N	N	N	N	N
Walton County, Georgia	N	N	N	N	N	N	2,718	91.9	20.0
Whitfield County, Georgia	N	N	N	N	N	N	19,153	39.9	3.7
HAWAII	15,453	86.8	24.9	166,296	95.3	26.9	77,881	91.2	23.0
Hawaii County, Hawaii	N	N	N	30,697	94.0	17.2	12,754	78.3	13.2
Honolulu County, Hawaii	10,356	96.0	30.4	108,435	95.7	31.4	49,676	95.6	28.4
Kauai County, Hawaii	N	N	N	9,246	95.7	18.9	4,397	90.8	16.8
Maui County, Hawaii	N	N	N	17,918	94.2	20.7	11,049	86.4	12.6
IDAHO	37,977	60.3	7.5	25,837	90.3	38.9	115,826	68.8	12.7
Ada County, Idaho	4,799	79.1	21.3	8,295	97.4	61.3	22,659	81.5	22.1
Bannock County, Idaho	N	N	N	N	N	N	4,063	85.0	21.1
Bonneville County, Idaho	N	N	N	N	N	N	7,828	74.2	16.9
Canyon County, Idaho	17,007	54.4	5.8	5,005	74.4	13.7	29,144	61.8	8.1
Kootenai County, Idaho	N	N	N	N	N	N	4,136	91.4	9.0
Twin Falls County, Idaho	N	N	N	N	N	N	7,600	55.6	8.3
ILLINOIS	422,033	68.1	13.4	144,592	90.6	39.0	1,256,316	71.3	16.8
Adams County, Illinois	N	N	N	N	N	N	N	N	N
Champaign County, Illinois	N	N	N	N	N	N	5,538	73.4	40.9
Cook County, Illinois	282,874	68.8	14.8	69,718	91.7	45.1	778,104	72.3	17.7
DeKalb County, Illinois	N	N	N	N	N	N	5,645	77.0	24.7
DuPage County, Illinois	17,762	66.6	7.2	12,705	95.7	41.0	74,577	76.6	19.4
Kane County, Illinois	34,561	62.0	7.8	7,945	80.8	33.0	93,030	60.9	13.0
Kankakee County, Illinois	N	N	N	N	N	N	5,670	72.9	11.1
Kendall County, Illinois	N	N	N	N	N	N	14,652	80.8	21.9
Lake County, Illinois	28,447	64.4	4.2	8,530	92.4	43.4	82,402	65.2	10.5
LaSalle County, Illinois	1,819	51.6	0.1	N	N	N	5,915	64.6	5.4
McHenry County, Illinois	2,439	64.4	19.8	N	N	N	22,641	75.4	17.2
McLean County, Illinois	N	N	N	N	N	N	3,902	85.7	31.2
Macon County, Illinois	N	N	N	N	N	N	1,106	83.5	24.7
Madison County, Illinois	N	N	N	N	N	N	4,737	81.6	25.1
Peoria County, Illinois	N	N	N	N	N	N	4,270	72.8	20.8
Rock Island County, Illinois	3,127	67.7	5.6	2,109	85.2	27.4	9,984	71.6	12.0
St. Clair County, Illinois	N	N	N	2,593	98.7	32.6	6,238	80.0	27.9
Sangamon County, Illinois	N	N	N	N	N	N	2,700	84.0	23.8
Tazewell County, Illinois	N	N	N	N	N	N	N	N	N
Vermilion County, Illinois	N	N	N	N	N	N	1,765	52.8	12.1
Will County, Illinois	22,598	68.3	12.3	8,395	83.3	27.9	67,858	72.2	14.1
Williamson County, Illinois	N	N	N	N	N	N	N	N	N
Winnebago County, Illinois	2,688	69.4	29.5	2,774	87.2	11.8	19,124	61.9	10.1
INDIANA	85,178	61.8	9.3	61,423	88.4	26.7	247,337	69.9	15.6
Allen County, Indiana	5,479	61.5	9.6	4,178	89.0	30.9	14,515	65.2	12.4
Bartholomew County, Indiana	N	N	N	N	N	N	2,964	72.4	37.4
Boone County, Indiana	N	N	N	N	N	N	N	N	N
Clark County, Indiana	N	N	N	N	N	N	3,463	57.8	33.8
Delaware County, Indiana	N	N	N	N	N	N	N	N	N
Elkhart County, Indiana	7,398	60.7	4.6	N	N	N	15,685	64.0	7.9
Floyd County, Indiana	N	N	N	N	N	N	N	N	N
Grant County, Indiana	N	N	N	N	N	N	N	N	N
Hamilton County, Indiana	N	N	N	N	N	N	8,038	83.1	38.3
Hancock County, Indiana	N	N	N	N	N	N	N	N	N
Hendricks County, Indiana	N	N	N	N	N	N	N	N	N
Howard County, Indiana	N	N	N	N	N	N	N	N	N
Johnson County, Indiana	N	N	N	N	N	N	N	N	N

N = Data for this geographic area cannot be displayed because the number of sample cases is too small.

Table C-2. Educational Attainment of the Population, by Selected Counties, 2019—*Continued*

(Number; percent; dollars.)

| State/County | Median earnings in the past 12 months (2019 inflation-adjusted dollars) | | | | | |
| | Population 25 years and over with earnings | | | | | |
	Total	Less than high school graduate	High school graduate (includes equivalency)	Some college or associate's degree	Bachelor's degree	Graduate or professional degree
GEORGIA—*(Continued)*						
Jackson County, Georgia	41,442	19,152	33,602	51,338	48,472	67,715
Lowndes County, Georgia	31,451	21,427	30,426	29,840	42,542	62,303
Muscogee County, Georgia	35,133	21,035	27,175	34,187	47,511	57,459
Newton County, Georgia	31,860	19,966	25,704	29,949	44,606	57,106
Paulding County, Georgia	43,848	30,886	41,132	42,224	50,023	67,004
Richmond County, Georgia	30,819	21,950	27,266	27,495	44,703	63,744
Rockdale County, Georgia	40,117	18,341	38,460	40,026	46,202	51,306
Spalding County, Georgia	33,390	24,790	30,894	36,254	37,470	46,717
Troup County, Georgia	35,027	31,653	23,983	32,450	51,145	47,180
Walker County, Georgia	31,032	23,802	31,296	30,790	43,581	48,727
Walton County, Georgia	39,449	26,992	32,579	38,411	51,527	72,974
Whitfield County, Georgia	31,970	30,134	31,675	31,057	49,291	64,217
HAWAII	44,557	31,620	35,573	41,842	52,183	72,035
Hawaii County, Hawaii	36,621	33,041	31,542	34,762	44,980	65,607
Honolulu County, Hawaii	47,223	31,092	35,300	44,436	55,489	75,908
Kauai County, Hawaii	41,827	32,208	40,531	41,762	44,572	55,788
Maui County, Hawaii	41,209	31,219	38,466	41,077	52,090	66,884
IDAHO	36,445	27,667	31,395	33,984	46,364	60,816
Ada County, Idaho	41,047	23,792	32,311	36,120	51,257	65,374
Bannock County, Idaho	32,479	26,824	27,169	31,199	38,432	65,048
Bonneville County, Idaho	36,013	26,631	27,725	31,807	48,123	90,672
Canyon County, Idaho	35,144	26,575	31,636	34,606	43,236	49,239
Kootenai County, Idaho	35,362	25,398	31,351	32,075	49,063	52,385
Twin Falls County, Idaho	40,393	38,884	37,341	31,002	45,664	52,135
ILLINOIS	45,015	27,186	32,304	39,400	60,357	76,363
Adams County, Illinois	36,494	30,016	32,303	31,998	42,437	61,658
Champaign County, Illinois	41,140	31,151	28,615	41,206	44,617	54,744
Cook County, Illinois	46,504	27,450	31,617	38,815	61,648	77,279
DeKalb County, Illinois	43,663	33,370	37,383	47,599	48,680	56,948
DuPage County, Illinois	53,538	30,809	36,360	42,165	65,172	87,291
Kane County, Illinois	43,715	29,854	35,905	41,187	64,923	78,569
Kankakee County, Illinois	40,840	21,969	32,411	39,405	55,405	68,841
Kendall County, Illinois	51,014	19,625	47,659	41,443	55,714	81,874
Lake County, Illinois	51,125	27,091	33,817	40,790	72,910	100,567
LaSalle County, Illinois	36,830	22,577	32,267	40,076	44,723	60,798
McHenry County, Illinois	49,783	32,425	40,810	42,291	65,286	71,450
McLean County, Illinois	47,426	20,324	35,143	40,989	55,386	61,505
Macon County, Illinois	40,140	24,524	32,357	40,022	47,125	53,442
Madison County, Illinois	43,205	21,794	31,020	40,619	54,274	76,476
Peoria County, Illinois	40,253	26,425	26,523	31,400	53,035	76,043
Rock Island County, Illinois	40,490	26,269	34,049	36,826	51,416	69,730
St. Clair County, Illinois	39,206	22,983	28,482	36,714	60,836	66,280
Sangamon County, Illinois	45,032	20,273	33,960	38,034	58,124	71,088
Tazewell County, Illinois	41,701	17,689	31,652	42,768	52,347	68,935
Vermilion County, Illinois	34,119	30,526	31,194	34,511	54,870	50,860
Will County, Illinois	50,731	27,960	37,814	45,611	61,838	81,761
Williamson County, Illinois	37,589	18,953	26,079	37,162	42,202	82,050
Winnebago County, Illinois	37,222	26,198	30,298	36,435	46,929	70,390
INDIANA	39,833	27,765	32,101	37,154	50,630	65,941
Allen County, Indiana	39,812	28,315	31,071	36,828	49,728	69,413
Bartholomew County, Indiana	41,656	21,870	35,777	30,435	57,207	67,750
Boone County, Indiana	50,680	24,932	34,434	46,027	72,496	98,951
Clark County, Indiana	37,200	25,522	31,715	35,941	47,324	51,714
Delaware County, Indiana	34,514	33,180	27,053	34,818	40,981	55,898
Elkhart County, Indiana	35,691	31,946	33,656	31,431	50,571	51,095
Floyd County, Indiana	41,044	31,800	30,872	38,568	53,542	66,920
Grant County, Indiana	33,777	20,970	33,652	31,666	43,142	49,464
Hamilton County, Indiana	61,265	36,748	35,036	47,411	63,627	95,318
Hancock County, Indiana	50,221	50,853	38,365	45,762	60,586	75,635
Hendricks County, Indiana	49,774	28,239	39,463	47,695	57,118	78,431
Howard County, Indiana	34,116	18,790	33,722	31,703	45,636	56,583
Johnson County, Indiana	45,938	25,891	35,361	41,407	58,705	65,837

N – Data for this geographic area cannot be displayed because the number of sample cases is too small.

Table C-2. Educational Attainment of the Population, by Selected Counties, 2019—*Continued*

(Number; percent; dollars.)

	Educational attainment by race/ethnicity, 25 years and over								
	Some other race alone			Two or more races			Hispanic or Latino (of any race)		
State/County	Total	High school graduate or more (percent)	Bachelor's degree or more (percent)	Total	High school graduate or more (percent)	Bachelor's degree or more (percent)	Total	High school graduate or more (percent)	Bachelor's degree or more (percent)
INDIANA—(*Continued*)									
Kosciusko County, Indiana	N	N	N	N	N	N	3,373	55.2	6.4
Lake County, Indiana	24,331	71.1	6.3	5,112	86.2	36.5	55,383	78.1	11.6
LaPorte County, Indiana	N	N	N	N	N	N	4,040	77.1	6.2
Madison County, Indiana	N	N	N	N	N	N	2,773	66.6	32.5
Marion County, Indiana	14,768	43.1	11.4	12,414	86.9	28.2	49,960	60.1	15.9
Monroe County, Indiana	N	N	N	N	N	N	N	N	N
Morgan County, Indiana	N	N	N	N	N	N	N	N	N
Porter County, Indiana	N	N	N	N	N	N	10,163	91.2	23.4
St. Joseph County, Indiana	4,829	62.9	18.3	4,176	92.6	18.8	11,794	70.3	26.0
Tippecanoe County, Indiana	N	N	N	N	N	N	7,716	62.1	18.9
Vanderburgh County, Indiana	N	N	N	N	N	N	2,530	83.3	12.0
Vigo County, Indiana	N	N	N	N	N	N	N	N	N
Wayne County, Indiana	N	N	N	N	N	N	N	N	N
IOWA	17,543	64.6	14.1	24,563	92.5	29.0	94,822	67.5	13.8
Black Hawk County, Iowa	N	N	N	N	N	N	2,757	83.4	28.5
Dallas County, Iowa	N	N	N	N	N	N	2,755	81.5	40.0
Dubuque County, Iowa	N	N	N	N	N	N	N	N	N
Johnson County, Iowa	N	N	N	N	N	N	4,181	80.1	31.2
Linn County, Iowa	N	N	N	N	N	N	3,896	86.7	20.5
Polk County, Iowa	2,907	50.3	4.6	3,738	88.0	39.0	20,189	63.2	9.4
Pottawattamie County, Iowa	N	N	N	N	N	N	3,273	68.5	23.2
Scott County, Iowa	N	N	N	N	N	N	6,291	85.5	24.2
Story County, Iowa	N	N	N	N	N	N	N	N	N
Woodbury County, Iowa	N	N	N	N	N	N	8,362	51.2	4.9
KANSAS	46,958	61.0	10.0	41,525	91.1	27.5	177,719	68.4	14.1
Butler County, Kansas	N	N	N	N	N	N	N	N	N
Douglas County, Kansas	N	N	N	N	N	N	3,723	75.5	40.1
Johnson County, Kansas	7,131	80.7	17.3	7,263	94.5	52.1	25,509	77.8	24.4
Leavenworth County, Kansas	N	N	N	N	N	N	3,155	79.3	9.0
Riley County, Kansas	N	N	N	N	N	N	N	N	N
Sedgwick County, Kansas	8,019	59.6	13.5	9,437	91.7	24.9	37,715	67.2	16.6
Shawnee County, Kansas	4,751	76.3	12.8	2,610	88.5	19.0	11,208	84.9	12.6
Wyandotte County, Kansas	9,896	54.4	8.9	2,470	90.5	24.9	24,716	57.2	8.2
KENTUCKY	21,419	56.3	11.3	32,799	86.5	26.8	84,517	70.3	19.7
Boone County, Kentucky	N	N	N	N	N	N	N	N	N
Bullitt County, Kentucky	N	N	N	N	N	N	N	N	N
Campbell County, Kentucky	N	N	N	N	N	N	N	N	N
Christian County, Kentucky	N	N	N	N	N	N	2,175	67.0	4.7
Daviess County, Kentucky	N	N	N	N	N	N	N	N	N
Fayette County, Kentucky	5,164	66.8	15.2	5,009	83.4	27.0	11,966	60.6	18.1
Hardin County, Kentucky	N	N	N	N	N	N	3,515	95.3	29.6
Jefferson County, Kentucky	2,241	70.4	32.5	6,360	96.5	37.1	25,232	82.4	29.1
Kenton County, Kentucky	N	N	N	N	N	N	2,394	49.2	24.2
McCracken County, Kentucky	N	N	N	N	N	N	N	N	N
Madison County, Kentucky	N	N	N	N	N	N	N	N	N
Oldham County, Kentucky	N	N	N	N	N	N	N	N	N
Warren County, Kentucky	N	N	N	N	N	N	3,663	55.3	18.0
LOUISIANA	39,604	68.8	13.6	41,559	87.2	26.7	145,024	73.6	17.4
Ascension Parish, Louisiana	N	N	N	N	N	N	N	N	N
Bossier Parish, Louisiana	N	N	N	N	N	N	5,024	60.3	7.6
Caddo Parish, Louisiana	N	N	N	2,509	93.2	19.0	3,106	84.3	25.9
Calcasieu Parish, Louisiana	N	N	N	N	N	N	4,680	67.3	20.9
East Baton Rouge Parish, Louisiana	4,747	68.6	15.9	N	N	N	9,908	78.5	23.5
Iberia Parish, Louisiana	N	N	N	N	N	N	N	N	N
Jefferson Parish, Louisiana	7,722	76.2	14.5	4,516	79.4	26.6	39,830	79.0	14.6
Lafayette Parish, Louisiana	N	N	N	N	N	N	6,309	57.7	14.0
Lafourche Parish, Louisiana	N	N	N	N	N	N	N	N	N
Livingston Parish, Louisiana	N	N	N	N	N	N	N	N	N
Orleans Parish, Louisiana	4,196	76.2	21.1	3,999	96.2	44.8	13,079	79.8	38.1
Ouachita Parish, Louisiana	N	N	N	N	N	N	2,015	69.5	12.2
Rapides Parish, Louisiana	N	N	N	N	N	N	N	N	N
St. Landry Parish, Louisiana	N	N	N	N	N	N	N	N	N

N = Data for this geographic area cannot be displayed because the number of sample cases is too small.

Table C-2. Educational Attainment of the Population, by Selected Counties, 2019—*Continued*

(Number; percent; dollars.)

State/County	Median earnings in the past 12 months (2019 inflation-adjusted dollars)					
		Population 25 years and over with earnings				
	Total	Less than high school graduate	High school graduate (includes equivalency)	Some college or associate's degree	Bachelor's degree	Graduate or professional degree
INDIANA—(*Continued*)						
Kosciusko County, Indiana	39,915	31,190	27,104	41,838	50,996	57,064
Lake County, Indiana	40,584	25,662	32,472	36,818	55,213	72,420
LaPorte County, Indiana	36,000	20,140	31,619	39,000	55,389	64,063
Madison County, Indiana	36,488	22,407	31,040	39,458	49,848	65,486
Marion County, Indiana	37,350	26,380	30,881	35,653	47,691	60,630
Monroe County, Indiana	36,450	30,863	28,668	32,014	36,584	57,105
Morgan County, Indiana	40,037	22,572	38,477	36,365	65,065	112,411
Porter County, Indiana	46,739	27,141	44,025	42,079	55,986	70,099
St. Joseph County, Indiana	36,920	26,780	31,869	31,984	42,987	59,942
Tippecanoe County, Indiana	37,527	26,312	30,560	37,872	43,656	52,092
Vanderburgh County, Indiana	36,246	20,774	30,896	31,801	48,262	61,645
Vigo County, Indiana	35,336	27,168	27,449	34,384	40,262	70,519
Wayne County, Indiana	31,358	30,984	28,233	31,168	39,087	53,859
IOWA	41,268	30,381	33,066	39,073	51,751	66,887
Black Hawk County, Iowa	39,558	31,138	31,605	38,476	49,888	70,171
Dallas County, Iowa	58,603	33,489	32,743	48,891	63,416	76,384
Dubuque County, Iowa	40,111	22,565	35,234	36,990	46,451	62,170
Johnson County, Iowa	46,590	22,466	32,136	37,858	51,097	66,510
Linn County, Iowa	45,102	23,221	35,503	41,211	56,029	74,108
Polk County, Iowa	45,499	29,514	33,743	40,722	60,022	71,578
Pottawattamie County, Iowa	40,008	35,102	31,506	36,594	46,235	60,682
Scott County, Iowa	44,852	24,097	35,127	39,593	55,300	75,403
Story County, Iowa	41,540	31,092	29,007	35,276	49,779	55,978
Woodbury County, Iowa	36,921	33,376	27,944	39,349	46,698	78,036
KANSAS	41,181	26,549	32,106	36,994	51,678	62,008
Butler County, Kansas	43,587	46,862	33,232	39,300	49,848	56,143
Douglas County, Kansas	41,294	22,574	30,627	36,243	46,222	58,816
Johnson County, Kansas	54,343	30,547	35,426	44,719	62,650	75,347
Leavenworth County, Kansas	45,111	31,265	30,530	45,129	60,072	61,864
Riley County, Kansas	36,812	17,329	27,898	33,612	45,271	50,213
Sedgwick County, Kansas	40,035	24,571	31,800	35,885	50,560	63,571
Shawnee County, Kansas	41,074	27,573	34,364	38,870	50,247	60,817
Wyandotte County, Kansas	32,557	24,632	33,853	31,684	49,071	56,013
KENTUCKY	37,674	24,631	31,313	35,326	50,711	60,270
Boone County, Kentucky	45,969	40,232	36,805	41,419	57,339	74,312
Bullitt County, Kentucky	43,649	31,194	37,813	42,170	60,510	59,903
Campbell County, Kentucky	45,701	35,093	36,992	36,127	51,131	62,057
Christian County, Kentucky	35,716	32,009	28,230	32,390	52,287	58,771
Daviess County, Kentucky	38,092	26,472	30,841	34,161	51,083	59,563
Fayette County, Kentucky	40,962	21,459	28,309	33,847	46,171	64,253
Hardin County, Kentucky	41,231	21,579	32,240	40,371	55,157	59,364
Jefferson County, Kentucky	40,715	23,787	31,319	36,819	51,068	64,295
Kenton County, Kentucky	43,694	25,935	35,296	44,573	54,593	63,259
McCracken County, Kentucky	33,769	33,859	30,205	27,191	49,235	57,706
Madison County, Kentucky	37,291	20,339	27,034	31,720	41,285	55,048
Oldham County, Kentucky	51,278	7,417	40,090	42,623	64,402	81,930
Warren County, Kentucky	36,400	25,307	26,686	34,338	48,991	55,218
LOUISIANA	37,599	22,913	30,786	35,064	50,699	60,992
Ascension Parish, Louisiana	51,732	27,058	36,278	47,779	77,417	59,959
Bossier Parish, Louisiana	34,217	19,656	27,637	35,058	47,082	60,428
Caddo Parish, Louisiana	36,238	16,304	29,938	31,556	47,307	58,165
Calcasieu Parish, Louisiana	39,457	27,782	34,667	35,963	46,207	65,522
East Baton Rouge Parish, Louisiana	41,113	26,164	29,267	35,834	52,271	64,074
Iberia Parish, Louisiana	35,972	26,763	32,051	33,943	52,219	43,723
Jefferson Parish, Louisiana	36,862	20,446	31,548	34,060	50,031	56,972
Lafayette Parish, Louisiana	41,377	20,612	30,605	39,552	50,840	70,834
Lafourche Parish, Louisiana	37,281	27,326	31,560	32,303	50,030	55,606
Livingston Parish, Louisiana	45,007	31,619	41,700	46,543	55,341	65,165
Orleans Parish, Louisiana	37,190	20,811	23,578	29,727	46,386	66,851
Ouachita Parish, Louisiana	34,106	22,532	25,011	35,951	45,386	66,261
Rapides Parish, Louisiana	36,737	20,366	34,986	33,893	50,771	66,738
St. Landry Parish, Louisiana	34,418	24,765	35,114	30,898	46,350	42,159

N = Data for this geographic area cannot be displayed because the number of sample cases is too small.

Table C-2. Educational Attainment of the Population, by Selected Counties, 2019—*Continued*

(Number; percent; dollars.)

	Educational attainment by race/ethnicity, 25 years and over								
	Some other race alone			Two or more races			Hispanic or Latino (of any race)		
State/County	Total	High school graduate or more (percent)	Bachelor's degree or more (percent)	Total	High school graduate or more (percent)	Bachelor's degree or more (percent)	Total	High school graduate or more (percent)	Bachelor's degree or more (percent)
LOUISIANA—(*Continued*)									
St. Tammany Parish, Louisiana	N	N	N	N	N	N	9,566	81.1	31.4
Tangipahoa Parish, Louisiana	N	N	N	N	N	N	N	N	N
Terrebonne Parish, Louisiana	N	N	N	N	N	N	N	N	N
MAINE	3,042	85.8	28.2	14,470	88.7	31.7	13,580	89.9	37.8
Androscoggin County, Maine	N	N	N	1,526	77.0	14.8	N	N	N
Aroostook County, Maine	N	N	N	N	N	N	N	N	N
Cumberland County, Maine	N	N	N	2,930	83.9	45.7	3,538	84.6	54.9
Kennebec County, Maine	N	N	N	N	N	N	N	N	N
Penobscot County, Maine	N	N	N	N	N	N	N	N	N
York County, Maine	N	N	N	N	N	N	N	N	N
MARYLAND	172,165	56.9	12.8	91,388	93.3	44.0	358,740	67.2	22.0
Allegany County, Maryland	N	N	N	N	N	N	N	N	N
Anne Arundel County, Maryland	6,928	79.2	33.7	11,473	93.5	41.3	25,573	81.2	31.5
Baltimore County, Maryland	9,801	71.6	21.5	10,780	98.9	40.6	25,411	76.8	25.9
Calvert County, Maryland	N	N	N	N	N	N	N	N	N
Carroll County, Maryland	N	N	N	N	N	N	3,523	95.0	33.3
Cecil County, Maryland	N	N	N	N	N	N	N	N	N
Charles County, Maryland	N	N	N	2,737	97.6	19.0	5,482	83.4	22.5
Frederick County, Maryland	2,026	61.5	14.0	3,395	86.1	39.3	15,062	63.2	23.4
Harford County, Maryland	N	N	N	3,002	100.0	28.2	7,524	89.4	29.9
Howard County, Maryland	2,672	98.6	48.9	5,620	88.8	57.0	12,811	78.6	37.5
Montgomery County, Maryland	63,011	57.4	12.8	21,430	93.9	58.1	124,170	67.3	23.4
Prince George's County, Maryland	72,512	48.8	5.7	14,886	93.8	41.5	98,075	53.4	9.8
St. Mary's County, Maryland	N	N	N	N	N	N	3,677	81.0	18.5
Washington County, Maryland	N	N	N	N	N	N	4,532	73.3	7.4
Wicomico County, Maryland	N	N	N	N	N	N	N	N	N
Baltimore city, Maryland	6,608	62.5	33.8	6,281	87.7	45.2	18,255	76.6	44.5
MASSACHUSETTS	180,134	71.8	17.0	113,285	83.8	40.5	486,528	73.2	20.8
Barnstable County, Massachusetts	N	N	N	N	N	N	4,560	60.1	25.6
Berkshire County, Massachusetts	N	N	N	1,761	89.2	32.0	2,984	75.2	22.1
Bristol County, Massachusetts	17,985	67.8	10.9	6,380	94.3	39.0	24,628	73.2	14.7
Essex County, Massachusetts	51,510	63.9	8.6	11,095	81.1	38.6	99,239	66.7	14.1
Franklin County, Massachusetts	N	N	N	N	N	N	N	N	N
Hampden County, Massachusetts	13,089	74.7	20.5	6,442	88.6	18.6	67,506	69.8	12.1
Hampshire County, Massachusetts	N	N	N	N	N	N	4,123	72.0	35.8
Middlesex County, Massachusetts	32,755	69.6	19.6	22,778	89.4	55.9	77,511	76.7	32.0
Norfolk County, Massachusetts	7,724	82.8	41.0	8,784	93.2	63.8	20,524	93.0	45.3
Plymouth County, Massachusetts	7,774	68.3	15.5	5,481	83.8	29.8	12,325	76.3	20.8
Suffolk County, Massachusetts	29,161	82.0	23.8	35,123	70.2	32.6	115,020	73.9	22.8
Worcester County, Massachusetts	15,007	84.1	19.4	8,266	92.2	28.7	56,072	75.6	15.0
MICHIGAN	64,422	68.1	16.5	118,032	90.1	30.0	273,449	75.6	21.6
Allegan County, Michigan	N	N	N	N	N	N	4,586	64.2	10.8
Bay County, Michigan	N	N	N	N	N	N	3,347	87.2	13.9
Berrien County, Michigan	N	N	N	N	N	N	4,958	83.1	28.8
Calhoun County, Michigan	N	N	N	2,588	92.2	25.2	4,104	85.6	8.7
Clinton County, Michigan	N	N	N	N	N	N	2,047	83.2	17.6
Eaton County, Michigan	N	N	N	N	N	N	3,438	96.2	15.9
Genesee County, Michigan	N	N	N	5,496	90.4	20.2	7,750	84.1	20.0
Grand Traverse County, Michigan	N	N	N	N	N	N	N	N	N
Ingham County, Michigan	N	N	N	3,755	87.3	36.1	12,360	88.7	28.4
Isabella County, Michigan	N	N	N	N	N	N	N	N	N
Jackson County, Michigan	N	N	N	1,779	88.1	15.2	2,822	88.9	30.3
Kalamazoo County, Michigan	N	N	N	4,441	90.9	31.4	5,860	78.3	37.2
Kent County, Michigan	11,265	54.0	14.1	10,711	93.1	30.8	35,050	61.5	19.9
Lapeer County, Michigan	N	N	N	N	N	N	2,131	56.8	3.5
Lenawee County, Michigan	N	N	N	N	N	N	4,395	69.2	17.0
Livingston County, Michigan	N	N	N	N	N	N	N	N	N
Macomb County, Michigan	2,956	70.8	15.3	10,094	90.6	33.8	13,558	74.6	15.5
Marquette County, Michigan	N	N	N	N	N	N	N	N	N
Midland County, Michigan	N	N	N	N	N	N	N	N	N
Monroe County, Michigan	N	N	N	N	N	N	3,105	94.7	28.7
Muskegon County, Michigan	N	N	N	N	N	N	5,175	79.5	11.0

N = Data for this geographic area cannot be displayed because the number of sample cases is too small.

Table C-2. Educational Attainment of the Population, by Selected Counties, 2019—*Continued*

(Number; percent; dollars.)

State/County	Median earnings in the past 12 months (2019 inflation-adjusted dollars)					
	Population 25 years and over with earnings					
	Total	Less than high school graduate	High school graduate (includes equivalency)	Some college or associate's degree	Bachelor's degree	Graduate or professional degree
LOUISIANA—(*Continued*)						
St. Tammany Parish, Louisiana	42,056	24,739	33,274	37,635	55,591	82,748
Tangipahoa Parish, Louisiana	34,217	13,427	29,274	31,876	56,469	50,691
Terrebonne Parish, Louisiana	35,819	49,261	31,510	31,140	38,737	41,341
MAINE	39,550	25,504	31,798	36,274	47,375	60,347
Androscoggin County, Maine	40,346	22,177	32,408	37,697	52,346	71,716
Aroostook County, Maine	33,660	20,009	27,310	33,180	45,518	51,820
Cumberland County, Maine	47,304	27,997	35,494	40,495	54,336	66,338
Kennebec County, Maine	39,374	29,941	35,198	35,926	46,239	65,043
Penobscot County, Maine	37,010	23,922	31,280	36,035	42,131	56,911
York County, Maine	41,290	40,292	34,565	37,367	50,999	51,638
MARYLAND	52,011	30,300	36,700	44,022	65,193	89,066
Allegany County, Maryland	35,134	14,714	27,189	30,125	49,358	57,767
Anne Arundel County, Maryland	60,638	35,396	43,113	50,650	70,835	92,115
Baltimore County, Maryland	50,507	26,578	36,317	45,240	58,410	78,562
Calvert County, Maryland	63,310	47,091	50,162	57,074	87,748	95,601
Carroll County, Maryland	57,490	26,662	40,507	50,535	76,376	81,558
Cecil County, Maryland	50,057	15,348	37,437	55,425	52,037	77,871
Charles County, Maryland	62,154	34,393	42,178	59,758	83,135	89,936
Frederick County, Maryland	56,037	32,253	37,207	48,117	69,072	83,903
Harford County, Maryland	57,973	38,736	42,249	50,120	67,511	89,391
Howard County, Maryland	72,512	30,761	41,019	46,924	76,448	102,249
Montgomery County, Maryland	60,143	26,314	31,987	40,741	70,639	101,602
Prince George's County, Maryland	50,115	34,076	37,743	44,790	65,063	84,382
St. Mary's County, Maryland	57,070	36,934	40,236	52,104	71,646	91,192
Washington County, Maryland	41,775	31,964	35,278	41,000	46,744	73,205
Wicomico County, Maryland	40,787	24,047	31,127	35,031	57,404	61,945
Baltimore city, Maryland	41,309	23,443	31,660	35,595	55,264	70,996
MASSACHUSETTS	52,470	30,693	39,463	42,066	65,373	85,717
Barnstable County, Massachusetts	46,841	31,304	41,056	40,459	50,594	67,826
Berkshire County, Massachusetts	40,666	24,133	36,565	36,280	42,775	61,968
Bristol County, Massachusetts	48,058	31,407	40,968	41,919	61,187	78,251
Essex County, Massachusetts	51,540	32,000	40,026	41,474	65,948	85,526
Franklin County, Massachusetts	37,038	25,779	31,149	36,246	42,500	62,511
Hampden County, Massachusetts	42,192	24,072	35,908	41,481	55,515	69,659
Hampshire County, Massachusetts	50,966	32,430	44,822	36,532	46,524	67,558
Middlesex County, Massachusetts	62,709	32,758	40,478	45,065	73,844	94,156
Norfolk County, Massachusetts	62,169	30,048	41,883	46,605	70,655	93,477
Plymouth County, Massachusetts	52,048	31,860	41,613	46,914	65,359	86,336
Suffolk County, Massachusetts	52,039	30,219	34,634	38,265	65,113	84,452
Worcester County, Massachusetts	50,804	30,308	39,710	42,336	63,145	82,073
MICHIGAN	40,450	23,192	31,028	36,272	54,634	71,623
Allegan County, Michigan	39,365	32,447	31,635	37,536	55,701	80,978
Bay County, Michigan	38,565	20,732	30,287	41,834	53,250	68,914
Berrien County, Michigan	36,802	17,118	28,937	36,909	51,060	56,178
Calhoun County, Michigan	36,148	26,401	32,472	36,345	43,871	61,381
Clinton County, Michigan	45,640	21,662	32,646	42,216	59,432	74,958
Eaton County, Michigan	43,849	17,721	32,468	41,823	53,790	66,497
Genesee County, Michigan	36,623	19,091	29,898	35,631	53,288	71,997
Grand Traverse County, Michigan	38,404	21,410	32,426	33,383	46,656	66,757
Ingham County, Michigan	37,697	24,194	29,666	32,028	47,291	67,020
Isabella County, Michigan	32,983	20,405	31,222	26,894	41,392	71,250
Jackson County, Michigan	40,155	19,931	33,414	37,393	55,706	66,800
Kalamazoo County, Michigan	38,532	26,608	31,052	35,146	40,773	71,460
Kent County, Michigan	40,619	24,965	31,833	36,176	49,976	67,176
Lapeer County, Michigan	39,678	23,930	31,753	41,679	62,931	72,413
Lenawee County, Michigan	35,302	27,007	30,608	32,910	50,102	61,053
Livingston County, Michigan	51,567	21,608	37,087	42,494	72,289	81,307
Macomb County, Michigan	41,269	23,783	31,461	40,398	57,332	74,625
Marquette County, Michigan	35,366	41,060	27,281	30,801	37,171	58,013
Midland County, Michigan	43,815	20,925	29,716	39,127	60,727	72,110
Monroe County, Michigan	46,554	17,121	37,211	41,376	60,981	65,618
Muskegon County, Michigan	35,424	22,486	31,812	32,263	50,817	60,838

N = Data for this geographic area cannot be displayed because the number of sample cases is too small.

Table C-2. Educational Attainment of the Population, by Selected Counties, 2019—*Continued*

(Number; percent; dollars.)

State/County	Educational attainment by race/ethnicity, 25 years and over								
	Some other race alone			Two or more races			Hispanic or Latino (of any race)		
	Total	High school graduate or more (percent)	Bachelor's degree or more (percent)	Total	High school graduate or more (percent)	Bachelor's degree or more (percent)	Total	High school graduate or more (percent)	Bachelor's degree or more (percent)
MICHIGAN—(*Continued*)									
Oakland County, Michigan	5,071	87.1	49.1	13,545	95.0	52.9	30,386	88.1	42.4
Ottawa County, Michigan	4,633	54.9	6.9	N	N	N	14,466	69.3	13.4
Saginaw County, Michigan	N	N	N	2,420	88.8	15.7	9,234	80.2	19.8
St. Clair County, Michigan	N	N	N	N	N	N	2,456	75.0	10.8
Shiawassee County, Michigan	N	N	N	N	N	N	N	N	N
Van Buren County, Michigan	N	N	N	N	N	N	4,429	68.3	6.6
Washtenaw County, Michigan	N	N	N	5,106	94.7	41.3	9,307	89.5	44.4
Wayne County, Michigan	20,630	60.7	8.9	19,565	85.4	30.1	56,703	66.7	14.2
MINNESOTA	57,270	66.2	16.8	67,207	94.2	31.2	158,254	75.0	22.8
Anoka County, Minnesota	3,455	54.4	7.4	4,352	98.0	34.6	8,742	67.1	21.0
Blue Earth County, Minnesota	N	N	N	N	N	N	N	N	N
Carver County, Minnesota	N	N	N	N	N	N	2,088	54.7	13.6
Crow Wing County, Minnesota	N	N	N	N	N	N	N	N	N
Dakota County, Minnesota	5,798	40.5	15.4	5,590	94.6	24.4	16,568	70.1	18.2
Hennepin County, Minnesota	21,525	68.0	18.0	19,283	92.6	41.0	45,966	75.9	29.7
Olmsted County, Minnesota	N	N	N	N	N	N	4,677	81.0	35.8
Ramsey County, Minnesota	5,266	78.6	31.7	8,065	95.4	33.6	21,541	80.8	24.0
Rice County, Minnesota	N	N	N	N	N	N	N	N	N
St. Louis County, Minnesota	N	N	N	2,649	97.3	21.7	2,062	76.5	41.7
Scott County, Minnesota	N	N	N	3,043	99.7	30.1	3,864	83.4	41.7
Sherburne County, Minnesota	N	N	N	N	N	N	N	N	N
Stearns County, Minnesota	N	N	N	N	N	N	2,247	81.2	15.4
Washington County, Minnesota	1,733	81.0	40.1	3,795	95.4	31.8	6,067	84.9	35.2
Wright County, Minnesota	N	N	N	N	N	N	N	N	N
MISSISSIPPI	14,862	53.4	12.4	15,831	87.2	27.7	46,120	67.8	11.8
DeSoto County, Mississippi	N	N	N	N	N	N	5,058	84.6	20.1
Forrest County, Mississippi	N	N	N	N	N	N	N	N	N
Harrison County, Mississippi	N	N	N	N	N	N	5,676	86.8	12.3
Hinds County, Mississippi	N	N	N	N	N	N	N	N	N
Jackson County, Mississippi	N	N	N	N	N	N	5,470	74.0	18.6
Jones County, Mississippi	N	N	N	N	N	N	N	N	N
Lauderdale County, Mississippi	N	N	N	N	N	N	N	N	N
Lee County, Mississippi	N	N	N	N	N	N	N	N	N
Madison County, Mississippi	N	N	N	N	N	N	N	N	N
Rankin County, Mississippi	N	N	N	N	N	N	N	N	N
MISSOURI	41,151	73.3	17.6	66,755	89.5	30.7	138,178	77.8	22.9
Boone County, Missouri	N	N	N	2,895	94.3	32.6	2,734	93.2	28.9
Buchanan County, Missouri	N	N	N	N	N	N	3,373	68.0	18.1
Cape Girardeau County, Missouri	N	N	N	N	N	N	N	N	N
Cass County, Missouri	N	N	N	N	N	N	N	N	N
Christian County, Missouri	N	N	N	N	N	N	N	N	N
Clay County, Missouri	4,636	78.2	6.7	3,872	87.2	25.9	10,070	81.9	16.8
Cole County, Missouri	N	N	N	N	N	N	1,687	85.6	22.7
Franklin County, Missouri	N	N	N	N	N	N	N	N	N
Greene County, Missouri	N	N	N	4,261	96.5	23.2	5,356	80.3	28.8
Jackson County, Missouri	14,135	70.4	15.5	9,363	91.6	31.8	33,795	74.1	21.2
Jasper County, Missouri	N	N	N	N	N	N	4,580	46.1	3.9
Jefferson County, Missouri	N	N	N	N	N	N	2,605	80.8	3.8
Platte County, Missouri	N	N	N	N	N	N	4,083	92.4	47.2
St. Charles County, Missouri	N	N	N	2,543	100.0	41.5	7,206	94.5	39.2
St. Francois County, Missouri	N	N	N	N	N	N	N	N	N
St. Louis County, Missouri	6,829	82.6	29.2	10,604	88.7	42.6	16,316	88.5	41.8
St. Louis city, Missouri	N	N	N	3,715	97.6	59.2	7,598	74.3	36.3
MONTANA	5,369	78.2	27.6	16,804	94.3	39.3	22,102	84.7	26.8
Cascade County, Montana	N	N	N	N	N	N	N	N	N
Flathead County, Montana	N	N	N	N	N	N	N	N	N
Gallatin County, Montana	N	N	N	N	N	N	N	N	N
Lewis and Clark County, Montana	N	N	N	N	N	N	N	N	N
Missoula County, Montana	N	N	N	N	N	N	N	N	N
Yellowstone County, Montana	N	N	N	N	N	N	4,811	78.0	13.8

N = Data for this geographic area cannot be displayed because the number of sample cases is too small.

Table C-2. Educational Attainment of the Population, by Selected Counties, 2019—*Continued*

(Number; percent; dollars.)

State/County	Median earnings in the past 12 months (2019 inflation-adjusted dollars)					
	Population 25 years and over with earnings					
	Total	Less than high school graduate	High school graduate (includes equivalency)	Some college or associate's degree	Bachelor's degree	Graduate or professional degree
MICHIGAN—(*Continued*)						
Oakland County, Michigan	51,786	25,244	31,801	37,278	66,654	86,140
Ottawa County, Michigan	41,890	30,223	31,268	39,537	54,667	67,426
Saginaw County, Michigan	33,792	20,547	27,956	30,999	47,446	66,296
St. Clair County, Michigan	39,859	21,515	31,718	40,063	50,471	70,660
Shiawassee County, Michigan	37,732	25,467	31,637	38,031	51,553	60,049
Van Buren County, Michigan	33,513	20,686	26,964	35,876	45,537	53,173
Washtenaw County, Michigan	50,444	15,879	31,396	36,306	56,316	71,793
Wayne County, Michigan	37,691	22,174	30,362	35,536	55,763	70,566
MINNESOTA	47,050	28,327	35,337	41,858	60,316	75,925
Anoka County, Minnesota	50,556	31,934	37,397	47,143	63,900	80,181
Blue Earth County, Minnesota	41,792	40,273	33,995	40,362	50,723	66,493
Carver County, Minnesota	59,722	32,027	41,591	48,073	75,114	89,466
Crow Wing County, Minnesota	38,610	24,569	30,665	41,294	45,313	67,013
Dakota County, Minnesota	51,544	21,838	36,548	45,146	65,828	82,004
Hennepin County, Minnesota	51,750	26,297	34,849	41,625	65,579	81,627
Olmsted County, Minnesota	51,812	25,830	36,425	41,362	61,884	77,306
Ramsey County, Minnesota	43,927	27,420	31,459	40,183	54,110	71,395
Rice County, Minnesota	45,219	33,510	39,579	40,566	51,908	75,507
St. Louis County, Minnesota	41,198	23,958	33,895	37,226	50,601	64,505
Scott County, Minnesota	56,227	40,921	41,870	50,767	74,527	81,269
Sherburne County, Minnesota	50,865	31,270	45,876	44,763	70,456	81,022
Stearns County, Minnesota	42,334	14,923	36,933	42,036	52,235	64,674
Washington County, Minnesota	54,748	30,678	35,119	46,882	66,759	90,640
Wright County, Minnesota	55,154	26,580	41,094	52,156	65,776	72,066
MISSISSIPPI	32,574	20,764	27,158	31,459	44,148	56,208
DeSoto County, Mississippi	43,277	22,897	35,472	40,830	56,358	61,295
Forrest County, Mississippi	27,052	18,791	25,199	26,466	34,697	51,282
Harrison County, Mississippi	36,350	25,747	30,764	30,288	49,168	55,247
Hinds County, Mississippi	31,230	20,481	25,648	27,102	40,354	51,934
Jackson County, Mississippi	37,883	30,322	27,700	37,223	44,059	82,319
Jones County, Mississippi	27,734	18,342	21,888	28,216	36,872	48,150
Lauderdale County, Mississippi	27,776	15,615	20,401	31,264	41,358	49,699
Lee County, Mississippi	36,645	22,230	28,529	36,309	46,476	81,955
Madison County, Mississippi	43,301	18,615	29,050	32,949	54,180	63,926
Rankin County, Mississippi	40,701	25,102	31,813	39,120	50,502	59,428
MISSOURI	40,078	24,831	31,297	36,127	51,217	63,368
Boone County, Missouri	42,396	23,226	30,691	36,504	47,381	61,623
Buchanan County, Missouri	35,638	17,017	30,875	34,434	42,391	62,740
Cape Girardeau County, Missouri	38,237	12,338	31,464	37,047	41,992	49,635
Cass County, Missouri	43,363	30,962	36,869	41,684	65,632	57,857
Christian County, Missouri	40,453	30,457	32,999	38,965	50,890	48,049
Clay County, Missouri	44,613	31,310	35,480	40,481	55,064	69,660
Cole County, Missouri	37,707	23,231	31,296	35,873	47,380	49,270
Franklin County, Missouri	39,752	26,382	29,921	41,458	50,249	71,857
Greene County, Missouri	37,270	23,001	32,293	31,298	42,996	51,774
Jackson County, Missouri	41,373	25,393	31,821	37,569	52,986	63,526
Jasper County, Missouri	29,870	18,190	25,708	29,539	38,657	49,012
Jefferson County, Missouri	41,346	24,761	35,260	42,272	53,689	61,279
Platte County, Missouri	51,115	19,019	33,940	41,866	60,517	72,435
St. Charles County, Missouri	51,237	29,415	36,302	43,826	64,165	76,557
St. Francois County, Missouri	28,524	16,517	19,834	30,398	41,296	57,762
St. Louis County, Missouri	47,224	25,691	30,159	38,280	59,940	77,471
St. Louis city, Missouri	40,796	26,286	31,454	32,632	51,423	59,009
MONTANA	36,953	27,804	30,843	33,040	42,150	58,287
Cascade County, Montana	35,077	35,179	27,266	30,583	44,731	71,473
Flathead County, Montana	36,814	22,672	35,302	32,408	40,590	55,850
Gallatin County, Montana	41,987	35,833	31,967	44,045	42,353	52,397
Lewis and Clark County, Montana	40,362	38,761	27,026	32,031	47,293	59,255
Missoula County, Montana	36,935	33,661	32,498	35,145	37,523	61,840
Yellowstone County, Montana	40,433	22,273	32,477	32,933	54,245	65,868

N = Data for this geographic area cannot be displayed because the number of sample cases is too small.

Table C-2. Educational Attainment of the Population, by Selected Counties, 2019—*Continued*

(Number; percent; dollars.)

	Educational attainment by race/ethnicity, 25 years and over								
	Some other race alone			Two or more races			Hispanic or Latino (of any race)		
State/County	Total	High school graduate or more (percent)	Bachelor's degree or more (percent)	Total	High school graduate or more (percent)	Bachelor's degree or more (percent)	Total	High school graduate or more (percent)	Bachelor's degree or more (percent)
NEBRASKA	26,006	60.7	7.7	18,136	94.8	30.4	106,780	63.2	13.4
Douglas County, Nebraska....................	4,738	79.0	11.6	7,286	96.8	44.9	34,976	63.5	13.9
Lancaster County, Nebraska..................	2,618	77.9	18.1	N	N	N	10,584	63.4	18.9
Sarpy County, Nebraska........................	N	N	N	N	N	N	9,536	82.3	20.6
NEVADA	190,619	62.8	8.8	66,882	89.1	24.9	512,330	67.0	10.6
Clark County, Nevada..........................	151,382	65.1	9.4	53,014	89.3	26.0	411,068	68.0	11.0
Washoe County, Nevada........................	27,808	50.8	7.0	8,426	90.1	27.2	64,837	60.8	10.4
NEW HAMPSHIRE.......................	5,977	86.1	18.2	12,804	88.8	32.1	29,638	78.7	25.0
Cheshire County, New Hampshire..........................	N	N	N	N	N	N	N	N	N
Grafton County, New Hampshire..........................	N	N	N	N	N	N	N	N	N
Hillsborough County, New Hampshire	3,651	87.4	21.4	4,691	88.6	32.6	16,809	69.3	16.1
Merrimack County, New Hampshire....................	N	N	N	N	N	N	N	N	N
Rockingham County, New Hampshire.................	N	N	N	N	N	N	6,314	88.9	41.0
Strafford County, New Hampshire................	N	N	N	N	N	N	1,829	100.0	31.2
NEW JERSEY	342,229	69.4	15.4	112,926	89.4	39.7	1,134,354	75.4	21.1
Atlantic County, New Jersey..................	14,096	67.6	18.0	4,785	93.7	27.1	29,073	70.5	19.0
Bergen County, New Jersey	19,044	72.9	20.0	13,730	89.0	43.9	126,560	83.5	33.2
Burlington County, New Jersey...............	5,576	90.0	24.7	8,292	98.2	31.9	22,491	89.3	24.1
Camden County, New Jersey..................	24,372	61.2	8.5	5,650	90.6	31.3	49,555	67.9	12.7
Cape May County, New Jersey	N	N	N	N	N	N	4,426	78.6	12.5
Cumberland County, New Jersey	6,511	60.2	1.4	N	N	N	26,449	56.8	7.3
Essex County, New Jersey....................	36,161	62.0	13.1	10,452	92.4	40.9	116,163	71.6	16.9
Gloucester County, New Jersey.............	3,505	71.0	21.8	2,601	89.9	36.7	10,568	71.3	25.6
Hudson County, New Jersey..................	43,824	72.5	20.1	15,694	88.8	46.6	192,070	74.7	22.3
Hunterdon County, New Jersey...............	N	N	N	N	N	N	5,344	67.4	28.3
Mercer County, New Jersey...................	9,752	50.9	15.1	3,434	94.8	41.4	38,579	67.2	20.5
Middlesex County, New Jersey...............	31,556	74.3	16.4	11,025	81.9	45.4	107,788	76.3	17.5
Monmouth County, New Jersey...............	8,424	83.4	14.3	5,369	86.0	38.1	38,875	84.7	23.8
Morris County, New Jersey	6,758	74.2	30.1	4,253	95.7	58.0	43,341	80.6	32.0
Ocean County, New Jersey....................	5,979	74.7	23.1	3,786	92.6	29.7	32,219	84.4	17.4
Passaic County, New Jersey..................	42,389	71.7	10.3	5,888	85.9	25.7	130,214	73.9	15.5
Salem County, New Jersey....................	N	N	N	N	N	N	3,084	77.2	8.9
Somerset County, New Jersey...............	14,395	84.1	17.8	N	N	N	30,197	79.7	25.5
Sussex County, New Jersey	N	N	N	N	N	N	7,867	83.7	29.9
Union County, New Jersey	65,627	66.8	14.8	6,763	89.6	43.1	113,075	71.3	19.8
Warren County, New Jersey...................	N	N	N	N	N	N	6,416	90.5	30.3
NEW MEXICO	126,817	74.0	12.8	33,989	91.5	26.5	630,721	78.0	16.5
Bernalillo County, New Mexico............	47,327	74.5	14.3	14,788	91.7	28.8	213,180	81.4	20.6
Chaves County, New Mexico	2,279	63.1	0.3	N	N	N	21,400	65.2	12.0
Doña Ana County, New Mexico	17,782	68.6	20.0	1,275	88.8	38.0	85,137	68.7	16.5
Lea County, New Mexico......................	N	N	N	N	N	N	22,744	64.6	9.5
McKinley County, New Mexico	N	N	N	N	N	N	5,479	86.0	15.5
Otero County, New Mexico....................	2,868	69.5	4.7	N	N	N	15,634	72.6	7.9
Sandoval County, New Mexico..............	6,680	91.7	16.5	3,289	96.3	27.0	36,580	90.9	25.6
San Juan County, New Mexico..............	N	N	N	N	N	N	13,933	83.3	9.0
Santa Fe County, New Mexico	7,747	70.1	9.4	2,730	93.8	37.8	50,306	76.6	15.7
Valencia County, New Mexico	N	N	N	N	N	N	27,830	84.2	14.7
NEW YORK	1,060,782	68.0	16.2	326,564	84.3	35.7	2,359,532	72.6	21.1
Albany County, New York......................	2,609	81.0	25.0	6,732	70.1	23.7	9,731	82.1	32.8
Bronx County, New York	265,986	67.9	14.7	35,446	74.7	22.8	502,485	68.3	14.9
Broome County, New York	N	N	N	N	N	N	3,540	79.0	16.5
Cattaraugus County, New York...............	N	N	N	N	N	N	N	N	N
Cayuga County, New York.....................	N	N	N	N	N	N	N	N	N
Chautauqua County, New York	N	N	N	N	N	N	4,678	71.7	23.6
Chemung County, New York..................	N	N	N	N	N	N	1,718	82.3	40.6
Clinton County, New York.....................	N	N	N	N	N	N	N	N	N
Dutchess County, New York	7,267	67.5	16.7	5,731	100.0	31.6	22,786	81.7	24.7
Erie County, New York..........................	13,279	70.2	14.9	7,952	88.0	40.8	28,216	78.8	22.5
Jefferson County, New York..................	N	N	N	2,140	99.4	22.1	3,808	88.0	18.0
Kings County, New York........................	142,179	60.3	14.5	49,168	87.0	46.4	314,231	69.4	20.1
Livingston County, New York	N	N	N	N	N	N	N	N	N

N = Data for this geographic area cannot be displayed because the number of sample cases is too small.

Table C-2. Educational Attainment of the Population, by Selected Counties, 2019—*Continued*

(Number; percent; dollars.)

State/County	Median earnings in the past 12 months (2019 inflation-adjusted dollars)					
	Population 25 years and over with earnings					
	Total	Less than high school graduate	High school graduate (includes equivalency)	Some college or associate's degree	Bachelor's degree	Graduate or professional degree
NEBRASKA	41,488	30,298	32,174	38,209	50,779	61,853
Douglas County, Nebraska	45,443	27,048	31,284	41,784	54,256	62,937
Lancaster County, Nebraska	41,297	29,100	31,521	37,024	48,366	56,931
Sarpy County, Nebraska	50,082	35,528	38,893	42,824	60,855	75,743
NEVADA	39,505	29,609	32,879	40,057	50,293	66,105
Clark County, Nevada	38,216	29,167	32,075	39,621	50,232	65,657
Washoe County, Nevada	41,585	28,897	36,887	41,158	50,635	68,116
NEW HAMPSHIRE	47,392	30,119	37,820	42,368	60,544	71,884
Cheshire County, New Hampshire	41,138	30,959	40,870	35,598	51,520	51,542
Grafton County, New Hampshire	40,281	30,056	28,311	35,669	41,706	72,030
Hillsborough County, New Hampshire	49,540	26,952	38,624	44,435	60,063	71,632
Merrimack County, New Hampshire	46,597	30,775	41,903	42,072	54,403	63,018
Rockingham County, New Hampshire	55,922	34,783	40,902	48,866	74,226	85,050
Strafford County, New Hampshire	45,900	26,872	31,838	45,800	62,113	67,538
NEW JERSEY	51,786	28,427	35,048	44,983	67,038	92,098
Atlantic County, New Jersey	40,128	29,371	32,302	36,228	57,090	77,039
Bergen County, New Jersey	61,970	30,380	37,194	51,463	71,627	100,653
Burlington County, New Jersey	54,053	24,986	38,510	45,596	69,192	86,785
Camden County, New Jersey	46,213	26,291	32,358	41,412	61,203	81,387
Cape May County, New Jersey	48,220	28,389	35,924	41,744	65,512	80,192
Cumberland County, New Jersey	32,949	25,298	27,817	43,342	60,278	66,051
Essex County, New Jersey	44,677	26,550	31,470	41,175	62,418	94,029
Gloucester County, New Jersey	52,124	29,842	37,859	46,528	65,748	80,701
Hudson County, New Jersey	51,675	27,394	30,436	41,495	69,494	100,364
Hunterdon County, New Jersey	63,745	27,001	41,363	43,867	80,907	97,478
Mercer County, New Jersey	51,410	31,497	31,788	43,734	66,587	84,405
Middlesex County, New Jersey	53,238	28,744	36,363	46,779	68,460	92,222
Monmouth County, New Jersey	57,731	26,953	40,145	45,245	69,573	90,871
Morris County, New Jersey	66,846	30,255	35,966	50,626	77,228	102,277
Ocean County, New Jersey	49,150	31,975	36,932	46,113	59,485	70,808
Passaic County, New Jersey	42,461	29,398	31,275	45,857	60,756	86,149
Salem County, New Jersey	41,434	25,417	30,395	41,622	60,324	80,216
Somerset County, New Jersey	66,329	26,864	40,530	54,946	71,910	103,214
Sussex County, New Jersey	57,646	39,405	43,797	50,933	74,750	91,257
Union County, New Jersey	48,091	27,410	35,785	41,551	61,960	93,171
Warren County, New Jersey	52,293	31,543	39,652	48,773	69,085	67,292
NEW MEXICO	35,284	21,016	29,002	32,187	45,109	62,501
Bernalillo County, New Mexico	38,597	21,033	30,296	34,133	47,625	67,398
Chaves County, New Mexico	33,309	22,363	30,106	26,361	50,013	65,510
Doña Ana County, New Mexico	29,557	15,555	24,658	27,187	37,665	58,442
Lea County, New Mexico	49,283	36,698	52,083	46,857	60,811	70,299
McKinley County, New Mexico	27,443	16,965	21,845	30,862	49,366	55,820
Otero County, New Mexico	26,096	12,964	18,681	29,390	40,356	77,133
Sandoval County, New Mexico	39,853	22,003	31,602	34,359	47,879	65,098
San Juan County, New Mexico	31,355	21,913	30,181	31,843	41,620	50,550
Santa Fe County, New Mexico	34,213	26,171	30,004	30,126	46,063	60,758
Valencia County, New Mexico	40,023	12,330	40,480	35,065	55,609	50,410
NEW YORK	47,645	26,036	33,401	41,421	62,699	81,041
Albany County, New York	51,157	18,438	32,164	44,678	61,481	71,722
Bronx County, New York	33,473	23,139	30,012	35,787	50,367	65,642
Broome County, New York	38,107	25,169	31,480	35,309	56,265	61,727
Cattaraugus County, New York	36,483	35,032	29,215	34,506	56,326	54,309
Cayuga County, New York	40,814	37,961	30,277	41,812	48,360	71,769
Chautauqua County, New York	37,649	32,719	31,118	35,306	45,767	61,206
Chemung County, New York	40,914	21,899	31,988	35,281	43,727	70,310
Clinton County, New York	41,623	30,490	35,583	39,519	51,423	61,115
Dutchess County, New York	50,542	24,833	31,877	44,541	60,206	89,567
Erie County, New York	42,404	21,432	33,646	38,867	52,476	65,006
Jefferson County, New York	40,033	20,225	32,122	36,306	50,086	64,464
Kings County, New York	47,345	24,669	32,597	41,214	67,050	80,260
Livingston County, New York	41,775	32,216	35,866	38,713	57,949	65,340

N = Data for this geographic area cannot be displayed because the number of sample cases is too small.

Table C-2. Educational Attainment of the Population, by Selected Counties, 2019—*Continued*

(Number; percent; dollars.)

	Educational attainment by race/ethnicity, 25 years and over								
	Some other race alone			Two or more races			Hispanic or Latino (of any race)		
State/County	Total	High school graduate or more (percent)	Bachelor's degree or more (percent)	Total	High school graduate or more (percent)	Bachelor's degree or more (percent)	Total	High school graduate or more (percent)	Bachelor's degree or more (percent)
NEW YORK —(*Continued*)									
Madison County, New York	N	N	N	N	N	N	N	N	N
Monroe County, New York	8,880	66.1	17.8	9,413	86.2	41.6	37,193	72.6	21.2
Nassau County, New York	59,204	71.7	18.4	22,375	80.2	34.7	145,253	75.2	26.1
New York County, New York	140,031	66.6	17.7	41,805	82.4	51.5	297,113	71.2	27.7
Niagara County, New York	N	N	N	3,573	85.3	22.2	3,750	95.3	29.2
Oneida County, New York	1,828	81.8	5.2	3,458	87.9	18.4	7,209	74.7	12.9
Onondaga County, New York	3,788	63.9	14.5	7,529	68.3	21.0	12,681	74.2	25.4
Ontario County, New York	N	N	N	N	N	N	2,934	74.8	20.2
Orange County, New York	14,695	77.0	14.7	7,275	85.8	22.6	46,978	80.5	22.9
Oswego County, New York	N	N	N	N	N	N	N	N	N
Putnam County, New York	4,098	70.8	21.6	N	N	N	11,021	81.4	31.9
Queens County, New York	214,700	71.5	16.2	50,866	85.9	34.0	420,903	74.5	19.5
Rensselaer County, New York	N	N	N	N	N	N	4,076	79.0	22.3
Richmond County, New York	11,092	73.7	27.2	4,529	99.2	30.5	52,903	75.5	23.3
Rockland County, New York	17,139	64.4	12.6	4,194	86.6	35.4	34,765	76.5	25.1
St. Lawrence County, New York	N	N	N	N	N	N	N	N	N
Saratoga County, New York	N	N	N	N	N	N	4,016	86.3	37.6
Schenectady County, New York	4,373	66.5	15.8	3,162	89.0	21.6	6,985	83.2	19.6
Steuben County, New York	N	N	N	N	N	N	N	N	N
Suffolk County, New York	52,093	68.9	14.1	15,874	89.6	33.9	174,444	74.9	17.7
Sullivan County, New York	N	N	N	N	N	N	7,475	60.6	9.7
Tompkins County, New York	N	N	N	N	N	N	N	N	N
Ulster County, New York	3,632	71.2	21.3	3,442	93.3	21.8	10,760	75.9	20.3
Warren County, New York	N	N	N	N	N	N	N	N	N
Wayne County, New York	N	N	N	N	N	N	N	N	N
Westchester County, New York	69,452	72.2	22.0	12,828	87.0	45.0	152,938	76.5	29.2
NORTH CAROLINA	185,783	53.6	11.4	110,659	89.9	33.6	513,662	62.8	17.0
Alamance County, North Carolina	4,039	59.7	7.9	N	N	N	10,622	52.1	10.3
Brunswick County, North Carolina	N	N	N	N	N	N	N	N	N
Buncombe County, North Carolina	N	N	N	N	N	N	9,446	70.7	19.9
Burke County, North Carolina	N	N	N	N	N	N	N	N	N
Cabarrus County, North Carolina	N	N	N	N	N	N	10,969	67.5	26.3
Caldwell County, North Carolina	N	N	N	N	N	N	2,005	74.7	12.8
Carteret County, North Carolina	N	N	N	N	N	N	N	N	N
Catawba County, North Carolina	N	N	N	N	N	N	8,263	58.5	15.1
Chatham County, North Carolina	N	N	N	N	N	N	4,196	62.5	11.5
Cleveland County, North Carolina	N	N	N	N	N	N	N	N	N
Craven County, North Carolina	N	N	N	N	N	N	N	N	N
Cumberland County, North Carolina	6,104	82.7	20.7	7,461	96.9	26.5	20,869	85.5	19.9
Davidson County, North Carolina	N	N	N	N	N	N	6,551	75.2	16.4
Durham County, North Carolina	5,272	64.9	31.5	N	N	N	22,150	48.3	16.9
Forsyth County, North Carolina	5,190	45.3	7.6	3,335	84.1	37.6	23,734	55.4	14.0
Franklin County, North Carolina	N	N	N	N	N	N	N	N	N
Gaston County, North Carolina	2,809	75.5	4.2	2,025	79.5	24.7	9,045	79.9	11.6
Guilford County, North Carolina	9,333	65.1	14.8	6,861	88.3	27.9	21,994	71.4	24.6
Harnett County, North Carolina	2,434	68.2	5.3	N	N	N	8,400	72.9	27.3
Henderson County, North Carolina	N	N	N	N	N	N	6,954	68.7	7.7
Iredell County, North Carolina	2,941	60.9	8.4	2,661	83.8	43.8	7,719	73.6	19.2
Johnston County, North Carolina	5,147	35.4	5.2	N	N	N	13,536	51.4	8.7
Lincoln County, North Carolina	N	N	N	N	N	N	3,863	75.2	22.5
Mecklenburg County, North Carolina	39,130	51.2	11.1	15,402	86.9	41.5	81,524	59.1	18.4
Moore County, North Carolina	N	N	N	N	N	N	3,403	60.0	30.1
Nash County, North Carolina	N	N	N	N	N	N	3,748	44.0	8.0
New Hanover County, North Carolina	N	N	N	N	N	N	6,659	81.8	26.6
Onslow County, North Carolina	N	N	N	N	N	N	11,394	85.4	27.6
Orange County, North Carolina	N	N	N	N	N	N	6,435	86.2	55.1
Pitt County, North Carolina	4,647	71.8	10.8	N	N	N	6,005	71.0	12.4
Randolph County, North Carolina	N	N	N	N	N	N	8,500	42.8	4.8
Robeson County, North Carolina	3,603	35.0	4.3	N	N	N	4,768	37.6	2.6
Rockingham County, North Carolina	N	N	N	N	N	N	N	N	N
Rowan County, North Carolina	N	N	N	N	N	N	6,858	50.5	12.7
Rutherford County, North Carolina	N	N	N	N	N	N	N	N	N
Surry County, North Carolina	N	N	N	N	N	N	3,847	61.9	10.3
Union County, North Carolina	N	N	N	N	N	N	13,423	61.0	17.3
Wake County, North Carolina	26,058	56.0	14.9	10,702	92.1	50.0	60,563	69.7	21.8

N = Data for this geographic area cannot be displayed because the number of sample cases is too small.

Table C-2. Educational Attainment of the Population, by Selected Counties, 2019—*Continued*

(Number; percent; dollars.)

State/County	Median earnings in the past 12 months (2019 inflation-adjusted dollars)					
	Population 25 years and over with earnings					
	Total	Less than high school graduate	High school graduate (includes equivalency)	Some college or associate's degree	Bachelor's degree	Graduate or professional degree
NEW YORK —(*Continued*)						
Madison County, New York	39,862	31,444	32,091	40,878	51,850	70,656
Monroe County, New York	43,241	25,759	31,222	36,659	51,988	65,298
Nassau County, New York	60,958	29,086	40,537	47,815	74,254	96,852
New York County, New York	72,404	22,839	31,618	39,545	85,699	110,007
Niagara County, New York	41,783	30,454	32,375	41,377	50,766	66,084
Oneida County, New York	41,846	25,754	35,359	39,578	51,985	56,535
Onondaga County, New York	43,673	24,610	31,838	40,313	52,253	66,879
Ontario County, New York	42,085	23,952	33,965	37,427	50,288	62,390
Orange County, New York	51,067	29,937	38,008	47,632	67,378	87,299
Oswego County, New York	40,186	30,425	32,486	36,874	51,568	60,851
Putnam County, New York	54,251	25,274	42,166	50,706	65,633	76,520
Queens County, New York	42,761	26,782	32,255	41,640	59,902	74,378
Rensselaer County, New York	46,681	26,615	31,697	46,525	59,101	70,093
Richmond County, New York	54,122	25,746	40,015	51,518	66,196	79,025
Rockland County, New York	52,136	25,822	40,210	48,655	65,921	83,130
St. Lawrence County, New York	38,426	21,877	30,165	37,276	55,369	60,697
Saratoga County, New York	53,879	26,415	39,262	42,140	62,444	83,683
Schenectady County, New York	42,156	35,233	30,074	40,666	58,910	75,823
Steuben County, New York	39,130	30,864	31,240	35,179	53,906	62,868
Suffolk County, New York	55,461	33,801	42,949	50,956	66,572	90,966
Sullivan County, New York	40,377	20,903	32,306	40,237	49,230	70,686
Tompkins County, New York	41,304	26,250	31,891	36,654	34,485	57,917
Ulster County, New York	42,745	24,612	37,240	36,932	48,972	70,101
Warren County, New York	46,251	31,156	38,264	42,460	60,766	66,228
Wayne County, New York	36,742	31,873	30,204	37,670	52,505	57,184
Westchester County, New York	61,702	28,886	36,973	46,380	76,994	101,664
NORTH CAROLINA	38,534	23,976	30,369	34,861	50,977	65,620
Alamance County, North Carolina	37,891	23,865	31,155	35,181	51,156	63,154
Brunswick County, North Carolina	33,535	18,871	25,646	31,289	46,421	55,483
Buncombe County, North Carolina	36,479	19,154	28,078	31,946	41,222	53,522
Burke County, North Carolina	31,996	21,441	32,745	29,095	42,183	50,574
Cabarrus County, North Carolina	41,287	36,077	28,871	35,827	55,031	72,092
Caldwell County, North Carolina	32,154	26,834	31,582	31,037	39,137	51,661
Carteret County, North Carolina	33,971	22,695	29,855	31,872	45,990	55,283
Catawba County, North Carolina	34,781	26,671	31,973	35,366	42,350	47,262
Chatham County, North Carolina	41,697	30,136	25,827	40,129	55,360	64,773
Cleveland County, North Carolina	30,970	25,489	26,947	31,963	44,993	58,996
Craven County, North Carolina	34,296	22,289	28,779	41,268	53,468	55,640
Cumberland County, North Carolina	32,114	22,293	26,753	30,801	41,872	61,644
Davidson County, North Carolina	36,920	22,420	35,025	35,069	50,246	60,572
Durham County, North Carolina	41,862	24,138	26,121	31,963	50,817	67,793
Forsyth County, North Carolina	36,899	22,341	28,413	32,352	49,400	61,678
Franklin County, North Carolina	37,209	24,626	32,068	35,038	66,526	51,712
Gaston County, North Carolina	37,759	24,015	29,384	37,036	54,583	56,507
Guilford County, North Carolina	37,276	22,459	28,721	32,101	47,884	60,768
Harnett County, North Carolina	36,230	24,215	27,938	35,711	49,930	62,296
Henderson County, North Carolina	36,027	25,581	31,471	36,221	41,394	53,288
Iredell County, North Carolina	40,084	30,113	35,522	36,294	57,891	61,252
Johnston County, North Carolina	41,952	26,836	40,346	41,675	50,441	57,077
Lincoln County, North Carolina	44,334	31,964	32,429	41,277	65,845	71,275
Mecklenburg County, North Carolina	43,387	24,627	30,170	36,397	58,669	75,772
Moore County, North Carolina	38,721	21,320	31,378	31,709	50,308	71,993
Nash County, North Carolina	35,974	38,320	34,573	30,330	48,015	30,629
New Hanover County, North Carolina	38,179	20,531	26,337	34,000	46,158	61,778
Onslow County, North Carolina	32,969	21,473	30,112	31,461	45,082	57,101
Orange County, North Carolina	46,099	26,613	29,242	35,101	46,549	71,603
Pitt County, North Carolina	37,242	17,167	28,925	35,268	52,013	58,514
Randolph County, North Carolina	33,473	22,013	31,188	38,144	41,789	47,300
Robeson County, North Carolina	30,782	28,452	28,271	26,831	45,499	53,113
Rockingham County, North Carolina	31,756	23,203	28,015	39,858	49,547	37,211
Rowan County, North Carolina	36,568	19,268	34,581	38,567	41,724	64,346
Rutherford County, North Carolina	33,694	30,870	26,241	31,004	51,049	65,293
Surry County, North Carolina	34,665	23,527	26,234	36,642	45,072	49,715
Union County, North Carolina	46,995	30,683	35,394	41,715	56,023	99,665
Wake County, North Carolina	50,840	21,995	30,868	40,158	64,951	77,743

N = Data for this geographic area cannot be displayed because the number of sample cases is too small.

Table C-2. Educational Attainment of the Population, by Selected Counties, 2019—*Continued*

(Number; percent; dollars.)

| | Educational attainment by race/ethnicity, 25 years and over | | | | | | | | |
| | Some other race alone | | | Two or more races | | | Hispanic or Latino (of any race) | | |
State/County	Total	High school graduate or more (percent)	Bachelor's degree or more (percent)	Total	High school graduate or more (percent)	Bachelor's degree or more (percent)	Total	High school graduate or more (percent)	Bachelor's degree or more (percent)
NORTH CAROLINA—(*Continued*)									
Wayne County, North Carolina	N	N	N	N	N	N	6,453	36.2	12.9
Wilkes County, North Carolina	N	N	N	N	N	N	N	N	N
Wilson County, North Carolina	N	N	N	N	N	N	N	N	N
NORTH DAKOTA	4,140	85.1	3.8	10,065	92.4	16.9	15,357	84.1	17.3
Burleigh County, North Dakota	N	N	N	N	N	N	N	N	N
Cass County, North Dakota	N	N	N	N	N	N	2,495	100.0	29.5
Grand Forks County, North Dakota	N	N	N	N	N	N	N	N	N
Ward County, North Dakota	N	N	N	N	N	N	N	N	N
OHIO	71,858	70.2	16.2	126,022	88.4	25.2	247,310	76.1	20.2
Allen County, Ohio	N	N	N	N	N	N	1,789	76.9	15.0
Ashtabula County, Ohio	N	N	N	N	N	N	N	N	N
Athens County, Ohio	N	N	N	N	N	N	N	N	N
Belmont County, Ohio	N	N	N	N	N	N	N	N	N
Butler County, Ohio	N	N	N	2,952	90.8	36.6	8,306	66.5	21.5
Clark County, Ohio	N	N	N	N	N	N	1,868	77.7	25.7
Clermont County, Ohio	N	N	N	N	N	N	2,157	83.8	36.1
Columbiana County, Ohio	N	N	N	N	N	N	N	N	N
Cuyahoga County, Ohio	12,963	69.4	14.0	13,076	91.1	27.4	44,421	73.4	16.9
Delaware County, Ohio	N	N	N	N	N	N	3,194	98.9	51.3
Erie County, Ohio	N	N	N	N	N	N	N	N	N
Fairfield County, Ohio	N	N	N	N	N	N	N	N	N
Franklin County, Ohio	15,672	67.9	16.6	20,445	90.9	40.2	37,985	73.7	27.7
Geauga County, Ohio	N	N	N	N	N	N	N	N	N
Greene County, Ohio	N	N	N	N	N	N	2,815	100.0	30.2
Hamilton County, Ohio	3,823	89.6	34.7	9,342	88.9	33.0	13,884	78.5	31.9
Hancock County, Ohio	N	N	N	N	N	N	2,275	71.4	10.0
Jefferson County, Ohio	N	N	N	N	N	N	N	N	N
Lake County, Ohio	N	N	N	N	N	N	5,167	64.6	10.9
Licking County, Ohio	N	N	N	N	N	N	N	N	N
Lorain County, Ohio	N	N	N	4,624	89.8	13.7	18,159	72.7	12.6
Lucas County, Ohio	4,676	58.0	13.8	6,916	77.9	14.1	16,281	79.7	14.9
Mahoning County, Ohio	N	N	N	2,782	85.0	12.4	8,402	64.9	10.5
Marion County, Ohio	N	N	N	N	N	N	N	N	N
Medina County, Ohio	N	N	N	N	N	N	2,209	83.9	29.7
Miami County, Ohio	N	N	N	N	N	N	N	N	N
Montgomery County, Ohio	4,324	68.8	14.0	7,834	86.1	17.8	8,553	65.8	15.3
Muskingum County, Ohio	N	N	N	N	N	N	N	N	N
Portage County, Ohio	N	N	N	N	N	N	N	N	N
Richland County, Ohio	N	N	N	N	N	N	N	N	N
Ross County, Ohio	N	N	N	1,386	95.7	10.4	N	N	N
Scioto County, Ohio	N	N	N	N	N	N	N	N	N
Stark County, Ohio	N	N	N	4,104	79.9	13.9	4,415	78.3	30.9
Summit County, Ohio	N	N	N	6,533	82.4	25.3	6,593	83.0	31.0
Trumbull County, Ohio	N	N	N	N	N	N	1,838	93.5	19.9
Tuscarawas County, Ohio	N	N	N	N	N	N	N	N	N
Warren County, Ohio	N	N	N	N	N	N	3,864	90.1	40.6
Wayne County, Ohio	N	N	N	N	N	N	N	N	N
Wood County, Ohio	N	N	N	N	N	N	3,803	77.4	25.5
OKLAHOMA	51,498	55.4	8.3	139,026	89.3	23.3	215,930	63.2	12.0
Canadian County, Oklahoma	N	N	N	3,102	83.9	20.8	7,515	50.0	15.1
Cleveland County, Oklahoma	N	N	N	8,054	94.5	30.5	13,586	78.5	27.8
Comanche County, Oklahoma	N	N	N	6,365	80.4	4.5	8,706	91.4	17.7
Creek County, Oklahoma	N	N	N	2,101	88.6	12.9	1,861	78.3	3.2
Muskogee County, Oklahoma	N	N	N	3,420	85.0	26.4	2,432	72.0	8.1
Oklahoma County, Oklahoma	13,369	53.3	6.7	20,338	92.7	33.1	68,273	55.4	11.9
Payne County, Oklahoma	N	N	N	2,071	91.5	22.4	N	N	N
Pottawatomie County, Oklahoma	N	N	N	1,383	97.3	16.8	1,839	80.2	9.6
Rogers County, Oklahoma	N	N	N	4,614	94.8	22.6	2,397	74.3	20.4
Tulsa County, Oklahoma	9,773	55.5	9.9	22,380	90.2	31.0	42,020	65.8	12.0
Wagoner County, Oklahoma	N	N	N	3,371	92.9	20.1	2,901	72.6	10.3
OREGON	85,411	62.5	12.5	103,053	91.4	32.6	301,623	68.9	16.0
Benton County, Oregon	N	N	N	N	N	N	3,223	78.2	34.4
Clackamas County, Oregon	6,641	72.0	18.3	7,879	93.7	37.0	20,450	70.8	17.3

N = Data for this geographic area cannot be displayed because the number of sample cases is too small.

Table C-2. Educational Attainment of the Population, by Selected Counties, 2019—*Continued*

(Number; percent; dollars.)

| State/County | Median earnings in the past 12 months (2019 inflation-adjusted dollars) | | | | | |
| | Population 25 years and over with earnings | | | | | |
	Total	Less than high school graduate	High school graduate (includes equivalency)	Some college or associate's degree	Bachelor's degree	Graduate or professional degree
NORTH CAROLINA—(*Continued*)						
Wayne County, North Carolina	31,944	19,343	30,229	32,429	37,840	56,165
Wilkes County, North Carolina	31,963	21,052	30,459	31,163	52,157	64,275
Wilson County, North Carolina	35,097	31,493	39,842	25,913	41,658	61,458
NORTH DAKOTA	43,865	28,756	34,343	41,818	51,854	61,288
Burleigh County, North Dakota	48,743	30,972	36,539	42,274	52,983	81,190
Cass County, North Dakota	42,886	22,929	27,631	39,653	53,592	55,753
Grand Forks County, North Dakota	44,516	87,905	32,848	42,449	50,192	57,830
Ward County, North Dakota	46,545	17,361	40,388	42,862	50,361	71,536
OHIO	40,586	24,836	31,514	36,821	53,680	71,180
Allen County, Ohio	37,012	26,123	30,039	41,131	43,810	69,223
Ashtabula County, Ohio	31,872	31,610	26,511	34,978	48,163	69,847
Athens County, Ohio	37,683	30,177	30,985	34,697	35,982	70,868
Belmont County, Ohio	30,820	14,764	27,068	34,375	50,148	54,909
Butler County, Ohio	46,153	22,791	36,841	40,299	61,760	76,352
Clark County, Ohio	34,627	22,497	30,091	35,944	50,948	65,441
Clermont County, Ohio	43,504	30,735	39,425	38,405	57,115	73,797
Columbiana County, Ohio	33,635	30,875	29,063	31,473	46,017	53,339
Cuyahoga County, Ohio	40,833	22,151	29,783	35,697	55,167	72,195
Delaware County, Ohio	60,417	23,578	31,222	48,750	81,231	89,118
Erie County, Ohio	34,291	17,646	31,502	34,238	43,568	47,845
Fairfield County, Ohio	42,343	20,167	31,938	41,724	51,653	76,261
Franklin County, Ohio	42,185	23,467	30,300	36,591	53,623	72,582
Geauga County, Ohio	46,392	41,367	30,875	40,922	60,009	81,676
Greene County, Ohio	42,469	17,170	33,236	35,149	50,659	82,158
Hamilton County, Ohio	42,359	24,016	31,302	36,605	54,891	76,541
Hancock County, Ohio	42,919	22,400	36,863	36,988	55,790	74,093
Jefferson County, Ohio	36,181	18,848	30,983	35,164	46,005	52,184
Lake County, Ohio	41,973	26,826	31,667	40,958	59,189	70,475
Licking County, Ohio	42,100	30,163	34,367	40,158	58,060	70,929
Lorain County, Ohio	41,403	21,661	31,486	41,361	60,290	57,374
Lucas County, Ohio	36,709	20,573	30,360	35,014	50,447	67,366
Mahoning County, Ohio	36,223	23,416	29,639	34,545	48,199	64,835
Marion County, Ohio	33,013	19,340	26,241	36,036	47,248	72,891
Medina County, Ohio	51,094	38,699	32,488	47,448	65,632	81,330
Miami County, Ohio	39,149	30,731	34,290	35,099	57,475	73,513
Montgomery County, Ohio	37,269	21,954	31,076	32,235	52,262	72,538
Muskingum County, Ohio	32,397	25,540	25,158	31,937	55,920	45,915
Portage County, Ohio	39,307	28,760	31,376	39,001	45,848	61,015
Richland County, Ohio	33,847	21,646	30,678	31,964	45,536	56,149
Ross County, Ohio	36,745	29,811	31,098	36,039	48,299	55,236
Scioto County, Ohio	40,067	27,160	31,907	35,896	55,554	61,115
Stark County, Ohio	37,030	26,095	31,676	34,314	52,568	72,671
Summit County, Ohio	39,075	25,867	31,105	34,973	56,021	66,905
Trumbull County, Ohio	36,154	24,664	31,233	35,715	42,299	60,998
Tuscarawas County, Ohio	35,559	40,115	31,745	28,100	52,575	61,405
Warren County, Ohio	54,825	32,050	35,110	50,094	67,400	88,781
Wayne County, Ohio	36,410	38,445	30,796	35,571	41,276	64,138
Wood County, Ohio	43,207	20,692	32,468	40,579	51,998	68,103
OKLAHOMA	38,088	24,760	31,766	35,955	47,828	61,092
Canadian County, Oklahoma	41,904	20,479	37,103	42,069	53,024	56,344
Cleveland County, Oklahoma	43,873	23,280	36,472	41,184	48,881	62,058
Comanche County, Oklahoma	31,262	16,559	28,205	32,165	30,639	41,582
Creek County, Oklahoma	37,012	29,726	34,455	35,546	42,510	59,900
Muskogee County, Oklahoma	35,436	26,842	30,632	30,905	41,678	56,356
Oklahoma County, Oklahoma	39,867	23,162	31,112	36,008	51,239	75,360
Payne County, Oklahoma	31,076	21,775	26,767	22,310	46,604	31,267
Pottawatomie County, Oklahoma	37,545	27,888	36,314	35,795	41,878	54,247
Rogers County, Oklahoma	41,547	34,375	36,379	41,643	44,521	62,207
Tulsa County, Oklahoma	40,223	25,504	32,074	35,708	50,557	64,958
Wagoner County, Oklahoma	42,936	37,885	36,672	42,310	50,910	60,595
OREGON	40,774	27,408	31,451	36,817	52,498	70,854
Benton County, Oregon	42,203	25,651	31,797	35,004	44,131	62,347
Clackamas County, Oregon	46,863	31,819	35,803	45,032	63,440	76,233

N = Data for this geographic area cannot be displayed because the number of sample cases is too small.

Table C-2. Educational Attainment of the Population, by Selected Counties, 2019—*Continued*

(Number; percent; dollars.)

	Educational attainment by race/ethnicity, 25 years and over								
	Some other race alone			Two or more races			Hispanic or Latino (of any race)		
State/County	Total	High school graduate or more (percent)	Bachelor's degree or more (percent)	Total	High school graduate or more (percent)	Bachelor's degree or more (percent)	Total	High school graduate or more (percent)	Bachelor's degree or more (percent)
OREGON—(*Continued*)									
Deschutes County, Oregon	N	N	N	3,311	100.0	23.3	8,788	79.0	18.6
Douglas County, Oregon	N	N	N	3,366	87.9	3.5	3,757	83.9	13.8
Jackson County, Oregon	N	N	N	N	N	N	15,139	65.8	19.0
Josephine County, Oregon	N	N	N	N	N	N	3,808	73.3	11.0
Klamath County, Oregon	N	N	N	N	N	N	4,981	76.0	12.2
Lane County, Oregon	7,579	69.5	12.0	9,603	94.5	38.4	18,720	81.5	20.0
Linn County, Oregon	N	N	N	3,836	73.5	19.2	6,314	66.8	12.0
Marion County, Oregon	15,533	44.9	10.5	10,173	84.0	27.4	47,637	61.2	11.5
Multnomah County, Oregon	12,769	61.8	18.1	23,516	96.2	45.2	56,205	67.6	24.7
Polk County, Oregon	N	N	N	N	N	N	5,897	80.6	26.3
Umatilla County, Oregon	N	N	N	1,765	94.2	16.3	11,167	71.2	11.5
Washington County, Oregon	20,176	72.9	12.0	13,547	91.2	43.0	55,160	73.5	13.2
Yamhill County, Oregon	N	N	N	N	N	N	10,132	56.9	11.2
PENNSYLVANIA	196,555	63.1	10.8	131,353	88.7	30.4	544,225	72.9	16.5
Adams County, Pennsylvania	N	N	N	N	N	N	3,528	60.9	1.7
Allegheny County, Pennsylvania	4,596	81.2	31.5	14,129	90.4	39.8	16,434	88.0	46.6
Armstrong County, Pennsylvania	N	N	N	N	N	N	N	N	N
Beaver County, Pennsylvania	N	N	N	N	N	N	1,845	71.8	17.5
Berks County, Pennsylvania	20,103	69.0	18.8	3,685	73.7	15.1	49,004	71.8	15.8
Blair County, Pennsylvania	N	N	N	N	N	N	N	N	N
Bucks County, Pennsylvania	7,674	54.0	9.2	6,001	94.7	32.1	21,018	72.1	17.5
Butler County, Pennsylvania	N	N	N	N	N	N	N	N	N
Cambria County, Pennsylvania	N	N	N	N	N	N	N	N	N
Carbon County, Pennsylvania	N	N	N	N	N	N	2,009	80.5	22.6
Centre County, Pennsylvania	N	N	N	N	N	N	2,891	90.7	66.7
Chester County, Pennsylvania	8,396	47.4	16.4	5,687	97.5	48.5	20,540	62.8	28.6
Clearfield County, Pennsylvania	N	N	N	N	N	N	N	N	N
Columbia County, Pennsylvania	N	N	N	N	N	N	N	N	N
Crawford County, Pennsylvania	N	N	N	N	N	N	N	N	N
Cumberland County, Pennsylvania	N	N	N	3,485	93.7	22.6	6,121	87.2	24.0
Dauphin County, Pennsylvania	N	N	N	3,383	95.3	29.3	13,499	77.0	18.1
Delaware County, Pennsylvania	4,543	63.8	20.7	5,508	95.8	34.4	12,208	76.8	24.0
Erie County, Pennsylvania	N	N	N	3,437	77.1	23.2	6,040	59.2	19.8
Fayette County, Pennsylvania	N	N	N	N	N	N	N	N	N
Franklin County, Pennsylvania	N	N	N	N	N	N	5,051	80.3	13.2
Indiana County, Pennsylvania	N	N	N	N	N	N	N	N	N
Lackawanna County, Pennsylvania	N	N	N	N	N	N	9,144	76.8	10.9
Lancaster County, Pennsylvania	9,615	65.0	4.6	6,762	77.9	26.6	32,346	72.5	12.0
Lawrence County, Pennsylvania	N	N	N	N	N	N	N	N	N
Lebanon County, Pennsylvania	5,409	61.3	4.7	N	N	N	10,334	64.2	8.0
Lehigh County, Pennsylvania	9,720	75.3	12.0	4,464	87.6	24.4	52,780	79.1	11.8
Luzerne County, Pennsylvania	9,983	65.3	9.4	2,552	90.5	22.6	22,314	70.9	9.3
Lycoming County, Pennsylvania	N	N	N	N	N	N	N	N	N
Mercer County, Pennsylvania	N	N	N	N	N	N	N	N	N
Monroe County, Pennsylvania	N	N	N	N	N	N	17,076	84.4	21.4
Montgomery County, Pennsylvania	5,183	72.5	16.4	7,209	97.2	50.9	24,592	79.6	29.4
Northampton County, Pennsylvania	7,781	60.7	6.8	3,790	89.9	42.3	24,292	77.9	15.2
Northumberland County, Pennsylvania	N	N	N	N	N	N	2,092	66.6	1.5
Philadelphia County, Pennsylvania	75,690	59.5	6.6	25,128	87.7	31.3	135,692	66.9	13.1
Schuylkill County, Pennsylvania	N	N	N	N	N	N	3,871	64.1	11.8
Somerset County, Pennsylvania	N	N	N	N	N	N	N	N	N
Washington County, Pennsylvania	N	N	N	N	N	N	N	N	N
Westmoreland County, Pennsylvania	N	N	N	N	N	N	2,403	81.9	31.8
York County, Pennsylvania	5,656	59.3	9.4	4,875	87.1	18.2	18,494	64.0	6.6
RHODE ISLAND	36,544	66.2	10.5	18,859	81.8	30.6	97,435	70.9	14.4
Kent County, Rhode Island	N	N	N	N	N	N	5,362	69.3	18.3
Newport County, Rhode Island	N	N	N	N	N	N	N	N	N
Providence County, Rhode Island	32,347	64.8	9.0	14,240	78.9	26.3	85,822	69.2	12.5
Washington County, Rhode Island	N	N	N	N	N	N	N	N	N
SOUTH CAROLINA	60,585	53.4	12.3	42,843	89.5	29.5	157,206	65.8	18.0
Aiken County, South Carolina	N	N	N	N	N	N	N	N	N
Anderson County, South Carolina	N	N	N	N	N	N	4,123	66.5	8.9
Beaufort County, South Carolina	N	N	N	N	N	N	11,079	69.3	14.0
Berkeley County, South Carolina	6,321	70.6	7.3	3,265	93.9	32.6	8,295	78.2	17.4
Charleston County, South Carolina	6,721	44.3	11.4	4,440	95.6	46.6	11,547	62.2	25.2

N = Data for this geographic area cannot be displayed because the number of sample cases is too small.

Table C-2. Educational Attainment of the Population, by Selected Counties, 2019—*Continued*

(Number; percent; dollars.)

State/County	Median earnings in the past 12 months (2019 inflation-adjusted dollars)					
	Population 25 years and over with earnings					
	Total	Less than high school graduate	High school graduate (includes equivalency)	Some college or associate's degree	Bachelor's degree	Graduate or professional degree
OREGON—*(Continued)*						
Deschutes County, Oregon	37,262	25,530	30,988	34,361	46,929	65,654
Douglas County, Oregon	31,578	27,687	28,160	30,778	49,616	55,133
Jackson County, Oregon	33,544	25,671	30,539	31,739	49,722	60,697
Josephine County, Oregon	30,097	30,089	21,942	29,392	38,506	73,322
Klamath County, Oregon	34,915	21,756	30,738	30,588	53,508	50,500
Lane County, Oregon	36,380	22,316	31,599	33,815	45,910	57,813
Linn County, Oregon	36,617	36,875	31,210	40,432	35,547	53,144
Marion County, Oregon	36,479	30,186	27,162	36,317	46,955	66,867
Multnomah County, Oregon	44,774	25,963	30,649	38,351	56,185	72,163
Polk County, Oregon	47,578	34,280	41,280	48,131	42,216	67,855
Umatilla County, Oregon	35,009	30,906	31,398	36,381	35,384	67,022
Washington County, Oregon	50,470	30,087	33,974	41,452	62,431	92,322
Yamhill County, Oregon	41,587	29,099	34,451	40,854	60,415	70,653
PENNSYLVANIA	42,229	26,343	32,567	39,075	55,326	73,805
Adams County, Pennsylvania	38,664	30,944	32,124	40,076	46,494	75,982
Allegheny County, Pennsylvania	47,309	22,066	32,366	39,998	56,870	73,404
Armstrong County, Pennsylvania	38,686	22,006	33,125	38,189	51,644	71,607
Beaver County, Pennsylvania	40,788	21,266	33,497	37,755	52,491	65,452
Berks County, Pennsylvania	41,642	31,090	36,526	40,274	53,943	67,762
Blair County, Pennsylvania	36,169	26,198	30,868	36,385	46,075	71,344
Bucks County, Pennsylvania	54,742	40,270	40,514	48,300	65,776	85,210
Butler County, Pennsylvania	46,945	25,534	35,693	41,397	62,342	80,328
Cambria County, Pennsylvania	36,635	22,197	30,307	36,005	47,254	62,677
Carbon County, Pennsylvania	38,280	12,743	38,497	36,525	45,957	71,331
Centre County, Pennsylvania	41,638	27,389	31,173	35,066	46,842	63,963
Chester County, Pennsylvania	60,112	31,022	37,073	45,623	74,874	100,597
Clearfield County, Pennsylvania	33,901	19,207	28,971	35,762	41,488	56,923
Columbia County, Pennsylvania	37,498	20,333	29,852	36,561	52,206	75,634
Crawford County, Pennsylvania	36,218	26,958	30,354	36,641	47,939	65,304
Cumberland County, Pennsylvania	48,681	31,104	35,961	41,344	61,082	74,262
Dauphin County, Pennsylvania	41,439	27,049	31,059	40,355	53,413	66,067
Delaware County, Pennsylvania	49,038	22,290	35,143	41,870	59,643	86,197
Erie County, Pennsylvania	36,145	18,268	30,790	31,961	45,989	59,256
Fayette County, Pennsylvania	37,192	19,983	32,189	37,080	51,052	71,158
Franklin County, Pennsylvania	39,827	35,175	35,000	40,982	45,791	61,785
Indiana County, Pennsylvania	36,603	33,840	34,053	37,529	32,157	52,243
Lackawanna County, Pennsylvania	37,485	20,867	30,878	31,936	49,180	62,105
Lancaster County, Pennsylvania	41,166	38,135	35,716	37,550	50,465	65,144
Lawrence County, Pennsylvania	37,178	20,654	30,080	36,455	51,589	64,225
Lebanon County, Pennsylvania	40,352	21,148	39,825	36,909	53,126	67,685
Lehigh County, Pennsylvania	39,142	25,371	33,720	35,500	56,976	81,558
Luzerne County, Pennsylvania	37,275	27,870	30,690	37,882	52,097	70,319
Lycoming County, Pennsylvania	35,823	26,548	31,378	34,079	42,542	67,044
Mercer County, Pennsylvania	37,875	25,249	31,250	35,064	53,420	63,669
Monroe County, Pennsylvania	40,822	31,551	37,313	37,307	46,186	74,820
Montgomery County, Pennsylvania	55,858	27,412	37,119	45,616	66,658	85,272
Northampton County, Pennsylvania	44,202	26,998	36,054	42,141	55,263	77,426
Northumberland County, Pennsylvania	35,941	30,486	30,753	35,527	52,004	58,969
Philadelphia County, Pennsylvania	37,417	22,981	28,214	33,318	50,803	68,897
Schuylkill County, Pennsylvania	40,153	27,289	36,019	36,798	51,380	66,549
Somerset County, Pennsylvania	36,254	20,617	34,774	32,435	52,368	47,798
Washington County, Pennsylvania	43,723	19,029	35,701	38,826	58,895	68,582
Westmoreland County, Pennsylvania	41,467	20,279	31,741	39,441	52,239	66,895
York County, Pennsylvania	44,329	23,852	36,667	42,427	59,943	72,119
RHODE ISLAND	46,060	31,893	36,883	40,363	57,398	76,827
Kent County, Rhode Island	48,861	37,543	37,200	45,507	60,289	77,072
Newport County, Rhode Island	49,528	31,702	35,713	36,748	61,084	81,230
Providence County, Rhode Island	42,421	31,869	36,635	40,002	54,150	71,118
Washington County, Rhode Island	51,243	30,801	38,960	36,781	60,927	84,862
SOUTH CAROLINA	37,727	23,085	30,592	35,994	50,734	60,788
Aiken County, South Carolina	38,396	20,226	31,929	37,843	45,853	76,167
Anderson County, South Carolina	35,251	25,175	31,298	33,390	40,836	72,240
Beaufort County, South Carolina	37,925	23,150	30,084	35,164	50,913	66,560
Berkeley County, South Carolina	41,525	30,220	36,838	40,796	52,102	59,563
Charleston County, South Carolina	47,671	18,115	31,278	41,226	58,547	73,768

N = Data for this geographic area cannot be displayed because the number of sample cases is too small.

Table C-2. Educational Attainment of the Population, by Selected Counties, 2019—*Continued*

(Number; percent; dollars.)

| | Educational attainment by race/ethnicity, 25 years and over | | | | | | | | |
| | Some other race alone | | | Two or more races | | | Hispanic or Latino (of any race) | | |
State/County	Total	High school graduate or more (percent)	Bachelor's degree or more (percent)	Total	High school graduate or more (percent)	Bachelor's degree or more (percent)	Total	High school graduate or more (percent)	Bachelor's degree or more (percent)
SOUTH CAROLINA—(*Continued*)									
Darlington County, South Carolina	N	N	N	N	N	N	N	N	N
Dorchester County, South Carolina	N	N	N	N	N	N	5,526	47.7	20.7
Florence County, South Carolina	N	N	N	N	N	N	N	N	N
Greenville County, South Carolina	10,823	48.1	12.8	4,983	76.2	29.1	27,064	67.1	18.8
Greenwood County, South Carolina	N	N	N	N	N	N	N	N	N
Horry County, South Carolina	N	N	N	2,732	97.5	37.4	11,815	50.2	12.3
Kershaw County, South Carolina	N	N	N	N	N	N	N	N	N
Lancaster County, South Carolina	N	N	N	N	N	N	N	N	N
Laurens County, South Carolina	N	N	N	N	N	N	N	N	N
Lexington County, South Carolina	N	N	N	2,140	84.3	9.2	9,805	55.2	11.4
Oconee County, South Carolina	N	N	N	N	N	N	2,713	58.8	23.5
Orangeburg County, South Carolina	N	N	N	N	N	N	N	N	N
Pickens County, South Carolina	N	N	N	N	N	N	2,524	91.6	39.9
Richland County, South Carolina	4,690	56.7	17.4	4,241	88.4	37.3	10,841	71.1	26.3
Spartanburg County, South Carolina	2,515	64.5	4.4	2,468	86.5	26.0	11,509	64.3	14.7
Sumter County, South Carolina	N	N	N	N	N	N	N	N	N
York County, South Carolina	N	N	N	N	N	N	9,713	81.7	22.7
SOUTH DAKOTA	3,771	71.1	34.0	9,997	88.5	24.2	16,720	80.8	25.5
Minnehaha County, South Dakota	N	N	N	2,200	89.8	16.0	5,213	81.0	27.5
Pennington County, South Dakota	N	N	N	N	N	N	N	N	N
TENNESSEE	52,512	56.8	16.6	56,291	88.3	31.2	188,951	63.1	18.5
Anderson County, Tennessee	N	N	N	N	N	N	N	N	N
Blount County, Tennessee	N	N	N	N	N	N	2,693	50.8	3.9
Bradley County, Tennessee	N	N	N	N	N	N	3,929	60.3	8.4
Davidson County, Tennessee	12,108	59.5	23.5	7,587	94.5	48.5	36,785	52.4	16.2
Greene County, Tennessee	N	N	N	N	N	N	N	N	N
Hamilton County, Tennessee	N	N	N	N	N	N	10,611	66.8	30.4
Knox County, Tennessee	N	N	N	4,384	94.9	28.3	10,828	63.0	22.1
Madison County, Tennessee	N	N	N	N	N	N	N	N	N
Maury County, Tennessee	N	N	N	N	N	N	N	N	N
Montgomery County, Tennessee	N	N	N	5,341	94.4	33.4	10,672	89.9	23.0
Putnam County, Tennessee	N	N	N	N	N	N	N	N	N
Robertson County, Tennessee	N	N	N	N	N	N	2,649	75.5	19.0
Rutherford County, Tennessee	N	N	N	N	N	N	13,629	74.7	27.4
Sevier County, Tennessee	N	N	N	N	N	N	N	N	N
Shelby County, Tennessee	10,554	45.6	16.8	7,211	82.3	31.7	28,935	55.1	15.7
Sullivan County, Tennessee	N	N	N	N	N	N	1,758	65.3	26.9
Sumner County, Tennessee	N	N	N	N	N	N	5,182	60.1	21.8
Washington County, Tennessee	N	N	N	N	N	N	N	N	N
Williamson County, Tennessee	N	N	N	N	N	N	6,564	90.1	29.7
Wilson County, Tennessee	N	N	N	N	N	N	N	N	N
TEXAS	1,030,092	62.0	12.7	357,572	88.3	33.4	6,538,918	68.3	16.1
Angelina County, Texas	N	N	N	N	N	N	10,259	60.6	15.8
Bastrop County, Texas	10,203	58.6	2.1	N	N	N	18,249	62.6	9.1
Bell County, Texas	6,606	81.4	19.2	6,875	98.2	19.9	49,184	81.1	21.4
Bexar County, Texas	88,402	71.4	16.2	37,674	88.2	34.1	737,436	76.4	18.0
Bowie County, Texas	N	N	N	N	N	N	4,002	65.9	4.2
Brazoria County, Texas	7,469	56.9	6.0	N	N	N	67,173	75.4	14.8
Brazos County, Texas	N	N	N	N	N	N	29,544	69.3	14.5
Cameron County, Texas	9,705	53.4	7.5	2,404	60.6	6.5	218,424	65.2	14.6
Collin County, Texas	14,664	82.9	25.5	11,488	96.1	54.0	89,714	75.9	27.2
Comal County, Texas	N	N	N	N	N	N	25,948	86.0	37.9
Coryell County, Texas	N	N	N	4,330	80.8	5.6	8,156	77.8	14.5
Dallas County, Texas	111,295	51.7	10.0	32,644	90.9	38.0	582,360	56.9	11.5
Denton County, Texas	11,318	68.9	21.6	13,642	87.2	41.0	97,389	74.7	27.7
Ector County, Texas	10,273	67.1	2.8	N	N	N	56,724	65.6	9.0
Ellis County, Texas	4,925	55.6	8.0	N	N	N	26,715	67.5	8.9
El Paso County, Texas	61,286	67.0	13.5	10,034	87.2	17.7	423,740	76.4	20.0
Fort Bend County, Texas	21,054	61.5	17.7	9,802	94.7	48.1	117,309	74.3	25.6
Galveston County, Texas	3,493	70.9	13.6	3,804	89.9	31.0	50,408	77.1	14.9
Grayson County, Texas	N	N	N	N	N	N	9,182	59.3	8.6
Gregg County, Texas	N	N	N	N	N	N	12,015	63.6	10.2
Guadalupe County, Texas	3,626	80.3	4.3	N	N	N	38,537	76.9	16.9
Harris County, Texas	263,937	59.9	13.1	59,692	90.9	37.2	1,168,898	64.3	15.3
Harrison County, Texas	N	N	N	N	N	N	4,124	58.3	2.6

N = Data for this geographic area cannot be displayed because the number of sample cases is too small.

Table C-2. Educational Attainment of the Population, by Selected Counties, 2019—*Continued*

(Number; percent; dollars.)

State/County	Median earnings in the past 12 months (2019 inflation-adjusted dollars)					
	Population 25 years and over with earnings					
	Total	Less than high school graduate	High school graduate (includes equivalency)	Some college or associate's degree	Bachelor's degree	Graduate or professional degree
SOUTH CAROLINA—(*Continued*)						
Darlington County, South Carolina	33,974	23,019	31,190	32,373	60,075	47,549
Dorchester County, South Carolina	41,375	27,571	36,767	39,962	50,962	66,462
Florence County, South Carolina	35,775	21,040	30,176	30,710	55,656	60,079
Greenville County, South Carolina	41,166	22,214	30,517	39,275	53,726	66,498
Greenwood County, South Carolina	31,296	17,358	27,808	32,363	38,622	45,849
Horry County, South Carolina	31,495	20,575	26,234	33,407	40,576	51,198
Kershaw County, South Carolina	40,016	29,010	35,708	35,584	47,957	55,973
Lancaster County, South Carolina	39,221	28,741	30,476	36,607	68,602	65,095
Laurens County, South Carolina	34,515	27,897	31,202	40,151	43,817	47,385
Lexington County, South Carolina	41,330	27,870	31,811	39,782	55,268	61,097
Oconee County, South Carolina	32,916	27,752	29,444	30,189	39,743	66,183
Orangeburg County, South Carolina	30,600	16,393	29,468	26,877	36,345	50,339
Pickens County, South Carolina	36,554	24,399	31,262	35,068	45,308	50,952
Richland County, South Carolina	39,536	17,349	26,986	32,232	46,698	57,106
Spartanburg County, South Carolina	37,404	28,618	31,903	36,253	50,523	55,117
Sumter County, South Carolina	35,355	23,687	31,885	32,065	50,203	52,634
York County, South Carolina	42,777	25,479	31,772	38,518	59,541	70,211
SOUTH DAKOTA	38,646	22,131	31,306	36,732	47,630	57,244
Minnehaha County, South Dakota	41,616	19,373	31,877	40,612	51,315	59,952
Pennington County, South Dakota	32,422	20,968	30,170	35,214	36,069	62,931
TENNESSEE	37,610	25,365	30,596	35,518	50,633	62,832
Anderson County, Tennessee	32,595	26,555	30,492	31,977	42,600	56,330
Blount County, Tennessee	38,238	24,110	34,179	36,655	51,808	49,530
Bradley County, Tennessee	34,014	24,951	28,461	32,528	47,871	61,417
Davidson County, Tennessee	42,293	26,731	29,168	36,924	52,211	63,017
Greene County, Tennessee	32,848	21,934	28,701	32,017	35,122	65,247
Hamilton County, Tennessee	38,230	25,085	26,129	34,137	52,356	62,633
Knox County, Tennessee	41,264	24,946	29,676	36,791	50,782	63,506
Madison County, Tennessee	36,294	27,516	30,660	36,493	47,764	51,372
Maury County, Tennessee	40,296	22,867	35,068	39,005	52,097	54,916
Montgomery County, Tennessee	39,079	13,574	33,597	36,155	41,419	64,435
Putnam County, Tennessee	34,158	20,935	29,768	33,866	41,042	60,096
Robertson County, Tennessee	40,050	36,044	32,388	37,362	49,203	70,359
Rutherford County, Tennessee	40,254	30,668	32,265	39,678	43,400	61,092
Sevier County, Tennessee	30,861	21,482	28,683	30,414	36,101	61,888
Shelby County, Tennessee	37,249	22,547	28,434	32,152	50,847	72,327
Sullivan County, Tennessee	35,078	22,019	27,535	32,610	46,629	61,321
Sumner County, Tennessee	41,933	28,795	36,747	39,491	56,032	65,479
Washington County, Tennessee	36,786	28,102	27,205	36,001	45,111	75,405
Williamson County, Tennessee	62,369	24,954	36,803	37,446	76,242	90,794
Wilson County, Tennessee	44,667	31,085	33,523	41,675	52,075	61,372
TEXAS	40,895	25,282	31,234	38,121	56,853	72,195
Angelina County, Texas	31,923	20,532	24,342	27,407	46,237	65,939
Bastrop County, Texas	32,468	21,823	30,818	34,962	45,350	52,310
Bell County, Texas	37,350	22,279	30,257	35,393	51,254	66,985
Bexar County, Texas	36,408	23,458	30,116	34,745	54,516	66,759
Bowie County, Texas	38,240	22,179	34,105	40,221	46,068	59,219
Brazoria County, Texas	56,331	31,577	42,178	50,987	71,627	86,146
Brazos County, Texas	39,408	24,274	32,392	32,516	47,606	65,999
Cameron County, Texas	26,953	17,834	26,405	28,040	46,324	61,143
Collin County, Texas	57,676	27,029	32,498	46,454	70,192	91,222
Comal County, Texas	51,229	23,315	35,348	49,204	63,666	60,418
Coryell County, Texas	32,357	22,643	31,062	32,849	39,338	62,213
Dallas County, Texas	40,190	27,069	30,001	38,386	60,265	74,212
Denton County, Texas	52,065	30,121	35,222	47,134	62,997	80,442
Ector County, Texas	45,199	29,139	46,905	42,463	62,286	65,322
Ellis County, Texas	42,319	29,182	38,415	45,240	56,072	71,662
El Paso County, Texas	31,720	16,872	26,133	30,514	48,330	60,270
Fort Bend County, Texas	51,711	29,714	32,308	41,290	70,017	100,713
Galveston County, Texas	50,284	29,674	32,125	45,227	61,059	71,434
Grayson County, Texas	35,465	21,210	30,299	40,039	49,643	56,369
Gregg County, Texas	36,463	22,295	32,647	36,334	47,497	57,468
Guadalupe County, Texas	39,285	24,984	30,500	40,817	57,289	60,413
Harris County, Texas	40,668	26,176	30,816	37,118	58,758	75,616
Harrison County, Texas	42,312	21,659	34,361	51,140	60,289	75,654

N = Data for this geographic area cannot be displayed because the number of sample cases is too small.

Table C-2. Educational Attainment of the Population, by Selected Counties, 2019—*Continued*

(Number; percent; dollars.)

State/County	Educational attainment by race/ethnicity, 25 years and over								
	Some other race alone			Two or more races			Hispanic or Latino (of any race)		
	Total	High school graduate or more (percent)	Bachelor's degree or more (percent)	Total	High school graduate or more (percent)	Bachelor's degree or more (percent)	Total	High school graduate or more (percent)	Bachelor's degree or more (percent)
TEXAS—(*Continued*)									
Hays County, Texas	4,030	88.9	8.6	N	N	N	50,600	80.3	17.0
Henderson County, Texas	N	N	N	N	N	N	5,609	59.9	5.2
Hidalgo County, Texas	66,058	54.9	16.4	6,308	65.0	20.2	444,385	65.1	17.1
Hunt County, Texas	N	N	N	N	N	N	7,869	56.0	5.1
Jefferson County, Texas	N	N	N	N	N	N	30,344	53.1	5.2
Johnson County, Texas	N	N	N	N	N	N	21,184	64.6	8.7
Kaufman County, Texas	2,154	41.1	0.0	N	N	N	15,311	63.5	10.3
Liberty County, Texas	N	N	N	N	N	N	12,172	51.5	4.6
Lubbock County, Texas	12,491	69.8	10.4	4,109	87.2	27.7	60,688	72.0	13.7
McLennan County, Texas	2,122	79.1	37.3	3,048	72.1	20.9	35,442	67.2	12.5
Midland County, Texas	16,297	71.7	13.5	N	N	N	45,278	74.2	13.8
Montgomery County, Texas	8,329	72.6	25.8	7,238	89.2	34.1	81,802	64.8	19.3
Nacogdoches County, Texas	N	N	N	N	N	N	5,872	53.3	10.8
Nueces County, Texas	5,404	83.7	12.7	N	N	N	144,259	78.2	17.0
Orange County, Texas	N	N	N	N	N	N	3,889	76.9	21.3
Parker County, Texas	N	N	N	N	N	N	9,343	61.4	18.5
Potter County, Texas	N	N	N	N	N	N	24,840	63.9	5.9
Randall County, Texas	N	N	N	N	N	N	16,843	82.7	22.9
Rockwall County, Texas	N	N	N	N	N	N	10,970	79.8	22.1
San Patricio County, Texas	N	N	N	N	N	N	23,312	72.1	9.3
Smith County, Texas	3,505	57.3	7.8	N	N	N	23,538	54.3	9.0
Tarrant County, Texas	91,818	58.6	10.7	23,568	90.8	34.2	334,745	67.1	17.0
Taylor County, Texas	4,405	82.2	15.1	N	N	N	18,171	80.7	16.0
Tom Green County, Texas	N	N	N	N	N	N	28,094	75.8	14.0
Travis County, Texas	56,198	64.7	12.8	24,842	85.4	47.2	257,335	73.4	28.0
Victoria County, Texas	N	N	N	N	N	N	24,152	71.8	9.4
Walker County, Texas	N	N	N	N	N	N	6,805	54.9	1.9
Webb County, Texas	3,685	76.8	31.3	N	N	N	146,733	64.5	18.7
Wichita County, Texas	N	N	N	N	N	N	13,874	68.9	9.9
Williamson County, Texas	6,703	92.4	21.2	8,890	92.9	44.0	84,792	83.5	24.8
Wise County, Texas	N	N	N	N	N	N	7,089	48.4	7.7
UTAH	70,693	65.9	12.0	37,008	93.7	35.2	233,666	74.8	15.6
Cache County, Utah	N	N	N	N	N	N	6,709	70.9	9.8
Davis County, Utah	3,356	90.0	18.2	3,688	98.4	38.1	17,706	81.8	16.9
Salt Lake County, Utah	48,477	63.8	10.8	16,848	95.1	35.5	114,281	73.1	16.1
Tooele County, Utah	N	N	N	N	N	N	5,449	85.5	13.2
Utah County, Utah	6,123	85.1	13.6	8,428	97.9	50.6	36,516	82.4	20.2
Washington County, Utah	N	N	N	N	N	N	9,754	78.3	11.8
Weber County, Utah	3,095	60.1	12.5	2,670	94.1	24.0	24,876	73.9	14.0
VERMONT	N	N	N	7,602	75.7	33.2	5,638	88.6	32.7
Chittenden County, Vermont	N	N	N	N	N	N	2,355	96.3	40.3
VIRGINIA	141,159	65.4	19.7	127,448	92.1	39.6	465,976	73.3	26.3
Albemarle County, Virginia	N	N	N	N	N	N	3,002	79.5	39.9
Arlington County, Virginia	5,662	70.0	25.4	6,180	100.0	80.6	24,880	73.8	42.3
Augusta County, Virginia	N	N	N	N	N	N	N	N	N
Bedford County, Virginia	N	N	N	N	N	N	N	N	N
Chesterfield County, Virginia	10,791	66.1	7.9	4,188	100.0	33.7	18,215	69.5	16.3
Fairfax County, Virginia	38,008	66.1	23.8	20,666	95.6	57.4	111,624	72.5	28.9
Fauquier County, Virginia	N	N	N	N	N	N	3,714	61.5	14.0
Frederick County, Virginia	N	N	N	N	N	N	4,618	74.1	9.3
Hanover County, Virginia	N	N	N	N	N	N	1,828	84.4	29.6
Henrico County, Virginia	N	N	N	6,773	94.1	43.7	10,792	76.1	26.3
James City County, Virginia	N	N	N	N	N	N	N	N	N
Loudoun County, Virginia	9,042	60.8	17.2	8,682	93.3	54.4	32,321	79.7	33.4
Montgomery County, Virginia	N	N	N	N	N	N	N	N	N
Prince William County, Virginia	18,325	51.5	10.9	9,982	87.6	40.7	64,797	66.9	19.7
Roanoke County, Virginia	N	N	N	N	N	N	N	N	N
Rockingham County, Virginia	N	N	N	N	N	N	3,267	65.9	10.9
Spotsylvania County, Virginia	4,286	52.7	21.6	2,505	82.4	43.0	7,864	63.1	23.7
Stafford County, Virginia	6,153	63.8	13.1	2,275	96.9	49.3	11,602	75.4	21.3
York County, Virginia	N	N	N	N	N	N	N	N	N
Alexandria city, Virginia	N	N	N	4,937	97.8	46.7	16,640	74.6	48.2
Chesapeake city, Virginia	N	N	N	N	N	N	8,648	82.0	31.1
Hampton city, Virginia	N	N	N	N	N	N	4,577	86.1	14.3
Lynchburg city, Virginia	N	N	N	N	N	N	N	N	N

N = Data for this geographic area cannot be displayed because the number of sample cases is too small.

Table C-2. Educational Attainment of the Population, by Selected Counties, 2019—*Continued*

(Number; percent; dollars.)

State/County	Median earnings in the past 12 months (2019 inflation-adjusted dollars)					
	Population 25 years and over with earnings					
	Total	Less than high school graduate	High school graduate (includes equivalency)	Some college or associate's degree	Bachelor's degree	Graduate or professional degree
TEXAS—*(Continued)*						
Hays County, Texas	41,585	28,976	37,274	35,444	55,273	60,303
Henderson County, Texas	31,909	28,053	30,465	39,835	38,643	52,329
Hidalgo County, Texas	26,683	18,186	22,172	29,903	42,751	58,895
Hunt County, Texas	40,637	27,762	30,679	45,647	51,418	71,505
Jefferson County, Texas	40,123	33,010	30,919	36,730	52,382	65,501
Johnson County, Texas	40,156	32,969	36,724	38,356	57,029	70,095
Kaufman County, Texas	43,707	31,081	37,130	49,729	51,760	60,473
Liberty County, Texas	38,934	22,986	36,901	36,338	56,376	67,203
Lubbock County, Texas	35,590	25,196	30,155	34,084	46,653	58,014
McLennan County, Texas	37,148	23,470	32,570	35,167	47,809	69,473
Midland County, Texas	47,944	20,883	40,672	44,764	55,322	65,433
Montgomery County, Texas	50,975	27,653	39,386	45,483	63,859	103,652
Nacogdoches County, Texas	35,157	25,490	27,077	31,941	39,572	62,936
Nueces County, Texas	36,551	25,159	30,814	36,593	51,845	61,938
Orange County, Texas	50,420	35,259	44,338	42,168	80,302	62,447
Parker County, Texas	42,072	27,488	36,542	41,675	60,865	82,277
Potter County, Texas	29,283	24,579	23,315	35,677	52,053	54,253
Randall County, Texas	43,722	25,622	36,376	36,589	51,762	68,683
Rockwall County, Texas	60,528	26,470	39,559	61,961	59,685	82,371
San Patricio County, Texas	36,074	22,306	29,595	37,936	51,266	50,247
Smith County, Texas	37,141	24,784	31,066	36,828	47,251	68,212
Tarrant County, Texas	44,209	28,808	32,651	41,095	58,421	75,465
Taylor County, Texas	32,994	25,275	26,885	32,158	47,458	60,609
Tom Green County, Texas	36,410	26,190	28,314	40,688	47,500	59,007
Travis County, Texas	49,891	24,257	30,836	41,850	60,241	75,785
Victoria County, Texas	37,753	15,821	34,362	40,524	51,074	60,235
Walker County, Texas	36,202	29,219	34,487	36,417	35,662	60,711
Webb County, Texas	31,866	20,111	31,143	31,533	56,976	66,974
Wichita County, Texas	32,577	23,681	29,001	31,325	46,972	59,226
Williamson County, Texas	48,119	24,493	32,795	46,511	60,211	81,444
Wise County, Texas	41,511	24,360	33,328	45,342	76,226	91,994
UTAH	41,679	28,028	34,667	37,247	51,611	76,099
Cache County, Utah	35,580	28,364	32,007	30,828	38,308	67,388
Davis County, Utah	46,616	22,396	35,801	38,393	57,531	86,548
Salt Lake County, Utah	42,350	28,523	34,787	38,925	53,617	73,832
Tooele County, Utah	50,643	30,916	49,427	45,910	51,534	76,806
Utah County, Utah	42,456	31,618	31,803	37,042	50,965	81,448
Washington County, Utah	36,873	26,549	31,299	34,638	44,223	65,375
Weber County, Utah	41,490	35,507	37,982	38,680	49,089	80,288
VERMONT	41,496	27,052	32,425	39,882	47,170	61,617
Chittenden County, Vermont	50,393	27,892	36,480	42,339	51,814	75,556
VIRGINIA	46,873	23,892	32,366	40,071	61,529	85,582
Albemarle County, Virginia	52,346	22,206	36,325	42,559	61,852	72,240
Arlington County, Virginia	80,929	22,278	30,220	50,335	82,029	105,244
Augusta County, Virginia	40,762	23,770	36,154	40,305	53,493	69,236
Bedford County, Virginia	43,089	19,685	40,777	40,156	55,698	62,042
Chesterfield County, Virginia	46,989	31,004	32,323	41,421	57,228	67,020
Fairfax County, Virginia	66,110	22,671	36,033	43,752	74,060	106,509
Fauquier County, Virginia	56,253	30,269	35,082	55,197	75,665	71,250
Frederick County, Virginia	46,068	17,354	31,970	48,402	61,434	71,135
Hanover County, Virginia	50,707	16,898	36,641	39,244	65,013	75,107
Henrico County, Virginia	43,689	25,002	32,272	37,423	60,114	71,375
James City County, Virginia	47,478	29,167	31,079	45,523	60,284	71,460
Loudoun County, Virginia	78,844	30,459	41,162	51,639	91,802	110,917
Montgomery County, Virginia	41,894	20,360	32,434	35,139	41,635	60,809
Prince William County, Virginia	52,301	26,576	38,421	48,810	60,020	90,940
Roanoke County, Virginia	47,145	21,822	35,500	42,269	57,036	71,411
Rockingham County, Virginia	38,296	27,002	33,233	40,590	47,542	57,276
Spotsylvania County, Virginia	49,291	23,850	35,834	48,709	65,264	76,061
Stafford County, Virginia	53,538	26,697	41,602	47,084	57,495	96,483
York County, Virginia	55,325	34,203	30,654	51,595	60,229	82,163
Alexandria city, Virginia	69,273	28,263	27,652	35,403	72,005	102,278
Chesapeake city, Virginia	44,290	21,101	35,967	41,195	55,410	74,792
Hampton city, Virginia	38,388	21,507	30,782	39,242	48,439	56,189
Lynchburg city, Virginia	36,160	31,930	30,440	34,124	40,974	45,178

N = Data for this geographic area cannot be displayed because the number of sample cases is too small.

Table C-2. Educational Attainment of the Population, by Selected Counties, 2019—*Continued*

(Number; percent; dollars.)

State/County	Educational attainment by race/ethnicity, 25 years and over								
	Some other race alone			Two or more races			Hispanic or Latino (of any race)		
	Total	High school graduate or more (percent)	Bachelor's degree or more (percent)	Total	High school graduate or more (percent)	Bachelor's degree or more (percent)	Total	High school graduate or more (percent)	Bachelor's degree or more (percent)
VIRGINIA—(*Continued*)									
Newport News city, Virginia	N	N	N	3,347	92.9	13.0	9,236	78.3	13.4
Norfolk city, Virginia	3,121	64.7	19.0	3,856	98.0	22.1	9,634	80.0	26.4
Portsmouth city, Virginia	N	N	N	N	N	N	N	N	N
Richmond city, Virginia	5,357	32.7	6.2	N	N	N	8,868	41.4	15.4
Roanoke city, Virginia	N	N	N	N	N	N	N	N	N
Suffolk city, Virginia	N	N	N	N	N	N	2,380	86.7	22.9
Virginia Beach city, Virginia	5,876	85.3	31.7	10,376	90.0	21.1	22,081	90.0	31.3
WASHINGTON	197,368	61.5	11.9	206,101	91.7	33.3	509,771	69.3	17.9
Benton County, Washington	8,800	48.6	3.1	3,594	95.2	56.8	22,282	70.0	11.2
Chelan County, Washington	7,627	35.8	3.6	N	N	N	11,091	46.9	7.6
Clallam County, Washington	N	N	N	N	N	N	3,103	84.5	26.5
Clark County, Washington	6,432	65.5	7.7	11,625	83.8	28.8	24,339	76.3	17.3
Cowlitz County, Washington	N	N	N	N	N	N	4,975	78.3	10.8
Franklin County, Washington	10,852	43.5	4.9	N	N	N	24,854	48.4	6.1
Grant County, Washington	11,561	50.3	3.4	N	N	N	19,953	48.9	8.8
Grays Harbor County, Washington	N	N	N	N	N	N	4,064	72.1	4.1
Island County, Washington	N	N	N	N	N	N	3,106	100.0	24.9
King County, Washington	57,114	64.4	16.9	68,744	94.0	44.7	126,288	73.5	28.1
Kitsap County, Washington	3,505	92.4	17.3	7,492	92.5	27.2	12,016	89.9	19.4
Lewis County, Washington	N	N	N	4,059	60.7	2.4	4,006	46.0	7.8
Mason County, Washington	N	N	N	N	N	N	3,320	62.0	2.8
Pierce County, Washington	19,088	74.3	16.5	32,456	91.7	26.5	52,006	79.2	19.1
Skagit County, Washington	5,438	70.8	0.7	2,028	91.3	23.5	11,796	63.9	8.4
Snohomish County, Washington	16,432	75.8	16.6	22,453	92.9	32.1	45,431	78.3	22.8
Spokane County, Washington	3,552	92.1	33.4	10,747	94.5	30.0	17,075	91.3	26.9
Thurston County, Washington	2,369	68.5	23.3	7,609	93.6	35.5	14,535	79.1	24.7
Whatcom County, Washington	N	N	N	6,095	94.5	29.9	10,871	78.2	28.9
Yakima County, Washington	19,445	48.7	8.9	4,071	83.5	24.0	61,804	49.5	5.6
WEST VIRGINIA	3,128	83.3	14.6	13,045	88.3	23.9	14,106	86.5	22.5
Berkeley County, West Virginia	N	N	N	N	N	N	N	N	N
Cabell County, West Virginia	N	N	N	N	N	N	N	N	N
Harrison County, West Virginia	N	N	N	N	N	N	N	N	N
Kanawha County, West Virginia	N	N	N	N	N	N	N	N	N
Monongalia County, West Virginia	N	N	N	N	N	N	N	N	N
Raleigh County, West Virginia	N	N	N	N	N	N	N	N	N
Wood County, West Virginia	N	N	N	N	N	N	N	N	N
WISCONSIN	69,021	65.0	13.4	48,265	94.0	31.5	210,204	70.9	15.6
Brown County, Wisconsin	3,839	44.8	6.0	3,032	84.1	24.2	10,824	61.7	10.1
Dane County, Wisconsin	4,356	69.8	23.4	4,775	94.4	57.4	18,006	73.4	28.4
Dodge County, Wisconsin	N	N	N	N	N	N	2,603	73.4	7.6
Eau Claire County, Wisconsin	N	N	N	N	N	N	N	N	N
Fond du Lac County, Wisconsin	N	N	N	N	N	N	N	N	N
Jefferson County, Wisconsin	N	N	N	N	N	N	3,172	77.6	15.3
Kenosha County, Wisconsin	N	N	N	N	N	N	11,730	83.8	12.0
La Crosse County, Wisconsin	N	N	N	N	N	N	N	N	N
Manitowoc County, Wisconsin	N	N	N	N	N	N	N	N	N
Marathon County, Wisconsin	N	N	N	N	N	N	2,076	49.5	3.1
Milwaukee County, Wisconsin	32,712	68.7	12.8	12,624	95.6	41.4	77,687	69.7	13.7
Outagamie County, Wisconsin	N	N	N	N	N	N	4,604	71.6	26.4
Ozaukee County, Wisconsin	N	N	N	N	N	N	N	N	N
Portage County, Wisconsin	N	N	N	N	N	N	N	N	N
Racine County, Wisconsin	N	N	N	N	N	N	13,667	69.5	12.2
Rock County, Wisconsin	4,413	68.2	12.1	N	N	N	6,472	74.8	16.1
St. Croix County, Wisconsin	N	N	N	N	N	N	N	N	N
Sheboygan County, Wisconsin	N	N	N	N	N	N	3,515	85.7	21.9
Walworth County, Wisconsin	N	N	N	N	N	N	5,557	60.0	8.8
Washington County, Wisconsin	N	N	N	N	N	N	2,262	76.4	19.0
Waukesha County, Wisconsin	N	N	N	N	N	N	10,815	73.9	20.3
Winnebago County, Wisconsin	N	N	N	N	N	N	4,130	50.8	4.5
Wood County, Wisconsin	N	N	N	N	N	N	N	N	N
WYOMING	6,722	82	4	5,495	91	20	30,212	81.3	11.3
Laramie County, Wyoming	N	N	N	N	N	N	8,178	84.1	10.6
Natrona County, Wyoming	N	N	N	N	N	N	3,679	66.6	5.8

N = Data for this geographic area cannot be displayed because the number of sample cases is too small.

Table C-2. Educational Attainment of the Population, by Selected Counties, 2019—*Continued*

(Number; percent; dollars.)

| State/County | Median earnings in the past 12 months (2019 inflation-adjusted dollars) | | | | | |
| | Population 25 years and over with earnings | | | | | |
	Total	Less than high school graduate	High school graduate (includes equivalency)	Some college or associate's degree	Bachelor's degree	Graduate or professional degree
VIRGINIA—(*Continued*)						
Newport News city, Virginia	37,752	24,795	32,776	36,886	48,391	62,072
Norfolk city, Virginia	35,567	23,070	30,898	31,901	44,606	59,419
Portsmouth city, Virginia	40,619	29,500	27,262	41,382	45,162	53,841
Richmond city, Virginia	36,183	19,216	22,482	31,454	50,716	65,211
Roanoke city, Virginia	34,179	19,454	22,239	35,590	50,210	57,174
Suffolk city, Virginia	45,885	29,175	40,168	40,983	51,421	80,831
Virginia Beach city, Virginia	45,290	19,431	32,399	39,846	55,072	66,439
WASHINGTON	48,567	30,627	36,441	42,030	62,447	86,167
Benton County, Washington	44,352	27,094	31,527	41,164	65,829	82,076
Chelan County, Washington	35,159	28,541	26,559	39,395	49,782	63,393
Clallam County, Washington	33,857	23,203	26,910	31,392	42,197	61,818
Clark County, Washington	46,225	31,271	36,770	41,845	60,399	75,119
Cowlitz County, Washington	39,160	32,352	30,500	41,808	50,309	59,639
Franklin County, Washington	35,855	26,479	36,536	42,952	66,275	71,997
Grant County, Washington	36,681	28,030	27,352	43,101	47,581	77,956
Grays Harbor County, Washington	35,738	29,875	31,323	35,402	50,578	71,426
Island County, Washington	41,878	30,656	36,928	41,718	37,418	62,098
King County, Washington	60,869	32,780	37,227	45,677	73,663	100,926
Kitsap County, Washington	47,331	31,165	35,856	44,819	61,218	78,595
Lewis County, Washington	40,209	22,319	32,455	41,320	45,321	80,878
Mason County, Washington	39,415	30,084	31,049	46,701	39,917	46,746
Pierce County, Washington	47,288	35,295	40,271	45,650	57,490	77,296
Skagit County, Washington	41,172	30,314	40,136	39,684	56,000	66,955
Snohomish County, Washington	52,059	36,870	42,621	46,134	69,638	90,718
Spokane County, Washington	40,344	26,739	31,574	36,810	51,032	67,385
Thurston County, Washington	45,452	22,313	31,969	40,796	53,592	79,087
Whatcom County, Washington	44,676	41,066	37,155	40,117	46,618	70,008
Yakima County, Washington	32,466	25,661	32,251	36,100	56,042	77,523
WEST VIRGINIA	35,440	20,200	30,573	32,380	45,304	58,802
Berkeley County, West Virginia	37,906	22,278	33,609	39,062	47,870	81,597
Cabell County, West Virginia	31,532	11,724	30,322	26,159	50,234	50,311
Harrison County, West Virginia	41,021	25,507	34,007	32,056	52,282	52,162
Kanawha County, West Virginia	35,260	24,023	26,540	32,725	47,088	64,238
Monongalia County, West Virginia	37,320	11,631	29,329	30,051	37,855	73,534
Raleigh County, West Virginia	32,684	9,120	27,718	31,928	37,826	46,358
Wood County, West Virginia	31,326	19,019	27,674	29,878	38,134	52,587
WISCONSIN	42,222	29,561	33,547	40,482	52,425	67,112
Brown County, Wisconsin	42,212	26,717	31,856	40,736	51,709	65,267
Dane County, Wisconsin	50,756	26,394	37,155	41,606	56,753	69,193
Dodge County, Wisconsin	41,913	36,871	37,203	41,709	50,474	68,211
Eau Claire County, Wisconsin	40,424	26,298	31,994	35,459	43,816	61,948
Fond du Lac County, Wisconsin	43,150	38,989	37,488	41,596	49,228	66,359
Jefferson County, Wisconsin	43,166	32,090	31,664	45,941	51,679	65,886
Kenosha County, Wisconsin	41,800	26,053	31,648	40,901	54,454	60,288
La Crosse County, Wisconsin	38,851	21,932	31,541	36,687	45,143	65,415
Manitowoc County, Wisconsin	40,302	24,138	33,045	39,121	56,092	63,259
Marathon County, Wisconsin	38,953	29,043	32,716	37,369	47,416	61,326
Milwaukee County, Wisconsin	41,274	25,757	31,127	40,214	51,935	67,381
Outagamie County, Wisconsin	42,069	23,478	38,691	38,674	48,185	68,567
Ozaukee County, Wisconsin	50,266	45,972	37,663	41,940	56,107	85,644
Portage County, Wisconsin	40,682	21,215	33,860	39,046	47,513	55,741
Racine County, Wisconsin	43,546	30,729	33,867	42,142	60,344	71,980
Rock County, Wisconsin	40,840	30,400	32,814	40,492	49,031	63,652
St. Croix County, Wisconsin	49,744	38,774	36,381	48,257	51,944	70,524
Sheboygan County, Wisconsin	41,485	32,761	36,928	37,104	56,501	63,385
Walworth County, Wisconsin	41,791	29,262	37,045	40,491	52,313	66,902
Washington County, Wisconsin	49,007	35,794	40,257	45,789	61,554	77,161
Waukesha County, Wisconsin	52,709	37,959	37,950	42,426	68,443	79,261
Winnebago County, Wisconsin	41,426	35,498	33,240	40,290	52,126	64,065
Wood County, Wisconsin	37,512	31,803	29,553	38,185	50,508	70,348
WYOMING	40,800	29,982	36,929	36,885	47,962	61,288
Laramie County, Wyoming	44,790	27,802	35,226	36,920	53,679	71,789
Natrona County, Wyoming	41,863	38,106	35,761	39,909	51,825	68,478

N = Data for this geographic area cannot be displayed because the number of sample cases is too small.

Table C-3. School Enrollment for the 20 Largest Public School Districts in Each State, by Grade Level, 2020–21

(Number.)

State/School District	Total students in all grades	Kindergarten	Grade 1	Grade 2	Grade 3	Grade 4	Grade 5
ALABAMA							
Auburn City	8,971	692	713	723	674	687	663
Autauga County	8,955	637	673	622	622	657	696
Baldwin County	30,210	2,003	2,235	2,137	2,216	2,272	2,246
Birmingham City	21,597	1,615	1,769	1,756	1,854	1,739	1,730
Cullman County	9,312	744	725	704	697	714	691
Decatur City	8,781	664	675	629	636	655	608
Elmore County	11,519	756	878	822	866	840	860
Hoover City	13,640	890	937	906	996	988	986
Huntsville City	23,514	1,689	1,732	1,758	1,785	1,763	1,813
Jefferson County	35,336	2,157	2,376	2,504	2,504	2,467	2,665
Lee County	9,310	666	602	646	668	693	689
Limestone County	13,041	881	913	856	919	889	946
Madison City	11,804	771	790	809	813	792	876
Madison County	19,142	1,301	1,375	1,300	1,343	1,420	1,436
Mobile County	52,460	3,658	4,107	4,026	3,934	3,934	4,018
Montgomery County	27,399	2,098	2,320	2,140	2,165	2,205	2,176
Shelby County	20,438	1,323	1,497	1,445	1,473	1,515	1,509
St Clair County	9,407	711	717	690	670	654	702
Tuscaloosa City	10,744	828	883	846	799	775	798
Tuscaloosa County	18,766	1,411	1,475	1,435	1,351	1,329	1,469
ALASKA							
Anchorage School District	41,856	2,869	3,084	3,154	3,134	3,183	3,162
Bering Strait School District	1,839	137	131	127	146	151	164
Chugach School District	694	67	51	58	48	55	62
Craig City School District	867	72	57	78	75	74	79
Delta/Greely School District	775	68	65	69	61	70	67
Denali Borough School District	1,206	74	87	89	91	70	90
Fairbanks North Star Borough School District	11,386	794	908	874	813	873	817
Galena City School District	9,366	837	844	810	812	800	727
Juneau Borough School District	4,124	230	310	298	282	320	284
Kenai Peninsula Borough School District	7,962	584	552	544	594	567	608
Ketchikan Gateway Borough School District	2,161	138	169	139	167	169	167
Kodiak Island Borough School District	2,294	160	179	193	169	168	189
Lower Kuskokwim School District	4,082	318	346	310	303	305	311
Lower Yukon School District	2,103	162	159	173	178	179	162
Matanuska-Susitna Borough School District	18,220	1,362	1,341	1,363	1,332	1,339	1,401
Nenana City School District	1,909	134	149	130	157	140	152
North Slope Borough School District	2,138	134	159	148	165	152	152
Northwest Arctic Borough School District	2,050	139	157	156	166	156	171
Sitka School District	1,151	72	76	82	79	91	79
Yukon-Koyukuk School District	4,331	311	358	338	362	342	328
ARIZONA							
Cartwright Elementary District	15,177	1,520	1,731	1,485	1,593	1,528	1,756
Chandler Unified District #80	43,790	2,309	2,588	2,695	2,844	2,859	2,931
Deer Valley Unified District	32,061	1,911	2,115	2,123	2,185	2,277	2,331
Dysart Unified District	23,011	1,337	1,436	1,422	1,555	1,593	1,553
Gilbert Unified District	32,661	2,024	2,217	2,170	2,265	2,105	2,292
Glendale Union High School District	16,462	X	X	X	X	X	X
Higley Unified School District	12,679	805	900	930	978	982	962
Kyrene Elementary District	15,632	1,372	1,562	1,634	1,662	1,656	1,728
Marana Unified District	12,395	773	876	898	857	855	843
Mesa Unified District	57,956	3,709	4,036	4,061	4,112	4,119	4,255
Paradise Valley Unified District	29,109	1,782	2,043	1,959	2,059	2,047	1,996
Peoria Unified School District	35,329	2,043	2,239	2,324	2,308	2,383	2,434
Phoenix Union High School District	27,037	X	X	X	X	X	X
Scottsdale Unified District	21,496	1,308	1,317	1,348	1,320	1,515	1,464
Sunnyside Unified District	14,942	993	1,045	1,081	1,062	1,064	1,146
Tempe Union High School District	12,868	X	X	X	X	X	X
Tolleson Union High School District	12,442	X	X	X	X	X	X
Tucson Unified District	41,898	2,715	3,048	3,090	2,971	3,137	3,087
Vail Unified District	13,642	839	900	848	944	1,019	1,009
Washington Elementary School District	20,511	1,829	2,165	2,145	2,185	2,182	2,251
ARKANSAS							
Benton School District	5,485	355	408	436	370	422	432
Bentonville School District	17,970	1,367	1,404	1,414	1,416	1,397	1,438
Bryant School District	9,353	602	703	687	695	718	718

NA = Not available.
X = Not applicable.

Table C-3. School Enrollment for the 20 Largest Public School Districts in Each State, by Grade Level, 2020–21—*Continued*

(Number.)

State/School District	Grade 6	Grade 7	Grade 8	Grade 9	Grade 10	Grade 11	Grade 12
ALABAMA							
Auburn City	682	718	672	712	705	677	643
Autauga County	761	741	698	710	724	649	617
Baldwin County	2,385	2,509	2,449	2,482	2,446	2,132	2,122
Birmingham City	1,684	1,694	1,540	1,487	1,444	1,316	1,221
Cullman County	708	726	741	734	699	658	655
Decatur City	694	719	660	659	682	605	578
Elmore County	938	905	862	985	944	797	757
Hoover City	1,091	1,134	1,092	1,100	1,094	1,102	1,111
Huntsville City	1,762	1,947	1,852	1,874	1,811	1,520	1,474
Jefferson County	2,786	2,861	3,025	3,003	2,827	2,807	2,720
Lee County	740	761	759	782	752	661	671
Limestone County	1,075	1,086	1,153	1,083	1,075	1,047	956
Madison City	847	864	916	998	1,016	1,019	999
Madison County	1,463	1,520	1,558	1,526	1,567	1,517	1,390
Mobile County	4,096	4,230	4,062	4,168	3,743	3,487	3,453
Montgomery County	2,213	2,316	2,152	2,345	1,822	1,520	1,550
Shelby County	1,623	1,737	1,714	1,733	1,632	1,566	1,567
St Clair County	689	790	701	755	721	712	620
Tuscaloosa City	829	786	779	813	701	673	711
Tuscaloosa County	1,487	1,354	1,493	1,381	1,378	1,277	1,243
ALASKA							
Anchorage School District	3,244	3,291	3,205	3,207	3,203	3,042	3,382
Bering Strait School District	140	139	130	120	122	111	109
Chugach School District	43	52	45	41	45	39	45
Craig City School District	76	86	63	71	44	41	47
Delta/Greely School District	56	66	57	49	47	47	42
Denali Borough School District	108	100	97	81	90	78	88
Fairbanks North Star Borough School District	888	924	909	848	801	928	806
Galena City School District	736	708	596	529	528	513	560
Juneau Borough School District	318	300	317	338	313	339	323
Kenai Peninsula Borough School District	664	588	639	655	595	579	610
Ketchikan Gateway Borough School District	154	174	163	140	161	165	149
Kodiak Island Borough School District	164	176	168	170	177	143	162
Lower Kuskokwim School District	308	289	295	440	268	241	248
Lower Yukon School District	170	148	157	150	134	116	146
Matanuska-Susitna Borough School District	1,397	1,393	1,420	1,472	1,400	1,364	1,218
Nenana City School District	131	133	122	105	116	215	145
North Slope Borough School District	171	160	139	146	150	134	140
Northwest Arctic Borough School District	165	149	181	129	135	110	129
Sitka School District	103	91	102	91	88	80	100
Yukon-Koyukuk School District	343	329	311	274	257	271	319
ARIZONA							
Cartwright Elementary District	1,725	1,802	1,770	X	X	X	X
Chandler Unified District #80	3,263	3,580	3,773	4,175	4,161	3,991	3,950
Deer Valley Unified District	2,411	2,504	2,673	2,809	2,809	2,642	2,475
Dysart Unified District	1,737	1,863	1,976	2,201	2,103	1,954	1,827
Gilbert Unified District	2,388	2,546	2,816	3,017	2,949	2,625	2,724
Glendale Union High School District	X	X	X	4,420	4,249	3,981	3,812
Higley Unified School District	994	977	976	1,097	1,020	961	939
Kyrene Elementary District	1,809	2,013	1,953	X	X	X	X
Marana Unified District	915	1,011	1,031	1,076	1,044	1,095	988
Mesa Unified District	4,504	4,751	4,779	5,592	5,164	3,964	3,632
Paradise Valley Unified District	2,288	2,235	2,331	2,556	2,483	2,484	2,513
Peoria Unified School District	2,491	2,757	2,832	3,506	3,423	3,077	2,928
Phoenix Union High School District	X	X	X	7,125	6,953	6,544	6,415
Scottsdale Unified District	1,534	1,614	1,674	1,974	2,136	1,956	2,063
Sunnyside Unified District	1,264	1,297	1,293	1,219	1,371	1,072	914
Tempe Union High School District	X	X	X	3,390	3,339	3,006	3,133
Tolleson Union High School District	X	X	X	3,376	3,326	2,998	2,742
Tucson Unified District	3,026	3,210	3,154	3,661	3,543	3,210	3,211
Vail Unified District	1,096	1,205	1,163	1,175	1,064	1,037	1,109
Washington Elementary School District	2,441	2,503	2,427	X	X	X	X
ARKANSAS							
Benton School District	445	428	487	400	435	417	386
Bentonville School District	1,467	1,394	1,426	1,323	1,375	1,273	1,258
Bryant School District	775	811	759	710	713	697	625

NA = Not available.
X = Not applicable.

Table C-3. School Enrollment for the 20 Largest Public School Districts in Each State, by Grade Level, 2020–21—*Continued*

(Number.)

State/School District	Total students in all grades	Kindergarten	Grade 1	Grade 2	Grade 3	Grade 4	Grade 5
ARKANSAS—*(Continued)*							
Cabot School District	10,471	714	732	747	787	746	769
Conway School District	10,035	742	769	793	763	771	768
El Dorado School District	4,150	346	343	290	300	258	315
Fayetteville School District	10,233	739	825	807	894	805	809
Fort Smith School District	14,361	983	1,065	1,027	1,008	1,046	1,106
Jonesboro School District	6,616	508	454	514	504	525	473
Lake Hamilton School District	4,342	290	287	333	305	277	331
Little Rock School District	21,612	1,568	1,715	1,729	1,653	1,704	1,676
North Little Rock School District	7,930	570	583	616	567	584	552
Pulaski County Special School District	11,742	799	860	788	825	837	843
Rogers School District	15,545	1,115	1,134	1,116	1,202	1,139	1,194
Russellville School District	5,361	409	416	395	402	378	347
Sheridan School District	4,183	302	284	306	320	327	324
Siloam Springs School District	4,294	283	305	301	332	318	315
Springdale School District	22,663	1,450	1,607	1,573	1,709	1,656	1,668
Van Buren School District	5,506	379	395	412	392	396	429
West Memphis School District	5,150	426	444	407	405	394	409
CALIFORNIA							
Capistrano Unified	43,719	2,836	2,827	2,851	2,939	3,049	3,142
Clovis Unified	42,790	3,302	3,022	3,091	3,130	3,218	3,228
Corona-Norco Unified	51,318	3,563	3,474	3,542	3,616	3,813	3,830
Elk Grove Unified	63,157	4,605	4,335	4,511	4,614	4,763	4,705
Fresno Unified	70,088	5,918	5,687	5,681	5,657	5,815	5,776
Garden Grove Unified	40,124	2,851	2,651	2,761	2,783	2,730	3,006
Irvine Unified	35,660	2,680	2,547	2,749	2,752	2,785	2,836
Kern High	42,370	X	X	X	X	X	X
Long Beach Unified	69,413	5,250	4,876	5,200	5,150	5,182	5,293
Los Angeles Unified	460,633	42,229	35,338	36,221	37,303	38,397	38,146
Poway Unified	35,663	2,953	2,520	2,547	2,514	2,691	2,621
Riverside Unified	39,443	2,960	2,708	2,770	2,753	2,950	2,819
Sacramento City Unified	40,711	2,856	3,115	3,149	3,186	3,254	3,291
San Bernardino City Unified	46,693	3,463	3,731	3,771	3,821	3,818	3,947
San Diego Unified	97,968	9,088	8,053	8,037	7,975	7,897	7,680
San Francisco Unified	51,790	4,413	4,191	4,165	4,195	4,292	4,013
San Juan Unified	39,218	2,947	2,901	2,942	2,834	2,925	2,987
Santa Ana Unified	44,271	3,278	2,858	2,983	3,225	3,215	3,232
Stockton Unified	36,190	2,521	2,748	2,917	2,893	2,965	2,908
Sweetwater Union High	37,060	0	0	0	0	0	0
COLORADO							
Academy School District No. 20	25,711	1,644	1,736	1,682	1,768	1,872	1,850
Adams 12 Five Star Schools	36,654	2,182	2,480	2,582	2,670	2,682	2,720
Aurora Joint District No. 28	37,907	2,544	2,834	2,832	2,866	2,863	2,958
Boulder Valley School District	29,240	1,529	1,840	1,844	1,977	2,034	2,080
Cherry Creek School District No. 5	54,184	3,330	3,470	3,799	3,744	3,857	3,975
Colorado Springs School District No. 11	23,885	1,557	1,758	1,776	1,729	1,765	1,794
Douglas County School District	62,979	4,016	4,289	4,362	4,531	4,509	4,624
El Paso County Colorado School District 49	23,984	1,387	1,449	1,442	1,411	1,456	1,448
GreeleySchool District No. 6	21,903	1,675	1,731	1,642	1,642	1,623	1,654
Harrison School District No. 2	11,177	851	973	892	883	884	913
Jefferson County School District	80,099	5,254	5,725	5,598	5,630	5,767	5,745
Littleton School District No. 6	14,132	867	910	886	953	957	960
Mesa County Valley School District No. 51	21,084	1,519	1,449	1,451	1,461	1,463	1,568
Poudre School District	29,418	1,914	2,034	2,054	2,155	2,155	2,137
Pueblo School District No. 60	15,219	1,015	1,163	1,151	1,128	1,166	1,246
School District 27J	19,203	1,372	1,406	1,426	1,423	1,419	1,475
School District No. 1	89,081	6,261	6,515	6,418	6,352	6,633	6,678
St. Vrain Valley School District	31,312	2,023	2,146	2,119	2,172	2,260	2,352
State Charter School Institute	20,749	1,686	1,655	1,665	1,650	1,636	1,697
Thompson School District	14,965	1,048	1,078	1,081	1,082	1,057	1,048
CONNECTICUT							
Bridgeport School District	19,276	1,341	1,588	1,522	1,512	1,607	1,443
Bristol School District	7,611	480	557	475	555	550	581
Capitol Region Education Council	8,792	581	585	579	595	591	590
Connecticut Technical Education and Career System	11,331	X	X	X	X	X	X
Danbury School District	11,813	803	907	894	935	883	919

NA = Not available.
X = Not applicable.

Table C-3. School Enrollment for the 20 Largest Public School Districts in Each State, by Grade Level, 2020–21—*Continued*

(Number.)

State/School District	Grade 6	Grade 7	Grade 8	Grade 9	Grade 10	Grade 11	Grade 12
ARKANSAS—(*Continued*)							
Cabot School District	758	805	851	849	842	822	749
Conway School District	770	799	777	738	760	718	681
El Dorado School District	314	324	346	304	346	334	301
Fayetteville School District	775	811	770	756	744	711	705
Fort Smith School District	1,033	1,180	1,134	1,041	1,100	1,074	1,025
Jonesboro School District	502	534	525	449	466	440	445
Lake Hamilton School District	388	358	355	326	360	312	313
Little Rock School District	1,601	1,623	1,582	1,623	1,534	1,443	1,294
North Little Rock School District	575	587	603	599	650	581	539
Pulaski County Special School District	902	907	922	959	974	938	868
Rogers School District	1,225	1,230	1,254	1,214	1,167	1,228	1,129
Russellville School District	450	434	415	388	387	408	371
Sheridan School District	317	337	364	341	319	287	275
Siloam Springs School District	350	325	345	355	334	328	282
Springdale School District	1,817	1,687	1,812	1,798	1,761	1,730	1,613
Van Buren School District	463	447	434	439	434	389	383
West Memphis School District	395	403	405	376	342	349	300
CALIFORNIA							
Capistrano Unified	3,148	3,344	3,677	3,786	4,148	3,838	4,134
Clovis Unified	3,209	3,432	3,512	3,507	3,400	3,462	3,277
Corona-Norco Unified	3,819	4,025	4,092	4,334	4,378	4,376	4,456
Elk Grove Unified	4,587	5,006	5,178	5,287	5,164	5,092	5,310
Fresno Unified	5,374	5,489	5,160	5,367	4,963	4,534	4,667
Garden Grove Unified	3,013	3,138	3,278	3,450	3,448	3,332	3,683
Irvine Unified	2,809	2,769	2,842	2,762	2,658	2,754	2,717
Kern High	X	X	X	10,983	10,535	10,288	10,564
Long Beach Unified	5,076	5,305	5,377	5,746	5,672	5,558	5,728
Los Angeles Unified	32,342	33,452	33,761	34,200	36,205	32,014	31,025
Poway Unified	2,614	2,717	2,799	2,938	2,897	2,851	3,001
Riverside Unified	2,932	3,269	3,210	3,496	3,243	3,213	3,120
Sacramento City Unified	3,213	3,130	3,305	3,232	3,104	2,925	2,951
San Bernardino City Unified	3,589	3,640	3,577	3,663	3,313	3,019	3,341
San Diego Unified	6,459	6,809	6,868	7,302	7,221	6,968	7,611
San Francisco Unified	3,403	3,500	3,600	3,670	4,166	4,152	4,030
San Juan Unified	2,752	3,058	3,039	3,377	3,203	3,091	3,162
Santa Ana Unified	3,330	3,580	3,576	3,803	3,756	3,650	3,785
Stockton Unified	2,698	2,829	2,853	2,877	2,767	2,639	2,575
Sweetwater Union High	0	4,702	5,246	6,662	6,660	6,539	7,251
COLORADO							
Academy School District No. 20	1,938	2,058	2,054	2,239	2,153	2,235	2,234
Adams 12 Five Star Schools	2,815	2,925	2,895	2,932	2,864	3,044	3,026
Aurora Joint District No. 28	3,177	3,014	2,980	2,621	2,549	2,400	2,758
Boulder Valley School District	2,175	2,254	2,356	2,609	2,537	2,606	2,670
Cherry Creek School District No. 5	4,211	4,320	4,337	4,472	4,356	4,372	4,578
Colorado Springs School District No. 11	1,636	1,723	1,729	1,871	1,744	1,767	2,186
Douglas County School District	4,989	5,040	5,264	4,975	5,002	5,027	5,149
El Paso County Colorado School District 49	1,513	1,489	1,502	1,818	2,175	2,501	4,067
Greeley School District No. 6	1,750	1,750	1,753	1,713	1,687	1,565	1,539
Harrison School District No. 2	936	952	943	828	791	690	641
Jefferson County School District	6,087	6,185	6,236	6,393	6,396	6,295	6,713
Littleton School District No. 6	1,014	1,023	1,112	1,220	1,249	1,244	1,339
Mesa County Valley School District No. 51	1,532	1,680	1,672	1,661	1,681	1,575	1,590
Poudre School District	2,283	2,321	2,333	2,410	2,283	2,304	2,388
Pueblo School District No. 60	1,125	1,276	1,117	1,116	1,083	963	1,081
School District 27J	1,523	1,571	1,572	1,479	1,430	1,320	1,256
School District No. 1	6,599	6,835	6,675	7,713	6,754	5,924	5,881
St. Vrain Valley School District	2,398	2,468	2,526	2,643	2,494	2,437	2,294
State Charter School Institute	1,645	1,571	1,535	1,406	1,370	1,351	1,706
Thompson School District	1,162	1,148	1,158	1,181	1,147	1,101	1,265
CONNECTICUT							
Bridgeport School District	1,567	1,378	1,476	1,374	1,404	1,112	1,202
Bristol School District	562	580	630	636	641	531	593
Capitol Region Education Council	697	713	688	617	596	568	495
Connecticut Technical Education and Career System	X	X	X	3,071	2,980	2,746	2,534
Danbury School District	923	969	942	988	814	780	849

NA = Not available.
X = Not applicable.

Table C-3. School Enrollment for the 20 Largest Public School Districts in Each State, by Grade Level, 2020–21—*Continued*

(Number.)

State/School District	Total students in all grades	Kindergarten	Grade 1	Grade 2	Grade 3	Grade 4	Grade 5
CONNECTICUT—*(Continued)*							
East Hartford School District.............................	6,546	429	457	466	480	459	455
Fairfield School District...................................	9,387	588	658	618	641	685	701
Greenwich School District................................	8,773	579	586	656	626	678	672
Hartford School District...................................	17,054	1,086	1,237	1,271	1,229	1,246	1,273
Manchester School District..............................	6,044	447	497	467	443	415	440
Meriden School District	8,072	570	647	608	639	663	665
New Britain School District	9,616	722	761	821	747	783	857
New Haven School District................................	19,827	1,161	1,406	1,389	1,406	1,454	1,465
Norwalk School District	11,509	737	824	824	821	765	833
Southington School District..............................	6,152	426	450	417	423	429	424
Stamford School District..................................	16,157	1,151	1,302	1,243	1,205	1,230	1,228
Stratford School District	6,632	363	449	453	475	482	510
Trumbull School District	6,719	422	459	470	464	484	501
Waterbury School District................................	18,374	1,336	1,447	1,499	1,453	1,377	1,463
West Hartford School District	9,117	583	624	639	621	653	650
DELAWARE							
Appoquinimink School District..........................	11,914	798	837	840	909	921	970
Brandywine School District..............................	10,405	671	736	728	840	797	795
Caesar Rodney School District..........................	7,960	542	569	579	625	649	608
Cape Henlopen School District..........................	5,892	409	463	445	459	433	460
Capital School District....................................	6,332	487	475	507	458	474	418
Christina School District	12,963	1,036	1,041	1,083	1,092	1,176	1,146
Colonial School District...................................	9,795	660	761	757	734	836	851
Delmar School District....................................	1,365	X	X	X	X	X	160
Indian River School District	10,592	762	782	841	853	842	857
Lake Forest School District	3,505	251	308	264	284	305	316
Laurel School District......................................	2,546	166	182	171	205	197	225
Milford School District....................................	4,214	346	327	307	308	348	340
MOT Charter School...	1,383	75	75	78	75	76	75
New Castle County Vocational-Technical School District	4,644	X	X	X	X	X	X
Newark Charter School	2,436	191	189	189	191	191	190
Odyssey Charter School	1,926	184	184	184	185	184	184
Red Clay Consolidated School District................	15,057	1,150	1,145	1,170	1,235	1,245	1,240
Seaford School District	3,224	244	232	266	251	264	283
Smyrna School District....................................	5,883	362	397	435	465	440	468
Woodbridge School District.............................	2,478	178	210	183	173	195	224
DISTRICT OF COLUMBIA							
BASIS DC PCS	664	X	X	X	X	X	135
Capital City PCS..	1,018	46	50	50	50	52	82
Center City PCS..	1,452	133	117	133	136	147	148
DC Prep PCS..	2,168	242	234	235	228	245	155
DC Scholars PCS	608	76	53	61	60	51	48
District of Columbia International School............	1,452	X	X	X	X	X	X
District of Columbia Public Schools...................	49,896	4,000	4,018	3,977	3,996	3,890	3,675
E.L. Haynes PCS...	1,199	52	51	53	49	54	58
Eagle Academy PCS...	706	141	118	140	118	X	X
Elsie Whitlow Stokes Community Freedom PCS .	585	95	95	82	48	47	42
Friendship PCS...	4,565	365	361	355	367	341	308
Ingenuity Prep PCS..	761	81	78	84	71	86	69
KIPP DC PCS	7,000	543	554	548	564	563	529
Meridian PCS...	605	68	56	60	59	58	60
Mundo Verde Bilingual PCS	955	185	187	89	86	79	66
Paul PCS...	726	X	X	X	X	X	X
Rocketship Education DC PCS...........................	1,525	246	231	235	193	138	111
Two Rivers PCS..	985	100	101	101	101	100	100
Washington Latin PCS	734	X	X	X	X	X	95
Washington Yu Ying PCS..................................	580	80	80	78	69	62	53
FLORIDA							
Brevard	70,996	4,884	5,119	4,998	5,185	5,148	5,155
Broward	260,235	16,438	18,364	18,665	19,095	19,812	19,594
Collier...	46,329	2,983	3,232	3,178	3,422	3,543	3,376
Duval..	126,815	9,561	9,963	10,197	10,257	10,447	9,726
Hillsborough	218,943	15,537	16,688	16,608	17,164	17,876	16,723
Lake	43,706	3,016	3,291	3,301	3,199	3,372	3,305
Lee	94,927	6,492	6,724	7,018	7,150	7,310	7,080

NA = Not available.
X = Not applicable.

Table C-3. School Enrollment for the 20 Largest Public School Districts in Each State, by Grade Level, 2020–21—Continued

(Number.)

State/School District	Grade 6	Grade 7	Grade 8	Grade 9	Grade 10	Grade 11	Grade 12
CONNECTICUT—(Continued)							
East Hartford School District	428	533	528	460	450	510	637
Fairfield School District	739	809	738	834	733	731	763
Greenwich School District	644	710	688	691	700	702	698
Hartford School District	1,270	1,267	1,359	1,356	1,260	997	1,122
Manchester School District	464	435	454	449	435	477	426
Meriden School District	579	599	569	610	619	612	585
New Britain School District	763	724	742	894	551	500	567
New Haven School District	1,540	1,601	1,576	1,692	1,497	1,283	1,258
Norwalk School District	881	846	902	1,006	1,010	973	902
Southington School District	489	500	468	483	541	508	508
Stamford School District	1,192	1,215	1,301	1,505	1,091	1,176	1,118
Stratford School District	498	551	550	565	527	512	565
Trumbull School District	464	543	528	554	506	572	556
Waterbury School District	1,438	1,397	1,464	1,557	1,212	1,160	1,065
West Hartford School District	655	707	724	760	731	755	808
DELAWARE							
Appoquinimink School District	988	933	977	875	890	900	899
Brandywine School District	821	889	845	871	840	715	669
Caesar Rodney School District	669	711	646	629	509	513	571
Cape Henlopen School District	432	466	453	502	422	418	399
Capital School District	478	505	477	554	473	442	434
Christina School District	1,089	1,126	1,012	820	747	593	637
Colonial School District	867	882	850	779	629	569	455
Delmar School District	192	187	197	171	159	151	146
Indian River School District	887	888	854	792	794	669	594
Lake Forest School District	321	282	300	240	193	196	185
Laurel School District	212	246	243	179	184	170	138
Milford School District	335	381	331	316	314	259	233
MOT Charter School	77	75	78	186	179	162	172
New Castle County Vocational-Technical School District	X	X	NA	1,251	1,166	1,144	1,083
Newark Charter School	191	191	190	189	186	179	169
Odyssey Charter School	184	175	178	83	72	69	60
Red Clay Consolidated School District	1,334	1,344	1,399	940	942	742	892
Seaford School District	292	275	275	240	229	166	183
Smyrna School District	499	537	491	469	433	400	375
Woodbridge School District	180	200	233	182	201	136	151
DISTRICT OF COLUMBIA							
BASIS DC PCS	128	118	71	71	49	53	39
Capital City PCS	85	83	85	114	82	86	77
Center City PCS	156	157	132	X	X	X	X
DC Prep PCS	148	124	112	X	X	X	X
DC Scholars PCS	59	46	46	X	X	X	X
District of Columbia International School	264	261	269	232	179	151	96
District of Columbia Public Schools	2,838	2,946	2,972	3,990	3,219	2,424	2,449
E.L. Haynes PCS	109	117	105	132	119	105	104
Eagle Academy PCS	X	X	X	X	X	X	X
Elsie Whitlow Stokes Community Freedom PCS	X	X	X	X	X	X	X
Friendship PCS	356	359	337	320	227	169	181
Ingenuity Prep PCS	75	77	X	X	X	X	X
KIPP DC PCS	512	506	486	332	290	261	227
Meridian PCS	57	46	47	X	X	X	X
Mundo Verde Bilingual PCS	X	X	X	X	X	X	X
Paul PCS	112	107	116	119	98	78	96
Rocketship Education DC PCS	X	X	X	X	X	X	X
Two Rivers PCS	109	50	45	X	X	X	X
Washington Latin PCS	94	97	95	91	104	81	77
Washington Yu Ying PCS	X	X	X	X	X	X	X
FLORIDA							
Brevard	5,389	5,889	5,709	5,859	6,107	5,423	4,704
Broward	19,951	20,370	20,556	20,426	20,261	19,759	21,162
Collier	3,623	3,839	3,700	3,877	3,682	3,881	3,466
Duval	10,157	9,764	9,354	10,036	10,040	8,086	7,106
Hillsborough	17,232	17,063	17,525	16,992	16,446	15,421	14,954
Lake	3,345	3,537	3,423	3,536	3,282	3,402	2,926
Lee	7,118	7,542	7,679	7,336	7,253	7,071	7,691

NA – Not available.
X = Not applicable.

Table C-3. School Enrollment for the 20 Largest Public School Districts in Each State, by Grade Level, 2020–21—Continued

(Number.)

State/School District	Total students in all grades	Kindergarten	Grade 1	Grade 2	Grade 3	Grade 4	Grade 5
FLORIDA—(Continued)							
Manatee	49,181	3,302	3,518	3,471	4,067	3,502	3,708
Miami-Dade	334,261	20,246	22,747	23,379	24,493	25,671	24,862
Orange	199,089	12,456	13,928	14,375	14,751	15,948	15,002
Osceola	68,640	4,368	4,741	4,762	5,080	5,133	5,116
Palm Beach	187,057	12,153	13,212	13,608	13,803	14,686	14,036
Pasco	77,125	5,226	5,595	5,595	5,578	6,177	5,818
Pinellas	96,068	6,542	6,818	6,901	6,888	7,043	6,943
Polk	100,495	6,956	7,477	7,407	7,318	8,028	7,523
Sarasota	42,618	2,623	2,967	2,941	3,096	3,250	3,154
Seminole	66,226	4,329	4,676	4,759	4,685	4,974	4,779
St. John's	44,550	2,815	3,094	3,052	3,304	3,220	3,299
St. Lucie	41,779	2,566	2,787	2,800	2,946	3,303	3,053
Volusia	61,088	3,899	4,394	4,436	4,343	4,482	4,650
GEORGIA							
Atlanta Public Schools	51,012	3,659	4,297	4,302	4,210	4,285	4,300
Bibb County	21,373	1,585	1,648	1,636	1,726	1,697	1,664
Cherokee County	41,373	2,603	2,781	2,900	2,928	2,965	3,017
Clayton County	52,149	3,039	3,754	3,881	3,880	3,981	4,094
Cobb County	107,379	6,463	7,502	7,407	7,710	7,871	8,076
Columbia County	28,266	1,911	1,966	2,040	2,035	2,144	2,181
Coweta County	22,241	1,370	1,535	1,571	1,513	1,603	1,568
DeKalb County	93,470	5,967	7,291	7,281	7,306	7,363	7,199
Douglas County	25,884	1,592	1,671	1,779	1,802	1,897	1,901
Fayette County	19,912	1,086	1,222	1,279	1,339	1,337	1,507
Forsyth County	51,152	3,263	3,327	3,669	3,664	3,887	4,123
Fulton County	90,300	5,125	5,982	6,131	6,342	6,455	6,739
Gwinnett County	177,401	10,820	11,882	12,292	12,747	12,923	13,120
Hall County	26,914	1,833	1,830	1,830	1,848	1,871	1,991
Henry County	42,388	2,405	2,739	2,702	2,778	2,977	3,133
Houston County	29,681	2,044	1,984	2,173	2,174	2,192	2,168
Muscogee County	30,757	2,155	2,272	2,313	2,359	2,333	2,399
Paulding County	29,966	1,885	2,058	2,149	2,161	2,189	2,306
Richmond County	29,093	1,996	2,260	2,214	2,291	2,229	2,249
Savannah-Chatham County	36,502	2,646	2,901	2,823	2,761	2,661	2,835
HAWAII							
Hawaii Department of Education	176,441	12,064	13,832	14,241	14,157	14,239	14,543
IDAHO							
Boise Independent District	23,703	1,454	1,552	1,547	1,635	1,637	1,793
Bonneville Joint District	13,230	963	901	941	976	970	963
Caldwell District	5,584	384	424	449	446	422	469
Cassia County Joint District	5,391	353	429	364	406	412	420
Coeur D'Alene District	10,011	606	718	747	735	786	805
Idaho Falls District	9,813	700	685	704	743	702	761
Jefferson County Joint District	6,287	468	432	489	476	460	467
Jerome Joint District	4,072	294	269	308	281	303	303
Joint School District No. 2	37,989	2,271	2,437	2,496	2,583	2,808	2,696
Kuna Joint District	5,416	367	371	380	350	370	370
Lakeland District	4,290	264	331	325	274	334	309
Lewiston Independent District	4,578	340	338	335	352	338	340
Madison District	5,370	389	392	413	374	400	381
Minidoka County Joint District	4,253	274	312	331	295	316	340
Nampa School District	14,899	1,013	1,167	1,100	1,122	1,134	1,141
Oneida County District	7,809	893	943	955	935	873	781
Pocatello District	11,885	813	809	831	804	878	862
Post Falls District	5,813	388	427	414	463	426	468
Twin Falls District	9,126	571	617	675	683	727	714
Vallivue School Distrct	8,916	584	685	672	626	664	670
ILLINOIS							
Aurora East USD 131	13,224	825	862	900	887	972	1,046
City of Chicago SD 299	341,382	21,844	23,778	23,671	24,122	25,382	25,372
CUSD 200	11,903	814	810	806	846	879	843
CUSD 300	20,216	1,273	1,363	1,337	1,425	1,467	1,472
CUSD 308	17,169	1,071	1,080	1,136	1,126	1,186	1,270
Indian Prairie CUSD 204	26,091	1,515	1,643	1,727	1,785	1,858	1,956
McLean County USD 5	12,536	810	889	898	847	975	927

NA = Not available.
X = Not applicable.

Table C-3. School Enrollment for the 20 Largest Public School Districts in Each State, by Grade Level, 2020–21—*Continued*

(Number.)

State/School District	Grade 6	Grade 7	Grade 8	Grade 9	Grade 10	Grade 11	Grade 12
FLORIDA (*Continued*)							
Manatee	3,713	4,023	4,069	3,976	3,742	3,587	3,444
Miami-Dade	26,154	26,843	26,471	27,029	26,356	25,581	26,280
Orange	15,281	15,991	15,574	16,480	15,551	15,589	15,760
Osceola	5,551	5,687	5,513	5,606	5,662	5,310	5,045
Palm Beach	14,488	15,077	14,648	14,976	14,609	14,087	14,546
Pasco	6,027	6,333	6,036	6,308	5,933	5,863	5,401
Pinellas	7,160	7,571	7,354	7,920	7,642	7,757	7,223
Polk	7,685	7,881	7,528	8,770	7,847	7,251	6,842
Sarasota	3,369	3,482	3,520	3,635	3,496	3,412	3,222
Seminole	5,337	5,231	4,906	6,037	5,472	5,384	4,727
St. John's	3,465	3,594	3,651	3,881	3,725	3,528	3,240
St. Lucie	3,166	3,380	3,415	3,592	3,498	3,341	3,470
Volusia	4,829	4,955	4,854	5,554	5,042	4,557	4,213
GEORGIA							
Atlanta Public Schools	4,150	3,828	3,923	3,876	3,424	2,987	2,617
Bibb County	1,702	1,671	1,620	1,771	1,471	1,226	1,131
Cherokee County	3,168	3,288	3,431	3,972	3,494	3,228	3,032
Clayton County	4,154	4,409	4,396	4,412	4,481	3,662	3,264
Cobb County	8,333	8,588	8,897	9,413	9,355	8,346	8,660
Columbia County	2,238	2,253	2,269	2,344	2,278	2,098	2,037
Coweta County	1,688	1,754	1,754	2,029	1,954	1,740	1,614
DeKalb County	7,283	7,192	7,207	8,242	6,650	6,087	5,862
Douglas County	2,117	2,146	2,182	2,331	2,266	2,070	1,962
Fayette County	1,541	1,634	1,610	1,867	1,735	1,699	1,696
Forsyth County	4,057	4,200	4,103	4,274	4,143	4,109	3,893
Fulton County	6,908	7,026	7,227	8,082	7,773	7,374	7,250
Gwinnett County	14,019	14,707	14,849	15,450	15,326	14,528	13,695
Hall County	2,089	2,256	2,308	2,414	2,541	1,952	1,795
Henry County	3,280	3,555	3,745	3,956	3,954	3,445	3,379
Houston County	2,319	2,356	2,396	2,424	2,286	2,141	1,964
Muscogee County	2,283	2,438	2,464	2,529	2,285	1,989	1,987
Paulding County	2,326	2,413	2,534	2,567	2,538	2,327	2,282
Richmond County	2,296	2,268	2,378	2,414	2,268	1,889	1,543
Savannah-Chatham County	3,029	2,987	2,816	3,165	2,578	1,881	1,848
HAWAII							
Hawaii Department of Education	11,216	14,118	13,765	14,710	13,794	12,371	11,185
IDAHO							
Boise Independent District	1,865	1,929	1,989	1,920	2,129	2,019	1,963
Bonneville Joint District	1,100	1,053	1,078	1,100	1,084	1,037	985
Caldwell District	381	436	446	445	446	365	406
Cassia County Joint District	418	418	450	422	438	393	406
Coeur D'Alene District	724	771	794	855	860	804	751
Idaho Falls District	739	838	830	763	776	675	755
Jefferson County Joint District	516	517	517	508	478	435	432
Jerome Joint District	333	345	323	359	326	304	288
Joint School District No. 2	2,904	3,148	3,213	3,348	3,304	3,166	3,235
Kuna Joint District	435	418	466	490	465	433	441
Lakeland District	305	369	366	341	359	348	338
Lewiston Independent District	315	362	331	386	366	365	339
Madison District	395	420	392	450	427	426	415
Minidoka County Joint District	339	395	337	355	340	296	271
Nampa School District	1,175	1,188	1,236	1,186	1,187	1,081	982
Oneida County District	736	617	549	236	167	59	61
Pocatello District	875	934	926	1,040	1,004	940	950
Post Falls District	449	458	504	458	448	436	429
Twin Falls District	728	775	781	761	682	726	599
Vallivue School District	653	751	786	727	714	671	613
ILLINOIS							
Aurora East USD 131	996	1,032	1,090	1,255	1,108	911	707
City of Chicago SD 299	26,256	27,041	27,058	25,799	27,305	26,193	26,122
CUSD 200	948	928	952	923	950	987	994
CUSD 300	1,547	1,619	1,598	1,738	1,713	1,556	1,624
CUSD 308	1,329	1,373	1,407	1,437	1,450	1,456	1,439
Indian Prairie CUSD 204	1,994	2,058	2,172	2,170	2,189	2,293	2,332
McLean County USD 5	892	1,018	1,028	1,025	961	936	971

NA = Not available.
X = Not applicable.

Table C-3. School Enrollment for the 20 Largest Public School Districts in Each State, by Grade Level, 2020–21—*Continued*

(Number.)

State/School District	Total students in all grades	Kindergarten	Grade 1	Grade 2	Grade 3	Grade 4	Grade 5
ILLINOIS—*(Continued)*							
Naperville CUSD 203	16,289	1,019	1,164	1,101	1,217	1,156	1,248
Palatine CCSD 15	11,540	1,035	1,104	1,249	1,164	1,199	1,205
Peoria SD 150	12,515	857	936	909	922	927	895
Plainfield SD 202	25,085	1,295	1,569	1,615	1,611	1,691	1,783
Rockford SD 205	26,739	1,791	1,969	1,898	1,878	2,003	1,902
Schaumburg CCSD 54	15,292	1,554	1,600	1,659	1,708	1,659	1,677
SD U-46	36,476	2,310	2,497	2,446	2,451	2,599	2,495
Springfield SD 186	13,483	978	995	1,003	1,004	1,012	978
St Charles CUSD 303	11,896	682	793	787	732	832	841
Township HSD 211	11,968	X	X	X	X	X	X
Township HSD 214	12,061	X	X	X	X	X	X
Valley View CUSD 365U	15,521	911	979	956	1,027	1,027	1,126
Waukegan CUSD 60	14,455	842	960	948	1,037	1,073	1,165
INDIANA							
Bartholomew Consolidated School Corp	11,474	843	860	867	854	805	846
Carmel Clay Schools	16,395	1,053	1,156	1,157	1,218	1,179	1,228
Elkhart Community Schools	11,939	849	927	853	894	874	897
Evansville Vanderburgh School Corp	22,191	1,533	1,588	1,559	1,682	1,599	1,724
Fort Wayne Community Schools	28,460	2,100	2,245	2,108	2,148	2,207	2,171
Franklin Township Community School Corp	10,587	837	797	782	818	765	781
Hamilton Southeastern Schools	21,760	1,306	1,550	1,532	1,554	1,589	1,610
Indianapolis Public Schools	22,928	1,654	1,899	1,828	1,889	1,872	1,917
MSD Lawrence Township	15,683	999	1,135	1,042	1,130	1,156	1,193
MSD Pike Township	10,919	692	842	712	808	813	829
MSD Warren Township	11,612	758	898	756	846	846	873
MSD Washington Township	10,888	650	803	756	775	747	818
MSD Wayne Township	16,473	1,074	1,229	1,111	1,222	1,263	1,225
New Albany-Floyd County Consolidated School Corp	11,524	783	876	783	855	848	830
Penn-Harris-Madison School Corp	11,488	724	795	830	858	846	760
Perry Township Schools	16,835	1,265	1,409	1,362	1,392	1,336	1,315
School City of Hammond	12,303	806	896	878	897	931	1,023
South Bend Community School Corp	16,297	1,083	1,172	1,190	1,198	1,180	1,152
Tippecanoe School Corp	13,464	1,085	1,048	1,011	1,098	1,009	1,106
Vigo County School Corp	13,674	1,142	1,128	1,047	1,044	1,014	1,044
IOWA							
Ankeny Community School District	12,188	917	940	907	896	942	899
Bettendorf Community School District	4,719	299	302	319	302	291	333
Cedar Falls Community School District	5,808	476	415	422	441	417	421
Cedar Rapids Community School District	15,786	1,136	1,121	1,090	1,092	1,097	1,113
College Community School District	5,669	388	365	366	401	390	437
Council Bluffs Community School District	8,910	611	648	688	650	626	646
Davenport Community School District	14,609	1,044	1,087	1,030	979	1,035	970
Des Moines Independent Community School District	31,720	2,193	2,340	2,270	2,268	2,259	2,245
Dubuque Community School District	10,746	728	777	707	710	734	741
Iowa City Community School District	14,428	1,027	1,016	1,085	1,086	1,058	1,129
Johnston Community School District	7,408	535	500	488	498	542	523
Linn-Mar Community School District	7,762	599	525	642	556	560	585
Marshalltown Community School District	5,076	352	326	332	359	349	371
Muscatine Community School District	4,778	305	342	311	281	283	341
Pleasant Valley Community School District	5,331	378	375	394	428	397	385
Sioux City Community School District	14,941	1,127	1,079	1,085	1,041	1,041	1,064
Southeast Polk Community School District	7,139	482	492	495	490	497	539
Waterloo Community School District	10,741	748	809	785	780	781	794
Waukee Community School District	11,781	909	975	1,004	947	948	927
West Des Moines Community School District	9,248	617	626	681	639	607	669
KANSAS							
Andover	8,737	362	666	807	734	826	744
Auburn Washburn	6,016	351	408	411	406	477	431
Blue Valley	22,148	1,391	1,511	1,544	1,554	1,602	1,684
De Soto	7,112	458	468	469	546	486	520
Derby	7,255	481	503	497	531	596	553
Dodge City	7,124	522	567	516	498	538	512
Garden City	7,370	558	516	494	464	522	564
Gardner Edgerton	5,831	411	402	437	455	429	448

NA = Not available.
X = Not applicable.

Table C-3. School Enrollment for the 20 Largest Public School Districts in Each State, by Grade Level, 2020–21—*Continued*

(Number.)

State/School District	Grade 6	Grade 7	Grade 8	Grade 9	Grade 10	Grade 11	Grade 12
ILLINOIS (*Continued*)							
Naperville CUSD 203	1,215	1,242	1,226	1,236	1,358	1,390	1,369
Palatine CCSD 15	1,275	1,368	1,409	X	X	X	X
Peoria SD 150	976	934	968	1,127	1,019	794	847
Plainfield SD 202	1,871	2,016	2,134	2,203	2,213	2,295	2,300
Rockford SD 205	2,040	2,080	1,996	2,522	2,095	1,655	1,450
Schaumburg CCSD 54	1,616	1,706	1,648	X	X	X	X
SD U-46	2,788	2,858	2,912	3,350	2,995	3,037	2,684
Springfield SD 186	972	1,041	1,005	1,269	998	923	771
St Charles CUSD 303	836	911	954	1,007	1,031	1,074	1,204
Township HSD 211	X	X	X	2,929	3,023	3,026	2,990
Township HSD 214	X	X	X	3,001	2,971	3,020	3,069
Valley View CUSD 365U	1,174	1,268	1,304	1,364	1,368	1,285	1,331
Waukegan CUSD 60	1,154	1,164	1,183	1,200	1,156	1,087	1,071
INDIANA							
Bartholomew Consolidated School Corp	868	838	850	963	972	901	819
Carmel Clay Schools	1,268	1,266	1,368	1,336	1,331	1,347	1,400
Elkhart Community Schools	949	962	999	920	886	861	783
Evansville Vanderburgh School Corp	1,647	1,746	1,767	1,797	1,727	1,668	1,605
Fort Wayne Community Schools	2,115	2,216	2,144	2,153	2,215	1,951	1,918
Franklin Township Community School Corp	840	843	837	817	767	770	695
Hamilton Southeastern Schools	1,730	1,744	1,766	1,782	1,804	1,709	1,713
Indianapolis Public Schools	1,940	1,844	1,730	1,440	1,472	1,465	1,278
MSD Lawrence Township	1,205	1,270	1,252	1,321	1,286	1,222	1,176
MSD Pike Township	889	940	902	918	869	830	775
MSD Warren Township	865	930	951	940	937	940	873
MSD Washington Township	821	835	841	955	969	934	896
MSD Wayne Township	1,313	1,315	1,261	1,365	1,294	1,322	1,405
New Albany-Floyd County Consolidated School Corp	864	916	921	996	964	897	869
Penn-Harris-Madison School Corp	872	858	879	871	881	848	830
Perry Township Schools	1,328	1,222	1,257	1,189	1,188	1,196	1,098
School City of Hammond	915	891	953	915	962	912	861
South Bend Community School Corp	1,211	1,209	1,228	1,301	1,213	1,233	1,245
Tippecanoe School Corp	1,085	1,092	1,075	1,047	982	924	902
Vigo County School Corp	1,056	1,049	1,049	1,066	1,008	1,000	926
IOWA							
Ankeny Community School District	911	981	889	905	908	874	895
Bettendorf Community School District	357	376	355	378	374	399	372
Cedar Falls Community School District	440	433	476	437	404	444	382
Cedar Rapids Community School District	1,111	1,179	1,156	1,223	1,273	1,197	1,158
College Community School District	454	420	457	445	434	423	409
Council Bluffs Community School District	672	656	623	660	672	623	710
Davenport Community School District	1,052	1,101	1,126	1,155	1,141	1,133	1,035
Des Moines Independent Community School District	2,277	2,344	2,400	2,383	2,302	2,323	2,633
Dubuque Community School District	748	814	841	712	807	772	903
Iowa City Community School District	1,016	1,098	1,096	1,095	1,030	1,119	1,092
Johnston Community School District	577	549	563	555	583	589	600
Linn-Mar Community School District	592	576	601	579	555	532	567
Marshalltown Community School District	390	420	396	395	396	371	376
Muscatine Community School District	357	373	362	387	382	342	378
Pleasant Valley Community School District	389	381	443	424	393	366	358
Sioux City Community School District	1,114	1,137	1,140	1,144	1,146	1,089	1,031
Southeast Polk Community School District	504	500	676	598	579	465	530
Waterloo Community School District	781	808	798	984	854	742	585
Waukee Community School District	927	895	899	871	786	755	736
West Des Moines Community School District	712	663	733	703	758	680	708
KANSAS							
Andover	829	730	792	540	537	461	491
Auburn Washburn	472	486	493	480	484	432	505
Blue Valley	1,653	1,693	1,800	1,787	1,756	1,928	1,852
De Soto	558	594	541	593	550	584	616
Derby	564	625	574	562	568	554	492
Dodge City	547	518	517	496	472	503	492
Garden City	531	527	591	624	540	514	454
Gardner Edgerton	426	475	477	413	479	407	399

NA = Not available.
X = Not applicable.

Table C-3. School Enrollment for the 20 Largest Public School Districts in Each State, by Grade Level, 2020–21—*Continued*

(Number.)

State/School District	Total students in all grades	Kindergarten	Grade 1	Grade 2	Grade 3	Grade 4	Grade 5
KANSAS—(*Continued*)							
Geary County Schools	7,041	674	678	553	610	562	531
Goddard	6,167	416	410	419	414	443	418
Kansas City	22,140	1,508	1,678	1,630	1,715	1,587	1,684
Lawrence	11,427	717	762	808	853	801	861
Maize	7,798	511	466	544	520	562	605
Manhattan-Ogden	6,675	483	480	463	489	460	478
Olathe	29,128	1,860	2,005	2,047	1,990	2,033	2,081
Salina	6,898	498	450	492	478	489	526
Shawnee Mission Pub Sch	26,117	1,820	1,869	1,891	1,989	1,957	1,887
Spring Hill	5,836	423	422	440	445	421	465
Topeka Public Schools	12,436	893	930	950	890	945	890
Wichita	46,908	3,309	3,395	3,492	3,449	3,546	3,647
KENTUCKY							
Boone County	20,280	1,298	1,434	1,498	1,337	1,515	1,558
Bullitt County	12,725	841	932	933	764	891	953
Christian County	8,219	610	652	625	558	589	629
Daviess County	11,102	708	842	831	747	812	822
Fayette County	41,203	2,823	3,135	3,124	2,773	3,199	3,102
Hardin County	14,655	965	1,087	1,055	910	1,040	1,016
Henderson County	7,044	450	564	485	437	478	485
Hopkins County	6,498	449	453	446	409	467	525
Jefferson County	95,911	6,876	7,369	7,231	6,335	7,350	7,381
Jessamine County	8,207	546	613	580	554	611	556
Kenton County	14,021	986	1,049	1,040	864	1,059	1,120
Laurel County	8,850	587	701	652	618	627	646
Madison County	11,045	749	784	838	756	849	815
McCracken County	6,905	515	531	510	464	496	521
Oldham County	12,416	793	797	890	820	916	911
Pike County	8,094	561	599	559	543	547	507
Pulaski County	8,294	580	551	575	515	580	581
Scott County	9,440	642	667	731	616	652	724
Shelby County	6,961	467	498	489	479	472	529
Warren County	16,860	1,178	1,296	1,255	1,095	1,258	1,234
LOUISIANA							
Acadia Parish	9,603	812	816	708	709	707	721
Ascension Parish	23,154	1,622	1,706	1,726	1,688	1,711	1,711
Bossier Parish	22,431	1,721	1,764	1,672	1,759	1,632	1,712
Caddo Parish	36,153	2,526	2,728	2,657	2,748	2,726	2,667
Calcasieu Parish	27,932	1,963	2,117	2,165	2,024	2,005	2,109
East Baton Rouge Parish	40,283	3,190	3,342	3,260	3,139	3,086	2,995
Iberia Parish	11,822	963	936	896	817	831	887
Jefferson Parish	48,160	3,538	3,847	3,770	3,780	3,721	3,678
Lafayette Parish	30,878	2,291	2,497	2,245	2,184	2,214	2,202
Lafourche Parish	14,393	1,050	1,142	1,079	1,050	1,017	1,041
Livingston Parish	25,687	1,918	1,992	1,915	1,846	1,839	1,886
Ouachita Parish	18,355	1,354	1,496	1,380	1,300	1,347	1,335
Rapides Parish	22,297	1,554	1,690	1,616	1,530	1,579	1,568
St. Charles Parish	9,460	660	751	726	670	670	688
St. Landry Parish	12,527	890	956	959	926	984	914
St. Tammany Parish	36,820	2,550	2,866	2,700	2,432	2,614	2,628
Tangipahoa Parish	19,549	1,404	1,476	1,441	1,409	1,462	1,316
Terrebonne Parish	16,563	1,229	1,246	1,169	1,214	1,216	1,234
Vermilion Parish	9,516	710	779	697	669	730	716
Vernon Parish	8,125	729	640	650	658	601	599
MAINE							
Auburn Public Schools	3,383	213	253	213	255	246	253
Bangor Public Schools	3,468	236	270	232	240	235	253
Biddeford Public Schools	2,346	180	191	176	148	162	198
Brunswick Public Schools	2,375	146	188	170	169	198	160
Gorham Public Schools	2,742	200	204	225	222	218	206
Lewiston Public Schools	5,184	401	381	372	379	366	368
Portland Public Schools	6,523	481	482	466	478	496	498
RSU 06/MSAD 06	3,429	243	240	248	250	229	233
RSU 14	3,139	205	252	244	230	214	240
RSU 17/MSAD 17	3,192	199	206	206	203	228	254
RSU 18	2,714	176	180	178	193	166	169

NA = Not available.
X = Not applicable.

Table C-3. School Enrollment for the 20 Largest Public School Districts in Each State, by Grade Level, 2020–21—Continued

(Number.)

State/School District	Grade 6	Grade 7	Grade 8	Grade 9	Grade 10	Grade 11	Grade 12
KANSAS—(Continued)							
Geary County Schools............................	510	488	493	398	408	339	335
Goddard..	503	568	572	505	477	450	463
Kansas City	1,688	1,721	1,712	1,770	1,649	1,396	1,339
Lawrence..	787	911	877	985	927	951	976
Maize..	650	614	633	589	586	617	561
Manhattan-Ogden.................................	501	503	547	496	513	477	509
Olathe..	2,129	2,282	2,392	2,324	2,343	2,326	2,350
Salina...	508	535	532	535	526	520	525
Shawnee Mission Pub Sch......................	1,934	2,067	1,926	2,198	2,035	2,000	1,916
Spring Hill..	456	445	481	435	388	412	417
Topeka Public Schools...........................	904	925	920	912	1,026	971	861
Wichita...	3,579	3,682	3,427	3,387	3,367	3,228	3,129
KENTUCKY							
Boone County	1,582	1,663	1,630	1,753	1,641	1,547	1,491
Bullitt County.......................................	1,022	1,091	1,058	1,027	1,003	954	1,048
Christian County	664	632	640	632	644	625	563
Daviess County	784	880	839	856	891	898	808
Fayette County	3,241	3,254	3,308	3,541	3,319	3,007	2,759
Hardin County	1,048	1,179	1,186	1,238	1,169	1,100	1,079
Henderson County	560	556	580	559	575	567	475
Hopkins County	519	553	560	564	520	440	430
Jefferson County...................................	7,309	7,439	7,514	7,881	7,946	6,997	6,366
Jessamine County..................................	675	679	699	709	646	578	539
Kenton County	1,125	1,102	1,142	1,128	1,151	1,081	969
Laurel County.......................................	712	712	660	761	704	688	613
Madison County	941	885	903	918	883	801	776
McCracken County.................................	506	520	532	589	550	465	489
Oldham County	968	1,047	985	1,054	1,048	1,025	989
Pike County..	609	600	651	638	662	615	579
Pulaski County......................................	651	631	655	682	713	654	620
Scott County	763	732	763	829	773	711	578
Shelby County.......................................	535	514	575	623	551	499	544
Warren County	1,228	1,314	1,273	1,391	1,358	1,235	1,092
LOUISIANA							
Acadia Parish	744	727	721	751	706	582	536
Ascension Parish	1,811	1,742	1,876	1,900	1,758	1,785	1,554
Bossier Parish.......................................	1,658	1,781	1,692	1,781	1,750	1,527	1,506
Caddo Parish..	2,765	2,749	2,679	3,000	2,938	2,603	2,567
Calcasieu Parish....................................	2,125	2,061	2,268	2,285	2,216	2,006	1,880
East Baton Rouge Parish........................	3,129	2,999	2,861	2,868	2,854	2,586	2,457
Iberia Parish...	963	877	943	938	853	809	754
Jefferson Parish....................................	3,776	3,801	3,600	3,721	3,475	3,071	2,796
Lafayette Parish....................................	2,359	2,436	2,274	2,655	2,640	2,423	1,913
Lafourche Parish...................................	1,108	1,137	1,140	1,068	1,125	963	848
Livingston Parish	1,976	2,098	2,132	2,126	1,973	1,804	1,634
Ouachita Parish.....................................	1,365	1,426	1,506	1,425	1,427	1,287	1,205
Rapides Parish......................................	1,658	1,687	1,699	1,781	1,679	1,676	1,506
St. Charles Parish	779	726	749	770	723	718	651
St. Landry Parish	968	953	923	1,158	871	895	690
St. Tammany Parish...............................	2,782	2,988	3,112	3,246	2,846	2,614	2,580
Tangipahoa Parish.................................	1,446	1,524	1,547	1,716	1,538	1,386	1,113
Terrebonne Parish.................................	1,270	1,356	1,228	1,444	1,151	1,092	995
Vermilion Parish....................................	729	742	786	717	692	613	567
Vernon Parish	680	625	620	564	513	482	462
MAINE							
Auburn Public Schools...........................	280	256	257	286	254	241	260
Bangor Public Schools...........................	237	264	258	274	286	288	301
Biddeford Public Schools........................	155	170	168	187	178	202	171
Brunswick Public Schools.......................	175	165	172	203	177	202	176
Gorham Public Schools	212	203	198	217	194	231	212
Lewiston Public Schools.........................	394	386	390	379	400	387	401
Portland Public Schools..........................	470	499	468	472	513	517	531
RSU 06/MSAD 06	266	272	255	260	265	306	300
RSU 14	212	285	280	226	248	232	239
RSU 17/MSAD 17	228	244	245	264	297	259	271
RSU 18	213	226	217	231	234	230	212

NA = Not available.
X = Not applicable.

Table C-3. School Enrollment for the 20 Largest Public School Districts in Each State, by Grade Level, 2020–21—*Continued*

(Number.)

State/School District	Total students in all grades	Kindergarten	Grade 1	Grade 2	Grade 3	Grade 4	Grade 5
MAINE—*(Continued)*							
RSU 21	2,494	132	160	142	177	162	169
RSU 57/MSAD 57	2,752	175	179	182	198	191	199
RSU 60/MSAD 60	2,931	195	194	211	223	203	227
RSU 75/MSAD 75	2,408	161	181	172	180	194	183
Saco Public Schools	2,782	195	209	176	187	181	197
Sanford Public Schools	3,107	188	222	220	196	217	233
Scarborough Public Schools	2,872	174	221	212	197	207	210
South Portland Public Schools	2,913	229	204	208	184	212	217
Westbrook Public Schools	2,369	170	192	168	182	181	195
MARYLAND							
Allegany County Public Schools	8,075	512	574	550	600	614	618
Anne Arundel County Public Schools	83,044	5,773	6,168	6,096	6,326	6,397	6,471
Baltimore City Public Schools	77,856	5,635	5,956	6,109	5,881	5,983	5,815
Baltimore County Public Schools	111,084	7,352	8,035	8,145	8,325	8,540	8,485
Calvert County Public Schools	15,292	943	1,002	1,015	1,013	1,146	1,079
Caroline County Public Schools	5,553	387	354	391	381	408	395
Carroll County Public Schools	24,568	1,678	1,748	1,723	1,783	1,749	1,803
Cecil County Public Schools	14,718	968	985	1,028	1,033	1,041	1,042
Charles County Public Schools	26,768	1,587	1,721	1,834	1,969	1,872	1,963
Dorchester County Public Schools	4,662	282	360	343	334	314	348
Frederick County Public Schools	43,221	2,792	3,015	3,039	3,051	3,210	3,204
Harford County Public Schools	37,333	2,593	2,741	2,607	2,663	2,775	2,759
Howard County Public Schools	57,293	3,634	3,919	4,115	4,067	4,327	4,273
Montgomery County Public Schools	160,564	10,347	11,399	11,573	11,622	11,858	12,100
Prince George's County Public Schools	131,646	8,639	9,885	9,860	9,997	10,154	10,361
Queen Anne's County Public Schools	7,395	473	478	476	495	556	504
St. Mary's County Public Schools	17,246	1,143	1,224	1,218	1,237	1,264	1,314
Washington County Public Schools	21,939	1,428	1,537	1,572	1,493	1,618	1,562
Wicomico County Public Schools	14,354	943	1,109	1,132	1,117	1,129	1,062
Worcester County Public Schools	6,711	405	451	445	454	497	492
MASSACHUSETTS							
Boston	48,112	3,244	3,508	3,635	3,637	3,583	3,306
Brockton	15,384	1,149	1,046	1,069	1,173	1,296	1,283
Brookline	6,891	488	501	505	545	495	543
Chicopee	6,850	412	464	459	505	552	528
Everett	6,883	363	532	490	536	517	524
Fall River	9,998	715	848	828	866	867	902
Framingham	8,733	660	659	794	688	722	723
Haverhill	7,771	472	585	606	651	641	643
Lawrence	12,842	730	951	1,012	1,016	1,044	1,074
Lexington	6,901	309	408	480	507	532	554
Lowell	14,023	1,019	1,108	1,219	1,116	1,172	1,109
Lynn	15,587	1,086	1,088	1,189	1,221	1,210	1,184
New Bedford	12,565	956	1,037	1,078	1,057	1,157	1,049
Newton	12,024	674	819	854	870	928	909
Plymouth	7,085	458	482	508	513	512	461
Quincy	9,480	677	743	747	718	689	676
Revere	7,166	471	561	557	555	565	560
Springfield	24,239	1,589	1,895	1,877	1,805	1,847	1,721
Taunton	7,735	518	569	570	596	597	612
Worcester	23,986	1,529	1,876	1,851	1,800	1,765	1,751
MICHIGAN							
Ann Arbor Public Schools	17,451	1,481	1,273	1,253	1,223	1,311	1,248
Chippewa Valley Schools	14,855	858	994	932	969	1,029	1,031
Dearborn City School District	20,417	1,407	1,420	1,400	1,382	1,512	1,492
Detroit Public Schools Community District	48,782	3,145	3,933	4,186	3,962	4,068	3,872
Farmington Public School District	9,108	644	722	669	683	659	646
Forest Hills Public Schools	9,365	623	656	656	649	673	710
Grand Rapids Public Schools	14,034	1,152	1,181	1,111	1,108	1,137	1,031
Kalamazoo Public Schools	12,581	906	995	1,012	960	992	975
Kentwood Public Schools	9,228	819	691	697	674	656	680
L'Anse Creuse Public Schools	9,881	665	675	691	681	752	649
Lansing Public School District	9,989	830	918	836	787	777	724
Livonia Public Schools School District	13,457	969	941	965	987	969	965
Plymouth-Canton Community Schools	16,632	1,036	984	1,066	1,074	1,183	1,135
Rochester Community School District	15,092	1,027	1,050	1,047	1,086	1,153	1,090

NA = Not available.
X = Not applicable.

Table C-3. School Enrollment for the 20 Largest Public School Districts in Each State, by Grade Level, 2020–21—*Continued*

(Number.)

State/School District	Grade 6	Grade 7	Grade 8	Grade 9	Grade 10	Grade 11	Grade 12
MAINE—*(Continued)*							
RSU 21	181	211	219	192	204	217	238
RSU 57/MSAD 57	210	226	221	231	216	213	231
RSU 60/MSAD 60	227	254	268	236	237	239	217
RSU 75/MSAD 75	214	182	177	182	185	197	178
Saco Public Schools	198	195	208	213	232	244	249
Sanford Public Schools	252	235	239	260	270	284	247
Scarborough Public Schools	246	251	212	216	228	252	246
South Portland Public Schools	234	218	241	224	228	225	232
Westbrook Public Schools	194	183	199	184	159	161	179
MARYLAND							
Allegany County Public Schools	617	618	618	634	573	607	608
Anne Arundel County Public Schools	6,531	6,512	6,538	6,463	6,330	5,878	5,632
Baltimore City Public Schools	6,061	5,977	5,782	7,239	5,799	4,458	4,345
Baltimore County Public Schools	8,605	8,758	8,621	8,477	8,962	7,759	8,143
Calvert County Public Schools	1,159	1,223	1,257	1,301	1,263	1,225	1,326
Caroline County Public Schools	397	453	456	493	405	381	407
Carroll County Public Schools	1,796	1,965	1,952	2,048	1,978	2,009	2,020
Cecil County Public Schools	1,152	1,192	1,182	1,252	1,139	1,101	1,107
Charles County Public Schools	2,009	2,136	2,233	2,284	2,236	2,102	2,093
Dorchester County Public Schools	374	391	374	430	347	330	265
Frederick County Public Schools	3,351	3,424	3,529	3,702	3,436	3,201	3,204
Harford County Public Schools	2,913	3,034	3,024	3,220	2,875	2,748	2,593
Howard County Public Schools	4,462	4,649	4,599	4,702	4,608	4,491	4,433
Montgomery County Public Schools	12,283	12,658	12,435	14,133	13,441	11,545	11,573
Prince George's County Public Schools	10,278	10,402	10,267	11,349	9,654	8,710	8,174
Queen Anne's County Public Schools	597	610	598	629	594	597	564
St. Mary's County Public Schools	1,294	1,363	1,419	1,456	1,375	1,157	1,260
Washington County Public Schools	1,631	1,692	1,834	1,817	1,683	1,655	1,620
Wicomico County Public Schools	1,054	1,103	1,107	1,056	1,076	1,013	983
Worcester County Public Schools	513	500	525	504	563	485	526
MASSACHUSETTS							
Boston	3,196	3,340	3,413	3,399	3,795	3,532	3,616
Brockton	1,218	1,240	1,326	1,096	1,228	981	1,009
Brookline	568	503	555	509	490	515	503
Chicopee	520	569	547	542	539	527	563
Everett	514	528	547	562	532	530	457
Fall River	784	828	810	567	644	564	552
Framingham	624	656	627	661	654	554	516
Haverhill	705	677	697	533	451	413	482
Lawrence	1,071	1,135	1,109	805	923	804	807
Lexington	567	601	625	550	599	582	530
Lowell	1,225	1,209	1,210	905	689	768	799
Lynn	1,138	1,211	1,208	1,160	1,318	1,286	1,064
New Bedford	981	1,026	1,066	788	805	719	560
Newton	998	956	949	928	978	1,017	990
Plymouth	535	532	608	616	580	578	559
Quincy	688	708	680	688	703	737	714
Revere	516	608	619	563	540	463	484
Springfield	1,630	1,742	1,708	2,049	1,848	1,608	1,559
Taunton	644	659	675	565	509	515	529
Worcester	1,834	1,761	1,733	1,935	1,849	1,766	1,683
MICHIGAN							
Ann Arbor Public Schools	1,262	1,211	1,244	1,424	1,448	1,498	1,510
Chippewa Valley Schools	1,075	1,171	1,235	1,375	1,300	1,423	1,352
Dearborn City School District	1,547	1,652	1,690	2,024	1,700	1,476	1,632
Detroit Public Schools Community District	3,552	3,345	3,462	4,058	3,963	3,418	3,378
Farmington Public School District	656	689	693	694	684	708	811
Forest Hills Public Schools	699	719	751	780	781	797	798
Grand Rapids Public Schools	1,150	1,151	1,157	1,097	969	892	783
Kalamazoo Public Schools	978	923	993	1,232	1,013	846	661
Kentwood Public Schools	632	635	674	782	829	645	662
L'Anse Creuse Public Schools	756	734	852	887	876	823	766
Lansing Public School District	737	719	715	980	761	605	473
Livonia Public Schools School District	916	1,082	1,061	1,063	1,046	1,138	1,131
Plymouth-Canton Community Schools	1,301	1,238	1,379	1,517	1,510	1,549	1,539
Rochester Community School District	1,132	1,138	1,199	1,230	1,243	1,241	1,244

NA = Not available.
X = Not applicable.

Table C-3. School Enrollment for the 20 Largest Public School Districts in Each State, by Grade Level, 2020–21—*Continued*

(Number.)

State/School District	Total students in all grades	Kindergarten	Grade 1	Grade 2	Grade 3	Grade 4	Grade 5
MICHIGAN—*(Continued)*							
Traverse City Area Public Schools	9,007	657	614	613	582	671	636
Troy School District	12,815	769	833	868	919	961	918
Utica Community Schools	25,701	1,728	1,814	1,772	1,837	1,820	1,829
Walled Lake Consolidated Schools	12,622	798	890	908	927	854	925
Warren Consolidated Schools	12,947	955	908	881	816	914	929
Wayne-Westland Community School District	9,652	582	722	692	705	687	646
MINNESOTA							
Anoka-Hennepin Public School District	37,719	2,154	2,573	2,591	2,534	2,583	2,690
Bloomington Public School District	10,139	601	641	678	666	679	724
Eastern Carver County Public School	9,485	695	714	689	695	685	651
Elk River School District	13,464	970	989	1,025	1,037	936	981
Lakeville Public School District	11,275	746	726	797	795	732	822
Mankato Public School District	8,693	592	625	644	648	623	682
Minneapolis Public School District	32,722	2,443	2,686	2,571	2,517	2,398	2,411
Minnetonka Public School District	11,106	862	801	858	806	841	863
Mounds View Public School District	11,806	833	810	868	834	841	858
North St. Paul-Maplewood Oakdale	10,352	684	712	723	716	663	676
Osseo Public School District	20,672	1,367	1,533	1,497	1,438	1,452	1,477
Prior Lake-Savage Area Schools	8,892	559	577	610	636	638	632
Robbinsdale Public School District	11,692	731	834	790	757	795	798
Rochester Public School District	17,474	1,258	1,252	1,240	1,259	1,268	1,267
Rosemount-Apple Valley-Eagan	29,156	1,848	2,097	2,125	2,119	2,107	2,124
South Washington County School District	19,001	1,223	1,368	1,334	1,332	1,399	1,427
St. Cloud Public School District	9,628	709	696	694	606	630	639
St. Paul Public School District	34,928	2,653	2,660	2,719	2,600	2,599	2,477
Wayzata Public School District	12,013	769	933	900	929	898	941
White Bear Lake School District	8,705	647	647	637	659	621	669
MISSISSIPPI							
Biloxi Public School District	5,952	422	489	447	396	468	397
Clinton Public School District	5,250	362	332	365	367	410	393
Desoto Co School District	34,067	2,153	2,430	2,475	2,428	2,516	2,521
Gulfport School District	6,367	494	506	548	501	465	484
Harrison Co School District	13,666	951	992	1,054	1,033	1,081	1,109
Hinds Co School District	5,364	313	347	340	402	399	381
Jackson Co School District	8,765	568	618	651	616	643	674
Jackson Public School District	20,401	1,229	1,514	1,457	1,669	1,940	1,258
Jones Co School District	8,073	611	586	607	574	570	557
Lamar County School District	10,298	715	772	717	739	748	722
Lauderdale Co School District	5,680	383	402	378	388	390	402
Lee County School District	6,389	421	521	482	463	476	484
Lowndes Co School District	5,173	344	363	351	372	354	389
Madison Co School District	12,988	897	959	901	960	903	944
Meridian Public Schools	4,940	355	440	370	368	453	299
Ocean Springs School District	5,739	346	436	390	404	415	431
Pascagoula-Gautier School District	6,508	422	459	449	452	487	468
Rankin Co School District	18,384	1,207	1,334	1,287	1,336	1,364	1,399
Tupelo Public School District	7,005	551	514	508	498	523	492
Vicksburg Warren School District	7,236	500	516	540	471	538	515
MISSOURI							
Blue Springs R-IV	14,687	1,025	1,096	1,052	1,065	1,041	1,106
Columbia 93	18,145	1,165	1,326	1,375	1,373	1,317	1,295
Ferguson-Florissant R-II	9,313	517	632	647	711	722	669
Fox C-6	11,022	726	763	765	809	829	870
Francis Howell R-III	16,936	1,086	1,246	1,220	1,185	1,292	1,273
Ft. Zumwalt R-II	17,310	1,089	1,136	1,205	1,128	1,221	1,238
Hazelwood	16,473	1,002	1,075	1,216	1,225	1,250	1,300
Independence 30	14,240	1,054	1,033	1,048	1,034	1,047	1,104
Kansas City 33	14,113	935	1,164	1,185	1,047	1,079	1,063
Lee's Summit R-VII	17,790	1,120	1,177	1,225	1,288	1,175	1,340
Liberty 53	12,632	815	835	904	888	904	917
Mehlville R-IX	9,969	635	710	667	738	701	742
North Kansas City 74	19,673	1,355	1,510	1,415	1,450	1,481	1,543
Park Hill	11,992	812	861	849	865	857	940
Parkway C-2	17,132	1,195	1,301	1,285	1,295	1,339	1,347
Rockwood R-VI	19,822	944	982	1,122	1,456	1,426	1,561
Springfield R-XII	23,731	1,534	1,710	1,666	1,681	1,683	1,692

NA = Not available.
X = Not applicable.

Table C-3. School Enrollment for the 20 Largest Public School Districts in Each State, by Grade Level, 2020–21—*Continued*

(Number.)

State/School District	Grade 6	Grade 7	Grade 8	Grade 9	Grade 10	Grade 11	Grade 12
MICHIGAN—*(Continued)*							
Traverse City Area Public Schools	611	699	661	815	747	828	837
Troy School District	894	997	1,048	1,119	1,099	1,110	1,144
Utica Community Schools	1,882	1,945	2,089	2,216	2,116	2,259	2,268
Walled Lake Consolidated Schools	969	965	937	1,051	1,029	1,001	1,167
Warren Consolidated Schools	992	1,027	1,017	1,052	1,089	1,110	1,168
Wayne-Westland Community School District	699	698	728	776	858	792	751
MINNESOTA							
Anoka-Hennepin Public School District	2,772	2,905	2,980	3,187	3,154	3,240	3,387
Bloomington Public School District	741	749	788	882	902	822	933
Eastern Carver County Public School	632	713	718	743	754	821	846
Elk River School District	977	1,058	1,035	1,023	1,045	1,053	1,068
Lakeville Public School District	868	874	890	999	935	933	969
Mankato Public School District	671	697	673	655	627	653	633
Minneapolis Public School District	2,250	2,245	2,307	2,409	2,416	2,374	2,814
Minnetonka Public School District	833	834	893	875	892	864	813
Mounds View Public School District	894	878	905	940	935	959	997
North St. Paul-Maplewood Oakdale	714	748	782	859	846	855	916
Osseo Public School District	1,469	1,569	1,477	1,671	1,637	1,725	1,762
Prior Lake-Savage Area Schools	697	713	760	744	725	710	762
Robbinsdale Public School District	798	889	891	912	989	980	1,090
Rochester Public School District	1,260	1,317	1,257	1,390	1,351	1,360	1,572
Rosemount-Apple Valley-Eagan	2,210	2,212	2,330	2,341	2,365	2,292	2,459
South Washington County School District	1,339	1,433	1,434	1,531	1,462	1,490	1,608
St. Cloud Public School District	628	659	694	722	770	811	919
St. Paul Public School District	2,389	2,428	2,405	2,682	2,563	2,583	2,977
Wayzata Public School District	952	878	960	883	958	948	921
White Bear Lake School District	680	691	695	620	592	555	733
MISSISSIPPI							
Biloxi Public School District	471	507	472	461	452	431	373
Clinton Public School District	465	451	448	422	413	369	361
Desoto Co School District	2,761	2,806	2,746	2,841	2,765	2,586	2,241
Gulfport School District	456	554	501	473	468	408	390
Harrison Co School District	1,211	1,201	1,170	1,074	1,041	857	836
Hinds Co School District	401	450	454	442	465	424	409
Jackson Co School District	679	721	739	719	658	709	612
Jackson Public School District	1,438	1,510	1,483	1,595	1,642	1,555	1,385
Jones Co School District	623	662	684	633	604	569	502
Lamar County School District	823	855	887	821	779	746	659
Lauderdale Co School District	421	462	499	454	520	452	436
Lee County School District	510	530	516	522	510	476	404
Lowndes Co School District	382	466	419	435	407	366	341
Madison Co School District	1,008	1,057	1,113	1,034	1,033	959	970
Meridian Public Schools	366	397	413	351	332	317	263
Ocean Springs School District	454	474	500	459	452	426	449
Pascagoula-Gautier School District	497	540	567	530	521	463	426
Rankin Co School District	1,434	1,554	1,530	1,517	1,432	1,362	1,299
Tupelo Public School District	564	538	545	497	519	500	391
Vicksburg Warren School District	534	592	584	550	531	512	451
MISSOURI							
Blue Springs R-IV	1,183	1,170	1,206	1,236	1,165	1,153	1,023
Columbia 93	1,371	1,428	1,436	1,417	1,452	1,446	1,305
Ferguson-Florissant R-II	762	790	792	746	682	709	670
Fox C-6	851	850	915	874	918	858	880
Francis Howell R-III	1,216	1,336	1,261	1,310	1,296	1,376	1,344
Ft. Zumwalt R-II	1,323	1,362	1,347	1,469	1,523	1,501	1,543
Hazelwood	1,271	1,373	1,386	1,297	1,241	1,239	1,121
Independence 30	1,080	1,095	1,112	1,103	1,098	950	955
Kansas City 33	979	948	997	1,115	1,034	880	908
Lee's Summit R-VII	1,354	1,434	1,461	1,479	1,453	1,491	1,497
Liberty 53	964	1,085	1,003	1,080	1,085	1,004	1,060
Mehlville R-IX	769	823	885	743	771	812	767
North Kansas City 74	1,508	1,570	1,615	1,599	1,571	1,512	1,543
Park Hill	936	937	920	964	899	923	926
Parkway C 2	1,274	1,323	1,343	1,355	1,343	1,341	1,391
Rockwood R-VI	1,584	1,601	1,651	1,734	1,823	1,771	1,775
Springfield R-XII	1,786	1,962	1,853	1,963	1,896	1,837	1,775

NA = Not available.
X = Not applicable.

Table C-3. School Enrollment for the 20 Largest Public School Districts in Each State, by Grade Level, 2020–21—*Continued*

(Number.)

State/School District	Total students in all grades	Kindergarten	Grade 1	Grade 2	Grade 3	Grade 4	Grade 5
MISSOURI—*(Continued)*							
St. Joseph	10,643	766	823	761	790	817	811
St. Louis City	19,299	1,430	1,569	1,534	1,482	1,466	1,490
Wentzville R-IV	17,400	1,149	1,246	1,251	1,247	1,403	1,294
MONTANA							
Belgrade Elem	2,297	226	257	258	250	252	248
Billings Elem	10,980	1,163	1,178	1,194	1,120	1,168	1,206
Billings H S	5,550	X	X	X	X	X	X
Bozeman Elem	4,464	452	483	465	478	510	504
Bozeman H S	2,389	X	X	X	X	X	X
Browning Elem	1,392	174	165	149	134	157	152
Butte Elem	2,948	354	352	306	332	323	329
Columbia Falls Elem	1,430	151	152	153	160	155	153
East Helena K-12	1,505	143	118	135	135	152	140
Flathead H S	2,952	X	X	X	X	X	X
Frenchtown K-12 Schools	1,345	92	76	84	94	105	98
Great Falls Elem	7,026	874	763	760	764	778	722
Great Falls H S	2,981	X	X	X	X	X	X
Hamilton K-12 Schools	1,498	129	96	99	95	105	103
Helena Elem	5,123	529	569	553	521	573	553
Helena H S	2,620	X	X	X	X	X	X
Hellgate Elem	1,473	164	167	161	154	153	159
Kalispell Elem	2,883	337	303	320	289	301	303
Missoula Elem	5,264	594	597	588	596	553	554
Missoula H S	3,717	X	X	X	X	X	X
NEBRASKA							
Bellevue Public Schools	9,386	645	688	652	667	641	700
Bennington Public Schools	3,589	341	323	279	336	294	283
Columbus Public Schools	4,159	286	282	304	324	269	325
Elkhorn Public Schools	10,642	793	835	847	802	867	786
Fremont Public Schools	4,868	370	353	361	309	361	325
Grand Island Public Schools	9,920	742	811	739	701	751	760
Gretna Public Schools	6,023	482	484	464	473	494	458
Hastings Public Schools	3,672	262	265	238	239	262	272
Kearney Public Schools	6,055	468	497	446	458	429	441
Lexington Public Schools	3,104	218	213	208	214	236	237
Lincoln Public Schools	41,674	2,871	2,927	2,959	2,984	3,053	3,033
Millard Public Schools	23,633	1,660	1,680	1,675	1,692	1,686	1,733
Norfolk Public Schools	4,444	326	320	312	282	319	314
North Platte Public Schools	3,919	247	264	253	271	267	298
Omaha Public Schools	51,914	3,773	3,816	3,886	3,879	3,616	3,876
Papillion La Vista Community Schools	11,831	783	812	785	858	827	886
Ralston Public Schools	3,210	244	203	236	234	234	228
Scottsbluff Public Schools	3,452	199	228	220	224	256	244
South Sioux City Community Schs	3,734	275	260	278	284	231	257
Westside Community Schools	6,091	392	446	417	409	422	426
NEVADA							
Carson City School District	7,787	523	544	560	574	543	579
Churchill County School District	3,200	218	214	216	244	248	231
Clark County School District	315,646	19,888	21,551	22,069	22,337	22,862	23,173
Correctional School District	38	X	X	X	X	X	X
Davidson Academy School District	234	X	X	X	X	X	NA
Douglas County School District	5,385	323	355	341	368	377	411
Elko County School District	9,608	658	743	773	641	687	739
Esmeralda County School District	101	14	4	10	7	9	12
Eureka County School District	324	24	24	34	15	24	35
Humboldt County School District	3,267	241	230	251	235	276	255
Lander County School District	1,027	81	77	69	74	87	74
Lincoln County School District	881	51	57	46	49	48	55
Lyon County School District	8,817	610	611	670	606	680	678
Mineral County School District	572	50	47	46	61	49	50
Nye County School District	5,353	336	373	354	362	386	379
Pershing County School District	637	55	54	51	59	56	45
State-Sponsored Charter Schools	53,223	4,450	4,774	4,713	4,604	4,558	4,508
Storey County School District	448	29	25	32	29	25	35
Washoe County School District	64,584	4,379	4,859	4,819	4,824	4,709	4,808
White Pine County School District	1,216	65	89	80	85	88	86

NA = Not available.
X = Not applicable.

Table C-3. School Enrollment for the 20 Largest Public School Districts in Each State, by Grade Level, 2020–21—*Continued*

(Number.)

State/School District	Grade 6	Grade 7	Grade 8	Grade 9	Grade 10	Grade 11	Grade 12
MISSOURI—(*Continued*)							
St. Joseph..	821	842	827	839	786	821	743
St. Louis City......................................	1,269	1,259	1,273	1,255	1,336	1,365	1,366
Wentzville R-IV....................................	1,389	1,387	1,389	1,401	1,357	1,283	1,260
MONTANA							
Belgrade Elem....................................	270	267	268	X	X	X	X
Billings Elem.....................................	1,208	1,368	1,375	X	X	X	X
Billings H S	X	X	X	1,455	1,387	1,454	1,254
Bozeman Elem...................................	538	553	481	X	X	X	X
Bozeman H S	X	X	X	702	592	567	528
Browning Elem...................................	160	157	144	X	X	X	X
Butte Elem..	305	335	312	X	X	X	X
Columbia Falls Elem...........................	152	184	170	X	X	X	X
East Helena K-12................................	140	136	146	125	135	0	0
Flathead H S......................................	X	X	X	814	773	706	659
Frenchtown K-12 Schools.....................	99	123	117	127	114	118	98
Great Falls Elem.................................	797	777	791	X	X	X	X
Great Falls H S	X	X	X	811	785	734	651
Hamilton K-12 Schools........................	108	119	134	142	130	122	111
Helena Elem......................................	607	617	567	X	X	X	X
Helena H S..	X	X	X	611	641	687	681
Hellgate Elem....................................	171	175	169	X	X	X	X
Kalispell Elem...................................	326	365	339	X	X	X	X
Missoula Elem...................................	611	581	580	X	X	X	X
Missoula H S.....................................	X	X	X	1,038	907	939	833
NEBRASKA							
Bellevue Public Schools......................	667	683	693	717	749	772	796
Bennington Public Schools...................	266	249	241	261	228	219	177
Columbus Public Schools.....................	274	285	291	332	296	334	363
Elkhorn Public Schools........................	819	850	748	784	752	738	686
Fremont Public Schools.......................	374	362	299	366	386	367	374
Grand Island Public Schools.................	759	751	703	638	670	600	659
Gretna Public Schools.........................	472	478	429	425	379	383	357
Hastings Public Schools.......................	241	260	210	282	274	248	299
Kearney Public Schools	416	421	392	417	377	422	382
Lexington Public Schools.....................	206	183	193	242	236	240	236
Lincoln Public Schools........................	3,230	3,110	2,902	3,094	3,162	3,196	3,477
Millard Public Schools........................	1,789	1,818	1,705	1,837	1,833	1,861	1,935
Norfolk Public Schools........................	332	312	316	336	325	325	362
North Platte Public Schools..................	303	297	293	287	302	304	311
Omaha Public Schools.........................	3,892	3,906	3,525	3,662	3,807	3,707	4,027
Papillion La Vista Community Schools......	900	965	841	993	948	940	971
Ralston Public Schools........................	241	249	242	228	237	242	273
Scottsbluff Public Schools....................	268	256	278	247	281	256	279
South Sioux City Community Schs	280	284	247	280	291	295	285
Westside Community Schools	459	512	457	518	507	491	509
NEVADA							
Carson City School District..................	610	620	668	649	627	589	582
Churchill County School District	248	266	243	266	225	246	221
Clark County School District.................	23,331	24,653	25,517	26,352	26,169	24,915	24,411
Correctional School District.................	0	0	0	1	11	14	12
Davidson Academy School District	11	32	48	48	29	28	38
Douglas County School District	398	430	432	463	458	455	470
Elko County School District..................	727	803	792	775	750	681	612
Esmeralda County School District..........	7	12	13	1	1	1	1
Eureka County School District...............	27	25	21	27	17	25	14
Humboldt County School District...........	241	299	242	280	222	233	190
Lander County School District	74	90	71	72	69	81	65
Lincoln County School District..............	61	56	57	71	76	89	73
Lyon County School District..................	682	742	767	720	678	674	618
Mineral County School District	35	34	35	40	33	29	31
Nye County School District	412	409	424	460	464	428	382
Pershing County School District	48	53	43	44	46	36	37
State-Sponsored Charter Schools..........	5,346	5,263	4,962	2,869	2,403	2,466	2,141
Storey County School District...............	33	40	42	40	45	35	36
Washoe County School District.............	4,769	5,123	5,285	5,359	5,205	4,977	4,775
White Pine County School District	96	80	90	109	97	93	109

NA = Not available.
X = Not applicable.

Table C-3. School Enrollment for the 20 Largest Public School Districts in Each State, by Grade Level, 2020–21—*Continued*

(Number.)

State/School District	Total students in all grades	Kindergarten	Grade 1	Grade 2	Grade 3	Grade 4	Grade 5
NEW HAMPSHIRE							
Bedford School District	4,266	177	250	302	291	320	341
Concord School District	4,093	242	258	264	261	284	280
Derry School District	3,133	274	321	291	323	349	354
Dover School District	3,846	183	254	226	255	256	293
Exeter Region Coop School District	2,633	X	X	X	X	X	X
Goffstown School District	2,767	126	168	168	163	181	164
Hudson School District	3,053	178	161	189	219	220	226
Keene School District	3,120	145	158	178	171	174	170
Londonderry School District	4,093	241	256	250	317	315	294
Manchester School District	12,410	747	961	932	950	1,015	928
Merrimack School District	3,582	197	259	276	238	243	280
Merrimack Valley School District	2,224	134	168	143	157	145	157
Milford School District	2,155	131	144	145	123	161	144
Nashua School District	10,239	562	699	735	737	752	749
Pinkerton Academy School District	3,160	X	X	X	X	X	X
Portsmouth School District	2,531	131	156	163	154	161	158
Rochester School District	4,098	261	278	296	288	306	281
Salem School District	3,519	242	260	237	249	250	269
Timberlane Regional School District	3,278	183	248	216	222	259	224
Windham School District	2,958	185	194	194	203	191	212
NEW JERSEY							
Bayonne School District	10,059	707	674	704	665	658	648
Cherry Hill School District	10,596	608	728	634	706	686	764
Clifton Public School District	10,514	616	703	717	745	729	737
Edison Township School District	16,632	936	1,150	1,222	1,342	1,308	1,306
Elizabeth Public Schools	28,090	1,792	1,803	1,817	1,865	1,842	1,845
Freehold Regional High School District	10,519	X	X	X	X	X	X
Hamilton Township Public School District	11,678	757	791	790	781	826	798
Jersey City Public Schools	26,782	1,843	1,866	1,786	1,827	1,749	1,674
New Brunswick School District	9,961	600	617	680	712	723	726
Newark Public School District	40,423	2,242	2,429	2,550	2,584	2,450	2,488
Passaic City School District	13,494	789	806	830	820	869	863
Paterson Public School District	25,937	1,560	1,850	1,674	1,721	1,659	1,746
Perth Amboy Public School District	10,786	694	769	775	770	767	770
Plainfield Public School District	9,744	645	657	695	628	575	663
Toms River Regional School District	14,618	754	932	908	954	958	1,003
Trenton Public Schools	14,708	1,181	1,213	1,163	1,079	957	1,030
Union City School District	13,101	836	873	858	864	874	841
Vineland Public School District	10,266	674	692	669	669	706	732
West Windsor-Plainsboro Regional School District	9,386	466	568	610	620	674	732
Woodbridge Township School District	13,860	858	1,016	1,000	984	941	929
NEW MEXICO							
Alamogordo Public Schools	5,572	382	431	420	427	404	426
Albuquerque Public Schools	83,031	5,217	5,705	5,762	5,831	6,011	6,188
Artesia Public Schools	3,741	322	273	285	283	281	267
Belen Consolidated Schools	3,667	220	260	268	253	294	267
Carlsbad Municipal Schools	8,847	650	680	719	668	697	692
Central Consolidated Schools	5,173	285	316	347	338	369	409
Clovis Municipal Schools	7,765	531	637	598	573	601	573
Deming Public Schools	5,115	297	349	369	371	356	367
Farmington Municipal Schools	10,768	707	765	734	725	723	784
Gadsden Independent Schools	12,844	763	847	880	871	941	953
Gallup-Mckinley Cty Schools	12,281	808	843	863	900	871	877
Grants-Cibola County Schools	3,206	200	243	220	221	238	229
Hobbs Municipal Schools	9,776	708	778	770	731	701	742
Las Cruces Public Schools	23,711	1,535	1,600	1,669	1,674	1,722	1,724
Los Alamos Public Schools	3,539	213	229	217	223	237	282
Los Lunas Public Schools	8,050	484	516	528	531	599	649
Lovington Municipal Schools	3,502	237	235	258	206	233	272
Rio Rancho Public Schools	16,807	1,052	1,106	1,104	1,181	1,201	1,282
Roswell Independent Schools	9,801	600	651	709	691	766	738
Santa Fe Public Schools	12,403	736	872	866	958	960	950
NEW YORK							
Buffalo City School District	31,428	2,004	2,251	2,251	2,248	2,172	2,206
New York City Geographic District # 2	60,446	2,690	2,644	2,552	2,628	2,539	2,483

NA = Not available.
X = Not applicable.

Table C-3. School Enrollment for the 20 Largest Public School Districts in Each State, by Grade Level, 2020–21—*Continued*

(Number.)

State/School District	Grade 6	Grade 7	Grade 8	Grade 9	Grade 10	Grade 11	Grade 12
NEW HAMPSHIRE							
Bedford School District................................	352	331	371	364	349	382	391
Concord School District................................	279	309	321	367	411	364	371
Derry School District...................................	337	383	420	1	1	1	4
Dover School District...................................	255	288	259	397	403	380	358
Exeter Region Coop School District	338	335	385	368	421	384	402
Goffstown School District	176	276	246	311	250	249	240
Hudson School District.................................	219	250	241	276	275	261	282
Keene School District...................................	220	245	233	357	337	345	324
Londonderry School District	269	329	294	323	381	351	384
Manchester School District............................	912	967	955	922	1,075	968	836
Merrimack School District	256	291	260	283	267	306	325
Merrimack Valley School District	143	174	200	180	208	200	190
Milford School District.................................	155	171	192	176	203	183	191
Nashua School District..................................	698	807	820	1,016	896	846	757
Pinkerton Academy School District.....................	X	X	X	929	755	773	693
Portsmouth School District.............................	165	179	183	249	273	289	267
Rochester School District	332	286	308	420	335	310	354
Salem School District...................................	257	259	284	285	289	295	262
Timberlane Regional School District	231	262	285	243	269	256	286
Windham School District	202	249	262	266	269	254	233
NEW JERSEY							
Bayonne School District................................	710	689	693	661	619	561	608
Cherry Hill School District.............................	737	827	837	866	834	891	873
Clifton Public School District	742	805	849	734	673	704	723
Edison Township School District........................	1,296	1,315	1,335	1,205	1,171	1,123	1,196
Elizabeth Public Schools...............................	1,906	1,871	1,954	1,878	1,795	1,826	1,405
Freehold Regional High School District.................	X	X	X	2,473	2,527	2,596	2,577
Hamilton Township Public School District	867	826	803	857	877	857	894
Jersey City Public Schools.............................	1,596	1,769	1,790	1,579	1,491	1,354	1,355
New Brunswick School District........................	749	688	682	828	557	526	516
Newark Public School District.........................	2,506	2,581	2,602	2,343	2,332	2,155	2,077
Passaic City School District	1,009	1,050	1,021	914	881	878	894
Paterson Public School District........................	1,794	1,788	1,796	1,371	1,364	1,355	1,436
Perth Amboy Public School District....................	774	760	744	660	732	605	509
Plainfield Public School District.......................	588	563	587	489	589	523	437
Toms River Regional School District....................	1,007	1,103	1,147	1,158	1,105	1,152	1,166
Trenton Public Schools	832	724	702	827	974	816	726
Union City School District..............................	807	817	872	850	906	897	821
Vineland Public School District........................	726	766	751	666	650	560	523
West Windsor-Plainsboro Regional School District	756	774	796	759	813	795	794
Woodbridge Township School District.................	1,035	1,048	1,055	987	950	1,085	1,030
NEW MEXICO							
Alamogordo Public Schools............................	435	447	427	437	413	376	374
Albuquerque Public Schools	6,147	6,414	6,561	8,383	7,553	6,150	5,514
Artesia Public Schools	303	296	297	272	289	248	263
Belen Consolidated Schools............................	329	288	303	298	273	268	294
Carlsbad Municipal Schools............................	693	732	670	644	601	603	571
Central Consolidated Schools	411	395	430	567	453	391	329
Clovis Municipal Schools	609	583	582	628	550	539	513
Deming Public Schools..................................	414	443	390	380	415	402	401
Farmington Municipal Schools.........................	842	947	873	915	879	843	833
Gadsden Independent Schools.........................	976	963	1,021	1,024	1,017	954	1,097
Gallup-Mckinley Cty Schools	915	1,004	960	966	1,026	964	847
Grants-Cibola County Schools	228	253	243	274	321	213	244
Hobbs Municipal Schools	824	777	827	747	707	655	640
Las Cruces Public Schools..............................	1,890	1,869	1,928	2,044	1,896	1,742	1,608
Los Alamos Public Schools.............................	282	299	295	276	306	322	263
Los Lunas Public Schools...............................	653	691	634	824	604	586	535
Lovington Municipal Schools...........................	241	317	322	284	317	258	210
Rio Rancho Public Schools..............................	1,213	1,329	1,332	1,421	1,388	1,297	1,324
Roswell Independent Schools..........................	832	789	826	874	707	654	660
Santa Fe Public Schools................................	1,059	885	922	1,025	994	912	839
NEW YORK							
Buffalo City School District	2,332	2,312	2,393	2,421	2,405	2,260	2,337
New York City Geographic District # 2	2,584	2,598	2,732	9,164	8,923	8,479	7,793

NA = Not available.
X = Not applicable.

Table C-3. School Enrollment for the 20 Largest Public School Districts in Each State, by Grade Level, 2020–21—Continued

(Number.)

State/School District	Total students in all grades	Kindergarten	Grade 1	Grade 2	Grade 3	Grade 4	Grade 5
NEW YORK—(Continued)							
New York City Geographic District # 8	25,994	1,640	1,814	1,842	1,880	1,939	2,083
New York City Geographic District # 9	31,384	1,744	2,190	2,260	2,366	2,451	2,536
New York City Geographic District #10	51,467	3,114	3,500	3,559	3,818	3,818	3,855
New York City Geographic District #11	36,296	2,377	2,622	2,874	2,819	2,874	3,063
New York City Geographic District #15	30,388	2,590	2,705	2,654	2,683	2,668	2,615
New York City Geographic District #20	50,119	3,705	3,799	3,718	4,115	3,965	3,843
New York City Geographic District #21	34,525	1,930	2,121	2,076	2,110	2,125	2,113
New York City Geographic District #22	33,200	2,293	2,469	2,473	2,547	2,524	2,601
New York City Geographic District #24	54,293	4,136	4,152	4,336	4,387	4,438	4,379
New York City Geographic District #25	36,061	2,689	2,786	2,770	2,840	2,769	2,582
New York City Geographic District #26	31,351	1,659	1,706	1,741	1,812	1,709	1,800
New York City Geographic District #27	43,540	2,779	3,071	3,096	3,107	3,189	3,231
New York City Geographic District #28	40,347	2,556	2,723	2,579	2,594	2,594	2,589
New York City Geographic District #29	24,957	1,810	2,052	2,129	2,114	2,153	2,295
New York City Geographic District #30	37,841	2,561	2,749	2,671	2,666	2,680	2,854
New York City Geographic District #31	62,857	4,093	4,349	4,261	4,497	4,536	4,569
Rochester City School District	24,898	1,358	1,748	1,843	1,756	1,886	1,820
Yonkers City School District	25,488	1,705	1,770	1,873	1,762	1,805	1,909
NORTH CAROLINA							
Alamance-Burlington Schools	21,931	1,376	1,618	1,643	1,596	1,654	1,703
Buncombe County Schools	22,298	1,529	1,759	1,642	1,648	1,715	1,622
Cabarrus County Schools	32,810	1,933	2,201	2,353	2,410	2,339	2,442
Charlotte-Mecklenburg Schools	142,733	9,705	10,328	10,636	10,676	10,690	10,992
Cumberland County Schools	49,278	3,364	3,951	3,688	3,591	3,796	3,802
Davidson County Schools	17,964	1,119	1,264	1,232	1,277	1,264	1,277
Durham Public Schools	32,005	2,172	2,407	2,416	2,350	2,357	2,445
Gaston County Schools	29,777	1,873	2,073	2,092	2,207	2,229	2,309
Guilford County Schools	70,047	4,381	5,018	5,010	5,116	4,945	5,166
Harnett County Schools	19,470	1,232	1,475	1,379	1,461	1,480	1,469
Iredell-Statesville Schools	20,163	1,253	1,338	1,275	1,404	1,408	1,446
Johnston County Public Schools	36,422	2,284	2,634	2,526	2,640	2,599	2,670
New Hanover County Schools	24,841	1,635	1,772	1,842	1,765	1,856	1,836
Onslow County Schools	26,269	1,954	2,108	2,143	2,040	2,094	2,041
Pitt County Schools	23,312	1,480	1,700	1,657	1,750	1,698	1,812
Public Schools of Robeson County	21,083	1,441	1,620	1,665	1,501	1,548	1,606
Rowan-Salisbury Schools	18,205	1,233	1,298	1,286	1,297	1,279	1,266
Union County Public Schools	40,207	2,164	2,545	2,593	2,708	2,858	3,014
Wake County Schools	159,802	10,406	11,427	11,324	11,672	11,968	12,216
Winston Salem / Forsyth County Schools	51,843	3,317	3,758	3,816	3,886	3,931	3,932
NORTH DAKOTA							
Belcourt 7	1,594	108	113	101	107	118	106
Beulah 27	719	55	70	51	52	53	70
Bismarck 1	13,433	1,035	1,000	1,005	995	986	982
Central Cass 17	953	68	79	69	77	69	72
Devils Lake 1	1,666	124	135	124	127	143	118
Dickinson 1	3,810	288	344	315	287	294	256
Fargo 1	11,304	758	927	873	869	848	866
Grafton 3	909	58	63	72	64	57	61
Grand Forks 1	7,567	592	594	541	583	548	549
Jamestown 1	2,206	138	176	144	154	141	153
Kindred 2	841	62	70	52	68	65	70
Mandan 1	4,095	346	317	359	301	287	305
Mckenzie Co 1	1,836	169	164	157	136	142	149
Minot 1	7,672	621	638	620	645	649	574
New Town 1	944	67	90	97	62	74	73
Valley City 2	1,060	69	86	67	74	75	74
Wahpeton 37	1,215	80	90	83	77	84	95
West Fargo 6	11,561	1,012	963	989	954	888	887
Williams County 8	729	78	80	86	93	74	85
Williston 1	4,297	372	351	328	355	324	323
OHIO							
Akron City	20,563	1,395	1,698	1,591	1,527	1,558	1,574
Cincinnati Public Schools	34,635	2,168	2,779	2,761	2,760	2,651	2,649
Cleveland Municipal	34,941	2,244	2,699	2,549	2,558	2,592	2,581
Columbus City School District	46,657	3,547	4,028	3,766	3,795	3,913	3,658
Dayton City	11,721	779	846	846	843	882	841
Dublin City	16,254	997	1,157	1,230	1,293	1,229	1,302

NA = Not available.
X = Not applicable.

Table C-3. School Enrollment for the 20 Largest Public School Districts in Each State, by Grade Level, 2020–21—*Continued*

(Number.)

State/School District	Grade 6	Grade 7	Grade 8	Grade 9	Grade 10	Grade 11	Grade 12
NEW YORK—*(Continued)*							
New York City Geographic District # 8	2,067	2,002	2,122	1,751	1,839	1,544	1,456
New York City Geographic District # 9	2,318	2,531	2,531	2,123	2,169	1,843	1,806
New York City Geographic District #10	3,749	3,637	3,815	4,069	3,955	3,622	3,455
New York City Geographic District #11	2,957	2,996	3,216	2,412	2,335	1,971	1,901
New York City Geographic District #15	2,123	2,054	2,178	1,514	1,793	1,572	1,471
New York City Geographic District #20	4,054	3,960	4,061	3,711	3,605	2,969	2,799
New York City Geographic District #21	3,212	3,053	3,095	3,239	3,212	2,418	2,370
New York City Geographic District #22	2,096	2,103	2,125	2,645	2,719	2,488	2,431
New York City Geographic District #24	4,077	4,289	4,334	3,533	3,544	3,055	3,171
New York City Geographic District #25	2,723	2,781	2,839	2,401	2,695	2,437	2,115
New York City Geographic District #26	1,935	1,985	2,169	3,880	3,420	3,181	2,962
New York City Geographic District #27	3,537	3,560	3,770	2,803	2,830	2,409	2,370
New York City Geographic District #28	2,502	2,577	2,574	3,857	3,745	3,514	3,365
New York City Geographic District #29	2,143	2,247	2,334	1,037	1,058	906	957
New York City Geographic District #30	3,020	3,036	3,154	2,818	2,542	2,195	2,227
New York City Geographic District #31	4,365	4,423	4,489	4,776	4,774	4,568	4,080
Rochester City School District	1,916	1,953	1,875	2,482	1,823	1,387	1,474
Yonkers City School District	1,932	1,989	1,992	1,816	1,722	1,766	1,807
NORTH CAROLINA							
Alamance-Burlington Schools	1,705	1,876	1,803	1,951	1,694	1,616	1,507
Buncombe County Schools	1,621	1,773	1,785	1,963	1,841	1,725	1,626
Cabarrus County Schools	2,705	2,711	2,812	2,878	2,896	2,495	2,520
Charlotte-Mecklenburg Schools	11,020	11,251	11,152	12,529	11,564	9,273	10,060
Cumberland County Schools	3,823	3,947	3,799	4,194	3,789	3,446	3,408
Davidson County Schools	1,432	1,462	1,480	1,590	1,551	1,451	1,408
Durham Public Schools	2,275	2,371	2,376	3,039	2,708	2,373	2,314
Gaston County Schools	2,436	2,388	2,462	2,600	2,438	2,173	2,174
Guilford County Schools	5,322	5,460	5,513	6,240	6,073	5,328	5,363
Harnett County Schools	1,581	1,545	1,644	1,732	1,534	1,367	1,425
Iredell-Statesville Schools	1,535	1,627	1,652	1,929	1,773	1,627	1,704
Johnston County Public Schools	2,959	2,965	3,049	3,242	3,012	2,792	2,683
New Hanover County Schools	1,829	1,790	2,046	2,347	2,172	1,932	1,882
Onslow County Schools	2,204	2,055	2,164	2,080	1,949	1,647	1,661
Pitt County Schools	1,901	1,942	1,831	2,024	1,849	1,674	1,626
Public Schools of Robeson County	1,705	1,763	1,690	1,822	1,670	1,353	1,322
Rowan-Salisbury Schools	1,450	1,506	1,490	1,667	1,486	1,323	1,423
Union County Public Schools	3,197	3,259	3,418	3,719	3,661	3,378	3,375
Wake County Schools	12,479	12,590	12,920	13,948	13,286	12,227	12,002
Winston Salem / Forsyth County Schools	4,121	4,148	4,141	4,382	4,079	3,047	3,931
NORTH DAKOTA							
Belcourt 7	107	128	125	140	147	144	114
Beulah 27	48	45	51	66	44	60	46
Bismarck 1	1,029	1,100	1,058	1,101	1,001	961	933
Central Cass 17	72	73	72	69	87	58	65
Devils Lake 1	123	129	138	133	115	113	117
Dickinson 1	296	289	268	278	272	268	245
Fargo 1	820	911	945	877	829	826	820
Grafton 3	61	79	60	70	53	64	73
Grand Forks 1	585	578	594	604	571	519	576
Jamestown 1	169	180	201	197	193	180	170
Kindred 2	74	61	59	76	51	51	55
Mandan 1	317	294	315	327	318	260	296
Mckenzie Co 1	146	144	136	123	135	107	103
Minot 1	600	542	607	519	525	506	483
New Town 1	83	75	57	97	71	51	40
Valley City 2	63	85	83	85	118	87	92
Wahpeton 37	79	109	104	121	96	104	74
West Fargo 6	927	888	827	842	776	748	733
Williams County 8	77	76	62	X	X	X	X
Williston 1	272	337	346	362	321	295	311
OHIO							
Akron City	1,607	1,513	1,548	1,538	1,532	1,548	1,495
Cincinnati Public Schools	2,577	2,539	2,666	2,798	2,806	2,338	1,949
Cleveland Municipal	2,539	2,360	2,511	3,401	3,017	2,445	2,488
Columbus City School District	3,465	3,203	3,344	4,813	3,237	2,672	2,053
Dayton City	862	768	785	1,273	993	823	774
Dublin City	1,248	1,247	1,289	1,318	1,285	1,239	1,298

NA = Not available.
X = Not applicable.

Table C-3. School Enrollment for the 20 Largest Public School Districts in Each State, by Grade Level, 2020–21—*Continued*

(Number.)

State/School District	Total students in all grades	Kindergarten	Grade 1	Grade 2	Grade 3	Grade 4	Grade 5
OHIO—*(Continued)*							
Fairfield City	9,708	669	641	732	678	740	736
Hamilton City	9,415	622	660	702	687	730	690
Hilliard City	16,027	1,020	1,158	1,139	1,179	1,145	1,194
Lakota Local	16,415	1,142	1,269	1,359	1,238	1,178	1,210
Mason City	10,267	564	655	677	706	758	775
Northwest Local	8,541	583	581	629	620	605	637
Ohio Virtual Academy	21,049	2,186	1,437	1,364	1,364	1,426	1,483
Olentangy Local	22,089	1,363	1,618	1,621	1,651	1,717	1,695
Parma City	9,318	586	598	588	617	587	599
Pickerington Local	10,454	619	725	726	757	777	773
South-Western City	21,654	1,376	1,531	1,582	1,633	1,620	1,705
Toledo City	22,312	1,637	1,735	1,621	1,593	1,632	1,673
Westerville City	14,576	899	1,108	1,037	1,097	1,052	1,088
Worthington City	10,530	755	841	886	758	751	736
OKLAHOMA							
Bartlesville	5,828	451	420	402	435	450	430
Bixby	6,560	443	491	517	507	475	518
Broken Arrow	18,619	1,242	1,384	1,333	1,384	1,245	1,394
Deer Creek	6,741	511	519	544	547	502	551
Edmond	23,496	1,571	1,686	1,648	1,650	1,671	1,657
Enid	7,390	547	565	549	537	554	508
Epic Blended Learning Charter	23,714	1,932	1,803	1,701	1,711	1,604	1,684
Epic One On One Charter School	35,731	2,441	2,333	2,393	2,347	2,363	2,454
Jenks	11,979	862	899	897	912	875	897
Lawton	12,897	1,013	1,088	979	904	899	847
Midwest City-Del City	11,044	776	820	841	799	803	813
Moore	23,390	1,688	1,708	1,708	1,752	1,588	1,739
Mustang	11,868	865	880	931	860	858	850
Norman	14,419	942	999	1,060	1,018	970	1,017
Oklahoma City	31,026	2,456	2,554	2,574	2,538	2,558	2,426
Owasso	9,035	577	619	615	664	664	667
Putnam City	17,829	1,239	1,340	1,313	1,262	1,364	1,351
Tulsa	32,569	2,498	2,634	2,602	2,534	2,627	2,469
Union	14,959	996	1,070	1,006	1,054	1,043	1,129
Yukon	8,158	524	582	597	593	572	587
OREGON							
Beaverton SD 48J	39,594	2,564	2,950	2,860	2,994	2,859	3,046
Bend-LaPine Administrative SD 1	17,543	1,114	1,220	1,220	1,265	1,341	1,342
Corvallis SD 509J	6,462	401	429	423	465	546	501
David Douglas SD 40	9,299	570	681	692	702	705	719
Eugene SD 4J	16,683	1,064	1,284	1,173	1,229	1,236	1,220
Greater Albany Public SD 8J	8,990	559	690	627	632	700	646
Gresham-Barlow SD 10J	11,661	716	770	791	852	863	869
Hillsboro SD 1J	19,407	1,295	1,430	1,471	1,472	1,405	1,458
Klamath County SD	6,784	491	527	509	496	562	561
Lake Oswego SD 7J	6,860	340	401	433	459	482	518
Medford SD 549C	13,962	890	1,038	1,070	1,060	1,127	1,117
North Clackamas SD 12	16,458	1,043	1,144	1,242	1,092	1,227	1,248
Oregon City SD 62	7,420	480	536	534	521	500	536
Portland SD 1J	46,965	3,251	3,717	3,741	3,647	3,755	3,767
Redmond SD 2J	7,070	422	479	451	469	472	464
Reynolds SD 7	10,560	720	844	840	830	846	899
Salem-Keizer SD 24J	39,906	2,450	2,780	2,942	2,837	2,992	3,150
Springfield SD 19	9,779	625	681	746	669	757	726
Tigard-Tualatin SD 23J	11,860	750	918	854	872	906	875
West Linn-Wilsonville SD 3J	9,302	544	586	604	642	639	737
PENNSYLVANIA							
Allentown City SD	16,231	1,027	1,243	1,271	1,208	1,241	1,312
Bethlehem Area SD	13,005	754	827	908	884	972	956
Central Bucks SD	17,571	813	1,126	1,198	1,277	1,293	1,302
Central Dauphin SD	11,894	761	971	937	946	943	964
Commonwealth Charter Academy CS	16,419	852	964	1,017	1,063	1,158	1,251
Council Rock SD	10,494	482	663	717	751	797	866
Cumberland Valley SD	9,403	625	722	707	732	779	728
Downingtown Area SD	12,909	743	793	891	945	967	963
Erie City SD	10,310	709	809	805	802	762	803
Hazleton Area SD	11,551	754	868	871	834	889	935

NA = Not available.
X = Not applicable.

Table C-3. School Enrollment for the 20 Largest Public School Districts in Each State, by Grade Level, 2020–21—*Continued*

(Number.)

State/School District	Grade 6	Grade 7	Grade 8	Grade 9	Grade 10	Grade 11	Grade 12
OHIO—*(Continued)*							
Fairfield City	765	790	787	812	836	689	688
Hamilton City	803	734	774	724	734	608	589
Hilliard City	1,205	1,260	1,291	1,366	1,370	1,250	1,278
Lakota Local	1,331	1,284	1,406	1,288	1,338	1,216	1,155
Mason City	801	837	904	857	850	888	897
Northwest Local	679	701	746	678	722	618	595
Ohio Virtual Academy	1,682	1,708	1,782	1,760	1,616	1,591	1,650
Olentangy Local	1,671	1,729	1,685	1,773	1,799	1,739	1,683
Parma City	697	679	747	852	841	840	895
Pickerington Local	825	850	898	882	888	767	868
South-Western City	1,651	1,765	1,704	1,954	1,716	1,541	1,570
Toledo City	1,715	1,645	1,762	1,610	1,622	1,585	1,560
Westerville City	1,133	1,130	1,116	1,298	1,233	1,167	1,112
Worthington City	735	810	830	795	749	779	852
OKLAHOMA							
Bartlesville	460	402	426	433	406	375	364
Bixby	516	495	514	498	472	449	435
Broken Arrow	1,464	1,403	1,445	1,378	1,361	1,311	1,300
Deer Creek	503	501	527	475	449	422	432
Edmond	1,750	1,854	1,779	1,914	1,846	1,715	1,690
Enid	544	550	533	589	546	511	444
Epic Blended Learning Charter	1,700	1,668	1,719	1,950	1,714	1,594	1,322
Epic One On One Charter School	2,467	2,574	2,595	3,307	3,164	3,000	2,337
Jenks	840	851	891	906	898	886	795
Lawton	877	952	967	940	914	891	883
Midwest City-Del City	855	815	842	867	793	757	817
Moore	1,796	1,813	1,873	1,774	1,757	1,733	1,678
Mustang	906	844	920	958	882	855	739
Norman	1,034	1,063	1,177	1,245	1,197	1,094	959
Oklahoma City	2,359	2,288	2,213	2,084	1,786	1,830	1,665
Owasso	713	693	704	739	695	722	672
Putnam City	1,331	1,366	1,296	1,248	1,226	1,287	1,284
Tulsa	2,341	2,280	2,289	2,328	1,961	2,068	2,123
Union	1,108	1,224	1,168	1,196	1,213	1,133	958
Yukon	589	649	669	650	665	593	558
OREGON							
Beaverton SD 48J	3,083	3,147	3,131	3,259	3,235	3,156	3,310
Bend-LaPine Administrative SD 1	1,375	1,396	1,494	1,542	1,442	1,417	1,375
Corvallis SD 509J	479	522	529	526	533	515	593
David Douglas SD 40	739	764	779	766	694	724	764
Eugene SD 4J	1,294	1,331	1,360	1,339	1,321	1,343	1,489
Greater Albany Public SD 8J	725	772	775	746	727	707	684
Gresham-Barlow SD 10J	852	912	957	1,001	991	976	1,111
Hillsboro SD 1J	1,558	1,560	1,533	1,511	1,605	1,505	1,604
Klamath County SD	566	584	536	504	534	473	451
Lake Oswego SD 7J	526	569	558	642	639	666	627
Medford SD 549C	1,130	1,175	1,166	1,056	1,034	1,069	1,030
North Clackamas SD 12	1,230	1,355	1,319	1,401	1,382	1,357	1,418
Oregon City SD 62	599	608	639	637	595	589	646
Portland SD 1J	3,607	3,658	3,716	3,434	3,482	3,466	3,724
Redmond SD 2J	579	530	604	647	630	653	670
Reynolds SD 7	889	923	808	788	722	656	795
Salem-Keizer SD 24J	3,130	3,350	3,319	3,417	3,145	3,128	3,266
Springfield SD 19	751	833	813	828	810	757	783
Tigard-Tualatin SD 23J	914	947	921	970	938	950	1,045
West Linn-Wilsonville SD 3J	758	758	847	813	813	784	777
PENNSYLVANIA							
Allentown City SD	1,283	1,306	1,254	1,250	1,409	1,261	1,166
Bethlehem Area SD	980	969	1,093	1,160	1,196	1,097	1,110
Central Bucks SD	1,373	1,446	1,486	1,481	1,536	1,602	1,638
Central Dauphin SD	985	1,038	963	885	841	826	834
Commonwealth Charter Academy CS	1,322	1,504	1,550	1,968	1,441	1,117	1,212
Council Rock SD	842	879	890	872	889	927	919
Cumberland Valley SD	762	760	754	721	731	728	654
Downingtown Area SD	1,079	1,048	1,083	1,154	1,082	1,049	1,112
Erie City SD	795	772	775	770	796	828	700
Hazleton Area SD	904	966	902	998	905	804	841

NA = Not available.
X = Not applicable.

Table C-3. School Enrollment for the 20 Largest Public School Districts in Each State, by Grade Level, 2020–21—*Continued*

(Number.)

State/School District	Total students in all grades	Kindergarten	Grade 1	Grade 2	Grade 3	Grade 4	Grade 5
PENNSYLVANIA—*(Continued)*							
Lancaster SD	10,384	758	818	812	770	881	761
North Penn SD	12,603	841	995	914	902	907	924
Parkland SD	9,541	582	664	723	739	681	727
Pennsbury SD	9,544	596	709	679	712	751	767
Pennsylvania Cyber CS	10,917	400	536	507	569	634	671
Philadelphia City SD	124,111	7,000	9,530	9,790	9,914	9,961	9,728
Pittsburgh SD	21,407	1,438	1,642	1,609	1,500	1,668	1,494
Reading SD	17,659	1,233	1,362	1,262	1,371	1,347	1,378
Upper Darby SD	12,420	788	892	933	971	985	960
West Chester Area SD	11,972	809	896	900	899	874	848
RHODE ISLAND							
Barrington	3,388	227	197	232	233	243	259
Bristol Warren	3,061	196	227	216	234	218	233
Central Falls	2,780	181	201	203	179	176	179
Chariho	3,143	172	208	197	190	225	201
Coventry	4,390	280	263	304	291	318	318
Cranston	10,403	703	675	746	736	757	727
Cumberland	4,602	299	318	332	328	349	332
East Greenwich	2,532	154	149	163	171	202	194
East Providence	5,041	310	346	339	357	380	387
Johnston	3,110	238	222	235	243	231	237
Lincoln	3,213	227	237	223	225	225	258
North Kingstown	3,923	223	254	256	230	245	271
North Providence	3,525	238	259	237	243	234	259
Pawtucket	8,450	538	640	647	655	657	661
Providence	22,440	1,236	1,601	1,677	1,665	1,672	1,756
South Kingstown	2,750	149	175	198	192	194	193
Warwick	8,140	565	598	610	605	624	592
West Warwick	3,551	257	253	273	282	274	275
Westerly	2,433	140	173	161	161	170	170
Woonsocket	5,742	384	491	447	444	430	473
SOUTH CAROLINA							
Aiken 01	22,538	1,569	1,744	1,583	1,677	1,653	1,655
Anderson 05	12,771	854	931	983	983	960	933
Beaufort 01	21,219	1,425	1,446	1,467	1,512	1,590	1,604
Berkeley 01	36,575	2,454	2,699	2,705	2,669	2,635	2,807
Charleston 01	48,330	3,602	3,736	3,722	3,730	3,714	3,647
Charter Institute at Erskine	23,750	1,548	1,511	1,450	1,524	1,528	1,565
Dorchester 02	24,684	1,586	1,758	1,718	1,722	1,743	1,852
Florence 01	15,186	1,048	1,076	1,064	1,172	1,143	1,154
Greenville 01	74,094	4,850	5,448	5,414	5,555	5,725	5,683
Horry 01	44,479	2,862	3,059	3,035	3,315	3,293	3,366
Lancaster 01	13,940	1,070	1,115	1,062	1,055	1,082	1,075
Lexington 01	27,072	1,778	1,890	2,028	1,974	1,956	2,093
Lexington 05	16,780	1,051	1,060	1,112	1,119	1,250	1,254
Pickens 01	15,689	1,126	1,131	1,114	1,187	1,147	1,099
Richland 01	22,202	1,625	1,730	1,663	1,692	1,679	1,671
Richland 02	27,761	1,764	1,869	1,893	1,987	2,053	2,052
SC Public Charter School District	15,773	1,066	1,107	1,116	1,069	1,079	1,131
Sumter 01	15,586	1,102	1,210	1,164	1,134	1,148	1,172
York 03	16,652	1,078	1,202	1,205	1,267	1,237	1,254
York 04	16,883	1,142	1,257	1,292	1,270	1,357	1,358
SOUTH DAKOTA							
Aberdeen School District 06-1	4,485	327	338	343	314	348	314
Belle Fourche School District 09-1	1,380	107	102	103	98	104	88
Brandon Valley School District 49-2	4,721	471	360	384	367	333	347
Brookings School District 05-1	3,346	288	255	229	257	266	243
Dakota Valley School District 61-8	1,377	99	84	105	112	112	108
Douglas School District 51-1	2,755	224	208	237	200	213	235
Harrisburg School District 41-2	5,457	516	483	426	472	450	438
Huron School District 02-2	2,766	219	239	221	234	234	240
Meade School District 46-1	3,006	254	235	225	221	238	261
Mitchell School District 17-2	2,775	252	192	180	194	210	184
Oglala Lakota County 65-1	1,807	123	143	155	153	137	169
Pierre School District 32-2	2,771	248	193	195	194	201	208
Rapid City Area School District 51-4	12,814	888	910	960	973	894	990
Sioux Falls School District 49-5	24,868	1,893	1,911	1,860	1,841	1,852	1,889

NA = Not available.
X = Not applicable.

Table C-3. School Enrollment for the 20 Largest Public School Districts in Each State, by Grade Level, 2020–21—*Continued*

(Number.)

State/School District	Grade 6	Grade 7	Grade 8	Grade 9	Grade 10	Grade 11	Grade 12
PENNSYLVANIA—*(Continued)*							
Lancaster SD	811	806	748	824	823	748	575
North Penn SD	991	1,015	1,001	1,047	1,045	1,026	995
Parkland SD	712	761	762	807	793	788	802
Pennsbury SD	774	824	841	702	660	758	771
Pennsylvania Cyber CS	826	916	1,023	1,425	1,181	1,175	1,054
Philadelphia City SD	9,217	9,365	9,420	10,182	10,402	9,484	8,625
Pittsburgh SD	1,558	1,658	1,636	1,631	1,565	1,478	1,572
Reading SD	1,366	1,361	1,339	1,733	1,417	1,129	1,013
Upper Darby SD	1,009	982	997	959	978	968	998
West Chester Area SD	956	958	929	940	978	979	1,006
RHODE ISLAND							
Barrington	260	279	305	286	286	241	298
Bristol Warren	232	248	228	266	236	217	279
Central Falls	202	214	210	165	242	210	223
Chariho	221	255	229	313	300	292	263
Coventry	354	323	361	379	350	366	360
Cranston	781	827	858	808	885	880	892
Cumberland	343	352	387	362	375	372	361
East Greenwich	225	196	220	192	209	205	216
East Providence	377	387	384	452	411	382	356
Johnston	251	265	259	207	193	189	232
Lincoln	267	265	252	276	230	237	225
North Kingstown	271	285	306	361	383	385	378
North Providence	266	287	296	277	284	290	297
Pawtucket	708	750	793	577	557	538	579
Providence	1,706	1,860	1,743	1,937	1,967	1,678	1,680
South Kingstown	227	205	220	252	224	230	243
Warwick	628	677	622	644	620	638	594
West Warwick	276	279	315	255	271	238	253
Westerly	210	200	203	190	186	197	213
Woonsocket	443	439	486	467	420	395	392
SOUTH CAROLINA							
Aiken 01	1,660	1,794	1,886	1,951	1,855	1,515	1,410
Anderson 05	1,007	1,037	1,026	1,127	957	835	741
Beaufort 01	1,609	1,673	1,654	1,970	1,675	1,495	1,394
Berkeley 01	2,947	3,040	2,919	2,800	2,626	2,653	2,418
Charleston 01	3,755	3,648	3,718	3,952	3,289	2,980	2,806
Charter Institute at Erskine	1,819	1,871	2,077	2,386	2,369	2,024	2,028
Dorchester 02	2,019	2,080	2,109	2,167	2,034	1,677	1,738
Florence 01	1,208	1,262	1,212	1,338	1,208	991	991
Greenville 01	5,966	6,201	6,118	6,261	5,675	5,026	4,732
Horry 01	3,615	3,663	3,750	3,966	3,413	3,180	2,827
Lancaster 01	1,126	1,156	1,090	1,121	1,089	882	821
Lexington 01	2,130	2,129	2,168	2,349	2,124	1,879	1,923
Lexington 05	1,262	1,296	1,466	1,489	1,407	1,388	1,263
Pickens 01	1,070	1,300	1,235	1,365	1,288	1,073	1,062
Richland 01	1,700	1,805	1,741	1,935	1,580	1,456	1,225
Richland 02	2,194	2,315	2,372	2,504	2,235	1,985	1,826
SC Public Charter School District	1,402	1,250	1,155	1,356	1,372	1,338	1,154
Sumter 01	1,254	1,238	1,255	1,287	1,297	956	921
York 03	1,350	1,358	1,352	1,380	1,246	1,282	1,052
York 04	1,361	1,351	1,382	1,413	1,271	1,178	1,130
SOUTH DAKOTA							
Aberdeen School District 06-1	338	367	375	349	336	350	383
Belle Fourche School District 09-1	112	101	98	122	124	108	113
Brandon Valley School District 49-2	359	350	359	343	389	315	305
Brookings School District 05-1	236	305	253	275	261	235	243
Dakota Valley School District 61-8	114	114	133	122	91	91	92
Douglas School District 51-1	232	203	227	242	211	180	143
Harrisburg School District 41-2	461	430	404	407	314	313	300
Huron School District 02-2	213	215	201	269	189	149	143
Meade School District 46-1	257	262	274	259	105	177	150
Mitchell School District 17-2	211	235	243	276	197	219	182
Oglala Lakota County 65-1	156	150	175	202	94	54	39
Pierre School District 32-2	232	236	245	232	213	204	170
Rapid City Area School District 51-4	995	976	1,093	1,315	1,025	914	762
Sioux Falls School District 49-5	1,910	1,848	1,860	2,111	1,009	1,629	1,468

NA – Not available.
X = Not applicable.

Table C-3. School Enrollment for the 20 Largest Public School Districts in Each State, by Grade Level, 2020–21—*Continued*

(Number.)

State/School District	Total students in all grades	Kindergarten	Grade 1	Grade 2	Grade 3	Grade 4	Grade 5
SOUTH DAKOTA—*(Continued)*							
Spearfish School District 40-2	2,345	158	144	158	151	189	192
Tea Area School District 41-5	2,061	196	166	154	166	171	187
Todd County School District 66-1	2,158	175	223	171	164	189	161
Watertown School District 14-4	3,953	291	260	301	270	278	290
West Central School District 49-7	1,384	129	104	104	94	85	99
Yankton School District 63-3	2,955	263	193	197	194	188	188
TENNESSEE							
Achievement School District	9,027	646	775	738	794	700	754
Blount County	10,399	768	803	766	771	730	781
Bradley County	9,701	684	688	708	725	693	681
Collierville	9,043	640	607	649	718	664	656
Davidson County	80,494	5,870	6,449	6,529	6,349	6,397	5,861
Hamblen County	10,210	713	734	761	750	752	730
Hamilton County	44,100	3,277	3,443	3,424	3,483	3,407	3,360
Knox County	59,169	4,080	4,220	4,232	4,553	4,315	4,326
Madison County	12,378	911	939	935	946	915	913
Maury County	12,734	1,017	923	972	907	995	948
Montgomery County	36,426	2,686	2,988	2,744	2,893	2,765	2,790
Putnam County	11,609	770	838	847	837	851	816
Robertson County	13,960	851	873	907	918	930	967
Rutherford County	47,186	2,738	2,738	2,818	2,826	2,883	2,933
Sevier County	14,140	1,005	1,078	1,053	1,010	1,061	1,055
Shelby County	110,780	8,070	8,811	8,942	8,684	8,794	8,660
Sumner County	29,588	2,048	2,138	2,121	2,126	2,367	2,281
Tipton County	10,393	722	766	722	719	726	727
Williamson County	39,817	2,394	2,608	2,704	2,759	2,864	2,947
Wilson County	18,444	1,154	1,235	1,222	1,291	1,226	1,233
TEXAS							
Aldine ISD	63,302	4,259	4,435	4,422	4,515	4,711	4,762
Arlington ISD	56,840	3,659	3,880	3,840	3,785	3,920	4,051
Austin ISD	74,871	5,664	5,761	5,683	5,602	5,538	5,478
Conroe ISD	64,563	4,296	4,606	4,609	4,658	4,660	4,974
Cypress-Fairbanks ISD	114,881	7,205	7,761	7,768	7,818	8,159	8,341
Dallas ISD	145,113	10,209	10,532	10,572	10,430	10,533	10,790
El Paso ISD	50,661	2,925	3,314	3,394	3,433	3,353	3,609
Fort Bend ISD	76,735	4,381	4,999	5,121	5,432	5,541	5,798
Fort Worth ISD	76,858	5,340	5,394	5,312	5,390	5,534	5,816
Frisco ISD	63,493	3,738	4,065	4,447	4,636	4,646	4,859
Garland ISD	53,921	3,312	3,623	3,666	3,809	3,741	3,911
Houston ISD	196,943	13,886	15,108	15,159	15,590	15,725	15,963
Idea Public Schools	62,158	6,736	6,669	6,161	5,035	4,073	3,900
Katy ISD	84,176	5,460	5,736	5,891	6,133	6,133	6,446
Klein ISD	52,824	3,082	3,441	3,529	3,686	3,797	3,857
Lewisville ISD	49,361	2,939	3,344	3,232	3,326	3,417	3,476
North East ISD	60,483	3,589	4,052	4,130	4,255	4,275	4,388
Northside ISD	103,151	6,636	6,958	7,155	7,103	7,669	7,773
Pasadena ISD	50,614	3,227	3,429	3,379	3,483	3,604	3,563
Plano ISD	50,154	3,103	3,303	3,509	3,559	3,591	3,761
UTAH							
Alpine District	82,800	5,667	5,814	5,913	5,896	5,930	6,027
American Preparatory Academy	5,329	497	488	523	523	514	542
Box Elder District	12,062	876	842	885	845	882	918
Cache District	19,214	1,268	1,316	1,344	1,365	1,408	1,388
Canyons District	34,383	2,177	2,426	2,371	2,372	2,378	2,567
Davis District	72,082	4,483	4,940	5,030	5,040	5,097	5,344
Granite District	63,430	3,911	4,499	4,591	4,420	4,550	4,660
Iron District	11,091	894	839	867	839	847	867
Jordan District	57,267	3,556	3,818	4,040	3,915	4,122	4,228
Logan City District	5,704	482	479	491	411	414	432
Murray District	6,175	419	460	446	437	439	479
Nebo District	35,912	2,537	2,541	2,578	2,604	2,753	2,704
Ogden City District	10,710	748	815	816	807	819	766
Provo District	13,575	907	946	959	911	970	971
Salt Lake District	20,798	1,278	1,447	1,462	1,429	1,539	1,474
Tooele District	21,535	1,575	1,731	1,701	1,741	1,736	1,690
Uintah District	6,787	472	507	497	469	498	543
Wasatch District	9,251	741	768	774	780	774	743

NA = Not available.
X = Not applicable.

Table C-3. School Enrollment for the 20 Largest Public School Districts in Each State, by Grade Level, 2020–21—*Continued*

(Number.)

State/School District	Grade 6	Grade 7	Grade 8	Grade 9	Grade 10	Grade 11	Grade 12
SOUTH DAKOTA—(*Continued*)							
Spearfish School District 40-2	179	214	225	195	190	192	158
Tea Area School District 41-5	181	157	162	151	123	127	120
Todd County School District 66-1	175	186	162	206	148	110	88
Watertown School District 14-4	293	322	309	355	301	306	276
West Central School District 49-7	104	104	105	112	119	120	105
Yankton School District 63-3	214	219	207	244	246	239	212
TENNESSEE							
Achievement School District	915	1,008	880	438	447	430	287
Blount County	779	839	854	812	800	785	757
Bradley County	667	747	751	773	764	790	781
Collierville	702	653	732	741	681	740	723
Davidson County	5,750	6,193	6,115	6,023	5,984	5,706	5,085
Hamblen County	768	773	896	800	810	768	705
Hamilton County	3,433	3,446	3,467	3,538	3,238	2,969	2,804
Knox County	4,492	4,495	4,744	4,842	4,634	4,504	4,489
Madison County	873	943	947	1,001	881	837	786
Maury County	937	999	1,046	1,003	941	861	852
Montgomery County	2,801	2,907	2,917	3,069	2,694	2,269	2,320
Putnam County	841	894	909	932	911	915	790
Robertson County	1,020	1,105	1,157	1,364	1,345	1,217	1,101
Rutherford County	3,510	4,519	4,499	4,587	4,400	4,185	3,956
Sevier County	1,063	1,129	1,152	1,176	1,057	1,037	1,046
Shelby County	8,198	8,424	8,157	8,535	7,879	7,051	6,775
Sumner County	2,281	2,352	2,387	2,402	2,260	2,271	2,117
Tipton County	810	829	851	830	802	795	752
Williamson County	2,965	3,096	3,169	3,550	3,529	3,438	3,250
Wilson County	1,264	1,352	1,335	1,850	1,799	1,642	1,598
TEXAS							
Aldine ISD	4,901	4,910	4,960	5,022	4,732	4,417	4,089
Arlington ISD	4,283	4,394	4,306	4,690	4,663	4,303	4,006
Austin ISD	5,431	5,405	5,425	5,755	5,623	4,979	4,974
Conroe ISD	5,113	5,139	5,170	5,085	5,222	4,837	4,501
Cypress-Fairbanks ISD	8,930	8,972	9,226	9,981	9,072	8,918	9,057
Dallas ISD	10,494	10,578	10,621	11,426	11,193	9,677	8,818
El Paso ISD	3,432	3,664	3,918	4,669	4,537	4,442	4,241
Fort Bend ISD	5,889	6,153	6,255	6,815	6,475	5,992	6,023
Fort Worth ISD	5,674	5,690	5,902	6,347	6,162	5,159	4,929
Frisco ISD	5,034	5,278	5,320	5,294	5,230	5,097	4,746
Garland ISD	4,065	4,354	4,347	4,405	4,671	4,119	4,015
Houston ISD	13,309	13,480	13,915	14,976	14,001	12,597	11,966
Idea Public Schools	6,143	5,529	4,691	3,350	2,577	1,995	1,463
Katy ISD	6,732	6,671	6,630	6,654	6,666	6,448	6,038
Klein ISD	4,244	4,207	4,325	4,732	4,384	4,184	4,077
Lewisville ISD	3,729	3,836	3,943	4,253	4,352	4,173	4,192
North East ISD	4,485	4,810	4,840	5,289	5,225	4,819	4,927
Northside ISD	7,728	7,960	8,282	8,595	8,384	7,921	7,358
Pasadena ISD	3,938	3,931	4,099	4,002	4,119	3,910	3,859
Plano ISD	3,809	4,005	4,046	3,921	4,028	4,049	4,126
UTAH							
Alpine District	6,196	6,679	6,718	6,447	6,557	6,518	6,449
American Preparatory Academy	493	492	434	306	205	167	145
Box Elder District	953	916	995	969	916	929	855
Cache District	1,431	1,452	1,492	1,655	1,566	1,609	1,492
Canyons District	2,629	2,685	2,717	2,914	3,029	2,682	2,625
Davis District	5,447	5,967	6,005	5,835	5,787	5,815	5,567
Granite District	4,899	5,105	5,077	5,110	5,107	4,838	4,814
Iron District	833	846	859	822	781	745	702
Jordan District	4,301	4,668	4,730	4,588	4,723	4,622	4,694
Logan City District	411	399	405	421	366	390	366
Murray District	452	489	519	495	484	490	466
Nebo District	2,773	2,854	2,901	2,814	2,857	2,615	2,705
Ogden City District	824	861	760	790	831	846	917
Provo District	1,009	1,020	1,127	1,112	1,104	1,094	1,149
Salt Lake District	1,592	1,547	1,586	1,765	1,730	1,688	1,778
Tooele District	1,680	1,663	1,572	1,734	1,511	1,489	1,371
Uintah District	545	558	553	584	473	470	462
Wasatch District	692	698	698	586	608	606	544

NA = Not available.
X = Not applicable.

Table C-3. School Enrollment for the 20 Largest Public School Districts in Each State, by Grade Level, 2020–21—*Continued*

(Number.)

State/School District	Total students in all grades	Kindergarten	Grade 1	Grade 2	Grade 3	Grade 4	Grade 5
UTAH—*(Continued)*							
Washington District	36,992	2,332	2,565	2,557	2,513	2,750	2,768
Weber District	32,423	2,109	2,177	2,221	2,312	2,363	2,481
VERMONT							
Addison Central Unified School District	1,742	116	122	115	125	116	115
Barre Unified Union School District #97	2,169	152	143	156	138	166	150
Burlington School District	3,591	228	232	253	224	264	248
Champlain Valley Unified School District	4,150	224	276	272	249	275	283
Colchester School District	2,361	158	151	155	174	154	138
Essex-Westford Educational Community Unified School District	3,831	222	256	230	250	221	255
Hartford School District	1,441	85	85	94	90	89	93
Harwood Unified School District	1,813	111	128	124	126	120	117
Kingdom East Unified Union School District	1,631	114	101	108	124	130	103
Lamoille South Unified Union School District #90	1,581	83	93	117	79	104	117
Maple Run Unified School District	2,597	151	168	180	188	174	168
Milton Incorporated School District	1,534	91	102	103	95	94	92
Missisquoi Valley School District #89	1,784	125	134	101	119	136	128
Mount Anthony UHSD #14	1,468	X	X	X	X	X	X
Mount Mansfield Unified Union School District #401	2,569	171	169	166	185	154	160
Rutland City School District	2,012	126	145	116	134	119	121
South Burlington School District	2,688	171	177	171	173	172	160
Taconic and Green Regional School District	1,611	74	103	92	96	105	103
Washington Central Unified Union School District #92	1,473	72	76	74	88	94	107
Windham Southeast Unified Union School District #96	2,353	138	145	154	141	155	140
VIRGINIA							
Alexandria City Public Schools	15,775	1,265	1,383	1,361	1,269	1,261	1,225
Arlington County Public Schools	26,831	1,963	2,099	2,177	2,118	2,018	2,047
Chesapeake City Public Schools	39,673	2,319	2,640	2,615	2,870	2,806	2,936
Chesterfield Co Public Schools	60,840	3,627	4,184	4,435	4,224	4,587	4,538
Fairfax County Public Schools	180,028	10,861	12,480	12,777	12,780	13,277	13,174
Frederick County Public Schools	13,521	908	917	940	971	941	989
Hampton City Public Schools	19,223	1,239	1,440	1,420	1,399	1,375	1,479
Hanover County Public Schools	16,519	947	1,067	1,091	1,116	1,198	1,224
Henrico County Public Schools	50,191	3,150	3,584	3,596	3,637	3,618	3,632
Loudoun County Public Schools	81,066	4,806	5,614	5,560	6,001	6,062	6,123
Newport News City Public Schools	27,113	1,835	2,113	2,070	2,047	2,053	2,099
Norfolk City Public Schools	27,955	2,082	2,235	2,196	2,191	2,192	2,158
Prince William County Public Schools	89,548	5,567	6,303	6,511	6,594	6,621	6,741
Richmond City Public Schools	28,225	2,208	2,343	2,241	2,473	2,297	2,296
Roanoke City Public Schools	13,853	1,004	1,088	1,076	1,069	1,045	1,045
Roanoke County Public Schools	13,690	882	884	962	912	959	1,040
Spotsylvania County Public Schools	23,025	1,362	1,562	1,548	1,599	1,669	1,716
Stafford County Public Schools	29,372	1,757	1,922	1,954	2,011	2,092	2,159
Suffolk City Public Schools	13,869	898	963	951	1,014	1,035	1,053
Virginia Beach City Public Schools	65,612	4,072	4,814	4,781	4,795	4,819	4,967
WASHINGTON							
Auburn School District	17,007	1,034	1,230	1,240	1,242	1,251	1,295
Bellevue School District	20,191	1,219	1,290	1,402	1,428	1,523	1,489
Bethel School District	20,076	1,346	1,481	1,508	1,509	1,541	1,553
Edmonds School District	20,851	1,445	1,534	1,555	1,513	1,484	1,546
Everett School District	20,226	1,446	1,547	1,652	1,570	1,556	1,522
Evergreen School District (Clark)	23,564	1,360	1,561	1,625	1,660	1,717	1,778
Federal Way School District	21,765	1,366	1,495	1,563	1,572	1,590	1,595
Highline School District	18,635	1,246	1,384	1,435	1,368	1,395	1,322
Issaquah School District	20,164	1,138	1,442	1,398	1,531	1,587	1,526
Kennewick School District	18,396	1,301	1,311	1,344	1,401	1,391	1,339
Kent School District	25,720	1,684	1,873	1,973	1,991	1,906	1,936
Lake Washington School District	30,964	2,098	2,403	2,557	2,494	2,546	2,549
Northshore School District	23,310	1,531	1,735	1,793	1,774	1,748	1,845
Pasco School District	18,614	1,274	1,323	1,391	1,378	1,403	1,452
Puyallup School District	22,398	1,407	1,676	1,598	1,611	1,649	1,709
Seattle School District No. 1	53,973	3,970	4,473	4,409	4,217	4,251	4,230
Spokane School District	28,280	1,901	2,191	2,275	2,194	2,149	2,266

NA = Not available.
X = Not applicable.

Table C-3. School Enrollment for the 20 Largest Public School Districts in Each State, by Grade Level, 2020–21—*Continued*

(Number.)

State/School District	Grade 6	Grade 7	Grade 8	Grade 9	Grade 10	Grade 11	Grade 12
UTAH—(*Continued*)							
Washington District	2,838	3,011	3,131	2,960	2,881	2,903	2,892
Weber District	2,499	2,783	2,710	2,603	2,620	2,582	2,636
VERMONT							
Addison Central Unified School District	113	123	135	116	162	135	105
Barre Unified Union School District #97	161	140	163	151	171	162	170
Burlington School District.....................................	219	276	259	240	275	255	243
Champlain Valley Unified School District	273	292	287	325	347	285	345
Colchester School District....................................	159	172	188	182	184	165	165
Essex-Westford Educational Community Unified School District	280	285	281	299	315	310	322
Hartford School District	97	94	104	121	136	122	124
Harwood Unified School District............................	131	125	138	118	123	117	128
Kingdom East Unified Union School District.........	124	125	131	135	136	135	119
Lamoille South Unified Union School District #90	112	150	124	116	142	109	106
Maple Run Unified School District	183	183	177	233	242	225	165
Milton Incorporated School District	108	116	106	133	115	118	124
Missisquoi Valley School District #89	121	135	126	120	151	140	127
Mount Anthony UHSD #14.....................................	126	228	217	227	273	201	196
Mount Mansfield Unified Union School District #401..............	152	170	195	191	213	187	201
Rutland City School District..................................	122	112	122	204	216	197	178
South Burlington School District...........................	147	166	189	236	218	227	211
Taconic and Green Regional School District...........	84	111	112	149	145	161	181
Washington Central Unified Union School District #92..................	97	124	116	124	117	141	115
Windham Southeast Unified Union School District #96	142	188	200	208	183	192	187
VIRGINIA							
Alexandria City Public Schools.............................	1,129	1,127	1,167	1,139	1,132	911	991
Arlington County Public Schools...........................	2,031	2,006	2,036	1,884	2,030	1,861	1,907
Chesapeake City Public Schools	3,106	3,171	3,309	3,346	3,365	3,256	3,276
Chesterfield Co Public Schools	4,834	4,763	4,957	5,114	5,102	4,832	4,796
Fairfax County Public Schools	13,553	14,289	14,175	14,678	14,993	14,800	14,713
Frederick County Public Schools..........................	1,045	1,088	1,174	1,163	1,090	1,075	1,102
Hampton City Public Schools................................	1,446	1,503	1,556	1,621	1,613	1,374	1,300
Hanover County Public Schools............................	1,294	1,322	1,355	1,447	1,430	1,428	1,427
Henrico County Public Schools.............................	3,808	3,982	4,031	4,420	4,135	3,918	3,707
Loudoun County Public Schools	6,352	6,698	6,760	6,640	6,747	6,679	6,546
Newport News City Public Schools	2,026	2,060	2,102	2,253	2,086	1,665	1,657
Norfolk City Public Schools..................................	2,159	2,067	2,054	2,291	2,017	1,442	1,593
Prince William County Public Schools	6,951	6,918	7,154	7,664	7,388	7,001	6,763
Richmond City Public Schools..............................	2,253	2,257	2,206	1,810	1,961	1,551	1,317
Roanoke City Public Schools	996	1,099	1,053	1,062	990	900	790
Roanoke County Public Schools	1,049	1,105	1,127	1,203	1,125	1,035	1,052
Spotsylvania County Public Schools	1,700	1,908	1,912	1,978	2,022	1,813	1,835
Stafford County Public Schools	2,243	2,424	2,449	2,561	2,541	2,304	2,481
Suffolk City Public Schools..................................	1,031	1,114	1,109	1,271	1,091	999	992
Virginia Beach City Public Schools.......................	5,068	5,181	5,090	5,453	5,328	4,933	4,988
WASHINGTON							
Auburn School District...	1,301	1,316	1,263	1,352	1,372	1,356	1,399
Bellevue School District	1,624	1,560	1,602	1,627	1,646	1,750	1,749
Bethel School District	1,563	1,610	1,611	1,517	1,458	1,458	1,593
Edmonds School District	1,536	1,644	1,558	1,556	1,560	1,622	1,900
Everett School District	1,592	1,618	1,506	1,489	1,438	1,489	1,460
Evergreen School District (Clark)	1,803	1,870	1,952	1,950	1,941	1,948	2,134
Federal Way School District	1,649	1,747	1,752	1,753	1,666	1,695	1,839
Highline School District	1,401	1,407	1,303	1,364	1,400	1,379	1,797
Issaquah School District	1,649	1,594	1,665	1,646	1,624	1,604	1,606
Kennewick School District	1,422	1,426	1,508	1,447	1,358	1,339	1,405
Kent School District	2,012	2,007	2,078	2,001	1,811	1,971	2,180
Lake Washington School District	2,389	2,457	2,390	2,274	2,234	2,130	2,094
Northshore School District...................................	1,759	1,844	1,758	1,866	1,764	1,715	1,850
Pasco School District...	1,502	1,497	1,470	1,472	1,437	1,333	1,481
Puyallup School District.......................................	1,899	1,738	1,784	1,741	1,697	1,747	1,802
Seattle School District No. 1	4,033	3,918	4,046	3,755	3,899	3,693	4,204
Spokane School District..	2,182	2,182	2,208	2,212	2,070	2,025	2,142

NA = Not available.
X = Not applicable.

Table C-3. School Enrollment for the 20 Largest Public School Districts in Each State, by Grade Level, 2020–21—*Continued*

(Number.)

State/School District	Total students in all grades	Kindergarten	Grade 1	Grade 2	Grade 3	Grade 4	Grade 5
WASHINGTON—(*Continued*)							
Tacoma School District	28,688	1,951	2,136	2,152	2,055	2,115	2,141
Vancouver School District	21,897	1,384	1,579	1,587	1,596	1,562	1,636
Yakima School District	15,858	1,030	1,147	1,168	1,185	1,141	1,201
WEST VIRGINIA							
Berkeley County Schools	19,278	1,386	1,188	1,437	1,350	1,373	1,404
Cabell County Schools	11,875	845	786	834	855	795	889
Fayette County Schools	5,688	363	356	421	403	416	443
Greenbrier County Schools	4,719	317	293	347	318	324	327
Harrison County Schools	10,111	674	592	710	665	709	727
Jackson County Schools	4,266	283	256	321	298	299	305
Jefferson County Schools	8,506	515	520	567	576	625	671
Kanawha County Schools	24,721	1,592	1,553	1,735	1,735	1,633	1,706
Logan County Schools	5,229	339	321	353	353	389	358
Marion County Schools	7,658	531	472	554	549	563	570
Marshall County Schools	4,320	317	257	309	333	328	315
Mercer County Schools	8,465	657	545	644	605	642	642
Mineral County Schools	4,001	258	233	302	307	280	310
Monongalia County Schools	11,113	789	734	768	800	820	756
Ohio County Schools	5,064	414	306	360	364	339	327
Preston County Schools	4,210	301	266	318	285	338	309
Putnam County Schools	9,147	632	575	631	620	676	625
Raleigh County Schools	10,869	678	670	803	759	846	846
Wayne County Schools	6,461	442	439	443	438	438	424
Wood County Schools	11,864	818	826	842	852	849	834
WISCONSIN							
Appleton Area School District	15,745	980	1,046	1,077	1,074	1,148	1,089
Eau Claire Area School District	11,008	772	772	782	714	753	720
Elmbrook School District	7,280	464	490	535	520	478	542
Fond du Lac School District	6,678	424	447	451	454	445	469
Green Bay Area Public School District	19,171	1,308	1,419	1,344	1,428	1,366	1,438
Janesville School District	9,574	650	661	609	587	582	638
Kenosha School District	19,244	1,173	1,323	1,266	1,354	1,327	1,335
Madison Metropolitan School District	26,151	1,893	1,966	1,858	1,839	1,831	1,836
Middleton-Cross Plains Area School District	7,410	489	466	512	496	533	525
Milwaukee School District	71,510	5,138	5,190	5,157	5,074	5,122	5,230
Neenah Joint School District	6,572	455	457	444	461	481	484
Oshkosh Area School District	9,191	591	623	636	672	611	658
Racine Unified School District	16,254	1,043	949	1,108	1,161	1,116	1,185
Sheboygan Area School District	9,663	666	615	654	653	697	637
Stevens Point Area Public School District	6,938	480	437	455	461	494	500
Sun Prairie Area School District	8,366	554	610	616	577	555	558
Waukesha School District	12,344	775	836	749	820	809	828
Wausau School District	7,786	495	509	473	493	566	563
Wauwatosa School District	6,917	431	467	432	453	447	457
West Allis-West Milwaukee School District	7,418	469	476	469	461	456	513
WYOMING							
Albany County School District #1	3,917	306	288	302	323	305	268
Big Horn County School District #1	1,837	111	112	135	131	122	143
Campbell County School District #1	8,567	720	613	603	657	626	688
Carbon County School District #1	1,680	139	126	117	124	126	137
Converse County School District #1	1,643	129	115	145	125	111	121
Fremont County School District # 1	1,705	117	101	112	117	120	135
Fremont County School District #25	2,311	184	158	169	184	130	171
Goshen County School District #1	1,606	118	117	109	119	125	106
Laramie County School District #1	13,994	1,019	1,011	1,034	1,015	1,039	1,128
Lincoln County School District #2	2,924	203	192	197	223	207	219
Natrona County School District #1	13,110	960	1,002	999	926	990	950
Niobrara County School District #1	1,397	95	109	103	86	100	115
Park County School District # 1	1,797	146	137	124	121	125	136
Park County School District # 6	1,974	153	143	146	166	141	135
Sheridan County School District #1	1,203	92	78	78	71	98	92
Sheridan County School District #2	3,519	276	270	239	254	274	281
Sweetwater County School District #1	5,141	390	373	392	361	387	399
Sweetwater County School District #2	2,359	196	174	139	161	171	165
Teton County School District #1	2,749	201	230	204	209	222	238
Uinta County School District #1	2,645	190	206	220	179	196	196

NA = Not available.
X = Not applicable.

Table C-3. School Enrollment for the 20 Largest Public School Districts in Each State, by Grade Level, 2020–21—*Continued*

(Number.)

State/School District	Grade 6	Grade 7	Grade 8	Grade 9	Grade 10	Grade 11	Grade 12
WASHINGTON—*(Continued)*							
Tacoma School District	2,136	2,241	2,284	2,192	2,091	2,154	2,154
Vancouver School District	1,740	1,784	1,813	1,761	1,726	1,690	1,790
Yakima School District	1,229	1,233	1,259	1,277	1,215	1,249	1,265
WEST VIRGINIA							
Berkeley County Schools	1,465	1,518	1,571	1,613	1,541	1,343	1,302
Cabell County Schools	866	907	882	984	895	863	840
Fayette County Schools	438	473	482	408	425	392	394
Greenbrier County Schools	367	377	371	382	369	337	315
Harrison County Schools	763	773	776	870	813	776	700
Jackson County Schools	327	347	344	349	341	297	298
Jefferson County Schools	658	689	733	682	736	684	617
Kanawha County Schools	1,873	1,943	1,905	2,284	2,010	1,822	1,751
Logan County Schools	371	399	414	439	476	406	383
Marion County Schools	572	595	554	602	578	524	542
Marshall County Schools	345	332	322	323	332	299	290
Mercer County Schools	669	695	656	668	594	552	529
Mineral County Schools	283	314	284	294	308	315	253
Monongalia County Schools	820	805	801	857	951	823	769
Ohio County Schools	385	387	382	390	400	376	352
Preston County Schools	317	332	328	348	313	283	265
Putnam County Schools	671	698	703	786	734	743	681
Raleigh County Schools	854	857	893	915	873	742	625
Wayne County Schools	497	508	527	502	484	466	452
Wood County Schools	888	905	892	980	961	905	774
WISCONSIN							
Appleton Area School District	1,205	1,150	1,180	1,160	1,207	1,244	1,357
Eau Claire Area School District	725	866	817	824	813	809	902
Elmbrook School District	552	571	536	622	623	680	621
Fond du Lac School District	486	490	514	493	511	510	529
Green Bay Area Public School District	1,379	1,498	1,469	1,377	1,297	1,371	1,429
Janesville School District	675	717	722	810	744	718	883
Kenosha School District	1,461	1,489	1,504	1,493	1,514	1,498	1,624
Madison Metropolitan School District	1,866	1,782	1,828	1,853	1,928	1,991	2,141
Middleton-Cross Plains Area School District	530	575	565	591	628	584	598
Milwaukee School District	5,194	5,176	5,120	6,189	4,989	4,659	4,066
Neenah Joint School District	482	444	485	496	506	508	493
Oshkosh Area School District	668	682	707	754	687	716	717
Racine Unified School District	1,190	1,141	1,261	1,249	1,246	1,283	1,370
Sheboygan Area School District	693	723	720	745	760	712	783
Stevens Point Area Public School District	523	499	509	530	534	522	516
Sun Prairie Area School District	610	629	625	632	638	605	629
Waukesha School District	878	850	936	1,019	1,008	1,082	1,122
Wausau School District	553	596	622	626	573	642	623
Wauwatosa School District	500	519	532	570	553	624	598
West Allis-West Milwaukee School District	550	615	580	633	590	630	643
WYOMING							
Albany County School District #1	299	321	281	333	301	281	277
Big Horn County School District #1	137	168	161	145	160	140	134
Campbell County School District #1	705	738	722	648	687	596	564
Carbon County School District #1	130	134	149	131	123	121	123
Converse County School District #1	127	121	109	139	135	140	126
Fremont County School District # 1	129	146	143	159	160	134	132
Fremont County School District #25	166	206	184	229	187	167	157
Goshen County School District #1	130	131	145	121	136	123	126
Laramie County School District #1	1,109	1,140	1,145	1,305	1,054	987	854
Lincoln County School District #2	239	249	261	231	235	229	239
Natrona County School District #1	986	988	1,051	1,012	1,015	939	936
Niobrara County School District #1	114	148	150	115	85	97	80
Park County School District # 1	140	130	141	165	149	130	153
Park County School District # 6	159	145	170	148	170	156	136
Sheridan County School District #1	101	94	116	105	94	99	85
Sheridan County School District #2	284	294	289	281	200	246	251
Sweetwater County School District #1	407	413	432	442	410	349	386
Sweetwater County School District #2	210	207	209	171	189	172	195
Teton County School District #1	225	220	231	212	196	192	169
Uinta County School District #1	219	215	207	197	206	200	214

NA – Not available.
X = Not applicable.

Table C-4. School Enrollment for the 20 Largest Public School Districts in Each State, by Race/Ethnicity, 2020–21

(Number; percent.)

State/County	Total students in all grades	White (percent)	Black or African American (percent)	Hispanic (percent)	Asian or Asian/ Pacific Islander (percent)	American Indian/ Alaska Native (percent)	Nat. Hawaiian or Other Pacific Islander (percent)	Two or More Races (percent)
ALABAMA								
Auburn City	8,971	56.2	22.5	7.0	11.1	-	-	3.2
Autauga County	8,955	63.8	27.1	4.3	2.0	0.3	0.1	2.5
Baldwin County	30,210	69.6	11.9	10.9	1.0	0.3	0.1	6.2
Birmingham City	21,597	1.2	88.7	8.9	0.1	0.3	0.1	0.5
Cullman County	9,312	82.9	0.7	9.6	0.1	0.2	0.3	6.3
Decatur City	8,781	33.5	29.5	31.2	1.0	0.2	0.1	4.5
Elmore County	11,519	65.6	27.2	2.5	0.8	0.4	0.1	3.3
Hoover City	13,640	55.0	23.5	8.5	7.2	0.1	-	5.8
Huntsville City	23,514	37.1	39.0	15.0	1.5	0.4	0.3	6.7
Jefferson County	35,336	35.1	50.8	12.1	0.5	0.2	0.1	1.3
Lee County	9,310	64.4	20.6	7.6	0.4	0.1	0.2	6.8
Limestone County	13,041	69.5	15.7	10.3	0.7	0.9	0.1	2.7
Madison City	11,804	58.4	19.3	7.3	9.1	0.6	0.2	5.1
Madison County	19,142	60.9	21.7	6.1	1.4	5.2	0.2	4.5
Mobile County	52,460	37.6	50.6	5.1	2.2	1.0	0.1	3.4
Montgomery County	27,399	7.9	78.5	7.7	3.6	1.3	0.2	0.8
Shelby County	20,438	69.0	16.9	9.3	2.0	0.2	0.1	2.4
St Clair County	9,407	81.0	9.3	5.8	0.7	0.1	0.1	3.1
Tuscaloosa City	10,744	22.9	67.8	5.6	1.8	0.3	0.2	1.4
Tuscaloosa County	18,766	57.7	29.7	10.6	0.7	0.3	0.1	0.9
ALASKA								
Anchorage School District	41,856	40.0	4.9	11.8	11.0	9.1	7.2	15.9
Bering Strait School District	1,839	1.1	0.3	0.2	0.1	98.0	-	0.2
Chugach School District	694	64.6	1.3	6.2	2.0	10.2	4.2	11.5
Craig City School District	867	54.8	1.8	2.3	2.4	16.5	1.5	20.6
Delta/Greely School District	775	76.9	0.6	10.1	0.5	3.2	1.8	6.8
Denali Borough School District	1,206	61.0	4.9	10.1	2.2	7.7	2.6	11.4
Fairbanks North Star Borough School District	11,386	56.5	4.0	9.6	2.1	8.7	1.3	17.9
Galena City School District	9,366	70.6	1.4	5.1	1.1	11.8	0.7	9.4
Juneau Borough School District	4,124	44.8	0.9	7.4	6.6	15.4	3.0	21.8
Kenai Peninsula Borough School District	7,962	72.9	0.5	4.3	1.0	7.8	0.3	13.1
Ketchikan Gateway Borough School District	2,161	50.4	0.9	1.8	9.3	30.9	1.0	5.7
Kodiak Island Borough School District	2,294	42.2	0.5	6.0	24.2	21.1	1.4	4.6
Lower Kuskokwim School District	4,082	3.1	0.1	0.3	0.3	95.9	-	0.2
Lower Yukon School District	2,103	0.6	-	-	-	98.0	-	1.3
Matanuska-Susitna Borough School District	18,220	67.8	0.8	7.3	1.2	8.5	0.8	13.8
Nenana City School District	1,909	67.0	2.4	3.3	2.0	12.0	1.7	11.7
North Slope Borough School District	2,138	1.5	0.5	-	5.4	78.0	3.1	11.5
Northwest Arctic Borough School District	2,050	2.1	0.3	0.3	0.2	92.1	0.2	4.7
Sitka School District	1,151	50.0	0.8	4.7	7.5	27.7	1.0	8.3
Yukon-Koyukuk School District	4,331	57.8	2.5	4.7	1.6	21.3	1.8	10.3
ARIZONA								
Cartwright Elementary District	15,177	2.6	5.6	89.3	0.4	1.2	0.1	0.8
Chandler Unified District #80	43,790	49.8	5.2	28.6	9.8	1.3	0.3	4.9
Deer Valley Unified District	32,061	66.4	3.8	20.9	3.9	1.0	0.4	3.7
Dysart Unified District	23,011	42.3	6.9	41.9	1.6	0.9	0.4	5.9
Gilbert Unified District	32,661	59.6	2.8	27.0	3.6	1.1	0.5	5.3
Glendale Union High School District	16,462	23.4	9.0	60.1	3.2	2.3	0.3	1.7
Higley Unified School District	12,679	62.7	4.8	21.5	3.6	0.9	0.5	6.1
Kyrene Elementary District	15,632	40.7	9.9	30.8	5.3	4.0	0.4	8.9
Marana Unified District	12,395	52.4	2.1	38.1	1.7	1.3	0.2	4.2
Mesa Unified District	57,956	40.0	4.6	46.0	1.2	4.3	0.8	3.1
Paradise Valley Unified District	29,109	54.2	3.7	32.4	3.5	1.2	0.2	4.8
Peoria Unified School District	35,329	50.6	5.0	35.9	2.7	0.9	0.3	4.6
Phoenix Union High School District	27,037	4.5	8.8	81.0	1.5	2.5	0.2	1.5
Scottsdale Unified District	21,496	62.7	4.4	23.1	5.3	2.6	0.2	1.7
Sunnyside Unified District	14,942	3.3	2.5	89.9	0.4	2.8	0.1	1.0
Tempe Union High School District	12,868	36.0	11.5	38.4	4.4	4.2	0.8	4.8
Tolleson Union High School District	12,442	7.0	9.2	78.4	2.1	1.0	0.3	2.0
Tucson Unified District	41,898	19.5	6.3	64.5	1.6	3.6	0.5	4.0
Vail Unified District	13,642	51.0	3.8	36.2	1.9	0.4	0.2	6.4
Washington Elementary School District	20,511	24.6	10.2	54.6	2.7	3.4	0.2	4.3

- = Zero or rounds to zero.
NA = Not available.

Table C-4. School Enrollment for the 20 Largest Public School Districts in Each State, by Race/Ethnicity, 2020–21—*Continued*

(Number; percent.)

State/County	Total students in all grades	White (percent)	Black or African American (percent)	Hispanic (percent)	Asian or Asian/ Pacific Islander (percent)	American Indian/ Alaska Native (percent)	Nat. Hawaiian or Other Pacific Islander (percent)	Two or More Races (percent)
ARKANSAS								
Benton School District	5,485	76.0	9.1	9.4	0.9	0.3	0.1	4.2
Bentonville School District	17,970	71.0	3.1	11.7	7.7	1.2	0.5	4.7
Bryant School District	9,353	62.0	18.1	15.4	1.9	0.1	0.1	2.3
Cabot School District	10,471	83.0	2.6	6.4	1.4	0.3	0.2	6.0
Conway School District	10,035	52.5	29.8	11.3	1.6	0.2	-	4.6
El Dorado School District	4,150	36.8	48.4	9.7	1.3	-	0.1	3.5
Fayetteville School District	10,233	65.3	9.8	12.3	2.9	0.4	1.5	7.8
Fort Smith School District	14,361	39.4	10.9	34.1	5.2	0.9	0.1	9.4
Jonesboro School District	6,616	33.5	46.9	14.1	0.6	0.2	NA	4.7
Lake Hamilton School District	4,342	76.3	3.7	12.5	0.5	0.4	0.1	6.4
Little Rock School District	21,612	19.3	60.6	15.7	3.2	0.3	0.1	0.8
North Little Rock School District	7,930	25.7	60.0	10.0	1.0	1.0	0.1	2.3
Pulaski County Special School District	11,742	39.2	44.3	9.7	2.5	0.4	-	3.9
Rogers School District	15,545	42.9	1.5	47.9	1.9	0.6	2.1	3.0
Russellville School District	5,361	61.2	6.4	25.6	1.5	0.2	0.1	4.9
Sheridan School District	4,183	87.5	2.5	5.9	1.3	0.3	NA	2.4
Siloam Springs School District	4,294	52.1	1.1	32.3	3.1	5.3	0.3	5.6
Springdale School District	22,663	32.3	2.2	48.3	1.5	0.5	13.4	1.8
Van Buren School District	5,506	67.3	2.8	18.9	2.4	1.4	0.2	6.9
West Memphis School District	5,150	20.4	76.3	1.8	0.3	-	-	1.2
CALIFORNIA								
Capistrano Unified	43,719	54.1	0.8	27.1	8.4	0.2	0.1	9.2
Clovis Unified	42,790	36.2	3.2	39.2	17.0	0.6	0.3	3.5
Corona-Norco Unified	51,318	22.5	5.8	53.6	14.5	0.3	0.4	2.8
Elk Grove Unified	63,157	17.4	10.9	27.6	32.6	0.4	1.8	9.3
Fresno Unified	70,088	8.4	8.0	69.0	11.1	0.6	0.4	2.5
Garden Grove Unified	40,124	6.7	0.6	53.0	36.6	0.1	0.4	2.7
Irvine Unified	35,660	25.6	1.9	11.7	50.9	0.1	0.2	9.4
Kern High	42,370	18.5	5.6	69.0	4.1	0.6	0.3	1.9
Long Beach Unified	69,413	12.5	12.6	58.2	10.6	0.2	1.2	4.7
Los Angeles Unified	460,633	10.5	7.6	73.6	5.9	0.1	0.2	2.0
Poway Unified	35,663	40.6	1.7	17.3	28.6	0.1	0.2	11.5
Riverside Unified	39,443	19.1	5.9	66.2	4.7	0.3	0.3	3.3
Sacramento City Unified	40,711	17.1	12.6	40.8	19.2	0.5	2.2	7.6
San Bernardino City Unified	46,693	4.7	9.7	80.8	1.7	0.3	0.4	2.4
San Diego Unified	97,968	23.7	7.3	44.2	14.8	0.3	0.4	9.4
San Francisco Unified	51,790	14.8	6.3	28.3	37.5	0.2	0.8	12.2
San Juan Unified	39,218	49.3	6.9	25.4	9.9	0.6	0.6	7.2
Santa Ana Unified	44,271	0.8	0.2	95.9	2.3	0.3	0.2	0.4
Stockton Unified	36,190	4.7	9.4	68.2	12.8	1.0	0.5	3.3
Sweetwater Union High	37,060	10.7	3.0	69.9	10.9	0.4	0.4	4.6
COLORADO								
Academy School District No. 20	25,711	69.8	2.9	14.8	4.3	0.4	0.3	7.5
Adams 12 Five Star Schools	36,654	44.5	1.6	43.2	5.7	0.4	0.1	4.4
Aurora Joint District No. 28	37,907	14.7	17.4	55.6	4.8	0.7	1.0	5.7
Boulder Valley School District	29,240	67.4	0.9	19.4	5.7	0.3	0.1	6.2
Cherry Creek School District No. 5	54,184	50.2	11.6	20.7	8.9	0.6	0.3	7.7
Colorado Springs School District No. 11	23,885	49.2	8.0	32.9	1.5	0.7	0.5	7.1
Douglas County School District	62,979	71.9	1.3	14.8	5.9	0.4	0.1	5.6
El Paso County Colorado School District 49	23,984	55.4	4.7	28.3	2.0	0.7	0.3	8.5
GreeleySchool District No. 6	21,903	30.3	2.7	62.4	2.3	0.3	0.2	1.8
Harrison School District No. 2	11,177	23.3	12.9	53.3	1.8	0.6	0.8	7.2
Jefferson County School District	80,099	66.2	1.3	24.6	3.1	0.5	0.2	4.1
Littleton School District No. 6	14,132	73.2	1.4	17.5	2.7	0.4	0.2	4.7
Mesa County Valley School District No. 51	21,084	69.6	0.5	24.4	0.8	0.6	0.2	3.9
Poudre School District	29,418	72.2	1.2	19.2	2.8	0.5	0.1	3.9
Pueblo School District No. 60	15,219	24.3	2.1	70.0	0.6	0.5	0.2	2.2
School District 27J	19,203	42.9	2.1	48.1	3.2	0.3	0.2	3.3
School District No. 1	89,081	25.7	13.5	52.5	3.2	0.7	0.5	4.0
St. Vrain Valley School District	31,312	62.3	0.9	30.0	3.3	0.3	0.1	3.0
State Charter School Institute	20,749	53.8	3.5	35.5	3.0	0.5	0.1	3.7
Thompson School District	14,965	71.0	1.0	22.4	1.1	0.5	0.1	3.9

- = Zero or rounds to zero.
NA = Not available.

Table C-4. School Enrollment for the 20 Largest Public School Districts in Each State, by Race/Ethnicity, 2020–21—*Continued*

(Number; percent.)

State/County	Total students in all grades	White (percent)	Black or African American (percent)	Hispanic (percent)	Asian or Asian/ Pacific Islander (percent)	American Indian/ Alaska Native (percent)	Nat. Hawaiian or Other Pacific Islander (percent)	Two or More Races (percent)
CONNECTICUT								
Bridgeport School District	19,276	10.9	31.4	53.3	2.3	0.7	0.1	1.3
Bristol School District	7,611	51.3	7.4	33.0	3.4	0.1	-	4.9
Capitol Region Education Council	8,792	18.7	29.9	40.2	5.6	0.2	0.1	5.2
Connecticut Technical Education and Career System	11,331	41.7	11.7	40.9	1.2	0.3	0.1	4.1
Danbury School District	11,813	31.2	7.4	52.5	6.2	0.1	-	2.5
East Hartford School District	6,546	11.3	30.1	50.0	4.2	0.2	0.2	3.9
Fairfield School District	9,387	74.5	2.6	11.9	6.1	0.1	-	4.9
Greenwich School District	8,773	60.8	2.3	22.3	8.7	0.2	-	5.6
Hartford School District	17,054	8.2	29.2	54.7	5.0	0.3	0.2	2.5
Manchester School District	6,044	33.2	24.3	31.0	8.4	0.4	0.2	2.5
Meriden School District	8,072	24.7	10.7	58.3	2.1	0.1	-	4.0
New Britain School District	9,616	16.3	10.7	66.9	2.1	0.1	-	3.8
New Haven School District	19,827	11.6	35.5	47.5	2.8	0.2	0.1	2.3
Norwalk School District	11,509	25.2	14.6	52.7	4.4	0.1	0.1	2.9
Southington School District	6,152	78.8	2.4	10.5	3.8	0.1	0.1	4.4
Stamford School District	16,157	29.3	14.0	45.9	7.0	0.1	0.1	3.7
Stratford School District	6,632	32.3	24.0	36.7	2.7	0.1	-	4.2
Trumbull School District	6,719	66.2	5.9	15.9	9.7	0.2	0.1	2.0
Waterbury School District	18,374	14.1	21.5	58.6	1.6	0.6	-	3.6
West Hartford School District	9,117	56.8	9.2	18.5	10.9	0.1	0.2	4.2
DELAWARE								
Appoquinimink School District	11,914	50.6	28.1	8.3	8.4	0.3	0.2	4.1
Brandywine School District	10,405	43.0	38.0	7.6	7.1	0.5	0.2	3.6
Caesar Rodney School District	7,960	52.7	26.6	9.1	3.2	0.3	0.2	7.9
Cape Henlopen School District	5,892	67.6	11.3	15.1	1.7	0.5	0.2	3.6
Capital School District	6,332	25.5	52.6	13.3	2.0	0.8	0.2	5.6
Christina School District	12,963	27.3	39.1	21.3	6.5	0.2	0.2	5.4
Colonial School District	9,795	26.6	44.6	21.5	2.6	0.3	0.3	4.0
Delmar School District	1,365	64.2	14.1	11.5	2.7	0.3	0.1	7.2
Indian River School District	10,592	46.5	10.9	36.9	1.1	0.4	0.1	4.1
Lake Forest School District	3,505	60.6	22.3	8.2	1.0	0.5	NA	7.4
Laurel School District	2,546	46.9	25.5	19.2	0.8	1.3	0.2	6.2
Milford School District	4,214	47.1	25.3	21.9	0.9	0.3	0.2	4.3
MOT Charter School	1,383	49.3	25.5	7.1	13.1	0.2	0.1	4.7
New Castle County Vocational-Technical School District	4,644	28.1	38.4	28.1	1.5	0.9	0.1	2.8
Newark Charter School	2,436	60.4	11.9	6.2	15.3	0.1	NA	6.0
Odyssey Charter School	1,926	45.4	23.0	7.3	18.8	0.5	0.3	4.8
Red Clay Consolidated School District	15,057	39.7	21.6	29.4	5.1	0.2	-	4.0
Seaford School District	3,224	31.2	35.4	25.8	0.7	0.1	-	6.7
Smyrna School District	5,883	56.7	29.5	8.2	1.4	0.4	0.1	3.7
Woodbridge School District	2,478	45.9	22.6	25.9	0.9	0.1	0.1	4.6
DISTRICT OF COLUMBIA								
BASIS DC PCS	664	46.4	25.8	9.9	7.2	0.2	NA	10.5
Capital City PCS	1,018	7.0	30.1	58.3	1.2	NA	NA	3.4
Center City PCS	1,452	0.6	72.4	22.0	0.5	0.2	NA	4.4
DC Prep PCS	2,168	0.7	89.0	6.6	0.2	0.1	-	3.3
DC Scholars PCS	608	0.2	95.9	1.6	NA	NA	NA	2.3
District of Columbia International School	1,452	16.9	31.1	41.1	2.8	0.5	0.1	7.6
District of Columbia Public Schools	49,896	16.6	57.9	20.5	2.0	0.1	0.1	2.9
E.L. Haynes PCS	1,199	7.6	35.5	51.8	0.5	1.3	0.3	3.1
Eagle Academy PCS	706	3.5	94.3	1.6	0.4	0.1	NA	NA
Elsie Whitlow Stokes Community Freedom PCS	585	24.3	46.7	15.4	1.5	0.2	NA	11.8
Friendship PCS	4,565	0.5	96.4	2.0	0.1	0.2	0.1	0.7
Ingenuity Prep PCS	761	NA	97.4	2.2	0.3	NA	0.1	NA
KIPP DC PCS	7,000	0.1	98.1	1.5	0.1	0.1	0.1	0.1
Meridian PCS	605	7.1	64.6	26.8	1.2	NA	NA	0.3
Mundo Verde Bilingual PCS	955	33.3	23.9	29.9	2.1	0.1	NA	10.7
Paul PCS	726	0.4	55.6	42.6	0.6	NA	NA	0.8
Rocketship Education DC PCS	1,525	0.3	95.4	2.6	0.1	0.4	0.1	1.1
Two Rivers PCS	985	26.1	57.2	6.6	1.2	0.1	NA	8.8
Washington Latin PCS	734	40.7	38.8	10.6	3.0	NA	NA	6.8
Washington Yu Ying PCS	580	25.7	34.3	6.6	9.8	NA	NA	23.6

- = Zero or rounds to zero.
NA = Not available.

Table C-4. School Enrollment for the 20 Largest Public School Districts in Each State, by Race/Ethnicity, 2020–21—*Continued*

(Number; percent.)

State/County	Total students in all grades	White (percent)	Black or African American (percent)	Hispanic (percent)	Asian or Asian/ Pacific Islander (percent)	American Indian/ Alaska Native (percent)	Nat. Hawaiian or Other Pacific Islander (percent)	Two or More Races (percent)
FLORIDA								
Brevard	70,996	59.6	14.7	15.3	2.2	0.2	0.2	7.9
Broward	260,235	18.3	38.9	36.1	3.7	0.2	0.2	2.6
Collier	46,329	32.0	11.3	52.6	1.5	0.3	0.1	2.3
Duval	126,815	32.2	42.6	14.8	4.5	0.4	0.3	5.2
Hillsborough	218,943	31.7	21.0	37.8	4.2	0.2	0.2	4.9
Lake	43,706	49.4	15.6	27.2	2.3	0.6	0.2	4.7
Lee	94,927	36.7	14.0	44.3	1.7	0.2	0.1	3.1
Manatee	49,181	44.4	13.4	35.7	2.0	0.1	0.1	4.3
Miami-Dade	334,261	6.4	19.1	72.7	1.1	-	-	0.6
Orange	199,089	24.6	24.4	43.3	4.7	0.2	0.3	2.4
Osceola	68,640	21.9	11.0	62.0	2.2	0.2	0.2	2.4
Palm Beach	187,057	29.1	27.8	36.3	3.1	0.7	0.1	2.8
Pasco	77,125	59.6	7.7	23.8	3.1	0.3	0.2	5.2
Pinellas	96,068	53.0	19.0	18.3	4.2	0.2	0.3	5.0
Polk	100,495	36.7	20.1	38.4	1.6	0.3	0.1	2.8
Sarasota	42,618	61.5	8.0	21.6	2.6	0.2	0.1	6.0
Seminole	66,226	46.4	14.4	28.9	5.7	0.2	0.2	4.2
St. John's	44,550	73.0	6.4	10.9	5.0	0.1	0.2	4.5
St. Lucie	41,779	30.1	31.1	32.7	1.5	0.2	0.1	4.3
Volusia	61,088	55.7	16.2	21.1	2.0	0.2	0.2	4.6
GEORGIA								
Atlanta Public Schools	51,012	16.3	72.2	7.6	1.1	0.2	0.1	2.6
Bibb County	21,373	12.1	77.7	5.8	1.3	0.1	-	2.9
Cherokee County	41,373	64.9	7.5	20.7	1.9	0.1	-	4.8
Clayton County	52,149	1.7	69.2	22.8	3.4	0.2	0.1	2.6
Cobb County	107,379	34.9	30.6	23.8	6.0	0.2	0.1	4.4
Columbia County	28,266	55.9	21.4	10.9	4.1	0.2	0.3	7.2
Coweta County	22,241	57.4	23.6	11.4	2.2	0.3	-	5.0
DeKalb County	93,470	11.4	59.3	19.7	6.9	0.4	0.1	2.3
Douglas County	25,884	19.8	54.9	18.3	1.3	0.2	0.2	5.2
Fayette County	19,912	44.6	29.5	13.0	6.6	0.3	0.1	5.8
Forsyth County	51,152	52.3	4.6	14.5	24.7	0.4	0.1	3.4
Fulton County	90,300	25.8	42.4	15.9	12.2	0.2	0.1	3.4
Gwinnett County	177,401	19.4	32.3	32.7	11.2	0.2	0.1	4.1
Hall County	26,914	45.4	4.6	46.2	1.2	0.1	0.1	2.5
Henry County	42,388	23.0	57.6	11.1	2.9	0.2	0.1	5.0
Houston County	29,681	42.0	38.4	10.4	2.5	0.2	0.1	6.5
Muscogee County	30,757	22.3	57.2	11.1	2.8	0.2	0.2	6.2
Paulding County	29,966	55.9	26.5	11.0	1.0	0.2	0.1	5.2
Richmond County	29,093	15.0	75.0	5.4	0.6	0.2	0.4	3.6
Savannah-Chatham County	36,502	22.0	57.7	12.3	2.3	0.2	0.2	5.2
HAWAII								
Hawaii Department of Education	176,441	11.3	1.4	16.8	26.4	0.2	26.6	17.4
IDAHO								
Boise Independent District	23,703	73.1	4.4	13.6	4.0	0.5	0.5	3.9
Bonneville Joint District	13,230	80.4	0.5	15.6	0.5	0.4	0.2	2.4
Caldwell District	5,584	34.2	0.4	61.5	0.2	0.6	0.4	2.8
Cassia County Joint District	5,391	62.3	0.4	35.6	0.3	0.3	0.1	1.0
Coeur D'Alene District	10,011	85.8	0.5	7.3	0.8	0.9	0.2	4.5
Idaho Falls District	9,813	71.7	0.5	23.0	0.8	0.5	0.1	3.4
Jefferson County Joint District	6,287	85.1	0.3	11.7	0.2	0.2	0.1	2.3
Jerome Joint District	4,072	42.6	0.2	55.7	0.2	0.6	0.2	0.5
Joint School District No. 2	37,989	79.1	1.9	11.3	2.3	0.5	0.4	4.5
Kuna Joint District	5,416	79.8	0.8	14.9	0.6	0.5	0.4	3.0
Lakeland District	4,290	88.4	0.2	5.5	0.3	0.7	0.1	4.8
Lewiston Independent District	4,578	87.5	0.5	4.4	0.4	1.4	0.2	5.5
Madison District	5,370	88.5	0.7	9.1	0.7	0.3	0.5	0.2
Minidoka County Joint District	4,253	49.6	0.2	48.9	0.1	0.3	0.2	0.7
Nampa School District	14,899	56.1	0.5	38.1	0.5	0.2	0.6	3.9
Oneida County District	7,809	87.8	0.6	10.3	0.9	0.4	0.1	-
Pocatello District	11,885	77.7	0.6	12.8	0.8	3.7	0.6	3.8

- = Zero or rounds to zero.
NA = Not available.

Table C-4. School Enrollment for the 20 Largest Public School Districts in Each State, by Race/Ethnicity, 2020–21—*Continued*

(Number; percent.)

State/County	Total students in all grades	White (percent)	Black or African American (percent)	Hispanic (percent)	Asian or Asian/ Pacific Islander (percent)	American Indian/ Alaska Native (percent)	Nat. Hawaiian or Other Pacific Islander (percent)	Two or More Races (percent)
IDAHO—(*Continued*)								
Post Falls District	5,813	87.3	0.7	7.0	0.6	0.9	0.4	3.1
Twin Falls District	9,126	69.5	2.9	22.1	2.1	0.6	0.7	2.1
Vallivue School Distrct	8,916	54.4	1.0	40.5	0.5	0.4	0.2	2.9
ILLINOIS								
Aurora East USD 131	13,224	2.9	7.0	87.6	0.6	0.4	0.2	1.3
City of Chicago SD 299	341,382	11.0	35.8	46.7	4.4	0.3	0.2	1.7
CUSD 200	11,903	62.7	6.3	17.4	8.6	0.1	0.2	4.7
CUSD 300	20,216	45.0	5.5	40.2	5.5	0.2	0.1	3.5
CUSD 308	17,169	53.4	9.8	24.2	7.8	0.2	-	4.6
Indian Prairie CUSD 204	26,091	37.6	9.0	12.7	34.9	0.2	0.1	5.5
McLean County USD 5	12,536	62.0	14.0	8.5	8.9	0.4	0.1	6.1
Naperville CUSD 203	16,289	60.5	4.8	11.1	17.8	0.1	0.1	5.5
Palatine CCSD 15	11,540	38.6	3.6	34.9	19.0	0.3	0.1	3.5
Peoria SD 150	12,515	20.0	56.4	12.2	1.2	0.3	0.2	9.7
Plainfield SD 202	25,085	51.9	11.8	24.7	6.9	0.3	0.1	4.3
Rockford SD 205	26,739	28.2	30.8	29.3	4.1	0.2	0.1	7.3
Schaumburg CCSD 54	15,292	39.6	5.9	23.4	26.7	0.3	0.1	4.0
SD U-46	36,476	24.9	6.2	55.9	8.4	1.1	0.2	3.3
Springfield SD 186	13,483	39.4	41.6	3.4	2.5	0.3	0.1	12.7
St Charles CUSD 303	11,896	74.3	1.4	13.2	7.1	0.4	0.1	3.4
Township HSD 211	11,968	42.7	5.8	26.3	21.5	0.2	0.1	3.3
Township HSD 214	12,061	52.5	2.1	34.0	8.2	0.1	0.1	2.9
Valley View CUSD 365U	15,521	21.5	21.0	46.0	6.6	0.1	0.1	4.6
Waukegan CUSD 60	14,455	3.2	13.2	79.3	1.4	0.9	0.1	1.9
INDIANA								
Bartholomew Consolidated School Corp	11,474	68.5	2.3	17.2	7.5	0.3	-	4.1
Carmel Clay Schools	16,395	70.6	3.5	3.5	15.3	0.1	0.2	6.9
Elkhart Community Schools	11,939	39.4	15.6	35.8	1.1	-	-	8.0
Evansville Vanderburgh School Corp	22,191	67.4	14.7	5.5	1.2	0.2	1.1	9.8
Fort Wayne Community Schools	28,460	38.5	25.0	19.7	6.5	0.2	0.1	10.0
Franklin Township Community School Corp	10,587	64.2	9.7	8.7	10.5	0.2	0.1	6.5
Hamilton Southeastern Schools	21,760	70.2	7.8	7.8	8.0	0.2	0.1	5.9
Indianapolis Public Schools	22,928	21.6	40.3	31.8	0.7	0.1	-	5.4
MSD Lawrence Township	15,683	19.7	44.7	27.4	1.0	0.1	0.1	7.1
MSD Pike Township	10,919	7.7	60.9	24.3	1.8	-	-	5.3
MSD Warren Township	11,612	18.9	54.8	17.7	0.5	0.1	0.1	7.9
MSD Washington Township	10,888	28.8	41.0	20.4	3.6	0.1	-	6.1
MSD Wayne Township	16,473	26.1	37.5	29.7	0.6	0.2	0.1	5.8
New Albany-Floyd County Consolidated School Corp	11,524	76.2	8.5	6.4	1.5	0.2	0.1	7.2
Penn-Harris-Madison School Corp	11,488	73.2	7.5	6.8	6.0	0.4	0.1	6.0
Perry Township Schools	16,835	39.4	8.6	15.9	30.9	0.1	-	5.0
School City of Hammond	12,303	11.7	35.6	47.8	0.2	0.1	-	4.5
South Bend Community School Corp	16,297	27.4	37.6	23.6	0.9	0.2	-	10.2
Tippecanoe School Corp	13,464	71.5	6.6	14.6	2.5	0.1	0.1	4.7
Vigo County School Corp	13,674	81.1	5.3	4.0	1.3	0.1	0.1	8.2
IOWA								
Ankeny Community School District	12,188	82.5	3.0	6.3	2.8	0.1	0.1	5.3
Bettendorf Community School District	4,719	73.0	8.6	10.0	2.2	0.2	NA	6.0
Cedar Falls Community School District	5,808	83.0	4.7	2.9	3.8	0.2	0.4	5.0
Cedar Rapids Community School District	15,786	60.3	19.4	7.6	2.2	0.2	0.3	9.9
College Community School District	5,669	76.1	9.7	5.9	1.2	0.1	0.4	6.5
Council Bluffs Community School District	8,910	75.8	3.7	14.9	0.9	0.6	0.3	3.7
Davenport Community School District	14,609	53.1	20.2	14.1	1.6	0.3	0.1	10.5
Des Moines Independent Community School District	31,720	35.4	20.6	28.4	8.2	0.4	0.2	6.8
Dubuque Community School District	10,746	76.1	9.8	4.8	1.0	0.1	2.4	5.7
Iowa City Community School District	14,428	54.2	21.6	12.3	5.7	0.2	0.1	5.9
Johnston Community School District	7,408	70.2	9.3	6.9	8.1	0.1	-	5.3
Linn-Mar Community School District	7,762	77.6	5.2	4.8	6.9	0.2	0.1	5.3
Marshalltown Community School District	5,076	32.5	3.3	53.4	7.3	0.6	0.2	2.8
Muscatine Community School District	4,778	61.1	4.4	29.4	0.9	0.3	0.1	3.9
Pleasant Valley Community School District	5,331	76.4	3.0	5.3	10.8	0.2	0.1	4.2
Sioux City Community School District	14,941	44.4	8.2	34.8	2.7	2.7	1.2	5.9
Southeast Polk Community School District	7,139	78.2	6.0	7.9	1.9	0.1	0.2	5.6

- = Zero or rounds to zero.
NA = Not available.

Table C-4. School Enrollment for the 20 Largest Public School Districts in Each State, by Race/Ethnicity, 2020–21—*Continued*

(Number; percent.)

State/County	Total students in all grades	White (percent)	Black or African American (percent)	Hispanic (percent)	Asian or Asian/ Pacific Islander (percent)	American Indian/ Alaska Native (percent)	Nat. Hawaiian or Other Pacific Islander (percent)	Two or More Races (percent)
IOWA—*(Continued)*								
Waterloo Community School District	10,741	44.9	27.7	12.2	3.3	0.2	2.5	9.3
Waukee Community School District	11,781	74.8	5.2	6.1	8.1	0.2	0.1	5.6
West Des Moines Community School District	9,248	59.5	10.4	16.1	7.5	0.3	0.1	6.1
KANSAS								
Andover	8,737	75.4	2.9	10.2	5.1	0.5	0.3	5.5
Auburn Washburn	6,016	74.1	4.4	8.5	3.5	0.4	0.1	9.1
Blue Valley	22,148	69.3	3.4	6.5	15.2	0.3	0.1	5.3
De Soto	7,112	82.0	3.1	8.8	2.3	0.2	0.1	3.6
Derby	7,255	66.8	4.3	16.0	3.8	1.1	0.2	7.8
Dodge City	7,124	15.8	1.8	79.5	0.9	0.3	NA	1.6
Garden City	7,370	19.3	3.4	70.9	4.4	0.1	-	1.8
Gardner Edgerton	5,831	78.2	4.0	10.5	1.6	0.3	0.1	5.3
Geary County Schools	7,041	46.9	17.0	19.6	1.9	0.7	2.6	11.2
Goddard	6,167	80.2	1.5	10.7	2.1	0.6	0.1	4.9
Kansas City	22,140	9.9	25.2	53.9	7.1	0.2	0.4	3.2
Lawrence	11,427	66.4	5.9	11.0	3.2	2.4	0.2	10.9
Maize	7,798	74.4	2.4	13.9	2.9	0.7	0.2	5.5
Manhattan-Ogden	6,675	63.7	8.0	14.7	4.1	0.4	0.4	8.6
Olathe	29,128	65.3	7.6	17.4	4.4	0.3	0.2	4.8
Salina	6,898	59.1	3.4	24.5	2.5	0.2	-	10.1
Shawnee Mission Pub Sch	26,117	62.8	8.9	19.5	2.5	0.3	0.1	5.9
Spring Hill	5,836	79.5	3.5	9.2	1.1	0.5	0.1	6.1
Topeka Public Schools	12,436	35.4	17.4	33.4	0.5	0.8	0.2	12.3
Wichita	46,908	30.8	19.9	36.1	4.5	0.0	0.2	7.6
KENTUCKY								
Boone County	20,280	76.8	6.0	9.6	2.3	0.1	0.5	4.7
Bullitt County	12,725	89.7	1.4	4.3	0.8	0.2	0.1	3.6
Christian County	8,219	49.4	34.1	7.8	0.6	0.4	0.3	7.5
Daviess County	11,102	79.8	3.4	7.0	4.5	0.2	0.1	4.9
Fayette County	41,203	47.3	23.2	18.4	4.9	0.2	0.1	6.0
Hardin County	14,655	66.5	13.3	8.8	1.5	0.2	0.6	9.0
Henderson County	7,044	75.7	8.8	5.7	0.5	0.1	0.4	8.8
Hopkins County	6,498	78.4	8.6	4.6	0.6	0.2	0.2	7.4
Jefferson County	95,911	40.2	36.8	12.6	4.7	0.1	0.1	5.4
Jessamine County	8,207	79.4	6.5	8.0	1.0	0.2	0.1	4.8
Kenton County	14,021	83.6	2.9	6.1	1.5	0.1	0.2	5.6
Laurel County	8,850	94.4	0.7	2.6	0.9	0.1	0.1	1.3
Madison County	11,045	84.6	4.1	5.1	0.8	0.2	0.1	5.1
McCracken County	6,905	82.8	6.0	4.9	1.4	0.2	-	4.8
Oldham County	12,416	84.1	2.3	7.2	2.0	0.1	-	4.3
Pike County	8,094	96.5	1.0	1.0	0.3		NA	1.2
Pulaski County	8,294	90.1	0.7	5.3	1.1	0.1	0.1	2.7
Scott County	9,440	78.1	6.2	9.8	0.9	0.1	0.1	4.8
Shelby County	6,961	64.1	6.6	22.7	0.7	0.1	0.1	5.6
Warren County	16,860	63.0	10.3	10.8	9.8	0.1	0.9	5.1
LOUISIANA								
Acadia Parish	9,603	66.4	24.3	4.0	0.1	0.2	NA	5.0
Ascension Parish	23,154	53.9	30.8	10.3	1.4	0.2	0.1	3.3
Bossier Parish	22,431	54.7	29.3	10.4	1.7	0.3	0.2	3.4
Caddo Parish	36,153	28.0	63.2	4.6	1.3	0.1	-	2.7
Calcasieu Parish	27,032	57.1	31.0	6.7	1.7	0.3	0.1	3.1
East Baton Rouge Parish	40,283	11.4	71.3	11.8	3.9	0.2	0.2	1.2
Iberia Parish	11,822	45.0	42.1	5.4	3.0	0.2	-	4.3
Jefferson Parish	48,160	23.7	36.6	32.1	4.7	0.4	-	2.6
Lafayette Parish	30,878	45.8	39.6	9.0	2.3	0.3	0.1	2.9
Lafourche Parish	14,393	61.5	19.6	8.5	0.9	3.1	0.1	6.4
Livingston Parish	25,687	77.7	10.3	9.4	1.0	0.2	0.1	1.3
Ouachita Parish	18,355	58.5	34.5	3.7	1.2	0.1	0.1	1.9
Rapides Parish	22,297	50.1	41.7	4.3	1.3	0.5	0.1	2.0
St. Charles Parish	9,460	53.7	32.7	8.6	1.3	0.3	0.1	3.3
St. Landry Parish	12,527	37.0	57.7	3.1	0.7	0.2	NA	1.3
St. Tammany Parish	36,820	67.0	19.4	8.3	1.4	0.3	0.1	3.4
Tangipahoa Parish	19,549	40.2	46.4	7.5	0.5	0.1	0.1	5.3

- = Zero or rounds to zero.
NA = Not available.

Table C-4. School Enrollment for the 20 Largest Public School Districts in Each State, by Race/Ethnicity, 2020–21—*Continued*

(Number; percent.)

State/County	Total students in all grades	White (percent)	Black or African American (percent)	Hispanic (percent)	Asian or Asian/ Pacific Islander (percent)	American Indian/ Alaska Native (percent)	Nat. Hawaiian or Other Pacific Islander (percent)	Two or More Races (percent)
LOUISIANA—(*Continued*)								
Terrebonne Parish	16,563	46.4	26.5	10.0	1.1	7.2	-	8.8
Vermilion Parish	9,516	70.3	19.0	4.0	2.3	0.1	-	4.3
Vernon Parish	8,125	68.0	13.7	9.4	0.8	0.7	0.8	6.6
MAINE								
Auburn Public Schools	3,383	82.4	9.8	3.4	1.3	0.3	0.1	2.7
Bangor Public Schools	3,468	82.2	3.5	4.3	2.1	1.5	0.1	6.4
Biddeford Public Schools	2,346	79.2	6.9	5.4	2.2	0.5	-	5.7
Brunswick Public Schools	2,375	84.3	2.8	4.4	1.9	0.2	0.2	6.4
Gorham Public Schools	2,742	90.0	1.9	2.7	2.0	0.1	0.1	3.2
Lewiston Public Schools	5,184	52.6	37.9	3.2	0.9	0.3	0.1	4.9
Portland Public Schools	6,523	52.1	28.5	8.4	4.4	0.2	-	6.3
RSU 06/MSAD 06	3,429	92.3	1.0	2.0	0.7	0.5	0.1	3.4
RSU 14	3,139	91.7	1.9	2.4	1.4	0.3	-	2.4
RSU 17/MSAD 17	3,192	92.7	0.6	2.4	0.7	0.4	-	3.1
RSU 18	2,714	93.8	0.7	2.1	0.4	0.3	-	2.7
RSU 21	2,494	92.0	1.2	2.4	1.9	0.5	0.2	1.8
RSU 57/MSAD 57	2,752	94.9	0.8	1.3	0.5	0.3	-	2.1
RSU 60/MSAD 60	2,931	92.3	0.5	2.6	1.0	0.1	-	3.5
RSU 75/MSAD 75	2,408	93.1	0.5	2.2	0.9	0.2	-	3.1
Saco Public Schools	2,782	87.4	3.3	2.8	2.7	0.1	0.1	3.5
Sanford Public Schools	3,107	88.8	1.6	3.1	1.6	0.2	0.1	4.6
Scarborough Public Schools	2,872	87.9	3.1	1.3	7.1	0.2	0.4	-
South Portland Public Schools	2,913	70.0	13.3	5.7	4.3	0.3	0.2	6.2
Westbrook Public Schools	2,369	69.1	17.5	4.2	5.1	0.2	0.1	3.7
MARYLAND								
Allegany County Public Schools	8,075	86.6	3.6	1.7	0.9	0.1	0.1	7.0
Anne Arundel County Public Schools	83,044	49.7	21.6	18.0	4.0	0.3	0.2	6.3
Baltimore City Public Schools	77,856	7.5	75.7	14.2	0.8	0.2	0.1	1.3
Baltimore County Public Schools	111,084	34.5	40.1	12.4	7.3	0.4	0.1	5.1
Calvert County Public Schools	15,292	68.6	13.4	6.7	1.5	0.2	0.1	9.4
Caroline County Public Schools	5,553	59.0	14.9	16.6	1.2	0.1	0.1	8.0
Carroll County Public Schools	24,568	81.0	4.3	7.4	3.0	0.2	0.3	3.9
Cecil County Public Schools	14,718	74.2	9.9	8.3	0.7	0.2	0.1	6.6
Charles County Public Schools	26,768	21.1	56.7	10.6	3.1	0.3	0.2	7.9
Dorchester County Public Schools	4,662	40.6	41.6	9.6	1.4	-	0.1	6.7
Frederick County Public Schools	43,221	54.9	13.4	19.0	6.2	0.3	0.2	6.0
Harford County Public Schools	37,333	60.8	20.2	8.0	3.4	0.3	0.2	7.2
Howard County Public Schools	57,293	32.8	24.7	12.4	23.3	0.2	0.1	6.3
Montgomery County Public Schools	160,564	25.8	21.8	32.8	14.3	0.2	0.1	5.0
Prince George's County Public Schools	131,646	3.7	55.3	36.5	2.8	0.3	0.2	1.3
Queen Anne's County Public Schools	7,395	76.7	5.9	10.3	1.1	0.1	-	5.9
St. Mary's County Public Schools	17,246	62.7	18.3	7.6	2.5	0.2	0.1	8.5
Washington County Public Schools	21,939	61.9	14.4	12.2	2.2	0.2	0.1	9.1
Wicomico County Public Schools	14,354	39.0	37.5	11.7	3.0	0.5	0.1	8.1
Worcester County Public Schools	6,711	64.6	18.5	8.3	1.7	0.1	-	6.6
MASSACHUSETTS								
Boston	48,112	15.2	29.3	42.4	9.1	0.3	0.2	3.4
Brockton	15,384	15.5	60.6	17.0	1.9	0.3	0.2	4.5
Brookline	6,891	52.1	6.2	10.8	19.9	-	0.1	10.8
Chicopee	6,850	49.2	4.5	40.8	2.0	-	-	3.4
Everett	6,883	18.4	14.9	59.2	5.4	0.3	0.1	1.6
Fall River	9,998	48.8	9.0	29.7	3.5	0.1	-	8.9
Framingham	8,733	47.9	6.8	36.2	4.4	0.1	0.1	4.5
Haverhill	7,771	50.3	5.3	40.1	1.8	0.2	0.1	2.1
Lawrence	12,842	3.3	1.2	93.7	1.2	-	NA	0.4
Lexington	6,901	42.2	3.9	4.8	41.8	0.1	-	7.3
Lowell	14,023	24.8	7.9	35.0	28.2	-	-	4.1
Lynn	15,587	13.0	8.2	67.6	7.6	0.3	-	3.2
New Bedford	12,565	38.2	13.5	41.7	0.8	0.4	0.1	5.3
Newton	12,024	59.2	4.6	8.2	20.0	0.1	0.1	7.7
Plymouth	7,085	85.1	2.2	6.6	1.0	0.2	-	4.8
Quincy	9,480	39.6	6.9	8.4	40.9	0.2	0.3	3.7
Revere	7,166	32.2	3.5	57.7	4.4	0.3	-	1.8

- = Zero or rounds to zero.
NA = Not available.

Table C-4. School Enrollment for the 20 Largest Public School Districts in Each State, by Race/Ethnicity, 2020–21—*Continued*

(Number; percent.)

State/County	Total students in all grades	White (percent)	Black or African American (percent)	Hispanic (percent)	Asian or Asian/ Pacific Islander (percent)	American Indian/ Alaska Native (percent)	Nat. Hawaiian or Other Pacific Islander (percent)	Two or More Races (percent)
MASSACHUSETTS—(*Continued*)								
Springfield	24,239	9.1	18.6	67.9	2.1	0.2	-	2.1
Taunton	7,735	60.2	19.2	13.5	1.1	0.3	0.2	5.6
Worcester	23,986	28.8	17.1	43.1	6.5	0.2	-	4.4
MICHIGAN								
Ann Arbor Public Schools	17,451	50.7	13.9	9.6	13.9	0.2	-	11.7
Chippewa Valley Schools	14,855	75.7	11.3	4.5	2.9	0.2	0.1	5.5
Dearborn City School District	20,417	94.0	2.7	1.7	1.2	0.1	0.1	0.2
Detroit Public Schools Community District	48,782	2.5	81.6	13.9	1.5	0.2	0.1	0.3
Farmington Public School District	9,108	49.4	24.9	4.4	15.9	0.4	0.1	5.0
Forest Hills Public Schools	9,365	78.8	3.0	4.2	8.4	0.1	-	5.4
Grand Rapids Public Schools	14,034	20.6	31.8	39.4	1.0	0.3	-	6.9
Kalamazoo Public Schools	12,581	34.8	38.6	13.9	1.2	0.2	-	11.2
Kentwood Public Schools	9,228	28.6	33.5	15.0	15.0	0.4	0.1	7.5
L'Anse Creuse Public Schools	9,881	72.7	14.6	4.3	1.2	0.1	0.1	7.1
Lansing Public School District	9,989	22.5	39.2	20.4	5.7	0.4	0.1	11.7
Livonia Public Schools School District	13,457	75.3	9.9	5.8	4.3	0.3	-	4.5
Plymouth-Canton Community Schools	16,632	65.9	10.0	4.6	14.6	0.3	0.1	4.6
Rochester Community School District	15,092	70.8	3.2	6.6	15.3	0.2	0.1	3.7
Traverse City Area Public Schools	9,007	88.1	1.2	4.3	1.4	1.5	0.1	3.4
Troy School District	12,815	48.4	4.5	3.9	39.0	0.1	0.2	3.8
Utica Community Schools	25,701	83.1	5.1	3.8	4.9	0.1	0.2	2.9
Walled Lake Consolidated Schools	12,622	74.0	8.8	6.4	6.6	0.2	0.1	3.9
Warren Consolidated Schools	12,947	64.6	13.2	1.6	16.3	0.2	0.1	4.0
Wayne-Westland Community School District	9,652	51.6	35.1	6.9	1.4	0.4	0.1	4.6
MINNESOTA								
Anoka-Hennepin Public School District	37,719	61.8	13.4	7.0	8.8	0.6	0.1	8.4
Bloomington Public School District	10,139	46.4	18.1	20.4	6.4	0.6	0.1	8.1
Eastern Carver County Public School	9,485	75.4	5.0	10.1	4.2	0.3	0.1	5.0
Elk River School District	13,464	84.5	3.9	3.8	2.2	0.3	0.1	5.3
Lakeville Public School District	11,275	76.7	4.9	7.0	5.4	0.3	0.1	5.6
Mankato Public School District	8,693	71.7	13.7	6.6	2.0	0.4	0.1	5.5
Minneapolis Public School District	32,722	36.9	33.3	17.1	4.4	2.6	0.1	5.5
Minnetonka Public School District	11,106	80.1	2.8	5.0	6.2	0.3	-	5.6
Mounds View Public School District	11,806	59.8	11.4	9.7	11.2	0.3	-	7.5
North St. Paul-Maplewood Oakdale	10,352	32.7	19.5	14.6	24.1	1.0	0.1	8.1
Osseo Public School District	20,672	40.6	24.8	9.6	16.5	0.7	-	7.7
Prior Lake-Savage Area Schools	8,892	77.2	5.7	5.6	5.2	0.7	NA	5.6
Robbinsdale Public School District	11,692	36.2	30.4	16.5	6.1	0.6	-	10.2
Rochester Public School District	17,474	56.3	15.0	11.4	9.6	0.4	0.1	7.3
Rosemount-Apple Valley-Eagan	29,156	59.9	13.5	10.5	8.5	0.4	0.1	7.2
South Washington County School District	19,001	64.4	8.5	8.5	11.4	0.4	-	6.8
St. Cloud Public School District	9,628	40.5	41.4	7.6	2.7	0.5	0.2	7.1
St. Paul Public School District	34,928	21.0	25.4	13.8	30.7	1.0	-	8.2
Wayzata Public School District	12,013	60.4	7.4	4.5	21.9	0.1	-	5.6
White Bear Lake School District	8,705	71.6	6.5	7.8	7.2	0.4	0.1	6.4
MISSISSIPPI								
Biloxi Public School District	5,952	39.4	33.5	16.3	3.6	0.3	0.3	6.7
Clinton Public School District	5,250	34.8	55.3	2.3	5.4	0.2	0.1	1.8
Desoto Co School District	34,067	46.1	38.9	4.7	1.8	0.1	0.1	8.3
Gulfport School District	6,367	34.3	52.8	8.2	1.3	0.2	0.2	3.0
Harrison Co School District	13,666	49.9	34.8	6.4	2.7	0.3	0.3	5.6
Hinds Co School District	5,364	9.3	87.9	1.8	0.1	0.1	-	0.8
Jackson Co School District	8,765	78.7	10.7	3.1	3.4	0.3	0.2	3.5
Jackson Public School District	20,401	1.3	95.0	2.4	0.1	-	-	1.2
Jones Co School District	8,073	63.0	19.6	11.8	0.6	1.0	NA	3.9
Lamar County School District	10,298	61.0	28.2	4.2	1.9	0.1	0.1	4.4
Lauderdale Co School District	5,680	62.5	31.0	2.9	1.0	-	0.1	2.6
Lee County School District	6,389	64.8	28.3	2.8	0.7	-	-	3.3
Lowndes Co School District	5,173	58.8	37.4	1.7	0.4	0.1	0.1	1.5
Madison Co School District	12,988	48.6	39.7	5.0	4.6	0.1	0.1	1.9
Meridian Public Schools	4,940	4.8	91.3	2.7	0.5	0.1	-	0.6
Ocean Springs School District	5,739	74.6	12.3	5.6	3.4	0.3	0.2	3.6
Pascagoula-Gautier School District	6,508	31.1	44.8	18.2	0.8	0.2	-	4.9

- = Zero or rounds to zero.
NA = Not available.

Table C-4. School Enrollment for the 20 Largest Public School Districts in Each State, by Race/Ethnicity, 2020–21—*Continued*

(Number; percent.)

State/County	Total students in all grades	White (percent)	Black or African American (percent)	Hispanic (percent)	Asian or Asian/ Pacific Islander (percent)	American Indian/ Alaska Native (percent)	Nat. Hawaiian or Other Pacific Islander (percent)	Two or More Races (percent)
MISSISSIPPI—*(Continued)*								
Rankin Co School District	18,384	67.5	24.6	3.1	1.5	0.1	-	3.1
Tupelo Public School District	7,005	33.8	52.0	6.8	2.4	-	-	4.9
Vicksburg Warren School District	7,236	32.1	63.6	1.5	1.0	0.1	0.1	1.6
MISSOURI								
Blue Springs R-IV	14,687	70.3	11.5	8.0	2.2	0.5	0.3	7.2
Columbia 93	18,145	57.1	20.6	7.0	5.3	0.4	0.2	9.3
Ferguson-Florissant R-II	9,313	8.1	82.4	3.7	0.2	0.1	0.1	5.5
Fox C-6	11,022	86.6	1.4	3.7	1.3	0.6	1.0	5.4
Francis Howell R-III	16,936	78.7	6.9	5.2	4.1	0.2	0.1	4.7
Ft. Zumwalt R-II	17,310	77.4	6.5	6.0	3.8	0.1	0.2	6.1
Hazelwood	16,473	13.7	80.5	2.5	0.8	0.1	0.2	2.1
Independence 30	14,240	51.6	14.0	21.6	0.8	0.5	0.9	10.6
Kansas City 33	14,113	10.5	53.9	27.4	4.2	0.1	2.2	1.7
Lee's Summit R-VII	17,790	74.3	12.6	2.8	2.4	0.2	0.2	7.5
Liberty 53	12,632	78.0	5.4	8.0	2.6	0.2	0.2	5.7
Mehlville R-IX	9,969	79.7	7.3	3.9	3.9	0.2	0.1	4.9
North Kansas City 74	19,673	54.8	14.8	14.8	3.4	0.2	1.3	10.8
Park Hill	11,992	66.1	12.7	10.4	3.2	0.5	1.2	5.9
Parkway C-2	17,132	58.5	15.7	5.3	13.9	0.3	0.1	6.2
Rockwood R-VI	19,822	76.0	7.6	3.9	8.7	0.2	0.1	3.6
Springfield R-XII	23,731	73.5	8.3	7.9	3.2	0.7	0.4	6.0
St. Joseph	10,643	70.3	6.4	10.2	2.1	0.3	1.4	9.2
St. Louis City	19,299	12.9	77.8	5.8	3.0	0.1	NA	0.5
Wentzville R-IV	17,400	81.0	6.7	5.4	2.0	0.1	-	4.7
MONTANA								
Belgrade Elem	2,297	86.9	0.2	8.1	0.2	1.2	-	3.3
Billings Elem	10,980	73.0	1.2	8.6	0.6	8.0	0.4	8.2
Billings H S	5,550	77.7	1.0	8.2	0.9	5.8	0.4	6.1
Bozeman Elem	4,464	84.5	0.5	7.6	1.3	1.5	0.1	4.4
Bozeman H S	2,389	87.6	0.7	6.4	1.7	1.0	0.1	2.5
Browning Elem	1,392	4.2	-	0.6	0.1	94.0	-	1.1
Butte Elem	2,948	86.2	0.3	7.0	0.4	1.7	0.1	4.2
Columbia Falls Elem	1,430	86.8	0.2	5.1	0.1	1.2	0.1	6.5
East Helena K-12	1,505	86.4	0.6	4.0	0.3	4.4	0.3	3.9
Flathead H S	2,952	91.1	0.6	3.5	1.1	1.5	0.3	1.9
Frenchtown K-12 Schools	1,345	86.6	0.5	4.5	1.3	2.2	0.4	4.4
Great Falls Elem	7,026	71.8	1.4	7.0	0.9	7.7	0.2	11.1
Great Falls H S	2,981	75.5	2.3	5.4	1.2	9.6	0.5	5.5
Hamilton K-12 Schools	1,498	87.6	0.3	5.7	0.4	0.9	0.3	4.9
Helena Elem	5,123	83.1	1.1	8.8	0.7	2.0	0.1	4.2
Helena H S	2,620	84.6	0.7	7.7	0.7	2.1	-	4.2
Hellgate Elem	1,473	83.4	0.2	4.1	2.0	2.3	0.2	7.7
Kalispell Elem	2,883	87.6	0.4	4.3	1.2	1.5	0.2	4.8
Missoula Elem	5,264	84.3	2.3	4.3	2.1	6.9	0.1	-
Missoula H S	3,717	85.3	2.1	3.7	2.2	6.5	0.2	-
NEBRASKA								
Bellevue Public Schools	9,386	65.9	8.1	15.9	2.0	0.7	0.5	7.0
Bennington Public Schools	3,589	86.6	3.3	4.6	1.5	0.2	-	3.7
Columbus Public Schools	4,159	53.1	1.7	42.2	0.7	0.8	-	1.4
Elkhorn Public Schools	10,642	84.4	1.7	4.3	6.0	0.2	0.2	3.1
Fremont Public Schools	4,868	58.5	1.4	37.7	0.5	0.4	0.3	1.3
Grand Island Public Schools	9,920	38.7	4.4	52.5	0.9	0.7	0.1	2.7
Gretna Public Schools	6,023	90.0	1.2	5.1	1.1	0.3	-	2.3
Hastings Public Schools	3,672	69.5	1.3	23.8	0.9	0.5	0.1	3.9
Kearney Public Schools	6,055	80.5	2.2	13.6	0.9	0.4	0.3	2.1
Lexington Public Schools	3,104	13.7	9.6	74.7	0.6	0.5	0.1	0.7
Lincoln Public Schools	41,674	64.2	6.8	14.9	4.8	0.6	0.1	8.7
Millard Public Schools	23,633	75.4	3.6	9.6	6.2	0.3	0.2	4.7
Norfolk Public Schools	4,444	63.4	1.6	27.2	0.8	1.8	-	5.2
North Platte Public Schools	3,919	76.6	1.7	16.4	0.9	0.7	0.1	3.7
Omaha Public Schools	51,914	24.4	24.7	37.3	6.9	0.8	0.1	5.8
Papillion La Vista Community Schools	11,831	74.7	5.0	11.7	2.5	0.3	0.2	5.7
Ralston Public Schools	3,210	48.7	6.4	36.7	1.0	0.5	0.4	6.4

- = Zero or rounds to zero.
NA = Not available.

Table C-4. School Enrollment for the 20 Largest Public School Districts in Each State, by Race/ Ethnicity, 2020–21—*Continued*

(Number; percent.)

State/County	Total students in all grades	White (percent)	Black or African American (percent)	Hispanic (percent)	Asian or Asian/ Pacific Islander (percent)	American Indian/ Alaska Native (percent)	Nat. Hawaiian or Other Pacific Islander (percent)	Two or More Races (percent)
NEBRASKA—(*Continued*)								
Scottsbluff Public Schools	3,452	49.1	0.8	44.8	0.7	2.7	0.1	1.9
South Sioux City Community Schs	3,734	16.7	9.5	63.6	2.9	2.9	1.2	3.2
Westside Community Schools	6,091	68.7	9.9	9.1	3.8	0.4	-	8.1
NEVADA								
Carson City School District	7,787	46.1	0.7	44.2	1.8	2.2	0.3	4.8
Churchill County School District	3,200	59.2	1.7	24.3	1.6	5.5	0.8	6.9
Clark County School District	315,646	22.3	15.3	47.2	6.0	0.3	1.6	7.2
Correctional School District	38	13.2	44.7	34.2	2.6	2.6	2.6	-
Davidson Academy School District	234	47.4	2.6	2.1	37.2	0.9	-	9.8
Douglas County School District	5,385	65.7	0.4	23.5	1.3	3.2	0.3	5.7
Elko County School District	9,608	55.0	0.9	34.0	0.7	6.1	0.3	2.5
Esmeralda County School District	101	51.5	1.0	35.6	-	5.9	-	5.9
Eureka County School District	324	77.5	-	13.0	-	4.3	0.3	4.9
Humboldt County School District	3,267	54.7	0.5	36.7	0.4	4.4	0.1	3.2
Lander County School District	1,027	59.1	0.3	33.2	0.6	3.3	0.1	3.4
Lincoln County School District	881	80.9	3.3	10.6	0.5	0.7	1.1	3.0
Lyon County School District	8,817	61.3	0.8	27.0	1.1	3.5	0.7	5.6
Mineral County School District	572	57.7	2.1	19.4	0.5	13.3	0.3	6.6
Nye County School District	5,353	55.7	3.5	30.8	1.2	1.2	1.0	6.7
Pershing County School District	637	46.8	1.1	34.9	0.5	8.3	0.2	8.3
State-Sponsored Charter Schools	53,223	34.7	11.9	35.0	7.7	0.4	1.6	8.7
Storey County School District	448	82.8	1.1	10.5	0.9	0.4	0.2	4.0
Washoe County School District	64,584	42.5	2.6	41.6	4.5	1.2	1.4	6.2
White Pine County School District	1,216	70.3	1.1	18.9	0.2	3.7	0.2	5.7
NEW HAMPSHIRE								
Bedford School District	4,266	80.8	1.1	3.0	8.0	0.2	0.1	6.9
Concord School District	4,093	79.6	9.7	2.9	7.1	0.7	NA	NA
Derry School District	3,133	86.8	1.7	5.9	1.2	0.4	0.1	4.0
Dover School District	3,846	81.1	2.2	2.9	7.5	0.1	0.1	6.1
Exeter Region Coop School District	2,633	90.8	0.9	2.2	3.6	0.5	0.2	1.8
Goffstown School District	2,767	89.4	1.3	3.8	1.5	0.4	0.1	3.6
Hudson School District	3,053	84.1	1.3	6.1	2.7	0.4	NA	5.5
Keene School District	3,120	87.7	1.3	3.1	2.6	0.9	0.3	4.0
Londonderry School District	4,093	89.2	1.0	4.6	1.9	0.1	0.1	3.1
Manchester School District	12,410	52.0	10.8	23.9	4.5	0.2	-	8.5
Merrimack School District	3,582	89.6	1.6	2.3	2.4	0.4	0.2	3.4
Merrimack Valley School District	2,224	92.5	2.2	1.8	1.3	0.2	0.1	1.8
Milford School District	2,155	88.1	1.7	4.4	1.0	0.2	0.3	4.3
Nashua School District	10,239	53.6	3.6	27.9	9.2	0.1	NA	5.7
Pinkerton Academy School District	3,160	89.0	0.9	4.3	2.1	0.3	0.1	3.3
Portsmouth School District	2,531	79.7	1.2	4.6	6.5	0.1	-	7.9
Rochester School District	4,098	87.8	1.2	3.5	1.8	0.1	-	5.6
Salem School District	3,519	80.3	1.1	10.7	3.6	0.1	-	4.3
Timberlane Regional School District	3,278	90.1	0.8	4.9	1.0	0.2	NA	3.0
Windham School District	2,958	80.5	0.8	4.5	4.9	NA	NA	9.3
NEW JERSEY								
Bayonne School District	10,059	40.4	11.0	36.7	8.0	0.2	0.3	3.4
Cherry Hill School District	10,596	55.2	8.8	13.5	17.3	0.1	0.2	4.8
Clifton Public School District	10,514	29.7	4.1	58.2	6.4	0.7	0.1	0.9
Edison Township School District	16,632	11.5	7.4	12.0	66.3	0.9	0.2	1.6
Elizabeth Public Schools	28,090	7.6	17.0	73.3	1.8	-	0.2	0.1
Freehold Regional High School District	10,519	71.8	3.4	14.1	8.9	0.1	0.2	1.7
Hamilton Township Public School District	11,678	40.9	17.0	34.7	3.7	0.1	0.1	3.5
Jersey City Public Schools	26,782	15.2	25.6	37.7	18.7	0.2	0.9	1.6
New Brunswick School District	9,961	0.7	7.2	91.2	0.4	0.1	-	0.3
Newark Public School District	40,423	7.4	39.0	52.3	0.9	0.3	0.2	-
Passaic City School District	13,494	1.0	4.0	93.0	1.6	0.1	0.1	0.1
Paterson Public School District	25,937	5.3	20.7	68.0	6.0	NA	-	NA
Perth Amboy Public School District	10,786	1.1	4.6	93.5	0.3	-	-	0.3
Plainfield Public School District	9,744	0.7	21.4	76.9	0.4	0.1	0.2	0.3
Toms River Regional School District	14,618	66.4	5.1	20.9	3.6	-	0.1	3.9
Trenton Public Schools	14,708	1.0	39.2	58.8	0.2	0.1	0.1	0.7
Union City School District	13,101	2.4	1.4	94.8	1.4	-	-	-

- = Zero or rounds to zero.
NA = Not available.

Table C-4. School Enrollment for the 20 Largest Public School Districts in Each State, by Race/Ethnicity, 2020–21—*Continued*

(Number; percent.)

State/County	Total students in all grades	White (percent)	Black or African American (percent)	Hispanic (percent)	Asian or Asian/ Pacific Islander (percent)	American Indian/ Alaska Native (percent)	Nat. Hawaiian or Other Pacific Islander (percent)	Two or More Races (percent)
NEW JERSEY—*(Continued)*								
Vineland Public School District	10,266	20.1	13.9	61.1	2.1	0.3	0.1	2.4
West Windsor-Plainsboro Regional School District	9,386	16.4	5.0	4.8	71.4	0.1	0.1	2.2
Woodbridge Township School District	13,860	31.6	10.5	26.0	30.2	-	NA	1.7
NEW MEXICO								
Alamogordo Public Schools	5,572	42.9	6.0	41.7	1.8	1.2	0.7	5.7
Albuquerque Public Schools	83,031	19.9	2.5	66.7	2.1	5.3	0.1	3.5
Artesia Public Schools	3,741	37.0	0.5	60.7	0.2	1.0	0.1	0.4
Belen Consolidated Schools	3,667	19.8	1.2	76.7	0.1	1.7	-	0.5
Carlsbad Municipal Schools	8,847	36.0	1.5	59.0	0.9	1.2	0.3	1.1
Central Consolidated Schools	5,173	4.6	0.2	4.9	0.7	86.0	-	3.6
Clovis Municipal Schools	7,765	27.0	5.8	63.0	0.7	0.3	0.2	3.0
Deming Public Schools	5,115	10.5	1.4	86.0	1.3	0.2	0.1	0.5
Farmington Municipal Schools	10,768	27.1	0.8	29.6	0.7	36.5	0.1	5.2
Gadsden Independent Schools	12,844	2.4	0.4	97.0	-	0.2	NA	NA
Gallup-Mckinley Cty Schools	12,281	6.9	0.5	18.4	1.0	71.1	0.2	1.8
Grants-Cibola County Schools	3,206	11.9	0.6	40.6	0.3	44.8	NA	1.7
Hobbs Municipal Schools	9,776	20.4	3.6	74.4	0.6	0.2	0.1	0.7
Las Cruces Public Schools	23,711	17.1	2.1	77.9	0.8	0.9	0.3	0.9
Los Alamos Public Schools	3,539	55.2	0.8	34.0	4.4	1.6	-	4.1
Los Lunas Public Schools	8,050	21.0	0.6	70.7	0.2	5.7	0.1	1.7
Lovington Municipal Schools	3,502	18.3	1.7	79.0	0.6	0.2	0.1	0.1
Rio Rancho Public Schools	16,807	29.4	1.9	58.1	1.2	4.0	0.1	5.4
Roswell Independent Schools	9,801	23.4	2.2	73.0	0.9	0.3	0.1	0.1
Santa Fe Public Schools	12,403	14.7	0.8	80.2	1.7	2.0	0.2	0.3
NEW YORK								
Buffalo City School District	31,428	18.9	44.4	20.4	11.3	0.5	0.1	4.5
New York City Geographic District # 2	60,446	26.3	13.8	32.6	21.7	0.6	0.4	4.7
New York City Geographic District # 8	25,994	5.7	21.0	64.7	6.3	1.2	0.4	0.6
New York City Geographic District # 9	31,384	1.5	26.7	69.2	1.1	0.7	0.3	0.5
New York City Geographic District #10	51,467	5.9	15.1	69.5	7.3	0.9	0.4	1.0
New York City Geographic District #11	36,296	8.8	36.3	43.9	8.2	1.3	0.5	1.0
New York City Geographic District #15	30,388	29.3	12.6	36.2	17.0	0.5	0.3	4.1
New York City Geographic District #20	50,119	24.3	2.4	27.6	44.0	0.4	0.3	1.0
New York City Geographic District #21	34,525	31.9	13.3	25.8	26.0	0.8	0.4	1.8
New York City Geographic District #22	33,200	31.7	27.8	15.8	21.1	0.9	0.8	1.9
New York City Geographic District #24	54,293	12.9	2.6	63.2	19.5	0.6	0.3	1.0
New York City Geographic District #25	36,061	11.0	6.3	31.0	49.1	0.6	0.3	1.7
New York City Geographic District #26	31,351	14.7	10.8	17.7	53.3	1.1	0.4	1.9
New York City Geographic District #27	43,540	10.3	21.7	40.4	20.9	4.3	1.1	1.4
New York City Geographic District #28	40,347	15.5	18.5	28.6	29.7	3.7	1.3	2.8
New York City Geographic District #29	24,957	2.4	56.6	18.3	16.2	4.1	1.0	1.5
New York City Geographic District #30	37,841	17.5	6.5	52.1	20.8	0.7	0.3	2.1
New York City Geographic District #31	62,857	42.7	12.5	29.4	12.6	0.5	0.3	2.2
Rochester City School District	24,898	9.3	53.3	32.8	2.9	0.2	0.1	1.5
Yonkers City School District	25,488	15.4	16.9	59.9	5.1	0.5	0.1	2.0
NORTH CAROLINA								
Alamance-Burlington Schools	21,931	40.2	24.0	28.0	1.6	0.3	0.1	5.8
Buncombe County Schools	22,298	67.7	7.0	18.8	1.2	0.3	0.4	4.5
Cabarrus County Schools	32,810	46.6	22.2	18.3	7.7	0.3	0.1	4.8
Charlotte-Mecklenburg Schools	142,733	25.5	36.6	27.4	7.5	0.2	0.1	2.7
Cumberland County Schools	49,278	26.9	45.6	14.9	1.9	1.4	0.5	8.8
Davidson County Schools	17,964	79.9	3.8	10.8	1.3	0.3	-	3.9
Durham Public Schools	32,005	19.3	41.0	33.1	2.1	0.2	0.1	4.3
Gaston County Schools	29,777	53.7	23.2	15.9	1.5	0.2	0.1	5.4
Guilford County Schools	70,047	29.0	41.8	17.2	6.9	0.4	0.2	4.5
Harnett County Schools	19,470	42.2	25.2	24.2	0.7	0.7	0.3	6.8
Iredell-Statesville Schools	20,163	62.6	13.9	15.2	3.1	0.1	0.1	4.9
Johnston County Public Schools	36,422	50.6	16.1	27.1	0.8	0.3	0.1	5.1
New Hanover County Schools	24,841	59.1	17.5	16.7	1.7	0.3	0.1	4.6
Onslow County Schools	26,269	55.6	17.1	16.1	1.2	0.4	0.4	9.2
Pitt County Schools	23,312	34.8	45.7	12.5	1.6	0.2	0.1	5.0
Public Schools of Robeson County	21,083	11.2	22.8	19.1	0.6	41.0	0.2	5.1
Rowan-Salisbury Schools	18,205	54.6	18.0	20.5	0.9	0.2	0.1	5.7

- = Zero or rounds to zero.
NA = Not available.

Table C-4. School Enrollment for the 20 Largest Public School Districts in Each State, by Race/Ethnicity, 2020–21—Continued

(Number; percent.)

State/County	Total students in all grades	White (percent)	Black or African American (percent)	Hispanic (percent)	Asian or Asian/ Pacific Islander (percent)	American Indian/ Alaska Native (percent)	Nat. Hawaiian or Other Pacific Islander (percent)	Two or More Races (percent)
NORTH CAROLINA—(Continued)								
Union County Public Schools	40,207	58.3	12.1	19.5	5.8	0.2	0.1	4.0
Wake County Schools	160,802	44.4	22.4	18.0	10.4	0.3	0.1	3.8
Winston Salem / Forsyth County Schools	51,843	35.4	29.0	27.9	2.7	0.1	0.1	4.7
NORTH DAKOTA								
Belcourt 7	1,594	1.5	0.2	0.3	NA	97.9	NA	0.1
Beulah 27	719	88.3	1.8	3.5	0.1	3.6	0.1	2.5
Bismarck 1	13,433	78.6	3.2	3.8	1.1	7.2	0.6	5.6
Central Cass 17	953	94.8	2.0	0.8	0.1	1.8	0.2	0.3
Devils Lake 1	1,666	63.9	1.1	2.6	0.2	30.3	NA	1.8
Dickinson 1	3,810	76.8	4.2	11.0	1.1	2.4	0.3	4.2
Fargo 1	11,304	70.1	13.1	5.3	4.1	2.5	0.2	4.6
Grafton 3	909	60.1	1.1	33.8	0.6	1.7	0.4	2.4
Grand Forks 1	7,567	67.5	6.6	8.8	3.8	3.9	0.2	9.2
Jamestown 1	2,206	85.0	3.2	4.9	0.6	0.8	0.1	5.3
Kindred 2	841	96.3	1.0	1.2	0.1	1.3	0.1	NA
Mandan 1	4,095	79.1	2.9	6.3	0.7	7.4	0.4	3.2
Mckenzie Co 1	1,836	69.4	3.3	20.3	1.7	3.3	0.3	1.6
Minot 1	7,672	73.5	6.6	8.8	1.1	3.9	0.2	5.8
New Town 1	944	4.7	0.7	4.8	1.4	88.1	NA	0.3
Valley City 2	1,060	87.0	1.7	4.2	0.8	1.9	0.2	4.3
Wahpeton 37	1,215	77.9	2.5	8.4	1.4	7.7	NA	2.1
West Fargo 6	11,561	70.7	15.1	4.1	3.7	1.8	0.1	4.5
Williams County 8	729	75.9	6.6	11.5	0.4	1.8	0.5	3.3
Williston 1	4,297	67.3	6.3	14.8	1.3	1.6	0.5	8.1
OHIO								
Akron City	20,563	29.6	46.7	4.8	8.8	-	0.1	9.9
Cincinnati Public Schools	34,635	21.9	61.7	8.6	1.3	0.1	0.1	6.3
Cleveland Municipal	34,941	14.9	63.9	16.9	1.2	0.2	0.2	2.8
Columbus City School District	46,657	21.5	53.0	14.2	3.4	0.2	0.1	7.6
Dayton City	11,721	23.1	65.1	6.3	0.3	0.1	0.1	5.0
Dublin City	16,254	58.8	5.6	7.7	21.5	0.1	-	6.2
Fairfield City	9,708	50.6	22.5	13.4	7.0	0.1	0.2	6.3
Hamilton City	9,415	61.0	12.2	19.2	0.6	0.2	0.6	6.1
Hilliard City	16,027	70.4	8.8	9.7	6.7	0.1	0.2	4.1
Lakota Local	16,415	63.6	12.4	9.8	7.9	0.1	0.1	6.1
Mason City	10,267	54.3	4.8	5.3	29.8	0.2	0.5	5.2
Northwest Local	8,541	43.6	32.9	6.4	5.2	0.1	0.1	11.8
Ohio Virtual Academy	21,049	67.9	15.0	7.6	1.1	0.3	0.1	8.0
Olentangy Local	22,089	69.0	4.4	4.2	15.9	0.3	-	6.2
Parma City	9,318	73.4	6.6	12.4	2.9	0.1	0.1	4.4
Pickerington Local	10,454	52.9	28.2	6.2	5.0	0.2	0.1	7.4
South-Western City	21,654	55.9	16.5	18.2	2.8	0.1	-	6.3
Toledo City	22,312	20.0	45.1	13.2	0.4	0.1	0.1	11.3
Westerville City	14,576	52.3	26.4	7.5	4.8	0.1	-	9.0
Worthington City	10,530	67.1	9.6	9.6	4.8	0.1	-	8.8
OKLAHOMA								
Bartlesville	5,828	53.0	3.4	12.0	3.1	11.7	0.1	16.7
Bixby	6,560	63.0	1.5	12.6	3.0	4.3	-	15.6
Broken Arrow	18,619	54.4	6.2	16.0	3.8	7.2	0.2	12.3
Deer Creek	6,741	63.6	7.2	9.3	7.9	5.2	0.3	6.5
Edmond	23,496	59.9	11.1	11.9	4.7	2.1	0.3	10.0
Enid	7,390	45.3	3.0	28.8	0.9	2.1	13.0	7.0
Epic Blended Learning Charter	23,714	44.6	16.3	16.7	0.8	2.9	0.1	18.6
Epic One On One Charter School	35,731	57.4	3.2	11.4	0.4	7.1	0.1	20.3
Jenks	11,979	51.7	6.7	13.0	15.4	11.7	0.1	1.6
Lawton	12,897	34.5	21.2	22.0	1.5	4.8	1.0	15.0
Midwest City-Del City	11,044	35.8	31.2	15.0	1.4	4.0	0.5	12.0
Moore	23,390	45.5	7.0	19.6	5.5	3.8	0.3	18.4
Mustang	11,868	60.1	4.4	15.2	4.8	4.5	0.2	10.9
Norman	14,419	55.4	6.7	16.3	3.2	4.3	0.2	13.9
Oklahoma City	31,026	12.0	19.2	58.4	1.9	2.3	0.4	5.9
Owasso	9,035	57.0	4.6	12.5	4.6	8.5	0.2	12.7
Putnam City	17,829	24.9	25.5	34.3	4.0	2.1	0.2	9.1

- = Zero or rounds to zero.
NA = Not available.

Table C-4. School Enrollment for the 20 Largest Public School Districts in Each State, by Race/Ethnicity, 2020–21—*Continued*

(Number; percent.)

State/County	Total students in all grades	White (percent)	Black or African American (percent)	Hispanic (percent)	Asian or Asian/ Pacific Islander (percent)	American Indian/ Alaska Native (percent)	Nat. Hawaiian or Other Pacific Islander (percent)	Two or More Races (percent)
OKLAHOMA—(*Continued*)								
Tulsa	32,569	23.0	22.9	36.7	1.6	4.7	0.8	10.3
Union	14,959	25.7	14.8	38.2	7.3	4.2	0.2	9.5
Yukon	8,158	61.7	4.3	17.7	2.4	3.3	0.1	10.4
OREGON								
Beaverton SD 48J	39,594	44.4	3.0	25.9	17.5	0.4	0.7	8.0
Bend-LaPine Administrative SD 1	17,543	81.3	0.7	12.1	1.3	0.5	0.2	3.9
Corvallis SD 509J	6,462	66.2	1.2	17.5	5.5	0.7	0.5	8.1
David Douglas SD 40	9,299	34.6	12.2	27.4	15.0	0.8	2.5	7.3
Eugene SD 4J	16,683	68.0	1.5	15.5	2.7	1.0	0.4	10.6
Greater Albany Public SD 8J	8,990	67.8	0.6	22.0	1.0	1.1	0.3	7.0
Gresham-Barlow SD 10J	11,661	54.4	3.5	29.6	3.0	0.9	1.0	7.3
Hillsboro SD 1J	19,407	41.9	2.4	40.0	6.8	0.6	0.7	7.4
Klamath County SD	6,784	64.9	0.9	20.5	0.8	5.5	0.3	7.1
Lake Oswego SD 7J	6,860	70.1	0.7	7.6	10.9	0.1	0.2	10.1
Medford SD 549C	13,962	64.2	0.8	27.3	1.2	0.6	0.7	5.0
North Clackamas SD 12	16,458	58.5	2.1	19.5	10.1	0.4	0.6	8.6
Oregon City SD 62	7,420	75.5	0.8	14.1	1.5	0.5	0.4	7.1
Portland SD 1J	46,965	55.7	8.7	16.4	6.1	0.5	0.8	11.3
Redmond SD 2J	7,070	74.1	0.5	19.5	0.7	0.8	0.3	4.0
Reynolds SD 7	10,560	29.9	9.8	42.5	7.2	0.7	2.8	6.9
Salem-Keizer SD 24J	39,906	43.4	1.4	44.0	2.1	0.7	2.5	5.8
Springfield SD 19	9,779	67.1	1.0	22.6	0.7	1.0	0.6	7.1
Tigard-Tualatin SD 23J	11,860	53.7	2.0	28.1	5.1	0.3	2.2	8.3
West Linn-Wilsonville SD 3J	9,302	72.4	0.8	12.5	4.5	0.3	0.5	9.1
PENNSYLVANIA								
Allentown City SD	16,231	8.2	13.3	72.7	1.0	0.1	0.2	4.5
Bethlehem Area SD	13,005	40.6	10.5	43.4	2.9	0.2	0.2	2.2
Central Bucks SD	17,571	78.9	1.4	7.1	9.2	0.1	-	3.3
Central Dauphin SD	11,894	45.2	21.0	12.8	12.2	0.2	-	8.6
Commonwealth Charter Academy CS	16,419	61.5	13.8	14.5	1.0	0.5	0.3	8.4
Council Rock SD	10,494	84.2	1.3	3.4	9.3	0.1	0.1	1.6
Cumberland Valley SD	9,403	67.9	3.4	5.6	17.7	0.5	0.1	4.9
Downingtown Area SD	12,909	71.8	2.8	5.2	16.4	0.1	0.1	3.6
Erie City SD	10,310	38.2	33.5	11.7	5.5	0.2	0.1	10.8
Hazleton Area SD	11,551	34.7	2.0	61.3	0.5	0.2	-	1.3
Lancaster SD	10,384	12.4	16.3	61.6	4.4	-	-	5.3
North Penn SD	12,603	56.8	9.0	6.3	20.3	0.1	0.1	7.5
Parkland SD	9,541	61.5	4.9	16.4	13.1	0.1	0.1	3.9
Pennsbury SD	9,544	73.6	5.8	7.0	6.9	0.2	-	6.5
Pennsylvania Cyber CS	10,917	74.4	10.5	4.7	1.6	0.2	0.1	8.5
Philadelphia City SD	124,111	14.5	48.0	22.9	9.6	0.2	0.1	4.7
Pittsburgh SD	21,407	30.8	51.6	4.5	3.8	0.1	0.1	9.2
Reading SD	17,659	5.1	7.2	85.7	0.3	0.1	-	1.6
Upper Darby SD	12,420	21.7	47.0	11.4	15.5	0.2	-	4.2
West Chester Area SD	11,972	74.2	4.6	8.9	8.6	0.1	0.1	3.6
RHODE ISLAND								
Barrington	3,388	81.3	1.5	4.5	7.3	0.1	NA	5.3
Bristol Warren	3,061	84.7	1.6	6.7	1.5	0.2	-	5.4
Central Falls	2,780	14.6	13.7	45.0	0.3	11.5	0.4	2.9
Chariho	3,143	91.0	0.5	2.8	0.4	1.4	0.1	3.8
Coventry	4,390	88.2	2.0	5.4	2.0	0.4	NA	2.1
Cranston	10,403	47.9	4.7	31.0	9.2	0.7	0.2	6.2
Cumberland	4,602	75.9	2.9	12.7	5.0	0.1	NA	3.4
East Greenwich	2,532	80.7	0.8	7.0	6.8	0.1	NA	4.7
East Providence	5,041	63.9	10.5	13.3	1.7	1.1	0.1	9.5
Johnston	3,110	64.8	5.8	24.7	3.2	0.4	0.1	1.1
Lincoln	3,213	80.0	4.7	8.2	3.7	0.1	0.6	2.6
North Kingstown	3,923	83.4	2.4	7.3	1.8	0.3	-	4.8
North Providence	3,525	53.7	13.8	23.3	3.4	0.3	0.1	5.4
Pawtucket	8,450	34.2	29.6	27.8	0.9	0.5	0.3	6.7
Providence	22,440	8.1	15.5	67.1	3.9	0.9	0.1	4.4
South Kingstown	2,750	81.5	2.1	5.6	2.0	2.7	0.1	6.0
Warwick	8,140	75.0	2.5	12.8	4.1	0.3	0.1	5.2

- = Zero or rounds to zero.
NA = Not available.

Table C-4. School Enrollment for the 20 Largest Public School Districts in Each State, by Race/Ethnicity, 2020–21—*Continued*

(Number; percent.)

State/County	Total students in all grades	White (percent)	Black or African American (percent)	Hispanic (percent)	Asian or Asian/ Pacific Islander (percent)	American Indian/ Alaska Native (percent)	Nat. Hawaiian or Other Pacific Islander (percent)	Two or More Races (percent)
RHODE ISLAND—*(Continued)*								
West Warwick	3,551	70.2	5.2	16.9	2.5	1.0	0.3	3.9
Westerly	2,433	78.1	1.1	9.7	2.2	1.4	0.1	7.3
Woonsocket	5,742	40.3	10.7	36.8	4.9	0.5	0.2	6.7
SOUTH CAROLINA								
Aiken 01	22,538	47.5	33.7	12.5	0.8	0.2	0.1	5.3
Anderson 05	12,771	49.1	32.9	8.9	1.6	0.1	-	7.4
Beaufort 01	21,219	38.5	25.5	29.6	1.3	0.2	0.1	4.9
Berkeley 01	36,575	47.8	28.0	14.7	1.6	0.2	0.1	7.6
Charleston 01	48,330	48.8	34.3	11.4	1.5	0.1	0.2	3.3
Charter Institute at Erskine	23,750	63.1	22.8	8.2	0.9	0.4	0.2	4.5
Dorchester 02	24,684	51.0	29.1	10.0	1.7	0.2	0.2	7.9
Florence 01	15,186	33.5	52.7	5.2	1.8	-	-	6.8
Greenville 01	74,094	51.2	23.0	18.3	2.5	0.4	0.2	4.5
Horry 01	44,479	60.0	18.0	14.4	1.3	0.3	0.2	5.7
Lancaster 01	13,940	57.0	26.1	10.6	1.7	0.2	0.1	4.3
Lexington 01	27,072	70.4	12.7	8.8	3.1	0.2	0.2	4.5
Lexington 05	16,780	55.8	28.3	6.1	3.0	0.2	0.3	6.2
Pickens 01	15,689	76.8	6.9	8.9	1.3	0.1	-	6.0
Richland 01	22,202	17.4	70.3	6.5	0.9	-	0.2	4.7
Richland 02	27,761	18.7	60.9	11.9	2.8	0.2	0.2	5.2
SC Public Charter School District	15,773	53.2	27.4	11.1	3.0	0.4	0.1	4.8
Sumter 01	15,586	28.1	62.7	4.5	1.2	0.2	0.2	3.1
York 03	16,652	40.7	40.5	11.1	1.3	1.2	0.1	5.0
York 04	16,883	65.0	10.8	10.3	8.2	0.2	0.1	5.4
SOUTH DAKOTA								
Aberdeen School District 06-1	4,485	76.0	1.8	7.3	3.9	5.6	0.2	5.2
Belle Fourche School District 09-1	1,380	85.4	0.1	7.2	-	2.5	-	4.9
Brandon Valley School District 49-2	4,721	85.9	4.0	3.4	1.7	0.8	0.1	4.1
Brookings School District 05-1	3,346	80.5	3.2	6.1	2.9	1.9	0.1	5.3
Dakota Valley School District 61-8	1,377	79.2	2.3	8.0	2.5	1.6	0.6	5.8
Douglas School District 51-1	2,755	69.5	2.4	9.7	1.3	6.5	0.3	10.3
Harrisburg School District 41 2	5,457	86.9	3.1	3.8	1.6	0.7	0.1	3.7
Huron School District 02-2	2,766	43.5	1.1	28.2	21.6	2.2	0.7	2.6
Meade School District 46-1	3,006	86.4	0.7	4.6	0.5	2.6	0.1	5.1
Mitchell School District 17-2	2,775	81.5	1.0	7.6	0.5	6.5	0.2	2.8
Oglala Lakota County 65-1	1,807	0.4	-	2.4	-	95.2	0.9	1.1
Pierre School District 32-2	2,771	69.9	0.6	4.6	0.9	14.5	-	9.5
Rapid City Area School District 51-4	12,814	61.2	1.2	8.6	1.3	17.0	0.1	10.7
Sioux Falls School District 49-5	24,868	59.4	13.2	13.1	3.2	4.5	0.1	6.5
Spearfish School District 40-2	2,345	87.9	0.6	5.0	1.2	2.1	0.3	2.9
Tea Area School District 41-5	2,061	85.7	2.1	5.0	0.5	1.6	-	5.0
Todd County School District 66-1	2,158	0.9	0.1	1.6	0.2	96.3	0.1	0.8
Watertown School District 14-4	3,953	84.9	0.6	6.2	0.7	4.0	0.1	4.6
West Central School District 49-7	1,384	91.5	1.4	1.6	0.3	3.0	0.1	2.2
Yankton School District 63-3	2,955	79.1	1.3	8.8	0.7	4.9	0.1	5.1
TENNESSEE								
Achievement School District	9,027	2.2	89.8	6.7	0.2	0.1	-	0.9
Blount County	10,399	87.6	1.6	6.9	0.4	0.4	-	3.0
Bradley County	9,701	85.5	2.9	7.2	0.5	0.1	-	3.7
Collierville	9,043	56.0	15.6	6.8	16.1	0.1	-	5.3
Davidson County	80,404	26.4	37.9	29.0	3.9	0.1	0.1	2.6
Hamblen County	10,210	59.6	2.9	30.3	1.1	0.1	0.5	5.5
Hamilton County	44,100	48.0	26.3	16.9	1.9	-	-	6.8
Knox County	59,169	67.8	13.1	11.3	2.4	0.2	0.1	5.2
Madison County	12,378	28.4	54.8	9.3	1.4	0.1	-	5.9
Maury County	12,734	65.5	17.5	13.3	1.0	0.1	0.1	2.5
Montgomery County	36,426	49.5	24.6	14.1	1.7	0.2	0.7	9.2
Putnam County	11,609	78.0	3.1	15.8	1.4	0.1	0.1	1.7
Robertson County	13,960	67.5	10.2	16.7	0.6	0.1	0.1	4.8
Rutherford County	47,186	55.4	17.9	17.6	4.4	0.2	0.1	4.3
Sevier County	14,140	78.5	1.1	17.1	1.3	0.3	0.1	1.6
Shelby County	110,780	6.0	73.4	15.9	1.1	0.1	-	3.5
Sumner County	29,588	73.9	10.6	9.9	2.0	0.3	0.1	3.2

- = Zero or rounds to zero.
NA = Not available.

Table C-4. School Enrollment for the 20 Largest Public School Districts in Each State, by Race/ Ethnicity, 2020–21—*Continued*

(Number; percent.)

State/County	Total students in all grades	White (percent)	Black or African American (percent)	Hispanic (percent)	Asian or Asian/ Pacific Islander (percent)	American Indian/ Alaska Native (percent)	Nat. Hawaiian or Other Pacific Islander (percent)	Two or More Races (percent)
TENNESSEE—(*Continued*)								
Tipton County..	10,393	68.9	21.9	4.1	0.6	0.2	0.1	4.1
Williamson County..	39,817	78.2	3.6	6.7	7.2	0.1	0.1	4.2
Wilson County..	18,444	77.5	8.0	7.9	3.1	0.2	0.2	3.0
TEXAS								
Aldine ISD...	63,302	2.1	22.0	73.6	1.0	0.2	0.2	0.8
Arlington ISD..	56,840	18.0	25.8	47.0	5.8	0.5	0.2	2.8
Austin ISD...	74,871	30.1	6.6	55.0	4.5	0.1	0.1	3.5
Conroe ISD..	64,563	44.5	8.7	37.9	4.9	0.4	0.2	3.3
Cypress-Fairbanks ISD....................................	114,881	22.7	19.3	44.7	9.5	0.8	0.1	3.0
Dallas ISD...	145,113	5.8	21.4	69.9	1.2	0.4	0.1	1.1
El Paso ISD..	50,661	8.6	3.3	84.5	1.3	0.2	0.4	1.9
Fort Bend ISD...	76,735	14.9	27.5	26.3	27.2	0.4	0.2	3.5
Fort Worth ISD..	76,858	11.0	21.0	64.3	1.7	0.1	0.1	1.7
Frisco ISD...	63,493	36.5	11.5	13.2	33.6	0.6	0.1	4.6
Garland ISD...	53,921	16.4	18.0	51.8	9.4	1.5	0.1	2.8
Houston ISD...	196,943	9.9	22.4	61.7	4.4	0.2	0.1	1.4
Idea Public Schools..	62,158	6.6	6.3	85.4	0.9	0.1	0.1	0.4
Katy ISD..	84,176	31.6	12.5	35.9	16.1	0.2	0.1	3.7
Klein ISD...	52,824	28.7	15.6	43.3	8.2	0.4	0.1	3.7
Lewisville ISD..	49,361	37.7	11.6	30.4	15.5	0.4	0.1	4.3
North East ISD...	60,483	23.9	7.3	60.6	3.9	0.2	0.1	3.9
Northside ISD...	103,151	17.9	6.8	68.3	3.5	0.1	0.2	3.2
Pasadena ISD...	50,614	5.3	7.7	83.2	3.0	0.1	0.1	0.7
Plano ISD..	50,154	31.5	13.1	26.5	24.3	0.3	0.1	4.3
UTAH								
Alpine District...	82,800	80.1	0.7	12.7	0.9	0.3	1.3	4.0
American Preparatory Academy..........................	5,329	38.2	3.9	36.7	17.3	0.2	1.7	1.9
Box Elder District...	12,062	85.2	0.3	11.3	0.4	0.6	0.4	1.7
Cache District..	19,214	85.5	0.5	10.0	0.7	0.7	0.5	2.0
Canyons District...	34,383	72.4	1.6	16.8	2.6	0.3	1.1	5.2
Davis District...	72,082	82.1	1.1	10.9	1.1	0.4	1.3	3.1
Granite District...	63,430	49.2	3.9	35.2	4.4	1.3	4.5	1.4
Iron District..	11,091	83.1	0.5	11.1	0.6	1.9	0.5	2.3
Jordan District...	57,267	74.1	1.1	16.6	1.7	0.3	1.8	4.4
Logan City District..	5,704	59.0	2.7	30.4	2.7	1.2	1.8	2.3
Murray District...	6,175	67.6	3.4	20.3	2.1	0.7	0.9	5.0
Nebo District..	35,912	81.7	0.5	13.4	0.3	0.3	0.7	3.1
Ogden City District...	10,710	42.2	2.0	50.9	0.7	0.8	0.5	3.0
Provo District...	13,575	58.4	1.1	30.2	1.9	0.8	3.6	4.1
Salt Lake District..	20,798	43.1	5.0	36.8	4.7	1.5	5.0	3.8
Tooele District..	21,535	82.3	0.7	12.8	0.5	0.6	1.0	2.0
Uintah District..	6,787	78.1	0.4	9.9	0.5	8.2	0.5	2.4
Wasatch District...	9,251	79.6	0.4	16.9	0.4	0.2	0.2	2.2
Washington District...	36,992	78.9	1.0	14.4	1.0	1.3	1.5	2.0
Weber District..	32,423	81.3	0.9	13.1	0.9	0.3	0.7	2.8
VERMONT								
Addison Central Unified School District..............	1,742	94.4	2.2	0.3	2.2	0.2	0.7	NA
Barre Unified Union School District #97..............	2,169	92.0	0.9	3.0	0.4	0.5	-	3.1
Burlington School District.................................	3,591	63.4	15.1	3.0	9.9	0.1	-	8.5
Champlain Valley Unified School District.............	4,150	88.8	2.5	2.6	3.1	0.1	0.1	2.8
Colchester School District.................................	2,361	86.4	4.5	2.6	5.4	0.6	0.5	NA
Essex-Westford Educational Community Unified School								
District...	3,831	81.0	2.4	5.4	5.4	0.2	0.3	5.4
Hartford School District....................................	1,441	89.9	1.1	3.5	0.8	NA	0.1	4.6
Harwood Unified School District.........................	1,813	95.7	0.4	0.9	0.6	0.1	NA	2.3
Kingdom East Unified Union School District..........	1,631	96.5	0.7	1.1	1.0	NA	0.1	0.6
Lamoille South Unified Union School District #90..........	1,581	90.6	2.3	3.6	1.3	0.1	0.2	1.9
Maple Run Unified School District......................	2,597	88.7	0.8	2.8	1.1	0.6	NA	6.0
Milton Incorporated School District.....................	1,534	90.2	3.3	1.6	1.9	0.7	0.1	2.3
Missisquoi Valley School District #89..................	1,784	79.7	0.3	1.6	0.2	1.7	NA	16.5
Mount Anthony UHSD #14.................................	1,468	90.7	1.7	3.1	0.9	NA	0.1	3.5
Mount Mansfield Unified Union School District #401.....	2,569	92.9	0.3	3.3	0.5	NA	NA	3.0
Rutland City School District..............................	2,012	87.1	2.4	3.7	1.2	0.2	-	5.3
South Burlington School District.........................	2,688	73.6	4.8	5.7	8.1	-	-	7.8
Taconic and Green Regional School District..........	1,611	91.2	1.6	3.7	1.3	NA	0.1	2.0

- = Zero or rounds to zero.
NA = Not available.

Table C-4. School Enrollment for the 20 Largest Public School Districts in Each State, by Race/Ethnicity, 2020–21—*Continued*

(Number; percent.)

State/County	Total students in all grades	White (percent)	Black or African American (percent)	Hispanic (percent)	Asian or Asian/ Pacific Islander (percent)	American Indian/ Alaska Native (percent)	Nat. Hawaiian or Other Pacific Islander (percent)	Two or More Races (percent)
VERMONT—*(Continued)*								
Washington Central Unified Union School District #92...	1,473	92.7	1.3	1.7	0.9	0.3	0.1	3.1
Windham Southeast Unified Union School District #96..	2,353	83.7	2.1	6.0	1.8	0.1	-	6.2
VIRGINIA								
Alexandria City Public Schools.................................	15,775	27.9	25.8	37.2	5.5	0.2	0.2	3.3
Arlington County Public Schools..............................	26,831	44.0	10.3	28.9	8.9	0.2	-	7.7
Chesapeake City Public Schools	39,673	44.4	32.4	11.3	2.9	0.3	0.2	8.5
Chesterfield Co Public Schools	60,840	46.1	26.3	18.7	3.4	0.2	0.2	5.2
Fairfax County Public Schools	180,028	36.8	10.0	27.1	19.8	0.3	0.1	5.9
Frederick County Public Schools..............................	13,521	67.8	4.4	20.6	1.9	0.2	0.2	5.0
Hampton City Public Schools...................................	19,223	21.7	60.3	6.9	1.7	0.3	0.3	8.8
Hanover County Public Schools...............................	16,519	76.6	9.5	6.2	2.4	0.3	-	5.0
Henrico County Public Schools................................	50,191	35.1	36.1	11.1	12.5	0.2	0.1	4.9
Loudoun County Public Schools	81,066	43.9	7.1	18.2	24.4	0.6	0.1	5.7
Newport News City Public Schools..........................	27,113	20.9	54.1	14.7	2.2	0.3	0.4	7.5
Norfolk City Public Schools.....................................	27,955	20.7	58.4	11.7	2.0	0.3	0.3	6.6
Prince William County Public Schools	89,548	28.0	20.3	35.7	9.7	0.2	0.2	5.9
Richmond City Public Schools.................................	28,225	21.0	55.4	18.5	1.6	0.2	-	3.4
Roanoke City Public Schools	13,853	32.2	43.0	15.8	3.2	0.3	0.1	5.5
Roanoke County Public Schools...............................	13,690	75.3	7.6	7.0	4.4	0.1	0.1	5.4
Spotsylvania County Public Schools.........................	23,025	49.8	19.0	20.0	2.8	0.2	0.2	7.9
Stafford County Public Schools	29,372	44.4	20.9	22.1	3.8	0.3	0.2	8.3
Suffolk City Public Schools.....................................	13,869	29.7	56.2	6.0	1.5	0.3	0.2	6.1
Virginia Beach City Public Schools..........................	65,612	46.2	23.5	12.9	6.3	0.2	0.5	10.4
WASHINGTON								
Auburn School District..	17,007	33.0	8.2	31.6	11.1	1.1	5.0	10.0
Bellevue School District	20,191	30.8	3.2	13.1	43.1	0.1	0.3	9.4
Bethel School District..	20,076	46.3	7.4	20.8	4.0	1.0	4.9	15.5
Edmonds School District	20,851	44.7	7.6	22.2	13.1	0.5	0.9	10.9
Everett School District	20,226	46.2	4.7	20.6	17.9	0.5	1.4	8.6
Evergreen School District (Clark).............................	23,564	52.5	2.9	26.3	6.1	0.4	2.3	9.2
Federal Way School District	21,765	22.1	16.0	32.9	11.8	0.4	5.6	11.0
Highline School District	18,635	18.2	15.1	39.7	15.0	0.7	3.5	7.7
Issaquah School District	20,164	46.7	2.1	9.2	33.1	0.2	0.2	8.5
Kennewick School District	18,396	51.5	1.9	39.2	1.9	0.3	0.3	4.9
Kent School District..	25,720	29.6	12.9	23.1	21.5	0.3	2.9	9.7
Lake Washington School District	30,964	43.9	2.1	10.6	35.0	0.2	0.1	8.1
Northshore School District.......................................	23,310	52.3	2.0	12.7	23.4	0.2	0.1	9.1
Pasco School District..	18,614	21.8	0.9	73.1	1.2	0.1	0.3	2.7
Puyallup School District..	22,398	53.4	5.4	18.5	6.0	1.0	2.3	13.4
Seattle School District No. 1	53,973	45.4	15.0	13.0	13.1	0.4	0.4	12.2
Spokane School District...	28,280	65.9	3.2	11.5	2.2	1.1	2.3	13.7
Tacoma School District..	28,688	35.9	13.1	21.8	8.9	1.0	3.3	16.0
Vancouver School District..	21,897	54.3	3.0	27.0	3.3	0.4	2.5	8.7
Yakima School District..	15,858	15.5	0.5	80.1	0.4	0.9	0.1	2.5
WEST VIRGINIA								
Berkeley County Schools	19,278	73.3	9.1	8.1	0.7	0.2	0.1	8.5
Cabell County Schools..	11,875	82.8	6.8	1.5	0.9	0.2	-	7.8
Fayette County Schools...	5,688	92.1	4.1	0.8	0.1	0.1	NA	2.9
Greenbrier County Schools	4,719	91.4	2.6	2.4	0.5	-	-	3.1
Harrison County Schools	10,111	92.6	1.5	1.7	0.8	-	-	3.4
Jackson County Schools	4,266	90.5	0.8	1.4	0.2	-	0.1	1.0
Jefferson County Schools	8,506	74.7	5.9	10.7	1.0	-	0.1	7.5
Kanawha County Schools...	24,721	81.7	10.2	1.0	1.2	0.1	0.1	5.8
Logan County Schools...	5,229	96.5	2.1	0.2	0.2	NA	NA	0.9
Marion County Schools..	7,658	90.1	4.2	1.1	0.5	0.1	0.1	3.9
Marshall County Schools..	4,320	95.7	0.7	0.8	0.2	0.1	-	2.4
Mercer County Schools..	8,465	83.6	8.9	1.1	0.4	0.1	-	5.0
Mineral County Schools...	4,001	92.5	3.7	0.8	0.4	NA	NA	2.5
Monongalia County Schools	11,113	85.5	3.5	2.4	3.0	0.1	0.1	5.2
Ohio County Schools...	5,064	84.9	6.5	1.3	0.8	0.1	-	6.5
Preston County Schools...	4,210	98.0	0.5	0.8	-	NA	NA	0.7
Putnam County Schools...	9,147	94.0	1.4	1.2	1.0	0.1	-	2.2
Raleigh County Schools...	10,869	85.2	7.9	1.3	0.6	-	0.1	5.0
Wayne County Schools..	6,461	97.7	0.9	0.5	0.2	-	-	0.7
Wood County Schools..	11,864	92.7	1.7	1.4	0.7	0.1	0.1	3.4

- = Zero or rounds to zero.
NA – Not available.

Table C-4. School Enrollment for the 20 Largest Public School Districts in Each State, by Race/ Ethnicity, 2020–21—*Continued*

(Number; percent.)

State/County	Total students in all grades	White (percent)	Black or African American (percent)	Hispanic (percent)	Asian or Asian/ Pacific Islander (percent)	American Indian/ Alaska Native (percent)	Nat. Hawaiian or Other Pacific Islander (percent)	Two or More Races (percent)
WISCONSIN								
Appleton Area School District	15,745	66.9	5.0	11.1	11.6	0.6	0.2	4.6
Eau Claire Area School District	11,008	75.4	2.6	6.2	9.9	0.6	0.2	5.2
Elmbrook School District	7,280	70.3	2.6	6.4	15.4	0.3	0.1	4.9
Fond du Lac School District	6,678	67.2	8.6	14.5	3.3	0.3	-	6.1
Green Bay Area Public School District	19,171	41.6	9.1	30.5	8.0	3.6	0.1	7.2
Janesville School District	9,574	70.0	5.4	14.6	2.3	0.3	-	7.4
Kenosha School District	19,244	47.8	13.5	29.6	1.8	0.2	0.1	7.1
Madison Metropolitan School District	26,151	41.0	18.1	23.0	8.4	0.2	0.1	9.3
Middleton-Cross Plains Area School District	7,410	67.9	4.9	9.2	12.2	0.3	0.1	5.5
Milwaukee School District	71,510	9.9	50.4	27.7	7.9	0.4	0.1	3.6
Neenah Joint School District	6,572	82.8	2.3	7.0	3.2	0.5	-	4.1
Oshkosh Area School District	9,191	73.9	6.6	6.2	7.6	0.4	-	5.2
Racine Unified School District	16,254	37.5	25.2	29.3	1.0	0.3	-	6.7
Sheboygan Area School District	9,663	48.6	4.6	20.9	18.4	0.1	-	7.3
Stevens Point Area Public School District	6,938	78.8	2.2	7.6	6.7	0.3	0.1	4.4
Sun Prairie Area School District	8,366	59.7	11.3	9.4	10.4	0.4	0.1	8.8
Waukesha School District	12,344	63.3	5.3	23.1	3.7	0.2	0.1	4.3
Wausau School District	7,786	63.7	2.2	6.8	20.3	0.6	0.1	6.2
Wauwatosa School District	6,917	62.6	17.7	8.4	4.3	0.1	-	6.9
West Allis-West Milwaukee School District	7,418	48.5	11.3	27.7	2.9	0.8	0.1	8.7
WYOMING								
Albany County School District #1	3,917	73.8	1.2	16.8	2.2	1.4	0.1	4.4
Big Horn County School District #1	1,837	81.9	1.0	11.3	0.3	1.2	-	4.3
Campbell County School District #1	8,567	83.1	0.9	12.2	0.7	2.0	0.1	1.0
Carbon County School District #1	1,680	59.8	1.1	34.3	1.3	1.2	0.1	2.2
Converse County School District #1	1,643	87.9	0.9	7.7	0.3	0.7	0.1	2.4
Fremont County School District # 1	1,705	74.6	0.3	5.7	0.9	10.4	0.1	8.0
Fremont County School District #25	2,311	61.1	0.3	11.9	0.6	19.3	0.1	6.7
Goshen County School District #1	1,606	80.4	0.8	14.1	0.3	1.2	0.1	3.1
Laramie County School District #1	13,994	68.8	2.4	21.8	1.0	0.7	0.3	5.1
Lincoln County School District #2	2,924	92.4	0.4	4.4	0.4	0.5	0.5	1.4
Natrona County School District #1	13,110	79.8	1.2	12.9	0.8	1.0	0.2	4.1
Niobrara County School District #1	1,397	79.5	0.7	16.3	0.6	1.6	0.4	0.8
Park County School District # 1	1,797	83.5	0.6	12.0	0.5	0.1	-	3.4
Park County School District # 6	1,974	91.9	0.5	3.3	0.9	0.5	0.2	2.8
Sheridan County School District #1	1,203	92.4	0.5	-	0.4	2.2	0.2	4.2
Sheridan County School District #2	3,519	88.0	0.3	7.2	0.6	0.9	0.1	2.8
Sweetwater County School District #1	5,141	67.4	0.9	26.2	0.6	0.5	0.2	4.2
Sweetwater County School District #2	2,359	81.5	0.3	14.8	0.2	0.3	0.1	2.9
Teton County School District #1	2,749	63.9	0.2	31.6	1.1	0.7	-	2.6
Uinta County School District #1	2645	78.1	0.5	17.7	0.3	0.5	0.2	2.6

- = Zero or rounds to zero.
NA = Not available.

NOTES AND DEFINITIONS: LOCAL AREA EDUCATION STATISTICS

Part C presents data items for the 20 largest school districts in each state, selected counties, county equivalents, and independent cities. The District of Columbia is included as both a county and a state.

TABLES C-2

Source: U.S. Census Bureau. *American Community Survey, 2019.* Tables S1701, S2701, S1501, B14004, and B14002. (ACS 1-Year Estimates) http://data.census.gov.

The educational attainment data in Table C-2 have been compiled from the detailed tables of the American Community Survey (2019 1-year) and can be found at data.census.gov on the Census Bureau's website.

Due to the impact of the COVID-19 pandemic on data collection for the ACS, the U.S. Census Bureau will not be releasing 2020 1-Year Estimates.

ACS data are subject to sampling error, which can be especially large in small geographic areas or small population groups. Margins of error can be found on the Census Bureau website.

ACS gathers demographic, social, economic, housing, and financial information about the nation's people and communities on a continuous basis, providing the detailed characteristics that have previously come from the sample long form of the decennial census.

GEOGRAPHIC IDENTIFICATION

A five-digit state and county code is assigned to each entity. The first two digits indicate the state; the remaining three identify the county. Within each state, the counties are numbered in alphabetical order, beginning with 001, with even numbers usually omitted. Independent cities follow the counties and begin with the number 510.

These codes have been established by the U.S. government as Federal Information Processing Standards and are often referred to as "FIPS codes." They are used by U.S. government agencies and many other organizations for data presentation. They are provided in this volume for use in matching the data given here with other data sources in which counties may be identified by FIPS codes.

Not all county equivalents are included in this publication.

County equivalents. In Louisiana, the primary divisions of the state are known as parishes rather than counties. In Alaska, the county equivalents are the organized boroughs, together with the census areas that were developed for general statistical purposes by the state of Alaska and the U.S. Census Bureau.

Independent cities. Independent cities are not included in any county; data are presented separately in this volume where available.

Maryland
  Baltimore (separate from Baltimore County)

Missouri
  St. Louis (separate from St. Louis County)

Virginia
  Alexandria
  Chesapeake
  Hampton
  Lynchburg
  Newport News
  Norfolk
  Portsmouth
  Richmond
  Roanoke
  Suffolk
  Virginia Beach

Highest Level of Educational Attainment. People are classified according to the highest degree or level of school completed. The order in which degrees were listed on the questionnaire suggested that doctorate degrees were "higher" than professional school degrees, which were "higher" than master's degrees. The question included instructions for people currently enrolled in school to report the level of the previous grade attended or the highest degree received. Respondents who did not report educational attainment or enrollment level were assigned the attainment of a person of the same age, race, Hispanic or Latino origin, occupation, and sex, where possible, who resided in the same area or nearby. Respondents who filled in more than one box were edited to the highest level or degree reported. The question included a response category that allowed respondents to report completing the 12th grade without receiving a high school diploma. It allowed people who received either a high school diploma or the equivalent, such as those who passed the Test of General Educational Development (GED) and did not attend college, to be reported as "high school graduate(s)."

High school diploma or less. This category includes all persons who have not received a high school diploma, as well as those high school graduates who never attended college.

High school diploma or more. This category includes people whose highest degree was a high school diploma or its equivalent, people who attended college but did not receive a degree, and people who received a college, university, or professional degree. People who reported completing the 12th grade but not receiving a diploma are not high school graduates.

Bachelor's degree or more. This category includes people whose highest degree was a bachelor's, master's, professional, or doctoral degree. Master's degrees include the traditional M.A. and M.S. degrees and field-specific degrees. Some examples of professional degrees include medicine, dentistry, chiropractic, optometry, osteopathic medicine, pharmacy, podiatry, veterinary medicine, law, and theology. Vocational and technical training, such as barber school training; business, trade, technical, and vocational schools; or other training for a specific trade are specifically excluded.

Public and private schools. Public and private schools include people who attended school during the reference period and who indicated they were enrolled by marking one of the questionnaire categories for either "public school, public college" or "private school, private college." Schools primarily supported and controlled by a federal, state, or local government are defined as public (including tribal schools). Those primarily supported and controlled by religious organizations or other private groups are considered private, as are home schools.

School enrollment. People were classified as enrolled in school if they reported attending a "regular" public or private school or college during the three months prior to the interview. The question included instructions to "include only nursery school or preschool, kindergarten, elementary school, and schooling which leads to a high school diploma or a college degree" as regular school or college. Respondents who did not answer the enrollment question were assigned the enrollment status and type of school of a person with the same age, sex, and race/Hispanic or Latino origin whose residence was in the same or a nearby area. All persons 3 years old and over are included.

TABLES C-1, C-3, AND C-4
Source: U.S. Department of Education, National Center for Education Statistics (NCES), Common Core of Data (CCD). Elementary/Secondary Information System (ElSi): 2020–2021 Popular Tables. https://nces.ed.gov/ccd/elsi.

The school district characteristics, enrollment numbers, and fiscal information in
tables C-1, C-3, and C-4 were compiled from
school-district level data within the Elemen-
tary/Secondary Information System (ElSi)
on the NCES website. The school district
characteristics and enrollment data are from
the 2020–21 school year. Fiscal data is from
the 2017–18 school year, which is the most
recent year available.

ElSi is an NCES web application that allows
users to quickly view public and private
school data and create custom tables and
charts using data from the Common Core
of Data (CCD) and Private School Survey
(PSS). ElSi utilizes variables that are frequently requested by users for producing
tables. It is a fast, easy way to obtain basic
statistical data on U.S. schools.

INDEX

INDEX